W9-DEM-475

1998 – 1999

V.I.P. ADDRESS BOOK

Edited by James M. Wiggins, Ph.D.

ASSOCIATED MEDIA COMPANIES, LTD.

1998 – 1999

V. I. P.

ADDRESS

BOOK

Library of Congress Catalog Card Number 96-656029
(ISSN 1043-0261)
The V.I.P. address book/edited by James M. Wiggins, Ph.D.
Bibliography: p.
Includes index.
1. Celebrities—Directories. 2. Celebrities—United States—Directories. 3. Social registers. 4. United States—Social registers.
I. Wiggins, James M., 1933- .   II. Title: VIP address book.
CT120.VI5 1990i   920'.0025'73 - dci   96-656029 (ISSN 1043-0261)
International Standard Book Number 0-938731-13-0
Manufactured in the United States of America

Table of Contents

The purpose of the V.I.P. ADDRESS BOOK is to provide readers with a means of reaching Very Important People — Celebrities, Government Officials, Business Leaders, Entertainers, Sports Stars, Scientists and Artists.

It is genuinely hoped that people will use this volume to write for information about an entrant's work or to express encouragement. Compliments and praise for one's efforts are always appreciated. Being at the top of one's chosen profession is no exception. And for those who are no longer active in a field, it is especially flattering to be contacted about one's past accomplishments.

Methodology

The determination of candidates for inclusion in this reference work is an on-going process. Committees of prominent and knowledgeable people review those included in the nine major areas (listed in bold below).

Public Service includes World Leaders, Government Officials (both U.S. and International), Law Enforcement Officials and Members of the Legal and Judicial Fields.

Adventure includes Military Leaders (both U.S. and International), Astronauts and Cosmonauts, Heroes and Explorers.

Business, Religion and Education includes Financial and Labor Leaders as well as Businesspeople and Nobel Prize Winners in Economics and Peace.

Life and Leisure includes Fashion Design, Modeling, Beauty and Health Care and Social and Political Activists.

Communications includes Columnists, Commentators, Editors and Publishers, along with Editorial and Comic Book Cartoonists.

Fine Arts includes Architects, Artists, Opera, Ballet and Dance Performers, Conductors, Concert Artists, Composers (both classical and popular), Writers, Photographers and Nobel Literature Laureates.

Science covers Nobel Prize winners in Chemistry, Medicine and Physics, Engineers, Inventors, Earth and Space Scientists, Psychologists and Psychiatrists, Medical and Research Scientists.

Entertainment includes stars of Radio, Stage and Screen, Musicians, Cinematographers, Producers and Directors.

Sports includes all major spectator and participatory sports.

The committees define the parameters of the people included and prepare a list of additions and deletions to the candidate list. The research staff checks and updates information daily.

Occupations and Titles

The category listed after an entrant's name is selected to best describe his/her most noteworthy accomplishment. No distinction is made as to whether the person still holds that position. It is felt that a person who made a name for herself/himself still retains that identity even if it was accomplished in the past.

How Addresses Are Obtained

The editors of the V.I.P. ADDRESS BOOK have made every effort possible to insure that the addresses listed are accurate and current. Once it is determined a person is eligible for inclusion in the book, that person is contacted to determine which address he/she prefers. If a person prefers a home address, it is included. If a person prefers a business address or one in care of an agent or representative, that address is included. If a person specifically asks that their name not be included, their name is omitted. Once an address is listed, we continue efforts to verify that the address has not changed. These efforts include random sampling of the entire database, follow-up on all returned mailings received including those received from users of the book and the National Change of Address database from the U.S. Postal Service.

Users of the book should realize that people's addresses are in a state of constant change. The U.S. Bureau of Statistics says that almost 20 percent of people move each year. Not only do people change places of residence, they may also change business affiliations. Businesses move their headquarters as well as downsizing, merging or selling portions of their companies. Athletes get traded or retire. Entertainers change agents or personal managers and television shows get canceled. Politicians leave office or run for new positions. In addition, there are deaths almost daily which affect the address listings.

National Change of Address Program

Our staff notes changes on a daily basis by watching television news shows and reading newspapers around the world. But we also take an extra step which no other directory or address book attempts. We match addresses of all U.S. listees with the U.S. Postal Service's National Change of Address program. The National Change of Address match is a process that compares mailing lists with more than 100 million address change cards filed by postal customers over the past three years. Address change information is provided for mailing list records that match with information from address change cards.

If a person/family/business moves, there are several factors which determine whether the National Change of Address program is effective. These include whether the mover filed an address change with the Postal Service, when the change was filed, whether the mover lived in an area covered by the automated address change systems (which includes more than 90 percent of the United States) and whether the name and address information in our files matches the information provided by the mover.

Bad Addresses/Corrections

We keep track not only of current addresses but outdated ones as well. Our files list more than 50,000 people and we have up to 20 addresses for some of the people in the book. We continually update our data base and you can help. We welcome information about bad addresses from users of the book.

Envelope Markings

On your outgoing letters, you should always write "Address Correction Requested" beneath your return address in a clear and noticeable manner. If you do this, postal workers are supposed to send the forwarding address for a nominal fee. While this may not always be successful, you can be reasonably sure it will not be provided if you have not requested an address correction.

V.I.P. Address Book Update

Realizing the ever changing aspect of addresses, we also publish the single volume V.I.P. ADDRESS BOOK UPDATE which is available mid-year for an additional fee. The UPDATE lists several thousand address changes and new addresses as well as informing users of the names of celebrities who pass away.

Recommendations for the Book

If you are interested in people who are not listed in the book, send us a letter with their name, address and biographical information. If these people are deemed worthy for inclusion, they may be listed in a future edition of the V.I.P. ADDRESS BOOK.

Until people stop moving or changing jobs (which will never happen), there are going to be address changes. We want to provide the best service possible and we think we have the highest percentage of accuracy of any directory or address book.

If you have suggestions for improving accuracy beyond random follow-ups, following daily news events, checking on all bad address notifications and using the Postal Service's National Change of Address service, let us know your ideas.

Forms of Address

An important part of writing to people - regardless of their positions - is to properly address envelopes and to use the correct salutations in the letters. Although the titles and positions of people listed in this directory are too numerous to cover, there are a number of people whose forms of address are worth noting. The table below is a guide to enhance the likelihood your letter will be received in a favorable light.

POSITION	ENVELOPE/ADDRESS	SALUTATION
Presidents of Countries	The President	Dear Mr/Madam President - - -
Vice Presidents of Countries	The Vice President	Dear Mr/Madam Vice President - - -
Cabinet Officers	The Honorable John/Jane Doe Secretary of - - -	Dear Mr/Madam Secretary - - -
Senators	The Honorable John/Jane Doe US Senator from - - -	Dear Mr/Ms Senator - - -
Representatives	The Honorable John/Jane Doe US Representative from - - -	Dear Mr/Ms Representative - - -
Judges	The Honorable John/Jane Doe, Judge, US - - - Court	Dear Judge - - -

Continued on page xii

1 9 9 8 – 1 9 9 9

V.I.P.
ADDRESS
BOOK

Publisher and Editor
James M. Wiggins, Ph.D.

President and Managing Editor
Adele M. Cooke

Vice President of Technical Affairs
Michael K. Maloy

Design Director
Lee Ann Nelson

Publisher
ASSOCIATED MEDIA COMPANIES
P.O. Box 489
Gleneden Beach, OR 97388-0489
United States of America

TABLE OF ABBREVIATIONS

A
AB	Alberta
AFB	Air Force Base
AK	Alaska
AL	Alabama
Aly	Alley
APO	Army Post Office
AR	Arkansas
Arc	Arcade
AS	American Samoa
Assn	Association
Assoc	Associates
Ave	Avenue
AZ	Arizona

B
BC	British Columbia
Bd	Board
Beds	Bedfordshire
Berks	Berkshire
Bldg	Building
Blvd	Boulevard
Br	Branch
Bros	Brothers
Bucks	Buckinghamshire
BWI	British West Indies
Byp	Bypass

C
CA	California
Cambs	Cambridgeshire
Cir	Circle
CM	Mariana Islands
CMH	Medal of Honor Winner
CO	Colorado
Co	Company
Corp	Corporation
Cres	Crescent
Cswy	Causeway
CT	Connecticut
Ct	Court
Ctr	Center
Ctrl	Central
Cts	Courts
CZ	Canal Zone

D
DC	District of Columbia
DE	Delaware
Dept	Department
Dis	District
Div	Division
Dr	Drive
Drwy	Driveway

E
E	East
Edin	Edinburghshire
Expy	Expressway
Ext	Extended, Extension

F
Fedn	Federation
FL	Florida
FPO	Fleet Post Office
Ft	Fort
Fwy	Freeway

G
GA	Georgia
Gdns	Gardens
Glos	Gloucestershire
Grp	Group
Grv	Grove
Gt	Great
GU	Guam

H
Hants	Hampshire
Herts	Hertfordshire
HI	Hawaii
HOF	Hall of Fame
Hts	Heights
Hwy	Highway
Hq	Headquarters

I
IA	Iowa
ID	Idaho
IL	Illinois
IN	Indiana
Inc	Incorporated
Inst	Institute
Int'l	International
Intercoll	Intercollegiate

J
Jr	Junior

K
KS	Kansas
KY	Kentucky

L
LA	Louisiana
Lancs	Lancashire
Lincs	Lincolnshire
Ln	Lane
Ltd	Limited

M		**R**	
MA	Massachusetts	Rep	Republic
MB	Manitoba	Rd	Road
MD	Maryland	RD	Rural Delivery
ME	Maine	RI	Rhode Island
MI	Michigan	RR	Rural Route
MN	Minnesota	Rt	Route
MO	Missouri		
Mon	Monmouthshire	**S**	
MS	Mississippi	S	South
MT	Montana	SC	South Carolina
Mt	Mount	SD	South Dakota
		SE	Southeast
N		SK	Saskatchewan
N	North	Spdwy	Speedway
NB	New Brunswick	Sq	Square
NC	North Carolina	St	Saint, Street
ND	North Dakota	SW	Southwest
NE	Northeast, Nebraska		
NF	Newfoundland	**T**	
NH	New Hampshire	TA	Tasmania
NJ	New Jersey	Ter	Territory
NM	New Mexico	Terr	Terrace
Northants	Northamptonshire	TN	Tennessee
Notts	Nottinghamshire	Tpke	Turnpike
NS	Nova Scotia	Trl	Trail
NSW	New South Wales	TX	Texas
NT	Northwest Territories		
NV	Nevada	**U**	
NW	Northwest	Univ	University
NY	New York	US	United States
		USSR	Russia
O		UT	Utah
OH	Ohio		
OK	Oklahoma	**V**	
ON	Ontario	VA	Virginia
OR	Oregon	VC	Victoria Cross Winner
Oxon	Oxfordshire	VI	Virgin Islands
		VIC	Victoria
P		VT	Vermont
PA	Pennsylvania		
PE	Prince Edward Island	**W**	
Pkwy	Parkway	W	West
Pl	Place	WA	Washington, Western Australia
Plz	Plaza	WI	Wisconsin
PO	Post Office	Worcs	Worcestershire
PQ	Providence of Quebec	WV	West Virginia
PR	Puerto Rico	WY	Wyoming
Prof	Professional		
Pt	Point	**X-Y-Z**	
		YK	Yukon Territory
Q		Yorks	Yorkshire
QLD	Queensland		

Foreign Ambassadors	His/Her Excellency John/Jane Doe	Dear Mr/Ms Ambassador - - -
Kings/Queens	His/Her Royal Highness - - - , King/Queen of - - -	Your Royal Highness - - -
Military Leaders (Attention should be given to the actual rank)	General/Admiral John/Jane Doe	Dear General/ Admiral - - -
Governors	The Honorable John/Jane Doe, Governor of - - -	Dear Governor - - -
Mayors	The Honorable John/Jane Doe, Mayor of - - -	Dear Mayor - - -
The Clergy Catholic		
The Pope	His Eminence the Pope - - -	Your Holiness - - -
Cardinals	His Eminence, John Cardinal Doe	Dear Your Eminence Cardinal
Episcopalian	The Rt Rev John Doe	Dear Bishop - - -
Protestant	The Rev John Doe	Dear Mr/Ms - - -
Eastern Orthodox Patriarch	His Holiness, the Patriarch - - -	Your Holiness - - -
Jewish	Rabbi John Doe	Dear Rabbi - - -

Forms of addresses can vary to almost impossible proportions. If you are a real stickler for proper protocol, you will need to obtain one of the many excellent reference books on etiquette or consult your local reference librarian for assistance.

Times are less formal so if you are polite and spell names correctly, your letter should be favorably received.

THE
DIRECTORY
OF
ADDRESS
LISTINGS

Although we have made every effort to provide
current correct addresses, we assume no responsibility
for addresses which become outdated.
Neither do we guarantee that people listed in the
book will personally answer their mail or
that they will respond to correspondence.

Aaker, Lee — *Actor*
Po Box 8013, Mammoth Lakes, CA 93546, USA

Aames, Willie — *Actor*
12821 Moorpark, #2, Studio City, CA 91604, USA

Aamodt, Kjetil Andre — *Skier*
Waldemar Thranes Gate 64-A, 0173 Oslo, Norway

Aaron, Henry L (Hank) — *Baseball Player, Executive*
1611 Adams Dr SW, Atlanta, GA 30311, USA

Aaron, Tommy — *Golfer*
440 E Lake Dr, Gainesville, GA 30506, USA

Aas, Roald — *Speed Skater*
Enebakkvn 252, 1187 Oslo 11, Norway

Aase, Donald W (Don) — *Baseball Player*
5055 Via Ricardo, Yorba Linda, CA 92886, USA

Abacha, Sani — *President, Nigeria; Army General*
%President's Office, State House, Ribadu Road, Ikoyi, Lagos, Nigeria

Abakanowicz, Magdalena — *Artist*
Ul Bzowa 1, 02-708 Warsaw, Poland

Abbado, Claudio — *Conductor*
Piazzetta Bossi 1, 20121 Milan, Italy

Abbatiello, Carmine — *Harness Racing Driver*
287 Highway 34 N, Colts Neck, NJ 07722, USA

Abbe, Elfriede M — *Artist*
Applewood, Manchester Center, VT 05255, USA

Abbot, Charles S — *Navy Admiral*
Commander, US 6th Fleet, Unit 50148, FPO, AE 09501, USA

Abbott, D Thomas — *Businessman*
%Savin Corp, 333 Ludlow St, Stamford, CT 06902, USA

Abbott, Diahnne — *Actress*
460 W Ave 46, Los Angeles, CA 90065, USA

Abbott, James A (Jim) — *Baseball Player*
%Anaheim Angels, Anaheim Stadium, PO Box 2000, Anaheim, CA 92803, USA

Abbott, Philip — *Actor*
%Dade/Schultz, 11846 Ventura Blvd, #100, Studio City, CA 91604, USA

Abbott, Preston S — *Psychologist*
1305 Namassin Road, Alexandria, VA 22308, USA

Abboud, A Robert — *Businessman*
%A Robert Abboud Co, 212 Stone Hill Center, Fox River Grove, IL 60021, USA

Abboud, Joseph M — *Fashion Designer*
650 5th Ave, #2700, New York, NY 10019, USA

Abdnor, James — *Senator, SD*
PO Box 217, Kennebec, SD 57544, USA

Abdrashitov, Vadim Y — *Movie Director*
3d Frunzenskaya 8, #211, 119270 Moscow, Russia

Abdul Ahad Mohmand — *Cosmonaut, Afghanistan*
%Potchta Kosmonavtov, Moskovskoi Oblasti, 141160 Syvisdny Goroduk, Russia

Abdul, Paula J — *Singer, Dancer*
14046 Aubrey Road, Beverly Hills, CA 90210, USA

Abdul-Jabbar, Kareem — *Basketball Player*
1436 Summitridge Dr, Beverly Hills, CA 90210, USA

Abdul-Rahim, Shareef — *Basketball Player*
%Vancouver Grizzlies, 288 Beatty St, #300, Vancouver BC V6B 2M1, Canada

Abdul-Rauf, Mahmoud — *Basketball Player*
%Sacramento Kings, 1 Sports Parkway, Sacramento, CA 95834, USA

Abdullah — *Prince, Jordan*
%Royal Palace, Ammam, Jordan

Abdullah Ibn Abdul Aziz — *Crown Prince, Saudi Arabia*
%Council of Ministers, Jeddah, Saudi Arabia

Abel, Joy — *Bowler*
PO Box 296, Lansing, IL 60438, USA

Abel, Robert, Jr — *Ophthalmologist*
1300 Harrison St, Wilmington, DE 19806, USA

Abel, Sidney G (Sid) — *Hockey Player, Coach*
26850 Halstead Road, Farmington Hills, MI 48331, USA

Abell, Murray R — *Pathologist*
%American Pathology Board, 5401 W Kennedy Blvd, Tampa, FL 33609, USA

Abelson, Alan — *Editor, Columnist*
%Barron's Magazine, Editorial Dept, 200 Liberty St, New York, NY 10281, USA

Abelson, Philip H — *Physicist*
4244 50th St NW, Washington, DC 20016, USA

Abelson, Robert P — *Psychiatrist*
1155 Whitney Ave, Hamden, CT 06517, USA

Aberastain, Jose M — *Ballet Instructor*
%Southern Methodist University, Dance Division, Dallas, TX 75275, USA

Aberconway of Bodnant, Charles M M — *Businessman*
25 Edgerton Terrace, London SW3, England

Abercrombie, John L — *Jazz Guitarist*
%Ted Kurland, 173 Brighton Ave, Boston, MA 02134, USA

Abernethy, Robert — *Commentator*
%NBC-TV, News Dept, 4001 Nebraska Ave NW, Washington, DC 20016, USA

Abert, Donald B — *Publisher*
%Milwaukee Journal, 333 W State St, Milwaukee, WI 53203, USA

Abiodun Oyewole — *Rap Artist (The Last Poets)*
%Agency Group, 1775 Broadway, #433, New York, NY 10019, USA

Ablon, Ralph E — *Businessman*
%Ogden Corp, 2 Pennsylvania Plaza, New York, NY 10121, USA

Abraham, Edward P — *Biochemist*
%Sir William Dunn School of Pathology, South Parks Road, Oxford, England

Abraham, F Murray — *Actor*
40 5th Ave, #2-C, New York, NY 10011, USA

Abraham, Seth — *Television Executive*
%Time Warner Sports, HBO, 1100 Ave of Americas, New York, NY 10036, USA

Abrahams, J H — *Businessman*
%Security Benefit Life, 700 SW Harrison St, Topeka, KS 66636, USA

Abram, Norm — *Television Entertainer*
%"This Old House" Show, PO Box 2284, South Bennington, VT 05407, USA

Abramovitz, Max — *Architect*
176 Honey Hollow Road, Pound Ridge, NY 10576, USA

Abramowitz, Morton I — *Diplomat*
800 25th St NW, Washington, DC 20037, USA

Abrams, Elliott — *Government Official*
%Hudson Institute, 1015 18th St NW, #200, Washington, DC 20036, USA

Abrams, Herbert L — *Radiologist*
714 Alvarado Row, Stanford, CA 94305, USA

Abrams, John N — *Army General*
Commanding General, V Corps, US Army Europe & 7th Army, APO, AE 09014, USA

Abramson, Jerry — *Mayor*
%Mayor's Office, City Hall, 601 W Jefferson St, Louisville, KY 40202, USA

Abramson, Leslie — *Attorney*
4929 Wilshire Blvd, Los Angeles, CA 90010, USA

Abrew, Frederick H — *Businessman*
%Equitable Resources, 420 Blvd of Allies, Pittsburgh, PA 15219, USA

Abril, Victoria — *Actress*
%Bresler Kelly Assoc, 15760 Ventura Blvd, #1730, Encino, CA 91436, USA

Abroms, Edward M — *Television Director, Executive*
%EMA Enterprises, 1866 Marlowe St, Thousand Oaks, CA 91360, USA

Abruzzo, Ray — *Actor*
20334 Pacific Coast Highway, Malibu, CA 90265, USA

Abshire, David M — *Diplomat*
%Strategic/International Studies Center, 1800 "K" St NW, Washington, DC 20006, USA

Abzug, Bella S — *Representative, NY*
2 5th Ave, New York, NY 10011, USA

Accola, Paul — *Skier*
Bolgenstr 17, 7270 Davos Platz, Switzerland

Acconci, Vito — *Conceptual Artist*
39 Pearl St, Brooklyn, NY 11201, USA

Acevedo, Hernan F — *Biochemist*
%Allegheny-Singer Research Institute, 320 E North Ave, Pittsburgh, PA 15212, USA

Achebe, Chinua — *Writer*
%Bard College, Language & Literature Dept, Annandale, NY 12504, USA

Achidi Achu, Simon — *Prime Minister, Cameroon Republic*
%Prime Minister's Office, Boite Postale 1057, Yaounde, Cameroon Republic

Acker, C Edward — *Businessman*
%Atlantic Coast Airlines, 515 Shaw Road, #A, Sterling, VA 20166, USA

Acker, Joseph E — *Cardiologist*
1307 Old Weisgarber Road, Knoxville, TN 37909, USA

Abelson - Acker

Acker, Sharon *Actress*
332 N Palm Dr, #401, Beverly Hills, CA 90210, USA
Ackeren, Robert V *Movie Director*
%Kurfurstendamm 132-A, 10711 Berlin, Germany
Ackerman, Bettye *Actress*
302 N Alpine Dr, Beverly Hills, CA 90210, USA
Ackermann, Rosemarie *Track Athlete*
Str der Jugend 72, 03050 Cottbus, Germany
Ackland, Joss *Actor*
%Susan Smith, 121 N San Vicente Blvd, Beverly Hills, CA 90211, USA
Ackley, Gardner *Government Official, Educator*
907 Berkshire Road, Ann Arbor, MI 48104, USA
Ackroyd, David *Actor*
273 N Many Lakes Dr, Kalispell, MT 59901, USA
Ackroyd, Peter *Writer*
%Anthony Sheil Assoc, 43 Doughty St, London WL1N 2LF, England
Acohido, Byron *Journalist*
%Seattle Times, Editorial Dept, Fairview Ave N & John St, Seattle, WA 98111, USA
Acton, Loren W *Astronaut*
108 W Arnold St, Bozeman, MT 59715, USA
Aczel, Janos D *Mathematician*
97 McCarron Crescent, Waterloo ON N2L 5M9, Canada
Ada, James *Governor, GU*
%Governor's Office, Government Offices, Agana, GU 96910, USA
Adair, Deborah *Actress*
%Paul Kohner, 9300 Wilshire Blvd, #555, Beverly Hills, CA 90212, USA
Adair, Paul N (Red) *Oil Well Fire Fighter*
%Red Adair Oil Well Fires & Blowouts Con, 5151 San Felipe St, Houston, TX 77056, USA
Adam, Robert *Architect*
Crooked Pightie, Crawley, Winchester, Hants SO21 2PN, England
Adam, Theo *Opera Singer*
Schillerstr 14, 01326 Dresden, Germany
Adamany, David W *Educator*
%Wayne State University, President's Office, Detroit, MI 48202, USA
Adamek, Donna *Bowler*
%Ladies Professional Bowlers Tour, 7171 Cherryvale Blvd, Rockford, IL 61112, USA
Adamle, Mike *Football Player, Sportscaster*
%ABC-TV, Sports Dept, 77 W 66th St, New York, NY 10023, USA
Adams, Alice *Writer*
2661 Clay St, San Francisco, CA 94115, USA
Adams, Alvan *Basketball Player*
5617 N Palo Cristi Road, Paradise Valley, AZ 85253, USA
Adams, Brock *Secretary, Transportation; Senator, WA*
1415 42nd Ave E, Seattle, WA 98112, USA
Adams, Brooke *Actress*
248 S Van Ness Ave, Los Angeles, CA 90004, USA
Adams, Bryan *Singer, Guitarist, Songwriter*
%Bruce Allen Talent, 406-68 Water St, Vancouver BC V6B 1A4, Canada
Adams, Charles J *Religious Leader*
%Progressive National Baptist Convention, 601 50th St NE, Washington, DC 20019, USA
Adams, Cindy *Movie Critic*
1050 5th Ave, New York, NY 10028, USA
Adams, Don *Actor*
2160 Century Park East, Los Angeles, CA 90067, USA
Adams, Douglas *Writer*
%Ed Victor Ltd, 162 Wardour St, London W1V 3AT, England
Adams, Edie *Actress*
8040 Okean Terrace, Los Angeles, CA 90046, USA
Adams, Edward (Eddie) *Photographer*
80 Warren St, #66, New York, NY 10007, USA
Adams, George R *Jazz Saxophonist, Flutist*
%Joel Chriss, 300 Mercer St, #3-J, New York, NY 10003, USA
Adams, Gerard (Gerry) *Political Leader, Northern Ireland*
%Sinn Fein/IRA, 51/55 Falls Road, Belfast BT 12, Northern Ireland
Adams, Greg *Hockey Player*
%Dallas Stars, StarCenter, 211 Cowboys Parkway, Dallas, TX 75063, USA
Adams, James L *Theologian*
3 Pooks Hill Road, #715, Bethesda, MD 20814, USA

Acker - Adams

Adams, Jane — *Actress*
17 Duke Dr, Rancho Mirage, CA 92270, USA

Adams, Joey — *Comedian, Writer*
%New York Post, 1211 Ave of Americas, #1900, New York, NY 10036, USA

Adams, John C — *Composer*
%Elektra Records, 75 Rockefeller Plaza, New York, NY 10019, USA

Adams, John H — *Religious Leader*
%African Methodist Church, Box 19039, Germantown Station, Philadelphia, PA 19138, USA

Adams, Julie — *Actress*
%Twentieth Century, 15315 Magnolia Blvd, #429, Sherman Oaks, CA 91403, USA

Adams, Julius — *Football Player, Coach*
2135 Jefferson Davis St, Macon, GA 31206, USA

Adams, Kenneth S (Bud) — *Football Executive*
%Tennessee Oilers, Hale Hall, Tennessee State University, Nashville, TN 37209, USA

Adams, Kim — *Actress*
%LA Talent, 8335 Sunset Blvd, #200, Los Angeles, CA 90069, USA

Adams, Lorraine — *Journalist*
%Washington Post, Editorial Dept, 1150 15th St, Washington, DC 20071, USA

Adams, Lucian — *WW II Army Hero (CMH)*
4323 Valleyfield Dr, San Antonio, TX 78222, USA

Adams, Mark — *Artist*
3816 22nd St, San Francisco, CA 94114, USA

Adams, Mary Kay — *Actress*
%Stone Manners, 8091 Selma Ave, Los Angeles, CA 90046, USA

Adams, Mason — *Actor*
2006 Stradella Road, Los Angeles, CA 90077, USA

Adams, Maud — *Actress*
2791 Ellison Dr, Beverly Hills, CA 90210, USA

Adams, Michael — *Basketball Player*
1860 Main St, Hartford, CT 06120, USA

Adams, Noah — *Commentator*
%National Public Radio, 635 Massachusetts Ave Nw, Washington, DC 20001, USA

Adams, Oleta — *Singer*
%Creative Artists Agency, 9830 Wilshire Blvd, Beverly Hills, CA 90212, USA

Adams, Pat — *Artist*
370 Elm St, Bennington, VT 05201, USA

Adams, Paul G, III — *Financier*
%First American BankShares, 15th & "H" Sts NW, Washington, DC 20005, USA

Adams, Richard — *Writer*
Benwell's, 26 Church St, Whitechurch, Hants RG28 7AR, England

Adams, Richard N — *Anthropologist*
%University of Texas, Anthropology Dept, Austin, TX 78712, USA

Adams, Robert — *Sculptor*
Rangers Hall, Great Maplestead, Halstead, Essex, England

Adams, Robert H — *Photographer*
306 Lincoln St, Longmont, CO 80501, USA

Adams, Robert M, Jr — *Anthropologist*
PO Box ZZ, Basalt, CO 81621, USA

Adams, Sam A — *Football Player*
12010 Hollystone Dr, Houston, TX 77070, USA

Adams, Scott — *Cartoonist (Dilbert)*
%Harper Business Publishers, 10 E 53rd St, New York, NY 10022, USA

Adams, Stanley T — *Korean War Army Hero (CMH)*
20454 Whistle Point Road, Bend, OR 97702, USA

Adams, Victoria — *Singer (Spice Girls)*
%Virgin Records, Kensal House, 533-79 Harrow Road, London W1O 4RH, England

Adams, William R — *Writer, Historian*
%Historic Property Assoc, PO Box 1002, St Augustine, FL 32085, USA

Adams-Sassoon, Beverly — *Model*
1923 Selby Ave, #203, Los Angeles, CA 90025, USA

Adamson, James C — *Astronaut*
%Lockheed Engineering & Science Co, 2625 Bay Area Blvd, Houston, TX 77058, USA

Adamson, John W — *Hematologist*
%New York Blood Center, 310 E 67th St, New York, NY 10021, USA

Adamson, Robert E, Jr — *Navy Admiral*
5102 Althea Dr, Annandale, VA 22003, USA

Adcock, Joseph W (Joe) — *Baseball Player*
PO Box 385, Coushatta, LA 71019, USA

Adderley, Nathaniel (Nat) — *Jazz Cornetist*
%Producers Inc, 11806 N 56th St, Tampa, FL 33617, USA

Adderly, Herbert A (Herb) — *Football Player*
8 Pelham Road, Philadelphia, PA 19119, USA

Addis, Don — *Cartoonist (Bent Offerings)*
%Creators Syndicate, 5777 W Century Blvd, #700, Los Angeles, CA 90045, USA

Ade, King Sunny — *Singer*
%Island Records, 400 Lafayette St, #500, New York, NY 10003, USA

Adel, Arthur — *Physicist*
610 N Bertrand St, Flagstaff, AZ 86001, USA

Adelman, Irma G — *Economist*
10 Rosemont Ave, Berkeley, CA 94708, USA

Adelman, Kenneth L — *Government Official*
%Int'l Contemporary Studies Institute, 4018 27th St N, Arlington, VA 22207, USA

Adelson, Mervyn L — *Television Executive*
1036 Cove Way, Beverly Hills, CA 90210, USA

Adey, Christopher — *Conductor*
137 Anson Road, Willesden Green NW2 4AH, England

Adhikary, Man Mohan — *Prime Minister, Nepal*
%Prime Minister's Office, Singhadurbar, Katmandu, Nepal

Adjani, Isabelle — *Actress*
%Association Des Amis, BP 166, 75523 Paris Cedex 11, France

Adjodhia, Jules — *Prime Minister, Suriname*
%Prime Minister's Office, Kleine Combeweg 1, Paramaribo, Suriname

Adleman, Leonard — *Computer Theorist*
%University of Southern California, Computer Math Dept, Los Angeles, CA 90089, USA

Adler, Jerry — *Actor*
%Paradigm Agency, 10100 Santa Monica Blvd, #2500, Los Angeles, CA 90067, USA

Adler, John — *Businessman*
%Adaptec, 691 S Milpitas Blvd, Milpitas, CA 95035, USA

Adler, Julius — *Biologist, Biochemist*
%University of Wisconsin, Biochemistry Dept, Madison, WI 53706, USA

Adler, Larry — *Concert Mouth Organist*
%MBA Literary Agents, 45 Fitzroy St, London W1, England

Adler, Lee — *Artist*
Lime Kiln Farm, Climax, NY 12042, USA

Adler, Lou — *Actor, Movie Director, Producer*
%Ode Sounds & Visuals, 3969 Villa Costera, Malibu, CA 90265, USA

Adler, Mortimer J — *Writer, Philosopher*
1320 N State Parkway, Chicago, IL 60610, USA

Adler, Renata — *Writer, Journalist*
PO Box 9, Danbury, CT 06813, USA

Adler, Richard — *Composer, Lyricist*
8 E 83rd St, New York, NY 10028, USA

Adni, Daniel — *Concert Pianist*
64-A Menelik Road, London NW2 3RH, England

Adolfo (Sardina) — *Fashion Designer*
%Adolfo Inc, 36 E 57th St, New York, NY 10022, USA

Adoor, Gopalakrishnan — *Movie Director*
Darsanam, Trivandrum, 695 017 Kerala, India

Adorf, Mario — *Actor*
Perlacher Str 28, 82031 Grunwald, Germany

Adrian, Barbara — *Artist*
420 E 64th St, New York, NY 10021, USA

Adriani, John — *Physician*
67 N Park Pl, New Orleans, LA 70124, USA

Adyebo, George Kosmas — *Prime Minister, Uganda*
%Prime Minister's Office, Kampala, Uganda

Aerle Taree (Taree Jones) — *Soul/Rap Artist (Arrested Development)*
%William Morris Agency, 1325 Ave of Americas, New York, NY 10019, USA

Afanasyev, Viktor M — *Cosmonaut*
%Potchta Kosmonavtov, Moskovskoi Oblasti, 141160 Syvisdny Goroduk, Russia

Affleck, Ben — *Actor*
%Paradigm Agency, 10100 Santa Monica Blvd, #2500, Los Angeles, CA 90067, USA

Afwerki, Issaias — *President, Eritrea*
%State Council, Asmara, Eritrea

Aga Khan IV, Prince Karim — *Spiritual Leader*
Aiglemont, 60270 Gouvieux, France

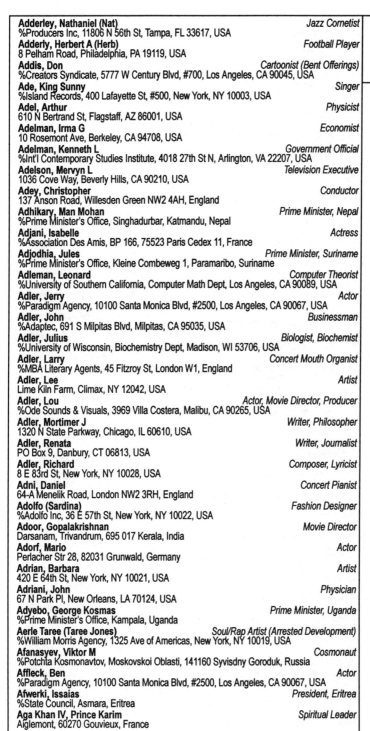

A

Adderley - Aga Khan IV

Agajanian, Benjamin (Ben) — *Football Player*
3940 E Broadway, Long Beach, CA 90803, USA

Agam, Yaacov — *Artist*
26 Rue Boulard, 75014 Paris, France

Agar, John — *Actor*
639 N Hollywood Way, Burbank, CA 91505, USA

Agase, Alexander G (Alex) — *Football Player, Coach*
1281 Pine Ridge Circle E, #C-2, Tarpon Spings, FL 34689, USA

Agassi, Andre — *Tennis Player*
8921 Andre Dr, Las Vegas, NV 89113, USA

Agee, Tommie L — *Baseball Player*
74 Candlelight Lane SW, Atlanta, GA 30331, USA

Aghayan, Ray — *Costume Designer*
431 S Fairfax Ave, #3, Los Angeles, CA 90036, USA

Agnelli, Giovanni — *Businessman*
%Fiat SpA, Corso G Marconi 10/20, 10125 Turin, Italy

Agnelli, Umberto — *Businessman*
%Fiat SpA, Corso G Marconi 10/20, 10125 Turin, Italy

Agnew, Harold M — *Physicist*
322 Punta Baja Dr, Solana Beach, CA 92075, USA

Agnew, James K — *Businessman*
%McCann Erikson Inc, 495 Lexington Ave, New York, NY 10017, USA

Agnew, M H Julian — *Art Dealer*
Egmere Farm House, Egmere near Walsingham, Norfolk, England

Agnew, Rudolph I J — *Businessman*
%Hanson PLC, 1 Grosvenor Place, London SW1, England

Agnos, Arthur C — *Mayor, San Francisco*
106 Dorchester Way, San Francisco, CA 94127, USA

Agoglia, John — *Television Executive*
%NBC Productions, NBC-TV, 30 Rockfeller Plaza, New York, NY 10112, USA

Agronsky, Martin — *Commentator*
%WUSA-TV, 4100 Wisconsin Ave NW, Washington, DC 20016, USA

Agt, Andries A M Van — *Prime Minister, Netherlands*
Europa House, 9-15 Sanbancho, Chiyodaku, Tokyo 102, Japan

Aguilera-Hellweg, Max — *Photographer*
510 W 110th St, #2-A, New York, NY 10025, USA

Aguirre, Mark — *Basketball Player, Executive*
7382 Silver Leaf Lane, West Bloomfield, MI 48322, USA

Agutter, Jenny — *Actress*
6884 Camrose Dr, Los Angeles, CA 90068, USA

Ahearn, Kevin — *Hockey Player*
174 Marlborough St, Boston, MA 02116, USA

Ahern, Bertie — *Prime Minister, Ireland*
%Prime Minister's Office, Upper Merrion St, Dublin 2, Ireland

Ahlfors, Lars V — *Mathematician*
160 Commonwealth Ave, Boston, MA 02116, USA

Ahlmann, Kaj — *Businessman*
%Employers Reinsurance Corp, 5200 Metcalf, Overland Park, KS 66202, USA

Ahmed, Khandakar M — *President, Bangladesh*
%Democratic League, 68 Jigatold, Dhaka 9, Bangladesh

Ahrends, Peter — *Architect*
%Ahrends Burton Koralek, 7 Chalcot Road, London NW1 8LH, England

Ahrens, Joseph — *Composer*
Huningerstr 26, 14195 Berlin, Germany

Ahronovitch, Yuri — *Conductor*
%Stockholm Philharmonic, Hotorget 8, Stockholm, Sweden

Ahtisaari, Martti — *President, Finland*
%Presidential Palace, Pohjoisesplandi 1, 00170 Helsinki 17, Finland

Aida, Takefumi — *Architect*
1-3-2 Okubo, Shinjukuku, Tokyo 169, Japan

Aida, Yukio — *Financier*
%Nomura Securities Co, 6-40-8 Shimo-Shakujii, Tokyo 103, Japan

Aidala, Thomas — *Architect*
387 Joost Ave, San Francisco, CA 94131, USA

Aiello, Danny — *Actor*
195 Surrey Court, Ramsey, NJ 07446, USA

Aiken, Joan D — *Writer*
Hermitage, Petworth, West Sussex GU28 OAB, England

Aiken, Michael T — *Educator*
%University of Illinois, Chancellor's Office, Champaign, IL 61801, USA

Aikman, Troy — *Football Player*
1000 Creekside Court, Irving, TX 75063, USA

Ailes, Roger E — *Publisher*
%Ailes Communications, 245 E 58th St, PH-C, New York, NY 10022, USA

Ailes, Stephen — *Government Official*
4521 Wetherill Road, Bethesda, MD 20816, USA

Aimee, Anouk — *Actress*
%Agents Associes Beaume, 201 Rue Faubourg St Honore, 75008 Paris, France

Ainge, Daniel B (Danny) — *Basketball Player, Coach*
%Phoenix Suns, 201 E Jefferson St, Phoenix, AZ 85004, USA

Aini, Mohsen Ahmed al- — *Prime Minister, Yemen*
%Yemen Arab Republic Embassy, 2600 Virginia Ave NW, #705, Washington, DC 20037, USA

Ainsleigh, H Gordon — *Distance Runner*
17119 Placer Hills Road, Meadow Vista, CA 95722, USA

Ainsworth-Land, George T — *Philosopher*
230 North St, Buffalo, NY 14201, USA

Airiana — *Circus Performer*
%Ringling Bros Barnum & Bailey Circus, 8607 Westwood Circle, Vienna, CA 22182, USA

Aishwarya Rajya Laxmi Devi Rana — *Queen, Nepal*
%Narayanhiti Royal Palace, Durbag Marg, Kathmandu, Nepal

Aitay, Victor — *Concert Violinist*
212 Oak Knoll Terrace, Highland Park, IL 60035, USA

Aitmatov, Chingiz T — *Writer*
Ulitsa Toktogula 98, #9, 720000 Biskek, Kyrgyzstan

Akalaitis, JoAnne — *Theater Director*
%Mabou Mimes, 150 1st Ave, New York, NY 10009, USA

Akashi, Yasushi — *Diplomat, Japan*
%Foreign Affairs Ministry, 2-2 Kasumigaseki, Chiyodaku, Tokyo, Japan

Akayev, Askar — *President, Kyrgyzstan*
%President's Office, Government House, 720003 Bishkek, Kyrgyzstan

Akbar, Taufik — *Astronaut, Indonesia*
Jalan Simp, Pahlawan III/24, Bandung 40124, Indonesia

Akebono (Chad Rowan) — *Sumo Wrestler*
%Azumazeki Stable, 4-6-4 Higashi Komagata, Rypgpku, Tokyo, Japan

Akers, Fred — *Football Coach*
%Purdue University, Athletic Dept, West Lafayette, IN 47907, USA

Akers, John F — *Businessman*
1 Sturges Highway, Westport, CT 06880, USA

Akers, Thomas D — *Astronaut*
%NASA, Johnson Space Center, 2101 NASA Road, Houston, TX 77058, USA

Akhmadulina, Bella — *Writer*
Chernyachovskogo Str 4, #37, 125319 Moscow, Russia

Akhmedov, Khan A — *Prime Minister, Turkmenistan*
%Council of Ministers, Vaiaku, Ashkabad, Turkmenistan

Akihito — *Emperor, Japan*
%Imperial Palace, 1-1 Chiyoda, Chiyodaku, Tokyo 100, Japan

Akins, James E — *Diplomat*
2904 Garfield Terrace, Washington, DC 20008, USA

Akins, Rhett — *Singer*
%Starstruck Entertainment, 40 Music Square W, Nashville, TN 37203, USA

Akira, Yeiri — *Businessman*
%Bridgestone Corp, 10-1-1 Kyobashi, Chuoku, Tokyo 104, Japan

Akiyama, Kazuyoshi — *Conductor*
%Columbia Artists Mgmt Inc, 165 W 57th St, New York, NY 10019, USA

Akiyama, Toyohiro — *Astronaut, Journalist*
%Tokyo Broadcasting Systems, 3-6-5 Akasaka, Minatoku, Tokyo 107, Japan

Akiyoshi, Toshiko — *Jazz Pianist, Composer, Bandleader*
38 W 94th St, New York, NY 10025, USA

Aksenov, Vladimir V — *Cosmonaut*
Astrakhansky Per 5, Kv 100, 129010 Moscow, Russia

Aksyonov, Vassily P — *Writer*
%George Mason University, English Dept, Fairfax, VA 22030, USA

Aladjem, Silvio — *Obstetrician, Gynecologist*
%Bronson Hospital, 252 E Lovell St, Kalamazoo, MI 49007, USA

Alaia, Azzeddine — *Fashion Designer*
18 Rue de la Verrerie, 75008 Paris, France

A

Aiken - Alaia

Alain, Marie-Claire — *Concert Organist*
1 Ave Jean-Jaures, 78580 Maule, France

Alan, Buddy — *Singer*
600 E Gilbert Dr, Tempe, AZ 85281, USA

Alarcon, Fabian — *President, Ecuador*
%President's Office, Gobierno Palacio, Garcia Moreno 1043, Quito, Ecuador

Alba, Jessica — *Actress*
%Bobby Ball Agency, 4342 Lankershim Blvd, Universal City, CA 91602, USA

Albanese, Licia — *Opera Singer*
Nathan Hale Dr, Wilson Point, South Norwalk, CT 06854, USA

Albeck, Stan — *Basketball Coach*
%Atlanta Hawks, 1 CNN Center, South Tower, Atlanta, GA 30303, USA

Albee, Arden L — *Geologist*
2040 Midlothian Dr, Altadena, CA 91001, USA

Albee, Edward F — *Writer*
14 Harrison St, New York, NY 10013, USA

Alberghetti, Anna Maria — *Singer, Actress*
10333 Chrysanthemum Lane, Los Angeles, CA 90077, USA

Albers, Hans — *Businessman*
%BASF AG, Carl-Bosch-Str 38, 78351 Ludwigshafen, Germany

Albert — *Prince, Monaco*
%Palais de Monaco, Boite Postale 518, 98015 Monacode Cedex, Monaco

Albert II — *King, Belgium*
%Koninklijk Palais, Rue de Brederode, 1000 Brussels, Belgium

Albert, Calvin — *Sculptor*
6525 Brandywine Dr S, Margate, FL 33063, USA

Albert, Carl B — *Representative, OK; Speaker*
1831 Word Road, McAlester, OK 74501, USA

Albert, Eddie — *Actor*
719 Amalfi Dr, Pacific Palisades, CA 90272, USA

Albert, Edward — *Actor*
Hawks Ranch, 27320 Winding Way, Malibu, CA 90265, USA

Albert, Frank C (Frankie) — *Football Player*
1 Stanford Dr, Rancho Mirage, CA 92270, USA

Albert, Ken — *Sportscaster*
%Fox TV, Sports Dept, 205 E 67th St, New York, NY 10021, USA

Alberts, Trev — *Football Player*
2709 Edgewood Dr, Cedar Falls, ID 50613, USA

Alberty, Robert A — *Chemist*
7 Old Dee Road, Cambridge, MA 02138, USA

Albicocco, Jean-Gabriel — *Movie Director*
%L'Alpicella, 171 Ave Frederic Mistral, 06250 Mougains, France

Albino, Judith E N — *Educator*
%University of Colorado, President's Office, Boulder, CO 80309, USA

Albita (Rodriguez) — *Singer*
%William Morris Agency, 1325 Ave of Americas, New York, NY 10019, USA

Albrecht, Gerd — *Conductor*
%Mariedi Anders Mgmt, 535 El Camino Del Mar, San Francisco, CA 94121, USA

Albrecht, Ronald F — *Anestheologist*
1020 Chestnut Ave, Wilmette, IL 60091, USA

Albright (Zsissly), Malvin Marr — *Artist*
1500 N Lake Shore Dr, Chicago, IL 60610, USA

Albright, Jack L — *Animal Scientist*
188 Blueberry Lane, West Lafayette, IN 47906, USA

Albright, Lola — *Actress*
PO Box 250070, Glendale, CA 91225, USA

Albright, Madeleine K — *Secretary, State*
%US State Department, 2201 "C" St NW, Washington, DC 20520, USA

Albright, Tenley E — *Figure Skater*
186 Windswept Way, Osterville, MA 02655, USA

Albuquerque, Lita — *Artist*
305 Boyd St, Los Angeles, CA 90013, USA

Albus, Jim — *Golfer*
8080 N Central Expressway, #1570, Dallas, TX 75206, USA

Alcott, Amy S — *Golfer*
1411 W 190th St, #500, Gardena, CA 90248, USA

Alda, Alan — *Actor*
%Martin Bregman Productions, 641 Lexington Ave, #1400, New York, NY 10022, USA

Alden, Ginger   *Model, Actress, Singer*
6554 Whitetail Lane, Memphis, TN 38115, USA
Alden, Norman   *Actor*
106 N Croft Ave, Los Angeles, CA 90048, USA
Alder, Berni J   *Theoretical Physicist*
%Lawrence Radiation Laboratory, PO Box 808, Livermore, CA 94551, USA
Alderman, Darrell   *Drag Racing Driver*
%D A Construction Co, 8145 Flemingsburg Road, Morehead, KY 40351, USA
Aldiss, Brian W   *Writer*
Woodlands, Foxcombe Road, Boars Hill, Oxford OX1 5DL, England
Aldred, Sophie   *Actress*
%McKenna & Grantham, 1-B Montagu Mews North, London W1H 1AJ, England
Aldredge, Theoni V   *Costume Designer*
425 Lafayette St, New York, NY 10003, USA
Aldridge, Donald O   *Air Force General*
%Aldridge Assoc, 159 Orange Blossom Circle, Folsom, CA 95630, USA
Aldridge, Edward C (Pete), Jr   *Government Official*
%Aerospace Corp, 2350 E El Segundo, El Segundo, CA 90245, USA
Aldrin, Edwin E (Buzz), Jr   *Astronaut*
%Starcraft Enterprises, 233 Emerald Bay, Laguna Beach, CA 92651, USA
Aleandro, Norma   *Actress*
Blanco Encalada 1150, 1428 Buenos Aires, Argentina
Alechinsky, Pierre   *Artist*
2 Bis Rue Henri Barbusse, 78380 Bougival, France
Alegre, Norberto Costa   *Prime Minister, Sao Tome & Principe*
%Prime Minister's Office, CP 38, Sao Tome, Sao Tome & Principe
Alekseev, Dimitri   *Concert Pianist*
%IMG Artists, 3 Burlington Lane, Chiswick, London W4 2TH, England
Aleksiy   *Religious Leader*
%Moscow Patriarchy, Chisty Per 5, Moscow, Russia
Aleman, Arnaldo   *President, Nicaragua*
%President's Office, Casa de Gobierno, Apartado 2398, Manuaga, Nicaragua
Alesana, Tofilau Eti   *Prime Minister, Western Samoa*
%Prime Minister's Office, PO Box 193, Apia, Western Samoa
Alesi, Jean   *Auto Racing Driver*
%Scuderia Ferrari, Via Ascari 55/57, 41053 Maranello (MO), Italy
Aletter, Frank   *Actor*
5430 Corbin Ave, Tarzana, CA 91356, USA
Alexander Karadjordjevic   *Crown Prince, Yugoslavia*
36 Park Lane, London W1Y 3LE, England
Alexander, A Lamar   *Secretary, Education; Governor, TN*
%Baker Worthington Crossley, 511 Union St, Nashville, TN 37219, USA
Alexander, Brooke   *Actress, Model*
%Abrams Artists, 9200 Sunset Blvd, #625, Los Angeles, CA 90069, USA
Alexander, Christopher   *Architect*
%University of California, Environmental Design College, Los Angeles, CA 90024, USA
Alexander, Clifford L   *Government Official*
%Alexander Assoc, 400 "C" St NE, Washington, DC 20002, USA
Alexander, Corey   *Basketball Player*
440 Alpha St, Waynesboro, VA 22980, USA
Alexander, Donald C   *Government Official*
2801 New Mexico Ave NW, Washington, DC 20007, USA
Alexander, Erika   *Actress*
%Warner Bros Ranch, 3701 Oak St, Burbank, CA 91505, USA
Alexander, Jane   *Actress, Government Official*
%William Morris Agency, 1350 Ave of Americas, New York, NY, USA
Alexander, Jason   *Actor*
6230 Wilshire Blvd, #A-103, Los Angeles, CA 90048, USA
Alexander, John   *Artist*
PO Box 600, Amagansett, NY 11930, USA
Alexander, Kenneth L   *Editorial Cartoonist*
1182 Glen Road, Lafayette, CA 94549, USA
Alexander, Khandi   *Actress*
%Agency For Performing Arts, 9200 Sunset Blvd, #900, Los Angeles, CA 90069, USA
Alexander, Leslie   *Basketball Executive*
%Houston Rockets, Summit, Greenway Plaza, #10, Houston, TX 77046, USA
Alexander, Monty   *Jazz Pianist*
%Abby Hoffer, 223 1/2 E 48th St, New York, NY 10017, USA

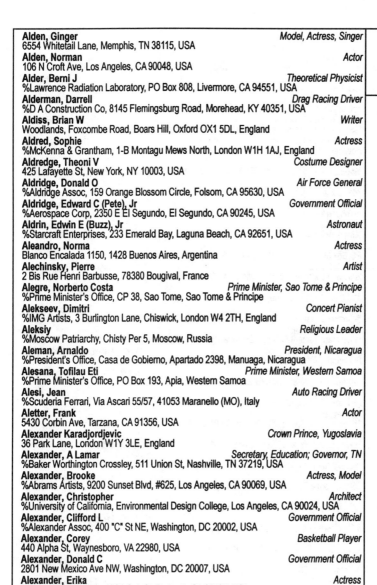

A

Alden - Alexander

Alexander, Norman E — *Businessman*
%Sequa Corp, 200 Park Ave, New York, NY 10166, USA

Alexander, R B — *Publisher*
%Business Week Magazine, 1221 Ave of Americas, New York, NY 10020, USA

Alexander, Robert S — *Financier*
%National Westminster Bank, 41 Lothbury, London EC2P 2BP, England

Alexander, Shana — *Journalist*
156 5th St, #617, New York, NY 10010, USA

Alexandrov, Alexander — *Cosmonaut, Bulgaria*
%Space Research Institute, 6 Moskovska St, BG-1000 Sofia, Bulgaria

Alexandrov, Alexander P — *Cosmonaut*
Hovanskaya Ul 3, #27, 129515 Moscow, Russia

Alexis, Kim — *Model*
%Manzella Personal Mgmt, 345 N Maple Dr, #185, Beverly Hills, CA 90210, USA

Alexrod, Albert — *Fencer*
701 Ardsley Road, Scarsdale, NY 10583, USA

Alfieri, Janet — *Cartoonist (Suburban Cowgirls)*
%Tribune Media Services, 435 N Michigan Ave, #1500, Chicago, IL 60611, USA

Alfiero, Sal H — *Businessman*
%Mark IV Industries, 501 John James Audubon Parkway, Amherst, NY 14228, USA

Alfonso, Kristian — *Actress*
PO Box 557, Brockton, MA 02403, USA

Alford, Steve — *Basketball Player, Coach*
2049 S Woodbury Ave, Springfield, MO 65809, USA

Alford, William — *Writer*
31 Athens St, Cambridge, MA 02138, USA

Alfredsson, Daniel — *Hockey Player*
%Ottawa Senators, 1000 Prom Palladium Dr, Kanata ON K2V 1A4, Canada

Alfredsson, Helen — *Golfer*
%Int'l Management Group, 1 Erieview Plaza, #1300, Cleveland, OH 44114, USA

Ali Haider Khan Bangash — *WW II Pakistan Army Hero (VC)*
PO Hangu, Tehsil Hangu, Distt Kohat Mohallah, Khan Bari, Pakistan

Ali, Kamal Hassan — *Prime Minister, Egypt; Army General*
110 Amar Ibn Yassar, Misr El Gadida, Egypt

Ali, Muhammad — *Boxer*
Ali Farm, PO Box 187, Berrien Springs, MI 49103, USA

Ali, Tatyana — *Actress*
16350 Ventura Blvd, #367, Encino, CA 91436, USA

Alice, Mary — *Actress*
%Abrams Artists, 9200 Sunset Blvd, #625, Los Angeles, CA 90069, USA

Alimo, Mark — *Actor*
%Craig Agency, 8485 Melrose Place, #E, Los Angeles, CA 90069, USA

Alioto, Joseph L — *Attorney, Mayor*
650 California St, #2500, San Francisco, CA 94108, USA

Alisha — *Singer*
%Brothers Mgmt, 141 Dunbar Ave, Fords, NJ 08863, USA

Aliyev, Geidar A — *President, Azerbaijan; Army General*
%President's Office, Parliament House, 370066 Baku, Azerbaijan

Allain, William A — *Governor, MS*
401 Capitol St, Jackson, MS 39201, USA

Allaire, Paul A — *Businessman*
%Xerox Corp, 800 Long Ridge Road, Stamford, CT 06902, USA

Allais, Maurice — *Nobel Economics Laureate*
15 Rue des Gate-Ceps, 92210 Saint Cloud, France

Allam, Mark W — *Veterinarian*
%Strath Haven, #809, Swathmore, PA 19081, USA

Allan, Jed — *Actor*
PO Box 5302, Blue Jay, CA 92317, USA

Allan, John D — *Businessman*
%Stelco, Toronto-Dominion Center, Toronto ON M5K 1J4, Canada

Allan, William — *Artist*
327 Melrose, Mill Valley, CA 94941, USA

Allard, Linda M — *Fashion Designer*
%Ellen Tracy Corp, 575 7th Ave, New York, NY 10018, USA

Allbritton, Joe L — *Financier*
%Perpetual Corp, 800 17th St NW, Washington, DC 20006, USA

Allen, Andrew M — *Astronaut*
%NASA, Johnson Space Center, 2101 NASA Road, Houston, TX 77058, USA

Allen, Betty *Classical, Opera Singer*
%Harlem School of Arts, 645 St Nicholas Ave, New York, NY 10030, USA
Allen, Bruce *Auto Racing Driver*
%Reger-Morrison Racing Engines, 1120 Enterprise Place, Arlington, TX 76001, USA
Allen, Chad *Actor*
6489 Cavalleri Road, #204, Malibu, CA 90265, USA
Allen, Corey *Actor, Director*
8642 Hollywood Blvd, Los Angeles, CA 90069, USA
Allen, Darryl F *Businessman*
%Trinova Corp, 3000 Strayer, Maumee, OH 43537, USA
Allen, Debbie *Singer, Dancer, Actress*
607 Marguerita Ave, Santa Monica, CA 90402, USA
Allen, Duane D *Singer (Oak Ridge Boys)*
329 Rockland Road, Hendersonville, TN 37075, USA
Allen, George F *Governor, VA*
%Governor's Offfice, State Capitol Building, Richmond, VA 23219, USA
Allen, Geri *Jazz Pianist, Composer*
%Jordan East, 9751 Gregory Way, Beverly Hills, CA 90212, USA
Allen, Herbert A *Financier*
%Allen & Co, 711 5th Ave, New York, NY 10022, USA
Allen, J Presson *Writer, Producer*
%Lewis Allen Productions, 1501 Broadway, #1614, New York, NY 10036, USA
Allen, Joan *Actress*
%International Creative Mgmt, 8942 Wilshire Blvd, Beverly Hills, CA 90211, USA
Allen, Joseph P, IV *Astronaut*
%Space Industries International, 800 Connecticut Ave NW, Washington, DC 20006, USA
Allen, Karen *Actress*
PO Box 237, Monterey, MA 01245, USA
Allen, Krista *Actress*
%Stone Manners, 8091 Selma Ave, Los Angeles, CA 90046, USA
Allen, Larry *Football Player*
2001 Piner Road, Santa Rosa, CA 95403, USA
Allen, Lew, Jr *Air Force General*
%Draper Laboratory, 555 Technology Square, Cambridge, MA 02139, USA
Allen, Marcus *Football Player*
433 Ward Parkway, #29, Kansas City, MO 64112, USA
Allen, Marty *Comedian*
8704 Carlitas Joy Court, Las Vegas, NV 89117, USA
Allen, Maryon P *Senator, AL*
3215 Cliff Road, Birmingham, AL 35205, USA
Allen, Nancy *Actress*
8154 Mulholland Terrace, Los Angeles, CA 90046, USA
Allen, Paul G *Co-Developer (PC Language)*
%Asymetrix Corp, 110 110th Ave NE, #530, Bellevue, WA 98004, USA
Allen, Ray *Basketball Player*
2095 Hillside Dr, Storrs, CT 06269, USA
Allen, Rex *Actor, Singer*
3061 N Hill Farm Dr, Tucson, AZ 85712, USA
Allen, Rex, Jr *Singer*
128 Pine Oak Dr, Hendersonville, TN 37075, USA
Allen, Richard V *Government Official*
905 16th St NW, Washington, DC 20006, USA
Allen, Robert E *Businessman*
%AT&T Co, 295 N Maple Ave, Basking Ridge, NJ 07920, USA
Allen, Scott *Figure Skater*
378 N Woodland St, Englewood, NJ 07631, USA
Allen, Sian Barbara *Actress*
1622 Sierra Bonita Ave, Los Angeles, CA 90046, USA
Allen, Steve *Comedian, Writer, Composer*
16185 Woodvale Road, Encino, CA 91436, USA
Allen, Terry *Football Player*
PO Box 8296, Columbia, SC 29202, USA
Allen, Thomas *Opera Singer*
%Lies Askonas Ltd, 186 Drury Lane, London WC2B 5RY, England
Allen, Tim *Actor*
1122 S Robertson Blvd, #15, Los Angeles, CA 90035, USA
Allen, W Wayne *Businessman*
%Phillips Petroleum, Phillips Bldg, 4th & Keeler Sts, Bartlesville, OK 74004, USA

Allen, Willard M — *Physician*
211 Key Highway, Baltimore, MD 21230, USA

Allen, William — *Editor*
%National Geographic Magazine, 17th & "M" NW, Washington, DC 20036, USA

Allen, Woody — *Actor, Comedian, Director*
930 5th Ave, New York, NY 10021, USA

Allende, Fernando — *Actor*
%William Morris Agency, 151 S El Camino Dr, Beverly Hills, CA 90212, USA

Allende, Isabel — *Writer*
15 Nightingale Lane, San Rafael, CA 94901, USA

Aller, Lawrence H — *Astronomer*
18118 W Kingsport Dr, Malibu, CA 90265, USA

Alley, Kirstie — *Actress*
%Wolf/Kasteller, 132 S Rodeo Dr, #300, Beverly Hills, CA 90212, USA

Alley, L Eugene (Gene) — *Baseball Player*
10236 Steuben Dr, Glen Allen, VA 23060, USA

Allfrey, Vincent G — *Biochemist*
24 Winthrop Court, Tenafly, NJ 07670, USA

Allimadi, E Otema — *Prime Minister, Uganda*
PO Box Gulu, Gulu District, Uganda

Allison, Dorothy — *Writer*
%E P Dutton Co, 375 Hudson St, New York, NY 10014, USA

Allison, Glenn — *Bowler*
1844 S Haster St, #138, Anaheim, CA 92802, USA

Allison, Mose J, Jr — *Jazz Pianist, Composer, Singer*
34 Dogwood Dr, Smithtown, NY 11787, USA

Allison, Robert J, Jr — *Businessman*
%Anadarko Petroleum, 17001 Northchase Dr, Houston, TX 77060, USA

Allison, Stacy — *Mountaineer*
7003 SE Reed College Place, Portland, OR 97202, USA

Allison, Wick — *Publisher*
4340 Versailles Ave, Dallas, TX 75205, USA

Alliss, Peter — *Sportscaster*
%Int'l Management Group, 1 Erieview Plaza, #1300, Cleveland, OH 44114, USA

Allman, Greg — *Singer, Songwriter*
%Allman Brothers Band Inc, 18 Tamworth Road, Waban, MA 02168, USA

Allott, Gordon L — *Senator, CO*
1764 Mesa Ridge Lane, Castle Rock, CO 80104, USA

Allouache, Merzak — *Movie Director*
Cite des Asphodeles, Bt D-15, 183 Ben Aknoun, Algiers, Algeria

Allred, Gloria R — *Attorney*
6300 Wilshire Blvd, #15, Los Angeles, CA 90048, USA

Allyson, June — *Actress*
1651 Foothill Road, Ojai, CA 93023, USA

Almen, Lowell G — *Religious Leader*
%Evangelical Lutheran Church, 8765 W Higgins Road, Chicago, IL 60631, USA

Almodovar, Pedro — *Movie Director*
El Deseo SA, Ruiz Perello 25, 28028 Madrid, Spain

Almond, Lincoln C — *Governor, RI*
%Governor's Office, 222 State House, Providence, RI 02903, USA

Almond, Marc — *Singer*
%Some Bizarre Agency, 166 New Cavendish St, London W1M 7FJ, England

Alois — *Hereditary-Prince, Liechtenstein*
%Schloss Vaduz, 9490 Vaduz, Liechtenstein

Alomar, Roberto V — *Baseball Player*
Urb Monserrate B-56, Box 367, Salinas, PR 00751, USA

Alomar, Santos C (Sandy), Jr — *Baseball Player*
PO Box 367, Salinas, PR 00751, USA

Alonso, Alicia — *Ballerina*
%Cuban National Ballet, Havana, Cuba

Alonso, Maria Conchita — *Actress, Singer*
PO Box 537, Beverly Hills, CA 90213, USA

Alonzo, John A — *Cinematographer*
310 Avondale Ave, Los Angeles, CA 90049, USA

Alou, Felipe R — *Baseball Player, Manager*
7263 Davit Circle, Lake Worth, FL 33467, USA

Alou, Moises — *Baseball Player*
975 Washington, #4-E, New York, NY 10456, USA

Alpert, Herb — *Musician*
31930 Pacific Coast Highway, Malibu, CA 90265, USA
Alphand, Luc — *Skier*
Chalet Le Balme, Chantemerie, 05330 Sierre Chavalier, France
Alpher, Ralph A — *Physicist*
2159 Orchard Park Dr, Niskayama, NY 12309, USA
Alport of Colchester, Cuthbert J M — *Government Official, England*
Cross House, Layer de la Haye, Colchester, Essex, England
Alsgaard, Thomas — *Cross Country Skier*
Lokkaveien 21, 1911 Flateby, Norway
Alston, Barbara — *Singer (The Crystals)*
%Mars Talent, 168 Orchid Dr, Pearl River, NY 10965, USA
Alston, Shirley — *Singer (The Shirelles)*
%Brothers Mgmt, 141 Dunbar Ave, Fords, NJ 08863, USA
Alt, Carol — *Model*
%Elite Model Mgmt, 111 E 22nd St, #200, New York, NY 10010, USA
Alt, John — *Football Player*
1 Scotch Pine Road, Saint Paul, MN 55127, USA
Altenberg, Wolfgang — *Army General, Germany*
Birkenhof 44, 28759 Brenen-St Magnus, Germany
Alter, Hobie — *Surfboard, Boat Designer*
PO Box 1008, Oceanside, CA 92051, USA
Altman, Jeff — *Actor*
5065 Calvin Ave, Tarzana, CA 91356, USA
Altman, Robert B — *Movie Director, Producer*
%Sandcastle 5 Productions, 502 Park Ave, #15-G, New York, NY 10022, USA
Altman, Scott D — *Astronaut*
15911 Manor Square Dr, Houston, TX 77062, USA
Altman, Sidney — *Nobel Chemistry Laureate*
%Yale University, Biology Dept, PO Box 6666, New Haven, CT 06520, USA
Altmeyer, Jeannine — *Opera Singer*
%Metropolitan Opera Assn, Lincoln Center Plaza, New York, NY 10023, USA
Altobelli, Joseph (Joe) — *Baseball Player*
10 Stonewell Dr, #3, Rochester, NY 14615, USA
Alvarado, Natividad (Naty) — *Handball Player*
%Equitable of Iowa, 2700 N Main, Santa Ana, CA 92705, USA
Alvarado, Trini — *Actress*
233 Park Ave S, #1000, New York, NY 10003, USA
Alvarez, Barry — *Football Coach*
%University of Wisconsin, Athletic Dept, Madison, WI 53711, USA
Alvary, Lorenzo — *Opera Singer*
205 W 57th St, New York, NY 10019, USA
Alvord, Joel B — *Businessman*
%Fleet Financial Group, 50 Kennedy Plaza, Providence, RI 02903, USA
Alworth, Lance D — *Football Player*
%Del Mar Corporate Center, 990 Highland Dr, #300, Solana Beach, CA 92075, USA
Amador, Jorge — *Writer*
Rua Alagoinhas 33, Rio Vermelho-Salvador, Bahia, Brazil
Amalfitano, J Joseph (Joe) — *Baseball Player*
265 Bowstring Dr, Sedona, AZ 86336, USA
Amandes, Tom — *Actor*
%Writers & Artists, 924 Westwood Blvd, #900, Los Angeles, CA 90024, USA
Amanpour, Christiane — *News Correspondent*
%Cable News Int'l, News Dept, 25 Rue de Ponthieu, 75008 Paris, France
Amara, Lucine — *Opera Singer*
260 West End Ave, #7-A, New York, NY 10023, USA
Amaral, Richard L (Rich) — *Baseball Player*
3132 Country Club Dr, Costa Mesa, CA 92626, USA
Amateau, Rodney — *Movie Director*
133 1/2 S Linden Dr, Beverly Hills, CA 90212, USA
Amato, Giuliano — *Prime Minister, Italy*
%Carmera dei Deputati, Piazza di Montecitorio, 00186 Rome, Italy
Amato, Joe — *Auto Racing Driver*
%Amato Racing, 44 Tunkhannuck Ave, Exter, PA 18643, USA
Amaya, Armando — *Sculptor*
Lopex 137, Depto 1, Mexico City 06070 CP, Mexico
Ambartsumian, Victor A — *Astrophysicist*
%Armenian Academy of Sciences, 24 Marshal Bagramian Ave, Erevan, Armenia

A

Alpert - Ambartsumian

Ambasz, Emilio *Architect*
%Emilio Ambasz Design Group, 636 Broadway, #1100, New York, NY 10012, USA

Amber *Singer*
%Famous Artists Agency, 1700 Broadway, #500, New York, NY 10019, USA

Ambler, Eric *Writer*
14 Bryanston Square, London W1H 7FF, England

Ambuehl, Cindy *Actress*
%Paul Kohner, 9300 Wilshire Blvd, #555, Beverly Hills, CA 90212, USA

Amdahl, Gene M *Computer Engineer, Businessman*
%Andor International, 17420 High St, Los Gatos, CA 95030, USA

Ameling, Elly *Opera Singer*
%Sheldon Soffer Mgmt, 130 W 56th St, New York, NY 10019, USA

Amend, Bill *Cartoonist (Fox Trot)*
%Universal Press Syndicate, 4520 Main St, Kansas City, KS 64111, USA

Amerman, John W *Businessman*
%Mattel Inc, 333 Continental Blvd, El Segundo, CA 90245, USA

Amery of Lustleigh, H Julian *Government Official, England*
112 Eaton Square, London SW1W 9AF, England

Ames, Bruce N *Biochemist*
1324 Spruce St, Berkeley, CA 94709, USA

Ames, Ed *Singer, Actor*
1457 Claridge Dr, Beverly Hills, CA 90210, USA

Ames, Frank Anthony *Concert Percussionist*
1235 Potamac St NW, Washington, DC 20007, USA

Ames, Rachel *Actress*
%Atkins Assoc, 303 S Crescent Heights Blvd, Los Angeles, CA 90048, USA

Amick, Madchen *Actress*
PO Box 48107, Los Angeles, CA 90048, USA

Amies, Hardy *Fashion Designer*
%Hardy Amies Ltd, 14 Savile Row, London SW1, England

Amin Dada, Idi *President, Uganda; Army Field Marshal*
PO Box 8948, Jidda 214942, Saudi Arabia

Amis, Martin *Writer, Journalist*
%Peters Fraser Dunlop, Chelsea Harbour, Lots Rd, London SW10 0XF, England

Amis, Suzy *Actress, Model*
%International Creative Mgmt, 8942 Wilshire Blvd, Beverly Hills, CA 90211, USA

Amitri, Del *Singer*
%Progressive Global Agency, PO Box 128288, Nashville, TN 37212, USA

Amling, Warren E *Football Player*
541 Eaton St, London, OH 43140, USA

Ammaccapane, Danielle *Golfer*
13214 N 13th St, Phoenix, AZ 85022, USA

Ammons, A R *Writer*
423 Cayuga Heights Road, Ithaca, NY 14850, USA

Amonte, Tony *Hockey Player*
142 Kilby St, Hingham, MA 02043, USA

Amory, Cleveland *Writer*
%Fund for the Animals, 200 W 57th St, New York, NY 10019, USA

Amos, John *Actor*
%Step and 1/2 Productions, PO Box 587, Califon, NJ 07830, USA

Amos, John B *Businessman*
%AFLAC Inc, AFLAC Center, 1932 Wynnton Road, Columbus, GA 31999, USA

Amos, Paul S *Financier*
%AFLAC Inc, AFLAC Center, 1932 Wynnton Road, Columbus, GA 31999, USA

Amos, Tori *Singer, Songwriter*
%Creative Artists Agency, 9830 Wilshire Blvd, Beverly Hills, CA 90212, USA

Amos, Wally (Famous) *Businessman*
%Rosica Mulhern Assoc, 627 Grove St, Ridgewood, NJ 07450, USA

Amram, David W, III *Jazz, Classical Composer, Conductor*
Peekskill Hollow Farm, Peekskill Hollow Road, Putnam Valley, NY 10579, USA

Amte, Baba *Religious Leader*
Anandwan 442914, Via Warora, Dist Chandrapur, Maharashtra, India

Ana-Alicia *Actress*
1148 4th St, #206, Santa Monica, CA 90403, USA

Anand Panyarachun *Prime Minister, Thailand*
Government House, Thanon Nakhon Pathom Road, Bangkok 10300, Thailand

Ananiashvili, Nina *Ballerina*
119270 Frunzenskaya Nab 46, #79, Moscow, Russia

Anathan, Mone, III — *Businessman*
%Filene's Basement Corp, 40 Walnut St, Wellesley, MA 02181, USA

Anaya, Toney — *Governor, NM*
%MALDEF, 634 S Spring, Los Angeles, CA 90014, USA

Anchia, Juan-Ruiz — *Cinematographer*
%Sanford-Beckett-Skouras, 1015 Gayley Ave, Los Angeles, CA 90024, USA

Anders, William A — *Astronaut, Air Force General*
%Apogee Group, PO Box 1630, Eastsound, WA 98245, USA

Andersen Watts, Teresa — *Sychronized Swimmer*
2582 Marsha Way, San Jose, CA 95125, USA

Andersen, Anthony L — *Businessman*
%H B Fuller Co, 2400 Energy Park Dr, St Paul, MN 55108, USA

Andersen, Elmer L — *Governor, MN; Businessman*
1483 Bussard Court, Arden Hills, MN 55112, USA

Andersen, Eric — *Singer, Songwriter*
%AGF Entertainment, 30 W 21st St, #700, New York, NY 10010, USA

Andersen, Greta — *Channel Swimmer*
19332 Brooktrail Lane, Huntington Beach, CA 92648, USA

Andersen, Hjalmar — *Speed Skater*
%Velferden for Handelsflaten, Trondheimsvn 2, 0560 Oslo 5, Norway

Andersen, John — *Publisher*
%Chicago Sun-Times, 401 N Wabash, Chicago, IL 60611, USA

Andersen, Ladell — *Basketball Coach*
3695 Mulberry Dr, St George, UT 84790, USA

Andersen, Linda — *Yachtswoman*
Aroysund, 3135 Torod, Norway

Andersen, Mogens — *Artist*
Strandagervej 28, 2900 Hellerup, Copenhagen, Denmark

Andersen, Morton — *Football Player*
5335 Pine Circle, Cumming, GA 30041, USA

Andersen, Reidar — *Ski Jumper*
%National Ski Hall of Fame, PO Box 191, Ishpeming, MI 49849, USA

Anderson Lee, Pamela — *Actress, Model*
31341 Mulholland Highway, Malibu, CA 90265, USA

Anderson, Barbara — *Actress*
PO Box 10118, Santa Fe, NM 87504, USA

Anderson, Beaufort T — *WW II Army Hero (CMH)*
22105 Ranchito Dr, Salinas, CA 93908, USA

Anderson, Beiron — *Model*
%Nina Blanchard, 957 N Cole Ave, Los Angeles, CA 90038, USA

Anderson, Bill — *Singer, Guitarist, Songwriter*
%Bill Anderson Enterprises, PO Box 888, Hermitage, TN 37076, USA

Anderson, Brad — *Drag Racing Driver*
%Brad Anderson Enterprises, 2356 1st Ave, La Verne, CA 91750, USA

Anderson, Bradley J (Brad) — *Cartoonist (Marmaduke)*
13022 Wood Harbour Dr, Montgomery, TX 77356, USA

Anderson, Brett — *Singer (Suede)*
PO Box 3431, London N1 7LW, England

Anderson, Daryl — *Actor*
%House of Representatives, 400 S Beverly Dr, #101, Beverly Hills, CA 90212, USA

Anderson, David P (Dave) — *Sportswriter*
8 Inness Road, Tenafly, NJ 07670, USA

Anderson, Derek — *Basketball Player*
%Cleveland Cavaliers, 2923 Statesboro Road, Richfield, OH 44286, USA

Anderson, Dick — *Football Player*
111 S St Joseph St, South Bend, IN 46601, USA

Anderson, Don L — *Geophysicist*
%California Institute of Technology, Geophysics Dept, Pasadena, CA 91125, USA

Anderson, Donny — *Football Player*
4516 Lovers Lane, #133, Dallas, TX 75225, USA

Anderson, Duwayne M — *Polar Scientist*
10240 NE 12th St, D-308, Bellevue, WA 98004, USA

Anderson, Edgar R (Andy), Jr — *Air Force General, Surgeon*
Surgeon General, HqUSAF, 170 Luke Ave, Bolling Air Force Base, DC 20332, USA

Anderson, Edward G (Ed), III — *Army General*
Commanding General, Space/Strategic Defense, Arlington, VA 22215, USA

Anderson, Erika — *Actress, Model*
%Artists Agency, 10000 Santa Monica Blvd, #305, Los Angeles, CA 90067, USA

A

Anathan - Anderson

Anderson - Anderson

Anderson, Ernestine I *Singer*
%Thomas Cassidy, 0366 Horseshoe Dr, Basalt, CO 81621, USA

Anderson, Gary L *Marksman*
%National Rifle Assn, 11250 Waples Mill Road, Fairfax, VA 22030, USA

Anderson, George L (Sparky) *Baseball Manager*
PO Box 6415, Thousand Oaks, CA 91359, USA

Anderson, Gerry *Television Director, Puppeteer*
%Gerry Anderson Magazine, 332 Lytham Road, Blackpool FY4 1DW, England

Anderson, Gillian *Actress*
%William Morris Agency, 151 S El Camino Dr, Beverly Hills, CA 90212, USA

Anderson, Greg *Basketball Player*
2525 Walnut Grove Court, Pearland, TX 77584, USA

Anderson, Harry *Actor*
422 292nd Ave NE, Fall City, WA 98024, USA

Anderson, Ian *Singer, Flutist (Jethro Tull)*
%Wooley, Maisson Ridge, 2 Wansdown Place, Fulham, London SW6, England

Anderson, Jack N *Columnist*
1200 Eton Court NW, Washington, DC 20007, USA

Anderson, James F *Religious Leader*
12001 Cottage Creek Court, Richmond, VA 23233, USA

Anderson, James G *Atmospheric Chemist*
%Harvard University, Earth-Planetary Physics Center, Cambridge, MA 02138, USA

Anderson, James W *Endocrinologist*
%University of Kentucky, Medical Center, Endocrinology Dept, Lexington, KY 40506, USA

Anderson, James W, III *Songwriter*
PO Box 888, Hermitage, TN 37076, USA

Anderson, John *Singer, Songwriter*
%Bobby Roberts Co, 909 Meadowlark Lane, Hendersonville, TN 37072, USA

Anderson, John B *Representative, Presidential Candidate*
%Nova University, Study of Law Center, Fort Lauderdale, FL 33314, USA

Anderson, John E *Attorney*
%Kindel & Anderson, 555 S Flower St, #2601, Los Angeles, CA 90071, USA

Anderson, John, Jr *Governor, KS*
16609 W 133rd, Olathe, KS 66062, USA

Anderson, Jon *Singer (Yes)*
%Sun Artists, 9 Hillgate St, London W8 7SP, England

Anderson, June *Opera Singer*
%Columbia Artists Mgmt Inc, 165 W 57th St, New York, NY 10019, USA

Anderson, Kenneth A (Kenny) *Football Player, Coach*
3 Cambridge Dr, Fort Mitchell, KY 41017, USA

Anderson, Kenny *Basketball Player*
270 N Canon Dr, #1289, Beverly Hills, CA 90210, USA

Anderson, Laurie *Performance Artist*
%Original Artists, 45 E 9th St, New York, NY 10003, USA

Anderson, Loni *Actress*
3355 Clarendon Road, Beverly Hills, CA 90210, USA

Anderson, Louie *Comedian, Actor*
109 N Sycamore Ave, Los Angeles, CA 90036, USA

Anderson, Lynn *Singer*
514 Fairlane Dr, Nashville, TN 37211, USA

Anderson, Lynn L *Financier*
%Frank Russell Trust, PO Box 1454, Tacoma, WA 98401, USA

Anderson, Melissa Sue *Actress*
1558 Will Geer Road, Topanga Canyon, CA 90290, USA

Anderson, Melody *Actress*
PO Box 350, New York, NY 10028, USA

Anderson, Michael *Singer, Songwriter*
%Brock Assoc, 7106 Moores Lane, #200, Brentwood, TN 37027, USA

Anderson, Michael H *Physicist*
%University of Colorado, Physics Dept, Boulder, CO 80309, USA

Anderson, Michael J *Movie Director*
%Paul Burford, 52 Yorkminster Road, North York ON M2P 1M3, Canada

Anderson, Mitchell *Actor*
%Badgley Connor, 9229 Sunset Blvd, #311, Los Angeles, CA 90069, USA

Anderson, N Christian, III *Editor, Publisher*
%Gazette Telegraph, 30 S Prospect St, Colorado Springs, CO 80903, USA

Anderson, Nick *Basketball Player*
530 E Central, #1002, Orlando, FL 32801, USA

Anderson, Nick — *Editorial Cartoonist*
%Courier-Journal, Editorial Dept, 525 W Broadway, Louisville, KY 40202, USA

Anderson, Peter J — *Financier*
%IDS Advisory Group, 80 S 8th St, Minneapolis, MN 55402, USA

Anderson, Philip W — *Nobel Physics Laureate*
%Princeton University, Physics Dept, Princeton, NJ 08544, USA

Anderson, Poul W — *Writer*
3 Las Palomas, Orinda, CA 94563, USA

Anderson, Randy — *Drag Racing Driver*
%Brad Anderson Enterprises, 2356 1st St, La Verne, CA 91750, USA

Anderson, Ray — *Jazz Trombonist, Cornetist, Trumpeter*
%Brad Simon Organization, 122 E 57th St, #400, New York, NY 10022, USA

Anderson, Reid B — *Ballet Dancer, Artistic Director*
%National Ballet of Canada, 157 King St E, Toronto ON M5C 1G9, Canada

Anderson, Richard — *Actor*
10120 Cielo Dr, Beverly Hills, CA 90210, USA

Anderson, Richard Dean — *Actor*
%Wolf/Kasteller, 132 S Rodeo Dr, #300, Beverly Hills, CA 90212, USA

Anderson, Robert G W — *Museum Director*
%British Museum, London WC1B 3DG, England

Anderson, Robert W — *Writer*
14 Sutton Place S, New York, NY 10022, USA

Anderson, Ross — *Journalist*
%Seattle Times, Editorial Dept, 1120 John St, Seattle, WA 98109, USA

Anderson, Shelly — *Drag Racing Driver*
%Brad Anderson Enterprises, 2356 1st St, La Verne, CA 91750, USA

Anderson, Terry — *Hostage, Journalist*
668 Oak Tree Road, Palisades, NY 10964, USA

Anderson, W French — *Biochemist, Geneticist*
%USC Medical School, 144 E Lake View Terrace, Los Angeles, CA 90039, USA

Anderson, Warren M — *Businessman*
270 Park Ave, New York, NY 10017, USA

Anderson, Webster — *Vietnam War Army Hero (CMH)*
Rt 2, Box 17-H, Winnsboro, SC 29180, USA

Anderson, Wendell R — *Governor/Senator, MN*
%Larkin & Hoffman, 1700 First Bank Plaza W, Minneapolis, MN 55402, USA

Anderson, Wessell — *Jazz Saxophonist*
%Fat City Artists, 1908 Chet Atkins Place, #502, Nashville, TN 37212, USA

Anderson, Weston — *Physicist*
%Varian Assoc, 611 Hansen Way, Palo Alto, CA 94304, USA

Anderson, William R — *Representative, TN; Navy Officer*
10505 Miller Road, Oakton, VA 22124, USA

Anderson, Willie — *Basketball Player*
%Toronto Raptors, 20 Bay St, #1702, Toronto ON M5J 2N8, Canada

Andersson, Bibi — *Actress*
%Open Road Stockholm-Sarajevo, PO Box 5037, 102 41 Stockholm, Sweden

Andersson, Harriet — *Actress*
Roslagsgatan 15, 113 55 Stockholm, Sweden

Andes, G Thomas — *Financier*
%Magna Group, 1401 S Brentwood Blvd, St Louis, MO 63144, USA

Andes, Karen — *Body Builder*
%G P Putnam's Sons, 200 Madison Ave, New York, NY 10016, USA

Andewelt, Roger B — *Judge*
%US Claims Court, 717 Madison Place NW, Washington, DC 20005, USA

Andov, Stojan — *President, Macedonia*
%President's Office, Dame Grueva 6, 91000 Skopje, Macedonia

Andre, Carl — *Sculptor*
PO Box 1001, Cooper Station, New York, NY 10249, USA

Andrean, Lee — *Businessman*
%Peoples Security Life Insurance, PO Box 61, Durham, NC 27702, USA

Andreas, Dwayne O — *Businessman*
%Archer Daniels Midland, 4666 Faries Parkway, Decatur, IL 62526, USA

Andreas, Ray A — *Businessman*
%Lubrizol Corp, 19400 Lakeland Blvd, Wickliffe, OH 44092, USA

Andreason, Larry — *Diver*
10874 Kyle St, Los Alamitos, CA 90720, USA

Andreef, Starr — *Actress*
%CNA Assoc, 1925 Century Park East, #750, Los Angeles, CA 90067, USA

Anderson - Andreef

Andreessen, Marc *Computer Software Designer*
%Netscape Communications, 501 E Middlefield Road, Mountain View, CA 94043, USA
Andreotti, Giulio *Prime Minister, Italy*
326 Corso Vittorio Emanuele, Rome, Italy
Andres Oteyza, Jose *Businessman*
%Pemex, Ave Marina Nacional 329, Mexico 17 DF, Mexico
Andress, Tuck *Jazz Guitarist (Tuck & Patti)*
%Q Entertainment, 584 N Larchmont Blvd, Los Angeles, CA 90004, USA
Andress, Ursula *Actress*
Lamonstr 9, 81679 Munich, Germany
Andretti, John *Auto Racing Driver*
7585 Ballinshire Dr S, Indianapolis, IN 46254, USA
Andretti, Mario *Auto Racing Driver*
53 Victory Lane, Nazareth, PA 18064, USA
Andretti, Michael M *Auto Racing Driver*
3310 Airport Road, Allentown, PA 18103, USA
Andrew *Prince, England*
Sunninghill Park, Windsor, England
Andrews, Andy *Comedian*
PO Box 17321, Nashville, TN 37217, USA
Andrews, Anthony *Actor*
%Peters Fraser Dunlop, Chelsea Harbour, Lots Rd, London SW10 0XF, England
Andrews, David *Actor*
2838 Lambert Dr, Los Angeles, CA 90068, USA
Andrews, Donna *Golfer*
PO Box 673, Richmond, VA 23206, USA
Andrews, Inez *Singer*
%Subrena Artists, 330 W 56th St, #18-M, New York, NY 10019, USA
Andrews, James *Sports Orthopedic Surgeon*
%American Sports Medicine Institute, 1313 13th St S, Birmingham, AL 35205, USA
Andrews, James E *Religious Leader*
%Presbyterian Church (USA), 100 Witherspoon St, Louisville, KY 40202, USA
Andrews, John H *Architect*
%John Andrews Int'l, 1017 Barrenjoey Road, Palm Beach NSW 2108, Australia
Andrews, Julie E *Actress, Singer*
PO Box 491668, Los Angeles, CA 90049, USA
Andrews, Mark *Senator, ND*
RR 1, PO Box 146, Mapleton, ND 58059, USA
Andrews, Patricia (Patti) *Singer (Andrews Sisters)*
9823 Aldea Ave, Northridge, CA 91325, USA
Andrews, Robert F *Religious Leader*
5536 N Roff Ave, Oklahoma City, OK 73112, USA
Andrews, Theresa *Swimmer*
2004 Homewood Road, Annapolis, MD 21402, USA
Andrews, Tige *Actor*
4914 Encino Terrace, Encino, CA 91316, USA
Andreychuck, Dave *Hockey Player*
%New Jersey Devils, Continental Arena, PO Box 504, East Rutherford, NJ 07073, USA
Androutsopoulos, Adamantios *Prime Minister, Greece*
63 Academias St, Athens, Greece
Andrus, Cecil D *Secretary, Interior; Governor, ID*
1280 Candleridge Road, Boise, ID 83712, USA
Andujar, Joaquin *Baseball Player*
Ave Lamiama Tio #47, San Pedro de Macoris, Dominican Republic
Ane, Charles T (Charlie), Jr *Football Player*
741 16th Ave, Honolulu, HI 96816, USA
Angel, Daniel D *Educator*
%Stephen F Austin State University, President's Office, Nacogdoches, TX 75962, USA
Angel, Heather H *Photographer*
Highways, 6 Vicarage Hill, Farnham, Surrey GU9 8HJ, England
Angel, J Roger P *Astronomer*
%University of Arizona, Steward Observatory, Tucson, AZ 85721, USA
Angel, Vanessa *Actress, Model*
%Agency For Performing Arts, 9200 Sunset Blvd, #900, Los Angeles, CA 90069, USA
Angell, Wayne D *Financier, Government Official*
%Bear Stearns Hires, 245 Park Ave, New York, NY 10167, USA
Angelopoulos, Theo *Movie Director*
Solmou 18, 106 82 Athens, Greece

Angelou, Maya — *Writer*
2720 Reynolda Road, #MB-9, Winston Salem, NC 27106, USA

Anger, Kenneth — *Movie Director*
354 E 91st St, #9, New York, NY 10128, USA

Angerer, Peter — *Biathlete*
Wagenau 2, 17326 Hammer, Germany

Angier, Natalie M — *Journalist*
%New York Times, Editorial Dept, 229 W 43rd St, New York, NY 10036, USA

Angle, Kurt — *Wrestler*
30 Standish Blvd, Mount Lebanon, PA 15228, USA

Anglin, Jennifer — *Actress*
651 N Kilkea Dr, Los Angeles, CA 90048, USA

Angotti, Lou — *Hockey Player*
2840 NE 14th St, #401-B, Pompano Beach, FL 33062, USA

Anguiano, Raul — *Artist*
Anaxagoras 1326, Colonia Narvate, Mexico City 13 DF, Mexico

Angus, Michael — *Businessman*
%Unilever PLC, PO Box 68, Unilever House, London EC4P 4BQ, England

Anhalt, Edward — *Movie Director, Writer*
500 Amalfi Dr, Pacific Palisades, CA 90272, USA

Aniston, Jennifer — *Actress*
%Creative Artists Agency, 9830 Wilshire Blvd, Beverly Hills, CA 90212, USA

Anjard, Ronald P, Sr — *Businessman, Engineering Consultant*
10942 Montego Dr, San Diego, CA 92124, USA

Anka, Paul — *Singer, Songwriter*
12078 Summit Circle, Beverly Hills, CA 90210, USA

Anlyan, William — *Surgeon*
First Union Plaza, 2200 W Main St, #1066, Durham, NC 27705, USA

Ann-Margret — *Actress, Singer, Dancer*
2707 Benedict Canyon Road, Beverly Hills, CA 90210, USA

Annakin, Kenneth (Ken) — *Movie Director*
1643 Lindacrest Dr, Beverly Hills, CA 90210, USA

Annan, Kofi A — *Secretary-General, United Nations*
%Secretary-General's Office, United Nations, 1 UN Plaza, New York, NY 10003, USA

Annand, Richard Wallace — *WW II British Army Hero (VC)*
Springwell House, Whitesmocks, Durham City DH1 4ZL, England

Annaud, Jean-Jacques — *Movie Director*
55 Rue de Varenne, 75007 Paris, France

Anne — *Princess, England*
%Gatecombe Park, Gloucestershire, England

Anne of Bourbon-Palma — *Queen, Romania*
%Villa Serena, 77 Chemin Louis-Degallier, 1290 Versoix-Geneva, Switzerland

Annenberg, Wallis — *Publisher*
10273 Century Woods Dr, Los Angeles, CA 90067, USA

Annenberg, Walter H — *Publisher, Diplomat*
71231 Tamarisk Lane, Rancho Mirage, CA 92270, USA

Annis, Francesca — *Actress*
2 Vicarage Court, London W8, England

Ansara, Edward — *Actor*
%Jack Scagnetti, 5118 Vineland Ave, #102, North Hollywood, CA 91601, USA

Ansara, Michael — *Actor*
4624 Park Mirasol, Calabasas, CA 91302, USA

Anspach, Susan — *Actress*
2369 Beach Ave, Venice, CA 90291, USA

Anspaugh, David — *Movie Director*
%International Creative Mgmt, 8942 Wilshire Blvd, Beverly Hills, CA 90211, USA

Ant, Adam — *Singer, Guitarist*
%Progressive Global Agency, PO Box 128288, Nashville, TN 37212, USA

Antes, Horst — *Artist*
Hohenbergstr 11, 19322 Karlsruhe, Germany

Anthony, Barbara Cox — *Businesswoman*
%Cox Enterprises, 1400 Lake Hearn Dr NE, Atlanta, GA 30319, USA

Anthony, Carl — *Environmentalist*
%Harvard University, Kennedy Government School, Cambridge, MA 02138, USA

Anthony, Earl R — *Bowler*
26649 NW Dairy Creek Road, Cornelius, OR 97113, USA

Anthony, Gerald — *Actor*
%Henderson/Hogan, 247 S Beverly Dr, #102, Beverly Hills, CA 90212, USA

A

Angelou - Anthony

A

Anthony, Greg — *Basketball Player*
520 S 4th St, Las Vegas, NV 89101, USA

Anthony, Lysette — *Actress*
125 W 76th St, #6-B, New York, NY 10023, USA

Anthony, Ray — *Orchestra Leader, Trumpeter*
9288 Kinglet Dr, Los Angeles, CA 90069, USA

Antin, Steven — *Writer, Actor*
%International Creative Mgmt, 8942 Wilshire Blvd, Beverly Hills, CA 90211, USA

Antoci, Mario J — *Financier*
%American Savings Bank, 17877 Von Karman Ave, Irvine, CA 92614, USA

Anton, Susan — *Actress*
16830 Ventura Blvd, #1616, Encino, CA 91436, USA

Antonakakis, Suzana M — *Architect*
Atelier 66, Em Benaki 118, Athens 114-73, Greece

Antonakos, Stephen — *Artist*
435 W Broadway, New York, NY 10012, USA

Antonelli, Ferdinando Cardinal — *Religious Leader*
Piazza S Calisto 16, 00153 Rome, Italy

Antonelli, John A (Johnny) — *Baseball Player*
PO Box 580, Pittsford, NY 14534, USA

Antonio — *Spanish Dancer*
Coslada 7, Madrid, Spain

Antonio, Lou — *Actor*
530 Gaylord Dr, Burbank, CA 91505, USA

Antonioni, Michelangelo — *Movie Director*
Via Vincenzo Tiberio 18, 00191 Rome, Italy

Antoun (Khouri), Bishop — *Religious Leader*
%Antiochian Orthodox Christian Archdiocese, 358 Mountain Rd, Englewood, NJ 07631, USA

Antsey, Chris — *Basketball Player*
%Dallas Mavericks, Reunion Arena, 777 Sports St, Dallas, TX 75207, USA

Antuofermo, Vito — *Boxer*
160-19 81st St, Howard Beach, NY 11414, USA

Anuszkiewicz, Richard J — *Artist*
76 Chestnut St, Englewood, NJ 07631, USA

Anwar, Gabrielle — *Actress*
%United Talent Agency, 9560 Wilshire Blvd, #500, Beverly Hills, CA 90212, USA

Aoi, Joichi — *Businessman*
%Toshiba Corp, 72 Horikawacho, Saiwaiku, Kawasaki 210, Japan

Aoki, Chieko N — *Businesswoman*
%Westin Hotels Co, Westin Building, 2001 6th Ave, Seattle, WA 98121, USA

Aoki, Isao — *Golfer*
%Int'l Management Group, 1 Erieview Plaza, #1300, Cleveland, OH 44114, USA

Aoki, Rocky — *Boat Racing Driver, Businessman*
%Benihana of Tokyo, 8685 NW 53rd Terrace, Miami, FL 33166, USA

Aouita, Said — *Track Athlete*
%Abdejil Bencheikh, 9 Rue Soivissi, Loubira, Rabat, Morocco

Aparicio, Luis E — *Baseball Player*
Calle 67, #26-82, Maracaibo, Venezuela

Apfalter, Heribert — *Businessman*
%Voest-Alpine, Muldenstr 5, 4010 Linz, Austria

Apodaca, Jerry — *Governor, NM*
1328 Camino Corrales, Santa Fe, NM 87505, USA

Appel, Karel — *Artist*
%Galerie Statler, 51 Rue de Seine, Paris, France

Appice, Carmine — *Drummer*
%Wyatt Mgmt Worldwide, 10797 Onyx Circle, Fountain Valley, CA 92708, USA

Apple, Fiona — *Singer, Songwriter*
%William Morris Agency, 151 S El Camino Dr, Beverly Hills, CA 90212, USA

Apple, Raymond W, Jr — *Journalist*
%New York Times, Editorial Dept, 1627 "I" St NW, Washington, DC 20006, USA

Appleby, Stuart — *Golfer*
%Professional Golfer's Assn, PO Box 109601, Palm Beach Gardens, FL 33410, USA

Applegate, Christina — *Actress*
20411 Chapter Dr, Woodland Hills, CA 91364, USA

Appleton, James R — *Educator*
%University of Redlands, President's Office, Redlands, CA 92373, USA

Appleton, Myra — *Editor*
%Cosmopolitan Magazine, Editorial Dept, 224 W 57th St, New York, NY 10019, USA

Anthony - Appleton

Appleton, Steven R *Businessman*
%Micron Technology, 2805 E Columbia Road, Boise, ID 83716, USA

Apps, Syl *Hockey Player*
185 Ontario St, #1303, Kingston ON K7L 2YZ, Canada

Apt, Jerome (Jay) *Astronaut*
4 Shadycourt Dr, Pittsburgh, PA 15232, USA

Apted, Michael D *Movie Director*
13176 Boca De Canon Lane, Los Angeles, CA 90049, USA

Aquilino, Thomas J, Jr *Judge*
%US Court of International Trade, 1 Federal Plaza, New York, NY 10278, USA

Aquino, Corazon C *President, Philippines*
Pius XVI Center, UN Center, Manila, Philippines

Arafat, Yasser *Palestine; Nobel Peace Laureate*
%PLO Chairman's Office, Gaza City, Gaza Strip, Palestine, Israel

Aragall, Giacomo *Opera Singer*
%Robert Lombardo, Harkness Plaza, 61 W 62nd St, #B-5, New York, NY 10023, USA

Aragon, Art *Boxer*
%Art Aragon Bail Bonds, 14444 Victory Blvd, Van Nuys, CA 91401, USA

Aragones, Sergio *Cartoonist (Mad Comics)*
PO Box 696, Ojai, CA 93024, USA

Arai, Kazuo *Businessman*
%Kao Corp, 14-10 Nihonbashi, Kayabacho, Chuoku, Tokyo 103, Japan

Araiza, Francisco *Opera Singer*
%Columbia Artists Mgmt Inc, 165 W 57th St, New York, NY 10019, USA

Arakawa, Ichiro *Businessman*
%Kanto Auto Works, Taura-Minatomachi, Yokosuka City 237, Japan

Arakawa, Toyozo *Pottery Maker*
4-101, O-Hatacho, Tokyo, Japan

Aramburu, Juan Carlos Cardinal *Religious Leader*
Arzobispado, Suipacha 1034, Buenos Aires 1008, Argentina

Arana Osorio, Carlos M *President, Guatemala; Army General*
%President's Office, Palacio Nacional, Guatemala City, Guatemala

Aranauskas, Leonas S *Architect*
%Glavmozarchitectura, Mayakovsky Square 1, 103001 Moscow, Russia

Araskog, Rand V *Businessman*
%ITT Corp, 1330 Ave of Americas, New York, NY 10019, USA

Arau, Alfonso *Movie Director*
%Productions AA, Privada Rafael Oliva 8, Coyoacan 04120, Mexico

Arazi, Efraim *Businessman*
%Electronics for Imaging, 2855 Campus Dr, San Mateo, CA 94403, USA

Arbanas, Frederick V *Football Player*
3350 SW Hook Road, Lee's Summit, MO 64082, USA

Arbeid, Murray *Fashion Designer*
202 Ebury St, London SW1W 8UN, England

Arber, Werner *Nobel Medicine Laureate*
70 Klingelbergstr, 4056 Basel, Switzerland

Arbour, Alan (Al) *Hockey Coach, Executive*
12 Donovan Dr, Cold Spring Harbor, NY 11724, USA

Arbulu Galliani, Guillermo *Prime Minister, Peru; Army General*
%Foreign Affairs Ministry, Lima, Peru

Arbus, Alan *Actor*
2208 N Beverly Glen, Los Angeles, CA 90077, USA

Arcain, Janet *Basketball Player*
%Houston Comets, 2 Greenway Plaza, #400, Houston, TX 77046, USA

Arcaro, G Edward (Eddie) *Thoroughbred Racing Jockey, Sportscaster*
11111 Biscayne Blvd, Miami, FL 33181, USA

Arce, Lisa *Volleyball Player*
%Women's Pro Volleyball Assn, 840 Apollo St, #204, El Segundo, CA 90245, USA

Archer, Anne *Actress*
13201 Old Oak Lane, Los Angeles, CA 90049, USA

Archer, Beverly *Actress*
%Judy Schoen, 606 N Larchmont Blvd, #309, Los Angeles, CA 90004, USA

Archer, Dennis W *Mayor*
%Mayor's Office, City-County Building, 2 Woodward Ave, Detroit, MI 48226, USA

Archer, George *Golfer*
774 Mays Blvd, #10-184, Incline Village, NV 89451, USA

Archer, Jeffrey H *Government Official, England; Writer*
93 Albert Embankment, London SE1, England

Archer, John — Writer
10901 176th Circle NE, #3601, Redmond, WA 98052, USA

Archerd, Army — Journalist
%Variety Magazine, Editorial Dept, 5700 Wilshire Blvd, Los Angeles, CA 90036, USA

Archibald, Joey — Boxer
75 E Ave, #1204, Pawtucket, RI 02860, USA

Archibald, Nathaniel (Nate) — Basketball Player
%Harlem Armory Homeless Shelter, 40 W 143rd St, New York, NY 10037, USA

Arciniega, Tomas A — Educator
%California State College, President's Office, Bakersfield, CA 93311, USA

Arciniegas, German — Writer, Diplomat
%Academia Colombiana de Histora, Calle 92, 10-21 Bogota, Colombia

Ard, William D (Bill) — Football Player
41 Vail Lane, Watchung, NJ 07060, USA

Ardalan, Nader — Architect
177 Milk St, Boston, MA 02109, USA

Ardant, Fanny — Actress
%Artmedia, 10 Ave George V, 75008 Paris, France

Arden, Jann — Singer, Songwriter
5647 Riverbend Road, Edmonton AB T6H 5F4, Canada

Arden, John — Writer
%Cassarotto, 60/66 Wardour St, London W1V 4ND, England

Arden, Toni — Singer
34-34 75th St, Jackson Heights, NY 11372, USA

Aregood, Richard L — Journalist
%Philadelphia Daily News, Editoral Dept, 400 N Broad St, Philadelphia, PA 19130, USA

Arens, Moshe — Government Official, Israel
49 Hagderot, Savyon, Israel

Aretsky, Ken — Restauranteur
%21 Club, 21 W 52nd St, New York, NY 10019, USA

Argento, Dominick — Composer
%University of Minnesota, Music Dept, Ferguson Hall, Minneapolis, MN 55455, USA

Argerich, Martha — Concert Pianist
%Goette Konzert Direktion, Colonnaden 70, 20354 Hamburg, Germany

Arian, David — Labor Leader
%International Longshoremen's Union, 1188 Franklin St, San Francisco, CA 94109, USA

Arias Sanchez, Oscar — President, Costa Rica; Nobel Laureate
%Arias Foundation for Peace, Apdo 8-6410-1000, San Jose, Costa Rica

Arias, Ricardo M — President, Panama
Apdo 4549, Panama City, Panama

Arinze, Francis Cardinal — Religious Leader
%Pontifical Council for Non-Christians, 00120 Vatican City

Ariyoshi, George R — Governor, HI
745 Fort St, #500, Honolulu, HI 96813, USA

Arizin, Paul J — Basketball Player
227 Lewis Road, Springfield, PA 19064, USA

Arkhipova, Irina K — Opera Singer
%Union of Musicians, Nezhdanovoy Str 2/14, #27, 103009 Moscow, Russia

Arkin, Adam — Actor
%International Creative Mgmt, 8942 Wilshire Blvd, Beverly Hills, CA 90211, USA

Arkin, Alan — Actor
21 E 40th St, #1705, New York, NY 10016, USA

Arkoff, Samuel Z — Movie Producer
3205 Oakdell Lane, Studio City, CA 91604, USA

Arledge, Roone P, Jr — Television Executive
535 Park Ave, #13-A, New York, NY 10021, USA

Arlen, Michael J — Writer
%New Yorker Magazine, Editorial Dept, 25 W 43rd St, New York, NY 10036, USA

Arm, Mark — Singer (Mudhoney)
%ICM/Twin Towers, 611 Broadway, #730, New York, NY 10012, USA

Armacost, Michael H — Diplomat
%US Embassy, 10-5-1 Akasaka, Minatoku, Tokyo, Japan

Arman — Sculptor
%Arman Studios, 430 Washington St, New York, NY 10013, USA

Armani, Giorgio — Fashion Designer
Palazzo Durini 24, 20122 Milan, Italy

Armas, Antonio R (Tony) — Baseball Player
Los Mercedes #37, P Piruto-Edo, Anzoatequi, Venezuela

Armatrading, Joan *Singer, Songwriter*
%Running Dog Mgmt, Lower Hampton Road, Sunbury, Middx TW16 5PR, England

Armedariz, Pedro, Jr *Actor*
%Diamond Artists, 215 N Barrington Ave, Los Angeles, CA 90049, USA

Armitage, Alison *Actress*
%Twentieth Century, 15315 Magnolia Blvd, #429, Sherman Oaks, CA 91403, USA

Armitage, Karole *Choreographer, Dancer*
350 W 21st St, New York, NY 10011, USA

Armitage, Kenneth *Artist*
22-A Avonmore Road, London W14 8RR, England

Armitage, Richard L *Government Official*
%Secretary's Office, Department of Army, Pentagon, Washington, DC 20310, USA

Arms, Russell *Actor, Singer*
2918 Davis Way, Palm Springs, CA 92262, USA

Armstrong, A James *Religious Leader*
%Broadway Methodist Church, 1100 W 42nd St, Indianapolis, IN 46208, USA

Armstrong, Anne L *Diplomat, Educator*
Armstrong Ranch, Armstrong, TX 78338, USA

Armstrong, B J *Basketball Player*
809 Union St, Pella, IA 50219, USA

Armstrong, Bess *Actress*
%William Morris Agency, 151 S El Camino Dr, Beverly Hills, CA 90212, USA

Armstrong, Billie Joe *Singer, Songwriter, Guitarist*
%Warner Bros Records, 3300 Warner Blvd, Burbank, CA 91505, USA

Armstrong, Bruce C *Football Player*
1035 Bedford Gardens Dr, Alpharetta, GA 30022, USA

Armstrong, Deborah (Debbie) *Skier*
1938 E Blaine, Seattle, WA 98112, USA

Armstrong, Garner Ted *Evangelist*
%Worldwide Church of God, PO Box 2525, Tyler, TX 75710, USA

Armstrong, George *Hockey Player*
22 St Cuthbert's Road, Toronto ON M4G 1V1, Canada

Armstrong, Gillian *Movie Director*
%William Morris Agency, 151 S El Camino Dr, Beverly Hills, CA 90212, USA

Armstrong, Lance *Cyclist*
%US Cycling Federation, 1750 E Boulder St, Colorado Springs, CO 80909, USA

Armstrong, Neil *Hockey Referee*
1169 Sherwood Trail, Sarnia ON N7V 2H3, Canada

Armstrong, Neil A *Astronaut*
%AIL Systems, Commack Road, Deer Park, NY 11297, USA

Armstrong, Otis *Football Player*
7183 S Newport Way, Englewood, CO 80112, USA

Armstrong, R G *Actor*
3856 Reklaw Dr, Studio City, CA 91604, USA

Armstrong, Robb *Cartoonist (Jump Start)*
%United Feature Syndicate, 200 Madison Ave, New York, NY 10016, USA

Armstrong, Thomas H W *Concert Organist*
1 East St, Olney, Bucks MK46 4AP, England

Armstrong, Valorie *Actress*
%Contemporary Artists, 1427 3rd St Promenade, #205, Santa Monica, CA 90401, USA

Arn, Edward *Governor, KS*
7373 E 29th St N, W-117, Wichita, KS 67226, USA

Arnaud, Jean-Loup *Government Official, France*
15 Quai Louis Bleriot, 75016 Paris, France

Arnaz, Desi, Jr *Actor*
525 Hotel Plaza, Boulder City, NV 89005, USA

Arnaz, Lucie *Actress*
RR 3, Flintlock Ridge Road, Katonah, NY 10536, USA

Arnell, Richard A S *Composer*
Benhall Lodge, Benhall, Suffolk IP17 1DJ, England

Arnesen, Liv *Polar Skier*
Trostevn 6, 1340 Bekkestua, Norway

Arness, James *Actor*
PO Box 49004, Los Angeles, CA 90049, USA

Arnett, Jon *Football Player*
PO Box 4077, Palos Verdes Estates, CA 90274, USA

Arnett, Peter *Commentator, Journalist*
%Cable News Network, News Dept, 820 1st St NE, Washington, DC 20002, USA

A

Arnette, Jeanetta *Actress*
466 N Harper Ave, Los Angeles, CA 90048, USA
Arnhold, Henry H *Financier*
%Arnhold & S Bleichroeder, 1345 Ave of Americas, #4300, New York, NY 10105, USA
Arnold, Andrew *Geneticist*
%Massachusetts General Hospital, Genetics Dept, Boston, MA 02114, USA
Arnold, Anna Bing *Philanthropist*
%Anna Bing Arnold Foundation, 9700 W Pico Blvd, Los Angeles, CA 90035, USA
Arnold, Ben *Singer*
%Golden Guru, 227 Pine St, Philadelphia, PA 19106, USA
Arnold, Debbie *Actress*
%M Arnold Mgmt, 12 Cambridge Park, East Twickenham, Middx TW1 2PF, England
Arnold, Edward (Eddy) *Singer*
PO Box 97, Franklin Road, Brentwood, TN 37024, USA
Arnold, Gary H *Movie Critic*
5133 N 1st St, Arlington, VA 22203, USA
Arnold, Harry L, Jr *Dermatologist, Writer*
250 Laurel St, #301, San Francisco, CA 94118, USA
Arnold, Jack *Businessman*
%Network Equipment Technologies, 800 Saginaw Dr, Redwood City, CA 94063, USA
Arnold, Jackson D *Navy Admiral*
Los Pinos, Box 185, Rancho Santa Fe, CA 92067, USA
Arnold, James R *Chemist*
%University of California, Space Institute, La Jolla, CA 92307, USA
Arnold, Malcolm *Composer*
%Faber Music Co, 3 Queen Square, London WC1N 3AU, England
Arnold, Murray *Basketball Coach*
%Western Kentucky University, Athletic Dept, Bowling Green, KY 42101, USA
Arnold, Stuart *Publisher*
%Fortune Magazine, Rockefeller Center, New York, NY 10020, USA
Arnold, Tom *Comedian, Actor*
PO Box 15458, Beverly Hills, CA 90209, USA
Arnoldi, Charles A *Artist*
721 Hampton Dr, Venice, CA 90291, USA
Arns, Paulo E Cardinal *Religious Leader*
Avenida Higienopolos 890, 01238 Sao Paulo, SP, Brazil
Aronson, Judi *Actress*
%Kazarian/Spencer, 11365 Ventura Blvd, #100, Studio City, CA 91604, USA
Arp, Halton C *Astronomer*
%Max Planck Physics/Radiology Institute, 84518 Garching Munich, Germany
Arpel, Adrien *Beauty Consultant*
666 5th Ave, New York, NY 10103, USA
Arpino, Gerald P *Choreographer*
%City Center Joffrey Ballet, 70 E Lake St, #1300, Chicago, IL 60601, USA
Arquette, David *Actor*
%International Creative Mgmt, 8942 Wilshire Blvd, Beverly Hills, CA 90211, USA
Arquette, Patricia *Actress*
%United Talent Agency, 9560 Wilshire Blvd, #500, Beverly Hills, CA 90212, USA
Arquette, Rosanna *Actress*
8033 Sunset Blvd, #16, Los Angeles, CA 90046, USA
Arrindell, Clement A *Governor General, St Kitts & Nevis*
Government House, Basseterre, St Kitts, St Kitts & Nevis
Arriola, Gus *Cartoonist (Gordo)*
PO Box 3275, Carmel, CA 93921, USA
Arrow, Kenneth J *Nobel Economics Laureate*
580 Constanzo St, Stanford, CA 94305, USA
Arroyo, Luis E *Baseball Player*
PO Box 354, Penuelas, PR 00624, USA
Arroyo, Martina *Opera Singer*
%Thea Dispeker, 59 E 54th St, New York, NY 10022, USA
Arteaga, Rosalia *President, Ecuador; Vice President*
%Vice President's Office, Gobierno Palacio, Garcia Moreno, Quito, Ecuador
Arthur, Beatrice *Actress*
2000 Old Ranch Road, Los Angeles, CA 90049, USA
Arthur, Maureen *Actress*
PO Box 280009, Northridge, CA 91328, USA
Arthur, Owen *Prime Minister, Barbados*
%Prime Minister's Office, Government House, Bridgetown, Barbados

Arnette - Arthur

Artschwager, Richard E *Artist*
PO Box 12, Hudson, NY 12534, USA

Artsebarsky, Anatoly *Cosmonaut*
%Potchta Kosmonavtov, Moskovskoi Oblasti, 141160 Syvisdny Goroduk, Russia

Artyukhin, Yuri P *Cosmonaut*
%Potchta Kosmonavtov, Moskovskoi Oblasti, 141160 Syvisdny Goroduk, Russia

Artzt, Alice J *Concert Guitarist*
180 Claremont Ave, #31, New York, NY 10027, USA

Artzt, Edwin L *Businessman*
%Procter & Gamble Co, 1 Procter & Gamble Plaza, Cincinnati, OH 45202, USA

Arum, Robert (Bob) *Boxing Promoter*
%Top Rank, 3900 Paradise Road, Las Vegas, NV 89109, USA

Arvesen, Nina *Actress*
950 Lake St, #2, Venice, CA 90291, USA

Arzu, Alvaro *President, Guatemala*
%President's Office, Palacio Nacional, Guatemala City, Guatamala

Asahina, Takashi *Conductor*
%Osaka Philharmonic, 1-1-44 Kishinosato-Nishinariku, Osaka 557, Japan

Asby, Joseph W *Air Force General*
Commander, Air Training Command, Randolph Air Force Base, TX 78150, USA

Asch, Peter *Water Polo Player*
54 Michael Lane, Orinda, CA 94563, USA

Aschenbrenner, Frank *Football Player*
16372 E Jacklin Dr, Fountain Hills, AZ 85268, USA

Ash, Mary Kay W *Businesswoman*
%Mary Kay Cosmetics, 16251 Dallas Parkway, Dallas, TX 75248, USA

Ash, Roy L *Businessman, Government Official*
655 Funchal Road, Los Angeles, CA 90077, USA

Ashbery, John L *Writer*
%Bard College, Language & Literature Dept, Annandale-On-Hudson, NY 12504, USA

Ashbrook, Dana *Actor*
7019 Melrose Ave, #332, Los Angeles, CA 90038, USA

Ashbrook, Daphne *Actress*
%Innovative Artists, 1999 Ave of Stars, #2850, Los Angeles, CA 90067, USA

Ashbury, Beverly A *Religious Leader*
%Vanderbilt University, Religious Affairs Office, Nashville, TN 37204, USA

Ashby, Jeffrey S *Astronaut*
%NASA, Johnson Space Center, 2101 NASA Road, Houston, TX 77058, USA

Ashdown, J J D (Paddy) *Government Official, England*
Vane Cottage, Norton Sub Hamdon, Somerset TA14 6SG, England

Ashenfelter, Horace, III *Track Athlete*
100 Hawthorne Ave, Glen Ridge, NJ 07028, USA

Asher, Barry *Bowler*
%Professional Bowlers Assn, 1720 Merriman Road, Akron, OH 44313, USA

Asher, Jane *Actress*
644 N Doheny Dr, Los Angeles, CA 90069, USA

Asher, Peter *Record Producer, Singer (Peter & Gordon)*
%Peter Asher Mgmt, 644 N Doheny Dr, Los Angeles, CA 90069, USA

Ashford, Evelyn *Track Athlete*
818 Plantation Lane, Walnut, CA 91789, USA

Ashford, Matthew *Actor*
7948 Blackburn, #5, Los Angeles, CA 90048, USA

Ashford, Nicholas (Nick) *Singer (Ashford & Simpson), Songwriter*
%Associated Booking Corp, 1995 Broadway, #501, New York, NY 10023, USA

Ashihara, Yoshinobu *Architect*
%Ashihara Architects, 31-15 Sakuragaokacho, Shibuyaku, Tokyo 150, Japan

Ashkenasi, Shmuel *Concert Pianist*
3800 N Lake Shore Dr, Chicago, IL 60613, USA

Ashkenazy, Vladimir D *Concert Pianist, Conductor*
Kappelistr 15, 6045 Meggen, Switzerland

Ashley *Model*
%Ford Model Agency, 344 E 59th St, New York, NY 10022, USA

Ashley, Elizabeth *Actress*
1223 N Ogden Dr, Los Angeles, CA 90046, USA

Ashley, John *Hockey Referee*
9-236 Kingswood Dr, Kitchener ON N2E 2K2, Canada

Ashley, Leon *Singer*
%Country Music Spectacular, 249 Bluegrass Dr, Hendersonville, TN 37075, USA

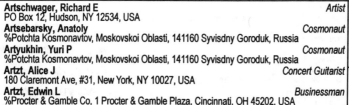

A

Artschwager - Ashley

Ashley, Merrill *Ballerina*
%New York City Ballet, Lincoln Center Plaza, New York, NY 10023, USA

Ashley, Robert *Composer*
%Brooklyn Academy of Music, 30 Lafayette Ave, New York, NY 10007, USA

Ashmore, Edward B *Navy Fleet Admiral, England*
%Naval Secretary, Ministry of Defense, London SW1, England

Ashmore, Harry S *Editor, Foundation Executive*
900 Calle De Los Amigos, #D-502, Santa Barbara, CA 93105, USA

Ashrawi, Hanan *Political Leader, Palestine*
%Bir Zeit University, PO Box 14, West Bank, Bir Zeit, Israel

Ashton, Harris J *Businessman*
%General Host, Metro Center, 1 Station Place, Stamford, CT 06902, USA

Ashton, John *Actor*
700 Hinsdale Dr, Fort Collins, CO 80526, USA

Ashton, Susan *Singer*
%Blanton/Harrell, 2910 Poston Ave, Nashville, TN 37203, USA

Ashworth, Gerald (Gerry) *Track Athlete*
7 Athena Circle, Andover, MA 01810, USA

Ashworth, Jeanne C *Speed Skater*
Whiteface Highway, Wilmington, NY 12997, USA

Askew, Reubin O *Governor, FL*
%Akerman Senterfitt Edson, 255 S Orange Ave, Orlando, FL 32801, USA

Askin, Leon *Actor*
PO Box 847, Beverly Hills, CA 90213, USA

Asmis, Herbert *Businessman*
%Schering, Mullerstr 170-178, 12487 Berlin, Germany

Asner, Edward *Actor*
12400 Ventura Blvd, #346, Studio City, CA 91604, USA

Assad, Hafez al- *President, Syria*
%President's Palace, Muharreen, Abu Rumanch, Al-Rashid St, Damascus, Syria

Assante, Armand *Actor*
367 Windsor Highway, New Windsor, NY 12553, USA

Assylmuratova, Altynai *Ballerina*
%Kirov Ballet Theatre, 1 Ploshchad Iskusstr, St Petersburg, Russia

Ast, Pat *Actress*
4439 Worster Ave, Studio City, CA 91604, USA

Astin, Allen V *Physicist*
5008 Battery Lane, Bethesda, MD 20814, USA

Astin, John *Actor, Director*
1271 Stoner Ave, #408, Los Angeles, CA 90025, USA

Astin, Mackenzie *Actor*
%William Morris Agency, 151 S El Camino Dr, Beverly Hills, CA 90212, USA

Astin, Sean *Actor*
5824 Norwich Ave, Van Nuys, CA 91411, USA

Astley, Thea *Writer*
PO Box 23, Cambewarra, NSW 2540, Australia

Astor, Brooke *Foundation Executive*
%Vincent Astor Foundation, 405 Park Ave, New York, NY 10022, USA

Asturaga, Nova *Government Official, Nicaragua*
%Permanent Mission of Nicaragua, 820 2nd Ave, #801, New York, NY 10017, USA

Asylmuratova, Altynai *Ballerina*
%Mariinsky Theater, Teatralnaya Pl 1, St Petersburg, Russia

Atchison, David W *Religious Leader*
%Southern Baptist Convention, 5452 Grannywhite Pike, Brentwood, TN 37027, USA

Atherton, Alfred L, Jr *Diplomat*
4301 Massachusetts Ave NW, #5003, Washington, DC 20016, USA

Atherton, David *Conductor*
%San Diego Symphony, 770 "B" St, #402, San Diego, CA 92101, USA

Atherton, Michael A *Cricketer*
%Lancashire County Cricket Club, Old Trafford, Manchester M16 0PX, England

Atherton, William *Actor*
5102 San Feliciano Dr, Woodland Hills, CA 91364, USA

Athow, Kirk L *Plant Pathologist*
2104 Crestview Court, Lafayette, IN 47905, USA

Atiyeh, Victor *Governor, OR*
%Victor Atiyeh Co, 519 SW Park Ave, #205, Portland, OR 97205, USA

Atkins, Chet *Guitarist*
1096 Lynwood Blvd, Nashville, TN 37215, USA

Atkins, Christopher — *Actor*
6934 Bevis Ave, Van Nuys, CA 91405, USA
Atkins, Douglas L (Doug) — *Football Player*
PO Box 14007, Knoxville, TN 37914, USA
Atkins, Eileen — *Actress*
%Duncan Heath, Paramount House, 162 Wardour, London W1V 3AT, England
Atkins, Robert C — *Nutritionist*
%M Evans Co, 216 E 49th St, New York, NY 10017, USA
Atkins, Thomas E — *WW II Army Hero (CMH)*
Rt 2, Box 433, Inman, SC 29349, USA
Atkins, Tom — *Actor*
%Paradigm Agency, 10100 Santa Monica Blvd, #2500, Los Angeles, CA 90067, USA
Atkinson, Richard C — *Educator*
%University of California System, 300 Lakeside Dr, Oakland, CA 94612, USA
Atkinson, Rick — *Journalist*
%Kansas City Times, Editorial Dept, 1729 Grand Ave, Kansas City, MO 64108, USA
Atkov, Oleg Y — *Cosmonaut*
%Potchta Kosmonavtov, Moskovskoi Oblasti, 141160 Syvisdny Goroduk, Russia
Atlantov, Vladimir — *Opera Singer*
%Bolshoi Theatre, Teatralnaya Pl 1, 103009 Moscow, Russia
Attenborough, David — *Television Broadcaster, Writer*
5 Park Road, Richmond, Surrey TW10 6NS, England
Attenborough, Richard S — *Actor, Director*
Beaver Lodge, Richmond Green, Surrey TW9 1NQ, England
Attkisson, Sharyl — *Commentator*
%Cable News Network, News Dept, 1050 Techwood Dr NW, Atlanta, GA 30318, USA
Attles, Al — *Basketball Player, Coach*
195 Villanova Dr, Oakland, CA 94611, USA
Atwood, J Leland — *Businessman*
PO Box 1587, Vista, CA 92085, USA
Atwood, Margaret E — *Writer*
%McClelland/Stewart, 481 University Ave, #900, Toronto ON M5G 2E9, Canada
Atwood, Susie (Sue) — *Swimmer*
6820 E Ocean Blvd, Long Beach, CA 90803, USA
Atzmon, Moshe — *Conductor*
Marignanostr 12, 4059 Basel, Switzerland
Auberjonois, Rene — *Actor*
448 S Arden Blvd, Los Angeles, CA 90020, USA
Aubert, Pierre — *President, Switzerland*
%Federal Dept of Foreign Affairs, Palais Federal, 3003 Berne, Switzerland
Aubrecht, Richard A — *Businessman*
%Moog Inc, Jamison Road, East Aurora, NY 14052, USA
Aubry, Cecile — *Actress*
Le Moulin Bleu, 6 Chemin Moulin Bleu, 91410 Saint-Cyr-Sous-Dourdan, France
Aubry, Eugene E — *Architect*
8021 Marina Isles Lane, Bradenton Beach, FL 34217, USA
Auchincloss, Louis S — *Writer*
1111 Park Ave, #14-D, New York, NY 10128, USA
Audran, Stephane — *Actress*
95 Bis Rue de Chezy, 92200 Neuilly-sur-Seine, France
Auel, Jean M — *Writer*
PO Box 430, Sherwood, OR 97140, USA
Auer, Peter L — *Plasma Physicist*
220 Devon Road, Ithaca, NY 14850, USA
Auerbach, Arnold J (Red) — *Basketball Coach, Executive*
PO Box 8607, Boston, MA 02114, USA
Auerbach, Frank — *Artist*
%Marlborough Fine Art Gallery, 6 Albermarle St, London W1X 4BY, England
Auerbach, Stanley I — *Ecologist*
24 Wildwood Dr, Oak Ridge, TN 37830, USA
Auermann, Nadia — *Model*
Via San Viottore 40, 20123 Milan, Italy
Auger, Brian — *Jazz Pianist*
8901 Melrose Ave, #201, West Hollywood, CA 90069, USA
Auger, Claudine — *Actress*
%William Morris Agency, 151 S El Camino Dr, Beverly Hills, CA 90212, USA
Auger, Pierre V — *Physicist*
12 Rue Emile Faguet, 75014 Paris, France

A

Atkins - Auger

A

Augmon - Avery

Augmon, Stacey 4212 Kessler Ridge Dr, Marietta, GA 30062, USA	*Basketball Player*
Augstein, Rudolf %Spiegel-Verloff Augstein, Brandstwiete 19, 20457 Hamburg, Germany	*Publisher*
August, Bille 2800 Lyngby, Denmark	*Movie Director*
Augustain, Ira %Diamond Artists, 215 N Barrington Ave, Los Angeles, CA 90049, USA	*Actor*
Augustine, Norman R %Lockheed Marietta Corp, 6801 Rockledge Dr, Bethesda, MD 20817, USA	*Businessman*
Auker, Eldon L 15 Sailfish Road, Vero Beach, FL 32960, USA	*Baseball Player*
Aulby, Mike 1591 Springmill Ponds Circle, Carmel, IN 46032, USA	*Bowler*
Ault, James M %United Methodist Church, 168 Mt Vernon St, Newtonville, MA 02165, USA	*Religious Leader*
Aumont, Jean-Pierre 4 Allee des Brouillards, 75018 Paris, France	*Actor*
Aung San Suu Kyi %National League for Democracy, 54-56 University Ave, Yangon, Myanmar	*Nobel Peace Laureate*
Aurand, Calvin W, Jr %Banta Corp, River Place, 225 Main St, Menasha, WI 54952, USA	*Businessman*
Auriemma, Geno %University of Connecticut, Athletc Dept, 2095 Hillside Road, Storrs, CT 06269, USA	*Basketball Coach*
Ausmus, Bradley D (Brad) 15 Newbridge Circle, Cheshire, CT 06410, USA	*Baseball Player*
Austin, Charles 514 Duncan Dr, San Marcus, TX 78666, USA	*Track Athlete*
Austin, Debbie 6733 Bittersweet Lane, Orlando, FL 32819, USA	*Golfer*
Austin, Denise %Getting Fit, PO Box 3771, San Clemente, CA 92674, USA	*Physical Fitness Instructor*
Austin, Karen 3356 Rowena Ave, #3, Los Angeles, CA 90027, USA	*Actress*
Austin, Patti 641 5th Ave, New York, NY 10022, USA	*Singer*
Austin, Teri 4245 Laurel Grove, Studio City, CA 91604, USA	*Actress*
Austin, Tracy 1751 Pinnacle Dr, #1500, McLean, VA 22102, USA	*Tennis Player*
Austregesilo de Athayde, Belarmino M Rua Cosme Velho 599, Rio de Janeiro RJ, Brazil	*Journalist*
Austrian, Robert %Univ of Pennsylvania, Med Center, 36th & Hamilton Walk, Philadelphia, PA 19130, USA	*Physician*
Auth, Tony %Philadelphia Inquirer, Editorial Dept, 400 N Broad St, Philadelphia, PA 19130, USA	*Editorial Cartoonist*
Autry, Alan %David Shapira, 15301 Ventura Blvd, #345, Sherman Oaks, CA 91403, USA	*Actor*
Autry, Gene 4383 Colfax Ave, Studio City, CA 91604, USA	*Actor, Singer, Baseball Executive*
Avalon, Frankie 4303 Spring Forest Lane, Westlake Village, CA 91362, USA	*Singer, Actor*
Avari, Erick %Henderson/Hogan, 247 S Beverly Dr, #102, Beverly Hills, CA 90212, USA	*Actor*
Avdelsayed, Gabriel %Coptic Orthodox Church, 427 West Side Ave, Jersey City, NJ 07304, USA	*Religious Leader*
Avdeyev, Sergei %Potchta Kosmonavtov, Moskovskoi Oblasti, 141160 Syvisdny Goroduk, Russia	*Cosmonaut*
Avedon, Richard (Dick) 407 E 75th St, New York, NY 10021, USA	*Photographer*
Averback, Hy 65 Old Ranch Road, Palm Desert, CA 92211, USA	*Movie Director*
Averitt, William (Bird) PO Box 1371, Hopkinsville, KY 42241, USA	*Basketball Player*
Avery, James %Abrams Artists, 9200 Sunset Blvd, #625, Los Angeles, CA 90069, USA	*Actor*
Avery, Margaret %Artists Agency, 10000 Santa Monica Blvd, #305, Los Angeles, CA 90067, USA	*Actress*

Avery, Phyllis *Actress*
609 Sterling Place, South Pasadena, CA 91030, USA
Avery, Steven T (Steve) *Baseball Player*
22138 Haig, Taylor, MI 48180, USA
Avery, Val *Actor*
84 Grove St, #19, New York, NY 10014, USA
Avery, William H *Governor, KS*
Rt 2, Wakefield, KS 67487, USA
Avery, William J *Businessman*
%Crown Cork & Seal, 9300 Ashton Road, Philadelphia, PA 19114, USA
Avida, Dan *Businessman*
%Electronics for Imaging, 2855 Campus Dr, San Mateo, CA 94403, USA
Avila, Roberto F G (Bobby) *Baseball Player*
Navegantes FR-19, Reforma-Veracruz, Mexico
Avildsen, John G *Movie Director*
45 E 89th St, #37-A, New York, NY 10128, USA
Awtrey, Dennis *Basketball Player*
1816 N 9th Ave, Phoenix, AZ 85007, USA
Ax, Emmanuel *Concert Pianist*
173 Riverside Dr, #12-G, New York, NY 10024, USA
Axelrod, Julius *Nobel Medicine Laureate*
10401 Grosvenor Place, Rockville, MD 20852, USA
Axton, Hoyt W *Singer, Songwriter*
103 Bedford St, #102, Hamilton, MT 59840, USA
Ay-O *Artist*
2-6-38 Matsuyama, Kiyoseshi, Tokyo, Japan
Ayckbourn, Alan *Writer*
%M Ramsay, 14-A Goodwins Court, St Martin's Lane, London WC2N 4LL, England
Aycock, Alice *Artist*
62 Green St, New York, NY 10012, USA
Ayers, Chuck *Cartoonist (Crankshaft)*
%Creators Syndicate, 5777 W Century Blvd, #700, Los Angeles, CA 90045, USA
Ayers, Richard H *Businessman*
%Stanley Works, 1000 Stanley Dr, New Britain, CT 06053, USA
Ayers, Roy *Jazz Vibist, Pianist, Singer*
%Associated Booking Corp, 1995 Broadway, #501, New York, NY 10023, USA
Aykroyd, Dan *Actor, Comedian*
1180 S Beverly Dr, #618, Los Angeles, CA 90035, USA
Azaria, Hank *Actor*
%Creative Artists Agency, 9830 Wilshire Blvd, Beverly Hills, CA 90212, USA
Azcarraga Milmo, Emilio *Publisher*
%Televisa SA, Avda Chapultepec 28, 06 724 Mexico City, Mexico
Azenberg, Emanuel *Theater Producer*
165 W 46th St, New York, NY 10036, USA
Azinger, Paul *Golfer*
7847 Chick Evans Place, Sarasota, FL 34240, USA
Aziz, Tariq *Prime Minister, Iraq*
%Prime Minister's Office, Karadat Mariam, Baghdad, Iraq
Azlan Muhibuddin Shan *Sultan, Malaysia*
%Sultan's Palace, Istana Bukit Serene, Kuala Lumpur, Malaysia
Aznar, Jose Maria *Prime Minister, Spain*
%Prime Minister's Office, Complejo de las Moncloa, 28071 Madrid, Spain
Aznavour, Charles *Singer, Actor, Songwriter*
12 Chemin du Chateau Blanc, 1231 Conches, Switzerland
Azoff, Irving *Record Company Executive*
%Warner Bros Records, 3300 Warner Blvd, Burbank, CA 91505, USA
Azuma, Norio *Artist*
276 Riverside Dr, New York, NY 10025, USA
Azuma, Takamitsu *Architect*
%Azuma Architects, 3-6-1 Minami-Aoyama Minatoku, Tokyo 107, Japan
Azzara, Candice *Actress*
%David Shapira, 15301 Ventura Blvd, #345, Sherman Oaks, CA 91403, USA

A

Avery - Azzara

Baba, Corneliu *Artist*
%Uniunea Artistilor Plastici, Str Nicolae Iorga 42, Bucharest, Romania

Baba, Encik Abdul Ghafar Bin *Prime Minister, Malaysia*
%Rural Development Ministry, Jalan Raja Laut, 50606 Kuala Lampur, Malaysia

Babangida, Ibrahim *Head of State, Nigeria; Army General*
Minna, Niger State, Nigeria

Babashoff, Jack *Swimmer*
4859 Monroe Ave, San Diego, CA 92115, USA

Babashoff, Shirley *Swimmer*
16260 Mercury Dr, Westminster, CA 92683, USA

Babb, Albert L *Biomedical Engineer*
3237 Lakewood Ave S, Seattle, WA 98144, USA

Babb-Sprague, Kristen *Synchronized Swimmer*
4677 Pine Valley Dr, Stockton, CA 95219, USA

Babbitt, Bruce E *Secretary, Interior*
%Interior Department, 1849 "C" St NW, Washington, DC 20240, USA

Babbitt, George T, Jr *Air Force General*
Commander, USAF Materiel Command, Wright-Patterson Air Force Base, OH 45433, USA

Babbitt, J Randolph *Labor Leader*
%Air Line Pilots Assn, 1625 Massachusetts Ave NW, Washington, DC 20036, USA

Babbitt, Milton B *Composer*
222 Western Way, Princeton, NJ 08540, USA

Babcock, Barbara *Actress*
530 W California Blvd, Pasadena, CA 91105, USA

Babcock, Horace W *Astronomer*
2189 N Altadena Dr, Altadena, CA 91001, USA

Babcock, Tim *Governor, MT*
%Ox Bow Ranch, PO Box 877, Helena, MT 59624, USA

Babenco, Hector E *Movie Director*
%International Creative Mgmt, 8942 Wilshire Blvd, Beverly Hills, CA 90211, USA

Babich, Bob *Football Player*
2717 Bay Canyon Court, San Diego, CA 92117, USA

Babilonia, Tai *Figure Skater*
13889 Valley Vista Blvd, Sherman Oaks, CA 91423, USA

Baby Oje *Soul/Rap Artist (Arrested Development)*
%William Morris Agency, 1325 Ave of Americas, New York, NY 10019, USA

Baca, Edward D (Ed) *Army General*
Chief, National Guard Bureau, HqUSA, Pentagon, Washington, DC 20310, USA

Baca, John *Vietnam War Army Hero (CMH)*
%Southern California College, Box 316, 55 Fair Dr, Costa Mesa, CA 92626, USA

Bacall, Lauren *Actress*
%Dakota Hotel, 1 W 72nd St, #43, New York, NY 10023, USA

Bach, Barbara *Actress*
1541 Ocean Ave, #200, Santa Monica, CA 90401, USA

Bach, Catherine *Actress*
15930 Woodvale Road, Encino, CA 91436, USA

Bach, Pamela *Actress*
%Marion Rosenberg, 8428 Melrose Place, #C, Los Angeles, CA 90069, USA

Bach, Richard *Writer*
%Dell Publishing, 1540 Broadway, New York, NY 10036, USA

Bach, Steven K *Movie Producer*
746 S Orange Dr, Los Angeles, CA 90036, USA

Bacharach, Burt *Composer, Musician*
10 Ocean Park Blvd, #4, Santa Monica, CA 90405, USA

Bachardy, Don *Writer*
145 Adelaide Dr, Santa Monica, CA 90402, USA

Bacher, Robert F *Physicist*
1300 Hot Springs Road, Montecito, CA 93108, USA

Bachrach, Louis F, Jr *Photographer*
%Bachrach Inc, 4 Strathmore Road, Natick, MA 01760, USA

Baciocco, Albert J, Jr *Navy Admiral*
747 Pitt St, Mount Pleasant, SC 29464, USA

Backe, John D *Entertainment Executive*
%Backe Group, 1646 W Chester Pike, Westtown, PA 19395, USA

Backman, Walter W (Wally) *Baseball Player*
PO Box 223, Ione, OR 97843, USA

Backus, Billy *Boxer*
308 N Main, Canastoga, NY 13032, USA

Backus, George E *Theoretical Geophysicist*
9362 La Jolla Farms Road, La Jolla, CA 92037, USA
Backus, John *Computer Programmer, Mathematician*
91 St Germaine Ave, San Francisco, CA 94114, USA
Backus, Sharon *Softball Coach*
%University of California, Athletic Dept, Los Angeles, CA 90024, USA
Bacon, Edmund N *Architect*
2117 Locust St, Philadelphia, PA 19103, USA
Bacon, James *Columnist*
10982 Topeka Dr, Northridge, CA 91326, USA
Bacon, Kevin *Actor*
285 Central Park West, New York, NY 10024, USA
Bacon, Nicky D *Vietnam War Army Hero (CMH)*
PO Box 9000, Conway, AR 72033, USA
Bacon, Roger F *Navy Admiral*
3103 W 109th Place, Westminster, CO 80030, USA
Bacot, J Carter *Financier*
48 Porter Place, Montclair, NJ 07042, USA
Bacquier, Gabriel *Opera Singer*
141 Rue de Rome, 75017 Paris, France
Bacs, Ludovic *Conductor, Composer*
31 D Golescu, Sc III, E7 V Ap 87, Bucharest 1, Romania
Bada, Jeffrey *Chemist*
%Scripps Institute of Oceanography, Chemistry Dept, La Jolla, CA 92093, USA
Badgro, Morris H (Red) *Football Player*
1010 E Temperance St, Kent, WA 98031, USA
Badham, John M *Movie Director*
288 Hot Springs Road, Montecito, CA 93108, USA
Badran, Mudar *Prime Minister, Jordan*
Shmaisani, Amman, Jordan
Badura-Skoda, Paul *Concert Pianist*
Zuckerkandlgass 14, 1190 Vienna, Austria
Baer, Gordy *Bowler*
5145 Arquilla Dr, Richton Park, IL 60471, USA
Baer, Max, Jr *Actor, Movie Producer, Director*
%Max Baer Productions, 10433 Wilshire Blvd, #103, Los Angeles, CA 90024, USA
Baer, Olaf *Opera Singer*
Olbersdorferstr 7, 01324 Dresden, Germany
Baer, Parley *Actor*
4967 Bilmoor Ave, Tarzana, CA 91356, USA
Baer, Robert J (Jacob) *Army General*
6213 Militia Court, Fairfax Station, VA 22039, USA
Baez, Joan *Singer, Songwriter*
%Diamonds & Rust Productions, PO Box 1026, Menlo Park, CA 94026, USA
Bafile, Corrado Cardinal *Religious Leader*
Via P Pancrazio Pfeiffer 10, 00193 Rome, Italy
Bagdasarian, Ross *Actor*
1465 Lindacrest Dr, Beverly Hills, CA 90210, USA
Baggett, Lee, Jr *Navy Admiral*
1650 Copa de Oro, La Jolla, CA 92037, USA
Baggetta, Vincent *Actor*
3928 Madelia Ave, Sherman Oaks, CA 91403, USA
Baggio, Roberto *Soccer Player*
%Federazione Giuoco Calcio, Via Gregorio Allegri 14, 00198 Rome, Italy
Bagian, James P *Astronaut*
%Somanetics Corp, 1653 E Maple Road, Troy, MI 48083, USA
Bagley, John *Basketball Player*
92 Harral Ave, Bridgeport, CT 06604, USA
Bagnall, Nigel T *Army Field Marshal, England*
%Royal Bank of England, 49 Charing Cross Road, London SW1A 2DX, England
Bagratyan, Grant A *Prime Minister, Armenia*
%Prime Minister's Office, Parliament Buildings, Yerevan, Armenia
Bagwell, Jeffrey R (Jeff) *Baseball Player*
2317 Drexel Dr, Houston, TX 77027, USA
Bagwell, Wendy *Singer*
%Harper Assoc, PO Box 144, Goodlettsville, TN 37070, USA
Bahcall, John N *Astrophysicist*
%Institute for Advanced Study, Natural Sciences School, Princeton, NJ 08540, USA

B

Backus - Bahcall

Bahns, Maxine *Actress, Model*
%Elite Model Mgmt, 111 E 22nd St, #200, New York, NY 10010, USA

Bahouth, Peter *Association Executive*
%Greenpeace, 1436 "U" St NW, Washington, DC 20009, USA

Bahr, Chris *Football Player*
200 Hylbert Road, Boalsburg, PA 16827, USA

Bahr, Egon *Government Official, West Germany*
%Institut fur Friedensforschung, Falkenstein 1, 22587 Hamburg, Germany

Bahr, Matt *Football Player*
53 Parkridge Lane, Pittsburgh, PA 15228, USA

Bahr, Morton *Labor Leader*
%Communications Workers Union, 501 3rd St NW, Washington, DC 20001, USA

Bahr, Walter *Soccer Player*
250 Elks Road, Boalsburg, PA 16827, USA

Bailar, Benjamin F *Government Official, Educator*
410 Walnut Road, Lake Forest, IL 60045, USA

Bailey, Colin *Businessman*
%Calgon Carbon Corp, 400 Calgon Carbon Dr, Pittsburgh, PA 15205, USA

Bailey, David *Photographer*
%Camera Eye Ltd, 24-26 Brownlow Mews, London WC1N 2LA, England

Bailey, F Lee *Attorney*
1400 Centre Park Blvd, #909, West Palm Beach, FL 33401, USA

Bailey, G W *Actor*
4972 Calvin Ave, Tarzana, CA 91356, USA

Bailey, Jerome H *Financier*
%Salomon Inc, 7 World Trade Center, New York, NY 10048, USA

Bailey, Jim *Actor, Singer*
5909 W Colgate Ave, Los Angeles, CA 90036, USA

Bailey, John *Cinematographer*
%United Talent Agency, 9560 Wilshire Blvd, #500, Beverly Hills, CA 90212, USA

Bailey, Johnny *Football Player*
6601 Dunlap St, #201, Houston, TX 77074, USA

Bailey, Keith E *Businessman*
%Williams Companies, 1 Williams Center, Tulsa, OK 74172, USA

Bailey, Leonard L *Heart Surgeon*
%Loma Linda University, Medical School, Loma Linda, CA 92350, USA

Bailey, Michael *Psychologist*
%Northwestern University, Psychology Dept, Evanston, IL 60208, USA

Bailey, Norman S *Opera Singer*
84 Warham Road, South Croydon, Surrey CR2 6LB, England

Bailey, Paul *Writer*
79 Davisville Road, London W12 9SH, England

Bailey, Philip *Singer (Earth Wind & Fire)*
%Performers of the World, 8901 Melrose Ave, #200, West Hollywood, CA 90069, USA

Bailey, Razzy *Singer, Songwriter*
%Doc Sedelmeier, PO Box 62, Geneva, NE 68361, USA

Bailey, Robert L *Businessman*
%State Auto Financial Corp, 518 E Broad St, Columbus, OH 43215, USA

Bailey, Thomas H *Financier*
%Janus Capital Corp, 100 Fillmore St, Denver, CO 80206, USA

Bailey, Thurl *Basketball Player*
9292 Horizon Vista Lane, Las Vegas, NV 89117, USA

Bailey, William *Artist*
223 E 10th St, New York, NY 10003, USA

Bailyn, Bernard *Writer, Historian*
170 Clifton St, Belmont, MA 02178, USA

Bain, Barbara *Actress*
1501 Skylark Lane, West Hollywood, CA 90069, USA

Bain, Conrad *Actor*
1230 Chickory Lane, Los Angeles, CA 90049, USA

Bainbridge, Beryl *Actress, Writer*
42 Albert St, London NW1 7NU, England

Baines, Harold D *Baseball Player*
PO Box 335, Saint Michaels, MD 21663, USA

Baio, Jimmy *Actor*
4333 Forman Ave, Toluca Lake, CA 91602, USA

Baio, Scott *Actor*
4333 Forman Ave, Toluca Lake, CA 91602, USA

Baird, Charles F — *Businessman*
PO Box 421, Bridgehampton, NY 11932, USA
Baird, Euan — *Businessman*
%Schlumberger Ltd, 277 Park Ave, New York, NY 10172, USA
Baird, James M — *Religious Leader*
%Presbyterian Church, PO Box 1428, Decatur, GA 30031, USA
Baird, Stuart — *Movie Diector*
%William Morris Agency, 151 S El Camino Dr, Beverly Hills, CA 90212, USA
Baird, William D, Jr — *Financier*
%Chemical Bank New Jersey, 2 Tower Center, East Brunswick, NJ 08816, USA
Baird, Zoe — *Attorney*
%Aetna Life & Casualty, 151 Farmington Ave, Hartford, CT 06156, USA
Baitz, Jon Robin — *Writer*
%William Morris Agency, 1325 Ave of Americas, New York, NY 10019, USA
Baiul, Oksana — *Figure Skater*
%International Skating Center, 1375 Hopmeadow St, Simsbury, CT 06070, USA
Baker Guadagnino, Kathy — *Golfer*
%Int'l Management Group, 1 Erieview Plaza, #1300, Cleveland, OH 44114, USA
Baker, Anita — *Singer*
8216 Tivoli Cove Dr, Las Vegas, NV 89128, USA
Baker, Blanche — *Actress*
70 Flower Ave, Hastings-on-Hudson, NY 10706, USA
Baker, Buck — *Auto Racing Driver*
1613 Runnymede Lane, Charlotte, NC 28211, USA
Baker, Buddy — *Auto Racing Driver*
4860 Moonlite Bay Dr, Sherrills Ford, NC 28673, USA
Baker, Carroll — *Actress*
630 Masselin Ave, #221, Los Angeles, CA 90036, USA
Baker, Diane — *Actress*
2733 Outpost Dr, Los Angeles, CA 90068, USA
Baker, Dylan — *Actor*
%International Creative Mgmt, 8942 Wilshire Blvd, Beverly Hills, CA 90211, USA
Baker, Ellen Shulman — *Astronaut*
%NASA, Johnson Space Center, 2101 NASA Road, Houston, TX 77058, USA
Baker, Eugene W — *Baseball Player*
2250 E 48th St, Davenport, IA 52807, USA
Baker, Frank — *Bowling Contributor*
13900 W Burleigh Road, Brookfield, WI 53005, USA
Baker, Ginger — *Drummer (Cream, Masters of Reality)*
%Twist Mgmt, 4230 Del Rey Ave, #621, Marina del Rey, CA 90292, USA
Baker, Graham — *Movie Director*
10 Buckingham St, London WC2, England
Baker, Howard H, Jr — *Senator, TN*
PO Box 8, Huntsville, TN 37756, USA
Baker, James A, III — *Secretary, State*
%Baker & Botts, 1299 Pennsylvania Ave NW, Washington, DC 20004, USA
Baker, James K — *Businessman*
%Arvin Industries, Noblitt Plaza, PO Box 3000, Columbus, IN 47202, USA
Baker, Janet — *Opera, Concert Singer*
%Ibbs & Tillett, 18-B Pindock Mews, London W9, England
Baker, Joe Don — *Actor*
23339 Hatteras St, Woodland Hills, CA 91367, USA
Baker, John F, Jr — *Vietnam War Army Hero (CMH)*
3832 Trogon Way, Las Vegas, NV 89103, USA
Baker, John H, Jr — *Football Player*
5 Farnham Park Dr, Houston, TX 77024, USA
Baker, John T — *Publisher*
%JAMA Magazine, 535 N Dearborn St, Chicago, IL 60610, USA
Baker, Johnnie B (Dusty) — *Baseball Player, Manager*
40 Livingston Terrace Dr, San Bruno, CA 94066, USA
Baker, Kathy — *Actress*
1146 N Central Ave, #163, Glendale, CA 91202, USA
Baker, Kendall L — *Educator*
%University of North Dakota, President's Office, Grand Forks, ND 58202, USA
Baker, Leslie M, Jr — *Financier*
%Wachovia Corp, 301 N Main St, Winston-Salem, NC 27101, USA
Baker, Margaret B — *Financier*
%First Options of Chicago, 440 S LaSalle, Chicago, IL 60605, USA

B

Baird - Baker

Baker, Mark — *Bowler*
665 Park Dr, #20, Costa Mesa, CA 92627, USA

Baker, Michael A (Mike) — *Astronaut*
%NASA, Johnson Space Center, 2101 NASA Road, Houston, TX 77058, USA

Baker, Nicholson — *Writer*
%Melanie Jackson Agency, 256 W 57th St, #1119, New York, NY 10019, USA

Baker, Paul T — *Anthropologist*
47-450 Lulani St, Kaneohe, HI 96744, USA

Baker, R Robinson — *Surgeon*
8717 McDonogh Road, McDonogh, MD 21208, USA

Baker, Robert — *Attorney*
%Baker Silberberg Keener, 2850 Ocean Park Blvd, Santa Monica, CA 90405, USA

Baker, Roy Ward — *Movie Director*
%Michael Whitehall, 125 Gloucester Road, London SW7 4TE, England

Baker, Russell W — *Journalist, Columnist*
%New York Times, Editorial Dept, 229 W 43rd St, New York, NY 10036, USA

Baker, Sherman — *Businessman*
%J Baker Inc, 555 Turnpike St, Canton, MA 02021, USA

Baker, Thomas A — *Air Force General*
Commander, 12th Air Force, E Gafford, Davis Mountain Air Force Base, AZ 85707, USA

Baker, Vernon J — *WW II Army Hero (CMH)*
%General Delivery, St Maries, ID 83861, USA

Baker, Vin — *Basketball Player*
153 Ayers Point Road, Old Saybrook, CT 06475, USA

Baker, W Thane — *Track Athlete*
6704 Saint John Court, Granbury, TX 76049, USA

Baker, Warren J — *Educator*
%California Poly University, President's Office, San Luis Obispo, CA 93407, USA

Baker, William (Bill) — *Hockey Player*
620 Sugar Bush Trail N, Brainerd, MN 56401, USA

Baker, William O — *Research Chemist*
%ATT Bell Telephone Laboratories, 600 Mountain Ave, Murray Hill, NJ 07974, USA

Baker-Finch, Ian — *Golfer*
%Int'l Management Group, 1 Erieview Plaza, #1300, Cleveland, OH 44114, USA

Bakis, Kirsten — *Writer*
%Farrar Straus Giroux, 19 Union Square W, New York, NY 10003, USA

Bakke, Brenda — *Actress*
21838 Encino Road, Topanga, CA 90290, USA

Bakken, Jim — *Football Player*
230 Glen Hollow Road, Madison, WI 53705, USA

Bakker Messner, Tammy Faye — *Religious Leader*
72727 Country Club Dr, Rancho Mirage, CA 92270, USA

Bakker, James O (Jim) — *Religious Leader*
%New Covenant Church, PO Box 987, Hendersonvlle, NC 28793, USA

Bakshi, Ralph — *Animator*
%Gang Tyre Ramer Brown, PO Box 4322, Los Angeles, CA 90078, USA

Bakula, Scott — *Actor*
%United Talent Agency, 9560 Wilshire Blvd, #500, Beverly Hills, CA 90212, USA

Balaguer Ricardo, Joaquin — *President, Dominican Republic*
%Partido Reformista, Ensanche La Fe, Santo Domingo, Dominican Republic

Balandin, Alexander N — *Cosmonaut*
%Potchta Kosmonavtov, Moskovskoi Oblasti, 141160 Syvisdny Goroduk, Russia

Balaski, Belinda — *Actress*
%Epstein-Wyckoff, 280 S Beverly Dr, #400, Beverly Hills, CA 90212, USA

Balassa, Sandor — *Composer*
14 Arnyas Str, Budapest 1121, Hungary

Balayan, Roman G — *Movie Director*
Gogolevskaya Str 37/2, #15, Kiev 252053, Ukraine

Balboa, Marcelo — *Soccer Player*
13139 Hedda Dr, Cerritos, CA 90703, USA

Balderstone, James S — *Businessman*
115 Mont Albert Road, Canterbury 3126, VIC, Australia

Baldessari, John — *Conceptual Artist*
2001 1/2 Main St, Santa Monica, CA 90405, USA

Balding, Rebecca — *Actress*
%Sanders Agency, 1204 Broadway, #304, New York, NY 10001, USA

Baldrige, Letitia — *Businesswoman*
%Letitia Baldrige Enterprises, PO Box 32287, Washington, DC 20007, USA

Baldschun, Jack E — *Baseball Player*
311 Erie Road, Green Bay, WI 54311, USA
Baldwin, Adam — *Actor*
1301 Caryle Ave, Santa Monica, CA 90402, USA
Baldwin, Alec — *Actor*
%Wolf/Kasteller, 132 S Rodeo Dr, #300, Beverly Hills, CA 90212, USA
Baldwin, Jack — *Auto Racing Driver*
4748 Balmoral Way, Marietta, GA 30068, USA
Baldwin, John A (Jack), Jr — *Navy Admiral*
6 N Liberty St, Nantucket, MA 02554, USA
Baldwin, Judy — *Actress*
%Twentieth Century, 15315 Magnolia Blvd, #429, Sherman Oaks, CA 91403, USA
Baldwin, Stephen — *Actor*
PO Box 447, Camillus, NY 13031, USA
Baldwin, William — *Actor*
%Creative Artists Agency, 9830 Wilshire Blvd, Beverly Hills, CA 90212, USA
Bale, Christian — *Actor*
685 McCowan Road, Box 66534, Toronto ON M1J 3NB, Canada
Balfanz, John C — *Ski Jumper*
7770 E Iliff Ave, #G, Denver, CO 80231, USA
Baliles, Gerald L — *Governor, VA*
%Hunton & Williams, PO Box 1535, Richmond, VA 23212, USA
Balin, Marty — *Singer, Songwriter*
%Joe Buchwald, 436 Belvedere St, San Francisco, CA 94117, USA
Balk, Fairuza — *Actress*
%Paul Kohner, 9300 Wilshire Blvd, #555, Beverly Hills, CA 90212, USA
Balkenhol, Klaus — *Equestrian Athlete*
Narzissenweg 11-A, 40723 Hilden, Germany
Ball, Robert M — *Government Official*
1776 Massachusetts Ave NW, Washington, DC 20036, USA
Balladur, Edouard — *Prime Minister, France*
35039 Marburg 1, France
Ballard, Carroll — *Movie Director*
PO Box 556, Mt Helena, CA 94574, USA
Ballard, Del, Jr — *Bowler*
%Professional Bowlers Assn, 1720 Merriman Road, Akron, OH 44313, USA
Ballard, Donald E — *Vietnam War Navy Hero (CMH)*
PO Box 34593, North Kansas City, MO 64116, USA
Ballard, Greg — *Basketball Player*
1791 Kirkwood Lane N, Plymouth, MN 55441, USA
Ballard, Hank — *Singer, Songwriter*
%Ambassadors of American Culture, 46 Las Cascades Road, #1, Orinda, CA 94563, USA
Ballard, J(ames) G(raham) — *Writer*
36 Old Charlton Road, Shepperton, Middx, England
Ballard, Joe N — *Army General*
Commanding General, Chief of Engineers, Fort Leonard Wood, MO 65473, USA
Ballard, Kaye — *Actress*
91475 Mashi Dr, Rancho Mirage, CA 92270, USA
Ballard, Robert D — *Oceanographer (Titanic Discoverer)*
%Mystic Oceano, Mystic, CT 06355, USA
Ballesteros, Seveiano (Seve) — *Golfer*
Ruiz Zorilla 16-20J, 39009 Santander, Spain
Ballestrero, Anastasio Cardinal — *Religious Leader*
Via Arcivescovado 12, 10121 Turin, Italy
Ballhaus, Michael — *Cinematographer*
PO Box 2230, Los Angeles, CA 90078, USA
Ballhaus, William F, Jr — *Aeronautical Engineer*
%Martin Marietta Civil Space & Communication Co, PO Box 179, Denver, CO 80201, USA
Ballou, Clinton E — *Biochemist*
%University of California, Chemistry Dept, Berkeley, CA 94720, USA
Ballou, Mark — *Actor*
145 Ave of Americas, #200, New York, NY 10013, USA
Balmaseda, Liz — *Journalist*
%Miami Herald, Editorial Dept, 1 Herald Plaza, Miami, FL 33132, USA
Balsam, Talia — *Actress*
%Innovative Artists, 1999 Ave of Stars, #2850, Los Angeles, CA 90067, USA
Balser, Glennon — *Religious Leader*
%Advent Christian Church, 6315 Studley Road, Mechanicsville, VA 23116, USA

B

Baldschun - Balser

Balsley, Philip E *Singer (Statler Brothers)*
%American Major Talent, PO Box 492, Hernando, MS 38632, USA

Balter, Sam *Basketball Player*
4124 Los Nietos Dr, Los Angeles, CA 90027, USA

Balthus *Artist*
Grand Chalet Rossiniere, Canton de Vaux, Switzerland

Baltimore, David *Nobel Medicine Laureate, Educator*
%California Institute of Technology, President's Office, Pasadena, CA 91125, USA

Baltron, Donna *Actress*
%CNA Assoc, 1925 Century Park East, #750, Los Angeles, CA 90067, USA

Baltsa, Agnes *Opera Singer*
%R Schultz Mgmt, Rutistr 52, 8044 Zurich-Gockhausen, Switzerland

Baltz, Lewis *Photographer*
11693 San Vicente Blvd, #527, Los Angeles, CA 90049, USA

Balukas, Jean *Billiards Player*
9818 4th Ave, Brooklyn, NY 11209, USA

Bama, Jim *Artist*
PO Box 148, Wapiti, WY 82450, USA

Bamberger, George I *Baseball Manager*
455 N Bath Club Blvd, North Redington Beach, FL 33708, USA

Banach, Ed *Wrestler*
2128 Country Club Blvd, Ames, IA 50014, USA

Banach, Lou *Wrestler*
3276 E Fairfax, Cleveland Heights, OH 44118, USA

Banachowski, Andy *Volleyball Player, Coach*
%University of California, Athletic Dept, Los Angeles, CA 90024, USA

Banana, Canaan S *President, Zimbabwe*
Burroughs House, PO Box 8136, Causeway, Zimbabwe

Banaszynski, Jacqui *Journalist*
%St Paul Pioneer Press Dispatch, Editorial Dept, 345 Cedar, St Paul, MN 55101, USA

Banazak, Pete *Football Player*
12400 Old Still Court, Ponte Verde, FL 32082, USA

Banbury, F H Frith *Theater Director*
18 Park St James, Prince Albert Road, London NW8 7LE, England

Bancroft, Anne *Actress*
2301 La Mesa Dr, Santa Monica, CA 90402, USA

Bancroft, Cameron *Actor*
1934 Londa Flora Dr, Los Angeles, CA 90077, USA

Bancroft, Ian P *Government Leader, England*
%House of Lords, Westminster, London SW1A 0PW, England

Bandaranaike, Sirimavo R D *Prime Minister, Sri Lanka*
301 T B Jayah Mawatha, Colombo 10, Sri Lanka

Banderas, Antonio *Actor*
201 S Rockingham Ave, Los Angeles, CA 90049, USA

Bando, Salvatore L (Sal) *Baseball Player*
104 W Juniper Lane, Mequon, WI 53092, USA

Bandy, Moe *Singer, Songwriter*
PO Box 748, Adkins, TX 78101, USA

Banfield, Edward C *Educator*
%Harvard University, Littauer Center, Cambridge, MA 02138, USA

Bangemann, Martin *Government Official, West Germany*
Sannentalstr 9, 72555 Metzingen, Germany

Bangerter, Hans E *Soccer Official*
Hubelgasse 25, 3065 Bolligen BE, Switzerland

Bangerter, Norman H *Governor, UT*
%NHB Construction Co, 2976 W 10000 S, South Jordan, UT 84095, USA

Bani-Sadr, Abolhassan *Prime Minister, Iran*
16 Ave Pont Royal, 94230 Cachan, France

Banier, Francois-Marie *Photographer*
%William Morrow Co, 1350 Ave of Americas, New York, NY 10016, USA

Bank, Aaron *WW II Army Hero*
239 Avenida Montalvo, San Clemente, CA 92672, USA

Banke, Paul *Boxer*
1926 Bobolink Way, Pomona, CA 91767, USA

Banks, David R *Businessman*
%Beverly Enterprises, 5111 Rogers Ave, Fort Smith, AR 72919, USA

Banks, Dennis *Indian Activist*
%General Delivery, Oglala, SD 57764, USA

Banks, Ernest (Ernie) — *Baseball Player*
16161 Ventura Blvd, #814, Encino, CA 91436, USA

Banks, Gene — *Basketball Player*
PO Box 1964, Greensboro, NC 27402, USA

Banks, Jonathan — *Actor*
909 Euclid St, #8, Santa Monica, CA 90403, USA

Banks, Kelcie — *Boxer*
3040 E Charleston Blvd, Las Vegas, NV 89104, USA

Banks, Steven — *Comedian*
%Gersh Agency, 232 N Canon Dr, Beverly Hills, CA 90210, USA

Banks, Ted — *Track Coach*
%Riverside Community College, Athletic Dept, Riverside, CA 92506, USA

Banks, Tyra — *Model, Actress*
730 N Eucalyptus Ave, #6, Inglewood, CA 90302, USA

Banks, Willie — *Track Athlete*
PO Box 4108, Salt Lake City, UT 84110, USA

Bannen, Ian — *Actor*
%London Mgmt, 2-4 Noel St, London W1V 3RB, England

Banner, Bob — *Movie Producer, Director*
461 S Maple Dr, Beverly Hills, CA 90212, USA

Bannister, Floyd F — *Baseball Player*
6701 Caball Dr, Paradise Valley, AZ 85253, USA

Bannister, Roger G — *Track Athlete, Neurologist*
21 Bardwell Road, Oxford OX2 6SV, England

Bannon, Jack — *Actor*
5923 Wilbur Ave, Tarzana, CA 91356, USA

Banois, Vincent J — *Football Player*
24256 J Tamarack Trail, Southfield, MI 48075, USA

Bantom, Mike — *Basketball Player, Executive*
%NBA Properties, Olympic Tower, 122 E 55th St, New York, NY 10022, USA

Banton, Julian W — *Financier*
%SouthTrust Bank of Alabama, 420 N 20th St, Birmingham, AL 35203, USA

Banzer Suarez, Hugo — *President, Bolovia; Army General*
%President's Office, Palacio de Gobierno, Plaza Murilla, La Paz, Bolivia

Baptiste, Marianne Jean — *Actress*
%Stephen Hatton, 83-93 Shepperton Road, London N1 3DF, England

Baquet, Dean P — *Journalist*
%New York Times, Editorial Dept, 229 W 43rd St, New York, NY 10036, USA

Bar-Josef, Ofer — *Archeologist*
%Harvard University, Archeology Dept, Cambridge, MA 02138, USA

Barak, Ehud — *Foreign Minister, Army General, Israel*
%Israel Labor Party, 16 Hayarkon St, Tel-Aviv 63571, Israel

Baranski, Christine — *Actress*
%International Creative Mgmt, 8942 Wilshire Blvd, Beverly Hills, CA 90211, USA

Barany, Istvan — *Swimmer*
I Attila Utca 87, 01012 Budapest, Hungary

Barba, Carlos — *Entertainment Executive*
%Univision Television Group, 9405 NW 41st St, Miami, FL 33178, USA

Barbakow, Jeffrey C — *Businessman*
%National Medical Enterprises, 2700 Colorado Ave, Santa Monica, CA 90404, USA

Barbara, Agatha — *President, Malta*
Wied Il-Ghajn St, Zabbar, Malta

Barbeau, Adrienne — *Actress, Singer*
PO Box 1839, Studio City, CA 91614, USA

Barber, Anthony P L — *Financier*
%Standard Chartered Bank, 10 Clements Lane, London EC4N 7AB, England

Barber, Bill — *Hockey Player*
PO Box 504, East Rutherford, NJ 07073, USA

Barber, Glynis — *Actress*
%Billy Marsh Agency, 19 Denmark St, London WC2H 8NA, England

Barber, Miller — *Golfer*
2637 Rivercrest Dr, Sherman, TX 75092, USA

Barber, Rex T — *WW II Army Air Corps Hero*
70460 NW Lower Bridge Way, Terrebonne, OR 97760, USA

Barber, Steven L (Steve) — *Baseball Player*
1517 Cushman Dr, Sierra Vista, AZ 85635, USA

Barber, William E — *Korean War Marine Corps Hero (CMH)*
15231 Chalon Circle, Irvine, CA 92604, USA

B

Banks - Barber

Barbera, Joseph (Joe) *Animator (Yogi Bear, Flintstones)*
12003 Briarvale Lane, Studio City, CA 91604, USA
Barbi, Shane *Model (Barbi Twins)*
29196 Heathercliff, #216-410, Malibu, CA 90265, USA
Barbi, Sia *Model (Barbi Twins)*
29169 Heathercliff, #216-410, Malibu, CA 90265, USA
Barbieri, Fedora *Opera Singer*
Viale Belfiore 9, Florence, Italy
Barbieri, Gato *Jazz Saxophonist*
200 W 51st St, #1410, New York, NY 10019, USA
Barbieri, Paula *Actress, Model*
PO Box 20483, Panama City, FL 32411, USA
Barbot, Ivan *Law Enforcement Official*
%Presidence Interpol, 50 Quai Achille Lignon, 69006 Lyon, France
Barbour, Haley *Political Leader*
%Republican National Committee, 310 1st St SE, Washington, DC 20002, USA
Barbour, John *Comedian, Writer*
54 Pine Isle Court, Henderson, NV 89014, USA
Barbutti, Pete *Jazz Trumpeter*
%Thomas Cassidy, 0366 Horseshoe Dr, Basalt, CO 81621, USA
Barclay, George M *Financier*
%Federal Home Loan Bank, 5605 N MacArthur Blvd, Irving, TX 75038, USA
Barco Vargas, Virgilio *President, Colombia*
%Colombian Embassy, 3 Hans Crescent, #3-A, London SW1X 0LR, England
Bard, Allen J *Chemist*
6202 Mountainclimb Dr, Austin, TX 78731, USA
Bardis, Panos D *Writer*
%University of Toledo, Sociology Dept, Toledo, OH 43606, USA
Bardot, Brigitte *Actress*
La Madrigue, 83990 St Tropez, Var, France
Bare, Bobby *Singer, Songwriter*
2401 Music Valley Dr, Nashville, TN 37214, USA
Bare, Richard L *Television Director*
700 Harbor Island Dr, Newport Beach, CA 92660, USA
Barenboim, Daniel *Conductor, Concert Pianist*
%Chicago Symphony Orchestra, 220 S Michigan Ave, Chicago, IL 60604, USA
Barfield, Jesse L *Baseball Player*
4208 Canterwood Dr, Houston, TX 77068, USA
Barfod, Hakon *Yachtsman*
Jon Ostensensv 15, 1360 Nesbru, Norway
Barfoot, Van T *WW II Army Hero (CMH)*
Leaning Oaks, Rt 1, Box 32-A, Ford, VA 23850, USA
Barker, Cliff *Basketball Player*
PO Box 113, Arcadia, IN 46030, USA
Barker, Clive *Writer, Movie Director*
9332 Readcrest Dr, Beverly Hills, CA 90210, USA
Barker, Horace A *Biochemist*
561 Santa Clara Ave, Berkeley, CA 94707, USA
Barker, Richard A *Religious Leader*
%Orthodox Presbyterian Church, PO Box P, Willow Grove, PA 19090, USA
Barker, Robert W (Bob) *Entertainer*
1851 Outpost Dr, Los Angeles, CA 90068, USA
Barkin, Ellen *Actress*
%Creative Artists Agency, 9830 Wilshire Blvd, Beverly Hills, CA 90212, USA
Barkley, Charles W *Basketball Player*
%Houston Rockets, Summit, Greenway Plaza, #10, Houston, TX 77046, USA
Barkley, Iran *Boxer*
2645 3rd Ave, Bronx, NY 10451, USA
Barkley, Richard C *Diplomat*
%US State Department, 2201 "C" St NW, Washington, DC 20520, USA
Barkman Tyler, Janie *Swimmer*
%Princeton University, Athletic Dept, Princeton, NJ 08544, USA
Barks, Carl *Cartoonist (Uncle Scrooge, Ducksburg)*
%Carl Barks Studios, PO Box 524, Grants Pass, OR 97528, USA
Barksdale, James (Jim) *Businessman*
%Netscape Communications, 501 E Middlefield Road, Mountain Valley, CA 94043, USA
Barletta, Joseph *Publisher*
%TV Guide Magazine, 100 Matsonford Road, Radnor, PA 19087, USA

Barletta, Nicolas Ardito	*President, Panama*
PO Box 7737, Panama City 9, Panama	
Barmore, Leon	*Basketball Coach*
%Louisiana Tech University, Athletic Dept, Ruston, LA 71272, USA	
Barnard, Christiaan N	*Heart Surgeon*
PO Box 6143, Welgemoed, 7538 Capetown, South Africa	
Barnes, Binnie	*Actress*
838 N Doheny Dr, #B, Los Angeles, CA 90069, USA	
Barnes, Clive A	*Dance, Theater Critic*
%New York Post, 1211 Avenue of Americas, New York, NY 10036, USA	
Barnes, Edward Larrabee	*Architect*
320 W 13th St, New York, NY 10014, USA	
Barnes, Erich	*Football Player*
255 W 85th St, New York, NY 10024, USA	
Barnes, Frank	*Baseball Player*
1508 Brazil St, Greenville, MS 38701, USA	
Barnes, Harry G, Jr	*Diplomat*
Hapenny Road, Peachum, VT 05862, USA	
Barnes, James E	*Businessman*
%Mapco Inc, PO Box 645, Tulsa, OK 74101, USA	
Barnes, Jhane E	*Fashion Designer*
%Jhane Barnes Inc, 575 7th Ave, New York, NY 10018, USA	
Barnes, Jimmy	*Singer*
%Premier Artists Pty, 9 Dundas Lane, Albert Park VIC 3206, Australia	
Barnes, Joanna	*Actress*
267 Middle Road, Santa Barbara, CA 93108, USA	
Barnes, Julian P	*Writer*
%A D Peters, 10 Buckingham St, London WC2H 6B0, England	
Barnes, Linda	*Writer*
%Delacorte Press, 1540 Broadway, New York, NY 10036, USA	
Barnes, Norm	*Hockey Player*
17 Meadow Crossing, Simsbury, CT 06070, USA	
Barnes, Priscilla	*Actress*
%HWA Talent, 1964 Westwood Blvd, #400, Los Angeles, CA 90025, USA	
Barnes, Robert H	*Psychiatrist*
%Texas Tech University Medical School, PO Box 4349, Lubbock, TX 79409, USA	
Barnes, Roosevelt	*Football Player*
922 E Belmont Dr, Fort wayne, IN 46806, USA	
Barnes, Wallace	*Businessman*
%Barnes Group, 123 Main St, Bristol, CT 06010, USA	
Barnet, Will	*Artist, Educator*
%National Arts Club, 15 Gramercy Park, New York, NY 10003, USA	
Barnett of Heywood & Royton, Joel B	*Government Official, England*
24 John Islip St, #92, London SW1, England	
Barnett, Dick	*Basketball Player*
PO Box 640194, San Francisco, CA 94164, USA	
Barnett, Gary	*Football Coach*
%Northwestern University, Athletic Dept, Evanston, IL 60208, USA	
Barnett, Jim	*Basketball Player*
7 Kittiwake Road, Orinda, CA 94563, USA	
Barnett, Jonathan	*Architect*
4501 Connecticut Ave NW, Washington, DC 20008, USA	
Barnett, Mandy	*Singer*
%Dan Cleary Mgmt, 1801 Ave of Stars, #1105, Los Angeles, CA 90067, USA	
Barnett, Sabrina	*Model*
%Next Model Mgmt, 23 Watts St, New York, NY 10013, USA	
Barnett, Steven (Steve)	*Water Polo Player*
433 Queens Court, Campbell, CA 95008, USA	
Barnett, Tommy	*Religious Leader*
%Phoenix First Assembly Church, 13613 N Cave Creek Road, Phoenix, AZ 85022, USA	
Barnette, Curtis H (Hank)	*Businessman*
%Bethlehem Steel, 1170 8th Ave, Bethlehem, PA 18018, USA	
Barnevik, Barney	*Businessman*
%ASEA AB, 721 83 Vasteras, Sweden	
Barnevik, Percy N	*Businessman*
%Skanska AB, 182 25 Danderyd, Stockholm, Sweden	
Barney, Lem	*Football Player*
23195 Laurel Valley, Southfield, MI 48034, USA	

B

Barletta - Barney

Barnidge, Tom	*Editor*
%Sporting News, Editorial Dept, 1212 N Lindbergh Blvd, St Louis, MO 63132, USA	
Barnum, Harvey C, Jr	*Vietnam War Marine Corps Hero (CMH)*
2101 Cabot's Point Lane, Reston, VA 20191, USA	
Baron Crespo, Enrique	*Government Official, Spain*
%European Parliament, 97/113 Rue Velliard, 1040 Brussels, Belgium	
Baron, Carolyn	*Editor*
%Dell Publishing, 666 5th Ave, New York, NY 10103, USA	
Barone, Anita	*Actress*
%Gersh Agency, 232 N Canon Dr, Beverly Hills, CA 90210, USA	
Barone, Richard	*Singer*
%Little Fishes Mgmt, 923 5th Ave, New York, NY 10021, USA	
Barr, Doug	*Actor*
PO Box 63, Rutherford, CA 94573, USA	
Barr, Julia	*Actress*
%St Laurent Assoc, Cherokee Station, PO Box 20191, New York, NY 10028, USA	
Barr, Murray L	*Anatomist, Geneticist*
411-312 Oxford St W, London ON N6H 4N7, Canada	
Barr, Nevada	*Writer*
%G P Putnam's Sons, 200 Madison Ave, New York, NY 10016, USA	
Barr, William P	*Attorney General*
%Shaw Pittman Potts Trowbridge, 2300 "N" St NW, Washington, DC 20037, USA	
Barrasso, Tom	*Hockey Player*
502 Hillside Dr, Sewickley, PA 15143, USA	
Barraud, Henry	*Composer*
1 Chemin de Presles, 94410 Saint-Maurice, France	
Barrault, Marie-Christine	*Actress*
19 Rue de Lisbonne, 75008 Paris, France	
Barre, Raymond	*Prime Minister, France*
4-6 Ave Emile-Acollas, 75007 Paris, France	
Barreto, Bruno	*Movie Director*
22 W 68th St, New York, NY 10023, USA	
Barrett, Charles S	*Physicist, Metallurgist*
%University of Denver, Metallurgy Materials Division, Denver, CO 80208, USA	
Barrett, Craig R	*Businessman*
%Intel Corp, 2200 Mission College Blvd, Santa Clara, CA 95054, USA	
Barrett, Ernie	*Basketball Player*
2824 Timbercreek Circle, Wichita, KS 67204, USA	
Barrett, Majel	*Actress*
PO Box 691370, West Hollywood, CA 90069, USA	
Barrett, Martin G (Marty)	*Baseball Manager*
9708 Buckhorn Dr, Las Vegas, NV 89134, USA	
Barrett, Rona	*Columnist, Commentator*
PO Box 1410, Beverly Hills, CA 90213, USA	
Barrett, Stan	*Auto Racing Driver*
Rocking K Ranch, Bishop, CA 93514, USA	
Barretto, Ray	*Jazz Percussionist, Conga Player*
%Creative Music Consultants, 181 Christie St, #300, New York, NY 10002, USA	
Barrie, Barbara	*Actress*
15 W 72nd St, #2-A, New York, NY 10023, USA	
Barris, Chuck	*Television Producer*
1990 Bundy Ave, Los Angeles, CA 90025, USA	
Barron, Donald J	*Financier*
%Midland Bank, Poultry, London EC2P 2BX, England	
Barron, Kenneth (Kenny)	*Jazz Pianist, Composer*
%Joanne Klein Entertainment, 130 W 28th St, New York, NY 10001, USA	
Barron, William W	*Governor, WV*
Nassau House, 301 N Ocean Blvd, #603, Pompano Beach, FL 33062, USA	
Barros, Dana	*Basketball Player*
17 Clarkwood St, Mattapan, MA 02126, USA	
Barrow, Robert H	*Marine Corps General*
HC 68, Box 409-R, Saint Francisville, LA 70775, USA	
Barrs, Jay	*Archer*
6395 Senoma Dr, Salt Lake City, UT 84121, USA	
Barry, A L	*Religious Leader*
%Lutheran Church - Missouri Synod, 421 S 2nd St, Elkhart, IN 46516, USA	
Barry, Brent	*Basketball Player*
%Los Angeles Clippers, Sports Arena, 3939 Figueroa St, Los Angeles, CA 90037, USA	

Barry, Claudje — *Singer*
%T-Best Talent Agency, 2001 Wayne Ave, #103, San Leandro, CA 94577, USA

Barry, Daniel T — *Astronaut*
%NASA, Johnson Space Center, 2101 NASA Road, Houston, TX 77058, USA

Barry, Dave — *Journalist*
%Miami Herald, Editorial Dept, 1 Herald Plaza, Miami, FL 33132, USA

Barry, David A — *Financier*
%Bariston Holdings, 1 International Place, Boston, MA 02110, USA

Barry, Gene — *Actor*
%Merlis Green, 10390 Santa Monica Blvd, Los Angeles, CA 90025, USA

Barry, John — *Composer*
540 Centre Island Road, Oyster Bay, NY 11771, USA

Barry, John J — *Labor Official*
%Int'l Brotherhood of Electrical Workers, 1125 15th St NW, Washington, DC 20005, USA

Barry, Jon — *Basketball Player*
5030 Paces Station Dr NW, Atlanta, GA 30339, USA

Barry, Len — *Singer (The Dovells)*
%Hot Hits Mgmt, 3096 Janice Circle, Chamblee, GA 30341, USA

Barry, Lynda — *Cartoonist (Ernie Pook's Comeck)*
PO Box 5286, Evanston, IL 60204, USA

Barry, Patricia — *Actress*
12742 Highwood St, Los Angeles, CA 90049, USA

Barry, Philip S, Jr — *Movie Producer, Writer*
PO Box 49895, Los Angeles, CA 90049, USA

Barry, Raymond J — *Actor*
%Metropolitan Talent Agency, 4526 Wilshire Blvd, Los Angeles, CA 90010, USA

Barry, Richard F D (Rick) — *Basketball Player, Sportscaster*
5240 Broadmoor Bluffs Dr, Colorado Springs, CO 80906, USA

Barry, Seymour (Sy) — *Cartoonist (Flash Gordon, Phantom)*
34 Saratoga Dr, Jericho, NY 11753, USA

Barrymore, Drew — *Actress*
612 N Sepulveda Blvd, #10, Los Angeles, CA 90049, USA

Barschall, Henry H — *Physicist*
1110 Tumalo Trail, Madison, WI 53711, USA

Barshai, Rudolf B — *Conductor*
Homberg Str 6, 4433 Ramlinsburg, Sweden

Barsotti, Charles — *Cartoonist*
%New Yorker Magazine, Editorial Dept, 20 W 43rd St, New York, NY 10036, USA

Barstow, Josephine — *Opera Singer*
%John Coast, 31 Sinclair Road, London W14 ONS, England

Bart, Lionel — *Composer, Lyricist*
8-10 Bulstrode St, London W1M 6AH, England

Bart, Peter B — *Editor*
2270 Betty Lane, Beverly Hills, CA 90210, USA

Bartel, Paul — *Actor, Director*
7860 Fareholm Dr, Los Angeles, CA 90046, USA

Barth, Robert — *Religious Leader*
%Churches of Christ in Christian Union, Box 30, Circleville, OH 43113, USA

Bartholomew, Patriarch — *Religious Leader*
Eastern Orthodox Church, Rum Ortoks Patrikhanesi, H Fener, Istanbul,Turkey

Bartholomew, Reginald — *Diplomat*
%US State Department, 2201 "C" St NW, Washington, DC 20520, USA

Bartholomew, Samuel W, Jr — *Attorney*
%Federal National Mortgage Assn, 1133 15th St NW, Washington, DC 20005, USA

Bartiromo, Maria — *Commentator*
%CBS-TV, News Dept, 51 W 52nd St, New York, NY 10019, USA

Bartkowski, Steve — *Football Player*
10745 Bell Road, Duluth, GA 30097, USA

Bartlett, Jennifer L — *Artist*
%Paula Cooper Gallery, 534 W 21st St, New York, NY 10011, USA

Bartlett, Jim — *Hockey*
8718 Chadwick Dr, Tampa, FL 33635, USA

Bartlett, Neil — *Chemist*
6 Oak Dr, Orinda, CA 94563, USA

Bartlett, Paul D — *Chemist*
%Brookhaven, 1010 Waltham St, #A-311, Lexington, MA 02173, USA

Bartlett, Thomas A — *Educator*
1209 SW 6th St, #904, Portland, OR 97204, USA

Bartley, Robert L *Editor*
%Wall Street Journal, Editorial Dept, 200 Liberty St, New York, NY 10281, USA

Bartoe, John-David F *Astronaut*
2121 Cabots Point Lane, Reston, VA 20191, USA

Bartoletti, Bruno *Conductor*
%Chicago Lyric Opera, 20 N Wacker Dr, Chicago, IL 60606, USA

Bartoli, Cecilia *Opera Singer*
%La Scala, Via Filodrammatici 2, 20100 Milan, Italy

Bartolo, Sal *Boxer*
422 Border St, East Boston, MA 02128, USA

Bartolome, Victor *Basketball Player*
1025 Rinconada Road, #A, Santa Barbara, CA 93101, USA

Barton, Derek H R *Nobel Chemistry Laureate*
%Texas A&M University, Chemistry Dept, College Station, TX 77843, USA

Barton, Eileen *Singer*
8740 Hickory Dr, Los Angeles, CA 90002, USA

Barton, Greg *Kayak Athlete*
6657 58th Ave NE, Seattle, WA 98115, USA

Barton, Harris *Football Player*
1156 Hamilton Ave, Palo Alto, CA 94301, USA

Barton, Jacqueline K *Chemist*
%California Institute of Technology, Chemistry Dept, Pasadena, CA 91125, USA

Barton, Lou Ann *Singer*
2010 Kinney Ave, Austin, TX 78704, USA

Barton, Peter *Actor*
2265 Westwood Blvd, #2619, Los Angeles, CA 90064, USA

Bartow, Gene *Basketball Coach*
%University of Alabama, Athletic Dept, Birmingham, AL 35294, USA

Bartowski, Steve *Football Player*
10745 Bell Road, Duluth, GA 30097, USA

Barty, Billy *Actor*
4502 Farmdale Ave, North Hollywood, CA 91602, USA

Baryshnikov, Mikhail *Ballet Dancer, Actor*
%American Ballet Theatre, 890 Broadway, New York, NY 10003, USA

Barzun, Jacques M *Educator*
1170 5th Ave, New York, NY 10029, USA

Basch, Harry *Actor*
920 1/2 S Serrano Ave, Los Angeles, CA 90006, USA

Baschnagel, Brian D *Football Player*
1823 Sunset Ridge Road, Glenview, IL 60025, USA

Basco, Dante *Actor*
%Don Buchwald, 9229 Sunset Blvd, #710, Los Angeles, CA 90069, USA

Bascom, Wes *Boxing*
4503 Adelaide, St Louis, MO 63115, USA

Baselitz, Georg *Artist*
Schloss Derneburg, 3201 Holle Bei Hildesheim, Germany

Bashir, Omar Hassan Ahmed *President, Sudan; Army General*
%Prime Minister's Office, Revolutionary Command Council, Khartoum, Sudan

Bashmet, Yuri A *Concert Viola Player*
Nezhdanovoy Str 7, #16, 103009 Moscow, Russia

Basia *Singer*
%Creative Artists Agency, 9830 Wilshire Blvd, Beverly Hills, CA 90212, USA

Basilio, Carmen *Boxer*
67 Boxwood Dr, Rochester, NY 14617, USA

Basinger, Kim *Actress*
%PMK Public Relations, 955 S Carillo Dr, #200, Los Angeles, CA 90048, USA

Baskin, Leonard *Artist*
PO Box 413, Leeds, MA 01053, USA

Basov, Nikolai G *Nobel Physics Laureate*
%Lebedev Physical Institute, 53 Lenin Prospect, Moscow, Russia

Basri, Gibor *Astronomer*
%University of California, Astronomy Dept, Berkeley, CA 94720, USA

Bass, Bob *Basketball Coach, Executive*
2266 Deerfield Dr, Fort Mill, SC 29715, USA

Bass, Fontella *Singer, Keyboardist*
%Cape Entertainment, 1181 NW 76th Ave, Fort Lauderdale, FL 33322, USA

Bass, Louis N *Agronomist, Plant Physiologist*
1117 Fairview Dr, Fort Collins, CO 80521, USA

Bass, Richard L (Dick) — *Football Player*
12801 Rosecrans Ave, #344, Norwalk, CA 90650, USA

Bass, Robert M — *Businessman*
%Bass Brothers Enterprises, 201 Main St, Fort Worth, TX 76102, USA

Basset, Brian — *Editorial Cartoonist, Cartoonist (Adam)*
%Seattle Times, Editorial Dept, Fairview Ave N & John St, Seattle, WA 98111, USA

Bassett, Angela — *Actress*
6427 1/2 Troost Ave, North Hollywood, CA 91606, USA

Bassett, Leslie R — *Composer*
1618 Harbal Dr, Ann Arbor, MI 48105, USA

Bassett, Tim — *Basketball Player*
445 Wyckoff Ave, Wyckoff, NJ 07481, USA

Bassett-Seguso, Carling — *Tennis Player*
%Women's Tennis Assn, 133 1st St NE, St Petersburg, FL 33701, USA

Bassey, Shirley — *Singer*
Villa Capricorn, 55 Via Campoine, 6816 Bissone, Switzerland

Basu, Asit Prakas — *Statistician*
1800 Valley Vista Court, Columbia, MO 65203, USA

Batalov, Aleksey V — *Movie Director*
%VGIK, Wilgelm Piek Str 3, 129226 Moscow, Russia

Batchelor, Joy E — *Animator*
%Educational Film Center, 5-7 Kean St, London WC2B 4AT, England

Bate, Anthony — *Actor*
%Al Parker, 55 Park Lane, London W1Y 3DD, England

Bateman, Jason — *Actor*
2623 2nd St, Santa Monica, CA 90405, USA

Bateman, Justine — *Actress*
11288 Ventura Blvd, #190, Studio City, CA 91604, USA

Bateman, Robert M — *Artist*
Box 115, Fulford Harbour BC V0S 1C0, Canada

Bateman, Walter R — *Businessman*
%Harleysville Mutual Insurance, 355 Maple Ave, Harleysville, PA 19438, USA

Bates, Alan — *Actor*
122 Hamilton Terrace, London NW8, England

Bates, Alfred — *Track Athlete*
1212 McKinley St, Philadelphia, PA 19111, USA

Bates, Charles C — *Oceanographer*
136 W La Pintura, Green Valley, AZ 85614, USA

Bates, Jared L (Jerry) — *Army General*
%Inspector General's Office, HqUSA, Pentagon, Washington, DC 20310, USA

Bates, Kathy — *Actress*
2829 W Shore Dr, Los Angeles, CA 90068, USA

Bates, Robert T — *Labor Leader*
%Railroad Signalmen Brotherhood, 601 W Golf Road, Mount Prospect, IL 60056, USA

Bateson, Mary Catherine — *Anthropologist*
10220 Bushman Dr, #211, Oakton, VA 22124, USA

Bathgate, Andy — *Hockey Player*
43 Brentwood Dr, Bramelea ON L6T 1R1, Canada

Batiz Campbell, Enrique — *Conductor*
Periferico Sur 5141, Col Fabela, Dele Tlalan, Mexico City DF 14030, Mexico

Batliner, Gerard — *Head of Government, Liechtenstein*
Am Schragen, Weg 2, 9490 Vaduz, Liechtenstein

Batt, Phil — *Governor, ID*
%Governor's Office, State Capitol, Boise, ID 83720, USA

Batten, William M — *Stock Exchange Executive*
7 Hadley Lane, Hilton Head Island, SC 29926, USA

Battey, Charles W — *Businessman*
%K N Energy, 370 Van Gordon Dr, Lakewood, CO 80228, USA

Battle, Hinton — *Dancer, Actor*
%Abrams Artists, 9200 Sunset Blvd, #625, Los Angeles, CA 90069, USA

Battle, Kathleen D — *Opera Singer*
%Columbia Artists Mgmt Inc, 165 W 57th St, New York, NY 10019, USA

Battle, Tony — *Basketball Player*
%Denver Nuggets, McNichols Arena, 1635 Clay St, Denver, CO 80204, USA

Bau, Sabine — *Fencer*
%Fecht-Stutzpunkt, Pestalozziallee 12, 97941 Tauberbischofsheim, Germany

Bauchau, Patrick — *Actor*
%Paul Kohner, 9300 Wilshire Blvd, #555, Beverly Hills, CA 90212, USA

B

Bass - Bauchau

Baudo, Serge — *Conductor*
Jas du Ferra, Chemin Charre, 13600 Ceyreste, France

Baudry, Patrick — *Spatinaut, France*
18 Ave Édouard-Belin, 31055 Toulouse, France

Bauer, Belinda — *Actress*
%House of Representatives, 400 S Beverly Dr, #101, Beverly Hills, CA 90212, USA

Bauer, Chris M — *Financier*
%Firstar Corp, 777 E Wisconsin Ave, Milwaukee, WI 53202, USA

Bauer, Erwin A — *Photographer*
PO Box 3730, Sequim, WA 98382, USA

Bauer, Henry A (Hank) — *Baseball Player, Manager*
11150 Alejo Place, San Diego, CA 92124, USA

Bauer, Jaime Lyn — *Actress*
%Tyler Kjar, 10643 Riverside Dr, Toluca Lake, CA 91602, USA

Bauer, Michelle — *Actress*
16032 Sherman Way, #73, Van Nuys, CA 91406, USA

Bauer, Peggy — *Photographer*
PO Box 3730, Sequim, WA 98382, USA

Bauer, Steven — *Actor*
5820 Wilshire Blvd, #400, Los Angeles, CA 90036, USA

Baugh Cole, Laura — *Golfer*
5225 Timberview Terrace, Orlando, FL 32819, USA

Baugh, John F — *Businessman*
%Sysco Corp, 1390 Enclave Parkway, Houston, TX 77077, USA

Baugh, Samuel A (Sammy) — *Football Player, Coach*
General Delivery, Rotan, TX 79546, USA

Baughan, Maxie C — *Football Player, Coach*
200 Sunset Park, Ithaca, NY 14850, USA

Baughman, J Ross — *Photographer*
2316 W Spruce St, Rogers, AR 72756, USA

Baulieu, Etienne-Emile — *Biochemist, Inventor*
%Laboratoire des Hormones, Hopital de Bicetre, Le Kremlin-Bicetre, France

Baum, Herbert M — *Businessman*
%Quaker State Corp, 225 E John Carpenter Freeway, Irving, TX 75062, USA

Baum, Warren C — *Economist*
%International Bank of Reconstruction, 1818 "H" St NW, Washington, DC 20433, USA

Baum, William W Cardinal — *Religious Leader*
Piazza della Citta, Lemonina 9, 00193 Rome, Italy

Bauman, G Duncan — *Publisher*
37 Conway Close Road, St Louis, MO 63124, USA

Bauman, Jon (Bowzer) — *Singer*
%Hallmark Entertainment, 8033 Sunset Blvd, #1000, Los Angeles, CA 90046, USA

Baumann, Alex — *Swimmer*
2617 Field St, Sudbury ON P3E 4X8, Canada

Baumann, Dieter — *Track Athlete*
Akazienweg 31, 89134 Blaustein, Germany

Baumann, Frank M — *Baseball Player*
7712 Sunray Lane, St Louis, MO 63123, USA

Baumbauer, Frank — *Theater Director*
%Deutsches Schauspielhaus, Kirchenallee 39, 20099 Hamburg, Germany

Baumgartner, Bruce — *Wrestler*
RR 2, Cambridge Springs, PA 16403, USA

Baumgartner, William — *Surgeon*
%Johns Hopkins Hospital, 600 N Wolfe St, Baltimore, MD 21287, USA

Bausch, Pina — *Dancer, Choreographer*
%Wuppertal Dance Theatre, Spinnstr 4, 42283 Wuppertal, Germany

Baute, Joseph A — *Businessman*
%Nashua Corp, 44 Franklin St, Nashua, NH 03060, USA

Bavasi, Emil Joseph (Buzzie) — *Baseball Executive*
PO Box 3292, La Jolla, CA 92038, USA

Bavasi, Peter J — *Baseball Executive*
%Telerate Sports Inc, 600 Plaza 2, Harborside, Jersey City, NJ 07311, USA

Baxandall, Lee — *Association Executive*
%Naturist Society, PO Box 132, Oshkosh, WI 54902, USA

Baxter, Frank E — *Financier*
%Jeffries Group, 11100 Santa Monica Blvd, Los Angeles, CA 90025, USA

Baxter, Glen — *Cartoonist*
%Aitken & Stone, 29 Fernshaw Road, London SW10 0TG, England

Baxter, James — *Animator*
%Dreamworks SKG, 100 Universal City Plaza, Universal City, CA 91608, USA

Baxter, Meredith — *Actress*
%William Morris Agency, 151 S El Camino Dr, Beverly Hills, CA 90212, USA

Baxter, William F — *Government Official*
%Stanford University, Law School, Stanford, CA 94305, USA

Bay, Howard — *Movie, Theater Designer*
159 W 53rd St, New York, NY 10019, USA

Bay, Willow — *Model*
%"Sunday GMA" Show, ABC-TV, News Dept, 77 W 66th St, New York, NY 10023, USA

Baye, Nathalie — *Actress*
%Artmedia, 10 Ave George V, 75008 Paris, France

Bayes, G E — *Religious Leader*
%Free Methodist Church, PO Box 535002, Winona Lake, IN 46590, USA

Bayh, Birch E, Jr — *Senator, IN*
%Bayh Connaughton Festerheim Malone, 1350 "I" St NW, Washington, DC 20005, USA

Bayi, Filbert — *Track Athlete*
PO Box 60240, Dar es Salaam, Tanzania

Bayle, Jean-Michel — *Motorcycle Racing Rider*
%General Delivery, Manosque, France

Baylor, Don E — *Baseball Player, Manager*
5 Fieldstone Lane, South Natick, MA 01760, USA

Baylor, Elgin G — *Basketball Player, Executive*
2480 Briarcrest Road, Beverly Hills, CA 90210, USA

Bazell, Robert J — *Commentator*
%NBC-TV, News Dept, 4001 Nebraska Ave NW, Washington, DC 20016, USA

Bazin, Marc L — *President, Haiti*
2-E Ave du Trvail, #8, Port-au-Prince, Haiti

Beach, Bill — *Bowling*
360 Reed St, Sharon, PA 16146, USA

Beach, Edward L — *WW II Navy Hero, Writer*
%Henry Holt Inc, 115 W 18th St, New York, NY 10011, USA

Beacham, Stephanie — *Actress*
79 High Ridge Road, Easton, CT 06612, USA

Beagle, Ron — *Football Player*
3830 San Ysidro Way, Sacramento, CA 95864, USA

Beal, Bernard B — *Financier*
%M R Beal Co, 565 5th Ave, New York, NY 10017, USA

Beal, Jack — *Artist*
HC 64, Box 83-A, Oneonta, NY 13820, USA

Beale, Betty — *Columnist*
2926 Garfield St NW, Washington, DC 20008, USA

Beall, Donald R — *Businessman*
%Rockwell International, PO Box 5090, Costa Mesa, CA 92628, USA

Beals, Vaughn L, Jr — *Businessman, Motorcycle Executive*
%Harley-Davidson Inc, 3700 W Juneau Ave, Milwaukee, WI 53208, USA

Beaman, Lee Anne — *Actress*
%Cavaleri Assoc, 405 Riverside Dr, #200, Burbank, CA 91506, USA

Beaman, Sally — *Writer*
%Bantam Books, 1540 Broadway, New York, NY 10036, USA

Bean, Alan L — *Astronaut*
9173 Briar Forest Dr, Houston, TX 77024, USA

Bean, Andy — *Golfer*
3300 Bridgefield Dr, Lakeland, FL 33803, USA

Bean, Orson — *Actor, Comedian*
444 Carroll Canal, Venice, CA 90291, USA

Bean, William Bennett — *Physician*
11 Rowland Court, Iowa City, IA 52246, USA

Beard, Alfred (Butch) — *Basketball Player; Coach*
1004 Afton Road, Louisville, KY 40222, USA

Beard, Amanda — *Swimmer*
3792 Carmel Ave, Irvine, CA 92606, USA

Beard, Frank — *Golfer*
73012 Skyward Way, Palm Desert, CA 92260, USA

Beard, Percy — *Track Athlete, Coach*
832 NW 22nd St, Gainesville, FL 32603, USA

Beard, Ralph — *Basketball Player*
7805 McCarthy Lane, Louisville, KY 40222, USA

B

Baxter - Beard

Beard, Ronald S *Attorney*
%Gibson Dunn Crutcher, 333 S Grand Ave, #4400, Los Angeles, CA 90071, USA

Bearden, H Eugene (Gene) *Baseball Player*
PO Box 176, Helena, AR 72342, USA

Bearse, Amanda *Actress*
15332 Antioch St, #143, Pacific Palisades, CA 90272, USA

Beart, Emmanuelle *Actress*
9 Rue Constant-Coquelin, 75007 Paris, France

Beart, Guy *Singer, Songwriter*
%Editions Temporel, 2 Rue Du Marquis de Mores, 92380 Garches, France

Beasley, Allyce *Actress*
147 N Windsor Blvd, Los Angeles, CA 90004, USA

Beasley, Bruce M *Artist*
322 Lewis St, Oakland, CA 94607, USA

Beasley, David *Governor, SC*
%Governor's Office, State Capitol, PO Box 11369, Columbia, SC 29211, USA

Beasley, Jere L *Governor, AL*
%Beasley Wilson Allen Mendelsohn, 207 Montgomery, #1000, Montgomery, AL 36104, USA

Beasley, Terry P *Football Player*
4449 Central Plank Road, Wetumpka, AL 36092, USA

Beathard, Bobby *Football Executive*
%San Diego Chargers, Jack Murphy Stadium, Box 609609, San Diego, CA 92160, USA

Beatrix *Queen, Netherlands*
Kasteel Drakesteijn, Lage Vuursche 3744 BA, Netherlands

Beattie, Ann *Writer*
%Janklow & Nesbit, 598 Madison Ave, New York, NY 10022, USA

Beattie, Bob *Skier*
%World Wide Ski Corp, 402 Pacific Ave, #D, Aspen, CO 81611, USA

Beatty, Jim *Track Athlete*
1515 LaRochelle Lane, Charlotte, NC 28226, USA

Beatty, Ned *Actor*
2706 N Beachwood Dr, Los Angeles, CA 90068, USA

Beatty, Warren *Actor, Director, Producer*
13671 Mulholland Dr, Beverly Hills, CA 90210, USA

Beatty, Zelmo *Basketball Player*
2808 120th Ave NE, Bellvue, WA 98005, USA

Beaupre, Don *Hockey Player*
5020 Scriver Road, Edina, MN 55436, USA

Beauvais, Garcelle *Model, Actress*
%Nina Blanchard, 957 N Cole Ave, Los Angeles, CA 90038, USA

Beavogui, Louis Lansana *Prime Minister, Guinea*
%Prime Minister's Office, Conakry, Guinea

Bebey, Francis *Guitarist, Composer*
18 Rue du Camp de L'Alouette, 25013 Paris, France

Becaud, Gilbert *Singer, Songwriter*
24 Rue de Longchamp, 75016 Paris, France

Becherer, Hans W *Businessman*
%Deere Co, John Deere Road, Moline, IL 61265, USA

Bechtel, Riley P *Businessman*
%Bechtel Group, 50 Beale St, San Francisco, CA 94105, USA

Bechtel, Stephen D, Jr *Businessman*
%Bechtel Group, 50 Beale St, San Francisco, CA 94105, USA

Bechtol, Hubert *Football Player*
7917 Taranto Dr, Austin, TX 78729, USA

Beck *Singer, Songwriter*
%William Morris Agency, 151 S El Camino Dr, Beverly Hills, CA 90212, USA

Beck Hilton, Kimberly *Actress*
28775 Sea Ranch Way, Malibu, CA 90265, USA

Beck, Aaron T *Psychiatrist*
3600 Market St, #700, Philadelphia, PA 19104, USA

Beck, Chip *Golfer*
327 Mayflower Road, Lake Forest, IL 60045, USA

Beck, Conrad *Composer*
St Johann Vorstadt, Basel, Switzerland

Beck, Ernest (Ernie) *Basketball Player*
1523 Brierwood Road, Havertown, PA 19083, USA

Beck, Jeff *Singer, Guitarist (Yardbirds)*
%Ernest Chapman, 11 Old South Lincoln's Inn, London WC2, England

Beck, John — *Actor*
12424 Wilshire Blvd, Los Angeles, CA 90025, USA
Beck, Marilyn M — *Columnist*
2152 El Roble Lane, Beverly Hills, CA 90210, USA
Beck, Mat — *Cinematographer*
%Dream Quest Images, 2635 Park Center Dr, Simi Valley, CA 93065, USA
Beck, Michael — *Actor*
%David Shapira, 15301 Ventura Blvd, #345, Sherman Oaks, CA 91403, USA
Beck, Rodney R (Rod) — *Baseball Player*
13531 Haynes St, Van Nuys, CA 91401, USA
Beckenbauer, Franz — *Soccer Player, Coach*
Am Lutzenberg 15, 6370 Kitzbuhel, Austria
Becker, Boris — *Tennis Player*
%Karl-Heinz Becker, Nusslocherstr 51, 69181 Leimen, Germany
Becker, Gary S — *Nobel Economics Laureate*
1308 E 58th St, Chicago, IL 60637, USA
Becker, George — *Labor Leader*
%United Steelworkers of America, 5 Gateway Center, Pittsburgh, PA 15222, USA
Becker, Harold — *Movie Director*
%Creative Artists Agency, 9830 Wilshire Blvd, Beverly Hills, CA 90212, USA
Becker, John A — *Financier*
%Firstar Corp, 777 W Wisconsin Ave, Milwaukee, WI 53233, USA
Becker, Margaret — *Singer, Guitarist*
%Jeff Roberts Assoc, 909 Meadowland Lane, Goodlettsville, TN 37072, USA
Becker, Quinn H — *Army General, Surgeon*
PO Box 2388, Dillon, CO 80435, USA
Becker, Richard G (Rick) — *Baseball Player*
1738 Roanoke, Aurora, IL 60506, USA
Becker, Robert J — *Allergist*
6 Oakbrook Club Dr, #J-101, Oak Brook, IL 60523, USA
Becker, Thomas — *Kayak Athlete*
Weststr 26, 42697 Solingen, Germany
Becket, MacDonald G — *Architect*
%Becket Group, 2501 Colorado Blvd, Santa Monica, CA 90404, USA
Beckett, Margaret M — *Government Official, England*
%House of Commons, Westminster, London SW1A 0AA, England
Beckinsale, Kate — *Actress*
%Peters Fraser Dunlop, Chelsea Harbour, Lots Rd, London SW10 0XF, England
Beckley, Gerry — *Singer, Guitarist (America)*
%Gallin-Morey, 345 N Maple Dr, #300, Beverly Hills, CA 90210, USA
Beckman, Arnold O — *Inventor (Acidity Testing Apparatus)*
%SmithKline Beckman Corp, 1 Franklin Plaza, Philadelphia, PA 19102, USA
Becton, C W — *Religious Leader*
%United Pentacostal Free Will Baptist Church, 8855 Dunn Rd, Hazelwood, MO 63042, USA
Becton, Henry P, Jr — *Businessman*
%WGBH-TV, 125 Western Ave, Allston, MA 02134, USA
Becton, Julius W, Jr — *Army General, Educator*
%Prairie View A&M University, President's Office, Prairie View, TX 77446, USA
Bedard, Irene — *Actress*
%Don Buchwald, 9229 Sunset Blvd, #710, Los Angeles, CA 90069, USA
Bedard, Myriam — *Biathlete*
3329 Pinecourt, Neufchatel PQ G2B 2E4, Canada
Bedelia, Bonnie — *Actress*
1021 Georgina Ave, Santa Monica, CA 90402, USA
Bedford, Brian — *Actor*
%Paradigm Agency, 10100 Santa Monica Blvd, #2500, Los Angeles, CA 90067, USA
Bedford, Sybille — *Writer*
%Messrs Coutts, 1 Old Park Lane, London W1Y 4BS, England
Bedi, Bisban Singh — *Cricketer*
Ispat Bhawan, Lodhi Road, New Delhi 3, India
Bedi, Kabir — *Actor*
%Conway Van Gelder Robinson, 18-21 Jermyn St, London SW1Y 6NB, England
Bedie, Henri Konan — *President, Cote D'Ivoire*
Blvd Clozel, Boite Postale 1354, Abidjan, Cote D'Ivoire
Bednarik, Charles P (Chuck) — *Football Player*
6379 Winding Road, Coppersburg, PA 18036, USA
Bednarski, John — *Hockey Player*
11 2nd St, Scottsville, NY 14546, USA

B

Bednorz, J Georg *Nobel Physics Laureate*
%IBM Research Laboratory, Saumerstr 4, 8803 Ruschlikon, Switzerland

Bedrosian, Stephen W (Steve) *Baseball Player*
3335 Gordon Road, Senoia, GA 30276, USA

Bedser, Alec V *Cricketer*
%Initial Cleaning Services, 33/34 Hoxton Sq, London N1 6NN, England

Beebe, Stephen A *Businessman*
%J R Simplot Co, 1 Capital Center, Boise, ID 83707, USA

Beeby, Clarence E *Architect*
%Hammond Beeby Babka, 400 N Wells St, Chicago, IL 60610, USA

Beedle, Lynn S *Civil Engineer*
102 Cedar Road, Hellertown, PA 18055, USA

Beene, Geoffrey *Fashion Designer*
%Geoffrey Beene Inc, 550 7th Ave, New York, NY 10018, USA

Beer, A M *Editor*
%The Spectator, Editorial Dept, 44 Frid St, Hamilton ON L8N 3G3, Canada

Beerbaum, Ludger *Equestrian Rider*
Altvaterweg 5, 86807 Buchloe, Germany

Beering, Steven C *Educator*
%Purdue University, President's Office, West Lafayette, IN 47907, USA

Beers, Gary *Bassist, Singer (INXS)*
8 Hayes St, #1, Neutral Bay 20891 NSW, Australia

Beeson, Jack H *Composer*
18 Seaforth Lane, Lloyd Neck, NY 11743, USA

Beeston, Paul M *Baseball Executive*
%President's Office, Major League Baseball, 350 Park Ave, New York, NY 10022, USA

Beevers, Harry *Biologist*
46 S Circle Dr, Santa Cruz, CA 95060, USA

Bega, Leslie *Actress*
%Don Buchwald, 9229 Sunset Blvd, #710, Los Angeles, CA 90069, USA

Begg, Varyl *Fleet Admiral, England*
Copyhold Cottage, Chilbolton, Stockbridge, Hants, England

Beggs, James M *Space Engineer, Government Official*
150 Vernon Ave, #410, Vernon Rockville, CT 06066, USA

Begley, Ed, Jr *Actor*
3850 Mound View Ave, Studio City, CA 91604, USA

Behenna, Richard K (Rick) *Baseball Player*
164 Bradford Station Dr, Sharpsburg, GA 30277, USA

Behle, Jochen *Cross Country Skier*
Sonnenhof 1, 34508 Willingen, Germany

Behm, Forrest A *Football Player*
3 Briarcliff Dr, Corning, NY 14830, USA

Behrend, Marc *Hockey Player*
1808 Savannah Way, Wauakee, WI 53597, USA

Behrendt, Jan *Luge Athlete*
Hanns-Eilser-Str 11, 98693 Ilmenau, Germany

Behrens, Hildegard *Opera Singer*
%Columbia Artists Mgmt Inc, 165 W 57th St, New York, NY 10019, USA

Behrens, Sam *Actor*
3546 Longridge Ave, Sherman Oaks, CA 91423, USA

Behrman, Richard E *Pediatrician*
15 Crest Road, Belvedere, CA 94920, USA

Beickler, Ferdinand *Businessman*
%Adam Opel AG, Bahnhofsplatz 1, 65428 Russelsheim, Germany

Beikirch, Gary B *Vietnam War Army Hero (CMH)*
468 Crosby Lane, Rochester, NY 14612, USA

Beilina, Nina *Concert Violinist*
400 W 43rd St, #7-D, New York, NY 10036, USA

Beitz, Berthold *Businessman*
Hugel 15, 45133 Essen, Germany

Bejart, Maurice J *Ballet Dancer, Choreographer*
%Bejart Ballet, Case Postale 25, 1000 Lausanne 22, Switzerland

Bel Geddes, Barbara *Actress*
15 Mill St, Putnam Valley, NY 10579, USA

Bela, Magyari *Cosmonaut, Hungary*
18885 P Alffy 7-11, Budapest, Hungary

Belafonte, Harry *Singer, Actor*
%Belafonte Road, Chatham, NY 12037, USA

Belaga, Julie — *Financier*
%Export-Import Bank, 811 Vermont Ave NW, Washington, DC 20571, USA
Belanger, Mark H — *Baseball Player*
2028 Pot Spring Road, Timonium, MD 21093, USA
Belcher, Timothy W (Tim) — *Baseball Player*
Spring St, Sparta, OH 43350, USA
Beldon, Sanford T — *Publisher*
%Prevention Magazine, 33 E Minor St, Emmaus, PA 18098, USA
Belenki, Valeri — *Gymnast*
Schillerstr 20, 73760 Ostfildern, Germany
Belford, Christina — *Actress*
12747 Riverside Dr, #208, North Hollywood, CA 91607, USA
Belichik, Bill — *Football Coach*
%New York Jets, 1000 Fulton Ave, Hempstead, NY 11550, USA
Belita — *Actress*
%Rose Cottage, Crabtree Gardens, 42 Crabtree Lane, London SW6 6LW, England
Beliveau, Jean A — *Hockey Player*
155 Victoria Ave, Longuevil PQ H4H 2J4, Canada
Belk, John M — *Businessman*
%Belk Stores Services, 2801 W Tyvola Road, Charlotte, NC 28217, USA
Bell, Archie — *Singer*
%Fat City Artists, 1908 Chet Atkins Place, #502, Nashville, TN 37212, USA
Bell, Bobby L, Sr — *Football Player*
10810 Oak St, Kansas City, MO 64114, USA
Bell, C Gordon — *Computer Designer*
%Microsoft Corp, 1 Microsoft Way, Redmond, WA 98052, USA
Bell, Catherine — *Actress*
%Ambrosio/Mortimer, 9150 Wilshire Blvd, #175, Beverly Hills, CA 90212, USA
Bell, Clyde R (Bob) — *Navy Admiral, Association Executive*
1301 Harney St, Omaha, NE 68102, USA
Bell, David E — *Economist, Government Official*
1 Waterhouse St, Cambridge, MA 02138, USA
Bell, David G (Buddy) — *Baseball Player*
9017 Decima St, Cincinnati, OH 45242, USA
Bell, Derek N — *Baseball Player*
9820 Bay Island Dr, Tampa, FL 33615, USA
Bell, Derrick A — *Attorney, Educator*
%New York University, Law School, 40 Washington Square S, New York, NY 10012, USA
Bell, Greg — *Track Athlete*
831 W Miami Ave, Logansport, IN 46947, USA
Bell, Griffin B — *Attorney General*
%King & Spalding, 2500 Trust Tower, 181 Peachtree St NE, Atlanta, GA 30303, USA
Bell, James D — *Diplomat*
14 Kite Hill Road, Santa Cruz, CA 95060, USA
Bell, Jay S — *Baseball Player*
3835 Cold Creek Dr, Valrico, FL 33594, USA
Bell, Jerry — *Baseball Executive*
%Minnesota Twins, 501 Chicago Ave S, Minneapolis, MN 55415, USA
Bell, Jorge A (George) — *Baseball Player*
Bario Rest Cle T #179, San Pedro de Macoris, Dominican Republic
Bell, Joshua — *Concert Violinist*
%IMG Artists, Media House, 3 Burlington Lane, London W4 2TH, England
Bell, Larry S — *Artist*
PO Box 4101, Taos, NM 87571, USA
Bell, Madison Smartt — *Writer*
%Pantheon Books, Random House Inc, 201 E 50th St, New York, NY 10022, USA
Bell, Sam — *Track Coach*
%Indiana University, Athletic Dept, Assembly Hall, Bloomington, IN 47405, USA
Bell, Tom — *Actor*
%Christina Shepherd, 84 Claverton St, London SW1 3AX, England
Bellamy, Carol — *Association Leader*
%United Nations Children's Fund, 1 UN Plaza, New York, NY 10003, USA
Bellamy, David — *Singer (Bellamy Brothers), Songwriter*
%Bellamy Brothers, 201 Restless Lane, Dade City, FL 33525, USA
Bellamy, David J — *Botanist, Writer, Broadcaster*
Mill House, Bedburn, Bishop Auckland, County Durham, England
Bellamy, Howard — *Singer (Bellamy Brothers), Songwriter*
%Bellamy Brothers, 201 Restless Lane, Dade City, FL 33525, USA

B

Belaga - Bellamy

Bellamy, Walt — *Basketball Player*
2884 Lakeshore Dr, College Park, GA 30337, USA

Belle, Albert J — *Baseball Player*
55 W Goethe St, #1226, Chicago, IL 60610, USA

Belle, Regina — *Singer*
PO Box 4450, New York, NY 10101, USA

Bellecourt, Vernon — *Social Activist, Association Executive*
%American Indian Movement, 1209 4th St SE, Minneapolis, MN 55414, USA

Beller, Kathleen — *Actress*
235 Metzgar St, Half Moon Bay, CA 94019, USA

Bellingham, Norman — *Canoist*
208 Morgan St NW, Washington, DC 20001, USA

Bellino, Joseph M (Joe) — *Football Player*
45 Hayden Lane, Bedford, MA 01730, USA

Bellisario, Donald P — *Television Producer*
%Broder Kurland Webb Uffner, 9242 Beverly Blvd, #200, Beverly Hills, CA 90210, USA

Belliveau, Cynthia — *Actress*
%K&K Entertainment, 1498 W Sunset Blvd, Los Angeles, CA 90026, USA

Bellmon, Henry — *Governor/Senator, OK*
Rt 1, Red Rock, OK 74651, USA

Bello, Maria — *Actress*
14 Driftwood St, #6, Venice, CA 90292, USA

Bellow, Saul C — *Nobel Literature Laureate*
745 Commonwealth Ave, Boston, MA 02215, USA

Bellows, James G — *Journalist, Television Producer*
2337 Canyonback Road, Los Angeles, CA 90049, USA

Bellson, Louis (Louie) — *Jazz Drummer*
12804 Raymer St, North Hollywood, CA 91605, USA

Bellucci, Monica — *Model*
%Elite Model Mgmt, 111 E 22nd St, #200, New York, NY 10010, USA

Bellwood, Pamela — *Actress*
7444 Woodrow Wilson Dr, Los Angeles, CA 90046, USA

Bellwood, Wesley E — *Businessman*
%Wynn's International, 500 N State College Blvd, Fullerton, CA 92831, USA

Belm, Michaela — *Model*
%Agentur Talents, Ohmstr 5, 80802 Munich, Germany

Belmondo, Jean-Paul — *Actor*
9 Rue des St Peres, 75007 Paris, France

Belohlavek, Jiri — *Conductor*
%Czechoslovakia Philharmonic, Alsovo Nabr 12, 11001 Prague, Czech Republic

Belote Hamlin, Melissa — *Swimmer*
7311 Exmore St, Springfield, VA 22150, USA

Belousova, Ludmila — *Figure Skater*
Chalet Hubel, 3818 Grindelwald, Switzerland

Belsted, John J G — *Government Official, England*
%House of Lords, Westminster, London SW1A 0PW, England

Beltran, Robert — *Actor*
2210 Talmadge St, Los Angeles, CA 90027, USA

Belucci, Monica — *Model*
%Elite Model Mgmt, 111 E 22nd St, #200, New York, NY 10010, USA

Belushi, James — *Actor*
%International Creative Mgmt, 8942 Wilshire Blvd, Beverly Hills, CA 90211, USA

Belzer, Richard — *Actor, Comedian*
%Agency For Performing Arts, 9200 Sunset Blvd, #900, Los Angeles, CA 90069, USA

Beman, Deane R — *Golfer, Golf Executive*
117 Carriage Lamp Way, Ponte Vedra Beach, FL 32082, USA

Ben Ali, Zine al-Abidine — *President, Tunisia; Army General*
%President's Office, Palais Presidentiel, Tunis, Tunisia

Benabib, Kim — *Writer*
%Harper Collins Publishers, 10 E 53rd St, New York, NY 10022, USA

Benacerraf, Baruj — *Nobel Medicine Laureate*
111 Perkins St, Boston, MA 02130, USA

Benade, Leo Edward — *Army General*
417 Pine Ridge Road, #A, Carthage, NC 28327, USA

Benard, Andre P J — *Businessman*
%Eurotunnel SA, Tour Franklin, Cedex 11, 92001 Paris-La-Defense 8, France

Benatar, Pat — *Singer, Songwriter*
2644 30th St, Santa Monica, CA 90405, USA

Benavidez, Roy P — *Vietnam War Army Hero (CMH)*
1700 Byrne St, El Campo, TX 77437, USA

Bench, John L (Johnny) — *Baseball Player*
661 Reisling Knoll, Cincinnati, OH 45226, USA

Benchley, Peter B — *Writer*
35 Boudinot St, Princeton, NJ 08540, USA

Benchoff, Dennis L (Den) — *Army General*
Deputy CG, US Material Command, 5001 Eisenhower Ave, Alexandria, VA 22304, USA

Bender, Gary N — *Sportscaster*
%TNT-TV, Sports Dept, 1050 Techwood Dr NW, Atlanta, GA 30318, USA

Bender, Myron L — *Chemist*
2514 Sheridan Road, Evanston, IL 60201, USA

Benedict, Dirk — *Actor*
PO Box 634, Bigfork, MT 59911, USA

Benedict, Manson — *Chemical Engineer*
108 Moorings Park Dr, #206-B, Naples, FL 34105, USA

Benedict, Paul — *Actor*
84 Rockland Place, Newton, MA 02164, USA

Benedict, William — *Actor*
1347 N Orange Grove Ave, Los Angeles, CA 90046, USA

Benes, Andrew C (Andy) — *Baseball Player*
PO Box 6607, Chesterfield, MO 63006, USA

Benetton, Luciano — *Businessman*
%Benetton SPA, Via Chiesa Ponzano 24, 31050 Ponzano Veneto, Italy

Benglis, Lynda — *Artist*
222 Bowery St, New York, NY 10012, USA

Bengston, Billy Al — *Artist*
805 Hampton Dr, Venice, CA 90291, USA

Benhamou, Eric A — *Businessman*
%ThreeCom Corp, 5400 Bayfront Plaza, Santa Clara, CA 95054, USA

Bening, Annette — *Actress*
13671 Mulholland Dr, Beverly Hills, CA 90210, USA

Benirschke, Rolf J — *Football Player*
PO Box 9922, Rancho Santa Fe, CA 92067, USA

Benjamin, Benoit — *Basketball Player*
%Toronto Raptors, 20 Bay St, #1702, Toronto ON M5J 2N8, Canada

Benjamin, Curtis G — *Publisher*
Kellogg Hill Road, Weston, CT 06880, USA

Benjamin, Guy — *Football Player*
19 W 456 Deerpath, Lemont, IL 60439, USA

Benjamin, Karl S — *Artist*
675 W 8th St, Claremont, CA 91711, USA

Benjamin, Leanne — *Ballerina*
%Royal Ballet, Bow St, London WC2E 9DD, England

Benjamin, Richard — *Actor, Director*
%Gersh Agency, 232 N Canon Dr, Beverly Hills, CA 90210, USA

Benn, Anthony N W (Tony) — *Government Official, England*
%House of Commons, Westminster, London SW1A 0AA, England

Bennack, Frank A, Jr — *Publisher*
%Hearst Corp, 959 8th Ave, New York, NY 10019, USA

Bennett, A L — *Basketball Player*
3446 S Gary Ave, Tulsa, OK 74105, USA

Bennett, Alan — *Writer, Actor*
%Peters Fraser Dunlop, Chelsea Harbour, Lots Rd, London SW10 0XF, England

Bennett, Bill — *Hockey*
146 Boston Neck Road, Narragansett, RI 02882, USA

Bennett, Bob — *Singer, Songwriter*
%Jeff Roberts Assoc, 909 Meadowland Lane, Goodlettsville, TN 37072, USA

Bennett, Brooke — *Swimmer*
2565 Bedford Mews Dr, West Palm Beach, FL 33414, USA

Bennett, Bruce (Herman Brix) — *Actor, Track Athlete*
2702 Forester Road, Los Angeles, CA 90064, USA

Bennett, Cornelius — *Football Player*
%Atlanta Falcons, 2745 Burnett Road, Suwanee, GA 30024, USA

Bennett, Harvey — *Hockey Player*
1096 Warwick Neck Ave, Warwick, RI 02889, USA

Bennett, Hywel — *Actor*
%James Sharkey, 21 Golden Square, London W1R 3PA, England

B

Benavidez - Bennett

Bennett, John — *Track Athlete*
1615 Gateway St S, Middletown, WI 53652, USA

Bennett, Nelson — *Skier*
807 S 20th Ave, Yakima, WA 98902, USA

Bennett, Ric — *Hockey Player*
1382 Brookwood Forest Blvd, #701, Jacksonville, FL 32225, USA

Bennett, Richard Rodney — *Composer*
%Lemon & Durbridge, 24 Pottery Lane, Holland Park, London W11 4LZ, England

Bennett, Robert (Bob) — *Swimmer*
70 Rivo Alto Canal, Long Beach, CA 90803, USA

Bennett, Robert F — *Governor, KS*
9535 Ash St, #211, Shawnee Mission, KS 66207, USA

Bennett, Robert S — *Attorney*
%Skadden Arps Slate Meagher Flom, 1440 New York Ave NW, Washington, DC 20005, USA

Bennett, Tony — *Singer*
%Tony Bennett Enterprises, 130 W 57th St, # 9-D, New York, NY 10019, USA

Bennett, Ward — *Interior Designer*
%Dakota Hotel, 1 W 72nd St, PH-A, New York, NY 10023, USA

Bennett, William J — *Secretary, Education*
%Hudson Institute, 4401 Ford Ave, Alexandria, VA 22302, USA

Bennis, Warren G — *Educator, Writer*
%University of Southern California, Management School, Los Angeles, CA 90007, USA

Bennitt, Brent M — *Navy Admiral*
Commander, Naval Air Force Pacific Fleet, NAS North Island, San Diego, CA 92135, USA

Benoit Samuelson, Joan — *Marathon Runner*
95 Lower Flying Point Road, Freeport, ME 04032, USA

Benoit, David — *Jazz Pianist*
%Fitzgerald-Hartley, 50 W Main St, Ventura, CA 93001, USA

Benoit, David — *Basketball Player*
%New Jersey Nets, Byrne Meadowlands Arena, East Rutherford, NJ 07073, USA

Benshoff, Janet — *Attorney, Women's Activist*
%Center for Reproductive Law & Policy, 120 Wall St, New York, NY 10005, USA

Benson, Andrew A — *Biochemist, Plant Physiologist*
6044 Folsom Dr, La Jolla, CA 92037, USA

Benson, George — *Jazz Guitarist*
%Fritz/Byers, 648 N Robertson Blvd, Los Angeles, CA 90069, USA

Benson, James M — *Businessman*
%Equitable Life Assurance Society, 1285 Ave of Americas, New York, NY 10019, USA

Benson, Johnny, Jr — *Auto Racing Driver*
3102 Bird Ave NE, Grand Rapids, MI 49525, USA

Benson, Kent — *Basketball Player*
1223 Benson Court, Bloomington, IN 47401, USA

Benson, Renaldo (Obie) — *Singer (Four Tops)*
%International Creative Mgmt, 40 W 57th St, New York, NY 10019, USA

Benson, Robby — *Actor*
PO Box 1305, Woodland Hills, CA 91365, USA

Benson, Sidney W — *Chemist*
1110 N Bundy Dr, Los Angeles, CA 90049, USA

Benson, Stephen R — *Editorial Cartoonist*
%Arizona Republic, Editorial Dept, PO Box 1950, Phoenix, AZ 85001, USA

Benson, Tom — *Football Executive*
%New Orleans Saints, 1500 Poydras St, New Orleans, LA 70112, USA

Bentley, Eric — *Writer*
194 Riverside Dr, New York, NY 10025, USA

Bentley, John — *Actor*
Wedgewood House, Peterworth, Sussex, England

Bentley, Stacey — *Body Builder*
PO Box 26, Santa Monica, CA 90406, USA

Benton, Barbi — *Model, Actress*
40 N 4th St, Carbondale, CO 81623, USA

Benton, David L (Dan), III — *Army General*
Chief of Staff, US European Command, APO, AE 09128, USA

Benton, Fletcher — *Artist*
250 Dore St, San Francisco, CA 94103, USA

Benton, Jim — *Football Player*
6200 Timber Ridge Dr, Pine Bluff, AR 71603, USA

Benton, Robert — *Movie Director*
%International Creative Mgmt, 40 W 57th St, New York, NY 10019, USA

Bentsen, Lloyd M, Jr *Secretary, Treasury*
%Verner Lipfert Bernhard, 901 15th St NW, #700, Washington, DC 20005, USA
Benvenuti, Nino *Boxer*
Via Giuseppe Ferrari 35, 00127 Rome, Italy
Benz, Amy *Golfer*
5570 Coach House Circle, #E, Boca Raton, FL 33486, USA
Benz, Sepp *Bobsled Athlete*
Kiefernweg 37, 8057 Zurich, Switzerland
Benzali, Daniel *Actor*
%Paul Kohner, 9300 Wilshire Blvd, #555, Beverly Hills, CA 90212, USA
Benzer, Seymour *Biologist*
2075 Robin Road, San Marino, CA 91108, USA
Benzi, Roberto *Conductor*
12 Villa St Foy, 92200 Neuilly-sur-Seine, France
Beran, Bruce *Coast Guard Admiral*
Commander, Pacific Area, US Coast Guard, Coast Guard Island, Alameda, CA 94501, USA
Beras Rojas, Octavio Antonio Cardinal *Religious Leader*
Arzobispade, Apartado 186, Santo Domingo, Dominican Republic
Berbick, Trevor *Boxer*
%Don King Productions, 501 Fairway Dr, Deerfield Beach, FL 33441, USA
Berce, Gene *Basketball Player*
509 Nadig Court, Fort Atkinson, WI 53538, USA
Bercu, Michaela *Model*
%Elite Model Mgmt, 111 E 22nd St, #200, New York, NY 10010, USA
Berdahl, Robert M *Educator*
%University of California, Chancellor's Office, Berkeley, CA 94720, USA
Bere, Jason P *Baseball*
17 Dorchester St, Wilmington, MA 01887, USA
Bere, Richard L *Businessman*
%Kroger Co, 1014 Vine St, Cincinnati, OH 45202, USA
Berenblum, Isaac *Pathologist*
%Weizmann Institute of Science, Pathology Dept, Rehovot, Israel
Berenger, Tom *Actor*
%Creative Artists Agency, 9830 Wilshire Blvd, Beverly Hills, CA 90212, USA
Berenson, Ken (Red) *Hockey Player, Coach*
3555 Daleview Dr, Ann Arbor, MI 48105, USA
Berenson, Marisa *Actress*
%Myriam Bru, 80 Ave Charles de Gaulle, 92200 Neuilly, France
Beresford, Bruce *Movie Director*
3 Marathon Road, #13, Darling Point, Sydney NSW, Australia
Beresford, Meg *Social Activist*
Abbey, Iona Community, Argull PA76 6SW, Scotland
Berezovi, Anatoli N *Cosmonaut*
%Potchta Kosmonavtov, Moskovskoi Oblasti, 141160 Syvisdny Goroduk, Russia
Berg, Bob *Jazz Saxophonist*
%International Music Network, 2 Main St, #400, Gloucester, MA 01930, USA
Berg, Dave *Cartoonist*
%Whitegate Features Syndicate, 71 Fawnce Dr, #1, Providence, RI 02906, USA
Berg, Elizabeth *Writer*
%Random House Inc, 201 E 50th St, New York, NY 10022, USA
Berg, Jeffrey S *Entertainment Executive*
%International Creative Mgmt, 8942 Wilshire Blvd, Beverly Hills, CA 90211, USA
Berg, Matraca *Singer, Songwriter*
%Mike Crowley Artist Mgmt, 602 Wayside Dr, Wimberley, TX 78676, USA
Berg, Patty *Golfer*
PO Box 1607, Fort Myers, FL 33902, USA
Berg, Paul *Nobel Chemistry Laureate*
%Stanford University Medical School, Beckman Center, Stanford, CA 94305, USA
Berg, Peter *Actor*
433 N Camden Dr, #500, Beverly Hills, CA 90210, USA
Berganza, Teresa *Opera Singer*
Cafeto #5, Madrid 7, Spain
Berge, Ole M *Labor Leader*
%Maintenance of Way Brotherhood, 12050 Woodward Ave, Detroit, MI 48203, USA
Berge, Pierre V G *Businessman*
%Yves Saint Laurent SA, 5 Ave Marceau, 75116 Paris, France
Bergen, Candice *Actress*
222 Central Park South, New York, NY 10019, USA

Bergen, Polly *Actress*
15 W 53rd St, #20-A, New York, NY 10019, USA

Bergen, William B *Aerospace Engineer*
%Aerospatiale, 37 Rue de Montmorency, 75016 Paris, France

Berger, Frank M *Biologist*
515 E 72nd St, New York, NY 10021, USA

Berger, Gerhard *Auto Racing Driver*
%Berger Motorsport, Postfach 1121, 9490 Vaduz, Austria

Berger, Helmut *Actor*
Pundterplatz 6, 80803 Munich, Germany

Berger, John *Writer*
Quincy, Mieussy, 74440 Taninges, France

Berger, Richard L *Entertainment Executive*
%Cinetropolis, 4540 W Valerio St, Burbank, CA 91505, USA

Berger, Samuel R *Government Official*
%National Security Council, Old Executive Office Building, Washington, DC 20505, USA

Berger, Senta *Actress*
Robert-Koch-Str 10, 12621 Grunewald, Germany

Berger, Thomas L *Writer*
PO Box 11, Palisades, NY 10964, USA

Bergere, Lee *Actor*
32 Beach Plum Way, Hampton, NH 03842, USA

Bergey, William E (Bill) *Football Player*
2 Hickory Lane, Chadds Ford, PA 19317, USA

Berggren, Jenny *Singer (Ace of Base)*
%Siljemark Promotion, Gardsvagen 2, 171 25 Solna, Sweden

Berggren, Jonas *Singer (Ace of Base)*
%Siljemark Promotion, Gardsvagen 2, 171 25 Solna, Sweden

Berggren, Malin *Singer (Ace of Base)*
%Siljemark Promotion, Gardsvagen 2, 171 25 Solna, Sweden

Berggren, Thommy *Actor*
%Swwedish Film Institute, PO Box 27126, 102 52, Stockholm, Sweden

Bergin, Michael *Model, Actor*
%Click Model Mgmt, 881 7th Ave, New York, NY 10019, USA

Bergin, Patrick *Actor*
%Caroline Dawson, 47 Courtfield Road, #9, London SW7 4DB, England

Bergland, Robert S *Secretary, Agriculture*
Rt 3, Roseau, MN 56751, USA

Berglund, Dennis C *Financier*
%Century Acceptance Corp, City Center Square, Kansas City, MO 64196, USA

Berglund, Paavo A E *Conductor*
Munkkiniemenranta 41, 00330 Helsinki 33, Finland

Bergman, Alan *Lyricist*
714 N Maple Dr, Beverly Hills, CA 90210, USA

Bergman, Andrew C *Writer, Movie Director*
555 W 57th St, #1230, New York, NY 10019, USA

Bergman, Ingmar *Movie Director*
%Swedish Film Institute, PO Box 27126, 102 52 Stockholm, Sweden

Bergman, Klaus *Businessman*
%Allegheny Power System, 12 E 49th St, #4900, New York, NY 10017, USA

Bergman, Marilyn K *Lyricist*
714 N Maple Dr, Beverly Hills, CA 90210, USA

Bergman, Martin *Movie Producer*
641 Lexington Ave, New York, NY 10022, USA

Bergman, Peter *Actor*
4799 White Oak Ave, Encino, CA 91316, USA

Bergman, Sandahl *Actress*
9903 Santa Monica Blvd, #274, Beverly Hills, CA 90212, USA

Bergmann, Arnfinn *Ski Jumper*
Nils Collett Vogtsv 58, 0765 Oslo 7, Norway

Bergonzi, Carlo *Opera Singer*
%A Ziliani ALCI, Via Paolo da Cannobio 2, 120122 Milan, Italy

Bergquist, Curt *Immunologist*
%Allergon AB, Valinge 2090, 262 92 Angelholm, Sweden

Bergsten, C Fred *Economist*
4106 Sleepy Hollow Road, Annandale, VA 22003, USA

Bergstrom, K Sune *Nobel Medicine Laureate*
%Karolinska Institute, Nobelkansli Box 60250, 104 01 Stockholm, Sweden

Berio, Luciano   *Composer*
Il Colombaio, Radicondoli, 53100 Siena, Italy
Beriosova, Svetlana   *Ballerina*
10 Palliser Court, Palliser Road, London W14, England
Berkeley, Michael F   *Composer*
%Rogers Coleridge White, 20 Powis Mews, London W11 1JN, England
Berkley, Elizabeth   *Actress, Model*
12400 Ventura Blvd, #122, Studio City, CA 91604, USA
Berkley, Stephen M   *Businessman*
%Quantum Corp, 500 McCarthy Blvd, Milpitas, CA 95035, USA
Berkley, William R   *Businessman*
%W R Berkley Corp, 165 Mason St, Greenwich, CT 06830, USA
Berkoff, David   *Swimmer*
%Harvard University, Athletic Dept, Cambridge, MA 02138, USA
Berkowitz, Bob   *Entertainer*
%CNBC-TV, 2200 Fletcher Ave, Fort Lee, NJ 07024, USA
Berlant, Anthony (Tony)   *Artist*
%Los Angeles Louver Gallery, 55 N Venice Blvd, Venice, CA 90291, USA
Berle, Milton   *Comedian*
%Media Artists Group, 8383 Wilshire Blvd, #954, Beverly Hills, CA 90211, USA
Berlin, Isaiah   *Philosopher*
Headington House, Old High St, Headington, Oxford OX3 9HU, England
Berliner, Robert W   *Physician*
36 Edgehill Terrace, New Haven, CT 06517, USA
Berlinger, Warren   *Actor*
10642 Arnel Place, Chatsworth, CA 91311, USA
Berlinsky, Dmitri   *Concert Violinist*
35 W 64th St, #7-F, New York, NY 10023, USA
Berlitz, Charles F   *Linguist, Writer, Archaeologist*
26 Minnetonka Road, Sea Ranch Lakes, FL 33308, USA
Berlusconi, Silvio   *Prime Minister, Italy*
Palazzo Chigi, Piazza Colonna 370, 00187 Rome, Italy
Berman, Chris   *Sportscaster*
%ESPN-TV, Sports Dept, ESPN Plaza, 935 Middle St, Bristol, CT 06010, USA
Berman, Julius   *Religious Leader, Attorney*
%Kaye Scholer Fierman, 425 Park Ave, New York, NY 10022, USA
Berman, Shelley   *Comedian, Actor*
268 Bell Canyon Road, Bell Canyon, CA 91307, USA
Bernadotte, Sigvard O F   *Craft, Industrial Designer*
Villagatan 10, Stockholm, Sweden
Bernard, Crystal   *Actress, Singer, Songwriter*
14014 Aubrey Road, Beverly Hills, CA 90210, USA
Bernard, Ed   *Actor*
PO Box 7965, Northridge, CA 91327, USA
Berners-Lee, Tom   *Computer Scientist*
%Massachusetts Institute of Technology, Computer Sci Lab, Cambridge, MA 02139, USA
Bernhard   *Prince, Netherlands*
%Soestdijk Palace, Baarn, Netherlands
Bernhard, Ruth   *Photographer*
2982 Clay St, San Francisco, CA 94115, USA
Bernhard, Sandra   *Actress*
%Gold Marshak Liedtke, 3500 W Olive Ave, #1400, Burbank, CA 91505, USA
Bernhardt, Glenn R   *Cartoonist*
PO Box 3772, Carmel, CA 93921, USA
Bernheimer, Martin   *Music Critic*
%Los Angeles Times, Editorial Dept, Times-Mirror Sq, Los Angeles, CA 90012, USA
Bernier, Sylvie   *Diver*
%Olympic Assn, Cite du Harve, Montreal PQ H3C 3R4, Canada
Berning, Susie Maxwell   *Golfer*
PO Box 321, Kailena Kona, HI 96745, USA
Bernsen, Corbin   *Actor*
11075 Santa Monica Blvd, #150, Los Angeles, CA 90025, USA
Bernstein, Carl   *Journalist*
%Janklow & Nesbit Assoc, 598 Madison Ave, New York, NY 10022, USA
Bernstein, Elmer   *Composer*
2715 Pearl St, Santa Monica, CA 90405, USA
Bernstein, Jay L   *Movie Producer, Agent*
%Jay Bernstein Productions, PO Box 1148, Beverly Hills, CA 90213, USA

B

Berio - Bernstein

Bernstein, Kenny	*Auto Racing Driver*
%King Racing, 1105 Seminole Dr, Richardson, TX 75080, USA	
Bernstein, Richard A	*Businessman*
%Western Publishing Group, 444 Madison Ave, New York, NY 10022, USA	
Bernstein, Robert L	*Publisher*
%John Wiley & Sons, 605 3rd Ave, New York, NY 10158, USA	
Berov, Lyuben	*Prime Minister, Bulgaria*
%Prime Minister's Office, 1 Dondukov Blvd, 1000 Sofia, Bulgaria	
Berra, Lawrence P (Yogi)	*Baseball Player, Manager*
19 Highland Ave, Montclair, NJ 07042, USA	
Berresford, Susan V	*Foundation Executive*
%Ford Foundation, 320 E 43rd St, New York, NY 10017, USA	
Berri, Claude	*Movie Director, Producer*
%Renn Productions, 10 Rue Lincoln, 75008 Paris, France	
Berridge, Elizabeth	*Actress*
%Judy Schoen, 606 N Larchmont Blvd, #309, Los Angeles, CA 90004, USA	
Berrigan, Daniel	*Clergyman, Social Activist*
220 W 98th St, #11-L, New York, NY 10025, USA	
Berroa, Geronimo E	*Baseball Player*
3681 Broadway, #23, New York, NY 10031, USA	
Berruti, Livio	*Track Athlete*
Via Avigliana 45, 10138 Torino, Italy	
Berry, Bill	*Skiing Writer*
839 N Center St, Reno, NV 89501, USA	
Berry, Bob	*Hockey Player, Coach, Executive*
41 Yorkshire Lane Court, St Louis, MO 63144, USA	
Berry, Charles E (Chuck)	*Singer, Songwriter*
Berry Park, 691 Buckner Road, Wentzville, MO 63385, USA	
Berry, Halle	*Actress, Model*
%Creative Artists Agency, 9830 Wilshire Blvd, Beverly Hills, CA 90212, USA	
Berry, Jan	*Singer (Jan & Dean), Songwriter*
%Jan & Dean Music Co, 1720 N Ross St, Santa Ana, CA 92706, USA	
Berry, Jim	*Editorial Cartoonist*
%NEA Syndicate, 200 Park Ave, New York, NY 10166, USA	
Berry, John	*Singer*
%Corlew-O'Grady Mgmt, 1102 18th Ave S, Nashville, TN 37212, USA	
Berry, Ken	*Actor*
15831 Foothill Blvd, Sylmar, CA 91342, USA	
Berry, Kevin	*Swimmer*
28 George St, Manly NSW 2295, Australia	
Berry, Michael J	*Chemist*
PO Box 1421, Pebble Beach, CA 93953, USA	
Berry, Richard S	*Chemist*
%University of Chicago, Chemistry Dept, 5317 S University Ave, Chicago, IL 60615, USA	
Berry, Sean R	*Baseball Player*
%Houston Astros, Astrodome, PO Box 288, Houston, TX 77001, USA	
Berry, Stephen J (Steve)	*Journalist*
4945 Reforma Road, Woodland Hls, CA 91364, USA	
Berry, Walter	*Basketball Player*
123 Fairmont Circle, Danville, VA 24541, USA	
Berry, Walter	*Opera Singer*
Kahlenbergerstr 82, 1190 Vienna, Austria	
Berry, Wendell E	*Writer, Ecologist*
River Road, Port Royal, KY 40058, USA	
Berryman, Michael	*Actor*
RR 3, Box 117-A, Clarkesville, AR 72830, USA	
Berson, Jerome A	*Chemist*
45 Bayberry Road, Hamden, CT 06517, USA	
Berst, David	*Sports Investigator*
%National Collegiate Athletic Assn, 6201 College Blvd, Overland Park, KS 66211, USA	
Bertelli, Angelo B	*Football Player*
22 Springdale Court, Clifton, NJ 07013, USA	
Bertil	*Prince, Sweden*
Hert Av Halland, Kungl Slottet, 111 30 Stockholm, Sweden	
Bertinelli, Valerie	*Actress*
PO Box 1984, Studio City, CA 91614, USA	
Bertini, Catherine	*Association Executive*
%World Food Programs, Via Cristoforo Colombo 426, 00145 Rome, Italy	

Bertoli, Paolo Cardinal — *Religious Leader*
Piazza della Citta Leonina 1, 00193 Rome, Italy

Bertolucci, Bernardo — *Movie Director*
Via Della Lungara 3, 00165 Rome, Italy

Berton, Pierre — *Writer, Historian*
%Pierre Berton Enterprises, 21 Sackville St, Toronto ON M5A 3E1, Canada

Bertrand, Frederic H — *Businessman*
%National Life Insurance, 1 National Life Dr, Montpelier, VT 05604, USA

Bertuccelli, Jean-Louis A — *Movie Director*
9 Rue Benard, 75014 Paris, France

Berwanger, John J (Jay) — *Football Player*
1245 Warren Ave, Downers Grove, IL 60515, USA

Bessmertnova, Natalia — *Ballerina*
%Bolshoi Theater, Teatralnya Pl 1, 103009 Moscow, Russia

Besson, Luc — *Movie Director*
%Films du Dauphin, 25 Rue Yves-Toudic, 75010 Paris, France

Best, James — *Actor*
433 Pinehill Blvd, Geneva, FL 32732, USA

Best, Pete — *Singer, Drummer (The Beatles)*
8 Hymans Green, West Derby, Liverpool 12, England

Best, Travis — *Basketball Player*
703 Bradley Road, Springfield, MA 01109, USA

Beswicke, Martine — *Actress*
%Goldey Co, 1156 S Carmelina Ave, #B, Los Angeles, CA 90049, USA

Bethe, Hans A — *Nobel Physics Laureate*
324 Savage Farm Dr, Ithaca, NY 14850, USA

Bethea, Elvin L — *Football Player*
16211 Leslie Lane, Missouri City, TX 77489, USA

Bethune, Zina — *Actress*
3096 Lake Hollywood Dr, Los Angeles, CA 90068, USA

Bethurem, Richard C — *Air Force General*
%HqAirSouth, PSC 813, Box 101, FPO, AE 09620, USA

Bettenhausen, Gary — *Auto Racing Driver*
2550 Tree Farm Road, Martinsville, IN 46151, USA

Bettger, Lyle — *Actor*
PO Box 1076, Pai, HI 96779, USA

Bettis, Jerome — *Football Player*
17600 Fairway Dr, Detroit, MI 48221, USA

Bettis, Valerie — *Dancer, Choreographer*
%Valerie Bettis Dance Studio, 22 W 15th St, New York, NY 10011, USA

Bettman, Gary B — *Hockey Executive*
%National Hockey League, 650 5th Ave, #3300, New York, NY 10019, USA

Bettmann, Otto L — *Photo Archivist*
The Forum, 3001 Deer Creek Blvd, #563, Deerfield Beach, FL 33442, USA

Betts, Virginia Trotter — *Labor Leader*
%American Nurses Assn, 600 Maryland Ave SW, Washington, DC 20024, USA

Betz Addie, Pauline — *Tennis Player*
%Bidwell Friends School, 3825 Wisconsin Ave NW, Washington, DC 20016, USA

Beuerlein, Steve — *Football Player*
%Carolina Panthers, Ericsson Stadium, 800 S Mint St, Charlotte, NC 28202, USA

Beutel, Bill — *Commentator*
%WABC-TV, News Dept, 7 Lincoln Square, New York, NY 10023, USA

Bevan, Timothy H — *Financier*
%Barclay's Bank, 54 Lombard St, London EC3P 3AH, England

Beverly, Joe E — *Financier*
%Synovus Financial Corp, 901 Front St, Columbus, GA 31901, USA

Bevilacqua, Anthony J Cardinal — *Religious Leader*
%Office of the Archbishop, 222 N 17th St, Philadelphia, PA 19103, USA

Bevill, Lisa — *Singer*
%Jeff Roberts, 206 Bluebird Dr, Goodlettsville, TN 37072, USA

Bevington, Terry P — *Baseball Manager*
18 S Clay St, Hinsdale, IL 60521, USA

Bevis, Leslie — *Actress*
%Epstein-Wyckoff, 280 S Beverly Dr, #400, Beverly Hills, CA 90212, USA

Bey, Richard — *Entertainer*
445 Park Ave, #1000, New York, NY 10022, USA

Beyer, Richard — *Businessman*
%National Semiconductor, 2900 Semiconductor Dr, Santa Clara, CA 95051, USA

Beymer, Richard — Actor
1818 N Fuller Ave, Los Angeles, CA 90046, USA

Bezombes, Roger — Artist
3 Quai Saint-Michel, 75005 Paris, France

Bhandari Ram, Subadar — WW II Indian Army Hero (VC)
Vill & Po Auhar, Teh Ghumarwin, Distt Bilaspur HP, India

Bhatarai, Krishna Prasad — Prime Minister, Nepal
%Congress Central Office, Baneshwar, Kathmandu, Nepal

Bhattacharya, Basu — Movie Director
%Gold Mist, 36 Carter Road, Bandra, Bombay 50, India

Bhutto, Benazir — Prime Minister, Pakistan
%Prime Minister's Office, Old State Bank Building, Islamabad, Pakistan

Bialik, Mayim — Actress
1529 N Cahuenga Blvd, #19, Los Angeles, CA 90028, USA

Bialosuknia, Wesley — Basketball Player
29 Bayberry Dr, Bristol, CTY 06010, USA

Bianchi, Al — Basketball Player, Coach
%Miami Heat, Miami Arena, 100 NE 3rd Ave, Miami, FL 33132, USA

Biasucci, Dean — Football Player
5545 Grey Feather Court, Westlake Village, CA 91362, USA

Bibb, John — Sportswriter
%Nashville Tennessean, Editorial Dept, 1100 Broadway, Nashville, TN 37203, USA

Bibby, James B (Jim) — Baseball Player
1840 S Coolwell Road, Madison Hts, VA 24572, USA

Bible, Geoffrey C — Businessman
%Philip Morris Companies, 120 Park Ave, New York, NY 10017, USA

Bich, Bruno — Businessman
%BIC Corp, 500 Bic Dr, Milford, CT 06460, USA

Bichette, A Dante — Baseball Player
968 Eastwood Dr, Golden, CO 80401, USA

Bickel, Stephen D — Businessman
%Variable Annuity Life, 2929 Allen Parkway, Houston, TX 77019, USA

Bickerstaff, Bernard T (Bernie) — Basketball Coach, Executive
%Washington Wizards, Capital Centre, 1 Truman Dr, Landover, MD 20785, USA

Bickett, Duane — Football Player
%Carolina Panthers, Ericsson Stadium, 800 S Mint St, Charlotte, NC 28202, USA

Bickford, Bruce — Track
73 Cedar St, Wellesley, MA 02181, USA

Biddle, Melvin E — WW II Army Hero (CMH)
918 Essex Dr, Anderson, IN 46013, USA

Bidwell, John G — Businessman
%Winterthur Reinsurance, 225 Liberty St, New York, NY 10281, USA

Bidwell, William V — Football Executive
%Arizona Cardinals, 8701 S Hardy Dr, Tempe, AZ 85284, USA

Bieber, Owen F — Labor Leader
%United Auto Workers Union, 8000 E Jefferson Ave, Detroit, MI 48214, USA

Biedenbach, Edward (Ed) — Basketball Player
1000 Sunset Dr, Asheville, NC 28804, USA

Biederman, Charles J — Artist
5840 Collischan Road, Red Wing, MN 55066, USA

Biegler, David W — Businessman
%Lone Star Gas Co, 301 S Harwood St, Dallas, TX 75201, USA

Biehler, Michele — Artist
%Quartersaw Gallery, 528 NW 12th, Portland, OR 97209, USA

Biehn, Michael — Actor
11220 Valley Spring Lane, North Hollywood, CA 91602, USA

Bieka, Silvestre Siale — Prime Minister, Equatorial Guinea
%Prime Minister's Office, Malabo, Equatorial Guinea

Bielecki, J Krzysztof — Prime Minister, Poland
%Prime Minister's Office, Ursad Rady Ministrow, 00-583 Warsaw, Poland

Bielecki, Michael J (Mike) — Baseball Player
5907 Foxhall Manor Dr, Baltimore, MD 21228, USA

Biellmann, Denise — Figure Skater
Im Brachli 25, 8053 Zurich, Switzerland

Bien, Lyle G — Navy Admiral
Deputy CinC, US Spce Command, Peterson Air Force Base, CO 80914, USA

Bieniemy, Eric — Football Player
15564 E Prentice Dr, Aurora, CO 80015, USA

Bies, Don — Golfer
%Int'l Management Group, 1 Erieview Plaza, #1300, Cleveland, OH 44114, USA

Bietila, Walter — Skier
%General Delivery, Iron Mountain, MI 49801, USA

Biffi, Giacomo Cardinal — Religious Leader
Archdiocese of Bologna, Via Altabella 6, 40126 Bologna, Italy

Biffle, Jerome — Track Athlete
3205 Monaco Parkway, Denver, CO 80207, USA

Bigeleisen, Jacob — Chemist
PO Box 217, Saint James, NY 11780, USA

Bigelow, Kathryn A — Movie Director
%Creative Artists Agency, 9830 Wilshire Blvd, Beverly Hills, CA 90212, USA

Biggio, Craig A — Baseball Player
141233 Woodville Gardens Dr, Houston, TX 77077, USA

Biggs, John H — Businessman
%TIAA-CREF, 730 3rd Ave, New York, NY 10017, USA

Biggs, Tyrell — Boxer
%Cross Country Concert Corp, 310 Madison Ave, New York, NY 10017, USA

Bigley, Thomas J — Navy Admiral
1329 Carpers Ferry Way, Vienna, VA 22182, USA

Bignotti, George — Auto Racing Mechanic
%Bignotti Enterprises, 7802 Eagle Creek Overlook Dr, Indianapolis, IN 46254, USA

Bijan — Fashion Designer
699 5th Ave, New York, NY 10022, USA

Bikel, Theodore — Actor, Singer
94 Honey Hill Road, Wilton, CT 06897, USA

Bildt, Carl — Prime Minister, Sweden
Stratradsbereduingen, 103 33 Stockholm, Sweden

Bileck, Pam — Gymnast
%SCATS, 5742 McFadden Ave, Huntington Beach, CA 92649, USA

Biletnikoff, Fred — Football Player, Coach
%Oakland Raiders, 1220 Harbor Bay Parkway, Alameda, CA 94502, USA

Bilheimer, Robert S — Religious Leader
15256 Knightwood Road, Cold Spring, MN 56320, USA

Bill, Tony — Producer, Director, Actor
%Market Street Productions, 73 Market St, Venice, CA 90291, USA

Biller, Morris (Moe) — Labor Leader
%American Postal Workers Union, 1300 "L" St NW, Washington, DC 20005, USA

Billingham, John W (Jack) — Baseball
8945 Lake Irma Pointe, Orlando, FL 32817, USA

Billings, Marland P — Geologist
Westside Road, RFD, North Conway, NH 03860, USA

Billingslea, Beau — Actor
6025 Sepulveda Blvd, #201, Van Nuys, CA 91411, USA

Billingsley, Barbara — Actress
PO Box 1320, Santa Monica, CA 90406, USA

Billingsley, Hobie — Diving Coach
%Indiana University, Athletic Dept, Bloomington, IN 47405, USA

Billingsley, Ray — Cartoonist (Curtis)
%King Features Syndicate, 235 E 45th St, New York, NY 10017, USA

Billington, James H — Writer, Historian, Librarian
%Library of Congress, 101 Independence Ave SE, Washington, DC 20540, USA

Billington, Kevin — Movie Director
30 Addison Ave, London W11 4QR, England

Billups, Chauncey — Basketball Player
%Boston Celtics, 151 Merrimac St, #500, Boston, MA 02114, USA

Bilson, Bruce — Television Director
%Downwind Enterprises, 12505 Sarah St, Studio City, CA 91604, USA

Bilson, Malcolm — Concert Pianist
132 N Sunset Dr, Ithaca, NY 14850, USA

Binder, John — Religious Leader
%North American Baptist Conference, 1 S 210 Summit, Oakbrook Terrace, IL 60181, USA

Binder, Theodore — Physician
Taos Canyon, Taos, NM 87571, USA

Bindley, William E — Businessman
%Bindley Western Industries, 4212 W 71st St, Indianapolis, IN 46268, USA

Bing, Dave — Basketball Player
%Bing Manufacturing, 1111 Rosedale Court, Detroit, MI 48211, USA

B

Bies - Bing

Bing, Ilse *Photographer*
210 Riverside Dr, #6-G, New York, NY 10025, USA

Bing, R H *Mathematician*
%University of Texas, Mathematics Dept, Austin, TX 78712, USA

Bingham, Barry, Jr *Editor, Publisher*
%Louisville Courier Journal & Times, 525 W Broadway, Louisville, KY 40202, USA

Binnig, Gerd K *Nobel Physics Laureate*
%IBM Research Laboratory, Saumerstr 4, 8803 Ruschlikon, Switzerland

Binns, Malcolm *Concert Pianist*
233 Court Road, Orpington, Kent BR6 9BY, England

Binoche, Juliette *Actress*
%Agency Marceline Lenoir, 99 Blvd Marlesherbes, 75008 Paris, France

Bintley, David *Choreographer*
%Royal Ballet, Bow St, London WC2E 9DD, England

Biondi, Frank J, Jr *Businessman*
%MCA Inc, 100 Universal City Plaza, Universal City, CA 91608, USA

Biondi, Matt *Swimmer*
%Nicholas A Biondi, 1404 Rimer Dr, Moraga, CA 94556, USA

Birch, L Charles *Zoologist*
5-A/73 Yarranabbe Road, Darling Point, NSW 2027, Australia

Birch, Thora *Actress*
%United Talent Agency, 9560 Wilshire Blvd, #500, Beverly Hills, CA 90212, USA

Birchard, Bruce *Religious Leader*
%Friends General Conference, 1216 Arch St, Philadelphia, PA 19107, USA

Birchby, Kenneth L *Financier*
%Hudson City Savings Bank, W 80 Century Road, Paramus, NJ 07652, USA

Bird, Caroline *Writer, Social Activist*
1600 S Eads St, #1024-S, Arlington, VA 22202, USA

Bird, Larry J *Basketball Player, Coach*
RR 1, Box 77-A, West Baden Springs, IN 47469, USA

Bird, Lester *Prime Minister, Antigua & Barbuda*
%Prime Minister's Office, Factory Road, St John's, Antigua

Birdsong, Otis *Basketball Player*
3202 Farrow Ave, Kansas City, KS 66104, USA

Birendra Bir Bikram Shah Dev *King, Nepal*
%Narayanhiti Royal Palace, Durbag Marg, Kathmandu, Nepal

Birk, Roger E *Businessman*
%Federal National Mortgage Assn, 3900 Wisconsin Ave NW, Washington, DC 20016, USA

Birkavs, Valdis *Prime Minister, Latvia*
%Prime Minister's Office, Brivibus Bulv 36, Riga 336170 PDP, Latvia

Birkerts, Gunnar *Architect*
%Gunnar Birkerts Assoc, 28105 Greenfield Road, Southfield, MI 48076, USA

Birkin, Jane *Actress*
28 Rue de la Tour, 75016 Paris, France

Birman, Len *Actor*
%Michael Mann Mgmt, 8380 Melrose Ave, #207, Los Angeles, CA 90069, USA

Birmingham, Stephen *Writer*
%Brandt & Brandt, 1501 Broadway, New York, NY 10036, USA

Birney, David *Actor*
20 Ocean Park Blvd, #118, Santa Monica, CA 90405, USA

Birney, Earle *Writer*
1204-130 Carlton St, Toronto ON M5A 4K3, Canada

Biroc, Joseph F *Cinematographer*
4427 Pettit Ave, Encino, CA 91316, USA

Birtwistle, Harrison *Composer*
%Allied Artists, 42 Montpelier Square, London SW7 1JZ, England

Bisher, J Furman *Sportswriter*
431 Lester Road, Fayetteville, GA 30215, USA

Bishop, Ed *Actor*
29 Sunbury Court Island, Sunbury-on-Thames, Middx TW16 5PP, England

Bishop, Elvin *Singer, Guitarist*
5028 Geary St, San Francisco, CA 94118, USA

Bishop, J Michael *Nobel Medicine Laureate*
%University of California, G W Hooper Foundation, San Francisco, CA 94143, USA

Bishop, Joey *Comedian*
534 Via Lido Nord, Newport Beach, CA 92663, USA

Bishop, Julie *Actress*
45134 Brest St, Mendocino, CA 95460, USA

Bishop, Stephen *Singer, Songwriter*
2310 Apollo Dr, Los Angeles, CA 90046, USA

Bisoglio, Val *Actor*
%House of Representatives, 400 S Beverly Dr, #101, Beverly Hills, CA 90212, USA

Bisplinghoff, Raymond L *Aeronautical Engineer*
%Tyco Laboratories, Tycor Park, Exeter, NH 03833, USA

Bissell, Charles O *Editorial Cartoonist*
4221 Farrar Ave, Nashville, TN 37215, USA

Bissell, Phil *Cartoonist*
5 Shetland Road, Rockport, MA 01966, USA

Bisset, Jacqueline *Actress*
1815 Benedict Canyon Dr, Beverly Hills, CA 90210, USA

Bissett, Josie *Actress*
10350 Wilshire Blvd, #502, Los Angeles, CA 90024, USA

Bista, Kirti Nidhi *Prime Minister, Nepal*
Gyaneshawor, Kathmandu, Nepal

Biswas, Abdul Rahmana *President, Bangladesh*
%President's Office, Old Sangsad Bhaban, 12 Bangabhaban, Dhaka, Bangladesh

Bittle, Ryan *Actor*
%Hollander Talent, 3518 Cahuenga Blvd, #103, Los Angeles, CA 90068, USA

Bittner, Armin *Skier*
Rauchbergstr 30, 83334 Izell, Germany

Bittner, Ronald L *Businessman*
%Frontier Corp, 180 S Clinton Ave, Rochester, NY 14646, USA

Biya, Paul *President, Cameroon Republic*
%Palais Presidentiel, Rue de L'Exploration, Yaounde, Cameroon Republic

Bizimungu, Pasteur *President, Rwanda*
%President's Office, Church St, Boite Postale 15, Kigali, Rwanda

Bizzy Bone *Rap Artist (Bone Thugs-N-Harmony)*
%Pyramid Entertainment, 89 5th Ave, #700, New York, NY 10003, USA

Bjedov-Gabrilo, Djurdjica *Swimmer*
Brace Santini 33, 5800 Split, Yugoslavia

Bjork *Singer, Songwriter*
18 Rue Des Fosses St Jacques, 75007 Paris, France

Bjork, Anita *Actress*
AB Baggensgatan 9, 1131 Stockholm, Sweden

Bjorklund, Anders *Neurologist*
%University of Lund, Neurology Dept, Lund, Sweden

Black, Cathleen P *Publisher*
%Hearst Corp, Magazine Division, 959 8th Ave, New York, NY 10019, USA

Black, Charles L, Jr *Attorney*
%Yale University, Law School, New Haven, CT 06520, USA

Black, Cilla *Singer, Actress*
%Hindworth Mgmt, Regent House, 235-241 Regent St, London W1V 3AU, England

Black, Clint *Singer, Songwriter*
%Left Bank Mgmt, 6255 Sunset Blvd, #1111, Los Angeles, CA 90028, USA

Black, Conrad M *Publisher*
%Hollinger Inc, 10 Toronto St, Toronto ON M5C 2B7, Canada

Black, Daniel J *Businessman*
%Carter-Wallace Inc, Burlington House, 1345 Ave of Americas, New York, NY 10105, USA

Black, James W *Nobel Medicine Laureate*
%University of Dundee, Pharmacology Dept, Dundee DD1 4HN, Scotland

Black, Joe Ed *Golf Executive*
%Professional Golfer's Assn, PO Box 109601, Palm Beach Gardens, FL 33410, USA

Black, Karen *Actress*
%Gold Marshak Liedtke, 3500 W Olive Ave, #1400, Burbank, CA 91505, USA

Black, Larry *Track Athlete*
14401 Pierce St, Miami, FL 33176, USA

Black, Lennox K *Businessman*
%Teleflex Inc, 630 W Germantown Pike, Plymouth Meeting, PA 19462, USA

Black, Leon D *Financier*
%Apollo Advisors, 2 Manhattanville Road, Purchase, NY 10577, USA

Black, Mary *Singer*
%Agency Group, 1775 Broadway, #433, New York, NY 10019, USA

Black, Robert P *Financier, Government Official*
10 Dahlgren Road, Richmond, VA 23233, USA

Black, Shirley Temple *Actress, Diplomat*
115 Lakeview Dr, Woodside, CA 94062, USA

B

Black, Stanley — *Conductor, Composer*
8 Linnell Close, London NW11, England

Blackburn, Charles L — *Businessman*
%Maxus Energy Corp, 717 N Harwood St, Dallas, TX 75201, USA

Blackburn, Greta — *Actress*
%Dade/Schultz, 11846 Ventura Blvd, #100, Studio City, CA 91604, USA

Blackledge, Todd A — *Football Player*
2711 Glenmont Dr NW, Canton, OH 44708, USA

Blackman, Honor — *Actress*
%Michael Ladkin Mgmt, 11 Southwick Mews, London W2 1JG, England

Blackman, Robert L (Bob) — *Football Coach*
8 Full Sweep, Palmetto Dr, Hilton Head Island, SC 29928, USA

Blackmore, Ritchie — *Singer, Guitarist*
%Performers of the World, 8901 Melrose Ave, #200, West Hollywood, CA 90069, USA

Blackmun, Harry A — *Supreme Court Justice*
%US Supreme Court, 1 1st St NE, Washington, DC 20543, USA

Blackwell, Harolyn — *Opera Singer*
%Columbia Artists Mgmt Inc, 165 W 57th St, New York, NY 10019, USA

Blackwell, Lloyd P — *Forester*
1212 Dubach St, Ruston, LA 71270, USA

Blackwell, Mr (Richard) — *Fashion Designer*
531 S Windsor, Los Angeles, CA 90020, USA

Blackwell, Otis — *Composer*
119 W 57th St, New York, NY 10019, USA

Blackwood, Nina — *Entertainer*
22968 Victory Blvd, #158, Woodland Hills, CA 91367, USA

Blacque, Taurean — *Actor*
5049 Rock Springs Road, Lithonia, GA 30038, USA

Blades, Arthur C — *Marine Corps General*
Deputy CofS Plans Policies Ops, HqUSMC, Navy Annex, Washington, DC 20380, USA

Blades, H Benedict (Bennie) — *Football Player*
1900 SW 70th Terrace, Plantation, FL 33317, USA

Blades, Ruben — *Singer, Songwriter, Actor*
1187 Coast Village Road, #1, Montecito, CA 93108, USA

Blaha, John E — *Astronaut*
%NASA, Johnson Space Center, 2101 NASA Road, Houston, TX 77058, USA

Blahnik, Manolo — *Fashion Designer*
49-51 Old Church Road, London SW3, England

Blair, Anthony C L (Tony) — *Prime Minister, England*
%Prime Minister's Office, 10 Downing St, London SW1A 2AA, England

Blair, Betsy — *Actress*
11 Chalcot Gardens, Englands Lane, London NW3 4YB, England

Blair, Bonnie — *Speed Skater*
306 White Pine Road, Delafield, WI 53018, USA

Blair, Dennis C — *Navy Admiral*
Director, Joint Staff, Joint Chiefs of Staff, Pentagon, Washington, DC 20318, USA

Blair, Janet — *Actress*
21650 Burbank Blvd, #107, Woodland Hills, CA 91367, USA

Blair, Linda — *Actress*
4709 Norwich Ave, Sherman Oaks, CA 91403, USA

Blair, Matthew A (Matt) — *Football Player*
12243 Nicollet Ave, Burnsville, MN 55337, USA

Blair, Paul L D — *Baseball Player*
48 Mamaroneck Ave, #30, White Plains, NY 10601, USA

Blair, William Draper, Jr — *Conservationist*
5006 Warren St NW, Washington, DC 20016, USA

Blair, William M, Jr — *Attorney, Diplomat*
2510 Foxhall Road NW, Washington, DC 20007, USA

Blair, William S — *Publisher*
RD 3, Brattleboro, VT 05301, USA

Blais, Madeleine H — *Journalist*
%Miami Herald, Editorial Dept, 1 Herald Plaza, Miami, FL 33132, USA

Blake, George R — *Editor*
%Cincinnati Enquirer, Editorial Dept, 617 Vine St, Cincinnati, OH 45202, USA

Blake, Jeff — *Football Player*
%Cincinnati Bengals, 1 Bengals Dr, Cincinnati, OH 45204, USA

Blake, John C — *Artist*
Oz Voorburgwal 131, 1012 ER Amsterdam, Netherlands

Blake, Julian W (Bud) _Cartoonist (Tiger)_
PO Box 146, Damariscotta, ME 04543, USA
Blake, Norman P, Jr _Businessman_
%USF&G, 100 Light St, Baltimore, MD 21202, USA
Blake, Peter _Yachtsman_
Emsworth, Hants, England
Blake, Peter _Architect_
140 Elm St, Branford, CT 06405, USA
Blake, Peter T _Artist_
%Waddington Galleries, 11 Cork St, London W1X 1PD, England
Blake, Robert _Actor_
%Breezy Productions, 11604 Dilling St, #8, North Hollywood, CA 91604, USA
Blake, Rockwell _Opera Singer_
1 Onondaga Lane, Plattsburgh, NY 12901, USA
Blake, Stephanie _Actress_
%First Artists, 10000 Riverside Dr, #10, Toluca Lake, CA 91602, USA
Blake, Whitney _Actress_
PO Box 6088, Malibu, CA 90264, USA
Blakeley, Ronee _Actress, Singer_
8033 Sunset Blvd, #693, Los Angeles, CA 90046, USA
Blakely, Ross M _Financier_
%Coast Federal Savings, 1000 Wilshire Blvd, Los Angeles, CA 90017, USA
Blakely, Susan _Actress, Model_
%Jaffe/Blakely Films, 421 N Rodeo Dr, #15-111, Beverly Hills, CA 90210, USA
Blakemore, Colin B _Neurophysiologist, Physiologist_
%University Laboratory of Physiology, Parks Road, Oxford OX1 3PT, England
Blakemore, Michael H _Theater Director, Actor, Writer_
18 Upper Park Road, London NW3 2UP, England
Blalack, Robert _Cinematographer_
12251 Huston St, North Hollywood, CA 91607, USA
Blalock, Jane _Golfer_
148 Brackett Road, Portsmouth, NH 03801, USA
Blanc, Georges _Chef_
Le Mere Blanc, 01540 Vonnas, Ain, France
Blanc, Raymond R A _Chef_
%Le Quat' Saisons, Church Road, Great Milton, Oxford OX44 7PD, England
Blancas, Homero _Golfer_
15303 Poplar Grove Dr, Houston, TX 77068, USA
Blanchard, Felix A (Doc) _Football Player_
30395 Olympus, Bulverde, TX 78163, USA
Blanchard, George S _Army General_
23 Dewberry Road, Whispering Pines, NC 28327, USA
Blanchard, James H _Financier_
%Synovus Financial Corp, 901 Front Ave, Columbus, GA 31901, USA
Blanchard, James J _Governor, MI; Diplomat_
%American Embassy, 100 Wellington St, Ottawa ON K1P 5T1, Canada
Blanchard, Kenneth _Writer, Business Consultant_
2048 Aldergrove, #B, Escondido, CA 92029, USA
Blanchard, Nina _Model Agency Executive_
3610 Wrightwood Dr, Studio City, CA 91604, USA
Blanchard, Terence _Jazz Trumpeter_
%Joel Chriss, 300 Mercer St, #3-J, New York, NY 10003, USA
Blanchard, Tim _Religious Leader_
%Conservative Baptist Assn, PO Box 66, Wheaton, IL 60189, USA
Blanck, Ronald R (Ron) _Army General, Surgeon_
%Surgeon General's Office, 5109 Leesburg Pike, Falls Church, VA 22041, USA
Blanco-Cervantes, Raul _President, Costa Rica_
Apdo 918, San Jose, Costa Rica
Bland, Bobby (Blue) _Singer_
108 N Auburndale St, #1010, Memphis, TN 38104, USA
Blanda, George F _Football Player_
1513 Stonegate Road, LaGrange Park, IL 60526, USA
Blankers-Koen, Fanny _Track Athlete_
%Olympic Committee, Surinamestraat 33, 2585 La Harve, Netherlands
Blankfield, Mark _Actor_
%Artists Group, 10100 Santa Monica Blvd, #2490, Los Angeles, CA 90067, USA
Blankley, Walter E _Businessman_
%Ametek Inc, Station Square, Paoli, PA 19301, USA

Blashford-Snell, John N	*Explorer*

%Scientific Exploration Soc, Motcome, Shaftesbury, Dorset SP7 9PB, England

Blass, Stephen R (Steve) *Baseball Player*
1756 Quigg Dr, Pittsburgh, PA 15241, USA

Blass, William R (Bill) *Fashion Designer*
%Bill Blass Ltd, 550 7th Ave, New York, NY 10018, USA

Blassie, Freddie *Wrestler*
215 W Hartdale Ave, Hartdale, NY 10530, USA

Blasucci, Richard *Actor*
10424 Bloomfield St, North Hollywood, CA 91602, USA

Blatnick, Jeff *Wrestler*
%Cowen Co, 80 State St, Albany, NY 12207, USA

Blatty, William Peter *Writer*
3025 Vista Linda Lane, Santa Barbara, CA 93108, USA

Blauner, Peter *Writer*
%Little Brown Co, 34 Beacon St, Boston, MA 02108, USA

Blauser, Jeffrey M (Jeff) *Baseball Player*
3005 Compton Court, Alpharetta, GA 30022, USA

Blaylock, Kenneth T *Labor Leader*
%American Government Employees Federation, 80 "F" St NW, Washington, DC 20001, USA

Blaylock, Mookie *Basketball Player*
%Atlanta Hawks, 1 CNN Center, South Tower, Atlanta, GA 30303, USA

Blazelowski, Carol *Basketball Player, Executive*
%New York Liberty, Madison Square Garden, 2 Penn Plaza, New York, NY 10121, USA

Bleak, David B *Korean War Army Hero (CMH)*
RR 1 Box 345, Arco, ID 83213, USA

Blech, Harry *Conductor*
The Owls, 70 Leopold Road, Wimbledon, London SW19 T5Q, England

Bleck, Max E *Businessman*
%Raytheon Co, 141 Spring St, Lexington, MA 02173, USA

Bledsoe, Drew *Football Player*
45 Tabway Lane, Bridgewater, MA 02324, USA

Bledsoe, Tempestt *Actress*
%Innovative Artists, 1999 Ave of Stars, #2850, Los Angeles, CA 90067, USA

Bleeth, Yasmine *Actress*
308 N Sycamore Ave, #202, Los Angeles, CA 90036, USA

Blegen, Judith *Opera Singer*
91 Central Park West, #1-B, New York, NY 10023, USA

Bleiberg, Robert M *Editor*
25 Central Park West, New York, NY 10023, USA

Bleier, Rocky *Football Player*
%Rocky Bleier Enterprises, 706 Ivy St, #2, Pittsburgh, PA 15232, USA

Bleifeld, Stanley *Sculptor*
27 Spring Valley Road, Weston, CT 06883, USA

Blessed, Brian *Actor*
%Vernon Conway, 5 Spring St, London W2 3RA, England

Blethen, Frank A *Publisher*
%Seattle Times, Fairview Ave N & John St, Seattle, WA 98111, USA

Blethen, John A *Publisher*
%Seattle Times, Fairview Ave N & John St, Seattle, WA 98111, USA

Blethyn, Brenda *Actress*
%International Creative Mgmt, 76 Oxford St, London W1N 0AX, England

Bley, Carla B *Composer, Jazz Pianist*
%Watt Works Inc, Grogkill Road, Willow, NY 12495, USA

Bley, Paul *Jazz Pianist, Composer*
%Soul Note Records, 810 7th Ave, New York, NY 10019, USA

Blick, Richard (Dick) *Swimmer*
2505 Tamarack Court, Kingsburg, CA 93631, USA

Blige, Mary J *Rapper, Singer*
%International Creative Mgmt, 40 W 57th St, New York, NY 10019, USA

Blinder, Alan S *Government Official, Financier*
%Princeton University, Economics Dept, Princeton, NJ 08544, USA

Blitzer, Wolf *Commentator*
%Cable News Network, News Dept, 820 1st St NE, Washington, DC 20002, USA

Blix, Hans M *Government Official*
%International Atomic Energy Agency, Wagramserstr 5, 1400 Vienna, Austria

Blobel, Gunter *Cell Biologist*
%Rockefeller University, Cell Biology Dept, 1230 York Ave, New York, NY 10021, USA

Bloch, Erich *Government Official, Scientist*
%National Science Foundation, 1800 "C" St NW, Washington, DC 20550, USA
Bloch, Henry W *Businessman*
%H & R Block Inc, 4410 Main St, Kansas City, MO 64111, USA
Bloch, Konrad E *Nobel Medicine Laureate*
%Harvard University, Chemistry Dept, 12 Oxford St, Cambridge, MA 02138, USA
Bloch, Thomas M *Businessman*
%H & R Block Inc, 4410 Main St, Kansas City, MO 64111, USA
Blochwitz, Hans-Peter *Opera Singer*
%Shaw Concerts, Lincoln Center Plaza, 1900 Broadway, #200, New York, NY 10023, USA
Block, Herbert L (Herblock) *Editorial Cartoonist*
%Washington Post Writers Group, 1150 15th St NW, Washington, DC 20071, USA
Block, James A *Businessman*
%Block Drug Co, 257 Cornelison Ave, Jersey City, NJ 07302, USA
Block, John R *Secretary, Agriculture*
%Nat Am Wholesale Grocers Assn, 201 Park Washington Ct, Falls Church, VA 22046, USA
Block, Lawrence *Writer*
299 W 12th St, #12-D, New York, NY 10014, USA
Block, Leonard N *Businessman*
%Block Drug Co, 257 Cornelison Ave, Jersey City, NJ 07302, USA
Block, Sherman *Law Enforcement Official*
%L A County Sheriffs Office, 4700 W Ramona Blvd, Monterey Park, CA 91754, USA
Block, Steven *Biophysicist*
%Princeton University, Biophysics Dept, Princeton, NJ 08544, USA
Blocker, John *Concert Pianist, Educator*
%University of California, School of Arts, Los Angeles, CA 90024, USA
Bloembergen, Nicolaas *Nobel Physics Laureate*
%Harvard University, Applied Physics Dept, Pierce Hall, Cambridge, MA 02138, USA
Blomstedt, Herbert T *Conductor*
%InterArtists, Frans Van Mierisstraat 43, 1071 RK Amsterdam, Netherlands
Blood, Edward J *Skier*
RFD 2, Beech Hill, Durham, NH 03824, USA
Bloodworth-Thomason, Linda *Television Producer, Screenwriter*
9220 Sunset Blvd, #311, Los Angeles, CA 90069, USA
Bloom, Alfred H *Educator*
%Swarthmore College, President's Office, Swarthmore, PA 19081, USA
Bloom, Anne *Actress*
%Abrams Artists, 9200 Sunset Blvd, #625, Los Angeles, CA 90069, USA
Bloom, Brian *Actor*
11 Croydon Court, Dix Hills, NY 11746, USA
Bloom, Claire *Actress*
%Conway Van Gelder Robinson, 18-21 Jermyn St, London SW1Y 6NB, England
Bloom, Lindsay *Actress*
PO Box 412, Weldon, CA 93283, USA
Bloom, Luka *Singer*
%Vector Mgmt, 48 Music Square E, Nashville, TN 37203, USA
Bloom, Ursula *Writer*
Newton House, Walls Dr, Ravenglass, Cumbria, England
Bloomfield, Sara *Museum Director*
%Holocaust Memorial Museum, 100 Raoul Wallenberg Pl SW, Washington, DC 20024, USA
Bloomquist, Robert O *Businessman*
%Lutheran Brotherhood, 625 4th Ave S, Minneapolis, MN 55415, USA
Blot, Harold W *Marine Corps General*
%Deputy CofS for Aviation, HqUSMC, 2 Navy Annex, Washington, DC 20370, USA
Blount, Lisa *Actress*
2060 Paramount Dr, Los Angeles, CA 90068, USA
Blount, Mel *Football Player, Executive*
108 Jamestown Dr, Pittsburgh, PA 15216, USA
Blount, Winton M, III *Businessman*
%Blount Inc, 4520 Executive Park Dr, Montgomery, AL 36116, USA
Blount, Winton M, Jr *Postmaster General, Businessman*
%Blount Inc, 4520 Executive Park Dr, Montgomery, AL 36116, USA
Blout, Elkan R *Biochemist*
1010 Memorial Dr, Cambridge, MA 02138, USA
Blow, Kurtis *Rap Artist*
%Headline Talent, 1650 Broadway, #508, New York, NY 10019, USA
Blue, Forrest *Football Player*
4451 Ashton Dr, Sacramento, CA 95864, USA

B

Bloch - Blue

Blue, Vida *Baseball Player*
PO Box 1449, Pleasanton, CA 94566, USA

Bluford, Guion S, Jr *Astronaut*
%NYMA Inc, 2001 Aerospace Parkway, Brook Park, OH 44142, USA

Bluhm, Kay *Kayak Athlete*
Bahnofstr 104, 14480 Potsdam, Germany

Blum, Arlene *Mountaineer*
%University of California, Biochemistry Dept, Berkeley, CA 94720, USA

Blumberg, Baruch S *Nobel Medicine Laureate*
%Fox Chase Cancer Center, 7701 Burholme Ave, Philadelphia, PA 19111, USA

Blume, Judy S *Writer*
%Harold Ober Assoc, 425 Madison Ave, New York, NY 10017, USA

Blume, Veronica *Model*
%Ford Model Agency, 344 E 59th St, New York, NY 10022, USA

Blumenthal, W Michael *Secretary, Treasury; Financier*
%Lazard Freres Co, 1 Rockefeller Plaza, New York, NY 10020, USA

Bluth, Ray *Bowler*
%Crestwood Bowl, 9822 Highway 66, Crestwood, MO 63126, USA

Bly, Robert E *Writer, Psychologist*
1904 Girard Ave S, Minneapolis, MN 55403, USA

Blyleven, R Bert *Baseball Player*
4745 E Ashfird Ave, Orange, CA 92867, USA

Blyth, Ann *Actress, Singer*
35325 Beach Road, #PH, Capistrano Beach, CA 92624, USA

Blyth, Myrna G *Editor*
%Ladies Home Journal, Editorial Dept, 100 Park Ave, New York, NY 10017, USA

Bo, Jurgen *Architect*
Lindevangsvej 22, 3460 Birkerod, Denmark

Boardman, Christopher M (Chris) *Cyclist*
Mozolowski & Murray, Bridgend Industrial Estate, Kinross KY13 7ER, England

Boardman, Thomas G *Financier*
%National Westminster Bank, 41 Lothbury, London EC2P 2BP, England

Boatman, Michael *Actor*
1571 S Kiowa Crest Dr, Diamond Bar, CA 91765, USA

Bobko, Karol J *Astronaut*
%Booz Allen Hamilton, 2525 Bay Area Blvd, #290, Houston, TX 77058, USA

BoBo, D J *Singer*
Postfach, 6242 Wauwil, Switzerland

Bocca, Julio *Ballet Dancer*
%FPS International, 150 Broadway, New York, NY 10038, USA

Boccardi, Louis D *Publisher*
%Associated Press Broadcast, 12 Norwick St, London EC4A 1BP, England

Bochco, Steven *Television Producer, Writer*
%Steven Bochco Productions, PO Box 900, Beverly Hills, CA 90213, USA

Bochner, Hart *Actor*
1746 Correa Way, Los Angeles, CA 90049, USA

Bochner, Lloyd *Actor*
42 Haldeman Road, Santa Monica, CA 90402, USA

Bochner, Salomon *Mathematician*
4100 Greenbriar Ave, #239, Houston, TX 77098, USA

Bochte, Bruce A *Baseball Player*
3688 Hastings Court, Lafayette, CA 94549, USA

Bochy, Bruce D *Baseball Player, Manager*
16144 Brittany Park Lane, Poway, CA 92064, USA

Bock, Edward J *Businessman, Football Player*
7 Huntleigh Woods, St Louis, MO 63131, USA

Bock, Jerry *Composer*
145 Wellington Ave, New Rochelle, NY 10804, USA

Bocuse, Paul *Restauranteur*
40 Rue de la Plage, 69660 Collonges-au-Mont d'Or, France

Boddicker, Michael J (Mike) *Baseball Player*
11324 W 121st Terrace, Overland Park, KS 66213, USA

Bode, Hendrick W *Research Engineer*
%Harvard University, Pierce Hall, Cambridge, MA 02138, USA

Bode, Ken *Commentator*
%"Washington Week in Review" Show, WETA-TV, Box 2626, Washington, DC 20013, USA

Bode, Rolf *Cinematographer*
PO Box 2230, Los Angeles, CA 90078, USA

Bodenstein, Dietrich H F A — *Biologist*
536 Valley Road, Charlottesville, VA 22903, USA

Bodine, Brett — *Auto Racing Driver*
18822 River Wind Lane, Davidson, NC 28036, USA

Bodine, Geoff — *Auto Racing Driver*
%GEB Racing, 6007 Victory Lane, Harrisburg, NC 28075, USA

Bodman, Samuel W, III — *Financier*
%Cabot Corp, 75 State St, Boston, MA 02109, USA

Bodmer, Walter F — *Geneticist*
%Imperial Cancer Research, Lincoln's Inn Fields, London WC2A 3PX, England

Bodner, David E — *Financier*
%Julius Baer Securities, 330 Madison Ave, New York, NY 10017, USA

Boede, Marvin J — *Labor Leader*
%Plumbing & Pipe Fitting Union, 901 Massachusetts NW, Washington, DC 20001, USA

Boeheim, Jim — *Basketball Coach*
%Syracuse University, Manley Field House, Syracuse, NY 13244, USA

Boehm, Gottfried K — *Writer, Art Historian*
Sevogelplatz 1, 4052 Basel, Switzerland

Boehne, Edward G — *Financier*
%Federal Reserve Bank, Independence Mall, 100 N 6th St, Philadelphia, PA 19106, USA

Boekelheide, Virgil C — *Chemist*
2017 Elk Dr, Eugene, OR 97403, USA

Boeker, Paul H — *Diplomat*
3701 Blacktorn Court, Chevy Chase, MD 20815, USA

Boerner, Jacqueline — *Speed Skater*
Bernhard-Bastlein-Str 55, 10367 Berlin, Germany

Boerwinkle, Tom — *Basketball Player*
%Chicago Bulls, 1901 W Madison St, Chicago, IL 60612, USA

Boesak, Allan — *Religious Leader, Social Activist*
PO Box 316, Kasselsvlei 7533, South Africa

Boeschenstein, William W — *Businessman*
3 Locust St, Perrysburg, OH 43551, USA

Boese, Lawrence E (Larry) — *Air Force General*
Commander, 11th Air Force, 5800 "G" St, Elmendorf Air Force Base, AK 99506, USA

Boesel, Raul — *Auto Racing Driver*
230 Island Dr, Miami, FL 33149, USA

Boesen, Dennis L — *Astronaut*
6613 Sandra Ave NE, Albuquerque, NM 87109, USA

Boettcher, Wilfried — *Conductor*
%Christopher Tennant, 11 Lawrence St, London SW3 5NB, England

Boetticher, Budd — *Movie Director*
23969 Green Haven Lane, Ramona, CA 92065, USA

Boeynants, Paul V D — *Prime Minister, Belgium*
41 Rue de Deux Eglises, 1040 Brussels, Belgium

Boff, Leonardo G D — *Theologian*
Pr M Leao 12/204, Alto Vale Encantado, 20531-350 Rio de Janeiro, Brazil

Bofill, Angela — *Singer*
1385 York Ave, #6-B, New York, NY 10021, USA

Bofill, Ricardo — *Architect*
%Taller de Arquitectura, 14 Ave de la Industria, 08960 Barcelona, Spain

Bofinger, Heinz — *Architect*
Biebricher Allee 49, 65187 Wiesbaden, Germany

Bogarde, Dirk — *Actor*
%Jonathan Altaras, 27 Floral St, London WC2E 9DP, England

Bogart, Paul — *Television, Movie Director*
1900 Ave of Stars, #1040, Los Angeles, CA 90067, USA

Bogdanovich, Peter — *Movie Director*
468 N Camden Dr, #200, Beverly Hills, CA 90210, USA

Boggs, J Caleb — *Governor/Senator, DE*
1203 Grinnell Road, Wilmington, DE 19803, USA

Boggs, Wade A — *Baseball Player*
6006 Windham Place, Tampa, FL 33647, USA

Bogguss, Suzy — *Singer, Songwriter, Guitarist*
%Ten Ten Mgmt, 33 Music Sq W, #110, Nashville, TN 37203, USA

Bogle, John C — *Financier*
%Vanguard Group, 1300 Morris Dr, Valley Forge, PA 19482, USA

Boglioli, Wendy — *Swimmer*
11 Iris St, Eatontown, NJ 07724, USA

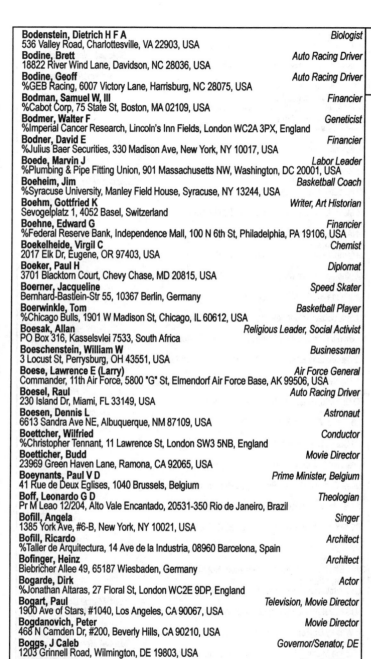

B

Bodenstein - Boglioli

Bogner, Willy *Fashion Designer*
%Bogner Film GmbH, Saint-Veit-Str 4, 81673 Munich, Germany
Bogorad, Lawrence *Biologist, Plant Physiologist*
%Harvard University, Biological Laboratories, Cambridge, MA 02138, USA
Bogosian, Eric *Performance Artist, Actor*
145 Hudson St, #9-W, New York, NY 10013, USA
Bogues, Tyrone (Muggsy) *Basketball Player*
%Charlotte Hornets, 1 Hive Dr, Charlotte, NC 28217, USA
Boguinskaia, Svetlana *Gymnast*
%Karolyi's World Gym, RR 12, Box 140, Huntsville, TX 77340, USA
Boh, Robert H *Financier*
%Hibernia Corp, 313 Carondelet St, New Orleans, LA 70130, USA
Bohan, Marc *Fashion Designer*
55 Rue Saint-Dominique, 75007 Paris, France
Bohannon, David D *Community Planner, Developer*
60 Hillsdale Mall, San Mateo, CA 94403, USA
Bohay, Heidi *Actress*
48 Main St, South Bound Brook, NJ 08880, USA
Bohlin, John D *Space Scientist*
%NASA, Solar & Heliospherics Physics Division, Washington, DC 22546, USA
Bohlin, Peter Q *Architect*
197 Parfitt Way SW, Bainbridge Island, WA 98110, USA
Bohlmann, Ralph A *Religious Leader*
%Lutheran Church Missouri Synod, 1333 S Kirkwood Road, St Louis, MO 63122, USA
Bohr, Aage N *Nobel Physics Laureate*
Strangade 34, 1-Sal, 1401 Copenhagen, Denmark
Bohrer, Corinne *Actress*
%Metropolitan Talent Agency, 4526 Wilshire Blvd, Los Angeles, CA 90010, USA
Boisset, Yves *Movie Director*
61 Blvd Inkerman, 92200 Neuilly-sur-Seine, France
Boitano, Brian *Figure Skater*
%Brian Boitano Enterprises, 101 1st St, #370, Los Altos, CA 94022, USA
Boiteux, Jean *Swimmer*
51 Ave de Merignac, 33200 Bordeaux, Cauderan, France
Boivin, Leo *Hockey Player*
PO Box 406, Prescott ON K0E 1T0, Canada
Bok, Bart J *Astronomer, Educator*
200 Sierra Vista Dr, Tucson, AZ 85719, USA
Bok, Chip *Editorial Cartoonist*
709 Castle Blvd, Akron, OH 44313, USA
Bok, Derek C *Educator*
%Harvard University, Law School, Cambridge, MA 02138, USA
Bok, Joan T *Businessman*
%New England Electric System, 25 Research Dr, Westborough, MA 01582, USA
Bok, Sissela *Philosopher*
75 Cambridge Parkway, #E-610, Cambridge, MA 02142, USA
Bokamper, Kim *Football Player*
301 NW 127th Ave, Plantation, FL 33325, USA
Bol, Manute *Basketball Player*
%Manute Bol's Restaurant, 1211 "U" St NW, Washington, DC 20009, USA
Bolack, Tom *Governor, NM*
3701 Bloomfield Highway, Farmington, NM 87401, USA
Bolcom, William E *Composer*
3080 Whitmore Lake Road, Ann Arbor, MI 48105, USA
Bolden, Charles F, Jr *Astronaut, Marine Corps General*
%US Naval Academy, Deputy Commandant's Office, Annapolis, MD 21402, USA
Bolen, David B *Diplomat*
26 Wesley Dr, Foxmeadow, Hockessin, DE 19707, USA
Boles, John *Baseball Manager, Executive*
%Florida Marlins, 100 NE 3rd Ave, Fort Lauderdale, FL 33301, USA
Bolger, James B (Jim) *Prime Minister, New Zealand*
%National Party, Parliament, Wellington, New Zealand
Bolin, Bert *Meteorologist*
%University of Stockholm, Meteorological Institute, Stockholm, Sweden
Bolkiah Mu'izuddin Waddaulah *Sultan, Brunei Darussalam*
Istana Darul Hana, Brunei Darussalam
Bolkvadze, Elisso *Concert Pianist*
%Hillyer International, Carnegie Mews, 211 W 56th St, New York, NY 10019, USA

Bolleau, Linda *Editorial Cartoonist*
%Frankfort State Journal, Editorial Dept, 321 W Main St, Frankfort, KY 40601, USA
Bollen, Roger *Cartoonist (Animal Crackers, Catfish)*
8964 Little St, Mentor, OH 44060, USA
Bollenbach, Stephen F *Businessman*
%Hilton Hotels Corp, 9336 Civic Center Dr, Beverly Hills, CA 90210, USA
Bolles, Richard N *Writer*
3044 Oakraider Dr, Alamo, CA 94507, USA
Bollettieri, Nick *Tennis Coach*
%Nick Bollettieri Tennis Academy, 5500 34th St W, Bradenton, FL 34210, USA
Bolling, Claude *Jazz Pianist, Composer*
%New Audiences Artist Mgmt, 155 W 57th St, #706, New York, NY 10019, USA
Bolling, Tiffany *Actress*
12483 Braddock Dr, Los Angeles, CA 90066, USA
Bollom, Daniel A *Businessman*
%WPS Resources Corp, 700 N Adams St, Green Bay, WI 54301, USA
Bologna, Joseph *Actor*
16830 Ventura Blvd, #326, Encino, CA 91436, USA
Bolt, Tommy *Golfer*
PO Box 5118, Akron, OH 44334, USA
Bolton, Michael *Singer, Songwriter*
PO Box 679, Branford, CT 06405, USA
Bolton-Holifield, Ruthie *Basketball Player*
%Sacramento Monarchs, Arco Arena, 1 Sports Parkway, Sacramento, CA 95834, USA
Bombassaro, Gerald *Labor Leader*
%Tile Marble & Granite Cutters Union, 801 N Pitt St, Alexandria, VA 22314, USA
Bon Jovi, Jon *Singer, Songwriter (Bon Jovi)*
%Bon Jovi Mgmt, 250 W 57th St, #603-5, New York, NY 10107, USA
Bonaduce, Danny *Actor, Singer*
%Music Expo, 812 W Darby Road, Haverton, PA 19083, USA
Bonaly, Surya *Figure Skater*
10 Impasse du Petit Champigny, 94500 Champigny, France
Bonamy, James *Singer*
%Hallmark Direction, 1905 Broadway, Nashville, TN 37203, USA
Bonanno, Louis *Actor*
PO Box 583, Laguna Beach, CA 92652, USA
Bonaventura, Celia *Hematologist*
%Duke University, Medical Center, Hematology Dept, Durham, NC 27708, USA
Bonaventura, Joseph *Hematologist*
%Duke University, Medical Center, Hematology Dept, Durham, NC 27708, USA
Bond, Alan *Businessman, Yachtsman*
89 Watkins Road, Dalkeith WA 6069, Australia
Bond, Edward *Writer*
Orchard Way, Great Wilbraham, Cambridge CB1 5KA, England
Bond, H Julian *Civil Rights Activist*
6002 34th Place NW, Washington, DC 20015, USA
Bond, Richard N *Political Leader*
%Republican National Committee, 310 1st St SE, Washington, DC 20002, USA
Bond, Tommy (Butch) *Actor*
14704 Road 36, Madera, CA 93638, USA
Bond, Victoria A *Conductor, Composer*
%Roanoke Symphony, PO Box 2433, Roanoke, VA 24010, USA
Bondar, Roberta *Astronaut, Canada*
%McMaster University, Health Science Center, Hamilton ON L8N 3Z5, Canada
Bondarenko, Larissa *Model*
%Elite Model Mgmt, 345 N Maple Dr, Beverly Hills, CA 90210, USA
Bonde, Peder *Businessman*
1 Farragut Square South, Washington, DC 20006, USA
Bonderman, David *Businessman*
%Continental Airlines, 2929 Allen Parkway, Houston, TX 77019, USA
Bondi, Hermann *Applied Mathematician*
60 Mill Lane, Impington, Cambridgeshire CB4 4XN, England
Bondlow, William F, Jr *Publisher*
%House & Garden Magazine, 350 Madison Ave, New York, NY 10017, USA
Bondra, Peter *Hockey Player*
%Washington Capitals, USAir Arena, 1 Truman Dr, Landover, MD 20785, USA
Bonds, Barry L *Baseball Player*
%San Francisco Giants, Candlestick Park, San Francisco, CA 94124, USA

Bonds, Bobby L — *Baseball Player*
175 Lyndhurst Ave, San Carlos, CA 94070, USA

Bonds, Gary U S — *Singer*
%Talent Consultants Int'l, 1560 Broadway, #1308, New York, NY 10036, USA

Bonerz, Peter — *Actor, Comedian, Director*
3637 Lowry Road, Los Angeles, CA 90027, USA

Bonet, Lisa — *Actress*
%Progressive Artists Agency, 400 S Beverly Dr, #216, Beverly Hills, CA 90212, USA

Bonet, Pep — *Architect*
C/Pujades 62, 08005 Barcelona, Spain

Bongiorno, John J — *Financier*
%Navistar Financial Corp, 2850 W Golf Road, Rolling Meadows, IL 60008, USA

Bongo, Albert-Bernard O — *President, Gabon*
%President's Office, Blvd de Independence, BP 546, Libreville, Gabon

Bonham, Ron — *Basketball Player*
8020 S Country Road 700-E, Selma, IN 47383, USA

Bonham, Tracy — *Singer, Songwriter*
%McGhee Entertainment, 8730 Sunset Blvd, #175, Los Angeles, CA 90069, USA

Bonham-Carter, Helena — *Actress*
7 West Heath Ave, London NW11 7S, England

Bonilla, Roberto M A (Bobby) — *Baseball Player*
390 Round Hill Road, Greenwich, CT 06831, USA

Bonin, Gordie — *Auto Racing Driver*
12471 Sanford St, Los Angeles, CA 90066, USA

Bonnefous, Jean-Pierre — *Ballet Dancer, Choreographer*
%Indiana University, Ballet Dept, Music School, Bloomington, IN 47405, USA

Bonnefoy, Yves J — *Writer*
%College de France, 11 Place Marcelin Berthelot, 75005 Paris, France

Bonner, James — *Biologist*
131 N El Molino Ave, #380, Pasadena, CA 91101, USA

Bonney, Barbara — *Opera Singer*
Gunnarsbyn, 671 94 Edane, Sweden

Bono (Paul Hewson) — *Singer, Songwriter (U-2)*
%Principle Mgmt, 30-32 Sir John Rogerson's Quay, Dublin 2, Ireland

Bono, Chastity — *Actress, Singer*
11825 Kling St, North Hollywood, CA 91607, USA

Bonoff, Karla — *Singer, Pianist, Songwriter*
%Performers of the World, 8901 Melrose Ave, #200, West Hollywood, CA 90069, USA

Bonsall, Joseph S (Joe), Jr — *Singer (Oak Ridge Boys)*
329 Rockland Road, Hendersonville, TN 37075, USA

Bonsignore, Joseph J — *Publisher*
%Smithsonian Magazine, 900 Jefferson Dr SW, Washington, DC 20560, USA

Bonsignore, Michael R — *Businessman*
%Honeywell Inc, PO Box 524, Minneapolis, MN 55440, USA

Bontemps, Ron — *Basketball Player*
133 S Illinois Ave, Morton, IL 61550, USA

Bonvicini, Joan — *Basketball Coach*
%University of Arizona, Athletic Dept, McKale Memorial Center, Tucson, AZ 85721, USA

Bonynge, Richard — *Conductor*
Chalet Monet, Rte de Sonloup, 1833 Les Avants, Switzerland

Boon, David C — *Cricketer*
%Australian Cricket Board, 90 Jollimont St, Victoria 3002, Australia

Boone, Debby — *Actress, Singer*
4334 Kester Ave, Sherman Oaks, CA 91403, USA

Boone, James T — *Financier*
%Grenada Sunburst System, 2000 Gateway, Grenada, MS 38901, USA

Boone, Mary — *Artist Representative*
420 W Broadway, New York, NY 10012, USA

Boone, Pat — *Actor, Singer*
904 N Beverly Dr, Beverly Hills, CA 90210, USA

Boone, Robert R (Bob) — *Baseball Player, Manager*
18571 Villa Dr, Villa Park, CA 92861, USA

Boorman, John — *Movie Director*
%Merlin Films, 16 Upper Pembroke St, Dublin 2, Ireland

Boorstin, Daniel J — *Writer, Historian*
3541 Ordway St NW, Washington, DC 20016, USA

Boosler, Elayne — *Comedienne*
11061 Wrightwood Lane, North Hollywood, CA 91604, USA

Booth, Adrian — *Actress*
3922 Glenridge Dr, Sherman Oaks, CA 91423, USA

Booth, George — *Cartoonist*
PO Box 1539, Stony Brook, NY 11790, USA

Booth, James — *Actor*
%Hillard/Elkins, 8306 Wilshire Blvd, #438, Beverly Hills, CA 90211, USA

Booth, John C — *Financier*
%Carnegie Capital Mgmt, 1228 Euclid Ave, Cleveland, OH 44115, USA

Booth, Keith — *Basketball Player*
%Chicago Bulls, 1901 W Madison St, Chicago, IL 60612, USA

Booth, Pat — *Writer*
%Crown Publishers, 225 Park Ave S, New York, NY 10003, USA

Boothe, Powers — *Actor*
23629 Long Valley Road, Hidden Hills, CA 91302, USA

Boozer, Emerson — *Football Player*
25 Windham Dr, Huntington Station, NY 11746, USA

Bordaberry Arocena, Juan M — *President, Uruguay*
Joaquin Suarez 2868, Montevideo, Uruguay

Bordick, Michael T (Mike) — *Baseball Player*
335 N Auburn Road, Auburn, ME 04210, USA

Boren, David L — *Governor/Senator, OK; Educator*
%University of Oklahoma, President's Office, Norman, OK 73019, USA

Borg Olivier, George — *Prime Minister, Malta*
%House of Representatives, Valletta, Malta

Borg, Bjorn R — *Tennis Player*
%Int'l Management Group, 1 Erieview Plaza, #1300, Cleveland, OH 44114, USA

Borg, Kim — *Opera Singer*
Osterbrogade 158, 2100 Copenhagen, Denmark

Borg, Robert (Bob) — *Equestrian Rider*
1955 Ray Road, Oxford, MI 48371, USA

Borge, Victor — *Pianist, Comedian*
Field Point Park, Greenwich, CT 06830, USA

Borghi, Frank — *Soccer Player*
5140 Dagget Ave, St Louis, MO 63110, USA

Borgman, James M (Jim) — *Editorial Cartoonist*
%Cincinnati Enquirer, Editorial Dept, 617 Vine St, Cincinnati, OH 45202, USA

Borgnine, Ernest — *Actor*
%Bensky Entertainment, 15030 Ventura Blvd, #343, Sherman Oaks, CA 91403, USA

Boris, James R — *Financier*
%Kemper Securities, 77 W Wacker Dr, Chicago, IL 60601, USA

Boris, Ruthanna — *Ballerina, Choreographer*
%Center for Dance, 555 Pierce St, #1033, Albany, CA 94706, USA

Bork, Robert H — *Judge*
%American Enterprise Institute, 1150 17th St NW, Washington, DC

Borkh, Inge — *Opera Singer*
Haus Weifblick, 9405 Wienacht, Switzerland

Borkowski, Francis T — *Educator*
%Applalachian State University, President's Office, Boone, NC 28606, USA

Borlaug, Norman E — *Nobel Peace Laureate*
15611 Ranchita Dr, Dallas, TX 75248, USA

Borman, Frank — *Businessman, Astronaut*
%Patlex Corp, 250 Cotorro Court, #A, Las Cruces, NM 88005, USA

Bornhuetter, Ronald L — *Businessman*
%NAC Re Corp, 1 Greenwich Plaza, Greenwich, CT 06830, USA

Bornstein, Rita — *Educator*
%Rollins College, President's College, Winter Park, FL 32789, USA

Bornstein, Steven M — *Television Executive*
%ESPN-TV, News Dept, ESPN Plaza, 935 Middle St, Bristol, CT 06010, USA

Borodina, Olga V — *Opera Singer*
%Mariinsky Opera Theater, Teatralnaya Ploshchad 1, St Petersburg, Russia

Borofsky, Jonathan — *Artist*
57 Market St, Venice, CA 90291, USA

Boros, Guy — *Golfer*
2900 NE 40th St, Fort Lauderdale, FL 33308, USA

Borowy, Henry L (Hank) — *Baseball Player*
Beacon Hill, Maryland Ave, #9-C, Point Pleasant Beach, NJ 08742, USA

Borra, Ermanno F — *Astrophysicist*
%Universite Laval, Cite Universitaire, Quebec PQ G1K 7P4, Canada

Borten, Per	*Prime Minister, Norway*
7095 Ler, Norway	
Boryla, Vince	*Basketball Player, Executive*
1900 E Gerald Place, #602, Englewood, CO 80112, USA	
Borysewicz, Eddy	*Cycling Coach*
%Cycling Velodrome, Balboa Park, San Diego, CA 92136, USA	
Borzov, Valeri F	*Track Athlete*
%Sport & Youth Ministry, Esplanadna St 42, 252023 Kiev 23, Ukraine	
Bosco, Philip	*Actor*
337 W 43rd St, #1-B, New York, NY 10036, USA	
Bose, Miguel	*Singer, Songwriter, Actor*
%WEA Records, Calle Lopez de Hoyoz 42, 28006 Madrid, Spain	
Boselli, Tony	*Football Player*
%Carolina Panthers, Ericsson Stadium, 800 S Mint St, Charlotte, NC 28202, USA	
Boskin, Michael J	*Government Official*
%Stanford University, Hoover Institution, Stanford, CA 94305, USA	
Bosley, Tom	*Actor*
%Burton Moss, 8827 Beverly Blvd, #L, Los Angeles, CA 90048, USA	
Bosman, Richard A (Dick)	*Baseball Player*
3511 Landmark Trail, Palm Harbor, FL 34684, USA	
Bossard, Andre	*Law Enforcement Official*
%Interpol, 26 Rue Armengaud, 92210 Saint-Cloud, France	
Bossen, David A	*Businessman*
%Measurex Corp, 1 Results Way, Cupertino, CA 95014, USA	
Bossidy, Lawrence A	*Businessman*
%AlliedSignal Inc, PO Box 4000, Morristown, NJ 07962, USA	
Bossier, Albert L, Jr	*Businessman*
%Avondale Industries, PO Box 50280, New Orleans, LA 70150, USA	
Bosson, Barbara	*Actress*
694 Amalfi Dr, Pacific Palisades, CA 90272, USA	
Bossy, Michael (Mike)	*Hockey Player*
3080 Carriefour, Laval PQ H7T 2K9, Canada	
Bostelle, Tom	*Artist*
%Aeolian Palace Gallery, PO Box 8, Pocopson, PA 19366, USA	
Bostic, Jeff	*Football Player*
1311 Westridge Road, Greensboro, NC 27410, USA	
Bostic, Keith	*Football Player*
%Indianapolis Colts, 7001 W 56th St, Indianapolis, IN 46254, USA	
Boston, Ralph	*Track Athlete*
2970 Clairmont Road, #285, Atlanta, GA 30329, USA	
Bostwick, Barry	*Actor*
170 S Mountain Road, New City, NY 10956, USA	
Boswell, David W (Dave)	*Baseball Player*
309 Roxbury Court, Joppa, MD 21085, USA	
Boswell, Thomas M	*Sportswriter*
%Washington Post, Sports Dept, 1150 15th St NW, Washington, DC 20071, USA	
Bosworth, Brian	*Football Player, Actor*
31721 Sea Level Dr, Malibu, CA 90265, USA	
Botelho, Carlos	*Artist*
Ave Joao XXI-3-3d-F, 1000 Lisbon, Portugal	
Botero, Fernando	*Artist*
5 Blvd du Palais, 75004 Paris, France	
Botha, Francois (Frans)	*Boxer*
%Don King Productions, 968 Pinehurst Dr, Las Vegas, NV 89109, USA	
Botha, Pieter W	*President, Prime Minister, South Africa*
Libertas, Bryntirion, Pretoria 0001, South Africa	
Botha, Roelof F	*Government Official, South Africa*
%Foreign Affairs Ministry, Union Bldgs, PB X-152, Cape Town, South Africa	
Botham, Ian T	*Cricketer*
%Durham County Cricket Club, Houghton-le-Spring DH4 5PH, England	
Botstein, Leon	*Educator*
%Bard College, President's Office, Annandale-on-Hudson, NY 12504, USA	
Bott, Raoul	*Mathematician*
1 Richdale Ave, #9, Cambridge, MA 02140, USA	
Bottari, Vic	*Football Player*
52 Esta Bueno, Orinda, CA 94563, USA	
Bottom, Joe	*Swimmer*
PO Box 5988, Napa, CA 94581, USA	

Bottoms, Joseph — *Actor*
%Agency For Performing Arts, 9200 Sunset Blvd, #900, Los Angeles, CA 90069, USA

Bottoms, Sam — *Actor*
4719 Willowcrest Ave, North Hollywood, CA 91602, USA

Bottoms, Timothy — *Actor*
532 Hot Springs Road, Santa Barbara, CA 93108, USA

Botts, Tom — *Track Coach*
210 E Ridgeley Road, Columbia, MO 65203, USA

Botwinick, Michael — *Museum Official*
%Newport Harbor Art Museum, 850 San Clemente Dr, Newport Beach, CA 92660, USA

Boubacar, Sidi Mohamed Ould — *Prime Minister, Mauritania*
%Prime Minister's Office, Nouakchott, Mauritania

Boucha, Henry — *Hockey Player*
314 Minnesota St, Warroad, MN 56763, USA

Bouchard, Dick — *Hockey Player*
1851 Geronimo Trail, Maitland, FL 32751, USA

Bouchard, Emile J (Butch) — *Hockey Player*
213 Marie-Victoria, Vercheres PQ J0L 2R0, Canada

Bouchard, Lucien — *Government Official, Canada*
%Gouvement du Quebec, 885 Grand Allee Est, Quebec PQ GLA 1A2, Canada

Boucher, Gaetan — *Speed Skater*
%Center Sportif, 3850 Edgar, St Hubert PQ J4T 368, Canada

Boucher, Pierre — *Photographer*
L'Ermitage, 7 Ave Massoul, Faremountiers, 77120 Coulomiers, France

Boudreau, Louis (Lou) — *Baseball Player, Manager*
415 Cedar Lane, Frankfort, IL 60423, USA

Bougas, Nick — *Cartoonist*
28 Martin Dr, Raynham, MA 02767, USA

Boulez, Pierre — *Composer, Conductor*
%IRCAM, 1 Place Igor Stravinsky, 75004 Paris, France

Boulting, John — *Movie Producer, Director*
%Charter Films, Twickenham Studios, Twickenham, Mddx TW1 2AW, England

Boulware, Peter — *Football Player*
%Baltimore Ravens, 200 St Paul Place, #2400, Baltimore, MD 21202, USA

Bouquet, Carole — *Actress*
%Agents Associes Beaume, 201 Rue Faubourg St Honore, 75008 Paris, France

Bourdeaux, Michael — *Religious Leader*
%Keston College, Heathfield Road, Keston, Kent BR2 6BA, England

Bourgeois, Louise — *Sculptor*
347 W 20th St, New York, NY 10011, USA

Bourgignon, Serge — *Movie Director*
18 Rue de General-Malterre, 75016 Paris, France

Bourjaily, Vance — *Writer*
Redbird Farm, Rt 3, Iowa City, IA 52240, USA

Bourland, Clifford — *Track Athlete*
380 S Carmelina Ave, Brentwood, CA 90049, USA

Bourne, Bob — *Hockey Player*
17 Darius Court, Dix Hills, NY 11746, USA

Bournissen, Chantal — *Skier*
1983 Evolene, Switzerland

Bourque, Pierre — *Horticulturist*
4101 E Sherbrooke St, Montreal PQ H1X 2B2, Canada

Bourque, Raymond (Ray) — *Hockey Player*
36 Boren Lane, Boxford, MA 01921, USA

Boushka, Dick — *Basketball Player*
402 S Lynwood St, Wichita, KS 67218, USA

Boussena, Sadek — *Government Official, Algeria*
%Ministry of Mines & Industry, 80 Rue Ahmad Ghermoul, Algiers, Algeria

Bouteflika, Abdul Aziz — *Government Official, Algeria*
138 Chemin Bachir Brahimi, El Biar, Algiers, Algeria

Bouton, James A (Jim) — *Baseball Player, Writer*
265 Cedar Lane, Teaneck, NJ 07666, USA

Boutros-Ghali, Boutros — *Secretary-General, United Nations*
2 Ave El Nil, Giza, Cairo, Egypt

Bouvet, Didier — *Skier*
%Bouvet-Sports, 74360 Abondance, France

Bouvia, Gloria — *Bowler*
685 NE 23rd Place, Gresham, OR 97030, USA

B

Bottoms - Bouvia

Bowa, Lawrence R (Larry) — *Baseball Player*
1029 Morris Ave, Bryn Mawr, PA 19010, USA

Bowden, Bobby — *Football Coach*
%Florida State University, Athletic Dept, Tallahassee, FL 32306, USA

Bowden, Hugh K — *Businessman*
%Canoca Ltd, Park House, 116 Park St, London W1Y 4NN, England

Bowden, Terry — *Football Coach*
%Auburn University, Athletic Complex, PO Box 351, Auburn, AL 36831, USA

Bowdler, William G — *Diplomat*
%US State Department, 2201 "C" St NW, Washington, DC 20520, USA

Bowe, David — *Actor*
%Karg/Weissenbach, 329 N Wetherly Dr, #101, Beverly Hills, CA 90211, USA

Bowe, Riddick L — *Boxer*
%Spencer Promptions, 36 Channing St NW, Washington, DC 20001, USA

Bowe, Rosemarie — *Actress*
321 St Pierre Road, Los Angeles, CA 90077, USA

Bowen, Ray M — *Educator*
%Texas A&M University, President's Office, College Station, TX 77843, USA

Bowen, Richard L — *Educator*
%Idaho State University, President's Office, Pocatello, ID 83209, USA

Bowen, William G — *Foundation Executive, Educator*
%Andrew Mellon Foundation, 140 E 62nd St, New York, NY 10021, USA

Bower, Antoinette — *Actress*
1529 N Beverly Glen Blvd, Los Angeles, CA 90077, USA

Bower, Johnny — *Hockey Player*
3937 Parkgate Dr, Mississauga ON L5N 7B4, Canada

Bower, Marvin D — *Businessman*
%State Farm Life Insurance, 1 State Farm Plaza, Bloomington, IL 61710, USA

Bower, Rodney A — *Labor Leader*
%Professional & Technical Engineers, 818 Roeder Road, Silver Spring, MD 20910, USA

Bowerman, William J (Bill) — *Businessman, Track Coach*
%Nike Inc, 1 SW Bowerman Dr, Beaverton, OR 97005, USA

Bowers, Bryan — *Singer, Guitarist*
%Klezmer Corp, PO Box 800, Mahopac, NY 10541, USA

Bowers, John W — *Religious Leader*
%Foursquare Gospel Int'l Church, 1100 Glendale Blvd, Los Angeles, CA 90026, USA

Bowersox, Kenneth D — *Astronaut*
%NASA, Johnson Space Center, 2101 NASA Road, Houston, TX 77058, USA

Bowie, David — *Singer, Actor*
%Isolar Entertainment, 641 5th Ave, #22-Q, New York, NY 10022, USA

Bowie, Lester — *Jazz Trumpeter, Composer*
%Joel Chriss, 300 Mercer St, #3-J, New York, NY 10003, USA

Bowie, Sam — *Basketball Player*
3509 Castlegate Court, Lexington, KY 40502, USA

Bowker, Albert H — *Educator*
1523 New Hampshire Ave NW, Washington, DC 20036, USA

Bowker, Judi — *Actress*
%Howes & Prior, 66 Berkeley House, Hay Hill, London W1X 7LH, England

Bowles, Erskine B — *Government Official*
%White House, 1600 Pennsylvania Ave NW, Washington, DC 20500, USA

Bowles, Paul F — *Composer, Writer*
2117 Tanger Socco, Tangier, Morocco

Bowlin, Michael R — *Businessman*
%Atlantic Richfield, 515 S Flower St, Los Angeles, CA 90071, USA

Bowlin, Patrick L — *Religious Leader*
%Open Bible Standard Churches, 2020 Bell Ave, Des Moines, IA 50315, USA

Bowman, Christopher — *Figure Skater*
5653 Kester Ave, Van Nuys, CA 91411, USA

Bowman, Frank L (Skip) — *Navy Admiral*
Director, Naval Nuclear Propulsion, Navy Department, Washington, DC 20362, USA

Bowman, Harry W — *Businessman*
%Outboard Marine, 100 Sea-Horse Dr, Waukegan, IL 60085, USA

Bowman, Scotty — *Hockey Coach, Executive*
%Detroit Red Wings, Joe Louis Arena, 600 Civic Center Dr, Detroit, MI 48226, USA

Bown, Jane H — *Photographer*
Parsonage Farm, Bentworth near Alton, Hants GU34 5RB, England

Bowsher, Charles A — *Government Official*
%General Accounting Office, 441 "G" St NW, Washington, DC 20548, USA

Bowyer, C Stuart — *Astronomer, Educator*
34 Seascape Dr, Muir Beach, CA 94965, USA

Boxberger, Loa — *Bowler*
PO Box 708, Russell, KS 67665, USA

Boxcar Willie — *Singer, Songwriter*
%Magic Promotions, 199 E Garfield Road, Aurora, OH 44202, USA

Boxer, Stanley R — *Artist*
37 E 18th St, New York, NY 10003, USA

Boxleitner, Bruce — *Actor*
23679 Calabasas Road, #181, Calabasas, CA 91302, USA

Boy George — *Singer*
7 Pepys Court, 84 The Chase, Clapham, London SW4 0NF, England

Boyan, William L — *Businessman*
%John Hancock Mutual Life, PO Box 111, Boston, MA 02117, USA

Boyce, Kim — *Singer*
%Sasser Entertainment, 2723 Westwood Dr, Nashville, TN 37204, USA

Boyd, Alan S — *Secretary, Transportation*
2301 Connecticut Ave NW, Washington, DC 20008, USA

Boyd, Arthur M B — *Artist*
Bundanon, PO Box 3343, North Nowra NSW 2541, Australia

Boyd, Malcolm — *Writer, Religious Leader*
%St Augustine-By-The-Sea Episcopal Church, 1227 4th St, Santa Monica, CA 90401, USA

Boyd, Richard A — *Labor Leader*
%Fraternal Order of Police, 2100 Gardiner Lane, Louisville, KY 40205, USA

Boyd, Tanya — *Actress*
%Amsel Eisenstadt Frazier, 6310 San Vicente Blvd, #401, Los Angeles, CA 90048, USA

Boyd, William C — *Biochemist*
80 E Concord St, Boston, MA 02118, USA

Boyer, Cletis L (Clete) — *Baseball Player*
100 Aleta Dr, Belleair Beach, FL 33786, USA

Boyer, Herbert W — *Biochemist, Genetics Engineer*
520 Summit Ave, Mill Valley, CA 94941, USA

Boyer, Paul D — *Biochemist*
PO Box 276, Thayne, WY 83127, USA

Boykoff, Harry — *Basketball Player*
11499 Thurston Circle, Los Angeles, CA 90049, USA

Boyle Clune, Charlotte — *Swimmer*
50 Brown's Grove, Box 31, Scottsville, NY 14546, USA

Boyle, Barbara D — *Movie Executive*
%Boyle-Taylor Productions, 5200 Lankershim Blvd, #700, North Hollywood, CA 91601, USA

Boyle, Danny — *Movie Director*
%International Creative Mgmt, 8942 Wilshire Blvd, Beverly Hills, CA 90211, USA

Boyle, Francis J — *Businessman*
%Westmoreland Coal Co, Bellevue, 200 S Broad St, Philadelphia, PA 19102, USA

Boyle, Jerry — *Sculptor*
%Jerry Boyle Studio, 926 3rd Ave, Longmont, CO 80501, USA

Boyle, Lara Flynn — *Actress*
12190 1/2 Ventura Blvd, #304, Studio City, CA 91604, USA

Boyle, Peter — *Actor*
130 East End Ave, New York, NY 10028, USA

Boyle, T Coraghessan — *Writer*
%University of Southern California, English Dept, Los Angeles, CA 90089, USA

Boynton, Sandra — *Graphic Artist*
%Recycled Paper Products, 3636 N Broadway, Chicago, IL 60613, USA

Brabham, Geoff — *Auto Racing Driver*
General Delivery, Noblesville, IN 46060, USA

Brabham, John A (Jack) — *Auto Racing Driver*
33 Central Road, Worcester Park, Surrey KT4 8EG, England

Bracco, Lorraine — *Actress*
%Innovative Artists, 1999 Ave of Stars, #2850, Los Angeles, CA 90067, USA

Brace, William F — *Geologist*
49 Liberty St, Concord, MA 01742, USA

Brack, Reginald K, Jr — *Publisher*
%Time Inc, Time-Life Building, Rockefeller Center, New York, NY 10020, USA

Bracken, Eddie — *Actor*
18 Fulton St, Weehauken, NJ 07087, USA

Bracken, Thomas A — *Financier*
%CoreStates (NJ) Bank, 370 Scotch Road, Pennington, NJ 08534, USA

Bradbury, Curt *Financier*
%Worthen Banking Corp, 200 W Capitol Ave, Little Rock, AR 72201, USA

Bradbury, Janette Lane *Actress*
1217 Summit North Dr NE, Atlanta, GA 30324, USA

Bradbury, Malcolm S *Writer*
14 Heigham Grove, Norwich NR2 3DQ, England

Bradbury, Ray D *Writer*
10265 Cheviot Dr, Los Angeles, CA 90064, USA

Brademas, John *Educator; Representative, NY*
%New York University, President's Emeritus Office, New York, NY 10012, USA

Braden, Vic *Tennis Coach*
22000 Trabuco Canyon Road, Trabuco Canyon, CA 92678, USA

Bradford, Barbara Taylor *Writer*
%Bradford Enterprises, 450 Park Ave, New York, NY 10022, USA

Bradford, James C *Financier*
%J C Bradford Co, 330 Commerce St, Nashville, TN 37201, USA

Bradford, Richard *Actor*
849 S Broadway, #75, Los Angeles, CA 90014, USA

Bradham, James A, Jr *Marine Corps General*
Deputy CofS Installations/Logistics, HqUSMC, 2 Naby Annex, Washington, DC 20370, USA

Bradlee, Benjamin C *Editor*
3014 "N" St NW, Washington, DC 20007, USA

Bradley, Brian *Hockey Player*
6417 MacLaurin Dr, Tampa, FL 33647, USA

Bradley, Bruce *Water Polo Player*
420 Ultimo Ave, Long Beach, CA 90814, USA

Bradley, Edward R (Ed) *Commentator*
%CBS-TV, News Dept, 524 W 57th St, New York, NY 10019, USA

Bradley, Gordon *Soccer Player, Coach*
%George Mason University, Athletic Dept, Fairfax, VA 22030, USA

Bradley, Michael (Mike) *Golfer*
5208 Twin Creeks Dr, Valrico, FL 33594, USA

Bradley, Patricia E (Pat) *Golfer*
PO Box 488, Camp Hill, PA 17001, USA

Bradley, Robert A *Physician*
2465 S Downing, Denver, CO 80210, USA

Bradley, Shawn *Basketball Player*
Highway 10, Box 744, Castle Dale, UT 84513, USA

Bradman, Donald G (Don) *Cricketer*
2 Holden St, Kensington Park, SA 5068, Australia

Bradshaw, John E *Writer, Theologian*
8383 Commerce Park Dr, #600, Houston, TX 77036, USA

Bradshaw, Terry *Football Player, Sportscaster*
1925 N Pearson Lane, Roanoke, TX 76262, USA

Brady, Charles E *Astronaut*
%NASA, Johnson Space Center, 2101 NASA Road, Houston, TX 77058, USA

Brady, James S *Government Official, Journalist*
%Handgun Control, 1225 "I" St NW, #1100, Washington, DC 20005, USA

Brady, Jerome D *Businessman*
%AM International, 431 Lakeview Court, #A, Mt Prospect, IL 60056, USA

Brady, Nicholas F *Secretary, Treasury; Senator, NJ*
Black River Road, Far Hills, NJ 07931, USA

Brady, Pat *Cartoonist*
%United Feature Syndicate, 200 Madison Ave, New York, NY 10016, USA

Brady, Patrick H *Vietnam War Army Hero (CMH), General*
2809 179th Ave E, Sumner, WA 98390, USA

Brady, Ray *Commentator*
%CBS-TV, News Dept, 524 W 57th St, New York, NY 10019, USA

Brady, Roscoe O *Neurogeneticist*
6026 Valerian Lane, Rockville, MD 20852, USA

Brady, Sarah *Social Activist*
%Handgun Control, 1225 "I" St NW, #1100, Washington, DC 20005, USA

Braeden, Eric *Actor*
13723 Romany Dr, Pacific Palisades, CA 90272, USA

Braga, Sonia *Actress*
295 Greenwich St, #11-B, New York, NY 10007, USA

Bragg, Billy *Singer*
%Sincere Mgmt, 421 Harrow Road, London W10 4RD, England

Bragg, Charles — *Artist*
%Woodland Graphics, 9713 Santa Monica Blvd, #216, Beverly Hills, CA 90210, USA
Bragg, Darrell B — *Nutritionist*
%University of British Columbia, Vancouver BC V6T 2AZ, Canada
Bragg, Don — *Track Athlete*
%D B Enterprises, PO Box 171, New Gretna, NJ 08224, USA
Bragg, Melvyn — *Writer*
12 Hampstead Hill Gardens, London NW3, England
Bragg, Richard (Rick) — *Journalist*
%New York Times, Editorial Dept, 229 W 43rd St, New York, NY 10036, USA
Brahaney, Tom — *Football Player*
17 Winchester Court, Midland, TX 79705, USA
Braidwood, Robert J — *Archaeologist, Anthropologist*
%University of Chicago, Oriental Institute, Chicago, IL 60637, USA
Brainin, Norbert — *Concert Violinist*
19 Prowse Ave, Busbey Heath, Herts, England
Bramble, Frank P — *Financier*
%First Maryland Bancorp, 25 S Charles St, Baltimore, MD 21201, USA
Bramble, Livingstone — *Boxer*
PO Box 4240, Kings Hill, St Croix, VI 00851, USA
Bramlett, David A (Dave) — *Army General*
Commanding General, Forces Command, Fort McPherson, GA 30330, USA
Bramlett, Delaney — *Singer, Guitarist (Delaney & Bonnie)*
10723 Johanna Ave, Sunland, CA 91040, USA
Branagh, Kenneth — *Actor, Director*
%Marmont Mgmt, Langham House, 302/8 Regent St, London W1R 5AL, England
Branca, John G — *Attorney*
%Ziffren Brittenham Branca, 1801 Century Park West, Los Angeles, CA 90067, USA
Branca, Ralph T J — *Baseball Player*
%National Pension, 1025 Westchester, White Plains, NY 10604, USA
Branch, Cliff — *Football Player, Coach*
112 William Circle, Cloverdale, CA 95425, USA
Branch, William B — *Writer*
53 Cortlandt Ave, New Rochelle, NY 10801, USA
Brand, Colette — *Aerials Skier*
Rigistr 24, 6340 Baar, Switzerland
Brand, Daniel (Dan) — *Wrestler*
4321 Bridgeview Dr, Oakland, CA 94602, USA
Brand, Joshua — *Television Producer*
%Creative Artists Agency, 9830 Wilshire Blvd, Beverly Hills, CA 90212, USA
Brand, Oscar — *Singer, Songwriter*
%Music Tree Artists, 1414 Pennsylvania Ave, Pittsburgh, PA 15233, USA
Brand, Vance D — *Astronaut*
%DFRC, PO Box 273, Edwards, CA 93523, USA
Brandauer, Klaus Maria — *Actor*
Bartensteingasse 8/9, 1010 Vienna, Austria
Brandenstein, Daniel C — *Astronaut*
%Loral Space Information Systems, 2450 S Shore Blvd, Houston, TX 77258, USA
Brandis, Jonathan — *Actor*
%Gersh Agency, 232 N Canon Dr, Beverly Hills, CA 90210, USA
Brando, Marlon — *Actor*
%International Creative Mgmt, 8942 Wilshire Blvd, Beverly Hills, CA 90211, USA
Brandon, Barbara — *Cartoonist*
%Universal Press Syndicate, 4900 Main St, #900, Kansas City, KS 64112, USA
Brandon, John — *Actor*
%Coast To Coast Talent, 4942 Vineland Ave, #200, North Hollywood, CA 91601, USA
Brandon, Michael — *Actor*
%London Mgmt, 2-4 Noel St, London W1V 3RB, England
Brandon, Terrell — *Basketball Player*
%Cleveland Cavaliers, 2923 Statesboro Road, Richfield, OH 44286, USA
Brands, Tom — *Wrestler*
4494 Taft Ave SE, Iowa City, IA 52240, USA
Brands, X — *Actor*
17171 Roscoe Blvd, #104, Northridge, CA 91325, USA
Brandt, Jon — *Singer, Bassist (Cheap Trick)*
%Ken Adamay, 3805 County Road "M", Middleton, WI 53562, USA
Brandt, Paul — *Singer*
%Creative Trust, 1910 Acklen Ave, Nashville, TN 37212, USA

B

Bragg - Brandt

Brandy (Norwood) *Singer, Actress*
536 E 169th St, Carson, CA 90746, USA

Branigan, Laura *Singer, Songwriter*
%Pyramid Entertainment, 89 5th Ave, #700, New York, NY 10003, USA

Branitzki, Heinz *Businessman*
%Porsche Dr Ing HCF, Porchenstr 42, 70435 Stuttgart, Germany

Brann, Alton J *Businessman*
%Litton Industries, 21240 Burbank Blvd, Woodland Hills, CA 91367, USA

Brannan, Charles F *Secretary, Agriculture*
3131 E Alameda Ave, Denver, CO 80209, USA

Brannon, Ronald *Religious Leader*
%Wesleyan Church, PO Box 50434, Indianapolis, IN 46250, USA

Branscomb, Lewis M *Physicist*
%Harvard University, Kennedy School of Government, Cambridge, MA 02138, USA

Branson, Richard *Businessman, Balloonist*
%Virgin Group, 120 Campden Hill Road, London W8 7AR, England

Branstad, Terry E *Governor, IA*
%Governor's Office, State Capitol Building, Des Moines, IA 50319, USA

Brant, Tim *Sportscaster*
%ABC-TV, Sports Dept, 77 W 66th St, New York, NY 10023, USA

Brathwaite, Edward *Writer*
%University of West Indies, History Dept, Mona, Kingston 7, Jamaica

Bratkowski, Zeke *Football Player, Coach*
51000 Fulton Ave, Hempstead, NY 11550, USA

Bratt, Benjamin *Actor*
%Creative Artists Agency, 9830 Wilshire Blvd, Beverly Hills, CA 90212, USA

Bratton, Joseph K *Army General*
%Ralph M Parsons Co, 100 W Walnut St, Pasadena, CA 91124, USA

Brauer, Arik *Artist*
%Joram Harel Mgmt, PO Box 28, 1182 Vienna, Austria

Brauer, Jerald C *Church Historian*
5620 S Blackstone Ave, Chicago, IL 60637, USA

Braugher, Andrew *Actor*
%United Talent Agency, 9560 Wilshire Blvd, #500, Beverly Hills, CA 90212, USA

Braun, Lillian Jackson *Writer*
%Blanche Gregory Inc, 2 Tudor Place, New York, NY 10017, USA

Braun, Neil S *Entertainment Executive*
%NBC-TV, Rockefeller Center, New York, NY 10112, USA

Braun, Pinkas *Actor, Theater Director*
Unterdorf, 8261 Hemishofen/SH, Switzerland

Braunn, Erik *Singer, Guitarist (Iron Butterfly)*
%Holiday Entertainment, 8803 Mayne St, Bellflower, CA 90706, USA

Braunwald, Eugene *Physician*
%Brigham & Women's Hospital, 75 Francis St, Boston, MA 02115, USA

Braver, Rita *Commentator*
%CBS-TV, News Dept, 2020 "M" St NW, Washington, DC 20036, USA

Brawne, Michael *Architect*
28 College Road, Bath BA1 5RR, England

Braxton, Anthony *Jazz Saxophonist, Composer*
%Berkeley Agency, 2608 9th St, Berkeley, CA 94710, USA

Braxton, Toni *Singer, Songwriter*
%Stiefel-Phillips, 9255 W Sunset Blvd, #610, Los Angeles, CA 90069, USA

Brazauskas, Algirdas *President, Lithuania*
%President's Office, Gedimino 53, Vilnius 232026, Lithuania

Brazelton, T Berry *Pediatrician*
23 Hawthorn St, Cambridge, MA 02138, USA

Brazil, Jeff *Journalist*
%Orlando Sentinel, Editorial Dept, 633 N Orange Ave, Orlando, FL 32801, USA

Brazil, John R *Educator*
%Bradley University, President's Office, Peoria, IL 61625, USA

Bready, Richard L *Businessman*
%Nortek Inc, 50 Kennedy Plaza, Providence, RI 02903, USA

Bream, Julian *Concert Guitarist*
%Shaw Concerts, Lincoln Center Plaza, 1900 Broadway, #200, New York, NY 10023, USA

Breathed, Berkeley *Cartoonist (Bloom County, Outland)*
%Washington Post Writers Group, 1150 15th St NW, Washington, DC 20071, USA

Breathitt, Edward T *Governor, KY*
%Wyatt Tarrant, Lexington Financial Center, 250 W Main, Lexington, KY 40507, USA

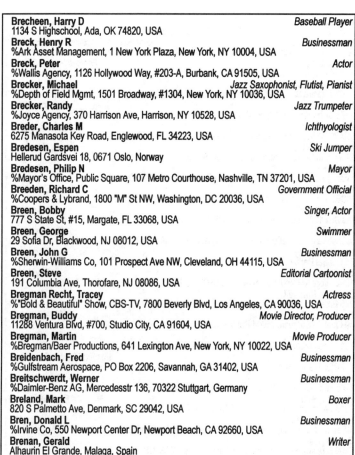

Brecheen, Harry D — *Baseball Player*
1134 S Highschool, Ada, OK 74820, USA

Breck, Henry R — *Businessman*
%Ark Asset Management, 1 New York Plaza, New York, NY 10004, USA

Breck, Peter — *Actor*
%Wallis Agency, 1126 Hollywood Way, #203-A, Burbank, CA 91505, USA

Brecker, Michael — *Jazz Saxophonist, Flutist, Pianist*
%Depth of Field Mgmt, 1501 Broadway, #1304, New York, NY 10036, USA

Brecker, Randy — *Jazz Trumpeter*
%Joyce Agency, 370 Harrison Ave, Harrison, NY 10528, USA

Breder, Charles M — *Ichthyologist*
6275 Manasota Key Road, Englewood, FL 34223, USA

Bredesen, Espen — *Ski Jumper*
Hellerud Gardsvei 18, 0671 Oslo, Norway

Bredesen, Philip N — *Mayor*
%Mayor's Office, Public Square, 107 Metro Courthouse, Nashville, TN 37201, USA

Breeden, Richard C — *Government Official*
%Coopers & Lybrand, 1800 "M" St NW, Washington, DC 20036, USA

Breen, Bobby — *Singer, Actor*
777 S State St, #15, Margate, FL 33068, USA

Breen, George — *Swimmer*
29 Sofia Dr, Blackwood, NJ 08012, USA

Breen, John G — *Businessman*
%Sherwin-Williams Co, 101 Prospect Ave NW, Cleveland, OH 44115, USA

Breen, Steve — *Editorial Cartoonist*
191 Columbia Ave, Thorofare, NJ 08086, USA

Bregman Recht, Tracey — *Actress*
%"Bold & Beautiful" Show, CBS-TV, 7800 Beverly Blvd, Los Angeles, CA 90036, USA

Bregman, Buddy — *Movie Director, Producer*
11288 Ventura Blvd, #700, Studio City, CA 91604, USA

Bregman, Martin — *Movie Producer*
%Bregman/Baer Productions, 641 Lexington Ave, New York, NY 10022, USA

Breidenbach, Fred — *Businessman*
%Gulfstream Aerospace, PO Box 2206, Savannah, GA 31402, USA

Breitschwerdt, Werner — *Businessman*
%Daimler-Benz AG, Mercedesstr 136, 70322 Stuttgart, Germany

Breland, Mark — *Boxer*
820 S Palmetto Ave, Denmark, SC 29042, USA

Bren, Donald L — *Businessman*
%Irvine Co, 550 Newport Center Dr, Newport Beach, CA 92660, USA

Brenan, Gerald — *Writer*
Alhaurin El Grande, Malaga, Spain

Brendel, Alfred — *Concert Pianist*
%Ingpen & Williams, 14 Kensington Court, London W8, England

Brenden, Hallgeir — *Nordic Skier*
2417 Torberget, Norway

Brendsel, Leland C — *Financier*
%Federal Home Loan Mortgage, 1700 "G" St NW, Washington, DC 20552, USA

Breneman, Curtis E — *Chemist*
38 Carlyle Ave, Troy, NY 12180, USA

Brennaman, Thom — *Sportscaster*
%Fox-TV, Sports Dept, PO Box 900, Beverly Hills, CA 90213, USA

Brennan, Bernard F — *Businessman*
%Montgomery Ward, 619 W Chicago Ave, Chicago, IL 60610, USA

Brennan, Christine — *Sportswriter*
%Washington Post, Sports Dept, 1150 15th Ave NW, Washington, DC 20071, USA

Brennan, Eileen — *Actress*
974 Mission Terrace, Camarillo, CA 93010, USA

Brennan, John J — *Financier*
%Vanguard Group, 1300 Morris Dr, Valley Forge, PA 19482, USA

Brennan, Joseph E — *Governor/Representative, ME*
104 Frances St, Portland, ME 04102, USA

Brennan, Maire — *Singer, Songwriter*
%Atlantic Records, 75 Rockefeller Plaza, New York, NY 10019, USA

Brennan, Melissa — *Actress*
6520 Platt Ave, #634, West Hills, CA 91307, USA

Brennan, Patrick E — *Businessman*
%Consolidated Papers Inc, 231 1st Ave S, Wisconsin Rapids, WI 54494, USA

Brennan, Peter J — *Secretary, Labor*
2100 Massachusetts Ave, Washington, DC 20008, USA

Brennan, Robert E — *Horse Racing Executive, Businessman*
%First Jersey Securities, 50 Broadway, #1401, New York, NY 10004, USA

Brennan, Terry — *Football Player, Coach*
1349 Chestnut St, Wilmette, IL 60091, USA

Brenneman, Amy — *Actress*
9150 Wilshire Blvd, #175, Beverly Hills, CA 90212, USA

Brenner, David — *Comedian*
1575 Silver King Dr, Aspen, CO 81611, USA

Brenner, Sydney — *Molecular Biologist*
%MRC Molecular Genetics Unit, Hills Road, Cambridge CB2 2QH, England

Brenner, Teddy — *Boxing Promoter*
24 W 55th St, #9-C, New York, NY 10019, USA

Brent, Eve — *Actress*
%Craig Agency, 8485 Melrose Place, #E, Los Angeles, CA 90069, USA

Brescia, Richard — *Radio Executive*
%CBS Inc, Radio Network, 51 W 52nd St, New York, NY 10019, USA

Bresee, Bobbie — *Actress*
PO Box 1222, Los Angeles, CA 90078, USA

Bresky, H H — *Businessman*
%Seaboard Corp, 200 Boylston St, Chestnut Hill, MA 02167, USA

Breslin, Jimmy — *Journalist*
75 Central Park West, New York, NY 10023, USA

Breslow, Lester — *Physician*
10926 Verano Road, Los Angeles, CA 90077, USA

Breslow, Ronald C — *Chemist*
275 Broad Ave, Englewood, NJ 07631, USA

Bresson, Robert — *Movie Director*
49 Quai de Bourbon, 75004 Paris, France

Brest, Martin — *Movie Director*
831 Paseo Miramar, Pacific Palisades, CA 90272, USA

Brett, George H — *Baseball Player, Executive*
PO Box 419969, Kansas City, MO 64141, USA

Breuer, Grit — *Track Athlete*
%Konrad-Adenauer-Str 16, 30823 Garbsen, Germany

Breunig, Bob — *Football Player*
9215 Westview Circle, Dallas, TX 75231, USA

Brewer, Albert P — *Governor, AL*
%Samford University, Law School, 800 Lakeshore Dr, Birmingham, AL 35229, USA

Brewer, Gay — *Golfer*
2100 Brookwood Road, Shawnee Mission, KS 66208, USA

Brewer, Jim T — *Basketball Player, Coach*
29710 Whitley Collins Dr, Rancho Palos Verdes, CA 90275, USA

Brewer, Leo — *Chemist*
15 Vista del Orinda, Orinda, CA 94563, USA

Brewer, Richard G — *Atomic Physicist*
%IBM Almaden Research Center, 650 Harry Road, San Jose, CA 95120, USA

Brewer, Rowanne — *Model*
%Elite Model Mgmt, 111 E 22nd St, #200, New York, NY 10010, USA

Brewer, Teresa — *Singer*
384 Pinebrook Blvd, New Rochelle, NY 10804, USA

Breyer, Stephen G — *Supreme Court Justice*
%US Supreme Court, 1 1st St NE, Washington, DC 20543, USA

Breytenbach, Breyten — *Writer, Political Activist*
%Harcourt Brace Co, 525 "B" St, San Diego, CA 92101, USA

Brialy, Jean-Claude — *Actor*
%Theatre des Bouffes Parisiens, 4 Rue Monsigny, 75002 Paris, France

Brian, Earl W — *Publisher*
%United Press International, 1400 "I" St NW, Washington, DC 20005, USA

Brice, William J — *Artist*
427 Beloit St, Los Angeles, CA 90049, USA

Brickell, Beth — *Movie Director*
PO Box 119, Paron, AR 72122, USA

Bricker, Neal S — *Physician*
2313 N 2nd Ave, Upland, CA 91784, USA

Brickhouse, John B (Jack) — *Sportscaster*
%WGN-Continental Broadcasting, 2501 W Bradley Place, Chicago, IL 60618, USA

Bricklin, Daniel S *Computer Software Designer (VisiCalc)*
%Slate Corp, 25 Needham St, Newton, MA 02161, USA

Brickman, Jim *Pianist*
%Edge Entertainment, 11288 Ventura Blvd, #606, Encino, CA 91604, USA

Brickman, Paul M *Movie Director*
4116 Holly Knoll Dr, Los Angeles, CA 90027, USA

Brickowski, Frank *Basketball Player*
132 Grove Place, San Antonio, TX 78209, USA

Bricusse, Leslie *Composer, Lyricist*
9903 Santa Monica Blvd, #112, Beverly Hills, CA 90212, USA

Bridges, Alan J S *Movie Director*
Wyndham House, 1 Wyndham St, Kemp Town, Brighton Sussex BN2 1AF, England

Bridges, Alicia *Singer, Songwriter*
%Talent Consultants Int'l, 1560 Broadway, #1308, New York, NY 10036, USA

Bridges, Beau *Actor*
5525 N Jed Smith Road, Hidden Hills, CA 91302, USA

Bridges, Bill *Basketball Player*
6205 Busch Dr, Malibu, CA 90265, USA

Bridges, Jeff *Actor*
11661 San Vicente Blvd, #910, Los Angeles, CA 90049, USA

Bridges, Lloyd *Actor*
225 Loring Ave, Los Angeles, CA 90024, USA

Bridges, Roy D, Jr *Astronaut, Air Force General*
%USAF Materials Command, Wright Patterson Air Force Base, Dayton, OH 45433, USA

Bridges, Todd A *Actor*
7550 Zombar Ave, #1, Van Nuys, CA 91406, USA

Bridgewater, Bernard A, Jr *Businessman*
%Brown Group, 8300 Maryland Ave, St Louis, MO 63105, USA

Briers, Richard *Comedian*
%Lorraine Hamilton, 24 Denmark St, London WC2H 8NA, England

Brigati, Eddie *Singer (The Youny Rascals)*
%Dassinger Creative, 32 Ardsley Road, #201, Montclair, NJ 07042, USA

Briggs of Lewes, Asa *Writer, Historian*
Caprons, Keere St, Lewes, Sussex, England

Briggs, Edward S *Navy Admiral*
3648 Lago Sereno, Escondido, CA 92029, USA

Briggs, Raymond R *Writer, Illustrator, Cartoonist*
Weston, Underhill Lane, Westmeston near Hassocks, Sussex, England

Briggs, Robert W *Biologist*
7128 Casitas Pass Road, Carpinteria, CA 93013, USA

Bright, Stanley J *Businessman*
%Iowa-Illinois Gas & Electric, 206 E 2nd St, Davenport, IA 52801, USA

Brightman, Sarah *Singer*
47 Greek St, London W1V 5LQ, England

Briles, Nelson K *Baseball Player*
1324 Clearview Dr, Greensburg, PA 15601, USA

Brill, Charlie *Actor*
3635 Wrightwood Dr, Studio City, CA 91604, USA

Brill, Steven *Editor, Publisher*
%American Lawyer Magazine, 600 3rd Ave, New York, NY 10016, USA

Brill, Winston J *Bacteriologist*
4134 Cherokee Dr, Madison, WI 53711, USA

Brillstein, Bernie *Television Producer, Agent*
%Brillstein/Grey, 9150 Wilshire Blvd, #350, Beverly Hills, CA 90212, USA

Brimley, Wilford *Actor*
B "7" Ranch, 10000 North, Lehi, UT 84043, USA

Brimmer, Andrew F *Government Official, Economist*
%Brimmer Co, 4400 MacArthur Blvd NW, Washington, DC 20007, USA

Brimsek, Frank *Hockey Player*
1017 13th St N, Virginia, MN 55792, USA

Brinckman, Donald W *Businessman*
%Safety-Kleen Corp, 1000 N Randall Road, Elgin, IL 60123, USA

Brinegar, Claude S *Secretary, Transportation; Businessman*
%Unocal Corp, 2101 Rosecrans Ave, #1200, El Segundo, CA 90245, USA

Brink, Andre P *Writer*
%University of Cape Town, Rondebosch 7700, South Africa

Brink, Frank, Jr *Biophysicist*
Pine Run, #E-1, Ferry & Iron Hill Roads, Doylestown, PA 18901, USA

B

Bricklin - Brink

Brink, K Robert	*Publisher*
%Town & Country Magazine, 1700 Broadway, New York, NY 10019, USA	
Brink, R Alexander	*Geneticist*
4237 Manitou Way, Madison, WI 53711, USA	
Brinker, Norman E	*Businessman*
%Brinker International, 6820 LBJ Freeway, Dallas, TX 75240, USA	
Brinkhous, Kenneth M	*Pathologist*
524 Dogwood Dr, Chapel Hill, NC 27516, USA	
Brinkley, Christie	*Model, Actress*
%Ford Model Agency, 344 E 59th St, New York, NY 10022, USA	
Brinkley, David	*Commentator*
%ABC-TV, News Dept, 1717 De Sales St NW, Washington, DC 20036, USA	
Brinson, Gary	*Financier*
%Brinson Partners, 209 S LaSalle St, Chicago, IL 60604, USA	
Brinster, Ralph L	*Reproductive Physiologist*
%University of Pennsylvania, Veterinary Medicine School, Philadelphia, PA 19104, USA	
Brisco, Valerie	*Track Athlete*
%USA Track & Field, PO Box 120, Indianapolis, IN 46206, USA	
Briscoe, Dolph	*Governor, TX*
338 Pecan St, Uvalde, TX 78801, USA	
Brisebois, Danielle	*Actress*
950 N Kings Road, Los Angeles, CA 90069, USA	
Briskin, Jacqueline	*Writer*
%Delacorte Press, 1540 Broadway, New York, NY 10036, USA	
Brisse, Leland V (Lou)	*Baseball Player*
1908 White Pine Dr, North Augusta, SC 29841, USA	
Brister, Bubby	*Football Player*
2749 Point Dr, Monroe, LA 71201, USA	
Bristow, Allan M	*Basketball Player, Coach, Executive*
3551 S Franklin St, Englewood, CO 80110, USA	
Britain, Radie	*Composer*
PO Box 17, Smithville, IN 47458, USA	
Britt, Mai	*Actress*
PO Box 525, Zephyr Cove, NV 89448, USA	
Brittan, Leon	*Government Official, England*
%European Communities Commission, 200 Rue de Loi, 1049 Brussels, Belgium	
Brittany, Morgan	*Actress, Model*
3434 Cornell Road, Agoura Hills, CA 91301, USA	
Britten, Roy J	*Geneticist*
%Kerckhoff Marine Laboratory, 101 Dahlia Ave, Corona del Mar, CA 92625, USA	
Brittenham, Harry	*Attorney*
%Ziffren Brittenham Branca, 1801 Century Park West, Los Angeles, CA 90067, USA	
Britton, Tony	*Actor*
%International Creative Mgmt, 76 Oxford St, London W1N 0AX, England	
Britz, Jerilyn	*Golfer*
%Ladies Professional Golf Assn, 2570 Volusia Ave, Daytona Beach, FL 32114, USA	
Brizan, George	*Prime Minister, Grenada*
%Prime Minister's Office, Botanical Gardens, Saint George's, Grenada	
Broad, Eli	*Businessman*
%SunAmerica Inc, 1 SunAmerica Center, 11601 Wilshire Blvd, Los Angeles, CA 90025, USA	
Broadbent, John Edward	*Government Official, Canada*
%House of Commons, Parliamentry Buildings, Ottawa ON K1A 0A6, Canada	
Broaddus, J Alfred, Jr	*Financier*
%Federal Reserve Bank, PO Box 27622, Richmond, VA 23261, USA	
Broadhead, James L	*Businessman*
%FPL Group, 700 Universe Blvd, Juno Beach, FL 33408, USA	
Broberg, Gus	*Basketball Player*
208 El Pueblo Way, Palm Beach, FL 33480, USA	
Broches, Aron	*Attorney*
2600 Tilden Place NW, Washington, DC 20008, USA	
Brochtrup, William (Bill)	*Actor*
%Agency For Performing Arts, 9200 Sunset Blvd, #900, Los Angeles, CA 90069, USA	
Brock, Louis C (Lou)	*Baseball Player*
11885 Lackland Road, St Louis, MO 63146, USA	
Brock, Stan	*Football Player*
34160 SW Peaks View Dr, Hillsboro, OR 97123, USA	
Brock, William E (Bill)	*Secretary of Labor; Senator, TN*
2029 Homewood Road, Annapolis, MD 21402, USA	

Brockert, Richard C — Labor Leader
%United Telegraph Workers, 701 Gude Dr, Rockville, MD 20850, USA

Brockhouse, Bertram N — Nobel Physics Laureate
PO Box 7338, Ancaster ON L9G 3N6, Canada

Brodbin, Kevin — Writer
%Creative Artists Agency, 9830 Wilshire Blvd, Beverly Hills, CA 90212, USA

Broder, David S — Columnist
4024 N 27th St, Arlington, VA 22207, USA

Broder, Samuel — Medical Administrator
%National Cancer Institute, 9000 Rockville Pike, Bethesda, MD 20892, USA

Broderick, Beth — Actress
%Innovative Artists, 1999 Ave of Stars, #2850, Los Angeles, CA 90067, USA

Broderick, Matthew — Actor
9056 Santa Monica Blvd, #110, Los Angeles, CA 90069, USA

Brodeur, Martin — Hockey Player
%New Jersey Devils, Continental Arena, PO Box 504, East Rutherford, NJ 07073, USA

Brodie, John — Football Player, Sportscaster, Golfer
2600 El Camino Real, Palo Alto, CA 94306, USA

Brody, Clark L — Concert Clarinetist
1621 Colfax St, Evanston, IL 60201, USA

Brody, Jane E — Journalist
%New York Times, Editorial Dept, 229 W 43rd St, New York, NY 10036, USA

Brody, Kenneth D — Financier
%Export-Import Bank, 811 Vermont Ave NW, Washington, DC 20571, USA

Brody, Lane — Singer
%Black Stallion Country Productions, PO Box 368, Tujunga, CA 91043, USA

Broeg, Robert W (Bob) — Sportswriter
%St Louis Post Dispatch, Editorial Dept, 900 N Tucker Blvd, St Louis, MO 63101, USA

Broelsch, Christopher E — Surgeon
%University of Chicago, Medical Center, Surgery Dept, Box 259, Chicago, IL 60690, USA

Broglio, Ernest G (Ernie) — Baseball Player
2838 Via Carmen, San Jose, CA 95124, USA

Brokaw, Norman R — Entertainment Executive
710 N Alta Dr, Beverly Hills, CA 90210, USA

Brokaw, Thomas J (Tom) — Commentator
941 Park Ave, #14-C, New York, NY 10028, USA

Brolin, James — Actor
PO Box 56927, Sherman Oaks, CA 91413, USA

Brolin, Josh — Actor
PO Box 56927, Sherman Oaks, CA 91413, USA

Bromfield, John — Actor
PO Box 2655, Lake Havasu City, AZ 86405, USA

Bromley, D Allan — Government Official, Physicist
35 Tokeneke Dr, North Haven, CT 06473, USA

Bromwich, John — Tennis Player
%International Tennis Hall of Fame, 194 Bellevue Ave, Newport, RI 02840, USA

Bronars, Edward J — Marine Corps General
3354 Rose Lane, Falls Church, VA 22042, USA

Bronfman, Charles R — Businessman, Baseball Executive
%Seagram Co, 1400 Peel St, Montreal PQ H3A 1S9, Canada

Bronfman, Edgar M — Businessman
%Joseph E Seagram & Sons, 375 Park Ave, New York, NY 10152, USA

Bronfman, Yefin — Concert Pianist
%International Creative Mgmt, 40 W 57th St, New York, NY 10019, USA

Bronson, Charles — Actor
PO Box 2644, Malibu, CA 90265, USA

Bronson, Oswald P, Sr — Educator
%Bethune-Cookman College, President's Office, Daytona Beach, FL 32114, USA

Bronson, Po — Writer
%Random House Inc, 201 E 50th St, New York, NY 10022, USA

Brook, Peter S P — Movie, Theater Director
%CICT, 9 Rue du Cirque, 75008 Paris, France

Brooke, Edward W — Senator, MA
2500 Virginia Ave NW, #301-S, Washington, DC 20037, USA

Brooke, Hillary — Actress
40 Via Casitas, Bonsall, CA 92003, USA

Brooke, Peter A — Financier
%Advent International, 101 Federal St, Boston, MA 02110, USA

B

Brooker, Gary *Singer (Procul Harem), Songwriter*
5 Cranley Gardens, London SW7, England

Brookes, Harvey *Physicist*
%Harvard University, Aiken Computation Laboratory, Cambridge, MA 02138, USA

Brookins, Gary *Editorial Cartoonist*
%Richmond Newspapers, Editorial Dept, PO Box 85333, Richmond, VA 23293, USA

Brookner, Anita *Writer*
68 Elm Park Gardens, #6, London SW10 9PB, England

Brooks, Albert *Actor, Director, Writer*
%Scotti Bros, 2114 Pico Blvd, Santa Monica, CA 90405, USA

Brooks, Avery *Actor*
360 Christopher Dr, Princeton, NJ 08540, USA

Brooks, Derrick *Football Player*
%Tampa Bay Buccaneers, 1 Buccaneer Place, Tampa, FL 33607, USA

Brooks, Diana D *Businesswoman*
%Sotheby's Holdings, 500 N Woodward Ave, Bloomfield Hills, MI 48304, USA

Brooks, Donald M *Fashion, Theater Designer*
158 E 70th St, New York, NY 10021, USA

Brooks, E R *Businessman*
%Central & South West Corp, 1616 Woodall Rogers Freeway, Dallas, TX 75202, USA

Brooks, Foster *Comedian*
%Covenant Agency, 6420 SW River Road, Hillsboro, OR 97123, USA

Brooks, Garth *Singer, Songwriter*
%GB Mgmt, 1111 17th Ave S, Nashville, TN 37212, USA

Brooks, Gwendolyn *Writer*
5530 S Shore Dr, #2-A, Chicago, IL 60637, USA

Brooks, Hadda *Singer, Pianist*
%Alan Eichler, 1862 Vista Del Mar St, Los Angeles, CA 90028, USA

Brooks, Harvey *Physicist*
46 Brewster St, #Y, Cambridge, MA 02138, USA

Brooks, Herb *Hockey Coach*
5423 Carlson Road, Shoreview, MN 55126, USA

Brooks, Hubert (Hubie) *Baseball Player*
15001 Olive St, Hesperia, CA 92345, USA

Brooks, James *Football Player*
%Baltimore Ravens, 200 St Paul Place, #2400, Baltimore, MD 21202, USA

Brooks, James C, Jr *Businessman*
%Life Insurance of Georgia, 5780 Powers Ferry Road NW, Atlanta, GA 30327, USA

Brooks, James L *Movie Director, Producer, Writer*
10380 Tennessee Ave, Los Angeles, CA 90064, USA

Brooks, Karen *Singer*
5408 Clear View Lane, Waterford, WI 53185, USA

Brooks, Kix *Singer (Brooks & Dunn), Songwriter*
%Titley-Spalding, 900 Division St, Nashville, TN 37203, USA

Brooks, Lala *Singer (The Crystals)*
%Mars Talent, 168 Orchid Dr, Pearl River, NY 10965, USA

Brooks, Mark *Golfer*
6608 Medinah Dr, Fort Worth, TX 76132, USA

Brooks, Mel *Movie Director, Actor*
2301 La Mesa Dr, Santa Monica, CA 90402, USA

Brooks, Michael *Basketball Player*
495 Bethany St, San Diego, CA 92114, USA

Brooks, Nathan *Boxer*
4606 E 147th St, Cleveland, OH 44128, USA

Brooks, Rand *Actor*
1 Rockefeller Plaza, #1528, New York, NY 10020, USA

Brooks, Randi *Actress, Model*
3205 Evergreen Point Road, Medina, WA 98039, USA

Brooks, Richard *Actor*
%Don Buchwald, 9229 Sunset Blvd, #710, Los Angeles, CA 90069, USA

Brookshier, Tom *Sportscaster, Football Player*
%WIP-Radio, Sports Dept, 19th & Walnut Sts, Philadelphia, PA 19103, USA

Brophy, Kevin *Actor*
15010 Hamlin St, Van Nuys, CA 91411, USA

Broshears, Robert *Sculptor*
%Robert Broshears Studio, 8020 NW Holly Road, Bremerton, WA 98312, USA

Brosnan, Pierce *Actor*
28011 Paquet Place, Malibu, CA 90265, USA

Brooker - Brosnan

Brostek, Bern — Football Player
%St Louis Rams, 100 N Broadway, #2100, St Louis, MO 63102, USA

Broten, Neal — Hockey Player
9704 Brassie Circle, Eden Prairie, MN 55347, USA

Brothers, Joyce D — Psychologist
1530 Palisade Ave, Fort Lee, NJ 07024, USA

Brough Clapp, Louise — Tennis Player
1808 Voluntary Road, Vista, CA 92084, USA

Broun, Heywood Hale — Sportscaster, Columnist
184 Plochman, Woodstock, NY 12498, USA

Brouwenstyn, Gerarda — Opera Singer
3 Bachplein, Amsterdam, Netherlands

Brown Heritage, Doris — Track Athlete
%Seattle Pacific College, Athletic Dept, Seattle, WA 98119, USA

Brown, Arthur E, Jr — Army General
18 Fairway Winds Place, Hilton Head Island, SC 29928, USA

Brown, Blair — Actress
434 W 20th St, #3, New York, NY 10011, USA

Brown, Bo — Cartoonist
218 Wyncote Road, Jenkintown, PA 19046, USA

Brown, Bob — Football Player
1200 Lakeshore Ave, Oakland, CA 94606, USA

Brown, Bobby — Singer, Dancer, Songwriter
%Tommy Brown, 66 Antone St, Atlanta, GA 30318, USA

Brown, Bruce — Photographer, Surfer
15550 Calle Real, Gaviota, CA 93117, USA

Brown, Bryan — Actor
%Creative Artists Agency, 9830 Wilshire Blvd, Beverly Hills, CA 90212, USA

Brown, Buck — Cartoonist
PO Box 122, Park Forest, IL 60466, USA

Brown, Carol Page — Rower
1321 35th Ave S, Seattle, WA 98144, USA

Brown, Chad — Football Player
%Seattle Seahawks, 11220 NE 53rd St, Kirkland, WA 98033, USA

Brown, Charles — Pianist, Singer
2870 Adeline St, #102, Berkeley, CA 94703, USA

Brown, Charles — Hockey Player
4677 Brassie Circle, Eagan, MN 55123, USA

Brown, Clancy — Actor
2569 Laurel Pass, Los Angeles, CA 90046, USA

Brown, Clarence (Gatemouth) — Singer, Guitarist
%Concerted Efforts, 50 Parsons St, Newtonville, MA 02165, USA

Brown, Curtis L, Jr — Astronaut
%NASA, Johnson Space Center, 2101 NASA Road, Houston, TX 77058, USA

Brown, Dale D — Basketball Coach, Sportscaster
%ESPN-TV, Sports Dept, ESPN Plaza, 935 Middle St, Bristol, CT 06010, USA

Brown, David — Movie Producer
%Zanuck/Brown Co, 200 W 57th St, New York, NY 10019, USA

Brown, Dee — Basketball Player
5105 Isleworth Country Club Dr, Windemere, FL 34786, USA

Brown, Denise Scott — Architect
%Venturi Scott Brown Assoc, 4236 Main St, Philadelphia, PA 19127, USA

Brown, Edmund G (Jerry), Jr — Governor, CA
%We the People, 200 Harrison St, Oakland, CA 94607, USA

Brown, Fred — Basketball Player, Coach
7202 79th Ave SE, Mercer Island, WA 98040, USA

Brown, Georg Stanford — Actor
2565 Greenvalley Road, Los Angeles, CA 90046, USA

Brown, George C, Jr — Football Player
860 Jamacha Road, #109, El Cajon, CA 92019, USA

Brown, Gordon — Government Official, England
%Chancellory of Exchequer, 11 Downing St, London SW1A 2AA, England

Brown, Harold — Secretary, Defense
%Strategic & Int'l Studies Center, 1800 "K" St NW, #1800, Washington, DC 20006, USA

Brown, Helen Gurley — Editor, Writer
1 W 81st St, #22-D, New York, NY 10024, USA

Brown, Herbert C — Nobel Chemistry Laureate
1840 Garden St, West Lafayette, IN 47906, USA

B

Brostek - Brown

Brown, Himan	*Director*
285 Central Park W, New York, NY 10024, USA	
Brown, Hubie	*Basketball Coach*
120 Foxridge Road NW, Atlanta, GA 30327, USA	
Brown, Isaac (Ike)	*Baseball Player*
Lincoln Court, #A-4, Lakeland, FL 33805, USA	
Brown, J Carter	*Businessman*
1201 Pennsylvania Ave NW, #621, Washington, DC 20004, USA	
Brown, J Cristopher (Cris)	*Baseball Player*
5015 Brighton Ave, Los Angeles, CA 90062, USA	
Brown, J Gordon	*Government Official, England*
%House of Commons, Westminster, London SW1A 0AA, England	
Brown, James	*Sportscaster*
%Fox-TV, Sports Dept, 205 E 67th St, New York, NY 10021, USA	
Brown, James	*Singer*
%James Brown Enterprises, 1217 W Medical Park Road, Augusta, GA 30909, USA	
Brown, James N (Jim)	*Football Player, Actor*
1851 Sunset Plaza Dr, Los Angeles, CA 90069, USA	
Brown, James R	*Air Force General*
1591 Stowe Road, Reston, VA 20194, USA	
Brown, Jim Ed	*Singer*
%Bill Deaton, 1300 Division St, #102, Nashville, TN 37203, USA	
Brown, Joe	*Boxer*
1615 N Broad St, New Orleans, LA 70119, USA	
Brown, John	*Basketball Player*
1329 N Florissant Road, St Louis, MO 63135, USA	
Brown, John Y, Jr	*Governor, KY*
PO Box 221130, Hollywood, FL 33022, USA	
Brown, Joseph W, Jr	*Businessman*
%Talegen Holdings, 1011 Western Ave, Seattle, WA 98104, USA	
Brown, Julie	*Comedienne, Actress*
11288 Ventura Blvd, #728, Studio City, CA 91604, USA	
Brown, Julie (Downtown)	*Entertainer*
%Agency For Performing Arts, 9200 Sunset Blvd, #900, Los Angeles, CA 90069, USA	
Brown, Junior	*Singer*
%FCC Mgmt, 209 10th Ave S, #322, Nashville, TN 37203, USA	
Brown, Kenneth J	*Labor Leader*
%Graphic Communications Int'l Union, 1900 "L" St NW, Washington, DC 20036, USA	
Brown, Kimberlin	*Actress*
%Pakula/King Assoc, 9229 Sunset Blvd, #315, Los Angeles, CA 90069, USA	
Brown, L Dean	*Diplomat*
3030 Cambridge Place, Washington, DC 20007, USA	
Brown, Larry	*Football Player*
%Oakland Raiders, 1220 Harbor Bay Parkway, Alameda, CA 94502, USA	
Brown, Larry	*Hockey Player*
5781 Eucalyptus Dr, Garden Valley, CA 95633, USA	
Brown, Lawrence H (Larry)	*Basketball Player, Coach*
%Philadelphia 76ers, Veterans Stadium, PO Box 25040, Philadelphia, PA 19147, USA	
Brown, Les	*Orchestra Leader*
735 Napoli Dr, Pacific Palisades, CA 90272, USA	
Brown, Lester R	*Ecologist*
%Worldwatch Institute, 1776 Massachusetts Ave NW, Washington, DC 20036, USA	
Brown, Mark N	*Astronaut*
%General Research Corp, Space Division, 2940 Presidential Dr, Fairborn, OH 45324, USA	
Brown, Melanie	*Singer (Spice Girls)*
%Virgin Records, Kensal House, 533-79 Harrow Road, London W1O 4RH, England	
Brown, Michael S	*Nobel Medicine Laureate*
5719 Redwood Lane, Dallas, TX 75209, USA	
Brown, Mike	*Football Executive*
%Cincinnati Bengals, 1 Bengals Dr, Cincinnati, OH 45204, USA	
Brown, Olivia	*Actress*
5856 College Ave, #139, Oakland, CA 94618, USA	
Brown, Owsley, II	*Businessman*
%Brown-Forman Corp, 850 Dixie Highway, Louisville, KY 40210, USA	
Brown, P J	*Basketball Player*
903 Beverly Dr, Carthage, TX 75633, USA	
Brown, Raymond M (Ray)	*Jazz Bassist*
PO Box 845, Concord, CA 94522, USA	

Brown, Rita Mae *Writer, Social Activist*
%Wendy Weill Agency, 232 Madison Ave, New York, NY 10016, USA
Brown, Robert McAfee *Religious Leader*
2090 Columbia Ave, Palo Alto, CA 94306, USA
Brown, Roger W *Social Psychologist*
100 Memorial Dr, Cambridge, MA 02142, USA
Brown, Ron J *Football Player, Track Athlete*
363 S Fairfax Ave, Los Angeles, CA 90036, USA
Brown, Roosevelt *Football Player*
153 Van Buskirk Ave, Teaneck, NJ 07666, USA
Brown, Ruth *Singer*
%Alan Eichler, 1862 Vista Del Mar St, Los Angeles, CA 90028, USA
Brown, Stephen L *Businessman*
%John Hancock Mutual Life, PO Box 111, Boston, MA 02117, USA
Brown, T Graham *Singer*
%Sarchett Mgmt, 115 16th Ave S, Nashville, TN 37203, USA
Brown, Timothy D (Tim) *Football Player*
%Oakland Raiders, 1220 Harbor Bay Parkway, Alameda, CA 94502, USA
Brown, Tina *Editor*
%New Yorker Magazine, Editorial Dept, 20 W 43rd St, New York, NY 10036, USA
Brown, Tom *Football Player*
%Pemberton Houston Willoughby, Bentall Center 4, Vancouver BC, Canada
Brown, Tracy *Ballerina*
%Royal Ballet, Bow St, London WC2E 9DD, England
Brown, Trisha *Choreographer, Dancer*
%Trisha Brown Dance Co, 211 W 61st St, New York, NY 10023, USA
Brown, Vanessa *Actress*
5914 Coldwater Canyon Ave, #5, North Hollywood, CA 91607, USA
Brown, W L Lyons, Jr *Businessman*
%Brown-Forman Corp, 850 Dixie Highway, Louisville, KY 40210, USA
Brown, Willie *Football Player, Coach*
27138 Lillegard Court, Tracy, CA 95376, USA
Brown, Willie L, Jr *Mayor*
%Mayor's Office, City Hall, 400 Van Ness Ave, San Francisco, CA 94102, USA
Browne, Herbert A, Jr *Navy Admiral*
Commander, US 3rd Fleet, FPO, AP 96601, USA
Browne, Jackson *Singer, Songwriter*
%Donald Miller Mgmt, 12746 Kling St, Studio City, CA 91604, USA
Browne, Leslie *Ballerina, Actress*
%American Ballet Theatre, 890 Broadway, New York, NY 10003, USA
Browne, Roscoe Lee *Actor*
465 W 57th St, #1-A, New York, NY 10019, USA
Browne, Secor D *Aviation Engineer, Government Official*
2101 "L" St NW, #207, Washington, DC 20037, USA
Browner, Carol M *Government Official*
%Environmental Protection Agency, 401 "M" St SW, Washington, DC 20024, USA
Browner, Ross *Football Player*
%Ross Browner Enterprises, 1135 Flamingo Dr SW, Atlanta, GA 30311, USA
Browning, Dominique *Editor*
%Mirabella Magazine, Editorial Dept, 200 Madison Ave, New York, NY 10016, USA
Browning, Edmond L *Religious Leader*
%Episcopal Church, 815 2nd Ave, New York, NY 10017, USA
Browning, John *Concert Pianist*
%Columbia Artists Mgmt Inc, 165 W 57th St, New York, NY 10019, USA
Browning, Kurt *Figure Skater*
%Royal Glenora Club, 11160 River Valley Road, Edmonton ON T5J 2G7, Canada
Browning, Ricou *Actor*
5221 SW 196th Lane, Fort Lauderdale, FL 33332, USA
Browning, Thomas L (Tom) *Baseball Player*
3094 Friars St, Covington, KY 41017, USA
Brownlow, Kevin *Movie Producer*
%Thames TV, Teddington Studios, Teddington, Middx, England
Brownmiller, Susan *Feminist Leader*
61 Jane St, New York, NY 10014, USA
Brownstein, Philip N *Government Official*
550 "N" St NW, Washington, DC 20001, USA
Broyles, Frank *Football Coach, Sportscaster*
%University of Arkansas, Broyles Athletic Complex, Fayetteville, AR 72701, USA

B

Brown - Broyles

Brozman, Jack L	*Financier*
%Century Acceptance Corp, City Center Square, Kansas City, MO 64196, USA	
Brubeck, David W (Dave)	*Jazz Pianist*
221 Millstone Road, Wilton, CT 06897, USA	
Brubeck, William H	*Government Official*
7 Linden St, Cambridge, MA 02138, USA	
Bruce, Aundray	*Football Player*
1730 Wentworth Dr, Montgomery, AL 36106, USA	
Bruce, Carol	*Actress, Singer*
1361 N Laurel Ave, #20, Los Angeles, CA 90046, USA	
Bruce, Jack	*Singer (Cream), Bassist, Songwriter*
%International Creative Mgmt, 40 W 57th St, New York, NY 10019, USA	
Bruce, Robert V	*Writer, Historian*
28 Evans Road, Madbury, NH 03820, USA	
Bruce, Thomas (Tom)	*Swimmer*
3258 Clearview Dr, Cupertino, CA 95993, USA	
Bruckheimer, Jerry	*Movie Producer*
%Simpson-Bruckheimer Productions, 500 S Buena Vista St, Burbank, CA 91521, USA	
Brudzinski, Bob	*Football Player*
2725 Hackney Road, Fort Lauderdale, FL 33331, USA	
Brueckner, Keith A	*Physicist*
7723 Ludington Place, La Jolla, CA 92037, USA	
Bruel, Patrick	*Singer*
%BMG, 17 Rue Soyer, 92200 Neuilly-Sur-Seine, France	
Bruen, John D	*Army General, Businessman*
6104 Greenlawn Court, Springfield, VA 22152, USA	
Brugger, Ernst	*President, Switzerland*
8625 Gossau ZH, Switzerland	
Bruggink, Eric G	*Judge*
%US Claims Court, 717 Madison Place NW, Washington, DC 20005, USA	
Bruguera, Sergi	*Tennis Player*
C'Escipion 42, 08023 Barcelona, Spain	
Brumback, Charles T	*Publisher*
%Tribune Co, 435 N Michigan Ave, Chicago, IL 60611, USA	
Brumfield, Jacob D	*Baseball Player*
43275 Tillman Dr, Hammond, LA 70403, USA	
Brunansky, Thomas A (Tom)	*Baseball Player*
15442 Via Penoles, San Diego, CA 92128, USA	
Brundage, Howard D	*Publisher*
PO Box 766, Lyne, CT 06371, USA	
Brundtland, Gro Harlem	*Prime Minister, Norway*
Det Norske Arbeiderparti, Youngstorget 2V, 0181 Oslo 1, Norway	
Brunell, Mark	*Football Player*
%Jacksonville Jaguars, 1 Stadium Place, Jacksonville, FL 32202, USA	
Bruner, Mike	*Swimmer*
1144 Derbyshire Dr, Cupertino, CA 95014, USA	
Brunet, Andre Joly	*Figure Skater*
2805 Boyne City Road, Boyne City, MI 49712, USA	
Brunhart, Hans	*Chief of Government, Liechtenstein*
%Government Palace, Regierungsgebaude, 9490 Vaduz, Liechtenstein	
Bruni, Carla	*Model*
%Women Inc, 107 Greene St, #200, New York, NY 10012, USA	
Brunner, J Terrance	*Association Executive*
%Better Government Assn, 230 N Michigan Ave, Chicago, IL 60601, USA	
Brunner, Jerome S	*Psychologist, Educator*
200 Mercer St, New York, NY 10012, USA	
Bruno, Franklin R (Frank)	*Boxer*
PO Box 2266, Brentwood, Essex CM15 0AQ, England	
Brunt, Jennifer	*Model*
%Elite Model Mgmt, 111 E 22nd St, #200, New York, NY 10010, USA	
Bruschi, Tedy	*Football Player*
%New England Patriots, Foxboro Stadium, Rt 1, Foxboro, MA 02035, USA	
Bruskin, Grisha	*Artist*
236 W 26th St, #705, New York, NY 10001, USA	
Bruton, John G	*Prime Minister, Ireland*
Cornelstown, Dunboyne, County Meath, Ireland	
Bry, Ellen	*Actress*
%Media Artists Group, 8383 Wilshire Blvd, #954, Beverly Hills, CA 90211, USA	

Bryan, Dora	*Actress*
11 Marine Parade, Brighton, Sussex, England	
Bryan, J Stewart, III	*Businessman*
%Media General Inc, PO Box 85333-C, Richmond, VA 23293, USA	
Bryan, John H, Jr	*Businessman*
%Sara Lee Corp, 3 First National Plaza, 70 W Madison St, Chicago, IL 60602, USA	
Bryan, John S, III	*Publisher*
%Media General Inc, PO Box 85333-C, Richmond, VA 23293, USA	
Bryan, Wright	*Journalist*
3747 Peachtree Road NE, #516, Atlanta, GA 30319, USA	
Bryan, Zachary Ty	*Actor*
9105 Carmelita Ave, #101, Beverly Hills, CA 90210, USA	
Bryant Clark, Rosalyn	*Track Athlete*
3901 Somerset Dr, Los Angeles, CA 90008, USA	
Bryant, Anita	*Singer, Social Activist*
PO Box 7300, Branson, MO 65615, USA	
Bryant, Brad	*Golfer*
11026 Lake Butler Blvd, Windermere, FL 34786, USA	
Bryant, Gay	*Editor*
34 Horatio St, New York, NY 10014, USA	
Bryant, Kelvin	*Football Player*
%Washington Redskins, 21300 Redskin Park Dr, Ashburn, VA 20147, USA	
Bryant, Kobe	*Basketball Player*
%Los Angeles Lakers, Forum, PO Box 10, Inglewood, CA 90306, USA	
Bryant, Mark	*Basketball Player*
107 Kirkwood Court, Sugar Land, TX 77478, USA	
Bryant, Michael	*Actor*
19 Deanhill Court, Upper Richmond Road, London SW14 7DJ, England	
Bryant, Ray	*Jazz Pianist*
%Corvalan-Condliffe, 1702 Clark Lane, #B, Redondo Beach, CA 90278, USA	
Brymer, Jack	*Concert Clarinetist*
Underwood, Ballards Farm Road, South Croydon, Surrey, England	
Bryson, John E	*Businessman*
%SCEcorp, 2244 Walnut Grove Ave, Rosemead, CA 91770, USA	
Bryson, Peabo	*Singer, Songwriter*
%Agency For Performing Arts, 9200 Sunset Blvd, #900, Los Angeles, CA 90069, USA	
Brzeska, Magdalena	*Rhythmic Gymnast*
%Vitesse Karcher GmbH, Porscestr 6, 70736 Fellbach, Germany	
Brzezinski, Zbigniew	*Government Official, Educator*
%Strategic & International Studies Center, 1800 "K" NW, Washington, DC 20006, USA	
Buatta, Mario	*Interior Designer*
120 E 80th St, New York, NY 10021, USA	
Bubas, Vic	*Basketball Coach*
133 Robert E Lee Lane, Bluffton, SC 29910, USA	
Bubka, Sergei N	*Track Athlete*
%Andresj Kulikowski, Vasavagen 13, 171 39 Solna, Sweden	
Buccellati, Giorgio	*Anthroploogist*
%University of California, Near Eastern Languages Dept, Los Angeles, CA 90024, USA	
Bucha, Paul W	*Vietnam War Army Hero (CMH)*
142 Wooster St, #4-A, New York, NY 10012, USA	
Buchanan, Edna	*Journalist*
%Miami Herald, Editorial Dept, 1 Herald Plaza, Miami, FL 33132, USA	
Buchanan, Ian	*Actor, Model*
%Gold Marshak Liedtke, 3500 W Olive Ave, #1400, Burbank, CA 91505, USA	
Buchanan, Isobel	*Opera Singer*
%Marks Mgmt, 14 New Burlington St, London W1X 1FF, England	
Buchanan, James M	*Nobel Economics Laureate*
%George Mason University, Study of Public Choice Center, Fairfax, VA 22030, USA	
Buchanan, Jensen	*Actress*
196 Columbia Heights, Brooklyn, NY 11201, USA	
Buchanan, John M	*Biochemist*
56 Meriam St, Lexington, MA 02173, USA	
Buchanan, Patrick J	*Commentator, Government Official*
1017 Savile Lane N, McLean, VA 22101, USA	
Buchanon, Willie	*Football Player*
227 Cottingham Court, Oceanside, CA 92054, USA	
Buchen, Philip W	*Attorney, Government Official*
800 25th Ave NW, Washington, DC 20037, USA	

B

Bucher, Lloyd M — *Navy Hero*
11296 Rostrata Hill, Poway, CA 92064, USA

Buchheim, Lothar-Gunther — *Actor*
Biersackstr 23, 82340 Feldafing, Germany

Buchholz, Douglas D (Doug) — *Army General*
Director, Command Communications, Joint Chiefs of Staff, Washington, DC 20318, USA

Buchholz, Horst — *Actor*
Kt Graubunden, 7078 Lenzerheide, Switzerland

Buchi, George H — *Chemist*
%Massachusetts Institute of Technology, Chemistry Dept, Cambridge, MA 02139, USA

Buchli, James F — *Astronaut*
%Boeing Defense/Space Group, ISSA, PO Box 58747, Houston, TX 77258, USA

Buchwald, Art — *Columnist*
4329 Hawthorne St NW, #W, Washington, DC 20016, USA

Buck, Detlev — *Movie Director*
%Agentur Sigrid Narjes, Goethestr 17, 80336 Munich, Germany

Buck, Jack — *Sportscaster*
PO Box 559, Salisbury, NC 28145, USA

Buck, Jason — *Football Player*
%Washington Redskins, 21300 Redskin Park Dr, Ashburn, VA 20147, USA

Buck, Joe — *Sportscaster*
%Fox-TV, Sports Dept, PO Box 900, Beverly Hills, CA 90213, USA

Buck, Robert T, Jr — *Museum Director*
%Brooklyn Museum, 200 Eastern Parkway, Brooklyn, NY 11238, USA

Buckingham, Gregory — *Swimmer*
338 Ridge Road, San Carlos, CA 94070, USA

Buckingham, Lindsey — *Guitarist, Singer (Fleetwood Mac)*
%Michael Brokaw Mgmt, 2934 Beverly Glen Circle, #383, Bel Air, CA 90077, USA

Buckley, Betty — *Actress, Singer*
%Innovative Artists, 1999 Ave of Stars, #2850, Los Angeles, CA 90067, USA

Buckley, Richard E — *Conductor*
87 Woods Road, Branchville, NJ 07826, USA

Buckley, Terrell — *Football Player*
%Miami Dolphins, 7500 SW 30th St, Davie, FL 33314, USA

Buckley, William F, Jr — *Commentator, Editor*
%National Review Magazine, 150 E 35th St, New York, NY 10016, USA

Buckner, Pam — *Bowler*
646 Utah St, Reno, NV 89506, USA

Buckner, William J (Bill) — *Baseball Player*
2425 W Victory Blvd, Meridian, ID 83642, USA

Buckson, David P — *Governor, DE*
110 N Main St, Camden, DE 19934, USA

Bucyk, John (Chief) — *Hockey Player*
17 Boren Lane, Boxford, MA 01921, USA

Budarin, Nikolai — *Cosmonaut*
%Potchta Kosmonavtov, Moskovskoi Oblasti, 141160 Syvisdny Goroduk, Russia

Budd Pieterse, Zola — *Track Athlete*
General Delivery, Bloemfontein, South Africa

Budd, Harold — *Composer, Poet*
%Opal/Warner Bros Records, 6834 Camrose Dr, Los Angeles, CA 90068, USA

Budd, Julie — *Actress, Singer*
%Herb Bernstein, 180 West End Ave, New York, NY 10023, USA

Budde, Ed — *Football Player*
1176 Cherry Lane, Kansas City, MO 64106, USA

Budge, J Donald (Don) — *Tennis Player*
PO Box 789, Dingman's Ferry, PA 18328, USA

Budig, Gene A — *Baseball Executive, Educator*
%American League, 350 Park Ave, #1800, New York, NY 10022, USA

Buehler, Judd — *Basketball Player*
4576 South Lane, Del Mar, CA 92014, USA

Bueno, Maria — *Tennis Player*
Rua Consolagao 3414, #10, 1001 Edificio Augustus, Sao Paulo, Brazil

Buerger, Martin J — *Mineralogist, Crystallographer*
Weston Road, Lincoln, MA 01773, USA

Buffet, Bernard — *Artist*
%Galerie Maurice Garnier, 6 Ave Matignon, 75008 Paris, France

Buffett, Jimmy — *Singer, Songwriter*
%HK Mgmt, 8900 Wilshire Blvd, #300, Beverly Hills, CA 90211, USA

Buffett, Warren E — *Businessman*
%Berkshire Hathaway, 1440 Kiewit Plaza, Omaha, NE 68131, USA

Buffkins, Archie Lee — *Performing Arts Administrator*
%Kennedy Center, Executive Suite, Washington, DC 20566, USA

Buffone, Douglas J (Doug) — *Football Player*
847 W Barry Ave, #G-A, Chicago, IL 60657, USA

Buffum, William B — *Diplomat*
%US Delegation, United Nations, New York, NY 10017, USA

Bufman, Zev — *Theater Producer*
520 Brickell Key Dr, #612, Miami, FL 33131, USA

Buford, Damon J — *Baseball Player*
15412 Valley Vista Blvd, Sherman Oaks, CA 91403, USA

Bugel, Joe — *Football Coach*
%Oakland Raiders, 1220 Harbor Bay Parkway, Alameda, CA 94502, USA

Bugliosi, Vincent T — *Attorney, Writer*
8530 Wilshire Blvd, #404, Beverly Hills, CA 90211, USA

Bugner, Joe — *Boxer*
C/22 Bucjingham St, Surry Hills NSW 201, Australia

Buhari, Muhammadu — *President, Nigeria; Army General*
%GRA, Daura, Katsina State, Nigeria

Buhl, Robert R (Bob) — *Baseball Player*
26 Laurel Oak Dr, Winter Haven, FL 33880, USA

Buhner, Jay C — *Baseball Player*
1420 NW Gilman Blvd, #2666, Issaquah, WA 98027, USA

Bujold, Genevieve — *Actress*
27258 Pacific Coast Highway, Malibu, CA 90265, USA

Buktenica, Raymond — *Actor*
11873 Rochester Ave, Los Angeles, CA 90025, USA

Buliach, Norman B (Norm) — *Football Player*
421 Lynn Dale Court, Hurst, TX 76054, USA

Bulifant, Joyce — *Actress*
301 Red Tail Court, Basalt, CO 81621, USA

Bull, John S — *Astronaut*
1674 Alexander Court, Los Altos, CA 94024, USA

Bull, Ronald D (Ronnie) — *Football Player*
2520 Park Ave, North Riverside, IL 60546, USA

Bullen, Voy M — *Religious Leader*
%Church of God, 1207 Willow Brook, Huntsville, AL 35802, USA

Bullins, Ed — *Writer*
425 Lafayette St, New York, NY 10003, USA

Bullitt, John C — *Attorney, Government Official*
%Shearman Sterling, 53 Wall St, New York, NY 10005, USA

Bullmann, Maik — *Greco-Roman Wrestler*
%AC Bavaria Goldbach, Postfach 1112, 63769 Goldbach, Germany

Bullock, Sandra — *Actress*
291 S La Cienega Blvd, #616, Beverly Hills, CA 90211, USA

Bullock, Theodore H — *Biologist*
3258 Caminito Ameca, La Jolla, CA 92037, USA

Bumbeck, David — *Artist*
Drew Lane, RD 3, Middlebury, VT 05753, USA

Bumbry, Alonzo B (Al) — *Baseball Player*
28 Tremblant Court, Lutherville, MO 21093, USA

Bumbry, Grace — *Opera Singer*
%Herbert Breslin, 119 W 57th St, New York, NY 10019, USA

Bumpus, Frederick J — *Businessman*
%Arkwright Mutual Insurance, 225 Wyman St, Waltham, MA 02154, USA

Bund, Karlheinz — *Businessman*
Huyssenallee 82-84, 45128 Essen Ruhr, Germany

Bundy, Brooke — *Actress*
833 N Martel Ave, Los Angeles, CA 90046, USA

Bundy, William P — *Government Official, Editor*
1087 Great Road, Princeton, NJ 08540, USA

Bunetta, Bill — *Bowler*
1176 E San Bruno, Fresno, CA 93710, USA

Bunge, Bettina — *Tennis Player*
2301 S Bayshore Dr, #14-D, Miami, FL 33133, USA

Bunker, Wallace E (Wally) — *Baseball Player*
RR 1, Box 182, Lowell, OH 45744, USA

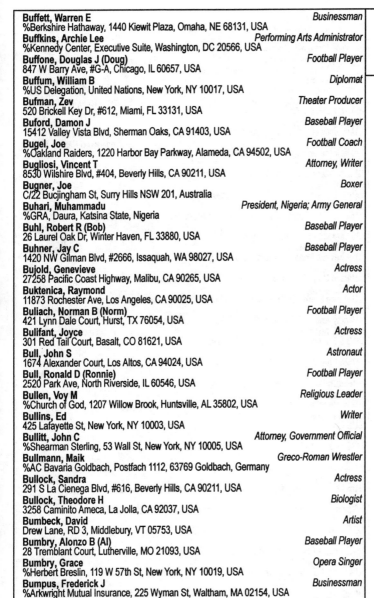

B

Buffett - Bunker

Bunnell, David *Editor, Publisher*
%PCW Communications, 555 DeHaro, San Francisco, CA 94107, USA

Bunnell, Dewey *Singer, Guitarist (America)*
%Gallin-Morey, 345 N Maple Dr, #300, Beverly Hills, CA 90210, USA

Bunning, James P D (Jim) *Representative, KY; Baseball Player*
1717 Dixie Highway, #180, Fort Wright, KY 41011, USA

Bunton, Emma *Singer (Spice Girls)*
%Virgin Records, Kensal House, 533-79 Harrow Road, London W1O 4RH, England

Buoniconti, Nicholas A (Nick) *Football Player, Businessman*
2665 S Bayshore Dr, #PH 2-B, Miami, FL 33133, USA

Burbidge, E Margaret P *Astronomer*
%University of California, Astrophysics Center, 9500 Gilman, La Jolla, CA 92093, USA

Burch, Elliot *Thoroughbred Racing Trainer*
420 Fair Hill Dr, #1, Elkton, MD 21921, USA

Burchhardt, Helmuth *Businessman*
%Eschweiler Bergwerks-Verein, 52134 Herzogenrath, Germany

Burchill, Thomas F (Tony) *Radio Executive*
%RKO General, 175 Ghent Road, Fairlawn, OH 44333, USA

Burchuladze, Paata *Opera Singer*
%Metropolitan Opera Assn, Lincoln Center Plaza, New York, NY 10023, USA

Burden, William A M *Diplomat, Financier*
820 5th Ave, New York, NY 10021, USA

Burdette, S Lewis (Lew) *Baseball Player*
2019 Beveva Road, Sarasota, FL 34232, USA

Burdge, Jeffrey J *Businessman*
%Harsco Corp, PO Box 8888, Camp Hill, PA 17001, USA

Burditt, Joyce *Writer*
%Ballatine Books, 201 E 50th St, New York, NY 10022, USA

Burdon, Eric *Singer (Animals); Songwriter*
%Variety Artists, 555 Chorro St, #A-1, San Luis Obispo, CA 93405, USA

Burford, Anne M *Government Official*
3853 S Hudson St, Denver, CO 80237, USA

Burford, Chris *Football Player*
377 2nd Tee Dr, Incline Village, NV 89451, USA

Burgee, John H *Architect*
Perelanda Farm, Skunks Misery Road, Millerton, NY 12546, USA

Burgess, Adrian *Mountaineer*
109 North St, Anderson, SC 29621, USA

Burgess, Greg *Track Athlete*
%US Olympic Committee, 1 Olympia Plaza, Colorado Springs, CO 80909, USA

Burgess, Neil *Electrical Engineer*
8425 Kugler Mill Road, Cincinnati, OH 45243, USA

Burgess, Robert K *Businessman*
%Pulte Corp, 33 Bloomfield Hills Parkway, Bloomfield Hills, MI 48304, USA

Burgess, Tony *Ecologist*
%US Geological Survey, 119 National Center, Reston, VA 22092, USA

Burgess, Warren D *Religious Leader*
%Reformed Church in America, 475 Riverside Dr, New York, NY 10115, USA

Burghoff, Gary *Actor*
4275 34th St S, #4, St Petersburg, FL 33711, USA

Burgi, Richard *Actor*
2622 Victoria Blvd, Laguna Beach, CA 92651, USA

Burgin, C David *Editor*
%Oakland Tribune, Editorial Dept, 409 13th St, Oakland, CA 94612, USA

Burhoe, Ralph Wendell *Theologian*
Montgomery Place, 5550 S Shore Dr, #715, Chicago, IL 60637, USA

Burke Hederman, Lynn *Swimmer*
26 White Oak Tree Road, Laurel Hollow, NY 11791, USA

Burke, Bernard F *Physicist, Astrophysicist*
10 Bloomfield St, Lexington, MA 02173, USA

Burke, Chris *Actor*
426 S Orange Grove Ave, Los Angeles, CA 90036, USA

Burke, Delta *Actress*
%Michael Hurwitz, 427 N Canon Dr, #215, Beverly Hills, CA 90210, USA

Burke, Jack, Sr *Golfer*
%Champions Golf Club, 13722 Champions Dr, Houston, TX 77069, USA

Burke, James *Commentator*
Henley House, Terrace Barnes, London SW13 0NP, England

Burke, James D — *Museum Director*
%St Louis Art Museum, Forest Park, St Louis, MO 63110, USA

Burke, James Lee — *Writer*
%Hyperion Press, 114 5th Ave, New York, NY 10011, USA

Burke, John F — *Surgeon, Educator*
984 Memorial Dr, #503, Cambridge, MA 02138, USA

Burke, Joseph — *Educator*
%La Salle University, President's Office, Philadelphia, PA 19141, USA

Burke, Joseph C — *Educator*
%State University of New York, Provost's Office, Albany, NY 12246, USA

Burke, Kelly Howard — *Air Force General*
%Stafford Burke Hecker, 1006 Cameron St, Alexandria, VA 22314, USA

Burke, Lloyd L — *Korean War Army Hero (CMH)*
700 Grand Point Dr, Hot Springs, AR 71901, USA

Burke, Michael D — *Businessman*
%Tesoro Petroleum, 8700 Tesoro Dr, San Antonio, TX 78217, USA

Burke, Paul Timothy — *Actor*
2217 Avenida Caballeros, Palm Springs, CA 92262, USA

Burke, Solomon — *Singer*
%Rodgers Redding, 1048 Tatnall St, Macon, GA 31201, USA

Burket, Harriet — *Editor*
700 John Ringling Blvd, Sarasota, FL 34236, USA

Burkett, John D — *Baseball Player*
104 Craydon Circle, Beaver, PA 15009, USA

Burkhalter, Edward A, Jr — *Navy Admiral*
4128 Fort Washington Place, Alexandria, VA 22304, USA

Burkhardt, Francois — *Architect*
3 Rue de Venise, 75004 Paris, France

Burkhardt, Lisa — *Sportscaster*
%Madison Square Garden Network, 4 Pennsylvania Plaza, New York, NY 10001, USA

Burkholder, Barry C — *Financier*
%Bank United of Texas, 3200 Southwest Freeway, Houston, TX 77027, USA

Burki, Fred A — *Labor Leader*
%United Retail Workers Union, 9865 W Roosevelt Road, Westchester, IL 60154, USA

Burkley, Dennis — *Actor*
5145 Costello Ave, Sherman Oaks, CA 91423, USA

Burks, Arthur W — *Applied Mathematician, Philosopher*
3445 Vintage Valley Road, Ann Arbor, MI 48105, USA

Burks, Ellis R — *Baseball Player*
4924 S Elizabeth, Englewood, CO 80110, USA

Burleson, Richard P (Rick) — *Baseball Player*
270 E Mira Verde Dr, La Habra Heights, CA 90631, USA

Burleson, Tom — *Basketball Player*
PO Box 861, Newland, NC 28657, USA

Burnell, Jocelyn — *Astronomer*
%Bell Open University, Physics Dept, Milton Keynes MK7 6AA, England

Burnes, Karen — *Commentator*
%CBS-TV, News Dept, 51 W 52nd St, New York, NY 10019, USA

Burnett, Carol — *Actress*
%Brillstein/Grey, 9150 Wilshire Blvd, #350, Beverly Hills, CA 90212, USA

Burnett, Howard J — *Educator*
%Washington & Jefferson College, President's Office, Washington, PA 15301, USA

Burnett, James E — *Government Official*
%Transportation Safety Board, 800 Independence Ave SW, Washington, DC 20594, USA

Burnett, Robert A — *Publisher*
%Meredith Corp, PO Box 400430, Des Moines, IA 50350, USA

Burnette, Rocky — *Singer*
1900 Ave of Stars, #2530, Los Angeles, CA 90067, USA

Burney, Leroy E — *Physician*
%Milbank Memorial Fund, 40 Wall St, New York, NY 10005, USA

Burnham, Duane L — *Businessman*
%Abbott Laboratories, 100 Abbott Park Road, Abbott Park, IL 60064, USA

Burns, Annie — *Singer (The Burns Sisters), Songwriter*
%Drake Assoc, 177 Woodland Ave, Westwood, NJ 07675, USA

Burns, Carroll D — *Businessman*
%Life Insurance of Georgia, 5780 Powers Ferry Road NW, Atlanta, GA 30327, USA

Burns, Edward — *Movie Director, Actor*
588 Broadway, #210, New York, NY 10012, USA

B

Burke - Burns

B

Burns, Eric *Television Entertainer*
%"Arts & Entertainment Revue" Show, 402 E 76th St, New York, NY 10021, USA

Burns, James MacGregor *Political Scientist, Historian*
High Mowing, Bee Hill Road, Williamstown, MA 01267, USA

Burns, Jeannie *Singer (The Burns Sisters), Songwriter*
%Drake Assoc, 177 Woodland Ave, Westwood, NJ 07675, USA

Burns, Jere, II *Actor*
PO Box 3596, Mammoth Lakes, CA 93546, USA

Burns, John F *Journalist*
%New York Times, Editorial Dept, 229 W 43rd St, New York, NY 10036, USA

Burns, John J *Air Force General*
23 Southwind Court, Niceville, FL 32578, USA

Burns, Kenneth L (Ken) *Documentary Director*
%Florentine Films, Maple Grove Road, Walpole, NH 03608, USA

Burns, M Anthony *Businessman*
%Ryder System Inc, 3600 NW 82nd Ave, Miami, FL 33166, USA

Burns, Marie *Singer (The Burns Sisters), Songwriter*
%Drake Assoc, 177 Woodland Ave, Westwood, NJ 07675, USA

Burns, Pat *Hockey Coach*
%Boston Bruins, 1 Fleet Center, 1 Accolyn Way, #250, Boston, MA 02114, USA

Burns, W L, Jr *Financier*
%CCB Financial Corp, 111 Corcoran St, Durham, NC 27701, USA

Burr, Craig L *Businessman*
%Burr Egan Deleage Co, 1 Post Office Square, Boston, MA 02109, USA

Burr, Robert *Actor*
%Goldey Co, 1156 S Carmelina Ave, #B, Los Angeles, CA 90049, USA

Burrell, Kenneth E (Kenny) *Jazz Guitarist, Composer*
%Tropix International, 163 W 3rd Ave, #143, New York, NY 10003, USA

Burrell, Leroy *Track Athlete*
%Santa Monica Track Club, 1801 Ocean Park Blvd, #112, Santa Monica, CA 90405, USA

Burrell, Scott *Basketball Player*
331 Evergreen Ave, Hamden, CT 06518, USA

Burris, Robert H *Biochemist*
1015 University Bay Dr, Madison, WI 53705, USA

Burroughs, Jeffrey A (Jeff) *Baseball Player*
6155 Laguna Court, Long Beach, CA 90803, USA

Burrows, Darren E *Actor*
%Writers & Artists, 924 Westwood Blvd, #900, Los Angeles, CA 90024, USA

Burrows, Eva *Religious Leader*
%Salvation Army Int'l, 101 Queen Victoria St, London EC4 4EP, England

Burrows, J Stuart *Opera Singer*
%John Coast Mgmt, 31 Sinclair Road, London W14 0NS, England

Burrows, Stephen *Fashion Designer*
10 W 57th St, New York, NY 10019, USA

Bursch, Daniel W *Astronaut*
%NASA, Johnson Space Center, 2101 NASA Road, Houston, TX 77058, USA

Burstyn, Ellen *Actress*
Ferry House, Washington Spring Road, Snedens Landing, Palisades, NY 10964, USA

Burt, Adam *Hockey Player*
8810 Tipsico Lake Road, Holly, MI 48442, USA

Burt, James M *WW II Army Hero (CMH)*
1621 Sherwood Road, Colony Park, Wyomissing, PA 19610, USA

Burt, Robert N *Businessman*
%FMC Corp, 200 E Randolph Dr, Chicago, IL 60601, USA

Burtis, Theodore A *Businessman*
%Sunbrook Conference Center, 601 Country Line Road, Wayne, PA 19087, USA

Burtnett, Wellington *Hockey Player*
1703 Pouliot Place, Welmington, MA 01887, USA

Burton, Brandie *Golfer*
%Int'l Management Group, 1 Erieview Plaza, #1300, Cleveland, OH 44114, USA

Burton, Charles *Transglobal Explorer*
27-A Leinster Square, London W2, England

Burton, Gary *Jazz Vibist*
%Berklee College of Music, 1140 Boylston St, Boston, MA 02215, USA

Burton, Jeff *Auto Racing Driver*
Rt 2, Box 885-C, Halifax, VA 24558, USA

Burton, Kate *Actress, Singer*
3600 Stewart Ave, Los Angeles, CA 90066, USA

Burns - Burton

Burton, Lance — *Illusionist*
%Monte Carlo Hotel, 3770 S Las Vegas Blvd, Las Vegas, NV 89109, USA
Burton, LeVar — *Actor*
%Peaceful Warrior Productions, 13601 Ventura Blvd, #209, Sherman Oaks, CA 91423, USA
Burton, Nelson, Jr — *Bowler*
133 Chippenham Lane, Clarkson Valley, MO 63005, USA
Burton, Robert G — *Publisher*
%World Color Press, 101 Park Ave, New York, NY 10178, USA
Burton, Ron — *Football Player*
%John Hancock Insurance, Community Affairs, 200 Clarendon St, Boston, MA 02116, USA
Burton, Scott — *Artist*
86 Thompson St, New York, NY 10012, USA
Burton, Steve — *Actor*
2211 Glyndon Ave, Venice, CA 90291, USA
Burton, Timothy W (Tim) — *Movie Director*
445 Redondo Ave, #7, Long Beach, CA 90814, USA
Burton, Wendell — *Actor*
2617 Ivanhill Terrace, Los Angeles, CA 90039, USA
Burton, Willie — *Basketball Player*
18900 Fleming St, Detroit, MI 48234, USA
Burts, Stephen L, Jr — *Financier*
%Synovus Financial Corp, 901 Front Ave, Columbus, GA 31901, USA
Burum, Stephen — *Cinematographer*
%Smith/Gosnell/Nicholson, 1515 Palisades Dr, #N, Pacific Palisades, CA 90272, USA
Bury, Pol — *Sculptor*
12 Vallee de la Taupe-Perdreauville, 78200 Mantes-La-Jolie, France
Busbee, George D — *Governor, GA*
%King & Spalding, 191 Peachtree St NW, #4900, Atlanta, GA 30303, USA
Busby, Jheryl — *Record Company Executive*
%Motown Records, 6255 Sunset Blvd, Los Angeles, CA 90028, USA
Busby, Steven L (Steve) — *Baseball Player*
%Texas Rangers, PO Box 901111, Arlington, TX 76004, USA
Buscaglia, F Leonardo (Leo) — *Educator*
%LFB Inc, PO Box 599, Glenbrook, NV 89413, USA
Busch, August A, III — *Businessman, Baseball Executive*
%Anheuser-Busch Cos, 1 Busch Place, St Louis, MO 63118, USA
Busemann, Frank — *Track Athlete*
Borkumstr 13-A, 45665 Recklinghausen, Germany
Buser, Martin — *Dog Sled Racer*
PO Box 520997, Big Lake, AK 99652, USA
Busey, Gary — *Actor*
18424 Coastline Dr, Malibu, CA 90265, USA
Busfield, Timothy — *Actor*
2416 "G" St, #D, Sacramento, CA 95816, USA
Bush, Barbara P — *Wife of US President*
9 West Oak Dr, Houston, TX 77056, USA
Bush, George H W — *President, USA*
9 West Oak Dr, Houston, TX 77056, USA
Bush, George H W, Jr — *Governor, TX*
%Governor's Office, State Capitol, PO Box 12428, Austin, TX 78711, USA
Bush, Jim — *Track Coach*
5106 Bounty Lane, Culver City, CA 90230, USA
Bush, Kate — *Singer, Songwriter*
20 Manchester Square, London W1, England
Bush, Lesley — *Diver*
83311 Overseas Highway, Islamorada, FL 33036, USA
Bush, Richard E — *WW II Marine Corps Hero (CMH)*
2200 Marshall Parkway, Waukegan, IL 60085, USA
Bush, Robert E — *WW II Navy Hero (CMH)*
3148 Madrona Beach Road NW, Olympia, WA 98502, USA
Bush, William Green — *Actor*
%Gold Marshak Liedtke, 3500 W Olive Ave, #1400, Burbank, CA 91505, USA
Bushinsky, Joseph M (Jay) — *Commentator*
Rehov Hatsafon 5, Savyon 56540, Israel
Bushland, Raymond C — *Entomologist*
200 Concord Plaza Dr, San Antonio, TX 78216, USA
Bushnell, Nolan K — *Businessman*
%Etak Inc, 1430 O'Brien Dr, Menlo Park, CA 94025, USA

B

Burton - Bushnell

Buss, Jerry H	*Basketball Executive*
1143 Summit Dr, Beverly Hills, CA 90210, USA	
Bussard, Robert W	*Physicist*
8505 Euclid Ave, #3, Manassas Park, VA 20111, USA	
Bussell, Darcey A	*Ballerina*
155 New King's Road, London SW6 4SJ, England	
Bustamante, Alfonso	*Government Official, Peru*
Urb Corpac, Calle 1 Oeste S/N, San Isidro, Lima 27, Peru	
Buster, John E	*Obstetrician*
%Harbor-UCLA Medical Center, PO Box 2910, Torrance, CA 90509, USA	
Butala, Tony	*Singer (The Lettermen)*
%ACT Mgmt, 13090 Hosler Ave, Chico, CA 95973, USA	
Butcher, Susan H	*Dog Sled Racer*
%Trail Breaker Kennel, 1 Eureka, Manley, AK 99756, USA	
Buthelezi, Chief Mangosuthu G	*Chief Minister, KwaZulu/Natal*
Private Bag X-01, Ulundi 3838, Kwazulu, South Africa	
Butkus, Dick	*Football Player, Actor*
%Epstein-Wyckoff, 280 S Beverly Dr, #400, Beverly Hills, CA 90212, USA	
Butler, Bill	*Cinematographer*
%Smith/Gosnell/Nicholson, 1515 Palisades Dr, #N, Pacific Palisades, CA 90272, USA	
Butler, Brett	*Comedienne*
%International Creative Mgmt, 8942 Wilshire Blvd, Beverly Hills, CA 90211, USA	
Butler, Brett M	*Baseball Player*
3248 Strathmore Dr, Duluth, GA 30096, USA	
Butler, Dan	*Actor*
%Gersh Agency, 232 N Canon Dr, Beverly Hills, CA 90210, USA	
Butler, Dean	*Actor*
1310 Westholme Ave, Los Angeles, CA 90024, USA	
Butler, Gilbert	*Financier*
%Butler Capital Corp, 767 5th Ave, New York, NY 10153, USA	
Butler, Jerry (Iceman)	*Singer, Songwriter*
%Jerry Butler Productions, 164 Woodstone Dr, Buffalo Grove, IL 60089, USA	
Butler, Michael C	*Financier, Producer*
%Laura Lizer Assoc, 12711 Ventura Blvd, #440, Studio City, CA 91604, USA	
Butler, Paul	*Astronomer*
%University of California, Astronomy Dept, Berkeley, CA 94720, USA	
Butler, Richard A	*Government Official, England*
Spencers, Great Yeldham, Essex CO9 4JG, England	
Butler, Robert	*Television Director*
650 Club View Dr, Los Angeles, CA 90024, USA	
Butler, Robert N	*Gerontologist*
%Mt Sinai Medical Center, Geriatrics Dept, 1 Levy Plaza, New York, NY 10029, USA	
Butler, Robert Olen	*Writer*
PO Box 4767, Lake Charles, LA 70606, USA	
Butler, Samuel C	*Attorney*
%Cravath Swain Moore, 825 8th Ave, New York, NY 10019, USA	
Butler, William E	*Businessman*
%Eaton Corp, Eaton Center, 1111 Superior Ave, Cleveland, OH 44114, USA	
Butler, Yancy	*Actress*
6154 Glen Tower, Los Angeles, CA 90068, USA	
Butor, Michel	*Writer*
A L'Ecart, Lucinges, 74380 Bonne, France	
Butsavage, Bernard	*Labor Leader*
%Molders & Allied Workers Union, 1225 E McMillan St, Cincinnati, OH 45206, USA	
Butterfield, Jack A	*Hockey Executive*
55 Pineridge Dr, Westfield, MA 01085, USA	
Buttner, Jean B	*Financier*
%Value Line Inc, 220 E 42nd St, New York, NY 10017, USA	
Button, Richard T (Dick)	*Figure Skater, Television Producer*
%Candid Productions, 250 W 57th St, #1818, New York, NY 10107, USA	
Buttons, Red	*Actor*
778 Tortuoso Way, Los Angeles, CA 90077, USA	
Butts, James	*Track Athlete*
16950 Belforest Dr, Carson, CA 90746, USA	
Butz, David R (Dave)	*Football Player*
65 Oak Grove Dr, Belleville, IL 62221, USA	
Butz, Earl	*Secretary, Agriculture*
2741 N Salisbury St, West Lafayette, IN 47906, USA	

Buxton, Charles I, II *Businessman*
%Federated Mutual Insurance, 121 E Park Square, Owatonna, MN 55060, USA
Buxton, Winslow H *Businessman*
%Pentair Inc, Waters Edge Plaza, 1500 Country Road B-2 W, St Paul, MN 55113, USA
Buyoya, Pierre *President, Burundi; Army Officer*
%President's Office, Bujumbura, Burundi
Buzzi, Ruth *Comedienne, Actress*
%Amsel Eisenstadt Frazier, 6310 San Vicente Blvd, #401, Los Angeles, CA 90048, USA
Byars, Betsy C *Writer*
126 Riverpoint Dr, Clemson, SC 29631, USA
Byars, Keith *Football Player*
%New England Patriots, Foxboro Stadium, Rt 1, Foxboro, MA 02035, USA
Byatt, Antonia Susan (A S) *Writer*
37 Rusholme Road, London SW15 3LF, England
Bychkov, Semyon *Conductor*
%Buffalo Symphony Orchestra, 71 Symphony Circle, Buffalo, NY 14201, USA
Byers, Walter *Athletic Association Executive*
PO Box 1525, Shawnee Mission, KS 66222, USA
Bykovsky, Valeri F *Cosmonaut*
%Potchta Kosmonavtov, Moskovskoi Oblasti, 141160 Syvisdny Goroduk, Russia
Byner, John *Actor*
%Gregg Purcott, 1 S Ocean Blvd, #316, Boca Raton, FL 33432, USA
Bynoe, Peter C B *Basketball Executive*
%Denver Nuggets, McNichols Arena, 1635 Clay St, Denver, CO 80204, USA
Byram, Cassandra *Actress*
12725 Ventura Blvd, #F, Studio City, CA 91604, USA
Byrd, Benjamin F, Jr *Physician*
4230 Harding Road, #609, Nashville, TN 37205, USA
Byrd, Charles L (Charlie) *Jazz, Classical Guitarist*
764 Fairview Ave, #E, Annapolis, MD 21403, USA
Byrd, David *Actor*
%Paradigm Agency, 10100 Santa Monica Blvd, #2500, Los Angeles, CA 90067, USA
Byrd, Gill *Football Player*
14555 Wildgrove Road, Poway, CA 92064, USA
Byrd, Harry F, Jr *Senator, VA*
%Rockingham Publishing Co, 2 N Kent St, Winchester, VA 22601, USA
Byrd, Michael *Businessman*
%Maxim Integrated Products, 120 San Gabriel Dr, Sunnyside, CA 94086, USA
Byrd, Tracy *Singer*
%Ritter/Carter, PO Box 128195, Nashville, TN 37212, USA
Byrne, Brendan T *Governor, NJ*
%Carella Byrne Bain Gilfillan Rhodes, Gateway 1, Newark, NJ 07102, USA
Byrne, David *Singer (Talking Heads), Songwriter*
7964 Willow Glen Road, Los Angeles, CA 90046, USA
Byrne, Gabriel *Actor*
%International Creative Mgmt, 76 Oxford St, London W1N 0AX, England
Byrne, Gerry *Publisher*
%Variety Inc, 5700 Wilshire Blvd, Los Angeles, CA 90036, USA
Byrne, John V *Educator*
%Oregon State University, President's Office, Corvallis, OR 97330, USA
Byrne, Thomas J (Tommy) *Baseball Player*
617 Shiretown Lane, Wake Forest, NC 27587, USA
Byrnes, Edd *Actor*
PO Box 1623, Beverly Hills, CA 90213, USA
Byron, Don *Jazz Clarinetist*
%Joel Chriss, 300 Mercer St, #3-J, New York, NY 10003, USA
Byron, Kathleen *Actress*
PO Box 130, Hove, East Sussex BN3 6QU, England
Byrum, John W *Movie Director*
7435 Woodrow Wilson Dr, Los Angeles, CA 90046, USA
Bywater, William H *Labor Leader*
%International Electronic Workers, 1126 16th St NW, Washington, DC 20036, USA

B

Buxton - Bywater

Caan, James *Actor*
%JEC Productions, 2029 Century Park East, #500, Los Angeles, CA 90067, USA

Caballe, Montserrat *Opera Singer*
%Carlos Caballe, Via Augusta 59, 08006 Barcelona, Spain

Cabana, Robert D *Astronaut*
%NASA, Johnson Space Center, 2101 NASA Road, Houston, TX 77058, USA

Cacoyannis, Michael *Movie, Theatre Director*
15 Mouson St, Athens 401, Greece

Caddell, Patrick H *Statistician*
%Cambridge Research Inc, 1625 "I" St NW, Washington, DC 20006, USA

Cade, J Robert *Medical Researcher, Inventor (Gatorade)*
%University of Florida Medical School, Physiology Dept, Gainesville, FL 32610, USA

Cade, Mossy *Football Player*
6112 N 67th Ave, #127, Glendale, AZ 85301, USA

Cadell, Ava *Actress*
3349 W Cahuenga Blvd, #2, Los Angeles, CA 90068, USA

Cadigan, Dave *Football Player*
83 Baldwin Ave, Point Lookout, NY 11569, USA

Cadmus, Paul *Artist, Etcher, Photographer*
PO Box 1255, Weston, CT 06883, USA

Cadorette, Mary *Actress*
%House of Representatives, 400 S Beverly Dr, #101, Beverly Hills, CA 90212, USA

Caesar, Shirley *Singer*
%Shirley Caesar Outreach Ministries, 606 W Club Blvd, Durham, NC 27701, USA

Caesar, Sid *Comedian, Actor*
1910 Loma Vista Dr, Beverly Hills, CA 90210, USA

Cafego, George *Football Player*
405 Kittredge Court, Knoxville, TN 37922, USA

Cafferata, Hector A, Jr *Korean War Marine Corps Hero (CMH)*
630 Dewey Ave, Alpha, NJ 08865, USA

Cagatay, Mustafa *Prime Minister, Cyprus Federated State*
60 Cumhuriyet Caddesi, Kyrenia, Cyprus

Cage, Michael *Basketball Player*
12629 N Tatum Blvd, #148, Phoenix, AZ 85032, USA

Cage, Nicolas *Actor*
%Brillstein/Grey, 9150 Wilshire Blvd, #350, Beverly Hills, CA 90212, USA

Caglayangil, Ihsan S *President, Turkey*
Sehit Ersan Caddesi 30/15, Cankaya, Ankara, Turkey

Cahill, John C *Businessman*
%Trans World Airlines, City Center, 515 N 6th St, St Louis, MO 63101, USA

Cahouet, Frank V *Financier*
%Mellon Bank Corp, 1 Mellon Bank Center, 500 Grant St, Pittsburgh, PA 15219, USA

Cain, Carl *Basketball Player*
1614 Carrie Ave, Des Moines, IA 50315, USA

Cain, Dean *Actor*
%Centre Films, 1019 Chautauqua Blvd, Pacific Palisades, CA 90272, USA

Cain, John Paul *Golfer*
1112 Nantucket Dr, #B, Houston, TX 77057, USA

Caine, Michael *Actor*
Rectory Farm House, Northstoke, Oxfordshire, England

Cairncross, Alexander K *Government Official, England; Economist*
14 Staverton Road, Oxford OX2 6XJ, England

Calcevecchia, Mark *Golfer*
1005 Alamanda Dr, North Palm Beach, FL 33408, USA

Calder, Iain W *Editor*
%National Enquirer, Editorial Dept, 600 SE Coast Ave, Lantana, FL 33464, USA

Calder, Nigel *Writer*
8 The Chase, Furnace Green, Crawley, West Sussex RH10 6HW, England

Caldera Rodriguez, Rafael *President, Venezuela*
Ave Urdaneta 33-2, Apdo 2060, Caracas, Venezuela

Calderon Fournier, Rafael A *President, Costa Rica*
%Casa Presidencial, Apdo 520-2010, San Jose 1000, Costa Rica

Calderon Sol, Armando *President, El Salvador*
%President's Office, Casa Presidencial, San Salvador, El Salvador

Calderone, Mary S *Physician*
%New York University, Health & Education Dept, 715 Broadway, New York, NY 10003, USA

Caldicott, Helen *Social Activist, Pediatrician*
%Physicians for Responsibility, 639 Massachusetts Ave, Cambridge, MA 02139, USA

Caldwell, Philip — *Businessman*
%Smith Barney Shearson, 200 Vesey St, New York, NY 10281, USA

Caldwell, R Michael (Mike) — *Baseball Player*
1645 Brook Run Dr, Raleigh, NC 27614, USA

Caldwell, Sarah — *Opera Producer, Conductor*
%Boston Opera Co, 539 Washington St, Boston, MA 02111, USA

Caldwell, William A — *Editor*
%Vineyard Gazette, Editorial Dept, S Summer St, Edgartown, MA 02539, USA

Caldwell, Zoe — *Actress*
%Whitehead-Stevens, 1501 Broadway, New York, NY 10036, USA

Cale, J J — *Singer, Guitarist*
%Rosebud Agency, PO Box 170429, San Francisco, CA 94117, USA

Cale, John — *Singer, Musician (Velvet Underground)*
%Performers of the World, 8901 Melrose Ave, #200, West Hollywood, CA 90069, USA

Calegari, Maria — *Ballerina*
%New York City Ballet, Lincoln Center Plaza, New York, NY 10023, USA

Calfa, Marian — *Prime Minister, Czech Republic*
%CTL Consulting, Premyslovska 28, Prague 3, Czech Republic

Calhoun, Jim — *Basketball Coach*
%University of Connecticut, Athletic Dept, 2111 Hillside Rd, Storrs, CT 06269, USA

Calhoun, Rory — *Actor*
PO Box 689, Morongo Valley, CA 92256, USA

Cali, Joseph — *Actor*
25750 Vista Verde Dr, Monte Nido, CA 91302, USA

Califano, Joseph A, Jr — *Secretary, Health Education & Welfare*
1775 Pennsylvania Ave NW, Washington, DC 20006, USA

Caligiuri, Paul — *Soccer Player*
12021 Wilshire Blvd, #741, Los Angeles, CA 90025, USA

Calipari, John — *Basketball Coach*
%New Jersey Nets, Byrne Meadowlands Arena, East Rutherford, NJ 07073, USA

Calisher, Hortense — *Writer*
%Candida Donadio, 231 W 22nd St, New York, NY 10011, USA

Call, Brandon — *Actor*
5918 Van Nuys Blvd, Van Nuys, CA 91401, USA

Callaghan of Cardiff, James — *Prime Minister, England*
%House of Lords, Westminster, London SW1A 0PW, England

Callaghan, James T — *Air Force General*
Commander, Air South, Box 101, Air South, FPO, AE 09620, USA

Callahan, Harry M — *Photographer*
145 15th St NE, #421, Atlanta, GA 30309, USA

Callahan, James T — *Actor*
13900 Tahiti Way, #206, Marina del Rey, CA 90292, USA

Callahan, John — *Actor*
342 N Alfred St, Los Angeles, CA 90048, USA

Callan, K — *Actress*
4957 Matilija Ave, Sherman Oaks, CA 91423, USA

Callan, Michael — *Actor*
1730 Camden Ave, #201, Los Angeles, CA 90025, USA

Callas, Charlie — *Comedian, Actor*
9000 Sunset Blvd, #502, Los Angeles, CA 90069, USA

Callaway, Paul Smith — *Concert Organist*
%Washington Cathedral, Mount St Alban, Washington, DC 20016, USA

Callaway, Thomas — *Actor*
%House of Representatives, 400 S Beverly Dr, #101, Beverly Hills, CA 90212, USA

Callejas, Rafael L — *President, Honduras*
%President's Office, 6-A Avda La Calle, Tegucigalpa, Honduras

Callen Jones, Gloria — *Swimmer*
1508 Chafton Road, Charleston, WV 25314, USA

Calley, John — *Entertainment Executive*
%Sony Pictures Entertainment, 10202 W Washington Blvd, Culver City, CA 90232, USA

Calloway, D Wayne — *Businessman*
%PepsiCo Inc, 700 Anderson Hill Road, Purchase, NY 10577, USA

Calugas, Jose, Sr — *WW II Army Hero (CMH)*
2907 Narrows Place, Tacoma, WA 98407, USA

Calverly, Ernie — *Basketball Player*
36 Hillside Road, Wakefield, RI 02879, USA

Calvert, James — *Actor*
6334 Hollywood Blvd, #303, Los Angeles, CA 90028, USA

Calvert, James F — *Navy Admiral, Writer*
PO Box 479, St Michael's, MD 21663, USA

Calvert, Phyllis — *Actress*
Argyll Lodge, Towersey, Thames, Oxon, England

Calvet, Corinne — *Actress*
%Pacific Plaza Towers, 1431 Ocean Ave, #109, Santa Monica, CA 90401, USA

Calvin, John — *Actor*
%Stone Manners, 8091 Selma Ave, Los Angeles, CA 90046, USA

Calvin, Mack — *Basketball Player, Coach*
%California State University, Athletic Dept, Carson, CA 90747, USA

Calvin, William H — *Neurobiologist*
%University of Washington, Neurobiology Dept, Seattle, WA 98195, USA

Calvo, Paul M — *Governor, GU*
%Governor's Office, Capitol Building, Agana, GU 96910, USA

Calvo-Sotelo Bustelo, Leopoldo — *Prime Minister, Spain*
Alcala 93, 28009 Madrid, Spain

Camacho, Hector — *Boxer*
4751 Yardarm Lane, Boynton Beach, FL 33436, USA

Camara, Helder P — *Religious Leader*
Rua Henrique Dias 208, Igreja Das Fronteiras, 50 070 Recife PE, Brazil

Camarillo, Richard J (Rich) — *Football Player*
1913 E South Fork Dr, Phoenix, AZ 85048, USA

Cambre, Ronald C — *Businessman*
%Newmont Mining, 1700 Lincoln St, Denver, CO 80203, USA

Camby, Marcus — *Basketball Player*
%ProServe, 1101 Woodrow Wilson Blvd, #1800, Arlington, VA 22209, USA

Camden, John — *Businessman*
%RMC Group, Coldgarbour Lane, Thorpe, Egham, Surrey TW20 8TD, England

Camdessus, Michel J — *Financier*
%International Monetary Fund, 700 19th St NW, Washington, DC 20431, USA

Camel, Marvin — *Boxer*
18331 Mansel Ave, Redondo Beach, CA 90278, USA

Cameron, Candance — *Actress*
8369 Sausalito Ave, West Hills, CA 91304, USA

Cameron, Dean — *Actor*
%Gold Marshak Liedtke, 3500 W Olive Ave, #1400, Burbank, CA 91505, USA

Cameron, Duncan — *Singer (Sawyer Brown)*
%TKO Artist Mgmt, 4219 Hillsboro Road, #318, Nashville, TN 37215, USA

Cameron, Gerry B — *Financier*
%US Bancorp, 111 SW 5th Ave, Portland, OR 97204, USA

Cameron, James — *Movie Director*
3201 Retreat Court, Malibu, CA 90265, USA

Cameron, Joanna — *Actress*
%Cameron Productions, PO Box 1011, Pebble Beach, CA 93953, USA

Cameron, Kenneth D — *Astronaut*
%NASA, Johnson Space Center, 2101 NASA Road, Houston, TX 77058, USA

Cameron, Kirk — *Actor*
PO Box 8665, Calabasas, CA 91372, USA

Cameron, Michelle — *Synchronized Swimmer*
Box 2, Site 1-SS-3, Calgary AL T3C 3N9, Canada

Camilli, Douglas J (Doug) — *Baseball Player*
2831 Hacienda St, San Mateo, CA 94403, USA

Camilo, Michel — *Jazz Pianist*
%Redondo Music, 590 West End Ave, #6, New York, NY 10024, USA

Caminiti, Kenneth G (Ken) — *Baseball Player*
2210 Quarter Path, Richmond, TX 77469, USA

Camp, Colleen — *Actress*
%Gersh Agency, 232 N Canon Dr, Beverly Hills, CA 90210, USA

Camp, John — *Journalist*
%St Paul Pioneer Press & Dispatch, 55 E 4th St, St Paul, MN 55101, USA

Camp, Steve — *Singer*
%Brokaw Co, 1106 16th Ave S, Nashville, TN 37212, USA

Campanella, Joseph — *Actor*
4647 Arcola Ave, North Hollywood, CA 91602, USA

Campbell, Alan — *Actor*
2554 Lincoln Blvd, #445, Venice, CA 90291, USA

Campbell, Allan McCulloch — *Biologist*
947 Mears Court, Stanford, CA 94305, USA

Campbell, Bill	*Mayor*
%Mayor's Office, City Hall, 55 Trinity Ave SW, Atlanta, GA 30335, USA	
Campbell, Bruce	*Actor*
212 Bell Canyon Road, Bell Canyon, CA 91307, USA	
Campbell, Charles J	*Businessman*
%Crystal Brands Inc, 404 5th Ave, New York, NY 10018, USA	
Campbell, Cheryl	*Actress*
%Michael Whitehall, 125 Gloucester Road, London SW7 4TE, England	
Campbell, Colin (Soupy)	*Hockey Coach*
%New York Rangers, Madison Square Garden, 2 Penn Plaza, New York, NY 10121, USA	
Campbell, Earl	*Football Player*
2937 Thousand Oaks, Austin, TX 78746, USA	
Campbell, Eldon	*Basketball Player*
17252 Hawthorne Blvd, #493, Torrance, CA 90504, USA	
Campbell, Frank B (Ted)	*Air Force General*
Cmdr, 12th Air Force, 5340 E Gafford, Davis Mountain Air Force Base, AZ 85707, USA	
Campbell, Gene	*Hockey Player*
1554 Wilshire Dr NE, Rochester, MN 55906, USA	
Campbell, Glen	*Singer*
28 Biltmore Estates, Phoenix, AZ 85016, USA	
Campbell, Hugh D	*Navy Admiral, Attorney*
%Judge Advocate General's Office, 200 Stovall St, Alexandria, VA 22332, USA	
Campbell, J Kermit	*Businessman*
%Herman Miller Inc, 855 E Main Ave, Zeeland, MI 49464, USA	
Campbell, Jack M	*Governor, NM*
PO Box 2208, Santa Fe, NM 87504, USA	
Campbell, James R	*Financier*
%Norwest Bank Minnesota, 6th & Marquette, Minneapolis, MN 55479, USA	
Campbell, Jim	*Hockey Player*
11 Carolyn Dr, Westborough, MA 01581, USA	
Campbell, John	*Harness Racing Driver*
%John D Campbell Stable, 823 Allison Dr, River Vale, NJ 07675, USA	
Campbell, Julia	*Actress*
%William Morris Agency, 151 S El Camino Dr, Beverly Hills, CA 90212, USA	
Campbell, Keith	*Biologist*
%Roslin Institute, Development/Reproduction Dept, Midlothian, Scotland	
Campbell, Kim	*Prime Minister, Canada*
24 Sussex Dr, Ottawa ON K1M OMS, Canada	
Campbell, Louis B	*Businessman*
%Textron Inc, 40 Westminster St, Providence, RI 02903, USA	
Campbell, Luther (Skywalker)	*Singer (2 Live Crew)*
%Famous Artists Agency, 1700 Broadway, #500, New York, NY 10019, USA	
Campbell, Marion	*Publisher*
%Atlantic Monthly Co, 745 Boylston St, Boston, MA 02116, USA	
Campbell, Milton	*Track Athlete*
1132 St Marks Place, Plainfield, NJ 07062, USA	
Campbell, Naomi	*Model, Singer, Actress*
%Women Inc, 107 Green St, New York, NY 10012, USA	
Campbell, Neve	*Actress*
%Performance Unlimited, 3-2401 Cliffe St, Courtenay BC V9N 2L5, Canada	
Campbell, Nicholas	*Actor*
1206 N Orange Grove, Los Angeles, CA 90046, USA	
Campbell, Patrick J	*Labor Leader*
%Carpenters & Joiners Union, 101 Constitution Ave NW, Washington, DC 20001, USA	
Campbell, Robert	*Architecture Critic*
%Boston Globe, Editorial Dept, 135 Morrissey Blvd, Boston, MA 02125, USA	
Campbell, Robert H	*Businessman*
%Sun Co, 10 Penn Center, 1801 Market St, Philadelphia, PA 19103, USA	
Campbell, Tevin	*Singer*
%Creative Artists Agency, 9830 Wilshire Blvd, Beverly Hills, CA 90212, USA	
Campbell, Tisha	*Actress*
%Writers & Artists, 924 Westwood Blvd, #900, Los Angeles, CA 90024, USA	
Campbell, Tony	*Basketball Player*
1445 Teaneck Road, Teaneck, NJ 07666, USA	
Campbell, William	*Actor*
21502 Velicate St, Woodland Hills, CA 91364, USA	
Campbell, William J	*Air Force General*
3267 Alex Findlay Place, Sarasota, FL 34240, USA	

C

Campbell - Campbell

Campbell, William R (Bill) — *Baseball Player*
133 S Hale St, Palatine, IL 60067, USA

Campion, Jane — *Movie Director*
%H Linstead Assoc, 9-13 Bronte Road, Bondi Junction NSW 2022, Australia

Campos, Antonio C — *Financier*
%Banco Central Hispano, 221 Ponce de Leon Ave, Hato Rey, PR 00917, USA

Canadeo, Tony — *Football Player*
1746 Carriage Court, Green Bay, WI 54304, USA

Canary, David — *Actor*
903 S Mansfield Ave, Los Angeles, CA 90036, USA

Canby, Vincent — *Movie Critic*
215 W 88th St, New York, NY 10024, USA

Candela, Felix — *Engineer, Architect*
6341 Wynbrook Way, Raleigh, NC 27612, USA

Candelaria, John R — *Baseball Player*
25732 Bucklestone Court, Laguna Hills, CA 92653, USA

Candeloro, Philippe — *Figure Skater*
42 Rue de Lourve, 75001 Paris, France

Candilis, Georges — *Architect*
17 Rue Campagne-Premiere, 75014 Paris, France

Candiotti, Tom — *Baseball Player*
5500 Sun Cloud Court, Concord, CA 94521, USA

Candoli, Conte — *Jazz Trumpeter*
%Thomas Cassidy, 0366 Horseshoe Dr, Basalt, CO 81621, USA

Canella, Guido — *Architect*
Via Revere 7, 20123 Milan, Italy

Canepa, John C — *Financier*
%Old Kent Financial, 1 Vandenberg Center, Grand Rapids, MI 49503, USA

Canestri, Giovanni Cardinal — *Religious Leader*
Archdiocese of Genoa-Bobbio, Piazza Matteotti 4, 16123 Genoa, Italy

Canfield, William N (Bill) — *Editorial Cartoonist*
143 Wayside Road, Tinton Falls, NJ 07724, USA

Canizales, Orlando — *Boxer*
807 Preston Road, Laredo, TX 78045, USA

Cannell, Stephen J — *Television Producer, Writer*
%Stephen J Cannell Productions, 7083 Hollywood Blvd, Los Angeles, CA 90028, USA

Cannon, Billy — *Football Player*
656 Lobdell Ave, Baton Rouge, LA 70806, USA

Cannon, Dyan — *Actress*
8033 Sunset Blvd, #254, Los Angeles, CA 90046, USA

Cannon, Freddy (Boom Boom) — *Singer, Songwriter*
%Cannon Productions, 18641 Cassandra St, Tarzana, CA 91356, USA

Cannon, Howard W — *Senator, NV*
6300 Evermay Dr, McLean, VA 22101, USA

Cannon, J D — *Actor*
%Gage Group, 9255 Sunset Blvd, #515, Los Angeles, CA 90069, USA

Cannon, Katherine — *Actress*
1310 Westholme Ave, Los Angeles, CA 90024, USA

Cannon, Robert H, Jr — *Aerospace Engineer*
%Stanford University, Aeronautics/Astronautics Dept, Stanford, CA 94305, USA

Canova, Diana — *Actress*
%Lemond, 5570 Old Highway 395 N, Carson City, NV 89707, USA

Canseco, Jose — *Baseball Player*
3025 Meadow Lane, Fort Lauderdale, FL 33331, USA

Cantalupo, James R — *Businessman*
%McDonald's Corp, 1 McDonald's Plaza, 1 Kroc Dr, Oak Brook, I 60523, USA

Cantarella, Paolo — *Businessman*
%Fiat SpA, Corso G Marconi 10/20, 10125 Turin, Italy

Cantlay, George G — *Army General*
501 Thomas Bransby, Kingsmill-on-the-James, Williamsburg, VA 23185, USA

Cantone, Vic — *Editorial Cartoonist*
%New York Daily News, Editorial Dept, 220 E 42nd St, New York, NY 10017, USA

Cantor, Charles R — *Molecular Biologist*
11 Bay St Road, #11, Boston, MA 02215, USA

Cantor, Tim — *Artist*
%Adrienne Editions, 377 Geary St, San Francisco, CA 94102, USA

Cantrell, Lana — *Singer*
300 E 71st St, New York, NY 10021, USA

Cantu, Carlos H *Businessman*
%ServiceMaster Cos, 1 ServiceMaster Road, Downers Grove, IL 60515, USA
Capa, Cornell *Photographer*
%International Center of Photography, 1130 5th Ave, New York, NY 10128, USA
Capalbo, Carmen C *Theater Producer, Director*
500 2nd Ave, New York, NY 10016, USA
Capecchi, Mario R *Biologist*
%University of Utah, Biology Dept, Salt Lake City, UT 84112, USA
Capen, Richard G, Jr *Publisher, Diplomat*
6077 San Elijo, Rancho Santa Fe, CA 92067, USA
Caperton, W Gaston, III *Governor, WV*
%Governor's Office, State Capitol, Charleston, WV 25305, USA
Capice, Philip C *Television Producer*
1359 Miller Dr, Los Angeles, CA 90069, USA
Capilla Perez, Joaquin *Diver*
Torres de Mixcoac, Lomas de Plateros, Mexico 19 DF, Mexico
Capleton *Singer*
%Agency Group, 1775 Broadway, #433, New York, NY 10019, USA
Caplin, Mortimer M *Government Official*
5610 Wisconsin Ave NW, #18-E, Bethesda, MD 20815, USA
Capobianco, Tito *Opera Director*
%Pittsburgh Opera Co, 711 Penn Ave, #800, Pittsburgh, PA 15222, USA
Caponera, John *Comedian*
%Messina/Baker/Miller, 7920 Sunset Blvd, #400, Los Angeles, CA 90046, USA
Caponi Young, Donna *Golfer*
2 Mack Road, Woburn, MA 01801, USA
Cappelletti, Gino *Football Player*
19 Louis Dr, Wellesley, MA 02181, USA
Cappelletti, John R *Football Player*
28791 Brant Lane, Laguna Niguel, CA 92677, USA
Capps, Steve *Computer Software Designer*
%Microsoft Corp, 1 Microsoft Way, Redmond, WA 98052, USA
Capps, Thomas E *Businessman*
%Dominion Resources, Riverfront Plaza West, 901 E Byrd St, Richmond, VA 23219, USA
Cappuccilli, Piero *Opera Singer*
%S A Gorlinsky, 33 Dover St, London W1X 4NJ, England
Capra, Frank, Jr *Movie Producer*
1447 S Jameson Lane, Santa Barbara, CA 93108, USA
Capra, Lee W (Buzz) *Baseball Player*
7112 Riverside Dr, Berwyn, IL 60402, USA
Capriati, Jennifer *Tennis Player*
5435 Blue Heron Lane, Wesley Chapel, FL 33543, USA
Caprio, Giuseppe Cardinal *Religious Leader*
Palazzo delle Congregazione Largo del Colonnato 3, 00193 Rome, Italy
Capshaw, Kate *Actress*
PO Box 869, Pacific Palisades, CA 90272, USA
Capucill, Terese *Dancer*
%Martha Graham Contemporary Dance Center, 316 E 63rd St, New York, NY 10021, USA
Cara, Irene *Singer*
%Talent Consultants Int'l, 1560 Broadway, #1308, New York, NY 10036, USA
Caras, Roger *Writer*
22108 Slab Bridge Road, Freeland, MD 21053, USA
Carasco, Joe (King) *Singer*
1851 Gulf Freeway S, #3, League City, TX 77573, USA
Caray, Harry C *Sportscaster*
%WGN-TV, Sports Dept, 2501 Bradley Place, Chicago, IL 60618, USA
Caray, Skip *Sportscaster*
%Turner Broadcasting System, 1050 Techwood Dr NW, Atlanta, GA 30318, USA
Carazo Odio, Rodrigo *President, Costa Rica; Educator*
%UN University for Peace, Rector's Office, Ciudad Colon, Costa Rica
Carbajal, Michael *Boxer*
914 E Filmore St, Phoenix, AZ 85006, USA
Carberry, Charles M *Attorney*
%Jones Davis Reeve Pogue, 599 Lexington Ave, New York, NY 10022, USA
Carberry, Deirdre *Ballerina*
%American Ballet Theater, 890 Broadway, New York, NY 10003, USA
Carberry, John Cardinal *Religious Leader*
4445 Lindell Blvd, St Louis, MO 63108, USA

C

Cantu - Carberry

Card, Michael *Banjoist, Pianist, Guitarist*
%Street Level Artists, 106 N Buffalo St, #200, Warsaw, IN 46580, USA

Carden, Joan M *Opera Singer*
%Jennifer Eddy, 596 St Kilda Road, #11, Melbourne 3004 VIC, Australia

Cardich, Augusto *Archeologist*
%University of La Plata, Archeology Dept, La Plata, Argentina

Cardiff, Jack *Cinematographer*
%L'Epine Smith Carney, Kent House, 87 Regent St, London W1R 7HF, England

Cardin, Pierre *Fashion Designer*
59 Rue Du Faubourg-Saint-Honore, 75008 Paris, France

Cardinale, Claudia *Actress*
Via Flaminia KW 77, Prima Porta, 00188 Rome, Italy

Cardona, Manuel *Physicist*
%Max-Planck-Institut, Heisenbergstr 1, 70569 Stuttgart, Germany

Cardoso, Fernando Henrique *President, Brazil*
Palacio do Planalto, Praca dos Tres Poderes, 70150 Brasilia DF, Brazil

Cardoza, Robert J *Association Executive*
%California State Automobile Assn, PO Box 422940, San Francisco, CA 94142, USA

Caretto-Brown, Patty *Swimmer*
16079 Mesquite Circle, Santa Ana, CA 92708, USA

Carew, Rodney C (Rod) *Baseball Player*
5144 E Crescent Dr, Anaheim, CA 92807, USA

Carey, D John *Businessman*
%Integrated Devices, 2975 Stender Way, Santa Clara, CA 95054, USA

Carey, Drew *Actor*
%Command Performance Entertainment, PO Box 31, Malverne, NY 11565, USA

Carey, George L *Archbishop, Canterbury*
%Lambeth Palace, London SE1 9JU, England

Carey, Harry, Jr *Actor*
PO Box 3256, Durango, CO 81302, USA

Carey, Hugh L *Governor, NY*
9 Prospect Place W, Brooklyn, NY 11217, USA

Carey, Jim *Hockey Player*
47 Kingman St, Weymouth, MA 02188, USA

Carey, John J *Businessman*
%Allendale Mutual Insurance, Allendale Park, Johnston, RI 02919, USA

Carey, Mariah *Singer*
%Horizon Ent, 421 W 54th St, #5, New York, NY 10019, USA

Carey, Michelle *Actress*
%H David Moss, 733 N Seward St, #PH, Los Angeles, CA 90038, USA

Carey, Philip *Actor*
427 N Canon Dr, #205, Beverly Hills, CA 90210, USA

Carey, Raymond B, Jr *Marine Corps General*
HqUSMC, 2 Navy Annex, Washington, DC 20380, USA

Carey, Richard E *Marine Corps General*
HqUSMC, 2 Navy Annex, Washington, DC 20380, USA

Carey, Ron *Actor*
419 N Larchmont Ave, Los Angeles, CA 90004, USA

Carey, Ronald R *Labor Official*
%International Teamsters Brotherhood, 25 Louisiana Ave NW, Washington, DC 20001, USA

Carey, William D *Publisher*
%Science Magazine, 1333 "H" St NW, 11th Floor, Washington, DC 20005, USA

Carey, William H *Religious Leader*
%National Gay Pentecostal Alliance, PO Box 1391, Schenectady, NY 12301, USA

Cargo, David F *Governor, NM*
6422 Concordia Road NE, Albuquerque, NM 87111, USA

Carillo, Mary *Sportscaster*
822 Boylston St, #203, Chestnut Hill, PA 02167, USA

Cariou, Len *Actor*
%Paradigm Agency, 10100 Santa Monica Blvd, #2500, Los Angeles, CA 90067, USA

Carithers, William, Jr *Physicist*
%Fermi Nat Acceleration Lab, D-Zero Collaboration, PO Box 500, Batavia, IL 60510, USA

Carl XVI Gustaf *King, Sweden*
Kungliga Slottet, Slottsbacken, 111 30 Stockholm, Sweden

Carle, Frankie *Pianist, Composer*
PO Box 7415, Mesa, AZ 85216, USA

Carlesimo, Pete J (P J) *Basketball Coach*
%Golden State Warriors, 7000 Coliseum Way, Oakland, CA 94621, USA

Carlile, Forbes — *Swimming Coach*
16 Cross St, Ryde NSW 2112, Australia

Carlin, George — *Comedian*
%Carlin Productions, 11911 San Vicente Blvd, #348, Los Angeles, CA 90049, USA

Carlin, John W — *Governor, KS*
18201 Allwood Terrace, Olney, MD 20832, USA

Carlin, Lynn — *Actress*
%David Shapira, 15301 Ventura Blvd, #345, Sherman Oaks, CA 91403, USA

Carlin, Thomas R — *Publisher*
%St Paul Pioneer Press, 55 E 4th St, St Paul, MN 55101, USA

Carling, William D C — *Rugby Player*
%Insights Ltd, 5 Chelsea Wharf, Lots Road, London SW10 0QJ, England

Carlisle, Belinda — *Singer, Songwriter*
23922 De Ville Way, Malibu, CA 90265, USA

Carlisle, Bob — *Singer, Songwriter*
%Ray Ware Artist Mgmt, 1102 W Main St, Franklin, TN 37064, USA

Carlisle, James — *Governor General, Antigua & Barbuda*
%Governor General's Office, Government House, St John's, Antigua

Carlisle, Kitty — *Singer, Actress*
32 E 64th St, New York, NY 10021, USA

Carlos, John — *Track Athlete*
68640 Tortuga Road, Cathedral City, CA 92234, USA

Carlot, Maxime — *Prime Minister, Vanuatu*
%Prime Minister's Office, PO Box 10, Port Vila, Vanuatu

Carlson, Arne H — *Governor, MN*
%Governor's Office, State Capitol Building, #130, Minneapolis, MN 55155, USA

Carlson, D H E — *Publisher*
%The Spectator, 44 Frid St, Hamilton ON L8N 3G3, Canada

Carlson, Dudley L — *Navy Admiral*
%Navy League, 2300 Wilson Blvd, Arlington, VA 22201, USA

Carlson, G Raymond — *Religious Leader*
%Assemblies of God, 1445 N Boonville Ave, Springfield, MO 65802, USA

Carlson, Jack W — *Association Executive*
%American Assn of Retired Persons, 1901 "K" St NW, Washington, DC 20006, USA

Carlson, John A — *Businessman*
%Cray Research, 655-A Lone Oak Dr, Eagan, MN 55121, USA

Carlson, Katrina — *Actress*
%Sara Bennett Agency, 6404 Hollywood Blvd, #316, Los Angeles, CA 90028, USA

Carlson, Linda — *Actress*
%Judy Schoen, 606 N Larchmont Blvd, #309, Los Angeles, CA 90004, USA

Carlson, Paulette — *Singer*
%Marathon Attractions, 24 Music Square W, #208, Nashville, TN 37203, USA

Carlsson, Ingvar G — *Prime Minister, Sweden*
Riksdagen, 100 12 Stockholm, Sweden

Carlton, Carl — *Singer*
%Randolph Enterprises, 26751 De Ville Way, Malibu, CA 90265, USA

Carlton, Paul K — *Air Force General*
2025 Shoreline Towers, 900 Gulf Shore Dr, Destin, FL 32541, USA

Carlton, Steven N (Steve) — *Baseball Player*
PO Box 736, Durango, CO 81302, USA

Carlucci, Dave — *Singer (Danny & The Juniors)*
%Joe Terry Mgmt, PO Box 1017, Turnersville, NJ 08012, USA

Carlucci, Frank C, III — *Businessman; Secretary, Defense*
%Carlyle Group, 1001 Pennsylvania Ave NW, Washington, DC 20004, USA

Carlyle, Joan H — *Opera Singer*
The Griffin, Ruthin Clwyd, North Wales, England

Carman — *Singer*
%Carman Ministries, PO Box 5093, Brentwood, TN 37024, USA

Carman, Gregory W — *Judge; Representative, NY*
%US Court of International Trade, 1 Federal Plaza, New York, NY 10278, USA

Carmen, Eric — *Singer, Songwriter*
%Carmen-Daniels Mgmt, 1015 N Doheny Dr, #1, Los Angeles, CA 90069, USA

Carmen, Julie — *Actress*
%Metropolitan Talent Agency, 4526 Wilshire Blvd, Los Angeles, CA 90010, USA

Carmichael, Harold — *Football Player*
38 Birch Lane, Glassboro, NJ 08028, USA

Carmichael, Ian — *Actor*
%London Mgmt, 2-4 Noel St, London W1V 3RB, England

C

Carlile - Carmichael

Carmody, Thomas R	*Businessman*
%American Business Products, PO Box 105684, Atlanta, GA 30348, USA	
Carnahan, Mel	*Governor, MO*
PO Box 698, Rolla, MO 65402, USA	
Carne, Jean	*Singer*
%Walt Reeder, 1516 Redwood Lane, Wynacote, PA 19095, USA	
Carne, Judy	*Comedienne*
2 Horatio St, #10-N, New York, NY 10014, USA	
Carner, JoAnne	*Golfer*
3030 S Ocean Blvd, Palm Beach, FL 33480, USA	
Carnes, Kim	*Singer, Songwriter*
2031 Old Natchez Trace, Franklin, TN 37069, USA	
Carnesale, Albert	*Educator*
%University of California, Chancellor's Office, Los Angeles, CA 90024, USA	
Carnesecca, Lou	*Basketball Coach*
%St John's University, Athletic Dept, Jamaica, NY 11439, USA	
Carnevale, Bernard L (Ben)	*Basketball Coach*
5109 Dorset Mews, Williamsburg, VA 23188, USA	
Carnevale, Mark	*Golfer*
24 Loggerhead Lane, Ponte Vedra, FL 32082, USA	
Carney, Art	*Actor*
143 Kingfisher Lane, Westbrook, CT 06498, USA	
Carney, John	*Football Player*
2823 Camino del Mar, Del Mar, CA 92014, USA	
Carney, Thomas P	*Army General*
Deputy Chief of Staff for Personnel, US Army, Washington, DC 20310, USA	
Carnoy, Martin	*Economist*
%Stanford University, Economic Studies Center, Stanford, CA 94305, USA	
Caro, Anthony	*Sculptor*
111 Frognal, Hampstead, London NW3, England	
Caro, Robert A	*Writer*
%Robert A Caro Assoc, 250 W 57th St, New York, NY 10107, USA	
Caroline	*Princess, Monaco*
La Maison de la Source, St Reme de Provence, France	
Caroline, J C	*Football Player*
2501 Stanford, Champaign, IL 61820, USA	
Caron, Leslie	*Actress*
6 Rue De Bellechaisse, 75007 Paris, France	
Carothers, Robert L	*Educator*
%University of Rhode Island, President's Office, Kingston, RI 02881, USA	
Carothers, Veronica	*Actress*
6182 Shawnee Road, Westminster, CA 92683, USA	
Carp, Daniel A	*Businessman*
%Eastman Kodak Co, 343 State St, Rochester, NY 14650, USA	
Carpenter, Bob	*Hockey Player*
PO Box 451, Alton Bay, NH 03810, USA	
Carpenter, Carleton	*Actor*
RD 2, Chardavoyne Road, Warwick, NY 10990, USA	
Carpenter, Dave	*Editorial Cartoonist*
PO Box 520, Emmetsburg, IA 50536, USA	
Carpenter, David R	*Businessman*
%Transamerica Occidental Life, 1150 S Olive St, Los Angeles, CA 90015, USA	
Carpenter, Edmund M	*Businessman*
%General Signal Corp, 1 High Ridge Park, Stamford, CT 06905, USA	
Carpenter, John H	*Movie Director*
%International Creative Mgmt, 8942 Wilshire Blvd, Beverly Hills, CA 90211, USA	
Carpenter, John M	*Opera Singer*
%Maurel Enterprises, 225 W 34th St, #1012, New York, NY 10122, USA	
Carpenter, John W, III	*Air Force General*
5100 John D Ryan Blvd, #2611, San Antonio, TX 78245, USA	
Carpenter, Liz	*Women's Activist*
116 Skyline Dr, Austin, TX 78746, USA	
Carpenter, M Scott	*Astronaut*
PO Box 3161, Vail, CO 81658, USA	
Carpenter, Marj C	*Religious Leader*
%Presbyterian Church (USA), 100 Witherspoon, Louisville, KY 40202, USA	
Carpenter, Mary Chapin	*Singer, Songwriter, Guitarist*
%Borman Entertainment, 1250 6th St, #401, Santa Monica, CA 90401, USA	

Carpenter, Richard — *Pianist, Singer, Songwriter*
9386 Raviller Dr, Downey, CA 90240, USA

Carpenter, Teresa — *Journalist*
%Village Voice, Editorial Dept, 36 Cooper Square, New York, NY 10003, USA

Carper, Thomas R — *Governor, DE*
%Governor's Office, Tatnall Building, Dover, DE 19901, USA

Carr of Hadley, L Robert — *Government Official, England*
14 North Court, Great Peter St, London SW1, England

Carr, Alan — *Movie Producer, Agent*
%Alan Carr Enterprises, PO Box 691670, Los Angeles, CA 90064, USA

Carr, Antoine — *Basketball Player*
%Utah Jazz, Delta Center, 301 W South Temple, Salt Lake City, UT 84101, USA

Carr, Austin — *Basketball Player*
32659 Allenbury Dr, Solon, OH 44139, USA

Carr, Caleb — *Writer*
%Random House, 201 E 50th St, New York, NY 10022, USA

Carr, Catherine (Cathy) — *Swimmer*
409 E 10th St, Davis, CA 95616, USA

Carr, Charles L G (Chuck), Jr — *Baseball Player*
%Florida Marlins, 100 NE 3rd Ave, Fort Lauderdale, FL 33301, USA

Carr, Darleen — *Actress*
1604 N Vista Ave, Los Angeles, CA 90046, USA

Carr, Gerald P (Jerry) — *Astronaut*
%CAMUS Inc, PO Box 919, Huntsville, AR 72740, USA

Carr, Henry — *Track Athlete*
11642 Beaverland St, Detroit, MI 48239, USA

Carr, Jane — *Actress*
6200 Mt Angelus Dr, Los Angeles, CA 90042, USA

Carr, Kenneth M — *Navy Admiral*
2322 Fort Scott Dr, Arlington, VA 22202, USA

Carr, Kenny — *Basketball Player*
24421 SW Valley View Dr, West Linn, OR 97068, USA

Carr, Michael Leon (M L) — *Basketball Player, Coach, Executive*
%Boston Celtics, 151 Merrimac St, #500, Boston, MA 02114, USA

Carr, Paul — *Actor*
%H David Moss, 733 N Seward St, #PH, Los Angeles, CA 90038, USA

Carr, Vikki — *Singer*
3102 Iron Stone Lane, San Antonio, TX 78230, USA

Carradine, David — *Actor*
%David Shapira, 15301 Ventura Blvd, #345, Sherman Oaks, CA 91403, USA

Carradine, Keith — *Actor, Singer, Songwriter*
PO Box 460, Placerville, CO 81430, USA

Carradine, Robert — *Actor*
355 S Grand Ave, #4150, Los Angeles, CA 90071, USA

Carreker, James — *Businessman*
%Aspect Telecommunications, 1730 Fox Dr, San Jose, CA 95131, USA

Carreno, Jose Manuel — *Ballet Dancer*
%Royal Ballet, Bow St, London WC2E 9DD, England

Carreno, Manuel — *Ballet Dancer*
%American Ballet Theatre, 890 Broadway, New York, NY 10003, USA

Carrera, Barbara — *Actress*
%Gold Marshak Liedtke, 3500 W Olive Ave, #1400, Burbank, CA 91505, USA

Carreras, Jose — *Opera Singer*
%Opera Caballe, Via Augusta 59, 08006 Barcelona, Spain

Carrere, Tia — *Actress*
816 N La Cienega Blvd, #8638, Los Angeles, CA 90069, USA

Carrey, Jim — *Actor*
%United Talent Agency, 9560 Wilshire Blvd, #500, Beverly Hills, CA 90212, USA

Carrier, George F — *Applied Mathematician*
Rice Spring Lane, Wayland, MA 01778, USA

Carrier, Mark A — *Football Player*
2895 Deerfield, #101, Lake Orion, MI 48360, USA

Carriere, Jean P J — *Writer*
Les Broussanes, Domessargues, 30350 Ledignan, France

Carriere, Mathieu — *Actor*
%Agentur Alexander, Lamontstr 9, 81679 Munich, Germany

Carrigg, James A — *Businessman*
%New York State Electric & Gas, 4500 Vestal Parkway E, Binghamton, NY 13902, USA

Carril, Pete — *Basketball Coach*
%Sacramento Kings, 1 Sports Parkway, Sacramento, CA 95834, USA

Carrillo, Elpidia — *Actress*
%Bresler Kelly Assoc, 15760 Ventura Blvd, #1730, Encino, CA 91436, USA

Carrington, Peter A R — *Government Official, England*
Manor House, Bledlow near Aylesbury, Bucks HP17 9PE, England

Carroll, Bruce — *Singer, Songwriter*
%William Morris Agency, 2100 West End Ave, #1000, Nashville, TN 37203, USA

Carroll, Charles A — *Businessman*
%Rubbermaid Inc, 1147 Akron Road, Wooster, OH 44691, USA

Carroll, Charles O (Chuck) — *Football Player*
%Carroll Rindal Kennedy Schuck, 1200 Westlake Ave N, Seattle, WA 98109, USA

Carroll, Diahann — *Singer, Actress*
%Sterling/Winters, 1900 Ave of Stars, #1640, Los Angeles, CA 90067, USA

Carroll, Earl W — *Labor Official*
%United Garment Workers of America, PO Box 239, Hermitage, TN 37076, USA

Carroll, Joe Barry — *Basketball Player*
%Denver Nuggets, McNichols Arena, 1635 Clay St, Denver, CO 80204, USA

Carroll, John — *Attorney*
%Rogers & Wells, 200 Park Ave, New York, NY 10166, USA

Carroll, John B — *Psychologist*
409 Elliott Road N, Chapel Hill, NC 27514, USA

Carroll, John S — *Editor*
%Baltimore Sun, Editorial Dept, 501 N Calvert St, Baltimore, MD 21202, USA

Carroll, Julian M — *Governor, KY*
%Carroll Assoc, 25 Fountain Place, Frankfort, KY 40601, USA

Carroll, Kent J — *Navy Admiral*
%Country Club of North Carolina, 1600 Morganton Road, #30-X, Pinehurst, NC 28374, USA

Carroll, L Vane, Jr — *Financier*
%Blazer Financial Services, 8900 Grand Oak Circle, Tampa, FL 33637, USA

Carroll, Leonard M — *Financier*
%Integra Financial Corp, PO Box 837, Pittsburgh, PA 15230, USA

Carroll, Lester — *Cartoonist (Our Boarding House)*
21100 Beachwood Dr, Rocky River, OH 44116, USA

Carroll, Pat — *Actress*
14 Old Tavern Lane, Harwich Port, MA 02646, USA

Carroll, Pete — *Football Coach*
%New England Patriots, Foxboro Stadium, Rt 1, Foxboro, MA 02035, USA

Carroll, Robert J — *Businessman*
%Laclede Gas Co, 720 Olive St, St Louis, MO 63101, USA

Carruth, John Campbell — *Businessman*
%TNT Freightways, 9700 Higgins Road, Rosemont, IL 60018, USA

Carruthers, Garrey E — *Governor, NM*
PO Box 7090, Las Cruces, NM 88006, USA

Carruthers, James H (Red) — *Skier*
8 Malone Ave, Garnerville, NY 10923, USA

Carruthers, Kitty — *Figure Skater*
22 E 71st St, New York, NY 10021, USA

Carruthers, Peter — *Figure Skater*
22 E 71st St, New York, NY 10021, USA

Carruthers, Robert — *Electrical Engineer*
11 Badgers Copse, Radley, Abingdon, Oxon OX14 3BQ, England

Carry, Julius J, III — *Actor*
%Innovative Artists, 1999 Ave of Stars, #2850, Los Angeles, CA 90067, USA

Carsey, Marcia L P — *Television Producer*
%Carsey-Warner Productions, 4024 Radford Ave, Bldg 3, Studio City, CA 91604, USA

Carson, David — *Movie Director*
10474 Santa Monica Blvd, Los Angeles, CA 90025, USA

Carson, David E A — *Financier*
%People's Bank, 850 Main St, Bridgeport, CT 06604, USA

Carson, John David — *Actor*
145 S Fairfax Ave, #310, Los Angeles, CA 90036, USA

Carson, Johnny — *Entertainer*
6962 Wildlife Road, Malibu, CA 90265, USA

Carson, William H (Willie) — *Thoroughbred Racing Jockey*
Minster House, Barnsley, Cirencester, Glos, England

Carter, Anthony — *Football Player*
69 Dunbar Road, Palm Beach Gardens, FL 33418, USA

Carter, Arthur L — *Publisher*
%Nation Magazine, 72 5th Ave, New York, NY 10011, USA

Carter, Benny — *Jazz Alto Saxophonist, Composer*
8321 Skyline Dr, Los Angeles, CA 90046, USA

Carter, Betty — *Singer, Songwriter*
%Bet-Car Booking, 307 Lake St, San Francisco, CA 94118, USA

Carter, Carlene — *Singer, Songwriter*
%Fitzgerald-Hartley, 1908 Wedgewood Dr, Nashville, TN 37212, USA

Carter, Clarence — *Singer*
%Insight Talent, 2300 E Independence Blvd, Charlotte, NC 28205, USA

Carter, Cris — *Football Player*
%Minnesota Vikings, 9520 Viking Dr, Eden Prairie, MN 55344, USA

Carter, Deana — *Singer, Songwriter*
%Left Bank Mgmt, 6255 Sunset Blvd, #1111, Los Angeles, CA 90028, USA

Carter, Dexter — *Football Player*
385 N Wolfe Road, #221, Sunnyvale, CA 94086, USA

Carter, Dixie — *Actress*
%Bresler Kelly Assoc, 15760 Ventura Blvd, #1730, Encino, CA 91436, USA

Carter, Don — *Bowler*
9895 SW 96th St, Miami, FL 33176, USA

Carter, Donald — *Basketball Executive*
%Dallas Mavericks, Reunion Arena, 777 Sports St, Dallas, TX 75207, USA

Carter, E Graydon — *Editor*
%Vanity Fair Magazine, Editorial Dept, 350 Madison Ave, New York, NY 10017, USA

Carter, Elliott C, Jr — *Composer*
31 W 12th St, New York, NY 10011, USA

Carter, Frank — *Labor Leader*
%Glass Molders Pottery Plastics Union, 608 E Baltimore Pike, Media, PA 19063, USA

Carter, Frederick J (Fred) — *Basketball Player, Coach*
777 W Germantown Pike, #1008, Plymouth Meeting, PA 19462, USA

Carter, G Emmett Cardinal — *Religious Leader*
%Archdiocese of Toronto, 355 Church St, Toronto ON M5B 1Z8, Canada

Carter, Gary E — *Baseball Player*
15 Huntly Dr, Palm Beach Gardens, FL 33418, USA

Carter, Herbert E — *Biochemist, Educator*
2401 Cerrada de Promesa, Tucson, AZ 85718, USA

Carter, Howard — *Basketball Player*
7572 Hanks Dr, Baton Rouge, LA 70812, USA

Carter, Jack — *Comedian, Actor*
1023 Chevy Chase Dr, Beverly Hills, CA 90210, USA

Carter, James — *Jazz Saxophonist*
%American International Artists, 315 E 62nd St, #600, New York, NY 10021, USA

Carter, James Earl (Jimmy), Jr — *President, USA*
%Carter Presidential Center, 1 Copenhill Ave NE, Atlanta, GA 30307, USA

Carter, John Mack — *Editor*
%Good Housekeeping Magazine, Editorial Dept, 959 8th Ave, New York, NY 10019, USA

Carter, Joseph C (Joe) — *Baseball Player*
3000 W 117th St, Leawood, KS 66211, USA

Carter, Ki-Jana — *Football Player*
254 Crosswind Dr, Westerville, OH 43081, USA

Carter, Lynda — *Actress*
9200 Harrington Dr, Potomac, MD 20854, USA

Carter, Marshall N — *Financier*
%State Street Bank & Trust, 225 Franklin St, Boston, MA 02110, USA

Carter, Mel — *Actor*
%Film Artists, 7080 Hollywood Blvd, #1118, Los Angeles, CA 90028, USA

Carter, Mel — *Singer*
%Bowen Agency, 504 W 168th St, New York, NY 10032, USA

Carter, Michael — *Football Player*
3324 Flintmont Dr, San Jose, CA 95148, USA

Carter, Nell — *Actress, Singer*
%Sterling/Winters, 1900 Ave of Stars, #1640, Los Angeles, CA 90067, USA

Carter, Powell F, Jr — *Navy Admiral*
699 Fillmore St, Harpers Ferry, WV 25425, USA

Carter, Ronald L (Ron) — *Jazz Bassist, Composer*
%Bridge Agency, 35 Clark St, A-5, Brooklyn, NY 11201, USA

Carter, Rosalynn S — *Wife of US President*
1 Woodland Dr, Plains, GA 31780, USA

C

Carter - Carter

Carter, Rubin *Football Player*
PO Box 1616, College Park, MD 20741, USA

Carter, Rubin (Hurricane) *Boxer*
1313 Brookedge Dr, Hamlin, NY 14464, USA

Carter, Thomas *Television Director*
10958 Strathmore Dr, Los Angeles, CA 90024, USA

Carter, W Hodding, III *Government Official*
211 S Saint Asaph St, Alexandria, VA 22314, USA

Carter, William G (Bill), III *Army General*
Chief of Staff, Allied Forces Southern Europe, APO, AE 09620, USA

Carteri, Rosana *Opera Singer*
%Angel Records, 810 7th Ave, New York, NY 10019, USA

Carteris, Gabrielle *Actress*
662 N Van Ness Ave, #305, Los Angeles, CA 90004, USA

Cartier-Bresson, Henri *Photographer*
%Magnum Photos, 5 Passage River, 75011 Paris, France

Cartland, Barbara H *Writer*
Camfield Place, Hatfield, Herts AL9 6JE, England

Cartwright, Angela *Actress*
4330 Bakman St, North Hollywood, CA 91602, USA

Cartwright, Bill *Basketball Player, Executive*
2222 Francisco Dr, #510, El Dorado Hills, CA 95762, USA

Cartwright, Carol A *Educator*
%Kent State University, President's Office, Kent, OH 44242, USA

Cartwright, Lynn *Actress*
%Don Gerler, 3349 Cahuenga Blvd W, #1, Los Angeles, CA 90068, USA

Cartwright, Nancy *Actress*
%Artists Group, 10100 Santa Monica Blvd, #2490, Los Angeles, CA 90067, USA

Cartwright, Veronica *Actress*
4342 Bakman Ave, North Hollywood, CA 91602, USA

Carty, Ricardo A J (Rico) *Baseball Player*
5 Ens Enriquillo, San Pedro de Macoris, Dominican Republic

Caruana, Patrick P (Pat) *Air Force General*
Vice Commander, Air Force Space Command, Peterson Air Force Base, CO 80914, USA

Caruso, Anthony *Actor*
1706 Mandeville Lane, Los Angeles, CA 90049, USA

Caruso, David *Actor*
%United Talent Agency, 9560 Wilshire Blvd, #500, Beverly Hills, CA 90212, USA

Caruso, Michael J *Editor*
%Los Angeles Magazine, 1888 Century Park West, Los Angeles, CA 90067, USA

Carvel, Elbert N *Governor, DE*
Clayton Ave, Laurel, DE 19956, USA

Carver, Brent *Actor*
%Live Entertainment, 1500 Broadway, #902, New York, NY 10036, USA

Carver, Johnny *Singer*
%House of Talent, 9 Lucy Lane, Sherwood, AR 72120, USA

Carver, Martin G *Businessman*
%Bandag Inc, Bandag Center, 2905 N Highway 61, Muscatine, IA 52761, USA

Carver, Randall *Actor*
%Tyler Kjar, 10643 Riverside Dr, Toluca Lake, CA 91602, USA

Carver, Richard M P *Army Field Marshal, England*
Wood End House, Wickham near Fareham, Hants PO17 6JZ, England

Carver, Shante *Football Player*
2152 E Rosarito Dr, Tempe, AZ 85281, USA

Carvey, Dana *Comedian*
775 E Blithedale Ave, #501, Mill Valley, CA 94941, USA

Carville, C James, Jr *Political Consultant*
%Carville Begala, 112 5th St SE, #112, Washington, DC 20003, USA

Cary, W Sterling *Religious Leader*
206 Lemoyne Parkway, Oak Park, IL 60302, USA

Casablancas, John *Model Agency Executive*
%Elite Model Mgmt, 111 E 22nd St, #200, New York, NY 10010, USA

Casadesus, Jean Claude *Conductor*
23 Blvd de la Liberte, 59800 Lille, France

Casals, Rosemary (Rosie) *Tennis Player*
%Sportswoman Inc, PO Box 537, Sausalito, CA 94966, USA

Casanova, Leonard J (Len) *Football Coach*
2611 Windsor Circle W, Eugene, OR 97405, USA

Casanova, Thomas R (Tommy) — *Football Player*
157 Fox Squirrel Lane, Crowley, LA 70526, USA

Casares, Rick — *Football Player*
5801 Marine St, Tampa, FL 33609, USA

Casaroli, Agostino Cardinal — *Religious Leader*
%Secretary of State's Office, 00120 Vatican City

Casbarian, John — *Architect*
%Taft Architects, 2444 Times Blvd, #320, Houston, TX 77005, USA

Case, Dean W — *Businessman*
%Reliance Insurance, 3 Benjamin Franklin Parkway, Philadelphia, PA 19102, USA

Case, Scott — *Football Player*
1262 Owen Circle, Buford, GA 30518, USA

Case, Walter, Jr — *Harness Racing Driver*
142 Summer St, Lisbon Falls, ME 04252, USA

Casey, Albert V — *Government Official, Businessman*
%Southern Methodist University, Cox Business School, Dallas, TX 75275, USA

Casey, Jeremiah E — *Financier*
%First Maryland Bancorp, 25 S Charles St, Baltimore, MD 21201, USA

Casey, John D — *Writer*
%University of Virginia, English Dept, Charlottesville, VA 22903, USA

Casey, Jon — *Hockey Player*
%St Louis Blues, Kiel Center, 1401 Clark Ave, St Louis, MO 63103, USA

Casey, Ronald B — *Journalist*
%Birmingham News, Editorial Dept, PO Box 2553, Birmingham, AL 35202, USA

Cash, Gerald C — *Governor General, Bahamas*
4 Bristol St, PO Box N-476, Nassau, Bahamas

Cash, Johnny — *Singer, Songwriter*
%House of Cash, 700 E Main St, Hendersonvlle, TN 37075, USA

Cash, June Carter — *Singer, Guitarist*
%House of Cash, 700 E Main St, Hendersonvlle, TN 37075, USA

Cash, Pat — *Tennis Player*
281 Clarence St, Sydney NSW 2000, Australia

Cash, R D — *Businessman*
%Questar Corp, 180 E 1st S, Salt Lake City, UT 84111, USA

Cash, Rosanne — *Singer, Songwriter*
%Danny Kahn, 326 Carlton Ave, #3, Brooklyn, NY 11205, USA

Cash, Tommy — *Singer, Songwriter*
%Capitol Mgmt, 1300 Division St, #200, Nashville, TN 37203, USA

Cashen, J Frank — *Baseball Executive*
%New York Mets, Shea Stadium, Flushing, NY 11368, USA

Cashman, John, Jr — *Thoroughbred Racing Executive*
PO Box 11889, Lexington, KY 40578, USA

Cashman, Wayne — *Hockey Player, Coach*
4 Oakwood Place, Voorhees, NJ 08043, USA

Casimir, Oye Mba — *Prime Minister, Gabon*
%Prime Minister's Office, Boite Postale 546, Libreville, Gabon

Caskey, C Thomas — *Geneticist, Biologist*
%Baylor College of Medicine, Molecular Genetics Dept, Houston, TX 77030, USA

Caslavska, Vera — *Gymnast*
SVS Sparta Prague, Korunovacni 29, Prague 7, Czech Republic

Casoria, Giuseppe Cardinal — *Religious Leader*
Via Pancrazio Pfeiffer 10, 00193 Rome, Italy

Casper, David J (Dave) — *Football Player*
291 Trappers Pass, Chanhassen, MN 55317, USA

Casper, Gerhard — *Educator*
%Stanford University, President's Office, Stanford, CA 94305, USA

Casper, John H — *Astronaut*
%NASA, Johnson Space Center, 2101 NASA Road, Houston, TX 77058, USA

Casper, William E (Billy) — *Golfer*
PO Box 1088, Chula Vista, CA 91912, USA

Caspersen, Finn M W — *Financier*
%Beneficial Corp, PO Box 1551, Wilmington, DE 19899, USA

Caspersson, Tobjorn O — *Biochemist, Cancer Specialist*
Emanuel Birkes Vag 2, 144 00 Ronninge, Sweden

Cass, Christopher — *Actor*
%Halpern Assoc, 12304 Santa Monica Blvd, #104, Los Angeles, CA 90025, USA

Cassady, Howard (Hopalong) — *Football Player*
539 Severn Ave, Tampa, FL 33606, USA

Casanova - Cassady

Cassavetes, Nick	*Actor, Director*
22223 Buena Ventura St, Woodland Hills, CA 91364, USA	
Cassel, Jean-Pierre	*Actor*
%International Creative Mgmt, 76 Oxford St, London W1N 0AX, England	
Cassel, Seymour	*Actor*
2800 Neilson Way, #1601, Santa Monica, CA 90405, USA	
Cassel, Walter	*Opera Singer*
%Indiana University, Music School, Bloomington, IN 47401, USA	
Casselio, Kathleen	*Opera Singer*
%Herbert Breslin, 119 W 57th St, New York, NY 10019, USA	
Cassell, Sam	*Basketball Player*
3315 Oakmont Dr, Sugar Land, TX 77479, USA	
Cassels, A James H	*Army Field Marshal, England*
Hamble End, Higham Road, Barrow, Bury Saint Edmunds, Suffolk, England	
Cassidy, David	*Actor, Singer*
3799 Las Vegas Blvd S, Las Vegas, NV 89109, USA	
Cassidy, Edward I Cardinal	*Religious Leader*
%Pontifical Council for Christian Unity, 00120 Vatican City	
Cassidy, Joanna	*Actress*
133 N Irving Blvd, Los Angeles, CA 90004, USA	
Cassidy, Patrick	*Actor*
701 N Oakhurst Dr, Beverly Hills, CA 90210, USA	
Cassidy, Shaun	*Actor, Singer*
19425 Shirley Court, Tarzana, CA 91356, USA	
Cassilly, Richard	*Opera Singer*
%Boston University, Music Dept, 855 Commonwealth Ave, Boston, MA 02215, USA	
Cassini, Oleg L	*Fashion Designer*
3 W 57th St, New York, NY 10019, USA	
Casson, Hugh Maxwell	*Architect*
6 Hereford Mansions, Hereford Road, London W2 5BA, England	
Castaneda, Carlos	*Writer, Anthropologist*
%University of California Press, 2121 Berkeley Way, Berkeley, CA 94704, USA	
Castaneda, Jorge A	*Government Official, Mexico*
Anillo Periferico Sur 3180, #1120, Jardines del Pedregal, 01900 Mexico	
Casteen, John T, III	*Educator*
%University of Virginia, President's Office, Charlottesville, VA 22906, USA	
Castel, Nico	*Opera Singer*
%RPA Mgmt, 4 Adelaide Lane, Washingtonville, NY 10992, USA	
Castelli, Leo	*Art Dealer*
%Leo Castelli Gallery, 420 W Broadway, New York, NY 10012, USA	
Castellini, Clateo	*Businessman*
%Becton Dickinson Co, 1 Becton Dr, Franklin Lakes, NJ 07417, USA	
Castilla, Vinicio S (Vinny)	*Baseball Player*
%Colorado Rockies, 2001 Blake St, Denver, CO 80205, USA	
Castille, Jeremiah	*Football Player*
%Praise & Worship Ministries, 701 26th Ave, Phoenix City, AL 36869, USA	
Castillo Lara, Rosalio Jose Cardinal	*Religious Leader*
%Pontifical Commission for Vatican City, 00120 Vatican City	
Castle of Blackburn, Barbara A	*Government Official, England*
%House of Lords, Westminster, London SW1A 0PW, England	
Castleman, E Riva	*Museum Curator*
%Museum of Modern Art, 11 W 53rd St, New York, NY 10019, USA	
Castro Ruz, Fidel	*President, Cuba*
%Palacio del Gobierno, Plaza de la Revolucion, Havana, Cuba	
Castro Ruz, Raul	*Prime Minister, Cuba; Army General*
%First Vice President's Office, Plaza de la Revolucion, Havana, Cuba	
Castro, Emilio	*Religious Leader*
%World Council of Churches, 475 Riverside Dr, New York, NY 10115, USA	
Castro, Raul H	*Governor, AZ*
1433 E Thomas St, Phoenix, AZ 85014, USA	
Catacosinos, William J	*Businessman*
%Long Island Lighting Co, 175 E Old Country Road, Hicksville, NY 11801, USA	
Catalano, Eduardo F	*Architect*
44 Grozier Road, Cambridge, MA 02138, USA	
Catalona, William J	*Urologist*
%Washington University School of Medicine, Urology Division, St Louis, MO 63110, USA	
Catanzaro, Tony	*Dancer*
1809 Ponce De Leon Blvd, Miami, FL 33134, USA	

Catell, Robert B — *Businessman*
%Brooklyn Union Gas, 1 Metrotech Center, Brooklyn, NY 11201, USA

Cates, Georgina — *Actress*
%William Morris Agency, 151 S El Camino Dr, Beverly Hills, CA 90212, USA

Cates, Gilbert — *Movie, Television Director, Producer*
%Gilbert Cates Productions, 10920 Wilshire Blvd, #600, Los Angeles, CA 90024, USA

Cates, Phoebe — *Actress*
1636 3rd Ave, #309, New York, NY 10128, USA

Cathcart, Patti — *Singer (Tuck & Patti)*
%Monterey International, 200 W Superior St, #202, Chicago, IL 60610, USA

Catlett, Mary Jo — *Actress*
4357 Farmdale Ave, North Hollywood, CA 91604, USA

Cato, Kelvin — *Basketball Player*
%Portland Trail Blazers, 1 N Center Court, #200, Portland, OR 97227, USA

Cato, Robert Milton — *Prime Minister, Saint Vincent*
PO Box 138, Ratho Mill, Saint Vincent & Grenadines

Caton-Jones, Michael — *Movie Director*
%Enigma Films, Pinewood Studios, Ivor Heath, Iver, Bucks SL0 0NH, England

Cattani, Richard J — *Publisher*
%Christian Science Monitor, 1 Norway St, Boston, MA 02115, USA

Catto of Cairncatto, Stephen G — *Financier*
%Morgan Grenfell Group, 23 Great Winchester St, London EC2P 2AX, England

Catto, Henry E, Jr — *Diplomat*
110 E Crockett St, San Antonio, TX 78205, USA

Cattrall, Kim — *Actress*
PO Box 492354, Los Angeles, CA 90049, USA

Caulfield, Lore — *Fashion Designer*
2228 Cotner Ave, Los Angeles, CA 90064, USA

Caulfield, Maxwell — *Actor*
340 E 64th St, #25, New York, NY 10021, USA

Caulo, Ralph D — *Publisher*
%Harcourt Brace Jovanovich, 6277 Sea Harbor Dr, Orlando, FL 32887, USA

Causewell, Duane — *Basketball Player*
%Sacramento Kings, 1 Sports Parkway, Sacramento, CA 95834, USA

Causley, Charles S — *Writer*
2 Cyprus Well, Launceston, Cornwall PL15 8BT, England

Cauthen, Steve — *Thoroughbred Racing Jockey*
%Cauthen Ranch, RFD, Boone County, Walton, KY 41094, USA

Cavaiani, Jon R — *Vietnam War Army Hero (CMH)*
10830 Yosemite Blvd, Waterford, CA 95386, USA

Cavanaugh, James H — *Government Official*
%White House, 1600 Pennsylvania Ave NW, Washington, DC 20500, USA

Cavanaugh, Joe — *Hockey Player*
25 Nathaniel Greene Dr, East Greenwich, RI 02818, USA

Cavanaugh, Page — *Musician*
5442 Woodman Ave, Van Nuys, CA 91401, USA

Cavaretta, Philip J (Phil) — *Baseball Player*
7225 Tara Dr, Villa Rica, GA 30180, USA

Cavazos, Lauro F — *Secretary, Education*
173 Annursnac Hill Road, Concord, MA 01742, USA

Cavett, Dick — *Entertainer*
%Conversation Co, 697 Middle Neck Road, Great Neck, NY 11023, USA

Cavezza, Carmen J — *Army General*
Commanding General, I Corps & Fort Lewis, Fort Lewis, WA 98433, USA

Cawley, Charles W — *Financier*
%MNBA America Bank, 1100 N King St, Wilmington, DE 19884, USA

Cawley, W Rex — *Track Athlete*
5850 Paseo de la Cumbre, Yorba Linda, CA 92887, USA

Cayetano, Benjamin J — *Governor, HI*
%Governor's Office, State Capitol Building, #500, Honolulu, HI 96813, USA

Cazenove, Christopher — *Actor*
32 Bolingbroke Grove, London SW11, England

Ce, Marco Cardinal — *Religious Leader*
%Divine Worship & Sacraments, Clergy, 00120 Vatican City

Ceballos, Cedric — *Basketball Player*
%Phoenix Suns, 201 E Jefferson St, Phoenix, AZ 85004, USA

Ceccato, Aldo — *Conductor*
Castel Gavarno, 24020 Scanzo BG, Italy

C

Catell - Ceccato

Cece, Joseph W *Publisher*
%TV Guide Magazine, 100 Matsonford Road, Radnor, PA 19087, USA

Cech, Thomas R *Nobel Chemistry Laureate*
%University of Colorado, Chemistry & Biochemistry Dept, Boulder, CO 80309, USA

Cedar, Paul *Religious Leader*
%Evangelical Free Church of America, 901 E 78th St, Minneapolis, MN 55420, USA

Cedeno, Cesar E *Baseball Player*
9919 Sagedowne Lane, Houston, TX 77089, USA

Cedras, Raoul *Army General, Haiti*
%Continental Riande Hotel, Panama City, Panama

Ceglarski, Leonard (Len) *Hockey Player, Coach*
61 Lantern Lane, Duxbury, MA 02332, USA

Cela, Camilio Jose *Nobel Literature Laureate*
Apartado de Correos 333, 19080 Guadalajara, Spain

Celant, Gerwano *Museum Curator*
%Solomon Guggenheim Museum, 1971 5th Ave, New York, NY 10128, USA

Celebrezze, Anthony J *Secretary, Health Education & Welfare*
%Porter Wright Morris Arthur, 41 High St, Columbus, OH 43215, USA

Celio, Nello *President, Switzerland*
Via Ronchi 13, Lugano, Switzerland

Cellucci, Paul *Governor, MA*
%Governor's Office, State House, Boston, MA 02133, USA

Celmins, Vija *Artist*
49 Crosby St, New York, NY 10012, USA

Cenac, Winston Francis *Prime Minister, Saint Lucia*
7 High St, Box 629, Castries, Saint Lucia

Cenker, Robert J *Astronaut*
%GORCA Inc, 155 Hickory Corner Road, East Windsor, NJ 08520, USA

Cennamo, Ralph *Labor Leader*
%Leather Plastics & Novelty Workers Union, 265 W 14th St, New York, NY 10011, USA

Cepeda, Orlando M *Baseball Player*
331 Brazelton Court, Suisan City, CA 94585, USA

Cerezo Arevalo, M Vinicio *President, Guatemala*
%President's Office, Palacio Nacional, Guatemala City, Guatemala

Cerf, Vinton G *Data Processing Executive*
%MCI Telecommunications Corp, 2100 Reston Parkway, Reston, VA 20191, USA

Cernan, Eugene A *Astronaut*
%Cernan Energy Corp, 900 Town & Country Lane, #300, Houston, TX 77024, USA

Cernik, Oldrich *Prime Minister, Czechoslovakia*
%Urban-Rural Municipalities Union, Pacovska 31, Prage 4, Czech Republic

Cerone, Richard (Rick) *Baseball Player*
63 Eisenhower, Cresskill, NJ 07626, USA

Cerruda, Ron *Golfer*
7 Foxbriar, Hilton Head, SC 29926, USA

Cervenka, Exene *Singer (X)*
%Performers of the World, 8901 Melrose Ave, #200, West Hollywood, CA 90069, USA

Cervi, Alfred N (Al) *Basketball Player*
177 Dunrovin Lane, Rochester, NY 14618, USA

Cesaire, Aime Ferdinand *Writer*
La Maire, 97200 Fort-de-France, Martinique, West Indies

Cetera, Peter *Singer, Bassist, Songwriter*
%Agency For Performing Arts, 9200 Sunset Blvd, #900, Los Angeles, CA 90069, USA

Cetlinski, Matt *Swimmer*
4290 Mediterranean Road, Lake Worth, FL 33461, USA

Cey, Ronald C (Ron) *Baseball Player*
22714 Creole Road, Woodland Hills, CA 91364, USA

Chaban-Delmas, Jacques M P *Prime Minister, France*
Marie de Bordeaux, Hotel de Ville, 33077 Bordeaux Cedex, France

Chabot, Herbert L *Judge*
%US Tax Court, 400 2nd St NW, Washington, DC 20217, USA

Chabrol, Claude *Movie Director, Producer*
%Jean Nainckrich, 31 Champs-Elysees, 75008 Paris, France

Chacon, Bobby *Boxer*
3165 Yard St, Oroville, CA 95966, USA

Chad (Stuart) *Singer (Chad & Jeremy)*
%Agency For Performing Arts, 9200 Sunset Blvd, #900, Los Angeles, CA 90069, USA

Chadirji, Rifat Kamil *Architect*
28 Troy Court, Kensington High St, London W8, England

Chadli, Bendjedid	*President, Algeria*
Palace Emir Abedelkader, Algiers, Algeria	
Chadnois, Lynn	*Football Player*
2048 Walden Court, Flint, MI 48532, USA	
Chadwick, Bill	*Hockey Referee*
Country Club Dr, Cutchogue, NY 11935, USA	
Chadwick, June	*Actress*
%Metropolitan Talent Agency, 4526 Wilshire Blvd, Los Angeles, CA 90010, USA	
Chadwick, Lynn R	*Sculptor*
Lypiatt Park, Stroud, Glos GL6 7LL, England	
Chadwick, Paul	*Cartoonist (Concrete)*
%Dark Horse Publishing, 10956 SE Main St, Milwaukie, OR 97216, USA	
Chadwick, Wallace L	*Construction Engineer*
4720 Pressley Road, Santa Rosa, CA 95404, USA	
Chafetz, Sidney	*Artist*
%Ohio State University, Art Dept, Columbus, OH 43210, USA	
Chailly, Riccardo	*Conductor*
Royal Concertgebrew, Jacob Obrechtstraat 51, 1071 KJ Amsterdam 41, Holland	
Chakiris, George	*Actor, Singer, Dancer*
7266 Clinton St, Los Angeles, CA 90036, USA	
Chalfont, A G (Arthur)	*Government Official, England*
%House of Lords, Westminster, London SW1A 0PW, England	
Challis, Christopher	*Cinematographer*
%Worldmark Productions, Old Studio, 18 Middle Row, London W1O 5AT, England	
Chalsty, John S	*Financier*
%Donaldson Lufkin Jenrette, 140 Broadway, New York, NY 10005, USA	
Chamberlain, David M	*Businessman*
%Genesco, Genesco Park, 1415 Murfreesboro Road, Nashville, TN 37217, USA	
Chamberlain, John A	*Sculptor*
%Ten Coconut Inc, 1315 10th St, Sarasota, FL 34236, USA	
Chamberlain, Joseph W	*Astronomer*
%Rice University, Space Physics & Astronomy Dept, Houston, TX 77001, USA	
Chamberlain, Owen	*Nobel Physics Laureate*
%University of California, Physics Dept, Berkeley, CA 94720, USA	
Chamberlain, Richard	*Actor*
3711 Round Top Dr, Honolulu, HI 96822, USA	
Chamberlain, Wilton N (Wilt)	*Basketball Player*
%Seymour Goldberg, 11111 Santa Monica Blvd, #1000, Los Angeles, CA 90025, USA	
Chambers, Anne Cox	*Businesswoman, Diplomat*
%Cox Enterprises, 1400 Lake Hearn Dr NE, Atlanta, GA 30319, USA	
Chambers, Paul	*Businessman*
1-A Frognal Gardens, Hampstead, London NW3, England	
Chambers, Tom	*Basketball Player*
3615 N Wolf Creek Dr, #1210, Eden, UT 84310, USA	
Chambers, Walter R	*Financier*
%Ohio Co, 155 E Broad St, Columbus, OH 43215, USA	
Chambliss, C Christopher (Chris)	*Baseball Player*
1 Braves Ave, Greenville, SC 29606, USA	
Champion, Marge	*Dancer, Actress*
484 W 43rd St, New York, NY 10036, USA	
Champlin, Charles D	*Movie Critic*
2169 Linda Flora Dr, Los Angeles, CA 90077, USA	
Chan Sy	*Premier, Kampuchea*
%Premier's Office, Phnom-Penh, People's Republic of Kampuchea	
Chan, Fred	*Businessman*
%ESS Technology, 46107 Landing Parkway, Fremont, CA 94538, USA	
Chan, Jackie	*Actor*
%Golden Harvest Studios, 145 Waterloo Road, Kowloon, Hong Kong, China	
Chan, Julius	*Prime Minister, Papua New Guinea*
PO Box 717, Rabaul, Papua New Guinea	
Chance, Britton	*Biophysicist, Educator*
4014 Pine St, Philadelphia, PA 19104, USA	
Chance, Larry	*Singer (The Earls)*
%JP Productions, 57 18th Ave, Ronkonkoma, NY 11779, USA	
Chance, W Dean	*Baseball Player*
9505 W Smithville Western, Wooster, OH 44691, USA	
Chancey, Malcolm B, Jr	*Financier*
%Liberty National BanCorp, 416 W Jefferson St, Louisville, KY 40202, USA	

C

Chadli - Chancey

Chandler, Alice *Educator*
%State University of New York, President's Office, New Paltz, NY 12561, USA

Chandler, Chris *Football Player*
%Atlanta Falcons, 2745 Burnett Road, Suwanee, GA 30024, USA

Chandler, Colby H *Businessman*
%Ford Motor Co, American Road, Dearborn, MI 48121, USA

Chandler, Gene *Singer*
%Headline Talent, 1650 Broadway, #508, New York, NY 10019, USA

Chandler, J Harold *Businessman*
%Provident Life & Accident, 1 Fountain Square, Chattanooga, TN 37402, USA

Chandler, Jeff *Boxer*
6242 Home St, Philadelphia, PA 19144, USA

Chandler, Kyle *Actor*
%Judy Schoen, 606 N Larchmont Blvd, #309, Los Angeles, CA 90004, USA

Chandler, Otis *Publisher*
%Times Mirror Co, Times Mirror Square, Los Angeles, CA 90053, USA

Chandler, Robert *Television News Executive*
21 Squaw Peak Road, Great Barrington, MA 01230, USA

Chandler, Wes *Football Player*
1562 E MerricK Dr, Deltona, FL 32738, USA

Chandola, Walter *Photographer*
%General Delivery, Annandale, NJ 08801, USA

Chandrasekhar, Bhagwat S *Cricketer*
571 31st Cross, 4th Block, Jayanagar, Bangalore 56011, India

Chanel, Tally *Actress*
%Don Gerler, 3349 Cahuenga Blvd W, #1, Los Angeles, CA 90068, USA

Chaney, Don *Basketball Player, Coach*
%New York Knicks, Madison Square Garden, 2 Penn Plaza, New York, NY 10121, USA

Chaney, John *Basketball Coach*
%Temple University, Athletic Dept, Philadelphia, PA 19122, USA

Chaney, William R *Businessman*
%Tiffany Co, 727 5th Ave, New York, NY 10022, USA

Chang, Jeannette *Publisher*
%Harper's Bazaar Magazine, 1700 Broadway, New York, NY 10019, USA

Chang, Michael *Tennis Player*
2657 Windmill Parkway, Henderson, NV 89014, USA

Chang, Morris *Businessman*
%Taiwan Semiconductor, Hsinchu Science Park, Taipei, Taiwan

Chang, Sarah *Concert Violinist*
%International Creative Mgmt, 40 W 57th St, New York, NY 10019, USA

Chang-Diaz, Franklin R *Astronaut*
%NASA, Johnson Space Center, 2101 NASA Road, Houston, TX 77058, USA

Channing, Carol *Actress, Singer*
9301 Flicker Way, Los Angeles, CA 90069, USA

Channing, Stockard *Actress*
1155 Park Ave, New York, NY 10128, USA

Chao, Elaine L *Association Official*
%United Way of America, 701 N Fairfax St, Alexandria, VA 22314, USA

Chao, Rosalind *Actress*
%Don Buchwald, 9229 Sunset Blvd, #710, Los Angeles, CA 90069, USA

Chapin, Dwight L *Publisher, Government Official*
%San Francisco Examiner, 110 5th St, San Francisco, CA 94103, USA

Chapin, Schuyler G *Opera Executive*
901 Lexington Ave, New York, NY 10021, USA

Chapin, Tom *Singer, Songwriter*
57 Piermont Place, Piermont, NY 10968, USA

Chaplin, Ben *Actor*
%London Mgmt, 2-4 Noel St, London W1V 3RB, England

Chaplin, Geraldine *Actress*
Manoir de Bau, Vevey, Switzerland

Chapman, Alvah H, Jr *Publisher*
%Knight-Ridder Inc, 1 Herald Plaza, Miami, FL 33132, USA

Chapman, Bruce K *Government Official*
%Discovery Institute, 1201 3rd Ave, #4000, Seattle, WA 98101, USA

Chapman, E T *WW II British Army Hero (VC)*
%Victoria Cross Society, Old Admiralty Bldg, London SW1A 2BE, England

Chapman, Gary *Songwriter*
%Blanton/Harrell, 2910 Posten Ave, Nashville, TN 37203, USA

Chapman, Judith — Actress
100 S Sunrise Way, #323, Palm Springs, CA 92262, USA
Chapman, Leonard F — Marine Corps General
311 Vassar Road, Alexandria, VA 22314, USA
Chapman, Max C, Jr — Financier
%Nomura Securities, 2 World Financial Center, 200 Liberty St, New York, NY 10281, USA
Chapman, Michael J — Movie Director, Cinematographer
%Gersh Agency, 232 N Canon Dr, Beverly Hills, CA 90210, USA
Chapman, Morris M — Religious Leader
%Southern Baptist Convention, 5452 Grannywhite Pike, Brentwood, TN 37027, USA
Chapman, Nathan A, Jr — Financier
%Chapman Co, 401 E Pratt St, Baltimore, MD 21202, USA
Chapman, Philip K — Astronaut
%Echo Canyon Software, 1000 Main St, Acton, MA 01720, USA
Chapman, Rex — Basketball Player
%Phoenix Suns, 201 E Jefferson St, Phoenix, AZ 85004, USA
Chapman, Samuel B (Sam) — Football Player
11 Andrew Dr, #39, Tiburon, CA 94920, USA
Chapman, Steven Curtis — Singer, Guitarist, Songwriter
%Creative Trust, 1910 Acklen Ave, Nashville, TN 37212, USA
Chapman, Tracy — Singer, Songwriter
%William Morris Agency, 151 S El Camino Dr, Beverly Hills, CA 90212, USA
Chapman, Wes — Ballet Dancer
%American Ballet Theater, 890 Broadway, New York, NY 10003, USA
Chapot, Frank — Equestrian Rider
1 Opie Road, Neshanic Station, NJ 08853, USA
Chappell, Fred D — Writer
305 Kensington Road, Greensboro, NC 27403, USA
Chappuis, Bob — Football Player
3115 Covington Lake Dr, Fort Wayne, IN 46804, USA
Chapuisat, Stephane — Soccer Player
%Borussia Dortmund Soccer Club, Strobelallee, 44139 Dortmund, Germany
Charbonneau, Patricia — Actress
%Don Buchwald, 9229 Sunset Blvd, #710, Los Angeles, CA 90069, USA
Charette, William R (Doc) — Korean War Navy Hero (CMH)
5237 Limberlost Dr, Lake Wales, FL 33853, USA
Chargaff, Erwin — Biochemist, Educator
350 Central Park West, #13-G, New York, NY 10025, USA
Charisse, Cyd — Actress, Dancer
10724 Wilshire Blvd, #1406, Los Angeles, CA 90024, USA
Charles — Prince of Wales, England
%Highgrove House, Doughton near Tetbury, Gloucs GL8 8TN, England
Charles, Bob — Golfer
%Int'l Management Group, 1 Erieview Plaza, #1300, Cleveland, OH 44114, USA
Charles, Caroline — Fashion Designer
56/57 Beauchamp Place, London SW3, England
Charles, Daedra — Basketball Player
%Los Angeles Sparks, Forum, 3900 W Manchester Ave, Inglewood, CA 90305, USA
Charles, Ken — Basketball Player
621 Putnam Ave, Brooklyn, NY 11221, USA
Charles, Lorenzo — Basketball Player
110 Collier Place, Cary, NC 27513, USA
Charles, M Eugenia — Prime Minister, Dominica
%Prime Minister's Office, Government House, Kennedy Ave, Roseau, Dominica
Charles, Nick — Sportscaster
%Cable News Network, News Dept, 1050 Techwood Dr NW, Atlanta, GA 30318, USA
Charles, Ray — Singer, Songwriter
%Ray Charles Enterprises, 2107 W Washington Blvd, #200, Los Angeles, CA 90018, USA
Charleson, Leslie — Actress
2314 Live Oak Dr E, Los Angeles, CA 90068, USA
Charlesworth, James H — Theologian
%Princeton Theological Seminary, Theology Dept, Princeton, NJ 08540, USA
Charlton, Robert (Bobby) — Soccer Player
Garthollerton, Cleford Road, Ollerton near Knutsford, Cheshire, England
Charmoli, Tony — Choreographer, Director
1271 Sunset Plaza Dr, Los Angeles, CA 90069, USA
Charnin, Martin — Theater Producer, Director, Lyricist
%Richard Ticktin, 1345 Ave of Americas, New York, NY 10105, USA

C

Chapman - Charnin

C

Charo *Singer, Flamenco Guitarist*
%Charo's Restaurant, PO Box 1007, Hanalei, Kauai, HI 96714, USA

Charpak, Georges *Nobel Physics Laureate*
37 Rue de la Plaine, 75020 Paris, France

Charren, Peggy *Television Executive, Consumer Activist*
%Action for Children's Television, PO Box 383090, Cambridge, MA 02238, USA

Chartoff, Melanie *Actress*
%Artists Agency, 10000 Santa Monica Blvd, #305, Los Angeles, CA 90067, USA

Chartoff, Robert *Movie Producer*
PO Box 3628, Granada Hills, CA 91394, USA

Charvet, David *Actor*
%"Baywatch" Show, 5433 Beethoven St, Los Angeles, CA 90066, USA

Chase, Alison *Dance Artistic Director*
%Pilolobus Dance Theater, PO Box 388, Washington Depot, CT 06794, USA

Chase, Barrie *Actress, Dancer*
3750 Beverly Ridge Dr, Sherman Oaks, CA 91423, USA

Chase, Bob *Labor Leader*
%National Education Assn, 1201 16th St NW, Washington, DC 20036, USA

Chase, Chevy *Comedian*
PO Box 257, Bedford, NY 10506, USA

Chase, John *Hockey Player*
30 Nanepashmet St, Marblehead, MA 01945, USA

Chase, Sylvia B *Commentator*
%ABC-TV, News Dept, 77 W 66th St, New York, NY 10023, USA

Chast, Roz *Cartoonist*
%New Yorker Magazine, Editorial Dept, 20 W 43rd St, New York, NY 10036, USA

Chastel, Andre *Writer*
30 Rue De Lubeck, 75116 Paris, France

Chatichai Choonhavan *Prime Minister, Army General, Thailand*
%Prime Minister's Office, Luke Luang Road, Bangkok 2, Thailand

Chatrier, Philippe *Tennis Executive*
7 Rue Allied Bruneau, 75016 Paris, France

Chauvel, Bernard L *Financier*
%Credit Agricole, 55 E Monroe St, Chicago, IL 60603, USA

Chauvire, Yvette *Ballerina*
21 Place di Commerce, 70015 Paris, France

Chaves, Richard *Actor*
%Media Artists Group, 8383 Wilshire Blvd, #954, Beverly Hills, CA 90211, USA

Chavez, Ignacio *Research Scientist*
Paseo de la Reforma 1310, Lomas, Mexico City 10 DF, Mexico

Chavez, Julio Cesar *Boxer*
539 Telegraph Canyon Rd, #253, Chula Vista, CA 91910, USA

Chavez, Martin *Mayor*
%Mayor's Office, City Hall, 400 Marque Ave, Albuquerque, NM 87103, USA

Chawla, Kalpana *Astronaut*
%Overset Methods Inc, 262 Warich Way, Los Altos, CA 94022, USA

Chayanne *Singer*
%Chagus Enterprises, 1717 N Bayshore Dr, #2146, Miami, FL 33132, USA

Chazov, Yevgeny I *Cardiologist*
%Cardiology Research Center, Cherepkovskaya Ul 15-A, 121552 Moscow, Russia

Cheadle, Don *Actor*
%International Creative Mgmt, 8942 Wilshire Blvd, Beverly Hills, CA 90211, USA

Cheaney, Calbert *Basketball Player*
5379 Stonehedge Dr, Evansville, IN 47715, USA

Checchi, Alfred *Businessman*
%Northwest Airlines, 5101 Northwest Dr, St Paul, MN 55111, USA

Checketts, David W *Basketball Executive*
%New York Knicks, Madison Square Garden, 2 Penn Plaza, New York, NY 10121, USA

Cheech (Richard A Marin) *Actor, Comedian (Cheech & Chong)*
%Joseph Mannis, 2029 Century Park East, #1200, Los Angeles, CA 90067, USA

Cheeks, Maurice *Basketball Player, Coach*
1083 S Park Terrace, Chicago, IL 60605, USA

Cheever, Eddie *Auto Racing Driver*
1054 S Starwood Dr, Aspen, CO 81611, USA

Cheevers, Gerry *Hockey Player, Executive; Sportscaster*
905 Lewis O'Gray Dr, Saugus, MA 01906, USA

Chelberg, Bruce S *Businessman*
%Whitman Corp, 3501 Algonwin, Rolling Meadows, IL 60008, USA

Chelberg, Robert D — *Army General*
%George C Marshall Security Studies Center, Unit 24502, APO, AE 09053, USA
Chelios, Christos K (Chris) — *Hockey Player*
%Chicago Blackhawks, United Center, 1901 W Madison St, Chicago, IL 60612, USA
Chen Xieyang — *Conductor*
%Shanghai Symphony Orchestra, 105 Hunan Road, Shanghai 200031, China
Chen Zuohuang — *Conductor*
%Wichita Symphony Orchestra, Concert Hall, 225 W Douglas St, Wichita, KS 67202, USA
Chen, Irvin S Y — *Medical Researcher*
%University of California, Med Center, Hematology Dept, Los Angeles, CA 90024, USA
Chen, Joan — *Actress*
2601 Filbert St, San Francisco, CA 94123, USA
Chen, Steve S — *Computer Engineer*
%Chen Systems Corp, 1414 W Hamilton Ave, Eau Claire, WI 54701, USA
Chenchikova, Olga — *Ballerina*
%Kirov Ballet Theatre, 1 Ploshchad Iskusstr, St Petersburg, Russia
Cheney, Lynne V — *Government Official*
%American Enterprise Institute, 1150 17th St NW, Washington, DC 20036, USA
Cheney, Richard B (Dick) — *Secretary, Defense*
%Halliburton Co, Lincoln Plaza, #3600, 500 N Akard St, Dallas, TX 75201, USA
Cher — *Actress, Singer*
%Bill Sammeth, PO Box 960, Beverly Hills, CA 90213, USA
Cherbrowski, Arthur K — *Navy Admiral*
Director, Space/Command/Control, Peterson Air Force Base, CO 80914, USA
Chereau, Patrice — *Movie, Opera, Theater Director*
%Nanterre-Amandiers, 7 Ave Pablo Picasso, 9200 Nanterre, France
Cherenkov, Pavel A — *Nobel Physics Laureate*
%Lebedev Physics Institute, Leninsky Prospekt 53, Moscow, Russia
Chermayeff, Peter — *Architect*
%Cambridge Seven Assoc, 1050 Massachusetts Ave, Cambridge, MA 02138, USA
Chern, Shiing-Shen — *Mathematician*
8336 Kent Court, El Cerrito, CA 94530, USA
Chernavin, Vladimir N — *Navy Admiral, Russia*
%Ministry of Defense, Kremlin, Staraya Pl 4, 103132 Moscow, Russia
Cherne, Leo — *Economist*
%Research Institute of America, 22 Cross Ridge Road, Chappaqua, NY 10514, USA
Chernier, Phil — *Basketball Player*
12121 Blue Flag Way, Columbia, MD 21044, USA
Chernomyrdin, Viktor S — *Prime Minister, Russia*
%Prime Minister's Office, Kremlin, Staraya Pl 4, 103132 Moscow, Russia
Chernov, Vladimir K — *Opera Singer*
%Columbia Artists Mgmt Inc, 165 W 57th St, New York, NY 10019, USA
Chernow, Ron — *Writer*
63 Joralemon St, Brooklyn, NY 11201, USA
Cherrelle — *Singer*
%Associated Booking Corp, 1995 Broadway, #501, New York, NY 10023, USA
Cherry, Bernard H — *Businessman*
%Oxbow Corp, 1601 Forum Place, West Palm Beach, FL 33401, USA
Cherry, Don S — *Hockey Player, Coach*
%Cherry's Grapevine, 1233 The Queensway, Etobicoke ON M8Z 1S1, Canada
Cherry, Neneh — *Singer*
PO Box 1622, London NW10 5TF, England
Chertok, Jack — *Movie Producer*
515 Ocean Ave, #305, Santa Monica, CA 90402, USA
Chesnutt, Mark — *Singer*
%BDM Co, 1106 16th Ave S, Nashville, TN 37212, USA
Chester, Colby — *Actor*
%Bauman Hiller, 5750 Wilshire Blvd, #512, Los Angeles, CA 90036, USA
Chester, Raymond T — *Football Player*
4722 Grass Valley Road, Oakland, CA 94605, USA
Chestnutt, Jane — *Editor*
%Woman's Day Magazine, Editorial Dept, 1515 Broadway, New York, NY 10036, USA
Chevallaz, Georges-Andre — *President, Switzerland*
1066 Epalinges, Switzerland
Chew, Geoffrey F — *Physicist*
10 Maybeck Twin Dr, Berkeley, CA 94708, USA
Chi Haotian — *General, China*
General Staff, Zhongyang Junshi Weiyuanhui, Beijing, China

Chia, Sandro *Artist*
Castello Romitorio, Montalcino, Siena, Italy

Chiadel, Dana *Kayak Athlete*
5302 Flanders Ave, Kensington, MD 20895, USA

Chiang-Kai Shek (Mayling Soong), Madame *Sociologist; Government Official, China*
Locust Valley, Lattingtown, NY 11560, USA

Chiao, Leroy *Astronaut*
%NASA, Johnson Space Center, 2101 NASA Road, Houston, TX 77058, USA

Chiara, Maria *Opera Singer*
%Columbia Artists Mgmt Inc, 165 W 57th St, New York, NY 10019, USA

Chiat, Jay *Art Director*
%Chiat/Day/Mojo Advertising, 340 Main St, Venice, CA 90291, USA

Chicago, Judy *Artist*
PO Box 5280, Santa Fe, NM 87502, USA

Chihara, Paul *Composer*
3815 W Olive Ave, #202, Burbank, CA 91505, USA

Chihuly, Dale P *Artist*
1124 Eastlake Ave, Seattle, WA 98109, USA

Chiklis, Michael *Actor*
%Moress/Nanas/Shea, 12424 Wilshire Blvd, #840, Los Angeles, CA 90025, USA

Child, Jane *Singer*
7095 Hollywood Blvd, #747, Los Angeles, CA 90028, USA

Child, Julia M *Food Expert, Writer*
103 Irving St, Cambridge, MA 02138, USA

Childers, Ernest *WW II Army Hero (CMH)*
13415 S 308 East Ave, Coweta, OK 74429, USA

Childress, Randolph *Basketball Player*
%Detroit Pistons, Palace, 2 Championship Dr, Auburn Hills, MI 48326, USA

Childress, Raymond C (Ray), Jr *Football Player*
17304 Club Hill Lane, Dallas, TX 75248, USA

Childs, Billy *Jazz Pianist*
%Open Door Mgmt, 15327 Sunset Blvd, #365, Pacific Palisades, CA 90272, USA

Childs, David M *Architect*
%Skidmore Owings Merrill, 220 E 42nd St, New York, NY 10017, USA

Childs, Toni *Singer, Songwriter*
%MFC Mgmt, 1342 S Stanley Ave, Los Angeles, CA 90019, USA

Chiles, Henry G (Hank), Jr *Navy Admiral*
6436 Pima St, Alexandria, VA 22312, USA

Chiles, Lawton M *Governor/Senator, FL*
%Governor's Office, State Capitol Building, Tallahassee, FL 32399, USA

Chiles, Linden *Actor*
2521 Topanga Skyline Dr, Topanga, CA 90290, USA

Chiles, Lois *Actress, Model*
644 San Lorenzo, Santa Monica, CA 90402, USA

Chillida Juantegui, Eduardo *Sculptor*
Intz-Enea, Puerto de Faro 26, 20008 San Sebastian, Spain

Chilstrom, Herbert W *Religious Leader*
%Evangelical Lutheran Church, 8765 W Higgins Road, Chicago, IL 60631, USA

Chilton, Alex *Singer (Box Tops)*
%Monterey Peninsula Artists, 509 Hartnell St, Monterey, CA 93940, USA

Chilton, Kevin P *Astronaut*
%NASA, Johnson Space Center, 2101 NASA Road, Houston, TX 77058, USA

Chiluba, Frederick T J *President, Zambia*
%President's Office, State House, PO Box 135, Lusaka, Zambia

Chino, Tetsuo *Businessman*
%Honda Motor Co, 1-1-2 Minami-Aoyama, Minatoku, Tokyo, Japan

Chirac, Jacques R *President, France*
%Palais de L'Elysee, 55-57 Rue de Faubourg St Honore, 75008 Paris, France

Chisholm, Melanie *Singer (Spice Girls)*
%Virgin Records, Kensal House, 533-79 Harrow Road, London W1O 4RH, England

Chisholm, Shirley A S *Representative, NY*
80 Wentworth Lane, Palm Coast, FL 32164, USA

Chisholm-Carrillo, Linda *Volleyball Player*
17213 Vose St, Van Nuys, CA 91406, USA

Chissano, Joaquim A *President, Mozambique*
%President's Office, Avda Julius Nyerere 2000, Maputo, Mozambique

Chitalada, Sot *Boxer*
%Home Express Co, 242/19 Moo 10, Sukhumvit Road, Cholburi 20210, Thailand

Chittister, Joan D — *Psychologist*
%St Scholastica Priory, 335 E 9th St, Erie, PA 16503, USA

Chitwood, Joey, Jr — *Stunt Car Driver*
4410 W Alva St, Tampa, FL 33614, USA

Chivers, Warren — *Skier*
%Vermont Academy, Saxtons River, WI 05154, USA

Chlumsky, Anna — *Actress*
%David S Lee, 641 W Lake St, #402, Chicago, IL 60661, USA

Cho, Margaret — *Actress, Comedienne*
345 N Maple Dr, #300, Beverly Hills, CA 90210, USA

Cho, Paul — *Evangelist*
%Full Gospel Central Church, Yoido Plaza, Seoul, South Korea

Choate, Clyde L — *WW II Army Hero (CMH)*
Rt 1, Anna, IL 62906, USA

Choate, Jerry D — *Businessman*
%Allstate Insurance, Allstate Plaza, Northbrook, IL 60062, USA

Chodorow, Marvin — *Physicist*
81 Pearce Mitchell Place, Stanford, CA 94305, USA

Chojnowska-Liskiewicz, Krystyna — *Yachtswoman*
Ul Norblina 29 M 50, 80 304 Gdansk-Oliwa, Poland

Chokachi, David — *Actor*
%William Morris Agency, 151 S El Camino Dr, Beverly Hills, CA 90212, USA

Chomsky, A Noam — *Linguistics Theorist*
15 Suzanne Road, Lexington, MA 02173, USA

Chomsky, Marvin J — *Television Director*
4707 Ocean Front Walk, Venice, CA 90292, USA

Chones, Jim — *Basketball Player*
32810 Creekside Dr, Pepper Pike, OH 44124, USA

Chong, Rae Dawn — *Actress*
PO Box 691600, Los Angeles, CA 90069, USA

Choppin, Purnell W — *Research Administrator*
2700 Calvert St NW, Washington, DC 20008, USA

Chopra, Deepak — *Writer*
%Sharp Institute, 9738 Lomas Santa Fe, Solano Beach, CA 92075, USA

Chorbajian, Herbert G — *Financier*
%Albank Financial Corp, 10 N Pearl St, Albany, NY 12207, USA

Chow, Amy — *Gymnast*
%West Valley Gymnastics School, 1190 Dell Ave, #1, Campbell, CA 95008, USA

Chretien, J J Jean — *Prime Minister, Canada*
%Prime Minister's Office, 24 Sussex Dr, Ottawa ON K1M 0MS, Canada

Chretien, Jean-Loup — *Spatinaut, France; Air Force General*
%CNES, 2 Place Maurice Quentin, 75039 Paris Cedex 01, France

Christensen, Kai — *Architect*
100 Vester Voldgade, 1552 Copenhagen V, Denmark

Christensen, Todd — *Football Player, Sportscaster*
%Management Team, 9507 Santa Monica Blvd, #304, Beverly Hills, CA 90210, USA

Christian, Claudia — *Actress*
%Paul Kohner, 9300 Wilshire Blvd, #555, Beverly Hills, CA 90212, USA

Christian, David (Dave) — *Hockey Player*
6806 Mallow Court, Springfield, VA 22152, USA

Christian, George E — *Government Official*
%George Christian Inc, 400 W 15th, #420, Austin, TX 78701, USA

Christian, Gordon — *Hockey Player*
604 Lake St NW, Warroad, MN 56763, USA

Christian, Roger — *Hockey Player*
508 Carrol St NW, Warroad, MN 56763, USA

Christian, William (Bill) — *Hockey Player*
502 Carrol St, Warroad, MN 56763, USA

Christian-Jacque — *Movie Director, Screenwriter*
42 Bis Rue de Paris, 92100 Boulogne-Billancourt, France

Christians, F Wilhelm — *Financier*
Konigsallee 51, 40212 Dusseldorf, Germany

Christie, Julie — *Actress, Model*
23 Linden Gardens, London W3, England

Christie, Linford — *Track Athlete*
Rosedale House, Rosedale Road, Richmond, Surrey TW9 2SZ, England

Christie, Lou — *Singer*
%Dartmouth Mgmt, 228 W 71st St, #1-E, New York, NY 10023, USA

Christie, William *Concert Harpsichordist*
Les Arts Florissants, 2 Rue de Leningrad, 75008 Paris, France

Christman, Daniel W (Dan) *Army General*
%US Military Academy, Superintendent's Office, West Point, NY 10996, USA

Christmas, George R *Marine Corps General*
Dep CofS, Manpower/Reserve Affairs, HqUSMC, Navy Annex, Washington, DC 20380, USA

Christo (Javacheff) *Sculptor*
48 Howard St, New York, NY 10013, USA

Christoff, Steven (Steve) *Hockey Player*
7260 Woodstock Dr, Bloomington, MN 55438, USA

Christopher, Dennis *Actor*
175 5th Ave, #2413, New York, NY 10010, USA

Christopher, Jordan *Actor*
300 Central Park West, New York, NY 10024, USA

Christopher, Robin *Actress*
%Century Artists, 1148 4th St, #206, Santa Monica, CA 90403, USA

Christopher, Thom *Actor*
%Ambrosio/Mortimer, 9150 Wilshire Blvd, #175, Beverly Hills, CA 90212, USA

Christopher, Warren M *Secretary, State*
%US State Department, 2201 "C" St NW, Washington, DC 20520, USA

Christopher, William *Actor*
PO Box 50698, Pasadena, CA 91115, USA

Christy, James W *Astronomer*
1720 W Niona Place, Tucson, AZ 85704, USA

Christy, Robert F *Physicist*
1230 Arden Road, Pasadena, CA 91106, USA

Chryssa *Sculptor*
565 Broadway, Soho, New York, NY 10012, USA

Chu, Paul C W *Physicist*
%University of Houston, Center for Superconductivity, Houston, TX 77204, USA

Chuan Leekpai *Prime Minister, Thailand*
%Prime Minister's Office, Gov't House, Luke Lang Road, Bangkok, Thailand

Chuck D *Rap Artist (Public Enemy)*
%Rush Artists, 1600 Varick St, New York, NY 10013, USA

Chung, Constance Y (Connie) *Commentator*
%Dakota Hotel, 1 W 72nd St, New York, NY 10023, USA

Chung, Kyung-Wha *Concert Violinist*
86 Hatton Garden, London EC1, England

Chung, Myung-Whun *Concert Pianist, Conductor*
%International Creative Mgmt, 40 W 57th St, New York, NY 10019, USA

Church, Emory (Bubba) *Baseball Player*
3304 Afton Circle, Birmingham, AL 35242, USA

Church, Sam *Labor Leader*
%United Mine Workers of America, 900 15th St NW, Washington, DC 20005, USA

Church, Thomas Haden *Actor*
%Creative Artists Agency, 9830 Wilshire Blvd, Beverly Hills, CA 90212, USA

Churches, Brady J *Businessman*
%Consolidated Stores, 1105 N Market St, Wilmington, DE 19801, USA

Churchill, Caryl *Writer*
%Cassarotto, 60/66 Wardour St, London W1V 4ND, England

Chute, Robert M *Biologist, Poet*
85 Echo Cove Lane, Poland, ME 04274, USA

Chuvalo, George *Boxer*
46 Goldwood Heights, Weston ON M9P 3M2, Canada

Chwast, Seymour *Artist*
%Push Pin Group, 67 Irving Place, New York, NY 10003, USA

Chygir, Mikhail *Prime Minister, Belarus*
%Ministers' Council, Government House, Dom Urada, 22010 Minsk, Belarus

Ciampi, Carlo A *Prime Minister, Italy*
%Palazzo Chigi, Piazza Colonna 370, 00187 Rome, Italy

Ciampi, Joe *Basketball Coach*
%Auburn University, Athletic Dept, Auburn, AL 36831, USA

Ciappi, Mario Luigi Cardinal *Religious Leader*
Via di Porto Angelica, #63, 00193 Rome, Italy

Ciccarelli, Dino *Hockey Player*
%Tampa Bay Lightning, Ice Palace, 401 Channelside Dr, Tampa, FL 33602, USA

Ciccolini, Aldo *Concert Pianist*
%IMG Artists, 22 E 71st St, New York, NY 10021, USA

Ciller, Tansu — *Prime Minister, Turkey*
T C, Basbakanlik, Ankara, Turkey

Cimino, Leonardo — *Actor*
%Michael Hartig Agency, 156 5th Ave, #820, New York, NY 10010, USA

Cimino, Michael — *Movie Director*
9015 Alto Cedro, Beverly Hills, CA 90210, USA

Cimoszewicz, Wlodzimierz — *Prime Minister, Poland*
%Ul Ursad Rady Ministrow, Ul Wiejska 4/8, 00-902 Warsaw, Poland

Cioffi, Charles — *Actor*
Glover Ave, Norwalk, CT 06850, USA

Ciriani, Henri — *Architect*
93 Rue de Montreuil, 75011 Paris, France

Cirici, Cristian — *Architect*
%Cirici Arquitecte, Carrer de Pujades 63 2-N, 08005 Barcelona, Spain

Cisneros, Evelyn — *Ballerina*
%San Francisco Ballet, 455 Franklin, San Francisco, CA 94102, USA

Cisneros, Henry G — *Secretary, Housing & Urban Development*
%Univision Inc, 6701 Center Dr W, Los Angeles, CA 90045, USA

Civalleri, Roberto — *Financier*
%First Los Angeles Bank, 2049 Century Park East, Los Angeles, CA 90067, USA

Civiletti, Benjamin R — *Attorney General*
%Mercantile Bank & Trust Bldg, #1800, 2 Hopkins Plaza, Baltimore, MD 21201, USA

Cizik, Robert — *Businessman*
%Cooper Industries, First City Tower, 1001 Fannin St, #4000, Houston, TX 77002, USA

Claes, Willy — *Government Official, Belgium*
Berkenlaan 23, 3500 Hasselt, Belgium

Claiborne Ortenberg, Elisabeth (Liz) — *Fashion Designer*
%Liz Claiborne Inc, 1441 Broadway, New York, NY 10018, USA

Claiborne, Craig — *Journalist, Food Expert*
30 Park Place, East Hampton, NY 11937, USA

Clampett, Bobby — *Golfer*
2615 Kildaire Farm Road, Cary, NC 27511, USA

Clancy, Edward B Cardinal — *Religious Leader*
Sydney Archdiocese, Polding House, 276 Pitt St, Sydney NSW 2000, Australia

Clancy, Gil — *Boxing Manager*
47 Morris Ave W, Malverne, NY 11565, USA

Clancy, Thomas J (Tom) — *Writer*
PO Box 800, Huntington, MD 10639, USA

Clanton, Jimmy — *Singer*
%Ken Keene, PO Box 1875, Gretna, LA 70054, USA

Clapp, Charles E, II — *Judge*
%US Tax Court, 400 2nd St NW, Washington, DC 20217, USA

Clapp, Gordon — *Actor*
%Paul Kohner, 9300 Wilshire Blvd, #555, Beverly Hills, CA 90212, USA

Clapp, Joseph M — *Businessman*
%Roadway Services, PO Box 5459, Akron, OH 44334, USA

Clapp, Nicholas R — *Explorer (Ubar), Movie Producer*
1551 S Robertson Blvd, Los Angeles, CA 90035, USA

Clapton, Eric — *Singer, Guitarist*
18 Harley House, Regents Park, London NW1, England

Clark, A James — *Businessman*
%Clark Construction Group, 7500 Old Georgetown Road, Bethesda, MD 20814, USA

Clark, Archie — *Basketball Player*
Wayne County Building, 600 Randolph St, #323, Detroit, MI 48226, USA

Clark, Bob — *Commentator*
%ABC-TV, News Dept, 1717 De Sales St NW, Washington, DC 20036, USA

Clark, C Joseph (Joe) — *Prime Minister, Canada*
707 7th Ave SW, #1300, Calgary AB T2P 3H6, Canada

Clark, Candy — *Actress*
5 Briar Hill Road, Montclair, NJ 07042, USA

Clark, Christie — *Actress*
435 S Ranch View Circle, #96, Anaheim, CA 92807, USA

Clark, Dane — *Actor*
%Osborne, 205 W 57th St, New York, NY 10019, USA

Clark, Dick C — *Senator, IA*
4424 Edmunds St NW, Washington, DC 20007, USA

Clark, Donald C — *Businessman*
%Household International, 2700 Sanders Road, Prospect Heights, IL 60070, USA

Clark, Dwight — *Football Player, Executive*
98 Inglewood Lane, Atherton, CA 94027, USA

Clark, Earl — *Diver*
1145 NE 126th St, #4, North Miami, FL 33161, USA

Clark, Eugenie — *Zoologist*
7817 Hampden Lane, Bethesda, MD 20814, USA

Clark, Gary M — *Businessman*
%Westinghouse Electric, Gateway Center, 11 Stanwix St, Pittsburgh, PA 15222, USA

Clark, Gene — *Singer, Percussionist (The Byrds)*
%Artists International Mgmt, 9850 Sandalfoot Road, #458, Boca Raton, FL 33428, USA

Clark, George W — *Physicist*
%Massachusetts Institute of Technology, Physics Dept, Cambridge, MA 02139, USA

Clark, Guy — *Singer, Songwriter*
%Keith Case Assoc, 59 Music Square W, Nashville, TN 37203, USA

Clark, J Desmond — *Anthropologist*
1941 Yosemite Road, Berkeley, CA 94707, USA

Clark, Jack A — *Baseball Player*
2708 Noffett Court, Plano, TX 75093, USA

Clark, James (Jim) — *Businessman*
%Netscape Communications, 501 E Middlefield Road, Mountain View, CA 94043, USA

Clark, Joe — *Educator*
225 Kingsberry Dr, Somerset, NJ 08873, USA

Clark, Kenneth B — *Psychologist*
17 Pinecrest Dr, Hastings-on-Hudson, NY 10706, USA

Clark, Malcolm D — *Businessman*
%Keystone International, 9600 W Gulf Bank Dr, Houston, TX 77040, USA

Clark, Marcia — *Prosecutor*
%William Morris Agency, 151 S El Camino Dr, Beverly Hills, CA 90212, USA

Clark, Mary Ellen — *Diver*
%Swimming Hall of Fame, 1 Hall of Fame Dr, Fort Lauderdale, FL 33316, USA

Clark, Mary Higgins — *Writer*
%Simon & Schuster, 1230 Ave of Americas, New York, NY 10020, USA

Clark, Matt — *Actor*
1199 Park Ave, #15-D, New York, NY 10128, USA

Clark, Peter B — *Publisher*
939 Coast Blvd, #16-E, La Jolla, CA 92037, USA

Clark, Petula — *Singer, Actress*
15 Chemin Rieu Colign, Geneva, Switzerland

Clark, Robert C — *Artist*
PO Box 597, Cambria, CA 93428, USA

Clark, Roy — *Singer, Guitarist*
%Roy Clark Productions, 3225 S Norwood Ave, Tulsa, OK 74135, USA

Clark, Steve — *Swimmer*
29 Martling Road, San Anselmo, CA 94960, USA

Clark, Susan — *Actress*
7943 Woodrow Wilson Dr, Los Angeles, CA 90046, USA

Clark, Vernon J — *Navy Admiral*
%Commander, Striking Fleet Atlantic Command, Unit 50148, FPO, AE 09501, USA

Clark, W Ramsey — *Attorney General*
36 E 12th St, New York, NY 10003, USA

Clark, Wesley K (Wes) — *Army General*
Supreme Allied Command, Supreme Hq, Allied Powers Europe, APO 09705, USA

Clark, William J — *Businessman*
%Massachusetts Mutual Life, 1295 State St, Springfield, MA 01111, USA

Clark, William N (Will), Jr — *Baseball Player*
504 Potomac Place, Southlake, TX 76092, USA

Clark, William P — *Secretary, Interior*
%Clark Co, 1031 Pine St, Paso Robles, CA 93446, USA

Clarke, Allan — *Singer, Musician (The Hollies)*
Hill Farm, Hackleton, Northantshire NN7 2DH, England

Clarke, Angela — *Actress*
7557 Mulholland Dr, Los Angeles, CA 90046, USA

Clarke, Arthur C — *Writer, Underwater Explorer*
Leslie's House, 25 Barnes Place, Colombo 07, Sri Lanka

Clarke, Brian Patrick — *Actor*
333 N Kenwood St, #D, Burbank, CA 91505, USA

Clarke, Cyril A — *Physician, Geneticist*
43 Caldy Road, West Kirby, Wirral, Merseyside L48 2HF, England

Clarke, Ellis E I — *President, Trinidad & Tobago*
%Queens Park Cricket Club, Port of Spain, Trinidad & Tobago

Clarke, Gilmore D — *Landscape Architect*
480 Park Ave, New York, NY 10022, USA

Clarke, Kenneth H — *Government Official, England*
%Chancellory of Exchequer, London, England

Clarke, Lenny — *Actor*
%Paradigm Agency, 10100 Santa Monica Blvd, #2500, Los Angeles, CA 90067, USA

Clarke, Martha — *Dancer, Choreographer*
%Sheldon Soffer Mgmt, 130 W 56th St, New York, NY 10019, USA

Clarke, Melinda — *Actress*
%Agency For Performing Arts, 9200 Sunset Blvd, #900, Los Angeles, CA 90069, USA

Clarke, Richard A — *Businessman*
%Pacific Gas & Electric, PO Box 770000, San Francisco, CA 94177, USA

Clarke, Robert E (Bobby) — *Hockey Player, Executive*
800 Albury Court, Moorestown, NJ 08057, USA

Clarke, Robert L — *Government Official*
%Bracewell & Patterson, 711 Louisiana St, #2900, Houston, TX 77002, USA

Clarke, Ron — *Track Athlete*
1 Bay St, Brighton VIC 3186, Australia

Clarke, Stanley M — *Jazz Bassist, Composer*
1807 Benedict Canyon Dr, Beverly Hills, CA 90210, USA

Clarkson, Lana — *Actress*
%LA Talent, 8335 Sunset Blvd, #200, Los Angeles, CA 90069, USA

Clarkson, Patricia — *Actress*
%Gersh Agency, 232 N Canon Dr, Beverly Hills, CA 90210, USA

Clary, Robert — *Actor*
1001 Sundial Lane, Beverly Hills, CA 90210, USA

Clatterbuck, Tamara — *Actress*
%House of Representatives, 400 S Beverly Dr, #101, Beverly Hills, CA 90212, USA

Clatworthy, Robert — *Sculptor*
Moelfre, Cynghordy, Landovery, Dyfed SA20 OUW Wales, England

Clausen, A W (Tom) — *Financier*
%BankAmerica Corp, 555 California St, San Francisco, CA 94104, USA

Clausen, R Mike, Jr — *Vietnam War Marine Corps Hero (CMH)*
PO Box 991, Ponchatoula, LA 70454, USA

Clauser, Francis H — *Aeronautical Engineer, Educator*
4072 Chevy Chase, Flintridge, CA 91011, USA

Clavel, Bernard — *Writer*
22 Rue Huyghens, 75014 Paris, France

Clay, Andrew — *Comedian, Actor*
%Gallin Morey, 345 N Maple Dr, #300, Beverly Hills, CA 90210, USA

Clay, Landon T — *Financier*
%Eaton Vance Corp, 24 Federal St, Boston, MA 02110, USA

Clayborn, Raymond — *Football Player*
11 Kings Road, Sharon, MA 02067, USA

Clayburgh, Jill — *Actress*
PO Box 18, Lakeville, CT 06039, USA

Clayderman, Richard — *Pianist*
%Gurthman Murtha, 450 7th Ave, #603, New York, NY 10123, USA

Clayman, Ralph V — *Surgeon*
%Barnes Hospital, Surgery Dept, 416 S Kingshighway Blvd, St Louis, MO 63110, USA

Clayton, Robert N — *Chemist, Educator*
5201 S Cornell Ave, Chicago, IL 60615, USA

Clayton, Royce S — *Baseball Player*
401 W Fairview Blvd, Inglewood, CA 90302, USA

Clayton-Thomas, David — *Singer (Blood Sweat & Tears)*
%Wolfman Jack Entertainment, Rt 1, PO Box 56, Belvidere, NC 27919, USA

Cleamons, Jim — *Basketball Player, Coach*
3067 Oak Spring Dr, Columbus, OH 43219, USA

Clearwater, Keith — *Golfer*
1077 E Bretonwoods Lane, Orem, UT 84097, USA

Cleary, Beverly A — *Writer*
%William Morrow, 1350 Ave of Americas, New York, NY 10016, USA

Cleary, Jon Stephen — *Writer*
%W Collins Ltd, 4 Eden Park, Waterloo Road, North Ryde NSW 2113, Australia

Cleary, Robert (Bob) — *Hockey Player*
18 Juniper Road, Weston, MA 02193, USA

C

Clarke - Cleary

Cleary, William (Bill) — *Hockey Player*
27 Kingswood Road, Auburndale, MA 02166, USA

Cleave, James H — *Financier*
%Marine Midland Banks, 1 Marine Midland Center, Buffalo, NY 14203, USA

Cleave, Mary L — *Astronaut*
%Goddard Space Flight Center, Hydrospheric Processes Lab, Greenbelt, MD 20771, USA

Cleaver, Alan — *Fashion Designer (Byblos)*
Via Vallone 11, Monte Conero, Sirolo, Italy

Cleaver, Vera — *Writer*
5119 N 13th St, Tampa, FL 33603, USA

Cledwyn (Hughes) of Penrhos — *Government Official, England*
Penmorfa, Trearddur, Holyhead, Gwynedd, Wales

Cleese, John — *Comedian, Writer*
82 Ladbroke Road, London W11 3NU, England

Clegg, Johnny — *Singer*
%Alive Enterprises, 3264 S Kihei Road, Kihei, HI 96753, USA

Cleghorne, Ellen — *Actress*
%Abrams Artists, 9200 Sunset Blvd, #625, Los Angeles, CA 90069, USA

Cleland, J Maxwell (Max) — *Senator, GA*
%Secretary of State's Office, 214 State Capital Building, Atlanta, GA 30334, USA

Clemens, Donella — *Religious Leader*
%Mennonite Church, 722 Main St, Newton, KS 67114, USA

Clemens, W Roger — *Baseball Player*
11535 Quail Hollow, Houston, TX 77024, USA

Clement, John — *Businessman*
Tuddenham Hall, Tuddenham, Ipswich, Suffolk IP6 9DD, England

Clemente, Carmine D — *Anatomist*
11737 Bellagio Road, Los Angeles, CA 90049, USA

Clemente, Francesco — *Artist*
684 Broadway, New York, NY 10012, USA

Clements, John Allen — *Physiologist*
%University of California, Cardiovascular Research Inst, San Francisco, CA 94143, USA

Clements, Lennie — *Golfer*
1714 Monterey Ave, Coronado, CA 92118, USA

Clements, Ronald F — *Animator*
%Walt Disney Productions, 500 S Buena Vista St, Burbank, CA 91521, USA

Clements, William P, Jr — *Governor, TX*
1901 N Akard St, Dallas, TX 75201, USA

Clemins, Archie R — *Navy Admiral*
CinC, US Pacific Fleet, Pearl Harbor, HI 96860, USA

Cleminson, James A S — *Businessman*
Loddon Hall, Hales, Norfolk NR14 6TB, England

Clendenin, John L — *Businessman*
%BellSouth Corp, 1155 Peachtree St NE, Atlanta, GA 30309, USA

Clennon, David — *Actor*
%Writers & Artists, 924 Westwood Blvd, #900, Los Angeles, CA 90024, USA

Cleobury, Nicholas R — *Conductor*
China Cottage, Church Lane, Petham, Canterbury, Kent CT4 5RD, England

Clerico, Christian — *Restauranteur*
%Lido-Normandie, 116 Bis Ave des Champs Elysees, 75008 Paris, France

Clerides, Glavkos J — *President, Cyprus*
%Presidential Palace, 5 Ioannis Clerides St, Nicosia, Cyprus

Clervoy, Jean-Francois — *Spatinaut, France*
%Europe Astronaut Center, Linder Hohe, Box 906096, 51127 Cologne, Germany

Cleveland, Ashley — *Singer, Songwriter*
%Blanton/Harrell, 2910 Posten Ave, Nashville, TN 37203, USA

Cleveland, J Harlan — *Diplomat, Educator*
46891 Grissom St, Sterling, VA 20165, USA

Clexton, Edward W, Jr — *Navy Admiral*
1054 Boston Post Road, Rye, NY 10580, USA

Cliburn, Van — *Concert Pianist*
455 Wilder Place, Shreveport, LA 71104, USA

Cliff, Jimmy — *Singer, Songwriter*
51 Lady Musgrave Road, Kingston, Jamaica

Clifford, Clark M — *Secretary, Defense*
9421 Rockville Pike, Bethesda, MD 20814, USA

Clifford, Joseph P — *Financier*
%TCF Financial Corp, 801 Marquette Ave, Minneapolis, MN 55402, USA

Clifford, Linda — *Singer*
%Talent Consultants Int'l, 1560 Broadway, #1308, New York, NY 10036, USA

Clifford, M Richard — *Astronaut*
%NASA, Johnson Space Center, 2101 NASA Road, Houston, TX 77058, USA

Clift, William B, III — *Photographer*
PO Box 6035, Santa Fe, NM 87502, USA

Cline, Martin J — *Physician, Educator*
%University of California, Med Center, Hematology Dept, Los Angeles, CA 90024, USA

Cline, Richard — *Cartoonist*
%New Yorker Magazine, Editorial Dept, 20 W 43rd St, New York, NY 10036, USA

Cline, Richard G — *Businessman*
%Nicor Inc, PO Box 3014, Naperville, IL 60566, USA

Cline, Robert S — *Businessman*
%Airborne Freight Corp, 3101 Western Ave, Seattle, WA 98121, USA

Clinger, Debra — *Actress*
1206 Chickasaw Dr, Brentwood, TN 37027, USA

Clingman, J Fully — *Businessman*
%H E Butt Grocery Co, 646 S Main Ave, San Antonio, TX 78204, USA

Clinton, George — *Singer*
%Absolute Artists, 530 Howard St, #200, San Francisco, CA 94105, USA

Clinton, Hillary Rodham — *Wife of US President*
%White House, 1600 Pennsylvania Ave NW, Washington, DC 20500, USA

Clinton, William J (Bill) — *President, USA*
%White House, 1600 Pennsylvania Ave NW, Washington, DC 20500, USA

Clinton-Davis of Hackney, Stanley C — *Government Official, England*
%J Berwin Co, 236 Gray's Inn Road, London WC1X 8HB, England

Clohessy, Robert — *Actor*
%Agency For Performing Arts, 9200 Sunset Blvd, #900, Los Angeles, CA 90069, USA

Cloninger, Tony L — *Baseball Player*
3182 Mack Ballard Road, Maiden, NC 28650, USA

Clooney, George — *Actor*
%William Morris Agency, 151 S El Camino Dr, Beverly Hills, CA 90212, USA

Clooney, Rosemary — *Singer, Actress*
1019 N Roxbury Dr, Beverly Hills, CA 90210, USA

Close, Charles T (Chuck) — *Artist*
271 Central Park West, New York, NY 10024, USA

Close, Eric — *Actor*
%Gersh Agency, 232 N Canon Dr, Beverly Hills, CA 90210, USA

Close, Glenn — *Actress*
PO Box 188, Bedford Hills, NY 10507, USA

Clotet, Lluis — *Architect*
%Studio PER, Caspe 151, Barcelona 08013, Spain

Clotworthy, Robert — *Actor*
%Amsel Eisenstadt Frazier, 6310 San Vicente Blvd, #401, Los Angeles, CA 90048, USA

Clotworthy, Robert (Bob) — *Diver*
HC 74 Box 22313, El Prado, NM 87529, USA

Cloud, Jack — *Football Player*
805 Janice Dr, Annapolis, MD 21403, USA

Clough, Charles E — *Businessman*
%Nashua Corp, 44 Franklin St, Nashua, NH 03060, USA

Clough, Charles M — *Businessman*
%Wyle Electronics, PO Box 19675, Irvine, CA 92623, USA

Clough, Gerald W — *Educator*
%Georgia Institute of Technology, President's Office, Atlanta, GA 30332, USA

Clough, Ray W, Jr — *Structural Engineer*
PO Box 4625, Sunriver, OR 97707, USA

Clow, Lee — *Businessman*
%Chiat/Day/Mojo Advertising, 340 Main St, Venice, CA 90291, USA

Clower, Jerry — *Comedian, Writer*
%Top Billing, 1222 16th Ave S, #24, Nashville, TN 37212, USA

Clyne, Patricia — *Fashion Designer*
353 W 39th St, New York, NY 10018, USA

Coachman Davis, Alice — *Track Athlete*
811 Gibson St, Tuskegee, AL 36083, USA

Coan, Gaylord O — *Businessman*
%Gold Kist Inc, 244 Perimeter Center Parkway NE, Atlanta, GA 30346, USA

Coase, Ronald H — *Nobel Economics Laureate*
%University of Chicago, Law School, 1111 E 60th St, Chicago, IL 60637, USA

C

Clifford - Coase

Coates, Phyllis *Actress*
PO Box 1969, Boyes Hot Springs, CA 95416, USA
Coats, Michael L *Astronaut*
%LORAL Space Information Systems, 1322 Space Park Dr, Houston, TX 77058, USA
Coats, William D *Businessman*
%Coats Patons, 155 St Vincent St, Glasgow G2 5PA, England
Cobb, Geraldyn M (Jerrie) *Astronaut*
%Jerrie Cobb Foundation, PO Box 5508, Sun City Center, FL 33571, USA
Cobb, Henry I *Architect*
%Pei Cobb Freed Partners, 600 Madison Ave, #900, New York, NY 10022, USA
Cobb, James R *Financier*
%First Commercial Corp, 400 W Capitol, Little Rock, AR 72201, USA
Cobb, Julie *Actress*
10437 Sarah St, North Hollywood, CA 91602, USA
Cobham, William C (Billy) *Jazz Drummer, Composer*
%Absolute Artists, 530 Howard St, #200, San Francisco, CA 94105, USA
Coblenz, Walter *Movie Director, Producer*
2348 Apollo Dr, Los Angeles, CA 90046, USA
Cobos, Jesus Lopez *Conductor*
%Cincinnati Symphony, 1241 Elm St, Cincinnati, OH 45210, USA
Coburn, Doris *Bowler*
130 Dalton Dr, Buffalo, NY 14223, USA
Coburn, James *Actor*
1601 Schuyler Road, Beverly Hills, CA 90210, USA
Coburn, John G *Army General*
Deputy Chief of Staff, Logistics, Hq USA, Pentagon, Washington, DC 20310, USA
Coca, Imogene *Comedienne*
%Joyce Agency, 370 Harrison Ave, Harrison, NY 10528, USA
Cochereau, Pierre *Concert Organist*
15 Bis Des Ursins, 75004 Paris, France
Cochran, Anita L *Astronomer*
%University of Texas, Astronomy Dept, Austin, TX 78712, USA
Cochran, Hank *Singer, Songwriter*
Rt 2, Box 438, Hunters Lake, Hendersonville, TN 37075, USA
Cochran, John *Commentator*
%ABC-TV, News Dept, 1717 De Sales St NW, Washington, DC 20036, USA
Cochran, Johnnie L, Jr *Attorney*
4929 Wilshire Blvd, #1010, Los Angeles, CA 90010, USA
Cochran, Leslie H *Educator*
%Youngstown State University, President's Office, Youngstown, OH 44555, USA
Cochran, Shannon *Actress*
%Geddes Agency, 1201 Greenacre Blvd, West Hollywood, CA 90046, USA
Cockburn, Bruce *Singer, Songwriter*
%Agency Group, 1775 Broadway, #433, New York, NY 10019, USA
Cocker, Joe *Singer*
%Creative Artists Agency, 9830 Wilshire Blvd, Beverly Hills, CA 90212, USA
Cockerell, Christopher S *Engineer, Inventor (Hovercraft)*
16 Prospect Place, Hythe, Southampton, Hants SO4 6AU, England
Cockrell, Kenneth D *Astronaut*
%NASA, Johnson Space Center, 2101 NASA Road, Houston, TX 77058, USA
Cockroft, Donald L (Don) *Football Player*
2377 Thornhill Dr, Colorado Springs, CO 80920, USA
Cocks of Hartcliffe, Michael F L *Government Official, England*
%House of Lords, Westminster, London SW1A 0PW, England
Cocks, W Burling (Burley) *Steeplechase Racing Trainer*
PO Box 512, Unionville, PA 19375, USA
Code, Arthur D *Astronomer*
%WUPPE Project, University of Wisconsin, Astronomy Dept, Madison, WI 53706, USA
Codrescu, Andrei *Writer*
%Louisiana State University, English Dept, Baton Rouge, LA 70803, USA
Cody, Iron Eyes *Actor*
4470 Sunset Dr, #503, Los Angeles, CA 90027, USA
Coe, David Allan *Singer, Guitarist, Songwriter*
PO Box 270188, Nashville, TN 37227, USA
Coe, George *Actor*
%Bauman Hiller, 5750 Wilshire Blvd, #512, Los Angeles, CA 90036, USA
Coe, Sebastian N *Track Athlete*
Starswood, High Barn Road, Effingham, Surrey KT24 5PW, England

Coe, Sue — Artist
%Galerie St Etienne, 24 W 57th St, New York, NY 10019, USA

Coe-Jones, Dawn — Golfer
8325 Riverboat Dr, Tampa, FL 33637, USA

Coelho, Susie — Actress
11759 Iowa Ave, Los Angeles, CA 90025, USA

Coen, Ethan — Movie Director, Screenwriter
%United Talent Agency, 9560 Wilshire Blvd, #500, Beverly Hills, CA 90212, USA

Coen, Joel — Movie Director, Screenwriter
%United Talent Agency, 9560 Wilshire Blvd, #500, Beverly Hills, CA 90212, USA

Coetzee, Gerrie — Boxer
%Catmac Carriers, PO Box 13510, Witfield 1467, South Africa

Coetzee, John M — Writer
PO Box 92, Rondebosch, Cape Province 7700, South Africa

Coffey, Paul — Hockey Player
%Philadelphia Flyers, CoreStates Center, Pattison Place, Philadelphia, PA 19148, USA

Coffey, Shelby, III — Editor
%Los Angeles Times, Editorial Dept, Times Mirror Square, Los Angeles, CA 90053, USA

Coffin, Fredrick — Actor
%Susan Smith, 121 N San Vicente Blvd, Beverly Hills, CA 90211, USA

Coffin, Tad — Equestrian Rider
%General Delivery, Strafford, VT 05072, USA

Coffin, Tristam — Writer
%Washington Spectator, PO Box 70023, Washington, DC 20088, USA

Coffin, William Sloane, Jr — Social Activist, Religious Leader
%SANE/Freeze, 55 Van Dyke Ave, Hartford, CT 06106, USA

Coffy, Robert Cardinal — Religious Leader
Archdiocese of Marseille, Marseille, France

Cogan, John F, Jr — Financier
%Pioneer Group, 60 State St, Boston, MA 02109, USA

Cogan, Kevin — Auto Racing Driver
205 Rocky Point Road, Palos Verdes Estates, CA 90274, USA

Coggan of Canterbury, F Donald — Religious Leader
28 Lions Hall, Saint Swithun St, Winchester SO23 9HW, England

Coghlan, Eamon — Track Athlete
%Int'l Management Group, 1 Erieview Plaza, #1300, Cleveland, OH 44114, USA

Coghlan, Paul — Businessman
%Linear Technology, 1630 McCarthy Blvd, Milpitas, CA 95035, USA

Cohan, Chris — Basketball Executive
%Golden State Warriors, 7000 Coliseum Way, Oakland, CA 94621, USA

Coheleach, Guy J — Artist
%Pandion Art, PO Box 96, Bernardsville, NJ 07924, USA

Cohen, Aaron — Space Administrator
1310 Essex Green, College Station, TX 77845, USA

Cohen, Alexander H — Movie Producer
25 W 54th St, #5-F, New York, NY 10019, USA

Cohen, Bennett R (Ben) — Businessman
%Ben & Jerry's Homemade, Rt 100, PO Box 240, Waterbury, VT 05676, USA

Cohen, Joseph — Television Executive
%Hughes Television Network, 4 Pennsylvania Plaza, New York, NY 10001, USA

Cohen, Larry — Movie Director
2111 Coldwater Canyon Dr, Beverly Hills, CA 90210, USA

Cohen, Leonard N — Writer, Singer, Songwriter
121 Leslie St, North York ON M3C 2J9, Canada

Cohen, Mary Ann — Judge
%US Tax Court, 400 2nd St NW, Washington, DC 20217, USA

Cohen, Morris — Metallurgist, Materials Scientist
491 Puritan Road, Swampscott, MA 01907, USA

Cohen, Rob — Movie Director
%Badham/Cohen Group, 100 Universal City Plaza, Universal City, CA 91608, USA

Cohen, Robert — Concert Cellist
%Intermusica Artists, 16 Duncan Terrace, London N1 8BZ, England

Cohen, Seymour S — Biochemist
10 Carrot Hill Road, Woods Hole, MA 02543, USA

Cohen, Sheldon S — Government Official
5518 Trent St, Chevy Chase, MD 20815, USA

Cohen, Stanley — Nobel Medicine Laureate
%Vanderbilt University, Medical Center, 1161 21st Ave, Nashville, TN 37232, USA

Cohen, Stanley N *Geneticist*
%Stanford University, Medical Center, Genetics Dept, Stanford, CA 94305, USA
Cohen, William S *Secretary, Defense; Senator, ME*
%Defense Department, Pentagon, Washington, DC 20301, USA
Cohn, Alfred (Al) *Bowler*
13918 S Clark St, Riverdale, IL 60827, USA
Cohn, Marc *Singer, Songwriter*
%MFC Mgmt, 1342 S Stanley Ave, Los Angeles, CA 90019, USA
Cohn, Mildred *Biochemist, Biophysicist*
747 Clarendon Road, Narbeth, PA 19104, USA
Cohn, Mindy *Actress*
913 18th St, #2, Santa Monica, CA 90403, USA
Cohn, Robert *Businessman*
%Octel Communications, 1001 Murphy Ranch Road, Milpitas, CA 95035, USA
Coia, Arthur A *Labor Leader*
%Laborers' International Union, 905 16th St NW, Washington, DC 20006, USA
Coker, Charles W, Jr *Businessman*
%Sonoco Products Co, N 2nd St, Hartsville, SC 29550, USA
Cokes, Curtis *Boxer*
618 Calcutta Dr, Dallas, TX 75241, USA
Colalillo, Mike *WW II Army Hero (CMH)*
3677 Riley Road, Duluth, MN 55803, USA
Colalucci, Gianluigi *Art Restorer*
%Office of Restoration, 00120 Vatican City
Colangelo, Jerry J *Basketball Executive*
%Phoenix Suns, 201 E Jefferson St, Phoenix, AZ 85004, USA
Colantoni, Enrico *Actor*
%Innovative Artists, 1999 Ave of Stars, #2850, Los Angeles, CA 90067, USA
Colasuonno, Louis C *Editor*
%New York Daily News, Editorial Dept, 220 E 42nd St, New York, NY 10017, USA
Colbert, Edwin H *Vertebrate Palaeontologist*
%Museum of Northern Arizona, 3101 N Fort Valley Road, Flagstaff, AZ 86001, USA
Colbert, Jim *Golfer*
222 S Rainbow Blvd, #218, Las Vegas, NV 89128, USA
Colbert, Robert *Actor*
%Thomas Talent Agency, 124 S Lasky Dr, #100, Beverly Hills, CA 90212, USA
Colborn, James W (Jim) *Baseball Player*
2932 Solimar Beach Dr, Ventura, CA 93001, USA
Colburn, Philip Wm *Businessman*
%Allen Group, 25101 Chagrin Blvd, Beachwood, OH 44122, USA
Cole, Artemas *Cartoonist*
RR 1, Box 3454, Rutland, VT 05701, USA
Cole, Bob *Sportscaster*
%Molstarr Communications, 250 Bloor St E, Toronto ON M4W 1E6, Canada
Cole, Dennis *Actor*
%Robert Cosden Agency, 3518 Cahuenga Blvd W, #216, Los Angeles 90068, USA
Cole, Eunice *Labor Leader*
%American Nurses Assn, 2420 Pershing Road, Kansas City, MO 64108, USA
Cole, Gary *Actor*
3855 Berry Dr, Studio City, CA 91604, USA
Cole, George *Actor*
%Joy Jameson Ltd, 2-19 The Plaza, 535 Kings Road, London SW10 0SZ, England
Cole, Johnnetta B *Educator*
%Spelman College, President's Office, Atlanta, GA 30314, USA
Cole, Kenneth S *Biophysicist*
2404 Loring St, San Diego, CA 92109, USA
Cole, Kimberly Lynn *Actress*
57 Comer Dr, Montgomery, AL 36018, USA
Cole, Lloyd *Singer (The Commotions), Songwriter*
%Agency Group, 1775 Broadway, #433, New York, NY 10019, USA
Cole, Michael *Actor*
6332 Costello Ave, Van Nuys, CA 91401, USA
Cole, Natalie *Singer*
%Dan Cleary, 1801 Ave of Stars, #1105, Los Angeles, CA 90067, USA
Cole, Olivia *Actress*
%Century Artists, 1148 4th St, #206, Santa Monica, CA 90403, USA
Cole, Tina *Actress*
3340 Sierra Oaks Dr, Sacramento, CA 95864, USA

Colella, Richard (Rick) — *Swimmer*
217 19th Place, Kirkland, WA 98033, USA

Coleman, Brian — *Artist*
241 22nd St, Santa Cruz, CA 95062, USA

Coleman, Catherine G — *Astronaut*
%NASA, Johnson Space Center, 2101 NASA Road, Houston, TX 77058, USA

Coleman, Cy — *Composer*
447 E 57th St, New York, NY 10022, USA

Coleman, Dabney — *Actor*
360 N Kenter Ave, Los Angeles, CA 90049, USA

Coleman, Daniel J — *Publisher*
%Popular Mechanics Magazine, 224 W 57th St, New York, NY 10019, USA

Coleman, Derrick D — *Basketball Player*
%Philadelphia 76ers, Veterans Stadium, PO Box 25040, Philadelphia, PA 19147, USA

Coleman, Don E — *Football Player*
424 McPherson Ave, Lansing, MI 48915, USA

Coleman, Gary — *Actor*
4710 Don Miguel Dr, Los Angeles, CA 90008, USA

Coleman, George E — *Jazz Saxophonist*
63 E 9th St, New York, NY 10003, USA

Coleman, Jack — *Actor*
4230 Colfax Ave, #304, Studio City, CA 91604, USA

Coleman, Leonard S, Jr — *Baseball Executive*
%National League, President's Office, 350 Park Ave, New York, NY 10022, USA

Coleman, Lester E — *Businessman*
%Lubrizol Corp, 29400 Lakeland Blvd, Wickliffe, OH 44092, USA

Coleman, Ornette — *Jazz Saxophonist, Composer*
%Monterey International, 200 W Superior, #202, Chicago, IL 60610, USA

Coleman, Peter T — *Governor, GU*
PO Box 1178, Pago Pago, AS 96799, USA

Coleman, Sidney R — *Physicist*
1 Richdale Ave, #12, Cambridge, MA 02140, USA

Coleman, Vincent M (Vince) — *Baseball Player*
7785 E Vaquero Dr, Scottsdale, AZ 85258, USA

Coleman, William T, Jr — *Secretary, Transportation*
%O'Melveny & Myers, 555 13th St NW, #500, Washington, DC 20004, USA

Colen, Beatrice — *Actress*
%Chasin Agency, 8899 Beverly Blvd, #716, Los Angeles, CA 90048, USA

Coles, Kim — *Actress*
325 Westbourne Dr, Los Angeles, CA 90048, USA

Coles, Robert M — *Psychiatrist*
%Harvard University Health Services, 75 Mount Auburn St, Cambridge, MA 02138, USA

Colescott, Warrington W — *Artist*
Rt 1, Hollandale, WI 53544, USA

Coley, Daryl — *Clarinetist, Pianist*
%Daryl Coley Ministries, 417 E Regent St, Inglewood, CA 90301, USA

Colgrass, Michael C — *Composer*
583 Palmerston Ave, Toronto ON M6G 2P6, Canada

Colicos, John — *Actor*
615 Yonge St, #401, Toronto ON M4Y 1Z5, Canada

Colin, Margaret — *Actress*
366 W 11th St, #PH-C, New York, NY 10014, USA

Coll, Stephen W — *Journalist*
%Washington Post, Editorial Dept, 1150 15th St NW, Washington, DC 20071, USA

Collard, Jean-Philippe — *Concert Pianist*
Boite Postal 210, 75426 Paris Cedex 09, France

Collen, Desire — *Medical Researcher*
%University of Leuven, Leuven, Belgium

Collen, Phil — *Guitarist (Def Leppard)*
%Q Prime Mgmt, 729 7th Ave, #1400, New York, NY 10019, USA

Collette, Buddy — *Jazz Musician*
900 S Sierra Bonita Ave, Los Angeles, CA 90036, USA

Colley, Ed — *Cartoonist (Suburban Cowgirls)*
%Tribune Media Services, 435 N Michigan Ave, #1500, Chicago, IL 60611, USA

Colley, Michael C — *Navy Admiral*
7849 Painted Daisy Dr, Springfield, VA 22152, USA

Collie, Mark — *Singer, Songwriter*
%Trifecta, 209 10th Ave S, #302, Nashville, TN 37203, USA

C

Colella - Collie

Collier, Lesley F *Ballerina*
%Royal Ballet Co, 155 Talgarth Road, London W14, England

Collins, Bootsy *Singer, Bassist*
%Performers of the World, 8901 Melrose Ave, #200, West Hollywood, CA 90069, USA

Collins, Bud *Sportscaster*
822 Boylston St, #203, Chestnut Hill, MA 02167, USA

Collins, Doug *Basketball Player, Coach*
275 Greenwood St, Birmingham, MI 48009, USA

Collins, Eileen M *Astronaut*
%NASA, Johnson Space Center, 2101 NASA Road, Houston, TX 77058, USA

Collins, Francis S *Geneticist*
%National Institutes of Health, 9000 Rockville Pike, Bethesda, MD 20892, USA

Collins, Gary *Actor*
2751 Hutton Dr, Beverly Hills, CA 90210, USA

Collins, George J *Financier*
%T Rowe Price Assoc, 100 E Pratt St, Baltimore, MD 21202, USA

Collins, Glen L *Football Player*
817 E River Place, Jackson, MS 39202, USA

Collins, Jack *Actor*
%Contemporary Artists, 1427 3rd St Promenade, #205, Santa Monica, CA 90401, USA

Collins, Jackie *Writer*
PO Box 5473, Glendale, CA 91221, USA

Collins, Joan *Actress*
16 Bulbecks Walk, S Woodham Ferrers, Chelmsford, Essex CM3 5ZN, England

Collins, John G *Financier*
%UJB Financial Corp, Carnegie Center, PO Box 2066, Princeton, NJ 08543, USA

Collins, John W *Businessman*
%Clorox Co, 1221 Broadway, Oakland, CA 94612, USA

Collins, Judy *Singer, Songwriter*
39 Wagon Wheel Road, Redding, CT 06896, USA

Collins, Kerry *Football Player*
2618 Flintgrove Road, Charlotte, NC 28226, USA

Collins, Larry *Writer*
La Biche Niche, 83350 Ramatuelle, France

Collins, Martha Layne *Governor, KY; Educator*
%St Catherine College, President's Office, St Catherine, KY 40061, USA

Collins, Marva *Educator*
%Westside Preparatory School, 4146 W Chicago Ave, Chicago, IL 60651, USA

Collins, Michael *Astronaut, Air Force General*
PO Box 600, Avon, NC 27915, USA

Collins, Patrick *Actor*
9200 Sunset Blvd, #702, Los Angeles, CA 90069, USA

Collins, Pauline *Actress*
%James Sharkey, 21 Golden Square, London W1R 3PA, England

Collins, Phil *Singer, Songwriter, Drummer*
%Hit & Run Mgmt, 25 Ives St, London SW3 2ND, England

Collins, Samuel C *Mechanical Engineer, Cryogenist*
12322 Riverview Road, Oxon Hill, MD 20744, USA

Collins, Stephen *Actor*
12960 Brentwood Terrace, Los Angeles, CA 90049, USA

Collins, Terry L *Baseball Manager*
%Anaheim Angels, Anaheim Stadium, PO Box 2000, Anaheim, CA 92803, USA

Collinsworth, Cris *Sportscaster*
%NBC-TV, Sports Dept, 30 Rockefeller Plaza, New York, NY 10112, USA

Collomb, Bertrand P *Businessman*
%LaFarge Corp, 11130 Sunrise Valley Dr, Reston, VA 20191, USA

Colnbrook of Waltham (H E G Atkins) *Government Official, England*
%House of Lords, Westminster, London SW1A 0PW, England

Colombo, Emilio *Prime Minister, Italy*
Via Aurelia 239, Rome, Italy

Colombo, Giovanni Cardinal *Religious Leader*
Palazzo Arcivescovile, Piazza Fontana 2, Milan, Italy

Colomby, Scott *Actor*
%Borinstein Oreck Bogart, 8271 Melrose Ave, #110, Los Angeles, CA 90046, USA

Colson, Charles W *Religious Leader, Watergate Figure*
%Prison Fellowship, PO Box 17500, Washington, DC 20041, USA

Colson, Elizabeth F *Anthropologist*
%University of California, Anthropology Dept, Berkeley, CA 94720, USA

Colt, Marshall _Actor_
333 Elm St, Denver, CO 80220, USA

Colter, Jessie _Singer_
1117 17th Ave S, Nashville, TN 37212, USA

Coltman, Charles L, III _Financier_
%CoreStates Financial Corp, Broad & Chestnut Sts, Philadelphia, PA 19101, USA

Colton, Frank B _Inventor (Oral Contraceptive)_
1418 E Beacon Dr, Gilbert, AZ 85234, USA

Coltrane, Robbie _Actor_
%Inspirational Artists, PO Box 1AS, London W1A 1AS, England

Columbu, Franco _Body Builder_
%Franco Columbu Productions, 2947 S Sepulveda Blvd, Los Angeles, CA 90064, USA

Columbus, Chris _Movie Director_
847 N Franklin Ave, River Forest, IL 60305, USA

Colussy, Dan A _Businessman_
%UNC Inc, 175 Admiral Cochrane Dr, Annapolis, MD 21401, USA

Colville, Alex _Artist_
408 Main St, Wolfville NS B0P 1XP, Canada

Colvin, Jack L _Actor_
%Century Artists, 1148 4th St, #206, Santa Monica, CA 90403, USA

Colvin, John O _Judge_
%US Tax Court, 400 2nd St NW, Washington, DC 20217, USA

Colvin, Shawn _Singer, Songwriter_
%AGF Entertainment, 30 W 21 St, #700, New York, NY 10010, USA

Colwell, John A _Association Executive, Physician_
%American Diabetes Assn, 1660 Duke St, Alexandria, VA 22314, USA

Colwell, Rita R _Microbiologist_
5110 River Hill Road, Bethesda, MD 20816, USA

Comaneci, Nadia _Gymnast_
4421 Hidden Hill Road, Norman, OK 73072, USA

Combes, Willard W _Editorial Cartoonist_
1266 Oakridge Dr, Cleveland, OH 44121, USA

Combs, Jeffrey _Actor_
13601 Ventura Blvd, #340, Sherman Oaks, CA 91423, USA

Comegys, Dallas _Basketball Player_
73 Water St, Park Forest, IL 60466, USA

Comer, Anjanette _Actress_
13701 Riverside Dr, #208, Sherman Oaks, CA 91423, USA

Comer, Clarence C _Businessman_
%Southdown Inc, 1200 Smith St, Houston, TX 77002, USA

Comer, Gary C _Businessman_
%Lands' End Inc, 1 Lands' End Lane, Dodgeville, WI 53595, USA

Comer, James P _Psychiatrist_
%Yale University, Child Study Center, 230 S Frontage Road, New Haven, CT 06519, USA

Comfort, Alexander (Alex) _Writer, Medical Biologist_
Fitzwarren House, Hornsey Lane, London N6 5LX, England

Comissiona, Sergiu _Conductor_
%Helsinki Philharmonic, Karamzininkatu 4, 00100 Helsinki, Finland

Commager, Henry Steele _Writer, Historian_
PO Box 2187, Amherst, MA 01004, USA

Commes, Thomas A _Businessman_
%Sherwin-Williams Co, 101 Prospect Ave NW, Cleveland, OH 44115, USA

Commoner, Barry _Plant Physiologist_
%Queens College, Biology of Natural Systems Center, Flushing, NY 11367, USA

Como, Perry _Singer, Actor_
%Roncom Productions, 305 Northern Blvd, #3-A, Great Neck, NY 11021, USA

Compagnoni, Deborah _Skier_
Via Frodonfo 3, Santa Catarina Valfurna, Italy

Compaore, Blaise _President, Burkina Faso_
%President's Office, Boite Postale 7031, Ouagadougou, Burkina Faso

Compton, Ann Woodruff _Commentator_
%ABC-TV, News Dept, 1717 DeSales St NW, Washington, DC 20036, USA

Compton, Denis C S _Cricket Player_
%Sunday Express, 245 Blackfriars Road, London SE1 9UX, England

Compton, John G M _Prime Minister, Saint Lucia_
%Prime Minister's Office, Laborie House, Castries, Saint Lucia

Compton, Joyce _Actress_
23388 Mulholland Dr, Woodland Hills, CA 91364, USA

Compton, Ronald E — *Businessman*
%Aetna Life & Casualty, 151 Farmington Ave, Hartford, CT 06156, USA

Comroe, Julius H, Jr — *Physiologist*
555 Laurent Road, Hillsborough, CA 94010, USA

Conable, Barber B, Jr — *Financier; Representative, NY*
%World Bank Group, 1818 "H" St NW, Washington, DC 20433, USA

Conant, Kenneth J — *Archaeologist*
3 Carlton Village, #T-105, Bedford, MA 01730, USA

Conaway, Cristi — *Actress*
PO Box 46515, Los Angeles, CA 90046, USA

Conaway, Jeff — *Actor*
3162 Durand Dr, Los Angeles, CA 90068, USA

Conboy, John J — *Television Producer*
%Major Clients Agency, 2121 Ave of Stars, Los Angeles, CA 90067, USA

Concepion, David I (Davey) — *Baseball Player*
Urb Los Caobos Botalon 5-D, 5-Piso-Maracay, Venezuela

Condit, Philip M — *Businessman*
%Boeing Co, 7755 Marginal Way, Seattle, WA 98108, USA

Condon, Paul — *Law Enforcement Official*
Metropolitan Police, New Scotland Yard, Broadway, London SW1H 0BG, England

Cone Vanderbush, Carin — *Swimmer*
116 Washington Road, #B, West Point, NY 10996, USA

Cone, David B — *Baseball Player*
17080 Harbour Point Dr, Fort Myers, FL 33908, USA

Conefry, John J, Jr — *Financier*
%Long Island Savings Bank, 201 Old Country Road, Melville, NY 11747, USA

Conforti, Gino — *Actor*
%Orange Grove Group, 12178 Ventura Blvd, #205, Studio City, CA 91604, USA

Conger, Harry M — *Businessman*
%Homestake Mining, 650 California St, San Francisco, CA 94108, USA

Conlan, Shane — *Football Player*
5 Carroll St, Frewsburg, NY 14738, USA

Conlee, John — *Singer*
%John Conlee Enterprises, 38 Music Square E, #117, Nashville, TN 37203, USA

Conley, Arthur — *Singer*
630 Oakstone Dr, Roswell, GA 30075, USA

Conley, Clare D — *Editor*
Hemlock Farms, Hawley, PA 18428, USA

Conley, D Eugene (Gene) — *Baseball, Basketball Player*
1 Farrington St, Foxboro, MA 02035, USA

Conley, Darlene — *Actress*
1840 S Beverly Glen Blvd, #501, Los Angeles, CA 90025, USA

Conley, Earl Thomas — *Singer, Songwriter*
%Entertainment Artists, 903 18th Ave S, Nashville, TN 37212, USA

Conley, Joe — *Actor*
PO Box 6487, Thousand Oaks, CA 91359, USA

Conley, Mike — *Track Athlete*
%University of Arkansas, Athletic Dept, Fayetteville, AR 72701, USA

Conlon, James J — *Conductor*
%Columbia Artists Mgmt Inc, 165 W 57th St, New York, NY 10019, USA

Conn, Didi — *Actress, Singer*
%Richard Gersh, Radio City Station, New York, NY 10019, USA

Connell, Elizabeth — *Opera Singer*
%S A Gorlinsky, 33 Dover St, London W1X 4NJ, England

Connell, Evan S, Jr — *Writer*
Fort Macy 13, 320 Artist Road, Santa Fe, NM 87501, USA

Connell, John MacFarlane — *Businessman*
%Distillers Co, 12 Torphechen St, Edinburgh EH3 8YT, Scotland

Connell, Thurman C — *Financier*
%Federal Home Loan Bank, 907 Walnut St, Des Moines, IA 50309, USA

Connelly, Jennifer — *Actress*
50 Bethel St, Cranston, RI 02920, USA

Connelly, Michael — *Writer*
%Little Brown, 34 Beacon St, Boston, MA 02108, USA

Conner, Bart — *Gymnast*
4421 Hidden Hill Road, Norman, OK 73072, USA

Conner, Bruce — *Artist*
45 Sussex St, San Francisco, CA 94131, USA

Conner, Finis F — *Businessman*
%Conner Peripherals, 3081 Zanker Road, San Jose, CA 95134, USA

Conner, Lester — *Basketball Player*
2545 Best Ave, Oakland, CA 94601, USA

Connery, Jason — *Actor*
%Joy Jameson, The Plaza, #219, 555 Kings Road, London SW10 0SZ, England

Connery, Sean — *Actor*
Casa Malibu, Fuente del Rodeo, Nueva Andalusia, Malaga, Spain

Connery, Vincent L — *Labor Leader*
%National Treasury Employees Union, 1730 "K" St NW, Washington, DC 20006, USA

Connick, Harry, Jr — *Pianist, Singer, Actor*
%Wilkins Mgmt, 323 Broadway, Cambridge, MA 02139, USA

Connick, Robert E — *Chemist*
50 Marguerita Road, Berkeley, CA 94707, USA

Conniff, Cal — *Skier*
157 Pleasantview Ave, Longmeadow, MA 01106, USA

Conniff, Ray — *Conductor, Composer*
2154 Hercules Dr, Los Angeles, CA 90046, USA

Connolly, Billy — *Actor*
%John Reid, Singes House, 32 Galena Road, London W6 0LT, England

Connolly, Eugene B, Jr — *Businessman*
%USG Corp, 125 S Franklin St, Chicago, IL 60606, USA

Connolly, Harold — *Track Athlete*
1029 Nowita Place, Venice, CA 90291, USA

Connolly, Norma — *Actress*
%Agency For Performing Arts, 9200 Sunset Blvd, #900, Los Angeles, CA 90069, USA

Connolly, Olga — *Track Athlete*
11027 Ocean Dr, Culver City, CA 90230, USA

Connor, Chris — *Singer*
%Lori Muscarelle Mgmt, 27 Prado Court, Toms River, NJ 08757, USA

Connor, George L — *Football Player*
235 E Walton Place, #5, Chicago, IL 60611, USA

Connor, John T — *Secretary, Commerce*
11854 Turtle Beach Road, North Palm Beach, FL 33408, USA

Connor, Joseph E — *Government Official, Businessman*
%UnderSecretary-Generals Office, United Nations, UN Plaza, New York, NY 10021, USA

Connor, Kenneth — *Actor*
%Peter Rogers Productions, Pinewood Films, Iver Heath SLO 0NH, England

Connor, Ralph — *Chemist*
9866 Highwood Court, Sun City, AZ 85373, USA

Connor, Richard L — *Publisher*
%Fort Worth Star-Telegram, 400 W 7th St, Fort Worth, TX 76102, USA

Connors, Carol — *Songwriter*
1709 Ferrari Dr, Beverly Hills, CA 90210, USA

Connors, James S (Jimmy) — *Tennis Player*
200 S Refugio Road, Santa Ynez, CA 93460, USA

Connors, Mike — *Actor*
4810 Louise Ave, Encino, CA 91316, USA

Conombo, Joseph I — *Prime Minister, Upper Volta*
Ave de la Liberte, BP 613, Dadoya, Ouagadougou, Burkina Faso

Conover, Lloyd H — *Inventor (Tetracycline)*
27 Old Barry Road, Quaker Hill, CT 06375, USA

Conrad Hefner, Kimberly — *Model*
10236 Charing Cross Road, Los Angeles, CA 90024, USA

Conrad, Charles (Pete), Jr — *Astronaut*
%McDonnell Douglas, 5301 Bolsa Ave, Huntington Beach, CA 92647, USA

Conrad, Fred — *Photographer*
%New York Times, Editorial Dept, 229 W 43rd St, New York, NY 10036, USA

Conrad, John H — *Astronaut*
%Hughes Aircraft Space Communications Group, Box 92919, Los Angeles, CA 90009, USA

Conrad, Paul F — *Editorial Cartoonist*
28649 Crestridge Road, Palos Verdes, CA 90275, USA

Conrad, Robert — *Actor*
PO Box 5237, Bear Valley, CA 95223, USA

Conradt, Judy — *Basketball Coach*
%University of Texas, Athletic Dept, Austin, TX 78712, USA

Conran, Jasper A T — *Fashion Designer*
49/50 Great Marlborough St, London W1V 1DB, England

C

Conran, Terence O — *Interior Designer*
512 Butler Wharf Building, 36 Shad Thames, London SE1 2YE, England

Conroy, D Patrick (Pat) — *Writer*
%Old New York Book Shop, PO Box 14027, Atlanta, GA 30324, USA

Conroy, Frank — *Writer*
%Houghton Mifflin, 215 Park Ave S, New York, NY 10003, USA

Consagra, Pietro — *Sculptor*
Via Cassia 1162, Rome, Italy

Considine, John — *Actor*
16 1/2 Red Coat Lane, Greenwich, CT 06830, USA

Considine, Tim — *Actor*
3708 Mountain View Ave, Los Angeles, CA 90066, USA

Constable, George — *Editor*
%Time-Life Books, Editorial Dept, Rockefeller Center, New York, NY 10020, USA

Constantine II — *King, Greece*
4 Linnell Dr, Hampstead Way, London NW11, England

Constantinescu, Emil — *President, Romania*
%President's Office, Calle Victoriei 49-53, Bucharest, Romania

Conte, John — *Actor*
75600 Beryl Dr, Indian Wells, CA 92210, USA

Conte, Lansana — *President, Guinea; Army General*
%President's Office, Conakry, Guinea

Conte, Lou — *Choreographer*
%Hubbard Street Dance Co, 218 S Wabash Ave, Chicago, IL 60604, USA

Conte, Richard L — *Businessman*
%Community Psychiatric Centers, 6600 W Charleston Blvd, Las Vegas, NV 89102, USA

Conti, Bill — *Composer*
117 Fremont Pl W, Los Angeles, CA 90005, USA

Conti, Tom — *Actor*
%Chatto & Linnit, Prince of Wales, Coventry St, London W1V 7FE, England

Contino, Dick — *Accordianist*
3355 Nahatan Way, Las Vegas, NV 89109, USA

Converse, Frank — *Actor*
%Artists Group, 10100 Santa Monica Blvd, #2490, Los Angeles, CA 90067, USA

Converse, Peggy — *Actress*
2525 Briarcrest Road, Beverly Hills, CA 90210, USA

Converse-Roberts, William — *Actor*
%Innovative Artists, 1999 Ave of Stars, #2850, Los Angeles, CA 90067, USA

Conway, Curtis — *Football Player*
1171 E 56th St, Los Angeles, CA 90011, USA

Conway, Gary — *Actor*
11240 Chimney Rock Road, Paso Robles, CA 93446, USA

Conway, James L — *Movie Director*
%Creative Artists Agency, 9830 Wilshire Blvd, Beverly Hills, CA 90212, USA

Conway, Jill K — *Writer, Historian*
65 Commonwealth Ave, #8-B, Boston, MA 02116, USA

Conway, Kevin — *Actor*
25 Century Park West, New York, NY 10023, USA

Conway, Tim — *Comedian*
%Tim Conway Enterprises, PO Box 17047, Encino, CA 91416, USA

Coobar, Abdulmegid — *Prime Minister, Libya*
Asadu El-Furat St 29, Garden City, Tripoli, Libya

Cooder, Ry — *Singer, Guitarist, Composer*
326 Entrada Dr, Santa Monica, CA 90402, USA

Coody, Charles — *Golfer*
%Int'l Management Group, 1 Erieview Plaza, #1300, Cleveland, OH 44114, USA

Coogan, Keith — *Actor*
1640 S Sepulveda Blvd, #218, Los Angeles, CA 90025, USA

Cook, Antoinette — *Government Official*
%Federal Communication Commission, 1919 "M" St NW, Washington, DC 20036, USA

Cook, Barbara — *Singer, Actress*
%JKE Services, 205 Lexington Ave, New York, NY 10016, USA

Cook, Beryl — *Artist*
3 Athenaeum St, The Hoe, Plymouth PL1 2RQ, England

Cook, Bruce — *Writer*
502 N Plymouth Blvd, Los Angeles, CA 90004, USA

Cook, Carole — *Comedienne, Actress*
8829 Ashcroft Ave, Los Angeles, CA 90048, USA

Cook, Don — *Golfer*
%Professional Golfer's Assn, PO Box 109601, Palm Beach Gardens, FL 33410, USA

Cook, G Bradford — *Stock Exchange Executive*
Woman Lake, Longville, MN 56655, USA

Cook, Jeffrey A (Jeff) — *Singer, Guitarist (Alabama)*
PO Box 35967, Fort Payne, AL 35967, USA

Cook, John — *Golfer*
1111 Tahquitz E, #203, Palm Springs, CA 92262, USA

Cook, Judy — *Bowler*
%Ladies Professional Bowlers Tour, 7171 Cherryvale Blvd, Rockford, IL 61112, USA

Cook, Lodwrick M — *Businessman*
%Atlantic Richfield, 515 S Flower St, Los Angeles, CA 90071, USA

Cook, Paul M — *Businessman*
%Raychem Corp, 300 Constitution Dr, Menlo Park, CA 94025, USA

Cook, Peter F C — *Architect*
54 Compayne Gardens, London NW6 3RY, England

Cook, Robert — *Opera Singer*
The Quavers, 53 Friars Ave, Fiern Barnet, London N2O OXG, England

Cook, Robert F (Robin) — *Government Official, England*
%House of Commons, Westminster, London SW1A 0AA, England

Cook, Robin — *Writer*
%Massachusetts Ear & Eye Infirmary, 243 Charles St, Boston, MA 02114, USA

Cook, Scott — *Businessman*
%Intuit Inc, PO Box 7850, Mountain View, CA 94039, USA

Cook, Stanton R — *Publisher*
%Tribune Co, 435 N Michigan Ave, Chicago, IL 60611, USA

Cooke, A Alistair — *Writer, Commentator*
1150 5th Ave, New York, NY 10128, USA

Cooke, Howard — *Governor General, Jamaica*
King's House, Hope Road, Kingston 10, Jamaica

Cooke, Janis — *Journalist*
%Washington Post, Editorial Dept, 1150 15th St NW, Washington, DC 20071, USA

Cooke, John P — *Rower*
290 Old Branchville Road, Ridgefield, CT 06877, USA

Cooks, Johnie — *Football Player*
%Baltimore Ravens, 200 St Paul Place, #2400, Baltimore, MD 21202, USA

Cooksey, Dave — *Religious Leader*
%Brethren Church, 524 College Ave, Ashland, OH 44805, USA

Cookson, Catherine A — *Writer*
White Lodge, 23 Glastonbury Grove, Newcastle Upon Tyne NE2 2HB, England

Cooley, Denton A — *Surgeon*
%Texas Heart Institution, 6621 Fannin St, Houston, TX 77030, USA

Coolidge, Charles H — *WW II Army Hero (CMH)*
1054 Balmoral Dr, Signal Mountain, TN 37377, USA

Coolidge, E David, III — *Financier*
%William Blair Co, 222 W Adams St, Chicago, IL 60606, USA

Coolidge, Harold J — *Conservationist*
38 Standley St, Beverly, MA 01915, USA

Coolidge, Martha — *Movie Director*
2129 Coldwater Canyon, Beverly Hills, CA 90210, USA

Coolio (Austin Ivey Jr) — *Rap Artist*
%Powermove, 1972 Outpost Circle, Los Angeles, CA 90068, USA

Coombe, George W — *Attorney*
%Graham & James, 1 Maritime Plaza, San Francisco, CA 94111, USA

Cooney, Joan Ganz — *Educator, Television Executive*
%Children's TV Workshop, 1 Lincoln Plaza, New York, NY 10023, USA

Cooper, Alexander — *Architect*
%Cooper Robertson & Partners, 311 W 43rd St, New York, NY 10036, USA

Cooper, Alice — *Singer, Songwriter*
4135 E Keim St, Paradise Valley, AZ 85253, USA

Cooper, Amy Levin — *Editor*
%Mademoiselle Magazine, Editorial Dept, 350 Madison Ave, New York, NY 10017, USA

Cooper, Arthur M — *Editor*
%Gentlemen's Quarterly Magazine, 350 Madison Ave, New York, NY 10017, USA

Cooper, Cecil C — *Baseball Player*
1431 Misty Bend, Katy, TX 77494, USA

Cooper, Charles G — *Marine Corps General*
3410 Barger Dr, Falls Church, VA 22044, USA

C

Cooper, Chris — *Actor*
%Paradigm Agency, 10100 Santa Monica Blvd, #2500, Los Angeles, CA 90067, USA

Cooper, Christin — *Skier*
1001 E Hyman Ave, Aspen, CO 81611, USA

Cooper, Cortz — *Religious Leader*
%Presbyterian Church in America, 1852 Century Place, Atlanta, GA 30345, USA

Cooper, Daniel L — *Navy Admiral*
121 Leisure Court, Wyomissing, PA 19610, USA

Cooper, David B — *Businessman*
%Edison Brothers Stores, 501 N Broadway, St Louis, MO 63102, USA

Cooper, Frederick E — *Businessman*
%Jones Davis Reavis, 1st Peachtree Center, 303 Peachtree St, Atlanta, GA 30308, USA

Cooper, Hal — *Television Director*
2651 Hutton Dr, Beverly Hills, CA 90210, USA

Cooper, Harry (Lighthouse) — *Golfer*
7 Verne Place, Hartsdale, NY 10530, USA

Cooper, Henry — *Boxer*
36 Brampton Grove, London NW4, England

Cooper, Imogen — *Concert Pianist*
%Van Walsum Mgmt, 26 Wadham Road, London SW15 2LR, England

Cooper, Jackie — *Movie Director, Actor*
9621 Royalton Dr, Beverly Hills, CA 90210, USA

Cooper, Jeanne — *Actress*
8401 Edwin Dr, Los Angeles, CA 90046, USA

Cooper, Jilly — *Writer*
%Desmond Elliott, 38 Bury St, London SW1Y 6AU, England

Cooper, Joel D — *Thoracic Surgeon*
%Washington University Medical School, Surgery Dept, St Louis, MO 63110, USA

Cooper, John — *Football Coach*
%Ohio State University, Athletic Dept, Columbus, OH 43210, USA

Cooper, John A D — *Physician*
4118 N River Road, Arlington, VA 22207, USA

Cooper, L Gordon, Jr — *Astronaut*
16303 Waterman Dr, #B, Van Nuys, CA 91406, USA

Cooper, Lance E — *Businessman*
%Iowa-Illinois Gas & Electric, 206 E 2nd St, Davenport, IA 52801, USA

Cooper, Leon N — *Nobel Physics Laureate*
49 Intervale Road, Providence, RI 02906, USA

Cooper, Lester I — *Television Producer*
45 S Morningside Dr, Westport, CT 06880, USA

Cooper, Paula — *Art Dealer*
%Paula Cooper Gallery, 534 W 21st St, New York, NY 10011, USA

Cooper, Ron — *Artist*
1310 Main St, Venice, CA 90291, USA

Cooper, Wayne — *Artist*
126 W 1025 S, Kouts, IN 46347, USA

Cooper, William A — *Financier*
%TCF Financial Corp, 801 Marquette Ave, Minneapolis, MN 55402, USA

Cooper, Wilma Lee — *Singer, Guitarist*
%Charles Rapp Enterprises, 1650 Broadway, #1410, New York, NY 10019, USA

Coor, Lattie F — *Educator*
%Arizona State University, President's Office, Tempe, AZ 85287, USA

Coords, Robert H — *Financier*
%SunBank/Miami, 777 Brickell Ave, Miami, FL 33131, USA

Coors, Joseph — *Businessman*
%Adolph Coors Co, 1221 Ford St, Golden, CO 80401, USA

Coors, William K — *Businessman*
%Adolph Coors Co, 1221 Ford St, Golden, CO 80401, USA

Coover, Robert — *Writer*
%Georges Borchardt Inc, 136 E 57th St, New York, NY 10022, USA

Cope, Derrike — *Auto Racing Driver*
%DC Enterprises, 19228 Betty Stough Road, Huntersville, NC 28078, USA

Cope, Julian — *Singer, Songwriter*
%International Talent Group, 729 7th Ave, #1600, New York, NY 10019, USA

Copeland, Al — *Powerboat Racing Driver, Businessman*
5001 Folse Dr, Metairie, LA 70006, USA

Copeland, Joan — *Actress*
%Alliance Talent, 9171 Wilshire Blvd, #441, Beverly Hills, CA 90210, USA

Copeland, Kenneth	*Evangelist*
%Kenneth Copeland Ministries, PO Box 2908, Fort Worth, TX 76113, USA	
Copeland, Lila	*Artist*
305 W 28th St, #21-E, New York, NY 10001, USA	
Copley, Helen K	*Publisher*
%Copley Press, 7776 Ivanhoe Ave, La Jolla, CA 92037, USA	
Copley, Teri	*Actress, Model*
5003 Coldwater Canyon Ave, Sherman Oaks, CA 91423, USA	
Copp, Daniel N	*Businessman*
%Circus Circus Enterprises, 2880 Las Vegas Blvd S, Las Vegas, NV 89109, USA	
Copperfield, David	*Illusionist*
515 Post Oak Blvd, #300, Houston, TX 77027, USA	
Copping, Allen A	*Educator*
%Louisiana State University System, President's Office, Baton Rouge, LA 70808, USA	
Coppola, Francis Ford	*Movie Director*
%Zoetrope Studios, 916 Kearny St, San Francisco, CA 94133, USA	
Coppola, Joseph R	*Businessman*
%Giddings & Lewis Inc, 142 Doty Road, Fond Du Lac, WI 54935, USA	
Cora, Jose M	*Baseball Player*
Calle 17, F-12 Villa Nueva, Caguas, PR 00625, USA	
Corbett, Gretchen	*Actress*
%SDB Partners, 1801 Ave of Stars, #902, Los Angeles, CA 90067, USA	
Corbett, Mike	*Rock Climber*
PO Box 917, Yosemite National Park, CA 95389, USA	
Corbett, Ronnie	*Comedian, Actor*
%International Artistes, 235 Regent St, London W1R 8AX, England	
Corbin, Barry	*Actor*
2113 Greta Lane, Fort Worth, TX 76120, USA	
Corbin, Tyrone	*Basketball Player*
%Atlanta Hawks, 1 CNN Center, South Tower, Atlanta, GA 30303, USA	
Corbus, William	*Football Player*
1100 Union St, #1100, San Francisco, CA 94109, USA	
Corby, Ellen	*Actress*
9024 Harratt St, Los Angeles, CA 90069, USA	
Corcoran, Kevin	*Actor*
8617 Balcom Ave, Northridge, CA 91325, USA	
Cord, Alex	*Actor*
335 N Maple Dr, #361, Beverly Hills, CA 90210, USA	
Corday, Barbara	*Entertainment Executive*
532 S Windsor Blvd, Los Angeles, CA 90020, USA	
Corday, Mara	*Actress, Model*
PO Box 800393, Valencia, CA 91380, USA	
Cordero, Angel T, Jr	*Thoroughbred Racing Jockey*
%New York Racing Assn, PO Box 90, Jamaica, NY 11417, USA	
Cordovez Zegers, Diego	*Government Official, Ecuador*
%Foreign Affairs Ministry, Avda 10 Agosta y Carrion, Quito, Ecuador	
Corea, Chick	*Jazz Pianist, Composer*
%Chick Corea Productions, 2635 Griffith Park Blvd, Los Angeles, CA 90039, USA	
Corey, Elias James	*Nobel Chemistry Laureate*
20 Avon Hill St, Cambridge, MA 02140, USA	
Corey, Irwin (Professor)	*Comedian*
58 Nassau Dr, Great Neck, NY 11021, USA	
Corey, Jeff	*Actor*
29445 Bluewater Road, Malibu, CA 90265, USA	
Corey, Jill	*Singer*
64 Division Ave, Levittown, NY 11756, USA	
Corfield, Kenneth G	*Businessman*
14 Elm Walk, Hampstead, London NW3 7UP, England	
Corgan, Billy	*Singer (Smashing Pumpkins), Songwriter*
%Cohen Brothers Mgmt, 8380 Melrose Ave, #311, Los Angeles, CA 90069, USA	
Corigliano, John P	*Composer*
365 West End Ave, New York, NY 10024, USA	
Corley, Al	*Actor*
3323 Corinth Ave, Los Angeles, CA 90066, USA	
Corley, Pat	*Actor*
%Contemporary Artists, 1427 3rd St Promenade, #205, Santa Monica, CA 90401, USA	
Cormack, Allan MacLeod	*Nobel Medicine Laureate*
18 Harrison St, Winchester, MA 01890, USA	

C

Copeland - Cormack

Corman, Avery	*Writer*
%International Creative Mgmt, 40 W 57th St, New York, NY 10019, USA	
Corman, Roger W	*Movie Director, Producer*
2501 La Mesa Dr, Santa Monica, CA 90402, USA	
Corn, Alfred	*Writer*
350 W 14th St, #6-A, New York, NY 10014, USA	
Corneille	*Artist*
%Society of Independent Artists, Cours la Reine, 75008 Paris, France	
Cornelis, Francois	*Businessman*
%Petrofina SA, Rue de l'Industrie 52, 1040 Brussels, Belgium	
Cornelius, Don	*Television Producer*
12685 Mulholland Dr, Beverly Hills, CA 90210, USA	
Cornelius, Helen	*Singer, Songwriter*
%Top Billing, 1222 16th Ave S, #24, Nashville, TN 37212, USA	
Cornell, Don	*Singer, Guitarist*
%Iris Cornell Productions, 100 Bayview Dr, #1521, North Miami Beach, FL 33160, USA	
Cornell, Harry M, Jr	*Businessman*
%Leggett & Platt Inc, PO Box 757, Carthage, MO 64836, USA	
Cornell, Lydia	*Actress*
142 S Bedford Dr, Beverly Hills, CA 90212, USA	
Cornelsen, Rufus	*Religious Leader*
415 S Chester Road, Swarthmore, PA 19081, USA	
Corness, Colin R	*Businessman*
%Redland, Redland House, Reigate, Surrey RH2 0SJ, England	
Cornforth, John W	*Nobel Chemistry Laureate*
Saxon Down, Cuilfail, Lewes, East Sussex BN7 2BE, England	
Cornog, Robert A	*Businessman*
%Snap-on Tools Corp, 2801 80th St, Kenosha, WI 53143, USA	
Cornthwaite, Robert	*Actor*
23388 Mulholland Dr, #12, Woodland Hills, CA 91364, USA	
Cornwell, Patricia D	*Writer*
500 Libbie Ave, #1-B, Richmond, VA 23226, USA	
Corr, Edwin G	*Diplomat*
544 Shawnee St, Norman, OK 73071, USA	
Correa, Charles M	*Architect*
Sonmarg, Napean Sea Road, Bombay 40006, India	
Correia, Carlos	*Prime Minister, Guinea-Bissau*
%Prime Minister's Office, Bissau, Guinea-Bissau	
Correll, A D	*Businessman*
%Georgia-Pacific Corp, 133 Peachtree St NE, Atlanta, GA 30303, USA	
Corretja, Alex	*Tennis Player*
%Assn of Tennis Professionals, 200 Tournament Players Rd, Ponte Vedra, FL 32082, USA	
Corri, Adrienne	*Actress*
%London Mgmt, 2-4 Noel St, London W1V 3RB, England	
Corrick, Ann Marjorie	*Journalist*
3050 Dover Dr, #56, Santa Cruz, CA 95065, USA	
Corridon-Mortell, Marie	*Swimmer*
13 Heritage Village, #A, Southbury, CT 06488, USA	
Corrigan, E Gerald	*Government Official, Financier*
%Goldman Sachs Co, 85 Broad St, New York, NY 10004, USA	
Corrigan, Wilfred J	*Businessman*
%LSI Logic, 1551 McCarthy Blvd, Milpitas, CA 95035, USA	
Corrigan-Maguire, Mairead	*Nobel Peace Laureate*
%Peace People Community, 224 Lisburn Road, Belfast BT9 6GE, North Ireland	
Corripio Ahumada, Ernesto Cardinal	*Religious Leader*
Apartado Postal 24-433, Mexico City 7 DF, Mexico	
Corry, Charles A	*Businessman*
%USX Corp, 600 Grant St, Pittsburgh, PA 15219, USA	
Corsaro, Frank A	*Theater, Opera Director*
33 Riverside Dr, New York, NY 10023, USA	
Corso, Gregory N	*Writer*
%New Directions, 80 8th Ave, New York, NY 10011, USA	
Corson, Dale R	*Physicist, Educator*
401 Savage Farm Dr, Ithaca, NY 14850, USA	
Corson, Fred P	*Religious Leader*
Cornwall Manor, Cornwall, PA 17016, USA	
Corson, Keith D	*Businessman*
%Coachmen Industries, 601 E Beardsley Ave, Elkhart, IN 46514, USA	

Corson, Shayne *Hockey Player*
%Montreal Canadiens, 1260 De la Gauchetiere W, Montreal PQ H3B 5E8, Canada
Corson, Thomas H *Businessman*
%Coachmen Industries, 601 E Beardsley Ave, Elkhart, IN 46514, USA
Cort, Bud *Actor*
2149 Lyric Ave, Los Angeles, CA 90027, USA
Cortes, Ron *Journalist*
%Philadelphia Inquirer, Editorial Dept, 400 N Broad St, Philadelphia, PA 19130, USA
Cortese, Dan *Actor*
15250 Ventura Blvd, #900, Sherman Oaks, CA 91403, USA
Cortese, Joe *Actor*
2065 Coldwater Canyon Dr, Beverly Hills, CA 90210, USA
Cortese, Valentina *Actress*
Pretta S Erasmo 6, 20121 Milan, Italy
Cortright, Edgar M, Jr *Aerospace Engineer*
9701 Calvin St, Northridge, CA 91324, USA
Corwin, Norman *Writer*
1840 Fairburn Ave, #302, Los Angeles, CA 90025, USA
Coryatt, Quentin *Football Player*
7941 Mallard Landing, Indianapolis, IN 46278, USA
Corzine, Dave *Basketball Player*
2311 N Champlain St, Arlington Heights, IL 60004, USA
Corzine, Jon S *Financier*
%Goldman Sachs Co, 85 Broad St, New York, NY 10004, USA
Cosbie, Douglas D (Doug) *Football Player*
1301 Brook Place, Mountain View, CA 94040, USA
Cosby, Bill *Actor, Comedian*
PO Box 4049, Santa Monica, CA 90411, USA
Coscarelli, Kate *Writer*
%Don Carter, PO Box 10927, Beverly Hills, CA 90213, USA
Cosgrave, Liam *Prime Minister, Ireland*
Beachpark, Templeogue County, Dublin, Ireland
Cosmatos, George P *Movie Director*
%International Creative Mgmt, 8942 Wilshire Blvd, Beverly Hills, CA 90211, USA
Cosmovici, Cristiano B *Astronaut, Italy*
%Istituto Fisica Spazio Interplanetario, CP 27, 00044 Frascati, Italy
Cossotto, Fiorenza *Opera Singer*
%Columbia Artists Mgmt Inc, 165 W 57th St, New York, NY 10019, USA
Cossutta, Carlo *Opera Singer*
%S A Gorlinsky, 33 Dover St, London W1X 4NJ, England
Costa, Gal *Singer*
%Performers of the World, 8901 Melrose Ave, #200, Los Angeles, CA 90069, USA
Costa, Mary *Opera Singer*
3340 Kingston Pike, #1, Knoxville, TN 37919, USA
Costa-Gavras, Konstaninos *Movie Director*
24 Rue Saint-Jacques, 75005 Paris, France
Costanza, Margaret (Midge) *Government Official*
4518 Agnes Ave, Studio City, CA 91607, USA
Costanzo, Robert *Actor*
%Gold Marshak Liedtke, 3500 W Olive Ave, #1400, Burbank, CA 91505, USA
Costas, Robert Q (Bob) *Sportscaster*
12813 Flushing Meadow Dr, St Louis, MO 63131, USA
Costello, Billy *Boxer*
%Roundouts Gardens, #71-H, Kingston, NY 12401, USA
Costello, Elvis *Singer, Songwriter*
%Riviera Global, 18 The Green, Richmond, Surrey TW9 1PY, England
Costello, John D *Coast Guard Admiral*
%US Coast Guard Pacific, Coast Guard Island, Alameda, CA 94501, USA
Costello, Larry *Basketball Player, Coach*
4263 Bay Beach Lane, #817-S, Fort Myers Beach, FL 33931, USA
Costello, Mariclare *Actress*
%Borinstein Oreck Bogart, 8271 Melrose Ave, #110, Los Angeles, CA 90046, USA
Costello, Murray *Hockey Player*
1600 James Nesmith Place, Gloucester ON K1B 5N4, Canada
Costello, Patty *Bowler*
715 S Crystal Lake Dr, Orlando, FL 32803, USA
Costelloe, Paul *Fashion Designer*
%Moygashel Mills, Dungannon BT71 7PB, Northern Ireland

Coster, Nicolas — *Actor*
1624 N Vista St, Los Angeles, CA 90046, USA

Costle, Douglas M — *Government Official, Educator*
%Harvard University, Public Health School, Cambridge, MA 02138, USA

Costner, Kevin — *Actor, Director*
PO Box 275, Montrose, CA 91021, USA

Cotchett, Joseph W — *Attorney*
840 Malcolm Road, Burlingame, CA 94010, USA

Cotlow, Lewis N — *Explorer*
132 Lakeshore Dr, North Palm Beach, FL 33408, USA

Cotrubas, Ileana — *Opera Singer*
%Royal Opera House, Covent Garden, Bow St, London WC2, England

Cotsworth, Stats — *Actor*
360 E 55th St, New York, NY 10022, USA

Cottee, Kay — *Yachtswoman*
%Showcase Productions, 113 Willoughby Road, Crows Nest NSW 2065, Australia

Cottet, Mia — *Actress*
%Metropolitan Talent Agency, 4526 Wilshire Blvd, Los Angeles, CA 90010, USA

Cotti, Flavio — *President, Switzerland*
%Foreign Affairs Dept, Bundeshaus-West, 3003 Berne, Switzerland

Cotting, James C — *Businessman*
%Navistar International, 455 N Cityfront Plaza Dr, Chicago, IL 60611, USA

Cottingham, Robert — *Artist*
PO Box 604, Blackman Road, Newtown, CT 06470, USA

Cotton, Francis E (Fran) — *Rugby Player*
Beechwood, Hulme Hall Road, Cheadle Hulme, Stockport, Che SK8 6JZ, England

Cotton, Frank A — *Chemist*
4101 Sand Creek Road, Bryan, TX 77808, USA

Cotton, James — *Singer, Harmonica Player*
%Antone's Records & Tapes, 609 W 6th St, #B, Austin, TX 78701, USA

Cotton, Josie — *Singer*
8406 Cresthill Road, Los Angeles, CA 90069, USA

Cottrell, Ralph — *Religious Leader*
%Baptist Missionary Assn, PO Box 1203, Van, TX 75790, USA

Couch, John C — *Businessman*
%Alexander & Baldwin Inc, 822 Bishop St, Honolulu, HI 96813, USA

Couch, John N — *Botanist*
1109 Carol Woods, Chapel Hill, NC 27514, USA

Coughlin, Bernard J — *Educator*
%Gonzaga University, Chancellor's Office, Spokane, WA 99258, USA

Coughlin, Tom — *Football Coach*
%Jacksonville Jaguars, 1 Stadium Place, Jacksonville, FL 32202, USA

Coulier, David — *Actor*
%Brillstein/Grey, 9150 Wilshire Blvd, #350, Beverly Hills, CA 90212, USA

Coulson, Catherine E — *Actress*
PO Box 158, Ashland, OR 97520, USA

Coulter, Arthur E (Art) — *Hockey Player*
500 Spanish Court Blvd, #203, Spanish Fort, AL 36527, USA

Coulter, David A — *Financier*
%BankAmerica Corp, 555 California St, San Francisco, CA 94104, USA

Coulter, Phil — *Singer*
%Maggie Cadden, 207 E 84th St, #206, New York, NY 10028, USA

Coulthard, David — *Auto Racing Driver*
%McLaren Int'l, Albert Dr, Woking, Surrey GU21 5JY, England

Counsilman, James E (DoC) — *Swimming Coach*
3602 William Court, Bloomington, IN 47401, USA

Countryman, Garl L — *Businessman*
%Liberty Mutual Insurance, 175 Berkeley St, Boston, MA 02116, USA

Counts, Mel — *Basketball Player*
1581 Matheny Road, Gervais, OR 97026, USA

Couples, Fred — *Golfer*
5609 Cradlerock Crest, Plano, TX 75093, USA

Courant, Ernest D — *Physicist*
109 Bay Ave, Bayport, NY 11705, USA

Couric, Katherine (Katie) — *Commentator*
1100 Park Ave, #15-A, New York, NY 10128, USA

Courier, James S (Jim), Jr — *Tennis Player*
306 E Southview Ave, Dade City, FL 33525, USA

Courlouris, George *Actor*
Chestnut Cottage, Vale of Heath, Hampstead, London NW3, England

Cournoyer, Yvan *Hockey Player*
4500 Promenade Paton, #128, Laval PQ H7W 4Y6, Canada

Courreges, Andre *Fashion Designer*
27 Rue Delabordere, 92 Neuilly-Sur-Seine, France

Court, Hazel *Actress*
%Taylor, 1111 San Vicente Blvd, Santa Monica, CA 90402, USA

Courtenay, Margaret *Actress*
%Barry Burnett, Grafton House, 2/3 Golden Square, London W1R 3AD, England

Courtenay, Tom *Actor*
%Michael Whitehall, 125 Gloucester Road, London SW7 4TE, England

Courtney, Tom *Track Athlete*
833 Wyndemere Way, Naples, FL 34105, USA

Cousin, Philip R *Religious Leader*
%Episcopal Church, 11th District Hq, PO Box 2970, Jacksonville, FL 32203, USA

Cousins, Ralph W *Royal Navy Admiral*
Leconfield House, Curzon St, London W1Y 8JR, England

Cousins, Robin *Figure Skater*
%Billy Marsh, 174-8 N Gower St, London NW1 2NB, England

Cousteau, Jean-Michel *Oceanographer*
%Cousteau Society, 870 Greenbriar Circle, #402, Chesapeake, VA 23320, USA

Cousy, Robert J (Bob) *Basketball Player*
427 Salisbury St, Worcester, MA 01609, USA

Coutinho, Antonio A R *Navy Admiral, Portugal*
Rua Carlos Malheiro Dias 18, 3 Esq, 1700 Lisbon, Portugal

Covay, Don *Singer, Songwriter*
%Rawstock, PO Box 2, Cambria Heights, NY 11411, USA

Cover, Franklin *Actor*
1422 N Sweetzer Ave, #402, Los Angeles, CA 90069, USA

Coverdale, David *Singer (Whitesnake, Deep Purple)*
%HK Mgmt, 8900 Wilshire Blvd, #300, Beverly Hills, CA 90211, USA

Coverly, Dave *Editorial Cartoonist*
%Bloomington Herald-Times, Editorial Dept, 1900 S Walnut, Bloomington, IN 47401, USA

Covert, James (Jimbo) *Football Player*
2679 Riviera Court, Weston, FL 33332, USA

Covey, Richard O *Astronaut*
%Unisys Space Systems, 600 Gemini Ave, Houston, TX 77058, USA

Covington, Warren *Orchestra Leader*
1735 Lake Cypress Dr, Safety Harbor, FL 34695, USA

Cowan, George A *Chemist*
%Santa Fe Institute, 1399 Hyde Park Road, Santa Fe, NM 87501, USA

Cowdrey, M Colin *Cricketer*
54 Lombard St, London EC3P 3AH, England

Cowens, Alfred E (Al) *Baseball Player*
1758 E 111th Place, Los Angeles, CA 90059, USA

Cowens, David W (Dave) *Basketball Player, Coach*
3420 Gray Moss Road, Charlotte, NC 28270, USA

Cowher, Bill *Football Coach*
313 Olde Chapel Trail, Pittsburgh, PA 15238, USA

Cowhill, William J *Navy Admiral*
1336 Elsinore Ave, McLean, VA 22102, USA

Cowie, Lennox L *Astronomer*
%University of Hawaii, Astronomy Dept, Honolulu, HI 96822, USA

Cowley, William M (Bill) *Hockey Player*
75 Sunnyside St, Ottawa ON, Canada

Cox, Allan V *Geophysicist*
%Stanford University, Earth Sciences School, Stanford, CA 94305, USA

Cox, Archibald *Attorney, Government Official*
%Harvard University, Law School, Cambridge, MA 02138, USA

Cox, Bryan *Football Player*
201 SW 85th Terrace, #102, Pembroke Pines, FL 33025, USA

Cox, Charles C *Government Official*
%Lexecon Inc, 332 S Michigan Ave, Chicago, IL 60604, USA

Cox, Courteney *Actress*
PO Box 49221, Los Angeles, CA 90049, USA

Cox, Danny B *Baseball Manager*
306 Feagin Mill Road, Warner Robbins, GA 31088, USA

C

Courlouris - Cox

Cox, David R — *Geneticist*
%Stanford University, Human Genome Center, Stanford, CA 94305, USA

Cox, Deborah — *Singer, Songwriter*
%Famous Artists Agency, 1700 Broadway, #500, New York, NY 10019, USA

Cox, G David — *Religious Leader*
%Church of God, Box 2420, Anderson, IN 46018, USA

Cox, Glenn A, Jr — *Businessman*
%WestStar Bank Building, 4th & Keeler, Bartlesville, OK 74004, USA

Cox, Harvey G, Jr — *Educator, Theologian*
%Harvard University, Divinity School, Cambridge, MA 02140, USA

Cox, John W — *Navy Admiral, Physician*
%Surgeon General's Office, Navy Department, Washington, DC 20372, USA

Cox, Lynne — *Distance Swimmer*
%Advanced Sport Research, 4141 Ball Road, #142, Cypress, CA 90630, USA

Cox, Mark — *Tennis Player*
The Oaks, Astead Woods Road, Astead, Surrey KT21 2ER, England

Cox, Paul — *Movie Director*
%Illumination Films, 1 Victoria Ave, Albert Park, VIC 3208, Australia

Cox, Robert J (Bobby) — *Baseball Manager, Executive*
4491 Chattahoochee Plantation, Marietta, GA 30067, USA

Cox, Ronny — *Actor*
%Concerted Efforts, 59 Parsons St, West Newton, MA 02165, USA

Cox, Stephen J — *Artist*
154 Barnsbury Road, Islington, London N1 0ER, England

Cox, Warren J — *Architect*
3111 "N" St NW, Washington, DC 20007, USA

Coyne, Frank J — *Businessman*
%General Accident Insurance, 436 Walnut St, Philadelphia, PA 19106, USA

Coyote, Peter — *Actor*
9 Rose Ave, Mill Valley, CA 94941, USA

Cozzarelli, Nicholas — *Biologist*
%University of California, Biology Dept, Berkeley, CA 94720, USA

Crable, Bob — *Football Player*
564 Miami Trace, Loveland, OH 45140, USA

Craddock, Billy (Crash) — *Singer, Songwriter*
%Al Embry, PO Box 23162, Nashville, TN 37202, USA

Craft, Christine — *Commentator*
%KRBK-TV, News Dept, 500 Media Place, Sacramento, CA 95815, USA

Craft, Clarence B — *WW II Army Hero (CMH)*
902 W 12th St, Fayetteville, AR 72701, USA

Craig of Radley, David B — *Royal Air Force Marshal, England*
%House of Lords, Westminster, London SW1A 0PW, England

Craig, Andrew B, III — *Financier*
%Boatmen's Bancshares, 800 Market St, St Louis, MO 63101, USA

Craig, Helen — *Actress*
%Beal, 205 W 54th St, New York, NY 10019, USA

Craig, James (Jim) — *Hockey Player*
15 Jyra Lane, North Easton, MA 02356, USA

Craig, Jenny — *Nutritionist*
PO Box 387910, La Jolla, CA 92038, USA

Craig, Michael — *Actor*
%Chatto & Linnit, Prince of Wales, Coventry St, London W1V 7FE, England

Craig, Roger — *Football Player*
271 Vista Verde Way, Portola Valley, CA 94028, USA

Craig, Roger L — *Baseball Player, Manager*
26658 San Felipe Ave, Warner Springs, GA 92086, USA

Craig, William — *Government Official, England*
23 Annadale Ave, Belfast BT7 3JJ, Northern Ireland

Craig, William (Bill) — *Swimmer*
PO Box 629, Newport Beach, CA 92661, USA

Craig, Yvonne — *Actress*
PO Box 827, Pacific Palisades, CA 90272, USA

Craighead, Frank C, Jr — *Ecologist*
%Craighead Environmental Research Institute, PO Box 156, Moose, WY 83012, USA

Crain, Jeanne — *Actress*
1029 Arbolado Road, Santa Barbara, CA 93103, USA

Crain, Keith E — *Publisher*
%Crain Communications, 1400 Woodbridge Ave, Detroit, MI 48207, USA

Crain, Rance — *Publisher*
%Crain Communications, 740 N Rush St, Chicago, IL 60611, USA

Crais, Robert — *Writer*
12829 Landale St, Studio City, CA 91604, USA

Cram, Donald J — *Nobel Chemistry Laureate*
405 Hilgard Ave, Los Angeles, CA 90095, USA

Cram, Steve — *Track Athlete*
%General Delivery, Jarrow, England

Cramer, Floyd — *Pianist, Composer*
3007 Old Martinsville Road, Greensboro, NC 27455, USA

Cramer, Grant — *Actor*
%Richard Sindell, 8271 Melrose Ave, #202, Los Angeles, CA 90046, USA

Cramer, Richard Ben — *Journalist*
%Philadelphia Inquirer, Editorial Dept, 400 N Broad St, Philadelphia, PA 19130, USA

Crampton, Barbara — *Actress*
%House of Representatives, 400 S Beverly Dr, #101, Beverly Hills, CA 90212, USA

Crampton, Bruce — *Golfer*
80472 Pebble Beach, La Quinta, CA 92253, USA

Crandall, Delmar W (Del) — *Baseball Player*
25 Rock Cliff Place, Pomona, CA 91766, USA

Crandall, Robert L — *Businessman*
%AMR Corp, PO Box 619616, Dallas-Fort Worth Airport, TX 75261, USA

Crane, Brian — *Cartoonist (Pickles)*
%Washington Post Writers Group, 1150 15th St NW, Washington, DC 20071, USA

Crane, Horace R — *Physicist*
830 Avon Road, Ann Arbor, MI 48104, USA

Crane, Irving D — *Pocket Billiards Player*
270 Yarmouth Road, Rochester, NY 14610, USA

Crane, Tony — *Actor*
%Abrams Artists, 9200 Sunset Blvd, #625, Los Angeles, CA 90069, USA

Cranston, Alan — *Senator, CA*
27080 W Fremont Road, Los Altos, CA 94022, USA

Cranston, Stewart E (Stu) — *Air Force General*
Commander, Air Force Test Center, 101 W D Ave, Elgin Air Force Base, FL 32542, USA

Cranz, Christl — *Skier*
Steibis 61, 87534 Oberstaufen, Germany

Craven, Matt — *Actor*
5033b Campo Road, Woodland Hls, CA 91364, USA

Craven, Wes — *Movie Director*
%Wes Craven Films, 10000 W Washington Blvd, #3011, Culver City, CA 90232, USA

Crawford, Bruce E — *Businessman, Opera Official*
%Omnicom Group, 437 Madison Ave, New York, NY 10022, USA

Crawford, Bryce L, Jr — *Chemist*
1545 Branston St, St Paul, MN 55108, USA

Crawford, Cindy — *Model*
%Wolf/Kasteller, 132 S Rodeo Dr, #300, Beverly Hills, CA 90212, USA

Crawford, Ellen — *Actress*
%Ambrosio/Mortimer, 9150 Wilshire Blvd, #175, Beverly Hills, CA 90212, USA

Crawford, Hank — *Jazz Saxophonist, Pianist, Composer*
%Maxine Harvard, 2227 Highway One, #251, North Brunswick, NJ 08902, USA

Crawford, Henry C (Shag) — *Baseball Umpire*
1530 Virginia Ave, Havertown, PA 19083, USA

Crawford, Joan — *Basketball Player*
1725 Mangard Lane, #323, Mount Prospect, IL 60056, USA

Crawford, Johnny — *Actor*
2440 El Contento Dr, Los Angeles, CA 90068, USA

Crawford, Marc — *Hockey Coach*
%Colorado Avalanche, McNichols Arena, 1635 Clay St, Denver, CO 80204, USA

Crawford, Michael — *Actor, Singer*
%Night Ayrton, 10 Argyll St, London W1V 1AB, England

Crawford, Randy — *Singer*
911 Park St SW, Grand Rapids, MI 49504, USA

Crawford, William A — *Diplomat*
4982 Sentinel Dr, #406, Bethesda, MD 20816, USA

Crawford, William J — *WW II Army Hero (CMH)*
Box 4, Palmer Lake, CO 80133, USA

Crawley, John B — *Publisher*
%Times Mirror Magazines, 2 Park Ave, New York, NY 10016, USA

C

Craxi, Benedetto — *Prime Minister, Italy*
Hammamet, Tunisia

Cray, Robert — *Singer, Guitarist*
%Rosebud Agency, PO Box 170429, San Francisco, CA 94117, USA

Crean, John C — *Businessman*
%Fleetwood Enterprises, 3125 Myers St, Riverside, CA 92503, USA

Creech, Wilbur L — *Air Force General*
20 Quail Run Road, Henderson, NV 89014, USA

Creekmur, Louis (Lou) — *Football Player*
7521 SW 1st St, Plantation, FL 33317, USA

Creeley, Robert W — *Writer*
PO Box 384, Waldoboro, ME 04572, USA

Creighton, John D — *Publisher*
%Toronto Sun, 333 King St E, Toronto ON M5A 3X5, Canada

Creighton, John O — *Astronaut*
%Boeing Commercial Airplane Group, PO Box 3707, Seattle, WA 98124, USA

Creighton, John W, Jr — *Businessman*
%Weyerhaeuser Co, 33663 Weyerhaeuser Ave S, Auburn, WA 98001, USA

Creme, Lol — *Singer, Guitarist (Godley & Creme)*
Heronden Hall, Tenferden, Kent, England

Cremins, Bobby — *Basketball Coach*
150 Bobby John Road, Atlanta, GA 30332, USA

Crenkovski, Branko — *Prime Minister, Macedonia*
%Prime Minister's Office, Dame Grueva 6, 9100 Skopje, Macedonia

Crenna, Richard — *Actor*
3941 Valley Meadow Road, Encino, CA 91436, USA

Crenshaw, Ben — *Golfer*
2905 San Gabriel St, #213, Austin, TX 78705, USA

Crenshaw, George — *Cartoonist*
%King Features Syndicate, 235 E 45th St, New York, NY 10017, USA

Crenshaw, Marshall — *Singer, Songwriter*
%Rascoff/Zysblat, 110 W 57th St, #300, New York, NY 10019, USA

Crespin, Regine — *Opera Singer*
%Musicaglotz, 3 Ave Frochet, 75009 Paris, France

Cresson, Edith — *Prime Minister, France*
Ville de Chatellerault, 86106 Chatellerault Cedex, France

Creutz, Edward C — *Physicist*
PO Box 2757, Rancho Santa Fe, CA 92067, USA

Crewdson, John M — *Journalist*
%Chicago Tribune, Editorial Dept, 435 N Michigan Ave, Chicago, IL 60611, USA

Crewe, Albert V — *Physicist*
8 Summitt Dr, Chesterton, IN 46304, USA

Crews, David — *Psychobiologist*
%University of Texas, Zoology Dept, Austin, TX 78712, USA

Crews, Harry E — *Writer*
%University of Florida, English Dept, Gainesville, FL 32611, USA

Crews, John R — *WW II Army Hero (CMH)*
1324 SW 54th St, Oklahoma City, OK 73119, USA

Crews, Phillip — *Chemist*
%University of California, Chemistry Dept, Santa Cruz, CA 99504, USA

Crewson, Wendy — *Actress*
%International Creative Mgmt, 40 W 57th St, New York, NY 10019, USA

Cribbs, Joe — *Football Player*
1555 Bent River Circle, Birmingham, AL 35216, USA

Crichton, J Michael — *Writer, Movie Director*
%Jenkins-McKay Inc, 433 N Camden Dr, #500, Beverly Hills, CA 90210, USA

Crick, Francis H C — *Nobel Medicine Laureate*
1792 Colgate Circle, La Jolla, CA 92037, USA

Crickhowell of Pont Esgob, Nicholas E — *Government Leader, England*
%House of Lords, Westminster, London SW1A 0PW, England

Crider, Missy — *Actress*
%Abrams Artists, 9200 Sunset Blvd, #625, Los Angeles, CA 90069, USA

Crier, Catherine — *Commentator*
%Cable News Network, News Dept, 1050 Techwood Dr NW, Atlanta, GA 30318, USA

Crile, Susan — *Artist*
168 W 86th St, New York, NY 10024, USA

Crim, Jack C — *Businessman*
%Talley Industries, 2702 N 44th St, Phoenix, AZ 85008, USA

Crippen, Robert L
%NASA Headquarters, Mail Code CD, Kennedy Space Center, FL 32899, USA *Astronaut*

Criqui, Don
%NBC-TV, Sports Dept, 30 Rockefeller Plaza, New York, NY 10112, USA *Sportscaster*

Crisostomo, Manny
%Pacific Daily News, PO Box DN, Agana, GU 96932, USA *Photographer*

Crisp, Quentin
46 E 3rd St, New York, NY 10003, USA *Actor*

Crisp, Terry A
9806 Bay Island Dr, Tampa, FL 33615, USA *Hockey Coach*

Criss, Peter
%McGhee Entertainment, 8730 Sunset Blvd, #195, Los Angeles CA 90069, USA *Singer, Drummer (Kiss)*

Crist, George B
%CBS-TV, News Dept, 51 W 52nd St, New York, NY 10019, USA *Marine Corps General*

Crist, Judith
180 Riverside Dr, New York, NY 10024, USA *Journalist*

Cristal, Linda
9129 Hazen Dr, Beverly Hills, CA 90210, USA *Actress*

Cristofer, Michael
%Richard Lovett, 9830 Wilshire Blvd, Beverly Hills, CA 90212, USA *Writer*

Cristol, Stanley J
2918 3rd St, Boulder, CO 80304, USA *Chemist*

Critchfield, Charles L
391 El Conejo, Los Alamos, NM 87544, USA *Physicist*

Critchfield, Jack B
%Florida Progress Corp, 1 Progress Plaza, St Petersburg, FL 33701, USA *Businessman*

Crocker, George A
Commanding General, I Corps, Fort Lewis, WA 98433, USA *Army General*

Crockett, Billy
%Billy Crockett Music, PO Box 161567, Austin, TX 78716, USA *Singer, Songwriter*

Crockett, Bruce L
%COMSAT Corp, 6560 Rock Spring Dr, Bethesda, MD 20817, USA *Businessman*

Croel, Mike
6565 S Syracuse Way, #1803, Englewood, CO 80111, USA *Football Player*

Crofts, Dash
%Nationwide Entertainment, 2756 N Green Valley Pkwy, #449, Las Vegas, NV 89014, USA *Singer (Seals & Crofts)*

Croll, Jimmy
420 Fair Hill Dr, #1, Elkton, MD 21921, USA *Thoroughbred Racing Trainer*

Cromwell, James
10110 Empryian Way, Los Angeles, CA 90067, USA *Actor*

Cromwell, Nolan
%Green Bay Packers, 1265 Lombardi Ave, Green Bay, WI 54304, USA *Football Player, Coach*

Cronbach, Lee J
850 Webster St, #623, Palo Alto, CA 94301, USA *Educator, Psychologist*

Cronenberg, David
%David Cronenberg Productions, 217 Avenue Road, Toronto ON M5R 2J3, Canada *Movie Director*

Cronin, James W
5825 S Dorchester St, Chicago, IL 60637, USA *Nobel Physics Laureate*

Cronkite, Eugene P
%Brookhaven National Laboratory, Medical Dept, Upton, NY 11973, USA *Physician*

Cronkite, Walter L, Jr
870 United Nations Plaza, #25-A, New York, NY 10017, USA *Commentator*

Cronyn, Hume
42 W 58th St, New York, NY 10019, USA *Actor*

Crosbie, John C
PO Box 9192, Station "B", St John's NF A1A 2X9, Canada *Political Leader, Canada*

Crosby, Cathy Lee
1223 Wilshire Blvd, #404, Santa Monica, CA 90403, USA *Actress*

Crosby, David
PO Box 9008, Solvang, CA 93464, USA *Singer (Byrds, Crosby Stills & Nash)*

Crosby, Denise
935 Embury St, Pacific Palisades, CA 90272, USA *Actress, Model*

Crosby, Gordon E, Jr
%USLife Corp, 125 Maiden Lane, New York, NY 10038, USA *Businessman*

Crosby, John O
%Santa Fe Opera, PO Box 2408, Santa Fe, NM 87504, USA *Conductor*

Crosby, Lucinda
4942 Vineland Ave, #200, North Hollywood, CA 91601, USA *Actress*

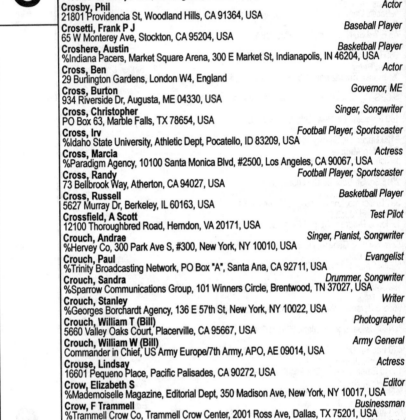

C

Crosby, Mary — *Actress*
5454 Gentry Ave, North Hollywood, CA 91607, USA

Crosby, Norm — *Comedian*
1400 Londonderry Place, Los Angeles, CA 90069, USA

Crosby, Phil — *Actor*
21801 Providencia St, Woodland Hills, CA 91364, USA

Crosetti, Frank P J — *Baseball Player*
65 W Monterey Ave, Stockton, CA 95204, USA

Croshere, Austin — *Basketball Player*
%Indiana Pacers, Market Square Arena, 300 E Market St, Indianapolis, IN 46204, USA

Cross, Ben — *Actor*
29 Burlington Gardens, London W4, England

Cross, Burton — *Governor, ME*
934 Riverside Dr, Augusta, ME 04330, USA

Cross, Christopher — *Singer, Songwriter*
PO Box 63, Marble Falls, TX 78654, USA

Cross, Irv — *Football Player, Sportscaster*
%Idaho State University, Athletic Dept, Pocatello, ID 83209, USA

Cross, Marcia — *Actress*
%Paradigm Agency, 10100 Santa Monica Blvd, #2500, Los Angeles, CA 90067, USA

Cross, Randy — *Football Player, Sportscaster*
73 Bellbrook Way, Atherton, CA 94027, USA

Cross, Russell — *Basketball Player*
5627 Murray Dr, Berkeley, IL 60163, USA

Crossfield, A Scott — *Test Pilot*
12100 Thoroughbred Road, Herndon, VA 20171, USA

Crouch, Andrae — *Singer, Pianist, Songwriter*
%Hervey Co, 300 Park Ave S, #300, New York, NY 10010, USA

Crouch, Paul — *Evangelist*
%Trinity Broadcasting Network, PO Box "A", Santa Ana, CA 92711, USA

Crouch, Sandra — *Drummer, Songwriter*
%Sparrow Communications Group, 101 Winners Circle, Brentwood, TN 37027, USA

Crouch, Stanley — *Writer*
%Georges Borchardt Agency, 136 E 57th St, New York, NY 10022, USA

Crouch, William T (Bill) — *Photographer*
5660 Valley Oaks Court, Placerville, CA 95667, USA

Crouch, William W (Bill) — *Army General*
Commander in Chief, US Army Europe/7th Army, APO, AE 09014, USA

Crouse, Lindsay — *Actress*
16601 Pequeno Place, Pacific Palisades, CA 90272, USA

Crow, Elizabeth S — *Editor*
%Mademoiselle Magazine, Editorial Dept, 350 Madison Ave, New York, NY 10017, USA

Crow, F Trammell — *Businessman*
%Trammell Crow Co, Trammell Crow Center, 2001 Ross Ave, Dallas, TX 75201, USA

Crow, James F — *Geneticist*
24 Glenway St, Madison, WI 53705, USA

Crow, John David — *Football Player, Coach*
%Texas A&M University, Athletic Dept, College Station, TX 77843, USA

Crow, Martin D — *Cricketer*
Millbrook Golf Resort, PO Box 160, Queenstown, New Zealand

Crow, Sheryl — *Singer, Songwriter*
%William Morris Agency, 1325 Ave of Americas, New York, NY 10019, USA

Crowe, Cameron — *Movie Director, Screenwriter*
%Creative Artists Agency, 9830 Wilshire Blvd, Beverly Hills, CA 90212, USA

Crowe, Phil — *Hockey Player*
PO Box 115, Willow Grove, PA 19090, USA

Crowe, Russell — *Actor*
%International Creative Mgmt, 8942 Wilshire Blvd, Beverly Hills, CA 90211, USA

Crowe, Tonya — *Actress*
13030 Mindanao Way, #4, Marina del Rey, CA 90292, USA

Crowe, William J, Jr — *Navy Admiral, Diplomat*
%American Embassy, 24/31 Grosvenor Square, London W1A 1AE, England

Crowell, Craven H, Jr — *Government Official*
%Tennessee Valley Authority, 400 W Summit Hill Dr, Knoxville, TN 37999, USA

Crowell, Donald W — *Financier*
%Crowell Weedon Co, 1 Wilshire Blvd, Los Angeles, CA 90017, USA

Crowell, Rodney J — *Singer, Songwriter*
%Gold Mountain, 1514 South St, #100, Nashville, TN 37212, USA

Crosby - Crowell

Crowley, Daniel — *Businessman*
%Foundation Health, 3400 Data Dr, Rancho Cordova, CA 95670, USA

Crowley, Joseph N — *Educator*
%University of Nevada, President's Office, Reno, NV 89557, USA

Crowley, Mart — *Writer*
8955 Beverly Blvd, Los Angeles, CA 90048, USA

Crowley, Patricia — *Actress*
150 W 56th St, #4603, New York, NY 10019, USA

Crown, David A — *Criminologist*
3344 Twin Lakes Lane, Sanibal, FL 33957, USA

Crowson, Richard — *Editorial Cartoonist*
%Wichita Eagle-Beacon, Editorial Dept, 825 E Douglas Ave, Wichita, KS 67202, USA

Crozier, William M, Jr — *Financier*
%BayBanks, 175 Federal St, Boston, MA 02110, USA

Crudup, Billy — *Actor*
%Writers & Artists, 924 Westwood Blvd, #900, Los Angeles, CA 90024, USA

Cruickshank, John A — *WW II Royal Air Force Hero (VC)*
34 Frogston Road W, Edinburgh EH10 7AJ, Scotland

Cruikshank, Thomas H — *Businessman*
%Halliburton Co, Lincoln Plaza, #3600, 500 N Akard St, Dallas, TX 75201, USA

Cruise, Tom — *Actor*
%Odin Productions, 253 26th St, #262, Santa Monica, CA 90402, USA

Crum, E Denzel (Denny) — *Basketball Coach*
9907 Spring Ridge Dr, Louisville, KY 40223, USA

Crumb, George H — *Composer*
240 Kirk Lane, Media, PA 19063, USA

Crumb, Robert — *Cartoonist (Keep on Truckin')*
%Fantagraphics Books, 7563 Lake City Way, Seattle, WA 98115, USA

Crumley, James R, Jr — *Religious Leader*
362 Little Creek Dr, Leesville, SC 29070, USA

Crutcher, Lawrence M — *Publisher*
%Book-of-the-Month Club, Rockefeller Center, New York, NY 10020, USA

Crutchfield, Edward E, Jr — *Financier*
%First Union Corp, 7815 Telegraph Road, Bloomington, MN 55438, USA

Crutzen, Paul — *Nobel Chemistry Laureate*
%Max Planck Chemistry Institute, J J Becher-Weg 27, 55128 Mainz, Germany

Cruyff, Johan — *Soccer Player, Coach*
%FC Barcelona, Aristides Maillol S/N, 08 028, Barcelona, Spain

Cruz Smith, Martin — *Writer*
%Random House, 201 E 50th St, New York, NY 10022, USA

Cruz, Celia — *Singer*
PO Box P-11007, Cambria Heights, NY 11411, USA

Cruz, Jose D — *Baseball Player*
B-15 Jardines Lafayette, Arroyo, PR 00615, USA

Cruz-Romo, Gilda — *Opera Singer*
1315 Lockhill-Selma Road, San Antonio, TX 78213, USA

Cryer, Gretchen — *Writer, Lyricist, Actress*
885 West End Ave, New York, NY 10025, USA

Cryer, Jon — *Actor*
%Media Artists Group, 8383 Wilshire Blvd, #954, Beverly Hills, CA 90211, USA

Cryner, Bobbie — *Singer*
%Lonesome Mgmt, 1313 16th Ave S, Nashville, TN 37212, USA

Crystal, Billy — *Actor, Comedian*
%Creative Artists Agency, 9830 Wilshire Blvd, Beverly Hills, CA 90212, USA

Crystal, Ronald G — *Molecular Biologist*
13712 Canal Vista Court, Potomac, MD 20854, USA

Csikszentmihalyi, Mihaly — *Psychologist*
%University of Chicago, Psychology Dept, Chicago, IL 60637, USA

Csonka, Larry — *Football Player*
37256 Hunter Camp Road, Lisbon, OH 44432, USA

Cua, Rick — *Singer, Pianist*
%Greg Menza, PO Box 1736, Columbia, TN 38402, USA

Cuckney, John G — *Financier*
%Brooke Bond Group, 45 Berkeley St, London EC4R 1DH, England

Cuellar, Miguel (Mike) — *Baseball Player*
5108 Louis Dr, El Paso, TX 79904, USA

Cuevas, Jose Luis — *Artist*
Galeana 109, San Angel Inn, Mexico City 20 DF, Mexico

Culbertson, Frank L, Jr — *Astronaut*
%NASA, Johnson Space Center, 2101 NASA Road, Houston, TX 77058, USA

Culbreath, Josh — *Track Athlete*
Central State University, Athletic Dept, Wilberforce, OH 45384, USA

Culkin, Macaulay — *Actor*
%William Morris Agency, 1325 Ave of Americas, New York, NY 10019, USA

Cullberg, Brigit R — *Choreographer*
Kommendorsgatan 8-C, 114 80 Stockholm, Sweden

Cullen, Brett — *Actor*
%Gersh Agency, 232 N Canon Dr, Beverly Hills, CA 90210, USA

Culligan, Joe — *Private Investigator, Writer*
%Research Investigative Services, 650 NE 126th St, Miami, FL 33161, USA

Cullinan, Edward H — *Architect*
The Wharf, Baldwin Terrace, London N1 7RU, England

Cullman, Edgar M, Jr — *Businessman*
%Culbro Corp, 387 Park Ave S, New York, NY 10016, USA

Cullman, Edgar M, Sr — *Businessman*
%Culbro Corp, 387 Park Ave S, New York, NY 10016, USA

Cullman, Joseph F, III — *Businessman*
%Philip Morris Companies, 100 Park Ave, New York, NY 10017, USA

Cullum, John — *Actor, Singer*
%International Creative Mgmt, 40 W 57th St, New York, NY 10019, USA

Cullum, Leo — *Cartoonist*
2900 Valmere Dr, Malibu, CA 90265, USA

Cullum, Mark E — *Editorial Cartoonist*
5401 Forest Acres Dr, Nashville, TN 37220, USA

Culp, Curley — *Football Player*
1779 Wells Branch Parkway, #110-B-309, Austin, TX 78728, USA

Culp, Robert — *Actor*
1270 Sunset Plaza Dr, Los Angeles, CA 90069, USA

Culver, John C — *Senator, IA*
5409 Spangler Ave, Bethesda, MD 20816, USA

Cumming, Ian M — *Businessman*
%Leucadia National Corp, 315 Park Ave S, New York, NY 10010, USA

Cummings, Burton — *Singer (The Guess Who), Songwriter*
%S L Feldman, 1505 W 2nd Ave, #200, Vancouver BC V6H 3Y4, Canada

Cummings, Constance — *Actress*
68 Old Church St, London SW3 6EP, England

Cummings, Quinn — *Actress*
%Pietragallo Agency, 398 Collins Dr, Pittsburgh, PA 15235, USA

Cummings, Ralph W — *Agriculturist*
812 Rosemont Ave, Raleigh, NC 27607, USA

Cummins, Peggy — *Actress*
17 Brockley Road, Bexhill-on-Sea, Sussex TN39 4TT, England

Cundey, Dean — *Cinematographer*
%Smith/Gosnell/Nicholson, 1515 Palisades Dr, #N, Pacific Palisades, CA 90272, USA

Cunniff, Jill — *Singer, Bassist (Luscious Jackson)*
%Metropolitan Entertainment, 2 Penn Plaza, #2600, New York, NY 10121, USA

Cunniff, John — *Hockey Coach*
%New Jersey Devils, Continental Arena, PO Box 504, East Rutherford, NJ 07073, USA

Cunningham, Bennie — *Football Player*
Helton St, PO Box 1147, Clemson, SC 29633, USA

Cunningham, Jeffrey M — *Publisher*
%Forbes Magazine, 60 5th Ave, New York, NY 10011, USA

Cunningham, John — *Test Pilot*
Canley, Kinsbourne Green, Harpenden, Herts, England

Cunningham, John A (Jack) — *Government Official, England*
%House of Commons, Westminster, London SW1A 0AA, England

Cunningham, John P — *Businessman*
%International Aluminum, 767 Monterey Pass Road, Monterey Park, CA 91754, USA

Cunningham, Liam — *Actor*
%Marina Martin Mgmt, 6-A Dunbury St, London N1 8JU, England

Cunningham, Merce — *Dancer, Choreographer*
55 Bethune St, New York, NY 10014, USA

Cunningham, R Walter — *Astronaut*
%Alcorn Ventures, 520 Post Oak Blvd, #130, Houston, TX 77027, USA

Cunningham, Randall — *Football Player, Sportscaster*
5020 Spanish Heights Dr, Las Vegas, NV 89113, USA

Cunningham, Sam — Football Player
7339 Marina Pacifica Dr N, Long Beach, CA 90803, USA

Cunningham, Sean S — Movie Director, Producer
4420 Hayvenhurst Ave, Encino, CA 91436, USA

Cunningham, Stephen — Astronaut
%Hughes Space/Communications Group, PO Box 92919, Los Angeles, CA 90009, USA

Cunningham, William J (Billy) — Basketball Player, Coach, Executive
PO Box 292, Gladwyne, PA 19035, USA

Cuomo, Andrew — Secretary, Housing & Urban Development
%Housing & Urban Development Department, 451 7th St SW, Washington, DC 20410, USA

Cuomo, Mario M — Governor, NY
%Wilkie Farr Gallagher, 153 E 53rd St, New York, NY 10022, USA

Cuozzo, Gary S — Football Player
911 Middletown Lincroft Road, Middletown, NJ 07748, USA

Cupit, Jacky — Golfer
8080 North Central Expressway, #1490, Dallas, TX 75206, USA

Curb, Mike — Record Producer
3907 W Alameda Ave, #2, Burbank, CA 91505, USA

Curbeam, Robert L, Jr — Astronaut
%NASA, Johnson Space Center, 2101 NASA Road, Houston, TX 77058, USA

Curd, Howard R — Businessman
%Jamesway Corp, 40 Hartz Way, Secaucus, NJ 07094, USA

Cureton, Thomas K — Swimming Contributor
501 E Washington, Urbana, IL 61801, USA

Curl, Robert F, Jr — Nobel Chemistry Laureate
1824 Bolsover St, Houston, TX 77005, USA

Curley, John J — Publisher
%Gannett Co, 1100 Wilson Blvd, Arlington, VA 22234, USA

Curley, Thomas — Publisher
%USA Today, 1000 Wilson Blvd, Arlington, VA 22209, USA

Curley, Walter J P, Jr — Diplomat, Financier
885 3rd Ave, #1200, New York, NY 10022, USA

Curnin, Thomas F — Attorney
%Cahill Gordon Reindel, 80 Pine St, New York, NY 10005, USA

Curran, Charles E — Theologian
%Southern Methodist University, Dallas Hall, Dallas, TX 75275, USA

Curran, Mike — Hockey Player
7615 Lanewood Lane, Maple Grove, MN 55311, USA

Currey, Francis S — WW II Army Hero (CMH)
RR 2, Box 185, Selkirk, NY 12158, USA

Currie, Louise — Actress
1317 Delresto Dr, Beverly Hills, CA 90210, USA

Currie, Peter — Businessman
%Netscape Communications, 501 E Middlefield Road, Mountain View, CA 94043, USA

Currie, Sondra — Actress
3951 Longridge Ave, Sherman Oaks, CA 91423, USA

Curris, Constantine W — Educator
%Clemson University, President's Office, Clemson, SC 29634, USA

Curry, Del — Basketball Player
263 Paine Run Road, Grottoes, VA 24441, USA

Curry, Denise — Basketball Player, Coach
%California State University, Athletic Dept, Fullerton, CA 92634, USA

Curry, Donald — Boxer
4189 Edwards St, Lancaster, TX 75134, USA

Curry, Eric — Football Player
1050 E Piedmont Road, #E-119, Marietta, GA 30062, USA

Curry, Tim — Singer, Actor
26666 Aberdeen Ave, Los Angeles, CA 90027, USA

Curtin, David S — Journalist
%Colorado Springs Gazette Telegraph, 30 S Prospect, Colorado Springs, CO 80903, USA

Curtin, David Y — Chemist
3 Montclair Road, Urbana, IL 61801, USA

Curtin, Jane — Actress
10450 Revuelta Way, Los Angeles, CA 90077, USA

Curtin, John J, Jr — Attorney
%Bingham Dana Gould, 150 Federal St, #3500, Boston, MA 02110, USA

Curtin, Phyllis — Opera Singer
%Boston University, School for Arts, Boston, MA 02215, USA

C

Cunningham - Curtin

Curtin, Valerie — *Actress*
%Creative Artists Agency, 9830 Wilshire Blvd, Beverly Hills, CA 90212, USA

Curtis Cuneo, Ann — *Swimmer*
35 Golden Hinde Blvd, San Rafael, CA 94903, USA

Curtis, Carl T — *Senator, NE*
Windsor Square, 1300 "G" St, #104-G, Lincoln, NE 68508, USA

Curtis, Daniel M (Dan) — *Movie Director*
143 S Rockingham Ave, Los Angeles, CA 90049, USA

Curtis, Isaac F — *Football Player*
711 Clinton Springs Ave, Cincinnati, OH 45229, USA

Curtis, Jamie Lee — *Actress*
%Creative Artists Agency, 9830 Wilshire Blvd, Beverly Hills, CA 90212, USA

Curtis, Keene — *Actor*
6363 Ivarene Ave, Los Angeles, CA 90068, USA

Curtis, Kelly — *Actress*
651 N Kikea Dr, Los Angeles, CA 90048, USA

Curtis, Kenneth M — *Governor, ME; Diplomat*
1154 Shore Road, Cape Elizabeth, ME 04107, USA

Curtis, Robin — *Actress*
%House of Representatives, 400 S Beverly Dr, #101, Beverly Hills, CA 90212, USA

Curtis, Todd — *Actor*
2046 14th St, #10, Santa Monica, CA 90405, USA

Curtis, Tony — *Actor*
11831 Folkstone Lane, Los Angeles, CA 90077, USA

Curtis-Hall, Vondie — *Actor*
%Gersh Agency, 232 N Canon Dr, Beverly Hills, CA 90210, USA

Cusack, Ann — *Actress*
%Innovative Artists, 1999 Ave of Stars, #2850, Los Angeles, CA 90067, USA

Cusack, Joan — *Actress*
540 N Lakeshore Dr, #722, Chicago, IL 60611, USA

Cusack, John — *Actor*
838 Sheridan, Evanston, IL 60202, USA

Cusack, Sinead — *Actress*
%Markham & Froggatt, Julian House, 4 Windmill St, London W1P 1HF, England

Cusick, John J — *Army General*
Director, Logistics, Joint Chiefs of Staff, Pentagon, Washington, DC 20318, USA

Cusick, Thomas A — *Financier*
%TCF Financial Corp, 801 Marquette Ave, Minneapolis, MN 55402, USA

Cussler, Clive E — *Writer*
7731 W 72nd Place, Arvada, CO 80005, USA

Cuthbeth, Betty — *Track Athlete*
4/7 Karara Close, Hall's Head, Mandurah WA 6210, Australia

Cutler, A Roden — *WW II Australian Army Hero (VC)*
22 Ginahgulla Road, Bellevue Hill NSW 2023, Australia

Cutler, Bruce — *Attorney*
41 Madison Ave, New York, NY 10010, USA

Cutler, Laurel — *Businesswoman*
%Foote Cone Belding, 767 5th Ave, New York, NY 10153, USA

Cutler, Lloyd N — *Government Official*
3115 "O" St NW, Washington, DC 20007, USA

Cutler, Walter L — *Diplomat*
%Meridian International Center, 1630 Crescent Place NW, Washington, DC 20009, USA

Cutter, Kiki — *Skier*
PO Box 1317, Carbondale, CO 81623, USA

Cutter, Lise — *Actress*
PO Box 1173, East Hampton, NY 11937, USA

Cutter, Slade — *Football Player*
5108 River Crescent Dr, Annapolis, MD 21401, USA

Cyert, Richard M — *Educator*
%Carnegie-Mellon University, GSIA Building, Pittsburgh, PA 15213, USA

Cypher, Jon — *Actor*
424 Manzanita Ave, Ventura, CA 93001, USA

Cyrus, Billy Ray — *Singer, Songwriter*
PO Box 1206, Franklin, TN 37065, USA

Czerny, Henry — *Actor*
%William Morris Agency, 151 S El Camino Dr, Beverly Hills, CA 90212, USA

Czrongursky, Jan — *Prime Minister, Slovakia*
%Prime Minister's Office, Nam Slobody 1, 81370 Bratislava, Slovakia

D'Abo, Maryam — *Actress*
%Gage Group, 9255 Sunset Blvd, #515, Los Angeles, CA 90069, USA

D'Abo, Olivia — *Actress*
%International Creative Mgmt, 8942 Wilshire Blvd, Beverly Hills, CA 90211, USA

D'Alemberte, Talbot (Sandy) — *Educator*
%Florida State University, President's Office, Tallahassee, FL 32306, USA

D'Amboise, Jacques J — *Dancer, Choreographer*
%National Dance Institute, 244 W 71st St, New York, NY 10023, USA

D'Ambrosio, Dominick — *Labor Leader*
%Allied Industrial Workers Union, 3520 W Oklahoma Ave, Milwaukee, WI 53215, USA

D'Amico, William D — *Bobsled Athlete*
30 Greenwood St, Lake Placid, NY 12946, USA

D'Angelo — *Singer*
%EMI America Records, 810 7th Ave, New York, NY 10019, USA

D'Angelo, Beverly — *Actress*
8033 Sunset Blvd, #247, Los Angeles, CA 90046, USA

D'Angio, Giulio J — *Radiation Therapist*
%Children's Hospital, 34th & Civic Center Blvd, Philadelphia, PA 19104, USA

D'Arbanville-Quinn, Patti — *Actress*
125 Main, Seacliff, NY 11579, USA

D'Arby, Terence Trent — *Singer*
%Creative Artists Agency, 9830 Wilshire Blvd, Beverly Hills, CA 90212, USA

D'Arcy, Margaretta — *Writer*
%M Ramsay, 14-A Goodwins Court, St Martin's Lane, London WC2N 4LL, England

D'Ascoli, Bernard — *Concert Pianist*
%Transart, 8 Bristol Gardens, London W9 2JG, England

D'Eath, Tom — *Boat Racing Driver*
2011 74th St NW, Bradenton, FL 34209, USA

D'Errico, Donna — *Model, Actress*
%Rael Co, 9255 Sunset Blvd, #425, Los Angeles, CA 90069, USA

D'Harnoncourt, Anne — *Museum Director*
%Philadelphia Museum of Art, 25th & Ben Franklin Parkway, Philadelphia, PA 19101, USA

D'Onofrio, Vincent — *Actor*
%International Creative Mgmt, 8942 Wilshire Blvd, Beverly Hills, CA 90211, USA

D'Oriola, Christian — *Fencer*
Valdebanne, Rt de Generac, 30 Nimes, France

D'Ornellas, Robert W — *Businessman*
%Del Monte Foods, 1 Market Plaza, San Francisco, CA 94105, USA

D'Rivera, Paquito — *Jazz Saxophonist*
%Tropijazz Talent Agency, 558 Broadway, #808, New York, NY 10012, USA

Da Brat — *Rap Artist*
%William Morris Agency, 1325 Ave of Americas, New York, NY 10019, USA

Dacre of Glanton (H R Trevor-Roper) — *Writer, Historian*
The Old Rectory, Didcot, Oxon, England

Daehlie, Bjorn — *Cross Country Skier*
Cathinka Guldbergs Veg 64, 2034 Holter, Norway

Dafoe, Willem — *Actor*
33 Wooster St, #200, New York, NY 10013, USA

Daggett, Tim — *Gymnast*
172 High Meadow Lane, West Springfield, MA 01089, USA

Dagworthy Prew, Wendy A — *Fashion Designer*
18 Melrose Terrace, London W6, England

Dahanayake, Wijeyananda — *Prime Minister, Ceylon*
225 Richmond Hill Road, Galle, Sri Lanka

Dahl, Arlene — *Actress*
%Dahlmark Productions, PO Box 116, Sparkill, NY 10976, USA

Dahl, Christopher — *Educator*
%State University of New York College, President's Office, Genesco, NY 14454, USA

Dahl, John — *Movie Director*
%United Talent Agency, 9560 Wilshire Blvd, #500, Beverly Hills, CA 90212, USA

Dahlgren, Edward C — *WW II Army Hero (CMH)*
Box 26, Mars Hill, ME 04758, USA

Dahlsten, Gunnar — *Businessman*
%Swedish Match, PO Box 16100, 103 22 Stockholm, Sweden

Dai Ailian — *Dancer, Choreographer*
Hua Qiao Gong Yu, #2-16, Hua Yuan Cun, Hai Dian, Beijing 100044, China

Daiches, David — *Writer*
12 Rothesay Place, Edinburgh EH3 7SQ, Scotland

D

D'Abo - Daiches

Dailey, Janet	*Writer*
%Janbill Ltd, PO Box 2197, Branson, MO 65616, USA	
Dailey, Peter H	*Diplomat*
%US State Department, 2201 "C" St NW, Washington, DC 20520, USA	
Daily, Bill	*Actor*
1331 Park Ave SW, #802, Albuquerque, NM 87102, USA	
Daily, E G	*Singer, Songwriter, Actress*
%T-Best Talent Agency, 2001 Wayne Ave, #103, San Leandro, CA 94577, USA	
Daily, Parker	*Religious Leader*
%Baptist Bible Fellowship International, PO Box 191, Springfield, MO 65801, USA	
Dainton, Frederick S	*Physical Chemist*
Fieldside, Water Eaton Lane, Kidlington, Oxford OX5 2PR, England	
Daio, Norberto J D C A	*Prime Minister, Sao Tome & Principe*
%Prime Minister's Office, CP 38, Sao Tome, Sao Tome & Principe	
Dake, Terrence R	*Marine Corps General*
Deputy Chief of Staff for Aviation, HqUSMC, Navy Annex, Washington, DC 20380, USA	
Dalai Lama, The	*Religious Leader; Nobel Peace Laureate*
Thekchen Choeling, McLeod Ganj 176219, Dharamsal, Himachal Pradesh, India	
Dalby, Dave	*Football Player*
3542 Argyle St, Napa, CA 94558, USA	
Dale, Bruce	*Photographer*
%National Geographic Magazine, 17th & "M" NW, Washington, DC 20001, USA	
Dale, Carroll	*Football Player*
PO Box 1449, Wise, VA 24293, USA	
Dale, Dick	*Singer, Guitarist*
PO Box 1713, Twenty-Nine Palms, CA 92277, USA	
Dale, Jim	*Actor*
26 Pembridge Villas, London W11, England	
Dale, William B	*Economist, Government Official*
6008 Landon Lane, Bethesda, MD 20817, USA	
Daler, Jiri	*Cyclist*
Jiraskova 43, 601 00 Brno, Czech Republic	
Dalessandro, Peter J	*WW II Army Hero (CMH)*
199 Old Niskyna Road, Latham, NY 12110, USA	
Daley, Richard M	*Mayor*
%Mayor's Office, City Hall, 121 N LaSalle St, Chicago, IL 60602, USA	
Daley, William N (Bill)	*Secretary, Commerce*
%Commerce Department, 14th St & Constitution Ave, Washington, DC 20230, USA	
Dalglish, Kenneth (Kenny)	*Soccer Player, Manager*
%FC Newcastle United, St James Park, Newcastle-Upon-Tyne NE1 4ST, England	
Dalhousie, Simon R	*Government Official, England*
Brechin Castle, Brechin DD7 6SH, Scotland	
Dali, Tracy	*Actress, Model*
%Victor Kruglov, 7060 Hollywood Blvd, #1220, Los Angeles, CA 90028, USA	
Dalis, Irene	*Opera Singer*
1731 Cherry Grove Dr, San Jose, CA 95125, USA	
Dallenbach, Wally	*Auto Racing Executive*
%Roush Racing, PO Box 1089, Liberty, NC 27298, USA	
Dallesandro, Joe	*Actor*
4400 Ambrose Ave, Los Angeles, CA 90027, USA	
Dalrymple, Jean V K	*Theater Producer*
150 W 55th St, New York, NY 10019, USA	
Dalrymple, Richard W	*Financier*
%Anchor Savings Bank, 400 W Sunrise Highway, Valley Stream, NY 11581, USA	
Dalton, Abby	*Actress*
PO Box 100, Mammoth Lakes, CA 93546, USA	
Dalton, James E	*Air Force General*
61 Misty Acres Road, Palos Verdes Peninsula, CA 90274, USA	
Dalton, John H	*Government Official*
3710 University Ave NW, Washington, DC 20016, USA	
Dalton, Lacy J	*Singer*
%LJD Enterprises, PO Box 1109, Mount Juliet, TN 37122, USA	
Dalton, Timothy	*Actor*
%James Sharkey, 21 Golden Square, London W1R 3PA, England	
Daltry, Roger	*Singer (The Who), Actor*
%Trinifold Mgmt, Harley House, 22 Marylebone Road, London NW1 4PR, England	
Daly, Cahal Brendan Cardinal	*Religious Leader*
Ara Coeli Cathedral Road, Armagh BT61 7QY, Northern Ireland	

Daly, Charles J (Chuck) — *Basketball Coach*
6625 Castlebury Dr, West Bloomfield, MI 48322, USA

Daly, John — *Movie Producer*
%Hemdale, 7960 Beverly Blvd, Los Angeles, CA 90048, USA

Daly, John — *Golfer*
13100 Worldgate Dr, #120, Herndon, VA 20170, USA

Daly, Michael J — *WW II Army Hero (CMH)*
155 Redding Road, Fairfield, CT 06430, USA

Daly, Robert A — *Entertainment Executive*
444 Loring Ave, Los Angeles, CA 90024, USA

Daly, Timothy — *Actor*
11718 Barrington Court, #252, Los Angeles, CA 90049, USA

Daly, Tyne — *Actress*
700 N Westknoll Dr, #302, Los Angeles, CA 90069, USA

Dam, Kenneth W — *Government Official*
%Universty of Chicago, Law School, 1111 E 60th St, Chicago, IL 60637, USA

Damas, Bertila — *Actress*
%Stone Manners, 8091 Selma Ave, Los Angeles, CA 90046, USA

Damasio, Antonio R — *Neurologist*
%University of Iowa Hospital, Neurology Dept, Iowa City, IA 52242, USA

Dame Edna (Barry Humphries) — *Comedian*
%Kate Feast, Primrose Hill Studios, Fitzroy Road, London NW1 8TR, England

Damian, Michael — *Actor*
%House of Representatives, 400 S Beverly Dr, #101, Beverly Hills, CA 90212, USA

Damiani, Damiano — *Movie Director*
Via Delle Terme Deciane 2, 00153 Rome, Italy

Dammeyer, Rodney F — *Businessman*
%Itel Corp, 2 N Riverside Plaza, Chicago, IL 60606, USA

Damon, Mark — *Actor*
2781 Benedict Canyon Dr, Beverly Hills, CA 90210, USA

Damon, Matt — *Actor*
%William Morris Agency, 151 S El Camino Dr, Beverly Hills, CA 90212, USA

Damon, Stuart — *Actor*
367 N Van Ness Ave, Los Angeles, CA 90004, USA

Damone, Vic — *Singer, Actor*
21700 Oxnard St, #400, Woodland Hills, CA 91367, USA

Dampier, Erick — *Basketball Player*
%Golden State Warriors, 7000 Coliseum Way, Oakland, CA 94621, USA

Dampier, Louie — *Basketball Player*
%Dampier Distributing, 2808 New Moody Lane, La Grange, KY 40031, USA

Dana, Bill — *Test Pilot*
%Ames Research Center, DFRF, PO Box 273, Edwards Air Force Base, CA 93523, USA

Dana, Bill — *Comedian*
PO Box 1792, Santa Monica, CA 90406, USA

Dana, Justin — *Actor*
13111 Ventura Blvd, #102, Studio City, CA 91604, USA

Danby, Gordon T — *Inventor (Magnetic Levitation Vehicle)*
%Brookhaven National Laboratory, Upton, NY 11973, USA

Dance, Charles — *Actor*
1311 N California St, Burbank, CA 91505, USA

Dancer, Stanley — *Harness Racing Driver*
RR 1, Box 2, New Egypt, NJ 08533, USA

Dancy, John — *Commentator*
%Harvard University, Kennedy Government School, Cambridge, MA 02138, USA

Dando, Evan — *Singer (Lemonheads)*
%Gold Mountain, 3575 Cahuenga Blvd W, #450, Los Angeles, CA 90068, USA

Dandridge, Bob — *Basketball Player*
1708 St Denis Ave, Norfolk, VA 23509, USA

Danes, Claire — *Actress*
%Innovative Artists, 1999 Ave of Stars, #2850, Los Angeles, CA 90067, USA

Danforth, Douglas D — *Baseball Executive, Businessman*
%Pittsburgh Pirates, Three Rivers Stadium, Pittsburgh, PA 15212, USA

Dangerfield, Rodney — *Comedian*
530 E 76th St, New York, NY 10021, USA

Daniel, Beth — *Golfer*
%Pros Inc, PO Box 673, Richmond, VA 23206, USA

Daniel, Margaret Truman — *Writer*
%Scott Meredith Literary Agency, 845 3rd Ave, New York, NY 10022, USA

D

Daly - Daniel

D

Daniel, Richard N — *Businessman*
%Handy & Harman, 555 Theodore Fremd Ave, #A, Rye, NY 10580, USA

Daniel-Lesur, J Y — *Composer*
101 Rue Sadi Carnot, 92800 Puteaux, France

Daniell, Averell E (Ave) — *Football Player*
1150 Bower Hill Road, #712-A, Pittsburgh, PA 15243, USA

Daniell, Martin H, Jr — *Coast Guard Admiral*
Commander, Pacific Area, Coast Guard Island, Alameda, CA 94501, USA

Daniell, Robert F — *Businessman*
%United Technologies Corp, United Technologies Building, Hartford, CT 06101, USA

Daniels, Antonio — *Basketball Player*
%Vancouver Grizzlies, 288 Beatty St, #300, Vancouver BC V6B 2M1, Canada

Daniels, Charlie — *Singer, Songwriter*
%CDB Mgmt, 17060 Central Pike, Lebanon, TN 37090, USA

Daniels, Cheryl — *Bowler*
18660 San Juan Dr, Detroit, MI 48221, USA

Daniels, Jeff — *Actor*
137 Park St, Chelsea, MI 48118, USA

Daniels, Mel — *Basketball Player*
19789 Centennial Road, Sheridan, IN 46069, USA

Daniels, William — *Actor*
12805 Hortense St, Studio City, CA 91604, USA

Daniels, William B — *Physicist*
283 Dallam Road, Newark, DE 19711, USA

Danielsen, Egil — *Track Athlete*
Roreks Gate 9, 2300 Hamar, Norway

Danielsson, Bengt F — *Anthropologist*
Box 558, Papette, Tahiti

Daniloff, Nicholas — *Journalist*
PO Box 892, Chester, VT 05143, USA

Danko, Rick — *Singer, Bassist (The Band)*
%Skyline Music, PO Box 31, Lancaster, NH 03584, USA

Dankworth, John — *Jazz Saxophonist, Composer, Bandleader*
Old Rectory, Wavendon, Milton Kenyes MK17 8LT, England

Danneels, Godfried Cardinal — *Religious Leader*
Aartsbisdom, Wollemarkt 15, 2800 Mechelen, Belgium

Dannemiller, John C — *Businessman*
%Bearings Inc, 3615 Euclid Ave, Cleveland, OH 44115, USA

Danner, Blythe — *Actress*
304 21st St, Santa Monica, CA 90402, USA

Danning, Harry — *Baseball Player*
212 Fox Chapel Court, Valparaiso, IN 46385, USA

Danning, Sybil — *Actress, Model*
611 S Catalina St, #220, Los Angeles, CA 90005, USA

Dano, Linda — *Actress*
%Shapiro-Lichtman, 8827 Beverly Blvd, Los Angeles, CA 90048, USA

Danson, Ted — *Actor*
165 Copper Cliff Lane, Sedona, AZ 86336, USA

Dante, Joe — *Movie Director*
2321 Holly Dr, Los Angeles, CA 90068, USA

Dantine, Nikki — *Actress*
707 N Palm Dr, Beverly Hills, CA 90210, USA

Dantley, Adrian — *Basketball Player, Coach*
%Towson State University, Athletic Dept, Towson, MD 21204, USA

Dantzig, George B — *Computer Scientist*
821 Tolman Dr, Stanford, CA 94305, USA

Dantzig, Rudi Van — *Choreographer*
%Het Nationale Ballet, Waterlooplein 22, 1011 PG Amsterdam, Netherlands

Danza, Tony — *Actor*
25000 Malibu Road, Malibu, CA 90265, USA

Danzig, Frederick P — *Editor*
%Advertising Age, Editorial Dept, 220 E 42nd St, New York, NY 10017, USA

Danziger, Jeff — *Editorial Cartoonist*
RFD, Plainfield, VT 05667, USA

Daphnis, Nassos — *Artist*
362 W Broadway, New York, NY 10013, USA

Darboven, Hanne — *Artist*
Am Burgberg 26, 21079 Hamburg, Germany

Daniel - Darboven

Darby, Kim — *Actress*
PO Box 1250, Studio City, cA 91614, USA

Dare, Yinka — *Basketball Player*
PO Box 523, Redding Ridge, CT 06876, USA

Darehshori, Nader F — *Publisher*
%Houghton Mifflin Co, 222 Berkeley St, Boston, MA 02116, USA

Darion, Joe — *Librettist, Lyricist*
PO Box 315, Pinnacle Road, Lynne, NH 03768, USA

Dark, Alvin R — *Baseball Player, Manager*
103 Cranberry Way, Easley, SC 29642, USA

Darling, Charles (Chuck) — *Basketball Player*
8066 S Kramerie Way, Englewood, CO 80112, USA

Darling, Jennifer — *Actress*
5006 Ventura Canyon Ave, Sherman Oaks, CA 91423, USA

Darling, Joan — *Actress*
33533 Shoreline Dr, Laguna Niguel, CA 92677, USA

Darling, Ronald M (Ron) — *Baseball Player*
19 Woodland St, Millbury, MA 01527, USA

Darman, Richard G — *Government Official*
1137 Crest Lane, McLean, VA 22101, USA

Darnall, Robert J — *Businessman*
%Inland Steel Industries, 30 W Monroe St, Chicago, IL 60603, USA

Darnton, John — *Journalist*
%New York Times, Editorial Dept, 229 W 43rd St, New York, NY 10036, USA

Darnton, Robert C — *Writer, Historian*
6 McCosh Circle, Princeton, NJ 08540, USA

Darragh, John K — *Businessman*
%Stanfast Inc, PO Box 1167, Dayton, OH 45401, USA

Darren, James — *Singer, Actor*
PO Box 1088, Beverly Hills, CA 90213, USA

Darrieux, Danielle — — *Actress*
%Nicole Cann, 1 Rue Alfred de Vigny, 75008 Paris, France

Darrow, Henry — *Actor*
15010 Ventura Blvd, #2314, Sherman Oaks, CA 91403, USA

Das Neves, Orlando — *Head of State, Sao Tome & Principe*
%Chief Executive's Office, Prago do Povo, Sao Tome, Sao Tome & Principe

Das, Alisha — *Actress*
%Innovative Artists, 1999 Ave of Stars, #2850, Los Angeles, CA 90067, USA

Dash, Leon D, Jr — *Journalist*
%Washington Post, Editorial Dept, 1150 15th Ave NW, Washington, DC 20071, USA

Dash, Samuel — *Attorney, Watergate Committee Counsel*
110 Newlands St, Chevy Chase, MD 20815, USA

Dash, Sarah — *Singer*
%Talent Consultants Int'l, 1560 Broadway, #1308, New York, NY 10036, USA

Dash, Stacey — *Actress*
%Michael Slessinger, 8730 Sunset Blvd, #220-W, Los Angeles, CA 90069, USA

Dassin, Jules — *Movie Director*
Athineon Efivon 8, Athens 11521, Greece

Dassler, Uwe — *Swimmer*
Stolze-Schrey-Str 6, 15745 Wilday, Germany

Datcher, Alex — *Actress*
%Paul Kohner, 9300 Wilshire Blvd, #555, Beverly Hills, CA 90212, USA

Dater, Judy L — *Photographer*
626 Middlefield Road, Palo Alto, CA 94301, USA

Daube, David — *Attorney, Educator*
%University of California, Law School, Berkeley, CA 94720, USA

Dauben, William G — *Chemist*
20 Eagle Hill, Kensington, CA 94707, USA

Daugherty, Bradley L (Brad) — *Basketball Player*
3777 Peachtree Road NE, #1432, Atlanta, GA 30319, USA

Dauline, Marie — *Singer (Zap Mama)*
%Luaka Bop, PO Box 652, Cooper Station, New York, NY 10276, USA

Daulton, Darren A — *Baseball Player*
5 Meadow Lane, Arkansas City, KS 67005, USA

Dausset, Jean B G — *Nobel Medicine Laureate*
9 Rue de Villersexel, 75007 Paris, France

Davalos, Richard — *Actor*
2311 Vista Gordo Dr, Los Angeles, CA 90026, USA

D

Darby - Davalos

Davenport, David — *Educator*
%Pepperdine University, President's Office, Malibu, CA 90265, USA

Davenport, Lindsey — *Tennis Player*
1440 Newporter Way, Newport Beach, CA 92660, USA

Davenport, Nigel — *Actor*
5 Ann's Close, Kinnerton St, London SW1, England

Davenport, Willie — *Track Athlete*
714 Millgate Place, Baton Rouge, LA 70808, USA

Davi, Robert — *Actor*
6568 Beachview Dr, #209, Rancho Palos Verdes, CA 90275, USA

Daviau, Allen — *Cinematographer*
2249 Bronson Hill Dr, Los Angeles, CA 90068, USA

David Mohato — *Crown Prince, Lesotho*
%Royal Palace, PO Box 524, Maseru, Lesotho

David, Edward E, Jr — *Underwater Sound Engineer*
%EED Inc, Box 435, Bedminster, NJ 07921, USA

David, George A L — *Businessman*
%United Technologies Corp, United Technologies Building, Hartford, CT 06101, USA

David, Hal — *Lyricist*
10430 Wilshire Blvd, Los Angeles, CA 90024, USA

David, Keith — *Actor*
1134 W 105th St, Los Angeles, CA 90044, USA

David, Peter — *Actor*
PO Box 239, Bayport, NY 11705, USA

David-Weill, Michel — *Financier*
%Lazard Freres Co, 1 Rockfeller Plaza, New York, NY 10020, USA

Davidovich, Bella — *Concert Pianist*
%Jacques Leiser, Dorchester Towers, 155 W 68th St, New York, NY 10023, USA

Davidovich, Lolita — *Actress*
%International Creative Mgmt, 8942 Wilshire Blvd, Beverly Hills, CA 90211, USA

Davidovsky, Mario — *Composer*
%Columbia University, Music Dept, New York, NY 10027, USA

Davidsen, Arthur F — *Astronomer*
%Johns Hopkins University, Astrophysical Sciences Center, Baltimore, MD 21218, USA

Davidson, Alfred E — *International Attorney*
5 Rue de la Manutention, 75116 Paris, France

Davidson, Ben E — *Football Player*
4737 Angels Point, La Mesa, CA 91941, USA

Davidson, Bruce — *Equestrian Rider*
Rt 842, Unionville, PA 19375, USA

Davidson, Eileen — *Actress*
13340 Galewood Dr, Sherman Oaks, CA 91423, USA

Davidson, George A, Jr — *Businessman*
%Consolidated Natural Gas, 625 Liberty Ave, Pittsburgh, PA 15222, USA

Davidson, Gordon — *Theater Producer, Director*
%Center Theatre Group, Mark Taper Forum, 135 N Grand, Los Angeles, CA 90012, USA

Davidson, Ian B — *Financier*
%D A Davidson Co, 8 3rd St N, Great Falls, MT 59401, USA

Davidson, Jaye — *Actor*
%International Creative Mgmt, 8942 Wilshire Blvd, Beverly Hills, CA 90211, USA

Davidson, Jim — *Actor*
%William Morris Agency, 151 S El Camino Dr, Beverly Hills, CA 90212, USA

Davidson, John — *Singer, Actor*
1624 Coriander Dr, #A, Costa Mesa, CA 92626, USA

Davidson, John — *Hockey Player*
12 Carey Dr, Bedford, NY 10506, USA

Davidson, Norman R — *Molecular Biologist*
318 E Laurel Ave, Sierra Madre, CA 91024, USA

Davidson, Ralph P — *Publisher*
494 Harbor Road, Southport, CT 06490, USA

Davidson, Richard K — *Businessman*
%Union Pacific Corp, Martin Tower, 8th & Eatons Aves, Bethlehem, PA 18018, USA

Davidson, Ronald C — *Physicist*
%Princeton University, Plasma Physics Laboratory, Princeton, NJ 08544, USA

Davidtz, Embeth — *Actress*
311 N Venice Blvd, #C, Venice, CA 90291, USA

Davie, Donald A — *Writer*
4 High St, Silverton, Exeter EX5 4JB, England

Davie, Robert (Bob) — *Football Coach*
%University of Notre Dame, Athletic Dept, PO Box 518, Notre Dame, IN 46556, USA

Davies, Charles W, Jr — *Businessman*
%Tultex Corp, 22 E Church St, Martinsville, VA 24112, USA

Davies, Dave — *Singer, Guitarist (Kinks)*
%Larry Page, 29 Ruston Mews, London W11 1RB, England

Davies, David R — *Biophysicist*
4224 Franklin St, Kensington, MD 20895, USA

Davies, Dennis Russell — *Conductor, Concert Pianist*
Am Wichelshof 24, 53111 Bonn, Germany

Davies, Gail — *Singer, Guitarist, Songwriter*
246 Cherokee Road, Nashville, TN 37205, USA

Davies, John G — *Judge, Swimmer*
520 Madeline Dr, Pasadena, CA 91105, USA

Davies, Lane — *Actor*
%Gold-Bouchard Mgmt, 201 N Robertson Blvd, #E, Beverly Hills, CA 90211, USA

Davies, Laura — *Golfer*
26 Tucker Road, Ottershaw, Surrey KT16 0HD, England

Davies, Linda — *Writer*
Calle Once 286, La Molona, Lima, Peru

Davies, Paul C W — *Mathematical Physicist*
%University of Adelaide, Math-Physics Dept, Adelaide SA 5005, Australia

Davies, Peter — *Biochemist*
%Albert Einstein College of Medicine, Biochemisty Dept, Bronx, NY 10461, USA

Davies, Peter Maxwell — *Composer*
%Judy Arnold, 50 Hogarth Road, London SW5 0PU, England

Davies, Raymond D (Ray) — *Singer, Guitarist (Kinks), Songwriter*
%Larry Page, 29 Rushton Mews, London W11 1RB, England

Davies, Richard T — *Diplomat*
3511 Leland St, Chevy Chase, MD 20815, USA

Davies, Ryland — *Opera Singer*
71 Fairmile Lane, Cobham, Surrey KT11 2DG, England

Davignon, Etienne — *Government Official; Businessman*
12 Ave Des Fleurs, 1150 Brussels, Belgium

Davis, A Dano — *Businessman*
%Winn-Dixie Stores, 5050 Edgewood Court, Jacksonville, FL 32254, USA

Davis, Allen (Al) — *Football Executive*
%Oakland Raiders, 1220 Harbor Bay Parkway, Alameda, CA 94502, USA

Davis, Allen L — *Financier*
%Provident Bank, 1 E 4th St, Cincinnati, OH 45202, USA

Davis, Andrew — *Movie Director*
%The Agency, 1800 Ave of Stars, #400, Los Angeles, CA 90067, USA

Davis, Andrew F — *Conductor*
%Harold Holt, 31 Sinclair Road, London W14 0NS, England

Davis, Angela Y — *Political Activist, Educator*
%University of California, Philosophy Dept, Santa Cruz, CA 15064, USA

Davis, Ann B — *Actress*
311 11th St, Ambridge, PA 15003, USA

Davis, Anthony — *Football Player*
9851 Oakwood Crest, Villa Park, CA 92861, USA

Davis, Anthony — *Jazz Pianist, Composer*
%American International Artists, 575 E 89th St, New York, NY 10128, USA

Davis, Antone — *Football Player*
9034 Village Green Blvd, Clermont, FL 34711, USA

Davis, Antonio — *Basketball Player*
625 Willow Glen Dr, El Paso, TX 79922, USA

Davis, Billy, Jr — *Singer (The Fifth Dimension)*
%Sterling/Winters, 1900 Ave of Stars, #1640, Los Angeles, CA 90067, USA

Davis, Carl — *Composer, Conductor*
99 Church Road, Barnes, London SW13 9HL, England

Davis, Clifton — *Actor*
141 Janine Dr, La Habra Heights, CA 90631, USA

Davis, Clive J — *Record Producer*
%Arista Records, 6 W 57th St, New York, NY 10019, USA

Davis, Colin R — *Conductor*
%Royal Opera House, Covent Garden, Bow St, London WC2, England

Davis, Dale — *Basketball Player*
PO Box 20885, Indianapolis, IN 46220, USA

D

D

Davis, Danny *Singer, Musician (The Nashville Brass)*
%Danny Davis Productions, PO Box 210317, Nashville, TN 37221, USA

Davis, Darrell L *Financier*
%Chrysler Financial Corp, 27777 Franklin Road, Southfield, MI 48034, USA

Davis, David (Dave) *Bowler*
%DeStasio, 710 Shore Road, Spring Lake Heights, NJ 07762, USA

Davis, Don *Golfer*
15910 FM 529, #219, Houston, TX 77095, USA

Davis, Don S *Actor*
%Gold Marshak Liedtke, 3500 W Olive Ave, #1400, Burbank, CA 91505, USA

Davis, Donald C *Navy Admiral*
5701 Rutgers Road, La Jolla, CA 92037, USA

Davis, Emanuel *Basketball Player*
%Houston Rockets, Summit, Greenway Plaza, #10, Houston, TX 77046, USA

Davis, Eric *Football Player*
5421 Country Club Parkway, San Jose, CA 95138, USA

Davis, Eric K *Baseball Player*
5616 Farmland Ave, Woodland Hills, CA 91367, USA

Davis, Errol B, Jr *Businessman*
%WPL Holdings, PO Box 2568, Madison, WI 53701, USA

Davis, Geena *Actress*
%Creative Artists Agency, 9830 Wilshire Blvd, Beverly Hills, CA 90212, USA

Davis, George K *Nutritional Biochemist*
2903 SW 2nd Court, Gainesville, FL 32601, USA

Davis, Glenn E *Baseball Player*
4882 Champions Way, Columbus, GA 31909, USA

Davis, Glenn H *Track Athlete*
801 Robinson Ave, Barberton, OH 44203, USA

Davis, Glenn W *Football Player*
4424 Bellingham Ave, Studio City, CA 91604, USA

Davis, H Thomas (Tommy) *Baseball Player*
9767 Whirlaway St, Alta Loma, CA 91737, USA

Davis, Hubert *Basketball Player*
140 Donegal Dr, Chapel Hill, NC 27514, USA

Davis, James B *Air Force General*
Chief of Staff, SHAPE, CMR 450, APO, AE 09705, USA

Davis, James H (Jimmie) *Governor, LA; Singer, Songwriter*
1331 Lakeridge Dr, Baton Rouge, LA 70802, USA

Davis, James O *Physician*
612 Maplewood Dr, Columbia, MO 65203, USA

Davis, James R (Jim) *Cartoonist (Garfield)*
%Fox Fires Restaurant, 3300 Chadham Lane, Muncie, IN 47304, USA

Davis, Jerry R *Businessman*
%Southern Pacific Transport, 1 Market Plaza, San Francisco, CA 94105, USA

Davis, Jesse *Jazz Saxophonist*
%Bridge Agency, 35 Clark St, #A-5, Brooklyn, NY 11201, USA

Davis, Josie *Actress*
12190 1/2 Ventura Blvd, Studio City, CA 91604, USA

Davis, Judy *Actress*
129 Bourke St, Woollomooloo, Sydney NSW 2011, Australia

Davis, Katherine W *Financier*
%Shelby Cullom Davis Co, 70 Pine St, New York, NY 10270, USA

Davis, Kristin *Actress*
%Flick East-West, 9057 Nemo St, #A, West Hollywood, CA 90069, USA

Davis, L Edward *Religious Leader*
%Evangelical Presbyterian Church, 26049 Five Mile Road, Detroit, MI 48239, USA

Davis, Linda *Singer*
%Starstruck Entertainment, 40 Music Square W, Nashville, TN 37203, USA

Davis, Mac *Singer, Songwriter, Actor*
759 Nimes Road, Los Angeles, CA 90077, USA

Davis, Mark M *Microbiologist*
%Stanford University, Medical Center, Microbiology Dept, Stanford, CA 94305, USA

Davis, Mark W *Baseball Player*
8038 E Tuckey Lane, Scottsdale, AZ 85250, USA

Davis, N Jan *Astronaut*
%NASA, Johnson Space Center, 2101 NASA Road, Houston, TX 77058, USA

Davis, Nathaniel *Diplomat*
1783 Longwood Ave, Claremont, CA 91711, USA

Davis, Ossie — *Actor*
44 Cortland Ave, New Rochelle, NY 10801, USA

Davis, Paul H (Butch) — *Football Coach*
%University of Miami, Athletic Dept, Coral Gables, FL 33146, USA

Davis, Phyllis — *Actress*
18319 Hart St, #11, Reseada, CA 91335, USA

Davis, Raymond G — *Korean Marine Corps Hero (CMH), General*
2530 Over Lake Ave, Stockbridge, GA 30281, USA

Davis, Raymond, Jr — *Chemist*
28 Bergen Lane, Blue Point, NY 11715, USA

Davis, Rennie — *Political Activist*
%Birth of a New Nation, 905 S Gilpin, Denver, CO 80209, USA

Davis, Richard — *Jazz Bassist*
%SRO Artists, PO Box 9532, Madison, WI 53715, USA

Davis, Robert T (Bobby), Jr — *Football Player*
3721 Eaglebrook Dr, Gastonia, NC 28056, USA

Davis, Ronald (Ron) — *Artist*
PO Box 276, Arroyo Hondo, NM 87513, USA

Davis, Russell S (Russ) — *Baseball Player*
3351 Crescent Dr, Hueytown, AL 35023, USA

Davis, Sammi — *Actress*
%Lou Coulson, 37 Berwick St, London W1V 3RF, England

Davis, Sammy L — *Vietnam War Army Hero (CMH)*
RR 2, Box 80-A, Flat Rock, IL 62427, USA

Davis, Scott — *Figure Skater*
1805 Beech Dr, Great Falls, MT 59404, USA

Davis, Skeeter — *Singer, Songwriter*
508 Seward Road, Brentwood, TN 37027, USA

Davis, Steve — *Snooker Player*
%Matchroom Snooker Ltd, 10 Western Road, Romford, Essex RM1 3JT, England

Davis, Terrell — *Football Player*
%Denver Broncos, 13655 E Dove Valley Parkway, Englewood, CO 80112, USA

Davis, Todd — *Actor*
245 S Keystone St, Burbank, CA 91506, USA

Davis, Tom — *Basketball Coach*
%University of Iowa, Athletic Dept, Iowa City, IA 52242, USA

Davis, Truman A — *Labor Leader*
%Congress of Industrial Unions, 303 Ridge St, Alton, IL 62002, USA

Davis, Tyrone — *Singer*
%Associated Booking Corp, 1995 Broadway, #501, New York, NY 10023, USA

Davis, Walt — *Track Athlete*
Rt 1, Box 2575, FM 841, Lufkin, TX 75901, USA

Davis, Walter P — *Basketball Player*
4500 S Monaco St, #1021, Denver, CO 80237, USA

Davis, Walter S — *Businessman*
%Davis & Kuelthau, 111 E Kilbourn Ave, Milwaukee, WI 53202, USA

Davis, William D (Willie) — *Football Player*
7352 Vista Del Mar, Playa del Rey, CA 90293, USA

Davis, William E — *Businessman*
%Niagara Mohawk Power, 300 Erie Blvd W, Syracuse, NY 13202, USA

Davis, William G — *Government Official, Canada*
%Tory Tory DesLauriers, Aetna Tower, #3000, Toronto ON M5K 1N2, Canada

Davis-Wrightsil, Clarissa — *Basketball Player*
%Columbus Quest, 7451 State Rt 161, Dublin, OH 43016, USA

Davison, Beverly C — *Religious Leader*
%American Baptist Churches, PO Box 851, Valley Forge, PA 19482, USA

Davison, Bruce — *Actor*
PO Box 57593, Sherman Oaks, CA 91413, USA

Davison, Fred C — *Foundation Executive, Educator*
%National Science Foundation, PO Box 15577, Augusta, GA 30919, USA

Davison, Peter — *Actor*
%Conway Van Gelder Robinson, 18-21 Jermyn St, London SW1Y 6NB, England

Dawber, Pam — *Actress*
%Wings Inc, 2236 Encinitas Blvd, #A, Encinitas, CA 92024, USA

Dawes, Dominque — *Gymnast*
129 Ritchie Ave, Silver Springs, MD 20910, USA

Dawes, Joseph — *Cartoonist*
20 Church Court, Closter, NJ 07624, USA

Dawkins, C Richard — *Biologist, Ethologist*
%Oxford University, New College, Oxford OX1 3BN, England

Dawkins, Johnny — *Basketball Player*
%Duke University, Athletic Dept, Durham, NC 27708, USA

Dawkins, Peter M (Pete) — *Football Player, Businessman*
178 Rumson Road, Rumson, NJ 07760, USA

Dawley, Joseph W (Joe) — *Artist*
13 Wholly St, Cranford, NJ 07016, USA

Dawson, Andre N — *Baseball Player*
6295 SW 58th Place, Miami, FL 33143, USA

Dawson, Buck — *Swimming Executive*
%Swimming Hall of Fame, 1 Hall of Fame Dr, Fort Lauderdale, FL 33316, USA

Dawson, Dermontti — *Football Player*
%Pittsburgh Steelers, 3 Rivers Stadium, 300 Stadium Circle, Pittsburgh, PA 15212, USA

Dawson, Henry A, Jr — *Judge*
%US Tax Court, 400 2nd St NW, Washington, DC 20217, USA

Dawson, Lenny (Len) — *Football Player, Sportscaster*
121 W 48th St, #1906, Kansas City, MO 64112, USA

Dawson, Richard — *Actor*
1117 Angelo Dr, Beverly Hills, CA 90210, USA

Day, Bill — *Editorial Cartoonist*
%Detroit Free Press, Editorial Dept, 321 W Lafayette Blvd, Detroit, MI 48226, USA

Day, Chon — *Cartoonist (Brother Sebastian)*
22 Cross St, Westerly, RI 02891, USA

Day, Doris — *Singer, Actress*
PO Box 223163, Carmel, CA 93922, USA

Day, George E (Bud) — *Vietnam War Air Force Hero (CMH)*
23 Bayshore Dr, Shalimar, FL 32579, USA

Day, Guy — *Businessman*
%Chiat/Day/Mojo Advertising, 340 Main St, Venice, CA 90291, USA

Day, Larraine — *Actress*
10313 Lauriston Ave, Los Angeles, CA 90025, USA

Day, Mary — *Ballet Executive*
%Washington Ballet, Kennedy Center, Washington, DC 20011, USA

Day, Peter R — *Agricultural Scientist*
394 Franklin Road, New Brunswick, NJ 08902, USA

Day, Robert — *Cartoonist*
%New Yorker Magazine, Editorial Dept, 20 W 43rd St, New York, NY 10036, USA

Day, Robin — *Journalist*
%BBC Studios, Lime Grove, London W12, England

Day, Thomas B — *Educator*
%San Diego State University, President's Office, San Diego, CA 92182, USA

Day, Todd — *Basketball Player*
%Miami Heat, Miami Arena, 100 NE 3rd Ave, Miami, FL 33132, USA

Day-George, Lynda — *Actress*
10310 Riverside Dr, #104, Toluca Lake, CA 91602, USA

Day-Lewis, Daniel — *Actor*
%Alastair Reid, 65 Connaught St, London W2, England

Dayne, Taylor — *Singer, Songwriter*
PO Box 476, Rockville Centre, NY 11571, USA

Days, Drews S, III — *Government Official*
%Yale University, Law School, New Haven, CT 06520, USA

De Agostini, Doris — *Skier*
6780 Airolo, Switzerland

De Angelis, Beverly — *Psychiatrist*
505 S Beverly Dr, #1017, Beverly Hills, CA 90212, USA

De Bakey, Michael E — *Surgeon*
%Baylor College of Medicine, Med Center, 1200 Moursund Ave, Houston, TX 77030, USA

De Benning, Burr — *Actor*
4235 Kingfisher Road, Calabasas, CA 91302, USA

De Blanc, Jefferson J — *WW II Marine Corps Hero (CMH)*
321 St Martin St, Saint Martinville, LA 70582, USA

De Blasis, Celeste — *Writer*
Kemper Campbell Ranch, #9, Victorville, CA 92392, USA

De Bont, Jan — *Cinematographer, Director*
%Gersh Agency, 232 N Canon Dr, Beverly Hills, CA 90210, USA

De Borchgrave, Arnaud — *Editor*
2141 Wyoming Ave NW, Washington, DC 20008, USA

De Branges, Louis — *Mathematician*
%Purdue University, Mathematics Dept, West Lafayette, IN 47907, USA
De Burgh, Chris — *Singer, Songwriter*
Bargy Castle, Tonhaggard, Wesxord, Ireland
De Camilli, Pietro — *Biologist*
%Yale University, School of Medicine, Cell Biology Dept, New Haven, CT 06512, USA
De Carlo, Yvonne — *Actress*
PO Box 250070, Glendale, CA 91225, USA
De Cordova, Frederick T — *Movie, Television Producer, Director*
1875 Carla Ridge, Beverly Hills, CA 90210, USA
De Deo, Joseph E (Joe) — *Businessman*
%Young & Rubicam, 285 Madison Ave, New York, NY 10017, USA
De Duve, Christian R — *Nobel Medicine Laureate*
80 Central Park West, New York, NY 10023, USA
De Frank, Vincent — *Conductor*
%Rhodes College of Music, 2000 N Parkway, Memphis, TN 38112, USA
De Freitas, Eric — *Bowler*
175 W 12th St, New York, NY 10011, USA
De Gaspe, Philippe — *Publisher*
%Canadian Living Magazine, 50 Holly St, Toronto ON M4S 3B3, Canada
De Gennes, Pierre-Gilles — *Nobel Physics Laureate*
11 Place Marcelin-Berthelot, 75005 Paris, France
De Givenchy, Hubert T — *Fashion Designer*
3 Ave George V, 75008 Paris, France
De Grazia, Sebastian — *Writer*
%Princeton University Press, PO Box 190, Princeton, NJ 08544, USA
De Hartog, Jan — *Writer*
%Harper Collins Publishers, 10 E 53rd St, New York, NY 10022, USA
De Haven, Gloria — *Actress*
88 Central Park West, #12-G, New York, NY 10023, USA
De Havilland, Olivia — *Actress*
3 Rue Benouville, 75016 Paris, France
De Jager, Cornelis — *Astronomer*
Zonnenburg 1, 352 NL Utrecht, Netherlands
De Kieweit, Cornelis W — *Writer, Historian*
22 Berkeley St, Rochester, NY 14607, USA
De Klerk, Frederik W — *President, South Africa; Nobel Laureate*
Tuynhuys, Cape Town 8000, South Africa
De Kok, Roger G — *Air Force General*
Commander, Space/Missile Systems Center, Los Angeles Air Force Base, CA 90245, USA
De La Billiere, Peter — *Army General, England*
%Coutts Co, 440 Strand, London WC2R 0QS, England
De La Cruz, Rosie — *Model*
%Next Model Mgmt, 23 Watts St, New York, NY 10013, USA
De la Falaise, Lucie — *Model*
%Elite Model Mgmt, 111 E 22nd St, #200, New York, NY 10010, USA
De La Fuente, Joel — *Actor*
%Ambrosio/Mortimer, 9150 Wilshire Blvd, #175, Beverly Hills, CA 90212, USA
De La Hoya, Oscar — *Boxer*
333 W Washington Blvd, Los Angeles, CA 90015, USA
De la Puente Raygada, Oscar — *Prime Minister, Peru*
%Prime Minister's Office, Urb Corpac, Calle 1 Oeste S/N, Lima, Peru
De La Rocha, Zack — *Singer (Rage Against the Machine)*
%William Morris Agency, 1325 Ave of Americas, New York, NY 10019, USA
De Larrocha, Alicia — *Concert Pianist*
Farmaceutic Carbonell, 46-48 Atic, Barcelona 34, Spain
De Laurentiis, Dino — *Movie Producer*
%De Laurentiis Entertainment, 8670 Wilshire Blvd, Beverly Hills, CA 90211, USA
De Leeuw, Ton — *Composer*
Costeruslaan 4, Hilversum, Netherlands
De Leon Carpio, Ramiro — *President, Guatemala*
%President's Office, Palacio Nacional, Guatemala City, Guatemala
De Los Angeles, Victoria — *Opera Singer*
Avenida de Pedralbes 57, 08034 Barcelona, Spain
De Lucchi, Michele — *Architect*
Via Cenisio 40, 20154 Milan, Italy
De Lue, Donald — *Sculptor*
82 Highland Ave, Leonardo, NJ 07737, USA

D

De Branges - De Lue

De Maiziere, Lothar — *Prime Minister, East Germany*
Am Treptower Park 31, 12435 Berlin, Germany

De Marco, Jean — *Sculptor*
Cervaro 03044, Prov-Frosinore, Italy

De Medeiros, Maria — *Actress*
%William Morris Agency, 151 S El Camino Dr, Beverly Hills, CA 90212, USA

De Ment, Jack — *Research Chemist*
%Oregon Health Care Center, 11325 NE Weidler St, #44, Portland, OR 97220, USA

De Merchant, Paul — *Religious Leader*
%Missionary Church, PO Box 9127, Fort Wayne, IN 46899, USA

De Mita, L Ciriaco — *Prime Minister, Italy*
%Partito Democrazia Cristiana, Piazza de Gesu 46, 00186 Rome, Italy

De Montebello, Philippe L — *Museum Executive*
%Metropolitan Museum of Art, 82nd St & 5th Ave, New York, NY 10028, USA

De Mornay, Rebecca — *Actress*
%J/P/M, 760 N La Cienega Blvd, #200, Los Angeles, CA 90069, USA

De Paiva, James — *Actor*
PO Box 11152, Greenwich, CT 06831, USA

De Palma, Brian R — *Movie Director*
270 N Canon Dr, #1195, Beverly Hills, CA 90210, USA

De Peyer, Gervase — *Concert Clarinetist, Conductor*
1250 S Washington St, Alexandria, VA 22314, USA

De Valois, Ninette — *Choreographer*
%Royal Ballet, Bow St, London WC2E 9DD, England

De Vicenzo, Roberto — *Golfer*
%Noni Lann, 5025 Veloz Ave, Tarzana, CA 91356, USA

De Waart, Edo — *Conductor*
Essenlaan 68, Rotterdam 3016, Netherlands

De Weldon, Felix — *Sculptor*
219 Randolph Place NE, Washington, DC 20002, USA

De Witt, Bryce S — *Physicist*
%University of Texas, Physics Dept, Austin, TX 78712, USA

De Witt, Joyce — *Actress*
1250 6th St, #403, Santa Monica, CA 90401, USA

De Young, Cliff — *Actor*
2143 Colby Ave, Los Angeles, CA 90025, USA

Deacon, Richard — *Sculptor*
%Margarete Roeder Gallery, 545 Broadway, New York, NY 10012, USA

Deacon, Terrence — *Neuroanatomist*
%Harvard University, Neuroanatomy Dept, Cambridge, MA 02138, USA

Deakins, Roger A — *Cinematographer*
23 Tavistock Terrace, London N19 4BZ, England

Deal, Kim — *Singer (Breeders)*
%Gold Mountain Ent, 3575 Cahuenga Blvd W, #450, Los Angeles, CA 90068, USA

Dean, Billy — *Singer*
PO Box 870689, Stone Mountain, GA 30087, USA

Dean, Christopher — *Ice Dancer*
PO Box 16, Beeston, Nottingham NG9, England

Dean, Clyde D — *Marine Corps General*
2014 Pineway Road, Martinsburg, WV 25401, USA

Dean, Eddie — *Singer, Actor*
32161 Sailview Lane, Westlake Village, CA 91361, USA

Dean, Frederick (Fred) — *Football Player, Coach*
%Howard University, Athletic Dept, PO Box 844, Washington, DC 20044, USA

Dean, Howard B — *Governor, VT*
%Governor's Office, Pavilion Office Building, Montpelier, VT 05609, USA

Dean, Howard M, Jr — *Businessman*
%Dean Foods, 3600 N River Road, Franklin Park, IL 60131, USA

Dean, Jimmy — *Singer*
8000 Centerview Parkway, #400, Cordova, TN 38018, USA

Dean, John G — *Diplomat*
29 Blvd Jules Sandeau, 75016 Paris, France

Dean, John W, III — *Watergate Figure*
9496 Rembert Lane, Beverly Hills, CA 90210, USA

Dean, Laura — *Choreographer, Composer*
%Dean Dance & Music Foundation, 552 Broadway, #400, New York, NY 10012, USA

Dean, Stafford R — *Opera Singer*
%Harrison Parrott, 12 Penzance Place, London W11 4PA, England

Deane, William Patrick — *Governor General, Australia*
%Government House, Canberra ACT 26000, Australia

Dearden, James — *Movie Director*
%International Creative Mgmt, 8942 Wilshire Blvd, Beverly Hills, CA 90211, USA

Deardurff-Schmidt, Deena — *Swimmer*
742 Murray Dr, El Cajon, CA 92020, USA

Dearie, Blossom — *Singer, Songwriter, Pianist*
%Daffodil Records, PO Box 21, East Durham, NY 12423, USA

Deas, Justin — *Actor*
%Paradigm Agency, 10100 Santa Monica Blvd, #2500, Los Angeles, CA 90067, USA

Deaver, Michael K — *Government Official*
%Edelman Public Relations Worldwide, 1420 "K" St NW, Washington, DC 20005, USA

DeBerg, Steve — *Football Player, Coach*
1806 W Jetton Ave, Tampa, FL 33606, USA

DeBold, Adolfo J — *Pathologist, Physiologist*
%Ottawa Civic Hospital, 1053 Carling Ave, Ottawa ON K1Y 4E9, Canada

Debre, Michel — *Prime Minister, France*
20 Rue Jacob, 75006 Paris, France

Debreu, Gerard — *Nobel Economics Laureate*
%University of California, Economics Dept, Berkeley, CA 94720, USA

DeBusschere, David A (Dave) — *Basketball Player*
136 Hampton Road, Garden City, NY 11530, USA

Deby, Idriss — *President, Chad*
%President's Office, N'Djamena, Chad

DeCamp, Rosemary — *Actress*
317 Camino de Los Colinas, Redondo Beach, CA 90277, USA

DeCarava, Roy — *Photographer*
%Hunter College, Photography Department, New York, NY 10021, USA

DeCastella, F Robert — *Track Athlete*
%Australian Institute of Sport, PO Box 176, Belconnen ACT 2616, Australia

Decherd, Robert W — *Businessman*
%A H Belo Corp, 400 S Record St, Dallas, TX 75202, USA

DeCinces, Douglas V (Doug) — *Baseball Player*
2 Leesburg Court, Newport Beach, CA 92660, USA

Decio, Arthur J — *Businessman*
%Skyline Corp, 2520 By-Pass Road, Elkhart, IN 46514, USA

DeCoster, Roger — *Motorcycle Racing Rider*
%MC Sports, 1919 Torrance Blvd, Torrance, CA 90501, USA

DeCrane, Alfred C, Jr — *Businessman*
55 Valley Road, Bronxville, NY 10708, USA

Decter, Midge — *Writer*
120 E 81st St, New York, NY 10028, USA

Dedeaux, Raoul M (Rod) — *Baseball Coach*
1430 S Eastman Ave, Los Angeles, CA 90023, USA

Dedini, Eldon L — *Cartoonist*
PO Box 1630, Monterey, CA 93942, USA

Dedkov, Anatoli I — *Cosmonaut*
%Potchta Kosmonavtov, Moskovskoi Oblasti, 141160 Syvisdny Goroduk, Russia

Dee, Donald (Don) — *Basketball Player*
1420 E 22nd Ave, North Kansas City, MO 64116, USA

Dee, Frances — *Actress*
Rt 3, Box 375, Camarillo, CA 93010, USA

Dee, Joey — *Singer*
%Horizon Mgmt, PO Box 8536, Endwell, NY 13762, USA

Dee, Ruby — *Actress*
44 Cortland Ave, New Rochelle, NY 10801, USA

Dee, Sandra — *Actress, Model*
880 Hilldale Ave, #15, Los Angeles, CA 90069, USA

Deeb, Gary — *Television Critic*
%Chicago Sun-Times, 401 N Wabash Ave, Chicago, IL 60611, USA

Deedes of Aldington, William F — *Government Official, England*
New Hayters, Aldington, Kent, England

Deependra Bir Bikram Shah Dev — *Crown Prince, Nepal*
%Narayanhiti Royal Palace, Durbag Marg, Kathmandu, Nepal

Deer, Ada E — *Government Official*
4615 N Park Ave, #405, Chevy Chase, MD 20815, USA

Deering, Anthony W — *Businessman*
%Rouse Co, 10275 Little Patuxent Parkway, Columbia, MD 21044, USA

D

Deane - Deering

Deering, John *Editorial Cartoonist*
6701 Westover Dr, Little Rock, AR 72207, USA

Dees, Archie *Basketball Player*
4405 N Hillview Dr, Bloomington, IN 47408, USA

Dees, Bowen C *Science Administrator*
140 N Camino Miramonte, Tucson, AZ 85716, USA

Dees, Rick *Radio Entertainer, Singer*
PO Box 4352, Los Angeles, CA 90078, USA

DeFeo, Ronald M *Businessman*
%Terex Corp, 500 Post Road E, Westport, CT 06880, USA

DeFigueiredo, Rui J P *Computer Engineer*
%University of California, Intelligent Sensors/Systems Lab, Irvine, CA 92717, USA

DeFleur, Lois B *Educator*
%State University of New York, President's Office, Binghamton, NY 13902, USA

Deford, Frank *Sportswriter*
Box 1109, Green Farms, CT 06436, USA

DeForest, Roy *Artist*
PO Box 47, Port Costa, CA 94569, USA

DeFrancisco, Joseph S (Joe) *Army General*
Chief of Staff, US Pacific Command, Camp H M Smith, HI 96861, USA

DeFranco, Buddy *Jazz Clarinetist*
22525 Coral Ave, Panama City, FL 32413, USA

DeFrantz, Anita *Sports Executive*
%US Olympic Committee, 1 Olympia Plaza, Colorado Springs, CO 80909, USA

DeGeneres, Ellen *Actress, Comedienne*
1122 S Roxbury Dr, Los Angeles, CA 90035, USA

DeHaan, Richard W *Religious Leader*
3000 Kraft Ave SE, Grand Rapids, MI 49512, USA

Dehaene, Jean-Luc *Prime Minister, Belgium*
%Prime Minister's Office, 16 Rue de la Loi, 1000 Brussels, Belgium

Dehere, Tony *Basketball Player*
%Sacramento Kings, 1 Sports Parkway, Sacramento, CA 95834, USA

Dehmelt, Hans G *Nobel Physics Laureate*
1600 43rd Ave E, Seattle, WA 98112, USA

Deighton, Leonard C (Len) *Writer*
Fairymount, Blackrock, Dundalk, County Louth, Ireland

Deihl, Richard H *Financier*
%H F Ahmanson Co, 4900 Rivergrade Road, Irwindale, CA 91706, USA

Deisenhofer, Johann *Nobel Chemistry Laureate*
%Howard Hughes Medical Institute, 5323 Harry Hines Blvd, Dallas, TX 75235, USA

Deja, Andreas *Animator*
%Walt Disney Studios, Animation Dept, 500 S Buena Vista St, Burbank, CA 91521, USA

DeJohnette, Jack *Jazz Drummer, Composer*
Silver Hollow Road, Willow, NY 11201, USA

DeJordy, Denis *Hockey Player*
472 Cherrin Des-Patriotes, St Charles PQ J0L 2G0, Canada

Dekker, Desmond *Singer*
%Free World Music, 230 12th St, #117, Miami Beach, FL 33139, USA

Del Negro, Vinny *Basketball Player*
36 Hickory, West Springfield, MA 01089, USA

Del Rio, Jack *Football Player*
134 Chanticleer Lane, Alamo, CA 94507, USA

Del Toro, Benicio *Actor*
%IFA Talent Agency, 8730 Sunset Blvd, #490, Los Angeles, CA 90069, USA

Del Tredici, David *Composer*
463 West St, #G-121, New York, NY 10014, USA

Delacote, Jacques *Conductor*
%IMG Artists, 3 Burlington Lane, Chiswick, London W4 2TH, England

DeLamielleure, Joe *Football Player*
4016 Cottonwood Dr, Durham, NC 27705, USA

Delamuraz, Jean-Pascal *President, Switzerland*
%Federal Chancellery, Bundeshaus-W, Bundesgasse, 3003 Berne, Switzerland

DeLancie, John *Actor*
1313 Brunswick Ave, South Pasadena, CA 91030, USA

Delaney, F James (Jim) *Track Athlete*
PO Box 331, Sun Valley, ID 83353, USA

Delaney, Kim *Actress, Model*
3435 Ocean Park Blvd, #201-N, Santa Monica, CA 90405, USA

Delaney, Shelagh	*Writer*
%Tess Sayle, 11 Jubilee Place, London SW3 3TE, England	
Delany, Dana	*Actress*
2522 Beverly Ave, Santa Monica, CA 90405, USA	
DeLap, Tony	*Artist*
225 Jasmine St, Corona del Mar, CA 92625, USA	
Delchamps, Randy	*Businessman*
%Delchamps Inc, 305 Delchamps Dr, Mobile, AL 36602, USA	
Deleage, Jean	*Businessman*
%Burr Egan Deleage Co, 1 Embarcadero Center, San Francisco, CA 94111, USA	
Delgado, Pedro	*Cyclist*
%General Delivery, Segovia, Spain	
DeLillo, Don	*Writer*
57 Rossmore Ave, Bronxville, NY 10708, USA	
Delk, Tony	*Basketball Player*
%Charlotte Hornets, 1 Hive Dr, Charlotte, NC 28217, USA	
Dell, Donald L	*Tennis Player, Attorney*
%ProServ Inc, 888 17th St NW, #1200, Washington, DC 20006, USA	
Dell, Michael S	*Businessman*
%Dell Computer, 9505 Arboretum Blvd, Austin, TX 78759, USA	
Della Casa-Debeljevic, Lisa	*Opera Singer*
Schloss Gottlieben, Thurgau, Switzerland	
Della Femina, Jerry	*Businessman*
%Jerry & Ketchum, 527 Madison Ave, New York, NY 10022, USA	
DelliBovi, Alfred A	*Financier*
%Federal Home Loan Bank, 7 World Trade Center, New York, NY 10048, USA	
Dellinger, Walter	*Educator, Attorney*
%Duke University, Law School, Durham, NC 27706, USA	
Dello Joio, Norman	*Composer*
PO Box 154, East Hampton, NY 11937, USA	
Delo, Ken	*Actor*
161 Avondale Dr, #93-8, Branson, MO 65616, USA	
Delon, Alain	*Actor*
%Leda Productions, 4 Rue Chambiges, 75008 Paris, France	
DeLong, Keith	*Football Player*
915 Fairway Oaks Lane, Knoxville, TN 37922, USA	
Delora, Jennifer	*Actress*
%Gilla Roos, 9744 Wilshire Blvd, #203, Beverly Hills, CA 90212, USA	
Deloria, Victor (Vine), Jr	*Indian Rights Activist*
%University of Colorado, History Dept, Box 234, Boulder, CO 80309, USA	
Delors, Jacques L J	*Government Official, France*
19 Blvd de Bercy, 75012 Paris, France	
Delpy, Julie	*Actress*
%Myriam Bru, IAC, Postfach 1105, 35112 Fronhausen, Germany	
DeLucas, Lawrence	*Astronaut*
%University of Alabama, Comprehensive Cancer Center, Birmingham, AL 35294, USA	
DeLuise, Dom	*Comedian*
1186 Corsica Dr, Pacific Palisades, CA 90272, USA	
DeLuise, Michael	*Actor*
1186 Corsica Dr, Pacific Palisades, CA 90272, USA	
DeLuise, Peter	*Actor*
1223 Wilshire Blvd, #411, Santa Monica, CA 90403, USA	
Delvecchio, Alex	*Hockey Player*
21186 Bridge St, #526, Southfield, MI 48034, USA	
Demarchelier, Patrick	*Photographer*
162 W 21st St, New York, NY 10011, USA	
DeMarco, Tony	*Boxer*
4929 N 40th St, Phoenix, AZ 85018, USA	
Demarest, Arthur A	*Archeologist*
%Vanderbilt University, Anthropology Dept, Nashville, TN 37235, USA	
Demars, Bruce	*Navy Admiral*
41 Manters Point Road, Plymouth, MA 02360, USA	
DeMent, Iris	*Singer, Songwriter*
%Myers Media, 250 W 57th St, #2316, New York, NY 10107, USA	
Demetriadis, Phokion	*Editorial Cartoonist*
3rd September St 174, Athens, Greece	
DeMeuse, Donald H	*Businessman*
%Fort Howard Corp, 1919 S Broadway, Green Bay, WI 54304, USA	

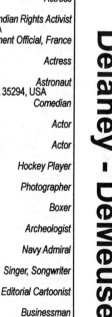

D

Delaney - DeMeuse

Demin, Lev S — *Cosmonaut*
%Potchta Kosmonavtov, Moskovskoi Oblasti, 141160 Syvisdny Goroduk, Russia

Demirel, Suleiman — *President, Turkey*
%President's Office, Cumhurbaskanlgi Kosku, Cankaya, Ankara, Turkey

Demme, Jonathan — *Movie Director*
%Creative Artists Agency, 9830 Wilshire Blvd, Beverly Hills, CA 90212, USA

Dempsey, J Rickard (Rick) — *Baseball Player*
1673 Crown Ridge Court, Westlake Village, CA 91362, USA

Dempsey, Jerry E — *Businessman*
%PPG Industries, 5 The Trillium, Pittsburgh, PA 15238, USA

Dempsey, John — *Cartoonist*
%Playboy Magazine, Reader Services, 680 N Lake Shore Dr, Chicago, IL 60611, USA

Dempsey, Patrick — *Actor*
2644 N Beachwood Dr, Los Angeles, CA 90068, USA

Dempsey, Tom — *Football Player*
%NADW, 1500 River Oaks Road W, Harahan, LA 70123, USA

Demus, Jorg — *Concert Pianist*
%LYRA, Doblinger Hauptstr 77-A/10, 1190 Vienna, Austria

Demuth, Richard H — *Attorney, Financier*
5404 Bradley Blvd, Bethesda, MD 20814, USA

Den Herder, Vern — *Football Player*
%General Delivery, Sioux Center, IA 51250, USA

Den Ouden, Willy — *Swimmer*
Goudsewagenstraat 23-B, Rotterdam, Holland

Den Tagayasu — *Choreographer*
%Ondekoza, Koda Performing Arts Co, Sado Island, Japan

Denard, Michael — *Ballet Dancer*
%Paris Opera Ballet, Place de l'Opera, 75009 Paris, France

DeNault, John B — *Businessman*
%Twentieth Century Insurance, 6301 Owensmouth Ave, Woodland Hills, CA 91367, USA

Dench, Judi — *Actress*
%Julian Belfarge, 46 Albermarle St, London W1X 4PP, England

Denenberg, Herbert S — *Educator, Government Official*
PO Box 7301, Saint Davids, PA 19087, USA

Denend, Les — *Businessman*
%Network General, 4200 Bohannon Dr, Menlo Park, CA 94025, USA

Denes, Agnes C — *Artist*
595 Broadway, New York, NY 10012, USA

Deneuve, Catherine — *Actress*
76 Rue Bonaparte, 75016 Paris, France

Denham, Maurice — *Actor*
44 Brunswick Gardens, #2, London W8, England

Denham, Robert E — *Financier*
%Salomon Inc, 7 World Trade Center, #4300, New York, NY 10048, USA

Denhardt, David T — *Biologist*
%Rutgers University, Nelson Biological Laboratories, Piscataway, NJ 08855, USA

DeNiro, Robert — *Actor*
9544 Hidden Valley Place, Beverly Hills, CA 90210, USA

Denison, Anthony — *Actor*
%Gersh Agency, 232 N Canon Dr, Beverly Hills, CA 90210, USA

Denisov, Edison V — *Composer*
Studentcheskaia 44/28, #35, 121165 Moscow, Russia

Denisse, Jean-Francois — *Astronomer*
48 Rue Monsieur Le Prince, 75006 Paris, France

Denker, Henry — *Writer*
241 Central Park West, New York, NY 10024, USA

Denlea, Leo E, Jr — *Businessman*
%Farmers Group, 4680 Wilshire Blvd, Los Angeles, CA 90010, USA

Dennehy, Brian — *Actor*
%Susan Smith, 121 N San Vicente Blvd, Beverly Hills, CA 90211, USA

Dennehy, Kathleen — *Actress*
%Susan Nathe, 8281 Melrose Ave, #200, Los Angeles, CA 90046, USA

Dennerlein, Barbara — *Jazz Organist*
Tsingtauer Str 66, 81827 Munich, Germany

Dennett, Daniel C — *Philosopher*
20 Ironwood Road, Andover, MA 01845, USA

Denning of Whitechurch, Alfred T — *Judge*
The Lawn, Whitechurch, Hants, England

Dennis, Cathy — *Pop Singer*
%William Morris Agency, 1325 Ave of Americas, New York, NY 10019, USA
Dennis, Donna F — *Sculptor*
131 Duane St, New York, NY 10013, USA
Dennison, Rachel — *Actress*
%Raymond Katz, 345 N Maple Dr, #205, Beverly Hills, CA 90210, USA
Denny, Floyd W, Jr — *Pediatrician*
9210 Dodsons Crossroads, Chapel Hill, NC 27516, USA
Denny, John A — *Baseball Player*
13430 E Camino la Cebadilla, Tucson, AZ 85749, USA
Denny, Martin — *Composer, Pianist*
6770 Hawaii Kai Dr, #402, Honolulu, HI 96825, USA
Denny, Robyn — *Artist*
66 Royal Mint St, London E1 8LG, England
Densen-Gerber, Judianne — *Psychiatrist, Social Activist*
%Odyssey Resources Inc, 5 Hedley Farms Road, Westport, CT 06880, USA
Densmore, John — *Drummer (Doors)*
49 Halderman Road, Santa Monica, CA 90402, USA
Dent, Frederick B — *Secretary, Commerce*
221 Montgomery St, Spartenburg, SC 29302, USA
Dent, Jim — *Golfer*
PO Box 22893, Tampa, FL 33622, USA
Dent, Richard L — *Football Player*
4453 RFD, Long Grove, IL 60047, USA
Dent, Russell E (Bucky) — *Baseball Player*
8895 Indian River Run, Boynton Beach, FL 33437, USA
Denton, Jeremiah A, Jr — *Senator, AL*
Rt 1, Box 305, Theodore, AL 36582, USA
Denton, Sandi (Pepa) — *Rap Artist (Salt-N-Pepa)*
%Next Plateau Records, 1650 Broadway, #1102, New York, NY 10019, USA
Denver, Bob — *Actor*
PO Box 269, Princeton, WV 24740, USA
Denver, John — *Singer, Songwriter*
PO Box 1587, Aspen, CO 81612, USA
DeOre, Bill — *Editorial Cartoonist*
%Dallas News, Editorial Dept, Communications Center, Dallas, TX 75265, USA
Depardieu, Gerard — *Actor*
4 Place de la Chapelle, 75800 Bougival, France
Depardon, Raymond — *Photographer*
18 Bis Rue Henri Barbusse, 75005 Paris, France
Depp, Johnny — *Actor, Director*
%International Creative Mgmt, 8942 Wilshire Blvd, Beverly Hills, CA 90211, USA
DePree, Max O — *Businessman*
%Herman Miller Inc, 855 E Main St, Zeeland, MI 49464, USA
DePreist, James A — *Conductor*
%Oregon Symphony, 711 SW Alder St, #200, Portland, OR 97205, USA
Der, Lambert — *Editorial Cartoonist*
%Houston Post, Editorial Dept, 4888 Loop Central Dr, #390, Houston, TX 77081, USA
Derbyshire, Andrew G — *Architect*
4 Sunnyfield, Hatfield, Herts AL9 5DX, England
Dercum, Max — *Skier*
PO Box 189, Dillon, CO 80435, USA
Derek, Bo — *Actress*
3275 Monticello, Santa Ynez, CA 93460, USA
Derek, John — *Actor*
3275 Monticello, Santa Ynez, CA 93460, USA
Dern, Bruce — *Actor*
23430 Malibu Colony Road, Malibu, CA 90265, USA
Dern, Laura — *Actress*
%Wolf/Kasteller, 132 S Rodeo Dr, #300, Beverly Hills, CA 90212, USA
Dernesch, Helga — *Opera Singer*
Neutorgasse 2/22, 1013 Vienna, Austria
DeRosa, Patricia — *Businesswoman*
%Gap Inc, 900 Cherry Ave, San Bruno, CA 94066, USA
DeRover, Jolanda — *Swimmer*
%Olympic Committee, Surinamestraat 33, 2514 La Harve, Netherlands
Derow, Peter A — *Publisher*
PO Box 534, Bedford, NY 10506, USA

D

D

Derr, Kenneth T	*Businessman*
%Chevron Corp, 555 Market St, San Francisco, CA 94105, USA	
Derricks, Cleavant	*Actor*
192 Lexington Ave, #1204, New York, NY 10016, USA	
Derrida, Jacques	*Philosopher*
%Ecole des Hautes Etudes, 54 Blvd Raspail, 75006 Paris, France	
Derringer, Rick	*Singer, Guitarist*
%Slatus Mgmt, 208 E 51st St, #151, New York, NY 10022, USA	
Dershowitz, Alan M	*Attorney, Educator*
%Harvard University, Law School, Cambridge, MA 02138, USA	
Derwinski, Edward J	*Secretary, Veterans Affairs*
%Derwinski Assoc, 1800 Diagonal Road, #600, Alexandria, VA 22314, USA	
Des'ree	*Singer*
%William Morris Agency, 1325 Ave of Americas, New York, NY 10019, USA	
Desai, Anita	*Writer*
%Alfred A Knopf Inc, 201 E 50th St, New York, NY 10022, USA	
DeSailly, Jean	*Actor*
53 Quai des Grands Augustins, 75006 Paris, France	
Desailly, Marcel	*Soccer Player*
%AC Milan, Via Turati 3, 20221 Milan, Italy	
DesBarres, John P	*Businessman*
%Transco Energy Co, 2800 Post Oak Blvd, Houston, TX 77056, USA	
Desch, Carl W	*Financier*
%Citibank (New York State), 99 Garnsey Road, Pittsford, NY 14534, USA	
Deschanel, Caleb	*Cinematographer*
7000 Romaine St, Los Angeles, CA 90038, USA	
Deschanel, Mary Jo	*Actress*
844 Chautauqua Blvd, Pacific Palisades, CA 90272, USA	
Deshays, Claudie	*Spatinaut, France*
%Hopital Cochin, Rhumatologie Dept, 75000 Paris, France	
DeShields, Delino L	*Baseball Player*
100 Shady Brook Walk, Fairburn, GA 30213, USA	
Desiderio, Robert	*Actor*
2934 1/2 Beverly Glen Circle, #30, Los Angeles, CA 90077, USA	
DeSimone, Livio D	*Businessman*
%Minnesota Mining (3-M), 3-M Center, St Paul, MN 55144, USA	
Desio, Ardito	*Explorer, Geologist*
Viale Maino 14, 20129 Milan, Italy	
Desjardins, Eric	*Hockey Player*
%Philadelphia Flyers, CoreStates Center, Pattison Place, Philadelphia, PA 19148, USA	
Deskur, Andrzej Maria Cardial	*Religious Leader*
%Council for Social Communications, 00120 Vatican City	
Desny, Ivan	*Actor*
Casa al Sole, 6612 Ascona-Collina, Switzerland	
Despotopoulos, Johannes (Jan)	*Architect*
Anapiron Polemou 7, 115 21 Athens, Greece	
Detmer, Ty	*Football Player*
900 South 906 East, Pleasant Grove, UT 84062, USA	
Detmers, Maruschka	*Actress*
%Myriam Bru, 80 Ave Charles de Gaulle, 92200 Neuilly Sur Seine, France	
Detweiler, David K	*Physiologist*
107 Macintosh Lane, North Wales, PA 19454, USA	
Detweiler, Robert C	*Educator*
%California State University, President's Office, Dominguez Hills, CA 90747, USA	
Deuba, Sher Sahadur	*Prime Minister, Nepal*
%Prime Minister's Office, Secretariat, Singh Dubar, Katmandu, Nepal	
Deukmejian, George	*Governor, CA*
%Sidley & Austin, 555 W 5th St, Los Angeles, CA 90013, USA	
Deuss, Walter	*Businessman*
%Kauflauskette Karstadt, Theodor-Althoff-Str 2, 45133 Essen, Germany	
Deutekom, Cristina	*Opera Singer*
Lancasterdreef 41, Dronten 8251 TG, Holland	
Deutsch, Patti	*Actress*
1811 San Ysidro Dr, Beverly Hills, CA 90210, USA	
Devan Nair, Chengara Veetil	*President, Singapore*
57 Notre Dame Road, Bedford, MA 01730, USA	
Devane, William	*Actor*
%International Creative Mgmt, 8942 Wilshire Blvd, Beverly Hills, CA 90211, USA	

Derr - Devane

DeVarona, Donna — *Swimmer, Sportscaster*
%ABC-TV, Sports Dept, 77 W 66th St, New York, NY 10023, USA

Devening, R Randolph — *Businessman*
%Doskocil Companies, 2601 Northwest Expressway, Oklahoma City, OK 73112, USA

Devers, Gail — *Track Athlete*
20214 Leadwell St, Canoga Park, CA 91306, USA

Deville, Michel — *Movie Director*
36 Rue Reinhardt, 92100 Boulogne, France

Devine, Dan — *Football Coach*
%Sun Angel Foundation, 3800 N Central Ave, #D-3, Phoenix, AZ 85012, USA

Devine, Harold — *Boxer*
8 Thayer Pond Dr, #7, North Oxford, MA 01537, USA

Devine, Loretta — *Actress*
5816 Ernest Ave, Los Angeles, CA 90034, USA

DeVita, Vincent T, Jr — *Oncologist*
%Yale Comprehensive Cancer Center, 333 Cedar St, New Haven, CT 06510, USA

DeVito, Danny — *Comedian, Actor, Director*
PO Box 491246, Los Angeles, CA 90049, USA

DeVito, Mathias J — *Businessman*
%Rouse Co, 10275 Little Patuxent Parkway, Columbia, MD 21044, USA

Devitt, John — *Swimmer*
46 Beacon Ave, Beacon Hill NSW 2100, Australia

Devlin, Bruce — *Golfer*
9274 E Sands Dr, Scottsdale, AZ 85255, USA

Devlin, John — *Actor*
825 N Crescent Heights Blvd, Los Angeles, CA 90046, USA

DeVol, Frank — *Composer, Conductor*
33791 Connemara Dr, San Juan Capistrano, CA 92675, USA

DeVos, Richard M — *Businessman*
%Amway Corp, 7575 E Fulton Road E, Ada, MI 49355, USA

DeVries, William C — *Surgeon*
201 Abraham Flexner Way, #1103, Louisville, KY 40202, USA

Dewar, Donald C — *Government Official, England*
23 Cleveden Road, Glasgow G12 OPQ, Scotland

Dewar, Jane E — *Editor*
%Legion Magazine, 359 Kent St, #504, Ottawa ON K2P 0R6, Canada

Dewar, Michael J S — *Chemist*
2431 NW 41st St, #5111, Gainesville, FL 32606, USA

Dewey, Duane E — *Korean War Marine Corps Hero (CMH)*
Rt 1, Box 494, Irons, MI 49644, USA

DeWilde, Edy — *Museum Director*
%Stedelijk Museum, Amsterdam, Netherlands

Dews, Peter B — *Psychiatrist*
181 Upland Road, Newtonville, MA 02160, USA

Dexmier, Jean-Yves — *Businessman*
%Octel Communications, 1001 Murphy Ranch Road, Milpitas, CA 95035, USA

Dexter, Peter W — *Writer*
%Sacramento Bee, Editorial Dept, 21st & "Q" Sts, Sacramento, CA 95852, USA

Dey, Susan — *Actress*
%Litke/Gale Madden, 366 N Gardner St, Los Angeles, CA 90036, USA

Dezhurov, Vladimir N — *Cosmonaut*
%Potchta Kosmonavtov, Moskovskoi Oblasti, 141160 Syvisdny Goroduk, Russia

Dezza, Paolo Cardinal — *Religious Leader*
Borgo Santo Spirito 4, 00195 Rome, Italy

Dhabhara, Firdaus S — *Neuroscientist*
%Rockefeller University, Neurology Dept, 1230 York Ave, New York, NY 10021, USA

Dhanapala, Jayantha — *Government Official, Sri Lanka*
%United Nations, Sri Lanka Delegation, United Nations Plaza, New York, NY 10007, USA

Dharmasakti, Sanya — *Prime Minister, Thailand*
15 Saukhumvit Road, Soi 41, Bangkok, Thailand

Di Beligiojoso, Lodovico B — *Architect*
%Studio Architetti BBPR, 2 Via Dei Chiostri, 20121 Milan, Italy

Di Meola, Al — *Jazz Guitarist*
%Don't Worry, 111 W 57th St, #1120, New York, NY 10019, USA

Di Sant'Angelo, Giorgio — *Fashion Designer*
20 W 57th St, New York, NY 10019, USA

Di Stefano, Giuseppe — *Opera Singer*
Via Palatino 10, 20148 Milan, Italy

D

DeVarona - Di Stefano

Di Suvero, Mark	*Sculptor*
PO Box 2218, Long Island, NY 11102, USA	
Diamandis, Peter G	*Publisher*
%Diamandis Communications, 1515 Broadway, New York, NY 10036, USA	
Diamandopoulos, Peter	*Educator*
%Adelphi University, President's Office, Garden City, NY 11530, USA	
Diamini, Obed	*Prime Minister, Swaziland*
%Prime Minister's Office, PO Box 395, Mbabane, Swaziland	
Diamond (Mike D), Michael	*Rapper (The Beastie Boys)*
%Gold Mountain, 3575 Cahuenga Blvd W, #450, Los Angeles, CA 90068, USA	
Diamond of Gloucester, John	*Government Official, England*
Aynhoe, Doggetts Wood Lane, Chalfont Saint Giles, Bucks, England	
Diamond, Abel J	*Architect*
2 Berkeley St, #600, Toronto ON M5A 2W3, Canada	
Diamond, David L	*Composer*
249 Edgerton St, Rochester, NY 14607, USA	
Diamond, Jared M	*Biologist*
%University of California Medical School, Physiology Dept, Los Angeles, CA 90024, USA	
Diamond, Marian C	*Neuroanatomist*
2583 Virginia St, Berkeley, CA 94709, USA	
Diamond, Neil	*Singer, Songwriter*
10345 W Olympic Blvd, #200, Los Angeles, CA 90064, USA	
Diamond, Seymour	*Physician*
%Diamond Headache Clinic, 467 W Deming Place, #500, Chicago, IL 60614, USA	
Diamont, Don	*Actor*
15045 Sheriew Place, Sherman Oaks, CA 91403, USA	
Diaz, Cameron	*Model, Actress*
345 N Maple Dr, #397, Beverly Hills, CA 90210, USA	
Diaz-Balart, Jose	*Commentator*
%"This Morning" Show, CBS-TV, News Dept, 51 W 52nd St, New York, NY 10019, USA	
DiBiaggio, John A	*Educator*
%Tufts University, President's Office, Medford, MA 02155, USA	
DiCamillo, Guy T	*Businessman*
%Polaroid Corp, 549 Technology Square, Cambridge, MA 02139, USA	
DiCaprio, Leonardo	*Actor*
%Baker/Winokur/Ryder, 405 S Beverly Dr, #500, Beverly Hills, CA 90212, USA	
DiCarlo, Dominick L	*Judge*
%US Court of International Trade, 1 Federal Plaza, New York, NY 10278, USA	
DiCenzo, George	*Actor*
RD 1, Box 728, Stone Hollow Farm, Pipersville, PA 18947, USA	
Dichter, Misha	*Concert Pianist*
%Shuman Assoc, 120 W 58th St, New York, NY 10019, USA	
Dick, Douglas	*Actor*
604 Gretna Green Way, Los Angeles, CA 90049, USA	
Dicke, Robert H	*Physicist*
321 Prospect Ave, Princeton, NJ 08540, USA	
Dickens, Jimmy	*Singer*
5010 W Concord, Brentwood, TN 37027, USA	
Dickenson, Gary	*Bowler*
501 Wade Martin Dr, Edmond, OK 73034, USA	
Dickerson, Eric	*Football Player*
26815 Mulholland Highway, Calabasas, CA 91302, USA	
Dickinson, Angie	*Actress*
1715 Carla Ridge, Beverly Hills, CA 90210, USA	
Dickinson, Bruce	*Singer (Iron Maiden)*
PO Box 391, London W4 1L2, England	
Dickinson, Gary	*Bowler*
%Professional Bowlers Assn, 1720 Merriman Road, Akron, OH 44313, USA	
Dickinson, Judy	*Golfer*
2907 Hill St, New Smyrna Beach, FL 32169, USA	
Dickinson, Peter	*Writer*
%Mysterious Press, Warner Books, 1271 6th Ave, New York, NY 10020, USA	
Dickson, Alan T	*Businessman*
%Ruddick Corp, 2 First Union Center, Charlotte, NC 28282, USA	
Dickson, Chris	*Yachtsman*
%Int'l Management Group, 1 Erieview Plaza, #1300, Cleveland, OH 44114, USA	
Dickson, Clarence	*Law Enforcement Official*
%Police Department, Metro Justice, 1351 NW 12th St, Miami, FL 33125, USA	

Dickson, Jennifer — Artist, Photographer
20 Osborne St, Ottawa ON K1S 4Z9, Canada
Dickson, Neil — Actor
%International Creative Mgmt, 76 Oxford St, London W1N 0AX, England
Diddley, Bo — Singer, Guitarist
PO Box 410, Archer, FL 32618, USA
Didion, Joan — Writer
%Janklow & Nesbitt, 598 Madison Ave, New York, NY 10022, USA
Diebold, John — Businessman
%Diebold Group, PO Box 515, Bedford Hills, NY 10507, USA
Diehl, Digby R — Journalist
788 S Lake Ave, Pasadena, CA 91106, USA
Diehl, John — Actor
13601 Ventura Blvd, #275, Sherman Oaks, CA 91423, USA
Diemeke, Enrique A — Conductor
%Flint Symphony Orchestra, 1026 E Kearsley St, Flint, MI 48503, USA
Diener, Theodor O — Plant Virologist
4530 Powder Mill Road, Beltsville, MD 20705, USA
Dierdof, Daniel L (Dan) — Football Player, Sportscaster
13302 Buckland Hall Road, Town and Country, MO 63131, USA
Dierker, Lawrence E (Larry) — Baseball Player, Manager
8318 N Tahoe Dr, Houston, TX 77040, USA
Dietrich, Dena — Actress
%Peter Strain, 8428 Melrose Place, Los Angeles, CA 90069, USA
Dietrich, William A (Bill) — Journalist
%Seattle Times, Editorial Dept, Fairview Ave N & John St, Seattle, WA 98111, USA
Diffie, Joe — Singer, Songwriter
%Image Management Group, 1009 16th Ave S, Nashville, TN 37212, USA
DiFranco, Ani — Singer, Songwriter, Musician
%Righteous Babe Mgmt, PO Box 95, Ellicott Station, Buffalo, NY 14205, USA
DiGregorio, Ernie — Basketball Player
60 Chestnut Ave, Narragansett, RI 02882, USA
Dilfer, Trent — Football Player
4875 N Backer Ave, #105, Fresno, CA 93726, USA
Dill, Guy — Artist
819 Milwood Ave, Venice, CA 90291, USA
Dill, Laddie John — Artist
1625 Electric Ave, Venice, CA 90291, USA
Dillard, Annie — Writer
%Russell Volkering, 50 W 29th St, New York, NY 10001, USA
Dillard, Harrison — Track Athlete
3449 Glencairn Road, Cleveland, OH 44122, USA
Dillard, Victoria — Actress
%Alliance Talent, 9171 Wilshire Blvd, #441, Beverly Hills, CA 90210, USA
Dillehay, Thomas (Tom) — Anthropologist
%University of Kentucky, Anthropology Dept, Lexington, KY 40506, USA
Diller, Barry — Entertainment Executive
1940 Coldwater Canyon Dr, Beverly Hills, CA 90210, USA
Diller, Phyllis — Comedienne, Actress
163 S Rockingham Road, Los Angeles, CA 90049, USA
Dillman, Bradford — Actor
770 Hot Springs Road, Santa Barbara, CA 93108, USA
Dillon, C Douglas — Secretary, Treasury
1330 Ave of Americas, #2700, New York, NY 10019, USA
Dillon, Matt — Actor
%Vic Ramos, 49 W 9th St, #5-B, New York, NY 10011, USA
Dillon, Melinda — Actress
29233 Heathercliff Road, #3, Malibu, CA 90265, USA
DiMaggio, Dominic P (Dom) — Baseball Player
162 Point Road, Marion, MA 02738, USA
DiMaggio, Joseph P (Joe) — Baseball Player
%Morris Engelberg, 3230 Stirling Road, Hollywood, FL 33021, USA
Dimas, Trent — Gymnast
%Gold Cup Gymnastics School, 6009 Carmel Ave NE, Albuquerque, NM 87113, USA
Dimbleby, David — Journalist, Commentator
14 King St, Richmond, Surrey TW9 1NF, England
Dimitrova, Ghena — Opera Singer
%KKN Enterprises, 277 West End Ave, #11-A, New York, NY 10023, USA

D

D

Dimon, James — *Businessman*
%Travelers Inc, 388 Greenwich St, New York, NY 10013, USA
DiNardo, Gerry — *Football Coach*
%Louisiana State University, Athletic Dept, Baton Rouge, LA 70803, USA
Dine, James — *Artist*
%Pace Gallery, 32 E 57th St, New York, NY 10022, USA
Dineen, Gary — *Hockey Player*
177 Sawmill Road, West Springfield, MA 01089, USA
Dineen, Kevin — *Hockey Player*
30 Rivermead, Avon, CT 06001, USA
Dineen, William P (Bill) — *Hockey Coach, Executive*
%Philadelphia Flyers, CoreStates Center, Pattison Place, Philadelphia, PA 19148, USA
Dinitz, Simcha — *Government Official, Israel*
40 Nayot, Jerusalem, Israel
Dion (DiMucci) — *Singer*
3099 NW 63rd St, Boca Raton, FL 33496, USA
Dion, Celine — *Singer*
%Feeling Productions, 1131 Leslie St, #555, Toronto ON M3C 3L8, Canada
Dionne, Joseph L — *Publisher*
%McGraw-Hill Inc, 1221 Ave of Americas, New York, NY 10020, USA
Dionne, Marcel — *Hockey Player*
PO Box 17013, Inglewood, CA 90308, USA
Diop, Majhemout — *President, Senegal*
210 HCM, Guediawaye, Dakar, Senegal
Diouf, Abdou — *President, Senegal*
%President's Office, Ave Roume, Boite Postale 168, Dakar, Senegal
DiPrete, Edward D — *Governor, RI*
555 Wilbur Ave, Cranston, RI 02921, USA
Dirda, Michael — *Journalist*
%Washington Post, 1150 15th Ave NW, Washington, DC 20071, USA
Disch, Thomas M — *Writer*
%Karpfinger Agency, 357 W 20th St, New York, NY 10011, USA
Dischinger, Terry — *Basketball Player*
1259 Lake Garden Court, Lake Oswego, OR 97034, USA
Disl, Uschi — *Biathlete*
Grosseglsee 16, 83623 Dietramszell, Germany
Disney, Anthea — *Editor*
%Harper Collins Publishers, 10 E 53rd St, New York, NY 10022, USA
Disney, Roy E — *Entertainment Executive*
%Shamrock Broadcasting, 4444 Lakeside Dr, Burbank, CA 91505, USA
Distel, Sacha — *Singer, Songwriter*
%Charley Marouani, 37 Rue Marbeuf, 75008 Paris, France
Ditka, Michael K (Mike) — *Football Player, Coach*
29 English Turn Dr, New Orleans, LA 70131, USA
Dittmer, Andreas — *Canoe Athlete*
Fischerbank 5, 17033 Neubrandenburg, Germany
Ditz, Nancy — *Track Athlete*
524 Moore Road, Woodside, CA 94062, USA
DiUlio, Albert J — *Educator*
%Marquette University, President's Office, Milwaukee, WI 53233, USA
Divac, Vlade — *Basketball Player*
%Charlotte Hornets, 1 Hive Dr, Charlotte, NC 28217, USA
Divine, Gary W — *Labor Leader*
%National Federation of Federal Employees, 1016 16th St, Washington, DC 20038, USA
Diwakar, R R — *Writer*
%Sri Arvind Krupa, 233 Sadashiv Nagar, Bangalore 560006, Karnataka, India
Dix, Drew D — *Vietnam War Army Hero (CMH)*
%Tundra Air, General Delivery, Manley Hot Springs, AR 99756, USA
Dixon, Alan J — *Senator, IL*
7606 Foley Dr, Belleville, IL 62223, USA
Dixon, Becky — *Sportscaster*
%ABC-TV, Sports Dept, 77 W 66th St, New York, NY 10023, USA
Dixon, Craig — *Track Athlete*
10630 Wellworth Ave, Los Angeles, CA 90024, USA
Dixon, D Jeremy — *Architect*
47 North Hill, Highgate, London N6, England
Dixon, Donna — *Actress*
7708 Woodrow Wilson Ave, Los Angeles, CA 90046, USA

Dixon, Floyd — *Singer, Pianist*
%Bon Ton West, PO Box 8406, Santa Cruz, CA 95061, USA

Dixon, Frank J — *Pathologist, Immunologist*
2355 Avenida de la Playa, La Jolla, CA 92037, USA

Dixon, Ivan — *Actor, Director*
8431 Compatible Way, #103, Charlotte, NC 28262, USA

Dixon, Robert J — *Air Force General*
29342 Ridgeview Terrace, Boerne, TX 78015, USA

Dixon, Rod — *Track Athlete*
22 Entrican Ave, Remuera, Auckland 5, New Zealand

Dixon, Thomas F — *Aerospace Engineer*
12 Beech Dr, Brunswick, ME 04011, USA

DJ Headliner (Timothy Barnwell) — *Soul/Rap Artist (Arrested Development)*
%William Morris Agency, 1325 Ave of Americas, New York, NY 10019, USA

Djerassi, Carl — *Inventor (Oral Contraceptive)*
%Stanford University, Chemistry Dept, Stanford, CA 94305, USA

Djerassi, Isaac — *Physician*
2034 Delancey Place, Philadelphia, PA 19103, USA

Djuranovic, Veselin — *President, Yugoslavia*
%Federal Executive Council, Bul Lenjina 2, 11075 Novi Belgrad, Yugoslavia

Dmytryk, Edward — *Movie Director*
3945 Westfall Dr, Encino, CA 91436, USA

Do Muoi — *Party Chairman, Vietnam*
%Chairman's Office, Council of Ministers, Hanoi, Vietnam

Do Nascimento, Alexandre Cardinal — *Religious Leader*
Arcebispado, CP 87, Luanda, Angola

Doan, Charles A — *Physician*
4935 Oletangy Blvd, Columbus, OH 43214, USA

Doar, John — *Attorney*
9 E 63rd St, New York, NY 10021, USA

Dobbin, Edmund J — *Educator*
%Villanova University, President's Office, Villanova, PA 19085, USA

Dobbs, Glenn — *Football Player*
7436 S Winston Place, Tulsa, OK 74136, USA

Dobbs, Lou — *Commentator*
%Cable News Network, News Dept, 820 1st St NE, Washington, DC 20002, USA

Dobbs, Mattiwilda — *Opera Singer*
1101 S Arlington Ridge Road, Arlington, VA 22202, USA

Dobek, Michelle — *Golfer*
292 Chicopee St, Chicopee, MA 01013, USA

Dobkin, Larry — *Movie Director, Actor*
1787 Old Ranch Road, Los Angeles, CA 90049, USA

Dobkins, Carl, Jr — *Singer*
%Ken Keane, PO Box 1875, Gretna, LA 70054, USA

Dobler, Conrad F — *Football Player*
8016 State Line Road, #201, Shawnee Mission, KS 66208, USA

Dobler, David — *Religious Leader*
%Presbyterian Church USA, 100 Witherspoon St, Louisville, KY 40202, USA

Dobson, James C — *Religious Leader*
%Focus on the Family, 8605 Explorer Dr, Colorado Springs, CO 80920, USA

Dobson, Kevin — *Actor*
PO Box 2388, Toluca Lake, CA 91610, USA

Dobson, Peter — *Actor*
1351 N Crescent Heights Blvd, #318, Los Angeles, CA 90046, USA

Doby, Lawrence E (Larry) — *Baseball Player*
45 Nishuane Road, Montclair, NJ 07042, USA

Dockser, William B — *Financier*
%CRIIMI MAE Inc, 1200 Rockville Pike, Rockville, MD 20852, USA

Dockstader, Frederick J — *Museum Director*
165 W 66th St, New York, NY 10023, USA

Doctorow, E L — *Writer*
170 Broadview Ave, New Rochelle, NY 10804, USA

Doda, Carol — *Exotic Dancer*
PO Box 387, Fremont, CA 94537, USA

Dodd, Carl H — *Korean War Army Hero (CMH)*
12 Mill Creek Road, Corbin, KY 40701, USA

Dodd, Deryl — *Singer, Songwriter*
%William Morris Agency, 2100 West End Ave, #1000, Nashville, TN 37203, USA

D

Dixon - Dodd

Dodd, Michael T (Mike) *Volleyball Player*
522 Virginia St, El Segundo, CA 90245, USA

Dodge, Brooks *Skier*
Box "C", Jackson, NH 03846, USA

Dods, Walter A, Jr *Financier*
%First Hawaiian Bank, 999 Bishop St, Honolulu, HI 96813, USA

Doenges, Bessie R *Writer*
%Russell & Volkening, 50 W 29th St, New York, NY 10001, USA

Doering, William V E *Chemist*
53 Francis Ave, Cambridge, MA 02138, USA

Doerr, Harriet *Writer*
%Liz Darhansoff, 1220 Park Ave, New York, NY 10128, USA

Doerr, Robert P (Bobby) *Baseball Player*
94449 Territorial Road, Junction City, OR 97448, USA

Doherty, Peter C *Nobel Medicine Laureate*
%St Jude Children's Research Hospital, Immunology Dept, Memphis, TN 38105, USA

Doherty, Shannen *Actress*
%The Agency, 1800 Ave of Stars, #400, Los Angeles, CA 90067, USA

Dohrmann, Fred G *Businessman*
%Winnebago Industries, PO Box 152, Forest City, IA 50436, USA

Doi, Takako *Government Official, Japan*
%Daini Giinkaikan, 2-1-2 Nagatacho, Chiyodaku, Tokyo, Japan

Doi, Takao *Astronaut, Japan*
%NASDA, 2-1-1 Sengen, Tukubashi, Ibaraki 303, Japan

Dokes, Michael *Boxer*
5151 Collins Ave, #522, Miami Beach, FL 33140, USA

Dolan, B(everly) F(ranklin) *Businessman*
%Textron Inc, 40 Westminster St, #10, Providence, RI 02903, USA

Dolan, Charles F *Television Executive*
%Cablevision Systems Corp, 1 Media Crossways, Woodbury, NY 11797, USA

Dolan, Ellen *Actress*
%Don Buchwald, 10 E 44th St, New York, NY 10017, USA

Dolan, Michael P *Government Official*
%Internal Revenue Service, 1111 Constitution Ave NW, Washington, DC 20224, USA

Dolan, Ronald V *Businessman*
%First Colony Corp, 700 Main St, Lynchburg, VA 24504, USA

Dolby, David C *Vietnam War Army Hero (CMH)*
Pekiomen Ave, PO Box 218, Oaks, PA 19456, USA

Dolby, Ray M *Inventor, Sound Engineer*
%Dolby Laboratories, 100 Potrero Ave, San Francisco, CA 94103, USA

Dolby, Thomas *Singer, Songwriter*
20 Manchester Square, London W1, England

Dolci, Danilo *Writer, Social Worker*
%Centro Iniziative Studi, Largo Scalia 5, Partinico/Palermo, Sicily, Italy

Dold, R Bruce *Journalist*
501 N Park Road, #HSE, La Grange Park, IL 60526, USA

Dole, Elizabeth H *Secretary, Transportation; Labor*
%Watergate South, 2510 Virginia Ave NW, #112, Washington, DC 20037, USA

Dole, Robert J *Senator, KS*
%Watergate South, 2510 Virginia Ave NW, #112, Washington, DC 20037, USA

Dole, Vincent P *Medical Researcher*
%Rockefeller University, 1230 York Ave, New York, NY 10021, USA

Doleman, Christopher J (Chris) *Football Player*
1025 Leadenhall St, Alpharetta, GA 30022, USA

Dolenz, Ami *Actress*
6058 St Clair Ave, North Hollywood, CA 91606, USA

Dolenz, Micky *Actor, Singer, Drummer (The Monkees)*
8369 Sausalito Ave, #A, West Hills, CA 91304, USA

Dolgen, Jonathan L *Entertainment Executive*
%Viacom Inc, 1515 Broadway, New York, NY 10036, USA

Doll, W Richard S *Epidemiologist*
12 Rawlison Road, Oxford OX2 6UE, England

Dollar, Linda *Volleyball Coach*
%Southwest Missouri State University, Athletic Dept, Springfield, MO 65804, USA

Dollfus, Audouin *Astronomer, Physicist*
%Observatoire de Paris, 5 Place Jules Janssen, 92195 Meudon, France

Dolmetsch, Carl F *Concert Recorder Player*
Jesses, Haslemere, Surrey, England

Dombasle, Arielle　　　　　　　　　　　　　　　*Actress*
%Agents Associes Beaume, 201 Rue Faubourg St Honore, 75008 Paris, France
Dombrowski, Jim　　　　　　　　　　　　　　*Football Player*
220 Evangeline Dr, Mandeville, LA 70471, USA
Domingo, Placido　　　　　　　　　　　　　　*Opera Singer*
150 Central Park South, New York, NY 10019, USA
Dominick, Peter H　　　　　　　　　　　　　　*Senator, CO*
5050 E Quincy St, Englewood, CO 80110, USA
Domino, Antoine (Fats)　　　　　　　　　　　*Singer, Pianist*
%New Orleans Entertainment, 3530 Rue Delphine, New Orleans, LA 70131, USA
Domnanovich, Joseph (Joe)　　　　　　　　　*Football Player*
3101 Lorna Road, #1112, Birmingham, AL 35216, USA
Donahue, Donald J　　　　　　　　　　　　　　*Businessman*
%Magma Copper Co, 6400 N Oracle Road, Tucson, AZ 85704, USA
Donahue, Elinor　　　　　　　　　　　　　　　*Actress*
4525 Lemp Ave, North Hollywood, CA 91602, USA
Donahue, Kenneth　　　　　　　　　　　　　*Museum Director*
245 S Westgate Ave, Los Angeles, CA 90049, USA
Donahue, Phil　　　　　　　　　　　　　　　*Entertainer*
244 Madison Ave, #707, New York, NY 10016, USA
Donahue, Terry　　　　　　　　*Football Coach, Sportscaster*
%CBS-TV, Sports Dept, 51 W 52nd St, New York, NY 10019, USA
Donahue, Thomas M　　　　　　　　　　　*Atmospheric Scientist*
1781 Arlington Blvd, Ann Arbor, MI 48104, USA
Donahue, Thomas R　　　　　　　　　　　　　*Labor Leader*
%American Federation of Labor, 815 16th St NW, Washington, DC 20006, USA
Donahue, Troy　　　　　　　　　　　　　　　　*Actor*
1022 Euclid Ave, #1, Santa Monica, CA 90403, USA
Donahue, William J　　　　　　　　　　　*Air Force General*
Cmmd, Communications/Information, HqUSAF, Pentagon, Washington, DC 20330, USA
Donald, David Herbert　　　　　　　　　　　　　*Writer*
PO Box 158, 41 Lincoln Road, Lincoln Center, MA 01773, USA
Donaldson of Kingsbridge, John G S　　*Government Official, England*
17 Edna St, London SW11 3DP, England
Donaldson of Lymington, John F　　　　　　　　　*Judge*
%Royal Courts of Justice, Strand, London WC2, England
Donaldson, James　　　　　　　　　　　　*Basketball Player*
2843 34th Ave W, Seattle, WA 98199, USA
Donaldson, Lou　　　　　　　*Jazz Saxophonist, Singer*
%Maxine Harvard, 2227 Highway One, #251, North Brunswick, NJ 08902, USA
Donaldson, Ray　　　　　　　　　　　　　　*Football Player*
31 Honeysuckle Road, Rome, GA 30165, USA
Donaldson, Roger　　　　　　　　　　　　　*Movie Director*
%Creative Artists Agency, 9830 Wilshire Blvd, Beverly Hills, CA 90212, USA
Donaldson, Samuel A (Sam)　　　　　　　　　*Commentator*
4452 Volta Place NW, Washington, DC 20007, USA
Donaldson, Simon K　　　　　　　　　　　　*Mathematician*
%Mathematical Institute, 24-25 Saint Giles, Oxford OX1 3LB, England
Donat, Peter　　　　　　　　　　　　　　　　*Actor*
PO Box 441, Wolfville NS B0P 1X0, Canada
Donath, Helen　　　　　　　　　　　　　　*Opera Singer*
Bergstr 5, 30900 Wedemark, Germany
Donatoni, Franco　　　　　　　　　　　　　　*Composer*
Via Bassini 39, 20133 Milan, Italy
Donegan, Dorothy　　　　　　　　　　　　　*Jazz Pianist*
%Abby Hoffer, 223 1/2 E 48th St, New York, NY 10017, USA
Donen, Stanley　　　　　　　　　　　　　　*Movie Director*
150 W 56th St, #5004, New York, NY 10019, USA
Donlan, Yolande　　　　　　　　　　　　　　　*Actress*
11 Mellina Place, London NW8, England
Donleavy, J(ames) P(atrick)　　　　　　　　　　　*Writer*
Levington Park, Mullingar, County Westmeath, Ireland
Donlon, Roger H C　　　　　*Vietnam War Army Hero (CMH)*
2101 Wilson Ave, Leavenworth, KS 66048, USA
Donner, Clive　　　　　　　　　　　　　　*Movie Director*
1466 N Kings Road, Los Angeles, CA 90069, USA
Donner, Jorn J　　　　　　　　　　　　　　*Movie Director*
Pohjoisranta 12, 00170 Helsinki 17, Finland

D

Dombasle - Donner

Donner, Richard D — *Movie Director*
%Creative Artists Agency, 9830 Wilshire Blvd, Beverly Hills, CA 90212, USA

Donohoe, Amanda — *Actress*
%Markham & Froggatt, Julian House, 4 Windmill St, London W1P 1HF, England

Donohoe, Peter — *Concert Pianist*
82 Hampton Lane, Solihull, West Midlands B91 2RS, England

Donoso, Jose — *Writer*
Calceite, Province of Teruel, Spain

Donovan (Leitch) — *Singer, Songwriter*
8528 Walnut Dr, Los Angeles, CA 90046, USA

Donovan, Alan B — *Educator*
%State University of New York College, President's Office, Oneonta, NY 13820, USA

Donovan, Anne — *Basketball Player, Coach*
%East Carolina University, Athletic Dept, Greenville, NC 27858, USA

Donovan, Arthur J (Art), Jr — *Football Player*
%Valley Country Club, 1512 Jeffers Road, Baltimore, MD 21204, USA

Donovan, Brian — *Journalist*
%Newsday, Editorial Dept, 235 Pinelawn Road, Melville, NY 11747, USA

Donovan, Elisa — *Actress*
%Silver Massetti Szatmary, 8730 Sunset Blvd, #480, Los Angeles, CA 90069, USA

Donovan, Francis R (Frank) — *Navy Admiral*
9216 Dellwood Dr, Vienna, VA 22180, USA

Donovan, Jason — *Singer, Actor*
38 Arthur St, South Yarra, Melbourne, VIC 3141, Australia

Donovan, Richard E (Dick) — *Baseball Player*
61 Deep Run Road, Cohasset, MA 02025, USA

Donovan, Tate — *Actor*
368 N Gardner St, Los Angeles, CA 90036, USA

Donvan, John — *Commentator*
%ABC-TV, News Dept, 77 W 66th St, New York, NY 10023, USA

Doob, Joseph L — *Mathematician*
101 W Windsor Road, #1104, Urbana, IL 61801, USA

Doob, Leonard W — *Psychologist*
6 Clark Road, Woodbridge, CT 06525, USA

Doody, Alison — *Actress*
%Julian Belfarge, 46 Albermarle St, London W1X 4PP, England

Doohan, James — *Actor*
%DoFame, PO Box 2800, Redmond, WA 98073, USA

Dooley, Paul — *Actor*
%Agency For Performing Arts, 9200 Sunset Blvd, #900, Los Angeles, CA 90069, USA

Dooley, Thomas — *Soccer Player*
6129 Heritage Lakes Dr, Hilliard, OH 43026, USA

Dooley, Vincent J (Vince) — *Football Coach, Administrator*
%University of Georgia, Athletic Dept, Athens, GA 30602, USA

Doran, Ann — *Actress*
1215 Bently Ave, Los Angeles, CA 90049, USA

Dore, Andre — *Hockey Player*
91 Ledge Lane, Stamford, CT 06905, USA

Dorff, Stephen — *Actor*
12985 Gale St, North Hollywood, CA 91604, USA

Dorfman, Ariel — *Writer*
%Duke University, International Studies Center, 2122 Campus Dr, Durham, NC 27706, USA

Dorfman, Dan — *Columnist, Commentator*
%"Dorfman Report" Show, CNBC, 51 W 52nd St, New York, NY 10019, USA

Dorfman, Henry S — *Businessman*
%Thorn Apple Valley Inc, 26999 Central Park Blvd, Southfield, MI 48076, USA

Dorfman, Joel M — *Businessman*
%Thorn Apple Valley, 26999 Central Park Blvd, Southfield, MI 48076, USA

Dorfmeister, Michaela — *Skier*
Quellenstr 12, 2763 Neusiedl, Austria

Dorio, Gabriella — *Track Athlete*
%Federation of Light Athletics, Viale Tiaiano 70, 00196 Rome, Italy

Dority, Douglas H — *Labor Leader*
%United Food & Commercial Workers Union, 1775 "K" St NW, Washington, DC 20006, USA

Dorman, Gerald D — *Physician*
2365 Village Lane, Orient, NY 11957, USA

Dorn, Michael — *Actor*
3751 Multiview Dr, Los Angeles, CA 90068, USA

Dorney, Keith R — Football Player
2450 Blucher Valley Road, Sebastopol, CA 95472, USA

Dorsett, Anthony D (Tony) — Football Player
6005 Kettering Court, Dallas, TX 75248, USA

Dorso, Betty McLauchlen — Model
444 N Camden Dr, Beverly Hills, CA 90210, USA

Dortort, David — Movie Producer
133 Udine Way, Los Angeles, CA 90077, USA

Dos Santos, Alexandre J M Cardinal — Religious Leader
Paco Arquiepiscopal, Avenida Eduardo Mondlane 1448, CP Maputo, Mozambique

Dos Santos, Jose Eduardo — President, Angola
%President's Office, Palacio do Povo, Luanda, Angola

Doshi, Balkkrishna V — Architect
Sangath, Thaltej Road, Almedabad 380 054, India

Doss, Desmond T — WW II Army Medical Corps Hero (CMH)
Rt 2, Box 307, Rising Fawn, GA 30738, USA

Dotrice, Roy — Actor
Talbot House, 98 St Martin's Lane, London WC2, England

Dotson, Richard E (Rich) — Baseball Player
%Hicks, 3410 Heatheridge Lane, Reno, NV 89509, USA

Dotson, Santana — Football Player
2800 Coachman Court, Green Bay, WI 54301, USA

Doty, Paul M — Biochemist
%Harvard University, John F Kennedy Government School, Cambridge, MA 02138, USA

Douaihy, Saliba — Artist
Vining Road, Windham, NY 12496, USA

Doubleday, Nelson — Publisher, Baseball Executive
%New York Mets, Shea Stadium, Flushing, NY 11368, USA

Doucet, Michael — Singer, Fiddler (BeauSoleil)
%Rosebud Agency, PO Box 170429, San Francisco, CA 94117, USA

Dougherty, Ed — Golfer
448 SW Fairway Vis, Port Saint Lucie, FL 34986, USA

Dougherty, William A, Jr — Navy Admiral
1505 Colonial Court, Arlington, VA 22209, USA

Douglas, Barry — Concert Pianist
%Terry Harrison Mgmt, 3 Clarendon Court, Charlbury Oxon OX7 3PS, England

Douglas, Cathleen — Lawyer, Conservationist
815 Connecticut Ave NW, Washington, DC 20006, USA

Douglas, Donna — Actress
PO Box 49455, Los Angeles, CA 90049, USA

Douglas, Herbert R — Businessman
%Jamesway Corp, 40 Hartz Way, Seacaucus, NJ 07094, USA

Douglas, James (Buster) — Boxer
465 Waterbury Court, #A, Gahanna, OH 43230, USA

Douglas, Kirk — Actor
805 N Rexford Dr, Beverly Hills, CA 90210, USA

Douglas, Leon — Basketball Player
PO Box 58, Leighton, AL 35646, USA

Douglas, Michael — Actor, Director, Producer
PO Box 49054, Los Angeles, CA 90049, USA

Douglas, Mike — Entertainer
1876 Chartley Road, Gates Mills, OH 44040, USA

Douglas, Mike — Singer (The Diamonds)
%Moments Mgmt, 520 Washington Blvd, #393, Marina del Rey, CA 90292, USA

Douglass, Bobby — Football Player
%Lettuce Entertain You Enterprises, 5419 N Sheridan Road, Chicago, IL 60640, USA

Douglass, Dale — Golfer
811 Simpson St, Fort Morgan, CO 80701, USA

Douglass, Robyn — Actress
10 Canterbury Court, Wilmette, IL 60091, USA

Dourda, Abu Zaid Umar — Prime Minister, Libya
%Prime Minister's Office, Bab el Aziziya Barracks, Tripoli, Libya

Dourif, Brad — Actor
PO Box 3762, Beverly Hills, CA 90212, USA

Dove, Billie — Actress
PO Box 5005, Rancho Mirage, CA 92270, USA

Dove, Rita F — Writer
1757 Lambs Road, Charlottesville, VA 22901, USA

D

Dove, Ronnie — *Singer*
%Jerry Patlow, 29276 Geraldine Court, Framington Hills, MI 48336, USA

Dow, Peggy — *Actress*
2121 S Yorktown Ave, Tulsa, OK 74114, USA

Dow, Tony — *Actor*
PO Box 1671, Topanga, CA 90290, USA

Dowdle, James C — *Businessman*
%Tribune Co, 435 N Michigan Ave, Chicago, IL 60611, USA

Dowdle, Walter R — *Microbiologist*
1708 Mason Mill Road, Atlanta, GA 30329, USA

Dowell, Anthony J — *Ballet Dancer*
%Royal Ballet, Bow St, London WC2E 9DD, England

Dowiyogo, Bernard — *President, Nauru*
%Parliament House, Government Offices, Yaren, Nauru

Dowler, Boyd H — *Football Player*
%Carolina Panthers, Ericsson Stadium, 800 S Mint St, Charlotte, NC 28202, USA

Dowling, Doris — *Actress*
9026 Elevado Ave, Los Angeles, CA 90069, USA

Dowling, John E — *Biologist, Neurobiologist*
%Biological Laboratories, 16 Divinity St, Cambridge, MA 02138, USA

Dowling, Robert J — *Editor, Publisher*
%Hollywood Reporter, 5055 Wilshire Blvd, Los Angeles, CA 90036, USA

Dowling, Vincent — *Theater Director, Playwright*
%Stepaside House, Box 30-A, East River Road, Huntington, MA 01050, USA

Down, Sarah — *Cartoonist (Betsey's Buddies)*
%Playboy Magazine, Reader Services, 680 N Lake Shore Dr, Chicago, IL 60611, USA

Downes, Edward — *Conductor*
%Royal Opera House, Covent Garden, London WC2E 9DD, England

Downes, Edward O D — *Music Historian*
1 W 72nd St, New York, NY 10023, USA

Downes, Terry — *Boxer*
Milestone, Milespit, Milespit Hill, London NW7, England

Downey, Michael — *Businessman*
%Nellcor, 4280 Hacienda Dr, Pleasanton, CA 94588, USA

Downey, Morton, Jr — *Entertainer*
8121 Georgia Ave, Silver Spring, MD 20910, USA

Downey, Robert J — *Movie Director*
55 West 900 S, Salt Lake City, UT 84101, USA

Downey, Robert, Jr — *Actor*
1350 1/2 N Harper Ave, Los Angeles, CA 90046, USA

Downey, Roma — *Actress*
2811 Arizona Ave, #2, Santa Monica, CA 90404, USA

Downie, Leonard, Jr — *Editor*
%Washington Post, Editorial Dept, 1150 15th St NW, Washington, DC 20071, USA

Downing, Alphonso E (Al) — *Baseball Player*
2800 Neilson Way, #412, Santa Monica, CA 90405, USA

Downing, Brian J — *Baseball Player*
8095 County Road 135, Celina, TX 75009, USA

Downing, George — *Surfer*
%Get Wet!, 3021 Waialae Ave, Honolulu, HI 96816, USA

Downing, Walt — *Football Player*
800 Everhard Road SW, #1501, North Canton, OH 44709, USA

Downs, Hugh — *Journalist*
%ABC-TV, News Dept, 157 Columbus Ave, New York, NY 10023, USA

Dowson, Philip M — *Architect*
%Arup Assoc, 37 Fitzroy Square, London W1P 6AA, England

Doyle, Francis C — *Financier*
%First National Bank (NO), 210 Barrone St, New Orleans, LA 70112, USA

Doyle, James H, Jr — *Navy Admiral*
5121 Baltan Road, Bethesda, MD 20816, USA

Dozier, James L — *Army General*
%David C Brown Enterprises, 2665 Oak Ridge Court, Fort Myers, FL 33901, USA

Dozier, Lamont — *Singer, Songwriter*
%McMullen Co, 9744 Wilshire Blvd, #301, Beverly Hills, CA 90212, USA

Dr Demento (Barret E Hansen) — *Radio Entertainer*
6102 Pimenta Ave, Lakewood, CA 90712, USA

Dr Dre (Andre Young) — *Rapper*
%Rush Artists, 1600 Varick St, New York, NY 10013, USA

Dr John *Jazz Pianist, Singer, Songwriter*
%Dream Street Mgmt, 1460 4th St, #205, Santa Monica, CA 90401, USA

Drabble, Margaret *Writer*
%Peters Fraser Dunlop, Chelsea Harbour, Lots Rd, London SW10 0XF, England

Drabek, Douglas D (Doug) *Baseball Player*
15 Ivy Pond Place, The Woodlands, TX 77381, USA

Drabowsky, Myron W (Moe) *Baseball Player*
4741 Oak Run Dr, Sarasota, FL 34243, USA

Draffen, Willis *Singer (Bloodstone)*
3642 Bales Ave, Kansas City, MO 64128, USA

Dragon, Daryl *Musician (The Captain & Tennille)*
7123 Franktown Road, Carson City, NV 89704, USA

Dragoti, Stan *Movie Director*
1800 Ave of Stars, #430, Los Angeles, CA 90067, USA

Drai, Victor *Movie Producer*
10527 Bellagio Road, Beverly Hills, CA 90210, USA

Drake, Betsy *Actress*
1717 Westridge Road, Los Angeles, CA 90049, USA

Drake, Frances *Actress*
1511 Summit Ridge Dr, Beverly Hills, CA 90210, USA

Drake, Frank D *Astronomer*
%Lick Observatory, University of California, Santa Cruz, CA 9064, USA

Drake, Judith *Actress*
%Twentieth Century, 15315 Magnolia Blvd, #429, Sherman Oaks, CA 91403, USA

Drake, Juel D *Labor Leader*
%Iron Workers Union, 1750 New York Ave NW, Washington, DC 20006, USA

Drake, Larry *Actor*
2293 Bronson Hill Dr, Los Angeles, CA 90068, USA

Drasner, Fred *Publisher*
%New York Daily News, 220 E 42nd St, New York, NY 10017, USA

Dravecky, David F (Dave) *Baseball Player*
19995 Chisholm Trail, Monument, CO 80132, USA

Draves, Vickie *Diver*
29591 Sea Horse Cove, Laguna Niguel, CA 92677, USA

Drechsler, Heike *Track Athlete*
Steubenstr 11, 07743 Jena, Germany

Dreesen, Tom *Comedian*
14538 Benefit St, #301, Sherman Oaks, CA 91403, USA

Dreier, R Chad *Businessman*
%Ryland Group, 1100 Broken Land Parkway, Columbia, MD 21044, USA

Drell, Sidney D *Physicist*
570 Alvarado Row, Stanford, CA 94305, USA

Drennen, William M *Judge*
%US Tax Court, 400 2nd St NW, Washington, DC 20217, USA

Drescher, Fran *Actress*
9336 W Washington Blvd, #R, Culver City, CA 90232, USA

Dresser, Paul A, Jr *Businessman*
%Chesapeake Corp, PO Box 2350, Richmond, VA 23218, USA

Dressler, Alan M *Astronomer*
%Carnegie Observatories, 813 Santa Barbara St, Pasadena, CA 91101, USA

Drew, Elizabeth H *Publisher*
%William Morrow, 1350 Ave of Americas, New York, NY 10016, USA

Drewitz, Henry *Financier*
%Astoria Federal Savings, Astoria Federal Plaza, Lake Success, NY 11042, USA

Drexler, Austin J *Museum Director*
%Museum of Modern Art, 11 W 53rd St, New York, NY 10019, USA

Drexler, Clyde *Basketball Player*
%Houston Rockets, Summit, Greenway Plaza, #10, Houston, TX 77046, USA

Drexler, Richard A *Businessman*
%Allied Products Corp, 10 S Riverside Plaza, Chicago, IL 60606, USA

Dreyfus, Lee S *Governor, WI*
PO Box 1776, Waukeska, WI 53187, USA

Dreyfuss, Richard *Actor*
2809 Nicholas Canyon Road, Los Angeles, CA 90046, USA

Drickamer, Harry G *Chemical Engineer*
304 E Pennsylvania St, Urbana, IL 61801, USA

Driedger, Florence G *Social Agency Executive*
3833 Montaigne St, Regina SK S4S 3J6, Canada

Driesell, Charles G (Lefty) *Basketball Coach*
%Georgia State University, Athletic Dept, Atlanta, GA 30303, USA
Driessen, Daniel (Dan) *Baseball Player*
97 Stoney Creek Road, Hilton Head Island, SC 29928, USA
Drinan, Robert F *Educator, Representative, MA*
%Georgetown University, 1507 Isherwood St NE, #1, Washington, DC 20002, USA
Driver, William J *Government Official*
215 W Columbia St, Falls Church, VA 22046, USA
Drnovsek, Janez *Prime Minister, Slovenia*
%Prime Minister's Office, Presemova St 8, 61000 Ljubljana, Slovenia
Drobney, Jaroslav *Tennis Player*
23 Kenilworth Court, Lower Richmond Road, London SW15 1EW, England
Droge, Pete *Singer, Songwriter*
%Curtis Mgmt, 417 Denny Way, #200, Seattle, WA 98109, USA
Dropo, Walter (Walt) *Baseball Player*
65 E India Row, Boston, MA 02110, USA
Drosdick, John G *Businessman*
%Ultramar Corp, 9830 Colonnade Blvd, San Antonio, TX 78230, USA
Drowley, Jesse R *WW II Army Hero (CMH)*
523 E Wabash Ave, Spokane, WA 99207, USA
Drucker, Daniel C *Engineer*
%University of Florida, Aerospace Engineering Building, Gainesville, FL 32611, USA
Drucker, Mort *Cartoonist (Ort)*
%Mad Magazine, 485 Madison Ave, New York, NY 10022, USA
Drucker, Peter F *Educator, Management Consultant, Writer*
636 Wellesley Dr, Claremont, CA 91711, USA
Druk, Mirchea *Prime Minister, Moldova*
Str 31 August 123, #7, 277012 Kishinev, Moldova
Drummond, Roscoe *Columnist*
6637 MacLean Dr, Olde Dominion Square, McLean, VA 22101, USA
Drury, Allen S *Writer*
PO Box 647, Tiburon, CA 94920, USA
Drury, James *Actor*
12755 Mill Ridge, #622, Cypress, TX 77429, USA
Dryden, Ken *Hockey Player*
1414 Rue Lambert-Closse, Montreal PQ H3N 1N2, Canada
Dryer, Fred *Football Player, Actor*
4117 Radford Ave, Studio City, CA 91604, USA
Dryke, Matt *Skeet Marksman*
4702 Davis Ave S, #2-B-102, Renton, WA 98055, USA
Drysdale, Cliff *Tennis Player*
%Landfall, 1801 Eastwood Road, #F, Wilmington, NC 28403, USA
Du Bain, Myron *Businessman*
%Fireman's Fund Insurance, 1 Market Plaza, #1200, San Francisco, CA 94105, USA
Du Bois, Ja'Net *Actress*
8306 Wilshire Blvd, #189, Beverly Hills, CA 90211, USA
Du Plessis, Christian *Opera Singer*
%Performing Arts, 1 Hinde St, London W1M 5RH, England
Du Pont, Pierre S, IV *Governor, DE*
%Richards Layton Finger, 1 Rodney Square, PO Box 551, Wilmington, DE 19899, USA
Dubbels, Britta *Model*
%Ford Model Agency, 344 E 59th St, New York, NY 10022, USA
Dubbie, Curtis *Religious Leader*
%Church of Brethren, 1451 Dundee Ave, Elgin, IL 60120, USA
Dube, Joseph (Joe) *Weightlifter*
8821 Eaton Ave, Jacksonville, FL 32211, USA
Dubia, John A *Army General*
Director, Army Staff, HqUSA, Pentagon, Washington, DC 20310, USA
Dubinbaum, Gail *Opera Singer*
%Metropolitan Opera Assn, Lincoln Center Plaza, New York, NY 10023, USA
Dubinin, Yuri V *Government Official, Russia*
%Ministry of Foreign Affairs, Smolenskaya-Sennaya 32/34, Moscow, Russia
DuBois, Marta *Actress*
%Artists Group, 10100 Santa Monica Blvd, #2490, Los Angeles, CA 90067, USA
DuBose, G Thomas *Labor Leader*
%United Transportation Union, 14600 Detroit Ave, Cleveland, OH 44107, USA
Ducasse, Alain *Chef*
%Louis XV Restaurant, Hotel de Paris, Monte Carlo, Monaco

Duchesnay, Isabelle   *Ice Dancer*
Im Steinach 30, 87561 Oberstdorf, Germany

Duchesnay, Paul   *Figure Skater*
%Bundesleistungszentrum, Rossbichstr 2-6, 87561 Oberstdorf, Germany

Duchesne, Steve   *Hockey Player*
%Ottawa Senators, 1000 Prom Palladium Dr, Kanata ON K2V 1A4, Canada

Duchin, Peter   *Jazz Pianist, Band Leader*
%Peter Duchin Orchestra, 305 Madison Ave, #956, New York, NY 10165, USA

Duchovny, David   *Actor*
%International Creative Mgmt, 8942 Wilshire Blvd, Beverly Hills, CA 90211, USA

DuCille, Michel   *Photographer*
5704 Lakeside Oak Lane, Burke, VA 22015, USA

Duckworth, Kevin   *Basketball Player*
%Los Angeles Clippers, Sports Arena, 3939 Figueroa St, Los Angeles, CA 90037, USA

Duderstadt, James J   *Government Official, Educator*
%National Science Foundation, 1800 "G" St NW, Washington, DC 20550, USA

Dudikoff, Michael   *Actor*
%Dudi Productions, 3037 Danalda Dr, Los Angeles, CA 90064, USA

Dudinskyaya, Natalia M   *Ballerina, Ballet Director*
2 Gogol St, #13, St Petersburg 191065, Russia

Dudley, Alfred E   *Businessman*
%First Brands Corp, 83 Wooster Heights Road, Danbury, CT 06810, USA

Dudley, Charles B, III   *Financier*
%Boatmen's Arkansas, 200 W Capitol Ave, Little Rock, AR 72201, USA

Dudley, Chris   *Basketball Player*
6621 Neptune Place, La Jolla, CA 92037, USA

Dudley, Jaquelin   *Microbiologist*
%University of Texas, Microbiology Dept, Austin, TX 78712, USA

Dudley, Rickey   *Football Player*
%Oakland Raiders, 1220 Harbor Bay Parkway, Alameda, CA 94502, USA

Dudley, William M (Bill)   *Football Player*
303 Barkley Court, Lynchburg, VA 24503, USA

Duenkel Fuldner, Virginia   *Swimmer*
707 Eisenhower, Monett, MO 65708, USA

Duerden, John H   *Businessman*
%Reebok International, 100 Technology Center Dr, Stoughton, MA 02072, USA

Duerson, Dave   *Football Player*
2605 Kelly Lane, Highland Park, IL 60035, USA

Duff, Dick   *Hockey Player*
7 Elwood Ave S, Mississauga ON L5G 3J6, Canada

Duff, John B   *Educator*
%Columbia College, President's Office, Chicago, IL 60605, USA

Duff, John E   *Sculptor*
7 Doyers St, New York, NY 10013, USA

Duff, Thomas M   *Businessman*
%Wellman Inc, 1040 Broad St, Shrewsbury, NJ 07702, USA

Duffy, Brian   *Astronaut*
%NASA, Johnson Space Center, 2101 NASA Road, Houston, TX 77058, USA

Duffy, Brian   *Editorial Cartoonist*
%Des Moines Register, Editorial Dept, PO Box 957, Des Moines, IA 50304, USA

Duffy, J C   *Cartoonist (Fusco Brothers)*
%Universal Press Syndicate, 4520 Main St, Kansas City, KS 64111, USA

Duffy, John   *Composer*
%Meet the Composer, 2112 Broadway, New York, NY 10023, USA

Duffy, Julia   *Actress*
%Lacey, 5699 Kanan Road, #285, Agoura, CA 91301, USA

Duffy, Karen   *Entertainer, Model*
%Ford Model Agency, 344 E 59th St, New York, NY 10022, USA

Duffy, Kenneth J   *Financier*
%Commercial Union, 1 Beacon St, Boston, MA 02108, USA

Duffy, Patrick   *Actor*
%Montana Power Inc, 10000 Washington Blvd, #411, Culver City, CA 90232, USA

Dufresne, John   *Writer*
%W W Norton, 500 5th Ave, New York, NY 10110, USA

Dugan, Alan   *Writer*
PO Box 97, Truro, MA 02666, USA

Dugan, Dennis   *Actor*
15611 Royal Oak Road, Encino, CA 91436, USA

D

Duchesnay - Dugan

Dugan, Michael J *Air Force General, Association Executive*
%National Multiple Sclerosis Society, 733 3rd Ave, New York, NY 10017, USA

Duggan, Ervin S *Broadcast Executive*
%Public Broadcasting Service, 1320 Braddock Place, Alexandria, VA 22314, USA

Dugger, John S *Artist*
501 3rd St, San Francisco, CA 94107, USA

Duguay, Ron *Hockey Player, Actor*
4359 Carina Ave, #533, Hammer ON P0M 1Y0, Canada

Duhe, A J *Football Player*
379 Coconut Circle, Fort Lauderdale, FL 33326, USA

Dukakis, Michael S *Governor, MA*
%Florida Atlantic University, InterGovernment Studies Dept, Boca Raton, FL 33437, USA

Dukakis, Olympia *Actress*
222 Upper Mountain Road, Montclair, NJ 07043, USA

Duke, Bill *Movie Director*
%Yagya Productions, PO Box 609, Pacific Palisades, CA 90272, USA

Duke, Charles M, Jr *Astronaut, Air Force General*
280 Lakeview, New Braunfels, TX 78130, USA

Duke, George *Jazz Keyboardist, Songwriter*
%Joyce Agency, 370 Harrison Ave, Harrison, NY 10528, USA

Duke, Patty *Actress*
5110 E Dodd Road, Hayden, ID 83835, USA

Dukes, David *Actor*
255 S Lorraine Blvd, Los Angeles, CA 90004, USA

Dukes, Walter *Basketball Player*
1980 Chicago Blvd, Detroit, MI 48206, USA

Dula, Brett M *Air Force General*
Vice Cdr, Air Combat Command, 205 Dodd, Langley Air Force Base, VA 23665, USA

Dulbecco, Renato *Nobel Medicine Laureate*
7525 Hillside Dr, La Jolla, CA 92037, USA

Dullea, Keir *Actor*
320 Fleming Lane, Fairfield, CT 06430, USA

Dulles, Avery R *Theologian*
%Fordham University, Jesuit Community, Bronx, NY 10458, USA

Dulo, Jane *Actress*
904 Hilldale Ave, #2, Los Angeles, CA 90069, USA

Dumars, Joe, III *Basketball Player*
3499 Franklin Road, Bloomfield Hills, MI 48302, USA

Dumart, Woody *Hockey*
36 Old Farm Road, Needham, MA 02192, USA

Dumas, Charley *Track Athlete*
10709 8th Ave, Inglewood, CA 90303, USA

Dumont, Sky *Actor*
%ZBF Agentur, Leopoldstr 19, 80802 Munich, Germany

Dunaway, Faye *Actress*
PO Box 15778, Beverly Hills, CA 90209, USA

Dunbar, Bonnie J *Astronaut*
%NASA, Johnson Space Center, 2101 NASA Road, Houston, TX 77058, USA

Duncan, Angus *Actor*
%Thomas Jennings, 28035 Dorothy Dr, #210-A, Agoura, CA 91301, USA

Duncan, Carmen *Actress*
%Marion Rosenberg, 8428 Melrose Place, #C, Los Angeles, CA 90069, USA

Duncan, Charles K *Navy Admiral*
813 1st St, Coronado, CA 92118, USA

Duncan, Charles W, Jr *Secretary, Energy*
9 Briarwood Court, Houston, TX 77019, USA

Duncan, Daniel Kablan *Prime Minister, Cote d'Ivoire*
%Prime Minister's Office, Boulevard Clozel, Abidjan, Cote d'Ivoire

Duncan, David Douglas *Photojournalist*
Castellaras Mouans-Sartoux 06370, France

Duncan, Mariano *Baseball Player*
Ingenio Angelina #137, San Pedro de Macoris, Dominican Republic

Duncan, Sandy *Actress*
44 W 77th St, #1-B, New York, NY 10024, USA

Duncan, William *Businessman*
%Rolls-Royce, 65 Buckingham Gate, London SW1E 6AT, England

Dundee, Angelo *Boxing Manager*
450 N Park Road, #800, Hollywood, FL 33021, USA

Dunderstadt, James *Educator*
%University of Michigan, President's Office, Ann Arbor, MI 48109, USA
Dungy, Tony *Football Coach*
%Tampa Bay Buccaneers, 1 Buccaneer Place, Tampa, FL 33607, USA
Dunham, Katherine *Dancer, Choreographer*
%Katherine Dunham Children's Workshop, 532 N 10th St, East St Louis, IL 62201, USA
Dunham, Russell E *WW II Army Hero (CMH)*
2144 Sunderland Road, Jerseyville, IL 62052, USA
Duning, George W *Composer*
PO Box 190, Borrego Springs, CA 92004, USA
Dunlap, Albert J *Businessman*
%Scott Paper Co, 1 Scott Plaza, Philadelphia, PA 19113, USA
Dunlap, Carla *Bodybuilder*
%Diamond, 732 Irvington Ave, Maplewood, NJ 07040, USA
Dunlap, Charles E *Businessman*
%Crown Central Petroleum, 1 N Charles, Baltimore, MD 21201, USA
Dunlap, Robert H *WW II Marine Corps Hero (CMH)*
615 N 6th St, Monmouth, IL 61462, USA
Dunleavy, Michael J (Mike) *Basketball Player, Coach*
5060 Foothills Dr, #G, Lake Oswego, OR 97034, USA
Dunlop, John T *Secretary, Labor*
509 Pleasant St, Belmont, MA 02178, USA
Dunn, Gregory *Publisher*
%Redbook Magazine, 224 W 57th St, New York, NY 10019, USA
Dunn, Halbert L *Statistician*
3637 Edelmar Terrace, Rossmoor Silver Spring, MD 20906, USA
Dunn, Holly *Singer, Songwriter*
PO Box 2525, Hendersonville, TN 37077, USA
Dunn, James Joseph *Publisher*
%Forbes Magazine, 60 5th Ave, New York, NY 10011, USA
Dunn, Martin *Editor*
%New York Daily News, Editorial Dept, 220 E 42nd St, New York, NY 10017, USA
Dunn, Mignon *Opera Singer*
%Columbia Artists Mgmt Inc, 165 W 57th St, New York, NY 10019, USA
Dunn, Mike *Auto Racing Driver*
%Circle A Racing, Rt 24, Box 537-A, Keeney Lane, York, PA 17406, USA
Dunn, Nora *Actress*
%Susan Smith, 121 N San Vicente Blvd, Beverly Hills, CA 90211, USA
Dunn, Ronnie *Singer (Brooks & Dunn), Songwriter*
%Titley-Spalding, 900 Division St, Nashville, TN 37203, USA
Dunn, Stephen L *Religious Leader*
%Churches of God General Conference, 7176 Glenmeadow Dr, Frederick, MD 21703, USA
Dunn, Susan *Opera Singer*
%Herbert Breslin, 119 W 57th St, New York, NY 10019, USA
Dunn, T R *Basketball Player*
1014 19th St SW, Birmingham, AL 35211, USA
Dunn, William G *Publisher*
%US News & World Report Magazine, 2400 "N" St NW, Washington, DC 20037, USA
Dunn, Winfield C *Governor, TN*
40 Concord Park E, Nashville, TN 37205, USA
Dunne, Dominick *Writer*
155 E 49th St, New York, NY 10017, USA
Dunne, Griffin *Actor, Producer*
445 Park Ave, #701, New York, NY 10022, USA
Dunne, John Gregory *Writer*
%Janklow & Nesbit, 598 Madison Ave, New York, NY 10022, USA
Dunnigan, Frank J *Publisher*
%Prentice-Hall, Rt 9-W, Englewood Cliffs, NJ 07632, USA
Dunnigan, T Kevin *Businessman*
%Thomas & Betts Corp, 1555 Lynnfield Ave, Memphis, TN 38119, USA
Dunning, Debbe *Actress*
8740 Oland Ave, Sun Valley, CA 91352, USA
Dunphy, Don *Boxing Sportscaster*
15 Sherry Hill Lane, Manhasset, NY 11030, USA
Dunphy, Jerry *Commentator*
%KCAL-TV, 5515 Melrose Ave, Los Angeles, CA 90038, USA
Dunphy, Marv *Volleyball Coach*
33370 Decker School Road, Malibu, CA 90265, USA

D

Dunderstadt - Dunphy

Dunphy, T J Dermot — *Businessman*
%Sealed Air Corp, Park 80 Plaza E, Saddle Park, NJ 07663, USA

Dunsmore, Barrie — *Commentator*
%ABC-TV, News Dept, 1717 De Sales St NW, Washington, DC 20036, USA

Dupont, Jacques — *Minister of State, Monaco*
%Minister of State's Office, Boite Postale 522, 98015 Monaco-Cedex, Monaco

DuPree, Billy Joe — *Football Player*
6235 Annapolis Lane, Dallas, TX 75214, USA

Dupree, Donald (Don) — *Bobsled Athlete*
3 Center St, Saranac Lake, NY 12983, USA

Duque, Pedro — *Astronaut*
%Europe Astronaut Center, Linder Hohe, Box 906096, 51127 Cologne, Germany

Duques, Henry C — *Businessman*
%First Data Corp, 401 Hackensack Ave, Hackensack, NJ 07601, USA

Duquette, Dan — *Baseball Executive*
%Montreal Expos, PO Box 500, Station "M", Montreal PQ H1V 3P2, Canada

Duran, Roberto — *Boxer*
Nuevo Reperto El Carmen, Panama

Durang, Christopher — *Writer*
%Helen Merrill Agency, 337 W 22nd St, New York, NY 10011, USA

Durant, Graham J — *Inventor (Antiulcer Compound)*
%Cambridge NeuroScience, 1 Kendall Square, Building 700, Cambridge, MA 02139, USA

Durante, Viviana P — *Ballerina*
20 Bristol Gardens, Little Venice, London W9, England

Durbin, Deanna — *Actress, Singer*
BP 3315, 75123 Paris Cedex 03, France

Durbin, Mike — *Bowler*
%Professional Bowlers Assn, 1720 Merriman Road, Akron, OH 44313, USA

Durbridge, Francis — *Writer*
4 Fairacres, Roehampton Lane, London SW15 5LX, England

Durham, G Robert — *Businessman*
%Walter Industries, 1500 N Dale Mabry Highway, Tampa, FL 33607, USA

Durham, Hugh — *Basketball Coach*
%Jacksonville University, Athletic Dept, Jacksonville, FL 32211, USA

Duritz, Adam — *Singer (Counting Crowes), Lyricist*
%Direct Mgmt, 947 N La Cienega Blvd, #G, Los Angeles, CA 90069, USA

Durkin, John A — *Senator, NH*
%Perito Duerk Carlson Pinco, 1140 Connecticut NW, Washington, DC 20036, USA

Durning, Charles — *Actor*
10590 Wilshire Blvd, #506, Los Angeles, CA 90024, USA

Durr Browning, Françoise — *Tennis Player*
195 Rue de Lourmel, 75015 Paris, France

Durrance, Samuel T — *Astronaut, Astronomer*
118 Warwick St, Lutherville, Timonium, MD 21093, USA

Durrant, Devin — *Basketball Player*
279 E Gold River Circle, Orem, UT 84057, USA

Durwood, Stanley H — *Entertainment Executive*
%AMC Entertainment, 106 W 14th St, Kansas City, MO 64105, USA

Dury, Ian — *Singer*
%Gold Artist Agency, 122 Holland Park Ave, London W11 4UA, England

Duryea, Terry — *Businessman*
%McAfee Assoc, 2805 Bowers Ave, Santa Clara, CA 95051, USA

Dusay, Debra — *Actress*
%Susan Nathe, 8281 Melrose Ave, #200, Los Angeles, CA 90046, USA

Dusay, Marj — *Actress*
1964 Westwood Blvd, #6-F, New York, NY 10025, USA

Dusenberry, Ann — *Actress*
1615 San Leandro Lane, Montecito, CA 93108, USA

Dussault, Nancy — *Actress*
12211 Iredell St, North Hollywood, CA 91604, USA

Dutilleux, Henri — *Composer*
12 Rue St Louis-en-l'Isle, 75004 Paris, France

Dutoit, Charles E — *Conductor*
%Montreal Symphony, 85 Sainte Catherine St W, Montreal PQ H2X 3P4, Canada

Dutt, Hank — *Violist (Kronos Quartet)*
%Kronos Quartet, 1235 9th Ave, San Francisco, CA 94122, USA

Dutton, Charles S — *Actor*
1201 Alta Loma Road, Los Angeles, CA 90069, USA

Dutton, John — *Football Player*
2701 Winding Hollow Lane, Plano, TX 75093, USA

Duva, Lou — *Boxing Promoter*
%Main Events, 811 Totowa Road, #100, Totowa, NJ 07512, USA

Duval, Helen — *Bowler*
1624 Posen Ave, Berkeley, CA 94707, USA

Duval, James — *Actor*
%Agency For Performing Arts, 9200 Sunset Blvd, #900, Los Angeles, CA 90069, USA

Duvall, Jed — *Commentator*
%ABC-TV, News Dept, 1717 De Sales St NW, Washington, DC 20036, USA

Duvall, Robert — *Actor*
PO Box 520, The Plains, VA 20198, USA

Duvall, Sammy — *Water Skier*
PO Box 871, Windermere, FL 34786, USA

Duvall, Shelley — *Actress*
PO Box 1660, Blanco, TX 78606, USA

Duvall-Hero, Camille — *Water Skier*
PO Box 871, Windermere, FL 34786, USA

Duvignaud, Jean — *Writer*
28 Rue Saint-Leonard, 1700 La Rochelle, France

Duvillard, Henri — *Skier*
Le Mont d'Arbois, 74120 Megere, France

Duwelius, Rick — *Volleyball Player*
345 W Juniper St, #5, San Diego, CA 92101, USA

Duwez, Pol E — *Applied Physicist*
1535 Oakdale St, Pasadena, CA 91106, USA

Dwight, Edward, Jr — *Astronaut*
4022 Montview Blvd, Denver, CO 80207, USA

Dworkin, Andrea — *Writer*
%Elaine Markson, 44 Greenwich Ave, New York, NY 10011, USA

Dworsky, Daniel L (Dan) — *Football Player, Architect*
%Daniel L Dworsky Assoc, 3530 Wilshire Blvd, #1000, Los Angeles, CA 90010, USA

Dye, John — *Actor*
%Gersh Agency, 232 N Canon Dr, Beverly Hills, CA 90210, USA

Dye, Lee — *Golf Course Architect*
%Dye Designs, 5500 E Yale Ave, Denver, CO 80222, USA

Dye, Nancy Schrom — *Educator*
%Oberlin College, President's Office, Oberlin, OH 44074, USA

Dyer, Hector — *Track Athlete*
1620 E Chapman, #214, Fullerton, CA 92831, USA

Dyer, Wayne W — *Psychologist*
%Hay House, PO Box 5100, Carlsbad, CA 92018, USA

Dyke, Charles W — *Army General, Association Executive*
%International Technical/Trade Assoc, 1330 Connecticut NW, Washington, DC 20036, USA

Dykes Bower, John — *Concert Organist*
4-Z Artillery Mansions, Westminster, London SW1, England

Dykstra, John — *Artist, Animator, Cinematographer*
15060 Encanto Dr, Sherman Oaks, CA 91403, USA

Dykstra, Lenny K (Len) — *Baseball Player*
236 Chester Road, Devon, PA 19333, USA

Dylan, Bob — *Singer, Songwriter*
PO Box 870, Cooper Station, New York, NY 10276, USA

Dysart, Richard — *Actor*
654 Copeland Court, Santa Monica, CA 90405, USA

Dyson, Freeman J — *Physicist, Writer*
105 Battle Road Circle, Princeton, NJ 08540, USA

Dystel, Oscar — *Publisher*
The Springs, Purchase Hills Dr, Purchase, NY 10577, USA

Dzau, Victor — *Medical Researcher*
%Stanford University Hospital, Cardiovascular Medicine Div, Stanford, CA 94305, USA

Dzeliwe — *Queen Regent, Swaziland*
%Royal Palace, Mbabane, Swaziland

Dzhanibekov, Vladimir A — *Cosmonaut, Air Force General*
%Potchta Kosmonavtov, Moskovskoi Oblasti, 141160 Syvisdny Goroduk, Russia

Dzundza, George — *Actor*
%Gersh Agency, 232 N Canon Dr, Beverly Hills, CA 90210, USA

D

Dutton - Dzundza

E

Eade, George J *Air Force General*
1131 Sunnyside Dr, Healdsburg, CA 95448, USA

Eads, George *Actor*
%William Morris Agency, 151 S El Camino Dr, Beverly Hills, CA 90212, USA

Eads, Ora Wilbert *Religious Leader*
%Christian Congregation, 804 W Hemlock St, LaFollette, TN 37766, USA

Eagleburger, Lawrence S *Secretary, State*
%Baker Worthington Assoc, 801 Pennsylvania Ave NW, #800, Washington, DC 20004, USA

Eagleson, Alan *Labor Leader, Hockey Executive*
%NHL Players Assn, 37 Maitland St, Toronto ON M4Y 1CB, Canada

Eagleton, Thomas F *Senator, MO*
%Thompson & Mitchell, 1 Mercantile Center, #3400, St Louis, MO 63101, USA

Eakes, Bobbie *Actress*
5420 Sylmar Dr, #202, Van Nuys, CA 91401, USA

Eakin, Richard R *Educator*
%East Carolina University, Chancellor's Office, Greenville, NC 27858, USA

Eanes, Antonio dos Santos R *President, Portugal; Army General*
%Partido Renovador Democratico, Travessa do Falo 9, 1200 Lisbon, Portugal

Earl, Anthony S *Governor, WI*
2918 Arbor Dr, Madison, WI 53711, USA

Earland, Charles *Jazz Organist, Saxophonist*
%Abby Hoffer, 223 1/2 E 48th St, New York, NY 10017, USA

Earle, Eyvind *Artist*
2900 Santa Lucia Ave, Carmel-by-the-Sea, CA 93923, USA

Earle, Steve *Singer, Songwriter, Guitarist*
%Press Network, 1018 17th Ave S, #1, Nashville, TN 37212, USA

Earle, Sylvia Alice *Oceanographer*
12812 Skyline Blvd, Oakland, CA 94619, USA

Early, Gerald L *Writer*
%Washington University, English Dept, St Louis, MO 63130, USA

Earnhardt, R Dale *Auto Racing Driver*
1951 Old Cuthbert Road, Cherry Hill, NJ 08034, USA

Easley, Bill *Jazz Saxophonist, Clarinetist, Flutist*
%Maxine Harvard, 2227 Highway One, #251, North Brunswick, NJ 08902, USA

Eason, Tony *Football Player*
851 Cocos Dr, San Marcos, CA 92069, USA

Easterbrook, Leslie *Actress, Singer*
5218 Bellingham Ave, Valley Village, CA 91607, USA

Easterly, David E *Businessman*
%Cox Enterprises, 1400 Lake Hearn Dr NE, Atlanta, GA 30319, USA

Eastman, Benjamin *Track Athlete*
1025 3100 Road, Hotchkiss, CO 81419, USA

Eastman, Dean E *Physicist*
170 Island Ave, Peaks Island, ME 04108, USA

Eastman, John *Attorney*
%Eastman & Eastman, 39 W 54th St, New York, NY 10019, USA

Eastman, Kevin *Cartoonist (Ninja Turtles)*
%Teenage Mutant Ninja Turtles, PO Box 417, Haydenville, MA 01039, USA

Easton, Bill *Track Coach*
1024 Mississippi St, Lawrence, KS 66044, USA

Easton, Michael *Actor*
%Michael Slessinger, 8730 Sunset Blvd, #220-W, Los Angeles, CA 90069, USA

Easton, Sheena *Singer*
%Emmis Mgmt, 4268 Hazeltine Ave, Sherman Oaks, CA 91423, USA

Eastwick-Field, Elizabeth *Architect*
Low Farm, Low Road, Denham, Eye, Suffolk IP21 5ET, England

Eastwood, Clint *Actor, Director*
%Malpaso Productions, 4000 Warner Blvd, Building 154, #206, Burbank, CA 91522, USA

Easum, Donald B *Diplomat*
801 West End Ave, #3-A, New York, NY 10025, USA

Eaton, Dan L *Hematologist*
%Genentech Inc, 460 Point San Bruno Blvd, South San Francisco, CA 94080, USA

Eaton, Don (Babtunde) *Rap Artist, Drummer (The Last Poets)*
%Agency Group, 1775 Broadway, #433, New York, NY 10019, USA

Eaton, John C *Composer*
4585 N Hartstrait Road, Bloomington, IN 47404, USA

Eaton, Mark *Basketball Player*
PO Box 980428, Park City, UT 84098, USA

Eade - Eaton

Eaton, Robert J — *Businessman*
%Chrysler Corp, 1200 Chrysler Dr, Highland Park, MI 48288, USA

Eaton, Shirley — *Actress*
8 Harley St, London W1N 2AB, England

Eban, Abba — *Government Official, Israel*
PO Box 394, Hertzelia, Israel

Ebb, Fred — *Lyricist, Librettist*
%San Remo Apts, 146 Central Park West, #14-D, New York, NY 10023, USA

Ebbers, Bernard J — *Businessman*
%LDDS Communications, 515 E Amite St, Jackson, MS 39201, USA

Eber, Lorenz — *Inventor (Mechanical Cable Drum Lifter)*
215 Shepard Way NW, Bainbridge Island, WA 98110, USA

Eberhart, Ralph E — *Air Force General*
Commander, US Forces Japan, Unit 5068, APO, AP 96328, USA

Eberhart, Richard — *Writer*
80 Lyme Road, #32, Kendal at Hanover, NH 03755, USA

Eberle, William D — *Government Official, Businessman*
13 Garland Road, Concord, MA 01742, USA

Ebersol, Dick — *Television Executive*
%NBC-TV, Sports Dept, 30 Rockefeller Plaza, New York, NY 10112, USA

Ebersole, Christine — *Actress, Singer*
%Hart, 1244 11th St, #A, Santa Monica, CA 90401, USA

Ebert, James D — *Embryologist, Biologist*
Winthrop House, 4100 N Charles St, Baltimore, MD 21218, USA

Ebert, Peter — *Opera Director*
Col di Mura, 06010 Lippiano, Italy

Ebert, Robert D — *Physician*
16 Brewster Road, Wayland, MA 01778, USA

Ebert, Roger J — *Movie Critic*
PO Box 146366, Chicago, IL 60614, USA

Ebina, Masao — *Financier*
%Nikko Securities, 1 World Financial Center, 200 Liberty St, New York, NY 10281, USA

Ebsen, Buddy — *Actor, Dancer*
605 Via Horquilla, Palos Verdes Estates, CA 90274, USA

Eccles of Chute, David M — *Government Official, England*
Dean Farm, Chute near Andover, Hants, England

Ecclestone, Bernie — *Auto Racing Executive*
%Formula One, 8 Rue de La Concorde, 70008 Paris, France

Ecclestone, Tim — *Hockey Player*
10095 Fairway Village Dr, Roswell, GA 30076, USA

Ecevit, Bulent — *Prime Minister, Turkey*
Or-An Sehri 69/5, Ankara, Turkey

Echeverria Alvarez, Luis — *President, Mexico*
Magnolia 131, San Jeronimo Lidice, Magdalena Contreras, CP 10200, Mexico

Eckersley, Dennis L — *Baseball Player*
39 Plympton Road, Sudbury, MA 01776, USA

Eckholdt, Steven — *Actor*
%Innovative Artists, 1999 Ave of Stars, #2850, Los Angeles, CA 90067, USA

Eco, Umberto — *Writer, Educator*
Piazza Castello 13, 20121 Milan, Italy

Edberg, Stefan — *Tennis Player*
Spinnaregatan 6, 593 00 Vastervik, Sweden

Eddy, Duane — *Singer, Songwriter, Guitarist*
%Fat City Artists, 1908 Chet Atkins Place, #502, Nashville, TN 37212, USA

Edell, Marc Z — *Attorney*
%Budd Larner Gross, 150 John F Kennedy Parkway, #1000, Short Hills, NJ 07078, USA

Edelman, Gerald M — *Nobel Medicine Laureate*
%Scripps Research Institute, Neurobiology Dept, La Jolla, CA 92037, USA

Edelman, Marian Wright — *Association Executive*
%Children's Defense Fund, 25 "E" St NW, Washington, DC 20001, USA

Edelmann, Otto K — *Opera Singer*
Breitenfurterstr 547, 1238 Wein-Kalksburg, Austria

Edelstein, Jean — *Artist*
48 Brooks Ave, Venice, CA 90291, USA

Edelstein, Victor — *Fashion Designer*
3 Stanhope Mews West, London SW7 5RB, England

Eden of Winton, John — *Government Official, England*
41 Victoria Road, London W8 5RH, England

E

Eaton - Eden of Winton

Eden, Barbara *Actress*
9816 Denbigh Dr, Beverly Hills, CA 90210, USA

Eder, Richard G *Journalist*
%Los Angeles Times, Editorial Dept, Times Mirror Sq, Los Angeles, CA 90053, USA

Ederle Reichenback, Gertrude (Trudy) *Marathon Swimmer*
4465 SW 37th Ave, Fort Lauderdale, FL 33312, USA

Edgar, Dave *Swimmer*
429 Seabreeze Blvd, #214, Fort Lauderdale, FL 33316, USA

Edge (Dave Evans), The *Guitarist (U-2), Singer*
%Principle Mgmt, 30-32 Sir John Rogersons Quay, Dublin 2, Ireland

Edison, Harry (Sweets) *Jazz Trumpeter*
%Jazz One, 44 Rio Vista Dr, Allendale, NJ 07401, USA

Edlen, Bengt *Astrophysicist*
%University of Lund, Physics Dept, Lund, Sweden

Edler, Inge G *Cardiologist*
%University Hospital, Cardiology Dept, Lund, Sweden

Edley, Christopher F *Association Director*
%United Negro College Fund, 500 E 62nd St, New York, NY 10021, USA

Edlund, Richard *Cinematographer*
%Boss Film Corp, 13335 Maxella Ave, Marina del Rey, CA 90292, USA

Edmiston, Mark M *Publisher*
%Jordan Edmiston Group, 885 3rd Ave, New York, NY 10022, USA

Edmond, John M *Marine Geochemist*
77 Massachusetts Ave, #E-34-201, Cambridge, MA 02139, USA

Edmonds, Kenneth (Babyface) *Singer, Songwriter, Record Producer*
%William Morris Agency, 151 S El Camino Dr, Beverly Hills, CA 90212, USA

Edmonds, Walter D *Writer*
27 River St, Concord, MA 01742, USA

Edmund-Davies, Herbert E *Judge*
5 Gray's Inn Square, London WC1R 5EU, England

Edmunds, Dave *Singer, Songwriter*
%Entertainment Services, Main Street Plaza 1000, #303, Voorhees, NJ 08043, USA

Edney, Leon A (Bud) *Navy Admiral*
233 Prince George St, Annapolis, MD 21401, USA

Edsall, John T *Biological Chemist*
985 Memorial Dr, #503, Cambridge, MA 02138, USA

Edson, Hilary *Actress*
%Kroll, 2211 Broadway, New York, NY 10024, USA

Eduardo dos Santos, Jose *President, Angola*
%President's Office, Palacio do Povo, Luanda, Angola

Edward *Prince, England*
%Buckingham Palace, London SW1A 1BA, England

Edwards, Anthony *Actor*
%United Talent Agency, 9560 Wilshire Blvd, #500, Beverly Hills, CA 90212, USA

Edwards, Barbara *Actress, Model*
%Hansen, 7767 Hollywood Blvd, #202, Los Angeles, CA 90046, USA

Edwards, Blake *Movie Director, Producer*
11777 San Vicente Blvd, #501, Los Angeles, CA 90049, USA

Edwards, Blue *Basketball Player*
%Vancouver Grizzlies, 288 Beatty St, #300, Vancouver BC V6B 2M1, Canada

Edwards, Charles C *Physician*
Keeney Park, 10666 N Torrey Pines Road, La Jolla, CA 92037, USA

Edwards, Charles C, Jr *Publisher*
%Des Moines Register & Tribune, 715 Locust St, Des Moines, IA 50309, USA

Edwards, Dennis *Singer (Temptations)*
%Bowen Agency, 504 W 168th St, New York, NY 10032, USA

Edwards, Don *Hockey Player*
609 E Maple Ave, El Segundo, CA 90245, USA

Edwards, Edwin W *Governor, LA*
8114 Walden Road, Baton Rouge, LA 70808, USA

Edwards, Gail *Actress*
%Gersh Agency, 232 N Canon Dr, Beverly Hills, CA 90210, USA

Edwards, Harry *Educator, Social Activist*
%University of California, Sociology Dept, Berkeley, CA 94720, USA

Edwards, James *Basketball Player*
3890 Lakeland Lane, Bloomfield Township, MI 48302, USA

Edwards, James B *Secretary, Energy; Governor, SC*
100 Venning St, Mount Pleasant, SC 29464, USA

Edwards, Jay — Basketball Player
121 N Washington St, #506, Marion, IN 46952, USA

Edwards, Jesse E — Cardiac Pathologist
1565 Edgcumbe Road, St Paul, MN 55116, USA

Edwards, Joe F, Jr — Astronaut
%NASA, Johnson Space Center, 2101 NASA Road, Houston, TX 77058, USA

Edwards, Jonathan — Singer, Songwriter
%Northern Lights, 161 Pantry Road, Sudbury, MA 01776, USA

Edwards, LaVell — Football Coach
%Brigham Young University, Athletic Dept, Provo, UT 84602, USA

Edwards, Lena F — Physician
821 Woodland Dr, Lakewood, NJ 08701, USA

Edwards, Ralph — Entertainer
6922 Hollywood Blvd, #415, Los Angeles, CA 90028, USA

Edwards, Robert A (Bob) — Commentator
%National Public Radio, News Dept, 635 Massachusetts NW, Washington, DC 20001, USA

Edwards, Robert G — Physiologist
Duck End Farm, Dry Drayton, Cambridge CB3 8DB, England

Edwards, Robert J — Editor
%Sunday Mirror, Editorial Dept, 33 Holborn, London EC1P 1DG, England

Edwards, Stephanie — Actress
8075 W 3rd St, #303, Los Angeles, CA 90048, USA

Edwards, Teresa — Basketball Player, Coach
Teresa Edwards Dr, Cairo, GA 31728, USA

Edwards, Theodore M (Teddy) — Jazz Saxphonist, Composer
%Antilles Records, Polygram, 3800 W Alameda Ave, #1500, Burbank, CA 91505, USA

Egal, Mohamed Ibrahim — Prime Minister, Somalia
PO Box 27, Via Asha, Mogadishu, Somalia

Egan, Jennifer — Writer
%Doubleday, 1540 Broadway, New York, NY 10036, USA

Egan, Peter — Actor
%James Sharkey, 21 Golden Square, London W1R 3PA, England

Egan, Richard J — Businessman
%EMC Corp, 171 South St, Hopkinton, MA 01748, USA

Egan, William P — Businessman
%Burr Egan Deleage Co, 1 Post Office Square, Boston, MA 02109, USA

Egdahl, Richard H — Surgeon
333 Commonwealth Ave, #23, Boston, MA 02115, USA

Ege, Julie — Actress
Vestre Nostegate 29, 3300 Hokksund, Norway

Egeberg, Roger O — Physician, Government Official
330 Independence St SW, 4039 North Bldg, Washington, DC 20547, USA

Egerszegi, Kristina — Swimmer
Feszti A Utca 4, 1032 Budapest, Hungary

Eggar, Samantha — Actress
15430 Mulholland Dr, Los Angeles, CA 90077, USA

Egger, Roscoe L (Roger), Jr — Government Official
3831 S Via de La Urraca, Green Valley, AZ 85614, USA

Eggert, Nicole — Actress
20591 Queens Park, Huntington Beach, CA 92646, USA

Eggleston, William — Photographer, Artist
%Robert Miller Gallery, 41 E 57th St, New York, NY 10022, USA

Egoyan, Atom — Movie Director
%Ego Film Artists, 80 Niagara St, Toronto ON M5V 1C5, Canada

Ehle, Jennifer — Actress
%International Creative Mgmt, 76 Oxford St, London W1N 0AX, England

Ehlers, Beth — Actress
%William Morris Agency, 151 S El Camino Dr, Beverly Hills, CA 90212, USA

Ehlers, Walter D — WW II Army Hero (CMH)
8382 Valley View, Buena Park, CA 90620, USA

Ehlo, Craig — Basketball Player
%Seattle Supersonics, 190 Queen Ave N, PO Box C-900911, Seattle, WA 98109, USA

Ehrenreich, Barbara — Women's Activist, Writer
%Farrar Straus Giroux, 19 Union Square W, New York, NY 10003, USA

Ehrlich, Paul R — Population Biologist
%Stanford University, Biological Sciences Dept, Stanford, CA 94305, USA

Ehrlich, S Paul, Jr — Physician
6512 Lakeview Dr, Falls Church, VA 22041, USA

Ehrlichman, John D — *Government Official*
2734 Peachtree Road NW, #C-102, Atlanta, GA 30305, USA

Ehrling, Sixten — *Conductor*
%Park Ten, 10 W 66th St, New York, NY 10023, USA

Eichelberger, Charles B — *Army General*
%California Microwave, 124 Sweetwater Oaks, Peachtree City, GA 30269, USA

Eichenfield, Samuel L — *Financier*
%GFC Financial, Dial Corporate Center, Phoenix, AZ 85077, USA

Eichhorn, Lisa — *Actress*
19 W 44th St, #1000, New York, NY 10036, USA

Eichner, Ira A — *Businessman*
%AAR Corp, 1111 Nicholas Blvd, Elk Grove Village, IL 60007, USA

Eickhoff, Gottfred — *Artist*
Frederiksholms Kanal 28-C, Copenhagen, Denmark

Eickmann, Kenneth G — *Air Force General*
Commander, Aeronautical Systems Ctr, Wright-Patterson Air Force Base, OH 45433, USA

Eigen, Manfred — *Nobel Chemistry Laureate*
%Max Planck Institute, Am Fassburg, 37077 Gottingen-Nikolausberg, Germany

Eigsti, Roger H — *Businessman*
%SAFECO Corp, SAFECO Plaza, Seattle, WA 98185, USA

Eikenberry, Jill — *Actress*
197 Oakdale Ave, Mill Valley, CA 94941, USA

Eilbacher, Lisa — *Actress*
4600 Petit Ave, Encino, CA 91436, USA

Eilber, Janet — *Actress*
%Irv Schechter, 9300 Wilshire Blvd, #410, Beverly Hills, CA 90212, USA

Eilenberg, Samuel — *Mathematician*
%Columbia University, Mathematics Dept, New York, NY 10027, USA

Eilts, Hermann F — *Diplomat*
67 Cleveland Road, Wellesley, MA 02181, USA

Einhorn, Edward M (Eddie) — *Baseball Executive*
%Chicago White Sox, 333 W 35th St, Chicago, IL 60616, USA

Einstein (Super Dave Osborn), Bob — *Actor*
%Super Dave Production, 10 Universal City Plaza, #3100, Universal City, CA 91608, USA

Eisen, Herman N — *Immunologist*
9 Homestead St, Waban, MA 02168, USA

Eisenberg, Kenneth S — *Restoration Expert*
1000 Connecticut Ave NW, Washington, DC 20036, USA

Eisenberg, Lee B — *Editor*
%Edison Project, 3286 N Park Blvd, Alcoa, TN 37701, USA

Eisenberg, Leon — *Psychiatrist*
9 Clement Circle, Cambridge, MA 02138, USA

Eisenman, Peter D — *Architect*
%Eisenman Architects, 40 W 25th St, New York, NY 10010, USA

Eisenmann, Ike — *Actor*
%Gage Group, 9255 Sunset Blvd, #515, Los Angeles, CA 90069, USA

Eisenreich, James M (Jim) — *Baseball Player*
1205 Arrowhead Trail, Blue Springs, MO 64015, USA

Eisley, Howard — *Basketball Player*
%Utah Jazz, Delta Center, 301 W South Temple, Salt Lake City, UT 84101, USA

Eisman, Hy — *Cartoonist*
99 Boulevard, Glen Rock, NJ 07452, USA

Eisner, Michael D — *Entertainment Executive*
%Walt Disney Co, 500 S Buena Vista St, Burbank, CA 91521, USA

Eisner, Thomas — *Biologist*
%Cornell University, Biological Sciences Dept, Ithaca, NY 14853, USA

Eisner, Will — *Cartoonist (The Spirit)*
%Poorhouse Press, 8333 W McNab Road, #114, Tamarac, FL 33321, USA

Eitan, Raphael — *Army General, Israel*
%Tsomet Party, Knesset, Tel-Aviv, Israel

Eitzel, Mark — *Singer, Songwriter*
%ICM/Twin Towers, 611 Broadway, #730, New York, NY 10012, USA

Eizenstat, Stuart E — *Government Official, Diplomat*
%Commerce Department, 14th St & Constitution Ave, Washington, DC 20230, USA

Ekandem, Dominic Cardinal — *Religious Leader*
PO Box 286, Garki, Abiya, Nigeria

Ekland, Britt — *Actress*
1888 N Crescent Heights Blvd, West Hollywood, CA 90069, USA

Eklund, A Sigvard — *Nuclear Physicist*
Krapfenwaldgasse 48, 1190 Vienna, Austria

El DeBarge — *Singer*
%Pyramid Entertainment, 89 5th Ave, #700, New York, NY 10003, USA

Elam, Jack — *Actor*
1257 Siskiyou Blvd, #222, Ashland, OR 97520, USA

Elcar, Dana — *Actor*
22920 Hatteras St, Woodland Hills, CA 91367, USA

Elder, Jeffrey L — *Businessman*
%Foundation Health, 3400 Data Dr, Rancho Cordova, CA 95670, USA

Elder, Mark P — *Conductor*
%National Opera, London Coliseum, London WC2N 4ES, England

Elder, R Lee — *Golfer*
%Lee Elder Enterprises, 4130 Palm-Aire Dr W, #302-B, Pompano Beach, FL 33069, USA

Elder, Will — *Cartoonist (Little Annie Fanny)*
311 Jutland Dr, #A, Cranbury, NJ 08512, USA

Elders, M Jocelyn — *Government Official, Pediatarician*
%University of Arkansas Medical School, Pediatrics Dept, Little Rock, AR 72205, USA

Eldredge, Todd — *Figure Skater*
6000 Revere Place, #H, Bloomfield, MI 48301, USA

Elegant, Robert S — *Writer*
Manor House, Middle Green near Langley, Bucks SL3 6BS, England

Eleniak, Erika — *Actress*
%William Morris Agency, 151 S El Camino Dr, Beverly Hills, CA 90212, USA

Elewonibi, Mohammed (Moe) — *Football Player*
%Buffalo Bills, 1 Bills Dr, Orchard Park, NY 14127, USA

Elfman, Danny — *Singer, Composer*
%Oingo Bongo Secret Society, PO Box 10815, Beverly Hills, CA 90213, USA

Elfman, Jenna — *Actress, Model*
%Michael Slessinger, 8730 Sunset Blvd, #220-W, Los Angeles, CA 90069, USA

Elfner, Albert H, III — *Financier*
%Keystone Group, 200 Berkeley St, Boston, MA 02116, USA

Elg, Taina — *Actress*
%Michael Hartig Agency, 114 E 28th St, New York, NY 10016, USA

Elgart, Larry J — *Orchestra Leader*
2065 Gulf of Mexico Dr, Longboat Key, FL 34228, USA

Elias, Eddie — *Bowling Executive*
4067 North Shore Dr, Akron, OH 44333, USA

Elias, Eliane — *Jazz Pianist, Composer*
%Bennett Morgan, 1282 Rt 376, Wappingers Falls, NY 12590, USA

Elias, Peter — *Electrical Engineer*
102 Raymond St, Cambridge, MA 02140, USA

Elias, Rosalind — *Opera Singer*
%Columbia Artists Mgmt Inc, 165 W 57th St, New York, NY 10019, USA

Elicker, Paul H — *Businessman*
5600 Wisconsin Ave, #19-D, Chevy Chase, MD 20815, USA

Elie, Mario — *Basketball Player*
6000 Reims Road, #3302, Houston, TX 77036, USA

Eliel, Ernest L — *Chemist*
725 Kenmore Road, Chapel Hill, NC 27514, USA

Elinson, Jack — *Sociomedical Scientist*
1181 E Laurelton Parkway, Teaneck, NJ 07666, USA

Elion, Gertrude B — *Nobel Medicine Laureate*
1 Banbury Lane, Chapel Hill, NC 27514, USA

Eliot, Jan — *Cartoonist*
%Universal Press Syndicate, 4400 Fairway Dr, Fairway, KS 66205, USA

Elish, Herbert — *Businessman*
%Weirton Steel Corp, 400 Three Springs Dr, Weirton, WV 26062, USA

Elisha, Walter Y — *Businessman*
%Springs Industries, 205 N White St, Fort Hill, SC 29715, USA

Elizabeth — *Queen Mother, Great Britain*
%Clarence House, London SW1A 1BA, England

Elizabeth II — *Queen, Great Britain & Northern Ireland*
%Buckingham Palace, London SW1A 1AA, England

Elizondo, Hector — *Actor*
5040 Noble Ave, Sherman Oaks, CA 91403, USA

Elkes, Joel — *Psychiatrist*
%University of Louisville, Psychiatry/Behavioral Sci Dept, Louisville, KY 40292, USA

E

Eklund - Elkes

E

Elkes, Terrence A	*Businessman*
%Apollo Partners, 350 Park Ave, New York, NY 10022, USA	
Elkington, Steve	*Golfer*
5114 FM 1960 W 1011, Houston, TX 77069, USA	
Elkins, Hillard	*Theater Producer*
1335 N Doheny Dr, Los Angeles, CA 90069, USA	
Ellard, Henry	*Football Player*
43405 Livery Square, Ashburn, VA 20147, USA	
Ellena, Jack	*Football Player*
%Mountain Meadow Ranch, PO Box 610, Susanville, CA 96130, USA	
Ellenstein, Robert	*Actor*
5215 Sepulveda Blvd, #23-F, Culver City, CA 90230, USA	
Ellenthal, Ira	*Publisher*
%New York Daily News, 220 E 42nd St, New York, NY 10017, USA	
Eller, Carl	*Football Player, Executive*
1035 Washburn Ave N, Minneapolis, MN 55411, USA	
Ellerbee, Linda	*Commentator*
%Lucky Duck Productions, 96 Morton St, #600, New York, NY 10014, USA	
Elliman, Donald M, Jr	*Publisher*
%Sports Illustrated Magazine, Rockefeller Center, New York, NY 10020, USA	
Elliman, Yvonne	*Singer*
%Talent Consultants Int'l, 1560 Broadway, #1308, New York, NY 10036, USA	
Elliot, Jane	*Actress*
%Judy Schoen, 606 N Larchmont Blvd, #309, Los Angeles, CA 90004, USA	
Elliot, Win	*Sportscaster*
14 October Place, Weston, CT 06883, USA	
Elliott, Bill	*Auto Racing Driver*
%Elliott Museum, PO Box 435, Dawsonville, GA 30534, USA	
Elliott, Chalmers (Bump)	*Football Player, Coach*
%University of Iowa, Athletic Dept, Iowa City, IA 52242, USA	
Elliott, David James	*Actor*
%United Talent Agency, 9560 Wilshire Blvd, #500, Beverly Hills, CA 90212, USA	
Elliott, Herb	*Track Athlete*
40 Porteous Road, Sorrento WA, Australia	
Elliott, Joe	*Singer (Def Leppard)*
%Q Prime Inc, 729 7th Ave, #1400, New York, NY 10019, USA	
Elliott, Jumbo	*Football Player*
%New York Jets, 1000 Fulton Ave, Hempstead, NY 11550, USA	
Elliott, Osborn	*Journalist*
36 E 72nd St, New York, NY 10021, USA	
Elliott, Patricia	*Actress*
%Ambrosio/Mortimer, 9150 Wilshire Blvd, #175, Beverly Hills, CA 90212, USA	
Elliott, Pete	*Football Player*
3003 Dunbarton Ave NW, Canton, OH 44708, USA	
Elliott, Sam	*Actor*
33050 Pacific Coast Highway, Malibu, CA 90265, USA	
Elliott, Sean	*Basketball Player*
3 Parman Place, San Antonio, TX 78230, USA	
Ellis, Albert	*Clinical Psychologist*
%Institute for Rational-Emotional Therapy, 45 E 65th St, New York, NY 10021, USA	
Ellis, Alton	*Singer*
27 McConnell House, Deeley Road, London SW8, England	
Ellis, Bret Easton	*Writer*
%International Creative Mgmt, 40 W 57th St, New York, NY 10019, USA	
Ellis, Dale	*Basketball Player*
18110 SE 41st Place, Bellevue, WA 98008, USA	
Ellis, Don	*Bowler*
34 Crestwood Circle, Sugar Land, TX 77478, USA	
Ellis, Elmer	*Writer, Historian*
3300 New Haven Ave, #223, Columbia, MO 65201, USA	
Ellis, Herb	*Jazz Guitarist*
%Thomas Cassidy, 0366 Horseshoe Dr, Basalt, CO 81621, USA	
Ellis, James O, Jr	*Navy Admiral*
%Deputy Chief, Plans/Policy/Ops, Navy Dept, Pentagon, Washington, DC 20350, USA	
Ellis, Janet	*Actress*
%Arlington Entertainments, 1/3 Charlotte St, London W1P 1HD, England	
Ellis, Jimmy	*Boxer*
8902 Loch Lea Lane, Louisville, KY 40291, USA	

Elkes - Ellis

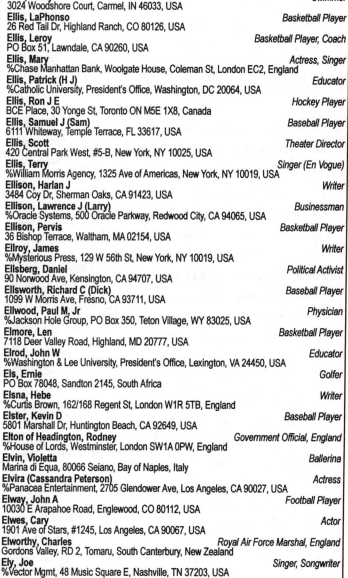

Ellis, Kathy	*Swimmer*
3024 Woodshore Court, Carmel, IN 46033, USA	
Ellis, LaPhonso	*Basketball Player*
26 Red Tail Dr, Highland Ranch, CO 80126, USA	
Ellis, Leroy	*Basketball Player, Coach*
PO Box 51, Lawndale, CA 90260, USA	
Ellis, Mary	*Actress, Singer*
%Chase Manhattan Bank, Woolgate House, Coleman St, London EC2, England	
Ellis, Patrick (H J)	*Educator*
%Catholic University, President's Office, Washington, DC 20064, USA	
Ellis, Ron J E	*Hockey Player*
BCE Place, 30 Yonge St, Toronto ON M5E 1X8, Canada	
Ellis, Samuel J (Sam)	*Baseball Player*
6111 Whiteway, Temple Terrace, FL 33617, USA	
Ellis, Scott	*Theater Director*
420 Central Park West, #5-B, New York, NY 10025, USA	
Ellis, Terry	*Singer (En Vogue)*
%William Morris Agency, 1325 Ave of Americas, New York, NY 10019, USA	
Ellison, Harlan J	*Writer*
3484 Coy Dr, Sherman Oaks, CA 91423, USA	
Ellison, Lawrence J (Larry)	*Businessman*
%Oracle Systems, 500 Oracle Parkway, Redwood City, CA 94065, USA	
Ellison, Pervis	*Basketball Player*
36 Bishop Terrace, Waltham, MA 02154, USA	
Ellroy, James	*Writer*
%Mysterious Press, 129 W 56th St, New York, NY 10019, USA	
Ellsberg, Daniel	*Political Activist*
90 Norwood Ave, Kensington, CA 94707, USA	
Ellsworth, Richard C (Dick)	*Baseball Player*
1099 W Morris Ave, Fresno, CA 93711, USA	
Ellwood, Paul M, Jr	*Physician*
%Jackson Hole Group, PO Box 350, Teton Village, WY 83025, USA	
Elmore, Len	*Basketball Player*
7118 Deer Valley Road, Highland, MD 20777, USA	
Elrod, John W	*Educator*
%Washington & Lee University, President's Office, Lexington, VA 24450, USA	
Els, Ernie	*Golfer*
PO Box 78048, Sandton 2145, South Africa	
Elsna, Hebe	*Writer*
%Curtis Brown, 162/168 Regent St, London W1R 5TB, England	
Elster, Kevin D	*Baseball Player*
5801 Marshall Dr, Huntington Beach, CA 92649, USA	
Elton of Headington, Rodney	*Government Official, England*
%House of Lords, Westminster, London SW1A 0PW, England	
Elvin, Violetta	*Ballerina*
Marina di Equa, 80066 Seiano, Bay of Naples, Italy	
Elvira (Cassandra Peterson)	*Actress*
%Panacea Entertainment, 2705 Glendower Ave, Los Angeles, CA 90027, USA	
Elway, John A	*Football Player*
10030 E Arapahoe Road, Englewood, CO 80112, USA	
Elwes, Cary	*Actor*
1901 Ave of Stars, #1245, Los Angeles, CA 90067, USA	
Elworthy, Charles	*Royal Air Force Marshal, England*
Gordons Valley, RD 2, Tomaru, South Canterbury, New Zealand	
Ely, Joe	*Singer, Songwriter*
%Vector Mgmt, 48 Music Square E, Nashville, TN 37203, USA	
Ely, Ron	*Actor*
4161 Mariposa Dr, Santa Barbara, CA 93110, USA	
Eman, J H A (Henny)	*Prime Minister, Aruba*
Arubaanse Volkspartij, Orangestad, Aruba	
Emanuel, Elizabeth F	*Fashion Designer*
44 Grove End Road, #7, London NW8 9NE, England	
Emanuels, Severinus D	*Prime Minister, Suriname*
98 Wassenaarse Weg, 2596 CZ The Hague, Netherlands	
Emberg, Kelly	*Actress, Model*
1608 N Poinsettia, Manhattan Beach, CA 90266, USA	
Embry, Wayne	*Basketball Player, Executive*
130 W Juniper Lane, Moreland Hills, OH 44022, USA	

E

Ellis - Embry

Emerson, Alice F *Educator*
%Andrew Mellon Foundation, 140 E 62nd St, New York, NY 10021, USA

Emerson, David F *Navy Admiral*
1777 Chelwood Circle, Charleston, SC 29407, USA

Emerson, Douglas *Actor*
1450 Belfast Dr, Los Angeles, CA 90069, USA

Emerson, J Martin *Labor Leader*
%American Federation of Musicians, 1501 Broadway, New York, NY 10036, USA

Emerson, Roy *Tennis Player*
2221 Alta Vista Dr, Newport Beach, CA 92660, USA

Emert, George H *Educator*
%Utah State University, President's Office, Logan, UT 84322, USA

Emery, John *Bobsled Athlete*
2001 Union St, San Francisco, CA 94123, USA

Emery, Kenneth O *Oceanographer*
35 Horseshoe Lane, North Falmouth, MA 02556, USA

Emery, Oren D *Religious Leader*
%Wesleyan International, 6060 Castleway West Dr, Indianapolis, IN 46250, USA

Emick, Jarrod *Actor*
%Gersh Agency, 232 N Canon Dr, Beverly Hills, CA 90210, USA

Emilio *Singer*
%Refugee Mgmt, 209 10th Ave S, #347 Cummins Station, Nashville, TN 37203, USA

Emmanuel *Singer*
%Hauser Entertainment, PO Box 978, Pico Rivera, CA 90660, USA

Emme *Model*
%Ford Model Agency, 344 E 59th St, New York, NY 10022, USA

Emmerich, Roland *Movie Director, Producer*
%20th Century Fox, 10202 W Pico Blvd, #58, Los Angeles, CA 90064, USA

Emmerton, Bill *Marathon Runner*
615 Ocean Ave, Santa Monica, CA 90402, USA

Emmett, John C *Inventor (Antiulcer Compound)*
Oak House, Hatfield Broad Oak, Bishop's Stortford, Herts CM22 7HG, England

Emmons, Howard W *Mechanical Engineer*
1010 Waltham St, #443-B, Lexington, MA 02173, USA

Emmott, Bill *Editor*
%Economist Magazine, 25 St James's St, London SW1A 1HG, England

Emtman, Steven C (Steve) *Football Player*
12509 35th Ave NE, Seattle, WA 98125, USA

Enberg, Dick *Sportscaster*
PO Box 710, Rancho Santa Fe, CA 92067, USA

Endacott, Paul *Basketball Player*
916 Cherokee Ave, Bartlesville, OK 74003, USA

Ender Grummt, Kornelia *Swimmer*
%DSV, Postfach 420140, 34070 Kassel, Germany

Enders, Anthony T *Financier*
%Brown Brothers Harriman, 59 Wall St, New York, NY 10005, USA

Engel, Albert E *Geologist*
%University of California, Scripps Institute, Geology Dept, La Jolla, CA 92093, USA

Engel, Georgia *Actress*
350 W 57th St, #10-E, New York, NY 10019, USA

Engelbart, Douglas C *Computer Scientist (Mouse Inventor)*
89 Catalpa Dr, Menlo Park, CA 94027, USA

Engelberger, Joseph F *Robotics Engineer*
%Transition Research Corp, 15 Durant Ave, Bethel, CT 06801, USA

Engelhardt, Thomas A *Editorial Cartoonist*
%St Louis Post-Dispatch, Editorial Dept, 900 N Tucker Blvd, St Louis, MO 63101, USA

Engen, Corey *Skier*
506 N 40 W, Lindon, UT 84042, USA

Engen, Donald D *Government Official*
809 Duke St, Alexandria, VA 22314, USA

Engen, Sverre *Skier*
9058 Green Hills Dr, Sandy, UT 84093, USA

Engholm, Bjorn *Government Official, Germany*
Jurgen-Wallenwever-Str 9, 23566 Lubeck, Germany

Engibous, Thomas J *Businessman*
%Texas Instruments, 13500 North Central Expressway, Dallas, TX 75243, USA

England, Anthony W *Astronaut, Geophysicist*
7949 Ridgeway Court, Dexter, MI 48130, USA

England, Richard *Architect*
26/1 Merchants St, Valletta, Malta
England, Ty *Singer*
%Bob Doyle, 1111 17th Ave S, Nashville, TN 37212, USA
Englander, Harold R *Dental Researcher*
11502 Whisper Bluff St, San Antonio, TX 78230, USA
Engle, Joe H *Astronaut, Air Force General*
3280 Cedar Heights Dr, Colorado Springs, CO 80904, USA
Englehart, Robert W (Bob), Jr *Editorial Cartoonist*
%Hartford Courant, Editorial Dept, 280 Broad St, Hartford, CT 06105, USA
Engler, John M *Governor, MI*
%Governor's Office, State Capitol Building, #200, Lansing, MI 48913, USA
English, Alex *Basketball Player*
596 Rimer Pond Road, Blythewood, SC 29016, USA
English, Diane *Writer*
%Shukovsky-English Ent, 4024 Radford Ave, Studio City, CA 91604, USA
English, Doug *Football Player*
4306 Benedict Lane, Austin, TX 78746, USA
English, Joseph T *Psychiatrist*
%St Vincents Hospital, 203 W 12th St, New York, NY 10011, USA
English, Lawrence P *Businessman*
%Connecticut General Life, 900 Cottage Grove Road, Bloomfield, CT 06002, USA
English, Michael *Singer*
PO Box 681598, Franklin, TN 37068, USA
Englund, Robert *Actor*
1616 Santa Cruz St, Laguna Beach, CA 92651, USA
Engstrom, Ted W *Association Executive*
%World Vision, 919 W Huntington Dr, Arcadia, CA 91007, USA
Enke-Kania, Karin *Speed Skater*
Tolstoistr 3, 01326 Dresden, Germany
Eno, Brian *Composer, Musician*
%Creative Artists Agency, 9830 Wilshire Blvd, Beverly Hills, CA 90212, USA
Enrico, Roger A *Businessman*
%PepsiCo Inc, 700 Anderson Hill Road, Purchase, NY 10577, USA
Enright, Dennis J *Writer, Educator*
35-A Viewfield Road, London SW18 5JD, England
Entremont, Philippe *Conductor, Concert Pianist*
14 Rue D'Alger, 75001 Paris, France
Entringer, James W *Businessman*
%Selective Insurance Group, 40 Wantage Ave, Branchville, NJ 07890, USA
Entwistle, John *Singer, Songwriter, Bassist (The Who)*
1704 Queens Court, Los Angeles, CA 90069, USA
Enzensberger, Hans M *Writer*
%Suhrkamp Verlag, Fach 2446, 60549 Frankfurt/Main, Germany
Ephron, Nora *Writer*
390 West End Ave, New York, NY 10024, USA
Epperson, Brenda *Actress*
%Lee, 403 Susana Ave, Redondo Beach, CA 90277, USA
Epple-Beck, Irene *Skier*
Aufmberg 235, 87637 Seeg, Germany
Epps, Omar *Actor*
%Gersh Agency, 232 N Canon Dr, Beverly Hills, CA 90210, USA
Epstein, Daniel M *Writer*
843 W University Parkway, Baltimore, MD 21210, USA
Epstein, Emmanuel *Plant Nutritionist*
%University of California, Land Air Water Resources Dept, Davis, CA 95616, USA
Epstein, Gabriel *Architect*
3 Rue Mazet, 75006 Paris, France
Epstein, Jason *Editor*
%Random House, 201 E 50th St, New York, NY 10022, USA
Epstein, Joseph *Writer, Educator*
522 Church St, #6-B, Evanston, IL 60201, USA
Erb, Donald *Composer*
4073 Bluestone Road, Cleveland, OH 44121, USA
Erb, Richard D *Government Official*
%International Monetary Fund, 700 19th St NW, Washington, DC 20431, USA
Erbakan, Necmettin *Prime Minister, Turkey*
%National Salvation Party, Balgat, Ankara, Turkey

E

England - Erbakan

E

Erbe, Norman — *Governor, IA*
915 Ashworth Road, #212, West Des Moines, IA 50265, USA

Erburu, Robert F — *Publisher, Businessman*
1518 Blue Jay Way, West Hollywood, CA 90069, USA

Erdman, Paul E — *Writer*
1817 Lytton Springs Road, Healdsburg, CA 95448, USA

Erdman, Richard — *Actor*
5655 Greenbush Ave, Van Nuys, CA 91401, USA

Erdrich, K Louise — *Writer*
PO Box 70, Cornish Flat, NH 03746, USA

Erhard, Werner — *est Founder*
1945 Franklin St, San Francisco, CA 94109, USA

Erhardt, Warren R — *Publisher*
455 Wakefield Dr, Metchen, NJ 08840, USA

Eric B — *Rap Artist (Eric B & Rakim)*
%Rush Artists, 1600 Varick St, New York, NY 10013, USA

Erickson, Arthur C — *Architect*
%Arthur Erickson Architects, 1672 W 1st Ave, Vancouver BC V6J 1G1, Canada

Erickson, Craig — *Football Player*
420 N Country Club Dr, Atlantis, FL 33462, USA

Erickson, Dennis — *Football Coach*
%Seattle Seahawks, 11220 NE 53rd St, Kirkland, WA 98033, USA

Erickson, Keith — *Basketball Player, Volleyball Player*
262 18th St, Santa Monica, CA 90402, USA

Erickson, Robert — *Composer*
%University of California, Music Dept, La Jolla, CA 92093, USA

Erickson, Scott G — *Baseball Player*
1183 Corral Ave, Sunnyvale, CA 94086, USA

Erickson, Steve — *Writer*
%Poseidon Press, 1230 Ave of Americas, New York, NY 10020, USA

Ericson, James D — *Businessman*
%Northwestern Mutual Life, 720 E Wisconsin Ave, Milwaukee, WI 53202, USA

Ericson, John — *Actor*
933 Camino De Chelly, Santa Fe, NM 87501, USA

Eriksen, Stein — *Skier*
7700 Stein Way, Park City, UT 84060, USA

Erikson, Raymond L — *Medical Researcher*
%Harvard University Medical School, 25 Shattuck St, Boston, MA 02115, USA

Erikson, Sheldon R — *Businessman*
%Western Co of North America, 5500 NW Central Dr, Houston, TX 77092, USA

Erixon, Jan — *Hockey Player*
PO Box 90111, Arlington, TX 76004, USA

Ermey, R Lee — *Actor*
%Metropolitan Talent Agency, 4526 Wilshire Blvd, Los Angeles, CA 90010, USA

Erni, Hans — *Artist*
6045 Meggen, Lucerne, Switzerland

Ernst, Richard R — *Nobel Chemistry Laureate*
Kurlistr 24, 8404 Winterthur, Switzerland

Eros, Peter — *Conductor*
222 Deervale Court, Vandalia, OH 45377, USA

Erroll of Hale, Frederick J — *Government Official, England*
%Bowater Corp, Bowater House, Knightsbridge, London SW1X 7LR, England

Erskine, Carl D — *Baseball Player*
6214 S Madison Ave, Anderson, IN 46013, USA

Erskine, Peter — *Jazz Drummer*
1727 Hill St, Santa Monica, CA 90405, USA

Erskine, Ralph — *Architect*
Gustav III's Vag, 170 11 Drottningholm, Sweden

Ertegun, Ahmet M — *Entertainment Executive*
%Atlantic Records, 75 Rockefeller Plaza, New York, NY 10019, USA

Ertl, Martina — *Skier*
Erthofe 17, 83661 Lenggries, Germany

Eruzione, Michael (Mike) — *Hockey Player*
28 Thornton St, Winthrop, MA 02152, USA

Erving, Julius W (Dr J) — *Basketball Player*
PO Box 8269, Cherry Hill, NJ 08002, USA

Ervolino, Frank — *Labor Leader*
%Laundry & Dry Cleaning Union, 107 Delaware Ave, Buffalo, NY 14202, USA

Erbe - Ervolino

Erwin, Bill *Actor*
%Dade/Schultz, 11846 Ventura Blvd, #100, Studio City, CA 91604, USA

Erwin, Henry E *WW II Army Air Corps Hero (CMH)*
Rt 2, Box 50, Leeds, AL 35094, USA

Erwitt, Elliott R *Photographer*
88 Central Park West, New York, NY 10023, USA

Erxleban, Russell *Football Player*
PO Box 164001, Austin, TX 78716, USA

Esaki, Leo *Nobel Physics Laureate*
Takezono 3-772, Tsukuba Ibaraki 305, Japan

Escalante, Jaime A *Educator*
%Hiram Johnson High School, 6879 14th Ave, Sacramento, CA 95820, USA

Eschenbach, Christoph *Conductor, Concert Pianist*
Maspalomas, Monte Leon 760625, Gran Canaria, Spain

Eschenmoser, Albert *Chemist*
Bergstra 9, 8700 Kusnacht (ZH), Switzerland

Esiason, Norman J (Boomer) *Football Player*
205 Fawn Court, East Islip, NY 11730, USA

Esmond, Carl *Actor*
576 Tigertail Road, Los Angeles, CA 90049, USA

Esperian, Kallen R *Opera Singer*
514 Lindseywood Cove, Memphis, TN 38117, USA

Espey, John *Writer*
PO Box 107, Topanga, CA 90290, USA

Esposito, Anthony J (Tony) *Hockey Player, Executive*
418 55th Ave, St Petersburg, FL 33706, USA

Esposito, Frank *Bowling Executive*
200 N State Route 17, Paramus, NJ 07652, USA

Esposito, Philip A (Phil) *Hockey Player, Executive*
401 Channelside Dr, Tampa, FL 33602, USA

Espy, A Michael (Mike) *Secretary, Agriculture*
154 Deertrail Lane, Madison, MS 39110, USA

Esquivel, Manuel *Prime Minister, Belize*
PO Box 165, Belize City, Belize

Esrey, William T *Businessman*
%Sprint Corp, 2300 Shawnee Mission Parkway, Westwood, KS 66205, USA

Esselborn, Bruce A *Businessman*
%Capsure Holdings, 2 N Riverside Plaza, Chicago, IL 60606, USA

Essex, David *Singer*
%London Mgmt, 2-4 Noel St, London W1V 3RB, England

Essex, Myron E *Microbiologist*
%Harvard School of Public Health, 665 Huntington Ave, Boston, MA 02115, USA

Essian, James S (Jim) *Baseball Manager*
134 Eckford, Troy, MI 48098, USA

Essman, Alyn V *Businessman*
%CPI Corp, 1706 Washington Ave, St Louis, MO 63103, USA

Esswood, Paul L V *Concert Singer*
Jasmine Cottage, 42 Ferring Lane, Ferring, West Sussex BN12 6QT, England

Esteban, Manuel A *Educator*
%California State University, President's Office, Chico, CA 95929, USA

Estefan, Emilio *Musician, Producer*
%Estefan Enterprises, 6205 SW 40th St, Miami, FL 33155, USA

Estefan, Gloria *Singer, Songwriter*
%Estefan Enterprises, 555 Jefferson Ave, Miami, FL 33139, USA

Estes, A Shawn *Baseball Player*
%Tim Estes, 974 Casey St, Gardnerville, NY 89410, USA

Estes, Bob *Golfer*
1821 Westlake Dr, #13-B, Austin, TX 78746, USA

Estes, Clarissa Pinkola *Psychologist*
%Ballantine Books, 201 E 50th St, New York, NY 10022, USA

Estes, Howell M, III *Air Force General*
CinC, USAF Space Command, Peterson Air Force Base, CO 80914, USA

Estes, Howell M, Jr *Air Force General, Businessman*
7603 Shadywood Road, Bethesda, MD 20817, USA

Estes, James *Cartoonist*
1103 Callahan St, Amarillo, TX 79106, USA

Estes, Robert *Actor*
910 Idaho Ave, Santa Monica, CA 90403, USA

E

Estes, Simon L *Opera Singer*
Hochstr 43, 8706 Feldmeilen, Switzerland

Estes, William K *Behavioral Scientist*
95 Irving St, Cambridge, MA 02138, USA

Esteve-Coll, Elizabeth *Museum Curator*
%Victoria & Albert Museum, South Kensington, London SW7 2RL, England

Estevez, Emilio *Actor, Director*
PO Box 4041, Malibu, CA 90264, USA

Estevez, Luis *Fashion Designer*
122 E 7th St, Los Angeles, CA 90014, USA

Estevez, Ramon *Actor*
837 Ocean Ave, #101, Santa Monica, CA 90403, USA

Estrada, Erik *Actor*
3768 Eureka Dr, North Hollywood, CA 91604, USA

Estrich, Susan R *Attorney*
%University of Southern California, Law Center, Los Angeles, CA 90089, USA

Estrin, Melvyn *Businessman*
%FoxMeyer Health Corp, 1220 Senlac Dr, Carrollton, TX 75006, USA

Eszterhas, Joseph A *Writer*
%William Morris Agency, 151 S El Camino Dr, Beverly Hills, CA 90212, USA

Etchegaray, Roger Cardinal *Religious Leader*
Piazza San Calisto, 00120 Vatican City

Etheridge, Melissa *Singer, Songwriter, Guitarist*
%W F Leopold Mgmt, 4425 Riverside Dr, #102, Burbank, CA 91505, USA

Ethridge, Mark F, III *Editor*
%Business Journal of Charlotte, 128 S Tryon St, #2200, Charlotte, NC 28202, USA

Etienne, Jean-Louis *Explorer*
%Think South, PO Box 4097, St Paul, MN 55104, USA

Etienne-Martin *Sculptor*
7 Rue Du Pot de Fer, 75005 Paris, France

Etrog, Sorel *Artist*
PO Box 5943, Station A, Toronto ON M5W 1P3, Canada

Etsel, Ed *Marksman*
%University of Virginia, Athletic Dept, Charlottesville, VA 22906, USA

Etter, Richard A *Financier*
%Bank of America Nevada, 300 S 4th St, Las Vegas, NV 89101, USA

Etzioni, Amitai W *Sociologist*
7110 Arran Place, Bethesda, MD 20817, USA

Etzwiler, Donnell D *Pediatrician*
%International Diabetes Center, 5000 W 39th St, Minneapolis, MN 55416, USA

Eubanks, Bob *Television Host*
5900 Highridge Road, Hidden Hills, CA 91302, USA

Eubanks, Kevin *Jazz Guitarist*
%Ted Kurland, 173 Brighton Ave, Boston, MA 02134, USA

Eure, Wesley *Actor*
PO Box 69405, Los Angeles, CA 90069, USA

Eustace, Joseph L *Governor General*
%Government House, Montrose, Saint Vincent & Grenadines

Evangelista, Linda *Model*
2640 Carmen Crest Dr, Los Angeles, CA 90068, USA

Evans, Anthony H *Educator*
%California State University, President's Office, San Bernardino, CA 92407, USA

Evans, Bill *Jazz Saxophonist, Keyboardist*
%Dept of Field Mgmt, 1501 Broadway, #1304, New York, NY 10036, USA

Evans, Brian *Basketball Player*
%Orlando Magic, Orlando Arena, 1 Magic Place, Orlando, FL 32801, USA

Evans, Dale *Actress*
15650 Seneca Road, Victorville, CA 92392, USA

Evans, Daniel J *Senator/Governor, WA, Educator*
%Daniel J Evans Assoc, 1111 3rd Ave, #3400, Seattle, WA 98101, USA

Evans, Darrell W *Baseball Player*
900 Sea Lane, #2, Corona del Mar, CA 92625, USA

Evans, Dick *Bowling Writer*
121 Morning Dove Court, Daytona Beach, FL 32119, USA

Evans, Dwayne *Track Athlete*
1923 E Caldwell St, Phoenix, AZ 85040, USA

Evans, Earl A, Jr *Biochemist*
1120 N Lake Shore Dr, Chicago, IL 60611, USA

Estes - Evans

Evans, Edward P — *Publisher*
712 5th Ave, #4900, New York, NY 10019, USA

Evans, Edwin C — *Physician*
500 Westover Dr NW, Atlanta, GA 30305, USA

Evans, Evans — *Actress*
3114 Abington Dr, Beverly Hills, CA 90210, USA

Evans, Faith — *Singer*
%William Morris Agency, 1325 Ave of Americas, New York, NY 10019, USA

Evans, Gene — *Actor*
PO Box 93, Medon, TN 38356, USA

Evans, Glen — *Molecular Biologist*
%Salk Institute, Molecular Biology Dept, PO Box 8500, San Diego, CA 92138, USA

Evans, Greg — *Cartoonist (Luann)*
216 Country Garden Lane, San Marcos, CA 92069, USA

Evans, Harold J — *Plant Physiologist*
14151 Redwood Court, Lake Oswego, OR 97034, USA

Evans, Harold M — *Editor*
%Random House, 201 E 50th St, New York, NY 10022, USA

Evans, J Handel — *Educator*
%San Jose State University, President's Office, San Jose, CA 95192, USA

Evans, J Thomas — *Wrestler*
607 S Fir Court, Broken Arrow, OK 74012, USA

Evans, Janet — *Swimmer*
8 Barnesburg, Dove Canyon, CA 92679, USA

Evans, John B — *Publisher*
%Murdoch Magazines, 755 2nd Ave, New York, NY 10017, USA

Evans, John R — *Foundation Executive*
%Rockefeller Foundation, 1133 Ave of Americas, New York, NY 10036, USA

Evans, John V — *Governor, ID*
%D L Evans Bank, 397 N Overland, Burley, ID 83318, USA

Evans, Kevin — *Businessman*
%Madge Networks, 2310 N 1st St, San Jose, CA 95131, USA

Evans, Lee — *Track Athlete*
%Quatar National Track Team, PO Box 7494, Dohar, Quatar

Evans, Linda — *Actress*
6714 Villa Madera Dr SW, Tacoma, WA 98499, USA

Evans, Mary Beth — *Actress*
PO Box 50105, Pasadena, CA 91115, USA

Evans, Michael — *Actor*
12530 Collins St, North Hollywood, CA 91607, USA

Evans, Raymond R (Ray) — *Football Player*
8449 Somerset Dr, Shawnee Mission, KS 66207, USA

Evans, Richard — *Sports Executive*
%Madison Square Garden, 4 Pennsylvania Plaza, New York, NY 10001, USA

Evans, Richard W — *Financier*
%Frost National Bank, 100 W Houston St, San Antonio, TX 78205, USA

Evans, Robert C — *Mountaineer*
Ardincaple, Capel Curig, Betws-y-Coed, Northern Wales, Wales

Evans, Robert E — *Financier*
%TCF Financial Corp, 801 Marquette Ave, Minneapolis, MN 55402, USA

Evans, Robert J (Bob) — *Movie Producer*
%Robert Evans Productions, Paramount Pictures, 5555 Melrose, Los Angeles, 90038, USA

Evans, Robert S — *Businessman*
%Crane Co, 100 1st Stamford Plaza, Stamford, CT 06902, USA

Evans, Ronald M — *Geneticist*
%Salk Institute, Gene Expression Laboratory, PO Box 85800, San Diego, CA 92186, USA

Evans, Rowland, Jr — *Columnist*
3125 "O" St NW, Washington, DC 20007, USA

Evans, Russell W — *Movie Producer*
Walnut Tree, Roehampton Gate, London SW15, England

Evans, Troy — *Actor*
PO Box 834, Lakeside, MT 59922, USA

Evans, Walker — *Truck, Off-Road Racing Driver*
%Walker Evans Racing, PO Box 2469, Riverside, CA 92516, USA

Evdokimova, Eva — *Ballerina*
%Gregori Productions, PO Box 1586, New York, NY 10150, USA

Eve, Trevor — *Actor*
%Julian Belfarge, 46 Albermarle St, London W1X 4PP, England

Everest, Frank K (Pete), Jr — *Test Pilot*
12440 E Barbary Coast Road, Tucson, AZ 85749, USA

Everett, Chad — *Actor*
5472 Island Forest Place, Westlake Village, CA 91362, USA

Everett, Danny — *Track Athlete*
%Santa Monica Track Club, 1801 Ocean Park Ave, #112, Santa Monica, CA 90405, USA

Everett, Doug — *Hockey Player*
10 Park St, Concord, NH 03301, USA

Everett, Jim — *Football Player*
%San Diego Chargers, Jack Murphy Stadium, Box 609609, San Diego, CA 92160, USA

Everett, Malcolm E, III — *Financier*
%First Union Corp, 1 First Union Center, Charlotte, NC 28288, USA

Everett, Rupert — *Actor*
%International Creative Mgmt, 76 Oxford St, London W1N 0AX, England

Everhard, Nancy — *Actress*
2751 Pelham Place, Los Angeles, CA 90068, USA

Everly, Donald (Don) — *Singer (Everly Brothers)*
PO Box 120725, Nashville, TN 37212, USA

Everly, Phil — *Singer (Everly Brothers)*
10414 Camarillo St, North Hollywood, CA 91602, USA

Evers, Charles — *Civil Rights Activist*
416 W Country Line Road, Tougaloo, MS 39174, USA

Evers, Jason — *Actor*
232 N Crescent Dr, #101, Beverly Hills, CA 90210, USA

Evers-Williams, Myrlie — *Association Executive*
%NAACP, 11718 Spring Haven Court, Ellicott City, MD 21042, USA

Eversley, Frederick J — *Sculptor*
1110 W Albert Kinney Blvd, Venice, CA 90291, USA

Everson, Corinna (Cory) — *Body Builder*
409 N Camden Dr, #205, Beverly Hills, CA 90210, USA

Evert, Christine M (Chris) — *Tennis Player*
701 NE 12th Ave, Fort Lauderdale, FL 33304, USA

Evigan, Greg — *Actor, Singer*
5472 Winnetka Ave, Woodland Hills, CA 91364, USA

Evora, Cesaria — *Singer*
%Monterey International, 200 W Superior, #202, Chicago, IL 60610, USA

Evren, Kenan — *President, Turkey; Army General*
Beyaz Ev Sokak 21, Armutalan, Marmaris, Turkey

Evron, Ephraim — *Government Official, Israel*
%Ministry of Foreign Affairs, Tel-Aviv, Israel

Ewald, Reinhold — *Astronaut, Germany*
%DLR Astronauterburo WT/AN, Linder Hohe, 51140 Cologne, Germany

Ewald, Robert H — *Businessman*
%Cray Research, 655-A Lone Oak Dr, Eagan, MN 55121, USA

Ewbank, Wilbur C (Weeb) — *Football Coach*
4160 Steamboat Bend E, #103, Fort Myers, FL 33919, USA

Ewing, Barbara — *Actress*
%Scott Marshall, 44 Perryn Road, London W3 7NA, England

Ewing, Maria L — *Opera Singer*
33 Bramerton St, London SW3, England

Ewing, Patrick A — *Basketball Player*
37 Summit St, Englewood Cliffs, NJ 07632, USA

Exum, Glenn — *Musician, Mountaineer*
PO Box 889, Thayne, WY 83127, USA

Eyadema, E Gnassingbe — *President, Togo; Army General*
%President's Office, Palais Presidentiel, Ave de la Marina, Lome, Togo

Eyes, Raymond — *Publisher*
%McCall's Magazine, 375 Lexington Ave, New York, NY 10017, USA

Eyre, Richard — *Movie, Theater, Television Director*
%Royal National Theater, South Bank, London SE1 9PX, England

Eysenck, Hans J — *Psychologist*
10 Dorchester Dr, London SE24, England

Eyskens, Mark — *Government Official, Belgium*
De Grunnelaan 23, 3001 Heverlee, Belgium

Eytchison, Ronald M — *Navy Admiral*
11 Prentice Lane, Signal Mountain, TN 37377, USA

Ezra, Derek — *Government Official, Businessman*
%House of Lords, Westminster, London SW1A 0PW, England

Fabares, Shelley *Actress, Singer*
MSC 826, PO Box 6010, Sherman Oaks, CA 91413, USA

Fabbricini, Tiziana *Opera Singer*
%Gianni Testa, Via Wrenteggio 31/6, 20146 Milan, Italy

Faber, Sandra M *Astronomer*
%Lick Observatory, Mount Hamilton, San Jose, CA 95140, USA

Fabi, Teo *Auto Racing Driver*
Via Bronzino 14, Milan, Italy

Fabian (Forte) *Singer*
1800 N Argyle Ave, #201, Los Angeles, CA 90028, USA

Fabian, John M *Astronaut*
%ANSER, Space Systems Dept, 1215 Jefferson Davis Highway, Arlington, VA 22202, USA

Fabio (Lanzoni) *Model, Actor*
PO Box 4, Inwood, NY 11696, USA

Fabiola Mora y Aragon, Dona *Queen Mother, Belgium*
%Royal Palace of Laeken, Laeken-Brussels, Belgium

Fabius, Laurent *Premier, France*
15 Place du Pantheon, 75005 Paris, France

Fabray, Nanette *Singer, Actress*
14350 W Sunset Blvd, Pacific Palisades, CA 90272, USA

Fabulous Moolah *Wrestler*
%TitanSports, 1241 E Main St, Stamford, CT 06902, USA

Face, Elroy L *Baseball Player*
608 Della Dr, #5-F, North Versailles, PA 15137, USA

Faddis, Jonathan (Jon) *Jazz Trumpeter, Flugelhorn Player*
%International Music Network, 2 Min St, #400, Gloucester, MA 01930, USA

Fadeyechev, Aleksei *Ballet Dancer*
%Bolshoi Theater, Teatralnaya Pl 1, 103009 Moscow, Russia

Fadeyechev, Nicolai B *Ballet Dancer*
%Bolshoi Theater, Teatralnaya Pl 1, 103009 Moscow, Russia

Fadiman, Clifton *Writer*
Beach Home 13, S S Plantation, PO Box 459, Captiva, FL 33924, USA

Fagan, Garth *Choreographer*
%State University of New York, Dance Dept, Brockport, NY 14420, USA

Fagan, John J *Labor Leader*
%International Teamsters Brotherhood, 25 Louisiana Ave NW, Washington, DC 20001, USA

Fagan, Kevin *Cartoonist (Drabble)*
26771 Ashford, Mission Viejo, CA 92692, USA

Fagen, Clifford B *Basketball Executive*
1021 Royal Saint George Dr, Naperville, IL 60563, USA

Fagen, Donald *Singer (Steely Dan); Songwriter*
%HK Mgmt, 8900 Wilshire Blvd, #300, Beverly Hills, CA 90211, USA

Fagerbakke, Bill *Actor*
1500 Will Geer Road, Topanga, CA 90290, USA

Faget, Maxime *Space Scientist*
%Space Industries International, 101 Courageous Dr, League City, TX 77573, USA

Faggin, Federico *Co-Inventor (Microprocessor)*
%Synaptics Inc, 2702 Orchard Parkway, San Jose, CA 95134, USA

Faggs Starr, Mae *Track Athlete*
10152 Shady Lane, Cincinnati, OH 45215, USA

Fagin, David K *Businessman*
%Golden Star Resources, 1990 N California Blvd, Walnut Creek, CA 94596, USA

Fahd Ibn Abdul Aziz *King, Saudi Arabia*
%Royal Palace, Royal Court, Riyadh, Saudi Arabia

Fahey, Jeff *Actor*
250 N Robertson Blvd, #518, Beverly Hills, CA 90211, USA

Fahn, Stanley *Neurologist*
%Columbia University, Neurology Dept, 710 W 168th St, New York, NY 10032, USA

Fahrenkopf, Frank J, Jr *Political Leader*
%Republican National Committee, 310 1st St SE, Washington, DC 20002, USA

Fain, Ferris R *Baseball Player*
PO Box 1357, Georgetown, CA 95634, USA

Fainsilber, Adrien *Architect*
7 Rue Salvador Allende, 92000 Nanterre, France

Fairbairn, Bruce *Actor*
%Century Artists, 1148 4th St, #206, Santa Monica, CA 90403, USA

Fairbanks, Douglas, Jr *Actor*
%Inverness Corp, 545 Madison Ave, New York, NY 10022, USA

F

Fabares - Fairbanks

Fairchild, Barbara — *Singer, Songwriter*
%Artist Direction Agency, 1017 16th Ave S, Nashville, TN 37212, USA

Fairchild, John B — *Publisher*
Chalet Bianchina, Talstr GR, 7250 Klosters, Switzerland

Fairchild, Morgan — *Actress*
3480 Blair Dr, Los Angeles, CA 90068, USA

Fairstein, Linda — *Writer, Attorney*
%Charles Scribner's Sons, 866 3rd Ave, New York, NY 10022, USA

Faison, Earl — *Football Player*
PO Box 711355, Santee, CA 92072, USA

Faith, Adam — *Singer, Actor*
Crockham Hill, Edenbridge, Kent, England

Faithfull, Marianne — *Singer, Songwriter, Actress*
Yew Tree Cottage, Aldridge, Berks, England

Fakir, Abdul (Duke) — *Singer (Four Tops)*
%International Creative Mgmt, 40 W 57th St, New York, NY 10019, USA

Falana, Lola — *Singer, Dancer*
%Capital Entertainment, 1201 "N" St NW, #A-5, Washington, DC 20005, USA

Falcao, Jose Freire Cardinal — *Religious Leader*
SHIS QL 12 Conj 12, Casa 01, 71 630-325 Brasilia, Brazil

Faldo, Nick — *Golfer*
%IMG, Pier House, Strand on Green, Chiswick, London W4 3NN, England

Falk, David B — *Sports Attorney*
%Falk Assoc, 5335 Wisconsin Ave NW, #850, Washington, DC 20015, USA

Falk, Lee H — *Cartoonist (Mandrake, Phantom)*
PO Box Z, Truro, MA 02666, USA

Falk, Paul — *Figure Skater*
Sybelstr 21, 40239 Dusseldorf, Germany

Falk, Peter — *Actor*
1004 N Roxbury Dr, Beverly Hills, CA 90210, USA

Falk, Randall M — *Religious Leader*
%Temple, 5015 Harding Road, Nashville, TN 37205, USA

Falkenburg McCrary, Jinx — *Model, Actress*
10 Shelter Rock Road, Manhasset, NY 11030, USA

Falkenstein, Claire — *Artist*
719 Ocean Front Walk, Venice, CA 90291, USA

Falkner, Keith — *Singer*
Low Cottages, Ilketshall Saint Margaraet, Bungay, Suffolk, England

Fallaci, Oriana — *Journalist*
%Rizzoli, 31 W 57th St, #400, New York, NY 10019, USA

Falldin, N O Thorbjorn — *Prime Minister, Sweden*
As, 870 16 Ramvik, Sweden

Fallon, William J — *Navy Admiral*
Dep CinC, US Atlantic Command, 1430 Mitscher Ave, Norfolk, VA 23551, USA

Fallows, James B — *Editor*
%US News & World Report, 2400 "N" St NW, Washington, DC 20037, USA

Falossi, David — *Artist*
%Adrienne Editions, 377 Geary St, San Francisco, CA 94102, USA

Faltings, Gerd — *Mathematician*
%Princeton University, Mathematics Dept, Princeton, NJ 08544, USA

Faludi, Susan C — *Journalist*
1032 Irving St, #204, San Francisco, CA 94122, USA

Falwell, Jerry L — *Religious Leader*
%Liberty Baptist Fellowship, 3765 Candler's Mountain Road, Lynchburg, VA 24502, USA

Fambrough, Charles — *Jazz Bassist*
%Zane Mgmt, The Bellvue, Broad & Walnut, Philadelphia, PA 19102, USA

Fanfani, Amintore — *Prime Minister, Italy*
Via XX Settembre 97, 00187 Rome, Italy

Fang Lizhi — *Astrophysicist; Political Activist*
%Cambridge University, Astronomy Institute, Cambridge, England

Fann, Al — *Actor*
6051 Hollywood Blvd, #207, Hollywood, CA 90028, USA

Fannin, Paul J — *Senator, AZ*
599 Orange Blossom Lane, Phoenix, AZ 85018, USA

Fanning, Katherine W — *Editor*
330 Beacon St, Boston, MA 02116, USA

Fanning, Mike — *Football Player*
6830 S Delaware Ave, Tulsa, OK 74136, USA

Fano, Ugo *Physicist*
5801 S Dorchester Ave, Chicago, IL 60637, USA

Faracy, Stephanie *Actress*
8765 Lookout Mountain Road, Los Angeles, CA 90046, USA

Faragalli, Lindy *Bowler*
113 N 5th Ave, Manville, NJ 08835, USA

Farenthold, Frances T *Women's Activist, Educator*
2929 Buffalo Speedway, #18-B, Houston, TX 77098, USA

Farentino, Debrah *Actress*
%Innovative Artists, 1999 Ave of Stars, #2850, Los Angeles, CA 90067, USA

Farentino, James *Actor*
1340 Londonderry Place, Los Angeles, CA 90069, USA

Fares, Muhammad Ahmed Al *Cosmonaut, Syria*
PO Box 1272, Aleppo, Syria

Fargis, Joe *Equestrian Rider*
11744 Marblestone Court, West Palm Beach, FL 33414, USA

Fargo, Donna *Singer*
%Prima-Donna Entertainment, PO Box 150527, Nashville, TN 37215, USA

Fargo, Thomas B *Navy Admiral*
Commander, US Naval Forces Mideast/5th Fleet, MacDill Air Force Base, FL 33621, USA

Farina, Battista (Pinin) *Industrial Designer*
%Pinitarina SpA, Via Lesna 78, 10095 Grugliasco, Turin, Italy

Farina, David *Religious Leader*
%Christian Church of North America, 41 Sherbrooke Road, Trenton, NJ 08638, USA

Farina, Dennis *Actor*
1201 Greenacre Ave, Los Angeles, CA 90046, USA

Farkas, Bertalan *Cosmonaut, Hungary*
A Magyar Koztarsasag, Kutato Urhajosa, Pf 25, 1885 Budapest, Hungary

Farkas, Ferenc *Composer*
Nagyatai-Utca 12, 1026 Budapest, Hungary

Farley, Carole *Opera, Concert Singer*
270 Riverside Dr, New York, NY 10025, USA

Farley, Chris *Comedian, Actor*
%Brillstein/Grey, 9150 Wilshire Blvd, #350, Beverly Hills, CA 90212, USA

Farley, William F *Businessman*
%Fruit of the Loom, Sears Tower, 233 S Wacker Dr, #500, Chicago, IL 60606, USA

Farlow, Talmadge H (Tal) *Jazz Guitarist*
%Richard A Barz, Rt 1, Box 91, Tannersville, PA 18372, USA

Farmer, Arthur S (Art) *Jazz Trumpeter, Flugelhorn Player*
%Joel Chriss, 300 Mercer St, #3-J, New York, NY 10003, USA

Farmer, James L, Jr *Civil Rights Activist*
3805 Guinea Station Road, Fredericksburg, VA 22408, USA

Farmer, Jim G *Financier*
%Boatmen's Arkansas, 200 W Capitol Ave, Little Rock, AR 72201, USA

Farmer, Richard G *Physician*
9126 Town Gate Lane, Bethesda, MD 20817, USA

Farnam, Walter E *Businessman*
%General Accident Insurance, 436 Walnut St, Philadelphia, PA 19106, USA

Farner, Donald S *Zoo Physiologist*
%University of Washington, Zoology Dept, Seattle, WA 98195, USA

Farner, Mark *Singer, Guitarist*
%Bobby Roberts, 909 Meadowlark Lane, Goodlettesville, TN 37072, USA

Farnsworth, Richard *Actor*
PO Box 215, Lincoln, NM 88338, USA

Farquhar, John W *Physician*
%Stanford University Med School, Disease Prevention Center, Stanford, CA 94305, USA

Farquhar, Robert W *Rocket Scientist*
%Johns Hopkins University, Applied Physics Laboratory, Laurel, MD 20723, USA

Farr, Bruce *Marine Architect*
%Bruce Farr Assoc, 613 3rd St, Annapolis, MD 21403, USA

Farr, Jaime *Actor*
99 Buckskin Road, Canoga Park, CA 91307, USA

Farr, Mel, Sr *Football Player*
4525 Lakeview Court, Bloomfield Hills, MI 48301, USA

Farrakhan, Louis *Religious Leader*
%Nation of Islam, 734 W 79th St, Chicago, IL 60620, USA

Farrar, Donald K *Businessman*
%Imo Industries, 1009 Lenox Dr, Lawrenceville, NJ 08648, USA

Farrar, Frank L *Governor, SD*
203 9th Ave, Britton, SD 57430, USA

Farrel, Franklin *Hockey Player*
89 Notch Hill Road, #223, North Bransford, CT 06471, USA

Farreley, Alexander *Governor, VI*
%Governor's Office, Government Offices, Charlotte Amalie, VI 00801, USA

Farrell, David C *Businessman*
%May Department Stores, 611 Olive St, St Louis, MO 63101, USA

Farrell, Eileen *Opera Singer*
72 Louis St, Staten Island, NY 10304, USA

Farrell, Joseph C *Businessman*
%Pittston Co, First Stamford Plaza, Stamford, CT 06912, USA

Farrell, Lawrence P, Jr *Air Force General*
Deputy CofS for Plans/Programs, HqUSAF, Pentagon, Washington, DC 20330, USA

Farrell, Mike *Actor*
PO Box 6010, MSC 828, Sherman Oaks, CA 91413, USA

Farrell, Sean *Football Player*
13711 Halliford Dr, Tampa, FL 33624, USA

Farrell, Sharon *Actress*
1619 Oak Dr, Topanga, CA 90290, USA

Farrell, Shea *Actor*
125 S Bowling Green Way, Los Angeles, CA 90049, USA

Farrell, Suzanne *Ballet Dancer*
%New York City Ballet, Lincoln Center Plaza, New York, NY 10023, USA

Farrell, Terence (Terry) *Architect*
17 Hatton St, London NW8 8PL, England

Farrell, Tommy *Actor*
5225 Riverton Ave, North Hollywood, CA 91601, USA

Farrell, W James *Businessman*
%Illinois Tool Works, 3600 W Lake Ave, Glenview, IL 60025, USA

Farrimond, Richard A *Astronaut, England*
95 Druid Stoke Ave, Stoke Bishop, Bristol BS9 1DE, England

Farrington, Bob *Harness Racing Driver*
Bruce Road, RR #1, Mokena, IL 60448, USA

Farrington, Jerry S *Businessman*
%Texas Utilities Co, 1601 Bryan St, Dallas, TX 75201, USA

Farris, Dionne *Singer*
%Creative Artists Agency, 9830 Wilshire Blvd, Beverly Hills, CA 90212, USA

Farris, Joseph *Cartoonist*
PO Box 4203, New York, NY 10017, USA

Farriss, Jon *Drummer, Singer (INXS)*
8 Hayes St, #1, Neutral Bay 20891 NSW, Australia

Farrow, Mia *Actress*
124 Henry Sanford Road, Bridgewater, CT 06752, USA

Fasanella, Ralph *Artist*
15 Chester St, Ardskey, NY 10502, USA

Fasi, Frank F *Mayor*
2054 Makiki St, Honolulu, HI 96822, USA

Fass, Horst *Photographer*
12 Norwich St, London EC4A, England

Fassbaender, Brigitte *Opera Singer*
%Jennifer Selby, Haiming 2, 83119 Obing, Germany

Fassel, Jim *Football Coach*
%New York Giants, Giants Stadium, East Rutherford, NJ 07073, USA

Fast, Darrell *Religious Leader*
%Mennonite Church General Conference, 722 Main St, Newton, KS 67114, USA

Fast, Howard M *Writer*
%Houghton Mifflin Co, 2 Park Ave, Boston, MA 02116, USA

Fauci, Anthony S *Immunologist*
3012 43rd St NW, Washington, DC 20016, USA

Faucon, Bernard *Photographer*
6 Rue Barbanegre, 75019 Paris, France

Faulk, Marshall *Football Player*
%Indianapolis Colts, 7001 W 56th St, Indianapolis, IN 46254, USA

Faulkner, John *Organic Chemist*
%Scripps Institution of Oceanography, La Jolla, CA 92093, USA

Faulkner, Sidney *Businessman*
%Oak Technology, 139 Kifer Court, Sunnyvale, CA 94086, USA

Faulstich, James R *Financier*
%Federal Home Loan Bank, 1501 4th Ave, Seattle, WA 98101, USA
Faure, Maurice H *Government Official, France*
28 Blvd Raspail, 75007 Paris, France
Faustino, David *Actor*
8075 W 3rd St, #303, Los Angeles, CA 90048, USA
Fauvet, Jacques *Editor*
5 Rue Louis-Boilly, 70016 Paris, France
Favier, Jean-Jacques *Spatinaut, France*
%CEREM, CENG, 53 Ave des Martyrs, 38041 Grenoble Cedex, France
Favre, Brett *Football Player*
3071 Gothic Court, Green Bay, WI 54313, USA
Fawcett, Don W *Anatomist*
1224 Lincoln Road, Missoula, MT 59802, USA
Fawcett, Farrah *Actress, Model*
9507 Heather Road, Beverly Hills, CA 90210, USA
Fawcett, Sherwood L *Research Physicist*
2820 Margate Road, Columbus, OH 43221, USA
Faxon, Brad *Golfer*
77 Rumstick Road, Barrington, RI 02806, USA
Fay, David B *Golf Executive*
%U S Golf Assn, Golf House, Liberty Corner Road, Far Hills, NJ 07931, USA
Fay, William M *Judge*
%US Tax Court, 400 2nd St NW, Washington, DC 20217, USA
Faye, Herbie *Actor*
1501 Kenneth Road, Glendale, CA 91201, USA
Fazio, Tom *Golf Course Architect*
%Fazio Golf Course Designers, 109 S Main St, Hendersonville, NC 28792, USA
Fazzini, Enrico *Neurologist*
%New York University, Medical Center, 550 1st Ave, New York, NY 10016, USA
Fears, Thomas (Tom) *Football Player*
126 24th St, Newport Beach, CA 92663, USA
Featherston, C Moxley *Judge*
%US Tax Court, 400 2nd St NW, Washington, DC 20217, USA
Feck, Luke M *Editor*
6880 Worthington Road, Westerville, OH 43082, USA
Federko, Bernie *Hockey Player*
2219 Devonsbrook Dr, Chesterfield, MO 63005, USA
Fedoseyev, Vladimir I *Conductor*
%Moscow House of Recording, Kachalova 24, 121069 Moscow, Russia
Feher, George *Physicist*
%University of California, Physics Dept, 9500 Gilman Dr, La Jolla, CA 92093, USA
Fehr, Donald M *Labor Leader*
%Major League Baseball Players Assn, 805 3rd Ave, New York, NY 10022, USA
Fehr, Rick *Golfer*
2014 222nd Ave NE, Redmond, WA 98053, USA
Fehr, Steve *Bowler*
6216 Highcedar Court, Cincinnati, OH 45233, USA
Feifel, Herman *Psychologist*
360 S Burnside Ave, Los Angeles, CA 90036, USA
Feiffer, Jules *Cartoonist*
RR 1, Box 440, Vineyard Haven, MA 02568, USA
Feigenbaum, Armand V *Businessman, Systems Engineer*
%General Systems, Berkshire Common, South St, Pittsfield, MA 01201, USA
Feigenbaum, Edward A *Computer Scientist*
1017 Cathcart Way, Stanford, CA 94305, USA
Feigenbaum, Mitchell J *Physicist*
%Cornell University, Physics Dept, Ithaca, NY 14853, USA
Feilden, Bernard M *Architect*
Stiffkey Old Hall, Wells-Next-to-the-Sea, Norfolk NR23 1QJ, England
Fein, Bernard *Businessman*
%United Industrial Corp, 18 E 48th St, New York, NY 10017, USA
Feininger, Andreas B L *Photographer*
5 E 22nd St, #15-P, New York, NY 10010, USA
Feinstein, A Richard *Physician*
164 Linden St, New Haven, CT 06511, USA
Feinstein, Michael *Singer, Pianist*
%International Creative Mgmt, 40 W 57th St, New York, NY 10019, USA

F

Felch, William C — *Physician*
26337 Carmelo St, Carmel, CA 93923, USA

Feld, Eliot — *Dancer, Choreographer*
%Feld Ballet, 890 Broadway, New York, NY 10003, USA

Feld, Kenneth — *Entertainment Executive*
%Ringling Bros Circus, 8607 Westwood Circle, Vienna, VA 22182, USA

Feldberg, Sumner L — *Businessman*
%TJX Companies, 770 Cochituate Road, Framingham, MA 01701, USA

Feldenkrais, Moshe — *Psychologist*
University of Tel-Aviv, Psychology Dept, Tel-Aviv, Israel

Felder, Don — *Singer, Guitarist (Eagles)*
PO Box 6051, Malibu, CA 90264, USA

Felder, Raoul Lionel — *Attorney*
437 Madison Ave, New York, NY 10022, USA

Feldman, Bella — *Artist*
12 Summit Lane, Berkeley, CA 94708, USA

Feldman, Corey — *Actor*
%Thomas, 3209 Tareco Dr, Los Angeles, CA 90068, USA

Feldman, Jerome M — *Physician*
%Duke University, Medical Center, Box 2963, Durham, NC 27715, USA

Feldman, Myer — *Government Official*
%Ginsberg Feldman Bress, 1250 Connecticut Ave NW, Washington, DC 20036, USA

Feldman, Sandra (Sandy) — *Labor Leader*
%American Federation of Teachers, 555 New Jersey Ave NW, Washington, DC 20001, USA

Feldon, Barbara — *Actress, Model*
14 E 74th St, New York, NY 10021, USA

Feldshuh, Tovah — *Actress*
322 Central Park West, #11-B, New York, NY 10025, USA

Feldstein, Martin S — *Government Official, Economist*
147 Clifton St, Belmont, MA 02178, USA

Felici, Pericle Cardinal — *Religious Leader*
Via Pfeiffer 10, 10093 Rome, Italy

Feliciano, Jose — *Singer, Guitarist*
%Peter Zaffina, 34 E Main St, Weston, CT 06880, USA

Felipe — *Crown Prince, Spain*
%Palacio de la Zarzuela, Madrid, Spain

Felisiak, Robert — *Fencer*
Kreuzberg 13, 97953 Konigheim, Germany

Felke, Petra — *Track Athlete*
%SC Motor Jena, Wollnitzevstr 42, 07749 Jena, Germany

Felker, Clay — *Editor*
322 E 57th St, New York, NY 10022, USA

Fell, Norman — *Actor*
4335 Marina City Dr, Marina del Rey, CA 90292, USA

Feller, Robert W A (Bob) — *Baseball Player*
PO Box 157, Gates Mill, OH 44040, USA

Fellows, Edith — *Actress*
2016 1/2 N Vista del Mar, Los Angeles, CA 90068, USA

Felsenstein, Lee — *Inventor (Portable Computer)*
2490 Greer Road, Palo Alto, CA 94303, USA

Felton, John — *Singer (The Diamonds)*
%Moments Mgmt, 520 Washington Blvd, #393, Marina del Rey, CA 90292, USA

Felton, Norman F — *Movie, Television Producer*
%Arena Productions, 23388 Mulholland Dr, Woodland Hills, CA 91364, USA

Felts, Narvel — *Singer, Songwriter*
2005 Narvel Felts Way, Maiden, MO 63863, USA

Felts, William R, Jr — *Physician*
1492 Hampton Hill Circle, McLean, VA 22101, USA

Feltsman, Vladimir — *Concert Pianist*
%Columbia Artists Mgmt Inc, 165 W 57th St, New York, NY 10019, USA

Fencik, Gary — *Football Player*
1134 W Schubert Ave, Chicago, IL 60614, USA

Fender, Freddy — *Singer, Songwriter, Guitarist*
PO Box 270540, Corpus Christi, TX 78427, USA

Fenech, Jeff — *Boxer*
PO Box 21, Hardys Bay, NSW 2257, Australia

Fenech-Adami, Edward — *Prime Minister, Malta*
%Education Ministry, Floriana, Auberge de Castille, Valleta, Malta

Fenical, William	*Organic Chemist*

Fenical, William — *Organic Chemist*
%Scripps Institution of Oceanography, Organic Chemistry Dept, La Jolla, CA 92093, USA

Fenimore, Robert (Bob) — *Football Player*
1214 Fairway Dr, Stillwater, OK 74074, USA

Fenley, Molissa — *Dancer, Choreographer*
%Molissa Fenley Dancers, PO Box 450, Prince Street Station, New York, NY 10012, USA

Fenn, Sherilyn — *Actress*
2934 N Beverly Glen Circle, #108, Sherman Oaks, CA 91403, USA

Fenswick, J Henry — *Editor*
%Modern Maturity Magazine, Editorial Dept, 3200 E Carson St, Lakewood, CA 90712, USA

Feoktistov, Konstantin P — *Cosmonaut*
%Potchta Kosmonavtov, Moskovskoi Oblasti, 141160 Syvisdny Goroduk, Russia

Fergason, James L (Jim) — *Inventor (Thermal Imaging Device)*
%Optical Shields Inc, 38930 Blacow Road, Fremont, CA 94536, USA

Ferguson Cullum, Cathy — *Swimmer*
17215 Palm St, Fountain Valley, CA 92708, USA

Ferguson, Charles A — *Editor*
1448 Joseph St, New Orleans, LA 70115, USA

Ferguson, Clarence C, Jr — *Diplomat, Lawyer*
%Harvard University, Law School, Cambridge, MA 02138, USA

Ferguson, Daniel C — *Businessman*
%Newell Co, Newell Center, 29 E Stephenson St, Freeport, IL 61032, USA

Ferguson, Frederick E — *Vietnam War Army Hero (CMH)*
106 E Stellar Parkway, Chandler, AZ 85226, USA

Ferguson, James (Jim) — *Water Polo Player*
26931 Whitehouse Road, Santa Clarita, CA 91351, USA

Ferguson, Jay — *Actor*
PO Box 57078, Sherman Oaks, CA 91413, USA

Ferguson, Joe — *Football Player, Coach*
3469 Par Court, Fayetteville, AR 72703, USA

Ferguson, Maynard — *Jazz Trumpeter*
PO Box 716, Ojai, CA 93024, USA

Ferguson, Ronald E — *Businessman*
%General Re Corp, 695 E Main St, Stamford, CT 06902, USA

Ferguson, Tom — *Rodeo Rider*
%General Delivery, Miami, OK 74354, USA

Ferguson, Vagas — *Football Player*
805 N 13th St, Richmond, IN 47374, USA

Ferguson, William C — *Businessman*
%Nynex Corp, 1095 Ave of Americas, New York, NY 10036, USA

Ferguson-Winn, Mabel — *Track Athlete*
2575 S Steele Road, #206, San Bernardino, CA 92408, USA

Fergusson, Frances D — *Educator*
%Vassar College, President's Office, Poughkeepsie, NY 12603, USA

Ferland, E James — *Businessman*
%Public Service Enterprise, 80 Park Plaza, Newark, NJ 07102, USA

Ferlinghetti, Lawrence — *Writer, Publisher*
%City Lights Booksellers, 261 Columbus Ave, San Francisco, CA 94133, USA

Fernandez Reyna, Leonel — *President, Dominican Republic*
%Ofica del Presidente, Santo Domingo DN, Dominican Republic

Fernandez, C Sidney (Sid) — *Baseball Player*
1011 Mokulua Dr, Kailua, HI 96734, USA

Fernandez, Juan — *Actor*
%Don Buchwald, 9229 Sunset Blvd, #710, Los Angeles, CA 90069, USA

Fernandez, Lisa — *Softball Player*
PO Box 121034, Lakewood, CA 90711, USA

Fernandez, Mario F — *Artist*
1415 5th St S, #A, Hopkins, MN 55343, USA

Fernandez, Mary Joe — *Tennis Player*
%Women's Tennis Assn, 133 1st St NE, St Petersburg, FL 33701, USA

Fernandez, O Antonio (Tony) — *Baseball Player*
Calle N-3, Restauracion, San Pedro de Macoris, Dominican Republic

Ferragamo, Vince — *Football Player*
6715 Horseshoe Road, Orange, CA 92869, USA

Ferrante, Art — *Pianist (Ferrante & Teicher)*
%Scott Smith, 12224 Avila Dr, Kansas City, MO 64145, USA

Ferrara, Abel — *Movie Director*
%William Morris Agency, 151 S El Camino Dr, Beverly Hills, CA 90212, USA

F

Fenical - Ferrara

Ferrara, Arthur V	*Businessman*
%Guardian Life Insurance, 201 Park Ave S, New York, NY 10003, USA	
Ferrare, Cristina	*Model, Entertainer*
1280 Stone Canyon Road, Los Angeles, CA 90077, USA	
Ferrari, Michael R, Jr	*Educator*
%Drake University, President's Office, Des Moines, IA 50311, USA	
Ferrari, Tina	*Dancer, Wrestler*
2901 S Las Vegas Blvd, Las Vegas, NV 89109, USA	
Ferraro, Geraldine A	*Representative, NY*
%Keck Mahin Cate Koehler, 220 E 42nd St, New York, NY 10017, USA	
Ferraro, John	*Football Player*
641 N Wilcox Ave, Los Angeles, CA 90004, USA	
Ferraro, Ray	*Hockey Player*
122 Oakridge, Unionville, CT 06085, USA	
Ferrazzi, Ferruccio	*Artist*
Piazza delle Muse, Via G G Porro 27, 00197 Rome, Italy	
Ferrazzi, Pierpaolo	*Kayak Athlete*
%EuroGrafica, Via del Progresso, 36035 Marano Vicenza, Italy	
Ferre, Gianfranco	*Fashion Designer*
Villa Della Spiga 19/A, 20121 Milan, Italy	
Ferrell Edmonson, Barbara	*Track Athlete*
239 N Hillcrest Dr, Inglewood, CA 90301, USA	
Ferrell, Conchata	*Actress*
1335 N Seward St, Los Angeles, CA 90028, USA	
Ferrell, Rachelle	*Singer*
%Dan Cleary Mgmt, 1801 Ave of Stars, #1105, Los Angeles, CA 90067, USA	
Ferrer, Lupita	*Actress*
904 N Bedford Dr, Beverly Hills, CA 90210, USA	
Ferrer, Mel	*Actor*
6590 Camino Caretta, Carpinteria, CA 93013, USA	
Ferrer, Miguel	*Actor*
%Gersh Agency, 232 N Canon Dr, Beverly Hills, CA 90210, USA	
Ferrero, Louis P	*Businessman*
PO Box 675744, Rancho Santa Fe, CA 92067, USA	
Ferrigno, Lou	*Actor, Bodybuilder*
PO Box 1671, Santa Monica, CA 90406, USA	
Ferris, John	*Swimmer*
1961 Klamath River Dr, Rancho Cordova, CA 95670, USA	
Ferriss, David M (Boo)	*Baseball Player*
510 Robinson Dr, Cleveland, MS 38732, USA	
Ferritor, Daniel E	*Educator*
%University of Arkansas, Chancellor's Office, Fayetteville, AR 72701, USA	
Ferron	*Singer, Songwriter*
%JR Productions, 4930 Paradise Dr, Tiburon, CA 94920, USA	
Ferry, Bryan	*Singer, Songwriter*
%Cohen Brothers Mgmt, 8380 Melrose Ave, #210, Los Angeles, CA 92805, USA	
Ferry, Danny	*Basketball Player*
%Cleveland Cavaliers, 2923 Statesboro Road, Richfield, OH 44286, USA	
Ferry, David	*Writer*
%Wellesley College, English Dept, Wellesley, MA 02181, USA	
Ferry, John D	*Chemist*
5015 Sheboygan Ave, #212, Madison, WI 53705, USA	
Feshbach, Herman	*Physicist*
5 Sedgwick Road, Cambridge, MA 02138, USA	
Festinger, Leon	*Psychologist*
37 W 12th St, New York, NY 10011, USA	
Fetisov, Viacheslav	*Hockey Player*
82 Cummings Circle, West Orange, NJ 07052, USA	
Fetterhoff, Robert	*Religious Leader*
%Fellowship of Grace Brethern, PO Box 386, Winona Lake, IN 46590, USA	
Fettman, Martin J	*Veterinarian, Astronaut*
%Colorado State University, Pathology Dept, Fort Collins, CO 80523, USA	
Feuer, Cy	*Theatrical, Movie Producer*
%Feuer & Martin, 630 Park Ave, New York, NY 10021, USA	
Feuillere, Edwige	*Actress*
141 Rue de Longchamp, 92200 Neuilly-Sur-Seine, France	
Feulner, Edwin J, Jr	*Foundation Executive*
%Heritage Foundation, 214 Massachusetts Ave NE, Washington, DC 20002, USA	

Fey, Michael *Cartoonist (Committed)*
%United Feature Syndicate, 200 Madison Ave, New York, NY 10016, USA
Fibiger, John A *Businessman*
%Transam Life Cos, 1159 S Olive St, Los Angeles, CA 90015, USA
Fichandler, Zelda *Theater Producer, Director*
%Arena Stages, 6th & Maine SW, Washington, DC 20024, USA
Fichtel-Mauritz, Anja *Fencer*
Drittigheimer Weg 26, 97941 Tauberbischofsheim, Germany
Fidrych, Mark S *Baseball Player*
260 West St, Northboro, MA 01532, USA
Fiechter, Jonathan L *Financier*
%Office of Thrift Supervision, 1700 "G" St NW, Washington, DC 20552, USA
Fiedler, Jens *Cyclist*
Bruno-Granz-Str 48, 09122 Chemnitz, Germany
Fiedler, John *Actor*
225 Adams St, #10-B, Brooklyn, NY 11201, USA
Fiedler, Leslie A *Writer, Critic*
154 Morris Ave, Buffalo, NY 14214, USA
Field, Chelsea *Actress*
%Troxell, 1001 Roscomare Road, Los Angeles, CA 90077, USA
Field, Frederick (Ted) *Entertainment Executive*
%Interscope Communications, 10900 Wilshire Blvd, Los Angeles, CA 90024, USA
Field, George B *Theoretical Astrophysicist*
%Harvard University Observatory, 60 Garden St, Cambridge, MA 02138, USA
Field, Helen *Opera Singer*
%Lies Askonas Ltd, 186 Drury Lane, London WC2B 5RY, England
Field, John W, Jr *Financier*
%J P Morgan Delaware, 902 Market St, Wilmingtonm, DE 19801, USA
Field, Marshall *Publisher*
%Field Corp, 333 W Wacker Dr, Chicago, IL 60606, USA
Field, Sally *Actress*
%Fogwood Films, PO Box 492417, Los Angeles, CA 90049, USA
Field, Shirley Ann *Actress*
%London Mgmt, 2-4 Noel St, London W1V 3RB, England
Fielder, Cecil G *Baseball Player*
700 Pinehurst Ave, Melbourne, FL 32940, USA
Fields, Debbi *Businesswoman*
%Mrs Fields Cookies, 462 Bearcat Dr, Salt Lake City, UT 84115, USA
Fields, Harold T, Jr *Army General*
126 Deer Run Strut, Enterprise, AL 36330, USA
Fields, Holly *Actress*
%David Shapira, 15301 Ventura Blvd, #345, Sherman Oaks, CA 91403, USA
Fields, Kim *Actress*
825 3/4 N Sweetzer Ave, Los Angeles, CA 90069, USA
Fiennes, Ralph *Actor*
%Larry Dalzell Assoc, 17 Broad Court, #12, London WC2B 5QN, England
Fiennes, Ranulph T-W *Transglobal Explorer*
Greenlands, Exford, Minehead, West Sussex, England
Fierstein, Harvey F *Writer, Actor*
1479 Carla Ridge Dr, Beverly Hills, CA 90210, USA
Fife, Bernard *Businessman*
%Standard Motor Products, 37-18 Northern Blvd, Long Island City, NY 11101, USA
Figg-Currier, Cindy *Golfer*
109 Blue Jay Dr, Austin, TX 78734, USA
Figgis, Mike *Movie Director*
%Steven R Pines, 520 Broadway, #600, Santa Monica, CA 90401, USA
Figini, Luigi *Architect*
Via Perone di S Martino 8, Milan, Italy
Figini, Michela *Skier*
6799 Prato-Leventina, Switzerland
Figueiredo, Joao Baptista de *President, Brazil; Army General*
Av Prefeito Mendes de Moraes 1400/802, S Conrado, Rio de Janeiro, Brazil
Figueres Olsen, Jose M *President, Costa Rica*
%President's Office, Apdo 520-2010, San Jose 1000, Costa Rica
Fikrig, Erol *Immunologist*
%Yale University, Medical Center, Infectious Disease Dept, New Haven, CT 06510, USA
Filatova, Ludmila P *Opera Singer*
Ryleyevastr 6, #13, St Petersburg, Russia

F

Filchock, Frank *Football Player*
1725 SW Fernwood Dr, Lake Oswego, OR 97034, USA
Filion, Herve *Harness Racing Driver*
104 Yale St, Roslyn Heights, NY 11577, USA
Filipacchi, Daniel *Publisher*
%Hachette Filipacchi, 2-6 Rue Ancelle, 92525 Neuilly-Sur-Seine, France
Filipchenko, Anatoly N *Cosmonaut; Air Force General*
%Potchta Kosmonavtov, Moskovskoi Oblasti, 141160 Syvisdny Goroduk, Russia
Fill, Dennis C *Businessman*
%Westmark International, 701 5th Ave, Seattle, WA 98104, USA
Filmus, Tully *Artist*
4 Fern Hill, Great Barrington, MA 01230, USA
Finch, Jon *Actor*
%Conway Van Gelder Robinson, 18-21 Jermyn St, London SW1Y 6NB, England
Finch, Larry *Basketball Player, Coach*
5962 Lake Tide Cove, Memphis, TN 38120, USA
Finchem, Timothy W *Golf Executive*
%Professional Golfer's Assn, Sawgrass, Ponte Vedra Beach, FL 32082, USA
Finder, Joseph *Writer*
%William Morrow, 1350 Ave of Americas, New York, NY 10016, USA
Findlay, Conn *Rower, Yachtsman*
1920 Oak Knoll, Belmont, CA 94002, USA
Fine, Travis *Actor*
%J Michael Bloom, 9255 Sunset Blvd, #710, Los Angeles, CA 90069, USA
Fingers, Roland G (Rollie) *Baseball Player*
4894 Eastcliff Court, San Diego, CA 92130, USA
Fink, Donald E *Editor*
%Aviation Week Magazine, 1221 Ave of Americas, New York, NY 10020, USA
Fink, Gerald R *Geneticist*
40 Alston Road, Chestnut Hill, MA 02167, USA
Finkel, Fyvush *Actor*
%Silver Massetti Szatmary, 8730 Sunset Blvd, #480, Los Angeles, CA 90069, USA
Finkel, Shelly *Boxing Promoter*
310 Madison Ave, #804, New York, NY 10017, USA
Finlay, Frank *Actor*
%Al Parker, 55 Park Lane, London W1Y 3DD, England
Finley, Charles E (Chuck) *Baseball Player*
1 Barrenger Court, Newport Beach, CA 92660, USA
Finley, Karen *Conceptual Artist*
%Kitchen Center for Video-Music-Dance, 512 W 9th, New York, NY 10018, USA
Finley, Michael *Basketball Player*
%Dallas Mavericks, Reunion Arena, 777 Sports St, Dallas, TX 75207, USA
Finley, Steven A (Steve) *Baseball Player*
2502 Ocean Front, Del Mar, CA 92014, USA
Finn, John W *WW II Navy Hero (CMH)*
Star Route, Box 17, Pine Valley, CA 91962, USA
Finn, Richard H *Financier*
%Transamerica Finance Group, 1150 S Olive St, Los Angeles, CA 90015, USA
Finn, Tim *Singer (Split Enz, Crowded House)*
%Grant Thomas Mgmt, 3 Mitchell Road, Rose Bay, Sydney NSW 2029, Australia
Finnane, Daniel F *Basketball Executive*
%Golden State Warriors, 7000 Coliseum Way, Oakland, CA 94621, USA
Finnbogagottir, Vigdis *President, Iceland*
%President's Office, Sto'marradshusini v/Laekjartog, Reykjavik, Iceland
Finnegan, John R, Sr *Editor*
%St Paul Pioneer Press Dispatch, 345 Cedar St, St Paul, MN 55101, USA
Finneran Rittenhouse, Sharon *Swimmer*
212 Harbor Dr, Santa Cruz, CA 95062, USA
Finneran, John G *Navy Admiral*
5600 Beam Court, Bethesda, MD 20817, USA
Finney, Albert *Actor*
39 Seymour Walk, London SW10, England
Finney, Allison *Golfer*
72750 Cactus Court, #A, Palm Desert, CA 92260, USA
Finney, Ross Lee *Composer*
35 Barranca Road, Los Alamos, NM 87544, USA
Finnie, Linda A *Concert Singer*
16 Golf Course, Girvan, Ayrshire KA26 9HW, England

Finster, Howard	*Artist*
Rt 2, Box 106-A, Summerville, GA 30747, USA	
Finsterwald, Dow	*Golfer*
%Broadmoor Golf Club, 1 Lake Circle, Colorado Springs, CO 80906, USA	
Fiondella, Robert W	*Businessman*
%Phoenix Home Mutual Life, 150 Bright Meadow Blvd, Enfield, CT 06082, USA	
Fiore, William J (Bill)	*Actor*
%Paradigm Agency, 10100 Santa Monica Blvd, #2500, Los Angeles, CA 90067, USA	
Fiorentino, Linda	*Actress*
%United Talent Agency, 9560 Wilshire Blvd, #500, Beverly Hills, CA 90212, USA	
Fiorillo, Elisa	*Opera Singer*
%Columbia Artists Mgmt Inc, 165 W 57th St, New York, NY 10019, USA	
Fippin, Cornelius J	*Financier*
%Golden 1 Credit Union, 6507 4th St, Sacramento, CA 95817, USA	
Fireman, Paul B	*Businessman*
%Reebok International, 100 Technology Center Dr, Stroughton, MA 02072, USA	
Firestone, Roy	*Sportscaster*
%Seizen/Wallach Productions, 257 Rodeo Dr, Beverly Hills, CA 90212, USA	
First, Neal	*Geneticist*
%University of Wisconsin, Genetics Dept, Madison, WI 53706, USA	
Firth, Peter	*Actor*
%Markham & Froggatt, Julian House, 4 Windmill St, London W1P 1HF, England	
Fischbach, Ephraim	*Physicist*
120 Pathway Lane, Lafayette, IN 47906, USA	
Fischer, Bill (Moose)	*Football Player*
1909 Prairie Ave, Ishpeming, MI 49849, USA	
Fischer, Birgit	*Kayak Athlete*
Kuckuckswald 11, 14532 Kleinmachnow, Germany	
Fischer, Edmond H	*Nobel Medicine Laureate*
5540 N Windermere Road, Seattle, WA 98105, USA	
Fischer, Ernst Otto	*Nobel Chemistry Laureate*
Sohnckestr 16, 81479 Munich, Germany	
Fischer, Gottfried B	*Publisher*
PO Box 237, Old Greenwich, CT 06870, USA	
Fischer, Ivan	*Conductor*
Nepkoztarsasag Utca 27, 1061 Budapest, Hungary	
Fischer, Lisa	*Singer*
%Alive Enterprises, 3264 S Kihei Road, Kihei, HI 96753, USA	
Fischer, Michael L	*Association Executive*
%California Coastal Conservancy, 1330 Broadway, #1100, Oakland, CA 94612, USA	
Fischer, Robert J (Bobby)	*Chess Player*
%US Chess Federation, 186 Rt 9-W, New Windsor, NY 12553, USA	
Fischer-Dieskau, Dietrich	*Opera, Concert Singer*
Lindenallee 22, 12587 Berlin, Germany	
Fischl, Eric	*Artist*
%Mary Boone Gallery, 417 W Broadway, New York, NY 10012, USA	
Fish, Howard M	*Air Force General*
%Loral Corp, 1725 Jefferson Davis Highway, Arlington, VA 22202, USA	
Fishburne, Laurence	*Actor*
%Helen Sugland, 4116 W Magnolia Blvd, #101, Burbank, CA 91505, USA	
Fishel, Richard	*Microbiologist*
%University of Vermont, Medical Center, Microbiology Dept, Burlington, VT 05405, USA	
Fisher, Anna L	*Astronaut*
%NASA, Johnson Space Center, 2101 NASA Road, Houston, TX 77058, USA	
Fisher, Bernard	*Surgeon*
5636 Aylesboro Ave, Pittsburgh, PA 15217, USA	
Fisher, Bernard F	*Vietnam War Air Force Hero (CMH)*
4200 King Road, Rt 1, Kuna, ID 83634, USA	
Fisher, Carrie	*Actress, Writer*
7985 Santa Monica Blvd, #109-336, Los Angeles, CA 90046, USA	
Fisher, Eddie	*Singer, Actor*
1000 North Point St, #1802, San Francisco, CA 94109, USA	
Fisher, Eddie G	*Baseball Player*
408 Cardinal Circle S, Altus, OK 73521, USA	
Fisher, Elder A (Bud)	*Bowling Executive*
7551 Brackenwood Circle N, Indianapolis, IN 46260, USA	
Fisher, Evan	*Singer (The Diamonds)*
%Moments Mgmt, 529 Washington Blvd, #393, Marina del Rey, CA 90292, USA	

F

Fisher, Frances *Actress*
2337 Roscomare Road, #2-174, Los Angeles, CA 90077, USA
Fisher, George A, Jr *Army General*
Chief of Staff, Forces Command, Fort McPherson, GA 30330, USA
Fisher, George M C *Businessman*
%Eastman Kodak, 343 State St, Rochester, NY 14650, USA
Fisher, Joel *Sculptor*
99 Commercial St, Brooklyn, NY 11222, USA
Fisher, Jules E *Theater Lighting Designer*
%Jules Fisher Enterprises, 126 5th Ave, New York, NY 10011, USA
Fisher, Mary *AIDS Activist*
%Charles Scribner's Sons, 866 3rd Ave, New York, NY 10022, USA
Fisher, Max M *Businessman*
2700 Fisher St, Detroit, MI 48217, USA
Fisher, Richard B *Financier*
%Morgan Stanley Group, 1251 Ave of Americas, New York, NY 10020, USA
Fisher, Rick *Lighting Designer*
%Royale Theater, 242 W 45th St, New York, NY 10036, USA
Fisher, Steve *Basketball Coach*
%University of Michigan, Crisler Arena, 1000 S State St, Ann Arbor, MI 48109, USA
Fisher, William F *Astronaut*
%Humana Hospital Clear Lake, 500 Medical Center Blvd, Webster, TX 77598, USA
Fishman, Michael *Actor*
1530 Bainum Dr, Topanga, CA 90290, USA
Fisk, Carlton E *Baseball Player*
16612 Catawba Road, Lockport, IL 60441, USA
Fisk, Pliny, III *Architect, Environmentalist*
8694 FM 969, Austin, TX 78724, USA
Fiske, Robert B, Jr *Attorney*
19 Juniper Road, Darien, CT 06820, USA
Fitch, Val L *Nobel Physics Laureate*
292 Hartley Ave, Princeton, NJ 08540, USA
Fitch, William C (Bill) *Basketball Coach*
%Los Angeles Clippers, Sports Arena, 3939 Figueroa St, Los Angeles, CA 90037, USA
Fites, Donald V *Businessman*
%Caterpillar Inc, 100 NE Adams St, Peoria, IL 61629, USA
Fitt of Bell's Hill, Gerard *Government Official, England*
%Irish Club, 82 Eaton Square, London SW1, England
Fittipaldi, Christian *Auto Racing Driver*
242 Alphaville Baruer, 064500 San Paul, Brazil
Fittipaldi, Emerson *Auto Racing Driver*
%Fittipaldi USA, 950 S Miami Ave, Miami, FL 33130, USA
Fitz, Raymond L *Educator*
%University of Dayton, President's Office, Dayton, OH 45469, USA
Fitzgerald, A Ernest *Government Efficiency Advocate*
%Air Force Management Systems, Pentagon, Washington, DC 20330, USA
FitzGerald, Frances *Writer*
%Simon & Schuster, 1230 Ave of Americas, New York, NY 10020, USA
FitzGerald, Garret *Prime Minister, Ireland*
%Dail Eireann, Leinster House, Kildare St, Dublin 2, Ireland
Fitzgerald, Geraldine *Actress*
%Lip Service, 4 Kingly St, London W1R 3RB, England
FitzGerald, Helen *Actress*
%Paul Kohner, 9300 Wilshire Blvd, #555, Beverly Hills, CA 90212, USA
Fitzgerald, Jack *Actor*
%William Kerwin Agency, 1605 N Cahuenga, #202, Los Angeles, CA 90028, USA
Fitzgerald, James B *Navy Admiral*
%Inspector General's Office, Washington Navy Yard, Washington, DC 20374, USA
Fitzgerald, James F *Basketball Executive*
%Golden State Warriors, 7000 Coliseum Way, Oakland, CA 94621, USA
Fitzgerald, Tara *Actress*
%Caroline Dawson, 47 Courtfield Road, #9, London SW7 4DB, England
Fitzgerald, Tom *Hockey Player*
6135 Vista Linda Lane, Boca Raton, FL 33433, USA
Fitzgerald, William A *Financier*
%Commercial Federal Corp, 2120 S 72nd St, Omaha, NE 68124, USA
Fitzgibbons, James M *Businessman*
%Fieldcrest Cannon Inc, 326 E Stadium Dr, Eden, NC 27288, USA

Fitzmaurice, David J — *Labor Leader*
%Electrical Radio & Machinists Union, 11256 156th St NW, Washington, DC 20005, USA
Fitzmaurice, Michael J — *Vietnam War Army Hero (CMH)*
Po Box 178, Hartford, SD 57033, USA
Fitzpatrick, Barry J — *Financier*
%First Virginia Banks, 6400 Arlington Blvd, Falls Church, VA 22042, USA
Fitzsimmons, Lowell (Cotton) — *Basketball Coach, Executive*
%Phoenix Suns, 201 E Jefferson St, Phoenix, AZ 85004, USA
Fitzsimonds, Roger L — *Financier*
%Firstar Corp, 777 E Wisconsin Ave, Milwaukee, WI 53202, USA
Fitzwater, Marlin — *Government Official*
851 Cedar Dr, Deale, MD 20751, USA
Fix, Oliver — *Kayak Athlete*
Ringstr 6, 86391 Stadtbergen, Germany
Fixman, Marshall — *Chemist*
%Colorado State University, Chemistry Dept, Fort Collins, CO 80523, USA
Fjeldstad, Oivin — *Conductor*
Damfaret 59, Bryn-Oslo 6, Norway
Flach, Ken — *Tennis Player, Coach*
%Vanderbilt University, Athletic Dept, Nashville, TN 37240, USA
Flach, Thomas — *Yachtsman (Soling)*
Johanna-Resch-Str 13, 12439 Berlin, Germany
Flack, Roberta — *Singer, Songwriter*
234 5th Ave, #504, New York, NY 10001, USA
Flade, H Klaus-Dietrich — *Cosmonaut, Germany*
Hennebuhlstr 2, 85051 Ingolstadt, Germany
Flagg, Fannie — *Comedienne*
1520 Willina Lane, Montecito, CA 93108, USA
Flaherty, John F (Red) — *Baseball Umpire*
9 Fowler Lane, Falmouth, MA 02540, USA
Flaherty, John T — *Baseball Player*
337 Svahn Dr, Valley Cottage, NY 10989, USA
Flaherty, Maureen — *Actress*
PO Box 7085, Moore, OK 73153, USA
Flaim, Eric — *Speed Skater*
%Eric Flaim's Motion Sports, 349 Newbury St, Boston, MA 02115, USA
Flaman, Fernie (Fern) — *Hockey Player*
29 Church St, Westwood, MA 02090, USA
Flanagan, Barry — *Sculptor*
5-E Fawe St, London E14 6PD, England
Flanagan, David T — *Businessman*
%Central Maine Power, Edison Dr, Augusta, ME 04330, USA
Flanagan, Fionnula — *Actress*
13438 Java Dr, Beverly Hills, CA 90210, USA
Flanagan, James L — *Research Engineer*
%Rutgers University, Computer Aids for Industry Center, Piscataway, NJ 08855, USA
Flanagan, Martin — *Financier*
%Franklin Resources, 777 Mariners Island Blvd, San Mateo, CA 94404, USA
Flanagan, Michael K (Mike) — *Baseball Player*
4901 Turtle Creek Trail, Oldsmar, FL 34677, USA
Flanagan, Tommy L — *Jazz Pianist*
139 W 82nd St, New York, NY 10024, USA
Flannery, Susan — *Actress*
789 Riven Rock Road, Santa Barbara, CA 93108, USA
Flannery, Thomas — *Editorial Cartoonist*
911 Dartmouth Glen Way, Baltimore, MD 21212, USA
Flatley, Michael — *Dancer*
%International Creative Mgmt, 8942 Wilshire Blvd, Beverly Hills, CA 90211, USA
Flatley, Patrick (Pat) — *Hockey Player*
1080 Washington Dr, Centerport, NY 11721, USA
Flatt, Lester — *Guitar, Mandolin, Banjo Player*
PO Box 647, Hendersonville, TN 37077, USA
Flavell, Richard A — *Immunologist*
%Yale University, Medical Center, Immunology Dept, New Haven, CT 06510, USA
Flavin, Jennifer — *Model*
100 SE 32nd Road, Miami, FL 33129, USA
Flavor Flav — *Rap Artist*
%Rush Artists, 1600 Varick St, New York, NY 10013, USA

F

Fitzmaurice - Flavor Flav

Fleck, Jack — *Golfer*
1368 Martin Loop, Magazine, AR 72943, USA

Fleetwood, Ken — *Fashion Designer*
14 Savile Row, London SW1, England

Fleetwood, Mick — *Drummer (Fleetwood Mac)*
%Courage Mgmt, 2899 Agoura Road, #582, Westlake, CA 91361, USA

Fleischer, Arthur, Jr — *Attorney*
%Fried Frank Harris Shriver Jacobson, 1 New York Plaza, New York, NY 10004, USA

Fleischer, Daniel — *Religious Leader*
%Church of Lutheran Confession, 460 75th Ave NE, Minneapolis, MN 55432, USA

Fleischer, Richard O — *Movie Director*
%Gersh Agency, 232 N Canon Dr, Beverly Hills, CA 90210, USA

Fleischmann, Martin — *Electrochemist*
Bury Lodge, Duck St, Tisbury, Wilts SP3 6LJ, England

Fleisher, Leon — *Concert Pianist, Conductor*
20 Merrymount Road, Baltimore, MD 21210, USA

Fleming Jenkins, Peggy — *Figure Skater*
16387 Aztec Ridge Dr, Los Gatos, CA 95030, USA

Fleming, James P — *Vietnam War Air Force Hero (CMH)*
PO Box 703, Longview, WA 98632, USA

Fleming, John M — *Businessman*
%Vauxhall Motors, Kimpton Road, Luton, Beds LU2 0SY, England

Fleming, Mac A — *Labor Leader*
%Maintenance of Ways Brotherhood, 26555 Evergreen Road, Southfield, MI 48076, USA

Fleming, Peter E, Jr — *Attorney*
%Curtis Mallet-Prevost Colt Mosle, 101 Park Ave, New York, NY 10178, USA

Fleming, Reg — *Hockey Player*
1605 E Central Road, #406-A, Arlington Heights, IL 60005, USA

Fleming, Renee — *Opera Singer*
%Columbia Artists Mgmt Inc, 165 W 57th St, New York, NY 10019, USA

Fleming, Rhonda — *Actress*
10281 Century Woods Dr, Los Angeles, CA 90067, USA

Fleming, Richard C D — *City Planner*
%Greater Denver Chamber of Commerce, 1445 Market St, Denver, CO 80202, USA

Fleming, Scott — *Government Official*
2750 Shasta Road, Berkeley, CA 94708, USA

Fleming, Vern — *Basketball Player*
12143 Pearl Bay Ridge, Indianapolis, IN 46236, USA

Flemming, William N (Bill) — *Sportscaster*
%ABC-TV, Sports Dept, 77 W 66th St, New York, NY 10023, USA

Fletcher, Arthur A — *Government Official*
%Commission on Civil Rights, 1121 Vermont Ave NW, Washington, DC 20005, USA

Fletcher, Charles M — *Physician, Research Scientist*
2 Coastguard Cottages, Newtown PO30 4PA, England

Fletcher, Colin — *Backpacker, Writer*
%Brandt & Brandt, 1501 Broadway, New York, NY 10036, USA

Fletcher, Louise — *Actress*
1520 Camden Ave, #105, Los Angeles, CA 90025, USA

Fletcher, Martin — *Commentator*
%NBC-TV, News Dept, 4001 Nebraska Ave NW, Washington, DC 20016, USA

Fletcher, Philip B — *Businessman*
%ConAgra Inc, 1 ConAgra Dr, Omaha, NE 68102, USA

Flexner, James T — *Writer*
530 E 86th St, New York, NY 10028, USA

Flindt, Flemming O — *Ballet Dancer, Choreographer*
%Dallas Ballet Assn, 1925 Elm St, #300, Dallas, TX 75201, USA

Flinn, Patrick L — *Financier*
%Bank South Corp, 55 Marietta St NW, Atlanta, GA 30303, USA

Flock, Tim — *Auto Racing Driver*
PO Box 560091, Charlotte, NC 28256, USA

Flom, Joseph H — *Attorney*
%Skadden Arps Slate Meagher Flom, 919 3rd Ave, New York, NY 10022, USA

Flood, Ann — *Actress*
15 E 91st St, New York, NY 10128, USA

Flood, Howard L — *Financier*
%FirstMerit Corp, 106 S Main St, Akron, OH 44308, USA

Flor, Claus Peter — *Conductor*
%Mariedl Anders Artists, 535 El Camino Del Mar, San Francisco, CA 94121, USA

Florek, Dann   *Actor*
%Silver Massetti Szatmary, 8730 Sunset Blvd, #480, Los Angeles, CA 90069, USA

Floren, Myron   *Accordionist*
26 Georgeff Road, Rolling Hills, CA 90274, USA

Flores, Patrick F   *Religious Leader*
%Archbishop's Residence, 2600 Woodlawn Ave, San Antonio, TX 78228, USA

Florio, James J (Jim)   *Governor; Representative, NJ*
%Mudge Rose Guthrie, Corporate Center 2, 180 Maiden Lane, New York, NY 10038, USA

Florio, Steven T   *Publisher*
%Conde Nast Publications, 350 Madison Ave, New York, NY 10017, USA

Florio, Thomas A   *Publisher*
%New Yorker Magazine, 20 W 43rd St, New York, NY 10036, USA

Flory, Med   *Actor*
6044 Ensign Ave, North Hollywood, CA 91606, USA

Flournoy, Craig   *Journalist*
%Dallas News, Editorial Dept, Communications Center, Dallas, TX 75265, USA

Flower, Joseph R   *Religious Leader*
%Assemblies of God, 1445 N Boonville Ave, Springfield, MO 65802, USA

Flowers of Queen's Gate, Brian H   *Physicist*
53 Athenaeum Road, London N2O 9AL, England

Floyd, Carlisle   *Composer*
4491 Yoakum Blvd, Houston, TX 77006, USA

Floyd, Eddie   *Singer, Songwriter*
%Talent Consultants Int'l, 1560 Broadway, #1308, New York, NY 10036, USA

Floyd, Eric (Sleepy)   *Basketball Player*
21 St Peters Walk, Sugar Land, TX 77479, USA

Floyd, Raymond (Ray)   *Golfer*
231 Royal Palm Way, #100, Palm Beach, FL 33480, USA

Fluckey, Eugene B   *WW II Navy Hero (CMH); Admiral*
1016 Sandpiper Lane, Annapolis, MD 21403, USA

Fluegel, Darlanne   *Actress*
PO Box 78, Beckwourth, CA 96129, USA

Flutie, Doug   *Football Player*
22 Chieftain Lane, Natick, MA 01760, USA

Flynn, William J   *Businessman*
%Mutual of America, 666 5th Ave, New York, NY 10103, USA

Flynn, William S   *Army General*
14 Annandale Road, Newport, RI 02840, USA

Flynt, Larry   *Publisher*
%Hustler Magazine, 9171 Wilshire Blvd, #300, Beverly Hills, CA 90210, USA

Fo, Dario   *Nobel Literature Laureate*
%Pietro Sciotto, Via Alessandria 4, 20144 Milan, Italy

Foale, C Michael   *Astronaut*
%NASA, Johnson Space Center, 2101 NASA Road, Houston, TX 77058, USA

Foale, Marion A   *Fashion Designer*
Church Farm, Orton-on-the-Hill near Atherstone, Warwicks, England

Fobes, John E   *Diplomat*
25 Beaverbrook Road, Asheville, NC 28804, USA

Foch, Nina   *Actress*
PO Box 1884, Beverly Hills, CA 90213, USA

Fock, Jeno   *Prime Minister, Hungary*
%Tech/Sciences Societies, Kossuth Lajos Ter 6/8, 1055 Budapest, Hungary

Fodor, Eugene N   *Concert Violinist*
22314 N Turkey Creek Road, Morrison, CO 80465, USA

Foeger, Luggi   *Skier*
%Christopher Foeger, 230 S Balsamina Way, Portola Valley, CA 94028, USA

Fogarty, Edward T   *Businessman*
%Tambrands Inc, 777 Westchester Ave, White Plains, NY 10604, USA

Fogarty, William M   *Navy Admiral*
Commander, Joint Task Force Middle East, FPO, New York, NY 09501, USA

Fogel, Robert W   *Nobel Economics Laureate*
%University of Chicago, Population Economics Center, Chicago, IL 60637, USA

Fogelberg, Dan   *Singer, Songwriter*
%HK Mgmt, 8900 Wilshire Blvd, #300, Beverly Hills, CA 90211, USA

Fogerty, John   *Singer, Songwriter*
14023 Aubrey Road, Beverly Hills, CA 90210, USA

Foggs, Edward L   *Religious Leader*
%Church of God, PO Box 2420, Anderson, IN 46018, USA

Fogler, Eddie *Basketball Coach*
%University of South Carolina, Athletic Dept, Columbia, SC 53233, USA

Fokin, Vitold *Prime Minister, Ukraine*
%Cabinet of Ministers, Government Building, Kiev, Ukraine

Foley, Dave *Actor*
%"NewsRadio" Show, NBC-TV, 3000 W Alameda Ave, Burbank, CA 91523, USA

Foley, Linda *Laber Leader*
%Newspaper Guild, 8611 2nd Ave, Silver Spring, MD 20910, USA

Foley, Maurice *Government Official, England*
Gillingham House, Gillingham St, London SW1, England

Foley, Robert F *Vietnam War Army Hero, General*
%CinC, US Army Military District, Fort Leslie J McNair, Washington, DC 20319, USA

Foley, Sylvester R, Jr *Navy Admiral*
50 Apple Hill Dr, Tewsbury, MA 01876, USA

Foley, Thomas S *Representative, WA; Speaker; Diplomat*
%US State Dept, 2201 "C" St NW, Washington, DC 20520, USA

Foley, William P, II *Businessman*
%CKE Restaurants, 1200 N Harbor Blvd, Anaheim, CA 92801, USA

Foligno, Mike *Hockey Player*
9705 The Maples, Clarence, NY 14031, USA

Folkenberg, Robert S *Religious Leader*
%Seventh-Day Adventists, 12501 Old Columbia Pike, Silver Spring, MD 20904, USA

Folkers, Karl A *Chemist*
PO Box 908, Austin, TX 78781, USA

Follett, Ken *Writer*
PO Box 708, London SW10 0DH, England

Follows, Megan *Actress*
%Susan Smith, 121 N San Vicente Blvd, Beverly Hills, CA 90211, USA

Folon, Jean-Michel *Artist*
Burcy, 77890 Beaumont-du-Gatinais, France

Folsom, Allan R *Writer*
%Little Brown, 34 Beacon St, Boston, MA 02108, USA

Folsom, James E (Jim), Jr *Governor, AL*
1221 Larkwood Dr NE, Cullman, AL 35055, USA

Folsome, Claire *Microbiologist*
%University of Hawaii, Microbiology Dept, Honolulu, HI 96822, USA

Fonda, Bridget *Actress*
%United Talent Agency, 9560 Wilshire Blvd, #500, Beverly Hills, CA 90212, USA

Fonda, Jane *Actress*
1 CNN Center NW, #1080, Atlanta, GA 30303, USA

Fonda, Peter *Actor*
%Pando Co, Rt 38, Box 2024, Livingston, MT 59047, USA

Fong, Hiram L *Senator, HI*
1102 Alewa Dr, Honolulu, HI 96817, USA

Fonseca, Caio *Artist*
%Charles Cowles, 420 W Broadway, New York, NY 10012, USA

Fontaine, Frank *Singer*
%Suffolk Marketing, 475 5th Ave, New York, NY 10017, USA

Fontaine, Joan *Actress*
PO Box 222600, Carmel, CA 93922, USA

Fontana, Wayne *Singer*
%Brian Cannon Mgmt, PO Box 81, Ruyton, Oldham, Manchester OL2 5DG, England

Fontes, Wayne *Football Coach*
626 Shellbourne Dr, Rochester Hills, MI 48309, USA

Fonville, Charles *Track Athlete*
2040 Walden Court, Flint, MI 48532, USA

Foot, Michael M *Government Official, England*
66 Pilgrims Road, London NW3, England

Foote, Dan *Editorial Cartoonist*
%Dallas Times Herald, Editorial Dept, Herald Sq, Dallas, TX 75202, USA

Foote, Edward T, II *Educator*
%University of Miami, President's Office, Coral Gables, FL 33124, USA

Foote, Horton *Writer*
95 Horatio St, #322, New York, NY 10014, USA

Foote, Shelby *Writer*
542 East Parkway S, Memphis, TN 38104, USA

Foote, William C *Businessman*
%USG Corp, 125 S Franklin St, Chicago, IL 60606, USA

Foray, June — *Actress*
22745 Erwin St, Woodland Hills, CA 91367, USA

Forbert, Steve — *Singer, Guitarist*
%Carter/Simonson, 315 W Ponce de Leon Ave, #755, Decatur, GA 30030, USA

Forbes, Bryan — *Movie Director, Screenwriter*
Bookshop, Virginia Water, Surrey, England

Forbes, Malcolm S (Steve), Jr — *Editor*
%Forbes Magazine, Editorial Dept, 60 5th Ave, New York, NY 10011, USA

Forbes, Michelle — *Actress*
%IFA Talent Agency, 8730 Sunset Blvd, #490, Los Angeles, CA 90069, USA

Forbes, Walter A — *Businessman*
%CUC International, 707 Summer St, Stamford, CT 06901, USA

Force, John — *Auto Racing Driver*
%John Force Racing, 22722 Old Canal Road, Yorba Linda, CA 92887, USA

Ford, Chris — *Basketball Player, Coach*
10113 N Vintage Court, Mequon, WI 53092, USA

Ford, Doug — *Golfer*
6241 Beaconwood Road, Lake Worth, FL 33467, USA

Ford, Edward C (Whitey) — *Baseball Player*
38 Schoolhouse Lane, Lake Success, NY 11020, USA

Ford, Eileen O — *Model Agency Executive*
%Ford Model Agency, 344 E 59th St, New York, NY 10022, USA

Ford, Elizabeth B (Betty) — *Wife of US President*
40365 Sand Dune Road, Rancho Mirage, CA 92270, USA

Ford, Faith — *Actress*
9460 Wilshire Blvd, #7, Beverly Hills, CA 90212, USA

Ford, Frankie — *Singer, Songwriter*
%Ken Keane Artists, PO Box 1875, Gretna, LA 70054, USA

Ford, Gerald J — *Financier*
%First Nationwide Bank, 135 Main St, San Francisco, CA 94105, USA

Ford, Gerald R, Jr — *President, USA*
40365 Sand Dune Road, Rancho Mirage, CA 92270, USA

Ford, Gerard W — *Model Agency Executive*
%Ford Model Agency, 344 E 59th St, New York, NY 10022, USA

Ford, Gilbert (Gil) — *Basketball Player*
30 Southpoint Lane, Ipswich, MA 01938, USA

Ford, Glenn — *Actor*
911 Oxford Way, Beverly Hills, CA 90210, USA

Ford, Harrison — *Actor*
3555 N Moose Wilson Road, Jackson Hole, WY 83001, USA

Ford, Larry C — *Gynecologic Oncologist*
%University of California Medical School, OB-Gyn Dept, Los Angeles, CA 90024, USA

Ford, Lita — *Singer*
128 Sinclair Ave, #3, Gardena, CA 91206, USA

Ford, Maria — *Actress*
%Arlene L Dayton Mgmt, 10119 Empryrian Way, #304, Los Angeles, CA 90067, USA

Ford, Phil — *Basketball Player*
12004 Iredell, Chapel Hill, NC 27514, USA

Ford, Phillip J (Phil) — *Air Force General*
%Commander, US 8th Air Force, 245 Davis Ave, Barksdale Air Force Base, LA 71110, USA

Ford, Richard — *Writer*
%Alfred A Knopf, 201 E 50th St, New York, NY 10022, USA

Ford, Ruth — *Actress*
%Dakota Hotel, 1 W 72nd St, New York, NY 10023, USA

Ford, William C, Jr — *Businessman*
%Ford Motor Co, American Road, Dearborn, MI 48121, USA

Fordice, D Kirkwood (Kirk), Jr — *Governor, MS*
%Governor's Office, State Capitol, PO Box 139, Jackson, MS 39205, USA

Foreman, Carol L T — *Government Official*
5408 Trent St, Chevy Chase, MD 20815, USA

Foreman, Charles (Chuck) — *Football Player*
7370 Stewart Dr, Eden Prairie, MN 55346, USA

Foreman, George — *Boxer*
7639 Pine Oak Dr, Humble, TX 77396, USA

Forget, Guy — *Tennis Player*
Rue des Pacs 2, 2000 Neuchatel, Switzerland

Forke, Farrah — *Actress*
%William Morris Agency, 151 S El Camino Dr, Beverly Hills, CA 90212, USA

Forlani, Arnaldo — *Prime Minister, Italy*
Piazzale Schumann 15, Rome, Italy

Forman, Milos — *Movie Director*
Hampshire House, 150 Central Park South, New York, NY 10019, USA

Forman, Stanley — *Photographer*
11 Shannon Lane, Beverly, MA 01915, USA

Forman, Tom — *Cartoonist (Motley's Crew)*
28947 Thousand Oaks Blvd, #120, Agoura Hills, CA 91301, USA

Formia, Osvaldo — *Harness Racing Trainer*
6501 Winfield Blvd, #A-10, Margate, FL 33063, USA

Fornos, Werner H — *Association Executive*
%Population Institute, 107 2nd St NE, Washington, DC 20002, USA

Forrest, Frederic — *Actor*
%Michael Wallach Mgmt, 9465 Wilshire Blvd, #405, Beverly Hills, CA 90212, USA

Forrest, Helen — *Singer*
1870 Camino Del Cielo, Glendale, CA 91208, USA

Forrest, Sally — *Actress*
1125 Angelo Dr, Beverly Hills, CA 90210, USA

Forrest, Steve — *Actor*
1065 Michael Lane, Pacific Palisades, CA 90272, USA

Forrestal, Robert P — *Financier, Government Official*
%Federal Reserve Bank, 104 Marietta St NW, Atlanta, GA 30303, USA

Forrester, James — *Medical Researcher*
%Cedars-Sinai Medical Center, 8700 Beverly Blvd, Los Angeles, CA 90048, USA

Forrester, Jay W — *Inventor (Digital Storage Device)*
%Massachusetts Institute of Technology, Management School, Cambridge, MA 02139, USA

Forrester, Maureen — *Concert Singer*
%Shaw Concerts, Lincoln Center Plaza, 1900 Broadway, #200, New York, NY 10023, USA

Forsberg, Peter — *Hockey Player*
%Colorado Avalanche, McNichols Arena, 1635 Clay St, Denver, CO 80204, USA

Forsch, Kenneth R (Ken) — *Baseball Player*
794 S Ridgeview Road, Anaheim, CA 92807, USA

Forsch, Robert H (Bob) — *Baseball Player*
1532 Highland Valley Circle, Chesterfield, MO 63005, USA

Forslund, Constance — *Actress*
165 W 46th St, #1109, New York, NY 10036, USA

Forsman, Dan — *Golfer*
88 West 4500 N, Provo, UT 84604, USA

Forster, Frederic J — *Financier*
%H F Ahmanson Co, 4900 Rivergrade Road, Irwindale, CA 91706, USA

Forster, K Dieter — *Religious Leader*
%Scientist Church of Christ, 175 Huntington Ave, Boston, MA 02115, USA

Forster, Peter H — *Businessman*
%DPL Inc, Courthouse Plaza SW, Dayton, OH 45402, USA

Forster, Robert — *Actor*
1115 Pine St, Santa Monica, CA 90405, USA

Forstmann, Theodore J — *Financier*
%Forstmann Little Co, 767 5th Ave, New York, NY 10153, USA

Forsyth, Bill — *Movie Director*
%Peters Fraser Dunlop, Chelsea Harbour, Lots Rd, London SW10 0XF, England

Forsyth, Bruce — *Comedian*
Kent House, Upper Ground, London SE1, England

Forsyth, Frederick — *Writer*
%Hutchinson Publishing Group, 3 Fitzroy Square, London W1P 6JD, England

Forsyth, Rosemary — *Actress*
1591 Benedict Canyon, Beverly Hills, CA 90210, USA

Forsythe, Henderson — *Actor*
3002 Willow Spring Court, Williamsburg, VA 23185, USA

Forsythe, John — *Actor*
3849 Roblar Ave, Santa Ynez, CA 93460, USA

Forsythe, William — *Actor*
%United Talent Agency, 9560 Wilshire Blvd, #500, Beverly Hills, CA 90212, USA

Fort, Edward B — *Educator*
%North Carolina A&T State University, Chancellor's Office, Greensboro, NC 27411, USA

Fort-Brescia, Bernardo — *Architect*
%Arquitectonica International, 550 Brickell Ave, #200, Miami, FL 33131, USA

Fortess, Karl E — *Artist*
311 Plochmann Lane, Woodstock, NY 12498, USA

Fortier, Claude — *Physiologist*
1014 De Grenoble, Ste-Foy, Quebec PQ G1V 2Z9, Canada
Fortune, Jimmy — *Singer (Statler Brothers)*
%American Major Talent, PO Box 492, Hernando, MS 38632, USA
Fosbury, Dick — *Track Athlete*
708 Cyn Run, Box 1791, Ketchum, ID 83340, USA
Foss, Joseph — *WW II Marine Hero (CMH); Governor, SD*
PO Box 566, Scottsdale, AZ 85252, USA
Foss, Lukas — *Composer, Conductor*
1140 5th Ave #4-B, New York, NY 10128, USA
Fossel, Jon S — *Financier*
%Oppenheimer Management, 2 World Trade Center, New York, NY 10048, USA
Fossey, Brigitte — *Actress*
18 Rue Troyon, 75017 Paris, France
Foster, Barry — *Football Player*
4604 Mill Springs Court, Colleyville, TX 76034, USA
Foster, Bill — *Basketball Coach*
%Virginia Polytechnic Institute, Athletic Dept, Blacksburg, VA 24061, USA
Foster, Bob — *Boxer*
913 Valencia NE, Albuquerque, NM 87108, USA
Foster, Brendan — *Track Athlete*
Whitegates, 31 Meadowfield Road, Stocksfield, Northumberland, England
Foster, Coy — *Balloonist*
5486 Glen Lakes Dr, Dallas, TX 75231, USA
Foster, David — *Songwriter, Musician*
PO Box 6228, Malibu, CA 90264, USA
Foster, George A — *Baseball Player*
%George Foster Pro Concepts, 15 E Putnam Ave, #320, Greenwich, CT 06830, USA
Foster, Jodie — *Actress, Director*
%International Creative Mgmt, 8942 Wilshire Blvd, Beverly Hills, CA 90211, USA
Foster, John S, Jr — *Physicist*
%TRW Inc, 1 Space Parkway, Redondo Beach, CA 90278, USA
Foster, Kent B — *Businessman*
%GTE Corp, 1 Stamford Forum, Stamford, CT 06901, USA
Foster, Lawrence — *Conductor*
%Harrison Parrott Ltd, 12 Penzance Place, London W11, England
Foster, Lisa-Raines — *Actress*
%Diamond Artists, 215 N Barrington Ave, Los Angeles, CA 90049, USA
Foster, M J — *Governor, LA*
%Governor's Office, PO Box 94004, Baton Rouge, LA 70804, USA
Foster, Meg — *Actress*
10866 Wilshire Blvd, #1100, Los Angeles, CA 90024, USA
Foster, Norman R — *Architect*
%Foster Assoc, Riverside 3, 22 Hester Road, London SW11 4AN, England
Foster, Radney — *Singer, Songwriter*
%Fitzgerald-Hartley, 1908 Wedgewood Ave, Nashville, TN 37212, USA
Foster, Todd — *Boxer*
2224 Beech Dr, Great Falls, MT 59404, USA
Foster, William C — *Government Official*
3304 "R" St NW, Washington, DC 20007, USA
Foster, William E (Bill) — *Basketball Coach*
152 Hollywood Dr, Coppell, TX 75019, USA
Foulkes, Llyn — *Artist*
6010 Eucalyptus Lane, Los Angeles, CA 90042, USA
Fountain, Peter D (Pete), Jr — *Jazz Clarinetist*
%Pete Fountain Productions, 237 N Peters St, #400, New Orleans, LA 70130, USA
Fouts, Daniel F (Dan) — *Football Player, Sportscaster*
%KPIX-TV, Sports Dept, 855 Battery St, San Francisco, CA 94111, USA
Fowden, Leslie — *Plant Chemist*
31 Southdown Road, Harpenden, Herts AL5 1PF, England
Fowler, Henry H — *Secretary, Treasury*
%Goldman Sachs Co, 85 Broad St, New York, NY 10004, USA
Fowler, Jim — *Actor*
%"Wild Kingdom", Mutual of Omaha, Mutual of Omaha Plaza, Omaha, NE 68175, USA
Fowler, Mark S — *Government Official*
%Latham & Watkins, 1001 Pennsylvania Ave NW, Washington, DC 20004, USA
Fowler, Michael — *Architect*
%Calder Fowler Styles Turner, PO Box 2692, Wellington, New Zealand

F

Fortier - Fowler

Fowler, Robert E, Jr — Businessman
%Vigoro Corp, 225 N Michigan Ave, Chicago, IL 60601, USA

Fowler, W Wyche, Jr — Senator, GA
%US State Department, 2201 "C" St NW, Washington, DC 20520, USA

Fowles, John R — Writer
%Anthony Sheil Assoc, 45 Doughty St, London WC1N 2LF, England

Fowley, Douglas — Actor
38510 Glen Abbey Lane, Murietta, CA 92562, USA

Fox, Allen — Tennis Player, Coach
%Pepperdine University, Athletic Dept, Malibu, CA 90265, USA

Fox, Bernard — Actor
145 S Fairfax Ave, #310, Los Angeles, CA 90036, USA

Fox, Bernard M — Businessman
%Northeast Utilities, PO Box 270, Hartford, CT 06141, USA

Fox, Charles I — Composer, Conductor
%William Morris Agency, 151 S El Camino Dr, Beverly Hills, CA 90212, USA

Fox, Edward — Actor
25 Maida Ave, London W2, England

Fox, Everett — Theologian
%Clark University, Jewish Studies Program, Worcester, MA 01610, USA

Fox, J Carter — Businessman
%Chesapeake Corp, PO Box 2350, Richmond, VA 23218, USA

Fox, James — Actor
3 Spencer Park Road, London SW18, England

Fox, Marye Anne — Organic Chemist
%University of Texas, Chemistry Dept, Austin, TX 78712, USA

Fox, Matthew — Religious Leader
%Grace Episcopal Cathedral, 1 Nob Hill Circle, San Francisco, CA 94108, USA

Fox, Maurice S — Molecular Biologist
983 Memorial Dr, #401, Cambridge, MA 02138, USA

Fox, Michael J — Actor
Lottery Hill Farm, South Woodstock, VT 05071, USA

Fox, Paula — Writer
%Robert Lescher, 67 Irving Place, New York, NY 10003, USA

Fox, Rick — Basketball Player
%Los Angeles Lakers, Forum, PO Box 10, Inglewood, CA 90306, USA

Fox, Samantha — Singer, Model
%Session Connection, 110-112 Disraeli Road, London SW15 2DX, England

Fox, Sheldon — Architect
%Kohn Pedersen Fox Assoc, 111 W 57th St, New York, NY 10019, USA

Fox, Sidney W — Biochemist
5433 Old Shell Road, #134, Mobile, AL 36608, USA

Fox, Stan — Auto Racing Driver
%Lemans Corp, 3501 Kennedy Road, PO Box 5222, Janesville, WI 53547, USA

Fox, Tim — Football Player
18 Shoreline Dr, Foxboro, MA 02035, USA

Fox, Vivica A — Actress
250 W 57th St, #2223, New York, NY 10107, USA

Fox, Wesley L — Vietnam War Marine Corps Hero (CMH)
OCS MCCOC, Development & Education Command, Quantico, VA 22134, USA

Fox, William F, Jr — Attorney
%Catholic University, Law School, Washington, DC 20064, USA

Foxworth, Robert — Actor
%Krisbo Productions, 9720 Wilshire Blvd, #300, Beverly Hills, CA 90212, USA

Foxworthy, Jeff — Comedian
%Parallel Entertainment, 8380 Melrose Ave, #310, Los Angeles, CA 90069, USA

Foy, Eddie, III — Actor
13332 McCormick St, Van Nuys, CA 91401, USA

Foyle, Adonal — Basketball Player
%Golden State Warriors, 7000 Coliseum Way, Oakland, CA 94621, USA

Foyt, A J, Jr — Auto Racing Driver
%AJF Enterprises, 6415 Toledo St, Houston, TX 77008, USA

Fradon, Dana — Cartoonist
RFD 2, Brushy Hill Road, Newtown, CT 06470, USA

Fraenkel-Conrat, Heinz L — Molecular Biologist
870 Grizzly Peak Blvd, Berkeley, CA 94708, USA

Frahm, Donald R — Businessman
%ITT Hartford, Hartford Plaza, Hartford, CT 06115, USA

Fraker, William A	*Cinematographer*
%Gersh Agency, 232 N Canon Dr, Beverly Hills, CA 90210, USA	
Frakes, Jonathan	*Actor*
9135 Hazen Dr, Beverly Hills, CA 90210, USA	
Frame, Janet	*Writer*
276 Glenfield Road, Auckland 10, New Zealand	
Frampton, Peter	*Singer, Songwriter, Guitarist*
8927 Byron Ave, Surfside, FL 33154, USA	
Franca, Celia	*Ballerina, Choreographer*
157 King St E, Toronto ON M5C 1G9, Canada	
France, Bill, Jr	*Auto Racing Executive*
%National Assn of Stock Car Racing, 1801 Speedway Blvd, Daytona Beach, FL 32114, USA	
France, Doug	*Football Player*
25993 Atherton Ave, Laguna Hills, CA 92653, USA	
Franciosa, Anthony (Tony)	*Actor*
567 Tigertail Road, Los Angeles, CA 90049, USA	
Francis, Anne	*Actress*
Po Box 3282, Palm Desert, CA 92261, USA	
Francis, Arlene	*Actress*
%Ritz Towers, 59th & Park Ave, New York, NY 10016, USA	
Francis, Clarence (Bevo)	*Basketball Player*
18340 Steubenville Pike Road, Salineville, OH 43945, USA	
Francis, Connie	*Singer, Actress*
6413 Nw 102nd Terrace, Parkland, FL 33076, USA	
Francis, Don	*Medical Researcher*
%Genentech Inc, 460 Point San Bruno Blvd, South San Francisco, CA 94080, USA	
Francis, Emile P	*Hockey Coach, Executive*
7220 Crystal Lake Dr, West Palm Beach, FL 33411, USA	
Francis, Fred	*Commentator*
%NBC-TV, News Dept, 4001 Nebraska Ave NW, Washington, DC 20016, USA	
Francis, Freddie	*Cinematographer*
12 The Chestnuts, Jersey Road, Osterley, Middx TW7 5QA, England	
Francis, Genie	*Actress*
9135 Hazen Dr, Beverly Hills, CA 90210, USA	
Francis, Harrison (Sam)	*Football Player*
2850 S Chambery Ave, Springfield, MO 65804, USA	
Francis, James	*Football Player*
7205 Robin, Texas City, TX 77591, USA	
Francis, Richard S (Dick)	*Writer*
PO Box 30866, Seven Mile Beach, Grand Cayman, West Indies	
Francis, Ron	*Hockey Player*
1550 Alaqua Dr, Sewickley, PA 15143, USA	
Francis, Russ	*Football Player*
PO Box 841, Santa Ynez, CA 93460, USA	
Francisco, George J	*Labor Leader*
%Fireman & Oilers Union, 1100 Circle 75 Parkway, Atlanta, GA 30339, USA	
Franck, George H	*Football Player*
2714 29th Ave, Rock Island, IL 61201, USA	
Franck, John M	*Businessman*
%Tultex Corp, 22 E Church St, Martinsville, VA 24112, USA	
Franco, John A	*Baseball Player*
111 Clifford Ave, Staten Island, NY 10304, USA	
Franco, Julio C	*Baseball Player*
651 NE 23rd Court, Pompano Beach, FL 33064, USA	
Francona, Terry J	*Baseball Manager*
958 Hunt Dr, Yardley, PA 19067, USA	
Frank, Anthony M	*Government Official, Financier*
%Independent Bancorp, 3800 N Central, Phoenix, AZ 85012, USA	
Frank, Diana	*Actress*
%The Agency, 1800 Ave of Stars, #400, Los Angeles, CA 90067, USA	
Frank, F Charles	*Physicist*
Orchard Cottage, Grove Road, Coombe Dingle, Bristol BS9 2RL, England	
Frank, Gerold	*Writer*
930 5th Ave, New York, NY 10021, USA	
Frank, Harold R	*Businessman*
%Applied Magnetics, 75 Robin Hill Road, Goleta, CA 93117, USA	
Frank, Jason David	*Actor*
%Media Artists Group, 8383 Wilshire Blvd, #954, Beverly Hills, CA 90211, USA	

F

Fraker - Frank

Frank, Jerome D	*Psychiatrist, Educator*
818 W 40th St, #K, Baltimore, MD 21211, USA	
Frank, Joe	*Radio Personality*
%KCRW-FM, 1900 Pico Blvd, Santa Monica, CA 90405, USA	
Frank, Neil L	*Meteorologist*
%National Hurricane Center, 1320 S Dixie Highway, Miami, FL 33146, USA	
Frank, Phil	*Cartoonist (Farley)*
500 Turley St, Sausalito, CA 94965, USA	
Frank, Reuven	*Television Producer*
%National Broadcasting Co, 30 Rockefeller Plaza, New York, NY 10112, USA	
Frank, Richard H	*Financier*
%World Bank Group, 1818 "H" St NW, Washington, DC 20433, USA	
Frank, Richard H	*Entertainment Executive*
%Comcast Corp, 1500 Market St, Philadelphia, PA 19102, USA	
Frank, Sarah	*Television Executive*
%BBC/Lionheart TV, Woodlands, 80 Wood Lane, London W12 0TT, England	
Franke, William A	*Businessman*
%America West Airlines, 51 W 3rd St, Tempe, AZ 85281, USA	
Frankel, Max	*Editor*
%New York Times, Editorial Dept, 229 W 43rd St, New York, NY 10036, USA	
Frankenheimer, John M	*Movie Director*
3114 Abington Dr, Beverly Hills, CA 90210, USA	
Frankenthaler, Helen	*Artist*
173 E 94th St, New York, NY 10128, USA	
Frankl, Peter	*Concert Pianist*
5 Gresham Gardens, London NW11 8NX, England	
Franklin, Aretha	*Singer*
16919 Stansbury, Detroit, MI 48235, USA	
Franklin, Barbara Hackman	*Secretary, Commerce*
1875 Perkins St, Bristol, CT 06010, USA	
Franklin, Bonnie	*Actress*
10635 Santa Monica Blvd, #130, Los Angeles, CA 90025, USA	
Franklin, Carl E	*Air Force General*
Commander, 9th Air Force, 524 Shaw Dr, Shaw Air Force Base, SC 29152, USA	
Franklin, Diane	*Actress*
2115 Topanga Skyline Dr, Topanga, CA 90290, USA	
Franklin, John	*Actor*
%Gilla Roos, 9744 Wilshire Blvd, #203, Beverly Hills, CA 90212, USA	
Franklin, John Hope	*Writer, Historian*
208 Pineview Road, Durham, NC 27707, USA	
Franklin, Jon D	*Journalist*
%University of Oregon, Journalism School, Eugene, OR 97403, USA	
Franklin, Pamela	*Actress*
1280 Sunset Plaza Dr, Los Angeles, CA 90069, USA	
Franklin, Richard C	*Businessman*
%Insurance Co (NA), 1601 Chestnut St, Philadelphia, PA 19192, USA	
Franklin, William	*Bowling Executive*
1039 La Casa Dr, San Marcus, CA 92069, USA	
Franklyn, Sabina	*Actress*
%CCA Mgmt, 4 Court Lodge, 48 Sloane Square, London SW1W 8AT, England	
Franks, Frederick M, Jr	*Army General*
Commanding General, US Army Training/Doctrine Command, Fort Monroe, VA 23651, USA	
Franks, Michael	*Singer, Songwriter, Guitarist*
%Agency For Performing Arts, 9200 Sunset Blvd, #900, Los Angeles, CA 90069, USA	
Franks, Tommy R (Tom)	*Army General*
Commanding General, 3rd Army, Fort McPherson, GA 30330, USA	
Frankston, Robert M	*Computer Software Designer (VisiCalc)*
%Slate Corp, 15035 N 73rd St, Scottsdale, AZ 85260, USA	
Frann, Mary	*Actress*
11365 Santa Monica Blvd, #130, Los Angeles, CA 90025, USA	
Fransioli, Thomas A	*Artist*
55 Dodges Row, Wenham, MA 01984, USA	
Franz, Dennis	*Actor*
11805 Bellagio Road, Los Angeles, CA 90049, USA	
Franz, Frederick W	*Religious Leader*
%Jehovah's Witnesses, 25 Columbia Heights, Brooklyn, NY 11201, USA	
Franz, Rodney T (Rod)	*Football Player*
1448 Engberg Court, Carmichael, CA 95608, USA	

Franzen, Jonathan — Writer
%Farrar Straus Giroux, 19 Union Square W, New York, NY 10003, USA
Franzen, Ulrich J — Architect
%Ulrich Franzen Assoc, 168 E 74th St, New York, NY 10021, USA
Frasca, Robert J — Architect
%Zimmer Gunsul Frasca, 320 SW Oak St, #500, Portland, OR 97204, USA
Frasconi, Antonio — Artist
26 Dock Road, South Norwalk, CT 06854, USA
Fraser Ware, Dawn — Swimmer
87 Birchgrove Road, Balmain NSW, Australia
Fraser, Antonia — Writer
%Curtis Brown, 162/168 Regent St, London W1R 5TB, England
Fraser, Brad — Writer
%Great North Artists Mgmt, 350 Dupont Ave, Toronto ON M5R 1V9, Canada
Fraser, Brendan — Actor
2118 Wilshire Blvd, #513, Santa Monica, CA 90403, USA
Fraser, Douglas — Labor Leader
%United Auto Workers, 8000 E Jefferson Ave, Detroit, MI 48214, USA
Fraser, Hugh — Actor
1 Northumberland Place, London W2 5BS, England
Fraser, Ian E — WW II British Royal Navy Hero (VC)
Innisfallen, 47 Warren Dr, Wallasey, Merseyside, England
Fraser, Malcolm — Prime Minister, Australia
ANZ Tower, #4400, 55 Collins St, Melbourne Vic 3000, Australia
Fraser, Neale — Tennis Player
%Tennis Australia, Private Bag 6060, Richmond South, 3121 Vic, Australia
Fratello, Michael R (Mike) — Basketball Coach
%Cleveland Cavaliers, 2923 Statesboro Road, Richfield, OH 44286, USA
Fratianne, Linda — Figure Skater
15691 Borgas Court, Moorpark, CA 93021, USA
Fraumeni, Joseph F, Jr — Cancer Researcher
%National Cancer Institute, Cancer Etiology Division, Bethesda, MD 20892, USA
Frayn, Michael — Writer
%Elaine Green Ltd, 31 Newington Glen, London N16 9PU, England
Frazer, Liz — Actress
42/43 Grafton House, 2/3 Golden Square, London W1, England
Frazetta, Frank — Artist
%Frazetta Art Museum, 82 S Courtland St, East Stroudsburg, PA 18301, USA
Frazier, Dallas — Singer, Songwriter
Rt 5, Box 133, Longhollow Pike, Gallatin, TN 37066, USA
Frazier, Herman — Track Athlete
9841 S 46th St, Phoenix, AZ 85044, USA
Frazier, Ian — Writer
%Farrar Straus Giroux, 19 Union Square W, New York, NY 10003, USA
Frazier, Joe — Boxer
2917 N Broad St, Philadelphia, PA 19132, USA
Frazier, Walt (Clyde) — Basketball Player
675 Flamingo Dr SW, Atlanta, GA 30311, USA
Frears, Stephen A — Movie Director
93 Talbot Road, London W2, England
Freberg, Stanley V (Stan) — Comedian
10450 Wilshire Blvd, #1-A, Los Angeles, CA 90024, USA
Freccia, Massimo — Conductor
25 Eaton Square, London SW1, England
Frederick, Sherman R — Editor
%Las Vegas Review-Journal, 1111 W Bonanza Road, Las Vegas, NV 89106, USA
Fredericks, Fred — Cartoonist (Mandrake the Magician)
Bridge Road, Box 475, Eastham, MA 02642, USA
Frederik Andre Henrik Christian — Prince, Denmark
%Amalienborg Palace, 1257 Copenhagen K, Denmark
Fredrickson, Donald S — Physician
6615 Bradley Blvd, Bethesda, MD 20817, USA
Fredriksson, Gert — Canoeist
Bruunsgat 13, 611 22 Nykoping, Sweden
Fredriksson, Marie — Singer, Songwriter (Roxette)
%Ema-Telstar, PO Box 1018, 181 21 Lidingo, Sweden
Free, World B — Basketball Player, Coach, Executive
%Philadelphia 76ers, Veterans Stadium, PO Box 25040, Philadelphia, PA 19147, USA

F

Franzen - Free

F

Freed, Curt R *Neurobiologist*
%University of Colorado Health Sciences Center, 4200 E 9th Ave, Denver, CO 80220, USA
Freed, James Ingo *Architect*
%Pei Cobb Freed Partners, 600 Madison Ave, New York, NY 10022, USA
Freedberg, Sydney J *Museum Curator*
3328 Reservoir Road, Washington, DC 20007, USA
Freedman, Alix M *Journalist*
%Wall Street Journal, Editorial Dept, 22 Cortlandt St, New York, NY 10007, USA
Freedman, Allen R *Financier*
%Fortis Inc, 1 World Trade Center, New York, NY 10048, USA
Freedman, Eric *Journalist*
%Detroit News, Editorial Dept, 615 Lafayette Blvd, Detroit, MI 48226, USA
Freedman, Gerald A *Theater, Opera Director*
%Theatre Julliard School, Lincoln Center Plaza, New York, NY 10023, USA
Freedman, James O *Educator*
%Dartmouth College, President's Office, Hanover, NH 03755, USA
Freedman, Michael H *Mathematician*
%University of California, Mathematics Dept, La Jolla, CA 92093, USA
Freedman, Wendy L *Astronomer, Astrophysicist*
%Carnegie Observatories, 813 Santa Barbara St, Pasadena, CA 91101, USA
Freeh, Louis J *Law Enforcement Official*
%Federal Bureau of Investigation, 9th & Pennsylvania NW, Washington, DC 20535, USA
Freehan, William A (Bill) *Baseball Player*
4248 Sunningdale Dr, Bloomfield Hills, MI 48302, USA
Freelon, Nnenna *Singer*
%Ted Kurland, 173 Brighton Ave, Boston, MA 02134, USA
Freeman, Al, Jr *Actor*
%Artists Agency, 10000 Santa Monica Blvd, #305, Los Angeles, CA 90067, USA
Freeman, Bobby *Singer*
%Holiday Entertainment, 8803 Mayne St, Bellflower, CA 90706, USA
Freeman, Charles W, Jr *Diplomat*
2805 31st St NW, Washington, DC 20008, USA
Freeman, Kathleen *Actress*
6247 Orion Ave, Van Nuys, CA 91411, USA
Freeman, Mona *Actress*
608 N Alpine Dr, Beverly Hills, CA 90210, USA
Freeman, Morgan *Actor*
2472 Broadway, #227, New York, NY 10025, USA
Freeman, Orville L *Secretary, Agriculture*
1101 S Arlington Ridge Road, Arlington, VA 22202, USA
Freeman, Russell D (Russ) *Jazz Pianist*
%Agency For Performing Arts, 9200 Sunset Blvd, #900, Los Angeles, CA 90069, USA
Freeman, Sandi *Commentator*
%Cable News Network, News Dept, 820 1st St NE, Washington, DC 20002, USA
Freeman, Yvette *Actress*
%Stone Manners, 8091 Selma Ave, Los Angeles, CA 90046, USA
Fregosi, James L (Jim) *Baseball Player, Manager*
1092 Copeland Court, Tarpon Springs, FL 34689, USA
Frehley, Ace *Singer, Guitarist (Kiss)*
%Kayos Productions, 16th W 19th St, #500, New York, NY 10011, USA
Frei Fruiz Tagle, Eduardo *President, Chile*
%President's Office, Palacio de la Monedo, Santiago, Chile
Frei, Emil, III *Physician*
%Dana-Farber Cancer Institute, 44 Binney St, Boston, MA 02115, USA
Freilberger, Marcus *Basketball Player*
14990 Hickory Green Court, Fort Myers, FL 33912, USA
Freilicher, Jane *Artist*
%Fishbach Gallery, 24 W 57th St, New York, NY 10019, USA
Freire, Paolo *Educator*
%World Council of Churches, Geneva, Switzerland
Freireich, Emil J *Physician*
%M D Anderson Medical Center, 1515 Holcombe Blvd, Houston, TX 77030, USA
Freis, Edward D *Physician*
4515 Willard Ave, Chevy Chase, MD 20815, USA
Fremaux, Louis J F *Conductor*
25 Edencroft, Wheeleys Road, Birmingham B15 2LW, England
French, Charles S *Plant Biologist*
1601 Gillespie St, Santa Barbara, CA 93101, USA

Freed - French

French, Leigh — *Actress*
1850 N Vista St, Los Angeles, CA 90046, USA

French, Marilyn — *Writer*
%Charlotte Sheedy Agency, 41 King St, New York, NY 10014, USA

French, Niki — *Singer*
%Famous Artists Agency, 1700 Broadway, #500, New York, NY 10019, USA

French, Paige — *Actress*
%Gersh Agency, 232 N Canon Dr, Beverly Hills, CA 90210, USA

Freni, Mirella — *Opera Singer*
%Columbia Artists Mgmt Inc, 165 W 57th St, New York, NY 10019, USA

Frerotte, Gus — *Football Player*
%Washington Redskins, 21300 Redskin Park Dr, Ashburn, VA 20147, USA

Fresno Lorrain, Juan Cardinal — *Religious Leader*
Erasmo Escala 1822, Santiago 30-D, Chile

Freud, Lucian — *Artist*
%James Kirkman, 46 Brompton Square, London SW3 2AF, England

Freund-Rosenthal, Miriam Kottler — *Religious Leader*
50 W 58th St, New York, NY 10019, USA

Frewer, Matt — *Actor*
6670 Wildlife Road, Malibu, CA 90265, USA

Frey, Glenn — *Singer (The Eagles), Songwriter, Actor*
5020 Brent Knoll Lane, Suwanee, GA 30024, USA

Frey, James G (Jim) — *Baseball Manager*
119 Versailles Circle, #A, Towson, MD 21204, USA

Freyndlikh, Alisa B — *Actress*
Rubinstein Str 11, #7, 191002 St Petersburg, Russia

Freytag, Arny — *Photographer*
22735 MacFarlane Dr, Woodland Hills, CA 91364, USA

Fribourg, Paul J — *Businessman*
%Continental Grain, 277 Park Ave, New York, NY 10172, USA

Frick, Gottlob — *Opera Singer*
Eichelberg-Haus Waldfrieden, 75248 Olbronn-Durrn, Germany

Fricke, Howard R — *Businessman*
%Security Benefit Insurance, 700 SW Harrison St, Topeka, KS 66603, USA

Fricke, Janie — *Singer*
%Janie Fricke Concerts, PO Box 798, Lancaster, TX 75146, USA

Fricker, Brenda — *Actress*
%Mayer Eden, Grafton House, #4, 2-3 Golden Square, London W1R 3AD, England

Frid, Jonathan — *Actor*
175 5th Ave, #2517, New York, NY 10010, USA

Friday, Elbert W, Jr — *Government Official*
%US National Weather Service, 1125 East-West Highway, Silver Spring, MD 20910, USA

Friday, Nancy — *Writer*
%Harper Collins Publishers, 10 E 53rd St, New York, NY 10022, USA

Fridell, Squire — *Actor*
7080 Hollywood Blvd, #704, Los Angeles, CA 90028, USA

Friderichs, Hans — *Businessman*
%AEG-Telefunken, Theodor-Stern-Kai 1, 60596 Frankfurt/Main, Germany

Fridovich, Irwin — *Biochemist*
3517 Courtland Dr, Durham, NC 27707, USA

Fried, Charles — *Government Official, Educator*
%Harvard University, Law School, Cambridge, MA 02138, USA

Fried, Josef — *Organic Chemist*
5717 S Kenwood Ave, Chicago, IL 60637, USA

Friedan, Betty — *Writer, Social Activist*
2022 Columbia Road NW, #414, Washington, DC 20009, USA

Friedkin, William — *Movie Director*
10451 Bellagio Road, Los Angeles, CA 90077, USA

Friedlander, Lee — *Artist, Photographer*
44 S Mountain Road, New City, NY 10956, USA

Friedman, Bruce Jay — *Writer*
Holly Lane, Water Mill, NY 11976, USA

Friedman, Emanuel A — *Medical Educator, Obstetrician*
%Beth-Israel Hospital, 330 Brookline Ave, Boston, MA 02215, USA

Friedman, Herbert — *Physicist*
2643 N Upshur St, Arlington, VA 22207, USA

Friedman, Jeffrey — *Molecular Geneticist*
%Rockefeller University, Hughes Medical Institute, New York, NY 10021, USA

F

Friedman, Jerome I — *Nobel Physics Laureate*
75 Greenough Circle, Brookline, MA 02146, USA

Friedman, Meyer — *Cardiologist*
160 San Carlos Ave, Sausalito, CA 94965, USA

Friedman, Milton — *Nobel Economics Laureate*
%Stanford University, Hoover Institution, Stanford, CA 94305, USA

Friedman, Philip — *Writer*
%Ivy Books, Random House Inc, 201 E 50th St, New York, NY 10022, USA

Friedman, Stephen — *Financier*
%Goldman Sachs Co, 85 Broad St, New York, NY 10004, USA

Friedman, Thomas L — *Journalist*
%New York Times, Editorial Dept, 229 W 43rd St, New York, NY 10036, USA

Friedman, Yona — *Architect*
33 Blvd Garibaldi, 75015 Paris, France

Friedmann, David — *Financier*
%Bank Leumi Trust, 579 5th Ave, New York, NY 10017, USA

Friel, Brian — *Writer*
Drumaweir House, Greencastle, County Donegal, Ireland

Friels, Colin — *Actor*
129 Brooke St, Woollomooloo, Sydney NSW 2011, Australia

Friend, Lionel — *Conductor*
136 Rosendale Road, London SE21 8LG, England

Friend, Patricia A — *Labor Leader*
%Flight Attendants Assn, 1625 Massachusetts Ave NW, Washington, DC 20036, USA

Friend, Richard H — *Chemist*
%Cavendish Laboratory, Chemistry Dept, Cambridge, England

Friend, Robert B (Bob) — *Baseball Player*
4 Salem Circle, Fox Chapel, PA 15238, USA

Friendly, Alfred W (Fred) — *Journalist*
%Columbia University, Journalism School, 475 Riverside Dr, New York, NY 10115, USA

Frierson, Daniel K — *Businessman*
%Dixie Yarns, 1100 S Watkins St, Chattanooga, TN 37404, USA

Friesen, David — *Jazz Bassist*
%Thomas Cassidy, 0366 Horseshoe Dr, Basalt, CO 81621, USA

Friesz, John — *Football Player*
1900 Marilyn Road, Rathdrum, ID 83858, USA

Frimout, Dirk D — *Astronaut, Belgium*
%D1/Nieuwe Ontwikkelingen, Bd E Jacqmainlaan 151, 1210 Brussels, Belgium

Frischman, Dan — *Actor*
717 N Ontario St, Burbank, CA 91505, USA

Frishberg, David L — *Jazz Singer, Pianist, Composer*
%Irvin Arthur, 9363 Wilshire Blvd, #212, Beverly Hills, CA 90210, USA

Frist, Thomas F, Jr — *Businessman*
%Columbia/HCA Healthcare Corp, 201 W Main St, Louisville, KY 40202, USA

Fritsch, Ted, Jr — *Football Player*
5014 Odins Way, Marietta, GA 30068, USA

Fritz, Harold A — *Vietnam War Army Hero (CMH)*
1017 W Scottwood Dr, Peoria, IL 61615, USA

Fritz, Nikki — *Actress*
%Don Gerler, 3349 Cahuenga Blvd W, #1, Los Angeles, CA 90068, USA

Frizzell, David — *Singer*
%Joe Taylor Artist Agency, 2802 Columbine Place, Nashville, TN 37204, USA

Froemming, Bruce N — *Baseball Umpire*
5045 Elk Court, Milwaukee, WI 53223, USA

Froese, Bob — *Hockey Player*
RR 30, Box 224, Lake Clear, NY 12945, USA

Frohnmayer, Dave — *Educator*
%University of Oregon, President's Office, Eugene, OR 97403, USA

Frohnmayer, John E — *Government Official*
100 Erik Dr, Bozeman, MT 59715, USA

Froines, John — *Social Activist, Educator*
%University of California, School of Public Health, Los Angeles, CA 90024, USA

Fromherz, Peter — *Biophysicist*
%Max Planck Biochemistry Institute, Biophysics Dept, Martinsried, Germany

Frommelt, Paul — *Skier*
%Liechtenstein Ski Federation, Vaduz, Liechtenstein

Fronczek, Vincent — *Photographer*
PO Box 425884, San Francisco, CA 94142, USA

Friedman - Fronczek

Frondel, Clifford *Mineralogist*
20 Beatrice Circle, Belmont, MA 02178, USA

Fronius, Hans *Artist*
Guggenbergasse 18, 2380 Perchtoldadorf Bei Vienna, Austria

Frosch, Robert A *Government Official, Space Administrator*
30495 Oakview Way, Birmingham, MI 48010, USA

Frost, David *Golfer*
11602 High Forest Dr, Dallas, TX 75230, USA

Frost, David P *Entertainer*
46 Egerton Crescent, London SW3, England

Frost, Lindsay *Actress*
310 Madison Ave, #232, New York, NY 10017, USA

Frost, Mark *Writer*
%Mark Frost Productions, PO Box 1723, North Hollywood, CA 91614, USA

Frost, Patrick B *Financier*
%Frost National Bank, 100 W Houston St, San Antonio, TX 78205, USA

Frost, Sadie *Actress*
%Burdett-Coutts, Riverside Studios, Crisp Road, London W6 9RL, England

Frost, T C *Financier*
%Cullen/Frost Bankers Inc, 100 W Houston St, San Antonio, TX 78205, USA

Fruedek, Jacques *Physicist*
2 Rue Jean-Francois Gerbillion, 70006 Paris, France

Fruh, Eugen *Artist*
Romergasse 9, 8001 Zurich, Switzerland

Fruhbeck de Burgos, Rafael *Conductor*
Reyes Magos 20, 28007 Madrid, Spain

Frumkin, Allan *Art Dealer*
%Frumklin/Adams Gallery, 1185 Park Ave, New York, NY 10128, USA

Fruton, Joseph S *Biochemist*
123 York St, New Haven, CT 06511, USA

Fry Irvin, Shirley *Tennis Player*
1970 Asylum Ave, West Hartford, CT 06117, USA

Fry, Arthur L *Inventor (Post-its)*
%Minnesota Mining (3-M), 3-M Center, Building 230-2S, St Paul, MN 55144, USA

Fry, Christopher *Writer*
Toft, East Dean near Chichester, Sussex, England

Fry, Hayden *Football Coach*
%University of Iowa, Athletic Dept, Iowa City, IA 52242, USA

Fry, Michael *Cartoonist (Committed, Over the Hedge)*
%United Feature Syndicate, 200 Madison Ave, New York, NY 10016, USA

Fry, Stephen *Comedian*
%Lorraine Hamilton, 76 Oxford St, London W1N 0AT, England

Fry, Thornton C *Mathematician*
500 Mohawk Dr, Boulder, CO 80303, USA

Fryar, Irving *Football Player*
7809 Galleon Court, Parkland, FL 33067, USA

Frye, Soliel Moon *Actress*
2713 N Keystone St, Burbank, CA 91504, USA

Fryman, D Travis *Baseball Player*
3201 Windmill Circle, Cantonment, FL 32533, USA

Fthenakis, Emanuel *Businessman*
%CEF Corp, PO Box 59708, Rockville, MD 20859, USA

Ftorek, Robbie *Hockey Player, Coach*
9 Barberry Way, Essex Falls, NY 07021, USA

Fuchs, Ann Sutherland *Publisher*
%Vogue Magazine, 350 Madison Ave, New York, NY 10017, USA

Fuchs, Joseph L *Publisher*
%Mademoiselle Magazine, 350 Madison Ave, New York, NY 10017, USA

Fuchs, Michael J *Television Executive*
%Home Box Office, 1100 Ave of Americas, New York, NY 10036, USA

Fuchs, Victor R *Economist*
796 Cedro Way, Stanford, CA 94305, USA

Fuchs, Vivian E *Explorer, Geologist*
106 Barton Road, Cambridge, Cambs CB3 9LH, England

Fuchsberger, Joachim *Actor*
Hubertusstr 62, 82031 Grunwald, Germany

Fudge, Alan *Actor*
355 S Rexford Dr, Beverly Hills, CA 90212, USA

Fuente, Luis	*Ballet Dancer*
98 Rue Lepic, 75018 Paris, France	
Fuentealba, Victor W	*Labor Leader*
4501 Arabia Ave, Baltimore, MD 21214, USA	
Fuentes, Carlos	*Writer*
%Harvard University, Latin American Studies Dept, Cambridge, MA 02138, USA	
Fuentes, Daisy	*Entertainer, Model*
%William Morris Agency, 151 S El Camino Dr, Beverly Hills, CA 90212, USA	
Fugard, Athol H	*Writer*
PO Box 5090, Walmer, Port Elizabeth, South Africa	
Fugate, Judith	*Ballerina*
%New York City Ballet, Lincoln Center Plaza, New York, NY 10023, USA	
Fuglesang, Christer	*Astronaut*
%Europe Astronaut Center, Linder Hohe, Box 906096, 51127 Cologne, Germany	
Fuhr, Grant	*Hockey Player*
40 Magnolia Dr, St Louis, MO 63124, USA	
Fujii, Keishi	*Financier*
%Bank of Tokyo, 3-2-1 Nihombasi Hongpkucho, Chuoku, Tokyo 103, Japan	
Fujimori, Alberto K	*President, Peru*
%President's Office, Palacio de Gobierno S/N, Plaza de Armas, Lima 1, Peru	
Fujimori, Tetsuo	*Financier*
%Dai-Ichi Kangyo Bank, 1-5-1 Uchisaiwaicho, Chiyodaku, Tokyo 100, Japan	
Fujimoto, Shun	*Businessman*
%Toyota Automobile Body, 100 Kanayama, Kariya City 448, Japan	
Fujinuma, Mototoshi	*Businessman*
%Sekisui Chemical, 2-4-4 Nishi-Tenma, Kitaku, Osaka 530, Japan	
Fujisaki, Akira	*Businessman*
%Sumitomo Metal Mining, 5-11-3 Shimbashi, Minatoku, Tokyo 105, Japan	
Fujita, Hiroyuki	*Microbiotics Engineer*
1-9-14 Senkawa, Toshimaku, Tokyo 171, Japan	
Fujiyoshi, Tsuguhide	*Businessman*
%Toray Industries, 2-2 Nihonbashi-Muromachi, Chuoku, Tokyo 103, Japan	
Fukui, Kenichi	*Nobel Chemistry Laureate*
%Fundamental Chemistry Inst, 34-4 Takano-Nishihiraki-cho, Kyoto 606, Japan	
Fuld, Richard S, Jr	*Financier*
%Lehman Brothers, 3 World Financial Center, New York, NY 10281, USA	
Fulford, Carlton W, Jr	*Marine Corps General*
CG, US Marine Expeditionary Force, FPO, AP 96602, USA	
Fulghum, Robert	*Religious Leader, Writer*
1015 Violeta Dr, Alhambra, CA 91801, USA	
Fuller, Bob B	*Writer*
37 Langton Way, London 5E3, England	
Fuller, Bonnie	*Editor*
%Cosmopolitan Magazine, Editorial Dept, 224 W 57th St, New York, NY 10019, USA	
Fuller, Charles	*Writer*
%William Morris Agency, 1325 Ave of Americas, New York, NY 10019, USA	
Fuller, Curtis D	*Jazz Trombonist*
%Denon Records, 135 W 50th St, #1915, New York, NY 10020, USA	
Fuller, E Keith	*Journalist*
%Associated Press, 50 Rockefeller Plaza, New York, NY 10020, USA	
Fuller, H Laurance	*Businessman*
%Amoco Corp, 200 E Randolph Dr, Chicago, IL 60601, USA	
Fuller, Jack W	*Editor, Publisher*
%Chicago Tribune, Editorial Dept, 435 N Michigan, Chicago, IL 60611, USA	
Fuller, Kathryn S	*Association Official*
%World Wildlife Fund, 1250 24th St NW, Washington, DC 20037, USA	
Fuller, Lawrence R	*Publisher*
%Argus Leader, PO Box 5034, Sioux Falls, SD 57117, USA	
Fuller, Millard	*Association Executive, Social Activist*
%Habitat for Humanity, 121 Habitat St, Americus, GA 31709, USA	
Fuller, Penny	*Actress*
12428 Hesby St, North Hollywood, CA 91607, USA	
Fuller, Robert (Bob)	*Actor*
5012 Auckland Ave, North Hollywood, CA 91601, USA	
Fuller, Samuel	*Movie Director*
7628 Woodrow Wilson Dr, Los Angeles, CA 90046, USA	
Fuller, Todd	*Basketball Player*
%Golden State Warriors, 7000 Coliseum Way, Oakland, CA 94621, USA	

Fuller, William H, Jr — *Football Player*
905 Chanticleer, Cherry Hill, NJ 08003, USA

Fullerton, C Gordon — *Astronaut*
%Ames/Dryden Research Facility, PO Box 273, Edwards Air Force Base, CA 93523, USA

Fullerton, Fiona — *Actress*
%London Mgmt, 2-4 Noel St, London W1V 3RB, England

Fullmer, Gene — *Boxer*
9250 S 2200 West, West Jordan, UT 84088, USA

Fulmer, Phillip — *Football Coach*
%University of Tennessee, Athletic Dept, Knoxville, TN 37996, USA

Fulton, Eileen — *Actress, Singer*
%"As the World Turns" Show, CBS-TV, 524 W 57nd St, New York, NY 10019, USA

Fulton, Robert D — *Governor, IA*
141 Hillcrest Road, Waterloo, IA 50701, USA

Funicello, Annette — *Actress, Singer*
16202 Sandy Lane, Encino, CA 91316, USA

Funk, Fred — *Golfer*
709 Spinnakers Reach Dr, Ponte Vedra, FL 32082, USA

Funkhouser, Paul W — *Businessman*
%Howell Corp, 1111 Fannin St, Houston, TX 77002, USA

Funt, Allen A — *Comedian, Television Producer*
PO Box 827, Monterey, CA 93942, USA

Furey, John — *Actor*
%House of Representatives, 400 S Beverly Dr, #101, Beverly Hills, CA 90212, USA

Furlan, Mira — *Actress*
PO Box 523093, Springfield, VA 22152, USA

Furlanetto, Ferruccio — *Opera Singer*
%Metropolitan Opera Assn, Lincoln Center Plaza, New York, NY 10023, USA

Furlong, Edward — *Actor*
10573 W Pico Blvd, #853, Los Angeles, CA 90064, USA

Furniss, Bruce — *Swimmer*
655 Westwood St, Anaheim Hills, CA 92807, USA

Furst, Stephen — *Actor*
3900 Huntercrest Court, Moorpark, CA 93021, USA

Furth, George — *Actor, Playwright*
%Bresler Kelly Assoc, 15760 Ventura Blvd, #1730, Encino, CA 91436, USA

Furth, Harold P — *Physicist*
36 Lake Lane, Princeton, NJ 08540, USA

Furth, Warren Wolfgang — *International Official*
13 Rt de Presinge, 1241 Puplinge, Geneva, Switzerland

Furuhashi, Hironshin — *Swimmer*
3-9-11 Nozawa, Setagayaku, Tokyo, Japan

Furukawa, Masaru — *Swimmer*
5-5-12 Shinohara Honmachi, Nadaku, Kobe, Japan

Furuseth, Ole Kristian — *Skier*
John Colletts Alle 74, 0854 Oslo, Norway

Furyk, Jim — *Golfer*
Rt 1, Box 259-A, Manheim, PA 17545, USA

Fusina, Chuck — *Football Player*
1548 King James St, Pittsburgh, PA 15237, USA

Fussell, Paul — *Writer, Educator*
1016 Spruce St, #2-F, Philadelphia, PA 19107, USA

Futch, Eddie — *Boxing Trainer*
5025 S Eastern Ave, #16-314, Las Vegas, NV 89119, USA

Futey, Bohdan A — *Judge*
%US Claims Court, 717 Madison Place NW, Washington, DC 20005, USA

Futrell, Mary H — *Labor Leader*
%George Washington University, Education School, Washington, DC 20052, USA

Futter, Ellen V — *Educator*
%American Museum of Natural History, Park Ave West & 79th St, New York, NY 10034, USA

Futterknecht, James O, Jr — *Businessman*
%Excel Industries, 1120 N Main St, Elkhart, IN 46514, USA

Futterman, Dan — *Actor*
%Gersh Agency, 232 N Canon Dr, Beverly Hills, CA 90210, USA

Futterman, Jack — *Businessman*
%Pathmark Stores, 301 Blair Road, Woodbridge, NJ 07095, USA

Fylstra, Daniel — *Computer Software Designer*
%Visicorp, 2895 Zanken Road, San Jose, CA 95134, USA

Gaarder, Jostein — *Philosopher*
Gullkroken 22-A, 0377 Oslo, Norway

Gabet, Sharon — *Actress*
222 E 44th St, New York, NY 10017, USA

Gable, Christopher — *Actor*
%Ken McReddie, 91 Regent St, London W1R 7TB, England

Gable, Dan — *Wrestler, Coach*
RR 2, Box 55, Iowa City, IA 52240, USA

Gabor, Zsa Zsa — *Actress*
1001 Bel Air Road, Los Angeles, CA 90077, USA

Gabreski, Francis S (Gabby) — *WW II Army Air Corps Hero*
106 Ryder Ave, Dix Hills, NY 11746, USA

Gabriel, John — *Actor*
130 W 42nd St, #1804, New York, NY 10036, USA

Gabriel, Juan — *Singer, Songwriter*
%Hauser Entertainment, PO Box 978, Pico Rivera, CA 90660, USA

Gabriel, Peter — *Singer, Songwriter*
%Gailforce Mgmt, 81-83 Walton St, London SW3 2HP, England

Gabriel, Roman — *Football Player*
%Roman Gabriel Sports Connection, 16817 McKee Road, Charlotte, NC 28278, USA

Gabrielle, Monique — *Model, Actress*
%Purrfect Productions, PO Box 430, Newbury Park, CA 91319, USA

Gaddafi, Mu'ammar Mohammad al- — *President, Libya; Army Colonel*
%President's Office, Bab el Aziziya Barracks, Tripoli, Libya

Gaddis, William — *Writer*
%Donadio & Ashworth, 121 W 27th St, #704, New York, NY 10001, USA

Gadsby, William A (Bill) — *Hockey Player*
28765 E Kalong Circle, Southfield, MI 48034, USA

Gaetti, Gary J — *Baseball Player*
7612 Rainwater Road, Raleigh, NC 27615, USA

Gaffney, F Andrew — *Astronaut*
6613 Chatsworth Place, Nashville, TN 37205, USA

Gage, Nicholas — *Columnist*
37 Nelson St, North Grafton, MA 01536, USA

Gage, Paul — *Computer Researcher*
%Crag Research, Highway 178 N, Chippewa Falls, WI 55402, USA

Gagne, Greg C — *Baseball Player*
746 Whetstone Hill Road, Somerset, MA 02726, USA

Gagnier, Holly — *Actress*
145 S Fairfax Ave, #310, Los Angeles, CA 90036, USA

Gagnon, Edouard Cardinal — *Religious Leader*
%Pontifical Family Council, Palazzo S Calisto, 00120 Vatican City

Gago, Jenny — *Actress*
%Metropolitan Talent Agency, 4526 Wilshire Blvd, Los Angeles, CA 90010, USA

Gahan, David — *Singer (Depeche Mode)*
%DMB&B Entertainment, 6500 Wilshire Blvd, #1000, Los Angeles, CA 90048, USA

Gaidukov, Sergei N — *Cosmonaut*
%Potchta Kosmonavtov, Moskovskoi Oblasti, 141160 Syvisdny Goroduk, Russia

Gail, Max — *Actor*
29451 Bluewater Road, Malibu, CA 90265, USA

Gaillard, Bob — *Basketball Coach*
50 Bonnie Brae Dr, Novato, CA 94949, USA

Gain, Bob — *Football Player*
11 Nokomis Dr, Timberlake Village, OH 44095, USA

Gaines, Boyd — *Actor, Singer*
%Duva/Flack, 200 W 57th St, #1407, New York, NY 10019, USA

Gaines, Ernest J — *Writer*
128 Buena Vista Blvd, Lafayette, LA 70503, USA

Gaines, James R — *Editor, Publisher*
%Time Warner Inc, Time Magazine, Rockefeller Center, New York, NY 10020, USA

Gaines, John R — *Thoroughbred Racing Breeder*
%Gainesway Farm, 3750 Paris Pike, Lexington, KY 40511, USA

Gaines, Rowdy — *Swimmer*
6800 Hawaii Kai Dr, Honolulu, HI 96825, USA

Gainey, Robert M (Bob) — *Hockey Player, Coach, Executive*
729 E Bethel School Road, Coppell, TX 75019, USA

Gaither, Bill — *Gospel Songwriter*
%Gaither Music Co, PO Box 737, Alexandria, IN 46001, USA

Gajdusek, D Carleton — *Nobel Medicine Laureate*
4316 Deer Spring Road, Middletown, MD 21769, USA

Gaje Ghale — *WW II India Army Hero (VC)*
Alexendre Lines, Almora 26301 UP, India

Galanos, James — *Fashion Designer*
2254 S Sepulveda Blvd, Los Angeles, CA 90064, USA

Galarraga, Andres J P — *Baseball Player*
Barrio Nuevo Chapellin, Clejon Soledad #5, Caracas, Venezuela

Galati, Frank J — *Stage, Opera Director*
1144 Michigan Ave, Evanston, IL 60202, USA

Galbraith, Clint — *Harness Racing Driver*
Rt 253, Box C, Scottsville, NY 14546, USA

Galbraith, Evan G — *Diplomat, Financier*
133 E 64th St, New York, NY 10021, USA

Galbraith, J Kenneth — *Government Official, Economist*
30 Francis Ave, Cambridge, MA 02138, USA

Galdikas, Birute M F — *Anthropologist*
%Orangutan Foundation International, 822 S Wellesley Ave, Los Angeles, CA 90049, USA

Gale, Robert P — *Medical Researcher*
2501 Roscomare Road, Los Angeles, CA 90077, USA

Galella, Ronald E (Ron) — *Photographer*
%Ron Galella Ltd, 12 Nelson Lane, Montville, NJ 07045, USA

Galer, Robert E — *WW II Marine Corps Hero (CMH), General*
5588 Southern Hills Dr, Frisco, TX 75034, USA

Galik, Denise — *Actress*
%Badgley Connor, 9229 Sunset Blvd, #311, Los Angeles, CA 90069, USA

Gall, Hugues — *Opera Executive*
%Theater National de l'Opera, Place de l'Opera, 75009 Paris, France

Gallagher — *Illusionist*
14984 Roan Court, West Palm Beach, FL 33414, USA

Gallagher, Helen — *Singer, Actress*
260 West End Ave, New York, NY 10023, USA

Gallagher, John — *Religious Leader*
%Advent Christian Church, PO Box 551, Presque Isle, ME 04769, USA

Gallagher, Megan — *Actress*
440 Landfair Ave, Los Angeles, CA 90024, USA

Gallagher, Peter — *Actor*
171 W 71st St, #3-A, New York, NY 10023, USA

Gallant, Mavis — *Writer*
14 Rue Jean Ferrandi, 75006 Paris, France

Gallardo, Camilio — *Actor*
%Innovative Artists, 1999 Ave of Stars, #2850, Los Angeles, CA 90067, USA

Gallardo, Silvana — *Actress*
201 Ruth Ave, Venice, CA 90291, USA

Gallarneau, Hugh — *Football Player*
2216 Maple Dr, Northbrook, IL 60062, USA

Gallatin, Harry J — *Basketball Player*
2010 Madison Ave, Edwardsville, IL 62025, USA

Gallego, Gina — *Actress*
%The Agency, 1800 Ave of Stars, #400, Los Angeles, CA 90067, USA

Galles, John — *Association Executive*
%National Small Business United, 1156 15th St NW, #1100, Washington, DC 20005, USA

Galley, Garry — *Hockey Player*
5 School Hill Lane, North Reading, MA 01864, USA

Gallison, Joe — *Actor*
PO Box 10187, Wilmington, NC 28405, USA

Gallo, Ernest — *Businessman*
%E&J Gallo Winery, 600 Yosemite Blvd, Modesto, CA 95354, USA

Gallo, Frank — *Sculptor*
%University of Illinois, Art Dept, Urbana, IL 61801, USA

Gallo, Lew — *Movie Director*
1421 Ambassador St, #101, Los Angeles, CA 90035, USA

Gallo, Robert C — *Research Scientist*
%Institute for Study of Viruses, University of Maryland, Baltimore, MD 21228, USA

Gallo, William V (Bill) — *Sports Cartoonist*
1 Mayflower Dr, Yonkers, NY 10710, USA

Galloway, Don — *Actor*
%J Miller, 1800 Century Park East, #300, Los Angeles, CA 90067, USA

G

Gallup, George H, II — *Statistician, Pollster*
53 Bank St, Princeton, NJ 08542, USA
Galotti, Ronald A — *Publisher*
%Hearst Magazines, 959 8th Ave, New York, NY 10019, USA
Galvin, James — *Writer*
%University of Iowa, Writers' Workshop, Iowa City, IA 52242, USA
Galvin, John R — *Army General*
114 South St, Medford, MA 02155, USA
Galvin, Robert W — *Businessman*
%Motorola Inc, 1303 E Algonquin Road, Schaumberg, IL 60196, USA
Galway, James — *Concert Flutist*
%IMG Artists, 3 Burlington Lane, London W4 2TH, England
Gam, Rita — *Actress*
180 W 58th St, #8-B, New York, NY 10019, USA
Gamache, Joey — *Boxer*
RR 2, Box 1680, 2 Easy St, Litchfield, ME 04350, USA
Gamba, Piero — *Conductor*
%Winnipeg Symphony Orchestra, 555 Main St, Winnipeg MB R3B 1C3, Canada
Gamble, Ed — *Editorial Cartoonist*
%Florida Times-Union, Editorial Dept, 1 Riverside Ave, Jacksonville, FL 32202, USA
Gamble, Kevin — *Basketball Player*
3112 Markwood Lane, Springfield, IL 62707, USA
Gamble, Patrick K — *Air Force General*
Commander, 11th Air Force, 5800 "G" St, Elmendorf Air Force Base, AK 99506, USA
Gambon, Michael — *Actor*
%Larry Dalzell Assoc, 17 Broad Court, #12, London WC2B 5QN, England
Gambrell, David H — *Senator, GA*
3205 Arden Road NW, Atlanta, GA 30305, USA
Gambril, Don — *Swimming Coach*
%University of Alabama, Athletic Dept, University, AL 35486, USA
Gambucci, Andre — *Hockey Player, Coach*
3 Poplar St, Colorado Springs, CO 80906, USA
Gammie, Anthony P — *Businessman*
%Bowater Inc, 55 E Campendown Way, Greenville, SC 29601, USA
Gammill, Lee M, Jr — *Businessman*
%New York Life & Annuity, 41 W 58th St, #10-C, New York, NY 10019, USA
Gammon, James — *Actor*
%Blake Agency, 415 N Camden Dr, #121, Beverly Hills, CA 90210, USA
Gamper, Albert R, Jr — *Financier*
%CIT Group Holdings, 650 CIT Dr, Livingston, NJ 07039, USA
Gandolfini, James — *Actor*
%Writers & Artists, 924 Westwood Blvd, #900, Los Angeles, CA 90024, USA
Gandrud, Robert P — *Businessman*
%Lutheran Brotherhood, 625 4th Ave S, Minneapolis, MN 55415, USA
Ganellin, C Robin — *Inventor (Antiulcer Compound)*
University College, Chemistry Dept, 20 Gordon St, London WC1H OAJ, England
Gangel, Jamie — *Commentator*
%NBC-TV, News Dept, 30 Rockefeller Plaza, New York, NY 10112, USA
Gangl, Kenneth R — *Financier*
%Case Finance Co, 700 State St, Racine, WI 53404, USA
Ganju Lama — *WW II India Army Hero (VC)*
Shangderpa House, 34 Singtam Ravangla Road, PO Ravangla, S Sikkim, India
Ganson, Arthur — *Sculptor*
%Massachusetts Institute of Technology, Compton Gallery, Cambridge, MA 02139, USA
Gant, Harry — *Auto Racing Driver*
Rt 3, Box 587, Taylorsville, NC 28681, USA
Gant, Richard — *Actor*
%Pakula/King, 9229 Sunset Blvd, #315, Los Angeles, CA 90069, USA
Gant, Ronald E (Ron) — *Baseball Player*
385 Nottingham Dr, Marietta, GA 30066, USA
Gantin, Bernardin Cardinal — *Religious Leader*
Piazzi S Calisto 16, 00153 Rome, Italy
Ganzel, Teresa — *Actress*
%Irv Schechter, 9300 Wilshire Blvd, #410, Beverly Hills, CA 90212, USA
Garabedian, Paul R — *Mathematician*
110 Bleecker St, New York, NY 10012, USA
Garagiola, Joe — *Sportscaster, Baseball Player*
6221 E Huntress Dr, Paradise Valley, AZ 85253, USA

Garas, Kaz — *Actor*
110 Glendale Ave, Oxnard, CA 93035, USA

Garba, Joseph N — *Army General; Diplomat, Nigeria*
%Foreign Affairs Ministry, 23 Marina, PMB 12600, Lagos, Nigeria

Garber, H Eugene (Gene) — *Baseball Player*
771 Stonemill Dr, Elizabethtown, PA 17022, USA

Garber, Terri — *Actress*
13606 Burbank Blvd, Van Nuys, CA 91401, USA

Garber, Victor — *Actor*
%Gersh Agency, 232 N Canon Dr, Beverly Hills, CA 90210, USA

Garberding, Larry G — *Businessman*
%Detroit Edison, 200 2nd Ave, Detroit, MI 48226, USA

Garci, Jose Luis — *Movie Director*
%Direccion General del Libro, Paseo de la Castellana 109, Madrid 16, Spain

Garcia Marquez, Gabriel — *Nobel Literature Laureate*
Fuego 144, Pedregal de San Angel, Mexico City DF, Mexico

Garcia, Andy — *Actor*
4323 Forman Ave, Toluca Lake, CA 91602, USA

Garcia, Carlos J — *Baseball Player*
%Toronto Blue Jays, 300 Bremner Blvd, Toronto ON M5V 3B3, Canada

Gardelli, Lamberto — *Conductor*
%Allied Artists, 42 Montpelier Square, London SW7 1J2, England

Gardiner, John Eliot — *Conductor*
Gore Farm, Ashmore, Salisbury, Wilts, England

Gardiner, Robert K A — *United Nations Official, Ghana*
PO Box 9274, The Airport, Accra, Ghana

Gardner, Cal — *Hockey Player*
41 Annesley Ave, Toronto ON M4G 2T5, Canada

Gardner, Carl — *Singer (The Coasters)*
%JP Productions, 57 18th Ave, Ronkonkoma, NY 11779, USA

Gardner, Dale A — *Astronaut*
1013 Sun Dr, Colorado Springs, CO 80906, USA

Gardner, David P — *Educator, Foundation Executive*
%Hewlett Foundation, 525 Middlefield Road, #200, Menlo Park, CA 94025, USA

Gardner, Guy S — *Astronaut*
%NASA Headquarters, Mail Code M-3, Washington, DC 20546, USA

Gardner, Howard E — *Psychologist, Neurobiologist*
%Harvard University, Graduate Education School, Cambridge, MA 02138, USA

Gardner, Jack (James H) — *Basketball Coach*
2486 Michigan Ave, Salt Lake City, UT 84108, USA

Gardner, John — *Ballet Dancer*
%American Ballet Theatre, 890 Broadway, New York, NY 10003, USA

Gardner, John W — *Secretary, Health Education & Welfare*
%Stanford University, Graduate Business School, Stanford, CA 94305, USA

Gardner, M Dozier — *Financier*
%Eaton Vance Corp, 24 Federal St, Boston, MA 02110, USA

Gardner, Philip J — *WW II British Army Hero (VC)*
Wakehurst, 19 Princes Crescent, Hove, Sussex BN3 4GS, England

Gardner, Randy — *Figure Skater*
4640 Glencoe Ave, #6, Marina del Rey, CA 90292, USA

Gardner, Richard N — *Diplomat*
1150 5th Ave, New York, NY 10128, USA

Gardner, Wilford R — *Physicist*
%University of California, Natural Resources College, Berkeley, CA 94720, USA

Gardner, William F (Bill) — *Baseball Manager*
35 Dayton Road, Waterford, CT 06385, USA

Gardner, William G — *Businessman*
%Apogee Enterprises, 7900 Xerxes Ave, Minneapolis, MN 55431, USA

Gare, Danny — *Hockey Player*
320 St Gregory Court, Buffalo, NY 14221, USA

Garfield, Allen — *Actor*
9931 Durant Dr, Beverly Hills, CA 90212, USA

Garfield, Brian W — *Writer*
345 N Maple Dr, #395, Beverly Hills, CA 90210, USA

Garfunkel, Art — *Singer, Actor*
9 E 79th St, New York, NY 10021, USA

Garland, Beverly — *Actress*
8014 Briar Summit Dr, Los Angeles, CA 90046, USA

G

Garas - Garland

Garland, George D — *Geophysicist*
%Academy of Science, 207 Queen St, Ottawa ON K1G OAO, Canada
Garlits, Don (Big Daddy) — *Drag Racing Driver*
%Garlits Racing Museum, 13700 SW 16th Ave, Ocala, FL 34473, USA
Garn, E Jacob (Jake) — *Senator, UT; Astronaut*
%Huntsman Chemical Corp, 2000 Eagle Gate Tower, Salt Lake City, UT 84111, USA
Garn, Stanley M — *Physical Anthropologist*
2410 Londonderry Road, Ann Arbor, MI 48104, USA
Garneau, Marc — *Astronaut, Canada*
6767 Route de Aeroport, Sainte-Hubert PQ J3Y 8Y9, Canada
Garneau, Robert M — *Businessman*
%Kaman Corp, 1332 Blue Hills Ave, Bloomfield, CT 06002, USA
Garner, C Kent — *Businessman*
%Dollar General Corp, 104 Woodmont Blvd, Nashville, TN 37205, USA
Garner, James — *Actor*
33 Oakmont Dr, Los Angeles, CA 90049, USA
Garner, Jay M — *Army General*
Asst Vice Chief of Staff, HqUSA, Pentagon, Washington, DC 20310, USA
Garner, Philip M (Phil) — *Baseball Player, Manager*
2451 Lake Village Dr, Kingwood, TX 77339, USA
Garner, Wendell R — *Psychologist*
48 Yowago Ave, Branford, CT 06405, USA
Garner, William S — *Editorial Cartoonist*
%Memphis Commercial Appeal, Editorial Dept, 495 Union Ave, Memphis, TN 38103, USA
Garnett, Kevin — *Basketball Player*
%Minnesota Timberwolves, Target Center, 600 1st Ave N, Minneapolis, MN 55403, USA
Garofalo, Janeane — *Actress*
%United Talent Agency, 9560 Wilshire Blvd, #500, Beverly Hills, CA 90212, USA
Garouste, Gerard — *Artist*
La Mesangere, 27810 Marcilly-sur-Eure, France
Garr, Ralph A — *Baseball Player*
7819 Chaseway Dr, Missouri City, TX 77489, USA
Garr, Teri — *Actress*
8686 Lookout Mountain Dr, Los Angeles, CA 90046, USA
Garrahy, J Joseph — *Governor, RI*
474 Ocean Road, Narragansett, RI 02882, USA
Garrels, Robert M — *Geologist*
%South Florida University, Marine Science Dept, St Petersburg, FL 33701, USA
Garrett, Betty — *Actress, Singer*
3231 Oakdell Road, Studio City, CA 91604, USA
Garrett, Brad — *Comedian, Actor*
%Abrams Artists, 9200 Sunset Blvd, #625, Los Angeles, CA 90069, USA
Garrett, George P, Jr — *Writer*
1845 Wayside Place, Charlottesville, VA 22903, USA
Garrett, H Lawrence, III — *Government Official*
3202 Cinch Ring Court, Oakton, VA 22124, USA
Garrett, Kenny — *Jazz Saxophonist*
%Robin Burgess Mgmt, 3225 Prytania St, New Orleans, LA 70115, USA
Garrett, Leif — *Actor, Singer*
11524 Amanda Dr, Studio City, CA 91604, USA
Garrett, Lila — *Movie Producer*
1245 Laurel Way, Beverly Hills, CA 90210, USA
Garrett, Mike — *Football Player, Sports Administrator*
%University of Southern California, Heritage Hall, Los Angeles, CA 90089, USA
Garrett, Pat — *Singer, Songwriter*
%Patrick Sickafus, PO Box 84, Strausstown, PA 19559, USA
Garrett, Wilbur E — *Editor*
%National Geographic Magazine, 17th & "M" Sts, Washington, DC 20036, USA
Garrett, William E — *Photographer*
209 Seneca Road, Great Falls, VA 22066, USA
Garriott, Owen K — *Astronaut*
111 Lost Tree Dr SW, Huntsville, AL 35824, USA
Garrison, John — *Hockey Player*
Old Concord Road, Lincoln, MA 01773, USA
Garrison, U Edwin — *Businessman*
%Thiokol Corp, 2475 Washington Blvd, Ogden, UT 84401, USA
Garrison, William R — *Businessman*
%CDI Corp, 1717 Arch St, Philadelphia, PA 19103, USA

Garrison-Jackson, Zina *Tennis Player*
PO Box 272305, Houston, TX 77277, USA
Garrity, Freddie *Singer*
16 Ascot Close, Congleton, Cheshire CW1Z 1LL, England
Garrum, Larry *Hockey Player*
987 Pleasant St, Framingham, MA 01701, USA
Garth, Jennie *Actress*
PO Box 5792, Sherman Oaks, CA 91413, USA
Gartner, Michael G *Television Executive, Publisher, Editor*
%Ames Daily Tribune, PO Box 380, Ames, IA 50010, USA
Gartner, Mike *Hockey Player*
981 Wayson Way, Davidsonville, MD 21035, USA
Garton, Daniel P, Sr *Businessman*
%Continental Airlines, 2929 Allen Parkway, Houston, TX 77019, USA
Gartzke, David G *Businessman*
%Minnesota Power, 30 W Superior St, Duluth, MN 55802, USA
Garver, Kathy *Actress*
%Robert Cosden Agency, 3518 Cahuenga Blvd W, #216, Los Angeles 90068, USA
Garver, Ned F *Baseball Player*
PO Box 114, Ney, OH 43549, USA
Garvey, Jane *Government Official*
%Federal Aviation Administration, 800 Independence Ave SW, Washington, DC 20591, USA
Garvey, Steven P (Steve) *Baseball Player*
11718 Barrington Court, #6, Los Angeles, CA 90049, USA
Garvin, Clifton C, Jr *Businessman*
33 Baldwin Farms, Greenwich, CT 06831, USA
Garwin, Richard L *Physicist*
%IBM Corp, Watson Research Center, PO Box 218, Yorktown Heights, NY 10598, USA
Gary, Cleveland *Football Player*
2431 Sw Danbury Lane, Palm City, FL 34990, USA
Gary, John *Singer*
7 Briarwood Circle, Richardson, TX 75080, USA
Gary, Lorraine *Actress*
1158 Tower Dr, Beverly Hills, CA 90210, USA
Gascoigne, Paul J *Soccer Player*
%Arran Gardner, Holborn Hall, London WC1X 8BY, England
Gaspari, Rich *Body Builder*
PO Box 29, Milltown, NJ 08850, USA
Gasparro, Frank *Sculptor*
216 Westwood Park Dr, Havertown, PA 19083, USA
Gasser, Michael J *Businessman*
%Greif Bros Corp, 425 Winter Road, Delaware, OH 43015, USA
Gassman, Vittorio *Actor*
Piazza S Alessio 32, 00191 Rome, Italy
Gastineau, Mark *Football Player*
9090 N 96th Place, Scottsdale, AZ 85258, USA
Gaston, Clarence E (Cito) *Baseball Player, Manager*
47 Melgund Road, Toronto ON M5R 2A1, Canada
Gately, George G *Cartoonist (Heathcliff)*
%Tribune Media Services, 435 N Michigan Ave, #1500, Chicago, IL 60611, USA
Gates, Charles C *Businessman*
%Gates Corp, 900 S Broadway St, Denver, CO 80209, USA
Gates, Daryl F *Law Enforcement Official*
756 Portoila Terrace, Los Angeles, CA 90042, USA
Gates, Henry Lewis, Jr *Educator*
%Harvard University, Afro-American Studies Dept, Cambridge, MA 02138, USA
Gates, Marshall De M, Jr *Chemist*
41 West Brook Road, Pittsburgh, PA 14534, USA
Gates, William (Pops) *Basketball Player*
2200 Madison Ave, #5-A, New York, NY 10037, USA
Gates, William H (Bill), III *Businessman*
%Microsoft Corp, 1 Microsoft Way, Redmond, WA 98052, USA
Gatlin, Larry W *Singer*
%Gatlin Enterprises, 7003 Chadwick Dr, #360, Brentwood, TN 37027, USA
Gatling, Chris *Basketball Player*
%New Jersey Nets, Byrne Meadowlands Arena, East Rutherford, NJ 07073, USA
Gatski, Frank *Football Player*
Rt 250, Grafton, WV 26354, USA

Garrison-Jackson - Gatski

G

Gatti, Jennifer — *Actress*
%SDB Partners, 1801 Ave of Stars, #902, Los Angeles, CA 90067, USA

Gatting, Michael W — *Cricketer*
%Middlesex Cricket Club, St John's Wood Road, London NW8 8QN, England

Gaudiani, Claire L — *Educator*
%Connecticut College, President's Office, New London, CT 06320, USA

Gaul, Gilbert M — *Journalist*
%Philadelphia Inquirer, Editorial Dept, 400 N Broad St, Philadelphia, PA 19130, USA

Gaulin, Jean — *Businessman*
%Ultramar Corp, 9830 Colonnade Blvd, San Antonio, TX 78230, USA

Gault, Stanley C — *Businessman*
%Goodyear Tire & Rubber, 1144 E Market St, Akron, OH 44316, USA

Gault, William Campbell — *Writer*
482 Vaquero Lane, Santa Barbara, CA 93111, USA

Gault, Willie — *Football Player*
33 26th Place, Venice, CA 90291, USA

Gaultier, Jean-Paul — *Fashion Designer*
%Gaultier Boutique, 2 Rue Vivien, 75006 Paris, France

Gautier, Dick — *Actor*
11333 Moorpark St, #59, North Hollywood, CA 91602, USA

Gavaskar, Sunil M — *Cricketer*
40 Sir Bhalchandra Road, #A, Dadar, Bombay 400014, India

Gavin, John — *Actor, Diplomat*
10263 Century Woods Dr, Los Angeles, CA 90067, USA

Gaviria Trujillo, Cesar — *President, Colombia*
%Organization of American States, 1889 "F" St NW, Washington, DC 20006, USA

Gavitt, Dave — *Basketball Executive*
%Boston Celtics, 151 Merrimac St, #500, Boston, MA 02114, USA

Gavrilov, Andrei V — *Concert Pianist*
%Harold Holt, 31 Sinclair Road, London W14 0NS, England

Gay, Gerald H — *Photographer*
2647 Perkins Lane W, Seattle, WA 98199, USA

Gay, Peter J — *Writer, Historian*
105 Blue Trail, Hamden, CT 06518, USA

Gayle, Crystal — *Singer*
%Gayle Enterprises, 51 Music Square E, Nashville, TN 37203, USA

Gayle, Jackie — *Comedian*
2155 San Ysidro Dr, Beverly Hills, CA 90210, USA

Gaylor, Noel — *Navy Admiral*
2111 Mason Hill Dr, Alexandria, VA 22306, USA

Gaylord, Edward L — *Publisher, Broadcast Executive*
%Oakland Publishing Co, 500 N Broadway, Oklahoma City, OK 73125, USA

Gaylord, Mitch — *Gymnast, Actor*
PO Box 15001, Beverly Hills, CA 90209, USA

Gaynes, George — *Actor*
3344 Campanil Dr, Santa Barbara, CA 93109, USA

Gaynor, Gloria — *Singer*
%Cliffside Music, PO Box 374, Fairview, NJ 07022, USA

Gaynor, Mitzi — *Actress, Dancer, Singer*
610 N Arden Dr, Beverly Hills, CA 90210, USA

Gayoom, Maumoon Abdul — *President, Maldives*
%President's Office, Marine Dr N, Male, Maldives

Gazzara, Ben — *Actor*
1080 Madison Ave, New York, NY 10028, USA

Geary, Anthony (Tony) — *Actor*
7010 Pacific View Dr, Los Angeles, CA 90068, USA

Geary, Cynthia — *Actress*
21121 Foxtail, Mission Viejo, CA 92692, USA

Gebel-Williams, Gunther — *Circus Animal Trainer*
%Ringling Bros Barnum & Bailey Circus, 8607 Westwood Circle, Vienna, VA 22182, USA

Gebrselassie, Haile — *Track Athlete*
%Ethiopian Athletic Federation, PO Box 3241, Addis Ababa, Ethiopia

Gedda, Nicolai — *Opera Singer*
%Shaw Concerts, Lincoln Center Plaza, 1900 Broadway, #200, New York, NY 10023, USA

Geddes, Jane — *Golfer*
118 S Westshore Blvd, #280, Tampa, FL 33609, USA

Gedrick, Jason — *Actor*
%IFA Talent Agency, 8730 Sunset Blvd, #490, Los Angeles, CA 90069, USA

Gee, E Gordon — *Educator*
%Ohio State University, President's Office, Columbus, OH 43210, USA

Gee, James D — *Religious Leader*
%Pentecostal Church of God, 4901 Pennsylvania, Joplin, MO 64804, USA

Geer, Dennis — *Financier*
%Federal Deposit Insurance, 550 17th St NW, Washington, DC 20429, USA

Geer, Ellen — *Actress*
21418 W Entrada Road, Topanga, CA 90290, USA

Geertz, Clifford J — *Anthropologist*
%Institute for Advanced Study, Social Science Dept, Princeton, NJ 08540, USA

Geeson, Judy — *Actress*
%MLR Ltd, 200 Fulham Road, London SW10 9PN, England

Geffen, David — *Movie, Record Producer*
%DreamWorks SKG, 100 Universal City Plaza, Universal City, CA 91608, USA

Gehman, Harold W, Jr — *Navy Admiral*
%Office of Vice Chief of Naval Operations, HqUSN, Pentagon, Washington, DC 20370, USA

Gehry, Frank O — *Architect*
%Frank Gehry Assoc, 1520-B Cloverfield Blvd, Santa Monica, CA 90404, USA

Geiberger, Al — *Golfer*
17700 NE 143rd Place, Woodinville, WA 98072, USA

Geiduschek, E Peter — *Biologist*
%University of California, Biology Dept, 9500 Gilman Dr, La Jolla, CA 92093, USA

Geier, Philip H, Jr — *Businessman*
%Interpublic Group, 1271 Ave of Americas, New York, NY 10020, USA

Geiger, Ken — *Photographer*
%Dallas Morning News, Communications Center, Dallas, TX 75265, USA

Geiger, Matt — *Basketball Player*
1692 Lago Vista Blvd, Palm Harbor, FL 34685, USA

Geingob, Hage G — *Prime Minister, Namibia*
%Prime Minister's Office, Private Bag 13338, Windhoek 9000, Namibia

Geis, Bernard — *Publisher*
500 5th Ave, #3600, New York, NY 10110, USA

Geithner, Paul H, Jr — *Financier*
%First Virginia Banks, 6400 Arlington Blvd, Falls Church, VA 22042, USA

Gelb, Bruce S — *Diplomat, Businessman*
%US Embassy, Belgium, APO, AE 09724, USA

Gelb, Richard L — *Businessman*
%Bristol-Myers Squibb, 345 Park Ave, New York, NY 10154, USA

Gelbart, Larry — *Movie, Television Producer; Writer*
807 N Alpine Dr, Beverly Hills, CA 90210, USA

Gelber, Jack — *Writer*
230 E 18th St, #1-C, New York, NY 10003, USA

Geldof, Bob — *Singer*
Davington Priory, Faversham, Kent, England

Gelin, Daniel — *Actor*
72 Ave de Chartres, 28570 Abondant, France

Gell-Mann, Murray — *Nobel Physics Laureate*
%California Institute of Technology, Physics Laboratory, Pasadena, CA 91125, USA

Gellar, Sarah Michelle — *Actress*
%Paradigm Agency, 10100 Santa Monica Blvd, #2500, Los Angeles, CA 90067, USA

Gellhorn, Martha — *Writer*
%Douglas Rae Mgmt, 28 Charing Cross Road, London WC2H 0DB, England

Gelman, Larry — *Actor*
5121 Greenbush Ave, Sherman Oaks, CA 91423, USA

Gemar, Charles D — *Astronaut*
%NASA, Johnson Space Center, 2101 NASA Road, Houston, TX 77058, USA

Gendron, George — *Editor*
%Inc Magazine, Editorial Dept, 38 Commercial Wharf, Boston, MA 02110, USA

Geneen, Harold S — *Businessman*
320 Park Ave, New York, NY 10022, USA

Gennaro, Peter — *Choreographer*
115 Central Park West, New York, NY 10023, USA

Genovese, Leonard — *Businessman*
%Genovese Drug Stores, 80 Marcus Dr, Melville, NY 11747, USA

Genovese, Peter J — *Financier*
%UMB Financial Corp, 1010 Grand Ave, St Louis, MO 64106, USA

Genscher, Hans-Dietrich — *Government Official, Germany*
Am Kottenforst 16, 5307 Wachtberg 3, Germany

G

Gee - Genscher

G

Gensler, M Arthur, Jr *Architect*
%Gensler & Assoc Architects, 550 Kearny St, San Francisco, CA 94108, USA

Gentile, Armond F *Financier*
%Beneficial Savings Bank, 1200 Chestnut St, Philadelphia, PA 19107, USA

Gentleman, John F *Businessman*
%ULLICO Inc, 111 Massachusetts Ave NW, Washington, DC 20001, USA

Gentner, Craig *Businessman*
%Network Equipment Technologies, 800 Saginaw Dr, Redwood City, CA 94063, USA

Gentry, Alvin *Basketball Coach*
%Miami Heat, Miami Arena, 100 NE 3rd Ave, Miami, FL 33132, USA

Gentry, Bobbie *Singer*
269 S Beverly Dr, #368, Beverly Hills, CA 90212, USA

Gentry, Teddy W *Singer, Guitarist (Alabama)*
PO Box 529, Fort Payne, AL 35968, USA

Geoffrin, Bernie (Boom Boom) *Hockey Player*
4431 Dobbs Ferry Crossing Dr, Marietta, GA 30068, USA

Geoffrion, Scott *Pro Stock Racing Driver*
592 Explorer St, #B, Brea, CA 92821, USA

Geoga, Douglas *Businessman*
%Hyatt Hotels Corp, 200 W Madison St, Chicago, IL 60606, USA

Georgantas, Astrides W *Financier*
%Chemical Bank New Jersey, 2 Tower Center, East Brunswick, NJ 08816, USA

George, Eddie *Football Player*
%Tennessee Oilers, Hale Hall, Tennessee State University, Nashville, TN 37209, USA

George, Elizabeth *Writer*
%Bantam Books, 1540 Broadway, New York, NY 10036, USA

George, Eric *Actor*
%Gage Group, 9255 Sunset Blvd, #515, Los Angeles, CA 90069, USA

George, Francis E *Religious Leader*
%Chicago Archdiocese, 1555 N State Parkway, Chicago, IL 60610, USA

George, James (Jim) *Weightlifter*
985 Merriman Road, Akron, OH 44303, USA

George, Jeff *Football Player*
1908 Schwier Court, Indianapolis, IN 46229, USA

George, Peter T *Weightlifter*
1441 Kapiolani Blvd, #520, Honolulu, HI 96814, USA

George, Phyllis *Commentator*
Cave Hill Place, Lexington, KY 40544, USA

George, Susan *Actress*
520 Washington Blvd, #187, Marina del Rey, CA 90292, USA

George, Tony *Motor Sports Executive*
%Indianapolis Motor Speedway, 4790 W 16th St, Speedway, IN 46222, USA

George, William D, Jr *Businessman*
%S C Johnson & Son, 1525 Howe St, Racine, WI 53403, USA

George, William W *Businessman*
%Medtronic Inc, 7000 Central Ave NE, Minneapolis, MN 55432, USA

Georges, John A *Businessman*
%International Paper, 2 Manhattanville Road, Purchase, NY 10577, USA

Georgian, Theodore J *Religious Leader*
%Orthodox Presbyterian Church, PO Box P, Willow Grove, PA 19090, USA

Georgije, Bishop *Religious Leader*
%Serbian Orthodox Church, Saint Sava Monastery, Box 519, Libertyville, IL 60048, USA

Georgine, Robert A *Businessman*
%ULLICO Inc, 111 Massachusetts Ave NW, Washington, DC 20001, USA

Georgius, John R *Financier*
%First Union Corp, 7815 Telegraph Road, Bloomington, MN 55438, USA

Gerard, Gil *Actor*
23679 Calabasas Road, #325, Calabasas, CA 91302, USA

Gerard, Jean Shevlin *Diplomat*
%American Embassy, 22 Blvd Emannanuel Servais, 2535 Luxembourg

Geraschenko, Victor V *Financier*
%Russian Central Bank, Neglinnaya St 12, 117049 Moscow, Russia

Gerber, H Joseph *Businessman*
%Gerber Scientific Inc, 83 Gerber Road W, South Windsor, CT 06074, USA

Gerber, Joel *Judge*
%US Tax Court, 400 2nd St NW, Washington, DC 20217, USA

Gere, Richard *Actor*
26 E 10th St, #PH, New York, NY 10003, USA

Gerety, Peter *Actor*
%Paradigm Agency, 10100 Santa Monica Blvd, #2500, Los Angeles, CA 90067, USA
Gerety, Tom, Jr *Educator*
%Amherst College, President's Office, Amherst, MA 01002, USA
Gerg-Leitner, Michaela *Skier*
Jachenauer Str 26, 83661 Lenggries, Germany
Gergiev, Valery A *Conductor*
%Kirov Opera, Mariinsky Theater, Teatralnaya Pl 1, St Petersburg, Russia
Geri, Joe *Football Player*
140 Chalfont Dr, Athens, GA 30606, USA
Gerlach, Gary *Publisher*
%Des Moines Register & Tribune, 715 Locust St, Des Moines, IA 50309, USA
Gerlach, John B *Businessman*
%Lancaster Colony Corp, 37 W Broad St, Columbus, OH 43215, USA
Gerlach, John B, Jr *Businessman*
%Lancaster Colony Corp, 37 W Broad St, Columbus, OH 43215, USA
German, William *Editor*
%San Francisco Chronicle, Editorial Dept, 901 Mission, San Francisco, CA 94103, USA
Germane, Geoffrey J *Mechanical Engineer*
%Brigham Young University, Mechanical Engineering Dept, Provo, UT 84602, USA
Germani, Fernando *Concert Organist*
Via Delle Terme Deciane 11, Rome, Italy
Germano, Lisa *Singer/Violinist*
%Artists & Audience Entertainment, 2112 Broadway, #600, New York, NY 10023, USA
Germeshausen, Bernhard *Bobsled Athlete*
Hinter Dem Salon 39, 99195 Schwansee, Germany
Gerner, Robert *Behavioral Psychiatrist*
%University of California, Neuropsychiatric Institute, Los Angeles, CA 90024, USA
Geronimo, Cesar F *Baseball Player*
120 W 97th St, #9-E, New York, NY 10025, USA
Gerring, Cathy *Golfer*
%Ladies Professional Golf Assn, 2570 Volusia Ave, Daytona Beach, FL 32114, USA
Gerry, Elbridge T *Harness Racing Executive, Businessman*
4 Laurel Lane, Locust Valley, NY 11560, USA
Gershon, Gina *Actress*
120 W 45th St, #3601, New York, NY 10036, USA
Gerson, Mark *Photographer*
3 Regal Lane, Regent's Park, London NW1 7TH, England
Gerson, Samuel J *Businessman*
%Filene's Basement Corp, 40 Walnut St, Wellesley, MA 02181, USA
Gerstell, A Frederick *Businessman*
%CalMat Co, 3200 San Fernando Road, Los Angeles, CA 90065, USA
Gerstner, Louis V, Jr *Businessman*
%IBM Corp, Old Orchard Road, Armonk, NY 10504, USA
Gerth, Donald R *Educator*
%California State University, President's Office, Sacramento, CA 95819, USA
Gertz, Jami *Actress*
%International Creative Mgmt, 8942 Wilshire Blvd, Beverly Hills, CA 90211, USA
Gervin, George *Basketball Player, Coach*
%San Antonio Spurs, 600 E Market St, #102, San Antonio, TX 78205, USA
Gerwick, Ben C, Jr *Construction Engineer*
5727 Country Club Dr, Oakland, CA 94618, USA
Gets, Malcolm *Actor*
%International Creative Mgmt, 8942 Wilshire Blvd, Beverly Hills, CA 90211, USA
Gettier, Glenn H, Jr *Businessman*
%Southwestern Life Corp, Lincoln Plaza, 500 N Akard St, Dallas, TX 75201, USA
Getty, Balthazar *Actor*
%William Morris Agency, 151 S El Camino Dr, Beverly Hills, CA 90212, USA
Getty, Estelle *Actress*
1240 N Wetherly Dr, Los Angeles, CA 90069, USA
Getty, Jeff *Baboon Marrow Transplant Recepient*
%ACT-UP Golden Gate, 519 Castro St, San Francisco, CA 94114, USA
Getz, John *Actor*
900 Galloway St, Pacific Palisades, CA 90272, USA
Geyer, George *Artist*
%Karl Bornstein Gallery, 1662 12th St, Santa Monica, CA 90404, USA
Geyer, Georgie Anne *Columnist*
%Plaza, 800 25th St NW, Washington, DC 20037, USA

G

Gerety - Geyer

Geyer, Hugh — *Singer (The Vogues)*
2218 Ridge Road, McKees Rocks, PA 15136, USA

Ghauri, Yasmine — *Model*
%Next Model Mgmt, 23 Watts St, New York, NY 10013, USA

Gheorghiu, Ion A — *Artist*
%Romanian Fine Arts Union, 21 Nicolae Iorga St, Bucharest 1, Romania

Ghiardi, John F L — *Economist, Government Official*
12 Park Overlook Court, Bethesda, MD 20817, USA

Ghiglia, Oscar A — *Concert Guitarist*
Helfembergstr 14, 4059 Basel, Switzerland

Ghiuselev, Nicola — *Opera Singer*
Villa Elpida, Sofia 1616, Bulgaria

Ghosh, Gautam — *Movie Director*
28/1A Gariahat Road, Block 5, #50, Calcutta 700029, India

Ghostley, Alice — *Actress*
3800 Reklaw Dr, Studio City, CA 91604, USA

Giacconi, Riccardo — *Astrophysicist*
3700 San Martin Dr, Baltimore, MD 21218, USA

Giacomin, Ed — *Hockey Player*
%New York Rangers, Madison Square Garden, 2 Penn Plaza, New York, NY 10121, USA

Giaever, Ivar — *Nobel Physics Laureate*
2080 Van Antwerp Road, Schenectady, NY 12309, USA

Giambalvo, Louis — *Actor*
%Judy Schoen, 606 N Larchmont Blvd, #309, Los Angeles, CA 90004, USA

Giambra, Joey — *Boxer*
3751 S Nellis Blvd, Las Vegas, NV 89121, USA

Gianelli, John — *Basketball Player*
PO Box 1097, Pinecrest, CA 95364, USA

Giannini, Giancarlo — *Actor*
%Mario & Vittorio Squillante, Via Mazzini 132, 00195 Rome, Italy

Gianulias, Nikki — *Bowler*
%Ladies Pro Bowlers Tour, 7171 Cherryvale Blvd, Rockford, IL 61112, USA

Giardello, Joey — *Boxer*
1214 Severn Ave, Cherry Hill, NJ 08002, USA

Gibb, Barry — *Singer (The Bee Gees), Songwriter*
1801 Bay Road, Miami Beach, FL 33139, USA

Gibb, Cynthia — *Actress*
1139 S Hill St, #177, Los Angeles, CA 90015, USA

Gibb, Maurice — *Singer (The Bee Gees), Songwriter*
1801 Bay Road, Miami Beach, FL 33139, USA

Gibb, Robin — *Singer (The Bee Gees), Songwriter*
1801 Bay Road, Miami Beach, FL 90012, USA

Gibberd, Frederick — *Architect*
The House, Marsh Lane, Old Harlow, Essex CM17 0NA, England

Gibbons, Billy — *Singer, Guitarist (ZZ Top)*
%Lone Wolf Mgmt, PO Box 16390, Austin, TX 78761, USA

Gibbons, John H (Jack) — *Government Official*
%Science/Technology Policy Office, Old Executive Building, Washington, DC 20500, USA

Gibbons, Leeza — *Entertainer*
PO Box 4321, Los Angeles, CA 90078, USA

Gibbons, Robert J — *Businessman*
%Franklin Life Insurance, 1 Franklin Square, Springfield, IL 62713, USA

Gibbs, Georgia — *Singer*
%Frank Gervasi, 965 5th Ave, New York, NY 10021, USA

Gibbs, Jake — *Football Player*
223 St Andrews Circle, Oxford, MS 38655, USA

Gibbs, Joe J — *Football Coach*
%Joe Gibbs Racing, 9900 Twin Lakes Parkway, Charlotte, NC 28269, USA

Gibbs, L Richard — *Cricketer*
276 Republic Park, Peter's Hall, EBD, Guyana

Gibbs, Lawrence B — *Government Official*
%Miller & Chevalier, 655 15th St NW, #900, Washington, DC 20005, USA

Gibbs, Marla — *Actress, Singer*
2323 W Martin Luther King Blvd, Los Angeles, CA 90008, USA

Gibbs, Patt — *Labor Leader*
%Flight Attendants Assn, 1625 Massachusetts Ave NW, Washington, DC 20036, USA

Gibbs, Terri — *Singer, Songwriter*
416 Gibbs Circle, Grovetown, GA 30813, USA

Gibbs, Terry   *Jazz Vibist, Drummer*
%Richard A Barz, Rt 1, Box 91, Tannersville, PA 18372, USA

Gibbs, Timothy   *Actor*
PO Box 8764, Calabasas, CA 91372, USA

Giblett, Eloise R   *Hematologist*
6533 53rd St NE, Seattle, WA 98115, USA

Gibran, Kahlil   *Sculptor*
160 W Canton St, Boston, MA 02118, USA

Gibron, Abe   *Football Player, Coach*
500 Ponce De Leon Blvd, Clearwater, FL 33756, USA

Gibson, Althea   *Tennis Player*
275 Prospect St, #768, East Orange, NJ 07017, USA

Gibson, Charles D   *Commentator*
%ABC-TV, News Dept, 77 W 66th St, New York, NY 10023, USA

Gibson, Christopher T   *Financier*
%Capstead Mortgage, 2001 Bryan Tower, Dallas, TX 75201, USA

Gibson, Deborah   *Singer*
300 Main St, #201, Huntington, NY 11743, USA

Gibson, Don   *Singer, Guitarist*
PO Box 50474, Nashville, TN 37205, USA

Gibson, Edward G   *Astronaut*
%Gibson International Corp, 7153 Tern Place, Carlsbad, CA 92009, USA

Gibson, Eleanor J   *Psychologist*
RD 1, Box 265-A, Middlebury, VT 05753, USA

Gibson, Everett K, Jr   *Geologist*
1015 Trowbridge Dr, Houston, TX 77062, USA

Gibson, Henry   *Actor*
26740 Latigo Shore Dr, Malibu, CA 90265, USA

Gibson, Kirk H   *Baseball Player*
17108 Mack Ave, Grosse Pointe, MI 48224, USA

Gibson, Mel   *Actor, Director*
%International Creative Mgmt, 8942 Wilshire Blvd, Beverly Hills, CA 90211, USA

Gibson, Quentin H   *Biochemist*
3 Woods End Road, Etna, NH 03750, USA

Gibson, Ralph H   *Photographer*
331 W Broadway, New York, NY 10013, USA

Gibson, Reginald W   *Judge*
%US Claims Court, 717 Madison Place NW, Washington, DC 20005, USA

Gibson, Robert (Bob)   *Baseball Player*
215 Belleview Road S, Belleview, NE 68005, USA

Gibson, Robert L (Hoot)   *Astronaut*
%NASA, Johnson Space Center, 2101 NASA Road, Houston, TX 77058, USA

Gibson, Thomas   *Actor*
%Alliance Talent, 9171 Wilshire Blvd, #441, Beverly Hills, CA 90210, USA

Gibson, William   *Writer*
%General Delivery, Stockbridge, MA 01262, USA

Gibson, William   *Photographer*
%Takarajima Books, 200 Varick St, New York, NY 10014, USA

Gidada, Negasso   *President, Ethiopia*
%President's Office, PO Box 5707, Addis Ababa, Ethiopia

Gideon, Raynold   *Actor, Writer*
3524 Multiview Dr, Los Angeles, CA 90068, USA

Gidley, Pamela   *Actress*
%Gersh Agency, 232 N Canon Dr, Beverly Hills, CA 90210, USA

Gidwitz, Gerald S   *Businessman*
%Helene Curtis Industries, 325 N Wells St, Chicago, IL 60610, USA

Gidwitz, Joseph L   *Businessman*
%Helene Curtis Industries, 325 N Wells St, Chicago, IL 60610, USA

Gidzenko, Yuri   *Cosmonaut*
%Potchta Kosmonavtov, Moskovskoi Oblasti, 141160 Syvisdny Goroduk, Russia

Giel, Paul R   *Football Player, Administrator*
13400 McGintz Road, Minneapolis, MN 55305, USA

Gielen, Michael A   *Conductor, Composer*
%Cincinnati Symphony, 1241 Elm St, Cincinnati, OH 45210, USA

Gielgud, John   *Actor*
South Pavilion, Wotton Underwood, Aylesbury Bucks HP18 0SB, England

Giella, Joseph   *Cartoonist (Mary Worth)*
191 Morris Dr, East Meadow, NY 11554, USA

G

Gibbs - Giella

G

Gierek, Edward *Premier, Poland*
Ustronie, Silesia, Poland

Gierer, Vincent A, Jr *Businessman*
%UST Inc, 100 W Putnam Ave, Greenwich, CT 06830, USA

Gierster, Hans *Conductor*
Hallerwiese 4, 90419 Nurenberg, Germany

Gifford, Frank N *Football Player, Sportscaster*
108 Cedar Cliff Road, Riverside, CT 06878, USA

Gifford, John *Businessman*
%Maxim Integrated Products, 120 San Gabriel Dr, Sunnywise, CA 94086, USA

Gifford, Kathie Lee *Entertainer*
108 Cedar Cliff Road, Riverside, CT 06878, USA

Gift, Roland *Singer (Fine Young Cannibals), Actor*
%Jonathan Altaras, 27 Floral St, London WC2E 9DP, England

Giguere, Russ *Singer, Guitarist (Association)*
%Variety Artists, 555 Chorro St, #A-1, San Luis Obispo, CA 93405, USA

Giheno, John *President, Papua New Guinea*
%Prime Minister's Office, Marera Hau, Port Moresby, Papua New Guinea

Gil, Gilberto *Singer, Songwriter*
%Performers of the World, 8901 Melrose Ave, #200, West Hollywood, CA 90069, USA

Gil, R Benjamin (Benji) *Baseball Player*
6532 Parkside Ave, San Diego, CA 92139, USA

Gilbert, Brad *Tennis Player*
%ProServe, 1101 Woodrow Wilson Blvd, #1800, Arlington, VA 22209, USA

Gilbert, Carl A *Businessman*
%Dravo Corp, 915 Penn Ave, Pittsburgh, PA 15222, USA

Gilbert, David *Financier*
%California Federal Bank, 5700 Wilshire Blvd, Los Angeles, CA 90036, USA

Gilbert, Felix *Writer, Historian*
266 Mercer Road, Princeton, NJ 08540, USA

Gilbert, J Freeman *Geophysicist*
780 Kalamath Dr, Del Mar, CA 92014, USA

Gilbert, Kenneth A *Concert Harpsichordist*
23 Cloitre Notre-Dame, 28000 Chartres, France

Gilbert, Lewis *Movie Director*
17 Sheldrake Place, Dutchess of Bedford Walk, London W8, England

Gilbert, Martin J *Writer, Historian*
7 Landsdowne Crescent, London W11, England

Gilbert, Melissa *Actress*
PO Box 57593, Sherman Oaks, CA 91413, USA

Gilbert, Richard W *Publisher*
%Des Molnes Register & Tribune, 715 Locust St, Des Moines, IA 50309, USA

Gilbert, Ronnie *Singer*
%Donna Korones Mgmt, PO Box 8388, Berkeley, CA 94707, USA

Gilbert, S J, Sr *Religious Leader*
%Baptist Convention of America, 6717 Centennial Blvd, Nashville, TN 37209, USA

Gilbert, Sara *Actress*
16254 High Valley Dr, Encino, CA 91346, USA

Gilbert, Walter *Nobel Chemistry Laureate*
15 Gray Gardens W, Cambridge, MA 02138, USA

Gilberto, Astrud *Singer*
%Absolute Artists, 530 Howard Ave, #200, San Francisco, CA 94105, USA

Gilbride, Kevin *Football Coach*
%San Diego Chargers, Jack Murphy Stadium, Box 609609, San Diego, CA 92160, USA

Gilchrist, Paul R *Religious Leader*
%Presbyterian Church in America, 1862 Century Place, Atlanta, GA 30345, USA

Gilday, Scott R *Financier*
%UAL Employees Credit Union, 125 E Algonquin Road, Arlington Heights, IL 60005, USA

Gilder, Bob *Golfer*
5934 NW Fairoaks Place, Corvallis, OR 97330, USA

Gilder, George F *Writer, Economist*
Main Road, Tyringham, MA 01264, USA

Giles, Jimmie *Football Player*
18124 Gunn Highway, Odessa, FL 33556, USA

Giles, Nancy *Actress*
12047 178th St, Jamaica, NY 11434, USA

Giles, William E *Editor*
667 College Hill Dr, Baton Rouge, LA 70808, USA

Giletti, Alain — *Figure Skater*
103 Place de L'Eglise, 74400 Chamonix, France

Gilgorov, Kiro — *President, Macedonia*
%President's Office, Skopje, Macedonia

Gill, Brendan — *Writer*
%New Yorker Magazine, 20 W 43rd St, New York, NY 10036, USA

Gill, George N — *Publisher*
%Louisville Courier-Journal & Times, 525 W Broadway, Louisville, KY 40202, USA

Gill, Johnny — *Singer, Songwriter*
4924 Balboa Blvd, #366, Encino, CA 91316, USA

Gill, Kendall — *Basketball Player*
%New Jersey Nets, Byrne Meadowlands Arena, East Rutherford, NJ 07073, USA

Gill, Vince — *Singer, Songwriter, Guitarist*
%Fitzgerald-Hartley, 1908 Wedgewood Ave, Nashville, TN 37212, USA

Gill, William A, Jr — *Labor Leader, Government Official*
15975 Cove Lane, Dumfries, VA 22026, USA

Gilles, Daniel — *Writer*
161 Ave Churchill, 1180 Brussels, Belgium

Gilles, Genevieve — *Actress*
%Dakota Hotel, 1 W 72nd St, New York, NY 10023, USA

Gillespie, Charles A, Jr — *Diplomat*
%US State Department, 2201 "C" St NW, Washington, DC 20520, USA

Gillespie, Rhondda — *Concert Pianist*
2 Princess Road, St Leonards-on-Sea, East Sussex TN37 6EL, England

Gillespie, Robert W — *Financier*
%KeyCorp, 127 Public Square, Cleveland, OH 44114, USA

Gillett, George — *Publisher*
%Gillett Group, 4400 Harding Road, Nashville, TN 37205, USA

Gillette, Anita — *Actress*
501 S Beverly Dr, #3, Beverly Hills, CA 90212, USA

Gilley, Mickey — *Singer, Songwriter*
%Gilley's Interests, PO Box 1242, Pasadena, TX 77501, USA

Gilliam, Armon — *Basketball Player*
3800 E Lincoln Dr, #34, Phoenix, AZ 85018, USA

Gilliam, Herm — *Basketball Player*
2701 Bon Air Ave, Winston-Salem, NC 27105, USA

Gilliam, Terry V — *Actor, Animator, Writer (Monty Python)*
%Poo Poo Pictures, 68-A Delancey St, Camden Town, London NW1 7RY, England

Gillies, Clark — *Hockey Player*
31 Stoneywell Court, Dix Hills, NY 11746, USA

Gilligan, John G — *Governor, OH*
%University of Notre Dame, Law School, Notre Dame, IN 46556, USA

Gillilan, William J, III — *Businessman*
%Centex Corp, PO Box 199000, Dallas, TX 75219, USA

Gillingham, Gale — *Football Player*
1201 W River Road, Little Falls, MN 56345, USA

Gillis, Malcolm — *Educator*
%Rice University, President's Office, Houston, TX 77251, USA

Gillman, Sid — *Football Coach*
2968 Playa Road, Carlsbad, CA 92009, USA

Gilman, Alfred G — *Nobel Medicine Laureate*
%Southwestern Medical Center, 5323 Harry Hines Blvd, Dallas, TX 75235, USA

Gilman, Dorothy — *Writer*
50 Whitney Glen, Westport, CT 06880, USA

Gilman, Henry — *Chemist*
3221 Oakland St, Ames, IA 50014, USA

Gilmartin, John A — *Businessman*
%Millipore Corp, 80 Ashby Road, Bedford, MA 01730, USA

Gilmartin, Raymond V — *Businessman*
%Merck Co, 1 Merck Dr, Whitehouse Station, NJ 08889, USA

Gilmer, Gary D — *Businessman*
%Hamilton Life Insurance, 32991 Hamilton Court, Farmington, MI 48334, USA

Gilmer, Harry — *Football Player*
7467 Highway "N", O'Fallon, MO 63366, USA

Gilmore, Artis — *Basketball Player*
8002 James Island Trail, Jacksonville, FL 32256, USA

Gilmore, Clarence P — *Editor*
19725 Creekround Ave, Baton Rouge, LA 70817, USA

G

Giletti - Gilmore

G

Gilmore, Jimmie Dale — *Singer, Songwriter*
%Mike Crowley Artists, 602 Wayside Dr, Wimberley, TX 78676, USA

Gilmore, Kenneth O — *Editor*
Charles Road, Mount Kisco, NY 10549, USA

Gilmour of Craigmillar, Ian — *Government Official, England*
Ferry House, Old Isleworth, Middx, England

Gilmour, Buddy — *Harness Racing Driver*
PO Box 812, Bellmore, NY 11710, USA

Gilmour, David — *Singer, Guitarist (Pink Floyd)*
43 Portland Road, London W11 4LJ, England

Gilmour, Doug — *Hockey Player*
%New Jersey Devils, Continental Arena, PO Box 504, East Rutherford, NJ 07073, USA

Gilroy, Frank D — *Writer*
6 Magnin Road, Monroe, NY 10950, USA

Gilruth, Robert R — *Aerospace Engineer*
2600 Barracks Road, #C-38, Charlottesville, VA 22901, USA

Gimbel, Norman — *Songwriter*
PO Box 50013, Santa Barbara, CA 93150, USA

Gimeno, Andres — *Tennis Player*
Paseo de la Bonanova 38, Barcelona 6, Spain

Ging, Jack — *Actor*
%Artists Agency, 10000 Santa Monica Blvd, #305, Los Angeles, CA 90067, USA

Ginibre, Jean-Louis — *Editor*
%Hachette Filipacchi, 1633 Broadway, New York, NY 10019, USA

Ginsburg, Ruth Bader — *Supreme Court Justice*
%US Supreme Court, 1 1st St NE, Washington, DC 20543, USA

Ginty, Robert — *Actor*
16133 Ventura Blvd, #800, Encino, CA 91436, USA

Ginzberg, Eli — *Economist*
845 West End Ave, New York, NY 10025, USA

Ginzton, Edward L — *Electrical Engineer, Businessman*
%Varian Assoc, 3100 Hansen Way, Palo Alto, CA 94304, USA

Giordano, Michele Cardinal — *Religious Leader*
Largo Donnaregina 22, 80138 Naples, Italy

Giovanni, Nikki E — *Writer*
%Virginia Polytechnic Institute, English Dept, Blacksburg, VA 24061, USA

Giraldi, Robert N (Bob) — *Movie Director*
%Giraldi Suarez, 581 6th Ave, New York, NY 10011, USA

Giraldo, Greg — *Actor*
%Creative Artists Agency, 9830 Wilshire Blvd, Beverly Hills, CA 90212, USA

Girardelli, Marc — *Skier*
%Alpenhotel Bodele, 6850 Dornbirn/Bodele, Austria

Girardi, Joseph E (Joe) — *Baseball Player*
1731 Aspen Dr, Lake Forest, IL 60045, USA

Girardot, Annie — *Actress*
%Editions Robert Laffont, 6 Place St-Sulpice, 75006 Paris, France

Giri, Tulsi — *Prime Minister, Nepal*
Jawakpurdham, District Dhanuka, Nepal

Giroux, Robert — *Publisher*
%Farrar Straus Giroux, 19 Union Square W, New York, NY 10003, USA

Giscard d'Estaing, Valery — *President, France*
11 Rue Benouville, 75116 Paris, France

Gish, Annabeth — *Actress*
25663 Buckhorne Dr, Calabasas, CA 91302, USA

Gismonti, Egberto — *Jazz Guitarist, Composer*
%International Music Network, 112 Washington St, Marblehead, MA 01945, USA

Giuliani, Rudolph W — *Mayor*
%Mayor's Office, Gracie Mansion, New York, NY 10007, USA

Giuliano, Tom — *Singer (The Happenings)*
7-12 Fairhaven Place, Fairlawn, NJ 07410, USA

Giulini, Carlo Maria — *Conductor*
%General Delivery, Bolzano, Italy

Giuranna, Bruno — *Concert Violist*
Via Bembo 96, 31011 Asolo TV, Italy

Givens, Ernest — *Football Player*
5293 61st Ave, South Bayway Island, St Petersburg, FL 33715, USA

Givens, Jack — *Basketball Player, Executive*
1536 Frazier Ave, Orlando, FL 32811, USA

Gilmore - Givens

Givens, Robin — *Actress*
451 S Harvard Blvd, #340, Los Angeles, CA 90020, USA
Gizyn, Louie — *Artist*
1161 NW Taylor Ave, Corvallis, OR 97330, USA
Glamack, George — *Basketball Player*
50 Pleasant Way, Rochester, NY 14622, USA
Glance, Harvey — *Track Athlete*
2408 Old Creek Road, Montgomery, AL 36117, USA
Glanville, Jerry — *Football Coach, Sportscaster*
%Fox-TV, Sports Dept, 205 E 67th St, New York, NY 10021, USA
Glaser, Donald A — *Nobel Physics Laureate*
%University of California, Molecular Biology Laboratory, Berkeley, CA 94720, USA
Glaser, Gabrielle (Gabby) — *Singer, Guitarist (Luscious Jackson)*
%Metropolitan Entertainment, 2 Penn Plaza, #2600, New York, NY 10121, USA
Glaser, Milton — *Graphic Artist*
%Milton Glaser Assoc, 207 E 32nd St, New York, NY 10016, USA
Glaser, Paul Michael — *Actor, Movie Director*
317 Georgina Ave, Santa Monica, CA 90402, USA
Glaser, Rob — *Businessman*
%Progressive Network, 10565 Old Placerville Road, Sacramento, CA 95827, USA
Glaser, Robert — *Psychologist*
%University of Pittsburgh, Psychology Dept, Pittsburgh, PA 15260, USA
Glaser, Robert J — *Foundation Executive*
%Lucille Markey Charitable Trust, 55 Middlefield Road, #130, Menlo Park, C 94027, USA
Glasgow, Vic (Wayne) — *Basketball Player*
6312 King Dr, Bartlesville, OK 74006, USA
Glashow, Sheldon Lee — *Nobel Physics Laureate*
30 Prescott St, Brookline, MA 02146, USA
Glaspie, April — *Diplomat*
%US State Department, 2201 "C" St NW, Washington, DC 20520, USA
Glass, David D — *Businessman*
%Wal-Mart Stores, 702 SW 8th St, Bentonville, AK 72712, USA
Glass, H Bentley — *Biologist*
PO Box 65, East Setauket, NY 11733, USA
Glass, Philip — *Composer*
231 2nd Ave, New York, NY 10003, USA
Glass, Ron — *Actor*
2485 Wild Oak Dr, Los Angeles, CA 90068, USA
Glass, William S (Bill) — *Football Player*
4299 Shiloh, Midlothian, TX 76065, USA
Glasser, Ira S — *Attorney, Legal Activist*
%American Civil Liberties Union, 132 W 43rd St, New York, NY 10036, USA
Glasser, James J — *Businessman*
%GATX Corp, 500 W Monroe St, Chicago, IL 60661, USA
Glasser, William — *Psychiatrist*
11633 San Vicente Blvd, Los Angeles, CA 90049, USA
Glavin, Denis Joseph — *Labor Leader*
%Electrical Radio & Machine Workers Union, 11 E 1st St, New York, NY 10003, USA
Glavine, Thomas M (Tom) — *Baseball Player*
8925 Old Southwick Pass, Alpharetta, GA 30022, USA
Glazkov, Yuri N — *Cosmonaut; Air Force General*
%Potchta Kosmonavtov, Moskovskoi Oblasti, 141160 Syvisdny Goroduk, Russia
Glazunov, Ilya S — *Artist*
Kalashny Per 2/10, #22-A, 103009 Moscow, Russia
Gleason, Andrew M — *Mathematician*
110 Larchwood Dr, Cambridge, MA 02138, USA
Gleason, Paul — *Actor*
%Stone Manners, 8091 Selma Ave, Los Angeles, CA 90046, USA
Glemp, Jozef Cardinal — *Religious Leader*
Sekretariat Prymasa, Kolski, Ul Miodowa 17, 00-246 Warsaw, Poland
Glenamara (Edward W Short) — *Government Official, England*
21 Priory Gardens, Corbridge, Northumberland, England
Glendening, Parris N — *Governor, MD*
%Governor's Office, State House, Annapolis, MD 21401, USA
Glenn, David W — *Financier*
%Federal Home Loan Mortgage, 8200 Jones Branch Dr, McLean, VA 22102, USA
Glenn, Scott — *Actor*
126 E De Vargas St, #1902, Santa Fe, NM 87501, USA

G

Glenn, Terry — *Football Player*
%New England Patriots, Foxboro Stadium, Rt 1, Foxboro, MA 02035, USA

Glenn, Wayne E — *Labor Leader*
%United Paperworkers Int'l Union, 3340 Perimeter Hill Dr, Nashville, TN 37211, USA

Glennan, Robert E, Jr — *Educator*
%Emporia State University, President's Office, Emporia, KS 66801, USA

Gless, Sharon — *Actress*
PO Box 48005, Los Angeles, CA 90048, USA

Glickman, Daniel R — *Secretary, Agriculture*
%Agriculture Department, 14th & Independence SW, Washington, DC 20250, USA

Glickman, Marty — *Sportscaster*
PO Box 559, Salisbury, NC 28145, USA

Glidden, Bob — *Auto Racing Driver*
%Glidden Racing, Rt 1, PO Box 236, Whiteland, IN 46184, USA

Glidden, Robert — *Educator*
%Ohio University, President's Office, Athens, OH 45701, USA

Glidewell, Iain — *Judge*
%Royal Courts of Justice, Strand, London WC2A 2LL, England

Glimcher, Arnold O (Arne) — *Art Dealer*
%Pace Gallery, 32 E 57th St, New York, NY 10022, USA

Glimm, James G — *Mathematician*
%State University of New York, Applied Math Dept, Stony Brook, NY 11794, USA

Glitman, Maynard W — *Diplomat*
%General Delivery, Jeffersonville, VT 05464, USA

Globus, Yoram — *Movie Producer*
%Pathe International, 8670 Wilshire Blvd, Beverly Hills, CA 90211, USA

Glossop, Peter — *Opera Singer*
End Cottage, 7 Gate Close, Hawkchurch near Axminster, Devon, England

Glover, Brian — *Actor*
%DeWolfe, Manfield House, 376/378 The Strand, London WC2R OLR, England

Glover, Bruce — *Actor*
11449 Woodbine St, Los Angeles, CA 90066, USA

Glover, Danny — *Actor*
PO Box 170069, San Francisco, CA 94117, USA

Glover, Jane A — *Conductor*
%Lies Askonas, 186 Drury Lane, London WC2B 5RY, England

Glover, John — *Actor*
453 W 16th St, New York, NY 10011, USA

Glover, Kevin — *Football Player*
303 Maro Road, Pasadena, MD 21122, USA

Glover, Richard (Rich) — *Football Player*
5097 Eppling Lane, San Jose, CA 95111, USA

Gluck, Louis — *Physician*
%University of California, Medical School, La Jolla, CA 92093, USA

Gluck, Louise E — *Writer*
Creamery Road, Plainfield, VA 05667, USA

Glynn, Carlin — *Actress*
1165 5th Ave, New York, NY 10029, USA

Glynn, Robert, Jr — *Businessman*
%Pacific Gas & Electric, PO Box 770000, San Francisco, CA 94177, USA

Gminski, Mike — *Basketball Player, Sportscaster*
1309 Canterbury Hill Circle, Charlotte, NC 28211, USA

Goalby, Bob — *Golfer*
5950 Town Hall Road, Belleville, IL 62223, USA

Godard, Jean-Luc — *Movie Director*
15 Rue du Nord, 1180 Roulle, Switzerland

Goddard, David R — *Biologist*
738-A I Walcott Dr, Philadelphia, PA 19118, USA

Goddard, John — *Explorer*
4224 Beulah Dr, La Canada, CA 91011, USA

Goddard, Samuel P, Jr — *Governor, AZ*
4724 E Camelback Canyon Dr, Phoenix, AZ 85018, USA

Godden, Rumer — *Writer*
Ardnacloich, Moniaive, Thornhill, Dumfriesshire D63 4HZ, Scotland

Godfrey, Paul V — *Publisher*
%Toronto Sun, 333 King St E, Toronto ON M5A 3X5, Canada

Godley & Creme — *Rock Music Group*
Heronden Hall, Tenferden, Kent, England

Godley, Georgina — *Fashion Designer*
%Georgina Godley London Ltd, 19-A All Saints Road, London W11 1HE, England

Godley, Kevin — *Singer, Drummer (Godley & Creme)*
Heronden, Tenferden, Kent, England

Godman, Jim — *Bowler*
1210 Shady Lane, Titusville, FL 32976, USA

Godmanis, Ivars — *Ministers Council Chairman, Latvia*
Bul Brivibas 26, 226170 Riga, Latvia

Godwin, Fay S — *Photographer*
%Fay Godwin Network, 3-4 Kirby St, London E4N 8TS, England

Godwin, Gail K — *Writer*
PO Box 946, Woodstock, NY 12498, USA

Godwin, Linda M — *Astronaut, Physicist*
%NASA, Johnson Space Center, 2101 NASA Road, Houston, TX 77058, USA

Godwin, Mills E, Jr — *Governor, VA*
2180 Partridge Place, Suffolk, VA 23433, USA

Goehr, Alexander — *Composer*
%University of Cambridge, Music Faculty, 11 West Road, Cambridge, England

Goellner, Marc-Kevin — *Tennis Athlete*
%Blau-Weiss Neuss, Tennishall Jahnstrasse, 41464 Neuss, Germany

Goergen, Robert G — *Businessman*
%XTRA Corp, 60 State St, Boston, MA 02109, USA

Goerke, Glenn A — *Educator*
%University of Houston, President's Office, Houston, TX 77204, USA

Goetz, Eric — *Yacht Builder*
%Eric Goetz Marine & Technology, 15 Broad Common Road, Bristol, RI 02809, USA

Goffe, William A — *Judge*
%US Tax Court, 400 2nd St NW, Washington, DC 20217, USA

Goffin, Gerry — *Lyricist*
9171 Hazen Dr, Beverly Hills, CA 90210, USA

Goh Chok Tong — *Prime Minister, Singapore*
%Prime Minister's Office, Istana Annexe, Singapore 0923, Singapore

Goheen, Robert F — *Educator, Diplomat*
1 Orchard Circle, Princeton, NJ 08540, USA

Going, Joanna — *Actress*
233 Park Ave S, #1000, New York, NY 10003, USA

Goitschel, Marielle — *Skier*
%Chalet Helrob, 73-Val D'Isere, France

Goizueta, Roberto C — *Businessman*
%Coca-Cola Co, 1 Coca-Cola Plaza, 310 North Ave NW, Atlanta, GA 30313, USA

Gola, Thomas J (Tom) — *Basketball Player*
15 Kings Oak Lane, Philadelphia, PA 19115, USA

Golan, Menahem — *Movie Producer*
%Cannon Film Group, 10000 Washington Blvd, Culver City, CA 90232, USA

Gold, Andrew — *Singer, Songwriter*
211 St Johns Road, Ridgefield, CT 06877, USA

Gold, Elon — *Comedian, Actor*
%United Talent Agency, 9560 Wilshire Blvd, #500, Beverly Hills, CA 90212, USA

Gold, Ernest — *Composer*
269 N Bellino Dr, Pacific Palisades, CA 90272, USA

Gold, Herbert — *Writer*
1051 Broadway, #A, San Francisco, CA 94133, USA

Gold, Jack — *Movie Director*
24 Wood Vale, London N1O 3DP, England

Gold, Joe — *Bodybuilder*
%World Gym, 2210 Main St, Santa Monica, CA 90405, USA

Gold, Missy — *Actress*
%Gold Marshak Liedtke, 3500 W Olive Ave, #1400, Burbank, CA 91505, USA

Gold, Thomas — *Astronomer, Physicist*
7 Pleasant Grove Lane, Ithaca, NY 14850, USA

Gold, Tracey — *Actress*
4619 Goodland Ave, Studio City, CA 91604, USA

Goldberg, Adam — *Actor*
%Somers Teitelbaum David, 1925 Century Park East, #2320, Los Angeles, CA 90067, USA

Goldberg, Bernard R — *Commentator*
%CBS-TV, News Dept, 51 W 52nd St, New York, NY 10019, USA

Goldberg, Danny — *Entertainment Executive*
%Warner Bros Records, 3300 Warner Blvd, Burbank, CA 91505, USA

Goldberg, Edward D — *Geochemist*
750 Val Sereno Dr, Encinitas, CA 92024, USA

Goldberg, Eric — *Animator*
%Walt Disney Studios, Animation Dept, 500 S Buena Vista St, Burbank, CA 91521, USA

Goldberg, Leonard — *Movie, Television Producer*
%Spectradyne Inc, 1501 N Plano Road, Richardson, TX 75081, USA

Goldberg, Marshall (Biggie) — *Football Player*
180 E Pearson St, #4202, Chicago, IL 60611, USA

Goldberg, Michael — *Artist*
222 Bowery Place, New York, NY 10012, USA

Goldberg, Stan — *Cartoonist (Archie)*
PO Box 604291, Flushing, NY 11360, USA

Goldberg, Whoopi — *Comedienne, Actress*
%Whoop Inc, 5555 Melrose Ave, #114, Los Angeles, CA 90038, USA

Goldberger, Paul J — *Journalist, Architecture Critic*
%New York Times, Editorial Dept, 229 W 43rd St, New York, NY 10036, USA

Goldblatt, Stephen — *Cinematographer*
%Smith/Gosnell/Nicholson, 1515 Palisades Dr, #N, Pacific Palisades, CA 90272, USA

Goldblum, Jeff — *Actor*
%International Creative Mgmt, 8942 Wilshire Blvd, Beverly Hills, CA 90211, USA

Golden, Diana — *Skier*
%Sharf Marketing Group, 822 Boylston St, #203, Chestnut Hill, MA 02167, USA

Golden, Harry — *Bowling Executive*
%Professional Bowlers Assn, 1720 Merriman Road, Akron, OH 44313, USA

Golden, Raymond L — *Financier*
%James D Wolfensohn Inc, 599 Lexington Ave, New York, NY 10022, USA

Golden, William Lee — *Singer (Oak Ridge Boys); Songwriter*
329 Rockland Road, Hendersonville, TN 37075, USA

Goldenson, Leonard H — *Television Executive*
%Capital Cities/ABC, 77 W 66th St, New York, NY 10023, USA

Goldhaber, Gertrude S — *Physicist*
91 S Gillette Ave, Bayport, NY 11705, USA

Goldhaber, Maurice — *Physicist*
91 S Gillette Ave, Bayport, NY 11705, USA

Goldhirsh, Bernard A — *Publisher*
%Inc Magazine, 38 Commercial Wharf, Boston, MA 02110, USA

Goldin, Daniel S — *Government Official, Space Administrator*
%National Aviation & Space Agency, Code A, 300 "E" St SW, Washington, DC 20024, USA

Goldin, Nan — *Photographer*
334 Bowry, New York, NY 10012, USA

Goldin, Ricky Paull — *Actor*
365 W 52nd St, #L-E, New York, NY 10019, USA

Golding, Susan — *Mayor*
%Mayor's Office, City Hall, 202 "C" St, San Diego, CA 92101, USA

Goldman, Bo — *Writer*
%Creative Artists Agency, 9830 Wilshire Blvd, Beverly Hills, CA 90212, USA

Goldman, James — *Writer*
%Barbara Deren, 965 5th Ave, New York, NY 10021, USA

Goldman, Robert I — *Financier*
%Congress Financial, 1133 Ave of Americas, New York, NY 10036, USA

Goldman, William — *Writer, Movie Director*
50 E 77th St, #30, New York, NY 10021, USA

Goldman-Rakic, Patricia — *Neuroscientist*
%Yale University Medical School, Neurology Dept, New Haven, CT

Goldmark, Peter C, Jr — *Foundation Executive*
%Rockefeller Foundation, 420 5th Ave, New York, NY 10018, USA

Goldovsky, Boris — *Concert Pianist, Opera Educator*
183 Clinton Road, Brookline, MA 02146, USA

Goldreich, Peter — *Astronomer*
471 S Catalina Ave, Pasadena, CA 91106, USA

Goldsboro, Bobby — *Singer, Songwriter*
%Jim Stephany Mgmt, 1021 Preston Dr, Nashville, TN 37206, USA

Goldsmith, Bram — *Financier*
%City National Corp, 400 N Roxbury Dr, Beverly Hills, CA 90210, USA

Goldsmith, Jerry — *Composer*
8491 Sunset Blvd, #492, West Hollywood, CA 90069, USA

Goldsmith, Judy — *Social Activist*
%National Organization for Women, 425 13th St NW, Washington, DC 20002, USA

Goldsmith, Olivia *Writer*
%Harper Collins Publishers, 10 E 53rd St, New York, NY 10022, USA
Goldstein, Abraham S *Attorney*
%Yale University, Law School, 127 Wall St, New Haven, CT 06511, USA
Goldstein, Allan L *Biochemist, Immunologist*
5053 Massachusetts Ave NW, Washington, DC 20016, USA
Goldstein, Avram *Pharmacologist*
735 Dolores St, Stanford, CA 94305, USA
Goldstein, Joseph L *Nobel Medicine Laureate*
%University of Texas, Medical Center, 5324 Harry Hines Blvd, Dallas, TX 75235, USA
Goldstein, Murray *Physician, Association Executive*
%United Cerebral Palsey Foundation, 1660 "L" St NW, #700, Washington, DC 20036, USA
Goldstein, Stanley P *Businessman*
%Melville Corp, 1 Theall Road, Rye, NY 10580, USA
Goldstine, Herman H *Mathematician*
1900 Rittenhouse Square, #13-B, Philadelphia, PA 19103, USA
Goldstone, Jeffrey *Physicist*
18 Orchard Road, Brookline, MA 02146, USA
Goldstone, Richard J *Judge*
PO Box 258, Bloemfontein 9300, South Africa
Goldstone, Steven F *Businessman*
%RJR Nabisco Holdings, 1301 Ave of Americas, New York, NY 10019, USA
Goldthwait, Bob (Bobcat) *Comedian*
3950 Fredonia Dr, Los Angeles, CA 90068, USA
Goldwater, Barry M *Senator, AZ*
6250 N Hogahn Dr, Paradise Valley, AZ 85253, USA
Goldwater, John L *Cartoonist (Archie)*
8 White Birch Lane, Scarsdale, NY 10583, USA
Goldwyn, Samuel J, Jr *Movie Producer*
%Samuel Goldwyn Co, 10203 Santa Monica Blvd, #500, Los Angeles, CA 90067, USA
Golembiewski, Billy *Bowler*
4966 Wise Road, Coleman, MI 48618, USA
Golic, Bob *Football Player, Sportscaster*
%NBC-TV, Sports Dept, 30 Rockefeller Plaza, New York, NY 10112, USA
Golimowski, David A *Astronomer*
%Johns Hopkins University, Astrophysical Sciences Center, Baltimore, MD 21218, USA
Golino, Valeria *Actress*
8033 W Sunset Blvd, #419, Los Angeles, CA 90046, USA
Golonka, Arlene *Actress*
17849 Duncan St, Reseda, CA 91335, USA
Golson, Benny *Jazz Saxophonist, Composer*
%Abby Hoffer, 223 1/2 E 48th St, New York, NY 10017, USA
Golub, Harvey *Businessman*
%American Express Co, American Express Tower, New York, NY 10285, USA
Golub, Leon A *Artist*
530 LaGuardia Place, New York, NY 10012, USA
Gomer, Robert *Chemist*
4824 S Kimbark Ave, Chicago, IL 60615, USA
Gomes, Francisco da Costa *President, Portugal; Army Marshal*
Ave Dos Eua 121-9-C, Lisbon, Portugal
Gomez, Edgar (Eddie) *Jazz Bassist*
%Integrity Talent, PO Box 961, Burlington, MA 01803, USA
Gomez, Jill *Opera Singer*
16 Milton Park, London N6 5QA, England
Gomez, Ruben C *Baseball Player*
N-43 Calle Luisa E, Toa Baja, PR 00949, USA
Gomory, Ralph E *Mathematician, Foundation Executive*
%Alfred P Sloan Foundation, 630 5th Ave, New York, NY 10111, USA
Gompf, Thomas (Tom) *Diver*
2716 Barret Ave, Plant City, FL 33567, USA
Goncalves, Vascos dos Santos *Prime Minister, Portugal; Army General*
Ave Estados Unidos da America 86, 5 Esq, 1700 Lison, Portugal
Goncz, Arpad *President, Hungary*
%President's Office, Kossuth Lajos Ter 1, 1055 Budapest, Hungary
Gonda, Leslie L *Financier*
%International Lease Finance, 1999 Ave of Stars, Los Angeles, CA 90067, USA
Gong Li *Actress, Model*
%Xi'an Film Studio, Xi'an City, Shaanxi Province, China

Gong Pin-Mei, Ignatius Cardinal — *Religious Leader*
128 Strawberry Hill Ave, Stamford, CT 06902, USA

Gonick, Larry — *Cartoonist*
247 Missouri St, San Francisco, CA 94107, USA

Gonshaw, Francesca — *Actress*
%Greg Mellard, 12 D'Arblay St, #200, London W1V 3FP, England

Gonzales, Dalmacio — *Opera Singer*
%Metropolitan Opera Assn, Lincoln Center Plaza, New York, NY 10023, USA

Gonzalez Marquez, Felipe — *Prime Minister, Spain*
%Prime Minister's Office, Complejo de la Moncloa, 28071 Madrid, Spain

Gonzalez Martin, Marcelo Cardinal — *Religious Leader*
Arco de Palacio 1, Toledo, Spain

Gonzalez, Alexander S (Alex) — *Baseball Player*
8620 SW 102nd Ave, Miami, FL 33173, USA

Gonzalez, Hector — *Religious Leader*
%Baptist Churches USA, PO Box 851, Valley Forge, PA 19482, USA

Gonzalez, Juan A — *Baseball Player*
Ext Catoni A-9, Vega Baja, PR 00693, USA

Gooch, Gerald — *Artist*
%Hansen Fuller Gallery, 228 Grant Ave, San Francisco, CA 94108, USA

Good, Hugh W — *Religious Leader*
%Primitive Advent Christian Church, 395 Frame Road, Elkview, WV 25071, USA

Good, Robert A — *Physician*
%All Children's Hospital, 801 6th St S, St Petersburg, FL 33701, USA

Goodacre Connick, Jill — *Model*
%Elite Model Mgmt, 111 E 22nd St, #200, New York, NY 10010, USA

Goodall, Caroline — *Actress*
%Jonathan Altaras, 27 Floral St, London WC2E 9DP, England

Goodall, Jack W — *Businessman*
%Foodmaker Inc, 9330 Balboa Ave, San Diego, CA 92123, USA

Goodall, Jane — *Ethologist, Primatologist*
%Jane Goodall Institute, PO Box 599, Ridgefield, CT 06877, USA

Goode, David R — *Businessman*
%Norfolk Southern Corp, 3 Commercial Place, Norfolk, VA 23510, USA

Goode, Joe — *Artist*
1645 Electric Ave, Venice, CA 90291, USA

Goode, Richard S — *Concert Pianist*
%Frank Salomon, 201 W 54th St, New York, NY 10019, USA

Goodell, Brian — *Swimmer*
13 Via Honesto, Rancho Santa Margarita, CA 92688, USA

Gooden, Dwight E — *Baseball Player*
6755 30th St S, St Petersburg, FL 33712, USA

Goodenough, Ward H — *Antropologist*
3300 Darby Road, #5306, Haverford, PA 19041, USA

Goodes, Melvin R — *Businessman*
%Warner-Lambert Co, 201 Tabor Road, Morris Plains, NJ 07950, USA

Goodeve, Charles P — *Physical Chemist*
38 Middleway, London NW11, England

Goodeve, Grant — *Actor*
21416 NE 68th Court, Redmond, WA 98053, USA

Goodfellow, Peter N — *Geneticist*
%Cancer Research Fund, Lincoln Inn Fields, London WC2A 3PX, England

Goodfriend, Lynda — *Actress*
%Cohen & Luckienbache, 740 N La Brea Ave, Los Angeles, CA 90038, USA

Gooding, Cuba, Jr — *Actor*
3200 Coldwater Canyon Ave, Studio City, CA 91604, USA

Goodman, Alfred — *Composer*
Bodenstedtstr 31, 81241 Munich, Germany

Goodman, Corey S — *Neurobiologist*
Howard Hughes Medical Institute, Molecular/Cell Biology Dept, Berkeley, CA 94720, USA

Goodman, Dody — *Comedienne*
%Ruth Webb, 13834 Magnolia Blvd, Sherman Oaks, CA 91423, USA

Goodman, Ellen H — *Columnist*
%Boston Globe, Editorial Dept, 135 Morrissey Blvd, Boston, MA 02125, USA

Goodman, John — *Actor*
%Creative Artists Agency, 9830 Wilshire Blvd, Beverly Hills, CA 90212, USA

Goodman, Julian — *Broadcast Executive*
%National Broadcasting Co, 30 Rockefeller Plaza, New York, NY 10112, USA

Goodman, Oscar	*Attorney*
520 S 4th St, Las Vegas, NV 89101, USA	
Goodpaster, Andrew J	*Army General*
%Atlantic Council, 1616 "H" St NW, Washington, DC 20006, USA	
Goodreault, Gene	*Football Player*
95 Colby St, Bradford, MA 01835, USA	
Goodrich, Gail	*Basketball Player*
147 Bryam Shore Road, Greenwich, CT 06830, USA	
Goodson, R Eugene	*Businessman*
%Oshkosh Truck, 2307 Oregon St, Oshkosh, WI 54901, USA	
Goodwin, Daniel L	*Financier*
%Inland Group, 2901 Butterfield Road, Oak Brook, IL 60523, USA	
Goodwin, Michael	*Labor Leader*
%Office & Professional Employees Union, 265 W 14th St, New York, NY 10011, USA	
Goodwin, Michael	*Actor*
%Susan Smith, 121 N San Vicente Blvd, Beverly Hills, CA 90211, USA	
Goodwin, Ron	*Composer, Conductor*
Black Nest Cottage, Hockford Lane, Br Com, Reading RG7 4RP, England	
Goodwin, V John	*Businessman*
%National Steel Corp, 4100 Edison Lakes Parkway, Mishawaka, IN 46545, USA	
Goody, Joan E	*Architect*
%Goody Clancy Assoc, 334 Boylston St, Boston, MA 02116, USA	
Goodyear, Scott	*Auto Racing Driver*
%Scott Goodyear Racing, PO Box 589, Carmel, IN 46032, USA	
Goolagong Cawley, Evonne	*Tennis Player*
%Int'l Management Group, 1 Erieview Plaza, #1300, Cleveland, OH 44114, USA	
Goosen, Don	*Boxing Promoter, Manager*
6320 Van Nuys Blvd, Van Nuys, CA 91401, USA	
Gorbachev, Mikhail S	*Gen Sec, USSR; Nobel Peace Laureate*
Leningradsky Prospekt 49, 125468 Moscow, Russia	
Gorbachev, Raisa M	*Wife of Russian Leader*
Leningradsky Prospekt 49, 125468 Moscow, Russia	
Gorbachev, Yuri	*Artist*
%Adrienne Editions, 377 Geary St, San Francisco, CA 94102, USA	
Gorbatko, Viktor V	*Cosmonaut; Air Force General*
%Potchta Kosmonavtov, Moskovskoi Oblasti, 141160 Syvisdny Goroduk, Russia	
Gorbunovs, Anatolijs V	*Chairman, Latvia*
%Supreme Council, 11 Jeraba St, PDP 226811 Riga, Latvia	
Gordeeva, Ekaterina	*Figure Skater*
%International Skating Center, 1375 Hopmeadow St, Simsbury, CT 06070, USA	
Gordeyev, Vyacheslav M	*Ballet Dancer, Choreographer*
Tverskaya Str 9, #78, 103009 Moscow, Russia	
Gordimer, Nadine	*Nobel Literature Laureate*
7 Frere Road, Parktown, Johannesburg 2193, South Africa	
Gordon, Barry	*Actor, Singer*
1912 Kaweah Dr, Pasadena, CA 91105, USA	
Gordon, Bridgette	*Basketball Player*
421 E Chelsea St, Deland, FL 32724, USA	
Gordon, David	*Choreographer*
%David Gordon/Pick Up Co, 131 Varick St, #901, New York, NY 10013, USA	
Gordon, Don	*Actor*
2095 Linda Flora Dr, Los Angeles, CA 90077, USA	
Gordon, Ed	*Commentator*
%NBC-TV, News Dept, 30 Rockefeller Plaza, New York, NY 10112, USA	
Gordon, Gerald	*Actor*
%Lichtman Co, 4439 Wortser Ave, Studio City, CA 91604, USA	
Gordon, Hannah	*Actress*
%Hutton Mgmt, 200 Fulham Road, London SW10 9PN, England	
Gordon, Jeff	*Auto Racing Driver*
18716 S Nautical Dr, Huntersville, NC 28078, USA	
Gordon, John A	*Air Force General*
%Central Intelligence Agency, Operations Dept, Washington, DC 20505, USA	
Gordon, Lancaster	*Basketball Player*
2022 Murray Ave, #1, Lousiville, KY 40205, USA	
Gordon, Lawrence	*Entertainment Executive*
%Largo Entertainment, 20th Century Fox, 10201 W Pico Blvd, Los Angeles, CA 90064, USA	
Gordon, Leo	*Actor*
9977 Wornom Ave, Sunland, CA 91040, USA	

G

Goodman - Gordon

Gordon, Lincoln	*Economist, Diplomat*
3069 University Terrace NW, Washington, DC 20016, USA	
Gordon, Mary C	*Writer*
%Viking Penguin, 375 Hudson St, New York, NY 10014, USA	
Gordon, Milton A	*Educator*
%California State University, President's Office, Fullerton, CA 99264, USA	
Gordon, Mita	*Governor General, Belize*
Belize House, Belnopan, Belize	
Gordon, Nathan G	*WW II Navy Hero (CMH)*
%Gordon & Gordon, PO Box 558, Morrilton, AR 72110, USA	
Gordon, Richard F, Jr	*Astronaut*
%Space Age America, 14126 Rosecrans Ave, Santa Fe Springs, CA 90670, USA	
Gordon, Robby	*Auto, Truck Racing Driver*
PO Box 2678, Orange, CA 92859, USA	
Gordon, Roger L	*Financier*
%SFFED Corp, 88 Kearny St, San Francisco, CA 94108, USA	
Gordon, Roscoe	*Singer, Guitarist, Pianist*
382 N Lemon Ave, Walnut, CA 91789, USA	
Gordon, William E	*Radio Physicist*
%Rice University, Space Physics Dept, PO Box 1892, Houston, TX 77251, USA	
Gordy, Berry, Jr	*Record Company Executive, Songwriter*
878 Stradella Road, Los Angeles, CA 90077, USA	
Gordy, John	*Football Player*
30100 Town Center Dr, #O-223, Laguna Niguel, CA 92677, USA	
Gordy, Walter	*Physicist*
2521 Perkins Road, Durham, NC 27706, USA	
Gore, Albert A	*Senator, TN*
%Gore Farms, Rt 2, Elmwood Road, Carthage, TN 37030, USA	
Gore, Albert A, Jr	*Vice President*
%Vice President's Office, Old Executive Office Bldg, Washington, DC 20501, USA	
Gore, Lesley	*Singer, Actress*
%Fox Entertainment, 1650 Broadway, #503, New York, NY 10019, USA	
Gorecki, Henryk M	*Composer*
Ul Feliksa Kona 4 M 1, 40-133 Katowice, Poland	
Goren, Shlomo	*Religious Leader, Army General*
Chief Rabbinate, Hechal Shlomo, Jerusalem, Israel	
Gorie, Dominic L	*Astronaut*
%NASA, Johnson Space Center, 2101 NASA Road, Houston, TX 77058, USA	
Goring, Marius	*Actor*
%Film Rights, Southbank House, Black Prince Road, London SE1 7SJ, England	
Goring, Robert T (Butch)	*Hockey Player*
PO Box 70065, Las Vegas, NV 89170, USA	
Gorman, Cliff	*Actor*
%Paradigm Agency, 200 W 57th St, #900, New York, NY 10019, USA	
Gorman, Joseph T	*Businessman*
%TRW Inc, 1900 Richmond Road, Cleveland, OH 44124, USA	
Gorman, Kenneth J	*Businessman*
%Atlantic Mutual Insurance, 45 Wall St, New York, NY 10005, USA	
Gorman, Patrick	*Actor*
%Dade/Schultz, 11846 Ventura Blvd, #100, Studio City, CA 91604, USA	
Gorman, R C	*Artist*
PO Box 1258, El Prado, NM 87529, USA	
Gorme, Eydie	*Singer*
820 Greenway Dr, Beverly Hills, CA 90210, USA	
Gormley, Dennis J	*Businessman*
%Federal-Mogul Corp, 26555 Northwestern Parkway, Southfield, MI 48034, USA	
Gorney, Karen Lynn	*Actress*
%Kroll, 390 West End Ave, New York, NY 10024, USA	
Gorouuch, Edward Lee	*Educator*
%University of Alaska, President's Office, Anchorage, AK 99508, USA	
Gorrell, Bob	*Editorial Cartoonist*
%Richmond Newspapers, Editorial Dept, PO Box 85333, Richmond, VA 23293, USA	
Gorrell, Fred	*Balloonist*
501 E Port Au Prince Lane, Phoenix, AZ 85022, USA	
Gorshin, Frank	*Comedian*
1740 El Camino Parocela, Palm Springs, CA 92264, USA	
Gorski, Mark	*Cyclist*
4503 N Pennsylvania St, Indianapolis, IN 46205, USA	

Gorter, Cornelis J — *Physicist*
Klobeniersburgwal 29, Amsterdam, Netherlands

Gortner, Marjoe — *Actor*
PO Box 46266, Los Angeles, CA 90046, USA

Gorton, John G — *Prime Minister, Australia*
8 Hamelin Crescent, Narrabundah ACT 2604, Australia

Gosdin, Vern — *Singer, Songwriter*
2509 W Marquette Ave, Tampa, FL 33614, USA

Gosling, James — *Computer Software Designer (Java)*
%Sun Microsystems, 2550 Garcia Ave, Mountain View, CA 94043, USA

Gosman, Abraham D — *Financier*
%Meditrust, 197 1st Ave, Needham Heights, MA 02194, USA

Goss, Robert F — *Labor Leader*
%Oil Chemical & Atomic International, 1636 Champa St, Denver, CO 80202, USA

Gossage, Richard M (Goose) — *Baseball Player*
35 Marland Dr, Colorado Springs, CO 80906, USA

Gossage, Thomas L — *Businessman*
%Hercules Inc, Hercules Plaza, Wilmington, DE 19894, USA

Gosselaar, Mark-Paul — *Actor*
27512 Wesley Way, Valencia, CA 91354, USA

Gosselin, Mario — *Hockey Player*
3758 Regal Vista Dr, Sherman Oaks, CA 91403, USA

Gossett, D Bruce — *Football Player*
6151 Oak Forest Way, San Jose, CA 95120, USA

Gossett, Louis, Jr — *Actor*
PO Box 57018, Sherman Oaks, CA 91413, USA

Gossick Crockatt, Sue — *Diver*
13768 Christian Barrett Dr, Moorpark, CA 93021, USA

Gottesman, David S — *Financier*
%First Manhattan Co, 437 Madison Ave, New York, NY 10022, USA

Gottfried, Brian — *Tennis Player*
4030 Inverrary Dr, Lauderhill, FL 33319, USA

Gottlieb, Michael — *Movie Director*
2436 Washington Ave, Santa Monica, CA 90403, USA

Gottlieb, Richard D — *Businessman*
%Lee Enterprises, 214 N Main St, Davenport, IA 52801, USA

Gottlieb, Robert A — *Editor, Publisher*
237 E 48th St, New York, NY 10017, USA

Gottschalk, Carl W — *Physician*
1300 Mason Farm Road, Chapel Hill, NC 27514, USA

Gottwald, Bruce C — *Businessman*
%Ethyl Corp, PO Box 2189, Richmond, VA 23217, USA

Gottwald, Bruce C, Jr — *Businessman*
%First Colony Corp, 700 Main St, Lynchburg, VA 24504, USA

Gottwald, John D — *Businessman*
%Tredegar Industries, 1100 Boulders Parkway, Richmond, VA 23225, USA

Gough, Michael — *Actor*
Torleigh Green Lane, Ashmore, Salisbury, Wilts SP5 5AQ, England

Gould Innes, Shane — *Swimmer*
General Delivery, Post Office, Margaret River 6285, Australia

Gould, Elliott — *Actor*
21250 Califa St, #201, Woodland Hills, CA 91367, USA

Gould, Harold — *Actor*
603 Ocean Ave, #4-East, Santa Monica, CA 90402, USA

Gould, Laurence M — *Geologist*
201 E Rudasill Road, Tucson, AZ 85704, USA

Gould, Stephen Jay — *Paleontologist*
%Museum of Comparative Zoology, Harvard University, Cambridge, MA 02138, USA

Gould, Thomas W — *WW II British Royal Navy Hero (VC)*
6 Howlands, Orton Gold Hay, Peterborough, Cambridgeshire, England

Gould, William B, IV — *Government Official*
%National Labor Relations Board, 1009 14th St NW, Washington, DC 20005, USA

Gouled Aptidon, Hassan — *President, Djibouti Republic*
%President's Office, 8-18 Ahmed Nessin St, Djibouti, Djibouti Republic

Goulet, Michel — *Hockey Player*
998 Principale, Peribonka PQ G0W 2G0, Canada

Goulet, Robert — *Singer, Actor*
3110 Monte Rosa Ave, Las Vegas, NV 89120, USA

G

Gorter - Goulet

Goulian, Mehran *Physician, Biochemist*
8433 Prestwick Dr, La Jolla, CA 92037, USA

Gourad Hamadou, Barkad *Prime Minister, Djibouti Republic*
%Prime Minister's Office, PO Box 2086, Djibouti, Djibouti Republic

Gourley, Roark *Artist*
%Roark Gourley Art Gallery, 33151 Paso Dr, South Laguna Beach, CA 92677, USA

Gouyon, Paul Cardinal *Religious Leader*
Ma Maison, 181 Rue Judaique, 33000 Bordeaux Cedex, France

Gowan, James *Architect*
2 Linden Gardens, London W2 4ES, England

Gowdy, Curt *Sportscaster*
300 Boylston St, #506, Boston, MA 02116, USA

Gowdy, Robert C *Financier*
%Commercial Union, 1 Beacon St, Boston, MA 02108, USA

Gower, Bob G *Businessman*
%Lyondell Petrochemical, 1221 McKinney St, Houston, TX 77010, USA

Gower, David I *Cricketer*
%David Gower Promotions, 6 George St, Nottingham NG1 3BE, England

Gowon, Yakub *President, Nigeria; Army General*
%University of Warwick, Politics Dept, Coventry CV4 7AL, England

Gowrie (A P G Hore-Ruthven), Earl of *Government Official, England*
%Arts Council, 14 Great Peter St, London SW1P 3NQ, England

Goycoechea, Sergio *Soccer Player*
%Argentine Football Assn, Via Monte 1366-76, 1053 Buenos Aires, Argentina

Gqozo, Oupa *Head of State, Ciskei; Army General*
%Military Council, Zwelitsha, Ciskei

Grabe, Ronald J *Astronaut*
%Orbital Science Corp, Launch Systems Group, 217000 Atlantic, Dulles, VA 20166, USA

Graber, Bill *Track Athlete*
1136 N Columbia Ave, Ontario, CA 91764, USA

Graber, Pierre *President, Switzerland*
1073 Savugny, Switzerland

Grabois, Neil R *Educator*
%Colgate University, President's Office, Hamilton, NY 13346, USA

Grabowski, James S (Jim) *Football Player*
1523 W Withorn Lane, Palatine, IL 60067, USA

Grace, Bud *Cartoonist (Ernie)*
PO Box 66, Oakton, VA 22124, USA

Gracen, Elizabeth *Actress*
%Metropolitan Talent Agency, 4526 Wilshire Blvd, Los Angeles, CA 90010, USA

Gracey, James S *Coast Guard Admiral, Businessman*
1141 21st St S, Arlington, VA 22202, USA

Grachev, Pavel S *Army Marshal, Russia*
%Defense Ministry, Novy Arbat 19, K-160 Moscow, Russia

Gracq, Julien *Writer*
3 Rue du Grenier a Del, 49410 St Florent Le Vieil, France

Grad, Harold *Mathematician*
248 Overlook Road, New Rochelle, NY 10804, USA

Grade of Elstree, Lew *Television Executive, Movie Producer*
Embassy House, Mayfair, 8 Queen St, London W1X 7PH, England

Grade, Jeffery T *Businessman*
%Harnischfeger Corp, 2855 S James Dr, New Berlin, WI 53151, USA

Gradishar, Randy *Football Player*
1111 Ash St, #209, Denver, CO 80220, USA

Grady, Don *Actor, Songwriter*
4444 Lankershim Blvd, #207, North Hollywood, CA 91602, USA

Grady, James T *Labor Leader*
%International Teamsters Brotherhood, 25 Louisiana Ave NW, Washington, DC 20001, USA

Grady, Wayne *Golfer*
1751 Pinnacle Dr, #1500, McLean, VA 22102, USA

Graf, Kathryn *Actress*
%Atkins Assoc, 303 S Crescent Heights Blvd, Los Angeles, CA 90048, USA

Graf, Steffi *Tennis Player*
Normannenstra 14, 68782 Bruhl, Germany

Graff, Randy *Actress*
%Marion Rosenberg, 8428 Melrose Place, #C, Los Angeles, CA 90069, USA

Graffin, Guillaume *Ballet Dancer*
%American Ballet Theatre, 890 Broadway, New York, NY 10003, USA

Graffman, Gary — *Concert Pianist*
PO Box 30, Tenafly, NJ 07670, USA

Grafton, Sue — *Writer*
PO Box 41447, Santa Barbara, CA 93140, USA

Graham, Alex — *Cartoonist (Fred Basset)*
%Tribune Media Services, 435 N Michigan Ave, #1500, Chicago, IL 60611, USA

Graham, Bruce J — *Architect*
%Graham & Graham, PO Box 8589, Hobe Sound, FL 33475, USA

Graham, Charles P — *Army General*
330 Martins Trail, Roswell, GA 30076, USA

Graham, David — *Golfer*
5619 Preston Fairways Dr, Dallas, TX 75252, USA

Graham, Dirk — *Hockey Player*
4 Elm Creek Dr, #103, Elmhurst, IL 60126, USA

Graham, Donald E — *Publisher*
%Washington Post Co, 1150 15th St NW, Washington, DC 20071, USA

Graham, Heather — *Actress*
28721 Timberlane St, Agoura Hills, CA 91301, USA

Graham, John R — *Astronomer*
%University of California, Astronomy Dept, Berkeley, CA 94720, USA

Graham, Jorie — *Writer*
%University of Iowa, Writers' Workshop, Iowa City, IA 55242, USA

Graham, Katharine M — *Businesswoman*
%Washington Post Co, 1150 15th St NW, Washington, DC 20071, USA

Graham, Lauren — *Actress*
%Writers & Artists, 924 Westwood Blvd, #900, Los Angeles, CA 90024, USA

Graham, Linda — *Bowler*
4147 E Seneca Ave, Des Moines, IA 50317, USA

Graham, Lou — *Golfer*
85 Concord Park W, Nashville, TN 37205, USA

Graham, Otto E, Jr — *Football Player, Coach*
2216 Riviera Dr, Sarasota, FL 34232, USA

Graham, Robert — *Sculptor*
35 Market St, Venice, CA 90291, USA

Graham, Robert — *Businessman*
%Novellus Systems, 3970 N 1st St, San Jose, CA 95134, USA

Graham, Virginia — *Commentator*
211 E 70th St, New York, NY 10021, USA

Graham, William B — *Businessman*
%Baxter International, 1 Baxter Parkway, Deerfield, IL 60015, USA

Graham, William F (Billy) — *Evangelist*
1300 Harmon Place, Minneapolis, MN 55403, USA

Graham, William R — *Government Official*
%Xsirius Inc, 1110 N Glebe Road, #620, Arlington, VA 22201, USA

Grahn, Nancy Lee — *Actress*
4910 Agnes Ave, North Hollywood, CA 91607, USA

Grainger, David W — *Businessman*
%W W Grainger Inc, 5500 W Howard St, Skokie, IL 60077, USA

Gralish, Tom — *Photographer*
105 Virginia Ave, Westmont, NJ 08108, USA

Gralla, Lawrence — *Publisher*
%Gralla Publications, 1515 Broadway, New York, NY 10036, USA

Gralla, Milton — *Publisher*
%Gralla Publications, 1515 Broadway, New York, NY 10036, USA

Gramm, Lou — *Singer (Foreigner)*
%Hard to Handle Mgmt, 1133 Broadway, #1301, New York, NY 10010, USA

Gramm, Wendy L — *Government Official*
%Commodity Futures Trading Commission, 2033 "K" St NW, Washington, DC 20581, USA

Grammer, Kathy — *Actress*
%Artists Agency, 10000 Santa Monica Blvd, #305, Los Angeles, CA 90067, USA

Grammer, Kelsey — *Actor*
3266 Cornell Road, Agoura Hills, CA 91301, USA

Granatelli, Andy — *Auto Racing Builder*
%TuneUp Masters, 21031 Ventura Blvd, Woodland Hills, CA 91364, USA

Grandin, Temple — *Animal Scientist*
2918 Silver Plume Dr, #C-3, Fort Collins, CO 80526, USA

Grandy, Fred — *Actor, Representative, IA*
9417 Spruce Tree Circle, Bethesda, MD 20814, USA

G

Graffman - Grandy

Grandy, John	*Royal Air Force Marshal, England*
%White's, St James's St, London SW1, England	
Granger, Farley	*Actor*
18 W 72nd St, #25-D, New York, NY 10023, USA	
Granlund, Paul T	*Sculptor*
%Adolphus College, Art Dept, St Peter, MN 56082, USA	
Granrud, Jerome H	*Army General*
Commanding General, US Army Japan/IX Corps, APO, AP 96343, USA	
Grant, Amy	*Singer, Songwriter*
Riverston Farm, Moran Road, Franklin, TN 37064, USA	
Grant, B Donald	*Television Executive*
%CBS Inc, Entertainment Group, 51 W 52nd St, New York, NY 10019, USA	
Grant, Boyd	*Basketball Coach*
%Colorado State University, Athletic Dept, Fort Collins, CO 80523, USA	
Grant, Brian	*Basketball Player*
505 N Green St, Georgetown, OH 45121, USA	
Grant, Deborah	*Actress*
%Larry Dalzall, 17 Broad Court, #12, London WC2B 5QN, England	
Grant, Eddy	*Singer, Songwriter*
155 Holland Park Dr, #D, London W11 4UX, England	
Grant, Faye	*Actress*
322 W 20th St, New York, NY 10011, USA	
Grant, Gogi	*Singer*
10323 Alamo Ave, #202, Los Angeles, CA 90064, USA	
Grant, Harvey	*Basketball Player*
%Washington Wizards, Capital Centre, 1 Truman Dr, Landover, MD 20785, USA	
Grant, Horace	*Basketball Player*
%Orlando Magic, Orlando Arena, 1 Magic Place, Orlando, FL 32801, USA	
Grant, Hugh	*Actor*
PO Box 8394, London SW7 2ZB, England	
Grant, Hugh	*Harness Racing Executive*
414 E 75th St, #4, Gainesville, FL 32604, USA	
Grant, James T (Mudcat)	*Baseball Player*
1020 S Dunsmuir Ave, Los Angeles, CA 90019, USA	
Grant, Jennifer	*Actress*
%Karg/Weissenbach, 329 N Wetherly Dr, #101, Beverly Hills, CA 90211, USA	
Grant, Lee	*Actress, Director*
610 West End Ave, #7-B, New York, NY 10024, USA	
Grant, Paul	*Basketball Player*
%Minnesota Timberwolves, Target Center, 600 1st Ave N, Minneapolis, MN 55403, USA	
Grant, Rodney A	*Actor*
%Omar, 526 N Larchmont Blvd, Los Angeles, CA 90004, USA	
Grant, Tom	*Jazz Musician*
%Brad Simon Organization, 122 E 57th St, New York, NY 10022, USA	
Grant, Toni	*Radio Psychologist*
610 S Ardmore Ave, Los Angeles, CA 90005, USA	
Grant, Verne E	*Biologist*
2811 Fresco Dr, Austin, TX 78731, USA	
Granville, Joseph	*Financier, Writer*
%Granville Market Letter, 2525 Market St, Kansas City, MO 64108, USA	
Granzow, Paul H	*Businessman*
%Standard Register Co, 626 Albany St, Dayton, OH 45408, USA	
Grappelli, Stephane	*Jazz Violinist*
87 Rue de Dunkerque, 75009 Paris, France	
Grass, Gunter	*Writer*
Niedstr 13, 12159 Berlin, Germany	
Grass, Martin L	*Businessman*
%Rite Aid Corp, 30 Hunter Lane, Camp Hill, PA 17011, USA	
Grassle, Karen	*Actress*
3717 Edmond Lane, Louisville, KY 40207, USA	
Grau, Shirley Ann	*Writer*
210 Baronne St, #1120, New Orleans, LA 70112, USA	
Graubard, Stephen R	*Writer, Historian, Editor*
8 Maple Ave, Cambridge, MA 02139, USA	
Graveline, Duane E	*Astronaut*
PO Box 92, Underhill Center, VT 05490, USA	
Graves, Adam	*Hockey Player*
%New York Rangers, Madison Square Garden, 2 Penn Plaza, New York, NY 10121, USA	

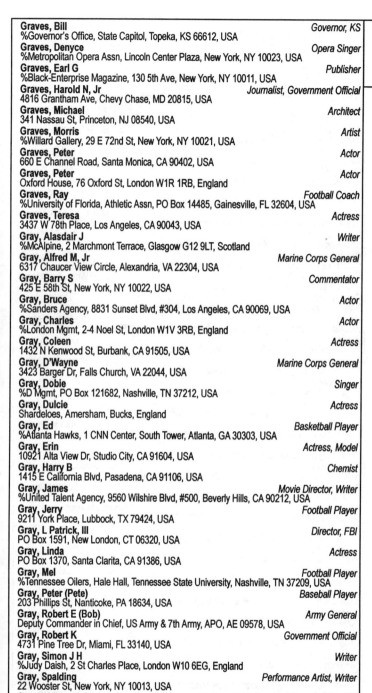

Graves, Bill *Governor, KS*
%Governor's Office, State Capitol, Topeka, KS 66612, USA
Graves, Denyce *Opera Singer*
%Metropolitan Opera Assn, Lincoln Center Plaza, New York, NY 10023, USA
Graves, Earl G *Publisher*
%Black-Enterprise Magazine, 130 5th Ave, New York, NY 10011, USA
Graves, Harold N, Jr *Journalist, Government Official*
4816 Grantham Ave, Chevy Chase, MD 20815, USA
Graves, Michael *Architect*
341 Nassau St, Princeton, NJ 08540, USA
Graves, Morris *Artist*
%Willard Gallery, 29 E 72nd St, New York, NY 10021, USA
Graves, Peter *Actor*
660 E Channel Road, Santa Monica, CA 90402, USA
Graves, Peter *Actor*
Oxford House, 76 Oxford St, London W1R 1RB, England
Graves, Ray *Football Coach*
%University of Florida, Athletic Assn, PO Box 14485, Gainesville, FL 32604, USA
Graves, Teresa *Actress*
3437 W 78th Place, Los Angeles, CA 90043, USA
Gray, Alasdair J *Writer*
%McAlpine, 2 Marchmont Terrace, Glasgow G12 9LT, Scotland
Gray, Alfred M, Jr *Marine Corps General*
6317 Chaucer View Circle, Alexandria, VA 22304, USA
Gray, Barry S *Commentator*
425 E 58th St, New York, NY 10022, USA
Gray, Bruce *Actor*
%Sanders Agency, 8831 Sunset Blvd, #304, Los Angeles, CA 90069, USA
Gray, Charles *Actor*
%London Mgmt, 2-4 Noel St, London W1V 3RB, England
Gray, Coleen *Actress*
1432 N Kenwood St, Burbank, CA 91505, USA
Gray, D'Wayne *Marine Corps General*
3423 Barger Dr, Falls Church, VA 22044, USA
Gray, Dobie *Singer*
%D Mgmt, PO Box 121682, Nashville, TN 37212, USA
Gray, Dulcie *Actress*
Shardeloes, Amersham, Bucks, England
Gray, Ed *Basketball Player*
%Atlanta Hawks, 1 CNN Center, South Tower, Atlanta, GA 30303, USA
Gray, Erin *Actress, Model*
10921 Alta View Dr, Studio City, CA 91604, USA
Gray, Harry B *Chemist*
1415 E California Blvd, Pasadena, CA 91106, USA
Gray, James *Movie Director, Writer*
%United Talent Agency, 9560 Wilshire Blvd, #500, Beverly Hills, CA 90212, USA
Gray, Jerry *Football Player*
9211 York Place, Lubbock, TX 79424, USA
Gray, L Patrick, III *Director, FBI*
PO Box 1591, New London, CT 06320, USA
Gray, Linda *Actress*
PO Box 1370, Santa Clarita, CA 91386, USA
Gray, Mel *Football Player*
%Tennessee Oilers, Hale Hall, Tennessee State University, Nashville, TN 37209, USA
Gray, Peter (Pete) *Baseball Player*
203 Phillips St, Nanticoke, PA 18634, USA
Gray, Robert E (Bob) *Army General*
Deputy Commander in Chief, US Army & 7th Army, APO, AE 09578, USA
Gray, Robert K *Government Official*
4731 Pine Tree Dr, Miami, FL 33140, USA
Gray, Simon J H *Writer*
%Judy Daish, 2 St Charles Place, London W10 6EG, England
Gray, Spalding *Performance Artist, Writer*
22 Wooster St, New York, NY 10013, USA
Gray, William H, III *Association Leader; Representative, PA*
%United Negro College Fund, 500 E 62nd St, New York, NY 10021, USA
Graydon, Michael J *Royal Air Chief Marshal, England*
%Lloyds Bank, Cox & King's Branch, 7 Pall Mall, London SW1Y 5NA, England

G

Graves - Graydon

Graysmith, Robert — *Editorial Cartoonist*
%San Francisco Chronicle, 901 Mission St, San Francisco, CA 94103, USA

Grayson, C Jackson, Jr — *Government Official, Educator*
123 N Post Oak Lane, Houston, TX 77024, USA

Grayson, Kathryn — *Singer, Actress*
%Terry M Hill, 6430 Variel Ave, #101, Woodland Hills, CA 91367, USA

Grazzola, Kenneth E — *Publisher*
%Aviation Week Magazine, 1221 Ave of Americas, New York, NY 10020, USA

Greatbatch, Wilson — *Inventor (Cardiac Pacemaker)*
%Wilson Greatbatch Prosthetics, 10871 Main St, Clarence, NY 14031, USA

Grebenshchikov, Boris — *Singer, Guitarist (Akvarium)*
2 Marata St, #3, 191 025 St Petersburg, Russia

Grechko, Georgi M — *Cosmonaut*
%Potchta Kosmonavtov, Moskovskoi Oblasti, 141160 Syvisdny Goroduk, Russia

Greco, Buddy — *Singer, Pianist*
%Cornell Productions, 100 Bayview Dr, #1521, North Miami Beach, FL 33160, USA

Greco, Emilio — *Sculptor*
Viale Cortina d'Ampezzo 132, 00135 Rome, Italy

Greco, Jose — *Dancer, Choreographer*
%Jose Greco Foundation, 866 United Nations Plaza, New York, NY 10017, USA

Greco, Juliette — *Actress, Singer*
%Maurice Maraouani, 37 Rue Marbeuf, 75008 Paris, France

Greco, Rosemarie B — *Financier*
%CoreStates Financial Corp, Centre Square Building, Philadelphia, PA 19101, USA

Greeley, Andrew M (Andy) — *Writer, Sociologist*
6030 S Ellis Ave, Chicago, IL 60637, USA

Greeley, William E — *Businessman*
%Valero Energy Corp, 530 McCullough Ave, San Antonio, TX 78215, USA

Green, A C — *Basketball Player*
%Dallas Mavericks, Reunion Arena, 777 Sports St, Dallas, TX 75207, USA

Green, Adolph — *Lyricist*
211 Central Park West, #19-E, New York, NY 10024, USA

Green, Al — *Singer, Songwriter*
%William Morris Agency, 1325 Ave of Americas, New York, NY 10019, USA

Green, Benny — *Jazz Pianist*
%Jazz Tree, 648 Broadway, #703, New York, NY 10012, USA

Green, Brian Austin — *Actor*
11333 Moorpark St, #27, Studio City, CA 91602, USA

Green, David — *Movie Director*
%International Creative Mgmt, 76 Oxford St, London W1N 0AX, England

Green, David E — *Chemist*
5339 Brody Dr, Madison, WI 53705, USA

Green, David T — *Inventor (Surgical Instruments)*
%US Surgical Corp, 150 Glover Ave, Norwalk, CT 06850, USA

Green, Dennis — *Football Coach*
%Minnesota Vikings, 9520 Viking Dr, Eden Prairie, MN 55344, USA

Green, G Dallas — *Baseball Manager, Executive*
548 S Guernsey Road, West Grove, PA 19390, USA

Green, Gerald — *Writer*
88 Arrowhead Trail, New Canaan, CT 06840, USA

Green, Hamilton — *Prime Minister, Guyana*
Plot "D" Lodge, Georgetown, Guyana

Green, Holcombe T, Jr — *Businessman*
%WestPoint Stevens, 400 W 10th St, West Point, GA 31833, USA

Green, Howard — *Cellular Physiologist*
%Harvard Medical School, Physiology & Biophysics Dept, Boston, MA 02115, USA

Green, Hubert — *Golfer*
PO Box 28030, Panama City, FL 32411, USA

Green, Hugh — *Football Player*
%Miami Dolphins, 7500 SW 30th St, Davie, FL 33314, USA

Green, Julian — *Writer*
%Editions Fayard, 75 Rue des Saints-Peres, 75006 Paris, France

Green, Kate — *Writer*
%Delacorte Press, 1540 Broadway, New York, NY 10036, USA

Green, Ken — *Golfer*
2875 Antietam Lane, West Palm Beach, FL 33409, USA

Green, Lucinda — *Equestrian Rider*
Appleshaw House, Andover, Hants, England

Green, Mark J *Activist, Attorney, Writer*
%Democracy Project, 530 E 90th St, #6-K, New York, NY 10128, USA
Green, Marshall *Diplomat*
5063 Millwood Lane NW, Washington, DC 20016, USA
Green, Maurice Spurgeon *Editor*
Hermitage, Twyford House, Hants, England
Green, Peter J F *Businessman*
85 Burton Court, London SW3 4SX, England
Green, Rick *Hockey Player*
RR 1, Peterborough ON K9J 6X2, Canada
Green, Tammie *Golfer*
%Ladies Professional Golf Assn, 2570 Volusia Ave, Daytona Beach, FL 32114, USA
Green, Tim *Sportscaster*
%Fox-TV, Sports Dept, PO Box 900, Beverly Hills, CA 90213, USA
Greenaway, Peter *Movie Director*
%Allarts Ltd, 387-B King St, London W6 9NH, England
Greenberg, Adam *Cinematographer*
%American Society of Cinematographers, 1782 N Orange Dr, Los Angeles, CA 90028, USA
Greenberg, Alan C *Financier*
%Bear Stearns Co, 245 Park Ave, New York, NY 10167, USA
Greenberg, Bernard *Biological Scientist, Entomologist*
1463 E 55th Place, Chicago, IL 60637, USA
Greenberg, Carl *Journalist*
6001 Canterbury Dr, Culver City, CA 90230, USA
Greenberg, Frank S *Businessman*
%Burlington Industries, PO Box 21207, Greensboro, NC 27420, USA
Greenberg, Jeffrey W *Businessman*
%American Home Assurance, 70 Pine St, New York, NY 10270, USA
Greenberg, Joseph H *Anthropologist*
860 Mayfield St, Stanford, CA 94305, USA
Greenberg, Robbie *Cinematographer*
%American Society of Cinematographers, 1782 N Orange Dr, Los Angeles, CA 90028, USA
Greenburg, Dan *Writer*
323 E 50th St, New York, NY 10022, USA
Greenburg, Paul *Journalist*
5900 Scenic Dr, Little Rock, AR 72207, USA
Greenbush, Rachel Lindsay *Actress*
%Gold Marshak Liedtke, 3500 W Olive Ave, #1400, Burbank, CA 91505, USA
Greenbush, Sidney Robin *Actress*
%Gold Marshak Liedtke, 3500 W Olive Ave, #1400, Burbank, CA 91505, USA
Greene of Harrow Weald, Sidney F *Labor Leader*
26 Kynaston Wood, Boxtree Road, Harrow Weald, Middx HA3 6UA, England
Greene Raine, Nancy *Skier*
%Nancy Greene Hotel, PO Box 418, Whistler/Blackcomb BC V0N 1B0, Canada
Greene, Charles E (Charlie) *Track Athlete*
11942 Gold Needle Way, Columbia, MD 21044, USA
Greene, Ellen *Actress, Singer*
%William Morris Agency, 151 S El Camino Dr, Beverly Hills, CA 90212, USA
Greene, Graham *Actor*
%Susan Smith, 121 N San Vicente Blvd, Beverly Hills, CA 90211, USA
Greene, Jack *Singer*
%Ace Productions, PO Box 428, Portland, TN 37148, USA
Greene, Jack P *Writer, Historian*
1606 Hishfield House, 4000 N Charles St, Baltimore, MD 21218, USA
Greene, Joseph (Mean Joe) *Football Player, Coach*
%Arizona Cardinals, 8701 S Hardy Dr, Tempe, AZ 85284, USA
Greene, Kevin *Football Player*
1162 Glenaire Dr, Santa Ana, CA 92705, USA
Greene, Leonard M *Inventor (Airplane Stall Warning Device)*
6 Hickory Road, Scarsdale, NY 10583, USA
Greene, Michele *Actress*
PO Box 29117, Los Angeles, CA 90029, USA
Greene, Robert B (Bob), Jr *Columnist*
%Chicago Tribune, Editorial Dept, 435 N Michigan Ave, Chicago, IL 60611, USA
Greene, Shecky *Comedian*
1642 S La Verne Way, Palm Springs, CA 92264, USA
Greenfield, James L *Journalist*
850 Park Ave, New York, NY 10021, USA

G

Green - Greenfield

Greenfield, Jerry *Businessman*
%Ben & Jerry's Homemade, Duxtown Common Plaza, Waterbury, CT 05676, USA

Greenfield, Meg *Journalist*
3318 "R" St NW, Washington, DC 20007, USA

Greenspan, Alan *Financier, Government Official*
%Federal Reserve Board, 20th St & Constitution Ave NW, Washington, DC 20551, USA

Greenspan, Bud *Producer, Director*
%Cappy Productions, 33 E 68th St, New York, NY 10021, USA

Greenstein, Jesse L *Astronomer*
1763 Royal Oaks Dr, #5-B, Duarte, CA 91010, USA

Greenwald, Gerald *Businessman*
%UAL Corp, 1200 Algonquin Road, Elk Grove Township, IL 60005, USA

Greenwald, Joseph A *Economist, Diplomat*
Town House, 8-5-25 Asaka, Minatoku, Tokyo 107, Japan

Greenwald, Milton *Paleontologist*
%University of California, Museum of Paleontology, Berkeley, CA 94720, USA

Greenwalt, T Jack *Medical Administrator*
328 Compton Hills Dr, Cincinnati, OH 45215, USA

Greenwell, Michael L (Mike) *Baseball Player*
12250 N River Road, Alva, FL 33920, USA

Greenwood, Bruce *Actor*
12414 Cascade Canyon Dr, Granada Hills, CA 91344, USA

Greenwood, David *Basketball Player*
12103 Turnberry, San Antonio, TX 78231, USA

Greenwood, Joan *Actress*
27 Slaidburn St, Chelsea, London SW10, England

Greenwood, L C *Football Player*
329 S Dallas Ave, Pittsburgh, PA 15208, USA

Greenwood, Lee *Singer, Songwriter*
%Blade Agency, 203 SW 3rd Ave, Gainesville, FL 37601, USA

Greenwood, Richard M *Businessman*
%Fidelity Federal Bank, 600 N Brand Blvd, Glendale, CA 91203, USA

Greer, C Scott *Businessman*
%Echlin Inc, 100 Double Beach Road, Branford, CT 06405, USA

Greer, Dabbs *Actor*
284 S Madison Ave, Pasadena, CA 91101, USA

Greer, David S *Internist*
%Brown University, Medicine Program, Box G-B221, Providence, RI 02901, USA

Greer, Germaine *Writer, Feminist*
%Atkin & Stone, 29 Fernshaw Road, London SW10 0TG, England

Greer, Gordon G *Editor*
%Better Homes & Gardens Magazine, 1716 Locust St, Des Moines, IA 50309, USA

Greer, Harold E (Hal) *Basketball Player*
2632 Beacon Hill Dr, #204, Auburn Hills, MI 48326, USA

Greer, Howard E *Navy Admiral*
8539 Prestwick Dr, La Jolla, CA 92037, USA

Greer, Jane *Actress*
966 Moraga Dr, Los Angeles, CA 90049, USA

Greer, Janet L *Nutritionist*
%University of Wisconsin, Nutritional Sciences Dept, Madison, WI 53706, USA

Greevy, Bernadette *Concert Singer*
Melrose, 672 Howth Road, Dublin 5, Ireland

Gregg, A Forrest *Football Player, Coach, Administrator*
2600 Zia Road, #H-4, Santa Fe, NM 87505, USA

Gregg, Hugh *Governor, NH*
RFD 5, 17 Gregg Road, Nashua, NH 03062, USA

Gregg, Julie *Actress*
12304 Santa Monica Blvd, #104, Los Angeles, CA 90025, USA

Gregg, Ricky Lynn *Singer*
%We Two Mgmt, 9 Music Square S, #335, Nashville, TN 37203, USA

Gregg, Stephen R *WW II Army Hero (CMH)*
130 Lexington Ave, Bayonne, NJ 07002, USA

Gregoire, Paul Cardinal *Religious Leader*
%Archbishopric, 2000 Rue Sherbrooke Quest, Montreal PQ H3H 1G4, Canada

Gregorio, Rose *Actress*
%Don Buchwald, 9229 Sunset Blvd, #710, Los Angeles, CA 90069, USA

Gregorios, Metropolitan Paulos M *Religious Leader*
%Orthodox Seminary, PO Box 98, Kottayam, Kerala 686001, India

Gregory, Bettina L — Commentator
%ABC-TV, News Dept, 1717 DeSales St NW, Washington, DC 20036, USA

Gregory, Cynthia — Ballet Dancer
%American Ballet Theatre, 890 Broadway, New York, NY 10003, USA

Gregory, Dick — Comedian, Social Activist
PO Box 3270, Plymouth, MA 02361, USA

Gregory, Frederick D — Astronaut
%National Aviation & Space Agency, Safety Quality, Code Q, Washington, DC 20546, USA

Gregory, James — Actor
55 Cathedral Rock Dr, #33, Sedona, AZ 86351, USA

Gregory, Kathy — Cartoonist
%Playboy Magazine, Reader Services, 680 N Lake Shore Dr, Chicago, IL 60611, USA

Gregory, Paul — Movie Producer
PO Box 38, Palm Springs, CA 92263, USA

Gregory, Richard — Religious Leader
%Independent Fundamental Churches, 2684 Meadow Ridge, Byron Center, MI 49315, USA

Gregory, Stephen — Actor
%Carey, 64 Thornton Ave, London W4 1QQ, England

Gregory, William G — Astronaut
%NASA, Johnson Space Center, 2101 NASA Road, Houston, TX 77058, USA

Gregory, William H — Editor
%Aviation Week Magazine, 1221 Ave of Americas, New York, NY 10020, USA

Grehl, Michael — Editor
%Memphis Commercial Appeal, Editorial Dept, 495 Union Ave, Memphis, TN 38103, USA

Greif, Michael — Theater Director
%La Jolla Playhouse, PO Box 12039, La Jolla, CA 92039, USA

Greiner, William R — Educator
%State University of New York, President's Office, Buffalo, NY 14221, USA

Greist, Kim — Actress
%Innovative Artists, 1999 Ave of Stars, #2850, Los Angeles, CA 90067, USA

Grentz, Theresa Shank — Basketball Coach
%University of Illinois, Athletic Dept, Champaign, IL 61820, USA

Gressette, L M, Jr — Businessman
%SCANA Corp, 1426 Main St, Columbia, SC 29201, USA

Gretzky, Wayne — Hockey Player
650 W Stafford Road, Thousand Oaks, CA 91361, USA

Grevey, Kevin — Basketball Player
466 River Bend Road, Great Falls, VA 22066, USA

Grewal, Alexi — Cyclist
PO Box 1620, Berthoud, CO 80513, USA

Grey, Beryl E — Ballerina
Fernhill, Priory Road, Forest Row, East Sussex RH18 5JE, England

Grey, Jennifer — Actress
%Creative Artists Agency, 9830 Wilshire Blvd, Beverly Hills, CA 90212, USA

Grey, Joel — Actor
9119 Thrasher Ave, Los Angeles, CA 90069, USA

Grey, Linda — Publisher
%Linda Grey Books, 201 E 50th St, New York, NY 10022, USA

Grey, Richard E — Businessman
%Tyco Toys, 6000 Midlantic Dr, Mount Laurel, NJ 08054, USA

Grey, Virginia — Actress
15101 Magnolia Blvd, #54, Sherman Oaks, CA 91403, USA

Greyeyes, Michael — Actor
%Gold Marshak Liedtke, 3500 W Olive Ave, #1400, Burbank, CA 91505, USA

Grich, Robert A (Bobby) — Baseball Player
206 Prospect Ave, Long Beach, CA 90803, USA

Grieco, Richard — Actor
2934 1/2 N Beverly Glen Circle, #252, Los Angeles, CA 90077, USA

Grieder, William — Journalist
%Simon & Schuster Inc, 1230 Ave of Americas, New York, NY 10020, USA

Griem, Helmut — Actor
Holbeinstr 4, 81677 Munich, Germany

Grier, Pam — Actress
PO Box 370958, Denver, CO 80237, USA

Grier, Roosevelt (Rosey) — Football Player, Actor
11656 Montana Ave, #301, Los Angeles, CA 90049, USA

Griese, Robert A (Bob) — Football Player, Sportscaster
4412 Santa Maria St, Coral Gables, FL 33146, USA

G

Gregory - Griese

Griesemer, John N	*Government Official*
RR 2, Box 204-B, Springfield, MO 65802, USA	
Grieve, Pierson M	*Businessman*
%Ecolab Inc, Ecolab Center, 370 Wabasha St N, St Paul, MN 55102, USA	
Griffey, G Kenneth (Ken)	*Baseball Player*
3942 Mack Road, #9, Fairfield, OH 45014, USA	
Griffey, G Kenneth (Ken), Jr	*Baseball Player*
1420 NW Gilman Blvd, #2717, Issawuah, WA 98027, USA	
Griffin, Archie	*Football Player*
4695 St Andrews Dr, Westerville, OH 43082, USA	
Griffin, Donald R	*Biologist*
Brookhaven, #A-212, 1010 Waltham St, Lexington, MA 02173, USA	
Griffin, Donald W	*Businessman*
%Olin Corp, PO Box 4500, Norwalk, CT 06856, USA	
Griffin, Eric	*Boxer*
PO Box 964, Jasper, TN 37347, USA	
Griffin, G Lee	*Financier*
%Premier Bancorp, 451 Florida St, Baton Rouge, LA 70801, USA	
Griffin, James Bennett	*Anthropologist*
5023 Wyandot Court, Bethesda, MD 20816, USA	
Griffin, Johnny	*Jazz Saxophonist*
%Joel Chriss, 300 Mercer St, #3-J, New York, NY 10003, USA	
Griffin, Merv E	*Entertainer*
%Merv Griffin Enterprises, 9860 Wilshire Blvd, Beverly Hills, CA 90210, USA	
Griffin, Robert P	*Senator, MI*
%Michigan Supreme Court, PO Box 30052, Lansing, MI 48909, USA	
Griffin, Thomas N, Jr	*Army General*
9749 S Park Circle, Fairfax Station, VA 22039, USA	
Griffith Joyner, Florence D	*Track Athlete*
%Flo-Jo Int'l, 27758 Santa Margarita Parkway, #385, Mission Viejo, CA 92691, USA	
Griffith, Andy	*Actor*
PO Box 1968, Manteo, NC 27954, USA	
Griffith, Bill	*Cartoonist (Zippy the Pinhead)*
%Innovative Artists, 1999 Ave of Stars, #2850, Los Angeles, CA 90067, USA	
Griffith, Darrell	*Basketball Player*
1300 Leighton Circle, Louisville, KY 40222, USA	
Griffith, Ed	*Actor*
8721 Santa Monica Blvd, #21, West Hollywood, CA 90069, USA	
Griffith, Emile	*Boxer*
110-14 Colfax St, Queens, NY 11429, USA	
Griffith, John C	*Air Force General*
Vice Commander, Education/Training Command, Randolph Air Force Base, TX 78150, USA	
Griffith, Melanie	*Actress, Model*
201 S Rockingham Ave, Los Angeles, CA 90049, USA	
Griffith, Nanci	*Singer, Songwriter*
%Gold Mountain, 1514 South St, #100, Nashville, TN 37212, USA	
Griffith, Thomas	*Editor*
25 East End Ave, New York, NY 10028, USA	
Griffith, Tom W	*Labor Leader*
%Rural Letter Carriers Assn, 1448 Duke St, #100, Alexandria, VA 22314, USA	
Griffiths, Phillip A	*Mathematician*
%Advanced Study Institute, Director's Office, Olden Lane, Princeton, NJ 08540, USA	
Grigson, Geoffrey	*Writer*
Broad Town Farm, Broad Town near Swindon, Wilts, England	
Grimaud, Helene	*Concert Pianist*
%Columbia Artists Mgmt Inc, 165 W 57th St, New York, NY 10019, USA	
Grimes, Martha	*Writer*
115 "D" St SE, #G-6, Washington, DC 20003, USA	
Grimes, Tammy	*Actress, Singer*
%Don Buchwald, 10 E 44th St, New York, NY 10017, USA	
Grimm, Russ	*Football Player, Coach*
3186 Mary Etta Lane, Herndon, VA 20171, USA	
Grimshaw, Nicholas T	*Architect*
1 Conway St, Fitzroy Square, London W1P 5HA, England	
Grinham Rawley, Judy	*Swimmer*
103 Green Lane, Northwood, Middx HA6 1AP, England	
Grinnell, Alan D	*Physiologist*
%University of California Medical School, Lewis Center, Los Angeles, CA 90024, USA	

Grinstead, Eugene A — *Navy Admiral*
%Director's Office, Defense Logistics Agency, Alexandria, VA 22314, USA

Grinstein, Gerald — *Businessman*
%Burlington Northern, Continental Plaza, 777 Main St, Fort Worth, TX 76102, USA

Grinville, Patrick — *Writer*
Academie Goncourt, 38 Rue du Faubourg St Jacques, 75014 Paris, France

Grisanti, Eugene P — *Businessman*
%International Flavors, 521 W 57th St, New York, NY 10019, USA

Grisez, Germain — *Theologian*
%Mount Saint Mary's College, Christian Ethics Dept, Emmitsburg, MD 21727, USA

Grisham, John — *Writer*
PO Box 1780, Oxford, MS 38655, USA

Grishin, Evgenii — *Speed Skater*
%Committee of Physical Culture, Skatertny Pl 4, Moscow, Russia

Grisman, David — *Mandolinist, Composer*
%C M Mgmt, 7957 Nita Ave, Canoga Park, CA 91304, USA

Grissom, Marquis D — *Baseball Player*
175 Cherokee Rose Lane, Fairburn, GA 30213, USA

Grisson, Steve — *Auto Racing Driver*
23110 S R 54-198, Lutz, FL 33549, USA

Grist, Reri — *Opera Singer*
%Columbia Artists Mgmt Inc, 165 W 57th St, New York, NY 10019, USA

Grizzard, George — *Actor*
400 E 54th St, New York, NY 10022, USA

Groat, Richard M (Dick) — *Baseball, Basketball Player*
%Champion Lakes, RR 1, PO Box 288, Bolivar, PA 15923, USA

Grodin, Charles — *Actor*
187 Chestnut Hill Road, Wilton, CT 06897, USA

Groebli, Werner (Mr Frick) — *Ice Skater*
PO Box 7886, Incline Village, NV 89452, USA

Groener, Harry — *Actor*
%Susan Smith, 121 N San Vicente Blvd, Beverly Hills, CA 90211, USA

Groening, Matthew (Matt) — *Cartoonist (Life in Hell, Simpsons)*
%"The Simpsons" Show, 10201 W Pico Blvd, Los Angeles, CA 90064, USA

Groer, Hans Hermann Cardinal — *Religious Leader*
Erzbischofliches, Wollzeile 2, 1010 Vienna, Austria

Grogan, Steve — *Football Player*
6 Country Club Lane, Foxborough, MA 02035, USA

Groh, David — *Actor*
301 N Canon Dr, #305, Beverly Hills, CA 90210, USA

Grondal, Benedikt — *Prime Minister, Iceland*
Hjallaland 26, 108 Reykjavik, Iceland

Gronk (Glugio Gronk Nicandro) — *Artist*
%Saxon-Lee Gallery, 7525 Beverly Blvd, Los Angeles, CA 90036, USA

Grooms, Charles R (Red) — *Artist*
85 Walker St, New York, NY 10013, USA

Gropp, Louis Oliver — *Editor*
140 Riverside Dr, #6-G, New York, NY 10024, USA

Grosbard, Ulu — *Movie Director*
29 W 10th St, New York, NY 10011, USA

Gross, Ludwik — *Physician*
%Veterans Administration Hospital, 130 W Kingsbridge Road, Bronx, NY 10468, USA

Gross, Michael — *Swimmer*
Paul-Ehrlich-Str 6, 60596 Frankfurt/Main, Germany

Gross, Michael — *Actor*
PO Box 522, La Canada, CA 91012, USA

Gross, Paul — *Actor*
55 Bloor St W, #222, Toronto ON M4W 1AS, Canada

Gross, Robert A — *Physicist*
14 Sunnyside Way, New Rochelle, NY 10804, USA

Gross, Terry R — *Commentator*
%WHYY-Radio, News Dept, Independence Mall W, Philadelphia, PA 19104, USA

Grossfeld, Stanley — *Photographer*
%Boston Globe, Editorial Dept, 135 Morrissey Blvd, Boston, MA 02125, USA

Grossman, Judith — *Writer*
%Warren Wilson College, English Dept, Swammanoa, NC 28778, USA

Grossman, Robert — *Illustrator*
19 Crosby St, New York, NY 10013, USA

G

Grinstead - Grossman

Grosvenor, Gilbert M *Foundation Executive, Publisher*
%National Geographic Society, 17th & "M" NW, Washington, DC 20036, USA

Grotowski, Jerzy *Theater Director*
%Centro Per la Sperimentazione, Via Manzoni 22, 56025 Pontedera, Italy

Grouch, Roger K *Astronaut*
%Life/Microgravity Sciences Office, NASA Headquarters, Washington, DC 20546, USA

Grout, James *Actor*
%Crouch Assoc, 59 Firth St, London W1V 5TA, England

Grove, Andrew S (Andy) *Businessman*
%Intel Corp, 2200 Mission College Blvd, Santa Clara, CA 95054, USA

Groza, Louis R (Lou) *Football Player*
287 Parkway Dr, Berea, OH 44017, USA

Grubbs, Gary *Actor*
%Paradigm Agency, 10100 Santa Monica Blvd, #2500, Los Angeles, CA 90067, USA

Gruber, Kelly W *Baseball Player*
3300 Bee Cave Road, #650-227, Austin, TX 78746, USA

Grubman, Allen J *Attorney*
%Grubman Indursky Schindler Goldstein, 152 W 57th St, New York, NY 10019, USA

Grudzielanek, Mark J *Baseball Player*
%Tom Grudzielanek, 550 E Mona Dr, Oak Creek, WI 53154, USA

Grum, Clifford J *Businessman*
%Temple-Inland Inc, 303 S Temple Dr, Diboll, TX 75941, USA

Grumbach, Melvin M *Physician*
%University of California, Med School, Pediatrics Dept, San Francisco, CA 94143, USA

Grummer, Elisabeth *Opera Singer*
Am Schlachtensee 104, 14163 Berlin, Germany

Grundfest, Joseph A *Government Official*
%Stanford University, Law School, Stanford, CA 94305, USA

Grundhofer, Jerry A *Financier*
%Star Banc Corp, 425 Walnut St, Cincinnati, OH 45202, USA

Grune, George V *Publisher, Foundation Executive*
PO Box 2348, Ponte Vedra, FL 32004, USA

Grunewald, Herbert *Businessman*
%Bayer AG, 17192 Leverkusen, Germany

Grunfeld, Ernie *Basketball Player, Executive*
507 Hampton Hills, Franklin Lakes, NJ 07417, USA

Grunsfeld, John M *Astronaut*
%NASA, Johnson Space Center, 2101 NASA Road, Houston, TX 77058, USA

Grunwald, Ernest M *Chemist*
%Brandeis University, Chemistry Dept, Waltham, MA 02154, USA

Grunwald, Henry A *Editor, Diplomat*
694 Madison Ave, New York, NY 10021, USA

Grushin, Pyotr D *Aviation Engineer*
%Academy of Sciences, 14 Lenisky Prospekt, Moscow, Russia

Grusin, Dave *Composer, Pianist*
%GRP Records, 555 W 57th St, New York, NY 10019, USA

Grutman, N Roy *Attorney*
%Grutman Miller Greenspoon Hendler, 505 Park Ave, New York, NY 10022, USA

Grzelecki, Frank E *Businessman*
%Handy & Harman, 555 Theodore Fremd Ave, #A, Rye, NY 10580, USA

Guadagnino, Kathy *Golfer*
%Ladies Professional Golf Assn, 2570 Volusia Ave, Daytona Beach, FL 32114, USA

Guardino, Harry *Actor*
2949 Via Vaquero, Palms Springs, CA 92262, USA

Guare, John *Writer*
%R Andrew Boose, 1 Dag Hammarskjold Plaza, New York, NY 10017, USA

Guarrera, Frank *Concert, Opera Singer*
4514 Latona Ave NE, Seattle, WA 98105, USA

Gubarev, Alexei A *Cosmonaut; Air Force General*
%Potchta Kosmonavtov, Moskovskoi Oblasti, 141160 Syvisdny Goroduk, Russia

Guber, Peter *Movie Producer*
%Mandaly Entertainment, 10202 W Washington Blvd, Culver City, CA 90232, USA

Guccione, Robert (Bob) *Publisher*
%Penthouse Magazine, 1965 Broadway, New York, NY 10023, USA

Guckel, Henry *Microbiotics Engineer*
%University of Wisconsin, Engineering Dept, Madison, WI 53706, USA

Gudelski, Leonard S *Financier*
%Hudson City Savings Bank, W 80 Century Road, Paramus, NJ 07652, USA

Guenther, Johnny — *Bowler*
23826 115th Place W, Woodway, WA 98020, USA

Guenther, Otto J — *Army General*
Director, Information Systems, HqUSA, Pentagon, Washington, DC 20310, USA

Guerard, Michel E — *Chef*
Les Pres d'Eugenie, 40320 Eugenie les Bains, France

Guerin, Bill — *Hockey Player*
39 W Colonial Road, Wibraham, MA 01905, USA

Guerin, Richie — *Basketball Player*
25 Bridle Path, West Hampton Beach, NY 11978, USA

Guerrero, Pedro — *Baseball Player*
4004 St Andrews Dr, Rio Rancho, NM 87124, USA

Guerrero, Roberto — *Auto Racing Driver*
31642 Via Cervantes, San Juan Capistrano, CA 92675, USA

Guest, Christopher — *Movie Director, Actor*
%Creative Artists Agency, 9830 Wilshire Blvd, Beverly Hills, CA 90212, USA

Guest, Douglas — *Concert Organist*
Gables, Minchinhampton, Glos GL6 9JE, England

Guffey, John W, Jr — *Businessman*
%Coltec Industries, 2550 W Tyvola Road, Charlotte, NC 28217, USA

Guglielmi, Ralph — *Football Player*
8501 White Pass Court, Potomac, MD 20854, USA

Gugliotta, Tom — *Basketball Player*
10963 Chapman Point, Eden Prairie, MN 55347, USA

Guida, Lou — *Harness Racing Breeder*
%General Delivery, Yardley, PA

Guidoni, Umberto — *Astronaut*
15010 Cobre Valley Dr, Houston, TX 77062, USA

Guidry, Ronald A (Ron) — *Baseball Player*
PO Box 278, Scott, LA 70583, USA

Guilbert, Ann — *Actress*
%Bauman Hiller, 5750 Wilshire Blvd, #512, Los Angeles, CA 90036, USA

Guilford, Joy Paul — *Psychologist*
PO Box 1288, Beverly Hills, CA 90213, USA

Guillaime, Raymond K — *Financier*
%Bank of Louisville, PO Box 1101, Louisville, KY 40201, USA

Guillaume, Robert — *Actor*
4709 Noeline Ave, Encino, CA 91436, USA

Guillem, Sylvie — *Ballerina*
%Royal Ballet, Bow St, London WC2E 9DD, England

Guillemin, Roger C L — *Nobel Medicine Laureate*
%Whittier Institute, 9894 Genesse Ave, La Jolla, CA 92037, USA

Guillen, Oswaldo J (Ozzie) — *Baseball Player*
%Cle San Jose 52, El Rodeo Del Tuy, Mirando, Venezuela

Guillerman, John — *Movie Director*
309 S Rockingham Ave, Los Angeles, CA 90049, USA

Guindon, Richard G — *Cartoonist (Guindon)*
321 W Lafayette Blvd, Detroit, MI 48226, USA

Guinier, Lani — *Attorney, Educator*
%University of Pennsylvania, Law School, 3400 Chestnut, Philadelphia, PA 19104, USA

Guinn, Kenny C — *Financier*
%Southwest Gas Corp, 5241 Spring Mountain Road, Las Vegas, NV 89150, USA

Guinness, A F B — *Businessman*
%Arthur Guinness & Sons, Park Royal Brewery, London NW10 7RR, England

Guinness, Alec — *Actor*
Kettlebrook Meadows, Steep Marsh, Petersfield, Hants, England

Guisewite, Cathy L — *Cartoonist (Cathy)*
4039 Camilla Ave, Studio City, CA 91604, USA

Guitar, Bonnie — *Singer, Guitarist*
%British & Int'l Artists, 500 Waterman Ave, #191, East Providence, RI 02914, USA

Guizar, Tito — *Guitarist, Actor*
Sierra Madre, 640 Lomas de Chapultepec, Mexico City DF 10-09999, Mexico

Gujral, Inder Kumar — *Prime Minister, India*
%Prime Minister's Officer, 1 Safdarjung Road, New Delhi 110011, India

Gulbinowicx, Henryk Roman Cardinal — *Religious Leader*
%Metropolita Wroclawski, Ul Katedraina 11, 50-328 Wroclaw, Poland

Guliyev, Faud — *Prime Minister, Azerbaijan*
%Prime Minister's Office, Parliament House, Baku, Azerbaijan

G

Gullickson, William L (Bill) — *Baseball Player*
300 Brentvale Lane, Brentwood, TN 37027, USA

Gullit, Ruud — *Soccer Player*
%FC Chelsea, Stamford Bridge, Fulham Road, London SW6 1HS, England

Gulliver, Harold — *Editor*
%Atlanta Constitution, Editorial Dept, 72 Marieta St NW, Atlanta, GA 30303, USA

Gulyas, Denes — *Opera Singer*
%Hungarian State Opera, Andrassy Utca 22, Budapest 1062, Hungary

Gumbel, Bryant C — *Commentator*
%CBS-TV, News Dept, 51 W 52nd St, New York, NY 10019, USA

Gumbel, Greg — *Sportscaster*
%NBC-TV, Sports Dept, 30 Rockefeller Plaza, New York, NY 10112, USA

Gumbiner, Robert — *Businessman*
%FHP International Corp, PO Box 25186, Santa Ana, CA 92799, USA

Gumede, Josiah Z — *President, Zimbabwe*
29 Barbour Fields, PO Mzilikazi, Bulawayo, Zimbabwe

Gund, Agnes — *Museum Executive*
%Musuem of Modern Art, 11 W 53rd St, New York, NY 10019, USA

Gundling, Beulah — *Synchronized Swimmer*
%Coral Ridge South, 3333 NE 34th St, #1517, Fort Lauderdale, FL 33308, USA

Gunn, James P — *Astronomer*
%Princeton University, Astrophysics Dept, Princeton, NJ 08544, USA

Gunn, Janet — *Actress*
%Don Buchwald, 9229 Sunset Blvd, #710, Los Angeles, CA 90069, USA

Gunn, Thomson W (Thom) — *Writer*
1216 Cole St, San Francisco, CA 94117, USA

Gunnell, Sally — *Track Athlete*
7 Old Patcham Mews, Old London Road, Brighton, East Sussex, England

Gunsalus, Irwin C — *Biochemist, Writer*
2316 Mulberry Court, Champaign, IL 61821, USA

Gunther, Dan — *Actor*
%Century Artists, 1148 4th St, #206, Santa Monica, CA 90403, USA

Guokas, Matt — *Basketball Coach, Executive*
26 Rodeo Dr, Burr Ridge, IL 60521, USA

Gupta, Sudhir — *Immunologist*
%University of California, Medicine Dept, Irvine, CA 92717, USA

Gur, Mordechai — *Army General, Israel*
25 Mishmeret St, Afeka, Tel-Aviv 69694, Israel

Gura, Larry C — *Baseball Player*
PO Box 94, Litchfield Park, AZ 85340, USA

Gurchenko, Ludmilla M — *Actress*
%Union of Cinematographists, Vasilyevskaya 13, 103056 Moscow, Russia

Gurney, A R, Jr — *Writer*
Wellers Bridge Road, Roxbury, CT 06783, USA

Gurney, Daniel S (Dan) — *Auto Racing Driver, Builder*
%All-American Racers Inc, 2334 S Broadway, Santa Ana, CA 92707, USA

Gurney, Hilda — *Equestrian Rider*
8430 Waters Road, Moorpark, CA 93021, USA

Gurraggchaa, Jugderdemidijn — *Cosmonaut, Mongolia; Air Force General*
Lyotchik Kosmonavt, MNR, Central Post Office Box 378, Ulan Bator, Mongolia

Gurwitch, Annabelle — *Actress*
%Ambrosio/Mortimer, 9150 Wilshire Blvd, #175, Beverly Hills, CA 90212, USA

Gusella, James — *Medical Researcher*
%Harvard Medical School, 25 Shattuck St, Boston, MA 02115, USA

Gushiken, Koji — *Gymnast*
%Nippon Physical Education College, Judo School, Tokyo, Japan

Guss, Louis — *Actor*
%Amsel Eisenstadt Frazier, 6310 San Vicente Blvd, #401, Los Angeles, CA 90048, USA

Gut, Rainer E — *Financier*
%CS First Boston, Park Ave Plaza, 55 E 52nd St, New York, NY 10055, USA

Gutensohn-Knopf, Katrin — *Skier*
Oberfeldweg 12, 83080 Oberaudorf, Germany

Guterres, Antonio — *Prime Minister, Portugal*
%Prime Minister's Office, Rua de Imprensa 8, 1300 Lisbon, Portugal

Guterson, David — *Writer*
%Vintage Books, 201 E 50th St, New York, NY 10022, USA

Guth, Alan H — *Physicist*
%Massachusetts Institute of Technology, Physics Dept, Cambridge, MA 02139, USA

Gullickson - Guth

Guth, John E, Jr	*Businessman*
%National-Standard Co, 1618 Terminal Road, Niles, MI 49120, USA	
Guth, Wilfried	*Financier*
%Deutsche Bank AG, Taunusanlage 12, 60262 Frankfurt/Main, Germany	
Guthman, Edwin O	*Editor*
%Philadelphia Inquirer, Editorial Dept, 400 N Broad St, Philadelphia, PA 19130, USA	
Guthrie, Arlo	*Singer, Songwriter*
The Farm, Washington, MA 01223, USA	
Guthrie, Jennifer	*Actress*
%Don Buchwald, 9229 Sunset Blvd, #710, Los Angeles, CA 90069, USA	
Gutierrez, Gerald A	*Theater Director*
%William Morris Agency, 1325 Ave of Americas, New York, NY 10019, USA	
Gutierrez, Gustavo	*Theologian*
Belisario Flores, 647 Lince, Ap 3090, Lima 100, Peru	
Gutierrez, Horacio	*Concert Pianist*
%Shaw Concerts, Lincoln Center Plaza, 1900 Broadway, #200, New York, NY 10023, USA	
Gutierrez, Sidney M	*Astronaut*
%Sandia National Laboratories, Strategic PO Box 5800, Albuquerque, NM 87185, USA	
Gutman, Natalia G	*Concert Cellist*
%Harold Holt, 31 Sinclair Road, London W14 0NS, England	
Gutman, Roy W	*Journalist*
13132 Curved Iron Road, Herndon, VA 20171, USA	
Gutowsky, Herbert S	*Physical Chemist*
202 W Delaware Ave, Urbana, IL 61801, USA	
Gutsche, Torsten	*Kayak Athlete*
Hans-Marchwitza-Ring 51, 14473 Potsdam, Germany	
Guttenberg, Steve	*Actor*
15237 Sunset Blvd, #48, Pacific Palisades, CA 90272, USA	
Guttman, Zoltan (Lou)	*Financier*
%New York Mercantile Exchange, 4 World Trade Center, New York, NY 10048, USA	
Gutton, Andre H G	*Architect*
3 Ave Vavin, 75006 Paris, France	
Guy, Billy	*Singer (Coasters)*
%Famous Artists Agency, 1700 Broadway, #500, New York, NY 10019, USA	
Guy, Buddy	*Singer, Guitarist*
%Cameron Organization, 2001 W Magnolia Blvd, Burbank, CA 91506, USA	
Guy, Jasmine	*Actress*
%Pantich, 21243 Ventura Blvd, #101, Woodland Hills, CA 91364, USA	
Guy, Ray	*Football Player*
1389 Wrightsboro Road NW, Thomson, GA 30824, USA	
Guy, William L	*Governor, ND*
3330 Prairiewood Dr W, Fargo, ND 58103, USA	
Guyer, David B	*Foundation Executive*
%Save the Children Foundation, Owyhee, NV 89832, USA	
Guyon, John C	*Educator*
%Southern Illinois University, President's Office, Carbondale, IL 62901, USA	
Guze, Samuel B	*Psychiatrist*
%Washington University, Medical School, Psychiatry Dept, St Louis, MO 63110, USA	
Guzy, Carol	*Photographer*
2145 Fort Scott Dr, Arlington, VA 22202, USA	
Gwathmey, Charles	*Architect*
%Gwathmey Siegel Architects, 475 10th Ave, New York, NY 10018, USA	
Gwinn, Mary Ann	*Journalist*
%Seattle Times, Editorial Dept, Fairview Ave N & John St, Seattle, WA 98111, USA	
Gwynn, Anthony K (Tony)	*Baseball Player*
15643 Boulder Ridge Lane, Poway, CA 92064, USA	
Gwynn, Darrell	*Auto Racing Driver*
4850 SW 52nd St, Davie, FL 33314, USA	
Gwynne, A Patrick	*Architect*
Homewood, Esher, Surrey KT10 9JL, England	
Gwynne, Anne	*Actress*
23388 Mulholland Dr, Woodland Hills, CA 91364, USA	
Gyll, J Soren	*Businessman*
%Volvo AB, 405 08 Goteborg, Sweden	
Gyllenhammar, Pehr G	*Businessman*
%Volvo AB, 405 08 Goteborg, Sweden	

G

Guth - Gyllenhammar

Haab, Larry D *Businessman*
%Illinova Corp, 500 S 27th St, Decatur, IL 62521, USA
Haacke, Hans C C *Artist*
%Cooper Union for Advancement of Science, Cooper Square, New York, NY 10003, USA
Haag, Rudolf *Physicist*
Oeltingsalle 20, 25421 Pinneberg, Germany
Haakon *Crown Prince, Norway*
Det Kongeligel Slottet, Drammensveien 1, 0010 Oslo, Norway
Haas, Andrew T *Labor Leader*
%Auto Aero & Agricultural Union, 1300 Connecticut NW, Washington, DC 20036, USA
Haas, Ernst *Photographer*
853 7th Ave, New York, NY 10019, USA
Haas, Freddie *Golfer*
147 E Oakridge Park, Metairie, LA 70005, USA
Haas, Jay *Golfer*
4 Tuscany Court, Greer, SC 29650, USA
Haas, Lukas *Actor*
%Wolf/Kasteller, 132 S Rodeo Dr, #300, Beverly Hills, CA 90212, USA
Haas, Richard J *Artist*
361 W 36th St, New York, NY 10018, USA
Haas, Robert D *Businessman*
%Levi Strauss Assoc, 1155 Battery St, San Francisco, CA 94111, USA
Haavelmo, Trygve *Nobel Economics Laureate*
%University of Oslo, PO Box 1072, Blindern, 0316 Oslo 3, Norway
Habash, George *Palestinian Leader*
Palais Essaada La Marsa, Tunis, Tunisia
Habel, Karl *Medical Researcher*
%Reading Institute of Rehabilitation, Rt 1, Box 252, Reading, PA 19607, USA
Haber, Bill *Entertainment Executive*
%Creative Artists Agency, 9830 Wilshire Blvd, Beverly Hills, CA 90212, USA
Haber, Norman *Inventor (Electromolecular Propulsion)*
%Haber Inc, 470 Main Road, Towaco, NJ 07082, USA
Habib, Munir *Cosmonaut, Syria*
%Potchta Kosmonavtov, Moskovskoi Oblasti, 141160 Syvisdny Goroduk, Russia
Habiger, Eugene E (Gene) *Air Force General*
CinC, US Strategic Command, 901 SAC Blvd, Offutt Air Force Base, NE 68113, USA
Hachette, Jean-Louis *Publisher*
79 Blvd Saint-Germain, 75006 Paris, France
Hack, Shelley *Actress, Model*
209 12th St, Santa Monica, CA 90402, USA
Hacken, Mark B *Businessman*
%FHP International Corp, PO Box 25186, Santa Ana, CA 92799, USA
Hackett, Buddy *Comedian, Actor*
800 N Whittier Dr, Beverly Hills, CA 90210, USA
Hackett, Martha *Actress*
%Vaughn D Hart, 8899 Beverly Blvd, #815, Los Angeles, CA 90048, USA
Hackford, Taylor *Movie Director*
2003 La Brea Terrace, Los Angeles, CA 90046, USA
Hackl, Georg *Luge Athlete*
Caftehaus Soamatl, Ramsauerstr 100, 83471 Berchtesgaden-Engedey, Germany
Hackman, Gene *Actor*
118 S Beverly Dr, #201, Beverly Hills, CA 90212, USA
Hackney, F Sheldon *Educator*
%Nat'l Endowment for Humanities, 1100 Pennsylvania NW, Washington, DC 20004, USA
Hackney, Roderick P *Architect*
St Peter's House, Windmill St, Macclesfield, Cheshire SK11 7HS, England
Hackwith, Scott *Singer, Guitarist (Dig); Songwriter*
%Overland Productions, 156 W 56th St, #500, New York, NY 10019, USA
Hackworth, David H *Korean, Vietnam Army Hero*
PO Box 430, Whitefish, MT 59937, USA
Haddon, Larry *Actor*
%Atkins Assoc, 303 S Crescent Heights Blvd, Los Angeles, CA 90048, USA
Haden, Charles E (Charlie) *Jazz Bassist, Composer*
%Merlin Co, 17609 Ventura Blvd, #212, Encino, CA 91316, USA
Haden, Pat *Football Player, Sportscaster*
1525 Wilson Ave, San Marino, CA 91108, USA
Hadl, John *Football Player*
4011 Vintage Court, Lawrence, KS 66047, USA

Hadlee, Richard J	*Cricketer*
PO Box 29186, Christchurch, New Zealand	
Hadley, Brett	*Actor*
5070 Woodley Ave, Encino, CA 91436, USA	
Hadley, Jerry	*Opera Singer*
%Lyric Arts Group, 204 W 10th St, New York, NY 10014, USA	
Hadley, Leonard A	*Businessman*
%Maytag Corp, 403 W 4th St N, Newton, IA 50208, USA	
Hadley, Tony	*Singer (Spandau Ballet)*
%International Talent Group, 729 7th Ave, #1600, New York, NY 10019, USA	
Haebler, Ingrid	*Concert Pianist*
%Ibbs & Tillett, 420-452 Edgware Road, London W2 1EG, England	
Haegg, Gunder	*Track Athlete*
%Swedish Olympic Committee, Idrottens Hus, 123 87 Farsta, Sweden	
Haendel, Ida	*Concert Violinist*
%Harold Holt, 31 Sinclair Road, London W14 0NS, England	
Haenicke, Diether H	*Educator*
%Western Michigan University, President's Office, Kalamazoo, MI 49008, USA	
Haensel, Vladimir	*Catalytic Chemist*
83 Larkspur Dr, Amherst, MA 01002, USA	
Haeusgen, Helmut	*Financier*
%Dresdner Bank, Jurgen-Ponto-Platz 1, 60329 Frankfurt/Main, Germany	
Hafner, Dudley H	*Foundation Executive*
%American Heart Assn, 7320 Greenville Ave, Dallas, TX 75231, USA	
Hafstein, Johann	*Prime Minister, Iceland*
Sjalfstaedisflokkurinn, Laufasvegi 46, Reykjavik, Iceland	
Haft, Herbert H	*Businessman*
%Dart Group, 3300 75th Ave, Landover, MD 20785, USA	
Hagan, Clifford O (Cliff)	*Basketball Player*
3637 Castlegate West Wynd, Lexington, KY 40502, USA	
Hagan, Molly	*Actress*
%Premiere Artists Agency, 8899 Beverly Blvd, #510, Los Angeles, CA 90048, USA	
Hagar, Sammy	*Singer, Songwriter, Guitarist*
PO Box 5395, Novato, CA 94948, USA	
Hagegard, Hakan	*Opera Singer*
Gunnarsbyn, 670 30 Edane, Sweden	
Hagemeister, Charles C	*Vietnam War Army Hero (CMH)*
811 N 16th Terrace Court, Leavenworth, KS 66048, USA	
Hagen, James A	*Businessman*
%Conrail Corp, 2001 Market St, Philadelphia, PA 19103, USA	
Hagen, Kevin	*Actor*
941 N Mansfield Ave, #C, Los Angeles, CA 90038, USA	
Hagen, Nina	*Singer*
%BMG Ariola Munich, Postfach 800149, 50670 Cologne, Germany	
Hagen, Uta	*Actress*
%Kroll, 390 West End Ave, New York, NY 10024, USA	
Hager, Robert	*Commentator*
%NBC-TV, News Dept, 4001 Nebraska Ave NW, Washington, DC 20016, USA	
Hagerty, Julie	*Actress*
%Innovative Artists, 1999 Ave of Stars, #2850, Los Angeles, CA 90067, USA	
Haggard, Merle	*Singer, Songwriter*
%HAG Inc, Box 536, Palo Cedro, CA 96073, USA	
Hagge, Marlene	*Golfer*
PO Box 570, La Quinta, CA 92253, USA	
Haggerty, Charles A	*Businessman*
%Western Digital Corp, 8105 Irvine Center Dr, Irvine, CA 92618, USA	
Haggerty, Dan	*Actor*
11684 Ventura Blvd, #211, Studio City, CA 91604, USA	
Haggerty, H B	*Actor*
%First Artists, 10000 Riverside Dr, #10, Toluca Lake, CA 91602, USA	
Haggerty, Tim	*Cartoonist (Ground Zero)*
%United Feature Syndicate, 200 Madison Ave, New York, NY 10016, USA	
Hagler, Marvin	*Boxer*
%Peter Devener, 75 Presidential Dr, #4, Quincy, MA 02169, USA	
Hagman, Larry	*Actor*
9950 Sulphur Mountain Road, Ojai, CA 93023, USA	
Hagn, Johanna	*Judo Athlete*
%ASG Elsdorf, Behrgasse 6, 50198 Elsdorf, Germany	

H

Hadlee - Hagn

Hague, William *Government Official, England*
%House of Commons, Westminster, London SW1A 0AA, England

Hahn, Carl H *Businessman*
%Volkswagenwerk AG, 78730 Wolfsburg, Germany

Hahn, Erwin L *Physicist*
69 Stevenson Ave, Berkeley, CA 94708, USA

Hahn, Hilary *Concert Violinist*
%Jascha Brodsky, Curtis Institute of Music, 1726 Locust St, Philadelphia, 19103, USA

Hahn, Jessica *Model, Actress*
6345 Balboa Blvd, #375, Encino, CA 91316, USA

Hahn, Michael J *Financier*
%Churchill Capital, 333 S 7th St, Minneapolis, MN 55402, USA

Haid, Charles *Actor*
4376 Forman Ave, North Hollywood, CA 91602, USA

Haig, Alexander M, Jr *Secretary, State; Army General*
1155 15th St NW, #800, Washington, DC 20005, USA

Haignere, Jean-Pierre *Spatinaut, France*
CNES, 2 Place Maurice Quentin, 75039 Paris Cedeux, France

Hailey, Arthur *Writer*
Lyford Cay, PO Box N-7776, Nassau, Bahamas

Hailsham of St Marylebone (Q M Hogg) *Government Official, England*
Corner House, Heathview Gardens, London SW15 OPW, England

Haim, Corey *Actor*
3209 Tareco Dr, Los Angeles, CA 90068, USA

Haimovitz, Matt *Concert Cellist*
%Columbia Artists Mgmt Inc, 165 W 57th St, New York, NY 10019, USA

Haines, Connie *Singer*
888 Mandalay Ave, #C-315, Clearwater, FL 33767, USA

Haines, George *Swimming Coach*
1218 Cordelia Ave, San Jose, CA 95129, USA

Haines, Randa *Movie Director*
1429 Avon Park Terrace, Los Angeles, CA 90026, USA

Haire, John E *Publisher*
%Time Magazine, Rockefeller Center, New York, NY 10020, USA

Hairston, Harold (Happy) *Basketball Player*
%Happy Hairston Youth Foundation, 1801 Ave of Stars, Los Angeles, CA 90067, USA

Hairston, Jester J *Composer*
5047 Valley Ridge Ave, Los Angeles, CA 90043, USA

Haise, Fred W, Jr *Astronaut*
14316 Tri City Beach Road, Baytown, TX 77520, USA

Haitink, Bernard *Conductor*
%Harold Holt, 31 Sinclair Road, London W14 0NS, England

Haje, Khrystyne *Actress*
PO Box 8750, Universal City, CA 91618, USA

Hakamada, Kunio *Businessman*
%Daido Steel, 11-18 Nishiki, Nakaku, Nagoya 460, Japan

Hakkinen, Mikka *Auto Racing Driver*
%McLaren International, Albert Dr, Woking, Surrey GU21 5UY, England

Hakulinen, Veikko *Nordic Skier*
%General Delivery, Valkeakoski, Finland

Halaby, Najeeb E *Businessman, Government Official*
175 Chain Bridge Road, McLean, VA 22101, USA

Halas, John *Animator*
%Educational Film Center, 5-7 Kean St, London WC2B 4AT, England

Halavalu Mata'aho *Queen, Tonga*
%The Palace, PO Box 6, Nuku'alofa, Tonga

Halberstam, David *Writer*
%William Morrow, 1350 Ave of Americas, New York, NY 10016, USA

Halbreich, Kathy *Museum Director*
%Walker Art Center, 725 Vineland Place, Minneapolis, MN 55403, USA

Haldorson, Burdette (burdie) *Basketball Player*
2422 Zane Place, Colorado Springs, CO 80909, USA

Hale, Barbara *Actress*
13351-D Riverside Dr, #261, Sherman Oaks, CA 91423, USA

Hale, Georgina *Actress*
74-A St John's Wood, High St, London NW8, England

Hale, James H *Publisher*
%Kansas City Star-Tribune, 1729 Grand Ave, Kansas City, MO 64108, USA

Hale, Roger E — Businessman
%LG&E Energy Corp, 220 W Main St, Louisville, KY 40202, USA

Haley, Charles L — Football Player
9538 E Valley Ranch Parkway, #1054, Irving, TX 75063, USA

Haley, Jack, Jr — Movie Director, Producer
1443 Devlin Dr, Los Angeles, CA 90069, USA

Haley, Maria — Financier
%Export-Import Bank, 811 Vermont Ave NW, Washington, DC 20571, USA

Halford, Rob — Singer (Judas Priest)
%International Creative Mgmt, 40 W 57th St, New York, NY 10019, USA

Hall Greff, Kaye — Swimmer
906 3rd St, Mukilteo, WA 98275, USA

Hall, A Stewart, Jr — Businessman
%Hughes Supply, 30 N Orange Ave, Orlando, FL 32801, USA

Hall, Alaina Reed — Actress
%Chasin Agency, 8899 Beverly Blvd, #716, Los Angeles, CA 90048, USA

Hall, Arnold A — Businessman
%Hawker Siddeley Group, 18 St James's Square, London SW1Y 4LJ, England

Hall, Arsenio — Entertainer
10989 Bluffside Dr, #3418, Studio City, CA 91604, USA

Hall, Bridget — Model
%IMG Models, 170 5th Ave, #1000, New York, NY 10010, USA

Hall, Charles — Inventor (Waterbed)
%Basic Designs, 5815 Bennett Valley Road, Santa Rosa, CA 95404, USA

Hall, Conrad L — Cinematographer
%G G Gundry Agency, 23715 Malibu Road, #383, Malibu, CA 90265, USA

Hall, Daryl — Singer (Hall & Oates), Songwriter
%Creative Artists Agency, 9830 Wilshire Blvd, Beverly Hills, CA 90212, USA

Hall, Deidre — Actress
215 Strada Corta Road, Los Angeles, CA 90077, USA

Hall, Delores — Singer, Actress
%Agency For Performing Arts, 888 7th Ave, New York, NY 10106, USA

Hall, Donald — Writer
Eagle Pond Farm, Danbury, NH 03230, USA

Hall, Donald J — Businessman
%Hallmark Cards, 2501 McGee St, Kansas City, MO 64108, USA

Hall, Edward T — Anthropologist, Writer
707 E Palace Ave, #13, Santa Fe, NM 87501, USA

Hall, Erv — Track Athlete
%Citicorp Mortgage, 670 Mason Ridge Center Dr, St Louis, MO 63141, USA

Hall, Fawn — Government Secretary
1568 Viewsite Dr, Los Angeles, CA 90069, USA

Hall, Floyd D — Businessman
%Kmart Corp, 3100 W Big Beaver Road, Troy, MI 48084, USA

Hall, Galen — Football Coach
%University of Florida, Athletic Dept, Gainesville, FL 32611, USA

Hall, Gary — Swimmer
6326 N 38th St, Phoenix, AZ 85253, USA

Hall, Gary C — Test Pilot, Engineer
PO Box 715, Rosamond, CA 93560, USA

Hall, Glenn — Hockey Player
PO Box 513, Stony Plain AB T0E 2GO, Canada

Hall, Gus — Political Party Official
%Communist Party of America, 215 W 23rd St, #700, New York, NY 10011, USA

Hall, Huntz — Actor
12512 Chandler Blvd, #307, North Hollywood, CA 91607, USA

Hall, James E (Jim) — Auto Race Car Builder, Driver
Rt 7, Box 640, Midland, TX 79706, USA

Hall, Jerry — Model, Actress
2 Munroe Terrace, London SW10 0DL, England

Hall, Jerry — Geneticist
%George Washington University, Med Center, 2300 "I" St NW, Washington, DC 20037, USA

Hall, Jim — Jazz Guitarist
%Jazz Tree, 648 Broadway, #703, New York, NY 10012, USA

Hall, Joe B — Basketball Coach
%Central Bank & Trust Co, 300 W Vine St, Lexington, KY 40507, USA

Hall, John B (Skip), Jr — Air Force General
Director for Plans, Pacific Air Forces, Hickam Air Force Base, HI 96853, USA

H

Hall, John R	*Businessman*
%Ashland Oil, 1000 Ashland Dr, Russell, KY 41169, USA	
Hall, Karen	*Writer*
9242 Beverly Dr, #200, Beverly Hills, CA 90210, USA	
Hall, Kevan	*Fashion Designer*
%Kevan Hall Studio, 756 S Spring St, #11-E, Los Angeles, CA 90014, USA	
Hall, Lani	*Singer*
31930 Pacific Coast Highway, Malibu, CA 90265, USA	
Hall, Lanny	*Educator*
%Hardin-Simmons University, President's Office, Abilene, TX 79698, USA	
Hall, Lawrence	*Physicist*
%University of California, Physics Dept, Berkeley, CA 94720, USA	
Hall, Llody M, Jr	*Religious Leader*
%Congregation Christian Churches National Assn, Box 1620, Oak Creek, MI 53154, USA	
Hall, Monty	*Entertainer*
519 N Arden Dr, Beverly Hills, CA 90210, USA	
Hall, Nigel J	*Artist*
11 Kensington Park Gardens, London W11 3HD, England	
Hall, Parker	*Football Player*
4712 Cole Road, Memphis, TN 38117, USA	
Hall, Peter R F	*Theater, Opera, Movie Director*
%Peter Hall Co, 18 Exeter St, London WC2E 7DU, England	
Hall, Samuel (Sam)	*Diver*
5759 Wilcke Way, Dayton, OH 45459, USA	
Hall, Sonny	*Labor Leader*
%Transport Workers Union, 80 West End Ave, New York, NY 10023, USA	
Hall, Tom T	*Singer, Songwriter*
%Tom T Hall Enterprises, PO Box 1246, Franklin, TN 37065, USA	
Hall, William E	*WW II Navy Hero (CMH)*
4131 Mercier St, Kansas City, MO 64111, USA	
Hall, William, Sr	*Bowler*
5108 N 126th Ave, Omaha, NE 68164, USA	
Hall-Garmes, Ruth	*Actress*
432 Alandele Ave, Los Angeles, CA 90036, USA	
Halla, Brian	*Businessman*
%National Semiconductor, 2900 Semiconductor Dr, Santa Clara, CA 95051, USA	
Hallahan, Charles	*Actor*
1975 W Silverlake Dr, Los Angeles, CA 90039, USA	
Hallet, Jim	*Golfer*
PO Box 1456, Ponte Vedra Beach, FL 32004, USA	
Hallier, Lori	*Actress*
%Epstein-Wyckoff, 280 S Beverly Dr, #400, Beverly Hills, CA 90212, USA	
Hallin, William P (Bill)	*Air Force General*
Deputy CofStaff, Installations/Logistics, HqUSAF, Pentagon, Washington, DC 20330, USA	
Halliwell, Geri	*Singer (Spice Girls)*
%Virgin Records, Kensal House, 533-79 Harrow Road, London W1O 4RH, England	
Hallstrom, Holly	*Model, Entertainer*
5757 Wilshire Blvd, #206, Los Angeles, CA 90036, USA	
Hallstrom, Lasse	*Movie Director*
%International Creative Mgmt, 8942 Wilshire Blvd, Beverly Hills, CA 90211, USA	
Hallyday, Estelle	*Model*
%Elite Model Mgmt, 111 E 22nd St, #200, New York, NY 10010, USA	
Hallyday, Johnny	*Singer*
6 Rue Deubigny, 75017 Paris, France	
Halperin, Bertrand I	*Physicist*
%Harvard University, Physics Dept, Cambridge, MA 02138, USA	
Halpern, Daniel	*Writer*
60 Pheasant Hill Road, Princeton, NJ 08540, USA	
Halpern, Jack	*Chemist*
5630 S Dorchester Ave, Chicago, IL 60637, USA	
Halpern, Merril M	*Financier*
%Charterhouse Group, 535 Madison Ave, New York, NY 10022, USA	
Halpern, Ralph M	*Businessman*
%Burton Group, 214 Oxford St, London W1N 9DF, England	
Halprin, Lawrence	*Landscape Architect, Planner*
444 Brannan St, San Francisco, CA 94107, USA	
Halsell, James D, Jr	*Astronaut*
%NASA, Johnson Space Center, 2101 NASA Road, Houston, TX 77058, USA	

Hall - Halsell

Halsey, Brett	*Actor*
141 N Grand Ave, Pasadena, CA 91103, USA	
Halver, John E	*Biochemist, Nutritionist*
16502 41st NE, Seattle, WA 98155, USA	
Ham, Jack R	*Football Player*
%Ham Enterprises, 509 Hegner Way, Sewickley, PA 15143, USA	
Hamann, H J	*Businessman*
%Schering, Mullerstr 170-178, 12487 Berlin, Germany	
Hamari, Julia	*Opera Singer*
Max Brod-Weg 14, 70437 Stuttgart, Germany	
Hamblen, Lapsley W, Jr	*Judge*
%US Tax Court, 400 2nd St NW, Washington, DC 20217, USA	
Hambling, Maggi	*Artist*
%Bernard Jacobson Gallery, 14-A Clifford St, London W1X 1RF, England	
Hambro, Leonid	*Concert Pianist*
%California Institute of Arts, Music Dept, Valencia, CA 91355, USA	
Hamburger, Michael P L	*Writer*
%John Johnson, 45/47 Clerkenwell Green, London EC1R 0HT, England	
Hamed, Nihad	*Religious Leader*
%Islamic Assn in US/Canada, 25351 Five Mile Road, Redford Township, MI 48239, USA	
Hamel, Veronica	*Actress, Model*
129 N Woodburn Dr, Los Angeles, CA 90049, USA	
Hamer, Jean Jerome Cardinal	*Religious Leader*
Piazza di S Uffizio 11, 00193 Rome, Italy	
Hamill, Dorothy S	*Figure Skater*
79490 Fairway Dr, Indian Wells, CA 92210, USA	
Hamill, Mark	*Actor*
PO Box 1051, Santa Monica, CA 90406, USA	
Hamill, W Pete	*Writer, Editor*
%New York Daily News, Editorial Dept, 220 E 42nd St, New York, NY 10017, USA	
Hamilton, Al	*Hockey Player*
2452 115th St, Edmonton AB T6J 3S1, Canada	
Hamilton, Ashley	*Actor*
10230 Wilshire Blvd, #1705, Los Angeles, CA 90024, USA	
Hamilton, Chico	*Jazz Drummer*
%Chico Hamilton Productions, 321 E 45th St, #PH-A, New York, NY 10017, USA	
Hamilton, David	*Photographer*
41 Blvd du Montparnasse, 75006 Paris, France	
Hamilton, Earl	*Artist*
%Gallery At Salishan, PO Box 148, Gleneden Beach, OR 97388, USA	
Hamilton, George	*Actor*
9255 Doheny Road, #2302, Los Angeles, CA 90069, USA	
Hamilton, George H	*Museum Director*
121 Gale Road, Williamstown, MA 01267, USA	
Hamilton, George, IV	*Singer, Songwriter, Guitarist*
%Fat City Artists, 1908 Chet Atkins Place, #502, Nashville, TN 37212, USA	
Hamilton, Guy	*Movie Director*
22 Mont Port, Puerto Andraitz, Mallorca, Baleares, Spain	
Hamilton, Linda	*Actress*
2400 Whitman Place, Los Angeles, CA 90068, USA	
Hamilton, Lisa Gay	*Actress*
%Paradigm Agency, 10100 Santa Monica Blvd, #2500, Los Angeles, CA 90067, USA	
Hamilton, Richard	*Artist*
Northend Farm, Northend, Oxon RG9 6LQ, England	
Hamilton, Scott S	*Figure Skater*
3674 W Amherst Ave, Denver, CO 80236, USA	
Hamilton, Suzanna	*Actress*
%Julian Belfarge, 46 Albermarle St, London W1X 4PP, England	
Hamilton, William	*Cartoonist, Writer*
115 E 89th St, #4-A, New York, NY 10128, USA	
Hamlin, Harry	*Actor*
PO Box 25578, Los Angeles, CA 90025, USA	
Hamlisch, Marvin	*Composer, Conductor*
970 Park Ave, #501, New York, NY 10028, USA	
Hamm, Charles J	*Financier*
%Independence Savings Bank, 195 Montague St, Brooklyn, NY 11201, USA	
Hamm, Richard L	*Religious Leader*
130 E Washington St, Indianapolis, IN 46204, USA	

Hammel, Eugene A — *Anthropologist*
%University of California, Anthroplogy Dept, Berkeley, CA 94720, USA

Hammer — *Rap Artist*
%Terrie Williams Agency, 1500 Broadway Front, #7, New York, NY 10036, USA

Hammer, Susan W — *Mayor*
%Mayor's Office, City Hall, 801 N 1st St, San Jose, CA 95110, USA

Hammett, Louis P — *Chemist*
288 Medford Leas, Medford, NJ 08055, USA

Hammond Innes, Ralph — *Writer*
Ayres End, Kersey by Ipswich, Suffolk 1P7 6EB, England

Hammond, Caleb D, Jr — *Publisher, Cartographer*
61 Woodland Road, Maplewood, NJ 07040, USA

Hammond, Darrell — *Comedian*
%United Talent Agency, 9560 Wilshire Blvd, #500, Beverly Hills, CA 90212, USA

Hammond, George S — *Chemist*
27 Timber Lane, Painted Post, NY 14870, USA

Hammond, James T — *Religious Leader*
%Pentecostal Free Will Baptist Church, PO Box 1568, Dunn, NC 28335, USA

Hammond, Jay S — *Governor, AK*
Lake Charles Lodge, Port Alsworth, AK 99652, USA

Hammond, Joan H — *Opera Singer*
Private Bag 101, Geelong, Mail Center, Victoria 3221, Australia

Hammond, John — *Singer*
%Rosebud Agency, PO Box 170429, San Francisco, CA 94117, USA

Hammond, L Blaine, Jr — *Astronaut*
2255 Broadlawn Dr, Houston, TX 77058, USA

Hammond, Tom — *Sportscaster*
%NBC-TV, Sports Dept, 30 Rockefeller Plaza, New York, NY 10112, USA

Hammons, David — *Sculptor*
%Exit Art, 578 Broadway, #800, New York, NY 10012, USA

Hammons, Roger — *Religious Leader*
%Primitive Advent Christian Church, 395 Frame Road, Elkview, WV 25071, USA

Hamnett, Katharine — *Fashion Designer*
%Katharine Hamnett Ltd, 202 New North Road, London N1, England

Hampel, Olaf — *Bobsled Athlete*
Pommenweg 2, 33689 Bielefeld, Germany

Hampel, Ronald C — *Businessman*
%Imperial Chemical Industries, 9 Millbank, London SW1P 3JF, England

Hampshire, Stuart — *Philosopher*
5 Beaumont Road, The Quarry, Headington, Oxford, England

Hampshire, Susan — *Actress*
%Chatto & Linnit, Prince of Wales, Coventry St, London W1V 7FE, England

Hampson, Thomas — *Opera Singer*
Starkfriedgasse 53, 1180 Vienna, Austria

Hampton, Christopher J — *Writer*
2 Kensington Park Gardens, London W11, England

Hampton, Henry E, Jr — *Movie, Television Producer*
%Backside Inc, 486 Shawmut Ave, Boston, MA 02118, USA

Hampton, James — *Actor*
5155 Valjean Ave, Encino, CA 91436, USA

Hampton, Lionel — *Jazz Vibist, Drummer, Pianist, Conductor*
20 W 64th St, #28-K, New York, NY 10023, USA

Hampton, Millard — *Track Athlete*
201 W Mission St, San Jose, CA 95110, USA

Hampton, Ralph C, Jr — *Religious Leader*
%Free Will Baptist Bible College, 3606 West End Ave, Nashville, TN 37205, USA

Hampton, Slide — *Jazz Trombonist*
%Charismic Productions, 2604 Mozart Place NW, Washington, DC 20009, USA

Hamrlik, Roman — *Hockey Player*
%Tampa Bay Lightning, Ice Palace, 401 Channelside Dr, Tampa, FL 33602, USA

Han Suyin — *Writer*
37 Montoie, Lausanne, Switzerland

Han, Maggie — *Actress*
%J Michael Bloom, 9255 Sunset Blvd, #710, Los Angeles, CA 90069, USA

Hanafusa, Hidesaburo — *Microbiologist*
%Rockefeller University, 1230 York Ave, New York, NY 10021, USA

Hanauer, Chip — *Speed Boat Racer*
%Hanauer Enterprises, 2702 NE 88th St, Seattle, WA 98115, USA

Hanbury-Tenison, Robin	*Explorer*
%Maidenwell, Cardinham, Bodmin, Cornwall PL3O 4DW, England	
Hancock, Herbert J (Herbie)	*Jazz Pianist, Composer*
%Kushnick Passick, 3 E 28th St, #600, New York, NY 10016, USA	
Hancock, John D	*Movie Director*
7355 N Fail Road, La Porte, IN 46350, USA	
Hancock, Walker K	*Artist*
Lanesville, PO Box 7133, Gloucester, MA 01930, USA	
Hancock, William P	*Navy Admiral*
Deputy CNO Logistics, HqUSN, Navy Department, Washington, DC 20350, USA	
Hand, Elbert O	*Businessman*
%Hartmarx Corp, 101 N Wacker Dr, Chicago, IL 60606, USA	
Hand, Jon	*Football Player*
11030 Queens Way, Carmel, IN 46032, USA	
Handelsman, J B	*Cartoonist*
%New Yorker Magazine, Editorial Dept, 20 W 43rd St, New York, NY 10036, USA	
Handelsman, Walt	*Editorial Cartoonist*
%New Orleans Times-Picayune, 3800 Howard Ave, New Orleans, LA 70140, USA	
Handke, Peter	*Writer*
%Farrar Straus Giroux, 19 Union Square W, New York, NY 10003, USA	
Handler, Ruth	*Businesswoman*
4701 Natick Ave, #204, Sherman Oaks, CA 91403, USA	
Handley, Vernon G	*Conductor*
Hen Gerrig, Pen-y-Fan near Monmouth, Gwent NP5 4RA, Wales	
Handlin, Oscar	*Writer, Historian*
18 Agassiz St, Cambridge, MA 02140, USA	
Hands, William A (Bill)	*Baseball Player*
Willow Terrace, Orient, NY 11957, USA	
Handy, James	*Actor*
%K&K Entertainment, 1498 W Sunset Blvd, Los Angeles, CA 90026, USA	
Handy, John	*Jazz Saxophonist*
%Integrity Talent, PO Box 961, Burlington, MA 01803, USA	
Haney, Lee	*Body Builder*
%Lee Haney Enterprises, 105 Trail Point Circle, Fairburn, GA 30213, USA	
Haney, R Lee	*Businessman*
%Orange & Rockland Utilities, 1 Blue Hill Plaza, Pearl River, NY 10965, USA	
Hanfmann, George M A	*Archaeologist*
%Harvard University, Fogg Art Museum, 32 Quincy St, Cambridge, MA 02138, USA	
Hanft, Ruth S	*Medical Researcher*
600 21st St NW, Washington, DC 20006, USA	
Hanin, Roger	*Actor*
9 Rue du Boccador, 75008 Paris, France	
Hanks, Tom	*Actor*
PO Box 1650, Pacific Palisades, CA 90272, USA	
Hanley, Edward T	*Labor Leader*
%Hotel-Restaurant Employees Union, 1219 28th St NW, Washington, DC 20007, USA	
Hanley, Frank	*Labor Leader*
%Int'l Union of Operating Engineers, 1125 17th St NW, Washington, DC 20036, USA	
Hanna, David S	*Financier*
%Bank of America Arizona, PO Box 16290, Phoenix, AZ 85011, USA	
Hanna, Sir Roland P	*Jazz Pianist*
%Abby Hoffer, 223 1/2 E 48th St, New York, NY 10017, USA	
Hanna, William D	*Animator (Flintstones, Yogi Bear)*
%Hanna-Barbera Productions, 3400 W Cahuenga Blvd, Los Angeles, CA 90068, USA	
Hannah, Bob	*Motorcycle Racing Rider*
%American Motorcycle Assn, PO Box 6114, Westerville, OH 43086, USA	
Hannah, Charles A (Charley)	*Football Player*
16057 Tampa Palms Blvd W, #201, Tampa, FL 33647, USA	
Hannah, Daryl	*Actress*
Columbia Plaza, Producers Building 8-153, Burbank, CA 91505, USA	
Hannah, John A	*Football Player*
42 Sabrina Road, Wellesley, MA 02181, USA	
Hannah, Thomas E	*Businessman*
%Collins & Aikman Corp, 701 McCullough Dr, Charlotte, NC 28262, USA	
Hannibal, Lars	*Concert Guitarist*
%Duo Concertante, Nordskraenten 3, 2980 Kokkedal, Denmark	
Hannula, Dick	*Swimming Coach*
1021 Westley Dr, Tacoma, WA 98465, USA	

H

Hanbury-Tenison - Hannula

Hannum, Alex — *Basketball Player, Coach*
130 Acacia Way, Coronado, CA 92118, USA

Hanover, Donna — *Commentator*
%Gracie Mansion, New York, NY 10007, USA

Hanratty, Terry — *Football Player*
22 Hunters Creek Lane, New Canaan, CT 06840, USA

Hans-Adam II — *Prince, Liechtenstein*
%Schloss Vaduz, 9490 Vaduz, Liechtenstein

Hansel, Stephen A — *Financier*
%Hibernia Corp, 313 Carondelet St, New Orleans, LA 70130, USA

Hansen, Alfred G — *Air Force General, Businessman*
%Lockheed Aero Systems, 86 S Cobb Dr, Marietta, GA 30063, USA

Hansen, Clifford P — *Governor/Senator, WY*
10821 W Venturi Dr, Sun City, AZ 85351, USA

Hansen, Darryl D — *Financier*
%Norwest Bank Iowa, 7th & Walnut Sts, Des Moines, IA 50309, USA

Hansen, Fred M — *Track Athlete*
909 Frostwood Dr, Houston, TX 77024, USA

Hansen, Jacqueline — *Track Athlete*
1133 9th St, Santa Monica, CA 90403, USA

Hansen, James E — *Meteorologist, Physicist*
%Goddard Institute for Space Studies, 2880 Broadway, New York, NY 10025, USA

Hansen, Kurt — *Businessman*
%Bayer, Surder Str 14, 51375 Leverkusen, Germany

Hansen, Patti — *Model*
Redlands, W Wittering, Chichester, Sussex, England

Hansen, Paul — *Businessman*
%Adaptec, 691 S Milpitas Blvd, Milpitas, CA 95035, USA

Hansen, Peter — *Actor*
%Stone Manners, 8091 Selma Ave, Los Angeles, CA 90046, USA

Hansen, Stephen C — *Financier*
%Dollar Bank, 3 Gateway Center, Pittsburgh, PA 15222, USA

Hansmeyer, Herbert — *Businessman*
%Fireman's Fund Insurance, 777 San Marin Dr, Novato, CA 94998, USA

Hanson of Edgerton, James E — *Businessman*
1 Grosvenor Place, London SW1X 7JH, England

Hanson, Carl T — *Navy Admiral*
900 Birdseye Road, Orient, NY 11967, USA

Hanson, Curtis — *Movie Director, Screenwriter*
%United Talent Agency, 9560 Wilshire Blvd, #500, Beverly Hills, CA 90212, USA

Hanson, William R — *Artist*
78 W Notre Dame St, Glens Falls, NY 12801, USA

Hanzlik, Bill — *Basketball Coach*
4825 S Vine St, Englewood, CO 80110, USA

Harad, George J — *Businessman*
%Boise Cascade Corp, 1111 Jefferson Square, Boise, ID 83702, USA

Harada, Masahiko (Fighting) — *Boxer*
2-21-5 Azabu-Juban, Minatoku, Tokyo 105, Japan

Harald V — *King, Norway*
Det Kongelige Slott, Drammensveien 1, 0010 Oslo, Norway

Harbaugh, Gregory J — *Astronaut*
%NASA, Johnson Space Center, 2101 NASA Road, Houston, TX 77058, USA

Harbaugh, Jim — *Football Player*
%Indianapolis Colts, 7001 W 56th St, Indianapolis, IN 46254, USA

Harbaugh, Robert E — *Neurosurgeon*
%Dartmouth-Hitchcock Medical Center, Surgery Dept, Hanover, NH 03756, USA

Harbison, John H — *Composer*
479 Franklin St, Cambridge, MA 02139, USA

Hard, Darlene — *Tennis Player*
22924 Erwin St, Woodland Hills, CA 91367, USA

Hardaway, Anfernee (Penny) — *Basketball Player*
%Orlando Magic, Orlando Arena, 1 Magic Place, Orlando, FL 32801, USA

Hardaway, Timothy D (Tim) — *Basketball Player*
10050 SW 62nd Ave, Miami, FL 33156, USA

Harden, Marcia Gay — *Actress*
1358 Woodbrook Lane, Southlake, TX 76092, USA

Harder, Melvin L (Mel) — *Baseball Player*
130 Center St, #6-A, Chardon, OH 44024, USA

Hardesty, David C, Jr — *Educator*
%West Virginia University, President's Office, Morgantown, WV 26506, USA

Hardgrove, Richard L — *Financier*
%First National Bank of Ohio, 106 S Main St, Akron, OH 44308, USA

Hardin, Clifford M — *Secretary, Agriculture*
10 Roan Lane, St Louis, MO 63124, USA

Hardin, Melora — *Actress*
%Paradigm Agency, 10100 Santa Monica Blvd, #2500, Los Angeles, CA 90067, USA

Hardin, Paul, III — *Educator*
%University of North Carolina, Chancellor's Office, Chapel Hill, NC 27599, USA

Harding, John Wesley — *Singer*
%Agency Group, 1775 Broadway, #433, New York, NY 10019, USA

Harding, Peter R — *Royal Air Force Marshal, England*
%Ministry of Defence, Whitehall, London SW1, England

Harding, Tonya — *Figure Skater*
121 SW Morrison St, #1100, Portland, OR 97204, USA

Hardison, Kadeem — *Actor*
19743 Valleyview Dr, Topanga, CA 90290, USA

Hardisty, Huntington — *Navy Admiral*
15 Highland St, #114, West Hartford, CT 06119, USA

Hardwick, Billy — *Bowler*
1576 S White Station, Memphis, TN 38117, USA

Hardwick, Elizabeth — *Writer*
15 W 67th St, New York, NY 10023, USA

Hardy, Francoise — *Singer, Songwriter*
13 Rue Halle, 75014 Paris, France

Hardy, Hugh — *Architect*
%Hardy Holzman Pfeiffer, 902 Broadway, New York, NY 10010, USA

Hardy, Kevin — *Football Player*
%Jacksonville Jaguars, 1 Stadium Place, Jacksonville, FL 32202, USA

Hardy, Mark — *Hockey Player*
220 21st St, #B, Manhattan Beach, CA 90266, USA

Hardy, Robert — *Actor*
Upper Bolney House, Upper Bolney, Henley-on-Thames, Oxon RG9 4AQ, England

Hardymon, James F — *Businessman*
%Textron Inc, 40 Westminster St, #10, Providence, RI 02903, USA

Hare, David — *Writer*
95 Linden Gardens, London WC2, England

Harewood, Dorian — *Actor*
810 Prospect Blvd, Pasadena, CA 91103, USA

Harewood, Nancy — *Actress*
%Metropolitan Talent Agency, 4526 Wilshire Blvd, Los Angeles, CA 90010, USA

Hargis, Billy James — *Clergyman*
Rose of Sharon Farm, Neosho, MO 64850, USA

Hargitay, Mariska — *Actress*
9274 Warbler Way, Los Angeles, CA 90069, USA

Hargrave, Robert L — *Businessman*
%Stewart & Stevenson Inc, 2707 North Loop W, Houston, TX 77008, USA

Hargrove, D Michael (Mike) — *Baseball Player, Manager*
20618 Carlton Ct, Strongsville, OH 44136, USA

Hargrove, Roy — *Jazz Trumpeter*
%Verve Records, Worldwide Plaza, 825 8th Ave, New York, NY 10019, USA

Haring, Robert W — *Editor*
%Tulsa World, Editorial Dept, 315 S Boulder Ave, Tulsa, OK 74103, USA

Hariri, Rafiq Al- — *Prime Minister, Lebanon*
%Prime Minister's Office, Serail, Place de L'Etoile, Beirut, Lebanon

Harker, David — *Biophysicist*
56 Lexington Ave, Buffalo, NY 14222, USA

Harkes, John — *Soccer Player*
1265 El Camino Real, Santa Clara, CA 95050, USA

Harket, Morten — *Singer (A-Ha)*
%Terry Slater, Thatched Cottage, Hollow Lane, Headley Downs, Hamp, England

Harkins, Kenneth R — *Judge*
%US Claims Court, 717 Madison Place NW, Washington, DC 20005, USA

Harkness, Ned — *Hockey Coach*
12 Fowler Ave, Glen Falls, NY 12801, USA

Harkness, Rebekah — *Philanthropist, Ballet Director*
4 E 75th St, New York, NY 10021, USA

Harlan, Jack R — *Plant Geneticist*
%University of Illinois, Agronomy Dept, Urbana, IL 61801, USA

Harlan, Kevin — *Sportscaster*
%Fox TV, Sports Dept, PO Box 900, Beverly Hills, CA 90213, USA

Harlan, Leonard M — *Financier*
%Castle Harlan Inc, 150 E 58th St, New York, NY 10155, USA

Harlin, Renny — *Movie Director*
%Midnight Sun Pictures, 8800 Sunset Blvd, #400, Los Angeles, CA 90069, USA

Harling, C Gene — *Financier*
%First Federal Michigan Corp, 1001 Woodward Ave, Detroit, MI 48226, USA

Harlow, Shalom — *Model*
%"House of Style" Show, MTV, 1515 Broadway, New York, NY 10036, USA

Harmon, James A — *Financier*
%Schroder Wertheim Co, Equitable Center, 787 7th Ave, New York, NY 10019, USA

Harmon, Kelly — *Actress*
13224 Old Oak Lane, Los Angeles, CA 90049, USA

Harmon, Mark — *Actor*
%Wings Inc, 2236 Encinitas Blvd, #A, Encinitas, CA 92024, USA

Harmon, Merle — *Sportscaster*
424 Lamar Blvd E, #210, Arlington, TX 76011, USA

Harmon, Ronnie — *Football Player*
13022 218th St, Laurelton, NY 11413, USA

Harms, Fred — *Businessman*
%ESS Technology, 46107 Landing Parkway, Fremont, CA 94538, USA

Harnden, Arthur (Art) — *Track Athlete*
7218 Pepper Ridge, Corpus Christi, TX 78413, USA

Harnell, Joe — *Composer, Conductor*
%ASCAP, 7920 Sunset Blvd, #300, Los Angeles, CA 90046, USA

Harness, William E — *Opera Singer*
2132 W 235th Place, Torrance, CA 90501, USA

Harnett, Gordon D — *Businessman*
%Brush Wellman Inc, 17876 St Clair Ave, Cleveland, OH 44110, USA

Harney, Paul — *Golfer*
72 Club Valley Dr, East Falmouth, MA 02536, USA

Harnick, Sheldon M — *Lyricist*
%Kraft Haiken Bell, 551 5th Ave, #900, New York, NY 10176, USA

Harnoncourt, Nikolaus — *Conductor*
38 Piaristangasse, 1080 Vienna, Austria

Harnoy, Ofra — *Concert Cellist*
122 Alfred Ave, Willowdale ON M2N 3H9, Canada

Harout, Magda — *Actress*
13452 Vose St, Van Nuys, CA 91405, USA

Harper, Alvin — *Football Player*
1304 Split Rock Lane, Fort Washington, MD 20744, USA

Harper, Billy — *Jazz Saxophonist*
%Joanne Klein, 130 W 28th St, New York, NY 10001, USA

Harper, Chandler — *Golfer*
4412 Gannon Road, Portsmouth, VA 23703, USA

Harper, Charles M — *Businessman*
%RJR Nabisco Holdings, 1301 Ave of Americas, New York, NY 10019, USA

Harper, Derek — *Basketball Player*
2214 Highpoint Circle, Carrolton, TX 75007, USA

Harper, Donald (Don) — *Diver*
1765 Lynnhaven Dr, Columbus, OH 43221, USA

Harper, Heather M — *Opera Singer*
20 Milverton Road, London NW6 7AS, England

Harper, Jessica — *Actress*
3454 Glorietta Place, Sherman Oaks, CA 91423, USA

Harper, Judson M — *Chemical Engineer*
1818 Westview Road, Fort Collins, CO 80524, USA

Harper, Ron — *Basketball Player*
1360 W 9th St, #220, Cleveland, OH 44113, USA

Harper, Ron — *Actor*
%Tisherman Agency, 6767 Forest Lawn Dr, #115, Los Angeles, CA 90068, USA

Harper, Tess — *Actress*
2271 Betty Lane, Beverly Hills, CA 90210, USA

Harper, Valerie — *Actress*
14 E 4th St, New York, NY 10012, USA

Harrah, Colbert D (Toby) 8828 Sandcastle Court, #A, Fort Worth, TX 76179, USA	*Baseball Player*
Harrar, J George 125 Puritan Dr, Scarsdale, NY 10583, USA	*Nutritionist*
Harrell, James A %University of Toledo, Geology Dept, Toledo, OH 43606, USA	*Geologist*
Harrell, Lynn M %International Management Group, 22 E 71st St, New York, NY 10021, USA	*Concert Cellist*
Harrell, Tom *Jazz Trumpeter, Flugelhorn Player* %Joel Chriss, 300 Mercer St, #3-J, New York, NY 10003, USA	
Harrelson, Derrell M (Bud) 25 Falcon Dr, Hauppauge, NY 11788, USA	*Baseball Player, Manager*
Harrelson, Kenneth S (Ken) 150 Crossways Park W, Woodbury, NY 11797, USA	*Baseball Player*
Harrelson, Woody 10780 Santa Monica Blvd, #280, Los Angeles, CA 90025, USA	*Actor*
Harrick, Jim %University of Rhode Island, Athletic Dept, Kingston, RI 02881, USA	*Basketball Coach*
Harrington, David %Kronos Quartet, 1235 9th Ave, San Francisco, CA 94122, USA	*Violinist (Kronos Quartet)*
Harrington, Donald J %St John's University, President's Office, Jamaica, NY 11439, USA	*Educator*
Harrington, John 6363 S Dexter St, Littleton, CO 80121, USA	*Hockey Player*
Harrington, Pat, Jr 730 Marzella Ave, Los Angeles, CA 90049, USA	*Actor*
Harrington, Robert 2609 Woodshade Ave, Kannapolic, NC 28127, USA	*Auto Racing Driver*
Harris, Barbara 823 W Montrose Ave, #100, Chicago, IL 60613, USA	*Actress*
Harris, Barbara C *Religious Leader, Social Activist* %Episcopal Diocese of Massachusetts, 138 Tremont St, Boston, MA 02111, USA	
Harris, Barry %Brad Simon Organization, 122 E 57th St, New York, NY 10022, USA	*Jazz Pianist*
Harris, Bernard A, Jr %NASA, Johnson Space Center, 2101 NASA Road, Houston, TX 77058, USA	*Astronaut*
Harris, Bill 12747 Riverside Dr, #208, Valley Village, CA 91607, USA	*Movie Critic*
Harris, Billy 12205-25 Richview Road, Islington ON M9A 4Y3, Canada	*Hockey Player*
Harris, Chauncy D 5649 S Blackstone Ave, Chicago, IL 60637, USA	*Geographer*
Harris, Cliff 722 Kentwood Dr, Rockwall, TX 75087, USA	*Football Player*
Harris, Danny %Iowa State University, Athletic Dept, Ames, IA 50011, USA	*Track Athlete*
Harris, Del %Los Angeles Lakers, Forum, PO Box 10, Inglewood, CA 90306, USA	*Basketball Coach*
Harris, Ed 9434 E Champagne Dr, Sun Lakes, AZ 85248, USA	*Actor*
Harris, Emmylou %Monty Hitchcock, PO Box 159007, Nashville, TN 37215, USA	*Singer*
Harris, Estelle %Gold Marshak Liedtke, 3500 W Olive Ave, #1400, Burbank, CA 91505, USA	*Actress*
Harris, Franco 995 Greentree Road, Pittsburgh, PA 15220, USA	*Football Player*
Harris, Joe Frank 712 West Ave, Cartersville, GA 30120, USA	*Governor, GA*
Harris, John R 24 Devonshire Place, London W1N 2BX, England	*Architect*
Harris, Jonathan 16830 Marmaduke Place, Encino, CA 91436, USA	*Actor*
Harris, Julie PO Box 1287, West Chatham, MA 02669, USA	*Actress*
Harris, King W %Pittway Corp, 200 S Wacker Dr, Chicago, IL 60606, USA	*Businessman*
Harris, Lew %Los Angeles Magazine, 1888 Century Park East, Los Angeles, CA 90067, USA	*Editor*

H

Harrah - Harris

H

Harris, Louis	*Statistician*
%Louis Harris Research, 152 E 38th St, New York, NY 10016, USA	
Harris, Mel	*Actress*
6300 Wilshire Blvd, #2110, Los Angeles, CA 90048, USA	
Harris, Neil Patrick	*Actor*
%Booh Schut, 11350 Ventura Blvd, #206, Studio City, CA 91604, USA	
Harris, Neison	*Businessman*
%Pittway Corp, 200 S Wacker Dr, Chicago, IL 60606, USA	
Harris, Peter	*Hematologist*
%John Radcliffe Hospital, MRC Molecular Hematology Unit, Oxford, England	
Harris, Richard	*Actor, Singer*
%Terence Baker, 17 Grove Hill Road, London SE5 8DF, England	
Harris, Richard H	*Radio Executive*
%Westinghouse Broadcasting, 565 5th Ave, New York, NY 10017, USA	
Harris, Ronald (Ronnie)	*Boxer*
1365 Glenview NE, North Canton, OH 44721, USA	
Harris, Rosemary	*Actress*
%International Creative Mgmt, 76 Oxford St, London W1N 0AX, England	
Harris, Sam	*Singer*
%T-Best Talent Agency, 2001 Wayne Ave, #103, San Leandro, CA 94577, USA	
Harris, Sidney	*Cartoonist*
135 W 70th St, #9-C, New York, NY 10023, USA	
Harris, Stephen	*Electrical Engineer, Applied Physicist*
%Stanford University, Ginzton Laboratory, Stanford, CA 94305, USA	
Harris, Thomas	*Writer*
%St Martin's Press, 175 5th Ave, New York, NY 10010, USA	
Harris, Tim	*Football Player*
%San Francisco 49ers, 4949 Centennial Blvd, Santa Clara, CA 95054, USA	
Harris, Virginia S	*Religious Leader*
%Church of Christ Scientist, 175 Huntington Ave, Boston, MA 02115, USA	
Harris-Stewart, Lusia (Lucy)	*Basketball Player*
1002 Cherry St, Greenwood, MS 38930, USA	
Harrison Breetzke, Joan	*Swimmer*
16 Clevedon Road, East London 5201, South Africa	
Harrison, E Hunter	*Businessman*
%Illinois Central Corp, 455 N Cityfront Plaza Dr, Chicago, IL 60611, USA	
Harrison, George	*Singer (The Beatles), Songwriter*
Friar Park Road, Henley-on-Thames, Oxfordshire, England	
Harrison, Gregory	*Actor*
%Catalina Productions, 11684 Ventura Blvd, #971, Studio City, CA 91604, USA	
Harrison, Jenilee	*Actress*
%Twentieth Century, 15315 Magnolia Blvd, #429, Sherman Oaks, CA 91403, USA	
Harrison, Ken L	*Businessman*
%Portland General Corp, 121 SW Salmon St, Portland, OR 97204, USA	
Harrison, Lester (Les)	*Basketball Executive*
134 Greystone Lane, #11, Rochester, NY 14618, USA	
Harrison, Mark	*Editor*
%The Gazette, 250 St Antoine St W, Montreal PQ H2Y 3R7, Canada	
Harrison, Noel	*Actor*
5-11 Mortimer St, London W1, England	
Harrison, Tony	*Writer*
%Peters Fraser Dunlop, Chelsea Harbour, Lots Rd, London SW10 0XF, England	
Harrison, William H	*Army General*
7302 Amber Lane SW, Tacoma, WA 98498, USA	
Harrold, Kathryn	*Actress*
241 Central Park S, #2-H, New York, NY 10019, USA	
Harry, Deborah A (Debbie)	*Singer, Songwriter, Actress*
%Overland Productions, 156 W 56th St, #500, New York, NY 10019, USA	
Harryhausen, Ray F	*Movie Director*
2 Ilchester Place, West Kensington, London W14 8AA, England	
Harsanyi, John C	*Nobel Economics Laureate*
%University of California, Business Administration School, Berkeley, CA 94720, USA	
Harsch, Joseph C	*Commentator*
275 Highland Dr, Jamestown, RI 02835, USA	
Harshman, Marv K	*Basketball Coach*
19221 90th Place NE, Bothell, WA 98011, USA	
Hart, Doris	*Tennis Player*
600 Biltmore Way, #306, Coral Gables, FL 33134, USA	

Harris - Hart

Hart, Freddie — Singer, Songwriter, Guitarist
%Tessier-Marsh, 505 Canton Pass, Madison, TN 37115, USA
Hart, Gary W — Senator, CO
PO Box 1988, Denver, CO 80201, USA
Hart, Herbert L A — Solicitor, Philosopher
11 Manor Place, Oxford, England
Hart, James W (Jim) — Football Player, Sports Administrator
745 E Park St, Carbondale, IL 62901, USA
Hart, John — Actor
35109 Highway 79, #134, Warner Springs, CA 92086, USA
Hart, John L (Johnny) — Cartoonist (BC, Wizard of Id)
%Creators Syndicate, 5777 W Century Blvd, #700, Los Angeles, CA 90045, USA
Hart, John R — Commentator
%International Creative Mgmt, 40 W 57th St, New York, NY 10019, USA
Hart, Leon J — Football Player
3904 Cotton Tail Lane, Birmingham, MI 48301, USA
Hart, Mary — Entertainer
9000 W Sunset Blvd, #16, Los Angeles, CA 90069, USA
Hart, Parker T — Diplomat
4705 Berkeley Terrace NW, Washington, DC 20007, USA
Hart, Roxanne — Actress
%International Creative Mgmt, 8942 Wilshire Blvd, Beverly Hills, CA 90211, USA
Hart, Stanley R — Geologist
53 Quonset Road, Falmouth, MA 02540, USA
Hart, Terry J — Astronaut
333 Woodloch Spings, Hawley, PA 18428, USA
Harte, Houston H — Publisher
%Harte-Hanks Communications, 200 Concord Plaza Dr, San Antonio, TX 78216, USA
Hartenstine, Mike — Football Player
322 Winchester Court, Lake Bluff, IL 60044, USA
Harter, Dick — Basketball Coach
%Indiana Pacers, Market Square Arena, 300 E Market St, Indianapolis, IN 46204, USA
Hartford, John C — Singer, Songwriter
%Keith Case, 59 Music Square W, Nashville, TN 37203, USA
Harth, Sidney — Concert Violinist
135 Westland Dr, Pittsburgh, PA 15217, USA
Hartigan, Grace — Artist
1701 1/2 Eastern Ave, Baltimore, MD 21231, USA
Hartke, Vance — Senator, IN
%Hartke & Hartke, 7637 Leesburg Pike, Falls Church, VA 22043, USA
Hartley, Harry J — Educator
%University of Connecticut, President's Office, Storrs, CT 06269, USA
Hartley, John T, Jr — Businessman
%Harris Corp, 1025 W NASA Blvd, Melbourne, FL 32919, USA
Hartley, Mariette — Actress
10110 Empryian Way, #304, Los Angeles, CA 90067, USA
Hartling, Poul — Prime Minister, Denmark
Emilievej 6E, 2920 Charlottenlund, Denmark
Hartman Black, Lisa — Actress
8606 Allenwood Road, Los Angeles, CA 90046, USA
Hartman, Arthur A — Diplomat
2738 McKinley St NW, Washington, DC 20015, USA
Hartman, David — Actor, Commentator
%Trascott Alyson Craig, 222 Cedar Lane, Teaneck, NJ 07666, USA
Hartman, George E — Architect
3525 Hamlet Place, Bethesda, MD 20815, USA
Hartman, Phil — Comedian. Actor
%Brillstein/Grey, 9150 Wilshire Blvd, #350, Beverly Hills, CA 90212, USA
Hartman, William C (Bill), Jr — Football Player
%National Life of Vermont, 1160 S Milledge Ave, #220, Athens, GA 30605, USA
Hartmann, Frederick W — Editor
%Florida Times-Union, Editorial Dept, 1 Riverside Ave, Jacksonville, FL 32202, USA
Hartmann, Robert T — Government Official
5001 Baltimore Ave, Bethesda, MD 20816, USA
Hartmann, Ulrich — Businessman
%VEBA AG, Bennigsenplatz 1, 40474 Dusseldorf, Germany
Hartog, Jan de — Writer
%Andrew Nurnberg Assoc, 45/47 Clerkenwell Green, London EC1R 0HT, England

H

Hart - Hartog

Hartong, Hendrik J, Jr *Businessman*
%Air Express International, 120 Tokeneke Road, Darien, CT 06820, USA

Hartsburg, Craig *Hockey Player, Coach*
%Chicago Blackhawks, United Center, 1901 W Madison St, Chicago, IL 60612, USA

Hartsfield, Henry W (Hank), Jr *Astronaut*
%NASA, Johnson Space Center, 2101 NASA Road, Houston, TX 77058, USA

Hartshorn, Terry *Businessman*
%Pacificare Health Systems, 5995 Plaza Dr, Cypress, CA 90630, USA

Hartung, James *Gymnast*
3621 Portia St, Lincoln, NE 68521, USA

Hartwell of Peterborough Court, Michael *Publisher*
Oving House, Whitechurch near Aylesbury, Bucks, England

Hartwig, Cleo *Sculptor*
5 W 16th St, New York, NY 10011, USA

Hartzog, George B, Jr *Government Official*
1643 Chain Bridge Road, McLean, VA 22101, USA

Hartzog, William W (Bill) *Army General*
Commanding General, US Army Training/Doctrine Command, Fort Monroe, VA 23651, USA

Harup, Karen *Swimmer*
Noerremarksvej 27, 2650 Hvidovre, Denmark

Harvey, Anthony *Movie Director*
%Arthur Greene, 101 Park Ave, #4300, New York, NY 10178, USA

Harvey, Cynthia *Ballerina*
%American Ballet Theater, 890 Broadway, New York, NY 10003, USA

Harvey, H Douglas (Doug) *Baseball Umpire*
16081 Mustang Dr, Springville, CA 93265, USA

Harvey, Paul *Commentator*
%Paulyanne, 1035 Park Ave, River Forest, IL 60305, USA

Harvey, Polly Jean (P J) *Singer, Guitarist, Songwriter*
%Shore Fire Media, 193 Joralemon St, Brooklyn, NY 11201, USA

Harvey, Raymond *Korean War Army Hero (CMH)*
8780 E McKellips Road, #380, Scottsdale, AZ 85257, USA

Harwell, William Earnest (Ernie) *Sportscaster*
141 Fernery Road, #A-6, Lakeland, FL 33809, USA

Hary, Armin *Track Athlete*
Scholss, 86911 Diessen/Ammersee, Germany

Hasch, J Bruce *Businessman*
%Peoples Energy Corp, 130 E Randolph Dr, Chicago, IL 60601, USA

Hase, Dagmar *Swimmer*
Niederndodeleber Str 14, 29110 Magdeburg, Germany

Hasegawa, Kenko *Businessman*
%Kawasaki Heavy Industries, 2-1-18 Nakamachidori, Chuoko, Kobe 650, Japan

Hasegawa, Norishige *Businessman*
%Sumitomo Chemical, 5-33-4 Kitahama, Chuoku, Osaka 541, Japan

Hasek, Dominik *Hockey Player*
28 Skylark Court, East Amherst, NY 14051, USA

Hasen, Irvin H *Cartoonist (Goldbergs, Dondi)*
68 E 79th St, New York, NY 10021, USA

Hashimoto, Ryutaro *Prime Minister, Japan*
%Prime Minister's Office, 1-6-1 Nagatocho, Tokyo 100, Japan

Haskell, Peter *Actor*
19924 Acre St, Northridge, CA 91324, USA

Haskins, Caryl P *Biophysicist*
Greenacres, 22 Green Acre Lane, Westport, CT 06880, USA

Haskins, Clem *Basketball Player, Coach*
2011 Pine Island Road, Hopkins, MN 55305, USA

Haskins, Don *Basketball Coach*
%University of Texas, Athletic Dept, El Paso, TX 79968, USA

Haskins, Samuel J (Sam) *Photographer*
PO Box 59, Wimbledon, London SW19, England

Haslam of Bolton, Robert *Businessman*
%House of Lords, Westminster, London SW1A 0PW, England

Hasler, Arthur D *Zoologist*
1233 Sweet Briar Road, Madison, WI 53705, USA

Hasluck, Paul M C *Government Official, Australia*
2 Adams Road, Dalkeith WA 6009, Australia

Hass, Robert *Writer*
%University of California, English Dept, Berkeley, CA 94720, USA

Hassan Ibn Talal	*Crown Prince, Jordan*
%Crown Prince's Office, Royal Palace, Amman, Jordan	
Hassan II	*King, Morocco*
%Royal Palais, Rabat, Morocco	
Hassanali, Noor Mohamed	*President, Trinidad & Tobago*
%President's House, St Ann's, Port of Spain, Trinidad & Tobago	
Hasselhoff, David	*Actor, Singer*
%J/S/O Mgmt, 11342 Dona Lisa Dr, Studio City, CA 91604, USA	
Hasselmo, Nils	*Educator*
%University of Minnesota, President's Office, Minneapolis, MN 55455, USA	
Hassenfeld, Alan G	*Businessman*
%Hasbro Inc, 1027 Newport Ave, Pawtucket, RI 02861, USA	
Hassett, Marilyn	*Actress*
%Contemporary Artists, 1427 3rd St Promenade, #205, Santa Monica, CA 90401, USA	
Hasso, Signe	*Actress*
582 S Orange Grove Ave, Los Angeles, CA 90036, USA	
Hasson, Maurice	*Concert Violinist*
18 West Heath Court, North End Road, London NW11, England	
Hast, Adele	*Editor*
%Newberry Library, 60 W Walton St, Chicago, IL 60610, USA	
Hastings, A Baird	*Chemist*
233 Prospect Ave, La Jolla, CA 92037, USA	
Hastings, Don	*Actor*
%Schneiderman Assoc, 400 Park Ave, New York, NY 10022, USA	
Hatch, Harold A	*Marine Corps General*
8655 White Beach Way, Vienna, VA 22182, USA	
Hatch, Henry J	*Army General*
%Law International Group, 1000 Abernathy Road NE, Atlanta, GA 30328, USA	
Hatch, Monroe W, Jr	*Air Force General*
%Air Force Assn, 1501 Lee Highway, Arlington, VA 22209, USA	
Hatch, Richard	*Actor*
12304 Santa Monica Blvd, #140, Los Angeles, CA 90025, USA	
Hatch, Robert W	*Businesman*
%Mohasco Corp, 4401 Fair Lakes Court, Fairfax, VA 22033, USA	
Hatchell, Sylvia	*Basketball Coach*
%University of North Carolina, Athletic Dept, Chapel Hill, NC 27515, USA	
Hatcher, Kevin	*Hockey Player*
%Pittsburgh Penguins, Civic Arena, Centre Ave, Pittsburgh, PA 15219, USA	
Hatcher, Teri	*Actress*
%William Morris Agency, 151 S El Camino Dr, Beverly Hills, CA 90212, USA	
Hatfield, Bobby	*Singer (Righteous Brothers)*
599 Camillo St, Sierra Madre, CA 91024, USA	
Hatfield, Hurd	*Actor*
Ballinterry House, Rathcormac, County Cork, Ireland	
Hatfield, Juliana	*Singer*
%ICM/Twin Towers, 611 Broadway, #730, New York, NY 10012, USA	
Hathaway, Derek C	*Businessman*
%Harsco Corp, PO Box 8888, Camp Hill, PA 17001, USA	
Hathaway, Stanley K	*Secretary, Interior; Governor, WY*
2424 Pioneer Ave, Cheyenne, WY 82001, USA	
Hathaway, William D	*Senator, ME*
80 Orchard St, Auburn, ME 04210, USA	
Hatsopoulos, George N	*Businessman*
%Thermo Electron Corp, 81 Wyman St, Waltham, MA 02154, USA	
Hatten, Tom	*Actor*
1759 Sunset Plaza Dr, Los Angeles, CA 90069, USA	
Hattersley, Roy S G	*Government Official, England*
%House of Commons, Westminster, London SW1A 0AA, England	
Hattestad, Stine Lise	*Moguls Skier*
Sundlia 1-B, 1315 Nesoya, Norway	
Hatton, Vernon	*Basketball Player*
PO Box 8405, Lexington, KY 40533, USA	
Hattori, Kunio	*Businessman*
%Bridgestone Corp, 1-10-1 Kyobashi, Chuoku, Tokyo 104, Japan	
Haub, Erivan	*Businessman*
%Unternehmensgruppe Tengelmann, Wissoll 5-43, 45478 Mulheim/Ruhr, Germany	
Hauck, Frederick H (Rick)	*Astronaut*
4602 Laverock Place NW, Washington, DC 20007, USA	

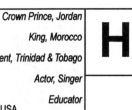

H

Hassan Ibn Talal - Hauck

H

Hauer, Rutger *Actor*
32 Sea Colony Dr, Santa Monica, CA 90405, USA

Haughey, Charles J *Prime Minister, Ireland*
Abbeville, Kinsakey, Malahide County Dublin, Ireland

Haugland, Aage *Opera Singer*
Skovbrinken 7, 3450 Allerod, Denmark

Hauk, A Andrew *Judge, Skier*
%US Court House, 312 N Spring St, Los Angeles, CA 90012, USA

Hauptman, Herbert A *Nobel Chemistry Laureate*
%Medical Foundation of Buffalo, 73 High St, Buffalo, NY 14203, USA

Hauptman, Michael *Radio Executive*
13 Carriage Road, Cos Cob, CT 06807, USA

Haurwitz, Bernhard *Meteorologist*
%Colorado State University, Atmospheric Science Dept, Fort Collins, CO 80523, USA

Hauser, Erich *Sculptor*
78628 Rottweil-Wurtt, Germany

Hauser, Wings *Actor*
9450 Chivers Ave, Sun Valley, CA 91352, USA

Havel, Richard J *Physician*
PO Box 1791, Ross, CA 94957, USA

Havel, Vaclav *President, Czech Republic; Playwright*
%Kancelar Prezidenta Republiky, Hradecek, 119 08 Prague 1, Czech Republic

Havelange, Jean M F G (Joao) *Soccer Executive*
Rua Prudente de Maroes 1700, #1001, 20420-042 Rio de Janiero, Brazil

Havens, Frank *Canoeist*
PO Box 55, Harborton, VA 23389, USA

Havens, Richie *Singer, Songwriter, Guitarist*
%ELO Productions, 123 W 44th St, New York, NY 10036, USA

Haver, June *Actress*
485 Halvern Dr, Los Angeles, CA 90049, USA

Havers, Nigel *Actor*
%Michael Whitehall, 125 Gloucester Road, London SW7 4TE, England

Haverty, Harold V *Businessman*
%Deluxe Corp, 1080 W Country Road "F", St Paul, MN 55126, USA

Havighurst, Clark C *Attorney, Educator*
3610 Dover Road, Durham, NC 27707, USA

Havlicek, John *Basketball Player*
24 Beech Road, Weston, MA 02193, USA

Havoc, June *Actress*
405 Old Long Ridge Road, Stamford, CT 06903, USA

Hawerchuk, Dale *Hockey Player*
%Philadelphia Flyers, CoreStates Center, Pattison Place, Philadelphia, PA 19148, USA

Hawk, John D *WW II Army Hero (CMH)*
3243 Solie Ave, Bremerton, WA 98310, USA

Hawke, Ethan *Actor*
1771 Broadway, #701, New York, NY 10019, USA

Hawke, Robert J L *Prime Minister, Australia*
Westfield Towers, #1300, 100 William St, Sydney NSW 2000, Australia

Hawkes, Christopher *Archaeologist*
19 Walton St, Oxford OX1 2HQ, England

Hawkes, John *Writer*
18 Everett Ave, Providence, RI 02906, USA

Hawking, Stephen W *Theoretical Physicist*
%University of Cambridge, Applied Math Dept, Cambridge CB3 9EW, England

Hawkins, Connie *Basketball Player, Executive*
%Phoenix Suns, 201 E Jefferson St, Phoenix, AZ 85004, USA

Hawkins, Dale *Singer, Songwriter*
4618 John F Kennedy Blvd, #107, North Little Rock, AR 72116, USA

Hawkins, Edwin *Vocal Group Leader*
%PAZ Entertainment, 2041 Locust St, Philadelphia, PA 19103, USA

Hawkins, Hersey *Basketball Player*
%Seattle Supersonics, 190 Queen Ave N, PO Box C-900911, Seattle, WA 98109, USA

Hawkins, M Andrew (Andy) *Baseball Player*
PO Box 8812, Waco, TX 76714, USA

Hawkins, Paula *Senator, FL*
1214 Park Ave N, Winter Park, FL 32789, USA

Hawkins, Ronnie *Singer*
%Backstage, 1-3015 Kennedy Road, Scarborough ON M1V 1E7, Canada

Hauer - Hawkins

Hawkins, Sophie B — Singer
%Q-Prime, 729 7th Ave, #1600, New York, NY 10019, USA

Hawkins, Tommy — Basketball Player
1745 Manzanita Park Ave, Malibu, CA 90265, USA

Hawkinson, Tim — Artist
%Ace Gallery, 5514 Wilshire Blvd, Los Angeles, CA 90036, USA

Hawks, Steve — Artist
%Hadley House, 1101 Hampshire Road S, Bloomington, MN 55438, USA

Hawley, Frank — Auto Racing Driver
%Frank Hawley Drag Racing School, County Road 225, Gainesville, FL 32609, USA

Hawley, Richard E (Dick) — Air Force General
Commander, Air Combat Cmd, 205 Dodd Blvd, Langley Air Force Base, VA 23665, USA

Hawley, Samuel W — Financier
%People's Bank, 850 Main St, Bridgeport, CT 06604, USA

Hawley, Steven A — Astronaut
3929 Walnut Pond Dr, Houston, TX 77059, USA

Hawn, Goldie — Actress
%Hawn-Sylbert Co, 500 S Buena Vista St, #10-D-06, Burbank, CA 91521, USA

Haworth, Jill — Actress
300 E 51st St, New York, NY 10022, USA

Haworth, Lionel — Aeronautical Engineer
10 Hazelwood Road, Sneryd Park, Bristol BS9 1PX, England

Hawpe, David V — Editor
%Louisville Courier-Journal, 525 W Broadway, Louisville, KY 40202, USA

Hawthorne, Nigel — Actor
Radwell Grange near Radwell, Baldock, Herts SG7 5EU, England

Hawthorne, William — Thermodynamics Engineer
%Churchill College, Engineering School, Cambridge CB3 0DS, England

Hayden, J Michael (Mike) — Governor, KS
%E C Mellick Agency, 406 State St, Atwood, KS 67730, USA

Hayden, Jim — Publisher
%Philadelphia Inquirer, 400 N Broad St, Philadelphia, PA 19130, USA

Hayden, Linda — Actress
%Michael Ladkin, 11 Southwick Mews, London W2 1JG, England

Hayden, Neil Steven — Publisher
749 Rivenwood Road, Franklin Lakes, NJ 07417, USA

Hayden, Tom — Political Activist (Chicago 7)
152 Wadsworth Ave, Santa Monica, CA 90405, USA

Hayden, William G — Governor General, Australia
16 East St, Ipswich, QLD 4305, Australia

Hayden, William J — Businessman
%Jaguar Cars Ltd, Browns Lane, Coventry, West Midlands CV5 9DR, England

Haydon Jones, Ann — Tennis Player
85 Westerfield Road, Edgloaston, Birmingham 15, England

Hayek, Salma — Actress, Model
%William Morris Agency, 151 S El Camino Dr, Beverly Hills, CA 90212, USA

Hayes, Bill — Singer
4528 Beck Ave, North Hollywood, CA 91602, USA

Hayes, Bob — Track Athlete, Football Player
13901 Preston Valley Place, Dallas, TX 75240, USA

Hayes, Charles A — Businessman
%Guilford Mills, 4925 W Market St, Greensboro, NC 27407, USA

Hayes, Denis A — Environmentalist
%Green Seal, PO Box 18237, Washington, DC 20036, USA

Hayes, Dennis C — Engineer, Co-Inventor (Modem)
%Hayes Microcomputer Products, PO Box 105203, Atlanta, GA 30348, USA

Hayes, Elvin — Basketball Player
252 Piney Point Road, Houston, TX 77024, USA

Hayes, Isaac — Composer, Singer, Actor
%Ron Moss, 2635 Griffith Park Blvd, Los Angeles, CA 90039, USA

Hayes, John B — Coast Guard Admiral
%Coast Guard Headquarters, 2100 2nd St SW, Washington, DC 20593, USA

Hayes, Louis S — Jazz Drummer
%Abby Hoffer, 223 1/2 E 48th St, New York, NY 10017, USA

Hayes, Peter Lind — Actor
3538 Pueblo Way, Las Vegas, NV 89109, USA

Hayes, Robert M — Social Activist
%National Coalition for the Homeless, 105 E 22nd St, New York, NY 10010, USA

H

Hawkins - Hayes

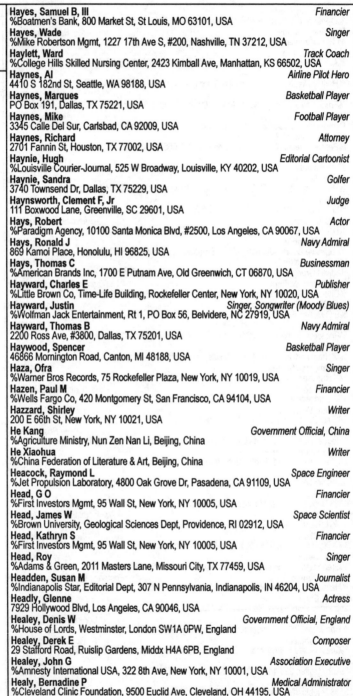

H

Hayes - Healy

Hayes, Samuel B, III — *Financier*
%Boatmen's Bank, 800 Market St, St Louis, MO 63101, USA
Hayes, Wade — *Singer*
%Mike Robertson Mgmt, 1227 17th Ave S, #200, Nashville, TN 37212, USA
Haylett, Ward — *Track Coach*
%College Hills Skilled Nursing Center, 2423 Kimball Ave, Manhattan, KS 66502, USA
Haynes, Al — *Airline Pilot Hero*
4410 S 182nd St, Seattle, WA 98188, USA
Haynes, Marques — *Basketball Player*
PO Box 191, Dallas, TX 75221, USA
Haynes, Mike — *Football Player*
3345 Calle Del Sur, Carlsbad, CA 92009, USA
Haynes, Richard — *Attorney*
2701 Fannin St, Houston, TX 77002, USA
Haynie, Hugh — *Editorial Cartoonist*
%Louisville Courier-Journal, 525 W Broadway, Louisville, KY 40202, USA
Haynie, Sandra — *Golfer*
3740 Townsend Dr, Dallas, TX 75229, USA
Haynsworth, Clement F, Jr — *Judge*
111 Boxwood Lane, Greenville, SC 29601, USA
Hays, Robert — *Actor*
%Paradigm Agency, 10100 Santa Monica Blvd, #2500, Los Angeles, CA 90067, USA
Hays, Ronald J — *Navy Admiral*
869 Kamoi Place, Honolulu, HI 96825, USA
Hays, Thomas C — *Businessman*
%American Brands Inc, 1700 E Putnam Ave, Old Greenwich, CT 06870, USA
Hayward, Charles E — *Publisher*
%Little Brown Co, Time-Life Building, Rockefeller Center, New York, NY 10020, USA
Hayward, Justin — *Singer, Songwriter (Moody Blues)*
%Wolfman Jack Entertainment, Rt 1, PO Box 56, Belvidere, NC 27919, USA
Hayward, Thomas B — *Navy Admiral*
2200 Ross Ave, #3800, Dallas, TX 75201, USA
Haywood, Spencer — *Basketball Player*
46866 Mornington Road, Canton, MI 48188, USA
Haza, Ofra — *Singer*
%Warner Bros Records, 75 Rockefeller Plaza, New York, NY 10019, USA
Hazen, Paul M — *Financier*
%Wells Fargo Co, 420 Montgomery St, San Francisco, CA 94104, USA
Hazzard, Shirley — *Writer*
200 E 66th St, New York, NY 10021, USA
He Kang — *Government Official, China*
%Agriculture Ministry, Nun Zen Nan Li, Beijing, China
He Xiaohua — *Writer*
%China Federation of Literature & Art, Beijing, China
Heacock, Raymond L — *Space Engineer*
%Jet Propulsion Laboratory, 4800 Oak Grove Dr, Pasadena, CA 91109, USA
Head, G O — *Financier*
%First Investors Mgmt, 95 Wall St, New York, NY 10005, USA
Head, James W — *Space Scientist*
%Brown University, Geological Sciences Dept, Providence, RI 02912, USA
Head, Kathryn S — *Financier*
%First Investors Mgmt, 95 Wall St, New York, NY 10005, USA
Head, Roy — *Singer*
%Adams & Green, 2011 Masters Lane, Missouri City, TX 77459, USA
Headden, Susan M — *Journalist*
%Indianapolis Star, Editorial Dept, 307 N Pennsylvania, Indianapolis, IN 46204, USA
Headly, Glenne — *Actress*
7929 Hollywood Blvd, Los Angeles, CA 90046, USA
Healey, Denis W — *Government Official, England*
%House of Lords, Westminster, London SW1A 0PW, England
Healey, Derek E — *Composer*
29 Stafford Road, Ruislip Gardens, Middx H4A 6PB, England
Healey, John G — *Association Executive*
%Amnesty International USA, 322 8th Ave, New York, NY 10001, USA
Healy, Bernadine P — *Medical Administrator*
%Cleveland Clinic Foundation, 9500 Euclid Ave, Cleveland, OH 44195, USA
Healy, Cornelius T — *Labor Leader*
%Plate Die Engravers Union, 228 S Swarthmore Ave, Ridley Park, PA 19078, USA

Healy, Jane E — *Journalist*
%Orlando Sentinel, Editorial Dept, 633 N Orange Ave, Orlando, FL 32801, USA

Healy, Jeremiah — *Writer*
%Pocket Books, 1230 Ave of Americas, New York, NY 10020, USA

Healy, Mary — *Actress*
3538 Pueblo Way, Las Vegas, NV 89109, USA

Healy, Patricia — *Actress*
%Silver Massetti Szatmary, 8730 Sunset Blvd, #480, Los Angeles, CA 90069, USA

Heaney, Robert A — *Financier*
%Chase Manhattan Corp, 1 Chase Manhattan Plaza, Wilmington, DE 19801, USA

Heaney, Seamus J — *Nobel Literature Laureate*
%Faber & Faber, 3 Queen Square, London WC1N 3RU, England

Heaps, Alvin E — *Labor Leader*
%Retail Wholesale Department Store Union, 30 E 29th St, New York, NY 10016, USA

Heard, G Alexander — *Educator*
2100 Golf Club Lane, Nashville, TN 37215, USA

Heard, Garfield (Gar) — *Basketball Player, Coach*
89 Timothy Circle, Radnor, PA 19087, USA

Heard, John — *Actor*
23215 Mariposa de Oro, Malibu, CA 90265, USA

Hearn, Chick — *Sportscaster, Basketball Executive*
%Los Angeles Lakers, Forum, PO Box 10, Inglewood, CA 90306, USA

Hearn, George — *Actor, Singer*
200 W 57th St, #900, New York, NY 10019, USA

Hearn, J Woodrow — *Religious Leader*
%United Methodist Church, PO Box 320, Nashville, TN 37202, USA

Hearn, James T (Jim) — *Baseball Player*
1678 Beverly Wood Court, Chamblee, GA 30341, USA

Hearn, Thomas K, Jr — *Educator*
%Wake Forest University, President's Office, Winston-Salem, NC 27109, USA

Hearnes, Warren E — *Governor, MO*
PO Box 349, Rt 3, Charleston, MO 63834, USA

Hearney, Richard D — *Marine Corps General*
%Assistant Commandant's Office, HqUSMC, 2 Navy Annex, Washington, DC 20370, USA

Hearns, Thomas (Tommy) — *Boxer*
19785 W 12 Mile Road, Southfield, MI 48076, USA

Hearst, Garrison — *Football Player*
3753 Augusta Road, Lincolnton, GA 30817, USA

Hearst, George R, Jr — *Publisher*
318 N Rockingham Ave, Los Angeles, CA 90049, USA

Hearst, Patricia C (Patty) — *Kidnap Victim*
110 5th St, San Francisco, CA 94103, USA

Hearst, Randolph A — *Publisher*
%Hearst Corp, 959 8th Ave, New York, NY 10019, USA

Hearst, Rick — *Actor*
10875 Kling St, North Hollywood, CA 91602, USA

Hearth, Donald P — *Aeronautical Engineer*
%Langley Research Center, NASA, Hampton, VA 23665, USA

Heath, Albert (Tootie) — *Jazz Drummer (Modern Jazz Quarter)*
%Ted Kurland, 173 Brighton Ave, Boston, MA 02134, USA

Heath, Edward R G — *Prime Minister, England*
%House of Commons, Westminster, London SW1A 0AA, England

Heath, Jimmy — *Jazz Saxophonist, Composer*
%Ted Kurland, 173 Brighton Ave, Boston, MA 02134, USA

Heath, Percy — *Jazz Bassist (Modern Jazz Quartet)*
%Ellen Levine Mgmt, 8033 Sunset Blvd, #1037, Los Angeles, CA 90046, USA

Heath-Stubbs, John F A — *Writer*
22 Artesian Road, London W2 5AR, England

Heathcote, Jud — *Basketball Coach*
5418 S Quail Ridge Circle, Spokane, WA 99223, USA

Hebert, Bobby J, Jr — *Football Player*
%Atlanta Falcons, 2745 Burnett Road, Suwanee, GA 30024, USA

Hebert, Guy — *Hockey Player*
%Anaheim Mighty Ducks, PO Box 2000, Gene Autry Way, Anaheim, CA 92803, USA

Hebert, Johnny — *Auto Racing Driver*
%Team Lotus, Kettering Hamm Hall, Wymondham, Norfolk NR18 7HW, England

Heche, Anne — *Actress*
6063 Scenic Ave, Los Angeles, CA 90068, USA

H

Healy - Heche

Hecht, Anthony E — *Writer*
4256 Nebraska Ave NW, Washington, DC 20016, USA

Hecht, Chic — *Senator, NV; Diplomat*
%US Embassy, Mosmar Building, Queen St, Nassau, Bahamas

Hecht, Duvall — *Rower*
729 Farad St, Costa Mesa, CA 92627, USA

Hecht, Jessica — *Actress*
%Ambrosio/Mortimer, 9150 Wilshire Blvd, #175, Beverly Hills, CA 90212, USA

Hechter, Daniel — *Fashion Designer*
4 Ave Ter Hoche, 75008 Paris, France

Heckart, Eileen — *Actress*
1223 Foxboro Dr, Norwalk, CT 06851, USA

Heckerling, Amy — *Movie Director*
1330 Schuyler Road, Beverly Hills, CA 90210, USA

Heckscher, August — *Writer*
333 E 68th St, New York, NY 10021, USA

Hedaya, Dan — *Actor*
%Gallin Morey, 345 N Maple Dr, #300, Beverly Hills, CA 90210, USA

Hedberg, Hollis D — *Petroleum Geologist*
118 Library Place, Princeton, NJ 08540, USA

Hedison, David — *Actor*
%Epstein/Wyckoff, 280 S Beverly Dr, #400, Beverly Hills, CA 90212, USA

Hedren, Tippi — *Actress*
6867 Soledad Canyon Road, Acton, CA 93510, USA

Hedrick, Jerry L — *Biochemist*
25280 Carlsbad Ave, Davis, CA 95616, USA

Hedrick, Joan D — *Writer*
%Trinity College, Women's Studies Program, Hartford, CT 06106, USA

Heeschen, David S — *Radio Astronomer*
2590 Earlysville Road, Earlysville, VA

Heffner, Ralph H — *Businessman*
%Agway Inc, 333 Butternut Dr, Dewitt, NY 13214, USA

Hefner, Christie A — *Publisher*
%Playboy Enterprises, 680 N Lake Shore Dr, Chicago, IL 60611, USA

Hefner, Hugh M — *Publisher, Editor*
10236 Charing Cross Road, Los Angeles, CA 90024, USA

Heft, Robert — *Flag Designer*
PO Box 131, Napoleon, OH 43545, USA

Hefti, Neal — *Composer*
%Encino Music, 9454 Wilshire Blvd, #405, Beverly Hills, CA 90212, USA

Hefty, Thomas R — *Businessman*
%United Wisconsin Services, 401 W Michigan St, Milwaukee, WI 53203, USA

Heger, Martin L — *Financier*
%Federal Home Loan Bank, 8259 Woodfield Crossing Blvd, Indianapolis, IN 46240, USA

Heggtveit, Ann Hamilton — *Skier*
%General Delivery, Grand Isle, VT 05458, USA

Hegyes, Robert — *Actor*
12206 Tweed Lane, Los Angeles, CA 90049, USA

Heidelberger, Charles — *Oncologist, Biochemist*
1495 Poppy Peak Dr, Pasadena, CA 91105, USA

Heiden, Beth — *Speed Skater*
3505 Blackhawk Dr, Madison, WI 53705, USA

Heiden, Eric A — *Speed Skater*
82 Sandburg Road, Sacramento, CA 95819, USA

Heigl, Katherine — *Actress, Model*
%Innovative Artists, 1999 Ave of Stars, #2850, Los Angeles, CA 90067, USA

Heilbroner, Robert L — *Economist*
830 Park Ave, New York, NY 10021, USA

Heilbrun (Amanda Cross), Carolyn G — *Writer*
%Columbia University, English Dept, Philosophy Hall, New York, NY 10027, USA

Heiliger, Bernhard — *Sculptor*
Kauzchensteig 8, 14195 Berlin, Germany

Heilmeier, George H — *Electronics Inventor*
%Bell Communications Research, 290 W Mount Pleasant Ave, Livingston, NJ 07039, USA

Heimbinder, Isaac — *Businessman*
%US Home Corp, 1800 West Loop S, Houston, TX 77027, USA

Heimbold, Charles A, Jr — *Businessman*
%Bristol-Myers Squibb, 345 Park Ave, New York, NY 10154, USA

Heimbuch, Babette	*Financier*
%FirstFed Financial Corp, 401 Wilshire Blvd, Santa Monica, CA 90401, USA	
Heimlich, Henry J	*Physician*
%Heimlich Institute, 2368 Victory Parkway, #410, Cincinnati, OH 45206, USA	
Heine, Jutta	*Track Athlete*
Blaue Muhle, 57614 Burglahr, Germany	
Heineken, Alfred H	*Businessman*
%Heineken Holding, 2-E Weteringplantsoen 5, 1017-ZD Amsterdam, Netherlands	
Heinemann, Stephen	*Neurobologist*
%Salk Biological Institute, 10010 N Torrey Pines Road, La Jolla, CA 92037, USA	
Heinsohn, Thomas W (Tom)	*Basketball Player, Coach*
406 Elliott St, Newton, MA 02164, USA	
Heinz, W C	*Sportswriter*
Nicholas Hill, Dorset, VT 05251, USA	
Heinze, Bernard T	*Conductor*
101 Victoria Road, Bellevue Hill, Sydney NSW, Australia	
Heinzer, Franz	*Skier*
Lauenen, 6432 Rickenbach/Schwyz, Switzerland	
Heiskell, Andrew	*Publisher*
870 United Nations Plaza, New York, NY 10017, USA	
Heiss Jenkins, Carol	*Figure Skater*
809 Lafayette Dr, Akron, OH 44303, USA	
Heist, L C	*Businessman*
%Champion International Corp, 1 Champion Plaza, Stamford, CT 06921, USA	
Heitmann, Scott K	*Financier*
%LaSalle Talman Bank, 135 S LaSalle St, Chicago, IL 60603, USA	
Hejduk, John Q	*Architect*
5721 Huxley Ave, Riverdale, NY 10471, USA	
Hekman, Peter M, Jr	*Navy Admiral*
Commander, Naval Sea Systems Command, Navy Dept, Washington, DC 20362, USA	
Held, Al	*Artist*
%Andre Emmerich Gallery, 41 E 57th St, New York, NY 10022, USA	
Held, Franklin (Bud)	*Track Athlete*
13367 Caminito Mar Villa, Del Mar, CA 92014, USA	
Held, Richard M	*Psychologist*
%Massachusetts Institute of Technology, Psychology Dept, Cambridge, MA 02139, USA	
Heldman, Gladys	*Tennis Contributor*
1002 Old Pecos Trail, Santa Fe, NM 87501, USA	
Helfer, Ricki Tigert	*Financier*
%Federal Deposit Insurance, 550 17th St NW, Washington, DC 20429, USA	
Helgenberger, Marg	*Actress*
1275 N Harper Ave, Los Angeles, CA 90046, USA	
Heliker, John	*Artist*
865 West End Ave, #3-C, New York, NY 10025, USA	
Helinski, Donald R	*Biologist*
%University of California, Molecular Genetics Center, La Jolla, CA 92093, USA	
Heller, Daniel M	*Attorney*
Israel Discount Bank Building, 14 NE 1st Ave, Miami, FL 33132, USA	
Heller, John H	*Research Scientist*
74 Horseshoe Road, Wilton, CT 06897, USA	
Heller, Joseph	*Writer*
%Simon & Schuster, 1230 Ave of Americas, New York, NY 10020, USA	
Hellerman, Fred	*Singer (Weavers), Songwriter*
83 Goodhill Road, Weston, CT 06883, USA	
Hellickson, Russ	*Wrestler*
%Ohio State University, Athletic Dept, Columbus, OH 43210, USA	
Helligbrodt, L William	*Businessman*
%Service Corp International, 1929 Allen Parkway, Houston, TX 77019, USA	
Helliwell, Robert A	*Radio Scientist*
2240 Page Mill Road, Palo Alto, CA 94304, USA	
Hellman, Monte	*Movie Director*
8588 Appian Way, Los Angeles, CA 90046, USA	
Hellman, Peter S	*Businessman*
%TRW Inc, 1900 Richmond Road, Cleveland, OH 44124, USA	
Hellmann, Martina	*Track Athlete*
Neue Leipziger Str 14, 04205 Leipzig, Germany	
Hellmuth, George F	*Architect*
5 Conway Lane, St Louis, MO 63124, USA	

H

Hellyer - Henderson

Hellyer, Paul T — *Government Official, Canada*
65 Harbour Square, #506, Toronto ON M5J 2L4, Canada
Helm, Levon — *Singer, Drummer (The Band); Actor*
%Ron Rainey, 315 S Beverly Dr, #206, Beverly Hills, CA 90212, USA
Helmond, Katherine — *Actress*
2035 Davies Way, Los Angeles, CA 90046, USA
Helmreich, Ernst J M — *Physiological Chemist*
%University of Wurzburg Biozentrum, Am Hubland, 97074 Wurzburg, Germany
Helms, Richard M — *Government Official*
%Safeer Co, 4649 Garfield St NW, Washington, DC 20007, USA
Helms, Susan J — *Astronaut*
%NASA, Johnson Space Center, 2101 NASA Road, Houston, TX 77058, USA
Helmsley, Leona M — *Businesswoman*
36 Central Park South, New York, NY 10019, USA
Heloise (Cruse Evans) — *Journalist*
PO Box 795000, San Antonio, TX 78279, USA
Helou, Charles — *President, Lebanon*
Kaslik, Jounieh, Lebanon
Helpern, Joan G — *Fashion Designer*
%Joan & David Helpern Inc, 4 W 58th St, New York, NY 10019, USA
Heltau, Michael — *Actor*
Sulzweg 11, 1190 Vienna, Austria
Helton, Bill D — *Businessman*
%Southwestern Public Service, Tyler & 6th, Amarillo, TX 79170, USA
Helvin, Marie — *Model*
%IMG, 23 Eyot Gardens, London W6 9TN, England
Hemingway, Mariel — *Model, Actress*
PO Box 2249, Ketchum, ID 83340, USA
Hemminghaus, Roger R — *Businessman*
%Diamond Shamrock R&M, 9830 Colonnade Blvd, San Antonio, TX 78230, USA
Hemmings, David — *Actor*
%Michael Whitehall, 125 Gloucester Road, London SW7 4TE, England
Hempel, Amy — *Writer*
%Charles Scribner's Sons, 866 3rd Ave, New York, NY 10022, USA
Hemphill, Shirley — *Actress*
PO Box 897, West Covina, CA 91793, USA
Hempstone, Smith, Jr — *Columnist, Diplomat*
7611 Fairfax Road, Bethesda, MD 20814, USA
Hemsley, Sherman — *Actor*
%Kenny Johnston, 15043 Valley Heart Dr, Sherman Oaks, CA 91403, USA
Hencken, John — *Swimmer*
10532 Tujunga Canyon Blvd, Tujunga, CA 91042, USA
Henderson, Alan — *Basketball Player*
%Atlanta Hawks, 1 CNN Center, South Tower, Atlanta, GA 30303, USA
Henderson, David L (Dave) — *Baseball Player*
6004 142nd Court SE, Bellvue, WA 98006, USA
Henderson, Donald A — *Epidemiologist*
3802 Greenway, Baltimore, MD 21218, USA
Henderson, Florence — *Actress, Singer*
%FHB Productions, PO Box 11295, Marina del Rey, CA 90295, USA
Henderson, George W, III — *Businessman*
%Burlington Industries, PO Box 21207, Greensboro, NC 27420, USA
Henderson, Gordon — *Fashion Designer*
%World Hong Kong, 80 W 40th St, New York, NY 10018, USA
Henderson, Greer F — *Businessman*
%USLife Corp, 125 Maiden Lane, New York, NY 10038, USA
Henderson, Horace E — *Government Official*
1100 Gough St, #15-F, San Francisco, CA 94109, USA
Henderson, J Nicholas — *Government Official, England*
6 Fairholt St, London SW7 1EG, England
Henderson, James A — *Businessman*
%Cummins Engine Co, PO Box 3005, Columbus, IN 47202, USA
Henderson, Joseph A (Joe) — *Jazz Saxophonist*
%Verve Records, Worldwide Plaza, 825 8th Ave, New York, NY 10019, USA
Henderson, Julia — *International Official*
1735 Forest Road, Venice, FL 34293, USA
Henderson, Mike — *Singer, Guitarist, Songwriter*
%Studio One Artists, 7010 Westmoreland Ave, #100, Tacoma Park, MD 20912, USA

Henderson, Paul *Journalist*
%Seattle Times, Editorial Dept, Fairview Ave N & John St, Seattle, WA 98111, USA
Henderson, Rickey H *Baseball Player*
10561 Englewood Dr, Oakland, CA 94605, USA
Henderson, Roy A *Financier*
%Bank of California, 400 California St, San Francisco, CA 94104, USA
Henderson, Skitch *Pianist, Conductor, Composer*
Hunt Hill Farm, 44 Upland Road, RFD 3, New Milford, CT 06776, USA
Henderson, Thomas (Tom) *Basketball Player*
14003 Piney Run Court, Houston, TX 77066, USA
Henderson, William D *Businessman*
%Smith Corona Corp, PO Box 2090, Cortland, NY 13045, USA
Hendricks, Barbara *Opera Singer*
%IMG Artists, 22 E 71st St, New York, NY 10021, USA
Hendricks, John S *Television Executive*
%Discovery Communications, 7700 Wisconsin Ave, Bethesda, MD 20814, USA
Hendricks, Jon *Singer*
%Virginia Wicks, 550 S Barrington Ave, #1306, Brentwood, CA 90049, USA
Hendricks, Theodore P (Ted) *Football Player*
1232 W Weston Dr, Arlington Heights, IL 60004, USA
Hendrix, Dennis R *Businessman*
%Panhandle Eastern Corp, 5400 Westheimer Court, Houston, TX 77056, USA
Hendrix, James R *WW II Army Hero (CMH)*
PO Box 164, Davenport, FL 33836, USA
Henion, John Q *Army General*
7713 Mesa Dr, Austin, TX 78731, USA
Henke, Nolan *Golfer*
19662 Lost Creek Dr, Fort Myers, FL 33912, USA
Henkel, Heike *Track Athlete*
Tannenbergstr 57, 51373 Leverkusen, Germany
Henkel, Konrad *Businessman*
%Degussa, Weissfrauenstr 9, 60311 Frankfurt/Main, Germany
Henkin, Louis *Attorney, Educator*
460 Riverside Dr, New York, NY 10027, USA
Henle, Gertrude *Virologist*
533 Ott Road, Bala-Cynwyd, PA 19004, USA
Henley, Don *Singer (The Eagles), Songwriter*
%Front Line Mgmt, 8900 Wilshire Blvd, #300, Beverly Hills, CA 90211, USA
Henley, Edward T *Labor Leader*
%Hotel & Restaurant Employees Union, 1219 28th St NW, Washington, DC 20007, USA
Henley, Elizabeth B (Beth) *Writer*
%William Morris Agency, 1325 Ave of Americas, New York, NY 10019, USA
Henley, Larry *Composer*
%Creative Directions, PO Box 335, Brentwood, TN 37024, USA
Henn, Mark *Animator (Little Mermaid)*
%Walt Disney Animation, PO Box 10200, Lake Buena Vista, FL 32830, USA
Henn, Walter *Architect*
Ramsachleite 13, 82418 Murnau, Germany
Henner, Marilu *Actress*
%William Morris Agency, 151 S El Camino Dr, Beverly Hills, CA 90212, USA
Hennessey, Tom *Bowler*
157 Forest Brook Lane, St Louis, MO 63146, USA
Hennessy, Jill *Actress, Model*
%William Morris Agency, 151 S El Camino Dr, Beverly Hills, CA 90212, USA
Hennessy, John B *Archaeologist*
%University of Sydney, Archaeology Dept, Sydney NSW 2006, Australia
Hennig, Frederick E *Businessman*
%Woolworth Corp, Woolworth Building, 233 Broadway, New York, NY 10279, USA
Henning, Doug *Illusionist*
6747 Odessa Ave, #105, Van Nuys, CA 91406, USA
Henning, Harold *Golfer*
1617 N Flagler Dr, #5-A, West Palm Beach, FL 33407, USA
Henning, John F, Jr *Publisher*
%Sunset Magazine, 80 Willow Road, Menlo Park, CA 94025, USA
Henning, Linda *Actress*
843 N Sycamore Ave, Los Angeles, CA 90038, USA
Henning, Lorne E *Hockey Player, Coach*
3171 Indian Creek Court, Buffalo Grove, IL 60089, USA

Henning-Walker, Anne — *Speed Skater*
9959 E Peakview Ave, Englewood, CO 80111, USA

Hennings, Chad — *Football Player*
913 Westwind Cove, Coppell, TX 75019, USA

Henrich, Thomas D (Tommy) — *Baseball Player*
1985 Shadow Valley Dr, Prescott, AZ 86301, USA

Henricks, Jon N — *Swimmer*
254 N Laurel Ave, Des Plaines, IL 60016, USA

Henricks, Terence T (Tom) — *Astronaut*
%NASA, Johnson Space Center, 2101 NASA Road, Houston, TX 77058, USA

Henrik — *Prince, Denmark*
%Amalienborg Palace, 1257 Copenhagen K, Denmark

Henriksen, Lance — *Actor*
9540 Dale St, Sunland, CA 91040, USA

Henriquez, Ron — *Actor*
PO Box 38027, Los Angeles, CA 90038, USA

Henry, Buck — *Actor, Screenwriter*
117 E 57th St, New York, NY 10022, USA

Henry, Carl F H — *Theologian*
1141 Hus Dr, #206, Watertown, WI 53098, USA

Henry, Clarence (Frog Man) — *Singer, Songwriter*
3309 Lawrence St, New Orleans, LA 70114, USA

Henry, Gloria — *Actress*
849 N Harper Ave, Los Angeles, CA 90046, USA

Henry, Gregg — *Actor*
8956 Appian Way, Los Angeles, CA 90046, USA

Henry, Joseph L — *Dentist*
309 Winchester St, #A, Newton Highlands, MA 02161, USA

Henry, Justin — *Actor*
2 Sackett Landing, Rye, NY 10580, USA

Henry, Kenneth (Ken) — *Speed Skater*
414 W Hawthorne Court, Lake Bluff, IL 60044, USA

Henry, Lenny — *Comedian*
%Luff, 294 Earls Court Road, London SW5 9BB, England

Henry, Pierre — *Composer*
32 Rue Toul, 75012 Paris, France

Henry, William H, Jr — *Publisher*
%Time-Life Books, Rockefeller Center, New York, NY 10020, USA

Henschel, Milton — *Religious Leader*
%Jehovah's Witnesses, 25 Columbia Heights, Brooklyn, NY 11201, USA

Hensel, Witold — *Archaeologist*
Ul Marszalkowska 84/92 M, 109 00-514 Warsaw, Poland

Hensley, Kirby J — *Religious Leader*
%Universal Life Church, 601 3rd St, Modesto, CA 95351, USA

Hensley, Pamela — *Actress*
9526 Dalegrove Dr, Beverly Hills, CA 90210, USA

Henson, Lisa — *Movie Producer*
%Columbia Pictures, 10202 W Washington Blvd, Culver City, CA 90232, USA

Henstridge, Natasha — *Actress, Model*
12190 1/2 Ventura Blvd, #331, Studio City, CA 91604, USA

Hentgen, Patrick G (Pat) — *Baseball Player*
14451 Knightsbridge Dr, Shelby Township, MI 48315, USA

Hentoff, Nathan I (Nat) — *Jazz Critic*
%Village Voice, Editorial Dept, 36 Cooper Square, New York, NY 10003, USA

Hentrich, Helmut — *Architect*
Dusseldorfer Str 67, 40545 Dusseldorf-Oberkassel, Germany

Henze, Hans Werner — *Composer, Conductor*
Weihergarten 1-5, 55116 Mainz, Germany

Hepburn, Katharine — *Actress*
350 5th Ave, #5019, New York, NY 10118, USA

Heppel, Leon A — *Biochemist*
%Cornell University, Biochemistry Dept, Ithaca, NY 14850, USA

Herb, Raymond G — *Physicist*
RR 1, Box 223-A, Middleton, WI 53704, USA

Herbert (Mr Wizard), Don — *Educator*
%"Mr Wizard's World" Show, PO Box 83, Canoga Park, CA 91305, USA

Herbert of Hemingford, Nicholas — *Publisher*
The Old Rectory, Hemingford Abbots, Huntington Cambs PE18 9AN, England

Herbert, Gavin S, Jr	*Businessman*
%Allergan Inc, 2525 Dupont Dr, Irvine, CA 92612, USA	
Herbert, Michael K	*Editor*
990 Grove St, Evanston, IL 60201, USA	
Herbert, Raymond E (Ray)	*Baseball Player*
9360 Taylors Turn, Stanwood, AL 35901, USA	
Herbert, Walter W (Wally)	*Explorer*
Old Vicarage, Vicarage Road, Stoke Gabriel, Devon TQ9 6QP, England	
Herbig, George H	*Astronomer*
%University of Hawaii, Astronomy Institute, 2680 Woodlawn Dr, Honolulu, HI 96822, USA	
Herbig, Gunther	*Conductor*
%Toronto Symphony, 60 Simcoe St, #C-116, Toronto ON MJ5 2H5, Canada	
Herd, Richard	*Actor*
4610 Worsten Ave, Sherman Oaks, CA 91423, USA	
Herda, Frank A	*Vietnam War Army Hero (CMH)*
PO Box 34239, Cleveland, OH 44134, USA	
Herincx, Raimund	*Opera Singer*
Monks' Vineyard, Larkbarrow, Shepton Mallet, Somerset BA4 4NR, England	
Herman (Paul Reubens), Pee Wee	*Actor*
PO Box 29373, Los Angeles, CA 90029, USA	
Herman, Alexis	*Secretary, Labor*
%Labor Department, 200 Constitution Ave NW, Washington, DC 20210, USA	
Herman, David J	*Businessman*
%Adam Opel AG, Bahnhofplatz 1, 65429 Russelsheim, Germany	
Herman, George E	*Commentator*
4500 "Q" Lane NW, Washington, DC 20007, USA	
Herman, Jerry	*Composer, Lyricist*
10847 Bellagio Road, Los Angeles, CA 90077, USA	
Hermann, Allen M	*Physicist*
2704 Lookout View Dr, Golden, CO 80401, USA	
Hermann, Mark	*Football Player*
8525 Tidewater Dr W, Indianapolis, IN 46236, USA	
Hermaszewski, Miroslav	*Cosmonaut, Poland; Air Force General*
Ul Czeczota 25, 02-650 Warsaw, Poland	
Hermlin, Stephan	*Writer*
Hermann-Hesse-Str 39, 13156 Berlin, Germany	
Hermon, John C	*Law Enforcement Official*
Warren Road, Donaghadee, County Down, Northern Ireland	
Herms, George	*Sculptor*
%Jack Rutberg Fine Arts, 357 N La Brea Ave, Los Angeles, CA 90036, USA	
Hern, Dick	*Thoroughbred Racing Trainer*
%West Ilsley Stables, West Ilsley, Newbury Berks RG16 0AE, England	
Hernandez Colon, Rafael	*Govenor, PR*
La Fortaleza, PO Box 82, Trujillo Alto, PR 00977, USA	
Hernandez, Amalia	*Dancer, Choreographer*
%Ballet Folklorico de Mexico, Palace of Belle Artes, Mexico City DF, Mexic	
Hernandez, Genaro	*Boxer*
24442 Ferrocarril, Mission Viejo, CA 92691, USA	
Hernandez, Guillermo (Willie)	*Baseball Player*
Bo Espina, Calle C Buzon 125, Aguada, PR 00602, USA	
Hernandez, Keith	*Baseball Player*
255 E 49th St, #28-D, New York, NY 10017, USA	
Hernandez, Manny	*Businessman*
%Cypress Semiconductor Corp, 3901 N 1st St, San Jose, CA 95134, USA	
Hernandez, Rodolfo P	*Korean War Army Hero (CMH)*
5328 Bluewater Place, College Lakes, Fayetteville, NC 28311, USA	
Herndon, Ty	*Singer*
%Image Mgmt, 1009 16th Ave S, Nashville, TN 37212, USA	
Heron, Patrick	*Artist*
Eagles Nest, Zennor near St Ives, Cornwall, England	
Herr, John C	*Immunologist*
%University of Virginia, Med Center, Immunology Dept, Charlottesville, VA 22903, USA	
Herr, Richard D	*Coast Guard Admiral*
%Vice Commandant's Office, USCG, 2100 2nd St SW, Washington, DC 20593, USA	
Herr, Thomas M (Tommy)	*Baseball Player*
1077 Olde Forge Crossing, Lancaster, PA 17601, USA	
Herrera, Carolina	*Fashion Designer*
%Carolina Herrera Ltd, 501 7th Ave, #1700, New York, NY 10018, USA	

H

Herbert - Herrera

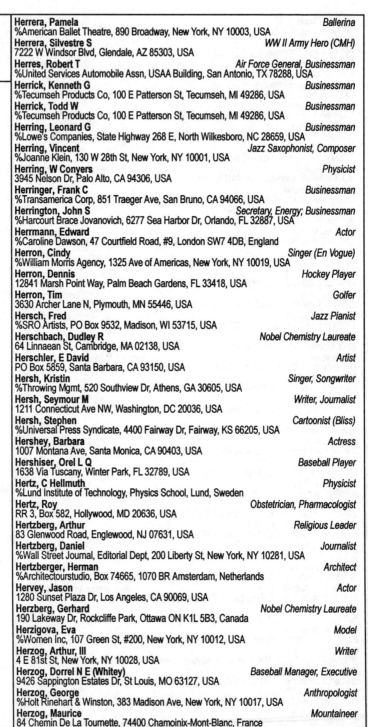

H

Herrera - Herzog

Herrera, Pamela *Ballerina*
%American Ballet Theatre, 890 Broadway, New York, NY 10003, USA

Herrera, Silvestre S *WW II Army Hero (CMH)*
7222 W Windsor Blvd, Glendale, AZ 85303, USA

Herres, Robert T *Air Force General, Businessman*
%United Services Automobile Assn, USAA Building, San Antonio, TX 78288, USA

Herrick, Kenneth G *Businessman*
%Tecumseh Products Co, 100 E Patterson St, Tecumseh, MI 49286, USA

Herrick, Todd W *Businessman*
%Tecumseh Products Co, 100 E Patterson St, Tecumseh, MI 49286, USA

Herring, Leonard G *Businessman*
%Lowe's Companies, State Highway 268 E, North Wilkesboro, NC 28659, USA

Herring, Vincent *Jazz Saxophonist, Composer*
%Joanne Klein, 130 W 28th St, New York, NY 10001, USA

Herring, W Conyers *Physicist*
3945 Nelson Dr, Palo Alto, CA 94306, USA

Herringer, Frank C *Businessman*
%Transamerica Corp, 851 Traeger Ave, San Bruno, CA 94066, USA

Herrington, John S *Secretary, Energy; Businessman*
%Harcourt Brace Jovanovich, 6277 Sea Harbor Dr, Orlando, FL 32887, USA

Herrmann, Edward *Actor*
%Caroline Dawson, 47 Courtfield Road, #9, London SW7 4DB, England

Herron, Cindy *Singer (En Vogue)*
%William Morris Agency, 1325 Ave of Americas, New York, NY 10019, USA

Herron, Dennis *Hockey Player*
12841 Marsh Point Way, Palm Beach Gardens, FL 33418, USA

Herron, Tim *Golfer*
3630 Archer Lane N, Plymouth, MN 55446, USA

Hersch, Fred *Jazz Pianist*
%SRO Artists, PO Box 9532, Madison, WI 53715, USA

Herschbach, Dudley R *Nobel Chemistry Laureate*
64 Linnaean St, Cambridge, MA 02138, USA

Herschler, E David *Artist*
PO Box 5859, Santa Barbara, CA 93150, USA

Hersh, Kristin *Singer, Songwriter*
%Throwing Mgmt, 520 Southview Dr, Athens, GA 30605, USA

Hersh, Seymour M *Writer, Journalist*
1211 Connecticut Ave NW, Washington, DC 20036, USA

Hersh, Stephen *Cartoonist (Bliss)*
%Universal Press Syndicate, 4400 Fairway Dr, Fairway, KS 66205, USA

Hershey, Barbara *Actress*
1007 Montana Ave, Santa Monica, CA 90403, USA

Hershiser, Orel L Q *Baseball Player*
1638 Via Tuscany, Winter Park, FL 32789, USA

Hertz, C Hellmuth *Physicist*
%Lund Institute of Technology, Physics School, Lund, Sweden

Hertz, Roy *Obstetrician, Pharmacologist*
RR 3, Box 582, Hollywood, MD 20636, USA

Hertzberg, Arthur *Religious Leader*
83 Glenwood Road, Englewood, NJ 07631, USA

Hertzberg, Daniel *Journalist*
%Wall Street Journal, Editorial Dept, 200 Liberty St, New York, NY 10281, USA

Hertzberger, Herman *Architect*
%Architectourstudio, Box 74665, 1070 BR Amsterdam, Netherlands

Hervey, Jason *Actor*
1280 Sunset Plaza Dr, Los Angeles, CA 90069, USA

Herzberg, Gerhard *Nobel Chemistry Laureate*
190 Lakeway Dr, Rockcliffe Park, Ottawa ON K1L 5B3, Canada

Herzigova, Eva *Model*
%Women Inc, 107 Green St, #200, New York, NY 10012, USA

Herzog, Arthur, III *Writer*
4 E 81st St, New York, NY 10028, USA

Herzog, Dorrel N E (Whitey) *Baseball Manager, Executive*
9426 Sappington Estates Dr, St Louis, MO 63127, USA

Herzog, George *Anthropologist*
%Holt Rinehart & Winston, 383 Madison Ave, New York, NY 10017, USA

Herzog, Maurice *Mountaineer*
84 Chemin De La Tournette, 74400 Chamoinix-Mont-Blanc, France

Herzog, Roman *President, Germany*
%President's Office, Kaiser-Friederich-Str 16, 53113 Bonn, Germany
Herzog, Werner *Movie Director*
%Herzog Film Productions, Turkenstr 91, 80799 Munich, Germany
Hesburgh, Theodore M *Educator*
%University of Notre Dame, Hesburgh Library, Notre Dame IN 46556, USA
Heseltine, Michael R D *Government Official, England*
Thenford House, near Banbury, Oxon OX17 2BX, England
Hess, Erika *Skier*
Aeschi, 6388 Gratenort, Switzerland
Hess, Leon *Businessman, Football Executive*
%Amerada Hess, 1185 Ave of Americas, New York, NY 10036, USA
Hesseman, Howard *Actor*
7146 La Pesa Dr, Los Angeles, CA 90068, USA
Hessler, Curtis A *Publisher*
%Times-Mirror Co, Times-Mirror Square, Los Angeles, CA 90053, USA
Hessler, Robert R *Oceanographer*
%Scripps Institute of Oceanography, Biodiversity Dept, La Jolla, CA 92037, USA
Heston, Charlton *Actor*
2859 Coldwater Canyon, Beverly Hills, CA 90210, USA
Hetfield, James *Singer, Guitarist (Metallica)*
%Q Prime Inc, 729 7th Ave, #1400, New York, NY 10019, USA
Hetrick, Jennifer *Actress*
2510 Canyon Dr, Los Angeles, CA 90068, USA
Hettich, Arthur M *Editor*
606 Shore Acres Dr, Mamaroneck, NY 10543, USA
Hetzel, Fred *Basketball Player*
218 Cornwall St NW, Leesburg, VA 20176, USA
Heuga, Jimmie *Skier*
%Jimmie Heuga Health Center, PO Box 5480, Avon, CO 81620, USA
Hewett, Christopher *Actor*
1422 N Sweetzer Ave, #110, Los Angeles, CA 90069, USA
Hewish, Anthony *Nobel Physics Laureate*
Pryor's Cottage, Kingston, Cambridge CB3 7NQ, England
Hewitt, Bob *Tennis Player*
%Pender Sports Corp, 29 Tower Road, Newton, MA 02164, USA
Hewitt, Don S *Television Producer*
%"Sixty Minutes" Show, CBS-TV, 555 W 57th St, New York, NY 10019, USA
Hewlett, William R *Inventor (Oscillarion Generator)*
%Hewlett-Packard Co, 3000 Hanover St, Palo Alto, CA 94304, USA
Hewson, John *Government Official, Australia*
%Parliament House, Canberra ACT 2600, Australia
Hextall, Dennis *Hockey Player*
2631 Harvest Hills Dr, Brighton, MI 48114, USA
Hextall, Ron *Hockey Player*
%Philadelphia Flyers, CoreStates Center, Pattison Place, Philadelphia, PA 19148, USA
Hey, J Stanley *Astronomer*
4 Shortlands Close, Eastbourne, East Sussex BN22 0JE, England
Heyerdahl, Thor *Explorer, Anthropologist*
Guimar, Tenerife, Canary Islands, Spain
Heyman, I Michael *Association Executive, Educator*
%Smithsonian Institution, 1000 Jefferson Dr SW, Washington, DC 20560, USA
Heyman, Richard *Geneticist*
%Ligand Pharmaceuticals, 9393 Town Center Dr, #100, San Diego, CA 92121, USA
Heyman, Samuel J *Businessman*
%GAF Corp, 1361 Alps Road, Wayne, NJ 07470, USA
Heyssel, Robert M *Physician*
230 Stoney Run Lane, Baltimore, MD 21210, USA
Heywood, Andrew *Television Producer*
%CBS-TV, News Dept, 51 W 52nd St, New York, NY 10019, USA
Heywood, Anne *Actress*
9966 Liebe Dr, Beverly Hills, CA 90210, USA
Hiassen, Carl *Writer, Journalist*
%Alfred A Knopf, 201 E 50th St, New York, NY 10022, USA
Hiatt, Andrew *Molecular Biologist*
%Scripps Research Foundation, 10666 N Torrey Pines Road, La Jolla, CA 92037, USA
Hiatt, John *Singer, Songwriter*
%Metropolitan Entertainment, 2 Penn Plaza, #2600, New York, NY 10121, USA

Hibbard, Dwight H — *Businessman*
%Cincinnati Bell, 201 E 4th St, Cincinnati, OH 45202, USA

Hibbler, Al — *Singer*
%Johnnie Martinelli, 888 8th Ave, New York, NY 10019, USA

Hick, Graeme A — *Cricketer*
%Worcestershire County Cricket Club, New Road, Worcester, England

Hickcox, Charlie — *Swimmer*
8315 Redfield Road, Scottsdale, AZ 85260, USA

Hicke, Bill — *Hockey Player*
20 Lancaster Place, Regina SK S4S 2Z4, Canada

Hickel, Walter J — *Secretary, Interior; Governor, AK*
935 W 5th Ave, Anchorage, AK 99501, USA

Hickey, James A Cardinal — *Religious Leader*
%Archdiocesan Pastoral Center, 5002 Eastern Ave, Washington, DC 20017, USA

Hickey, Maurice — *Publisher*
%Denver Post, 650 15th St, Denver, CO 80202, USA

Hickland, Catherine — *Actress*
247 S Beverly Dr, #102, Beverly Hills, CA 90212, USA

Hickman, Dwayne — *Actor*
812 16th St, #1, Santa Monica, CA 90403, USA

Hickman, Fred — *Sportscaster*
%Cable News Network, News Dept, 1050 Techwood Dr NW, Atlanta, GA 30318, USA

Hickox, Richard S — *Conductor*
35 Ellington St, London N7 8PN, England

Hicks, Catherine — *Actress*
15422 Brownwood Place, Los Angeles, CA 90077, USA

Hicks, Dan — *Sportscaster*
%NBC-TV, Sports Dept, 30 Rockefeller Plaza, New York, NY 10112, USA

Hicks, Dan — *Singer*
%CT Mgmt, PO Box 5481, Mill Valley, CA 94942, USA

Hicks, John — *Football Player*
3287 Green Cook Road, Johnstown, OH 43031, USA

Hicks, John — *Jazz Pianist*
%John Penny Enterprises, 484 Lexington St, Waltham, MA 02154, USA

Hicks, Scott — *Movie Director*
%Creative Artists Agency, 9830 Wilshire Blvd, Beverly Hills, CA 90212, USA

Hicks, Scottie B — *Labor Leader*
%National Rural Letter Carriers Assn, 1630 Duke St, Alexandria, VA 22314, USA

Hickson, Joan — *Actress*
%Plunket Greene, 21 Golden Square, London W1R 3PA, England

Hidalgo, John — *Government Official*
%Mays Valentine Davenport Moore, 1899 "L" St NW, Washington, DC 20036, USA

Hieb, Richard J — *Astronaut*
%Allied Signal Technical Services, 7515 Mission Dr, Lanham, MD 20706, USA

Hiebert, Erwin N — *Writer, Historian*
40 Payson Road, Belmont, MA 02178, USA

Hier, Marvin — *Religious Leader, Social Activist*
%Simon Wiesenthal Holocaust Center, 9766 W Pico Blvd, Los Angeles, CA 90035, USA

Hieronymus, Clara W — *Journalist*
1011 Spring St, Savannah, TN 38372, USA

Higdon, Bruce — *Cartoonist*
2631 Birdsong Ave, Murfreesboro, TN 37129, USA

Higdon, Ernest D — *Labor Leader*
%Coopers International Union, 400 Sherburn Lane, #207, Louisville, KY 40207, USA

Higgins, Bertie — *Singer, Songwriter*
%Miles Bell, 707 18th Ave S, Nashville, TN 37203, USA

Higgins, Chester, Jr — *Photographer*
%New York Times, Editorial Dept, 229 W 43rd St, New York, NY 10036, USA

Higgins, George G — *Religious Leader*
%Catholic University of America, Curley Hall, Washington, DC 20064, USA

Higgins, George V — *Writer*
15 Brush Hill Lane, Milton, MA 02186, USA

Higgins, Jack — *Editorial Cartoonist*
%Chicago Sun-Times, Editorial Dept, 401 N Wabash Ave, Chicago, IL 60611, USA

Higgins, Jack — *Writer*
September Tide, Mont de la Roque, Jersey, Channel Islands, England

Higgins, Joel — *Actor*
5008 Sanlo Place, Woodland Hills, CA 91364, USA

Higgins, John — Swimmer, Swimming Coach
40 Williams Dr, Annapolis, MD 21401, USA

Higgins, Stephen E — Law Enforcement Official
%Alcohol Tobacco Firearms Bureau, 650 Massachusetts NW, Washington, DC 20001, USA

Higginson, John — Pathologist
9650 Rockville Pike, Bethesda, MD 20814, USA

Higham, John — Historian
309 Tuscany Road, Baltimore, MD 21210, USA

Hightower, John B — Museum Director
101 Museum Parkway, Newport News, VA 23606, USA

Higuera, Teodoro V — Baseball Player
%Milwaukee Brewers, County Stadium, 201 S 46th St, Milwaukee, WI 53214, USA

Hijikata, Takeshi — Businessman
%Sumitomo Chemical, 5-33-4 Kitahama, Chuoku, Osaka 541, Japan

Hijuelos, Oscar — Writer
%Hofstra University, English Dept, 10000 Fulton Ave, Hempstead, NY 11550, USA

Hilbe, Alfred J — Head of Government, Liechtenstein
9494 Schaan, Garsill 11, Liechtenstein

Hilbert, Stephen C — Businessman
%Conseco, PO Box 1911, Carmel, IN 46032, USA

Hildegarde — Singer
230 E 48th St, New York, NY 10017, USA

Hildreth, Eugene A — Physician
%Reading Hospital/Medical Center, PO Box 16052, Reading, PA 19612, USA

Hilfiger, Tommy — Fashion Designer
%Tommy Hilfiger USA, 25 W 39th St, #1300, New York, NY 10018, USA

Hilgard, Ernest R — Psychologist
850 Webster St, #518, Palo Alto, CA 94301, USA

Hilgenberg, Jay — Football Player
1296 Kimmer Court, Lake Forest, IL 60045, USA

Hilger, Rusty — Football Player
1145 SW 78th Terrace, Oklahoma City, OK 73139, USA

Hilger, Wolfgang — Businessman
%Hoechst AG, Postfach 800320, 65903 Frankfurt, Germany

Hill of Luton, Baron — Government Official, Journalist
5 Bamville Wood, East Common, Harpenden, Herts, England

Hill Smith, Marilyn — Opera Singer
%Music International, 13 Ardilaun Road, Highbury, London N5 2QR, England

Hill, A Alan — Government Official
102 Coleman Dr, San Rafael, CA 94901, USA

Hill, A Derek — Artist
%National Art Collections Fund, 20 John Islip St, London SW1, England

Hill, Anita — Educator
%Oklahoma University, Law School, Norman, OK 73069, USA

Hill, Arthur — Actor
1515 Club View Dr, Los Angeles, CA 90024, USA

Hill, Brian — Basketball Coach
%Vancouver Grizzlies, 288 Beatty St, #300, Vancouver BC V6B 2M1, Canada

Hill, Calvin — Football Player, Executive
%Dallas Cowboys, 1 Cowboys Parkway, Irving, TX 75063, USA

Hill, Damon — Auto Racing Driver
PO Box 100, Nelson, Lanscashire BB9 8AQ, England

Hill, Dan — Singer, Songwriter
%Paquin Entertainment, 1067 Sherwin Road, Winnipeg MB R3H 0TB, Canada

Hill, Daniel W (Dan) — Football Player
171 Montrose Dr, Dunbarton, Durham, NC 27707, USA

Hill, Dave — Golfer
%Eddie Elias Enterprises, 1720 Merriman Road, #5118, Akron, OH 44313, USA

Hill, Draper — Editorial Cartoonist
368 Washington Road, Grosse Pointe, MI 48230, USA

Hill, Drew — Football Player
37 Westgate Park Lane, Newnan, GA 30263, USA

Hill, Dusty — Singer, Bassist (ZZ Top)
%Lone Wolf Mgmt, PO Box 163690, Austin, TX 78716, USA

Hill, Faith — Singer
480 Glen Arbor Circle, Cordova, TN 38018, USA

Hill, Gary — Artist
%Cornish College of the Arts Galleries, 710 E Roy St, Seattle, WA 98102, USA

H

Higgins - Hill

	Hill, George Roy	*Movie Director*
	%Pan Arts Productions, 59 E 54th St, #73, New York, NY 10022, USA	
	Hill, Grant	*Basketball Player*
	10300 Walker Lake Dr, Great Falls, VA 22066, USA	
	Hill, Jesse	*Singer*
	1210 Caffin Ave, New Orleans, LA 70117, USA	

Hill, George Roy — *Movie Director*
%Pan Arts Productions, 59 E 54th St, #73, New York, NY 10022, USA

Hill, Grant — *Basketball Player*
10300 Walker Lake Dr, Great Falls, VA 22066, USA

Hill, Jesse — *Singer*
1210 Caffin Ave, New Orleans, LA 70117, USA

Hill, Jim — *Sportscaster*
%ABC-TV, Sports Dept, 77 W 66th St, New York, NY 10023, USA

Hill, Kent A — *Football Player*
630 Hawthorne Place, Fayetteville, GA 30214, USA

Hill, Lauryn — *Rap Artist (The Fugees)*
%Writers & Artists, 924 Westwood Blvd, #900, Los Angeles, CA 90024, USA

Hill, Phil — *Auto Racing Driver*
266 20th St, Santa Monica, CA 90402, USA

Hill, Richard — *Businessman*
%Novellus Systems, 5790 N 1st St, San Jose, CA 94134, USA

Hill, Robert L — *Biochemist*
%Duke University, Medical Center, Biochemistry Dept, Durham, NC 27710, USA

Hill, Ron — *Track Athlete*
PO Box 11, Hyde, Cheshire SK14 1RD, England

Hill, Steven — *Actor*
18 Jill Lane, Monsey, NY 10952, USA

Hill, Susan E — *Writer*
Longmoor Farmhouse, Ebrington, Chipping Campden, Glos GL55 6NW, England

Hill, Terence — *Actor*
%Nobody Inc, 200 W DeVargas, #1, Santa Fe, NM 87501, USA

Hill, Terrell L — *Biophysicist, Chemist*
433 Logan St, Santa Cruz, CA 95062, USA

Hill, Thomas (Tom) — *Track Athlete*
428 Elmcrest Dr, Norman, OK 73071, USA

Hill, Virgil — *Boxer*
117 Santa Gertrudis Dr, Bismarck, ND 58501, USA

Hill, Virgil L, Jr — *Navy Admiral*
14 Fariston Road, Wayne, PA 19087, USA

Hill, Walter — *Movie Director*
836 Greenway Dr, Beverly Hills, CA 90210, USA

Hill-Norton, Peter J — *Navy Fleet Admiral, England*
Cass Cottage, Hyde, Fordingbridge, Hampshire, England

Hillaby, John — *Writer*
%Constable Co, Lanchesters, 102 Fulham Palace Road, London W6 9ER, England

Hillary, Edmund P — *Mountaineer, Explorer*
278-A Remuera Road, Auckland SE2, New Zealand

Hille, Einar — *Mathematician*
8862 La Jolla Scenic Dr N, La Jolla, CA 92037, USA

Hillebrecht, Rudolf F H — *Architect*
Gneiststr 7, 30169 Hanover, Germany

Hillel, Shlomo — *Government Official, Israel*
%Knesset, Jerusalem, Israel

Hilleman, Maurice R — *Virologist*
%Merck Institute for Therapeutic Research, West Point, PA 19486, USA

Hillenbrand, Daniel A — *Businessman*
%Hillenbrand Industries, 700 State Rt 46 E, Batesville, IN 47006, USA

Hillenbrand, Martin J — *Diplomat*
%University of Georgia, Global Policy Studies Center, Athens, GA 30602, USA

Hillenbrand, W August — *Businessman*
%Hillenbrand Industries, 700 State Rt 46 E, Batesville, IN 47006, USA

Hiller, Arthur — *Movie Director*
1218 Benedict Canyon, Beverly Hills, CA 90210, USA

Hiller, Susan — *Artist*
%Gimpel Fils, 30 Davies St, London W1, England

Hiller, Wendy — *Actress*
Spindles, Stratton Road, Beaconsfield, Bucks, England

Hillerman, John — *Actor*
PO Box 218, Blue Jay, CA 92317, USA

Hillerman, Tony — *Writer*
1632 Francisca Road NW, Albuquerque, NM 87107, USA

Hillery, Patrick J — *President, Ireland*
Grasmere, Greenfield Road, Sutton, Dublin 13, Ireland

Hill - Hillery

Hillier, James — *Inventor (Electron Lens Corrector)*
22 Arreton Road, Princeton, NJ 08540, USA

Hillis, W Daniel (Danny) — *Computer Scientist*
%Thinking Machines Corp, 14 Crosby Dr, Bedford, MA 01730, USA

Hillman, Chris — *Singer, Bassist (The Byrds), Songwriter*
PO Box 729, Ojai, CA 93024, USA

Hills, Carla A — *Secretary, Housing & Urban Development*
%Hills Co, 1200 19th St NW, Washington, DC 20036, USA

Hills, Lee — *Publisher, Editor*
%Knight-Ridder Newspapers, 1 Herald Plaza, Miami, FL 33132, USA

Hills, Roderick M — *Government Official*
%Mudge Rose Guthrie Alexander Ferdon, 1200 19th St NW, Washington, DC 20036, USA

Hilmers, David C — *Astronaut*
18502 Point Lookout Dr, Houston, TX 77058, USA

Hilsman, Roger — *Diplomat*
251 Hamburg Cove, Lyme, CT 06371, USA

Hilton, Barron — *Businessman*
%Hilton Hotels Corp, 9336 Civic Center Dr, Beverly Hills, CA 90210, USA

Hilton, Janet — *Concert Clarinetist*
Holly House, East Downs Road, Bowdon, Altrincham, Cheshire WA14 2LH, Engla

Himmelfarb, Gertrude — *Writer, Historian*
%City University of New York, Graduate School, New York, NY 10036, USA

Hinault, Bernard — *Cyclist*
Ouest Levure, 7 Rue de la Sauvaie, 21 Sud-Est, 35000 Rennes, France

Hinckley, Gordon B — *Religious Leader*
%Church of Latter Day Saints, 50 E North Temple, Salt Lake City, UT 84150, USA

Hindman, Earl — *Actor*
%"Home Improvment" Show, Disney TV, 500 S Buena Vista St, Burbank, CA 91521, USA

Hinds, Bruce J — *Test Pilot*
5915 Alleppo Lane, Palmdale, CA 93551, USA

Hinds, Samuel A A — *President, Guyana*
%Prime Minister's Office, Public Buildings, Georgetown, Guyana

Hinds, William E — *Cartoonist (Tank McNamara)*
1301 Spring Oaks Circle, Houston, TX 77055, USA

Hine, Maynard K — *Dentist*
1121 W Michigan St, Indianapolis, IN 46202, USA

Hine, Patrick — *Royal Air Force Marshal, England*
%Lloyd's Bank, Cox's & Kings, 7 Pall Mall, London SW1 5NA, England

Hiner, Glen H — *Businessman*
%Owens-Corning Fiberglas, Fiberglas Tower, Toledo, OH 43659, USA

Hines, Gregory — *Dancer, Actor*
377 W 11th St, #PH, New York, NY 10014, USA

Hines, Jerome — *Opera Singer*
%Shaw Concerts, Lincoln Center Plaza, 1900 Broadway, #200, New York, NY 10023, USA

Hines, Patrick — *Actor*
46 W 95th St, New York, NY 10025, USA

Hingis, Martina — *Tennis Player*
Seidenbaum, 9477 Trubbach, Sweden

Hingle, Pat — *Actor*
PO Box 2228, Carolina Beach, NC 28428, USA

Hingsen, Jurgen — *Track Athlete*
655 Circle Dr, Santa Barbara, CA 93108, USA

Hino, Kazuyoshi — *Fashion Designer*
%Hino & Malee Inc, 3701 N Ravenswood Ave, Chicago, IL 60613, USA

Hinojosa, Ricardo H — *Judge*
%US District Court, PO Box 5007, McAllen, TX 78502, USA

Hinojosa, Tish — *Singer, Songwriter*
%Craig Barker Mgmt, 2712 Sherwood Lane, Austin, TX 78704, USA

Hinshaw, Horton C — *Physician*
400 Deer Valley Road, #41, San Rafael, CA 94903, USA

Hinson, Larry — *Golfer*
RR 4, Box 397, Douglas, GA 31533, USA

Hinson, Roy — *Basketball Player*
4272 State Highway 27, Monmouth Junction, NJ 08852, USA

Hinson, Walter F, III — *Financier*
%Coral Gables Federal Savings, PO Box 1000, Pompano Beach, FL 33061, USA

Hinton of Bankside, Christopher — *Government Official, England; Engineer*
Tiverton Lodge, Dulwich Common, London SG2 7EW, England

H

Hillier - Hinton of Bankside

Hinton, Christopher J (Chris)	*Football Player*
5136 Falcon Chase Lane, Atlanta, GA 30342, USA	
Hinton, Leslie F	*Television Executive*
%Fox Television Stations, 5746 Sunset Blvd, Los Angeles, CA 90028, USA	
Hinton, Milton J (Judge)	*Jazz Bassist*
%Thomas Cassidy, 0366 Horseshoe Dr, Basalt, CO 81621, USA	
Hinton, S E	*Writer*
%Delacorte Press, 1540 Broadway, New York, NY 10036, USA	
Hinton, Sam	*Singer, Songwriter*
9420 La Jolla Shores Dr, La Jolla, CA 92037, USA	
Hiort, Esbjorn	*Architect*
%Bel Colles Farm, Parkvej 6, 2960 Rungsted Kyst, Denmark	
Hird, Thora	*Actress*
Old Loft, 21 Leinster Mews, Lancaster Gate, London W2 3EX, England	
Hiro, Keitaro	*Businessman*
%Kubota Ltd, 2-47 Shikitsuhigashi, Naniwaku, Osaka 556, Japan	
Hirsch, Elroy (Crazy Legs)	*Football Player*
50 Oak Creek Trail, Madison, WI 53717, USA	
Hirsch, Gary D	*Businessman*
%Penn Traffic Co, 1200 State Fair Blvd, Syracuse, NY 13209, USA	
Hirsch, Judd	*Actor*
888 7th Ave, #602, New York, NY 10106, USA	
Hirsch, Laurence E	*Businessman*
%Centex Corp, PO Box 199000, Dallas, TX 75219, USA	
Hirsch, Leon C	*Businessman*
%US Surgical Corp, 150 Glover Ave, Norwalk, CT 06850, USA	
Hirschfeld, Albert (Al)	*Artist, Illustrator*
122 E 95th St, New York, NY 10128, USA	
Hirschfield, Gerald J	*Cinematographer*
425 Ashland St, Ashland, OR 97520, USA	
Hirschmann, Ralph F	*Chemist*
740 Palmer Place, Blue Bell, PA 19422, USA	
Hirst, Damien	*Sculptor*
%Gagosian Gallery, 980 Madison Ave, #PH, New York, NY 10021, USA	
Hirt, Al	*Jazz Trumpeter*
1920 Frankel Ave, Metairie, LA 70003, USA	
Hirt, F William	*Businessman*
%Erie Insurance Group, 100 Erie Insurance Place, Erie, PA 16530, USA	
Hisle, Larry E	*Baseball Player*
312 Saddleworth Court W, Mequon, WI 53092, USA	
Hitchcock, Ken	*Hockey Coach*
%Dallas Stars, StarCenter, 211 Cowboys Parkway, Dallas, TX 75063, USA	
Hitchcock, Russell	*Singer (Air Supply)*
PO Box 25909, Los Angeles, CA 90025, USA	
Hitchings, George H	*Nobel Medicine Laureate*
%Burroughs Wellcome Co, PO Box 13398, Research Triangle, NC 27709, USA	
Hite, Ronald V (Ron)	*Army General*
Deputy Director, Acquisition Corps, HqUSA, Pentagon, Washington, DC 20310, USA	
Hite, Shere D	*Writer*
PO Box 1037, New York, NY 10028, USA	
Hitt, John C	*Educator*
%University of Central Florida, President's Office, Orlando, FL 32816, USA	
Hix, Charles	*Fashion Expert, Writer*
%Simon & Schuster, 1230 Ave of Americas, New York, NY 10020, USA	
Hlass, I Jerry	*Aeronautical Engineer*
%National Space Technology Laboratories, NSTL Station, MS 39529, USA	
Hlinka, Nichol	*Ballerina*
%New York City Ballet, Lincoln Center Plaza, New York, NY 10023, USA	
Hnatyshyn, Ramon J	*Governor General, Canada*
724 Saskatchewan Crescent East, Saskatoon SK S7N 0L2, Canada	
Ho, David	*Medical Researcher*
%Aaron Diamond AIDS Research Center, 455 1st Ave, New York, NY 10016, USA	
Ho, Donald T (Don)	*Singer*
277 Lewers St, Honolulu, HI 96815, USA	
Ho, Tao	*Architect*
Upper Deck, North Point West, Passenger Ferry Pier, North Point, Hong Kong	
Ho, Ya-Ming	*Biochemist*
%Massachusetts Institute of Technology, Biology Dept, Cambridge, MA 02139, USA	

Hoag, Charles — *Basketball Player*
2927 SW Foxcroft Court, #2, Topeka, KS 66614, USA

Hoag, David H — *Businessman*
%LTV Corp, 200 Public Square, Cleveland, OH 44114, USA

Hoag, Peter C — *Test Pilot*
%McDonnell Douglas, M/C 1064850, PO Box 516, St Louis, MO 63166, USA

Hoagland, Edward — *Writer*
RR 1, Box 2977, Bennington, VT 05201, USA

Hoagland, Jimmie L (Jim) — *Journalist*
%Washington Post, Editorial Dept, 1150 15th St NW, Washington, DC 20071, USA

Hoagland, Mahlon B — *Biochemist*
Academy Road, Thetford, VT 05074, USA

Hoaglin, Fred — *Football Player, Coach*
4308 Hanover Park Dr, Jacksonville, FL 32224, USA

Hoar, Joseph P — *Marine Corps General*
%Commander, US Central Command, MacDill Air Force Base, FL 33621, USA

Hoban, Russell C — *Writer*
%David Higham, Golden Square, 5-8 Lower John St, London W1R 4HA, England

Hobart, Nick — *Cartoonist*
133 Indiana Ave, New Port Richey, FL 33552, USA

Hobbs, Becky — *Singer*
%Gratton Stephens, 9 Music Square S, #231, Nashville, TN 37203, USA

Hobbs, Franklin (Fritz) — *Rower*
151 E 79th St, New York, NY 10021, USA

Hobson, Allan — *Neuroscientist*
%Harvard University, Sleep Laboratory, Cambridge, MA 02138, USA

Hobson, Clell L (Butch) — *Baseball Player, Manager*
5415 Nelson Road, Fairhope, AL 36532, USA

Hobson, Valerie — *Writer*
Old Barn Cottage, Upton Grey, Basinstoke, Hampshire RG25 2RM, England

Hoch, Scott — *Golfer*
8800 Lake Sheen Court, Orlando, FL 32836, USA

Hochhuth, Rolf — *Writer*
PO Box 661, 4002 Basel, Switzerland

Hochstrasser, Robin M — *Chemist*
%University of Pennsylvania, Chemistry Dept, Philadelphia, PA 19104, USA

Hock, Dee Ward — *Businessman*
%Visa International, 900 Metro Center Blvd, Foster City, CA 94404, USA

Hockaday, Irvine O, Jr — *Businessman*
%Hallmark Cards, 2501 McGee St, Kansas City, MO 64108, USA

Hockenberry, John — *Commentator*
%"Day One" Show, 147 Columbus Ave, New York, NY 10023, USA

Hockett, Charles F — *Anthropologist*
145 N Sunset Dr, Ithaca, NY 14850, USA

Hockney, David — *Artist*
7508 Santa Monica Blvd, Los Angeles, CA 90046, USA

Hodder, Kenneth — *Religious Leader*
%Salvation Army, 615 Slaters Lane, Alexandria, VA 22314, USA

Hodder, William A — *Businessman*
%Donaldson Co, 1400 W 94th St, Minneapolis, MN 55431, USA

Hoddinott, Alun — *Composer*
86 Mill Road, Lisvane, Cardiff CF4 5UG, Wales

Hodel, Donald P — *Secretary, Energy; Labor*
%Christian Coalition, 100 Venterville Turnpike, Virginia Beach, VA 23463, USA

Hodge, Charlie — *Hockey Player*
19856 44th St, Langley BC V3A 3E2, Canada

Hodge, Kate — *Actress*
%J Michael Bloom, 9255 Sunset Blvd, #710, Los Angeles, CA 90069, USA

Hodge, Ken, Sr — *Hockey Player*
1115 Main St, Lynnfield, MA 01940, USA

Hodges, Bill — *Basketball Coach*
%Georgia College, Athletic Dept, Milledgeville, GA 31061, USA

Hodges, Carl N — *Environmental Scientist*
%University of Arizona, Environmental Research Laboratory, Tucson, AZ 85721, USA

Hodges, Mike — *Movie Director*
Wesley Farm, Durweston, Blanford Forum, Dorset DT11 0QG, England

Hodges, Robert H, Jr — *Judge*
%US Claims Court, 717 Madison Place NW, Washington, DC 20005, USA

Hodgkin, Alan Lloyd *Nobel Medicine Laureate*
%Cambridge University, Physiology Lab, Downing St, Cambridge, England
Hodgkin, Howard *Artist*
32 Coptic St, London WC1, England
Hodgson, James D *Secretary, Labor*
10132 Hillgrove Dr, Beverly Hills, CA 90210, USA
Hodgson, Thomas R *Businessman*
%Abbott Laboratories, 100 Abbott Park Road, Abbott Park, IL 60064, USA
Hodler, Marc *Ski Executive*
%Int'l Ski Federation, Worbstr 210, 3073 Gumligen B Bern, Switzerland
Hodowal, John R *Businessman*
%IPALCO Enterprises, 25 Monument Circle, Indianapolis, IN 46204, USA
Hoeft, William F (Billy) *Baseball Player*
2243 S Huron Parkway, Ann Arbor, MI 48104, USA
Hoegh, Leo A *Governor, IA*
1472 W Desert Hills Dr, Green Valley, AZ 85614, USA
Hoenig, Thomas M *Financier*
%Federal Reserve Bank, 925 Grand Ave, Kansas City, MO 64198, USA
Hoepner, Theodore J *Financier*
%SunBank, 200 S Orange Ave, Orlando, FL 32801, USA
Hoerni, Jean A *Electronics Consultant*
302 Lakeside Ave S, Seattle, WA 98144, USA
Hoest, Bunny *Cartoonist (Lockhorns)*
%William Hoest Enterprises, 27 Watch Way, Lloyd Neck, Huntington, NY 11743, USA
Hoff, James E *Educator*
%Xavier University, President's Office, Cincinnati, OH 45207, USA
Hoff, Marcian E (Ted), Jr *Co-Inventor (Microprocessor)*
12226 Colina Dr, Los Altos, CA 94024, USA
Hoff, Philip H *Governor, VT*
%Hoff Wilson Powell Lang, PO Box 567, Burlington, VT 05402, USA
Hoff, Sydney (Syd) *Writer, Cartoonist (Laugh It Off)*
PO Box 2463, Miami Beach, FL 33140, USA
Hoffman, Alan J *Mathematician*
%IBM Research Center, Box 218, Yorktown Heights, NY 10598, USA
Hoffman, Alice *Writer*
3 Hurlbut St, Cambridge, MA 02138, USA
Hoffman, Basil *Actor*
4456 Cromwell Ave, Los Angeles, CA 90027, USA
Hoffman, Dustin *Actor*
315 E 65th St, New York, NY 10021, USA
Hoffman, Grace *Singer*
Bergstr 19, 72666 Neckartailfingen, Germany
Hoffman, Jeffrey A *Astronaut*
%NASA, Johnson Space Center, 2101 NASA Road, Houston, TX 77058, USA
Hoffman, Ted, Jr *Bowling Executive*
1568 Partarian Way, San Jose, CA 95129, USA
Hoffman, William M *Writer, Lyricist*
190 Prince St, New York, NY 10012, USA
Hoffmann, Frank (Nordy) *Football Player*
400 N Capitol St NW, #327, Washington, DC 20001, USA
Hoffmann, Jorg *Swimmer*
Saarmunder Str 74, 14478 Potsdam, Germany
Hoffmann, Roald *Nobel Chemistry Laureate*
4 Sugarbush Lane, Ithaca, NY 14850, USA
Hoffs, Susanna *Singer (The Bangles)*
%Stiefel-Phillips Ent, 9720 Wilshire Blvd, #400, Beverly Hills, CA 90212, USA
Hoflehner, Rudolf *Artist*
Ottensteinstr 62, 2344 Maria Enzersdorf, Austria
Hofman, Leonard J *Religious Leader*
%Christian Reformed Church, 2850 Kalamazoo Ave SE, Grand Rapids, MI 49508, USA
Hofmann, Detlef *Kayak Athlete*
Saarlandstr 164, 76187 Karlsruhe, Germany
Hofmann, Douglas *Artist*
8602 Saxon Circle, Baltimore, MD 21236, USA
Hofmann, Isabella *Actress*
%Susan Smith, 121 N San Vicente Blvd, Beverly Hills, CA 90211, USA
Hofmann, Peter *Opera Singer*
%Mgmt Studio Vierhofen, Alte Dortstr 74, 21444 Vierhofen, Germany

Hofstatter, Peter R — *Psychologist*
Lehmkuhleweg 16, 21614 Buxtehude, Germany

Hogan, A Paul — *Editor*
%Tampa Tribune, Editorial Dept, 202 S Parker St, Tampa, FL 33606, USA

Hogan, Craig — *Astronomer*
%University of Washington, Astronomy Dept, Seattle, WA 98195, USA

Hogan, Hulk — *Wrestler, Actor*
130 Willadel Dr, Belair, FL 33756, USA

Hogan, Jack — *Actor*
%Alex Brewis, 12429 Laurel Terrace Dr, Studio City, CA 91604, USA

Hogan, Paul — *Actor*
1472 Rising Glen Road, Los Angeles, CA 90069, USA

Hogan, Robert — *Actor*
%Borinstein-Oreck-Bogart, 8271 Melrose, #110, Los Angeles, CA 90046, USA

Hogarth, A Paul — *Artist*
%Tessa Sayle, 11 Jubilee Place, London SW3 3TE, England

Hogestyn, Drake — *Actor*
%Gage Group, 9255 Sunset Blvd, #515, Los Angeles, CA 90069, USA

Hogg, James R — *Navy Admiral*
Prescott Farm, 2556 W Main Road, Portsmouth, RI 02871, USA

Hogg, Sonya — *Basketball Coach*
%Baylor University, Athletic Dept, Waco, TX 76798, USA

Hoggard, Jay — *Jazz Vibist*
%Creative Music Consultants, 181 Christie St, #300, New York, NY 10002, USA

Hogwood, Christopher J H — *Concert Harpsichordist, Conductor*
10 Brookside, Cambridge CB2 1JE, England

Hohenberg, John — *Journalist, Educator*
7118 Sheffield Dr, Knoxville, TN 37909, USA

Hohmann, John — *Anthropologist*
%Louis Berger Assoc, 1110 E Missouri Ave, #200, Phoenix, AZ 85014, USA

Hohn, Harry G — *Businessman*
%New York Life Insurance, 41 W 58th St, #10-C, New York, NY 10019, USA

Hoiby, Lee — *Composer, Concert Pianist*
800 Rock Valley Road, Long Eddy, NY 12760, USA

Hoiles, Christopher A (Chris) — *Baseball PLayer*
888688 Jersey City Road, Wayne, OH 43466, USA

Holbrook, Bill — *Cartoonist (Safe Havens)*
1321 Weatherstone Way, Atlanta, GA 30324, USA

Holbrook, Hal — *Actor*
9100 Hazen Dr, Beverly Hills, CA 90210, USA

Holbrook, Terry — *Hockey Player*
8799 Arrowood Dr, Mentor, OH 44060, USA

Holbrooke, Richard C — *Diplomat*
%US State Department, 2201 "C" St NW, Washington, DC 20520, USA

Holden, Rebecca — *Actress, Singer*
%Box Office, 1010 16th Ave S, Nashville, TN 37212, USA

Holden-Brown, Derrick — *Businessman*
Copse House, Milford-on-Sea, Lymington, Hants, England

Holder, Geoffrey — *Actor, Dancer*
565 Broadway, New York, NY 10012, USA

Holder, Leonard D (Don), Jr — *Army General*
Commanding General, Army Combined Arms Center, Fort Leavenworth, KS 66027, USA

Holder, Richard G — *Businessman*
%Reynolds Metals, 6603 W Broad St, Richmond, VA 23230, USA

Holderness of Bishop Wilton — *Government Official, England*
65 Les Collines De Guerrevieille, 83120 Ste Maxime, France

Holdorf, Willi — *Track Athlete*
%Adidas KG, 91074 Herzogenaurach, Germany

Holdsclaw, Chamique — *Basketball Player*
%University of Tennessee, Athletic Dept, Knoxville, TN 37996, USA

Holdsworth, G Trevor — *Businessman*
%British Satellite Broadcasting, Queenstown Road, London SW8 4NQ, England

Holftreter, Johannes F C — *Zoologist*
29 Knolltop Dr, Rochester, NY 14610, USA

Holgate, Martin W — *Biologist*
%IUCN, 28 Rue Mauverney, 1196 Gland, Switzerland

Holl, Steven M — *Architect*
%Steven Holl Architects, 435 Hudson St, #500, New York, NY 10014, USA

H

Holladay, Wilhelmina Cole *Museum Official*
%National Museum of Women in Arts, 1250 New York NW, Washington, DC 20005, USA

Holland, Heinrich D *Geologist*
%Harvard University, Hoffman Laboratory, Cambridge, MA 02138, USA

Holland, John B *Businessman*
%Fruit of the Loom, Sears Tower, 233 S Wacker Dr, Chicago, IL 60606, USA

Holland, John R *Religious Leader*
%Foursquare Gospel Int'l Church, 1910 W Sunset Blvd, Los Angeles, CA 90026, USA

Holland, Terry *Basketball Coach, Administrator*
%Davidson College, Athletic Dept, Davidson, NC 28036, USA

Holland, Tom *Artist*
%San Francisco Art Institute, 800 Chestnut St, San Francisco, CA 94133, USA

Holland, Willard R, Jr *Businessman*
%Ohio Edison, 76 S Main St, Akron, OH 44308, USA

Hollander, John *Writer*
%Yale University, English Dept, New Haven, CT 06520, USA

Hollander, Lorin *Concert Pianist*
210 W 101st St, #PH, New York, NY 10025, USA

Hollander, Nicole *Cartoonist (Sylvia)*
%Sylvia Syndicate, 1440 N Dayton St, Chicago, IL 60622, USA

Holldobler, Berthold K *Writer, Biologist, Zoologist*
%Harvard University, Biology Dept, Cambridge, MA 02138, USA

Hollein, Hans *Architect*
Eiskellerstr 1, 40213 Dusseldorf, Germany

Hollen, Stanley C *Financier*
%Golden 1 Credit Union, 6507 4th Ave, Sacramento, CA 95817, USA

Hollerer, Walter F *Writer*
Heerstr 99, 14055 Berlin, Germany

Holliday, Fred *Actor*
4610 Forman Ave, North Hollywood, CA 91602, USA

Holliday, Jennifer *Singer, Actress*
%Atlantic Entertainment, 1125 Atlantic Ave, #700, Atlantic City, NJ 08401, USA

Holliday, Kene *Actor*
%Paul Kohner, 9300 Wilshire Blvd, #555, Beverly Hills, CA 90212, USA

Holliday, Polly *Actress, Singer*
201 E 17th St, #23-H, New York, NY 10003, USA

Holliger, Heinz *Concert Oboist, Composer*
%Ingpen & Williams, 14 Kensington Court, London W8, England

Holliman, Earl *Actor*
PO Box 1969, Studio City, CA 91614, USA

Hollings, Michael R *Religious Leader*
St Mary of Angels, Moorhouse Road, Bayswater, London W2 5DJ, England

Hollins, Lionel *Basketball Player*
1834 S Newberry Lane, Tempe, AZ 85281, USA

Holloway, Brian *Football Player*
Star Rt, Box 9, Stephentown, NY 12168, USA

Holloway, James L, III *Navy Admiral*
1694 Epping Farms Lane, Annapolis, MD 21401, USA

Holloway, Loleatta *Singer*
%Fat City Artists, 1908 Chet Atkins Place, #502, Nashville, TN 37212, USA

Holloway, Randy *Football Player*
%New England Patriots, Foxboro Stadium, Rt 1, Foxboro, MA 02035, USA

Holly, Lauren *Actress*
13601 Ventura Blvd, #99, Sherman Oaks, CA 91423, USA

Hollyday, Christopher *Jazz Saxophonist*
%Ted Kurland, 173 Brighton Ave, Boston, MA 02134, USA

Holm Whalen, Eleanor *Swimmer*
1800 NE 114th St, #1503, North Miami, FL 33181, USA

Holm, Celeste *Actress*
88 Central Park West, New York, NY 10023, USA

Holm, Ian *Actor*
%Julian Belfarge, 46 Albermarle St, London W1X 4PP, England

Holm, Jeanne M *Air Force General*
2707 Thyme Dr, Edgewater, MD 21037, USA

Holm, Joan *Bowler*
5829 N Magnolia Ave, Chicago, IL 60660, USA

Holm, Richard H *Chemist*
483 Pleasant St, #10, Belmont, MA 02178, USA

Holladay - Holm

Holman, C Ray — *Businessman*
%Mallinckrodt Group, 7733 Forsyth Blvd, St Louis, MO 63105, USA

Holman, Marshall — *Bowler*
%Professional Bowlers Assn, 1720 Merriman Road, Akron, OH 44313, USA

Holman, Ralph T — *Biochemist*
1403 2nd Ave SW, Austin, MN 55912, USA

Holmboe, Vagn — *Composer*
Holmboevej 4-6, Ramlose, 3200 Helsinge, Denmark

Holmes, Clint — *Singer*
%Conversation Co, 697 Middle Neck Road, Great Neck, NY 11023, USA

Holmes, D Brainerd — *Space Engineer, Businessman*
%Bay Colony Corp Center, 950 Winter St, #4350, Waltham, MA 02154, USA

Holmes, Ernie — *Football Player*
Rt 1, Box 124, Wiergate, TX 75977, USA

Holmes, Jennifer — *Actress*
PO Box 6303, Carmel, CA 93921, USA

Holmes, Larry — *Boxer*
896 Sheridan Dr, Easton, PA 18045, USA

Holmes, Ruppert — *Singer, Songwriter*
%Mars Talent, 168 Orchid Dr, Pearl River, NY 10965, USA

Holmes, Thomas F (Tommy) — *Baseball Player*
1 Pine Dr, Woodbury, NY 11797, USA

Holmgren, Mike — *Football Coach*
%Green Bay Packers, 1265 Lombardi Ave, Green Bay, WI 54304, USA

Holmgren, Paul — *Hockey Player, Coach*
415 Firetown Road, Simsbury, CT 06070, USA

Holmquest, Donald L — *Astronaut*
%Holmquest Assoc, 1617 Ash Valley Dr, Nashville, TN 37215, USA

Holmstrom, Carl — *Skier*
1703 E 3rd St, #101, Duluth, MN 55812, USA

Holomisa, Bantu — *President, Transkei; General*
%President's Office, Military Council, Umtata, Transkei

Holovak, Mike — *Football Player, Coach, Executive*
3432 Highlands Bridge Road, Sarasota, FL 34235, USA

Holroyd, Michael — *Writer*
85 St Marks Road, London W10 6JS England

Holst, Per — *Movie Producer*
%Per Holst Film A/S, Rentemestervej 69-A, 2400 Copenhagen NV, Denmark

Holt, Glenn L — *Labor Leader*
%Metal Workers Union, 5578 Montgomery Road, Cincinnati, OH 45212, USA

Holtermann, E Louis, Jr — *Publisher*
%Glamour Magazine, 350 Madison Ave, New York, NY 10017, USA

Holton, A Linwood, Jr — *Governor, VA*
6010 Claiborne Dr, McLean, VA 22101, USA

Holton, Gerald — *Physicist*
64 Francis Ave, Cambridge, MA 02138, USA

Holton, Robert J — *Labor Leader*
%Plasterers/Cement Masons International Assn, 1125 17th NW, Washington, DC 20036, USA

Holtz, Louis L (Lou) — *Football Coach*
9209 Cromwell Park Place, Orlando, FL 32827, USA

Holtzman, Jerome — *Sportswriter*
1225 Forest Ave, Evanston, IL 60202, USA

Holtzman, Kenneth D (Ken) — *Baseball Player*
115 Valley Trail Dr, #A, Ballwin, MO 63011, USA

Holtzman, Wayne H — *Psychologist*
3300 Foothill Dr, Austin, TX 78731, USA

Holub, E J — *Football Player*
Mullendore Cross Bell Ranch, RR 1, Copan, OK 74022, USA

Holum, Dianne — *Speed Skater*
2418 W Willowood Dr, Waukesha, WI 53188, USA

Holum, Kristin — *Speedskater*
2418 W Willowood Dr, Waukesha, WI 53188, USA

Holyfield, Evander — *Boxer*
794 Highway 279, Fairburn, GA 30213, USA

Holz, Ernest W — *Religious Leader*
%Salvation Army, Commander's Office, 120 W 14th St, New York, NY 10011, USA

Holzer, Jenny — *Artist*
245 Eldridge St, New York, NY 10002, USA

H	**Holzman, Malcolm** %Hardy Holzman Pfeiffer, 902 Broadway, New York, NY 10010, USA	*Architect*
	Holzman, William (Red) 408 Ocean Point Ave, Cedarhurst, NY 11516, USA	*Basketball Coach*
	Homeier, Skip 247 N Castellana, Palm Desert, CA 92260, USA	*Actor*

Holzman, Malcolm — *Architect*
%Hardy Holzman Pfeiffer, 902 Broadway, New York, NY 10010, USA

Holzman, William (Red) — *Basketball Coach*
408 Ocean Point Ave, Cedarhurst, NY 11516, USA

Homeier, Skip — *Actor*
247 N Castellana, Palm Desert, CA 92260, USA

Homes, A M — *Writer*
%Charles Scribner's Sons, 866 3rd Ave, New York, NY 10022, USA

Homfeld, Conrad — *Equestrian Rider*
%Sandron, 11744 Marblestone Court, West Palm Beach, FL 33414, USA

Honderich, Beland H — *Publisher*
%Toronto Star, 1 Yonge St, Toronto ON M5E 1E6, Canada

Honderich, John H — *Editor*
%Toronto Star, Editorial Dept, 1 Yonge St, Toronto ON M5E 1E6, Canada

Honea, T Milton — *Businessman*
%NorAm Energy, 1600 Smith St, Houston, TX 77002, USA

Honegger, Fritz — *President, Switzerland*
Schloss-Str 29, 8803 Ruschlikon, Switzerland

Honeycutt, Frederick W (Rick) — *Baseball Player*
207 Forrest Road, Fort Oglethorpe, GA 30742, USA

Honeycutt, Van B — *Businessman*
%Computer Sciences Corp, 2100 E Grand Ave, El Segundo, CA 90245, USA

Honeyghan, Lloyd — *Boxer*
50 Barnfield Wood Road, Park Langley, Beckenham, Kent, England

Honeyman, Janice — *Actress*
8-A Seymour St, Westdene, Johannesburg 2092, South Africa

Hong, James — *Actor*
11684 Ventura Blvd, #948, Studio City, CA 91604, USA

Honig, Edwin — *Writer*
%Brown University, English Dept, Providence, RI 02912, USA

Hood, Leroy E — *Biologist*
6411 NE Windermere Road, Seattle, WA 98105, USA

Hood, Robert — *Editor*
%Boys Life Magazine, Editorial Dept, 1325 Walnut Hill Lane, Irving, TX 75038, USA

Hood, Robin — *Golfer*
4017 Southern Charm Court, Arlington, TX 76016, USA

Hooglandt, Jan D — *Businessman*
%Hoogovens Group, 1970 CA Nijmegen, Netherlands

Hook, Harold S — *Businessman*
%American General Corp, 2929 Allen Parkway, Houston, TX 77019, USA

Hooker, Charles R — *Artist*
28 Whippingham Road, Brighton, Sussex BN2 3PG, England

Hooker, John Lee — *Singer, Songwriter, Guitarist*
%Rosebud Agency, PO Box 170429, San Francisco, CA 94117, USA

Hooks, Bell — *Writer*
291 W 12th St, New York, NY 10014, USA

Hooks, Benjamin L — *Civil Rights Activist*
200 Wagner Place, #407-8, Memphis, TN 38103, USA

Hooks, Jan — *Actress*
%William Morris Agency, 151 S El Camino Dr, Beverly Hills, CA 90212, USA

Hooks, Robert — *Actor*
145 N Valley St, Burbank, CA 91505, USA

Hookstratten, Edward G — *Attorney*
%Ed Hookstratten Mgmt, 9536 Wilshire Blvd, #500, Beverly Hills, CA 90212, USA

Hooper, C Darrow — *Track Athlete*
10909 Strait Lane, Dallas, TX 75229, USA

Hoops, Alan R — *Businessman*
%PacifiCare Health Systems, 5995 Plaza Dr, Cypress, CA 90630, USA

Hooten, Burt C — *Baseball Player*
3619 Granby Court, San Antonio, TX 78217, USA

Hoover, Dick — *Bowler*
112 Melody Dr, Copley, OH 44321, USA

Hoover, William R — *Businessman*
%Computer Sciences Corp, 2100 E Grand Ave, El Segundo, CA 90245, USA

Hope, Alec — *Writer*
66 Arthur Circle, Forrest ACT, Australia

Hope, Bob — *Comedian*
10346 Moorpark St, North Hollywood, CA 91602, USA

Holzman - Hope

Hope, Leslie — *Actress*
%Metropolitan Talent Agency, 4526 Wilshire Blvd, Los Angeles, CA 90010, USA

Hope, Maurice — *Boxer*
582 Kingsland Road, London E8, England

Hopfield, John J — *Biophysicist*
%California Institute of Technology, Chemistry/Biology Dept, Pasadena, CA 91125, USA

Hopkins, Anthony — *Actor*
%Creative Artists Agency, 9830 Wilshire Blvd, Beverly Hills, CA 90212, USA

Hopkins, Bo — *Actor*
6628 Ethel Ave, North Hollywood, CA 91606, USA

Hopkins, Godfrey T — *Photographer*
Wilmington Cottage, Wilmington Road, Seaford, E Sussex BN25 2EH, England

Hopkins, Jan — *Commentator*
%"Moneyline", CNN, News Dept, 1050 Techwood Dr NW, Atlanta, GA 30318, USA

Hopkins, Linda — *Singer*
2055 N Ivar St, #PH-21, Los Angeles, CA 90068, USA

Hopkins, Michael J — *Architect*
27 Broadley Terrace, London NW1 6LG, England

Hopkins, Telma — *Actress, Singer*
%Innovative Artists, 1999 Ave of Stars, #2850, Los Angeles, CA 90067, USA

Hopp, John L (Johnny) — *Baseball Player*
1914 Ave "M", Scottsbluff, NE 69361, USA

Hoppe, Wolfgang — *Bobsled Athlete*
Dieterstedter Str 11, 99510 Apolda, Germany

Hopper, Dennis — *Actor, Director*
330 Indiana Ave, Venice, CA 90291, USA

Hopson, Dennis — *Basketball Player*
7229 Donnybrook Dr, Dublin, OH 43017, USA

Horecker, Bernard L — *Biochemist*
1621 Sand Castle Road, Sanibel Island, FL 33957, USA

Horgan, Patrick — *Actor*
201 E 89th St, New York, NY 10128, USA

Horlock, John H — *Mechanical Engineer, Educator*
2 The Avenue, Ampthill, Bedford MK45 2NR, England

Horn, Carol — *Fashion Designer*
575 7th Ave, New York, NY 10018, USA

Horn, Charles G — *Businessman*
%Fieldcrest Cannon Inc, 326 E Stadium Dr, Eden, NC 27288, USA

Horn, Gyula — *Prime Minister, Hungary*
%Parliament, Kossuth Lajos Ter 1/3, 1055 Budapest, Hungary

Horn, Karen N — *Financier*
%Banc One Cleveland, PO Box 91308, Cleveland, OH 44101, USA

Horn, Marian Blank — *Judge*
%US Claims Court, 717 Madison Place NW, Washington, DC 20005, USA

Horn, Paul J — *Jazz Flutist, Saxophonist*
4601 Leyns Road, Victoria BC V8N 3A1, Canada

Horn, Shirley — *Singer*
473 Four Seasons Dr, Charlottesville, VA 22901, USA

Hornacek, Jeff — *Basketball Player*
%Utah Jazz, Delta Center, 301 W South Temple, Salt Lake City, UT 84101, USA

Horne, Donald R — *Writer*
53 Grosvenor St, Woollahra, Sydney NSW, Australia

Horne, Jimmy Bo — *Singer, Dancer*
%Talent Consultants Int'l, 1560 Broadway, #1308, New York, NY 10036, USA

Horne, Lena — *Singer, Actress*
%Volney Apts, 23 E 74th St, New York, NY 10021, USA

Horne, Marilyn — *Opera Singer*
%Columbia Artists Mgmt Inc, 165 W 57th St, New York, NY 10019, USA

Horneber, Petra — *Markswoman*
Ringstr 77, 85402 Kranzberg, Germany

Horner, Charles A — *Air Force General*
2824 Jack Nicklaus Way, Shalimar, FL 32579, USA

Horner, Freeman V — *WW II Army Hero (CMH)*
1501 Doubletree Dr, Columbus, GA 31904, USA

Horner, J Robert (Bob) — *Baseball Player*
209 Steeplechase Dr, Irving, TX 75062, USA

Horner, James — *Composer*
728 Brooktree Road, Pacific Palisades, CA 90272, USA

H

Hope - Horner

Horner, John R (Jack) — *Palentologist*
%Museum of the Rockies, Montana State University, Bozeman, MT 59717, USA

Horner, Martina S — *Educator, Businesswoman*
%TIAA-CREF, 730 3rd Ave, New York, NY 10017, USA

Horner, Red — *Hockey Player*
Brantford Smoke, 69-79 S Market St, Brantford ON N3T 5R2, Canada

Hornig, Donald F — *Chemist*
16 Longfellow Park, Cambridge, MA 02138, USA

Hornsby, Bruce — *Singer, Pianist*
PO Box 3545, Williamsburg, VA 23187, USA

Hornung, Paul V — *Football Player*
5800 Creighton Hill Road, Louisville, KY 40207, USA

Horovitz (King Ad-Rock), Adam — *Rap Artist (Beastie Boys)*
%Gold Mountain, 3575 Cahuenga Blvd W, #450, Los Angeles, CA 90068, USA

Horovitz, Israel A — *Writer*
146 W 11th St, New York, NY 10011, USA

Horovitz, Joseph — *Composer*
%Royal College of Music, Prince Consort Road, London SW7 2BS, England

Horowitz, David C — *Commentator*
4267 Marina City Dr, #810, Marina Del Rey, CA 90292, USA

Horowitz, David H — *Businessman*
141 E 72nd St, New York, NY 10021, USA

Horowitz, Jerome P — *Medical Researcher*
%Michigan Cancer Foundation, 110 E Warren Ave, Detroit, MI 48201, USA

Horowitz, Norman H — *Biologist*
2495 Brighton Road, Pasadena, CA 91104, USA

Horowitz, Paul — *Physician*
111 Chilton St, Cambridge, MA 02138, USA

Horowitz, Scott J — *Astronaut*
%NASA, Johnson Space Center, 2101 NASA Road, Houston, TX 77058, USA

Horrocks, Jane — *Actress*
%Peters Fraser Dunlop, Chelsea Harbour, Lots Rd, London SW10 0XF, England

Horry, Robert — *Basketball Player*
3323 Medinah Court, Sugar Land, TX 77479, USA

Horsford, Anna Maria — *Actress*
PO Box 48082, Los Angeles, CA 90048, USA

Horsley, Lee A — *Actor*
15054 E Dartmouth Ave, Aurora, CO 80014, USA

Horsley, Richard D — *Financier*
%Regions Financial Corp, 417 N 20th St, Birmingham, AL 35203, USA

Horton, Frank E — *Educator*
%University of Toledo, President's Office, Toledo, OH 43606, USA

Horton, Peter — *Actor*
409 Santa Monica Blvd, #PH, Santa Monica, CA 90401, USA

Horton, Robert — *Actor*
5317 Andasol Ave, Encino, CA 91316, USA

Horton, William W (Willie) — *Baseball Player*
%Reid, 15124 Warwick, Detroit, MI 48223, USA

Horvath, Bronko — *Hockey Player*
27 Oliver St, South Yarmouth, MA 02664, USA

Hoskins, Bob — *Actor*
30 Steele Road, London NW3 4RE, England

Hossein, Robert — *Actor, Theater Director*
%Ghislaine De Wing, 10 Rue Du Docteur Roux, 75015 Paris, France

Hostak, Al — *Boxer*
10436 21st Ave SW, Seattle, WA 98146, USA

Hostetler, Jeff W — *Football Player*
%Washington Redskins, 21300 Redskin Park Dr, Ashburn, VA 20147, USA

Hostetter, G Richard — *Religious Leader*
%Presbyterian Church in America, 1852 Century Place, Atlanta, GA 30345, USA

Hotani, Hirokazu — *Microbiotics Engineer*
%Teikyo University, Biosciences Dept, Toyosatodai, Utsunomiya 320, Japan

Hotard, Edgar G — *Businessman*
%Praxair Inc, 39 Old Ridgebury Road, Danbury, CT 06810, USA

Hotchkiss, Rollin D — *Bacterial Physiologist*
%State University of New York, Biology Dept, Albany, NY 12222, USA

Hottel, Hoyt C — *Chemical Engineer*
27 Cambridge St, Winchester, MA 01890, USA

Hottelet, Richard C — *Commentator*
120 Chestnut Hill Road, Wilton, CT 06897, USA

Hotter, Hans — *Opera Singer*
%Bayerische Staatsoper, Portiastr 8, 81545 Munich, Germany

Hou Runyu — *Conductor*
1710-3-602 Huai-Hai-Zhong Road, Shanghai, China

Hou, Ya-Ming — *Biologist*
%Massachusetts Institute of Technology, Biology Dept, Cambridge, MA 02139, USA

Houbregs, Bob — *Basketball Player*
2401 Summit Lake Shore Road NW, Olympia, WA 98502, USA

Hough, Charles O (Charlie) — *Baseball Player*
2266 Shade Tree Circle, Brea, CA 92821, USA

Hough, John — *Movie Director*
8 Queen St, Mayfair, London W1, England

Hough, Richard — *Writer*
31 Meadowbank, London NW3 1AY, England

Hough, Stephen A G — *Concert Pianist*
%Harrison/Parrott, 12 Penzance Place, London W11 4PA England

Houghton of Sowerby, Douglas — *Government Official, England*
110 Marsham Court, London SW1, England

Houghton, James R — *Businessman*
%Corning Inc, Houghton Park, Corning, NY 14831, USA

Houghton, John — *Physicist*
%Rutherford Appleton Laboratory, Chilton, Didcot Oxon OX11 0QX, England

Houghton, Katherine — *Actress*
134 Steele Road, West Hartford, CT 06119, USA

Hougland, Bill — *Basketball Player*
504 Canyon Dr, Lawrence, KS 66049, USA

Houk, Ralph G — *Baseball Manager*
3000 Plantation Road, Winter Haven, FL 33884, USA

Hounsfield, Godfrey N — *Nobel Medicine Laureate*
15 Crane Park Road, Whitton, Twickenham, Middx, England

House, Karen Eliot — *Journalist*
%Wall Street Journal, Editorial Dept, 22 Cortlandt St, New York, NY 10007, USA

Housley, Phil — *Hockey Player*
%Washington Capitals, USAir Arena, 1 Truman Dr, Landover, MD 20785, USA

Houston, Allan — *Basketball Player*
%New York Knicks, Madison Square Garden, 2 Penn Plaza, New York, NY 10121, USA

Houston, Byron — *Basketball Player*
1732 Lionsgate Circle, Bethany, OK 73008, USA

Houston, Cissy — *Singer*
2160 N Central Road, Fort Lee, NJ 07024, USA

Houston, James A — *Writer*
24 Main St, Stonington, CT 06378, USA

Houston, Jim — *Football Player*
3625 Hughestown Dr, Akron, OH 44333, USA

Houston, Ken — *Football Player*
3603 Forest Village Dr, Kingwood, TX 77339, USA

Houston, Penelope — *Singer*
%Houston Mgmt, 3450 3rd St, Building 2-A, San Francisco, CA 94124, USA

Houston, Thelma — *Singer*
4296 Mt Vernon Dr, Los Angeles, CA 90008, USA

Houston, Wade — *Basketball Coach*
%University of Tennessee, Athletic Dept, Knoxville, TN 37901, USA

Houston, Whitney — *Singer*
%Nippy Inc, 2160 N Central Road, Fort Lee, NJ 07024, USA

Houtte, Jean Van — *Prime Minister, Belgium*
54 Blvd St Michel, Brussels, Belgium

Hove, Andrew C, Jr — *Financier*
%Federal Deposit Insurance, 550 17th St NW, Washington, DC 20429, USA

Hovhaness, Alan — *Composer*
%C F Peters Corp, 373 Park Ave S, New York, NY 10016, USA

Hoving, Thomas — *Museum Director, Editor*
%Hoving Assoc, 150 E 73rd St, New York NY 10021, USA

Hovsepian, Vatche — *Religious Leader*
%Armenian Church of America (West), 1201 N Vine St, Los Angeles, CA 90038, USA

Howard, Adina — *Singer*
%International Creative Mgmt, 40 W 57th St, New York, NY 10019, USA

H

Hottelet - Howard

H

Howard - Howe

Howard, Alan	*Actor*
%Julian Belfarge, 46 Albermarle St, London W1X 4PP, England	
Howard, Ann	*Opera Singer*
%Stafford Law Assoc, 26 Mayfield Road, Weybridge, Surrey KT13 8XB, England	
Howard, Desmond	*Football Player*
3206 Alpine Dr, Ann Arbor, MI 48108, USA	
Howard, Frank O	*Baseball Player*
12087 Caminito Campana, San Diego, CA 92128, USA	
Howard, George	*Bowler*
8415 Brookwood Dr, Portage, MI 49024, USA	
Howard, George	*Jazz Saxophonist*
%David Rubinson, PO Box 411197, San Francisco, CA 94141, USA	
Howard, Greg	*Cartoonist (Sally Forth)*
3403 W 28th St, Minneapolis, MN 55416, USA	
Howard, Harry N	*Historian*
6508 Greentree Road, Bradley Hills Grove, Bethesda, MD 20817, USA	
Howard, Jack R	*Publisher*
%Scripps-Howard Newspapers, 200 Park Ave, New York, NY 10166, USA	
Howard, James J, III	*Businessman*
%Northern States Power, 414 Nicollett Mall, Minneapolis, MN 55401, USA	
Howard, James Newton	*Composer*
%Gorfaine/Schwarz/Roberts, 3301 Barham Blvd, #201, Los Angeles, CA 90068, USA	
Howard, Jan	*Singer*
%Joe Taylor Artist Agency, 2802 Columbine Place, Nashville, TN 37204, USA	
Howard, John	*Prime Minister, Australia*
%Prime Minister's Office, Parliament House, Canbera ACT 2600, Australia	
Howard, Juwan	*Basketball Player*
3057 Signature Blvd, #E, Ann Arbor, MI 48103, USA	
Howard, Ken	*Actor*
%Ken Howard Productions, 59 E 54th St, #22, New York, NY 10022, USA	
Howard, Michael	*Government Official, England*
%House of Commons, Westminster, London SW1A 0AA, England	
Howard, Rance	*Actor*
4286 Clybourn Ave, Burbank, CA 91505, USA	
Howard, Richard	*Writer*
23 Waverly Place, #5-X, New York, NY 10003, USA	
Howard, Robert L	*Vietnam War Army Hero (CMH)*
8450 Cambridge St, #1203, Houston, TX 77054, USA	
Howard, Ron	*Actor, Director*
%Imagine Entertainment, 1925 Century Park East, #2300, Los Angeles, CA 90067, USA	
Howard, Sherri	*Track Athlete*
14059 Bridle Ridge Road, Sylmar, CA 91342, USA	
Howard, Susan	*Actress*
PO Box 1456, Boerne, TX 78006, USA	
Howard, William W, Jr	*Association Executive*
%National Wildlife Federation, 8925 Leesburg Pike, Vienna, VA 22184, USA	
Howarth, Thomas	*Architect*
%University of Toronto, 230 College St, Toronto ON M5S 1R1, Canada	
Howatch, Susan	*Writer*
%Aitken & Stone, 29 Fernshaw Road, London SW10 0TG, England	
Howe of Aberavon, R E Geoffrey	*Government Official, England*
%Barclays Bank, Cavendish Square Branch, 4 Vere St, London W1, England	
Howe, Arthur	*Journalist*
%Philadelphia Inquirer, Editorial Dept, 400 N Broad St, Philadelphia, PA 19130, USA	
Howe, Arthur H (Art)	*Baseball Player, Manager*
711 Kahlddon Court, Houston, TX 77079, USA	
Howe, G Woodson	*Editor*
%Omaha World-Herald, Editorial Dept, World-Herald Square, Omaha, NE 68102, USA	
Howe, Gordon (Gordie)	*Hockey Player*
6645 Peninsula Dr, Traverse City, MI 49686, USA	
Howe, Jonathan T	*Navy Admiral*
3946 Saint Johns Ave, #123, Jacksonville, FL 32205, USA	
Howe, Mark	*Hockey Player, Executive*
564 Provencal Place, Bloomfield Hills, MI 48302, USA	
Howe, Oscar	*Artist*
128 Walker St, Vermillion, SD 57069, USA	
Howe, Robert W	*Businessman*
%Mapco Inc, PO Box 645, Tulsa, OK 74101, USA	

Howe, Stanley M — *Businessman*
%HON Industries, 414 E 3rd St, Muscatine, IA 52761, USA

Howe, Steven R (Steve) — *Baseball Player*
PO Box 1355, Warsaw, IN 46581, USA

Howe, Tina — *Writer*
333 West End Ave, New York, NY 10023, USA

Howell, Bailey — *Basketball Player*
1989 S Montgomery St, Strakville, MS 39759, USA

Howell, C Thomas — *Actor*
15919 Tuba St, North Hills, CA 91343, USA

Howell, Francis C — *Anthropologist*
1994 San Antonio Ave, Berkeley, CA 94707, USA

Howell, Harry — *Hockey Player*
21 Bruce St, Hamilton ON L8P 3M5, Canada

Howell, Jefferson D, Jr — *Marine Corps General*
Commander, USMC Forces Pacific, Box 64108, Camp Smith, HI 96861, USA

Howell, John R — *Financier*
%UJB Financial Corp, Carnegie Center, PO Box 2066, Princeton, NJ 08543, USA

Howell, Margaret — *Fashion Designer*
5 Garden House, 8 Battersea Park Road, London SW8, England

Howell, Margaret — *Actress*
%Chateau/Billings Agency, 5657 Wilshire Blvd, #340, Los Angeles, CA 90036, USA

Howell, Paul N — *Businessman*
%Howell Corp, 1111 Fannin St, Houston, TX 77002, USA

Howell, W Nathaniel, III — *Diplomat*
%US State Department, 2201 "C" St NW, Washington, DC 20520, USA

Howell, William R — *Businessman*
%J C Penney Co, PO Box 10001, Dallas, TX 75301, USA

Howells, Anne E — *Opera Singer*
Milestone, Broom Close, Esher, Surrey, England

Howells, William W — *Anthropologist*
11 Lawrence Lane, Kittery Point, ME 03905, USA

Howes, Sally Ann — *Actress, Siger*
%Saraband, 265 Liverpool Road, Islington, London N1 1LX, England

Howland, Beth — *Actress*
255 Amalfi Dr, Santa Monica, CA 90402, USA

Howley, Charles L (Chuck) — *Football Player*
%Howley Uniform Rental Inc, 5422 Redfield St, Dallas, TX 75235, USA

Howson, Robert E — *Businessman*
%McDermott International, 1450 Poydras St, New Orleans, LA 70112, USA

Hoyle, Fred — *Astronomer, Mathematician*
%Royal Society, 6 Carlton House Terrace, London SW1Y 5AG, England

Hoyt, D Lamarr — *Baseball Player*
31 Pointe Lane, Prosperity, SC 29127, USA

Hoyt, Henry H, Jr — *Businessman*
%Carter-Wallace Inc, Burlington House, 1345 Ave of Americas, New York, NY 10105, USA

Hoyte, Hugh Desmond — *President, Guyana*
14 North Road, Bourda, Georgetown, Guyana

Hrabosky, Alan T (Al) — *Baseball Player, Sportscaster*
16216 Pepper View Court, Chesterfield, MO 63005, USA

Hrawi, Elias — *President, Lebanon*
%President's Office, Palais de Baebda, Beirut, Lebanon

Hrbek, Kent A — *Baseball Player*
2611 W 112th St, Bloomington, MN 55431, USA

Hrkac, Tony — *Hockey Player*
9 Dunleith Dr, St Louis, MO 63131, USA

Hrudey, Kelly — *Hockey Player*
%San Jose Sharks, San Jose Arena, 525 W Santa Clara St, San Jose, CA 95113, USA

Hruska, Roman L — *Senator, NE*
2139 S 38th St, Omaha, NE 68105, USA

Hsuan, John — *Businessman*
%United Microelectronics, Hsinchu Science Park, Taipei, Taiwan

Hu Jintao — *Government Official, China*
%Communist Party Central Committee, 1 Jhony Nan Hai, Beijing, China

Hu Qili — *Government Official, China*
%Chinese Communist Party, Beijing, China

Huarte, John — *Football Player*
1448 E Northshore Dr, Tempe, AZ 85283, USA

Hubbard, Elizabeth	*Actress*
165 W 46th St, #1214, New York, NY 10036, USA	
Hubbard, Frederick D (Freddie)	*Jazz Trumpeter, Composer*
%Merlin Co, 17609 Ventura Blvd, #212, Encino, CA 91316, USA	
Hubbard, Gregg	*Singer (Sawyer Brown)*
%TKO Artist Mgmt, 4213 Hillsboro Road, #318, Nashville, TN 37215, USA	
Hubbard, John	*Artist*
Chilcombe House, Chilcombe near Bridport, Dorset, England	
Hubbard, Phil	*Basketball Player, Coach*
%Atlanta Hawks, 1 CNN Center, South Tower, Atlanta, GA 30303, USA	
Hubble, Don W	*Businessman*
%National Service Industries, 1420 Peachtree St NE, Atlanta, GA 30309, USA	
Hubel, David H	*Nobel Medicine Laureate*
98 Collins Road, Newton, MA 02168, USA	
Hubenthal, Karl	*Editorial Cartoonist*
5536 Via La Mesa, #A, Laguna Hills, CA 92653, USA	
Huber, Anke	*Tennis Player*
Dieselstr 10, 76689 Karlsdorf-Neuthard, Germany	
Huber, Robert	*Nobel Chemistry Laureate*
%Planck Biochemie Institut, Am Klopferspitz, 82152 Martinsried, Germany	
Hubley, Faith E	*Animator*
%Hubley Studio, 2575 Palisade Ave, #12-L, Riverdale, NY 10463, USA	
Hubley, Season	*Actress*
46 Wavecrest Ave, Venice, CA 90291, USA	
Hubley, Whip	*Actor*
%Agency For Performing Arts, 9200 Sunset Blvd, #900, Los Angeles, CA 90069, USA	
Huckabee, Michael (Mike)	*Governor, AR*
%Governor's Office, 205 State Capitol Building, Little Rock, AR 72201, USA	
Huckstep, Ronald L	*Orthopedic Surgeon*
108 Sugarloaf Crescent, Castlecrag, Syndey NSW 2068, Australia	
Huddleston, David	*Actor*
%J Michael Bloom, 9255 Sunset Blvd, #710, Los Angeles, CA 90069, USA	
Huddleston, Trevor	*Religious Leader*
%House of Resurrection, Mirfield, W Yorks WF14 OBN, England	
Huddleston, Walter D	*Senator, KY*
Seminole Road, Elizabethtown, KY 42701, USA	
Hudecek, Vaclav	*Concert Violinist*
Londynska 25, 120 00 Prague 2, Czech Republic	
Hudner, Thomas J, Jr	*Korean War Navy Hero (CMH)*
31 Allen Farm Lane, Concord, MA 01742, USA	
Hudson, Bannus B	*Businessman*
%US Shoe Corp, 1 Eastwood Dr, Cincinnati, OH 45227, USA	
Hudson, C B, Jr	*Businessman*
%Liberty National Life, PO Box 2612, Birmingham, AL 35202, USA	
Hudson, Clifford G	*Financier*
%Securities Investor Protection, 805 15th St NW, Washington, DC 20005, USA	
Hudson, Ernie	*Actor*
5711 Hoback Glen Road, Hidden Hills, CA 91302, USA	
Hudson, Hugh	*Movie Director*
%Hudson Films Ltd, 11 Queensgate Place Mews, London SW7 5BG, England	
Hudson, James	*Psychiatrist*
%Harvard Medical School, 25 Shattuck St, Boston, MA 02115, USA	
Hudson, James T	*Businessman*
%Hudson Foods Inc, 1225 Hudson Road, Rogers, AR 72756, USA	
Hudson, Lou	*Basketball Player*
1589 Little Kate Road, Park City, UT 84060, USA	
Hudson, Michael T	*Businessman*
%Hudson Foods Inc, 1225 Hudson Road, Rogers, AR 72756, USA	
Hudson, Sally	*Skier*
PO Box 2343, Olympic Valley, CA 96146, USA	
Huebner, Robert J	*Medical Research Scientist*
12100 Whippoorwil Lane, Rockville, MD 20852, USA	
Huff, Kenneth W (Ken)	*Football Player*
105 Blackford Court, Durham, NC 27712, USA	
Huff, Sam	*Football Player*
824 Emerald Dr, Wellington, VA 22308, USA	
Huffington, Arianna	*Writer*
3005 45th St NW, Washington, DC 30016, USA	

Hufstedler, Shirley M *Secretary, Education*
%Hufstedler Kaus Ettinger, 355 S Grand Ave, Los Angeles, CA 90071, USA

Huggard, E Douglas *Businessman*
%Atlantic Energy, 6801 Black Horse Pike, Pleasantville, NJ 08234, USA

Huggins, Bob *Basketball Coach*
207 Beecher Hall, Cincinnati, OH 45221, USA

Hughes, Barnard *Actor*
1244 11th St, #A, Santa Monica, CA 90401, USA

Hughes, Finola *Actress*
4234 S Bel Air Dr, La Canada, CA 91011, USA

Hughes, H Richard *Architect*
47 Chiswick Quay, London W4 3UR, England

Hughes, Harold E *Senator, NJ*
%Democratic National Committee, 1625 Massachusetts NW, Washington, DC 20036, USA

Hughes, Harry R *Governor, MD*
%Patton Boggs Blow, 250 W Pratt St, #1100, Baltimore, MD 21201, USA

Hughes, John W *Movie Director, Screenwriter*
%Hughes Entertainment, 1 E Westminster Road, Lake Forest, IL 60045, USA

Hughes, Kathleen *Actress*
%Atkins Assoc, 303 S Crescent Heights Blvd, Los Angeles, CA 90048, USA

Hughes, Keith W *Financier*
%Associated Corp (NA), 250 Carpenter Freeway, Dallas, TX 75266, USA

Hughes, Ken *Movie Director*
2218 N Beachwood Dr, #301, Los Angeles, CA 90068, USA

Hughes, Louis R *Businessman*
%General Motors AG, Postfach, 8152 Glattbrugg, Switzerland

Hughes, Merv *Cricketer*
%Australian Cricket Board, 90 Jollimant St, Melbourne VIC 3002, Australia

Hughes, Patrick M (Pat) *Army General*
Director, Defense Intelligence Agency, Pentagon, Washington, DC 20340, USA

Hughes, Richard H (Dick) *Baseball Player*
PO Box 598, Stephens, AR 71764, USA

Hughes, Robert S F *Art Critic*
143 Prince St, New York, NY 10012, USA

Hughes, Ted *Writer*
%Faber & Faber, 3 Queen Square, London WC1N 3AN, England

Hughes, Thomas J, Jr *Navy Admiral*
5167 Myers Mill Road, Jeffersonton, VA 22724, USA

Hughes, Wendy *Actress*
129 Bourke St, Woolloomooloo, Sydney NSW 2011, Australia

Hughes-Fulford, Millie *Astronaut*
%Veterans Affairs Dept, Medical Center, 4150 Clement St, San Francisco, CA 94121, USA

Hugstedt, Petter *Ski Jumper*
3600 Kongsberg, Norway

Huguenin, G Richard *Inventor (Portable Gun Detector Camera)*
%Millitech Corp, South Deerfield, MA 01373, USA

Huizenga, H Wayne *Businessman*
%Blockbuster Entertainment, 901 E Las Olas Blvd, Fort Lauderdale, FL 33301, USA

Huizenga, John R *Nuclear Chemist*
43 McMichael Dr, Pinehurst, NC 28374, USA

Hulce, Tom *Actor*
2305 Stanley Hills Dr, Los Angeles, CA 90046, USA

Hull, Brett A *Hockey Player*
%St Louis Blues, Kiel Center, 1401 Clark Ave, St Louis, MO 63103, USA

Hull, Don *Olympic Official*
%US Olympic Committee, 1 Olympia Plaza, Colorado Springs, CO 80909, USA

Hull, Jane *Governor, AZ*
%Governor's Office, State Capitol, West Wing, Phoenix, AZ

Hull, Kent *Football Player*
RR 1 Box 574-B, Greenwood, MS 38930, USA

Hull, Robert M (Bobby) *Hockey Player*
1439 S Indiana Ave, Chicago, IL 60605, USA

Hulme, Denis *Auto Racing Driver*
CI-6, RDTE Puke, Bay of Plenny, New Zealand

Hulse, Russell A *Nobel Physics Laureate*
%Princeton University, Plasma Physics Laboratory, Princeton, NJ 08544, USA

Humann, L Phillip *Financier*
%SunTrust Banks, 22 Park Place NE, Atlanta, GA 30303, USA

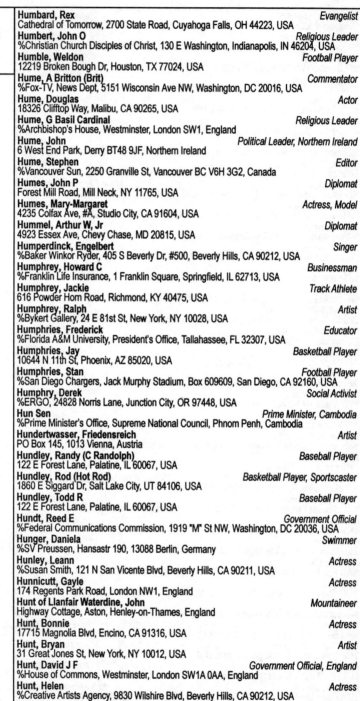

H

Humbard, Rex — *Evangelist*
Cathedral of Tomorrow, 2700 State Road, Cuyahoga Falls, OH 44223, USA

Humbert, John O — *Religious Leader*
%Christian Church Disciples of Christ, 130 E Washington, Indianapolis, IN 46204, USA

Humble, Weldon — *Football Player*
12219 Broken Bough Dr, Houston, TX 77024, USA

Hume, A Britton (Brit) — *Commentator*
%Fox-TV, News Dept, 5151 Wisconsin Ave NW, Washington, DC 20016, USA

Hume, Douglas — *Actor*
18326 Clifftop Way, Malibu, CA 90265, USA

Hume, G Basil Cardinal — *Religious Leader*
%Archbishop's House, Westminster, London SW1, England

Hume, John — *Political Leader, Northern Ireland*
6 West End Park, Derry BT48 9JF, Northern Ireland

Hume, Stephen — *Editor*
%Vancouver Sun, 2250 Granville St, Vancouver BC V6H 3G2, Canada

Humes, John P — *Diplomat*
Forest Mill Road, Mill Neck, NY 11765, USA

Humes, Mary-Margaret — *Actress, Model*
4235 Colfax Ave, #A, Studio City, CA 91604, USA

Hummel, Arthur W, Jr — *Diplomat*
4923 Essex Ave, Chevy Chase, MD 20815, USA

Humperdinck, Engelbert — *Singer*
%Baker Winkor Ryder, 405 S Beverly Dr, #500, Beverly Hills, CA 90212, USA

Humphrey, Howard C — *Businessman*
%Franklin Life Insurance, 1 Franklin Square, Springfield, IL 62713, USA

Humphrey, Jackie — *Track Athlete*
616 Powder Horn Road, Richmond, KY 40475, USA

Humphrey, Ralph — *Artist*
%Bykert Gallery, 24 E 81st St, New York, NY 10028, USA

Humphries, Frederick — *Educator*
%Florida A&M University, President's Office, Tallahassee, FL 32307, USA

Humphries, Jay — *Basketball Player*
10644 N 11th St, Phoenix, AZ 85020, USA

Humphries, Stan — *Football Player*
%San Diego Chargers, Jack Murphy Stadium, Box 609609, San Diego, CA 92160, USA

Humphry, Derek — *Social Activist*
%ERGO, 24828 Norris Lane, Junction City, OR 97448, USA

Hun Sen — *Prime Minister, Cambodia*
%Prime Minister's Office, Supreme National Council, Phnom Penh, Cambodia

Hundertwasser, Friedensreich — *Artist*
PO Box 145, 1013 Vienna, Austria

Hundley, Randy (C Randolph) — *Baseball Player*
122 E Forest Lane, Palatine, IL 60067, USA

Hundley, Rod (Hot Rod) — *Basketball Player, Sportscaster*
1860 E Siggard Dr, Salt Lake City, UT 84106, USA

Hundley, Todd R — *Baseball Player*
122 E Forest Lane, Palatine, IL 60067, USA

Hundt, Reed E — *Government Official*
%Federal Communications Commission, 1919 "M" St NW, Washington, DC 20036, USA

Hunger, Daniela — *Swimmer*
%SV Preussen, Hansastr 190, 13088 Berlin, Germany

Hunley, Leann — *Actress*
%Susan Smith, 121 N San Vicente Blvd, Beverly Hills, CA 90211, USA

Hunnicutt, Gayle — *Actress*
174 Regents Park Road, London NW1, England

Hunt of Llanfair Waterdine, John — *Mountaineer*
Highway Cottage, Aston, Henley-on-Thames, England

Hunt, Bonnie — *Actress*
17715 Magnolia Blvd, Encino, CA 91316, USA

Hunt, Bryan — *Artist*
31 Great Jones St, New York, NY 10012, USA

Hunt, David J F — *Government Official, England*
%House of Commons, Westminster, London SW1A 0AA, England

Hunt, Helen — *Actress*
%Creative Artists Agency, 9830 Wilshire Blvd, Beverly Hills, CA 90212, USA

Hunt, James B, Jr — *Governor, NC*
%Governor's Office, State Capitol, Raleigh, NC 27611, USA

Humbard - Hunt

Hunt, John R
Religious Leader
%Evangelical Covenant Church, 5101 N Francisco Ave, Chicago, IL 60625, USA

Hunt, Lamar
Football, Tennis, Soccer Executive
Thanksgiving Tower, 1601 Elm St, #2800, Dallas, TX 75201, USA

Hunt, Marsha
Actress
13131 Magnolia Blvd, Van Nuys, CA 91423, USA

Hunt, Nelson Bunker
Businessman
%Hunt Resources Corp, 1st International Building, #3600, Dallas, TX 75270, USA

Hunt, Nicholas S
Royal Navy Admiral, Businessman
%Eurotunnel, 111 Buckingham Palace Road, London SW1W 0ST, England

Hunt, Richard
Sculptor
1017 W Lill Ave, Chicago, IL 60614, USA

Hunt, Robert M
Publisher
%New York Daily News, 220 E 42nd St, New York, NY 10017, USA

Hunt, Ronald K (Ron)
Baseball Player
2806 Jackson Road, Wentzville, MO 63385, USA

Hunten, Donald M
Astronomer
10 Calle Corta, Tucson, AZ 85716, USA

Hunter (Ed McBain), Evan
Writer
324 Main Ave, #339, Norwalk, CT 06851, USA

Hunter, Dale
Hockey Player
2220 Hunt Valley Way, Gambrills, MD 21054, USA

Hunter, Holly
Actress
1223 Wilshire Blvd, #668, Santa Monica, CA 90403, USA

Hunter, James A (Jim Catfish)
Baseball Player
RR 1, Box 895, Hertford, NC 27944, USA

Hunter, Jesse
Singer, Guitarist
%Moress Nanas Shea, 1209 16th Ave S, Nashville, TN 37212, USA

Hunter, Jim
Skier
%Jungle Jim Hunter Mgmt, 864 Woodpark Way SW, Calgary AB T2W 2V8, Canada

Hunter, Kaki
Actress
%Gersh Agency, 232 N Canon Dr, Beverly Hills, CA 90210, USA

Hunter, Kim
Actress
42 Commerce St, New York, NY 10014, USA

Hunter, Lindsey
Basketball Player
%Detroit Pistons, Palace, 2 Championship Dr, Auburn Hills, MI 48326, USA

Hunter, R Alan
Businessman
%Stanley Works, 1000 Stanley Dr, New Britain, CT 06053, USA

Hunter, Rachel
Model
23 Beverly Park, Beverly Hills, CA 90210, USA

Hunter, Rita
Opera Singer
Cornways, 70 Embercourt Road, Thams Ditton, Surrey KT7 0LW, England

Hunter, Robert D
Financier
%Chase Manhattan Corp, 1 Chase Manhattan Plaza, Wilmington, DE 19801, USA

Hunter, Tab
Actor, Singer
223 N Guadalupe St, #292, Santa Fe, NM 87501, USA

Hunter-Gault, Charlayne
Commentator
%"MacNeil/Lehrer News Hour" Show, 2700 S Quincy St, #250, Arlington, VA 22206, USA

Hunthausen, Raymond G
Religious Leader
%Catholic Archdiocese of Seattle, 910 Marion, Seattle, WA 98104, USA

Huntington, Ellery C
Football Player
219 Wolfe St, Alexandria, VA 22314, USA

Huntington, Lawrence S
Financier
%Fiduciary Trust Co, 2 World Trade Center, New York, NY 10048, USA

Huntsman, Stanley H
Track Coach
5532 Timbercrest Trail, Knoxville, TN 37909, USA

Hunyadfi, Steven
Swimming Coach
838 Ridgewood Dr, #12, Fort Wayne, IN 46805, USA

Hunyady, Emese
Speed Skater
Beim Spitzriegel 1/2/9, 2500 Baden, Austria

Huo Yaobang
General Secretary, China
%Communist Party Central Committee, Zhongguo Gongchan Dang, Beijing, China

Hupp, Robert P
Religious Leader, Social Worker
%Father Flanagan's Boys Home, Boys Town, NE 68010, USA

Huppert, Isabelle
Actress
%Artmedia Varieties, 40 Rue Francois, 75008 Paris, France

Hurd, Douglas R
Government Official, England
5 Mitford Cottages, Westwell, Burford, Oxon, England

H

Hunt – Hurd

H

Hurd, Gale Anne	*Movie Producer*
%Pacific Western Productions, 270 N Canon Dr, #1195, Beverly Hills, CA 90210, USA	
Hurd, Joseph E (Joe)	*Air Force General*
Commander, 7th Air Force, Unit 2047, APO, AP 96278, USA	
Hurford, Peter J	*Concert Organist*
Broom House, St Bernard's Road, St Albans, Herts AL3 5RA, England	
Hurlburt, Wendell F	*Businessman*
%Esterline Technologies, 10800 NE 8th St, Bellevue, WA 98004, USA	
Hurley, Alfred F	*Writer, Historian*
%University of North Texas, President's Office, Denton, TX 76203, USA	
Hurley, Bobby	*Basketball Player*
728 Bridgeside Dr, Sacramento, CA 95831, USA	
Hurley, Denis E	*Religious Leader*
%Emanuel Catholic Cathedral, Cathedral Road, Durban 4001, South Africa	
Hurley, Elizabeth	*Actress, Model*
3 Cromwell Place, London DW 2JE, England	
Hurn, David	*Photographer*
Prospect Cottage, Tintern, Gwent, Wales	
Hurnik, Ilja	*Concert Pianist*
Narodni Trida 35, 11000 Prague 1, Czech Republic	
Hurt, Frank	*Labor Leader*
%Bakery Confectionery Tobacco Union, 10401 Connecticut, Kensington, MD 20895, USA	
Hurt, John	*Actor*
%Julian Belfarge, 46 Albermarle St, London W1X 4PP, England	
Hurt, Mary Beth	*Actress*
1619 Broadway, #900, New York, NY 10019, USA	
Hurt, William	*Actor*
370 Lexington Ave, #808, New York, NY 10017, USA	
Hurvich, Leo M	*Psychologist*
%University of Pennsylvania, Psychology Dept, Philadelphia, PA 19104, USA	
Hurwitz, Charles E	*Businessman*
%Maxxam Inc, PO Box 572887, Houston, TX 77257, USA	
Hurwitz, Emanuel	*Concert Violinist*
25 Dollis Ave, London N3 1DA, England	
Hurwitz, Jerard	*Molecular Biologist*
%Einstein College of Medicine, Yeshiva University, Bronx, NY 10461, USA	
Husa, Karel J	*Composer, Conductor*
1032 Hanshaw Road, Ithaca, NY 14850, USA	
Husband, Rick D	*Astronaut*
%NASA, Johnson Space Center, 2101 NASA Road, Houston, TX 77058, USA	
Husen, Torsten	*Educator*
%Int'l Educational Institute, Armfeltsgatan 10, 115 34 Stockholm, Sweden	
Huseynov, Surat	*Prime Minister, Azerbaijan*
%Prime Minister's Office, Baku, Azerbaijan	
Husky, Ferlin	*Singer, Songwriter*
%Richard Davis, 1030 N Woodland Dr, Kansas City, MO 64118, USA	
Hussein At-Takriti, Saddam	*President, Iraq*
%Revolutionary Command Council, Al-Sijoud Majalis, Baghdad, Iraq	
Hussein Ibn Talal	*King, Jordan*
%Royal Palace, Amman, Jordan	
Hussey, Olivia	*Actress*
PO Box 2507, Canyon Country, CA 91386, USA	
Hussey, Ruth	*Actress*
3361 Don Pablo Dr, Carlsbad, CA 92008, USA	
Huston, Anjelica	*Actress*
57 Windward Ave, Venice, CA 90291, USA	
Huston, John	*Golfer*
307 Lakeview Dr, Tarpon Springs, FL 34689, USA	
Hutcherson, Robert (Bobby)	*Jazz Vibist*
%Abby Hoffer, 223 1/2 E 48th St, New York, NY 10017, USA	
Hutchins, Will	*Actor*
PO Box 371, Glen Head, NY 11545, USA	
Hutchinson, Barbara	*Labor Leader*
%American Federation of Labor, 815 15th St NW, Washington, DC 20005, USA	
Hutchinson, Frederick E	*Educator*
%University of Maine, President's Office, Orono, ME 04469, USA	
Hutchinson, J Maxwell	*Architect*
10 St Augustine's Road, London NW1 9RN, England	

Hutchinson, Pemberton — *Businessman*
%Westmoreland Coal, Bellvue, 2 N Cascade Ave, Colorado Spings, CO 80903, USA
Hutchinson, W R — *Financier*
%Amoco Credit Corp, 200 E Randolph Dr, Chicago, IL 60601, USA
Hutchison, Clyde A, Jr — *Chemist*
%University of Chicago, Searle Laboratory, Chemistry Dept, Chicago, IL 60637, USA
Huth, Edward J — *Editor, Physician*
1124 Morris Ave, Bryn Mawr, PA 19010, USA
Hutson, Don — *Businessman*
%TIG Insurance, 5205 N O'Connor Blvd, Irving, TX 75039, USA
Hutt, Peter B — *Attorney*
%Covington & Burling, 1201 Pennsylvania Ave NW, Washington, DC 20004, USA
Hutton, Betty — *Actress, Singer*
1350 N Highland Place, Newport, RI 02840, USA
Hutton, Edward L — *Businessman*
%Chemed Corp, Chemed Center, 255 E 5th St, Cincinnati, OH 45202, USA
Hutton, Lauren — *Model, Actress*
382 Lafayette St, #6, New York, NY 10003, USA
Hutton, Ralph — *Swimmer*
%Vancouver Police Department, 312 Main St, Vancouver BC, Canada
Hutton, Timothy — *Actor*
RR 2, Box 331-B, Cushman Road, Patterson, NY 12563, USA
Huxley, Andrew F — *Nobel Medicine Laureate*
Master's Lodge, Trinity College, Cambridge CB2 1TQ, England
Huxley, Laura — *Therapist, Writer*
6233 Mulholland Dr, Los Angeles, CA 90068, USA
Huxtable, Ada Louise — *Architectural Critic*
969 Park Ave, New York, NY 10028, USA
Huyck, Willard — *Movie Director*
39 Oakmont Dr, Los Angeles, CA 90049, USA
Hvorostovsky, Dmitri — *Opera Singer*
%Metropolitan Opera Assn, Lincoln Center Plaza, New York, NY 10023, USA
Hwang, David Henry — *Writer*
70 W 36th St, #501, New York, NY 10018, USA
Hyams, Joseph I (Joe), Jr — *Writer*
10375 Wilshire Blvd, #4-D, Los Angeles, CA 90024, USA
Hyams, Peter — *Movie Director*
307 N Bristol Ave, Los Angeles, CA 90049, USA
Hyatt, Joel Z — *Attorney, Businessman*
%Hyatt Legal Services, 1215 Superior Ave E, Cleveland, OH 44114, USA
Hybl, William J — *Sports Official*
%US Olympic Committee, 1 Olympia Plaza, Colorado Springs, CO 80909, USA
Hyde-White, Alex — *Actor*
%Artists Group, 10100 Santa Monica Blvd, #2490, Los Angeles, CA 90067, USA
Hyer, Martha — *Actress*
4100 W Alameda Ave, #204, Toluca Lake, CA 91505, USA
Hyland, Brian — *Singer*
%Stone Buffalo, PO Box 101, Helendale, CA 92342, USA
Hyland, William G — *Government Official*
%Council on Foreign Relations, 58 E 68th St, New York, NY 10021, USA
Hylton, Thomas J — *Journalist*
%Pottstown Mercury, Editorial Dept, Hanover & King Sts, Pottstown, PA 19464, USA
Hyman, Earle — *Actor*
%Manhattan Towers, 484 W 43rd St, #33-E, New York, NY 10036, USA
Hyman, Morton P — *Businessman*
%Overseas Shipholding Group, 1114 Ave of Americas, New York, NY 10036, USA
Hyman, Richard R (Dick) — *Jazz Pianist, Composer*
%Abby Hoffer, 223 1/2 E 48th St, New York, NY 10017, USA
Hynde, Chrissie — *Singer, Guitarist, Songwriter*
%Premier Talent, 3 E 54th St, #1100, New York, NY 10022, USA
Hynes, Samuel — *Writer*
130 Moore St, Princeton, NJ 08540, USA
Hynter, Nicholas R — *Theater Director*
%National Theatre, South Bank, London SE1 9PX, England
Hyser, Joyce — *Actress*
%Artists Agency, 10000 Santa Monica Blvd, #305, Los Angeles, CA 90067, USA

H

Hutchinson - Hyser

I

Iacobellis, Sam F *Businessman, Aeronautical Engineer*
%Rockwell International, PO Box 5090, Costa Mesa, CA 92628, USA
Iacocca, Lido A (Lee) *Businessman*
30 Scenic Oaks Dr N, Bloomfield Hills, MI 48304, USA
Iaconio, Frank *Auto Racing Driver*
250 US Highway 206, Flanders, NJ 07836, USA
Iafrate, Al A *Hockey Player*
27480 Five Mile Road, Livonia, MI 48154, USA
Iakovos, Primate Archbishop *Religious Leader*
%Greek Orthodox Archdiocese, 8-10 E 79th St, New York, NY 10021, USA
Ian, Janis *Singer, Songwriter*
%Senior Mgmt, PO Box 218200, Nashville, TN 37221, USA
Ibbetson, Arthur *Cinematographer*
%Tanglewood, Chalfont Lane, Chorlry Wood, Herts, England
Ibrahim, Abdullah (Dollar Brand) *Jazz Pianist, Composer*
%Xippi Productions, Benjamin House, 81 Ardmore Road, West Hartford, CT 06119, USA
Ibrahim, Barre Mainassara *Head of State, Niger; Army Officer*
%Head of State's Office, Presidential Palace, Niamey, Niger
Ibuka, Masaru *Inventor, Businessman*
%Sony Corp, 6-7-35 Kitashinagawa, Shinagawaku, Tokyo 141, Japan
Icahn, Carl C *Businessman*
%Icahn Co, 100 S Bedford Road, Mount Kisco, NY 10549, USA
Ice Cube (O'Shea Jackson) *Rap Artist*
%It's Happening Now Presents, PO Box 8073, Pittsburg, CA 94565, USA
Ice T (Tracy Marrow) *Rap Artist, Actor*
2287 Sunset Plaza Dr, Los Angeles, CA 90069, USA
Ickx, Jacky *Auto Racing Driver*
171 Chaussee de la Hulpe, 1170 Brussels, Belgium
Idei, Nobuyuki *Businessman*
%Sony Corp, 6-7-35 Kitashinagawa, Shingawaku, Tokyo 141, Japan
Idle, Eric *Comedian (Monty Python), Actor*
%Mayday Mgmt, 68-A Delancey St, Camden Town, London NW1 7RY, England
Idol, Billy *Singer, Songwriter*
%East End Mgmt, 8209 Melrose Ave, #200, Los Angeles, CA 90046, USA
Iger, Robert A *Broadcast Executive*
%Capital Cities/ABC, 77 W 66th St, New York, NY 10023, USA
Iglesias, Enrique *Singer*
%Fernan Martinez, 601 Brickell Key Dr, Miami, FL 33131, USA
Iglesias, Julio *Singer*
5 Indian Creek Dr, Miami, FL 33154, USA
Ignatow, David *Writer*
PO Box 1458, East Hampton, NY 11937, USA
Ihnatowicz, Zbigniew *Architect*
Ul Mokotowska 31 M 15, 00-560 Warsaw, Poland
Ikagawa, Tadaichi *Financier*
%Sumitomo Bank of California, 320 California St, San Francisco, CA 94104, USA
Ike, Reverend *Evangelist*
4140 Broadway, New York, NY 10033, USA
Ikeda, Daisaku *Religious Leader*
%Soka Gakkai, 32 Shinanomachi, Shinjuku, Tokyo 160, Japan
Ikola, Willard *Hockey Player, Coach*
5697 Green Circle Drive, #316, Minnetonka, MN 55343, USA
Ilchman, Alice Stone *Educator*
%Sarah Lawrence College, President's Office, Bronxville, NY 10708, USA
Iley, Barbara *Actress*
%Paradigm Agency, 10100 Santa Monica Blvd, #2500, Los Angeles, CA 90067, USA
Ilg, Raymond P *Navy Admiral*
5504 Teak Court, Alexandria, VA 22309, USA
Ilgauskas, Zydrunas *Basketball Player*
%Cleveland Cavaliers, 2923 Statesboro Road, Richfield, OH 44286, USA
Iliescu, Ion *President, Romania*
R 71341, Piata, Victoriei 1, Bucharest, Romania
Illich, Ivan *Educator, Writer, Theologian*
Apdo Postal 1-479, 62001 Cuernavaca, Morelos, Mexico
Illmann, Margaret *Ballerina*
%National Ballet of Canada, 157 E King St, Toronto ON M5C 1G9, Canada
Imai, Kenji *Architect*
4-12-28 Kitazawa, Setagayaku, Tokyo, Japan

Iacobellis - Imai

Imai, Nobuko *Concert Viola Player*
%Harrison Mgmt, Clarendon Court, Park St, Charlbury Oxon OX7 3PS, England
Imamura, Shohei *Movie Director*
%Toei Co, 3-2-17 Ginza, Chuoku, Tokyo 104, Japan
Iman (Abudulmajid) *Model*
639 N Larchmont Blvd, #207, Los Angeles, CA 90004, USA
Imbert, Peter M *Law Enforcement Official*
%New Scotland Yard, Broadway, London SW1H 0BG, England
Imbrie, Andrew W *Composer*
2625 Rose St, Berkeley, CA 94708, USA
Imhoff, Darrall *Basketball Player*
1824 Ridgley Blvd, Eugene, OR 97401, USA
Imhoff, Gary *Actor*
%Samantha Group, 300 S Raymond Ave, Pasadena, CA 91105, USA
Imie, John F, Jr *Businessman*
%Unocal Corp, 2101 Rosecrans Ave, #1200, El Segundo, CA 90245, USA
Immerfall, Daniel (Dan) *Speedskater*
214 Glenway St, Madison, WI 53705, USA
Imshenetsky, Aleksandr A *Microbiologist*
%Russian Academy of Sciences, Profsoyuznaya Ul 7, Moscow, Russia
Imus, Don *Radio Entertainer*
%WFAN-Radio, 34-12 36th St, Long Island City, NY 11106, USA
Inaba, Kosaku *Businessman*
%Ishikawajima-Harima, 2-1 Ohtemachi, Tokyo 100, Japan
Inai, Yoshihiro *Businessman*
%Mitsubishi Metal, 1-5-2 Otemachi, Chiyodaku, Tokyo 100, Japan
Inatome, Rick *Businessman*
%InaCom Corp, 10810 Farnam Dr, Omaha, NE 68154, USA
Inbal, Eliahu *Conductor*
%Hessischer Rundfunk, Bertramstr 8, 60320 Frankfurt/Main, Germany
Incaviglia, Peter J (Pete) *Baseball Player*
PO Box 526, Pebble Beach, CA 93953, USA
Indiana, Robert *Artist*
Star of Hope, Vinalhaven, ME 04863, USA
Indurain, Miguel *Cyclist*
%Banesto, Avenida Bajona 37, 31011 Pamplona, Spain
Infante, Lindy *Football Coach*
%Indianapolis Colts, 7001 W 56th St, Indianapolis, IN 46254, USA
Infill, O Urcille, Jr *Religious Leader*
%African Methodist Church, Box 19039, Germantown Station, Philadelphia, PA 19138, USA
Inge, Peter A *Army General, England*
%Barclays Bank, Market Place, Leyburn, North Yorkshire DL8 5BQ, England
Ingels, Marty *Actor, Comedian*
%Ingels Entertainment, 8127 Melrose Ave, West Hollywood, CA 90046, USA
Ingersoll, Mary *Actress*
%Whitaker Agency, 4924 Vineland Ave, North Hollywood, CA 91601, USA
Ingersoll, Ralph, II *Publisher*
%Ingersoll Publications, PO Box 1869, Lakeville, CT 06039, USA
Inghram, Mark G *Physicist*
3077 Lakeshore Ave, Holland, MI 49424, USA
Ingle, Doug *Singer, Keyboardist (Iron Butterfly)*
%Holiday Entertainment, 8803 Mayne St, Bellflower, CA 90706, USA
Ingle, John *Actor*
%Artists Group, 10100 Santa Monica Blvd, #2490, Los Angeles, CA 90067, USA
Ingle, Robert D *Editor*
%San Jose Mercury News, Editorial Dept, 750 Ridder Park Dr, San Jose, CA 95131, USA
Ingman, Einar H, Jr *Korean War Army Hero (CMH)*
W-4053 N Silver Lake Road, Irma, WI 54442, USA
Ingraham, Hubert A *Prime Minister, Bahamas*
%Prime Minister's Office, Whitfield Center, Box CB-10980, Nassau, Bahamas
Ingram, A John *Surgeon*
190 Belle Meade Lane, Memphis, TN 38117, USA
Ingram, James *Singer, Songwriter*
867 Muirfield Road, Los Angeles, CA 90005, USA
Ingram, Lonnie *Microbiologist*
%University of Florida, Microbiology/Cell Science Dept, Gainesville, FL 32611, USA
Ingram, Vernon M *Biochemist*
%Massachusetts Institute of Technology, Biochemistry Dept, Cambridge, MA 02139, USA

Ingrao, Pietro *Government Official, Italy*
%Centro Studie Iniziative Per La Reforma, Via Della Vite 13, Rome, Italy
Ingrassia, Paul J *Journalist*
111 Division Ave, New Providence, NJ 07974, USA
Ingrid *Queen, Denmark*
%Amalienborg Palaca, 1257 Copenhagen K, Denmark
Ingstad, Anne Stine *Writer, Explorer*
Vettalivei 24, 0389 Oslo 3, Norway
Ingstad, Helge M *Explorer*
Vettalivei 24, 0389 Oslo 3, Norway
Inkster, Juli *Golfer*
23140 Mora Glen Dr, Los Altos, CA 94024, USA
Inman, Bobby Ray *Navy Admiral, Government Official*
3300 Bee Cave Road, #650-221, Austin, TX 78746, USA
Inman, John *Actor*
%Nick Thomas Artistes, 11-13 Broad Court, London WC2B 5QN, England
Inman, John *Golfer*
355 Carybell Lane, Alpharetta, GA 30004, USA
Innauer, Toni *Ski Jumper, Coach*
Steinbruckstr 8/II, 6024 Innsburck, Austria
Innaurato, Albert F *Writer*
325 W 22nd St, New York, NY 10011, USA
Innes, Laura *Actress*
%Don Buchwald, 9229 Sunset Blvd, #710, Los Angeles, CA 90069, USA
Innis, Roy E A *Civil Rights Activist*
%Congress of Racial Equality, 310 Cooper Square, New York, NY 10003, USA
Innocenti, Antonio Cardinal *Religious Leader*
%Pontifical Commission, 00120 Vatican City
inogradov, Pavel *Cosmonaut*
%Potchta Kosmonavtov, Moskovskoi Oblasti, 141160 Syvisdny Goroduk, Russia
Inoue, Shinya *Biologist, Photographer*
%Marine Biological Laboratory, 167 Water St, Woods Hole, MA 02543, USA
Inoue, Yuichi *Artist*
Ohkamiyashiki, 2475-2 Kurami, Samakawamachi 253-01, Kozagun, Kam, Japan
Inskeep, J Jerry, Jr *Financier*
%Columbia Management, 1300 SW 6th St, Portland, OR 97201, USA
Insko, Del *Harness Racing Driver*
Rt 1, Box 65, South Beloit, IL 61080, USA
Insley, Will *Artist*
231 Bowery, New York, NY 10002, USA
Insolia, Anthony *Editor*
%Newsday, Editorial Dept, 235 Pinelawn, Melville, NY 11747, USA
Ioannisiani, Bagrat K *Astronomer*
%State Institute of Optics, St Petersburg, Russia
Ipcar, Dahlov *Illustrator, Artist*
HCR-33, PO Box 432, Bath, ME 04530, USA
Ippolito, Angelo *Artist*
Powderhouse Road, Box 45, Vestal, NY 13851, USA
Irani, Ray R *Businessman*
%Occidental Petroleum, 10889 Wilshire Blvd, Los Angeles, CA 90024, USA
Irbe, Arturs *Hockey Player*
%Vancouver Canucks, 800 Griffiths Way, Vancouver BC V6B 6G1, Canada
Iredale, Randle W *Architect*
1151 W 8th Ave, Vancouver BC V6H 1C5, Canada
Ireland, Kathy *Model, Actress*
%Sterling/Winters, 1900 Ave of Stars, #1640, Los Angeles, CA 90067, USA
Ireland, Patricia *Association Executive*
%National Organization for Women, 1000 16th St NW, Washington, DC 20036, USA
Iris, Donnie *Singer, Songwriter*
807 Darlington Road, Beaver Falls, PA 15010, USA
Irizarry, Vincent *Actor*
%David Shapira, 15301 Ventura Blvd, #345, Sherman Oaks, CA 91403, USA
Irons, Jeremy *Actor*
%Hutton Mgmt, 200 Fulham Road, London SW10 9PN, England
Ironside, Michael *Actor*
%Gold Marshak Liedtke, 3500 W Olive Ave, #1400, Burbank, CA 91505, USA
Irrera, Dom *Comedian, Actor*
%Metropolitan Talent Agency, 4526 Wilshire Blvd, Los Angeles, CA 90010, USA

Irvan, Ernie	Auto Racing Driver
80 Lowe Ave, Concord, NC 28027, USA	
Irvin, John	Movie Director
6 Lower Common South, London SW15 1BP, England	
Irvin, Michael J	Football Player
2339 Aberdeen Bend, Carrollton, TX 75007, USA	
Irvin, Monford M (Monte)	Baseball Player
11 Douglas Court S, Homosassa, FL 34446, USA	
Irving, Amy	Actress
11693 San Vicente Blvd, #335, Los Angeles, CA 90049, USA	
Irving, Stu	Hockey Player
93 Hart St, Beverly Farms, MA 01915, USA	
Irwin, Bill	Entertainer, Clown
56 7th Ave, #4-E, New York, NY 10011, USA	
Irwin, Elaine	Model
%Ford Model Agency, 344 E 59th St, New York, NY 10022, USA	
Irwin, Hale S	Golfer
%Hale Irwin Golf Service, 9909 Clayton Road, St Louis, MO 63124, USA	
Irwin, Malcolm R	Biologist
4720 Regent St, Madison, WI 53705, USA	
Irwin, Paul G	Association Executive
%Humane Society of the United States, 2100 "L" St NW, Washington, DC 20037, USA	
Irwin, Robert W	Artist
%Pace Gallery, 32 E 57th St, New York, NY 10022, USA	
Isaacs, Jeremy I	Opera Director
%Royal Opera House, Covent Garden, Bow St, London WC2 7Q4, England	
Isaacs, John (Speed)	Basketball Player
1412 Crotona Ave, Bronx, NY 10456, USA	
Isaacs, Susan	Writer
%Harper Collins Publishers, 10 E 53rd St, New York, NY 10022, USA	
Isaacson, Julius	Labor Leader
%Novelty & Production Workers Union, 1815 Franklin Ave, Valley Stream, NY 11581, USA	
Isaak, Chris	Singer, Songwriter, Actor
PO Box 547, Larkspur, CA 94977, USA	
Isaak, Russell	Businessman
%CPI Corp, 1706 Washington Ave, St Louis, MO 63103, USA	
Isacksen, Peter	Actor
4635 Placidia Ave, North Hollywood, CA 91602, USA	
Isard, Walter	Regional Economist
3218 Garrett Road, Drexel Hill, PA 19026, USA	
Isenberg, Eugene M	Businessman
%Nabors Industries, 515 W Greens Road, Houston, TX 77067, USA	
Isenburger, Eric	Artist
140 E 56th St, New York, NY 10022, USA	
Ishibashi, Kanichiro	Businessman
%Bridgestone Corp, 1-10-1 Kyobashi, Chuoku, Tokyo 104, Japan	
Ishida, Jim	Actor
871 N Vail Ave, Montebello, CA 90640, USA	
Ishiguro, Kazuo	Writer
%Faber & Faber Ltd, 3 Queens Square, London WC1N 3AO, England	
Ishihara, Shintaro	Government Official, Japan
%Liberal Democratic Party, Diet, Tokyo, Japan	
Ishihara, Takashi	Businessman
%Nissan Motor, 6-17-1 Ginza, Chuoku, Tokyo 104, Japan	
Ishii, Kazuhiro	Architect
4-14-27 Akasaka, Minatoku, Tokyo 107, Japan	
Ishimaru, Akira	Electrical Engineer
2913 165th Place NE, Bellevue, WA 98008, USA	
Ishizaka, Kimishige	Allergist
%Allergy/Immunology Institute, 11149 N Torrey Pines Road, La Jolla, CA 92037, USA	
Ishizaka, Teruko	Allergist
%Good Samaritan Hospital, 5601 Loch Raven Blvd, Baltimore, MD 21239, USA	
Iskander, Fazil A	Writer
Krasnoarmeiskaya Str 23, #104, 125319 Moscow, Russia	
Isley, Ronald (Ron)	Singer
%Ron Weisner Mgmt, PO Box 261640, Encino, CA 91426, USA	
Ismail, Ahmed Sultan	Mechanical Engineer
43 Ahmed Abdel Aziz St, Dokki, Cairo, Egypt	

I

Irvan - Ismail

Ismail, Raghib (Rocket) *Football Player*
26 Mountainwood Dr, Mountain Top, PA 18707, USA
Isom, Gerald A *Businessman*
%Insurance Co (NA), 1601 Chestnut St, Philadelphia, PA 19192, USA
Ison, Christopher J *Journalist*
%Minneapolis-St Paul Star Tribune, 425 Portland Ave, Minneapolis, MN 55488, USA
Isozaki, Arata *Architect*
%Arata Assoc, 6-17-9 Akasaka, Minatoku, Tokyo 107, Japan
Issel, Daniel P (Dan) *Basketball Player, Coach, Executive*
10163 E Woodbury Road, Englewood, CO 80111, USA
Istock, Verne G *Financier*
%NBD Bancorp, 611 Woodward Ave, Detroit, MI 48226, USA
Istomin, Eugene G *Concert Pianist*
225 W 71st St, New York, NY 10023, USA
Itami, Juzo *Movie Director*
%Itami Productions, Sekaeya Bldg, 4-8-6 Akasaka, Minatoku, Tokyo, Japan
Ito, Lance *Judge*
%Los Angeles Superior Court, 210 W Temple St, Los Angeles, CA 90012, USA
Ito, Masatoshi *Businessman*
%Southland Corp, 2711 N Haskell Ave, Dallas, TX 75204, USA
Ito, Masayoshi *Government Official, Japan*
1-28-3 Chitose-Dai, Setagayaku, Tokyo 157, Japan
Ito, Midori *Figure Skater*
%Skating Federation, Kryshi Taaikukan 1-1-1, Shibuyaku, Tokyo 10, Japan
Ito, Robert *Actor*
%Chateau/Billings Agency, 5657 Wilshire Blvd, #340, Los Angeles, CA 90036, USA
Ito, Shinsui *Artist*
Kita-Kamakura, Kanagawa Prefecture, Japan
Itoh, Junji *Businessman*
%Kanebo Ltd, 5-90-1 Tomobuchicho, Miyakojimaku, Osaka 534, Japan
Iue, Satoshi *Businessman*
%Sanyo Electric Co, 2-18 Keihan-Hondori, Moriguchi City 570, Japan
Ivan, Thomas N (Tommy) *Hockey Executive*
557 N King Muir Road, Lake Forest, IL 60045, USA
Ivanchenkov, Alexander S *Cosmonaut*
%Potchta Kosmonavtov, Moskovskoi Oblasti, 141160 Syvisdny Goroduk, Russia
Ivanisevic, Goran *Tennis Player*
Alijnoviceva 28, 58000 Split, Yugoslavia
Iverson, Allen *Basketball Player*
%Philadelphia 76ers, Veterans Stadium, PO Box 25040, Philadelphia, PA 19147, USA
Iverson, F Kenneth *Businessman*
%Nucor Corp, 2100 Rexford Road, Charlotte, NC 28211, USA
Ives, J Atwood *Businessman*
%Eastern Enterprises, 9 Riverside Road, Weston, MA 02193, USA
Ivester, M Douglas *Businessman*
%Coca-Cola Co, 1 Coca-Cola Plaza, 310 North Ave NW, Atlanta, GA 30313, USA
Ivey, Dana *Actress*
%Paradigm Agency, 10100 Santa Monica Blvd, #2500, Los Angeles, CA 90067, USA
Ivey, James B (Jim) *Editorial Cartoonist*
2605 Curry Ford Road, Orlando, FL 32806, USA
Ivey, Judith *Actress*
4470 W Sunset Blvd, #131, Los Angeles, CA 90027, USA
Ivins, Marsha S *Astronaut*
%NASA, Johnson Space Center, 2101 NASA Road, Houston, TX 77058, USA
Ivins, Molly *Commentator, Columnist*
%CBS-TV, News Dept, 51 W 52nd St, New York, NY 10019, USA
Ivory, James F *Movie Director, Producer*
%Merchant-Ivory Productions, 46 Lexington St, London W1P 3LH, England
Iwago, Mitsuaki *Photographer*
Edelhof Daichi Building, #2-F, 8 Honsio-cho, Shinjukaku, Tokyo 160, Japan
Iwata, Kazuo *Businessman*
%Toshiba Corp, 72 Horikawacho, Sawwaiku, Kawasaki 210, Japan
Iwerks, Donald W *Entertainment Executive*
%Iwerks Entertainment, PO Box 7744, Burbank, CA 91510, USA
Izetbegovic, Alija *Co-President, Bosnia-Herzegovina*
%President's Office, Marsala Titz 7-A, 71000 Sarajevo, Bosnia-Herzegovina

Jablonski, Henryk President of Council, Poland
Ul Filtrowa 61 M 4, 02-056 Warsaw, Poland
Jackee (Harry) Actress
8649 Metz Place, Los Angeles, CA 90069, USA
Jacklin, Tony Golfer
10952 Egret Pointe Lane, West Palm Beach, FL 33412, USA
Jackson, Alan Singer, Songwriter
%Chip Peay, 1101 17th Ave S, Nashville, TN 37212, USA
Jackson, Anne Actress
90 Riverside Dr, New York, NY 10024, USA
Jackson, Arthur J WW II Marine Corps Hero (CMH)
1290 E Spring Court, Boise, ID 83712, USA
Jackson, Betty Fashion Designer
33 Tottenham St, London W1, England
Jackson, Bobby Basketball Player
%Seattle Supersonics, 190 Queen Ave N, PO Box C-900911, Seattle, WA 98109, USA
Jackson, Chuck Singer
%Headline Talent, 1650 Broadway, #508, New York, NY 10019, USA
Jackson, Danny L Baseball Player
%Philadelphia Phillies, Veterans Stadium, PO Box 7575, Philadelphia, PA 19101, USA
Jackson, Daryl S Architect
161 Hoham St, East Melbourne, VIC 3002, Australia
Jackson, Doris Singer (The Shirelles)
%Nationwide Entertainment, 2756 N Green Valley Pkwy, #449, Las Vegas, NV 89014, USA
Jackson, Freddie Singer
%Pyramid Entertainment, 89 5th Ave, #700, New York, NY 10003, USA
Jackson, Glenda Actress
51 Harvey Road, Blackheath, London SE3, England
Jackson, Harold Journalist
%Birmingham News, Editorial Dept, 2200 N 4th Ave N, Birmingham, AL 35203, USA
Jackson, Harry A Artist
PO Box 2836, Cody, WY 82414, USA
Jackson, Janet Singer, Actress, Dancer
%Creative Artists Agency, 9830 Wilshire Blvd, Beverly Hills, CA 90212, USA
Jackson, Jeremy Actor
%Mary Grady, 4444 Lankershim Blvd, #207, North Hollywood, CA 91602, USA
Jackson, Jermaine Singer, Songwriter
4641 Hayvenhurst Dr, Encino, CA 91436, USA
Jackson, Jesse L Evangelist, Civil Rights Activist
%Operation Push, 930 E 50th St, Chicago, IL 60615, USA
Jackson, Jim Basketball Player
%Philadelphia 76ers, Veterans Stadium, PO Box 25040, Philadelphia, PA 19147, USA
Jackson, Joe Singer, Songwriter
%Basement Music, Trinity House, 6 Pembridge Road, London W11, England
Jackson, Joe M Vietnam War Air Force Hero (CMH)
25320 38th Ave S, Kent, WA 98032, USA
Jackson, John David Boxer
7045 Holly Park Dr S, #436, Seattle, WA 98118, USA
Jackson, Kate Actress
624 N Rodeo Dr, Beverly Hills, CA 90210, USA
Jackson, Keith J Football Player
11 Chenal Circle, Little Rock, AR 72211, USA
Jackson, Keith M Sportscaster
%ABC-TV, Sports Dept, 77 W 66th St, New York, NY 10023, USA
Jackson, Larry R Labor Leader
%Grain Millers Federation, 4949 Olson Memorial Parkway, Minneapolis, MN 55422, USA
Jackson, LaToya Singer
%Leonard Fink, 30 Daniel Low Terrace, #3-R, Staten Island, NY 10301, USA
Jackson, Mark Basketball Player
11423 197th St, St Albans, NY 11412, USA
Jackson, Mary Actress
2055 Grace Ave, Los Angeles, CA 90068, USA
Jackson, Michael Singer, Songwriter, Actor
%MJJ Productions, 9255 W Sunset Blvd, #1100, Los Angeles, CA 90069, USA
Jackson, Millie Singer, Songwriter, Actor
%Associated Booking Corp, 1995 Broadway, #501, New York, NY 10023, USA
Jackson, Milton (Bags) Jazz Pianist
%Ted Kurland, 173 Brighton Ave, Boston, MA 02134, USA

J

Jablonski - Jackson

Jackson, Peter — *Movie Director*
%International Creative Mgmt, 8942 Wilshire Blvd, Beverly Hills, CA 90211, USA
Jackson, Philip — *Actor*
%Markham & Froggatt, Julian House, 4 Windmill St, London W1P 1HF, England
Jackson, Philip D (Phil) — *Basketball Player, Coach*
1200 Valley Road, Bannockburn, IL 60015, USA
Jackson, R Graham — *Architect*
%Calhoun Tungate Jackson Dill Architects, 6200 Savoy Dr, Houston, TX 77036, USA
Jackson, Rebbie — *Singer, Songwriter*
4641 Hayvenhurst Dr, Encino, CA 91436, USA
Jackson, Reginald M (Reggie) — *Baseball Player*
305 Amador Ave, Seaside, CA 93955, USA
Jackson, Rickey — *Football Player*
23 Rosedown Dr, Destrehan, LA 70047, USA
Jackson, Ronald Shannon — *Jazz Drummer*
%Worldwide Jazz, 1128 Broadway, #425, New York, NY 10010, USA
Jackson, Rose — *Actress*
%Judy Schoen, 606 N Larchmont Blvd, #309, Los Angeles, CA 90004, USA
Jackson, Roy I — *International Civil Servant*
%Food/Agriculture Organization, Via delle Terme di Caracalla, Rome, Italy
Jackson, Samuel L — *Actor*
5128 Encino Ave, Encino, CA 91316, USA
Jackson, Sherry — *Actress*
4933 Encino Ave, Encino, CA 91316, USA
Jackson, Stonewall — *Singer, Songwriter*
6007 Cloverland Dr, Brentwood, TN 37027, USA
Jackson, Stoney — *Actor*
%Agency For Performing Arts, 9200 Sunset Blvd, #900, Los Angeles, CA 90069, USA
Jackson, Tito — *Singer*
23725 Long Valley Road, Hidden Hills, CA 91302, USA
Jackson, Victoria — *Actress*
14631 Belgowan Road, #2-5, Hialeah, FL 33016, USA
Jackson, Vincent E (Bo) — *Football, Baseball Player*
1765 Old Shell Road, Mobile, AL 36604, USA
Jackson, Wanda — *Singer*
10326 Greenbriar Parkway, Oklahoma City, OK 73159, USA
Jacob, Francois — *Nobel Medicine Laureate*
%Institut Pasteur, 25 Rue du Dr Roux, 75015 Paris, France
Jacob, Irene — *Actress*
%Nicole Cann, 1 Rue Alfred de Vigny, 75008 Paris, France
Jacob, John E — *Civil Rights Activist*
%National Urban League, 120 Wall St, #700, New York, NY 10005, USA
Jacob, Katerina — *Actress*
%Agentur Doris Mattes, Merzstr 14, 81679 Munich, Germany
Jacob, Stanley W — *Surgeon*
1055 SW Westwood Court, Portland, OR 97201, USA
Jacobi, Derek — *Actor*
%International Creative Mgmt, 76 Oxford St, London W1N 0AX, England
Jacobi, Lou — *Actor*
240 Central Park South, New York, NY 10019, USA
Jacobs, Jack H — *Vietnam War Army Hero (CMH)*
%Bankers Trust Co, 1 Appold St, London EC2A 2HE, England
Jacobs, Jane — *Writer*
%Random House Inc, 201 E 50th St, New York, NY 10022, USA
Jacobs, Jim — *Writer*
%International Creative Mgmt, 40 W 57th St, New York, NY 10019, USA
Jacobs, Julien I — *Judge*
%US Tax Court, 400 2nd St NW, Washington, DC 20217, USA
Jacobs, Lawrence-Hilton — *Actor*
3804 Evans St, #2, Los Angeles, CA 90027, USA
Jacobs, Marc — *Fashion Designer*
%Marc Jacobs Co, 113 Spring St, #300, New York, NY 10012, USA
Jacobs, Norman J — *Publisher*
%Century Publishing Co, 990 Grove St, Evanston, IL 60201, USA
Jacobs, Wilfred E — *Governor General, Antigua & Barbuda*
Government House, St John's, Antigua
Jacobsen, James C — *Businessman*
%Kellwood Co, 600 Kellwood Parkway, St Louis, MO 63017, USA

Jacobsen, Peter — *Golfer*
16 Dover Way, Lake Oswego, OR 97034, USA

Jacobsen, Steven C — *Microbiotics Engineer*
%University of Utah, Engineering Design Center, Salt Lake City, UT 84112, USA

Jacobson, A Thurl — *Petroleum Geologist*
1734 N Oak Crest Dr, Orem, UT 84097, USA

Jacobson, Herbert L — *Diplomat, Journalist*
Apartado 160, Escazu, Costa Rica

Jacobson, Nathan — *Mathematician*
2 Prospect Court, Hamden, CT 06517, USA

Jacoby, Scott — *Actor*
PO Box 461100, Los Angeles, CA 90046, USA

Jacot, Michele — *Skier*
Residence du Brevent, 74 Chamonix, France

Jacquet, Illinois — *Jazz Saxophonist*
%Bowen Agency, 504 W 168th St, New York, NY 10032, USA

Jacquot, Pierre E — *Army General, France*
15 Ave de Villars, 75007 Paris, France

Jacuzzi, Roy — *Businessman*
%Jacuzzi Whirlpool Bath, 2121 N California Blvd, Walnut Creek, CA 94596, USA

Jadot, Jean L O — *Religious Leader*
Ave de l'Atlantique 71-B-12, Brussels 1150, Belgium

Jaeckin, Just — *Movie Director*
8 Villa Mequillet, 92200 Neuilly/Seine, France

Jaeger, Andrea — *Tennis Player*
%Kids Stuff Foundation, Silver Lining Ranch, PO Box 10970, Aspen, CO 81612, USA

Jaffe, Arthur M — *Mathematical Physicist*
27 Lancaster St, Cambridge, MA 02140, USA

Jaffe, Harold W — *Epidemiologist*
%Centers for Disease Control, 1600 Clifton Road, Atlanta, GA 30333, USA

Jaffe, Rona — *Writer*
%Janklow & Nesbit Assoc, 598 Madison Ave, New York, NY 10022, USA

Jaffe, Stanley R — *Entertainment Executive*
152 W 57th St, #5200-F, New York, NY 10019, USA

Jaffe, Susan — *Ballerina*
%American Ballet Theatre, 890 Broadway, New York, NY 10003, USA

Jagan, Janet — *Prime Minister, Guyana*
%Prime Minister's Office, Public Buildings, Georgetown, Guyana

Jagendorf, Andre T — *Plant Physiologist*
309 Brookfield Road, Ithaca, NY 14850, USA

Jager, Tom — *Swimmer*
64 Ramble Wood Blvd, Tijeras, NM 87059, USA

Jagge, Finn Christian — *Skier*
Michelets Vei 108, 1320 Stabekk, Norway

Jagger, Bianca — *Actress, Model*
530 Park Ave, #18-D, New York, NY 10021, USA

Jagger, Mick — *Singer, Harmonicist (The Rolling Stones)*
Cheyne Walk, Chelsea, London SW3, England

Jaglom, Henry — *Movie Director*
9165 W Sunset Blvd, #300, Los Angeles, CA 90069, USA

Jagr, Jaromir — *Hockey Player*
300 Auditorium Place, #9, Pittsburgh, PA 15219, USA

Jahan, Marine — *Actress, Dancer*
%Media Artists Group, 8383 Wilshire Blvd, #954, Beverly Hills, CA 90211, USA

Jahn, Helmut — *Architect*
224 S Michigan Ave, Chicago, IL 60604, USA

Jahn, Sigmund — *Cosmonaut, East Germany; General*
Fontanestr 35, 15344 Strausberg, Germany

Jaidah, Ali Mohammed — *Government Official, Qatar*
%Qatar Petroleum Corp, PO Box 3212, Doha, Qatar

Jakel, Bernd — *Yachtsman (Soling)*
Salvador-Allende-Str 48, 12559 Berlin, Germany

Jakes, John — *Writer*
34 Brams Point Road, Hilton Head, SC 29926, USA

Jaki, Stanley L — *Physicist, Theologian*
PO Box 167, Princeton, NJ 08542, USA

Jakobovits, Immanuel — *Religious Leader*
%Rabbi's Residence, Adler House, Tavistock Square, London WC1, England

J

Jacobsen - Jakobovits

Jakobson, Maggie *Actress*
%Writers & Artists, 924 Westwood Blvd, #900, Los Angeles, CA 90024, USA

Jakobson, Max *Journalist; Government Official, Finland*
Rahapajankatu 3B 17, 00160 Helsinki 16, Finland

Jakosits, Michael *Marksman*
Karlsbergstr 140, 66424 Homburg/Saar, Germany

Jalloud, Abdul Salam *Prime Minister, Libya*
%General Secretariat, General People's Congress, Tripoli, Libya

Jamail, Joseph D, Jr *Attorney*
%Jamail & Kolius, 500 Dallas St, #3434, Houston, TX 77002, USA

Jamal, Ahmad *Jazz Pianist*
%Shubra Productions, PO Box 295, Ashley Falls, MA 01222, USA

Jambor, Agi *Concert Pianist*
%Beethoven Apartments, 1518 Park Ave, #104-N, Baltimore, MD 21217, USA

Jamerson, James L (Jim) *Air Force General*
Deputy CinC, US European Command, Unit 30400, Box 1000, APO, AE 09128, USA

James of Holland Park, Phyllis D *Writer*
%Elaine Green Ltd, 37-A Goldhawk Road, London W12 SQQ, England

James, Anthony *Actor*
%CNA, 1925 Century Park East, #750, Los Angeles, CA 90067, USA

James, Bob *Jazz Keyboardist, Composer*
%Monterey International, 200 W Superior, #202, Chicago, IL 60610, USA

James, Brion *Actor*
%Agency For Performing Arts, 9200 Sunset Blvd, #900, Los Angeles, CA 90069, USA

James, Cheryl (Salt) *Rap Artist*
%Next Plateau Records, 1650 Broadway, #1103, New York, NY 10019, USA

James, Clifton *Actor*
500 W 43rd St, #25-D, New York, NY 10036, USA

James, Clive V L *Broadcaster, Journalist*
%A D Peters, 10 Buckingham St, London WC2H 6B0, England

James, D Clayton *Writer, Historian*
106 Wagon Wheel Trail, Moneta, VA 24121, USA

James, Edison *Prime Minister, Dominica*
%Prime Minister's Office, Government House, Kennedy Ave, Rosseau, Dominica

James, Etta *Singer*
PO Box 5025, Gardena, CA 90249, USA

James, Forrest H (Fob), Jr *Governor, AL*
%Governor's Office, State Capitol, 11 Union St, Montgomery, AL 36130, USA

James, G Larry *Track Athlete*
%Stockton State College, Athletic Dept, Pomona, NJ 08240, USA

James, Gene A *Businessman*
%CF Industries, 1 Salem Lake Dr, Long Grove, IL 60047, USA

James, Geraldine *Actress*
%Julian Belfarge, 46 Albermarle St, London W1X 4PP, England

James, Harold L *Geologist*
%US Geological Survey, 1617 Washington St, Port Townsend, WA 98368, USA

James, John *Actor*
PO Box 3248, Hilton Head Island, SC 29928, USA

James, Joni *Singer*
%Alan Eichler, 1862 Vista del Mar St, Los Angeles, CA 90028, USA

James, Kate *Model*
%Men/Women Agency, 107 Greene St, #200, New York, NY 10012, USA

James, P D *Writer*
%Elaine Greene Ltd, 37-A Goldhawk Road, London W12 8QQ, England

James, Rick *Singer, Songwriter*
%Richard Walters, 421 S Beverly Dr, #800, Beverly Hills, CA 90212, USA

James, Sheryl *Journalist*
%St Petersburg Times, Editorial Dept, 490 1st Ave, St Petersburg, FL 33731, USA

James, Stanislaus A *Governor General, St Lucia*
Government House, The Morue, Castries, St Lucia

James, Steve W *Actor*
%Artists Agency, 10000 Santa Monica Blvd, #305, Los Angeles, CA 90067, USA

James-Rodman, Charmayne *Rodeo Rider*
%General Delivery, Clayton, NM 88415, USA

Jameson, Betty *Golfer*
%Ladies Professional Golf Assn, 2570 Volusia Ave, Daytona Beach, FL 32114, USA

Jamieson, David A *WW II British Army Hero (VC)*
Drove House, Thornham, Hunstanton, Norfolk, England

Jamieson, John K	*Businessman*
601 Jefferson St, #975, Houston, TX 77002, USA	
Jamison, Judith	*Dancer, Dance Director, Choreographer*
2000 Broadway, #2-B, New York, NY 10023, USA	
Jance, J A	*Writer*
%William Morrow Co, 1350 Ave of Americas, New York, NY 10016, USA	
Jancso, Miklos	*Movie Director*
Solyom Laszlo Utca 17, 1022 Budapest II, Hungary	
Janeway, Elizabeth H	*Writer*
350 E 79th St, New York, NY 10021, USA	
Janeway, Michael C	*Editor*
%Northwestern University, Fisk Hall, Evanston, IL 60201, USA	
Janeway, Richard	*Physician*
PO Box 188, Blowing Rock, NC 28605, USA	
Janis, Conrad	*Actor, Jazz Trombonist*
1434 N Genesee Ave, Los Angeles, CA 90046, USA	
Janklow, Morton L	*Literary Agent, Attorney*
%Morton L Janklow Assoc, 598 Madison Ave, New York, NY 10022, USA	
Jankowski, Gene F	*Television Executive*
%American Film Institute, 901 15th St NW, #700, Washington, DC 20005, USA	
Janney, Craig	*Hockey Player*
3 Overhill Road, Enfield, CT 06082, USA	
Janofsky, Leonard S	*Law Enforcement Official*
661 Thayer Ave, Los Angeles, CA 90024, USA	
Janowitz, Gundula	*Opera Singer*
%Vienna Staatsoper, Opernring 2, 10100 Vienna, Austria	
Janowitz, Tama	*Writer*
%Pocket Books, 1230 Ave of Americas, New York, NY 10020, USA	
Jansen, Daniel E (Dan)	*Speed Skater*
5040 S 76th St, Greenfield, WI 53220, USA	
Jansen, Lawrence J (Larry)	*Baseball Player*
3207 NW Highway 47, Forest Grove, OR 97116, USA	
Jansen, Raymond A	*Publisher*
%Newsday Inc, 235 Pinelawn Road, Melville, NY 11747, USA	
Jansons, Maris	*Conductor*
%Oslo Philharmonic, PO Box 1607, 0119 Oslo, Norway	
Janss, William C	*Businessman*
PO Box 107, Sun Valley, ID 83353, USA	
Janssen, Famke	*Actress, Model*
%United Talent Agency, 9560 Wilshire Blvd, #500, Beverly Hills, CA 90212, USA	
January, Don	*Golfer*
14316 Hughes Lane, Dallas, TX 75240, USA	
January, Lois	*Actress*
225 N Crescent Dr, #103, Beverly Hills, CA 90210, USA	
Jany, Alex	*Swimmer*
104 Blvd Livon, 13007 Marseille, France	
Janzen, Edmund	*Religious Leader*
%General Conference of Mennonite Brethren, 8000 W 21st St, Wichita, KS 67205, USA	
Janzen, Lee	*Golfer*
7512 Dr Phillips Blvd, #50-906, Orlando, FL 32819, USA	
Jaquish, John E	*Air Force General*
Assistant for Acquisition, HqUSAF, Pentagon, Washington, DC 20330, USA	
Jardine, Alan C (Al)	*Singer, Guitarist (The Beach Boys)*
PO Box 36, Big Sur, CA 93920, USA	
Jarman, Claude, Jr	*Actor*
11 Dos Encinas, Orinda, CA 94563, USA	
Jarre, Maurice A	*Composer*
27011 Sea Vista Dr, Malibu, CA 90265, USA	
Jarreau, Al	*Singer*
%Patrick Rains, 1543 7th St, #3, Santa Monica, CA 90401, USA	
Jarrett, Dale	*Auto Racing Driver*
PO Box 564, Conover, NC 28613, USA	
Jarrett, Keith	*Jazz Pianist, Composer*
%DL Media, PO Box 2728, Bala Cynwyd, PA 19004, USA	
Jarrett, Will	*Editor*
%Dallas Times Herald, Editorial Dept, Herald Square, Dallas, TX 75202, USA	
Jarriel, Thomas E (Tom)	*Commentator*
%ABC-TV, News Dept, 77 W 66th St, New York, NY 10023, USA	

J

Jamieson - Jarriel

Jarring, Gunnar — *Government Official, Sweden*
Pontus Ols Vaeg 7, 260 40 Viken, Sweden

Jarrott, Charles — *Movie Director*
4314 Marina City Dr, #418, Marina del Rey, CA 90292, USA

Jarryd, Anders — *Tennis Player*
Maaneskoldsgatan 37, 531 00 Lidkoping, Sweden

Jaruzelski, Wojciech — *President, Poland/ Army General*
Ul Ikara 5, Warsaw, Poland

Jarvi, Neeme — *Conductor*
PO Box 305, Sea Bright, NJ 07760, USA

Jarvik, Robert K — *Heart Surgeon*
%University of Utah Medical College, Surgery Dept, Salt Lake City, UT 84102, USA

Jarvis, Graham — *Actor*
15351 Via De Las Olas, #531, Pacific Palisades, CA 90272, USA

Jason, Sybil — *Actress*
PO Box 40024, Studio City, CA 91614, USA

Jasrai, Puntsagiin — *Prime Minister, Mongolia*
%Prime Minister's Office, Ulan Bator, Mongolia

Jastremski, Chet — *Swimmer*
2611 Olcott Blvd, Bloomington, IN 47401, USA

Jastrow, Robert — *Physicist, Writer*
%Wilson Observatory, 740 Holladay Road, Pasadena, CA 91106, USA

Jastrow, Terry L — *Movie Director*
13201 Old Oak Lane, Los Angeles, CA 90049, USA

Jatoi, Ghulan Mustafa — *Prime Minister, Pakistan*
%Jatoi House, 18 Khayaban-E-Shamsheer Housing, #V, Karachi, Pakistan

Jaudes, Robert C — *Businessman*
%Laclede Gas, 720 Olive St, St Louis, MO 63101, USA

Javan, Ali — *Physicist*
12 Hawthorne St, Cambridge, MA 02138, USA

Javierre Ortas, Antonio M Cardinal — *Religious Leader*
%Biblioteca Apostolica Vatican, 00120 Vatican City

Jawara, Dawda K — *President, Gambia*
%President's Office, State House, Banjul, Gambia

Jaworski, Ronald V (Ron) — *Football Player, Sportscaster*
8 Silver Hill Lane, West Berlin, NJ 08043, USA

Jay, John — *Ski Photographer*
PO Box 3131, Rancho Santa Fe, CA 92067, USA

Jay, Joseph R (Joey) — *Baseball Player*
7209 Battenwood Court, Tampa, FL 33615, USA

Jay, Peter — *Government Official, England*
39 Castlebar Road, London W5 2DJ, England

Jay, Ricky — *Illusionist*
%W&V Dailey Booksellers, 8216 Melrose Ave, Los Angeles, CA 90046, USA

Jayawardene, Junius Richard — *President, Sri Lanka*
66 Ward Place, Colombo 7, Sri Lanka

Jayston, Michael — *Actor*
%Michael Whitehall, 125 Gloucester Road, London SW7 4TE, England

Jean — *Grand Duke, Luxembourg*
%Palais Grand-Ducal, Marche-Aux-Herbes, 1728 Luxembourg-Ville, Luxembourg

Jean, Gloria — *Actress, Singer*
20309 Leadwell, Canoga Park, CA 91306, USA

Jeangerard, Bob — *Basketball Player*
1930 Belmont Ave, San Carlos, CA 94070, USA

Jeanmaire, Zizi — *Ballet Dancer, Actress*
22 Rue de la Paix, 75002 Paris, France

Jeannette, Harry (Buddy) — *Basketball Player*
2 New Castle Dr, #8, Nashua, NH 03060, USA

Jeanrenaud, Joan — *Cellist (Kronos Quartet)*
%Kronos Quartet, 1235 9th Ave, San Francisco, CA 94122, USA

Jeantot, Philippe — *Yachtsman, Explorer*
%General Delivery, Quimper, France

Jeffcoat, Jim — *Football Player*
%Buffalo Bills, 1 Bills Dr, Orchard Park, NY 14127, USA

Jefferson, George — *Track Athlete*
9414 Petit Circle, Ventura, CA 93004, USA

Jefferson, Margo — *Journalist*
%New York Times, Editorial Dept, 229 W 43rd St, New York, NY 10036, USA

Jeffreys, Anne — *Actress*
%Sterling, 121 S Bentley Ave, Los Angeles, CA 90049, USA

Jeffreys, Harold — *Astronomer*
160 Huntingdon Road, Cambridge CB3 0LB, England

Jeffries, Herb — *Singer, Actor*
%Thomas Cassidy, 0366 Horseshoe Dr, Basalt, CO 81621, USA

Jeffries, John T — *Astronomer*
1652 E Camino Cielo, Tucson, AZ 85718, USA

Jeffries, Lionel — *Actor, Director*
%International Creative Mgmt, 76 Oxford St, London W1N 0AX, England

Jellicoe, George P J R — *Government Official, England*
97 Onslow Square, London SW7, England

Jemison, Mae C — *Astronaut*
PO Box 580317, Houston, TX 77258, USA

Jemison, Theodore J — *Religious Leader*
%National Baptist Convention USA, 1620 White's Creek Pike, Nashville, TN 37207, USA

Jencks, William P — *Biochemist*
11 Revere St, Lexington, MA 02173, USA

Jenes, Theodore G, Jr — *Army General*
809 169th Place SW, Lynwood, WA 98037, USA

Jenifer, Franklyn G — *Educator*
%University of Texas at Dallas, President's Office, Richardson, TX 75083, USA

Jenkin of Roding, Patrick F — *Government Official, England*
703 Howard House, Dolphin Square, London SW1V 3PQ, England

Jenkins of Hillhead, Roy H — *Government Official, England*
2 Kensington Park Gardens, London W11 3BH, England

Jenkins, Alfred le Sesne — *Diplomat*
Stalsama High Knob, PO Box 586, Front Royal, VA 22630, USA

Jenkins, Bill — *Auto Racing Driver*
%Jenkins Competition, 153 Pennsylvania Ave, Malvern, PA 19355, USA

Jenkins, Daniel — *Actor*
%Silver Massetti Szatmary, 8730 Sunset Blvd, #480, Los Angeles, CA 90069, USA

Jenkins, Don J — *Vietnam War Army Hero (CMH)*
3783 Bowling Green Road, Morgantown, KY 42261, USA

Jenkins, Ferguson A (Fergie), Jr — *Baseball Player*
PO Box 1202, Guthrie, OK 73044, USA

Jenkins, George — *Stage Designer, Movie Art Director*
740 Kingman Ave, Santa Monica, CA 90402, USA

Jenkins, Hayes Alan — *Figure Skater*
809 Lafayette Dr, Akron, OH 44303, USA

Jenkins, Jackie (Butch) — *Actor*
Rt 6, Box 541-G, Fairview, NC 28730, USA

Jenkins, Loren — *Journalist*
%Washington Post, Editorial Dept, 1150 15th St NW, Washington, DC 20071, USA

Jenkins, Paul — *Artist*
%Imago Terrae, PO Box 6833, Yorkville Station, New York, NY 10128, USA

Jenner, Bruce — *Track Athlete, Actor*
25254 Eldorado Meadow Road, Hidden Hills, CA 91302, USA

Jennings, Christopher R — *Financier*
%Dauphin Deposit Corp, 213 Market St, Harrisburg, PA 17101, USA

Jennings, Dave — *Football Player*
1 Briarcliff Road, Upper Saddle River, NJ 07458, USA

Jennings, Delbert O — *Vietnam War Army Hero (CMH)*
640 9th Ave, #A, Honolulu, HI 96816, USA

Jennings, Drue — *Businessman*
%Kansas City Power & Light, 1201 Walnut St, Kansas City, MO 64106, USA

Jennings, Elizabeth — *Writer*
%David Higham Assoc, 5-8 Lower John St, London W1R 4HA, England

Jennings, Jesse D — *Anthropologist*
21801 Siletz Highway, Siletz, OR 97380, USA

Jennings, Joseph L, Jr — *Businessman*
%WestPoint Stevens, 400 W 10th St, West Point, GA 31833, USA

Jennings, Lynn — *Track Athlete*
17 Cushing Road, Newmarket, NH 03857, USA

Jennings, Peter C — *Commentator*
%ABC-TV, News Dept, 77 W 66th St, New York, NY 10023, USA

Jennings, Waylon — *Singer, Songwriter*
%Waylon Jennings Enterprises, 1117 17th Ave S, Nashville, TN 37212, USA

Jenrette, Richard H		*Businessman*
67 E 93rd St, New York, NY 10128, USA		
Jens, Salome		*Actress*
9400 Readcrest Dr, Beverly Hills, CA 90210, USA		
Jens, Walter		*Writer*
Sonnenstr 5, 72076 Tubingen, Germany		
Jensen, Arthur R		*Educational Psychologist*
30 Canyon View Dr, Orinda, CA 94563, USA		
Jensen, Elwood V		*Biochemist*
%Hormone/Fertility Research Inst, Grandweg 64, 22529 Hamburg, Germany		
Jensen, James		*Geologist*
%Brigham Young University, Geology Dept, Provo, UT 84602, USA		
Jensen, Karen		*Actress*
111 S Kings Road, Los Angeles, CA 90048, USA		
Jensen, Robert P		*Businessman*
%Jostens Inc, 5501 Norman Center Dr, Minneapolis, MN 55437, USA		
Jepsen, Roger W		*Senator, IA*
608 W Mulberry Lane, Long Grove, IA 52756, USA		
Jeremy (Clyde)		*Singer (Chad & Jeremy)*
%Agency For Performing Arts, 9200 Sunset Blvd, #900, Los Angeles, CA 90069, USA		
Jergens, Adele		*Actress, Model*
32108 Village, #32, Camarillo, CA 93012, USA		
Jermoluk, Thomas A		*Businessman*
%Silicon Graphics, 2011 N Shoreline Blvd, Mountain View, CA 94043, USA		
Jernberg, Sixten		*Skier*
Fritidsby 780, 64 Lima, Sweden		
Jernigan, Tamara E (Tammy)		*Astronaut*
%NASA, Johnson Space Center, 2101 NASA Road, Houston, TX 77058, USA		
Jerome, Jerrold V		*Businessman*
%Unitrin Co, 1 E Wacker Dr, Chicago, IL 60601, USA		
Jerusalem, Siegfried		*Opera Singer*
Sudring 9, 90542 Eckental, Germany		
Jessee, Michael A		*Financier*
%Federal Home Loan Bank, 1 Financial Center, Boston, MA 02111, USA		
Jeter, Bob		*Football Player*
7147 S Paxton Ave, Chicago, IL 60649, USA		
Jeter, Derek		*Baseball Player*
2415 Cumberland St, Kalamazoo, MI 49006, USA		
Jeter, Gary		*Football Player*
32725 Shadowbrook Dr, Solon, OH 44139, USA		
Jeter, Michael		*Actor*
4571 N Figueroa St, #20, Los Angeles, CA 90065, USA		
Jethroe, Samuel (Sam)		*Baseball Player*
2312 German St, Erie, PA 16503, USA		
Jett, Brent W		*Astronaut*
%NASA, Johnson Space Center, 2101 NASA Road, Houston, TX 77058, USA		
Jett, Joan		*Singer, Songwriter*
%Jett Lag, 155 E 55th St, #6-H, New York, NY 10022, USA		
Jewell		*Singer, Songwriter*
PO Box 33494, San Diego, CA 92183, USA		
Jewison, Norman F		*Movie Director, Producer*
3000 Olympic Blvd, #1314, Santa Monica, CA 90404, USA		
Jhabvala, Ruth Prawer		*Writer*
400 E 52nd St, New York, NY 10022, USA		
Jia, Li		*Hematologist*
%Duke University, Medical Center, Hematology Dept, Durham, NC 27708, USA		
Jiang Tiefeng		*Artist*
%Fingerhut Gallery, 690 Bridgeway, Sausalito, CA 94965, USA		
Jiang Zemin		*President, China*
%General Secretary's Office, Zhonganahai, Beijing, China		
Jiles, Pamela (Pam)		*Track Athlete*
1653 N Broad Ave, New Orleans, LA 70119, USA		
Jillian, Ann		*Actress*
4241 Woodcliffe Road, Sherman Oaks, CA 91403, USA		
Jimenez, Flaco		*Accordianist*
%Pilot Mgmt, 209 10th Ave S, #509, Nashville, TN 37203, USA		
Jiminez, Joe		*Golfer*
29243 Enchanted Glen, Boeme, TX 78015, USA		

Jirsa, Ron — *Basketball Coach*
%University of Georgia, Athletic Dept, Athens, GA 30613, USA

Jiscke, Martin C — *Educator*
%Iowa State University, President's Office, Ames, IA 50011, USA

Joanou, Phil — *Movie Director*
%Creative Artists Agency, 9830 Wilshire Blvd, Beverly Hills, CA 90212, USA

Job, Brian — *Swimmer*
PO Box 70427, Sunnyvale, CA 94086, USA

Jobe, Edward B — *Businessman*
%American Re, 555 College Road E, Princeton, NJ 08540, USA

Jobe, Frank W — *Sports Orthopedic Surgeon*
%Kerlan-Jobe Orthopedic Clinic, 501 E Hardy St, #200, Inglewood, CA 90301, USA

Jobert, Michel — *Government Official, France*
21 Quai Alphonse-Le Gallo, 92100 Boulogne-Billancourt, France

Jobs, Steven P — *Businessman*
%Pixar, 1001 W Cutting Blvd, Richmond, CA 94804, USA

Joel, Billy — *Singer, Songwriter*
%Maritime Music, 280 Elm St, Southampton, NY 11968, USA

Joffe, Roland I V — *Movie Director, Producer*
2934 1/2 N Beverly Glen Circle, #270, Los Angeles, CA 90077, USA

Jofre, Eder — *Boxer*
Alamo de Ministero Rocha, Azevedo 373, C Cesar 21-15, Sao Paulo, Brazil

Johanos, Donald — *Conductor*
%Honolulu Symphony, 677 Ala Moana Blvd, #615, Honolulu, HI 96813, USA

Johanson, Donald C — *Anthropologist*
1288 9th St, Berkeley, CA 94710, USA

Johansson, E Lennart V — *Businessman*
Rakegaton 9, 41320 Goteborg, Sweden

John Paul II, John — *Religious Leader*
Palazzo Apostolico, 00120 Vatican City

John, Caspar — *Fleet Admiral, England*
Trethewey, Mousehole, Penzance, Cornwall, England

John, David D — *Museum Official, Explorer*
7 Cyncoed Ave, Cardiff CF2 6ST, Wales

John, Elton — *Singer, Songwriter*
%John Reid, Singes House, 32 Galena Road, London W6 0LT, England

John, Thomas E (Tommy) — *Baseball Player*
6202 Seton House Lane, Charlotte, NC 28277, USA

John-Roger (Hinkins) — *Religious Leader*
%John Roger Foundation, 2101 Wilshire Blvd, Santa Monica, CA 90403, USA

Johncock, Gordon — *Auto Racing Driver*
1042 Becker Road, Hastings, MI 49058, USA

Johns, Charley E — *Governor, FL*
%Community State Bank, 131 S Walnut St, Starke, FL 32091, USA

Johns, Glynis — *Actress*
11645 Gorham Ave, #309, Los Angeles, CA 90049, USA

Johns, Jasper — *Artist*
225 E Houston St, New York, NY 10002, USA

Johns, Lori — *Drag Racing Driver*
4418 Congressional Dr, Corpus Christi, TX 78413, USA

Johns, Mervyn — *Actor*
%Richards, 42 Hazlebury Road, London SW6, England

Johnson, A Clark, Jr — *Businessman*
%Union Texas Inc, 1330 Post Oak Blvd, Houston, TX 77056, USA

Johnson, Alexander (Alex) — *Baseball Player*
7650 Grand River Ave, Detroit, MI 48204, USA

Johnson, Amy Jo — *Actress*
%Premiere Artists Agency, 8899 Beverly Blvd, #510, Los Angeles, CA 90048, USA

Johnson, Anne-Marie — *Actress*
2606 Ivan Hill Terrace, Los Angeles, CA 90039, USA

Johnson, Arte — *Comedian, Actor*
2725 Bottlebrush Dr, Los Angeles, CA 90077, USA

Johnson, Avery — *Basketball Player*
%San Antonio Spurs, 600 E Market St, #102, San Antonio, TX 78205, USA

Johnson, Axel A — *Businessman*
%A Johnson & Co HAB, 103 75 Stockholm, Sweden

Johnson, Ben — *Track Athlete*
40 Oak Ave, Richmond Hill ON L4C 6R7, Canada

J

Jirsa - Johnson

Johnson, Betsey L — *Fashion Designer*
%Betsey Johnson Co, 209 W 38th St, New York, NY 10018, USA

Johnson, Beverly — *Model, Actress*
%Beverly Glen Enterprises, 250 W 40th St, #400, New York, NY 10018, USA

Johnson, Bill — *Skier*
472-750 Richmond Road, Susanville, CA 96130, USA

Johnson, Billy (White Shoes) — *Football Player*
3701 Whitney Place, Duluth, GA 30096, USA

Johnson, Brad — *Model, Actor*
%More/Medavoy, 7920 W Sunset Blvd, #400, Los Angeles, CA 90036, USA

Johnson, Brian — *Singer (AC/DC)*
11 Leominster Road, Morden, Surrey SA4 6HN, England

Johnson, Brooks — *Track Coach*
%Stanford University, Athletic Dept, Stanford, CA 94305, USA

Johnson, Butch — *Football Player*
%Denver Broncos, 13655 E Dove Valley Parkway, Englewood, CO 80112, USA

Johnson, Charles — *Writer*
%University of Washington, English Dept, Seattle, WA 98105, USA

Johnson, Charles — *Football Player*
%Pittsburgh Steelers, 3 Rivers Stadium, 300 Stadium Circle, Pittsburgh, PA 15212, USA

Johnson, Charles (Charlie) — *Basketball Player*
2301 Lake Tahoe Blvd, #851, South Lake Tahoe, CA 96150, USA

Johnson, Charles B — *Financier*
%Franklin Resources, 777 Mariners Island Blvd, San Mateo, CA 94404, USA

Johnson, Chris — *Golfer*
%Ladies Professional Golf Assn, 2570 Volusia Ave, Daytona Beach, FL 32114, USA

Johnson, Claudia A (Lady Bird) — *Wife of US President*
LBJ Ranch, Stonewall, TX 78671, USA

Johnson, Cletus — *Artist*
%Leo Castelli Gallery, 420 W Broadway, New York, NY 10012, USA

Johnson, Darrell D — *Baseball Manager*
65 Willotta Dr, Suisun City, CA 94585, USA

Johnson, Dave — *Track Athlete*
%Azusa Pacific University, PO Box 2713, Azusa, CA 91702, USA

Johnson, Dave — *Labor Leader*
%United Garment Workers, 4207 Lebanon Road, Hermitage, TN 37076, USA

Johnson, David A (Davey) — *Baseball Manager*
1064 Howell Branch Road, Winter Park, FL 32789, USA

Johnson, David W — *Businessman*
%Campbell Soup, Campbell Place, Camden, NJ 08103, USA

Johnson, Dennis — *Basketball Player*
8901 Jonathan Manor Dr, Orlando, FL 32819, USA

Johnson, Don — *Actor*
231 N Orchard Dr, Burbank, CA 91506, USA

Johnson, Donald J (Don) — *Bowler*
716 Ann Dr, Las Vegas, NV 89107, USA

Johnson, Earvin (Magic) — *Basketball Player, Coach*
Beverly Estates, 13100 Mulholland Dr, Beverly Hills, CA 90210, USA

Johnson, Eddie — *Basketball Player*
6133 N 61st Place, Paradise Valley, AZ 85253, USA

Johnson, Edward C, III — *Financier*
%FMR Corp, 82 Devonshire St, Boston, MA 02109, USA

Johnson, Eric — *Singer*
%Joe Priesnitz Artist Mgmt, PO Box 5249, Austin, TX 78763, USA

Johnson, Erik E — *Businessman*
%International Shipbuilding, 650 Poydras St, New Orleans, LA 70130, USA

Johnson, Ervin — *Basketball Player*
%Denver Nuggets, McNichols Arena, 1635 Clay St, Denver, CO 80204, USA

Johnson, F Ross — *Businessman*
%RJM Associates, 200 Galleria Parkway, #970, Atlanta, GA 30339, USA

Johnson, G Griffith, Jr — *Government Official*
300 Locust Ave, Annapolis, MD 21401, USA

Johnson, Gary — *Governor, NM*
%Governor's Office, State Capitol, Santa Fe, NM 87503, USA

Johnson, Gary — *Football Player*
450 Oliver Road, Haughton, LA 71037, USA

Johnson, Georgann — *Actress*
218 N Glenroy Place, Los Angeles, CA 90049, USA

Johnson, George W   *Educator*
%George Mason University, President's Office, Fairfax, VA 22030, USA
Johnson, Glendon E   *Businessman*
%John Alden Financial Corp, 7300 Corporate Center Dr, Miami, FL 33126, USA
Johnson, Hansford T   *Air Force General*
%USAA Capital Corp, 9800 Fredericksburg Road, San Antonio, TX 78284, USA
Johnson, Harold   *Boxer*
6101 Morris St, Philadelphia, PA 19144, USA
Johnson, Haynes B   *Journalist*
%George Washington University, Communications Studies Ctr, Washington, DC 20052, USA
Johnson, Hazel W   *Army General*
%Army Nurse Corps, Army Dept, Pentagon, Washington, DC 20310, USA
Johnson, Howard B   *Businessman*
%Howard Johnson Co, 1 Howard Johnson Plaza, Boston, MA 02125, USA
Johnson, Howard M (Hojo)   *Baseball Player*
14371 Twisted Branch Road, Poway, CA 92064, USA
Johnson, J J   *Jazz Trombonist, Composer*
4001 Murietta Ave, Sherman Oaks, CA 91423, USA
Johnson, James A   *Financier*
%Federal National Mortgage Assn, 3900 Wisconsin Ave NW, Washington, DC 20016, USA
Johnson, James E (Johnnie)   *WW II Royal Air Force Hero, England*
Stables, Hargate Hall, Buxton, Derbyshire SK17 8TA, England
Johnson, Jannette   *Skier*
PO Box 901, Sun Valley, ID 83353, USA
Johnson, Jay L   *Navy Admiral*
%Office of Chief of Naval Operations, Pentagon, Washington, DC 20370, USA
Johnson, Jenna   *Swimmer, Coach*
%University of Tennessee, Athletic Dept, PO Box 15016, Knoxville, TN 37901, USA
Johnson, Jerome L   *Navy Admiral*
%Navy-Marine Corps Relief Society, 801 N Randolph St, Arlington, VA 22203, USA
Johnson, Jimmy   *Football Player*
656 Amaranth Blvd, Mill Valley, CA 94941, USA
Johnson, Jimmy   *Football Coach*
%Miami Dolphins, 7500 SW 30th St, Davie, FL 33314, USA
Johnson, Joel W   *Businessman*
%Hormel Foods Corp, 1 Hormel Place, Austin, MN 55912, USA
Johnson, John G, Jr   *Businessman*
%Safety-Kleen Corp, 1000 N Randall Road, Elgin, IL 60123, USA
Johnson, John H   *Publisher*
%Johnson Publishing Co, 820 S Michigan Ave, Chicago, IL 60605, USA
Johnson, John Henry   *Football Player*
1543 East Blvd, #3, Cleveland, OH 44106, USA
Johnson, Johnnie   *Football Player*
98 Country Club Dr, La Grange, TX 78945, USA
Johnson, Johnnie   *Singer, Pianist, Songwriter*
%Talent Source, 1560 Broadway, #1308, New York, NY 10036, USA
Johnson, Joseph E, III   *Physician*
%The Philadelphian, 2401 Pennsylvania Ave, #15-C-44, Philadelphia, PA 19130, USA
Johnson, Junior   *Auto Racing Driver, Builder*
%Johnson Assoc, Rt 2, PO Box 162, Ronda, NC 28670, USA
Johnson, Keith   *Labor Leader*
%Woodworkers of America Union, 1622 N Lombard St, Portland, OR 97217, USA
Johnson, Kevin   *Basketball Player*
%Phoenix Suns, 201 E Jefferson St, Phoenix, AZ 85004, USA
Johnson, Keyshawn   *Football Player*
%New York Jets, 1000 Fulton Ave, Hempstead, NY 11550, USA
Johnson, Lamont   *Movie Director*
935 Mesa Road, Monterey, CA 93940, USA
Johnson, Larry D   *Basketball Player*
%New York Knicks, Madison Square Garden, 2 Penn Plaza, New York, NY 10121, USA
Johnson, Laura   *Actress*
1917 Weepah Way, Los Angeles, CA 90046, USA
Johnson, Leon W   *WW II Air Force Hero (CMH), General*
2550 N Bonanza Ave, Tucson, AZ 85749, USA
Johnson, Lynn-Holly   *Actress*
%Cavaleri, 405 W Riverside Dr, #2, Burbank, CA 91506, USA
Johnson, Manuel H, Jr   *Economist, Government Official*
%George Mason University, Global Market Studies Center, Fairfax, VA 22030, USA

J

Johnson - Johnson

Johnson, Mark *Hockey Player, Coach*
58 Princeton Place, Wayne, NJ 07470, USA

Johnson, Marvin *Boxer*
5452 Turfway Circle, Indianapolis, IN 46228, USA

Johnson, Michael *Track Athlete*
15851 Dallas Parkway, #500, Dallas, TX 75248, USA

Johnson, Michael *Singer*
%Fred Kewley, 1711 18th Ave S, #D-4, Nashville, TN 37212, USA

Johnson, Michelle *Actress, Model*
1322 Shadybrook Dr, Beverly Hills, CA 90210, USA

Johnson, Monica *Writer*
%Innovative Artists, 1999 Ave of Stars, #2850, Los Angeles, CA 90067, USA

Johnson, Nicholas *Attorney, Writer*
PO Box 1876, Iowa City, IA 52244, USA

Johnson, Niels W *Businessman*
%International Shipbuilding, 650 Poydras St, New Orleans, LA 70130, USA

Johnson, Ora J *Religious Leader*
%General Assn of General Baptists, 100 Stinson Dr, Popular Bluff, MO 63901, USA

Johnson, Oscar G *WW II Army Hero (CMH)*
121 Garfield St, Iron Mountain, MI 49802, USA

Johnson, Paul *Hockey Player*
65 Duck Pond Road, West St Paul, MN 55118, USA

Johnson, Paul B *Historian, Journalist*
Coach House, Over Stowey near Bridgewater, Somerset TA5 1HA, England

Johnson, Penny *Actress*
%Susan Smith, 121 N San Vicente Blvd, Beverly Hills, CA 90211, USA

Johnson, Pepper *Football Player*
%New York Jets, 1000 Fulton Ave, Hempstead, NY 11550, USA

Johnson, Philip C *Architect*
%John Burgee Architects, 885 3rd Ave, New York, NY 10022, USA

Johnson, R E *Labor Leader*
%Train Dispatchers Assn, 1370 Ontario St, #1040, Cleveland, OH 44113, USA

Johnson, Rafer *Track Athlete, Actor*
%Special Olympics California, 6071 Bristol Parkway, #100, Culver City, CA 90230, USA

Johnson, Ralph E *Architect*
%Perkins & Will, 330 N Wabash Ave, #3600, Chicago, IL 60611, USA

Johnson, Randall D (Randy) *Baseball Player*
16110 SE Cougar Mountain Way, Bellevue, WA 98006, USA

Johnson, Richard *Actor*
%Conway Van Gelder Robinson, 18-21 Jermyn St, London SW1Y 6NB, England

Johnson, Richard J V *Publisher*
%Houston Chronicle, 801 Texas St, Houston, TX 77002, USA

Johnson, Robert L *Entertainment Executive*
%Black Entertainment TV, 1900 "W" Place NE, Washington, DC 20018, USA

Johnson, Roger W *Government Official, Businessman*
%General Services Administration, 18th & "F" Sts NW, Washington, DC 20405, USA

Johnson, Ron *Football Player*
226 Summit Ave, Summit, NJ 07901, USA

Johnson, Roy *Labor Leader*
%Roofers & Waterproofers Union, 1125 17th St NW, Washington, DC 20036, USA

Johnson, Russell *Actor*
PO Box 3135, La Jolla, CA 92038, USA

Johnson, S(ankey) A(nton) *Businessman*
2310 Huntington Point Road W, Wayzata, MN 55391, USA

Johnson, Samuel C *Businessman*
%S C Johnson & Son, 1525 Howe St, Racine, WI 53403, USA

Johnson, Sonia *Women's, Religious Activist*
3318 2nd St S, Arlington, VA 22204, USA

Johnson, Steve *Basketball Player*
2425 NE Alameda St, Portland, OR 97212, USA

Johnson, Syl *Singer, Songwriter*
%Blue Sky Artists, 761 N Washington Ave, Minneapolis, MN 55401, USA

Johnson, Thomas S *Financier*
%GreenPoint Bank, 1981 Marcus Ave, New Hyde Park, NY 11042, USA

Johnson, Tim *Football Player*
%Washington Redskins, 21300 Redskin Park Dr, Ashburn, VA 20147, USA

Johnson, Tom *Hockey Player*
80 Holden Road, Sterling, MA 01564, USA

Johnson, Torrence V — *Astronomer*
%Jet Propulsion Laboratory, 4800 Oak Grove Dr, Pasadena, CA 91109, USA
Johnson, Van — *Actor*
%Studio Artists, 305 W 52nd St, #1-H, New York, NY 10019, USA
Johnson, Virginia — *Ballerina*
133 W 71st St, New York, NY 10023, USA
Johnson, Virginia E — *Sex Therapist, Psychologist*
%Johnson & Masters Institute, Campbell Plaza, 59th & Arsenal, St Louis, MO 63118, USA
Johnson, W Thomas (Tom), Jr — *Television Executive*
%Cable News Network, 1 CNN Center, Atlanta, GA 30303, USA
Johnson, Warren — *Drag Racing Driver*
%Warren Johnson Enterprises, PO Box 1294, Duluth, GA 30096, USA
Johnson, Warren C — *Chemist*
946 Bellclair Road SE, Grand Rapids, MI 49506, USA
Johnson, William B — *Businessman*
%Ritz-Carlton Hotels, 3414 Peachtree Road NE, #300, Atlanta, GA 30326, USA
Johnston McKay, Mary H — *Astronaut*
%University of Tennessee, Space Institute, Tullahoma, TN 37388, USA
Johnston, Alastair — *Sports Agent*
%International Mgmt Group, 75490 Fairway Dr, Indian Wells, CA 92210, USA
Johnston, Allen H — *Religious Leader*
%Bishop's House, 3 Wymer Terrace, PO Box 21, Hamilton, New Zealand
Johnston, Bruce — *Singer (The Beach Boys)*
%Boulder Creek, 4860 San Jacinto Circle, #F, Fallbrook, CA 92028, USA
Johnston, Cathy — *Golfer*
%Ladies Professional Golf Assn, 2570 Volusia Ave, Daytona Beach, FL 32114, USA
Johnston, Darryl (Moose) — *Football Player*
1115 S Meadow Creek Circle, #2054, Irving, TX 75038, USA
Johnston, Douglas — *Publisher*
%Vanity Fair Magazine, 350 Madison Ave, New York, NY 10017, USA
Johnston, Edward J (Eddie) — *Hockey Player, Coach, Executive*
20 Blueberry Lane, Reading, PA 19610, USA
Johnston, Freedy — *Singer, Songwriter*
%Hornblow Group, Washington Springs Road, Palisades, NY 10964, USA
Johnston, Harold S — *Chemist*
285 Franklin St, Harrisonburg, VA 22801, USA
Johnston, Joe — *Movie Director*
665 S Madison Ave, Pasadena, CA 91106, USA
Johnston, John Dennis — *Actor*
%SDB Partners, 1801 Ave of Stars, #902, Los Angeles, CA 90067, USA
Johnston, Kristen — *Actress*
8033 W Sunset Blvd, #4020, Los Angeles, CA 90046, USA
Johnston, Lynn — *Cartoonist (For Better or For Worse)*
%Universal Press Syndicate, 4900 Main St, #900, Kansas City, KS 64112, USA
Johnston, Lynn H — *Businessman*
%Life Insurance of Georgia, 5780 Powers Ferry Road NW, Atlanta, GA 30327, USA
Johnstone, John W, Jr — *Businessman*
%Olin Corp, PO Box 4500, Norwalk, CT 06856, USA
Johore — *Sultan, Malaysia*
%Istana Bukit Serene, Johore Bahru, Johore, Malaysia
Johung, John — *Businessman*
%Fritz, 706 Mission St, San Francisco, CA 94103, USA
Joiner, Charlie — *Football Player, Coach*
%Buffalo Bills, 1 Bills Dr, Orchard Park, NY 14127, USA
Joklik, W Karl — *Microbiologist*
%Duke University, Medical Center, Microbiology/Immunology Dept, Durham, NC 27710, USA
Joli, France — *Singer*
%Brothers Mgmt, 141 Dunbar Ave, Fords, NJ 08863, USA
Jolie, Angelina — *Actress*
13340 Galewood Dr, Sherman Oaks, CA 91423, USA
Jolly, Allison — *Yachtswoman*
3913 Calle Real, San Clemente, CA 92673, USA
Jonckheer, Efrain — *Prime Minister, Netherlands Antilles*
%Royal Netherlands Embassy, Calle 21, Avda 10, San Jose, Costa Rica
Jones (Imamu Amiri Baraka), LeRoi — *Writer*
%State University of New York, Afro-American Studies Dept, Stony Brook, NY 11794, USA
Jones, Alex S — *Journalist*
225 W 86th St, #309, New York, NY 10024, USA

J

Johnson - Jones

Jones, Alfred — Boxer
19303 Patton St, Detroit, MI 48219, USA

Jones, Allen — Artist
41 Charterhouse Square, London EC1M 6EA, England

Jones, Arthur — Inventor (Nautilus Exercise Machine)
%MedX, 1155 NE 77th St, Ocala, FL 34479, USA

Jones, Ben J — Prime Minister, Grenada
Archibald Ave, St George's, Grenada

Jones, Bert — Football Player
%Mid-States Wood Preservers, PO Box 298, Simsboro, LA 71275, USA

Jones, Bill T — Choreographer
%Bill T Jones/Arnie Zane Dance Co, 853 Broadway, #1706, New York, NY 10003, USA

Jones, Bobby — Basketball Player
5109 Panview Dr, Mathews, NC 28105, USA

Jones, Booker T — Singer, Pianist (Booker T & The MG's)
%Concerted Efforts, 59 Parsons St, West Newton, MA 02165, USA

Jones, Brent — Football Player
5279 Blackhawk Dr, Danville, CA 94506, USA

Jones, Breyton J (Bobby) — Baseball Player
%New York Mets, Shea Stadium, Flushing, NY 11368, USA

Jones, Catherine Zeta — Actress
%International Creative Mgmt, 76 Oxford St, London W1N 0AX, England

Jones, Charles M (Chuck) — Animator (Road Runner, Pepe le Pew)
PO Box 2319, Costa Mesa, CA 92628, USA

Jones, Charles W — Labor Leader
%Brotherhood of Boilermakers, 753 8th Ave, Kansas City, KS 66105, USA

Jones, Charlie — Sportscaster
8080 El Paseo Grande, La Jolla, CA 92037, USA

Jones, Claude Earl — Actor
%Henderson/Hogan, 247 S Beverly Dr, #102, Beverly Hills, CA 90212, USA

Jones, Courtney J L — Figure Skating Executive
%National Skating Assn, 15-27 Gee St, London EC1V 3RE, England

Jones, Cranston E — Editor
8 E 96th St, New York, NY 10128, USA

Jones, D Michael — Financier
%West One Bancorp, 101 S Capitol Blvd, Boise, ID 83702, USA

Jones, D Paul, Jr — Financier
%Compass BancShares, 15 S 20th St, Birmingham, AL 35233, USA

Jones, Dale P — Businessman
%Halliburton Co, Lincoln Plaza, 500 N Akard St, Dallas, TX 75201, USA

Jones, David (Deacon) — Football Player, Executive
%Calgary Stampeders, 1817 Crowchild Trail NW, Calgary AB T2M 4R6, Canada

Jones, David A — Businessman
%Humana Corp, 500 W Main St, Louisville, KY 40202, USA

Jones, David C — Businessman
%National Education Corp, 2601 Main St, #700, Irvine, CA 92614, USA

Jones, Davy — Singer, Guitarist (The Monkees)
%Nationwide Entertainment, 2756 N Green Valley Pkwy, #449, Las Vegas, NV 89014, USA

Jones, Dean — Actor, Singer
5055 Casa Dr, Tarzana, CA 91356, USA

Jones, Dean M — Cricketer
%Durham Club, Mercantile Road, Houghton-Le-Sring, Durham DH4 5PH, England

Jones, Dennis A — Navy Admiral
Deputy CinC, US Strategic Command, Offutt Air Force Base, NE 68113, USA

Jones, Dontae — Basketball Player
%New York Knicks, Madison Square Garden, 2 Penn Plaza, New York, NY 10121, USA

Jones, Dwight — Basketball Player
17122 Silverthorne Lane, Spring, TX 77379, USA

Jones, E Edward — Religious Leader
%Baptist Convention of America, 777 S R L Thornton Freeway, Dallas, TX 75203, USA

Jones, E Fay — Architect
1330 N Hillcrest St, Fayetteville, AR 72703, USA

Jones, Earl — Track Athlete
15114 Petroskey Ave, Detroit, MI 48238, USA

Jones, Ed (Too Tall) — Football Player
1 Lost Valley Dr, Dallas, TX 75234, USA

Jones, Eddie — Basketball Player
22297 SW 62nd Ave, Boca Raton, FL 33428, USA

Jones, Eddie *Actor*
%Gage Group, 9255 Sunset Blvd, #515, Los Angeles, CA 90069, USA

Jones, Elvin R *Jazz Drummer, Bandleader*
%Keiko Jones Mgmt, 415 Central Park West, New York, NY 10025, USA

Jones, George *Singer, Songwriter*
RR 3, Box 150, Murphy, NC 28906, USA

Jones, Geraint I *Conductor*
Long House, Arkley Lane, Barnet Road, Arkley, Herts, England

Jones, Grace *Model, Actress, Singer*
%Pyramid Entertainment Group, 89 5th Ave, #7QO, New York, NY 10003, USA

Jones, Grandpa *Comedian, Singer*
172 Happy Valley Road, Goodlettsville, TN 37072, USA

Jones, Greg *Skier*
PO Box 500, Tahoe City, CA 96145, USA

Jones, Gwyneth *Opera Singer*
PO Box 556, 8037 Zurich, Switzerland

Jones, Hayes *Track Athlete*
1040 James K Blvd, Pontiac, MI 48341, USA

Jones, Henry *Actor*
502 9th St, Santa Monica, CA 90402, USA

Jones, Henry (Hank) *Jazz Pianist*
%Joel Chriss, 300 Mercer St, #3-J, New York, NY 10003, USA

Jones, Howard *Singer, Songwriter*
Box 185, High Wycom, Bucks HP11 2E2, England

Jones, Jack *Singer*
78-825 Osage Trail, Indian Wells, CA 92210, USA

Jones, James Earl *Actor*
PO Box 610, Pawling, NY 12564, USA

Jones, James L (Jack) *Labor Leader*
74 Ruskin Park House, Champion Hill, London SE5, England

Jones, James L, Jr *Marine Corps General*
Office of Secretary of Defense, Pentagon, Washington, DC 20301, USA

Jones, Janet *Actress*
9100 Wilshire Blvd, #1000-W, Beverly Hills, CA 90212, USA

Jones, Jeff *Basketball Coach*
%University of Virginia, Athletic Dept, Charlottesville, VA 22903, USA

Jones, Jeffrey *Actor*
7336 Santa Monica Blvd, #691, Los Angeles, CA 90046, USA

Jones, Jennifer *Actress*
264 N Glenroy Ave, Los Angeles, CA 90049, USA

Jones, Jenny *Entertainer, Comedienne*
%Jenny Jones Show, NBC-Tower, 454 N Columbus Dr, #400, Chicago, IL 60611, USA

Jones, Jerrauld C (Jerry) *Football Executive*
%Dallas Cowboys, 1 Cowboys Parkway, Irving, TX 75063, USA

Jones, John E *Businessman*
%CBI Industries, 1501 N Division St, Plainfield, IL 60544, USA

Jones, John Paul *Sculptor*
22370 3rd Ave, South Laguna, CA 92677, USA

Jones, Johnny (Lam) *Football Player, Track Athlete*
4748 Old Bent Tree Lane, Dallas, TX 75287, USA

Jones, Jonah *Jazz Trumpeter*
%Counterpoint/Concerts, 8051 Shalom Dr, Spring Hill, FL 34606, USA

Jones, K C (Robert) *Basketball Player, Coach*
379 Boston Post Road, #302, Springfield, MA 01109, USA

Jones, L Q *Actor*
2144 1/2 N Cahuenga Blvd, Los Angeles, CA 90068, USA

Jones, Landon Y *Editor*
%People Magazine, Editorial Dept, Rockefeller Center, New York, NY 10020, USA

Jones, Larry W (Chipper) *Baseball Player*
1001 Tullamore Place, Alpharetta, GA 30022, USA

Jones, Leilani *Actress*
%Writers & Artists, 924 Westwood Blvd, #900, Los Angeles, CA 90024, USA

Jones, Lou *Track Athlete*
14 Winyah Terrace, New Rochelle, NY 10801, USA

Jones, Lyle V *Psychologist*
RR 7, Pittsboro, NC 27312, USA

Jones, Marcia Mae *Actress*
4541 Hazeltine, #4, Sherman Oaks, CA 91423, USA

Jones, Marian	*Track Athlete*
%University of North Carolina, Athletic Dept, Chapel Hill, NC 27599, USA	
Jones, Marvin	*Football Player*
8891 NW 193rd St, Miami, FL 33157, USA	
Jones, Mary Ellen	*Biochemist*
%University of North Carolina, Biochemistry Dept, Chapel Hill, NC 27599, USA	
Jones, Maxine	*Singer (En Vogue)*
%William Morris Agency, 1325 Ave of Americas, New York, NY 10019, USA	
Jones, Mick	*Guitarist (Clash, Foreigner)*
%Hard to Handle Mgmt, 1133 Broadway, #1301, New York, NY 10010, USA	
Jones, Parnelli	*Auto Racing Driver, Builder*
PO Box "W", Torrance, CA 90508, USA	
Jones, Philip M	*Concert Trumpeter*
14 Hamilton Terrace, London NW8 9UG, England	
Jones, Pirkle	*Photographer*
663 Lovell Ave, Mill Valley, CA 94941, USA	
Jones, Quincy D, Jr	*Composer, Conductor*
%Quincy Jones Productions, 3800 Barham Blvd, #503, Los Angeles, CA 90068, USA	
Jones, Randall L (Randy)	*Baseball Player*
2638 Cranston Dr, Escondido, CA 92025, USA	
Jones, Randy	*Publisher*
%Esquire Magazine, 250 W 55th St, New York, NY 10019, USA	
Jones, Reginald V	*Physicist*
8 Queen's Terrace, Aberdeen AB1 1XL, Scotland	
Jones, Renee	*Actress*
11300 W Olympic Blvd, #870, Los Angeles, CA 90064, USA	
Jones, Richard M	*Businessman*
%Savings/Profit Sharing Fund, Sears Tower, Chicago, IL 60606, USA	
Jones, Rickie Lee	*Singer, Songwriter*
%Gold Mountain, 3575 Cahuenga Blvd W, #450, Los Angeles, CA 90068, USA	
Jones, Robert T	*Aerospace Scientist*
25005 La Loma Dr, Los Altos, CA 94022, USA	
Jones, Robert Trent	*Golf Course Architect*
PO Box 1908, Pinehurst, NC 28370, USA	
Jones, Rosie	*Golfer*
509 Lake Dr, Villa Rica, GA 30180, USA	
Jones, Roy, Jr	*Boxer*
%Stanley Levin, 226 S Palafox Place, Pensacola, FL 32501, USA	
Jones, Samuel (Sam)	*Basketball Player*
15417 Tierra Dr, Wheaton, MD 20906, USA	
Jones, Shirley	*Actress, Singer*
701 N Oakhurst Dr, Beverly Hills, CA 90210, USA	
Jones, Stephen	*Attorney*
%Jones & Wyatt, PO Box 472, Enid, OK 73702, USA	
Jones, Steve	*Golfer*
5420 E Claire Dr, Scottsdale, AZ 85254, USA	
Jones, Steven	*Physicist*
%Brigham Young University, Physics Dept, Provo, UT 84602, USA	
Jones, Terry	*Animator, Director (Monty Python)*
%Mayday Mgmt, 68-A Delancy St, London NW1 7RY, England	
Jones, Thomas D	*Astronaut*
%NASA, Johnson Space Center, 2101 NASA Road, Houston, TX 77058, USA	
Jones, Thomas V	*Businessman*
1050 Moraga Dr, Los Angeles, CA 90049, USA	
Jones, Thomas W	*Businessman*
%TIAA-CREF, 730 3rd Ave, New York, NY 10017, USA	
Jones, Tom	*Singer*
363 Copa de Oro Road, Los Angeles, CA 90077, USA	
Jones, Tommy Lee	*Actor*
PO Box 966, San Saba, TX 76877, USA	
Jones, Wallace (Wah-Wah)	*Basketball Player*
512 Chinoe Road, Lexington, KY 40502, USA	
Jones, Walter	*Football Player*
%Seattle Seahawks, 11220 NE 53rd St, Kirkland, WA 98033, USA	
Jones, Will (Dub)	*Singer (The Coasters)*
%Famous Artists Agency, 1700 Broadway, #500, New York, NY 10019, USA	
Jones, William (Dub)	*Football Player*
326 Glendale, Ruston, LA 71270, USA	

Jones, William K — Marine Corps General
1211 Huntly Place, Alexandria, VA 22307, USA
Jong, Erica M — Writer
%K D Burrows, 425 Park Ave, New York, NY 10022, USA
Jonsen, Albert R — Physician
%University of Washington Medical School, Medical Ethics Dept, Seattle, WA 98195, USA
Joost, Edwin D (Eddie) — Baseball Player
303 Belhaven Circle, Santa Rosa, CA 95409, USA
Jopling, T Michael — Government Official, England
Clyder Howe Cottage, Windermere, Cumbria, England
Jordan, Charles M — Automobile Designer
PO Box 8330, Rancho Santa Fe, CA 92067, USA
Jordan, Don — Boxer
5100 2nd Ave, Los Angeles, CA 90043, USA
Jordan, Don D — Businessman
%Houston Industries, 4400 Post Oak Park, Houston, TX 77027, USA
Jordan, Eddie — Basketball Coach
1431 Kingswood Dr, #214, Roseville, CA 95678, USA
Jordan, Glenn — Movie Director
9401 Wilshire Blvd, #700, Beverly Hills, CA 90212, USA
Jordan, I King — Educator
%Gallaudet University, President's Office, 800 Florida NW, Washington, DC 20001, USA
Jordan, Jerry L — Financier
%Federal Reserve Bank, 1455 E 6th St, Cleveland, OH 44114, USA
Jordan, Kathy — Tennis Player
1604 Union St, San Francisco, CA 94123, USA
Jordan, Lee Roy — Football Player
%Redwood Lumber Co, 2425 Burbank St, Dallas, TX 75235, USA
Jordan, Michael H — Businessman
%Westinghouse Electric, Gateway Center, 11 Stanwix St, Pittsburgh, PA 15222, USA
Jordan, Michael J — Basketball Player
2700 Point Dr, Highland Park, IL 60035, USA
Jordan, Montell — Singer
%Shock Ink, PO Box 448, Pelham, NY 10803, USA
Jordan, Neil P — Movie Director
6 Sorrento Terrace, Dalkey, County Dublin, Ireland
Jordan, Payton — Track Coach
439 Knoll Dr, Los Altos, CA 94024, USA
Jordan, Stanley — Jazz Guitarist
%David Rubinson, PO Box 411197, San Francisco, CA 94141, USA
Jordan, Steven R (Steve) — Football Player
581 W San Marcos Dr, Chandler, AZ 85224, USA
Jordan, Vernon E, Jr — Civil Rights Activist
%Akin Gump Strauss Hauer, 1333 New Hampshire Ave NW, Washington, DC 20036, USA
Jorgensen, Anker — Prime Minister, Denmark
Borgbjergvej 1, 2450 SV Copenhagen, Denmark
Jorginho — Soccer Player
Rua Levi Carreiro 420, Barra de Tijuca, Brazil
Jorndt, L Daniel — Businessman
%Walgreen Co, 200 Wilmot Road, Deerfield, IL 60015, USA
Jose, Jose — Singer
%Promociones Bustelo, Brusela 10, #105, Colonia Juarez DF 06600, Mexico
Josefowicz, Leila — Concert Violinist
%Jascha Brodsky, Curtis Institute of Music, 1726 Locust, Philadelphia, PA 19103, USA
Joseph, Curtis — Hockey Player
%Edmonton Oilers, 11230 110th St, Edmonton AB T5G 3GB, Canada
Joseph, Joseph E, III — Physician
%University of Michigan, Taubman Center, Ann Arbor, MI 48109, USA
Joseph, Marcel P — Businessman
%Augat Inc, PO Box 2510, Attleboro Falls, MA 02763, USA
Joseph, Stephen — Physician
%New York City Department of Health, 125 Worth St, New York, NY 10013, USA
Josephine Charlotte — Princess, Luxembourg
Grand Ducal Palace, Luxembourg, Luxembourg
Josephs, Wilfred — Composer
4 Grand Union Walk, Kentish Town Rd, Camden Town, London NW1 9LP, England
Josephson, Brian D — Nobel Physics Laureate
%Cavendish Laboratory, Madingley Road, Cambridge CB3 0HE, England

J

Jones - Josephson

Josephson, Erland *Actor*
%Royal Dramatic Theater, Nybroplan, Box 5037, 102 41 Stockholm, Sweden

Josephson, Karen *Synchronized Swimmer*
1923 Junction Dr, Concord, CA 94518, USA

Josephson, Marvin *Entertainment Executive*
%International Creative Mgmt, 40 W 57th St, New York, NY 10019, USA

Josephson, Sarah *Synchronized Swimmer*
1923 Junction Dr, Concord, CA 94518, USA

Joslin, Roger S *Businessman*
%State Farm Fire & Casualty, 112 E Washington St, Bloomington, IL 61701, USA

Jospin, Lionel *Prime Minister, France*
Prime Minister's Office, 57 Rue de Vareene, 75700 Paris, France

Joubert, Beverly *Photographer*
%National Geographic Magazine, 17th & "M" Sts NW, Washington, DC 20036, USA

Joubert, Dereck *Photographer*
%National Geographic Magazine, 17th & "M" Sts NW, Washington, DC 20036, USA

Joulwan, George A *Army General*
Supreme Allied Command, Supreme Hq, Allied Powers Europe, APO, AP 09705, USA

Jourdan, Louis *Actor*
1139 Maybrook Dr, Beverly Hills, CA 90210, USA

Jovanovich, Peter W *Publisher*
%MacMillan Inc, 1177 Ave of Americas, #1965, New York, NY 10036, USA

Joyce, Andrea *Sportscaster*
%Home Box Office, Sports Dept, 1100 Ave of Americas, New York, NY 10036, USA

Joyce, Brenda *Actress*
61040 S Queens Dr, #44, Bend, OR 97702, USA

Joyce, Edward M *Television Executive*
%CBS Inc, 51 W 52nd St, New York, NY 10019, USA

Joyce, Elaine *Actress*
%Twentieth Century, 15315 Magnolia Blvd, #429, Sherman Oaks, CA 91403, USA

Joyce, Joan *Softball Player, Golfer*
160 Euclid Ave, Stratford, CT 06497, USA

Joyce, John T *Labor Leader*
%Bricklayers & Allied Craftsmen, 815 15th St NW, Washington, DC 20005, USA

Joyce, William *Artist, Writer*
3302 Centenary Blvd, Shreveport, LA 71104, USA

Joyce, William H *Businessman*
%Union Carbide, 39 Old Ridgebury Road, Danbury, CT 06817, USA

Joyner, Al *Track Athlete*
21214 Leadwell St, Canoga Park, CA 91304, USA

Joyner, Michelle *Actress*
%Alliance Talent, 9171 Wilshire Blvd, #441, Beverly Hills, CA 90210, USA

Joyner, Seth *Football Player*
%Green Bay Packers, 1265 Lombardi Ave, Green Bay, WI 54304, USA

Joyner, Wallace K (Wally) *Baseball Player*
PO Box 512, Rancho Santa Fe, CA 92067, USA

Joyner-Kersee, Jacqueline (Jackie) *Track Athlete*
21214 Leadwell St, Canoga Park, CA 91304, USA

Jozwiak, Brian J *Football Player, Coach*
51 Rohor Ave, Buckhannon, WV 26201, USA

Juan Carlos I *King, Spain*
%Palacio de la Zarzuela, 28671 Madrid, Spain

Juantorena, Alberto *Track Athlete*
%National Institute for Sports, Sports City, Havana, Cuba

Jubany Arnau, Narciso Cardinal *Religious Leader*
%Arquebisbe de Barcelone, Bisbe Irurita 5, 08002 Barcelona, Spain

Juckes, Gordon W *Hockey Executive*
1475 Avenue B, Big Pine Key, FL 33043, USA

Judd, Ashley *Actress*
PO Box 680339, Franklin, TN 37068, USA

Judd, Howard L *Obstetrician*
%University of California, Medical Center, OB-Gyn Dept, Los Angeles, CA 90024, USA

Judd, Naomi *Singer (The Judds), Songwriter*
1749 Mallory Lane, Franklin, TN 37068, USA

Judd, Wynonna *Singer (The Judds)*
%Judd House, 325 Bridge St, Franklin, TN 37064, USA

Judge, Mike *Animator (Beavis & Butt-Head)*
%"Beavis & Butt-Head" Show, MTV-TV, 1515 Broadway, New York, NY 10036, USA

Judge, Thomas L — *Governor, MT*
579 Diehl Dr, Helena, MT 59601, USA

Judkins, Jeff — *Basketball Coach*
%University of Utah, Athletic Dept, Salt Lake City, UT 84112, USA

Jugnauth, Anerood — *Prime Minister, Mauritius*
%Government House, New Government Center, Port Louis, Mauritius

Juhl, Finn — *Furniture Designer*
%Kratvaenget 15, 2920 Chartottenlund, Denmark

Julian, Alexander, II — *Fashion Designer*
%Alexander Julian Inc, 63 Copps Hill Road, Ridgefield, CT 06877, USA

Julian, Janet — *Actress*
%Borinstein Oreck Bogart, 8271 Melrose Ave, #110, Los Angeles, CA 90046, USA

Julien, Max — *Actor*
6051 Fulton Ave, Van Nuys, CA 91401, USA

Jumagulov, Apas — *Prime Minister, Kyrgyzstan*
%Prime Minister's Office, Government House, 720003 Bishkek, Kyrgyzstan

Jumblatt, Walid — *Government Official, Lebanon*
%Druze Headquarters, Mokhtara, Lebanon

Jump, Gordon — *Actor*
3285 Minnesota Ave, Costa Mesa, CA 92626, USA

Jumper, John P — *Air Force General*
Commander, 9th Air Force, 524 Shaw Dr, Shaw Air Force Base, SC 29152, USA

Jumper, John P — *Air Force General*
Deputy CofStaff, Air & Space Ops, HqUSAF, Pentagon, Washington, DC 20330, USA

Junck, Mary — *Publisher*
%Baltimore Sun Co, 501 N Calvert St, Baltimore, MD 21202, USA

Juncker, Jean-Claude — *Prime Minister, Luxembourg*
Hotel de Bourgogne, 4 Rue de la Congregation, 2910 Luxembourg

Juneau, Joe — *Hockey Player*
%Washington Capitals, USAir Arena, 1 Truman Dr, Landover, MD 20785, USA

Juneau, Pierre — *Government Official, Canada*
%Canadian Broadcast Co, 1500 Bronson Ave, Ottawa ON N1G 3J5, Canada

Jung, Ernst — *Writer*
88515 Lagenensligen/Wiltlingen, Germany

Jung, Richard — *Neurologist*
Waldhofstr 42, 71691 Freiburg, Germany

Junger, Ernst — *Writer*
88515 Langenenslinger, Germany

Junior, E J — *Football Player*
2681 Laguna Way, Miramar, FL 33025, USA

Juno — *Glass Maker*
%Lynn Howe Architectural Glass Design, 5753 Landregan St, Emeryville, CA 94608, USA

Juppe, Alain M — *Prime Minister, France*
37 Quai D'Orsay, 75700 Paris, France

Juran, Joseph M — *Engineer, Management Consultant*
%Juran Institute, 11 River Road, Wilton, CT 06897, USA

Jurasik, Peter — *Actor*
969 1/2 Manzanita St, Los Angeles, CA 90029, USA

Jurgensen, Christian A (Sonny), III — *Football Player*
PO Box 53, Mount Vernon, VA 22121, USA

Jurick, Geoffrey — *Businessman*
%Emerson Radio Corp, 9 Entin Road, Parsippany, NJ 07054, USA

Jurinac, Sena — *Opera Singer*
%State Opera House, Opernring 2, 10100 Vienna, Austria

Just, Walter — *Publisher*
%Milwaukee Journal, 333 W State St, Milwaukee, WI 53203, USA

Just, Ward S — *Writer*
36 Ave Junot, Paris, France

Justice, Charlie (Choo Choo) — *Football Player*
PO Box 819, Cherryville, NC 28021, USA

Justice, David C — *Baseball Player*
PO Box 56647, Atlanta, GA 30343, USA

Justice, Donald R — *Writer*
338 Rocky Shore Dr, Iowa City, IA 52246, USA

J

Judge - Justice

K

Kaassorla, Irene — *Psychologist*
10231 Charing Cross Road, Los Angeles, CA 90024, USA

Kaat, James L (Jim) — *Baseball Player*
2806 SE Dune Dr, #1208, Stuart, FL 34996, USA

Kabore, Marc-Christian — *Prime Minister, Burkina Faso*
%Prime Minister's Office, Ouagadougou, Burkina Faso

Kabua, Amata — *President, Marshall Islands*
%President's Office, Cabinet Building, PO Box 2, Majuro, Marshall Islands

Kaczmarek, Jane — *Actress*
304 E 65th St, #5-A, New York, NY 10021, USA

Kadanoff, Leo P — *Physicist*
5421 Cornell Ave, Chicago, IL 60615, USA

Kadare, Ismael — *Writer*
%Editions Fayard, 75 Rue De St Peres, 75006 Paris, France

Kadenyuk, Leonid — *Cosmonaut*
%Potchta Kosmonavtov, Moskovskoi Oblasti, 141160 Syvisdny Goroduk, Russia

Kadish, Mike — *Football Player*
5485 Red Bank Road, Galena, OH 43021, USA

Kadish, Ronald T (Ron) — *Air Force General*
Commander, Electronic Systems Center, Hanscom Air Force Base, MA 01731, USA

Kadison, Joshua — *Singer, Songwriter, Pianist*
%Nick Bode, 1265 Electric Ave, Venice, CA 90291, USA

Kael, Pauline — *Writer*
2 Berkshire Heights Road, Great Barrington, MA 01230, USA

Kaestle, Carl F — *Writer, Historian*
35 Charlesfield St, Providence, RI 02906, USA

Kafelnikov, Yevgeny — *Tennis Player*
%Int'l Management Group, 1 Erieview Plaza, #1300, Cleveland, OH 44114, USA

Kafi, Ali — *President, Algeria*
%President's Office, Council of State, Al-Mouradia, Algiers, Algeria

Kagame, Paul — *Army General, Rwanda*
%Vice Chairman's Office, Church St, Kigali, Rwanda

Kagan, Jeremy Paul — *Movie Director*
2024 N Curson Ave, Los Angeles, CA 90046, USA

Kagge, Erling — *Polar Skier*
Munkedamsveien 86, 0270 Oslo, Norway

Kagoshima, Juzo — *Dollmaker*
1-14 Toyotamakami, Nerimaku, Tokyo, Japan

Kahana, Aron — *Financier*
%Israel Discount Bank (NY), 511 5th Ave, New York, NY 10017, USA

Kahane, Jeffrey — *Concert Pianist*
%IMG Artists, 22 E 71st St, New York, NY 10021, USA

Kahn, Alfred E — *Government Official, Economist*
221 Savage Farm Dr, Ithaca, NY 14850, USA

Kahn, Jenette S — *Publisher*
%DC Comics, 1325 Ave of Americas, New York, NY 10019, USA

Kahn, Madeline — *Actress*
975 Park Ave, #9-A, New York, NY 10028, USA

Kaifu, Toshiki — *Prime Minister, Japan*
%House of Representatives, Diet, Tokyo, Japan

Kailbourne, Erland E — *Financier*
%Fleet Bank, Kiernan Plaza, Albany, NY 12207, USA

Kain, Karin A — *Ballet Dancer*
%National Ballet of Canada, 157 E King St, Toronto ON M5C 1G9, Canada

Kairamo, Kari — *Businessman*
%Nokia Group, Mikonkatu 15 A, 00101 Helsinki 10, Finland

Kaiser, A Dale — *Biochemist*
832 Santa Fe Ave, Stanford, CA 94305, USA

Kaiser, Philip M — *Diplomat*
%SRI International, 1611 N Kent St, Arlington, VA 22209, USA

Kaiserman, William — *Fashion Designer*
29 W 56th St, New York, NY 10019, USA

Kaji, Gautam S — *Financier*
%World Bank Group, 1818 "H" St NW, Washington, DC 20433, USA

Kaku, Ryuzaburo — *Businessman*
%Canon Inc, 2-7-1 Nishi-Shinku, Shinjuku, Tokyo 169, Japan

Kalainov, Samuel C — *Businessman*
%American Mutual Life, 611 5th Ave, Des Moines, IA 50309, USA

Kalangis, Ike *Financier*
%Boatmen's Sunwest, 303 Roma Ave NW, Albuquerque, NM 87102, USA
Kalb, Marvin *Commentator, Educator*
%Harvard University, Barone Center, 79 John F Kennedy St, Cambridge, MA 02138, USA
Kalber, Floyd *Commentator*
%NBC-TV, News Dept, 30 Rockefeller Plaza, New York, NY 10112, USA
Kalember, Patricia *Actress*
324 W 83rd St, #3-B, New York, NY 10024, USA
Kaleri, Alexander Y *Cosmonaut*
141 160 Svyosdny Gorodok, Moskovskoi Oblasti, Potchta Kosmonavtor, Russia
Kalikow, Peter S *Publisher*
%H J Kalikow Co, 101 Park Ave, New York, NY 10178, USA
Kalina, Mike *Chef*
%"Travelin' Gourmet" Show, PBS-TV, 1320 Braddock Place, Alexandria, VA 22314, USA
Kalina, Richard *Artist*
44 King St, New York, NY 10014, USA
Kaline, Albert W (Al) *Baseball Player*
945 Timberlake Dr, Bloomfield Hills, MI 48302, USA
Kalish, Martin *Labor Leader*
%School Administrators Federation, 853 Broadway, New York, NY 10003, USA
Kalish, Robert P *Financier*
%Government National Mortgage Assn, 451 7th St SW, Washington, DC 20410, USA
Kalitta, Connie *Drag Racing Driver*
%Kalitta Flying Service, 843 Willow Run Airport, Ypsilanti, MI 48198, USA
Kall (Kevin Kallaugher) *Editorial Cartoonist*
%Baltimore Sun, Editorial Dept, 501 N Calvert St, Baltimore, MD 21202, USA
Kallen, Kitty *Singer*
35 Winthrop Place, Englewood, NJ 07631, USA
Kallman, Donald H *Businessman*
%Manhattan Industries, 1114 Ave of Americas, New York, NY 10036, USA
Kalule, Ayub *Boxer*
%Palle, Skjulet, Bagsvaert 12, Copenhagen 2850, Denmark
Kamal El-Ganzoury *Prime Minister, Egypt*
%Prime Minister's Office, Heliopolis, Cairo, Egypt
Kamali, Norma *Fashion Designer*
%OMO Norma Kamali, 11 W 56th St, New York, NY 10019, USA
Kaman, Charles H *Businessman*
%Kaman Corp, 1332 Blue Hills Ave, Bloomfield, CT 06002, USA
Kamarck, Martin A *Financier*
%Export-Import Bank, 811 Vermont Ave NW, Washington, DC 20571, USA
Kamb, Alexander *Geneticist*
1103 E 600 South, Salt Lake City, UT 84102, USA
Kamberg, Kenneth E *Financier*
%Coral Gables Federal Savings, PO Box 1000, Pompano Beach, FL 33061, USA
Kamen, Harry P *Businessman*
%Metropolitan Life Insurance, 1 Madison Ave, New York, NY 10010, USA
Kamen, Martin D *Chemist*
Casa Burinda, #B-58, 300 Hot Springs Road, Montecito, CA 93108, USA
Kamen, Michael *Composer, Conductor*
%Gorfaine/Schwarz/Roberts, 3301 Barham Blvd, #201, Los Angeles, CA 90068, USA
Kamerschen, Robert J *Businessman*
%ADVO Inc, 1 Univac Lane, Windsor, CT 06095, USA
Kaminsky, Arthur C *Sports Attorney*
%Athletes & Artists, 888 7th Ave, #3700, New York, NY 10106, USA
Kamm, Henry *Journalist*
%New York Times, Editorial Dept, 229 W 43rd St, New York, NY 10036, USA
Kamoze, Ini *Singer*
%Famous Artists Agency, 1700 Broadway, #500, New York, NY 10019, USA
Kampelman, Max M *Government Official, Diplomat*
3154 Highland Place NW, Washington, DC 20008, USA
Kampouris, Emmanuel A *Businessman*
%American Standard, 1 Centennial Place, Piscataway, NJ 08854, USA
Kamu, Okko *Conductor*
%Svensk Konsertdirektion Ab, Box 5076, 402 22 Goteborg, Sweden
Kan, Yuet Wai *Geneticist*
20 Yerba Buena Ave, San Francisco, CA 94127, USA
Kanaly, Steve *Actor*
838 Foothill Lane, Ojai, CA 93023, USA

K

Kalangis - Kanaly

K

Kananin, Roman G — *Architect*
%Joint-Stock Co Mosprojekt, 13/14 1 Brestkaya Str, 125190 Moscow, Russia

Kanao, Minoru — *Businessman*
%Nippon Kokan, 1-1-2 Marunouchi, Chiyodaku, Tokyo 100, Japan

Kandel, Eric R — *Neurobiologist*
9 Sigma Place, Riverdale, NY 10471, USA

Kander, John H — *Composer*
12203 Octagon St, Los Angeles, CA 90049, USA

Kane Elson, Marion — *Synchronized Swimmer*
4669 Badger Road, Santa Rosa, CA 95409, USA

Kane, Big Daddy — *Rap Artist, Lyricist*
%Rush Artists, 1600 Varick St, New York, NY 10013, USA

Kane, Bob — *Cartoonist (Batman)*
8455 Fountain Ave, #725, Los Angeles, CA 90069, USA

Kane, Carol — *Actress*
8205 Santa Monica Blvd, #1426, Los Angeles, CA 90046, USA

Kane, Douglas C — *Businessman*
%MDU Resources Group, 400 N 4th St, Bismarck, ND 58501, USA

Kane, James — *Labor Leader*
%United Electrical Workers Union, 11 E 51st St, New York, NY 10022, USA

Kane, Joseph N — *Writer, Historian*
%H W Wilson Co, 950 University Ave, Bronx, NY 10452, USA

Kane, Nick — *Singer (The Mavericks)*
%AstroMedia, 1620 16th Ave S, Nashville, TN 37212, USA

Kaneda, Masaichi — *Baseball Player*
%Nippon Television, 14 Nibancho, Chiyodaku, Tokyo 102, Japan

Kaneko, Hisashi — *Businessman*
%NEC Corp, 5-33-1 Shiba, Minatoku, Tokyo 108, Japan

Kanew, Jeffrey R — *Movie Director*
%Gersh Agency, 232 N Canon Dr, Beverly Hills, CA 90210, USA

Kang Song San — *Prime Minister, North Korea*
%Prime Minister's Office, Pyongyang, North Korea

Kanin, Fay — *Writer*
653 Ocean Front Walk, Santa Monica, CA 90402, USA

Kanin, Garson — *Writer, Movie Director*
200 W 57th St, #1203, New York, NY 10019, USA

Kann Valar, Paula — *Skier*
PO Box 906, Franconia, NH 03580, USA

Kann, Peter R — *Businessman, Publisher, Journalist*
%Dow Jones Co, 200 Liberty St, New York, NY 10281, USA

Kannenberg, Bernd — *Track Athlete*
Sportschule, 87527 Sonthofen/Allgau, Germany

Kanovitz, Howard — *Artist*
463 Broome St, New York, NY 10013, USA

Kanter, Hal — *Movie, TV Producer; Screenwriter*
%Hecox Horn Wheeler, 4730 Woodman Ave, Sherman Oaks, CA 91423, USA

Kantner, Paul — *Guitarist (Jefferson Airplane, Starship)*
%Bill Thompson Mgmt, 2051 3rd St, San Francisco, CA 94107, USA

Kantor, Michael (Mickey) — *Government Official*
%Office of US Trade Representative, 600 17th St NW, Washington, DC 20508, USA

Kantrowitz, Adrian — *Heart Surgeon*
70 Gallogly Road, Pontiac, MI 48326, USA

Kantrowitz, Arthur R — *Physicist*
4 Downing Road, Hanover, NH 03755, USA

Kapioitas, John — *Businessman*
%ITT Sheraton Corp, 60 State St, Boston, MA 02109, USA

Kaplan, Gabe — *Actor, Comedian*
9551 Hidden Valley Road, Beverly Hills, CA 90210, USA

Kaplan, Jonathan S — *Movie Director*
8275 Kirkwood Dr, Los Angeles, CA 90046, USA

Kaplan, Justin — *Writer*
16 Francis Ave, Cambridge, MA 02138, USA

Kaplan, Marvin — *Actor*
PO Box 1522, Burbank, CA 91507, USA

Kaplan, Nathan O — *Biochemist*
8587 La Jolla Scenic Dr, La Jolla, CA 92037, USA

Kaplan, Richard — *Editor*
%Star Magazine, Editoral Dept, 660 White Plains Road, Tarrytown, NY 10591, USA

Kaplansky, Irving *Mathematician*
%Mathematical Sciences Research Institute, 100 Centennial Dr, Berkeley, CA 94720, USA
Kaplow, Herbert E *Commentator*
211 N Van Buren St, Falls Church, VA 22046, USA
Kapoor, Anish *Sculptor*
33 Coleherne Road, London SW10, England
Kapoor, Shashi *Actor*
%Film Valas, Janki Kutir, Juhu Church Road, Bombay 400049, India
Kapor, Mitchell D *Computer Programer*
%Electronic Frontier Foundation, 238 Main St, Cambridge, MA 02142, USA
Kapp, Joe *Football Player, Coach*
233 Edelen Ave, Los Gatos, CA 95030, USA
Kaprisky, Valerie *Actress*
%Artmedia, 10 Ave George V, 75008 Paris, France
Kapture, Mitzi *Actress*
4924 Balboa Blvd, #407, Encino, CA 91316, USA
Karageorghis, Vassos *Archaeologist*
%Foundation Anastasios Leventis, 28 Sofoulis St, Nicosia, Cyprus
Karan, Donna *Fashion Designer*
%Donna Karan Co, 550 7th Ave, New York, NY 10018, USA
Karathanasis, Sotirios K *Medical Researcher*
%Harvard Medical School, 25 Shattuck St, Boston, MA 02115, USA
Karcher, Carl *Businessman*
%Carl Karcher Enterprises, 1200 N Harbor Blvd, Anaheim, CA 92801, USA
Karelskaya, Rimma K *Ballerina*
%Bolshoi Theater, Teatralnaya Pl 1, 103009 Moscow, Russia
Karg, Uschi *Model*
%Ford Model Agency, 344 E 59th St, New York, NY 10022, USA
Karim-Lamrani, Mohammed *Prime Minister, Morocco*
Rue Du Mont Saint Michel, Anfa Superieur, Casablanca 21300, Morocco
Karimov, Islam M *President, Uzbekistan*
%President's Office, Pl V 1 Lenina, Tashkent B, Uzbekistan
Karina, Anna *Actress*
%JFPM, 11 Rue Chanez, 75781 Paris, France
Kariya, Paul *Hockey Player*
%Anaheim Mighty Ducks, PO Box 2000, Gene Autry Way, Anaheim, CA 92803, USA
Karl, George *Basketball Coach*
2833 134th Ave NE, Bellevue, WA 98005, USA
Karle, Isabella *Chemist*
6304 Lakeview Dr, Falls Church, VA 22041, USA
Karle, Jerome *Nobel Chemistry Laureate*
US Navy Structure of Matter Research Laboratory, Code 6030, Washington, DC 20375, USA
Karlen, John *Actor*
911 2nd St, #16, Santa Monica, CA 90403, USA
Karlin, Samuel *Mathematician*
%Stanford University, Mathematics Dept, Stanford, CA 94305, USA
Karling, John S *Mycologist*
1219 Tuckahoe Lane, West Lafayette, IN 47906, USA
Karlstad, Geir *Speed Skater*
Hamarveien 5-A, 1472 Fjellhamar, Norway
Karlzen, Mary *Singer, Songwriter*
%Little Big Man, 39-A Gramercy Park N, #1-C, New York, NY 10010, USA
Karmi, Ram *Architect*
%Karmi Architects, 5 Ben-Zion Blvd, Tel-Aviv, Israel
Karmi-Melamede, Ada *Architect*
%Karmi Architects, 5 Ben-Zion Blvd, Tel Aviv, Israel
Karn, Richard *Actor*
%Contemporary Artists, 1427 3rd St Promenade, #205, Santa Monica, CA 90401, USA
Karnes, David K *Senator, NE*
%Kutak Rock, Omaha Building, 1650 Farnam St, Omaha, NE 68102, USA
Karnow, Stanley *Writer, Historian*
10850 Spring Knolls Dr, Potomac, MD 20854, USA
Karolyi, Bela *Gymnastics Coach*
%Karolyi's World Gym, RR 12, Box 140, Huntsville, TX 77340, USA
Karoui, Hamed *Prime Minister, Tunisia*
%Prime Minister's Office, Place du Gouvernement, Tunis, Tunisia
Karp, David *Writer*
300 E 56th St, #3-C, New York, NY 10022, USA

K

Kaplansky - Karp

K

Karpati, Gyorgy *Water Polo Player*
Il Liva Utca 1, 1025 Budapest, Hungary
Karpatkin, Rhoda H *Publisher*
%Consumer Reports Magazine, 101 Truman Ave, Yonkers, NY 10703, USA
Karplus, Martin *Chemist*
%Harvard University, Chemistry Dept, Cambridge, MA 02138, USA
Karpov, Anatoly *Chess Player*
%Russian Chess Federation, Luzhnetskaya 8, 119270 Moscow, Russia
Karr, Mary *Writer*
%Syracuse University, English Dept, Syracuse, NY 13244, USA
Karras, Alex G *Football Player, Actor*
7943 Woodrow Wilson Dr, Los Angeles, CA 90046, USA
Karrass, Chester L *Writer*
1633 Stanford St, Santa Monica, CA 90404, USA
Karros, Eric P *Baseball Player*
PO Box 2380, Manhattan Beach, CA 90267, USA
Karsh, Yousuf *Photographer*
%Chateau Laurier Hotel, #660, 1 Rideau St, Ottawa ON K1N 8S7, Canada
Kasaks, Sally Frame *Businesswoman*
%AnnTaylor Stores, 142 W 57th St, New York, NY 10019, USA
Kasatkina, Natalya K *Ballerina, Choreographer*
St Karietny Riad, H 5/10, B 37, Moscow, Russia
Kasatonov, Alexei *Hockey Player*
153 Eagle Rock Way, Montclair, NJ 07042, USA
Kasdan, Lawrence E *Movie Director*
%United Talent Agency, 9560 Wilshire Blvd, #500, Beverly Hills, CA 90212, USA
Kasem, Casey *Entertainer, Actor*
138 N Mapleton Dr, Los Angeles, CA 90077, USA
Kasem, Jean *Actress*
138 N Mapleton Dr, Los Angeles, CA 90077, USA
Kaser, Helmut A *Soccer Executive*
Hitzigweg 11, 8032 Zurich, Switzerland
Kash, Lawrence S *Financier*
%Boston Co, 1 Boston Place, Boston, MA 02108, USA
Kasha, Al *Composer*
9249 Burton Way, #404, Beverly Hills, CA 90210, USA
Kashiwagi, Yusuke *Financier*
%Bank of Tokyo, 1-6-3 Nihombashi, Hongokucho, Chuoku, Tokyo 106, Japan
Kashnow, Richard *Businessman*
%Raychem Corp, 300 Constitution Dr, Menlo Park, CA 94025, USA
Kaske, Karlheinz *Businessman*
%Siemens AG, Wittelsbacherplatz 2, 80333 Munich, Germany
Kaskey, Raymond J *Sculptor*
%Portlandia Productions, PO Box 25658, Portland, OR 97298, USA
Kasle, Donald H *Financier*
%Bank One Dayton, Kettering Tower, Dayton, OH 45401, USA
Kasparaitis, Darius *Hockey Player*
48 Steers Ave, Northport, NY 11768, USA
Kasparov, Garri K *Chess Player*
%Russian Chess Federation, Luzhnetskaya 8, 119270 Moscow, Russia
Kasper, Steve *Hockey Player, Coach*
156 Lancaster Road, North Andover, MA 01845, USA
Kasrashvili, Makvala *Opera Singer*
%Bolshoi Theater, Teatralnaya Pl 1, 103 009 Moscow, Russia
Kassell, Carl *Commentator*
%National Public Radio, 635 Massachusetts Ave, Washington, DC 20001, USA
Kassirer, Jerome P *Physician, Editor*
%New England Journal of Medicine, 1440 Main St, Waltham, MA 02154, USA
Kassorla, Irene C *Psychologist*
PO Box 11001, Beverly Hills, CA 90213, USA
Kassulke, Karl *Football Player*
%Bethel College, Athletic Dept, St Paul, MN 55112, USA
Kasten, G Frederick, Jr *Businessman*
%Robert W Baird Co, 777 E Wisconsin Ave, Milwaukee, WI 53202, USA
Kasten, Robert W, Jr *Senator, WI*
%Strategic/International Studies Center, 1800 "K" St NW, Washington, DC 20006, USA
Kasten, Stan *Baseball, Basketball Executive*
%Atlanta Braves, Atlanta-Fulton County Stadium, PO Box 4064, Atlanta, GA 30302, USA

Karpati - Kasten

Kastner, Elliott — *Movie Producer*
%Winkast Films, Pinewood Studios, Iver Heath, Iver SLO ONH, England
Katayama, Nihachiro — *Businessman*
%Mitsubishi Electric, 2-2-3 Marunouchi, Chiyodaku, Tokyo 100, Japan
Katchor, Ben — *Cartoonist*
%Little Brown Co, 34 Beacon St, Boston, MA 02108, USA
Kates, Robert W — *Geographer*
RR 1, Box 169-B, Ellsworth, ME 04605, USA
Katims, Milton — *Conductor, Concert Violinist*
Fairway Estates, 8001 Sand Point Way NE, Seattle, WA 98115, USA
Katin, Peter — *Concert Pianist*
%Maureen Lunn, Top Farm, Parish Lane, Hedgerley, Bucks SL2 3JH, England
Katleman, Harris L — *Entertainment Executive*
%Mark Goodson Productions, 5750 Wilshire Blvd, #475, Los Angeles, CA 90036, USA
Katritzky, Alan R — *Chemist*
1221 SW 21st Ave, Gainesville, FL 32601, USA
Katt, William — *Actor*
23508 Canzonet St, Woodland Hls, CA 91367, USA
Katz, Abraham — *Diplomat*
%US Council for International Business, 1212 Ave of Americas, New York, NY 10036, USA
Katz, Alex — *Artist*
435 W Broadway, New York, NY 10012, USA
Katz, Bernard — *Nobel Medicine Laureate*
%University College, Biophysics Dept, Gower St, London WC1, England
Katz, Douglas J (Doug) — *Navy Admiral*
1530 Gordon Cove Dr, Annapolis, MD 21403, USA
Katz, Harold — *Basketball Executive*
%Philadelphia 76ers, Veterans Stadium, PO Box 25040, Philadelphia, PA 19147, USA
Katz, Hilda — *Artist*
915 West End Ave, #5-D, New York, NY 10025, USA
Katz, Lillian Hochberg — *Businesswoman*
%Lillian Vernon Corp, 543 Main St, New Rochelle, NY 10801, USA
Katz, Michael — *Pediatrician*
%March of Dimes Foundation, 1275 Mamaroneck Ave, White Plains, NY 10605, USA
Katz, Omri — *Actor*
%J H Productions, 23679 Calabasas Road, #333, Calabasas, CA 91302, USA
Katz, Samuel L — *Pediatrician*
1917 Wildcat Creek Road, Chapel Hill, NC 27516, USA
Katz, Sydney L — *Businessman*
%Grossman's Inc, 45 Dan Road, Canton, MA 02021, USA
Katz, Tonnie L — *Editor*
%Orange County Register, Editorial Dept, 625 N Grand Ave, Santa Ana, CA 92701, USA
Katzenbach, John — *Writer*
%Ballatine Books, 201 E 50th St, New York, NY 10022, USA
Katzenbach, Nicholas deB — *Attorney General*
906 The Great Road, Princeton, NJ 08540, USA
Katzenberg, Jeffrey — *Entertainment Executive*
%DreamWorks SKG, 100 Universal City Plaza, Universal City, CA 91608, USA
Katzir, Ephraim — *President, Israel*
%Weizmann Institute of Science, PO Box 26, Rehovot, Israel
Katzman, Jerry — *Entertainment Executive*
%William Morris Agency, 151 S El Camino Dr, Beverly Hills, CA 90212, USA
Kaufman, Henry — *Financier*
%Henry Kaufman Co, 65 E 55th St, New York, NY 10022, USA
Kaufman, Napoleon — *Football Player*
520 N "M" St, #1, Lompoc, CA 93436, USA
Kaufman, Philip — *Movie Director*
%Creative Artists Agency, 9830 Wilshire Blvd, Beverly Hills, CA 90212, USA
Kaufman, Victor A — *Entertainment Executive*
%Savoy Entertainment, 152 W 57th St, New York, NY 10019, USA
Kaufmann, Bob — *Basketball Player*
1677 Rivermist Dr, Lilburn, GA 30047, USA
Kauzmann, Walter J — *Chemist*
301 N Harrison St, #152, Princeton, NJ 08540, USA
Kavanaugh, Kenneth W (Ken) — *Football Player*
4907 Palm Aire Dr, Sarasota, FL 34243, USA
Kavandi, Janet L — *Astronaut*
%NASA, Johnson Space Center, 2101 NASA Road, Houston, TX 77058, USA

K

Kastner - Kavandi

Kavner, Julie *Actress*
25154 Malibu Road, #2, Malibu, CA 90265, USA

Kawai, Ryoichi *Businessman*
%Komatsu Ltd, 2-3-6 Akasaka, Minatoku, Tokyo 107, Japan

Kawakami, Tetsuro *Businessman*
%Sumitomo Electric Industries, 5-15 Kitahama, Higashiku, Osaka 541, Japan

Kawakubo, Rei *Fashion Designer*
%Comme des Garcons, 5-11-5 Minamiaoyama, Minatoku, Tokyo, Japan

Kawawa, Rashidi M *Prime Minister, Tanzania*
%Ministry of Defense, Dar es Salaam, Tanzania

Kay, Dianne *Actress*
1559 Palisades Dr, Pacific Palisades, CA 90272, USA

Kay, John *Singer, Guitarist (Steppenwolf)*
%Paradise Artists, 108 E Matilija St, Ojai, CA 93023, USA

Kaye, Judy *Actress, Singer*
870 N Vine St, #G, Los Angeles, CA 90038, USA

Kaysen, Carl *Economist*
41 Holden St, Cambridge, MA 02138, USA

Kayser, Elmer L *Writer, Historian*
2921 34th St NW, Washington, DC 20008, USA

Kazan, Elia *Movie Director*
174 E 95th St, New York, NY 10128, USA

Kazan, Lainie *Singer*
%Richard Gordon, 1222 N Olive Dr, Los Angeles, CA 90069, USA

Kazankina, Tatyana *Track Athlete*
Hoshimina St, 111211 St Petersburg, Russia

Kazarnovskaya, Lubov Y *Opera Singer*
Hohenbergstr 50, 1120 Vienna, Austria

Kazin, Alfred *Writer*
%City University of New York, English Dept, 33 W 42nd St, New York, NY 10036, USA

Kazmaier, Richard W (Dick), Jr *Football Player*
261 Park Lane, Concord, MA 01742, USA

Keach, Stacy *Actor*
3969 Longridge Road, Sherman Oaks, CA 91423, USA

Keady, Gene *Basketball Coach*
%Purdue University, Mackey Arena, West Lafayette, IN 47907, USA

Kean, Jane *Actress*
28128 W Pacific Coast Highway, Malibu, CA 90265, USA

Kean, Thomas H *Governor, NJ, Educator*
%Drew University, President's Office, 36 Madison Ave, Madison, NJ 07940, USA

Keanan, Staci *Actress*
%Abrams Artists, 9200 Sunset Blvd, #625, Los Angeles, CA 90069, USA

Keane, Bil *Cartoonist (Family Circus)*
5815 E Joshua Tree Lane, Paradise Valley, AZ 85253, USA

Keane, Glen *Animator*
%Walt Disney Studios, Animation Dept, 500 S Buena Vista St, Burbank, CA 91521, USA

Keane, John M (Jack) *Army General*
Commanding General, XVIII Airborne Corps, Fort Bragg, NC 28307, USA

Keane, Kerrie *Actress*
%SDB Partners, 1801 Ave of Stars, #902, Los Angeles, CA 90067, USA

Kear, David *Geologist*
14 Christiana Grover, Lower Hutt, Ohope, Wellington, New Zealand

Kearns Goodwin, Doris *Writer, Historian*
%General Delivery, Concord, MA 01742, USA

Kearns, David T *Government Official, Businessman*
%Education Department, 400 Maryland Ave SW, Washington, DC 20202, USA

Kearns, Dennis *Hockey Player*
605 King Georges Way, West Vancouver BC V7S 1S2, Canada

Keathley, George *Movie Director*
%Missouri Repertory Theater, 4949 Cherry St, Kansas City, MO 64110, USA

Keating, Charles *Actor*
%Don Buchwald, 10 E 44th St, New York, NY 10017, USA

Keating, Edward *Photographer*
%New York Times, Editorial Dept, 229 W 43rd St, New York, NY 10036, USA

Keating, Frank *Governor, OK*
%Governor's Office, State Capitol Building, Oklahoma City, OK 73105, USA

Keating, H R F *Writer*
35 Northumberland Place, London W2 5AS, England

Keating, Paul J — *Prime Minister, Australia*
%Prime Minister's Office, Parliament House, Canberra ACT 2600, Australia
Keaton, Diane — *Actress*
%William Morris Agency, 1325 Ave of Americas, New York, NY 10019, USA
Keaton, Michael — *Actor*
11901 Santa Monica Blvd, #547, Los Angeles, CA 90025, USA
Keb' Mo' — *Singer, Songwriter*
%MB Mgmt, 8439 W Sunset Blvd, #105, West Hollywood, CA 90069, USA
Kebich, Vyacheslau F — *Prime Minister, Belarus*
%Council of Ministers, Government House, Dom Urada, 220010 Minsk, Belarus
Keck, Donald B — *Inventor (Silica Optical Waveguide)*
2877 Chequers Circle, Big Flats, NY 14814, USA
Keck, Howard B — *Philanthropist*
%Keck Foundation, 555 S Flower St, #3640, Los Angeles, CA 90071, USA
Kedah — *Sultan, Kedah*
Alor Setar, Kedah, Malaysia
Kedrova, Lila — *Actress*
50 Forest Manor Road, #3, Willowdale ON M2J 1M1, Canada
Keefe, Adam — *Basketball Player*
6138 Oak Canyon Dr, Salt Lake City, UT 84121, USA
Keefe, Mike — *Editorial Cartoonist*
%Denver Post, Editorial Dept, PO Box 1709, Denver, CO 80201, USA
Keefer, Don — *Actor*
4146 Allott Ave, Sherman Oaks, CA 91423, USA
Keegan, Gerald C — *Financier*
%Greater NY Savings Bank, 1 Pennsylvania Plaza, New York, NY 10119, USA
Keegan, John — *Writer, Historian*
%Jonathan Cape, 32 Bedford Square, London WC1B 3EL, England
Keel, Alton G, Jr — *Diplomat, Businessman*
%Carlyle International, 1001 Pennsylvania Ave NW, Washington, DC 20004, USA
Keel, Howard — *Singer, Actor*
394 Red River Road, Palm Desert, CA 92211, USA
Keeler, William H Cardinal — *Religious Leader*
%National Conference of Catholic Bishops, 3211 4th St, Washington, DC 20017, USA
Keeley, Robert V — *Diplomat*
3814 Livingston St NW, Washington, DC 20015, USA
Keen, Robert Earl — *Singer, Songwriter*
%Eight Twenty-Three Mgmt, 305 Park Lane, Austin, TX 78704, USA
Keen, Sam — *Writer, Philosopher*
16331 Norrbom Road, Sonoma, CA 95476, USA
Keenan, Joseph D — *Labor Leader*
2727 29th St NW, Washington, DC 20008, USA
Keeshan, Bob — *Actor (Captain Kangaroo)*
PO Box 1243, Norwich, VT 05055, USA
Keezer, Geoff — *Jazz Pianist*
%Jazz Tree, 648 Broadway, #703, New York, NY 10012, USA
Kegel, Oliver — *Canoist*
Am Bogen 23, 13589 Berlin, Germany
Kehoe, Micholas B (Nick), III — *Air Force General*
Deputy Chairman, NATO Military Committee, PSC 80, Box 300, APO, AE 09724, USA
Keightley, David N — *Writer, Historian*
%University of California, History Dept, Berkeley, CA 94720, USA
Keillor, Garrison E — *Writer, Broadcaster*
%A Prairie Home Companion, 45 7th St E, Saint Paul, MN 55101, USA
Keim, Jenny — *Diver*
%Ron O'Brien, Swimming Hall of Fame, 1 Hall of Fame Dr, Ft Lauderdale, FL 33316, USA
Keiser, Robert L — *Businessman*
%Oryx Energy, 13155 Noel Road, Dallas, TX 75240, USA
Keita, Salif — *Singer, Composer*
%International Music Network, 2 Main St, #400, Gloucester, MA 01930, USA
Keitel, Harvey — *Actor*
110 Hudson St, #9-A, New York, NY 10013, USA
Keith, Damon J — *Judge*
%US Court of Appeals, US Courthouse, 231 W Lafayette Blvd, Detroit, MI 48226, USA
Keith, David — *Actor*
9595 Wilshire Blvd, #801, Beverly Hills, CA 90212, USA
Keith, Louis — *Physician*
333 E Superior St, #476, Chicago, IL 60611, USA

Keith, Penelope	*Actress*
66 Berkeley House, Hay Hill, London SW3, England	
Keith, Toby	*Singer*
%TKO Artist Mgmt, 4219 Hillsboro Road, #318, Nashville, TN 37215, USA	
Kekalainen, Jarmo	*Hockey Player*
145 Hillcrest Road, Needham, MA 02192, USA	
Keleti, Agnes	*Gynmast*
%Wingate Institute for Physical Education & Sport, Matanya 42902, Israel	
Kelker-Kelly, Robert	*Actor*
%Judy Schoen, 606 N Larchmont Blvd, #309, Los Angeles, CA 90004, USA	
Kell, George C	*Baseball Player*
PO Box 158, Swifton, AR 72471, USA	
Kellaway, Roger	*Composer*
%Pat Phillips Mgmt, 520 E 81st St, #PH-C, New York, NY 10028, USA	
Kelleher, Herbert D	*Businessman*
%Southwest Airlines, PO Box 36611, 2702 Love Field Dr, Dallas, TX 75235, USA	
Kellen, Stephen M	*Financier*
%Arnhold & S Bleichroeder, 1345 Ave of Americas, #4300, New York, NY 10105, USA	
Keller, Bill	*Journalist*
%New York Times, Editorial Dept, 229 W 43rd St, New York, NY 10036, USA	
Keller, Erhard	*Speed Skater*
Sudliche Munchneustr 6-A, 82031 Grunwald, Germany	
Keller, John	*Basketball Player*
608 Cheyenne View Dr, Great Bend, KS 67530, USA	
Keller, Joseph B	*Mathematician*
820 Sonoma Terrace, Stanford, CA 94305, USA	
Keller, Leonard B	*Vietnam War Army Hero (CMH)*
310 Majzun Road, Milton, FL 32570, USA	
Keller, Marthe	*Actress*
%Lemonstr 9, 81679 Munich, Germany	
Keller, Mary Page	*Actress*
%William Morris Agency, 151 S El Camino Dr, Beverly Hills, CA 90212, USA	
Kellerman, Faye	*Writer*
%Karpfinger Agency, 357 W 20th St, New York, NY 10011, USA	
Kellerman, Jonathan S	*Writer*
%Karpfinger Agency, 357 W 20th St, New York, NY 10011, USA	
Kellerman, Sally	*Actress*
7944 Woodrow Wilson Dr, Los Angeles, CA 90046, USA	
Kellermann, Susan	*Actress*
%Blake Agency, 415 N Camden Dr, #121, Beverly Hills, CA 90210, USA	
Kelley, David E	*Television Producer, Screenwriter*
2210 Wilshire Blvd, #998, Santa Monica, CA 90403, USA	
Kelley, DeForest	*Actor*
%Lincoln Enterprises, 14710 Arminta St, Van Nuys, CA 91402, USA	
Kelley, Edward F	*Physicist*
%National Standards & Technology Institute, Rt I-270, Gaithersburg, MD 20878, USA	
Kelley, Edward W, Jr	*Financier, Government Official*
%Federal Reserve Board, 20th St & Constitution Ave NE, Washington, DC 20551, USA	
Kelley, Gaynor N	*Businessman*
%Perkin-Elmer Corp, 761 Main Ave, Norwalk, CT 06859, USA	
Kelley, Harold H	*Psychologist*
21634 Rambla Vista St, Malibu, CA 90265, USA	
Kelley, Jay W	*Air Force General*
Commander, Air University, 55 LeMay Plaza S, Maxwell Air Force Base, AL 36112, USA	
Kelley, John A (Marathon)	*Marathon Runner*
136 Cedar Hill Road, East Dennis, MA 02641, USA	
Kelley, Kitty	*Writer*
1228 Eton Court NW, Washington, DC 20007, USA	
Kelley, Lawrence M (Larry)	*Football Player*
5917 Strickland Place, Pensacola, FL 32506, USA	
Kelley, Mike	*Sculptor*
2472 Eastman Ave, #35-36, Ventura, CA 93003, USA	
Kelley, Paul X	*Marine Corps General*
1600 N Oak St, #1619, Arlington, VA 22209, USA	
Kelley, Robert	*Businessman*
%Noble Affiliates, 110 W Broadway, Ardmore, OK 73401, USA	
Kelley, Sheila	*Actress*
2910 N Beachwood Dr, Los Angeles, CA 90068, USA	

Kelley, Steve — *Editorial Cartoonist*
%San Diego Union, 350 Camino de la Reina, PO Box 191, San Diego, CA 92112, USA
Kelley, Thomas G — *Vietnam War Navy Hero (CMH)*
8772 Cloudleap Court, #31, Columbia, MD 21045, USA
Kelley, William G — *Businessman*
%Consolidated Stores, 1105 N Market St, Wilmington, DE 19801, USA
Kellogg, Clark — *Basketball Player, Sportscaster*
691 Lookout Ridge Dr, Westerville, OH 43082, USA
Kelly, Daniel Hugh — *Actor*
%Innovative Artists, 1999 Ave of Stars, #2850, Los Angeles, CA 90067, USA
Kelly, Donald P — *Businessman*
%Envirodyne Industries, 701 Harger Road, Hinsdale, IL 60523, USA
Kelly, Eamon M — *Educator*
%Tulane University, President's Office, New Orleans, LA 70118, USA
Kelly, Edmund F — *Businessman*
%Liberty Mutual Insurance, 175 Berkeley St, Boston, MA 02116, USA
Kelly, Ellsworth — *Artist*
RD, PO Box 170-B, Chatham, NY 12037, USA
Kelly, J Thomas (Tom) — *Baseball Player, Manager*
%Minnesota Twins, 501 Chicago Ave S, Minneapolis, MN 55415, USA
Kelly, James E (Jim) — *Football Player*
44 Hillsboro Dr, Orchard Park, NY 14127, USA
Kelly, James P — *Businessman*
%United Parcel Service, 55 Glenlake Parkway NE, Atlanta, GA 30328, USA
Kelly, John — *Singer (Kelly Family)*
%Kel-Life Gmbh, Auenweg 173, 51063 Cologne, Germany
Kelly, John F — *Businessman*
%Alaska Air Group, 19300 Pacific Highway S, Seattle, WA 98188, USA
Kelly, John H — *Diplomat*
%US State Department, 2201 "C" St NW, Washington, DC 20520, USA
Kelly, Leonard (Red) — *Hockey Player*
5915 Airport Road, #820, Mississauga ON L4V 1T1, Canada
Kelly, Leroy — *Football Player*
74 Club House Dr, Willingboro, NJ 08046, USA
Kelly, Moira — *Actress*
501 N Spaulding Ave, #5, Los Angeles, CA 90036, USA
Kelly, Paul — *Singer, Songwriter*
%Premier Artists Pty, 9 Dundas Lane, Albert Park VIC 3206, Australia
Kelly, Paula — *Actress, Dancer*
7020 La Presa Dr, Los Angeles, CA 90068, USA
Kelly, R — *Rap Artist, Songwriter*
%Famous Artists Agency, 1700 Broadway, #500, New York, NY 10019, USA
Kelly, Thomas — *Writer*
%Alfred A Knopf Inc, 201 E 50th St, New York, NY 10022, USA
Kelly, Thomas J, III — *Photographer*
PO Box 2208, Sanatoga Branch, Pottstown, PA 19464, USA
Kelly, Thomas W — *Army General*
%George Washington University, Engineering School, Washington, DC 20052, USA
Kelly, William R — *Businessman*
%Kelly Services, 999 W Big Beaver Road, Troy, MI 48084, USA
Kelman, Arthur — *Plant Pathologist*
615 Yarmouth Road, Raleigh, NC 27607, USA
Kelman, Charles D — *Ophthalmologist*
Empire State Building, 350 5th Ave, #2100, New York, NY 10118, USA
Kelsey, Frances O — *Pharmacologist*
%Federal Drug Administration, 5600 Fishers Lane, Rockville, MD 20852, USA
Kelsey, Linda — *Actress*
1116 S Alvera St, Los Angeles, CA 90035, USA
Kelso, Frank B, II — *Navy Admiral*
7794 Turlock Road, Springfield, VA 22153, USA
Kemal, Yashar — *Writer*
PK 14 Basinkoy, Istanbul, Turkey
Kemble, Edwin C — *Physicist*
8 Ash Street Place, Cambridge, MA 02138, USA
Kemme, Thomas — *Labor Leader*
%Stove Furnance & Appliance Union, 2929 S Jefferson Ave, St Louis, MO 63118, USA
Kemp, Jack F — *Secretary, Housing & Urban Development*
%Empower America, 1776 "I" St NW, #800, Washington, DC 20006, USA

K

Kelley - Kemp

Kemp, Jeremy	*Actor*
%Marina Martin, 6-A Danbury St, London N1 8JU, England	
Kemp, Shawn T	*Basketball Player*
4034 35th Ave W, Seattle, WA 98199, USA	
Kemp, Steve F	*Baseball Player*
171 Linden Court, Pittsburgh, PA 15237, USA	
Kemp-Welch, John	*Financier*
Little Hallingbury Place, Bishop's Stortford, Herts CM22 7RE, England	
Kemper, David W, II	*Financier*
%Commerce Bancshares, 1000 Walnut St, Kansas City, MO 64106, USA	
Kemper, Jonathan	*Financier*
%Commerce Bancshares, 1000 Walnut St, Kansas City, MO 64106, USA	
Kemper, R Crosby	*Financier*
%UMB Financial Corp, 1010 Grand Ave, Kansas City, MO 64106, USA	
Kemper, Randolph E (Randy)	*Fashion Designer*
%Randy Kemper Corp, 530 7th Ave, #1400, New York, NY 10018, USA	
Kemper, Victor J	*Cinematographer*
10313 Pico Blvd, Los Angeles, CA 90064, USA	
Kempf, Cecil J	*Navy Admiral*
831 Olive Ave, Coronado, CA 92118, USA	
Kempner, Walter	*Nutritionist*
1505 Virginia Ave, Durham, NC 27705, USA	
Kendal, Felicity	*Actress*
%Chatto & Linnit, Prince of Wales, Coventry St, London W1V 7FE, England	
Kendall, Barbara	*Yachtswoman*
%Kendall Distributing, 82-B Great South Road, Auckland, New Zealand	
Kendall, Bruce	*Boardsailor*
6 Pedersen Place, Bucklands Beach, Auckland, New Zealand	
Kendall, Donald M	*Businessman*
%PepsiCo Inc, Anderson Hill Road, Purchase, NY 10577, USA	
Kendall, Henry W	*Nobel Physics Laureate*
%Massachusetts Institute of Technology, Physics Dept, Cambridge, MA 02139, USA	
Kendall, Suzy	*Actress*
Dentham House, #44, The Mount, Hampstead NW3, England	
Kendall, Tom	*Auto Racing Driver*
412 Highland Ave, Manhattan Beach, CA 90266, USA	
Kendler, Bob	*Handball, Raquetball Player*
%US Handball Assn, 4101 Dempster St, Skokie, IL 60076, USA	
Kendrew, John C	*Nobel Chemistry Laureate*
The Old Guildhall, 4 Church Lane, Linton, Cambridge CB1 6JX, England	
Kendrick, Rodney	*Singer, Jazz Pianist, Composer*
%Carolyn McClair, 410 W 53rd St, #128-C, New York, NY 10019, USA	
Keneally, Thomas M	*Writer*
24 The Serpentine, Bilgola Beach NSW 2107, Australia	
Kenilorea, Peter	*Prime Minister, Solomon Islands*
%Foreign Affairs Ministry, Honiara, Guadalcanal, Solomon Islands	
Kenn, Mike	*Football Player*
360 Bardolier, Alpharetta, GA 30022, USA	
Kenna, E Douglas (Doug)	*Businessman, Football Player*
%Carlisle Companies, 250 S Clinton, Syracuse, NY 13202, USA	
Kenna, Edward	*WW II Australian Army Hero (VC)*
121 Coleraine Road, Hamilton VIC 3300, Australia	
Kennan, George F	*Diplomat, Writer*
%Institute for Advanced Study, Princeton, NJ 08540, USA	
Kenneally, John P	*WW II Irish Army Hero (VC)*
7 Station Lane, Lapworth, Warwks, England	
Kennedy, Anthony M	*Supreme Court Justice*
%US Supreme Court, 1 1st St NE, Washington, DC 20543, USA	
Kennedy, Burt R	*Movie Director*
%Brigade Productions, 13138 Magnolia Blvd, Sherman Oaks, CA 91423, USA	
Kennedy, Claudia J	*Army General*
Deputy Assistant for Intelligence, HqUSA, Pentagon, Washington, DC 20310, USA	
Kennedy, Cortez	*Football Player*
43 Union, Wilson, AR 72395, USA	
Kennedy, D James	*Religious Leader*
%Coral Ridge Presbyterian Church, 5554 N Federal Hwy, Fort Lauderdale, FL 33308, USA	
Kennedy, David M	*Secretary, Treasury*
3838 Ruth Dr, Salt Lake City, UT 84124, USA	

Kennedy, Donald — *Educator*
%Stanford University, International Studies Institute, Stanford, CA 94305, USA
Kennedy, Eugene P — *Biological Chemist*
221 Mt Auburn St, Cambridge, MA 02138, USA
Kennedy, Forbes — *Hockey Player*
178 Kensington Road, Charlottetown, Prince Edward Island, Canada
Kennedy, George — *Actor*
%Paradigm Agency, 10100 Santa Monica Blvd, #2500, Los Angeles, CA 90067, USA
Kennedy, James C — *Businessman*
%Cox Enterprises, 1400 Lake Hearn Dr NE, Atlanta, GA 30319, USA
Kennedy, Jamie — *Actress*
%Agency For Performing Arts, 9200 Sunset Blvd, #900, Los Angeles, CA 90069, USA
Kennedy, Jayne — *Actress*
224 Barbour St, Playa Del Rey, CA 90293, USA
Kennedy, Joey D (Joe), Jr — *Journalist*
%Birmingham News, Editorial Dept, 2200 4th Ave N, Birmingham, AL 35203, USA
Kennedy, John F, Jr — *Editor*
%George Magazine, 1633 Broadway, #4100, New York, NY 10019, USA
Kennedy, John Milton — *Actor*
7100 Balboa Blvd, #606, Van Nuys, CA 91406, USA
Kennedy, John R, Jr — *Businessman*
%Federal Paper Board Co, 75 Chestnut Ridge Road, Montvale, NJ 07645, USA
Kennedy, Kevin C — *Baseball Manager*
5040 Cascade, Tarzana, CA 91356, USA
Kennedy, Leon Isaac — *Actor*
859 N Hollywood Way, #384, Burbank, CA 91505, USA
Kennedy, Lincoln — *Football Player*
%Oakland Raiders, 1220 Harbor Bay Parkway, Alameda, CA 94502, USA
Kennedy, Mimi — *Actress*
%Agency For Performing Arts, 9200 Sunset Blvd, #900, Los Angeles, CA 90069, USA
Kennedy, Nigel — *Concert Violinist*
%Pamela Esterson, 81 Landor Road, London SW9 9RT, England
Kennedy, Randall — *Attorney, Educator*
%Harvard University, Law School, Cambridge, MA 02138, USA
Kennedy, Robert D — *Businessman*
%Union Carbide, 39 Old Ridgbury Road, Danbury, CT 06817, USA
Kennedy, Ted (Teeder) — *Hockey Player*
13 Dixie Ave, Box 21, Niagara-on-the-Lake ON L0S 1J0, Canada
Kennedy, Terrence E (Terry) — *Baseball Player*
PO Box 30460, Mesa, AZ 85275, USA
Kennedy, Tom — *Television Host*
%William Morris Agency, 151 S El Camino Dr, Beverly Hills, CA 90212, USA
Kennedy, William J — *Writer*
%State University of New York, English Dept, Albany, NY 12468, USA
Kennedy, X J — *Writer*
4 Fern Way, Bedford, MA 01730, USA
Kennerly, David Hume — *Photographer*
1015 18th St, Santa Monica, CA 90403, USA
Kennet of Dene, Wayland Y — *Government Official, England*
%House of Lords, Westminster, London SW1A 0PW, England
Kennibrew, Dee Dee — *Singer (The Crystals)*
%Mars Talent, 168 Orchid Dr, Pearl River, NY 10965, USA
Kenny G — *Saxophonist*
2600 Benedict Canyon, Beverly Hills, CA 90210, USA
Kenny, Michael — *Sculptor*
71 Stepney Green, London E1 3LE, England
Kenny, Shirley Strum — *Educator*
%State University of New York, President's Office, Stony Brook, NY 11794, USA
Kensit, Patsy — *Actress*
14 Lambton Place, Nottinghill, London W11 2SH, England
Kent, Allegra — *Ballerina*
%New York City Ballet, Lincoln Center Plaza, New York, NY 10023, USA
Kent, Arthur — *Commentator*
%A K's O K, Box 695, New Hartford, CT 06057, USA
Kent, Bruce — *Social Activist*
%Nuclear Disarmament Campaign, 22-24 Underwood St, London N1 7JG, England
Kent, Geoffrey C — *Businessman*
Hill House, Gonalston, Nottingham NG14 7JA, England

K

Kennedy - Kent

Kent, Jean — *Actress*
%London Mgmt, 2-4 Noel St, London W1V 3RB, England

Kent, Jeffrey A (Jeff) — *Baseball Player*
%San Francisco Giants, Candlestick Park, San Francisco, CA 94124, USA

Kent, Jonathan — *Theater Director*
%International Creative Mgmt, 76 Oxford St, London W1N 0AX, England

Kent, Julie — *Ballerina*
%American Ballet Theatre, 890 Broadway, New York, NY 10003, USA

Kent, Peter — *Geologist*
43 Trinity Court, Gray's Inn Road, London WC1, England

Kentner, Louis P — *Concert Pianist*
1 Mallord St, London SW3, England

Kenty, Hilmer — *Boxer*
%Escot Boxing, 15260 Bretton Dr, Detroit, MI 48223, USA

Kenyon, Alfred K — *Businessman*
%Kemper Corp, 1 Kemper Dr, Long Grove, IL 60049, USA

Kenyon, Mel — *Auto Racing Driver*
2645 S 25th West, Lebanon, IN 46052, USA

Kenzle, Leila — *Actress*
%William Morris Agency, 151 S El Camino Dr, Beverly Hills, CA 90212, USA

Kenzo (Takada) — *Fashion Designer*
3 Place des Victories, 75001 Paris, France

Keogh, James — *Government Official*
Byram Dr, Belle Haven, Greenwich, CT 06830, USA

Keohane, Nannerl O — *Educator*
%Duke University, President's Office, Durham, NC 27706, USA

Keon, Dave — *Hockey Player*
115 Blackenwood Road, Palm Beach Gardens, FL 33418, USA

Keough, Donald R — *Financier*
%Allen & Co, 711 5th Ave, New York, NY 10022, USA

Kepes, Gyorgy — *Artist*
PO Box 1423, Wellfleet, MA 02667, USA

Kerber, James R — *Businessman*
%Southwestern Life, Lincoln Plaza, 500 N Akard St, Dallas, TX 75201, USA

Kercheval, Ken — *Actor*
PO Box 325, Goshen, KY 40026, USA

Kerekou, Mathieu A — *President, Benin; Army General*
%President's Office, Boite Postale 2020, Cotonou, Benin

Keresztes, K Sandor — *Architect*
Fo Utca 44/50, 1011 Budapest, Hungary

Kerkorian, Kirk — *Businessman*
%Kirk Kerkorian Enterprises, 3500 Las Vegas Blvd S, Las Vegas, NV 89109, USA

Kern, Geof — *Photographer*
1355 Conant St, Dallas, TX 75207, USA

Kern, Rex W — *Football Player*
4648 Stonehaven Dr, Columbus, OH 43220, USA

Kerns, David V, Jr — *Microbiotics Engineer*
%Vanderbilt University, Electrical Engineering Dept, Nashville, TN 37235, USA

Kerns, Joanna — *Actress*
PO Box 49216, Los Angeles, CA 90049, USA

Kerr, Clark — *Educator*
8300 Buckingham Dr, El Cerrito, CA 94530, USA

Kerr, Deborah — *Actress*
Los Monteros, 29600 Marbella, Malaga, Spain

Kerr, Donald M, Jr — *Physicist*
%Science Applications International, 1241 Cave St, La Jolla, CA 92037, USA

Kerr, Jean — *Writer*
1 Beach Ave, Larchmont Manor, NY 10538, USA

Kerr, John (Red) — *Basketball Player, Sportscaster*
120 S Riverside Plaza, #2100, Chicago, IL 60606, USA

Kerr, Judy — *Actress*
4139 Tujunga Ave, Studio City, CA 91604, USA

Kerr, Pat — *Fashion Designer*
%Pat Kerr Inc, 200 Wagner Place, Memphis, TN 38103, USA

Kerr, Tim — *Hockey Player, Coach*
%Springfield Indians, PO Box 4896, Springfield, MA 01101, USA

Kerr, William T — *Businessman*
%Meredith Corp, PO Box 400430, Des Moines, IA 50350, USA

Kerrigan, Nancy — Figure Skater
7 Cedar Ave, Stoneham, MA 02180, USA

Kersey, Jerome — Basketball Player
%Los Angeles Lakers, Forum, PO Box 10, Inglewood, CA 90306, USA

Kersh, David — Singer
%Trifecta Entertainment, 209 10th Ave S, #302, Nashville, TN 37203, USA

Kershaw, Doug — Singer, Fiddler
%Doc Holiday Productions, 10 Luanita Lane, Newport News, VA 23606, USA

Kershaw, Sammy — Singer
%Lucks Mgmt, PO Box 121135, Nashville, TN 37212, USA

Kershner, Irvin — Movie Director
424 Sycamore Road, Santa Monica, CA 90402, USA

Kerwin, Brian — Actor
304 W 81st St, #2, New York, NY 10024, USA

Kerwin, Joseph P — Astronaut
1802 Royal Fern Court, Houston, TX 77062, USA

Kerwin, Lance — Actor
PO Box 237, Lake Elsinore, CA 92531, USA

Kerwin, Larkin — Physicist
Canadian Space Agency, 500 Blvd Rene-Levesque, Montreal PQ H2Z 1Z7, Canada

Kesey, Ken — Writer
Rt 8, Box 477, Pleasant Hill, OR 97455, USA

Kesner, Jillian — Actress
%William Carroll, 139 N San Fernando Rd, #A, Burbank, CA 91502, USA

Kessel, Barney — Jazz Guitarist, Composer
1136 Madison Ave, San Diego, CA 92116, USA

Kessler, Bob — Basketball Player
1304 Forest Glen Court, Bloomfield Hills, MI 48304, USA

Kessler, David A — Physician, Government Official
%Yale University, Medical School, New Haven, CT 06510, USA

Kestelman, Sara — Actress
%Shepherdswell Productions, 34 S Molton St, London W1, England

Kesten, Hermann — Writer
Im Tiefen Boden 25, 4059 Basel, Switzerland

Kestner, Boyd — Actor
%Metropolitan Talent Agency, 4526 Wilshire Blvd, Los Angeles, CA 90010, USA

Ketchum, Hal — Singer, Songwriter
%Flood Bumstead McCready McCarthy, 1700 Hayes St, Nashville, TN 37203, USA

Ketchum, Howard — Color Engineer
3800 Washington Road, West Palm Beach, FL 33405, USA

Kety, Seymour S — Physiologist, Pscholobiolgist
%National Institutes of Health, 9000 Rockville Pike, Bethesda, MD 20892, USA

Kevorkian, Jack — Medical Activist
4870 Lockhart St, West Bloomfield, MI 48323, USA

Key, James E (Jimmy) — Baseball Player
59 Arverne Court, Lutherville, MD 21093, USA

Key, Ted — Cartoonist (Hazel)
1694 Glenhardie Road, Wayne, PA 19087, USA

Keyes, Evelyn — Actress
999 N Doheny Dr, #509, Los Angeles, CA 90069, USA

Keyes, James H — Businessman
%Johnson Controls, 5757 N Green Bay Ave, Milwaukee, WI 53209, USA

Keyes, Leroy — Football Player
6156 Pleasant Ave, Pennsauken, NJ 08110, USA

Keyes, Robert W — Physicist, Engineer
%IBM Research Division, PO Box 218, Yorktown Heights, NY 10598, USA

Keyser, F Ray, Jr — Governor, VT
64 Warner Ave, Proctor, VT 05765, USA

Keyser, Richard L — Businessman
%W W Grainger Inc, 5500 W Howard St, Skokie, IL 60077, USA

Keyworth, George A, II — Government Official
%Keyworth Meyer International, PO Box 25566, Washington, DC 20007, USA

Khajag Barsamian — Religious Leader
%Armenian Church of America, Eastern Diocese, 630 2nd Ave, New York, NY 10016, USA

Khaled (Hadj Brahim) — Singer
%Mango/Polygram Records, Worldwide Plaza, 825 8th Ave, New York, N 10019, USA

Khalifa al-Thani, Hamad Bin — Prime Minister, Qatar; Prince
%Royal Palace, PO Box 923, Doha, Qatar

K

K

Khalifa, Sheikh Hamad bin Isa al- *Crown Prince, Bahrain*
%Crown Prince's Office, Rifa's Palace, Manama, Bahrain

Khalifa, Sheikh Isa bin Sulman al- *Emir, Bahrain*
%Rifa's Palace, Manama, Bahrain

Khalifa, Sheikh Khalifa bin Sulman al- *Prime Minister, Bahrain*
%Prime Minister's Office, Government House, Government Rd, Manama, Bahrain

Khalil, Mustafa *Prime Minister, Egypt*
9-A El Maahad El Swisry St, Zamalek, Cairo, Egypt

Khamenei, Hojatolislam Sayyed Ali *President, Iran*
%Religious Leader's Office, Teheran, Iran

Khamtai Siphandon *Prime Minister, Laos; Army General*
%Prime Minister's Office, Council of Ministers, Vientiane, Laos

Khan, Ali Akbar *Composer, Sarod Player*
%Ali Akabar Music College, 215 West End Ave, San Rafael, CA 94901, USA

Khan, Chaka *Singer, Actress*
%Pyramid Entertainment, 89 5th Ave, #700, New York, NY 10003, USA

Khan, Gulam Ishaq *President, Pakistan*
3-B University Town, Jamrud Road, Peshawar, Pakistan

Khan, Inamullah *Religious Leader*
%Muslim Congress, D-26, Block 8, Gulshan-E-Iqbal, Karachi 75300, Pakistan

Khan, Niazi Imran *Cricketer*
%Shankat Khanum Memorial Trust, 29 Shah Jamal, Lahore 546000, Pakistan

Khanh, Emanuelle *Fashion Designer*
%Emanuelle Khanh International, 45 Ave Victor Hugo, 75116 Paris, France

Khanzadian, Vahan *Opera Singer*
3604 Broadway, #2-N, New York, NY 10031, USA

Khashoggi, Adnan M *Businessman*
La Baraka, Marbella, Spain

Khatami, Mohammad *President, Iran*
%President's Office, Dr Ali Shariati Ave, Teheran, Iran

Khatib, Ahmed al- *President, Syria*
%Syrian Ba'ath Party, Damascus, Syria

Khavin, Vladimir Y *Architect*
%Glavmosarchitectura, Mayakovsky Square 1, 103001 Moscow, Russia

Khayat, Robert *Educator*
%University of Mississippi, Chancellor's Office, University, MS 38677, USA

Kheel, Theodore W *Labor Mediator*
280 Park Ave, New York, NY 10017, USA

Khokhlov, Boris *Ballet Dancer*
Myaskovsky St 11-13, #102, 121019 Moscow, Russia

Khoraiche, Antoine Pierre Cardinal *Religious Leader*
Patriarcat Maronite, Dimane, Lebanon

Khorana, Har Gobind *Nobel Medicine Laureate*
%Massachusetts Institute of Technology, Biology Dept, Cambridge, MA 02139, USA

Khrennikov, Tikhon N *Composer*
Plotnikov Per 10/28, #19, 121200 Moscow, Russia

Khrunov, Yevgeni V *Cosmonaut*
%Potchta Kosmonavtov, Moskovskoi Oblasti, 141160 Syvisdny Goroduk, Russia

Khvorostovsky, Dimitri A *Opera Singer*
%Elen Victorova, Mosfilmovskaya 26, #5, Moscow, Russia

Kibrick, Anne *Medical Educator*
381 Clinton Road, Brookline, MA 02146, USA

Kid Creole *Singer*
%Ron Rainey, 315 S Beverly Dr, #208, Beverly Hills, CA 90212, USA

Kidd, Billy *Skier*
PO Box 1178, Steamboat Springs, CO 80477, USA

Kidd, Jason *Basketball Player*
11160 Elvessa St, Oakland, CA 94605, USA

Kidd, Michael *Choreographer, Dancer*
%William Morris Agency, 1325 Ave of Americas, New York, NY 10019, USA

Kidder Lee, Barbara *Skier*
1308 W Highland, Phoenix, AZ 85013, USA

Kidder, C Robert *Businessman*
%Borden Inc, 180 E Broad St, Columbus, OH 43215, USA

Kidder, Margot *Actress*
220 Pine Creek Road, Livingston, MT 59047, USA

Kidder, Tracy *Writer*
%George Borchardt, 136 E 57th St, New York, NY 10022, USA

Khalifa - Kidder

Kidjo, Angelique — *Singer*
%International Music Network, 2 Main St, #400, Gloucester, MA 01930, USA

Kidman, Nicole — *Actress*
335 N Maple Dr, #135, Beverly Hills, CA 90210, USA

Kiechel, Walter, III — *Editor*
%Fortune Magazine, Editorial Dept, 1291 Ave of Americas, New York, NY 10020, USA

Kiedis, Anthony — *Singer (Red Hot Chili Peppers)*
3120 Hollyridge Dr, Los Angeles, CA 90068, USA

Kiefer, Adolph — *Swimmer, Coach*
42125 N Hunt Club Road, Wadsworth, IL 60083, USA

Kiehl, Marina — *Skier*
Engadinerstr 2, 81475 Munich, Germany

Kiehl, Stuart — *Cinematographer*
PO Box 2341, Sausalito, CA 94966, USA

Kiel, Richard — *Actor*
40356 Oak Park Way, #T, Oakhurst, CA 93644, USA

Kiermayer, Susanne — *Markswoman*
Amthofplatz 5, 94259 Kirchberg, Germany

Kiernan, Charles E — *Businessman*
%Duracell International, Berkshire Corporate Park, Bethel, CT 06801, USA

Kiesler, Charles A — *Educator*
%University of Missouri, Chancellor's Office, Columbia, MO 65211, USA

Kight Wingard, Lenore — *Swimmer*
6281 Cary Ave, Cincinnati, OH 45224, USA

Kihune, Robert K U — *Navy Admiral*
1597 Haloloke St, Hilo, HI 96720, USA

Kiick, James F (Jim) — *Football Player*
8190 SW 28th St, Davie, FL 33328, USA

Kikuchi, Rioko — *Astronaut, Photographer*
%Tokyo Broadcasting System, 5-3-6 Akasaka, Minatoku, Tokyo 107-06, Japan

Kikutake, Kiyonori — *Architect*
1-11-15 Otsuka, Bunkyoku, Tokyo, Japan

Kilbourne, Wendy — *Actress*
9300 Wilshire Blvd, #410, Beverly Hills, CA 90212, USA

Kilburn, Terry — *Actor*
%Meadowbrook Theatre, Oakland University, Walton & Squirrel, Rochester, MI 48063, USA

Kilby, Jack S — *Inventor (Microchip)*
7723 Midbury St, Dallas, TX 75230, USA

Kilcline, Thomas J — *Navy Admiral*
%Retired Officers Assn, 201 N Washington St, Alexandria, VA 22314, USA

Kiley, Richard — *Actor, Singer*
Ryerson Road, Warwick, NY 10990, USA

Kilgallon, Robert D — *Environmental Researcher*
662 Park Ave, Meadville, PA 16335, USA

Kilgore, Al — *Cartoonist*
216-55 113th Dr, Queens Village, NY 11429, USA

Killanin, Michael M — *Olympics Official*
St Annins, Spiddal, County Galway, Ireland

Killebrew, Harmon C — *Baseball Player*
PO Box 14550, Scottsdale, AZ 85267, USA

Killinger, Kerry K — *Financier*
%Washington Mutual Savings, 1201 3rd Ave, Seattle, WA 98101, USA

Killip, Christopher D — *Photographer*
20 Wood Terrace, Bill Quay, Gateshead NE10 OUD, England

Killy, Jean-Claude — *Skier*
13 Chemin Bellefontaine, 1223 Cologny-GE, Switzerland

Kilmer, Val — *Actor*
%Wolf/Kasteller, 132 S Rodeo Dr, #300, Beverly Hills, CA 90212, USA

Kilpatrick, James J, Jr — *Columnist*
White Walnut Hill, Woodville, VA 22749, USA

Kilpatrick, Lincoln — *Actor*
6330 Simpson Ave, #8, North Hollywood, CA 91606, USA

Kilzer, Louis C (Lon) — *Journalist*
%Minneapolis-St Paul Star-Tribune, 425 Portland Ave, Minneapolis, MN 55488, USA

Kim Dae Jung — *Political Leader, South Korea*
%Democracy Party, 51-5 Yonggang-dong, Mapol, ku, Seoul 150101, South Korea

Kim Jong II — *President, North Korea; Army Marshal*
%President's Office, Central Committee, Pyongyang, North Korea

K

Kidjo - Kim Jong II

K

Kim Jong Pil *President, South Korea; Army General*
340-38, Sindang 4-Dongku, Seoul, South Korea

Kim Woo-Choong *Businessman*
%Daewoo Industrial Group, 541-5 Ga Namdaemunro, Seoul, South Korea

Kim Young Sam *President, South Korea*
%President's Office, Chong Wa Dae, 1 Sejong-no, Seoul, South Korea

Kim, Jacqueline *Actress*
%Paradigm Agency, 10100 Santa Monica Blvd, #2500, Los Angeles, CA 90067, USA

Kim, Nelli V *Gymnast*
%Russian Sports Council, Skaternyi Per 4, Moscow, Russia

Kim, Stephan S Cardinal *Religious Leader*
Archbishop's House, 2-KA 1 Myong Dong, Chungku, Seoul 100, South Korea

Kimball, Dick *Diver, Diving Coach*
%University of Michigan, Athletic Dept, Ann Arbor, MI 48109, USA

Kimball, Ward *Animator, Director*
8910 Ardendale Ave, San Gabriel, CA 91775, USA

Kimball, Warren F *Writer, Historian*
19 Larsen Road, Somerset, NJ 08873, USA

Kimbrough, Charles *Actor, Singer*
%Silver Massetti Szatmary, 8730 Sunset Blvd, #480, Los Angeles, CA 90069, USA

Kimbrough, John C *Football Player*
11659 Pescara Road, Rancho Cucamonga, CA 91701, USA

Kimery, James L *Association Executive*
%Veterans of Foreign Wars, 405 W 34th St, Kansas City, MO 64111, USA

Kimmelman, Michael *Art Critic*
%New York Times, 229 W 43rd St, New York, NY 10036, USA

Kimmins, Kenneth *Actor*
%J Michael Bloom, 9255 Sunset Blvd, #710, Los Angeles, CA 90069, USA

Kimura, Kazuo *Industrial Designer*
%Japan Design Foundation, 2-2 Cenba Chuo, Higashiku, Osaka 541, Japan

Kimura, Motoo *Geneticist, Biologist*
%Institute of Genetics, Yata 1, 111, Mishima, Shizuokaken 411, Japan

Kinard, Terry *Football Player*
19 English St, Sumter, SC 29150, USA

Kincaid, Aron *Actor*
12307 Ventura Blvd, #C, North Hollywood, CA 91604, USA

Kincaid, Jamaica *Writer*
%New Yorker Magazine, 25 W 43rd St, New York, NY 10036, USA

Kincses, Veronika *Opera Singer*
%Hungarian State Opera, Andrassy Utca 22, 1061 Budapest, Hungary

Kind, Peter A *Army General*
Director, Information Systems, OSA, Washington, DC 20310, USA

Kind, Richard *Actor*
%Gersh Agency, 232 N Canon Dr, Beverly Hills, CA 90210, USA

Kind, Roslyn *Actress, Singer*
8871 Burton Way, #303, Los Angeles, CA 90048, USA

Kinder, Melvyn *Psychologist*
1951 San Ysidro Dr, Beverly Hills, CA 90210, USA

Kinder, Richard D *Businessman*
%Enron Corp, PO Box 1188, Houston, TX 77251, USA

Kindleberger, Charles P *Economist*
Brookhaven, #A-406, 1010 Waltham St, Lexington, KY 02173, USA

Kindred, David A *Sportswriter*
%Atlanta Constitution, 72 Marietta St, Atlanta, GA 30303, USA

Kiner, Ralph M *Baseball Player, Sportscaster*
271 Silver Spur Trail, Palm Desert, CA 92260, USA

King Hogue, Micki *Diver*
3509 Colt Neck Lane, Lexington, KY 40502, USA

King of Wartnaby, John Leonard *Businessman*
Ensearch House, 8 St James's Square, London SW1Y 4JU, England

King, Alan *Comedian*
%William Morris Agency, 151 S El Camino Dr, Beverly Hills, CA 90212, USA

King, Angus *Governor, ME*
%Governor's Office, Blaine House, Augusta, ME 04333, USA

King, B B *Singer, Guitarist*
%Sidney Seidenberg, 1414 6th Ave, New York, NY 10019, USA

King, Ben E *Singer*
%Randy Irwin, 7231 Radio Road, #158, Naples, FL 34104, USA

King, Bernard 780 Apple Ridge Road, Franklin Lakes, NJ 07417, USA	*Basketball Player*
King, Betsy %General Delivery, Limekiln, PA 19535, USA	*Golfer*
King, Billie Jean %World Team Tennis, 445 N Wells St, #404, Chicago, IL 60610, USA	*Tennis Player*
King, Bruce PO Box 83, Stanley, NM 87056, USA	*Governor, NM*
King, Carole Robinson Bar Ranch, Stanley, ID 83278, USA	*Composer, Singer*
King, Cheryl %CLInc Talent, 843 N Sycamore Ave, Los Angeles, CA 90038, USA	*Actress*
King, Claude %House of Talent, 9 Lucy Lane, Sherwood, AR 72120, USA	*Singer, Guitarist*
King, Coretta S 671 Beckwith St SW, Atlanta, GA 30314, USA	*Civil Rights Leader*
King, Dana %CBS-TV, News Dept, 524 W 57th St, New York, NY 10019, USA	*Commentator*
King, Dennis 3857 26th St, San Francisco, CA 94131, USA	*Artist*
King, Derek 8 Indian Club Road, Northport, NY 11768, USA	*Hockey Player*
King, Dexter Scott %M L King Nonviolent Social Change Center, 449 Auburn Ave NE, Atlanta, GA 30312, USA	*Association Executive*
King, Don %Don King Productions, 968 Pinehurst Dr, Las Vegas, NV 89109, USA	*Boxing Promoter*
King, Edward J %A J Lane Co, 1500 Worcester Road, Framingham, MA 01702, USA	*Governor, MA*
King, Evelyn (Champagne) %Nationwide Entertainment, 2756 N Green Valley Pkwy, #449, Las Vegas, NV 89014, USA	*Singer*
King, Francis H 19 Gordon Place, London W8 4JE, England	*Writer*
King, Gordon D 2641 Highwood Dr, Roseville, CA 95661, USA	*Football Player*
King, Ivan R %University of California, Astronomy Dept, Berkeley, CA 94720, USA	*Astronomer*
King, James A %Columbia Artists Mgmt Inc, 165 W 57th St, New York, NY 10019, USA	*Opera Singer*
King, James B %Seattle Times, Editorial Dept, Fairview Ave N & John St, Seattle, WA 98111, USA	*Editor*
King, Jeff 230 Park Highway, Healy, AK 99743, USA	*Dog Sled Racer*
King, John W Kennedy Hill Road, RD 1, Goffstown, NH 03045, USA	*Governor, NH*
King, Larry 10801 Lockwood Dr, #230, Silver Spring, MD 20901, USA	*Commentator*
King, Mary-Claire %University of Washington, Medical School, Genetics Dept, Seattle, WA 98195, USA	*Geneticist*
King, Michael %King World Productions, 1700 Broadway, New York, NY 10019, USA	*Television Executive*
King, Morgana %Bowen Agency, 504 W 168th St, New York, NY 10032, USA	*Singer, Actress*
King, Olin B %SCI Systems Inc, 2101 W Clinton Ave, Huntsville, AL 35805, USA	*Businessman*
King, Pee Wee %Ressier, 505 Canton Pass, Madison, TN 37115, USA	*Singer, Songwriter*
King, Perry 3647 Wrightwood Dr, Studio City, CA 91604, USA	*Actor*
King, Phillip %New Rowan Gallery, 25 Dover St, London W1X 3PA, England	*Sculptor*
King, Roger %King World Productions, 1700 Broadway, New York, NY 10019, USA	*Television Executive*
King, Stacey 5340 Prairie Crossing, Long Grove, IL 60047, USA	*Basketball Player*
King, Stephen E %Juliann Eugley, 49 Florida Ave, Bangor, ME 04401, USA	*Writer*
King, Thomas J (Tom) %House of Commons, Westminster, London SW1A 0AA, England	*Government Official, England*

K

King - King

K

King, Thomas L	*Businessman*
%Standex International, 6 Manor Parkway, Salem, NH 03079, USA	
King, Tony	*Actor*
1333 N Sweetzer, #2-G, Los Angeles, CA 90069, USA	
King, Woodie, Jr	*Theater Producer*
417 Convent Ave, New York, NY 10031, USA	
King, Zalman	*Movie Director*
308 Alta Ave, Santa Monica, CA 90402, USA	
Kingdom, Roger	*Track Athlete*
322 Mall Blvd, #303, Monroeville, PA 15146, USA	
Kingman, David A (Dave)	*Baseball Player*
PO Box 11771, Zephyr Cove, NV 89448, USA	
Kingman, Dong	*Artist*
21 W 58th St, New York, NY 10019, USA	
Kings Norton (Harold R Cox)	*Engineer, Scientist*
Westcote House, Chipping Campden, Glos, England	
Kingsbury-Smith, Joseph	*Journalist*
1701 Pennsylvania Ave NW, Washington, DC 20006, USA	
Kingsley, Ben	*Actor*
New Penworth House, Stratford Upon Avon, Warwickshire OV3 7QX, England	
Kingsolver, Barbara E	*Writer*
PO Box 31870, Tucson, AZ 85751, USA	
Kingston, Alex	*Actress*
%J Michael Bloom, 9255 Sunset Blvd, #710, Los Angeles, CA 90069, USA	
Kingston, Maxine Hong	*Writer*
%University of California, English Dept, Berkeley, CA 94720, USA	
Kinkel, Klaus	*Government Official, Germany*
%Auswartigen Amt, Adenauerallee 101, 53113 Bonn, Germany	
Kinmont Boothe, Jill	*Skier*
Rt 1, Box 11, 310 Sunland Dr, Bishop, CA 93514, USA	
Kinmont, Kathleen	*Actress*
6651 Vineland Ave, North Hollywood, CA 91606, USA	
Kinnear, George E R, II	*Navy Admiral*
%New England Digital Corp, 7 New England Executive Park, Burlington, MA 01803, USA	
Kinnear, Greg	*Actor*
2677 La Cuesta Dr, Los Angeles, CA 90046, USA	
Kinnear, James W, III	*Businessman*
%Ten Standard Forum, PO Box 120, Stamford, CT 06904, USA	
Kinnell, Galway	*Writer*
RFD, Sheffield, VT 05866, USA	
Kinney, Kathy	*Actress*
%Michael Slessinger, 8730 Sunset Blvd, #220-W, Los Angeles, CA 90069, USA	
Kinney, Terry	*Actor*
%Gersh Agency, 232 N Canon Dr, Beverly Hills, CA 90210, USA	
Kinnock, Neil G	*Government Official, England*
%House of Commons, Westminster, London SW1A 0AA, England	
Kinoshita, Keisuke	*Movie Director*
1366 Tsujido, Fujisawa, Kanagawa Prefecture, Japan	
Kinsella, John	*Swimmer*
631 E 6th St, Hinsdale, IL 60521, USA	
Kinsella, Thomas	*Writer*
Killalane, Laragh, County Wicklow, Ireland	
Kinsella, W P	*Writer*
PO Box 2162, Blaine, WA 98231, USA	
Kinser, Steve	*Auto Racing Driver*
%King Racing, 1105 Seminole Dr, Richardson, TX 75080, USA	
Kinsey, Stan	*Entertainment Executive*
%Iwerks Entertainment, PO Box 7744, Burbank, CA 91510, USA	
Kinshofer-Guthlein, Crista	*Skier*
Munchnerstr 44, 83026 Rosenheim, Germany	
Kinskey, Leonid	*Actor*
15009 N Tamarack Lane, Fountain Hill, AZ 85268, USA	
Kinski, Nastassja	*Actress*
1000 Bel Air Place, Los Angeles, CA 90077, USA	
Kinsler, Richard	*Publisher*
%Playboy Magazine, 680 N Lake Shore Dr, Chicago, IL 60611, USA	
Kinsley, Michael E	*Editor, Commentator*
520 2nd Ave S, Kirkland, WA 98033, USA	

King - Kinsley

Kinsman, T Jim — *Vietnam War Army Hero (CMH)*
111 Howe Road E, Winlock, WA 98596, USA

Kinzer, Joseph W (Joe) — *Army General*
Commanding General, 5th Army, Fort Sam Houston, TX 78234, USA

Kiplinger, Austin H — *Publisher*
1729 "H" St NW, Washington, DC 20006, USA

Kipnis, Igor — *Concert Harpsichordist*
20 Drummer Lane, West Redding, CT 06896, USA

Kipniss, Robert — *Artist*
26 E 33rd St, New York, NY 10016, USA

Kiraly, Charles F (Karch) — *Volleyball Player, Coach*
%ProServe, 1101 Woodrow Wilson Blvd, #1800, Arlington, VA 22209, USA

Kirby, Bruce — *Actor*
629 N Orlando Ave, #3, Los Angeles, CA 90048, USA

Kirby, Bruno — *Actor*
%Metropolitan Talent Agency, 4526 Wilshire Blvd, Los Angeles, CA 90010, USA

Kirby, Durwood — *Actor*
Rt 7, Box 374, Sherman, CT 06784, USA

Kirby, F M — *Businessman*
%Alleghany Corp, Park Avenue Plaza, 55 E 52nd St, New York, NY 10055, USA

Kirby, Ronald H — *Architect*
PO Box 337, Melville, 2109 Johannesburg, South Africa

Kirchbach, Gunar — *Canoe Athlete*
Georgi-Dobrowolski-Str 10, 15517 Furstenwalde, Germany

Kirchhoff, Ulrich — *Equestrian Rider*
Hoven 258, 48720 Rosendahl, Germany

Kirchner, Leon — *Composer*
%Harvard University, Music Dept, Cambridge, MA 02138, USA

Kirchner, Mark — *Biathlete*
Hauptstr 74-A, 98749 Scheibe-Alsbach, Germany

Kirchschlager, Rudolf — *President, Austria*
Anderg 9, 1170 Vienna, Austria

Kirgo, George — *Actor, Screenwriter*
178 N Carmelina Ave, Los Angeles, CA 90049, USA

Kirk, Claude R, Jr — *Governor, FL*
%Kirk Co, 1180 Gator Trail, West Palm Beach, FL 33409, USA

Kirk, Phyllis — *Actress*
321 S Beverly Dr, #M, Beverly Hills, CA 90212, USA

Kirk, Rahsaan Roland — *Jazz Musician*
%Atlantic Records, 9229 Sunset Blvd, #900, Los Angeles, CA 90069, USA

Kirk, Walt, Jr — *Basketball Player*
2355 Coventry Parkway, #B-202, Dubuque, IA 52001, USA

Kirkby, Emma — *Concert Singer*
%Consort of Music, 54-A Leamington Road Villas, London W11 1HT, England

Kirkeby, Per — *Artist*
%Margarete Roeder Gallery, 545 Broadway, New York, NY 10012, USA

Kirkland, Gelsey — *Ballerina*
500 Mount Tailac Court, Roseville, CA 95747, USA

Kirkland, Kenny — *Jazz Pianist, Synthesizer Player*
%M-Squared Mgmt, 666 3rd Ave, #1400, New York, NY 10017, USA

Kirkland, Sally — *Actress*
17 E 89th St, New York, NY 10128, USA

Kirkman, Rick — *Cartoonist (Baby Blues)*
%Creators Syndicate, 5777 W Century Blvd, #700, Los Angeles, CA 90045, USA

Kirkpatrick, Clayton — *Editor*
471 Stagecoach Run, Glen Ellyn, IL 60137, USA

Kirkpatrick, Jeane J — *Government Official*
6812 Granby St, Bethesda, MD 20817, USA

Kirkpatrick, Ralph — *Concert Harpsichordist*
Old Quarry, Guilford, CT 06437, USA

Kirkup, James — *Writer*
%British Monomarks, BM-Box 2780, London WC1V 6XX, England

Kirrane, John (Jack) — *Hockey Player*
3 Country Road, Brookline, MA 02146, USA

Kirsch, Stan — *Actor*
%William Morris Agency, 151 S El Camino Dr, Beverly Hills, CA 90212, USA

Kirschner, Carl — *Educator*
%Rutgers State University College, President's Office, New Brunswick, NJ 08093, USA

K

Kinsman - Kirschner

Kirschner, David   *Entertainment Executive*
%Hanna-Barbera Productions, 3400 W Cahuenga Blvd, Los Angeles, CA 90068, USA
Kirschstein, Ruth L   *Physician*
%National Institutes of Health, 9000 Rockville Pike, Bethesda, MD 20892, USA
Kirshbaum, Laurence J   *Publisher*
%Warner Books, Time-Life Building, Rockefeller Center, New York, NY 10020, USA
Kirshbaum, Ralph   *Concert Cellist*
%Columbia Artists Mgmt Inc, 165 W 57th St, New York, NY 10019, USA
Kirszenstein Szewinska, Irena   *Track Athlete*
Ul Bagno 5 m 80, 00-112 Warsaw, Poland
Kirwan, William E, II   *Educator*
%University of Maryland, President's Office, College Park, MD 20742, USA
Kisabaka, Lisa   *Track Athlete*
Franz-Hitze-Str 22, 51372 Leverkusen, Germany
Kiser, Terry   *Actor*
%Bauman Hiller, 5750 Wilshire Blvd, #512, Los Angeles, CA 90036, USA
Kishlansky, Mark A   *Writer, Historian*
%Harvard University, History Dept, Cambridge, MA 02138, USA
Kisio, Kelly   *Hockey Player*
3 Tulip Tree Lane, Mamaroneck, NY 10543, USA
Kison, Bruce E   *Baseball Player*
1403 Riverside Circle, Bradenton, FL 33529, USA
Kissin, Evgeni I   *Concert Pianist*
%Harold Holt, 31 Sinclair Road, London W14 0NS, England
Kissinger, Henry A   *Secretary, State; Nobel Peace Laureate*
River House, 435 E 52nd St, New York, NY 10022, USA
Kissling, Conny   *Freestyle Skier*
Hubel, 3254 Messen, Switzerland
Kissling, Walter   *Businessman*
%H B Fuller Co, 2400 Energy Park Dr, St Paul, MN 55108, USA
Kistler, Darci   *Ballerina*
%New York City Ballet, Lincoln Center Plaza, New York, NY 10023, USA
Kitaen, Tawny   *Actress*
650 Town Center Dr, #1000, Costa Mesa, CA 92626, USA
Kitaj, R B   *Artist*
%Marlborough Fine Art, 6 Albemarle St, London W1, England
Kitaro   *Musician, Composer*
%Agency For Performing Arts, 9200 Sunset Blvd, #900, Los Angeles, CA 90069, USA
Kitayenko, Dmitri G   *Conductor*
%Moscow Philharmonic, Moscow Conservatory, Moscow, Russia
Kitbunchu, M Michai Cardinal   *Religious Leader*
%Assumption Cathedral, 51 Oriental Ave, Bangkok 10500, Thailand
Kite, Greg   *Basketball Player*
1267 Waterwitch Cove Circle, Orlando, FL 32806, USA
Kite, Thomas O (Tom), Jr   *Golfer*
6000 Long Champ Court, Austin, TX 78746, USA
Kitora, Fumio   *Financier*
%Daiwa Bank Trust, 75 Rockefeller Plaza, New York, NY 10019, USA
Kitt, A J   *Skier*
15 Hidden Valley Road, Rochester, NY 14624, USA
Kitt, Eartha   *Singer, Actress*
125 Boulder Ridge Road, Scarsdale, NY 10583, USA
Kittel, Charles   *Physicist*
%University of California, Physics Dept, Berkeley, CA 94720, USA
Kittinger, Joe   *Parachutist, Balloonist*
300 N Main St, Las Vegas, NV 89101, USA
Kittle, Ronald D (Ron)   *Baseball Player*
742 N Old Suman Road, Valparaiso, IN 46383, USA
Kittles, Kerry   *Basketball Player*
%New Jersey Nets, Byrne Meadowlands Arena, East Rutherford, NJ 07073, USA
Kitzhaber, John   *Governor, OR*
%Governor's Office, State Capitol, #224, Salem, OR 97301, USA
Kizer, Carolyn A   *Writer*
%University of Arizona, English Dept, Tucson, AZ 85721, USA
Kizim, Leonid D   *Cosmonaut; Air Force General*
%Mojaysky Military School, Russian Space Forces, St Petersburg, Russia
Kjus, Lasse   *Skier*
Rugdeveien 2-C, 1404 Siggerud, Norway

Klabunde, Charles S — Artist
68 W 3rd St, New York, NY 10012, USA
Klammer, Franz — Skier
Mooswald 22, 9712 Friesach/Ktn, Austria
Klatsky, Bruce J — Businessman
%Phillips-Van Heusen Corp, 1290 Ave of Americas, New York, NY 10104, USA
Klatte, Gunther — Businessman
%Rheinische Braunkohlenwerke, Stuttgenweg 2, 50935 Cologne, Germany
Klaus, Josef — Chancellor, Austria
Osterreichische Volkspartei, 1 Karntnerstr 51, Vienna, Austria
Klaus, Vaclav — Prime Minister, Czech Republic
%Prime Minister's Office, Nabr E Benese 4, 118 01 Prague, Czech Republic
Klausner, Richard — Biologist
%National Cancer Institute, 9000 Rockville Pike, Bethesda, MD 20892, USA
Klaw, Spencer — Editor
280 Cream Hill Road, West Cornwall, CT 06796, USA
Klebanoff, Michael — Businessman
%OMI Corp, 90 Park Ave, New York, NY 10016, USA
Klebe, Giselher — Composer
Bruchstr 16, 32756 Detmold, Germany
Klecko, Joe — Football Player
105 Stella Lane, Aston, PA 19014, USA
Klees, Christian — Marksman
%Eutiner Sportschutzen, Schutzenweg 26, 23701 Eutin, Germany
Kleiber, Carlos — Conductor
Max-Joseph-Platz 2, 80539 Munich, Germany
Kleihues, Josef P — Architect
Schlickweg 4, 14129 Berlin, Germany
Klein, Calvin R — Fashion Designer
%Calvin Klein Industries, 205 W 39th St, New York, NY 10018, USA
Klein, David — Geneticist
%National Child Health Institute, 9000 Rockville Pike, Bethesda, MD 20892, USA
Klein, George — Tumor Biologist
Kottlavagen 10, 181 61 Lidingo, Sweden
Klein, Heinrich J — Businessman
%Carl-Zeiss-Stiftung, Postfach 1369, 73447 Oberkochen, Germany
Klein, Herbert G — Publisher, Government Official
%Copley Press, 350 Camino de Reina, San Diego, CA 92108, USA
Klein, Joe — Journalist, Writer
%Newsweek Magazine, Editorial Dept, 251 W 57th St, New York, NY 10019, USA
Klein, Lawrence R — Nobel Economics Laureate
1317 Medford Road, Wynnewood, PA 19096, USA
Klein, Lester A — Urologist
%Scripps Clinic, Urology Dept, 10666 N Torrey Pines Road, La Jolla, CA 92037, USA
Klein, Robert — Entertainer
67 Ridge Crest Road, Briarcliff, NY 10510, USA
Klein, Yves — Artist
%Marisa del Re Gallery, 41 E 57th St, New York, NY 10022, USA
Kleindienst, Richard G — Attorney General
%Favour Moore Wilhelmsen, 1580 Plaza W, Prescott, AZ 86302, USA
Kleinert, Harold E — Microsurgeon
225 Abraham Flexner Way, Louisville, KY 40202, USA
Kleinman, Arthur M — Anthropologist
%Harvard University, Anthropology Dept, Cambridge, MA 02138, USA
Kleinrock, Leonard — Computer Scientist
318 N Rockingham Ave, Los Angeles, CA 90049, USA
Klemmer, John — Jazz Saxophonist
%Boardman, 10548 Clearwood Court, Los Angeles, CA 90077, USA
Klemperer, Werner — Actor
44 W 62nd St, #1000, New York, NY 10023, USA
Klemperer, William — Chemist
53 Shattuck Road, Watertown, MA 02172, USA
Klemt, Becky — Attorney
%Pence & MacMillan, PO Box 1285, Laramie, WY 82073, USA
Klensch, Else — Fashion Commentator
%Cable News Network, News Dept, 1050 Techwood Dr NW, Atlanta, GA 30318, USA
Kleppe, Thomas S — Secretary, Interior
7100 Darby Road, Bethesda, MD 20817, USA

K

Klesko, Ryan A — *Baseball Player*
9219 Nickles Blvd, Boynton Beach, FL 33436, USA

Klestil, Thomas — *President, Austria*
Prasidentschaftskanzlei, Hofburg, 1014 Vienna, Austria

Kliesmet, Robert B — *Labor Leader*
%Union of Police Assns, 815 16th St NW, #307, Washington, DC 20006, USA

Kliks, Rudolf R — *Architect*
%Russian Chamber of Commerce, Ul Kuibysheva 6, Moscow, Russia

Klima, Viktor — *Chancellor, Austria*
%Chancellor's Office, Balljausplatz 2, 1014 Vienna, Austria

Klimke, Reiner — *Equestrian Rider*
Krumme Str 3, 48143 Munster, Germany

Klimuk, Pyotr I — *Cosmonaut, Air Force General*
%Potchta Kosmonavtov, Moskovskoi Oblasti, 141160 Syvisdny Goroduk, Russia

Kline, Kevin — *Actor*
1636 3rd Ave, #309, New York, NY 10128, USA

Kling, Richard W — *Businessman*
%IDS Life Insurance, PO Box 5144, Albany, NY 12205, USA

Klingensmith, Michael J — *Publisher*
%Entertainment Weekly Magazine, Rockefeller Center, New York, NY 10020, USA

Klinger, Georgette — *Beauty Consultant*
131 S Rodeo Dr, #102, Beverly Hills, CA 90212, USA

Klinsmann, Jurgen — *Soccer Player*
%Tottenham Hotspurs, 748 High St, Tottenham, London W1V 3RB, England

Kljusev, Nikola — *Prime Minister, Macedonia*
%Prime Minister's Office, Dame Grueva 6, 91000 Skopje, Macedonia

Klotz, Irving M — *Chemist, Biochemist*
2515 Pioneer Road, Evanston, IL 60201, USA

Klous, Patricia — *Actress*
18096 Karen Dr, Encino, CA 91316, USA

Klug, Aaron — *Nobel Chemistry Laureate*
%Medical Research Council Centre, Hills Road, Cambridge CB2 2QH, England

Klugh, Earl — *Jazz Guitarist*
%Agency For Performing Arts, 9200 Sunset Blvd, #900, Los Angeles, CA 90069, USA

Klugman, Jack — *Actor*
22548 W Pacific Coast Highway, #110, Malibu, CA 90265, USA

Klutznick, Philip M — *Secretary, Commerce*
875 N Michigan Ave, #4044, Chicago, IL 60611, USA

Klyszewski, Waclaw — *Architect*
Ul Gornoslaska 16, M 15-A, 00-432 Warsaw, Poland

Knape Lindberg, Ulrike — *Diver*
Drostvagen 7, 691 33 Karlskoga, Sweden

Knapp, Charles B — *Educator*
%University of Georgia, President's Office, Athens, GA 30602, USA

Knapp, Cleon T — *Publisher*
%Talewood Corp, 10100 Santa Monica Blvd, #2000, Los Angeles, CA 90067, USA

Knapp, John W — *Educator, Army General*
%Virginia Military Institute, Superintendent's Office, Lexington, VA 24450, USA

Knapp, Stefan — *Artist*
The Studio, Sandhills, Godalming, Surrey, England

Knappenberger, Alton W — *WW II Army Hero (CMH)*
PO Box 364, Main St, Schwenksville, PA 19473, USA

Knauss, Hans — *Skier*
Fastenberg 60, 8970 Schladming, Austria

Kneale, R Bryan C — *Sculptor*
10-A Muswell Road, London N10 2BG, England

Knebel, John A — *Secretary, Agriculture*
1418 Laburnum St, McLean, VA 22101, USA

Knepper, Robert W (Bob) — *Baseball Player*
627 Forest View Way, Monument, CO 80132, USA

Kness, Richard M — *Opera Singer*
240 Central Park South, #3-N, New York, NY 10019, USA

Kneuer, Cameo — *Physical Fitness Expert*
%Starshape by Cameo, 2554 Lincoln Blvd, #640, Marina del Rey, CA 90291, USA

Knievel, Evel — *Motorcycle Stunt Rider*
160 E Flamingo Road, Las Vegas, NV 89109, USA

Knight Pulliam, Keshia — *Actress*
PO Box 866, Teaneck, NJ 07666, USA

Knight, Andrew S B	*Editor*
%News International, PO Box 495, Virginia St, London W1 9XY, England	
Knight, Billy	*Basketball Player*
7411 Perrier Dr, Indianapolis, IN 46278, USA	
Knight, Brevin	*Basketball Player*
%Cleveland Cavaliers, 2923 Statesboro Road, Richfield, OH 44286, USA	
Knight, C Ray	*Baseball Player, Manager*
2308 Tara Dr, Albany, GA 31707, USA	
Knight, Charles F	*Businessman*
%Emerson Electric Co, 8000 W Florissant Ave, St Louis, MO 63136, USA	
Knight, Christopher	*Actor*
7738 Chandelee Place, Los Angeles, CA 90046, USA	
Knight, Don	*Actor*
%Don Gerler, 3349 Cahuenga Blvd W, #1, Los Angeles, CA 90068, USA	
Knight, Gladys	*Singer*
%Pyramid Entertainment, 89 5th Ave, #700, New York, NY 10003, USA	
Knight, Jean	*Singer*
%Ken Keene Artists, PO Box 1875, Gretna, LA 70054, USA	
Knight, Michael E	*Actor*
%Paradigm Agency, 10100 Santa Monica Blvd, #2500, Los Angeles, CA 90067, USA	
Knight, Philip H	*Businessman*
%Nike Inc, 1 Bowerman Dr, Beaverton, OR 97005, USA	
Knight, Robert M (Bobby)	*Basketball Coach*
7411 Broadview Dr, Indianapolis, IN 46227, USA	
Knight, Shirley	*Actress*
1548 N Orange Ave, Los Angeles, CA 90046, USA	
Knight, Travis	*Basketball Player*
%Boston Celtics, 151 Merrimac St, #500, Boston, MA 02114, USA	
Knight, William J (Pete)	*Test Pilot*
1008 W Avenue M-14, #G, Palmdale, CA 93551, USA	
Knipling, Edward F	*Entomologist*
2623 Military Road, Arlington, VA 22207, USA	
Knoblauch, E Charles (Chuck)	*Baseball Player*
101 Westcott, #1105, Houston, TX 77007, USA	
Knodel, William C	*Businessman*
%Vista Chemical Co, 900 Threadneedle St, Houston, TX 77079, USA	
Knol, Monique	*Cyclist*
Draarlier 6, 3766 Et Soest, Holland	
Knoll, Jozsef	*Pharmacologist*
%Semmelweis Medical University, Pharmacology Dept, 1089 Budapest, Hungary	
Knopfler, Mark	*Singer, Guitarist (Dire Straits)*
%Damage Mgmt, 16 Lamberton Place, London W11 2SH, England	
Knopoff, Leon	*Geophysicist*
%University of California, Geophysics Institute, Los Angeles, CA 90024, USA	
Knostman, Dick	*Basketball Player*
13760 Tabequache Road, Nathrop, CO 80236, USA	
Knotts, Don	*Comedian*
1854 S Beverly Glen Blvd, #402, Los Angeles, CA 90025, USA	
Knowles, Michael R	*Medical Researcher*
%University of North Carolina, Medical School, Chapel Hill, NC 27599, USA	
Knowles, Tony	*Governor, AK*
%Governor's Office, State Capitol Building, Juneau, AK 99811, USA	
Knowlton, Richard L	*Businessman*
%Hormel Foods Corp, 1 Hormel Place, Austin, MN 55912, USA	
Knowlton, Steve R	*Skier*
%Palmer Yeager Assoc, 6600 E Hampden Ave, #210, Denver, CO 80224, USA	
Knox, Buddy	*Singer, Songwriter*
RR 3, C-10 Evans, Armstrong BC VOE 1BO, Canada	
Knox, Elyse	*Actress*
320 N Gunston Ave, Los Angeles, CA 90049, USA	
Knox, Northrup R	*Financier*
%Marine Midland Banks, 1 Marine Midland Center, Buffalo, NY 14203, USA	
Knox, Terence	*Actor*
%International Creative Mgmt, 8942 Wilshire Blvd, Beverly Hills, CA 90211, USA	
Knox-Johnson, Robin	*Yachtsman*
26 Sefton St, Putney, London SW15, England	
Knudsen, Arthur G	*Skier*
311 Blaine Ave, Racine, WI 53405, USA	

K

Knight - Knudsen

Knudsen, Conrad C — *Businessman*
%MacMillan Bloedel Ltd, 925 W Georgia St, Vancouver BC V6E 3R9, Canada

Knudson, Alfred G, Jr — *Geneticist*
%Institute for Cancer Research, 7701 Burlhome Ave, Philadelphia, PA 19111, USA

Knudson, Darrell G — *Financier*
%Fourth Financial Corp, 100 N Broadway, Wichita, KS 67202, USA

Knudson, Thomas J — *Journalist*
%Sacramento Bee, Editorial Dept, 21st & "Q" Sts, Sacramento, CA 95852, USA

Knussen, S Oliver — *Conductor, Composer*
%Faber Music, 3 Queen Square, London WC1, England

Knuth, Donald E — *Computer Scientist*
%Stanford University, Computer Sciences Dept, Stanford, CA 94305, USA

Knutson, Ronald — *Religious Leader*
%Free Lutheran Congregations Assn, 402 W 11th St, Canton, SD 57013, USA

Kobayashi, Hisao — *Financier*
%CUT Group Holdings, 650 CIT Dr, Livingston, NJ 07039, USA

Kobayashi, Kaoru — *Businessman*
%Matsushita Electric Works, 1048 Kadomashi, Osaka 571, Japan

Kober, Jeff — *Actor*
2248 Panorama Terrace, Los Angeles, CA 90039, USA

Koch, Bill — *Cross Country Skier*
PO Box 59, Greenview, CA 96037, USA

Koch, Charles G — *Businessman*
%Koch Industries, PO Box 2256, Wichita, KS 67201, USA

Koch, Charles John — *Financier*
%Charter One Financial, 1215 Superior Ave, Cleveland, OH 44114, USA

Koch, David A — *Businessman*
%Graco Inc, 4050 Olson Memorial Parkway, Minneapolis, MN 55422, USA

Koch, Desmond (Des) — *Track Athlete*
23296 Gilmore St, Canoga Park, CA 91307, USA

Koch, Ed — *Artist*
395 E 46th Ave, Eugene, OR 97405, USA

Koch, Edward I — *Mayor*
%Robinson Silverman Pearce, 1290 Ave of Americas, New York, NY 10104, USA

Koch, Greg — *Football Player*
4412 Darsey St, Bellaire, TX 77401, USA

Koch, Howard W — *Movie Producer, Director*
704 N Crescent Dr, Beverly Hills, CA 90210, USA

Koch, James V — *Educator*
%Old Dominion University, President's Office, Norfolk, VA 23529, USA

Koch, William I — *Yachtsman, Businessman*
%Oxbow Corp, 1601 Forum Place, West Palm Beach, FL 33401, USA

Kocherga, Anatoli I — *Opera Singer*
Gogolevskaya 37/2/47, 254053 Kiev, Russia

Kochi, Jay K — *Chemist*
4372 Faculty Lane, Houston, TX 77004, USA

Kocsis, Zoltan — *Concert Pianist, Composer*
Narcisa Utca 29, 1126 Budapest, Hungary

Koda, Cub — *Singer, Songwriter, Guitarist*
523 E Liberty, Ann Arbor, MI 48104, USA

Kodes, Jan — *Tennis Player*
Na Berance 18, 160 00 Prague 6/Dejvioe, Czech Republic

Kodjo, Edem — *Prime Minister, Togo*
%Prime Minister's Office, Boite Postale 1161, Lome, Togo

Koehn, George W — *Financier*
%SunBank of Tampa Bay, PO Box 3303, Tampa, FL 33601, USA

Koelle, George B — *Pharmacologist*
205 College Ave, Swarthmore, PA 19081, USA

Koen, Karleen — *Writer*
%Random House Inc, 201 E 50th St, New York, NY 10022, USA

Koenekamp, Fred — *Cinematographer*
9756 Shoshine Ave, Northridge, CA 91325, USA

Koenig, Harold B — *Navy Admiral, Surgeon*
Chief, Bureau of Medicine/Surgery, Navy Department, Washington, DC 20372, USA

Koenig, Pierre — *Architect*
12221 Dorothy St, Los Angeles, CA 90049, USA

Koenig, Walter — *Actor*
PO Box 4395, North Hollywood, CA 91617, USA

Koenigswald, G H Ralph von *Paleoanthropologist*
%Senckenberg Museum, Senckenberganlage 25, 60325 Frankfurt/Maim, Germany

Kogan, Richard J *Businessman*
%Schering-Plough Corp, 1 Giraldo Farms, Madison, NJ 07940, USA

Kohde-Kilsch, Claudia *Tennis Player*
Elsa-Brandstrom-Str 22, 66119 Saarbrucken, Germany

Kohl, Helmut *Chancellor, Germany*
Marbacherstr 11, 78351 Ludwigshafen/Rhein-Obbersheim, Germany

Kohlberg, Jerome, Jr *Financier*
%Kohlberg Co, 111 Radio Circle, Mount Kisco, NY 10549, USA

Kohler, Herbert V, Jr *Businessman*
%Kohler Co, 444 Highland Dr, Kohler, WI 53044, USA

Kohler, Jurgen *Soccer Player*
%Borussia Dortmund, Postfach 100509, 44005 Dortmund, Germany

Kohlsaat, Peter *Cartoonist (Single Slices)*
5282 Greenwood Road, Duluth, MN 55804, USA

Kohn, A Eugene *Architect*
%Kohn Pedersen Fox Assoc, 111 W 57th St, New York, NY 10019, USA

Kohn, Walter *Physicist*
%University of California, Physics Dept, Santa Barbara, CA 93106, USA

Kohner, Susan *Actress*
710 Park Ave, #14-E, New York, NY 10021, USA

Kohoutek, Lubos *Astronomer*
Corthumstr 5, 21029 Hamburg, Germany

Kojac, George *Swimmer*
10 Snoozing Tree Lane, Parsippany, NJ 07054, USA

Kojis, Don *Basketball Player*
7652 Stevenson Way, San Diego, CA 92120, USA

Kok Oudegeest, Mary *Swimmer*
%Escuela Nacional de Natacion, Izarra, Alava, Spain

Kok, Wim *Prime Minister, Netherlands*
%Prime Minister's Office, Binnehof 20, 2500 EA The Hague, Netherlands

Kokonin, Vladimir *Opera, Ballet Administrator*
%Bolshoi Theater, Teatralnaya Pl 1, 103009 Moscow, Russia

Kolar, Jiri *Writer, Artist*
61 Rue Olivier-Metra, 75020 Paris, France

Kolb Thomas, Claudia *Swimmer, Coach*
%Stanford University, Athletic Dept, Stanford, CA 94305, USA

Kolb, David L *Businessman*
%Mohawk Industries, 1755 The Exchange, Atlanta, GA 30339, USA

Kolbert, Kathryn *Attorney*
%Center for Reproductive Law & Policy, 120 Wall St, New York, NY 10005, USA

Kolehmainen, Mikko *Kayak Athlete*
Poppelitie 18, 50130 Mikkeli, Finland

Kolff, Willem J *Inventor (Soft-Shelled Mushroom Heart)*
2894 Crestview Dr, Salt Lake City, UT 84108, USA

Kolingba, Andre *President, Central African Republic*
%Palais de la Renaissance, Bangui, Central African Republic

Koller, Arnold *President, Switzerland*
Federal Chancellery, Bundeshaus-West, Bundesgasse, 3003 Berne, Switzerland

Koller, William *Medical Researcher*
%University of Kansas, School of Medicine, Lawrence, KS 66045, USA

Kollias, Konstantinos V *Prime Minister, Greece*
124 Vassil Sophias St, Ampelokipi, Athens, Greece

Kollner, Eberhard *Cosmonaut, East Germany*
An der Trainierbahn 7, 115366 Neuenhagen, Germany

Kollo, Rene *Opera Singer*
%Metropol Theater, Friedrichstr 101-102, 10117 Berlin, Germany

Kolm, Henry V *Electrical Engineer (Magnetic Train)*
Weir Meadow Road, Wayland, MA 01778, USA

Kolodner, Richard D *Biochemist, Cancer Researcher*
%Dana-Farber Cancer Institute, 44 Binney St, Boston, MA 02115, USA

Kolpakova, Irina A *Ballerina*
%American Ballet Theatre, 890 Broadway, New York, NY 10003, USA

Kolsti, Paul *Editorial Cartoonist*
%Dallas News, Editorial Dept, Communications Center, Dallas, TX 75265, USA

Kolvenbach, Peter-Hans *Religious Leader*
Borgo Santo Spirito 5, CP 6139, 00195 Rome, Italy

K

Koenigswald - Kolvenbach

Komack, James — *Television Producer, Director*
10380 Wilshire Blvd, #1001, Los Angeles, CA 90024, USA

Komar, Vitaly — *Artist*
%Ronald Freeman Fine Arts, 31 Mercer St, New York, NY 10013, USA

Komarkova, Vera — *Mountaineer*
%University of Colorado, INSTAAR, Boulder, CO 80302, USA

Komenich, Kim — *Photographer*
3 Vicksburg St, San Francisco, CA 94114, USA

Komer, Robert W — *Diplomat*
1211 Villsmsy Blvd, Alexandria, VA 22307, USA

Kominsky, Cheryl — *Bowler*
%Ladies Professional Bowlers Tour, 7171 Cherryvale Blvd, Rockford, IL 61112, USA

Komleva, Gabriela T — *Ballerina*
Fontanka River 116, #34, 198005 St Petersburg, Russia

Komlos, Peter — *Concert Violinist*
Torokvesz Utca 94, 1025 Budapest, Hungary

Komunyakaa, Yusef — *Writer*
%Indiana University, English Dept, Bloomington, IN 47405, USA

Konare, Alpha Oumar — *President, Mali*
%President's Office, Boite Postale 1463, Bamako, Mali

Koncak, Jon — *Basketball Player*
4688 Northside Dr NW, Atlanta, GA 30327, USA

Konchalovsky, Andrei — *Movie Director*
%Creative Artists Agency, 9830 Wilshire Blvd, Beverly Hills, CA 90212, USA

Kondakova, Yelena V — *Cosmonaut*
%Scientific Industrial Assn, Ulica Lenina 4-A, 141070 Kaliningrad, Russia

Kondratyeva, Maria V — *Ballerina*
%Bolshoi Theater, Teatralnaya Pl 1, 103009 Moscow, Russia

Konig, Franz Cardinal — *Religious Leader*
Erzbischofliches Sekretariat, Rotenturmstr 2, 1010 Vienna, Austria

Konitz, Lee — *Jazz Saxophonist*
%Paradise Artists, 108 E Matilija St, Ojai, CA 93023, USA

Kono, Tamio (Tommy) — *Weightlifter*
98-2025 Hopaki, Honolulu, HI 96814, USA

Konrad, John H — *Astronaut*
%Hughes Space-Communications Group, PO Box 92919, Los Angeles, CA 90009, USA

Konstantinidis, Aris — *Architect*
4 Vasilissis Sofias Blvd, 106 74 Athens, Greece

Konstantinov, Vladimir — *Hockey Player*
4329 Cherry Hill Dr, West Bloomfield, MI 48323, USA

Kontos, Chris — *Hockey Player*
3800 W Manchester Blvd, Inglewood, CA 90301, USA

Kontos, Constantine W — *Government Official*
3606 Warren St NW, Washington, DC 20008, USA

Koons, Fred B — *Financier*
%Chase Home Mortgage, PO Box 15700, Tampa, FL 33684, USA

Koons, Jeff — *Artist*
600 Broadway, New York, NY 10012, USA

Koontz, Dean R — *Writer*
PO Box 9529, Newport Beach, CA 92658, USA

Koontz, Richard H — *Businessman*
%Bowne Co, 345 Hudson St, New York, NY 10014, USA

Koop, C Everett — *Physician, Pediatrician*
%Dartmouth College, Medical Center, Koop Institute, Hanover, NH 03755, USA

Koopmans-Kint, Cor — *Swimmer*
Pacific Sands C'Van Park, Nambucca Heads NSW 2448, Australia

Koosman, Jerry M — *Baseball Player*
805 Main Road, Independence, MO 64056, USA

Kopell, Bernie — *Actor*
19413 Olivos Dr, Tarzana, CA 91356, USA

Kopins, Karen — *Actress*
%Sutton Barth Vennari, 145 S Fairfax Ave, #310, Los Angeles, CA 90036, USA

Kopit, Arthur — *Writer*
5 Glen Hill Road, Wilton, CT 06897, USA

Koplovitz, Kay — *Television Executive*
%USA Network, 1230 Ave of Americas, #1800, New York, NY 10020, USA

Kopp, Wendy — *Association Executive*
%Teach for America Foundation, PO Box 5114, New York, NY 10185, USA

Koppel, Ted — *Commentator*
%ABC-TV, News Dept, 1717 De Sales St NW, Washington, DC 20036, USA

Koppelman, Chaim — *Artist*
498 Broome St, New York, NY 10013, USA

Kopper, Hilmar — *Financier*
%Deutsche Bank AG, Taunusanlage 12, 60325 Frankfurt/Main, Germany

Koprowski, Hilary — *Microbiologist*
334 Fairhill Road, Wynnewood, PA 19096, USA

Korbut, Olga V — *Gymnast*
4705 Masters Court, Duluth, GA 30136, USA

Kord, Kazimierz — *Conductor*
%International Creative Mgmt, 40 W 57th St, New York, NY 10019, USA

Korda, Michael V — *Writer*
%Simon & Schuster Inc, 1230 Ave of Americas, New York, NY 10020, USA

Korell, Mark L — *Financier*
%GMAC Mortgage, 8360 Old York Road, Elkins Park, PA 19027, USA

Koren, Edward B — *Cartoonist*
%New Yorker Magazine, Editorial Dept, 20 W 43rd St, New York, NY 10036, USA

Korf, Mia — *Actress*
%Paradigm Agency, 10100 Santa Monica Blvd, #2500, Los Angeles, CA 90067, USA

Korjus, Tapio — *Track Athlete*
%General Delivery, Lapua, Finland

Korman, Harvey — *Comedian*
1136 Stradella Road, Los Angeles, CA 90077, USA

Korman, Lewis J — *Entertainment Executive*
%Savoy Entertainment, 152 W 57th St, New York, NY 10019, USA

Korman, Maxime Carlot — *Prime Minister, Vanuatu*
%Prime Minister's Office, PO Box 110, Port Vila, Vanuatu

Korn, Lester B — *Businessman*
237 Park Ave, New York, NY 10017, USA

Kornberg, Arthur — *Nobel Medicine Laureate*
365 Golden Oak Dr, Portola Valley, CA 94028, USA

Kornberg, Hans L — *Biochemist*
Master's Lodge, Christ College, Cambridge CB2 3BU, England

Korner, Jules G, III — *Judge*
%US Tax Court, 400 2nd St NW, Washington, DC 20217, USA

Koroma, Johnny Paul — *Head of State, Sierra Leone*
State House, Independence Ave, Freetown, Sierra Leone

Koroma, Sorie Ibrahim — *Prime Minister, Sierra Leone*
%First Vice President's Office, Tower Hill, Freetown, Sierra Leone

Korot, Alla — *Actress*
%Paradigm Agency, 10100 Santa Monica Blvd, #2500, Los Angeles, CA 90067, USA

Korowi, Wiwa — *Governor General, Papua New Guinea*
Government House, Konedobu, Box 79, Port Moresby, Boroko, Papua New Guinea

Korpan, Richard — *Businessman*
%Florida Progress Corp, 1 Progress Plaza, St Petersburg, FL 33701, USA

Korry, Edward M — *Diplomat*
RR 2, Stonington, CT 06378, USA

Kors, Michael — *Fashion Designer*
119 W 24th St, #900, New York, NY 10011, USA

Korth, Fred — *Government Official*
1700 "K" St NW, #501, Washington, DC 20006, USA

Korvald, Lars — *Prime Minister, Norway*
Vinkelgaten 6, 3050 Mjondalen, Norway

Kosar, Bernie, Jr — *Football Player*
6969 Ron Park Place, Youngstown, OH 44512, USA

Koshalek, Richard — *Museum Director*
%Museum of Contemporary Art, 250 S Grand Ave, Los Angeles, CA 90012, USA

Koshiro, Matsumoto, IV — *Kabuki Actor*
%Kabukiza Theatre, 12-15-4 Ginza, Chuoku, Tokyo 104, Japan

Koshland, Daniel E, Jr — *Biochemist*
3991 Happy Valley Road, Lafayette, CA 94549, USA

Kosler, Zdenek — *Conductor*
Nad Sarkou 35, 16000 Prague 6, Czech Republic

Koslow, Lauren — *Actress*
%Irv Schechter, 9300 Wilshire Blvd, #410, Beverly Hills, CA 90212, USA

Kosner, Edward A — *Editor*
%Esquire Magazine, Editorial Dept, 250 W 55th St, New York, NY 10019, USA

K

Koppel - Kosner

K

Koss, Johann Olav	*Speed Skater*
Dagaliveien 21, 0387 Oslo, Norway	
Koss, John C	*Television Inventor*
%Koss Corp, 4129 N Port Washington Ave, Milwaukee, WI 53212, USA	
Kostadinova, Stefka	*Track Athlete*
Rue Anghel Kantchev 4, 1000 Sofia, Bulgaria	
Kosterlitz, Hans W	*Pharmacist*
16 Glendor Terrace, Cults, Aberdeen AB1 9HX, Scotland	
Kostner, Isolde	*Skier*
General Delivery, Hortisei BZ, Italy	
Kosuth, Joseph	*Artist*
591 Broadway, New York, NY 10012, USA	
Kotcheff, W Theodore (Ted)	*Movie Director*
%Ted Kotcheff Productions, 13451 Firth Dr, Beverly Hills, CA 90210, USA	
Kotlarek, Gene	*Ski Jumper*
4811 W 89th Way, Westminster, CO 80030, USA	
Kotlarek, George	*Skier*
330 N Arlington Ave, #512, Duluth, MN 55811, USA	
Kotler, Steven	*Financier*
%Schroder Wertheim Co, Equitable Center, 787 7th Ave, New York, NY 10019, USA	
Kotsonis, Ieronymous	*Religious Leader*
%Archdiocese of Athens, Hatzichristou 8, Athens 402, Greece 53212, USA	
Kott, Jan K	*Writer, Educator*
29 Quaker Path, Stony Brook, NY 11790, USA	
Kottke, Leo	*Singer, Songwriter, Guitarist*
PO Box 7308, Carmel, CA 93921, USA	
Kotto, Yaphet	*Actor*
%Artists Group, 10100 Santa Monica Blvd, #2490, Los Angeles, CA 90067, USA	
Kotulak, Ronald	*Editor*
%Chicago Tribune, Editorial Dept, 435 N Michigan Ave, Chicago, IL 60611, USA	
Kotz, John	*Basketball Player*
4818 Bayfield Terrace, Madison, WI 53705, USA	
Kotzky, Alex S	*Cartoonist (Apartment 3-G)*
203-17 56th Ave, Bayside, NY 11364, USA	
Kouchner, Bernard	*Physician*
%L'Action D'Humanitaire, 56-60 Rue de la Glaciere, 75640 Paris, France	
Koufax, Sanford (Sandy)	*Baseball Player*
PO Box 8306, Vero Beach, FL 32963, USA	
Koumakoye, Kassire D	*Prime Minister, Chad*
%Prime Minister's Office, N'Djamena, Chad	
Kourpias, George J	*Labor Leader*
%International Machinists Assn, 9000 Machinist Place, Upper Marlboro, MD 20772, USA	
Koushouris, John L	*Television Executive*
%Hughes Television Network, 4 Pennsylvania Plaza, New York, NY 10001, USA	
Kovac, Vladimir	*President, Slovakia*
%President's Office, Nam Slobody 1, 813 70 Bratislava, Slovakia	
Kovacevich, Richard M	*Financier*
%Norwest Corp, 1200 Peavey Building, 6th & Marquette, Minneapolis, MN 55403, USA	
Kovacevich, Stephen	*Concert Pianist*
%Van Walsum Mgmt, 26 Wadham Road, London SW15 2LR, England	
Kovach, William	*Editor*
%Harvard University, Nieman Fellows Program, Cambridge, MA 02138, USA	
Kovacic, Ernst	*Concert Violinist*
%Tennant Artists' Mgmt, 39 Tadema Road, #2, London SW10 0PY, England	
Kovacic-Ciro, Zdravko	*Water Polo Player*
JP Kamova 57, 51000 Rijeka, Yugoslavia	
Kovacs, Andras	*Movie Director*
Magyar Jakobinusok Tere 2/3, 1122 Budapest, Hungary	
Kovacs, Denes	*Concert Violinist*
Iranyi Utca 12, Budapest V, Hungary	
Kovacs, Laszlo	*Cinematographer*
%American Society of Cinematographers, 1782 N Orange Dr, Los Angeles, CA 90028, USA	
Kovalenok, Vladimir S	*Cosmonaut, Air Force General*
3 Ap 22, Hovanskaya St, 129515 Moscow, Russia	
Kove, Martin	*Actor*
19155 Rosita St, Tarzana, CA 91356, USA	
Kowal, Charles T	*Astronomer*
%Space Telescope Science Institute, Homewood Campus, Baltimore, MD 21218, USA	

Koss - Kowal

V.I.P. Address Book

Kowalczyk, Ed *Singer, Guitarist (Live)*
%Peter Freedman, 1790 Broadway, #1316, New York, NY 10019, USA
Kowalski, Phil *Singer (The Diamonds)*
%Moments Mgmt, 520 Washington Blvd, #393, Marina del Rey, CA 90292, USA
Kowalski, Ted *Singer (The Diamonds)*
%Moments Mgmt, 520 Washington Blvd, #393, Marina del Rey, CA 90292, USA
Koz, Dave *Jazz Saxophonist, Flutist*
%Vision Mgmt, 7958 Beverly Dr, Los Angeles, CA 90048, USA
Kozak, Harley Jane *Actress*
8383 Wyndham Road, Los Angeles, CA 90046, USA
Kozlova, Valentina *Ballerina*
%New York City Ballet, Lincoln Center Plaza, New York, NY 10023, USA
Kozlowski, L Dennis *Businessman*
%Tyco International, 3 Tyco Park, Exeter, NH 03833, USA
Kozlowski, Linda *Actress*
%Writers & Artists, 924 Westwood Blvd, #900, Los Angeles, CA 90024, USA
Kozol, Jonathan *Writer*
PO Box 145, Byfield, MA 01922, USA
Krabbe, Jeroen *Actor*
Van Eeghaustraat 107, 1071 EZ Amsterdam, Netherlands
Krabbe, Katrin *Track Athlete*
Am Jahnstadion, 17033 Neubrandenburg, Germany
Krackow, Jurgen *Businessman*
Schumannstr 100, 40237 Dusseldorf, Germany
Kraft, Christopher C, Jr *Space Administrator*
%Rockwell International Systems Division, 555 Gemini Ave, Houston, TX 77058, USA
Kraft, Greg *Golfer*
14820 Rue de Bayonne, #302, Clearwater, FL 33762, USA
Kraft, Leo A *Composer*
9 Dunster Road, Great Neck, NY 11021, USA
Kraft, Robert *Composer*
4722 Noeline Ave, Encino, CA 91436, USA
Kraft, Robert P *Astrophysicist*
%University of California, Lick Observatory, Santa Cruz, CA 95064, USA
Krajisnik, Momcilo *Co-President, Bosnia-Herzegovina*
%President's Office, Marsala Titz 7-A, 71000 Sarajevo, Bosnia-Herzegovina
Krall, Diana *Singer*
%Jazz Tree, 648 Broadway, #703, New York, NY 10012, USA
Kramek, Robert E *Coast Guard Admiral*
Commandant, US Coast Guard, 2100 2nd St SW, Washington, DC 20593, USA
Kramer, Billy J *Singer*
%Entity Entertainment, 875 Ave of Americas, #1908, New York, NY 10001, USA
Kramer, Gerald (Jerry) *Football Player*
Rt 1, Highway 95, PO Box 370, Parma, ID 83660, USA
Kramer, Jack *Tennis Player, Promoter*
231 N Glenroy Place, Los Angeles, CA 90049, USA
Kramer, Joel R *Editor*
%Minneapolis Star Tribune, 425 Portland Ave, Minneapolis, MN 55488, USA
Kramer, John H (Jack) *Baseball Player*
2126 Pauline St, New Orleans, LA 70117, USA
Kramer, Larry *Social Activist, Writer*
%Gay Men's Health Crisis, 119 W 24th St, New York, NY 10011, USA
Kramer, Ron *Football Player*
10153 Walnut Shores Dr, Fenton, MI 48430, USA
Kramer, Stanley E *Movie Director*
5230 Shira Dr, Valley Village, CA 91607, USA
Kramer, Stepfanie *Actress*
8455 Beverly Blvd, #505, Los Angeles, CA 90048, USA
Kramer, Tommy *Football Player*
9 Carefree Lane, San Antonio, TX 78257, USA
Krantz, Judith T *Writer*
%Thorndike Press, PO Box 159, Thorndike, ME 04986, USA
Krasniqi, Luan *Boxer*
Oschleweg 10, 78628 Rottweil, Germany
Krasnoff, Eric *Businessman*
%Pall Corp, 2200 Northern Blvd, East Hills, NY 11548, USA
Krasnow, Robert A *Record Executive*
%Nonesuch Records, 75 Rockefeller Plaza, New York, NY 10019, USA

K

Krasny, Yuri *Artist*
%Sloane Gallery, Oxford Office Building, 1612 17th St, Denver, CO 80202, USA

Kratochvilova, Jarmila *Track Athlete*
Goleuv Jenikov, 582 82, Czechoslovakia

Kratzert, Bill *Golfer*
12289 Arbor Dr, Ponte Vedra, FL 32082, USA

Kraus, Alfredo *Opera Singer*
61 W 62nd St, #6-F, New York, NY 10023, USA

Kraus, Otakar *Opera Singer*
223 Hamlet Gardens, London W6, England

Krause, Chester L *Publisher*
%Krause Publications, 700 E State St, Iola, WI 54990, USA

Krause, Jerome R (Jerry) *Basketball Executive*
%Chicago Bulls, 1901 W Madison St, Chicago, IL 60612, USA

Krause, Paul J *Football Player*
18099 Judicial Way N, Lakeville, MN 55044, USA

Krause, Richard M *Immunologist*
4000 Cathedral Ave NW, #413-B, Washington, DC 20016, USA

Kraushaar, William L *Physicist*
462 Togstad Glen, Madison, WI 53711, USA

Krauskopf, Konrad B *Geologist*
806 La Mesa Dr, Menlo Park, CA 94028, USA

Krauss, Alison *Singer, Fiddler*
%Keith Case Mgmt, 59 Music Square W, Nashville, TN 37203, USA

Krausse, Stefan *Luge Athlete*
Heinrich-Hertz-Str 39, 98693 Ilmenau, Germany

Krauthammer, Charles *Columnist*
%Washington Post Writers Group, 1150 15th St NW, Washington, DC 20071, USA

Kravchuk, Leonid M *President, Ukraine*
%President's Office, Bankivska Ul 11, 252009 Kiev, Ukraine

Kravis, Henry *Financier*
%Kohlberg Kravis Roberts Co, 9 W 57th St, New York, NY 10019, USA

Kravitz, Lenny *Singer, Songwriter, Guitarist*
14681 Harrison St, Miami, FL 33176, USA

Krayer, Otto H *Pharmacologist*
4140 E Cooper St, Tucson, AZ 85711, USA

Krayzie Bone *Rap Artist (Bone Thugs-N-Harmony)*
%Pyramid Entertainment, 89 5th Ave, #700, New York, NY 10003, USA

Krebs, Edwin G *Nobel Medicine Laureate*
%University of Washington, Hughes Medical Institute, Seattle, WA 98195, USA

Krebs, Robert D *Businessman*
%Santa Fe Southern Pacific, 1700 E Golf Road, #700, Schaumburg, IL 60173, USA

Krebs, Susan *Actress*
722 Marco Place, Venice, CA 90291, USA

Kredel, Elmar Maria *Religious Leader*
Obere Karolinenstra 5, 96033 Bamber, Germany

Kregel, Kevin R *Astronaut*
%NASA, Johnson Space Center, 2101 NASA Road, Houston, TX 77058, USA

Krehbiel, Frederick A, II *Businessman*
%Molex Inc, 222 Wellington Court, Lisle, IL 60532, USA

Kreile, Reinhold *Businessman*
%Friedrich Flick Group, Monchenwerther Str 15, 40545 Dusseldorf, Germany

Krekich, Alexander J *Navy Admiral*
Commander, Surface Force Pacific, 2421 Vella Lavella Road, San Diego, CA 92155, USA

Krementz, Jill *Photographer*
%Dial Books Young, 375 Hudson St, New York, NY 10014, USA

Kremer, Gidon *Concert Violinist*
%International Creative Mgmt, 40 W 57th St, New York, NY 10019, USA

Krens, Thomas *Museum Administrator*
%Solomon R Guggenheim Museum, 1071 5th Ave, New York, NY 10128, USA

Krentz (Amanda Quick), Jayne Ann *Writer*
%Axelrod Agency, 66 Church St, Lenox, MA 01240, USA

Krenz, Egon *Chairman, East Germany*
Majakowskiweg 9, 13156 Berlin, Germany

Krenz, Jan *Composer, Conductor*
Al 1 Armii Wojska Polskiego 16/38, 00-582 Warsaw, Poland

Kreps, Juanita M *Secretary, Commerce*
1407 W Pettigrew St, Durham, NC 27705, USA

Krasny - Kreps

Kresa, Kent — *Businessman*
%Northrop Corp, 1840 Century Park East, Los Angeles, CA 90067, USA

Kreskin — *Illusionist*
PO Box 1383, West Caldwell, NJ 07007, USA

Kretchmer, Arthur — *Editor*
%Playboy Magazine, Editorial Dept, 680 N Lake Shore Dr, Chicago, IL 60611, USA

Kriangsak Chomanan — *Prime Minister, Thailand; Army General*
%National Assembly, Bangkok, Thailand

Krieg, Arthur M — *Immunologist*
%University of Iowa, College of Medicine, Immunology Dept, Iowa City, IA 52242, USA

Krieg, Dave — *Football Player*
%Tennessee Oilers, Hale Hall, Tennessee State University, Nashville, TN 37209, USA

Kriegel, David I — *Businessman*
%Drug Emporium, 155 Hidden Ravines Dr, Powell, OH 43065, USA

Kriek, Johan — *Tennis Player*
9220 Bonita Beach Road, #200, Bonita Springs, FL 34135, USA

Krier, Leon — *Architect*
16 Belsize Park, London NW3, England

Krige, Alice — *Actress*
10816 Lindbrook Dr, Los Angeles, CA 90024, USA

Krikalev, Sergei K — *Cosmonaut*
%Potchta Kosmonavtov, Moskovskoi Oblasti, 141160 Syvisdny Goroduk, Russia

Krim, Mathilde — *Philanthropist*
%Amer Foundation for AIDS Research, 5900 Wilshire Blvd, Los Angeles, CA 90036, USA

Krimsky, John, Jr — *Sports Executive*
%US Olympic Committee, 1 Olympia Plaza, Colorado Springs, CO 80909, USA

Krinsky, Paul L — *Coast Guard Admiral*
%US Merchant Marine Academy, Superintendent's Office, Kings Point, NY 11024, USA

Kriss, Gerard A — *Astronomer*
%Johns Hopkins University, Astronomy Dept, Baltimore, MD 21218, USA

Kristel, Sylvia — *Actress*
%Edrick/Rich Mgmt, 2400 Whitman Place, Los Angeles, CA 90068, USA

Kristen, Marta — *Actress*
11766 Wilshire Blvd, #516, Los Angeles, CA 90025, USA

Kristiansen, Ingrid — *Track Athlete*
Nils Collett Vogts Vei 51-B, 0765 Oslo, Norway

Kristof, Kathy M — *Columnist*
%Los Angeles Times, Editorial Dept, Times Mirror Square, Los Angeles, CA 90053, USA

Kristof, Nicholas D — *Journalist*
%New York Times, Editorial Dept, 229 W 43rd St, New York, NY 10036, USA

Kristofferson, Kris — *Singer, Songwriter, Actor*
PO Box 2147, Malibu, CA 90265, USA

Kristol, Irving — *Educator*
%Public Interest Magazine, 1112 16th St NW, Washington, DC 20036, USA

Kriwet, Heinz — *Businessman*
%Thyssen AG, Kaiser-Wilhelm-Str 100, 47166 Duisburg, Germany

Kroc, Joan B — *Businesswoman*
%Joan B Kroc Foundation, 8989 Villa La Jolla Dr, La Jolla, CA 92037, USA

Kroeger, Gary — *Actor*
%Agency For Performing Arts, 9200 Sunset Blvd, #900, Los Angeles, CA 90069, USA

Krofft, Marty — *Puppeteer*
700 Greentree Road, Pacific Palisades, CA 90272, USA

Krofft, Sid — *Puppeteer*
7710 Woodrow Wilson Dr, Los Angeles, CA 90046, USA

Kroft, Steve — *Commentator*
%CBS-TV, News Dept, 51 W 52nd St, New York, NY 10019, USA

Krogman, Wilton — *Physical Anthropologist*
1127 Spring Grove Ave, Lancaster, PA 17603, USA

Kroll, Alexander S (Alex) — *Football Player, Businessman*
%Young & Rubicam, 285 Madison Ave, New York, NY 10017, USA

Kroll, Lucien — *Architect*
Ave Louis Berlaimont 20, Boite 9, 1160 Brussels, Belgium

Kromm, Richard — *Hockey Player*
35469 Banbry St, Livonia, MI 48152, USA

Kronberger, Petra — *Skier*
Ellmautal 37, 5452 Pfarrwerfen, Austria

Krone, Julie — *Thoroughbred Racing Jockey*
%Monmouth Park Race Track, Oceanport Ave, Oceanport, NJ 07757, USA

Krongard, A B — *Financier*
%Alex Brown & Sons, 1 South St, Baltimore, MD 21202, USA

Kroon, Ciro D — *Prime Minister, Netherlands Antilles*
%Banco Mercantil Venezolano, PO Box 565, Willenstad, Netherlands Antilles

Kropfeld, Jim — *Boat Racing Driver*
%Hydroplanes Inc, 9117 Zoellner Dr, Cincinnati, OH 45251, USA

Kross, Walter (Walt) — *Air Force General*
Commander, US Transportation Command, Scott Air Force Base, IL 62225, USA

Kroto, Harold W — *Nobel Chemistry Laureate*
%Sussex University, Chemistry Dept, Falmer, Brighton BN1 9QJ, England

KRS-One — *Rap Artist*
%Famous Artists Agency, 1700 Broadway, #500, New York, NY 10019, USA

Krueger, Charles A (Charlie) — *Football Player*
4691 Clayton Road, Concord, CA 94521, USA

Krueger, Robert C — *Senator, TX; Diplomat*
%US Embassy-Burundi, State Department, 2201 "C" St NW, Washington, DC 20522, USA

Kruger, Hardy — *Actor*
Albert-Beit-Weg, 20149 Hamburg, Germany

Kruger, Lou — *Basketball Coach*
%University of Illinois, Athletic Dept, Assembly Hall, Champaign, IL 61820, USA

Kruger, Pit — *Actor*
Geleitstr 10, 60599 Frankfurt/Main, Germany

Krugman, Wilton — *Physical Anthropologist*
1127 Spring Grove Ave, Lancaster, PA 17603, USA

Krulak, Charles C — *Marine Corps General*
%Commandant's Office, HqUSMC, 2 Navy Annex, Washington, DC 20380, USA

Krulwich, Robert — *Commentator*
%CBS-TV, News Dept, 524 W 57th St, New York, NY 10019, USA

Krumrie, Tim — *Football Player*
%Cincinnati Bengals, 1 Bengals Dr, Cincinnati, OH 45204, USA

Kruschen, Jack — *Actor*
PO Box 10143, Canoga Park, CA 91309, USA

Kruse, Earl J — *Labor Leader*
%Roofers/Waterproofers/Allied Workers, 1125 17th St NW, Washington, DC 20036, USA

Kruse, Martin — *Religious Leader*
Neue Grunstr 19-20, 10179 Berlin, Germany

Krypreos, Nick — *Hockey Player*
9209 Copenhaven Dr, Potomac, MD 20854, USA

Kryuchkov, Vasiliy D — *Government Official, Ukraine*
4 Vinogradniy St, #74, Kiev, Ukraine

Krzyzewski, Mike — *Basketball Coach*
%Duke University, Cameron Indoor Stadium, Durham, NC 27706, USA

Kuban, Bob — *Singer, Drummer*
17626 Lasiandra Dr, Chesterfield, MO 63005, USA

Kubasov, Valery N — *Cosmonaut*
%Potchta Kosmonavtov, Moskovskoi Oblasti, 141160 Syvisdny Goroduk, Russia

Kubek, Anthony C (Tony) — *Baseball Player, Sportscaster*
8323 North Shore Road, Menasha, WI 54952, USA

Kubiak, Gary — *Football Player, Coach*
4330 Preserve Parkway S, Littleton, CO 80121, USA

Kubler-Ross, Elisabeth — *Physician, Writer*
%Celestial Arts Publishing, PO Box 7327, Berkeley, CA 94707, USA

Kubrick, Stanley — *Movie Director*
PO Box 123, Borehamwood, Herts, England

Kucan, Milan — *President, Slovenia*
%President's Office, Erjavcera 17, 61000 Ljubljana, Slovenia

Kucharski, John M — *Businessman*
%EG&G Inc, 45 William St, Wellesley, MA 02181, USA

Kuchma, Leonid D — *President, Ukraine*
%President's Office, Bankivska Ul 11, 252009 Kiev, Ukraine

Kudelka, James — *Choreographer*
%National Ballet of Canada, 157 E King St, Toronto ON M5C 1G9, Canada

Kudelski, Bob — *Hockey Player*
110 Coronet Circle, Feeding Hills, MA 01030, USA

Kudlow, Lawrence A — *Government Official, Economist*
%Bear Stearns Co, 245 Park Ave, New York, NY 10167, USA

Kudrna, Julius — *Canoeist*
Sekaninova 36, 120 00 Prague 2, Czech Republic

Kudrow, Lisa — *Actress*
1314 17th St, Santa Monica, CA 90404, USA

Kufeldt, James — *Businessman*
%Winn-Dixie Stores, 5050 Edgewood Court, Jacksonville, FL 32254, USA

Kuharic, Franjo Cardinal — *Religious Leader*
%Archdiocese of Zagreb, 41101 Zagreb, Yugoslavia

Kuhaulua, Jesse — *Sumo Wrestler*
%Azumazeki Stable, 4-6-4 Higashi Komagata, Ryogoku, Tokyo, Japan

Kuhlmann, Kathleen M — *Opera Singer*
37 Sydenham Park Road, London SE26, England

Kuhn, Bowie K — *Baseball Executive*
%Wilkie Farr Gallagher, 1 Citicorp Center, 153 E 53rd St, New York, NY 10022, USA

Kuhn, Steve — *Jazz Pianist, Composer*
%Berkeley Agency, 2608 9th St, Berkeley, CA 94710, USA

Kuhnen, Harald — *Businessman*
%Thyssen AG, Kaiser-Wilhelm-Str 100, 31089 Duisburg, Germany

Kukoc, Toni — *Basketball Player*
1850 Hybernia Dr, Highland Park, IL 60035, USA

Kulikov, Viktor G — *Army Marshal, USSR*
%Defense Ministry, Krasnopresnenskaya Nab 2, 103116 Moscow, Russia

Kulkarni, Shrinivas R — *Astronomer*
%California Institute of Technology, Astronomy Dept, Pasadena, CA 91125, USA

Kull, Lorenz A — *Businessman*
%Science Applications Int'l, 10260 Campus Point Dr, San Diego, CA 92121, USA

Kullberg, John F — *Association Executive*
%Society for Prevention of Cruelty to Animals, 441 E 92nd, New York, NY 10128, USA

Kumar, Sanjay — *Businessman*
%Computer Associates Int'l, 1 Computer Associates Plaza, Islandia, NY 11788, USA

Kumaratunga, Chandrika B — *Prime Minister, Sri Lanka*
%President's Office, Republic Square, Sri Jayewardenepura Kotte, Sri Lanka

Kume, Yutaka — *Businessman*
%Nissan Motor Co, 6-17-1 Ginza, Chuoku, Tokyo 104, Japan

Kumin, Maxine W — *Writer*
Joppa Road, Warner, NH 03278, USA

Kummer, Glenn F — *Businessman*
%Fleetwood Enterprises, 3125 Myers St, Riverside, CA 92503, USA

Kump, Ernest J — *Architect*
17 Rue Chanoinesse, 75004 Paris, France

Kundera, Milan — *Writer*
%University of Rennes, 6 Ave Gaston Berger, 35043 Rennes, France

Kundla, John — *Basketball Coach*
4519 Zenith Ave N, Minneapolis, MN 55422, USA

Kung, Hans — *Theologian*
Waldhauserstr 23, 72076 Tubingen, Germany

Kung, Patrick C — *Pharmacologist*
%T Cell Sciences, 119 4th Ave, Needham, MA 02194, USA

Kunin, Madeline M — *Governor, VT*
%National Arts-Humanities Foundation, 1100 Pennsylvania, Washington, DC 20004, USA

Kunisch, Robert D — *Businessman*
%PHH Corp, 11333 McCormick Road, Hunt Valley, MD 21031, USA

Kunitz, Stanley J — *Writer*
37 W 12th St, New York, NY 10011, USA

Kunkel, Louis M — *Pediatrician*
%Children's Hospital, 300 Longwood Ave, Boston, MA 02115, USA

Kunkle, John F — *Religious Leader*
%Evangelical Methodist Church, 3000 W Kellogg Dr, Wichita, KS 67213, USA

Kunnert, Kevin — *Basketball Player*
8286 SW Qilderland Court, Tigard, OR 97224, USA

Kunz, George J — *Football Player*
8215 S Bermuda Road, Las Vegas, NV 89123, USA

Kunzel, Erich, Jr — *Conductor*
%Cincinnati Symphony, Music Hall, 1241 Elm St, Cincinnati, OH 45210, USA

Kupchak, Mitch — *Basketball Player*
156 N Gunston Dr, Los Angeles, CA 90049, USA

Kupcinet, Irv — *Columnist*
%Chicago Sun-Times, Editorial Dept, 401 N Wabash Ave, Chicago, IL 60611, USA

Kupcinet, Kari — *Actress*
1651 N Dayton St, #202, Chicago, IL 60614, USA

K

Kudrow - Kupcinet

Kupfer, Carl *Ophthalmologist*
%National Eye Institute, 9000 Rockville Pike, Bethesda, MD 20892, USA

Kupfer, Harry *Opera Director*
%Komische Oper, Behrenstr 55-57, 10117 Berlin, Germany

Kupferberg, Sabine *Ballerina*
%Dans Theater 3, Scheldoldoekshaven 60, 2511 EN Gravenhage, Netherlands

Kuranari, Tadashi *Government Official, Japan*
2-18-12 Daita, Setangayaku, Tokyo 155, Japan

Kureishi, Hanif *Writer*
81 Comeragh Road, London W14 9HS, England

Kurland, Robert A (Bob) *Basketball Player*
1200 Brookside Parkway, Bartlesville, OK 74006, USA

Kurokawa, Kisho *Architect*
Aoyama Bldg, #11-F, 1-2-3 Kita Aoyama, Minatoku, Tokyo, Japan

Kurosawa, Akira *Movie Director*
%Kurosawa Production, 3-2-1 Kirigaoka Midoriku, Yokohama, Japan

Kurri, Jari *Hockey Player*
%Colorado Avalanche, McNichols Arena, 1635 Clay St, Denver, CO 80204, USA

Kurtenbach, Orland *Hockey Player*
12745 25A Ave, Surrey BC V4A 5S5, Canada

Kurtz, Swoosie *Actress*
320 Central Park West, New York, NY 10025, USA

Kurtzig, Sandra L *Businesswoman*
%ASK Group Inc, 2525 Augustine Dr, #200, Santa Clara, CA 95054, USA

Kurtzwell, John *Businessman*
%Read-Rite, 345 Los Coches St, Milpitas, CA 95035, USA

Kurz, Herbert *Businessman*
%Presidential Life Insurance, 69 Lydecker St, Nyack, NY 10960, USA

Kurzweil, Raymond *Inventor*
%Kurzweil Applied Intelligence, 411 Waverly Oaks Road, Waltham, MA 02154, USA

Kuschak, Metropolitan Andrei *Religious Leader*
%Ukranian Orthodox Church in America, 3 Davenport Ave, New Rochelle, NY 10805, USA

Kuse, James R *Businessman*
%Georgia Gulf Corp, 400 Perimeter Center Terrace, Atlanta, GA 30346, USA

Kushner, Robert E *Artist*
%Reinhold-Brown Gallery, 26 E 78th St, New York, NY 10021, USA

Kushner, Tony *Writer*
%Joyce Ketay Agency, 334 W 89th St, New York, NY 10024, USA

Kuter, Kay E *Actor*
6207 Satsuma Ave, North Hollywood, CA 91606, USA

Kutner, Malcolm J (Mal) *Football Player*
3 River Hollow Lane, Houston, TX 77027, USA

Kuttner, Robert *Journalist*
%Alfred A Knopf Inc, 201 E 50th St, New York, NY 10022, USA

Kuttner, Stephan G *Writer, Historian*
2270 Le Conte Ave, #601, Berkeley, CA 94709, USA

Kutyna, Donald J *Businessman, Air Force General*
%Loral Corp, Advanced Space Systems Division, 600 3rd Ave, New York, NY 10016, USA

Kuykendall, John W *Educator*
%Davidson College, President's Office, Davidson, NC 28036, USA

Kuznetsov, Vacheslav *Government Official, Belarus*
%Chairman's Office, Dom Pravitelstva, Minsk 220 010, Belarus

Kwalick, Ted *Football Player*
755 Purdie Court, Santa Clara, CA 95051, USA

Kwan, Michelle *Figure Skater*
44450 Pinetree Dr, #103, Plymouth, MI 48170, USA

Kwan, Nancy *Actress*
%Contemporary Artists, 1427 3rd St Promenade, #205, Santa Monica, CA 90401, USA

Kwasniewski, Aleksander *President, Poland*
%Kancelaria Prezydenta RP, Ul Wiejska 4/8, 00-902 Warsaw, Poland

Kwoh, Yik San *Electrical Engineer*
%Memorial Medical Center, PO Box 1428, Long Beach, CA 90801, USA

Kylian, Jiri *Ballet Dancer*
%Dance Theatre, Scheldeldoekshaven 60, 2511 EN Gravenhage, Netherlands

Kyo, Machiko *Actress*
Olimpia Copu, 6-35 Jingumae, Shibuyaku, Tokyo, Japan

Kyprianou, Spyros *President, Cyprus*
Antistaseos 1, Engomi, Nicosia, Cyprus

L'Engle, Madeleine — *Writer*
%Crosswicks, Goshen, CT 06756, USA

La Beef, Sleepy — *Singer*
484 Lexington St, Waltham, MA 02154, USA

La Belle, Patti — *Singer*
1212 Grennox Road, Wynnewood, PA 19096, USA

La Fosse, Robert — *Choreographer*
%New York City Ballet, Lincoln Center Plaza, New York, NY 10023, USA

La Paglia, Anthony — *Actor*
%International Creative Mgmt, 8942 Wilshire Blvd, Beverly Hills, CA 90211, USA

La Planche, Rosemary — *Actress*
13914 Hartsook St, Sherman Oaks, CA 91423, USA

La Plante, Lynda — *Writer*
%Random House, 201 E 50th St, New York, NY 10022, USA

La Rosa, Julius — *Singer*
67 Sycamore Lane, Irvington, NY 10533, USA

La Sala, James — *Labor Leader*
%Amalgamated Transit Union, 5025 Wisconsin Ave NW, Washington, DC 20016, USA

La Salle, Eriq — *Actor*
PO Box 2369, Beverly Hills, CA 90213, USA

La Scola, Judith — *Artist*
%Compositions Gallery, 317 Sutter St, San Francisco, CA 94108, USA

Laage, Gerhart — *Architect*
Weidenallee 26-A, 20357 Hamburg, Germany

Laar, Mart — *Prime Minister, Estonia*
%Prime Minister's Office, Lossi Plats 1-A, Tallinn 0100, Estonia

Laatasi, Kamuta — *Prime Minister, Tuvalu*
%Prime Minister's Office, Vaiaku, Funafuti, Tuvalu

Labaff, Ernie — *Labor Leader*
%Aluminum Brick Glass Workers Union, 3362 Hollenberg, Bridgeton, MO 63044, USA

Labeque, Katia — *Concert Pianist*
%Columbia Artists Mgmt Inc, 165 W 57th St, New York, NY 10019, USA

Labeque, Marielle — *Concert Pianist*
%Columbia Artists Mgmt Inc, 165 W 57th St, New York, NY 10019, USA

Labis, Attilo — *Ballet Dancer, Choreographer*
36 Rue du Chemin-de-fer, 78380 Bougival, France

LaBoa, Guy A J — *Army General*
Commanding General, 1st Army, Fort Gillem, GA 30050, USA

Labonte, Bobby — *Auto Racing Driver*
Rt 1, PO Box 607, Trinity, NC 27370, USA

Labonte, Terry — *Auto Racing Driver*
PO Box 843, Trinity, NC 27370, USA

Labre, Yvon — *Hockey Player*
1827 Peachtree Lane, Bowie, MD 20721, USA

Labrecque, Thomas G — *Financier*
%Chase Manhattan Corp, 270 Park Ave, New York, NY 10017, USA

Labyorteaux, Matthew — *Actor*
4555 Mariota Ave, Toluca Lake, CA 91602, USA

Labyorteaux, Patrick — *Actor*
8916 Ashcroft Ave, Los Angeles, CA 90048, USA

Lace, Jerry E — *Figure Skating Executive*
1701 N Nevada Ave, Colorado Springs, CO 80907, USA

Lacey, Deborah — *Actress*
%House of Representatives, 400 S Beverly Dr, #101, Beverly Hills, CA 90212, USA

Lach, Elmer J — *Hockey Player*
89 Bayview Ave, Pointe Claire PQ M9S 5C4, Canada

Lachance, Mike — *Harness Racing Driver*
109 Robertson Dr, Wyckoff, NJ 07481, USA

LaChapelle, David — *Photographer*
%Simon & Schuster, 1230 Ave of Americas, New York, NY 10020, USA

Lachemann, Marcel E — *Baseball Player, Manager*
7275 Seay Lane, Penryn, CA 95663, USA

Lachemann, Rene G — *Baseball Player, Manager*
7500 E Boulders Parkway, #68, Scottsdale, AZ 85262, USA

Lachey, James M (Jim) — *Football Player*
1427 Roxbury Road, #G, Columbus, OH 43212, USA

Lachiman Gurung — *WW II Nepal Army Hero (VC)*
Village Dahakhani, Village Development, Conmelle, Ward 4, Chitwan, Nepal

L

L'Engle - Lachiman Gurung

Lackey, Brad — *Motorcycle Racing Rider*
%Badco, 35 Monument Plaza, Pleasant Hill, CA 94523, USA

Laclavere, Georges — *Geophysicist*
53 Ave de Breteuil, 70075 Paris, France

Laclotte, Michel R — *Museum Director*
%Musee du Louvre, 4 Quai des Tuileries, 75041 Paris Cedex 1, France

Lacombe, Henri — *Oceanographer*
20 Bis Ave de Lattre de Tassigny, 92340 Bourg-La-Reine, France

Lacoste, Catherine — *Golfer*
Calle B-6, #4, El Soto de la Moraleja Alcobendas, Madrid, Spain

Lacroix, Andre — *Hockey Player*
1307 Ocean Ave, Brigantine, NJ 08203, USA

Lacroix, Christian M M — *Fashion Designer*
73 Rue du Faubourg St Honore, 75008 Paris, France

Lacy, Linwood A, Jr — *Businessman*
%Ingram Industries, 4400 Harding Road, Nashville, TN 37205, USA

Lacy, Steve — *Jazz Saxophonist, Composer*
%BMG, 1133 Ave of Americas, New York, NY 10036, USA

Lacy, Venus — *Basketball Player*
%Long Beach StingRays, 6378 E Pacific Coast Highway, #D, Long Beach, CA 90803, USA

Lacy, William H — *Financier*
%MGIC Investment Corp, 250 E Kilbourn Ave, Milwaukee, WI 53202, USA

Ladd, Alan W, Jr — *Movie Producer*
706 N Elm Dr, Beverly Hills, CA 90210, USA

Ladd, Cheryl — *Actress*
PO Box 1329, Santa Ynez, CA 93460, USA

Ladd, Diane — *Actress*
PO Box 17111, Beverly Hills, CA 90209, USA

Ladd, Margaret — *Actress*
444 21st St, Santa Monica, CA 90402, USA

Laderman, Ezra — *Composer*
%Yale University, Music School, New Haven, CT 06520, USA

Laettner, Christian — *Basketball Player*
1225 Church Road, Angola, NY 14006, USA

Laffer, Arthur — *Economist*
24255 Pacific Coast Highway, Malibu, CA 90263, USA

Lafleur, Guy — *Hockey Player*
%Montreal Canadiens, 1260 De la Gauchetiere W, Montreal PQ H3B 5E8, Canada

Lafontaine, Oskar — *Political Leader, Germany*
Staatskanzle, Am Ludwigsplatz 14, 66117 Saarbrucken, Germany

LaFontaine, Pat — *Hockey Player*
%Buffalo Sabres, Marine Midland Arena, 1 Seymour Knox Plaza, Buffalo, NY 14210, USA

Lagattuta, Bill — *Commentator*
%CBS-TV, News Dept, 7800 Beverly Blvd, Los Angeles, CA 90036, USA

Lagerfeld, Karl — *Fashion Designer*
14 Blvd de la Madeleine, 75008 Paris, France

Laghi, Pio Cardinal — *Religious Leader*
%Catholic Education Congregation, Piazza Pio XII 3, 00193 Rome, Italy

Laguna, Frederica de — *Anthropologist*
3300 Darby Road, #1310, Haverford, PA 19041, USA

LaHaie, Dick — *Auto Racing Driver*
%Dick LaHaie Racing, 14155 Wood Road, Lansing, MI 48906, USA

Lahav, Gideon — *Financier*
%Israel Discount Bank (NY), 511 5th Ave, New York, NY 10017, USA

Lahti, Christine — *Actress*
%International Creative Mgmt, 8942 Wilshire Blvd, Beverly Hills, CA 90211, USA

Lai, Francis — *Composer*
23 Rue Franklin, 75016 Paris, France

Laimbeer, Bill — *Basketball Player*
4310 S Bay Dr, Orchard Lake, MI 48323, USA

Laine, Cleo — *Singer*
%International Artists, 235 Regent St, London W1R 8AX, England

Laine, Frankie — *Singer, Songwriter*
352 San Gorgonio St, San Diego, CA 92106, USA

Laingen, L Bruce — *Diplomat*
5627 Old Chester Road, Bethesda, MD 20814, USA

Laird, Melvin R — *Secretary, Defense; Businessman*
%COMSAT Corp, 6560 Rock Spring Dr, Bethesda, MD 20817, USA

Laird, Peter *Cartoonist (Ninja Turtles)*
%Teenage Mutant Ninja Turtles, PO Box 417, Haydenville, MA 01039, USA
Laird, Ron *Track Athlete*
4706 Diane Dr, Astabula, OH 44004, USA
Laithwaite, Eric R *Electrical Engineer*
%Imperial College, Electrical Engineering Dept, London SW7 2BT, England
Laitman, Jeffrey *Anatomist*
%Mt Sinai Medical Center, Anatomy Dept, 1 Gustave Levy Place, New York, NY 10029, USA
Lake, Carnell *Football Player*
2627 Woodmont Lane, Wexford, PA 15090, USA
Lake, James A *Molecular Biologist*
%University of California, Molecular Biology Institute, Los Angeles, CA 90024, USA
Lake, Oliver E *Jazz Saxophonist, Synthesizer Player*
%Brad Simon Organization, 122 E 57th St, New York, NY 10022, USA
Lake, Ricki *Actress*
%Ricki Lake Show, 16202 Jamaica Ave, Jamaica, NY 11432, USA
Lake, W Anthony K *Director, CIA*
%National Security Council, Old Executive Office Building, Washington, DC 20506, USA
Laker, Frederick A *Businessman*
Princess Tower, West Sunrise, Box F-207, Freeport, Grand Bahamas, Bahamas
Laker, Jim *Cricketer*
Oak End, 9 Portinscale Road, Putney, London SW15, England
Lakes, Gary *Opera Singer*
%Herbert Barrett Mgmt, 1776 Broadway, New York, NY 10019, USA
Lakoue, Enoch Devant *Prime Minister, Central African Republic*
%Prime Minister's Office, Bangui, Central African Republic
LaLanne, Jack *Physical Fitness Expert*
%BeFit Enterprises, PO Box 1023, San Luis Obispo, CA 93406, USA
Laliberte-Bourque, Andree *Museum Director*
%Musee du Quebec, 1 Ave Wolfe-Montcalm, Quebec PQ G1R 5H3, Canada
Lalli, Frank *Editor*
%Money Magazine, Editorial Dept, Rockefeller Center, New York, NY 10020, USA
LaMaina, Lawrence J, Jr *Financier*
%Dauphin Deposit Corp, 213 Market St, Harrisburg, PA 17101, USA
Lamar, Dwight (Bo) *Basketball Player*
103 Claire St, Lafayette, LA 70507, USA
Lamarr, Hedy *Actress*
568 Orange Dr, #47, Altamonte Springs, FL 32701, USA
Lamas, Lorenzo *Actor*
3727 W Magnolia Blvd, #807, Burbank, CA 91505, USA
Lamb, Brian *Entertainment Executive*
%C-SPAN, 400 N Capitol St NW, Washington, DC 20001, USA
Lamb, Dennis *Diplomat*
19 Rue de Franqueville, 75016 Paris, France
Lamb, Willis E, Jr *Nobel Physics Laureate*
%University of Arizona, Optical Sciences Center, Tucson, AZ 85721, USA
Lambert, Christopher *Actor*
9 Ave Trempley, C/Lui, 1209 Geneva, Switzerland
Lambert, Jack *Football Player*
RR 2, Box 101-A, Worthington, PA 16262, USA
Lambert, Phyllis *Architect*
%Centre d'Architecture, 1920 Rue Baile, Montreal PQ H3H 2S6, Canada
Lambro, Phillip *Composer, Pianist*
%Trigram Music, 1888 Century Park East, #10, Los Angeles, CA 90067, USA
Lambsdorff, Otto *Government Official, West Germany*
Fritz-Erler-Str 23, 53113 Bonn, Germany
Lamm, Richard D *Governor, CO*
400 E 8th Ave, Denver, CO 80203, USA
Lamm, Robert *Singer, Keyboardist (Chicago)*
%Air Tight Mgmt, 115 West Road, Winchester Center, CT 06098, USA
Lamond, Pierre *Businessman*
%Cypress Semiconductor, 3901 N 1st St, San Jose, CA 95134, USA
Lamonica, Darryl *Football Player*
8796 N 6th St, Fresno, CA 93720, USA
Lamonica, Roberto de *Artist*
Rua Anibal de Mendanca 180, AP 202, Rio de Janeiro ZC-37 RJ, Brazil
Lamont, Gene W *Baseball Manager*
4966 Fallcrest Circle, Sarasota, FL 34233, USA

L

Laird - Lamont

Lamont, Norman S H *Government Official, England*
%House of Commons, Westminster, London SW1A 0AA, England

LaMotta, Jake *Boxer*
400 E 57th St, New York, NY 10022, USA

LaMotta, Vikki *Model*
235 Beacon Dr, Phoenixville, PA 19460, USA

Lamp, Jeff *Basketball Player*
1089 Normandy Hill Lane, Encinitas, CA 92024, USA

Lamparski, Richard *Writer*
2653 Puesta Del Sol, Santa Barbara, CA 93105, USA

Lampert, Zohra *Actress*
666 West End Ave, New York, NY 10025, USA

Lamphers, Gilbert H *Businessman*
%Illinois Central Corp, 455 N Cityfront Plaza Dr, Chicago, IL 60611, USA

Lampton, Michael *Astronaut*
%University of California, Space Science Laboratory, Berkeley, CA 94720, USA

Lance, T Bert *Government Official*
409 E Line St, PO Box 637, Calhoun, GA 30701, USA

Lanchbery, John A *Conductor*
17 Harwicke Road, London W4 5EA, England

Landau, Irvin *Editor*
%Consumer Reports Magazine, 101 Truman Ave, Yonkers, NY 10703, USA

Landau, Jacob *Artist*
2 Pine Dr, Roosevelt, NJ 08555, USA

Landau, Martin *Actor*
7455 Palo Vista Dr, Los Angeles, CA 90046, USA

Landau, Saul *Writer*
%Institute for Policy Studies, 1601 Connecticut Ave NW, Washington, DC 20009, USA

Landazuri Ricketts, Juan Cardinal *Religious Leader*
Arzobispado, Plazo de Armas, Apartado Postal 1512, Lima 100, Peru

Landeck, Armin *Artist*
RD 1, Litchfield, CT 06759, USA

Lander, Benjamin *Educator*
%American University, President's Office, Washington, DC 20016, USA

Lander, David L *Actor*
4138 Pulido Court, Calabasas, CA 91302, USA

Landers (Eppie Lederer), Ann *Columnist*
%Chicago Tribune, 435 N Michigan Ave, Chicago, IL 60611, USA

Landers, Andy *Basketball Coach*
%University of Georgia, Athletic Dept, Athens, GA 30602, USA

Landers, Audrey *Actress, Singer*
%Media Artists Group, 8383 Wilshire Blvd, #954, Beverly Hills, CA 90211, USA

Landers, Judy *Actress*
%Media Artists Group, 8383 Wilshire Blvd, #954, Beverly Hills, CA 90211, USA

Landes, David S *Writer, Historian*
24 Highland St, Cambridge, MA 02138, USA

Landes, Michael *Actor*
%Gersh Agency, 232 N Canon Dr, Beverly Hills, CA 90210, USA

Landesberg, Steve *Actor*
%Rick Bernstein Enterprises, 12725 Ventura Blvd, #E, Studio City, CA 91604, USA

Landguth, Daniel P *Businessman*
%Black Hills Corp, PO Box 1400, Rapid City, SD 57709, USA

Landis, John D *Movie Director*
835 Loma Vista Dr, Beverly Hills, CA 90210, USA

Lando, Joe *Actor*
%William Morris Agency, 151 S El Camino Dr, Beverly Hills, CA 90212, USA

Landon, Howard *Writer*
Chateau de Foncoussieres, 81800 Rabastens, Tarn, France

Landon, R Kirk *Businessman*
%American Bankers Insurance, 11222 Quail Roost Dr, Miami, FL 33157, USA

Landrieu, Moon *Secretary, Housing & Urban Development*
4301 S Prieur St, New Orleans, LA 70125, USA

Landry, Greg *Football Player, Coach*
%Detroit Lions, Silverdome, 1200 Featherstone Road, Pontiac, MI 48342, USA

Landry, Karen *Actress*
%Paradigm Agency, 10100 Santa Monica Blvd, #2500, Los Angeles, CA 90067, USA

Landry, Thomas W (Tom) *Football Executive*
%Landry Investment Co, 8411 Preston Road, #720, Dallas, TX 75225, USA

Landsburg, Valerie — *Actress*
22745 Chamera Lane, Topanga Canyon, CA 90290, USA

Lane, Abbe — *Singer, Actress*
444 N Faring Road, Los Angeles, CA 90077, USA

Lane, Charles — *Actor*
321 Gretna Green Way, Los Angeles, CA 90049, USA

Lane, Cristy — *Singer*
1225 Apache Lane, Madison, TN 37115, USA

Lane, Diane — *Actress*
111 W 40th St, #2000, New York, NY 10018, USA

Lane, John R (Jack) — *Museum Curator*
%San Francisco Museum of Modern Art, 151 3rd St, San Francisco, CA 94103, USA

Lane, Kenneth Jay — *Fashion Designer*
%Kenneth Jay Lane Inc, 20 W 37th St, New York, NY 10018, USA

Lane, Lawrence W, Jr — *Publisher, Diplomat*
3000 Sandhill Road, #215, Menlo Park, CA 94025, USA

Lane, Melvin B — *Publisher*
99 Tallwood Court, Menlo Park, CA 94027, USA

Lane, Mike — *Editorial Cartoonist*
%Baltimore Evening Sun, Editorial Dept, 501 N Calvert St, Baltimore, MD 21202, USA

Lane, Nathan — *Actor, Singer*
246 W 44th St, New York, NY 10036, USA

Lane, Richard (Night Train) — *Football Player*
18100 Meyers Road, Detroit, MI 48235, USA

Laney, James T — *Educator, Diplomat*
2080 Renault Lane NE, Atlanta, GA 30345, USA

Lang, Andrew — *Basketball Player*
115 W Grandview Road, Phoenix, AZ 85023, USA

Lang, Anton — *Plant Physiologist*
1305 Dana Dr, Oxford, OH 45056, USA

Lang, Belinda — *Actress*
%Ken McReddie, 91 Regent St, London W1R 7TB, England

Lang, Doreen — *Actress*
%Susan Smith, 121 N San Vicente Blvd, Beverly Hills, CA 90211, USA

Lang, Ed — *Photographer*
%Elysium Growth Press, 814 Robinson Road, Topanga, CA 90290, USA

Lang, George C — *Vietnam War Army Hero (CMH)*
3786 Clark St, Seaford, NY 11783, USA

Lang, Jack — *Government Official, France*
17 Place des Vosges, 75004 Paris, France

Lang, Jack — *Sportswriter*
%Baseball Writers' Assn, 36 Brookfield Road, Fort Salonga, NY 11768, USA

Lang, June — *Actress*
12756 Kahlenberg Lane, North Hollywood, CA 91607, USA

lang, k d — *Singer, Actress*
%Bumstead Productions, 1616 W 3rd Ave, #200, Vancouver BC V6J 1K2, Canada

Lang, Katherine Kelly — *Actress, Model*
317 S Carmelina Ave, Los Angeles, CA 90049, USA

Lang, Pearl — *Dancer, Choreographer*
382 Central Park West, New York, NY 10025, USA

Langbo, Arnold G — *Businessman*
%Kellogg Co, 1 Kellogg Square, 235 Porter St, Battle Creek, MI 49014, USA

Langdon, Harry — *Photographer*
PO Box 16816, Beverly Hills, CA 90209, USA

Langdon, Michael — *Opera Singer*
34 Warnham Court, Grand Ave, Hove, Sussex, England

Langdon, Sue Ane — *Actress*
24115 Long Valley Road, Calabasas, CA 91302, USA

Lange, David R — *Prime Minister, New Zealand*
14 Ambury Road, Mangere Bridge, Auckland, New Zealand

Lange, Hope — *Actress*
803 Bramble Way, Los Angeles, CA 90049, USA

Lange, Jessica — *Actress*
%Creative Artists Agency, 9830 Wilshire Blvd, Beverly Hills, CA 90212, USA

Lange, Ted — *Actor*
7651 Reseda Blvd, #69, Reseda, CA 91335, USA

Lange, Thomas — *Rowing Athlete*
%Ratzeburger Ruderclub, Domhof 57, 23909 Ratzeburg, Germany

L

Landsburg - Lange

Langella, Frank — *Actor*
%Innovative Artists, 1999 Ave of Stars, #2850, Los Angeles, CA 90067, USA

Langenkamp, Heather — *Actress*
4238 Ocean View Dr, Malibu, CA 90265, USA

Langer, A J — *Actress*
%Gersh Agency, 232 N Canon Dr, Beverly Hills, CA 90210, USA

Langer, Bernhard — *Golfer*
1120 SW 21st Lane, Boca Raton, FL 33486, USA

Langer, James J (Jim) — *Football Player*
4111 McKay Road N, Brainerd, MN 56401, USA

Langford, Frances — *Singer, Actress*
PO Box 96, Jensen Beach, FL 34958, USA

Langford, John — *Aeronautical Engineer*
%Aurora Flight Sciences, 9950 Wakeman Dr, Manassas, VA 20110, USA

Langham, Michael — *Theater Director*
%Julliard School, Drama Division, 144 W 66th St, New York, NY 10023, USA

Langley, H Desmond A — *Governor General, Bermuda; Army General*
%Governor's Office, 11 Langton Hill, Pembroke, Hamilton HM 13, Bermuda

Langley, Roger — *Skier*
Broad St, Barre, MA 01005, USA

Langlois, Albert, Jr — *Hockey Player*
23503 Heritage Oak Court, Santa Clarita, CA 91321, USA

Langlois, Lisa — *Actress*
9105 Carmelita Ave, #1, Beverly Hills, CA 90210, USA

Langston, J William — *Neurologist*
%Parkinson's Foundation, 2444 Moorpark Ave, San Jose, CA 95128, USA

Langston, Mark E — *Baseball Player*
4801 Copa de Oro, Anaheim, CA 92807, USA

Langway, Rod — *Hockey Player*
12802 Thistle Blossom Way, Upper Marlboro, MD 20772, USA

Lanier, Hal (Harold C) — *Baseball Manager*
19380 SW 90th Lane Road, Dunnellon, FL 34432, USA

Lanier, J Hicks — *Businessman*
%Oxford Industries, 222 Piedmont Ave NE, Atlanta, GA 30308, USA

Lanier, Max (H Max) — *Baseball Player*
11250 SW Rio Vista Dr, Dunnellon, FL 31630, USA

Lanier, Robert C — *Mayor*
%Mayor's Office, 901 Bagby St, #300, Houston, TX 77002, USA

Lanier, Robert J (Bob) — *Basketball Player, Coach*
%National Basketball Assn, Operations Dept, 645 5th Ave, New York, NY 10022, USA

Lanier, Willie E — *Football Player*
2911 W Brigstock Road, Midlothian, VA 23113, USA

Lanin, Lester — *Orchestra Leader*
%Ted Schmidt Assoc, 6278 N Federal Highway, #274, Fort Lauderdale, FL 33308, USA

Lanker, Brian — *Photographer*
1993 Kimberly Dr, Eugene, OR 97405, USA

Lankford, Kim — *Actress*
%House of Representatives, 400 S Beverly Dr, #101, Beverly Hills, CA 90212, USA

Lansbury, Angela — *Actress, Singer*
635 N Bonhill Road, Los Angeles, CA 90049, USA

Lansdowne, J Fenwick — *Artist*
941 Victoria Ave, Victoria BC V8S 4N6, Canada

Lansford, Carney R — *Baseball Player*
RR 1 Box 66, Baker City, OR 97814, USA

Lansing, Sherry L — *Movie Producer*
10451 Bellagio Road, Los Angeles, CA 90077, USA

Lanvin, Bernard — *Fashion Designer*
22 Rue du Faubourg St Honore, 70008 Paris, France

Lanz, David — *Pianist*
%Siddons Assoc, 14930 Ventura Blvd, #205, Sherman Oaks, CA 91403, USA

Lanza, Frank C — *Businessman*
%Loral Corp, 600 3rd Ave, New York, NY 10016, USA

Laoretti, Larry — *Golfer*
10567 Whooping Crane Way, Palm City, FL 34990, USA

Laperriere, Jacques — *Hockey Player, Coach*
1983 Nice Chomedey Estate, Laval PQ H7S 1G5, Canada

Lapham, Lewis H — *Editor*
%Harper's Magazine, Editorial Dept, 666 Broadway, New York, NY 10012, USA

Lapidus, Alan — *Architect*
%Lapidus Assoc, 43 W 61st St, New York, NY 10023, USA
Lapidus, Edmond (Ted) — *Fashion Designer*
35 Rue Francois 1er, 75008 Paris, France
Lapierre, Dominique — *Writer, Historian*
Les Bignoles, 8350 Ramatuelle, France
Lapine, James E — *Writer, Theater Director*
85 Mill River Road, South Salem, NY 10590, USA
LaPlaca, Alison — *Actress*
8380 Melrose Ave, #207, Los Angeles, CA 90069, USA
Lapointe, Guy — *Hockey Player*
4568 E Rue des Bosquets, St Augustin PQ 6A3 1C4, Canada
LaPorte, Danny — *Motorcycle Racing Rider*
949 Via Del Monte, Palos Verdes Estates, CA 90274, USA
Laporte, William F — *Businessman*
%American Home Products, 5 Giraldo Farms, Madison, NJ 07940, USA
Laposata, Joseph S — *Army General*
%Battle Monuments Commission, 20 Massachusetts, Washington, DC 20314, USA
Lapotaire, Jane — *Actress*
92 Oxford Gardens, #C, London W10, England
Lappas, Steve — *Basketball Coach*
%Villanova University, Athletic Dept, Villanova, PA 19085, USA
Laprade, Edgar — *Hockey Player*
12 Shuniah St, Thunder Bay ON P7A 2Y8, Canada
Laquer, Walter — *Writer, Historian*
%Georgetown University, Strategic Studies, 1800 "K" St NW, Washington, DC 20006, USA
Laragh, John H — *Physician, Educator*
435 E 70th St, New York, NY 10021, USA
Larch, John — *Actor*
4506 Varna Ave, Sherman Oaks, CA 91423, USA
Lardner, George, Jr — *Journalist*
%Washington Post, Editorial Dept, 1150 15th St NW, Washington, DC 20071, USA
Lardner, Ring W, Jr — *Writer*
55 Central Park West, New York, NY 10023, USA
Lardy, Henry A — *Biochemist*
1829 Thorstrand Road, Madison, WI 53705, USA
Laredo, Ruth — *Concert Pianist*
%Sony/Columbia/CBS Records, 51 W 52nd St, New York, NY 10019, USA
Large, David C — *Writer, Historian*
721 W Koch St, Bozeman, MT 59715, USA
Large, James M, Jr — *Financier*
%Anchor BanCorp, 1420 Broadway, Hewlett, NY 11557, USA
Largent, Steve — *Football Player; Representative, OK*
%US House of Representatives, Cannon Office Building, Washington, DC 20515, USA
Larkin, Barry L — *Baseball Player*
9178 Solon Dr, Cincinnati, OH 45242, USA
Larkin, Raymond, Jr — *Businessman*
%Nellcor, 4280 Hacienda Dr, Pleasanton, CA 94588, USA
Larmore, Jennifer — *Opera Singer*
%Metropolitan Opera Assn, Lincoln Center Plaza, New York, NY 10023, USA
LaRoche, Philippe — *Aerial Skier*
%Club de Ski Acrobatique, Lac Beauport PQ G0A 20Q, Canada
LaRocque, Gene R — *Government Official, Navy Admiral*
3140 Davenport St NW, Washington, DC 20008, USA
Larose, Claude — *Hockey Player*
33 Wickhams Fancy, Collinsville, CT 06022, USA
LaRouche, Lyndon H, Jr — *Political Activist*
%Executive Intelligence Review, PO Box 17390, Washington, DC 20041, USA
Larouche, Pierre — *Hockey Player*
116 Lancaster Ave, Pittsburgh, PA 15228, USA
Larrabee, Martin G — *Biophysicist*
4227 Long Green Road, Glen Arm, MD 21057, USA
Larrabee, Mike — *Track Athlete*
815 S Blosser Road, Santa Maria, CA 93458, USA
Larroquette, John — *Actor*
PO Box 6910, Malibu, CA 90264, USA
Larry, Wendy — *Basketball Coach*
%Old Dominion University, Athletic Dept, Norfolk, VA 23529, USA

L

Lapidus - Larry

Larsen, Art — *Tennis Player*
203 Lorraine Blvd, San Leandro, CA 94577, USA
Larsen, Bruce — *Editor*
%Vancouver Sun, 2250 Granville St, Vancouver BC V6H 3G2, Canada
Larsen, Don J — *Baseball Player*
PO Box 2863, Hayden Lake, ID 83835, USA
Larsen, Gary L — *Football Player*
4612 141st Court SE, Bellevue, WA 98006, USA
Larsen, Libby — *Composer*
2205 Kenwood Parkway, Minneapolis, MN 55405, USA
Larsen, Paul E — *Religious Leader*
%Evangelical Convenant Church, 5101 N Francisco Ave, Chicago, IL 60625, USA
Larsen, Ralph S — *Businessman*
%Johnson & Johnson, 1 Johnson & Johnson Plaza, New Brunswick, NJ 08904, USA
Larsen, Terrence A — *Financier*
%CoreStates Financial Corp, Broad & Chestnut Sts, Philadelphia, PA 19101, USA
Larson, April U — *Religious Leader*
%Evangelical Lutheran Church, PO Box 4900, Rochester, MN 55903, USA
Larson, Bill — *Businessman*
%McAfee Assoc, 2805 Bowers Ave, Santa Clara, CA 95051, USA
Larson, Charles R (Chuck) — *Navy Admiral*
%US Naval Academy, Superintendent's Office, Annapolis, MD 21402, USA
Larson, Eric — *Publisher*
%TV Guide Magazine, 100 Matsonford Road, Radnor, PA 19087, USA
Larson, Gary — *Cartoonist (Far Side)*
%Universal Press Syndicate, 4520 Main St, Kansas City, KS 64111, USA
Larson, Glen — *Television Producer*
351 Delfern Dr, Los Angeles, CA 90077, USA
Larson, Jack — *Actor*
449 Skyewiay Road N, Los Angeles, CA 90049, USA
Larson, Jill — *Actress*
%Innovative Artists, 1999 Ave of Stars, #2850, Los Angeles, CA 90067, USA
Larson, Lance — *Swimmer*
41 Balboa Coves, Newport Beach, CA 92663, USA
Larson, Nicolette — *Singer, Songwriter*
%Rick Alter, 1018 17th Ave S, #12, Nashville, TN 37212, USA
Larson, Wolf — *Actor*
10600 Holmann Ave, #1, Los Angeles, CA 90024, USA
LaRue, Eva — *Actress*
%Innovative Artists, 1999 Ave of Stars, #2850, Los Angeles, CA 90067, USA
LaRue, Florence — *Singer (The Fifth Dimension), Actress*
%Sterling/Winters, 1900 Ave of Stars, #1640, Los Angeles, CA 90067, USA
LaRussa, Anthony (Tony), Jr — *Baseball Manager*
4349 Dunsmore Ave, #3, Tampa, FL 33611, USA
LaRusso, Rudy — *Basketball Player*
%Los Angeles Lakers, Forum, PO Box 10, Inglewood, CA 90306, USA
Lary, Yale — *Football Player*
9366 Lansdale Road, Fort Worth, TX 76116, USA
LaSalle, Denise — *Singer*
%Rodgers Redding, 1048 Tatnall St, Macon, GA 31201, USA
Lasdun, Denys L — *Architect*
146 Grosvenor Road, London SW1V 3JY, England
Lash, Bill — *Skier*
2600 2nd Ave, #1707, Seattle, WA 98121, USA
Lasker, Dee Dee — *Golfer*
12237 Carmel Vista Road, #261, San Diego, CA 92130, USA
Lasorda, Thomas C (Tommy) — *Baseball Manager, Executive*
1473 W Maxzim Ave, Fullerton, CA 92833, USA
Lassally, Walter — *Cinematographer*
The Abbey, Eye, Suffolk, England
Lassaw, Ibram — *Sculptor*
PO Box 487, East Hampton, NY 11937, USA
Lasser, Louise — *Actress, Comedienne*
200 E 71st St, #20-C, New York, NY 10021, USA
Lasseter, John — *Movie Director, Animator*
%Pixar, 1001 W Cutting Blvd, Richmond, CA 94804, USA
Lassez, Sarah — *Actress*
%Innovative Artists, 1999 Ave of Stars, #2850, Los Angeles, CA 90067, USA

Lasswell, Fred	*Cartoonist (Barney Google)*
1111 N Westshore Blvd, #604, Tampa, FL 33607, USA	
Last, James	*Orchestra Leader*
Schone Aussicht 16, 22085 Hamburg, Germany	
Laster, Danny B	*Animal Research Scientist*
%Hruska Meat Animal Research Center, PO Box 166, Clay Center, NE 68933, USA	
Laster, Ralph W, Jr	*Businessman*
%AmVestors Financial Corp, 415 SW 8th Ave, Topeka, KS 66603, USA	
Laswell, Bill	*Record Producer*
%Axiom/Island Records, 400 Lafayette St, #500, New York, NY 10003, USA	
Laszlo, Andrew	*Cinematographer*
%Smith/Gosnell/Nicholson, 1515 Palisades Dr, #N, Pacific Palisades, CA 90272, USA	
Lateef, Yusef	*Jazz Saxophonist, Flutist, Composer*
%Rhino Records, 10635 Santa Monica Blvd, Los Angeles, CA 90025, USA	
Latham, David	*Astronomer*
%Harvard University, Astronomy Dept, Cambridge, MA 02138, USA	
Latham, Louise	*Actress*
2125 Piedras Dr, Santa Barbara, CA 93108, USA	
Lathiere, Bernard	*Businessman*
%Airbus-Industrie, 5 Ave de Villiers, 75017 Paris, France	
Latimore	*Singer*
%Rodgers Redding, 1048 Tatnall St, Macon, GA 31201, USA	
Latimore, Joseph	*Actor*
%Paul Kohner, 9300 Wilshire Blvd, #555, Beverly Hills, CA 90212, USA	
Latiolais, Rene L	*Businessman*
%Freeport-McMoRan Inc, 1615 Poydras St, New Orleans, LA 70112, USA	
Lattisaw, Stacy	*Singer*
%Walter Reeder, 1516 Redwood Lane, Wyncote, PA 19095, USA	
Lattner, Johnny	*Football Player*
933 Wenonah Ave S, Oak Park, IL 60304, USA	
Laub, Larry	*Bowler*
%Professional Bowlers Assn, 1720 Merriman Road, Akron, OH 44313, USA	
Lauda, Andreas-Nikolaus (Niki)	*Auto Racing Driver*
5322 Hof/Salzburg, Austria	
Lauder, Estee	*Businesswoman*
%Estee Lauder Companies, 767 5th Ave, New York, NY 10153, USA	
Lauder, Leonard A	*Businessman*
%Estee Lauder Companies, 767 5th Ave, New York, NY 10153, USA	
Lauder, Ronald S	*Communications Executive, Diplomat*
%Estee Lauder Companies, 767 5th Ave, New York, NY 10153, USA	
Lauderdale, Jim	*Singer*
%Press Network, 1018 17th Ave S, #1, Nashville, TN 37212, USA	
Lauderdale, Priest	*Basketball Player*
%Atlanta Hawks, 1 CNN Center, South Tower, Atlanta, GA 30303, USA	
Lauer, Andrew	*Actor*
%Brillstein/Grey, 9150 Wilshire Blvd, #350, Beverly Hills, CA 90212, USA	
Lauer, Martin	*Track Athlete*
Hardstr 41, 77886 Lauf, Germany	
Lauer, Matt	*Commentator*
%"Today" Show, NBC-TV, 30 Rockefeller Plaza, New York, NY 10112, USA	
Lauer, Tod R	*Astronomer*
6471 N Tierra de Las Catalina, Tucson, AZ 85718, USA	
Laughlin, James	*Publisher*
Meadow House, Mountain Road, Norfolk, CT 06058, USA	
Laughlin, John	*Actor*
11815 Magnolia Blvd, #2, North Hollywood, CA 91607, USA	
Laughlin, Tom	*Actor, Director*
PO Box 25355, Los Angeles, CA 90025, USA	
Lauper, Cyndi	*Singer, Songwriter*
640 Lee Road, #116, Wayne, PA 19087, USA	
Laurance, Matthew	*Actor*
1951 Hillcrest Road, Los Angeles, CA 90068, USA	
Laurance, Ray	*Businessman*
%Occidental Petroleum, 10889 Wilshire Blvd, Los Angeles, CA 90024, USA	
Laurel, Salvador H	*Prime Minister, Philippines*
Partido Nacionalista Ng Philipinas, Manila, Philippines	
Lauren, Ralph	*Fashion Designer*
1107 5th Ave, New York, NY 10128, USA	

L

Lasswell - Lauren

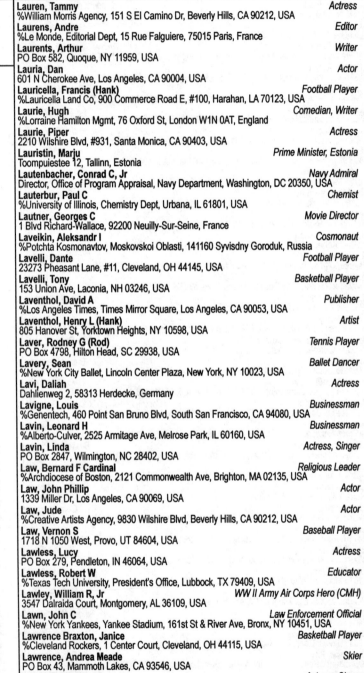

Lauren, Tammy — *Actress*
%William Morris Agency, 151 S El Camino Dr, Beverly Hills, CA 90212, USA

Laurens, Andre — *Editor*
%Le Monde, Editorial Dept, 15 Rue Falguiere, 75015 Paris, France

Laurents, Arthur — *Writer*
PO Box 582, Quoque, NY 11959, USA

Lauria, Dan — *Actor*
601 N Cherokee Ave, Los Angeles, CA 90004, USA

Lauricella, Francis (Hank) — *Football Player*
%Lauricella Land Co, 900 Commerce Road E, #100, Harahan, LA 70123, USA

Laurie, Hugh — *Comedian, Writer*
%Lorraine Hamilton Mgmt, 76 Oxford St, London W1N 0AT, England

Laurie, Piper — *Actress*
2210 Wilshire Blvd, #931, Santa Monica, CA 90403, USA

Lauristin, Marju — *Prime Minister, Estonia*
Toompuiestee 12, Tallinn, Estonia

Lautenbacher, Conrad C, Jr — *Navy Admiral*
Director, Office of Program Appraisal, Navy Department, Washington, DC 20350, USA

Lauterbur, Paul C — *Chemist*
%University of Illinois, Chemistry Dept, Urbana, IL 61801, USA

Lautner, Georges C — *Movie Director*
1 Blvd Richard-Wallace, 92200 Neuilly-Sur-Seine, France

Laveikin, Aleksandr I — *Cosmonaut*
%Potchta Kosmonavtov, Moskovskoi Oblasti, 141160 Syvisdny Goroduk, Russia

Lavelli, Dante — *Football Player*
23273 Pheasant Lane, #11, Cleveland, OH 44145, USA

Lavelli, Tony — *Basketball Player*
153 Union Ave, Laconia, NH 03246, USA

Laventhol, David A — *Publisher*
%Los Angeles Times, Times Mirror Square, Los Angeles, CA 90053, USA

Laventhol, Henry L (Hank) — *Artist*
805 Hanover St, Yorktown Heights, NY 10598, USA

Laver, Rodney G (Rod) — *Tennis Player*
PO Box 4798, Hilton Head, SC 29938, USA

Lavery, Sean — *Ballet Dancer*
%New York City Ballet, Lincoln Center Plaza, New York, NY 10023, USA

Lavi, Daliah — *Actress*
Dahlienweg 2, 58313 Herdecke, Germany

Lavigne, Louis — *Businessman*
%Genentech, 460 Point San Bruno Blvd, South San Francisco, CA 94080, USA

Lavin, Leonard H — *Businessman*
%Alberto-Culver, 2525 Armitage Ave, Melrose Park, IL 60160, USA

Lavin, Linda — *Actress, Singer*
PO Box 2847, Wilmington, NC 28402, USA

Law, Bernard F Cardinal — *Religious Leader*
%Archdiocese of Boston, 2121 Commonwealth Ave, Brighton, MA 02135, USA

Law, John Phillip — *Actor*
1339 Miller Dr, Los Angeles, CA 90069, USA

Law, Jude — *Actor*
%Creative Artists Agency, 9830 Wilshire Blvd, Beverly Hills, CA 90212, USA

Law, Vernon S — *Baseball Player*
1718 N 1050 West, Provo, UT 84604, USA

Lawless, Lucy — *Actress*
PO Box 279, Pendleton, IN 46064, USA

Lawless, Robert W — *Educator*
%Texas Tech University, President's Office, Lubbock, TX 79409, USA

Lawley, William R, Jr — *WW II Army Air Corps Hero (CMH)*
3547 Dalraida Court, Montgomery, AL 36109, USA

Lawn, John C — *Law Enforcement Official*
%New York Yankees, Yankee Stadium, 161st St & River Ave, Bronx, NY 10451, USA

Lawrence Braxton, Janice — *Basketball Player*
%Cleveland Rockers, 1 Center Court, Cleveland, OH 44115, USA

Lawrence, Andrea Meade — *Skier*
PO Box 43, Mammoth Lakes, CA 93546, USA

Lawrence, Carol — *Actress, Singer*
12337 Ridge Circle, Los Angeles, CA 90049, USA

Lawrence, Cynthia — *Opera Singer*
%Herbert Breslin, 119 W 57th St, New York, NY 10019, USA

Lauren - Lawrence

Lawrence, David, Jr — *Publisher*
%Miami Herald, 1 Herald Plaza, Miami, FL 33132, USA

Lawrence, Francis L — *Educator*
%Rutgers University, President's Office, New Brunswick, NJ 08903, USA

Lawrence, Henry — *Football Player*
6330 Green Valley Circle, #309, Culver City, CA 90230, USA

Lawrence, Henry S — *Physician, Immunologist*
343 E 30th St, New York, NY 10016, USA

Lawrence, Jacob — *Artist*
4316 37th Ave NE, Seattle, WA 98105, USA

Lawrence, Jerome — *Writer*
21506 Las Flores Mesa Dr, Malibu, CA 90265, USA

Lawrence, Joey — *Actor*
%Stiletto Entertainment, 5443 Beethoven St, Los Angeles, CA 90066, USA

Lawrence, Kenneth G — *Businessman*
%PECO Energy Co, 2301 Market St, Philadelphia, PA 19103, USA

Lawrence, Marc — *Actor*
14016 Bora Bora Way, #G-124, Marina del Rey, CA 90292, USA

Lawrence, Martin — *Comedian*
3130 Benedict Canyon, Beverly Hills, CA 90210, USA

Lawrence, Matthew — *Actor*
%FHL Co, 19722 Trull Brook Dr, Tarzana, CA 91356, USA

Lawrence, Robert S — *Physician*
4000 N Charles St, #1112, Baltimore, MD 21218, USA

Lawrence, Sharon — *Actress*
PO Box 462048, Los Angeles, CA 90046, USA

Lawrence, Steve — *Singer*
820 Greenway Dr, Beverly Hills, CA 90210, USA

Lawrence, Tracy — *Singer, Songwriter*
%TLE Mgmt, 1100 17th Ave S, Nashville, TN 37212, USA

Lawrence, Vicki — *Actress, Singer*
6000 Lido Ave, Long Beach, CA 90803, USA

Lawrence, Wendy B — *Astronaut*
%NASA, Johnson Space Center, 2101 NASA Road, Houston, TX 77058, USA

Lawrence, William P — *Navy Admiral*
303 Kyle Road, Crownsville, MD 21032, USA

Laws, Ronnie — *Jazz Saxophonist*
%Performers of the World, 8901 Melrose Ave, #200, West Hollywood, CA 90069, USA

Lawson of Blaby, Nigel — *Government Official, England*
32 Sutherland Walk, London SE17, England

Lawson, A Lowell — *Businessman*
%E-Systems Inc, 6250 LBJ Freeway, Dallas, TX 75240, USA

Lawson, Richard — *Actor*
4279 Clybourn Ave, Toluca Lake, CA 91602, USA

Lawson, Richard L — *Air Force General*
6910 Clifton Road, Clifton, VA 20124, USA

Lawton, Mary — *Cartoonist (Nowhere to Hide)*
%Chronicle Features, 901 Mission St, San Francisco, CA 94103, USA

Lawwill, Theodore — *Ophthalmologist*
7609 Tallwood Road, Prospect, KY 40059, USA

Lax, John — *Hockey Player*
3 Greendale Lane, Harwich, MA 02645, USA

Lax, Melvin — *Physicist*
12 High St, Summit, NJ 07901, USA

Lax, Peter D — *Mathematician*
%New York University, Courant Mathematics Institute, New York, NY 10012, USA

Laxalt, Paul — *Governor/Senator, NV*
%Laxalt Washington Willard, 1455 Pennsylvania NW, #975, Washington, DC 20004, USA

Laxness, Halldor — *Nobel Literature Laureate*
Gljufrasteini, 270 Mosfellsbaer, Iceland

Lay, Kenneth L — *Businessman*
%Enron Corp, PO Box 1188, Houston, TX 77251, USA

Layden, Francis P (Frank) — *Basketball Coach, Executive*
%Utah Jazz, Delta Center, 301 W South Temple, Salt Lake City, UT 84101, USA

Laynie, Tamrat — *Prime Minister, Ethiopia*
%Prime Minister's Office, PO Box 1013, Addis Ababa, Ethiopia

Layzie Bone — *Rap Artist (Bone Thugs-N-Harmony)*
%Pyramid Entertainment, 89 5th Ave, #700, New York, NY 10003, USA

L

Lawrence - Layzie Bone

Lazar, Laurence *Religious Leader*
%Romanian Orthodox Episcopate, 2522 Grey Tower Road, Jackson, MI 49201, USA

Lazarenko, Pavlo *Prime Minister, Ukraine*
%Prime Minister's Office, Government Building, Kiev 252008, Ukraine

Lazarev, Alexander N *Conductor*
%Christopher Tennant Artists, 39 Tadema Road, #2, London SW10 0PY, England

Lazarus, Charles *Businessman*
%Toys "R" Us Inc, 461 From Road, Paramus, NJ 07652, USA

Lazenby, George *Actor*
PO Box 55306, Sherman Oaks, CA 91413, USA

Lazier, Buddy *Auto Racing Driver*
%Performance Marketing, 1545 W 4th Ave, Vancouver BC V6U 1L6, Canada

Lazuktin, Alexander *Cosmonaut*
%Potchta Kosmonavtov, Moskovskoi Oblasti, 141160 Syvisdny Goroduk, Russia

Le Beauf, Sabrina *Actress*
354 Indiana Ave, Venice, CA 90291, USA

Le Bon, Simon *Singer, Songwriter (Duran Duran)*
25 Tewkesbury Ave, Pinner, Middx, England

Le Bon, Yasmin *Model*
25 Tewkesbury Ave, Pinner, Middx, England

Le Brun, Christopher M *Artist*
%Nigel Greenwood, 4 New Burlington St, London W1X 1FE, England

Le Carre (David J M Cornwell), John *Writer*
Tregiffian, Saint Buryan, Penzance, Cornwall, England

Le Duc Anh *President, Vietnam; Army General*
%President's Office, Hoang Hoa Tham, Hanoi, Vietnam

Le Mat, Paul *Actor*
1100 N Alta Loma Road, #805, West Hollywood, CA 90069, USA

Le Mesurier, John *Actor*
56 Barron's Keep, London W14, England

Le Pelley, Guernsey *Editorial Cartoonist*
35 Saint Germain St, Boston, MA 02115, USA

Le Roy, Gloria *Actress*
%Gold Marshak Liedtke, 3500 W Olive Ave, #1400, Burbank, CA 91505, USA

Le Vier, Anthony W (Tony) *Test Pilot*
%SAFE, 5108 Solliden Lane, La Canada, CA 91011, USA

Le Witt, Sol *Artist*
%Multiples Inc, 41 E 57th St, New York, NY 10022, USA

Lea, Charles W (Charlie) *Baseball Manager*
900 Peterson Lake Road, Collierville, TN 38017, USA

Leach, Henry C *Royal Navy Fleet Admiral, England*
Wonston Lea, Winchester, Hants SO21 3LS, England

Leach, Penelope *Child Psychologist*
3 Tanza Lane, London NW3 2UA, England

Leach, Robin *Television Producer, Entertainer*
1 Dag Hammarskjold Plaza, #2100, New York, NY, 10017, USA

Leach, Sheryl *Animator (Barney)*
%Lyons Group, 300 E Bethany Road, Allen, TX 75002, USA

Leachman, Cloris *Actress*
2045 Mandeville Canyon, Los Angeles, CA 90049, USA

Leader, George M *Governor, PA*
%Country Meadows, 830 Cherry Dr, Hershey, PA 17033, USA

Leaf, Alexander *Physician*
1 Curtis Circle, Winchester, MA 01890, USA

Leahy, Pat *Football Player*
717 Chamber Lane, St Louis, MO 63137, USA

Leakey, Richard E F *Paleonotolgist*
PO Box 24926, Nairobi, Kenya

Leaks, Roosevelt *Football Player*
8907 N Plaza Court, Austin, TX 78753, USA

Lear, Evelyn *Opera Singer*
414 Sailboat Circle, Fort Lauderdale, FL 33326, USA

Lear, Norman M *Television Producer, Director*
991 N Alpine Dr, Beverly Hills, CA 90210, USA

Learned, Michael *Actress*
1600 N Beverly Dr, Beverly Hills, CA 90210, USA

Leary, Denis *Comedian*
%William Morris Agency, 151 S El Camino Dr, Beverly Hills, CA 90212, USA

Leatherdale, Douglas W *Businessman*
%St Paul Companies, 385 Washington St, St Paul, MN 55102, USA

Leavitt, Michael O *Governor, UT*
%Governor's Office, State Capitol, #210, Salt Lake City, UT 84114, USA

Leavitt, Phil *Singer (The Diamonds)*
%Moments Mgmt, 520 Washington Blvd, #393, Marina del Rey, CA 90292, USA

Lebadang *Artist*
%Owl Gallery, 465 Powell St, San Francisco, CA 94102, USA

LeBaron, Dean *Financier*
%Batterymarch Financial, 200 Clarendon St, Boston, MA 02116, USA

LeBaron, Edward W (Eddie), Jr *Football Player*
%Pillsbury Madison Sutro, 400 Capitol Mall, #1700, Sacramento, CA 95814, USA

Lebedev, Valentin V *Cosmonaut*
%Potchta Kosmonavtov, Moskovskoi Oblasti, 141160 Syvisdny Goroduk, Russia

LeBel, Robert (Bob) *Hockey Executive*
25 Rue Saint Pierre, Cite de Chambly PQ J3L 1L7, Canada

LeBlanc, James E *Financier*
%Whirlpool Financial Corp, 553 Benson Road, Benton Harbor, MI 49022, USA

LeBlanc, Matt *Actor*
%United Talent Agency, 9560 Wilshire Blvd, #500, Beverly Hills, CA 90212, USA

LeBlanc, Raymond A *Businessman*
%Keystone International, 9600 W Gulf Bank Dr, Houston, TX 77040, USA

LeBlanc, Sherri *Ballerina*
%New York City Ballet, Lincoln Center Plaza, New York, NY 10023, USA

LeBow, Bennett S *Businessman*
%Brooke Group, 100 SE 2nd St, Miami, FL 33131, USA

Lebowitz, Fran *Writer*
%Random House, 201 E 50th St, New York, NY 10022, USA

Lebowitz, Joel L *Mathematician*
%Rutgers University, Mathematics Dept, New Brunswick, NJ 08903, USA

Leboyer, Frederick *Physician*
%Georges Borchardt, 136 E 57th St, New York, NY 10022, USA

LeBrock, Kelly *Actress, Model*
344 E 59th St, New York, NY 10022, USA

Leburton, Edmond *Prime Minister, Belgium*
%Ministre D'Etat, 36 Clos de Hesbaye, 4300 Waremme, Belgium

LeClair, J M *Businessman*
%Grand Trunk Corp, 1333 Brewery Park Blvd, Detroit, MI 48207, USA

LeClair, Jim *Football Player*
RR 3, Box 761, McGregor, MN 56469, USA

LeClair, John *Hockey Player*
RD 2, Freeeborn St, St Albans, VT 05478, USA

Leconte, Henri *Tennis Player*
58 Chemin Hauts-Crets, 1223 Cologny, Switzerland

Ledbetter, Donald N *Labor Leader*
%Postal Supervisors Assn, 490 L'Enfant Plaza SW, Washington, DC 20024, USA

Leder, Philip *Geneticist*
%Harvard University Medical School, 25 Shattuck St, Boston, MA 02115, USA

Lederberg, Joshua *Nobel Medicine Laureate*
%Rockefeller University, President's Office, 1230 York Ave, New York, NY 10021, USA

Lederer, Francis *Actor*
23134 Sherman Way, Canoga Park, CA 91307, USA

Lederer, Jerome *Aerospace Engineer*
468 Calle Cadiz, #D, Laguna Beach, CA 92653, USA

Lederman, Leon M *Nobel Physics Laureate*
34 Overbrook Road, Dobbs Ferry, NY 10522, USA

Ledford, Frank F, Jr *Army General*
%Southwest Foundation for Biomedical Research, Box 760549, San Antonio, TX 78245,

Ledley, Robert S *Inventor (Diagnostic X-Ray Systems)*
%Georgetown University, National Biomed Research Center, Washington, DC 20007, USA

LeDoux, Chris *Singer, Rodeo Rider*
4205 Hillsboro Road, #208, Nashville, TN 37215, USA

Lee Kuan Yew *Prime Minister, Singapore*
Senior Minister's Office, Istana Annexe, Istana, Singapore 0923, Singapore

Lee Teng-Hui *President, Taiwan*
%President's Office, Chung-King South Road, Section 1, Taipei 100, Taiwan

Lee, Anna *Actress*
4031 Hollyline Ave, Sherman Oaks, CA 91423, USA

L

Leatherdale - Lee

Lee, Bertram M *Basketball Executive*
%Denver Nuggets, McNichols Arena, 1635 Clay St, Denver, CO 80204, USA

Lee, Beverly *Singer (The Shirelles)*
%Bevi Corp, PO Box 100, Clifton, NJ 07011, USA

Lee, Brenda *Singer*
%Brenda Lee Productions, 2174 Carson St, Nashville, TN 37211, USA

Lee, Butch *Basketball Player*
PO Box 7145, #320, Ponce, PR 00732, USA

Lee, Catherine J *Artist*
283 Bemis St, San Francisco, CA 94131, USA

Lee, Chang-Rae *Writer*
%International Creative Mgmt, 40 W 57th St, New York, NY 10019, USA

Lee, Charles R *Businessman*
%GTE Corp, 1 Stamford Forum, Stamford, CT 06901, USA

Lee, Chester M *Space Engineer*
8540 Westown Way, Vienna, VA 22182, USA

Lee, Christopher *Actor*
5 Sandown House, Wheat Field Terrace, London W4, England

Lee, Daniel R *Businessman*
%Mirage Resorts, 3400 Las Vegas Blvd S, Las Vegas, NV 89109, USA

Lee, David H *Astronomer, Writer*
%Plenum Publishing Group, 233 Spring St, New York, NY 10013, USA

Lee, David M *Nobel Physics Laureate*
%Cornell University, Physics Dept, Clark Hall, Ithaca, NY 14853, USA

Lee, Dickey *Singer*
%Mars Talent, 168 Orchid Dr, Pearl River, NY 10965, USA

Lee, Dorothy *Actress*
2664 Narcissus Dr, San Diego, CA 92106, USA

Lee, Geddy *Singer, Bassist (Rush)*
%SRO Mgmt, 189 Carlton St, Toronto ON M5A 2K7, Canada

Lee, Gordon (Porky) *Actor*
7110 Highway 2, #22, Commerce City, CO 80022, USA

Lee, H Douglas *Educator*
%Stetson University, President's Office, Deland, FL 32720, USA

Lee, Howard V *Vietnam War Marine Corps Hero (CMH)*
529 King Arthur Dr, Virginia Beach, VA 23464, USA

Lee, J Bracken *Governor, UT*
1538 Devonshire Dr, Salt Lake Cty, UT 84108, USA

Lee, Jared B *Cartoonist*
%Jared B Lee Studio, 2942 Hamilton Road, Lebanon, OH 45036, USA

Lee, Jason Scott *Actor*
PO Box 1083, Pearl City, HI 96782, USA

Lee, Joe R *Businessman*
%General Mills, PO Box 1113, Minneapolis, MN 55440, USA

Lee, Johnny *Singer, Songwriter*
%WIFT Mgmt, PO Box 1644, Dickinson, TX 77539, USA

Lee, Jonna *Actress*
%Dremann, 13219 Albers Place, Van Nuys, CA 91401, USA

Lee, Keith *Basketball Player*
3617 Clearbrook St, Memphis, TN 38118, USA

Lee, Mark C *Astronaut*
%NASA, Johnson Space Center, 2101 NASA Road, Houston, TX 77058, USA

Lee, Michelle *Actress*
830 Birchwood Dr, Los Angeles, CA 90024, USA

Lee, Peggy *Singer, Actress*
11404 Bellagio Road, Los Angeles, CA 90049, USA

Lee, Raphael C *Surgeon*
%Massachusetts Institute Technology, Engineering Dept, Cambridge, MA 02139, USA

Lee, Ron *Basketball Player*
16 Andrew Ave, Hull, MA 02045, USA

Lee, Ruta *Actress*
2623 Laurel Canyon Road, Los Angeles, CA 90046, USA

Lee, Samuel (Sammy) *Diver, Coach*
16537 Harbour Lane, Huntington Beach, CA 92649, USA

Lee, Sheryl *Actress*
331 N Martel Ave, Los Angeles, CA 90036, USA

Lee, Spike *Movie Director*
%Forty Acres & A Mule Filmworks, 124 DeKalb Ave, #2, Brooklyn, NY 11217, USA

Lee, Stan — *Publisher, Cartoonist*
%Marvel Entertainment, 1440 S Sepulveda Blvd, #114, Los Angeles, CA 90025, USA

Lee, Thornton S — *Baseball Player*
9101 E Palm Tree Dr, Tucson, AZ 85710, USA

Lee, Tommy — *Drummer, Singer (Motley Crue)*
31341 Mulholland Highway, Malibu, CA 90265, USA

Lee, Tsung-Dao — *Nobel Physics Laureate*
25 Claremont Ave, New York, NY 10027, USA

Lee, Vernon R — *Religious Leader*
%Wyatt Baptist Church, 4621 W Hillsboro St, El Dorado, AR 71730, USA

Lee, William F (Bill) — *Baseball Player*
RR 1, Box 145, Craftsburg, VT 05826, USA

Lee, Yuan T — *Nobel Chemistry Laureate*
%University of California, Chemistry Dept, Berkeley, CA 94720, USA

Leeds, Phil — *Actor*
7135 Hollywood Blvd, #102, Los Angeles, CA 90046, USA

Leek, Sybil — *Self-Acclaimed Witch*
%Prentice-Hall, Rt 9-W, Englewood Cliffs, NJ 07632, USA

Leestma, David C — *Astronaut*
%NASA, Johnson Space Center, 2101 NASA Road, Houston, TX 77058, USA

Leetch, Brian — *Hockey Player*
29 Stratton Dr, Cheshire, CT 06410, USA

Leeves, Jane — *Actress*
21724 Ventura Blvd, #212, Woodland Hills, CA 91364, USA

Lefebvre, James K (Jim) — *Baseball Manager*
9120 N 106th Place, Scottsdale, AZ 85258, USA

Legace, Jean-Guy — *Hockey Player*
126 Casa Grande Lane, Santa Rosa Beach, FL 32459, USA

LeGault, Lance — *Actor*
16105-8H Victory Blvd, #382, Van Nuys, CA 91406, USA

Leghari, Farooq A — *President, Pakistan*
%President's Office, Awan-e-Sadr, Mall Road, Islamabad, Pakistan

Legorreta Vilchis, Ricardo — *Architect*
%Palacio de Versalles, #285-A, C Lomas Reforma, Mexico City 10 DF, Mexico

Legrand, Michel — *Composer*
%F Sharp Productions, 157 W 57th St, New York, NY 10019, USA

LeGuin, Ursula K — *Writer*
%Virginia Kidd, Box 278, Milford, PA 18337, USA

Leguizano, John — *Actor*
%William Morris Agency, 151 S El Camino Dr, Beverly Hills, CA 90212, USA

Lehane, Dennis — *Writer*
%William Morrow, 1350 Ave of Americas, New York, NY 10016, USA

Lehman, Ronald F, II — *Government Official*
693 Encina Grande Dr, Palo Alto, CA 94306, USA

Lehman, Tom — *Golfer*
3834 2nd Ave, La Crescenta, CA 91214, USA

Lehmann, Edie — *Actress*
PO Box 7217, Northridge, CA 91327, USA

Lehmann, Jens — *Cyclist*
Breite Str 4, 04317 Leipzig, Germany

Lehmann, Michael — *Movie Director*
%Creative Artists Agency, 9830 Wilshire Blvd, Beverly Hills, CA 90212, USA

Lehmberg, Stanford E — *Writer, Historian*
2300 S Willow Lane, Minneapolis, MN 55416, USA

Lehn, Jean-Marie P — *Nobel Chemistry Laureate*
21 Rue d'Oslo, 67000 Strasbourg, France

Lehninger, Albert L — *Biochemist*
15020 Tanyard Road, Sparks, MD 21152, USA

Lehrer, James C (Jim) — *Commentator*
1775 Broadway, #608, New York, NY 10019, USA

Lehrer, Robert I — *Molecular Biologist*
%University of California, Med Center, Hematology Dept, Los Angeles, CA 90024, USA

Lehrer, Thomas A (Tom) — *Entertainer*
%Cowell College, University of California, Santa Cruz, CA 95064, USA

Lehtinen, Dexter — *Attorney, Government Official*
%US Attorney's Office, Justice Dept, 155 S Miami Ave, Miami, FL 33130, USA

Leibman, Ron — *Actor*
10530 Strathmore Dr, Los Angeles, CA 90024, USA

L

Lee - Leibman

Leibovitz - LeMond

Leibovitz, Annie	*Photographer*
%Annie Leibovitz Studio, 55 Vandam St, New York, NY 10013, USA	
Leifer, Carol	*Comedienne, Actress*
1123 N Flores St, #17, Los Angeles, CA 90069, USA	
Leiferkus, Sergei P	*Opera Singer*
5 The Paddocks, Abberbury Road, Iffley, Oxford OX4 4ET, England	
Leifheit, Sylvia	*Model*
%Agentur Reed, Treppendorfer Weg 13, 12527 Berlin, Germany	
Leigh, Barbara	*Actress*
PO Box 246, Los Angeles, CA 90078, USA	
Leigh, Janet	*Actress*
1625 Summitridge Dr, Beverly Hills, CA 90210, USA	
Leigh, Jennifer Jason	*Actress*
%Edrick/Rich Mgmt, 2400 Whitman Place, Los Angeles, CA 90068, USA	
Leigh, Mike	*Movie, Theater Director*
8 Earlham Grove, London N22, England	
Leigh, Mitch	*Composer*
29 W 57th St, #1000, New York, NY 10019, USA	
Leighton, Laura	*Actress*
%United Talent Agency, 9560 Wilshire Blvd, #500, Beverly Hills, CA 90212, USA	
Leighton, Robert B	*Physicist*
%California Institute of Technology, Physics Dept, Pasadena, CA 91125, USA	
Leija, (Jesse) James	*Boxer*
9735 Richey Otis Way, San Antonio, TX 78223, USA	
Leimkuehler, Paul	*Amputee Skier, Businessman*
351 Darbys Run, Bay Village, OH 44140, USA	
Leisure, David	*Actor*
14071 Roblar Road, Sherman Oaks, CA 91423, USA	
Lejeune, Michael L	*Government Official*
80 Conejo Road, Santa Barbara, CA 93103, USA	
Lekang, Anton	*Ski Jumper*
47 Pratt St, Winsted, CT 06098, USA	
Lelouch, Claude	*Movie Director*
15 Ave Hoche, 75008 Paris, France	
Lelyveld, Joseph	*Editor*
%New York Times, Editorial Dept, 229 W 43rd St, New York, NY 10036, USA	
Lem, Stanislaw	*Writer*
%Franz Rottensteiner, Marchettigasse 9/17, 1060 Vienna, Austria	
Lemaire, Jacques	*Hockey Player, Coach*
32 Du Chene, Vaudrevil Sur Le Lac PQ H7V 5V5, Canada	
Lembeck, Michael	*Actor*
9171 Wilshire Blvd, #436, Beverly Hills, CA 90210, USA	
Lemelson, Jerome H	*Inventor*
48 Parkside Dr, Princeton, NJ 08540, USA	
Lemieux, Claude	*Hockey Player*
23 Ralph Road, West Orange, NJ 07052, USA	
Lemieux, Jocelyn	*Hockey Player*
609 London Court, Buffalo Grove, IL 60089, USA	
Lemieux, Joseph H	*Businessman*
%Owens-Illinois Inc, 1 Sea Gate, Toledo, OH 43604, USA	
Lemieux, Mario	*Hockey Player*
630 Academy St, Sewickley, PA 15143, USA	
Lemke, Mark A	*Baseball Player*
10060 High Falls Pointe, Alpharetta, GA 30022, USA	
Lemmon, Chris	*Actor*
80 Murray St, South Gastonbury, CT 06073, USA	
Lemmon, Jack	*Actor*
%Jalem Productions, 141 S El Camino Dr, #201, Beverly Hills, CA 90212, USA	
Lemon, Chester E (Chet)	*Baseball Player*
PO Box 951436, Lake Mary, FL 32795, USA	
Lemon, Meadowlark	*Basketball Player*
13610 N Scottsdale Road, #1026, Scottsdale, AZ 85254, USA	
Lemon, Peter C	*Vietnam War Army Hero (CMH)*
595 Saddlemountain Road, Colorado Springs, CO 80919, USA	
Lemon, Robert G (Bob)	*Baseball Player, Manager*
1141 Clairborne Dr, Long Beach, CA 90807, USA	
LeMond, Greg	*Cyclist*
%Greg LeMond Pro Centers, 5250 Neil Road, #101, Reno, NV 89502, USA	

Lemons, A E (Abe) — *Basketball Coach*
%Oklahoma City University, Athletic Dept, Oklahoma City, OK 73106, USA

Lemos, Richie — *Boxer*
18658 Klum Place, Rowland Heights, CA 91748, USA

Lemper, Ute — *Singer, Actress, Dancer*
%Les Visiteurs du Soir, 40 Rue de la Folie Regnault, 75011 Paris, France

Lenahan, Edward P — *Publisher*
%Fortune Magazine, Rockefeller Center, New York, NY 10020, USA

Lenard, Michael B — *Sports Executive*
%US Olympic Committee, 1 Olympia Plaza, Colorado Springs, CO 80909, USA

Lendl, Ivan — *Tennis Player*
400 5 1/2 Mile Road, Goshen, CT 06756, USA

Lenfant, Claude J M — *Physician*
%National Heart Institute, 9000 Rockville Pike, Bethesda, MD 20892, USA

Lenihan, Brian J — *Government Official, Ireland*
24 Park View, Castleknock, County Dublin, Ireland

Lenk, Maria — *Swimmer*
Rua Cupertino Durao 16, Leblon, Rio de Janeiro 22441, Brazil

Lenk, Thomas — *Sculptor*
Gemeinde Braunsbach, 7176 Schloss Tierberg, Germany

Lenkin, Melvin — *Financier*
%Columbia First Bank, 1560 Wilson Blvd, Arlington, VA 22209, USA

Lennon, Julian — *Singer, Songwriter*
%Agency For Performing Arts, 9200 Sunset Blvd, #900, Los Angeles, CA 90069, USA

Lennon, Sean — *Singer*
%Dakota Hotel, 1 W 72nd St, New York, NY 10023, USA

Lennox, Annie — *Singer (Eurythmics), Songwriter*
28 Alexander St, London W2, England

Leno, Jay — *Comedian*
1151 Tower Dr, Beverly Hills, CA 90210, USA

Lenoir, William B — *Astronaut*
%Booz-Allen Hamilton Inc, 4330 E West Highway, Bethesda, MD 20814, USA

Lenska, Rula — *Model, Actress*
306-16 Euston Road, London NW13, England

Lenz, Kay — *Actress*
5719 Allott Ave, Van Nuys, CA 91401, USA

Lenzie, Charles A — *Businessman*
%Nevada Power Co, 6226 W Sahara Ave, Las Vegas, NV 89151, USA

Leo, Melissa — *Actress*
%Agency For Performing Arts, 9200 Sunset Blvd, #900, Los Angeles, CA 90069, USA

Leonard, Bob (Slick) — *Basketball Player, Coach*
1241 Hillcrest Dr, Carmel, IN 46033, USA

Leonard, Dennis P — *Baseball Player*
4102 Evergreen Lane, Blue Springs, MO 64015, USA

Leonard, Elmore — *Writer*
2192 Yarmouth Road, Bloomfield Village, MI 48301, USA

Leonard, Hugh — *Writer*
Theros, Coliemore Road, Dalkey, County Dublin, Ireland

Leonard, Joanne — *Photographer*
%University of Michigan, Art Dept, Ann Arbor, MI 48109, USA

Leonard, Justin — *Golfer*
3304 Dartmouth Ave, Dallas, TX 75205, USA

Leonard, Ray C (Sugar Ray) — *Boxer*
4401 East-West Highway, #303, Bethesda, MD 20814, USA

Leonard, Robert Sean — *Actor*
%William Morris Agency, 151 S El Camino Dr, Beverly Hills, CA 90212, USA

Leonard, Walter F (Buck) — *Baseball Player*
605 Atlantic Ave, Rocky Mount, NC 27801, USA

Leone, Giovanni — *Prime Minister, Italy*
%Senato, Piazzi Madama 1, 00186 Rome, Italy

Leonetti, Matthew — *Cinematographer*
%Innovative Artists, 1999 Ave of Stars, #2850, Los Angeles, CA 90067, USA

Leonhart, William — *Diplomat*
2618 30th St NW, Washington, DC 20008, USA

Leoni, Tea — *Actress*
2300 W Victory Blvd, Burbank, CA 91506, USA

Leonis, John M — *Businessman*
%Litton Industries, 21240 Burbank Blvd, Woodland Hills, CA 91367, USA

Leonov, Aleksei A — *Cosmonaut, Air Force General*
%Chetek Corp, Varvarka Str 15, 103 012 Moscow, Russia

Leontief, Wassily — *Nobel Economics Laureate*
%New York University, Economic Analysis Institute, New York, NY 10003, USA

Leopold, Luna B — *Hydraulic Engineer*
400 Vermont Ave, Berkeley, CA 94707, USA

Lepage, Robert — *Actor*
%Union of Artistes, 1290 Rue St Denis, Montreal PQ H2X 3J7, Canada

Leppard, Raymond J — *Conductor*
%Indianapolis Symphony, 45 Monument Circle, Indianapolis, IN 46204, USA

Lerach, William (Bill) — *Attorney*
%Milberg Weiss Hynes Lerach, 1600 W Broadway, #1800, San Diego, CA 92101, USA

Lerner, Alfred — *Financier*
%MBNA Corp, 1100 N King St, Wilmington, DE 19884, USA

Lerner, Michael — *Actor*
%Gersh Agency, 232 N Canon Dr, Beverly Hills, CA 90210, USA

Leser, Bernard H — *Publisher*
%Conde Nast Publications, Conde Nast Bldg, 350 Madison Ave, New York, NY 10017, USA

Leser, Lawrence A — *Businessman*
%E W Scripps Co, 312 Walnut St, Cincinnati, OH 45202, USA

Lesh, Phil — *Bassist (Grateful Dead)*
PO Box 1073, San Rafael, CA 94915, USA

Leslie, Bethel — *Actress*
393 West End Ave, #11-C, New York, NY 10024, USA

Leslie, Fred W — *Astronaut*
%NASA, Johnson Space Center, 2101 NASA Road, Houston, TX 77058, USA

Leslie, Joan — *Actress*
2228 N Catalina St, Los Angeles, CA 90027, USA

Leslie, Lisa — *Basketball Player, Model*
14492 Yukon Ave, Hawthorne, CA 90250, USA

Lesser, Len — *Actor*
934 N Evergreen St, Burbank, CA 91505, USA

Lessing, Doris M — *Writer*
11 Kingscroft Road, #3, London NW2 3QE, England

Lester, Darrell — *Football Player*
3103 Meadow Oaks Dr, Temple, TX 76502, USA

Lester, Ketty — *Actress, Singer*
5931 Comey Ave, Los Angeles, CA 90034, USA

Lester, Mark L — *Movie Director*
17268 Camino Yatasto, Pacific Palisades, CA 90272, USA

Lester, Richard (Dick) — *Movie Director*
River Lane, Petersham, Surrey, England

Leto, Jared — *Actor*
%Innovative Artists, 1999 Ave of Stars, #2850, Los Angeles, CA 90067, USA

Letsie III — *King, Lesotho*
%Royal Palace, PO Box 524, Maseru, Lesotho

Lett, Leon — *Football Player*
10715 N MacArthur Blvd, #149, Irving, TX 75063, USA

Letterman, David — *Entertainer, Comedian*
%Worldwide Pants, 1697 Broadway, New York, NY 10019, USA

Leva, James R — *Businessman*
%General Public Utilities, 100 Interspace Parkway, Parsippany, NJ 07054, USA

LeVan, David M — *Businessman*
%Conrail Corp, 2001 Market St, Philadelphia, PA 19103, USA

LeVay, Simon — *Neuroscientist*
970 Palm Ave, West Hollywood, CA 90069, USA

Levenson, Harvey S — *Businessman*
%Kaman Corp, 1332 Blue Hills Ave, Bloomfield, CT 06002, USA

Leventhal, Kathy Neisloss — *Publisher*
%Vanity Fair Magazine, Conde Nast Building, 350 Madison Ave, New York, NY 10017, USA

Levert, Eddie — *Singer (The O'Jays)*
%Associated Booking Corp, 1995 Broadway, #501, New York, NY 10023, USA

Levert, Gerald — *Singer, Songwriter*
%Associated Booking Corp, 1995 Broadway, #501, New York, NY 10023, USA

Levertow, Denise — *Writer*
%New Directions Publishers, 80 8th Ave, New York, NY 10011, USA

Levi, Edward H — *Attorney General*
4950 Chicago Beach Dr, Chicago, IL 60615, USA

Levi, Wayne	*Golfer*
17 Ironwood Road, New Hartford, NY 13413, USA	
Levi-Montalcini, Rita	*Nobel Medicine Laureate*
%Cell Biology Institute, Piazzale Aldo Moro 7, 00185 Rome, Italy	
Levi-Strauss, Claude	*Anthropologist*
2 Rue Des Marronniers, 75016 Paris, France	
Levin, Gerald M	*Businessman*
%Time Warner Inc, 75 Rockefeller Plaza, New York, NY 10019, USA	
Levin, Ira	*Writer*
%Harry Ober Agency, 425 Madison Ave, New York, NY 10017, USA	
Levin, Richard C	*Educator*
%Yale University, President's Office, New Haven, CT 06520, USA	
Levin, Wilbur A	*Financier*
%Independence Savings Bank, 195 Montague St, Brooklyn, NY 11201, USA	
Levine, David	*Artist, Caricaturist*
161 Henry St, Brooklyn, NY 11201, USA	
Levine, Ellen R	*Editor*
%Good Housekeeping Magazine, 959 8th Ave, New York, NY 10019, USA	
Levine, Irving R	*Commentator*
%Lynn University, International Studies/Economics Dept, Boca Raton, FL 33431, USA	
Levine, Jack	*Artist*
68 Morton St, New York, NY 10014, USA	
Levine, James	*Conductor*
%Metropolitan Opera Assn, Lincoln Center Plaza, New York, NY 10023, USA	
Levine, Philip	*Writer*
2335 University Blvd, #2, Houston, TX 77005, USA	
Levine, Rachmiel	*Endocrinologist*
2024 Canyon Road, Arcadia, CA 91006, USA	
Levine, S Robert	*Businessman*
%Cabletron Systems, 35 Industrial Way, Rochester, NH 03867, USA	
Levine, Seymour	*Psychobiologist*
508 Summerbreeze Dr, Newark, DE 19702, USA	
Levine, Ted	*Actor*
%Innovative Artists, 1999 Ave of Stars, #2850, Los Angeles, CA 90067, USA	
Levingston, Cliff	*Basketball Player*
%Denver Nuggets, McNichols Arena, 1635 Clay St, Denver, CO 80204, USA	
Levingstone, Ken	*Government Official, England*
%House of Commons, Westminster, London SW1A 0AA, England	
Levinson, Barry	*Movie Director*
%Creative Artists Agency, 9830 Wilshire Blvd, Beverly Hills, CA 90212, USA	
Levinthal, Cyrus	*Biologist*
%Columbia University, Biological Sciences Dept, New York, NY 10027, USA	
Levitow, John L	*Vietnam War Air Force Hero (CMH)*
PO Box 741, Rocky Hill, CT 06067, USA	
Levy, Bernard-Henri	*Philosopher*
%Editions Bernans Grasset, 61 Rue des Saints-Penes, 75006 Paris, France	
Levy, David	*Government Official, Israel*
%Foreign Affairs Ministry, Hakirya, Romema, Jerusalem, Israel	
Levy, David	*Astronomer*
%Mount Palomar Observatory, Palomar Mountain, Mount Palomar, CA 92060, USA	
Levy, Irvin L	*Businessman*
%NCH Corp, 2727 Chemsearch Blvd, Irving, TX 75062, USA	
Levy, Joseph W	*Businessman*
%Gottschalks Inc, 7 River Park Place E, Fresno, CA 93720, USA	
Levy, Leon	*Financier*
%Odyssey Partners, 31 W 52nd St, New York, NY 10019, USA	
Levy, Leonard W	*Writer, Historian*
1025 Timberline Terrace, Ashland, OR 97520, USA	
Levy, Lester A	*Businessman*
%NCH Corp, 2727 Chemsearch Blvd, Irving, TX 75062, USA	
Levy, Marvin D (Marv)	*Football Coach*
%Buffalo Bills, 1 Bills Dr, Orchard Park, NY 14127, USA	
Levy, Michael R	*Publisher*
%Texas Monthly Magazine, PO Box 1569, Austin, TX 78767, USA	
Levy, Paul	*Editor*
2014 7th Court S, Lake Worth, FL 33461, USA	
Levy, Robert I	*Physician*
%Wyeth-Ayest Laboratories, PO Box 8299, Philadelphia, PA 19101, USA	

L

Levi - Levy

Lewin of Greenwich, Terence T *Royal Navy Fleet Admiral, England*
%House of Lords, Westminster, London SW1A 0PW, England

LeWinter, Nancy Nadler *Publisher*
%Esquire Magazine, 250 W 55th St, New York, NY 10019, USA

Lewis (Christianni Brand), Mary *Writer*
88 Maida Vale, London W9, England

Lewis, Al *Actor*
PO Box 277, New York, NY 10044, USA

Lewis, Albert *Football Player*
5456 Blackhawk Dr, Danville, CA 94506, USA

Lewis, Allen *Government Official, Saint Lucia*
Beaver Lodge, The Morn, PO Box 1076, Castries, Saint Lucia, West Indies

Lewis, Andrew L (Drew), Jr *Secretary, Transportation; Businessman*
%Union Pacific Corp, Martin Tower, 8th & Eaton Aves, Bethlehem, PA 18018, USA

Lewis, Anthony *Columnist*
%New York Times, Editorial Dept, 2 Faneuil Hall, Boston, MA 02109, USA

Lewis, Barbara *Singer*
%Hello Stranger Productions, PO Box 300488, Fern Park, FL 32730, USA

Lewis, Bobby *Singer*
%Neal Hollander, 9936 Majoraca Place, Boca Raton, FL 33434, USA

Lewis, Charlotte *Actress*
%Agency For Performing Arts, 9200 Sunset Blvd, #900, Los Angeles, CA 90069, USA

Lewis, David Levering *Writer*
%Rutgers University, History Dept, East Rutherford, NJ 08903, USA

Lewis, Dawnn *Actress*
PO Box 56718, Sherman Oaks, CA 91413, USA

Lewis, Edward B *Nobel Medicine Laureate*
%California Institute of Technology, Biology Dept, Pasadena, CA 91125, USA

Lewis, Emmanuel *Actor*
1900 Ave of Stars, #2800, Los Angeles, CA 90067, USA

Lewis, F Carlton (Carl) *Track Athlete*
PO Box 571990, Houston, TX 77257, USA

Lewis, Flora *Writer, Journalist*
%New York Times, Editorial Dept, 229 W 43rd St, New York, NY 10036, USA

Lewis, Gary *Singer (Gary Lewis & The Playboys)*
701 Balin Court, Nashville, TN 37221, USA

Lewis, Geoffrey *Actor*
6120 Shirley Ave, Tarzana, CA 91356, USA

Lewis, Huey *Singer, Actor*
%Bob Brown Mgmt, PO Box 779, Mill Valley, CA 94942, USA

Lewis, Jason *Actor*
%International Creative Mgmt, 8942 Wilshire Blvd, Beverly Hills, CA 90211, USA

Lewis, Jerome A *Businessman*
%Princeps Partners, 1775 Sherman St, Denver, CO 80203, USA

Lewis, Jerry *Comedian, Director*
1701 Waldman Ave, Las Vegas, NV 89102, USA

Lewis, Jerry Lee *Singer, Pianist, Composer*
Lewis Farms, Nesbit, MS 38651, USA

Lewis, John *Jazz Pianist, Composer*
%Ted Kurland, 173 Brighton Ave, Boston, MA 02134, USA

Lewis, John C, Jr *Businessman*
%Amdahl Corp, 1250 E Arques Ave, Sunnyvale, CA 94086, USA

Lewis, Juliette *Actress*
%William Morris Agency, 151 S El Camino Dr, Beverly Hills, CA 90212, USA

Lewis, Lennox *Boxer*
%Champion Enterprises, 84 Greens Lanes, London N16 9EJ, England

Lewis, Marilyn W *Businessman*
%American Water Works, 1025 Laurel Oak Road, Voorhees, NJ 08043, USA

Lewis, Monica *Singer*
%Lang, 1100 Alta Loma Road, #16-A, Los Angeles, CA 90069, USA

Lewis, Ramsey *Jazz Pianist, Composer*
%Gardner Howard Ring, 16601 Ventura Blvd, #508, Encino, CA 91436, USA

Lewis, Ray *Football Player*
%Baltimore Ravens, 200 St Paul Place, #2400, Baltimore, MD 21202, USA

Lewis, Richard *Acotr, Comedian*
8001 Hemet Place, Los Angeles, CA 90046, USA

Lewis, Russell T *Publisher*
%New York Times, 229 W 43rd St, New York, NY 10036, USA

Lewis, Samuel W *Diplomat*
%US Institute for Peace, 4701 Willard Ave, #1216, Bethesda, MD 20815, USA
Lewis, Shari *Ventriloquist, Puppeteer*
603 N Alta Dr, Beverly Hills, CA 90210, USA
Lewis, Vicki *Actress, Comedienne*
%William Morris Agency, 151 S El Camino Dr, Beverly Hills, CA 90212, USA
Lewis, Victor *Jazz Drummer*
%Joanne Klein, 130 W 28th St, New York, NY 10001, USA
Lewit-Nirenberg, Julie *Publisher*
%Mademoiselle Magazine, 350 Madison Ave, New York, NY 10017, USA
Lewitt, Sol *Artist*
20 Pratt St, Chester, CT 06412, USA
Lewitzky, Bella *Dancer, Choreographer*
%Lewitzky Dance Co, 3594 Multiview Dr, Los Angeles, CA 90068, USA
Leye, Jean-Marie *President, Vanuatu*
%President's Office, Vila, Vanuatu
Leygue, Louis Georges *Sculptor*
6 Rue de Docteur Blanche, 75016 Paris, France
Leyland, James R (Jim) *Baseball Manager*
30 Midway Road, Pittsburgh, PA 15216, USA
Leyritz, James J (Jim) *Baseball Player*
7911 Egungton Court, Cincinnati, OH 45255, USA
Leyton, John *Actor, Singer*
53 Keyes House, Dolphin Square, London SW1V 3NA, England
Leyva, Nicholas T (Nick) *Baseball Manager*
1098 Tilghman Road, Wayne, PA 19087, USA
Lezy, Normand G (Norm) *Air Force General*
Deputy Military Manpower/Personnel Police, Defense Dept, Washington, DC 20301, USA
Li Ka-Shing *Businessman*
%Hutchison Whampoa, Hutchison House, 10 Harvard Road, Hong Kong, China
Li Lanqing *Government Official, China*
%Communist Party Central Committee, Zhong Nan Hai, Beijing, China
Li Peng *Premier, China*
%Communist Party Central Committee, Zhong Nan Hai, Beijing, China
Li, Choh H *Biochemist*
901 Arlington Ave, Berkeley, CA 94707, USA
Li, Frederick *Molecular Biologist*
%Dana-Farber Cancer Institute, 44 Binney St, Boston, MA 02115, USA
Liacouras, Peter J *Educator*
%Temple University, President's Office, Philadelphia, PA 19122, USA
Liaklev, Reidar *Speed Skater*
2770 Jaren, Norway
Liberman, Alexander *Editor, Artist*
%Conde Nast Publications, 350 Madison Ave, New York, NY 10017, USA
Libertini, Richard *Actor*
2313 McKinley Ave, Venice, CA 90291, USA
Lichfield, Earl of (T Patrick J A) *Photographer*
133 Oxford Gardens, London 10 6NE, England
Licht, Jeremy *Actor*
4355 Clybourn Ave, Toluca Lake, CA 91602, USA
Lichtenberg, Byron K *Astronaut*
%Omega Aerospace Inc, 728 Wolfsnare Crescent, Virginia Beach, VA 23454, USA
Lichtenstein, Harvey *Musical Director*
%Brooklyn Academy of Music, 30 Lafayette Ave, Brooklyn, NY 11217, USA
Lick, Dennis *Football Player*
6140 S Knox Ave, Chicago, IL 60629, USA
Liddy, G Gordon *Watergate Figure*
9909 E Joshua Tree Lane, #E, Scottsdale, AZ 85253, USA
Liddy, Richard A *Businessman*
%General American Life, 700 Market St, St Louis, MO 63101, USA
Lidov, Arthur *Artist*
Pleasant Ridge Road, Poughquag, NY 12570, USA
Lidow, Eric *Businessman*
%International Rectifier Corp, 233 Kansas St, El Segundo, CA 90245, USA
Lidstrom, Nicklas *Hockey Player*
%Detroit Red Wings, Joe Louis Arena, 600 Civic Center Dr, Detroit, MI 48226, USA
Lieber, Larry *Cartoonist (Amazing Spider-Man)*
%Marvel Comics Group, 387 Park Ave S, New York, NY 10016, USA

L

Lewis - Lieber

Lieberman, Seymour *Biochemist*
%St Luke's-Roosevelt Health Science Institute, 432 W 58th St, New York, NY 10019, USA

Lieberman, William S *Museum Curator*
%Metropolitan Museum of Art, 5th Ave & 82nd St, New York, NY 10028, USA

Lieberman-Cline, Nancy *Basketball Player*
6616 Dupper Court, Dallas, TX 75252, USA

Liebeskind, John *Brain Surgeon, Psychologist*
%University of California, Medical Center, Surgery Dept, Los Angeles, CA 90024, USA

Liebman, David *Jazz Saxophonist*
%Richard A Barz, Rt 1, Box 91, Tannersville, PA 18372, USA

Liebowitz, Leo *Businessman*
%Getty Petroleum Corp, 125 Jericho Turnpike, Jericho, NY 11753, USA

Liefeld, Rob *Cartoonist (Youngblood)*
%Image Comics, 1440 N Harbor Blvd, #305, Fullerton, CA 92835, USA

Lien Chan *Prime Minister, Taiwan*
%Prime Minister's Office, 1 Chunghsiano East Road, Sec 1, Taipei, Taiwan

Lien, Jennifer *Actress*
1700 Varilla Dr, West Covina, CA 91792, USA

Lienhard, Bill *Basketball Player*
1320 Lawrence Ave, Lawrence, KS 66049, USA

Liepa, Adris *Ballet Dancer*
%Kirov Ballet Theatre, 1 Pl Iskusstr, St Petersburg, Russia

Lietzke, Bruce *Golfer*
5716 Arcady Place, Plano, TX 75093, USA

Lifford, Tina *Actress*
%Ambrosio/Mortimer, 9150 Wilshire Blvd, #175, Beverly Hills, CA 90212, USA

Lifvendahl, Harold R *Publisher*
%Orlando Sentinel, 633 N Orange Ave, Orlando, FL 32801, USA

Ligeti, Gyorgy S *Composer*
Himmelhofgasse 34, 1130 Vienna, Austria

Light, Judith *Actress*
2930 Beverly Glen Circle, #30, Los Angeles, CA 90077, USA

Light, Murray B *Editor*
%Buffalo News, Editorial Dept, 1 News Plaza, Buffalo, NY 14203, USA

Lightfoot, Gordon *Singer, Songwriter*
1365 Yonge St, #207, Toronto ON M4T 2P7, Canada

Lightner, Candy *Social Activist*
%Berman Co, 607 14th St NW, Washington, DC 20005, USA

Liguori, Frank N *Businessman*
%Olsten Corp, 175 Broad Hollow Road, Melville, NY 11747, USA

Likens, Gene E *Ecologist*
%Ecosystem Studies Institute, New Botanical Gardens, Box AB, Millbrook, NY 12545, USA

Likins, Peter W *Educator*
%Lehigh University, President's Office, Bethlehem, PA 18015, USA

Lilic, Zoran *President, Yugoslavia*
%President's Office, Bul Lenjina 2, 11 070 Novi Belgrade, Yugoslavia

Lilienfeld, Abraham M *Epidemiologist*
3203 Old Post Dr, Pikesville, MD 21208, USA

Lill, John R *Concert Pianist*
%Harold Holt, 31 Sinclair Road, London W14 0NS, England

Lillee, Dennis K *Cricketer*
%WACA Ground, Nelson Crescent, East Perth 6000 WA, Australia

Lillehei, C Walton *Surgeon*
73 Otis Lane, St Paul, MN 55104, USA

Lilley, James R *Diplomat*
7301 Maple Ave, Bethesda, MD 20815, USA

Lillie, John M *Businessman*
%American President Cos, 1111 Broadway, Oakland, CA 94607, USA

Lilly, John C *Dolphin Researcher*
%Human/Dolphin Foundation, 11930 Oceanaire Lane, Malibu, CA 90265, USA

Lilly, Robert L (Bob) *Football Player*
104 Aster Circle, Georgetown, TX 78628, USA

Lima, Luis *Opera Singer*
1950 Redondela Dr, Rancho Palos Verdes, CA 90275, USA

Limbaugh, Rush *Entertainer*
PO Box 526, New York, NY 10028, USA

Lime, Yvonne *Actress*
16071 Royal Oak Road, Encino, CA 91436, USA

Lin Ching-Hsia — *Actress*
%Taiwan Cinema-Drama Assn, 196 Chunghua Road, 10/F, Sec 1 Taipei, Taiwan
Lin, Bridget — *Actress*
8 Fei Ngo Shan Road, Kowloon, Hong Kong, China
Lin, Chia-Chiao — *Applied Mathematician*
%Massachusetts Institute of Technology, Mathematics Dept, Cambridge, MA 02139, USA
Lin, Cho-Liang — *Concert Violinist*
473 West End Ave, #15-A, New York, NY 10024, USA
Lin, Maya Ying — *Sculptor, Achitect*
%Sidney Janis Gallery, 110 W 57th St, New York, NY 10019, USA
Lin, Tsung-Yi — *Psychiatrist*
6287 MacDonald St, Vancouver BC V6N 1E7, Canada
Lin, Tung Yen — *Civil Engineer*
8701 Don Carol Dr, El Cerrito, CA 94530, USA
Linander, Nils — *Businessman*
%Saab-Scania, 581 88 Linkoping, Sweden
Lincoln, Abbey — *Singer, Songwriter*
645 West End Ave, New York, NY 10025, USA
Lincoln, Keith P — *Football Player*
SE 770 Ridgeview Court, Pullman, WA 99163, USA
Lind, Don L — *Astronaut*
%Utah State University, Physics Dept, Logan, UT 84322, USA
Lind, Geoffrey E — *Financier*
%UMB Financial Corp, 1010 Grand Ave, St Louis, MO 64106, USA
Lind, Joan — *Rowing Athlete*
240 Euclid Ave, Long Beach, CA 90803, USA
Lind, Marshall L — *Educator*
%University of Alaska Southeast, Chancellor's Office, Juneau, AK 99801, USA
Lindbergh, Anne Morrow — *Writer*
PO Box 157, Peacham, VT 05862, USA
Linden, Hal — *Actor*
416 N Bristol Ave, Los Angeles, CA 90049, USA
Linder, Kate — *Actress*
9111 Wonderland Ave, Los Angeles, CA 90046, USA
Lindgren, Astrid — *Writer*
Dalagatan 46, 113 24 Stockholm, Sweden
Lindh, Hilary — *Skier*
PO Box 33036, Juneau, AK 99803, USA
Lindig, Bill M — *Businessman*
%SYSCO Corp, 1390 Enclave Parkway, Houston, TX 77077, USA
Lindley, Audra — *Actress*
200 N Swall Dr, #PH-58, Beverly Hills, CA 90211, USA
Lindner, Carl H — *Businessman*
%Chiquita Brands International, 250 E 5th St, Cincinnati, OH 45202, USA
Lindner, Keith E — *Businessman*
%Chiquita Brands International, 250 E 5th St, Cincinnati, OH 45202, USA
Lindner, William G — *Labor Leader*
%Transport Workers Union, 80 West End Ave, New York, NY 10023, USA
Lindros, Eric — *Hockey Player*
%Philadelphia Flyers, CoreStates Center, Pattison Place, Philadelphia, PA 19148, USA
Lindroth, Eric — *Water Polo Player*
13151 Dufresne Place, San Diego, CA 92129, USA
Lindsay, Jack — *Writer*
56 Maids Causeway, Cambridge, England
Lindsay, Mark — *Singer, Songwriter*
%North River Entertainment, PO Box 210, Elk City, ID 83525, USA
Lindsay, Robert — *Actor, Singer*
%William Morris Agency, 31/32 Soho Square, London W1V 5DG, England
Lindsay, Ted — *Hockey Player*
398 Longford Dr, Rochester Hills, MI 48309, USA
Lindsey, George — *Actor, Singer*
%Artists Agency, 10000 Santa Monica Blvd, #305, Los Angeles, CA 90067, USA
Lindsey, Johanna — *Writer*
%William Morrow, 1350 Ave of Americas, New York, NY 10016, USA
Lindsey, Lawrence B — *Financier, Government Official*
%Federal Reserve Board, 20th St & Constitution NW, Washington, DC 20551, USA
Lindsey, Steven W — *Astronaut*
%NASA, Johnson Space Center, 2101 NASA Road, Houston, TX 77058, USA

L

Lin Ching-Hsia - Lindsey

Lindsley, Donald B	*Psychologist, Physiologist*
471 23rd St, Santa Monica, CA 90402, USA	
Lindstrand, Per	*Balloonist*
%Thunder & Colt, Maesbury Road, Oswestry, Shropshire SY10 8HA, England	
Lindvall, Olle	*Neurologist*
%University of Lund, Medical Cell Research Dept, 233 62 Lund, Sweden	
Lindwall, Raymond R	*Cricketer*
3 Wentworth Court, Endeavour St, Mt Ommaney, Brisbane 4074 QLD, Australia	
Lineker, Gary W	*Soccer Player*
19 John Charnwood Ave, Westone, Northampton NN3 3DX, England	
Linenger, Jerry M	*Astronaut*
%NASA, Johnson Space Center, 2101 NASA Road, Houston, TX 77058, USA	
Liney, John	*Cartoonist (Henry)*
%King Features Syndicate, 235 E 45th St, New York, NY 10017, USA	
Ling, James J	*Businessman*
5950 Lindenshire Lane, #307, Dallas, TX 75230, USA	
Link, Arthur A	*Governor, ND*
2201 Grimsrud Dr, Bismarck, ND 58501, USA	
Link, O Winston	*Photographer*
%Thomas H Garver, PO Box 3493, Madison, WI 53704, USA	
Linkert, Lo	*Cartoonist*
1333 Vivian Way, Port Coquitlam BC, Canada	
Linkletter, Art	*Entertainer*
1100 Bel Air Road, Los Angeles, CA 90077, USA	
Linkletter, John A	*Editor*
%Popular Mechanics Magazine, Editorial Dept, 224 W 57th St, New York, NY 10019, USA	
Linn, Teri Ann	*Actress*
4267 Marina City Dr, #312, Marina del Rey, CA 90292, USA	
Linn-Baker, Mark	*Actor*
%Jaime Harvey, 2700 Neilson Way, #1624, Santa Monica, CA 90405, USA	
Linnehan, Richard M	*Astronaut*
%NASA, Johnson Space Center, 2101 NASA Road, Houston, TX 77058, USA	
Linney, Laura	*Actress*
145 W 45th St, #1204, New York, NY 10036, USA	
Linseman, Ken	*Hockey Player*
1200 Busleton Pike, #6, Feasterville Trevose, PA 19053, USA	
Linson, Art	*Movie Director, Producer*
%Art Linson Productions, Warner Bros, 4000 Warner Blvd, Burbank, CA 91522, USA	
Linteris, Gregory T	*Astronaut*
%National Standards/Technology Institute, Gaithersburg, MD 20877, USA	
Linville, Joanne	*Actress*
3148 Fryman Road, Studio City, CA 91604, USA	
Linville, Larry	*Actor*
%Robert Cosden Agency, 3518 Cahuenga Blvd W, #216, Los Angeles 90068, USA	
Lionetti, Donald M	*Army General*
Commanding General, US Army Space/Strategic Defense Cmd, Arlington, VA 22215, USA	
Liotta, Ray	*Actor*
16829 Monte Hermosa Dr, Pacific Palisades, CA 90272, USA	
Lipinski, Ann Marie	*Journalist*
%Chicago Tribune, Editorial Dept, 435 N Michigan Ave, Chicago, IL 60611, USA	
Lipinski, Tara	*Figure Skater*
%US Figure Skating Assn, 20 1st St, Colorado Springs, CO 80906, USA	
Lipkin, Gerald H	*Financier*
%Valley National Bancorp, 1445 Valley Road, Wayne, NJ 07470, USA	
Lipovsek, Marjana	*Opera Singer*
Rottmaygrasse 16, 5020 Salzburg, Austria	
Lipp, Robert I	*Financier*
%Travelers Inc, 388 Greenwich St, New York, NY 10013, USA	
Lipper, Kenneth	*Financier*
%Lipper Co, 101 Park Ave, New York, NY 10178, USA	
Lippold, Richard	*Artist*
PO Box 248, Locust Valley, NY 11560, USA	
Lipponen, Paavo	*Prime Minister, Finland*
%Prime Minister's Office, Aleksanterinkatu, 00170 Helsinki, Finland	
Lipps, Louis	*Football Player*
276 Annex Dr, Reserve, LA 70084, USA	
Lipscomb, William N, Jr	*Nobel Chemistry Laureate*
%Harvard University, Gibbs Chemical Laboratory, Cambridge, MA 02138, USA	

Lipset, Seymour M *Sociologist*
900 N Stafford St, #2131, Arlington, VA 22203, USA

Lipsett, Mortimer B *Physician*
%National Institutes of Health, 9000 Rockville Pike, Bethesda, MD 20892, USA

Lipsey, Stanford *Publisher*
%Buffalo News, 1 News Plaza, Buffalo, NY 14203, USA

Lipshutz, Bruce H *Organic Chemist*
%University of California, Chemistry Dept, Santa Barbara, CA 93106, USA

Lipson, D Herbert *Publisher*
%Philadelphia Magazine, 1500 Walnut St, Philadelphia, PA 19102, USA

Lipton, Martin *Attorney*
%Wachtell Lipton Rosen Katz, 51 W 52nd St, New York, NY 10019, USA

Lipton, Peggy *Actress*
2576 Benedict Canyon Dr, Beverly Hills, CA 90210, USA

Liquori, Marty *Track Athlete, Sportscaster*
2915 NW 58th Blvd, Gainesville, FL 32606, USA

Lisa Lisa (Lisa Velez) *Singer (Lisa Lisa & Cult Jam)*
%Talent Consultants Int'l, 1560 Broadway, #1308, New York, NY 10036, USA

Lisi, Virna *Actress*
Via di Filomarino 4, Rome, Italy

Lissouba, Pascal *President, Congo*
%President's Office, Palace du Peuple, Brazzaville, Congo

List, Robert F *Governor, NV*
50 W Liberty St, #210, Reno, NV 89501, USA

Lister, Alton *Basketball Player*
233 Hudson Bay, Alameda, CA 94502, USA

Listowel (William F Hare), Earl of *Government Official, England*
10 Downshire Hill, London NW3, England

Lithgow, John *Actor*
1319 Warnall Ave, Los Angeles, CA 90024, USA

Little Anthony (Gordine) *Singer*
%Entity Communications, 874 Ave of Americas, #1908, New York, NY 10001, USA

Little Eva *Singer*
%Cape Entertainment, 1161 NW 76th Ave, Fort Lauderdale, FL 33322, USA

Little Milton *Singer, Guitarist*
%Camil Productions, 2101 E 79th St, #5, Chicago, IL 60649, USA

Little Richard (Penniman) *Singer*
%Hyatt Sunset Hotel, 8401 W Sunset Blvd, Los Angeles, CA 90069, USA

Little Steven *Singer*
%Premier Talent, 3 E 54th St, #1100, New York, NY 10022, USA

Little, Bernard L (Bernie) *Boat Racing Driver, Owner*
%Little Co, 3232 Maine Ave, Lakeland, FL 33801, USA

Little, Carole *Fashion Designer*
%Carole Little Inc, PO Box 77917, Los Angeles, CA 90007, USA

Little, Charles L *Labor Leader*
%United Transportation Union, 14600 Detroit Ave, Cleveland, OH 44107, USA

Little, David L *Football Player*
10460 SW 140th St, Miami, FL 33176, USA

Little, Floyd D *Football Player*
31315 22nd Ave SW, Federal Way, WA 98023, USA

Little, Larry *Football Player, Coach*
5310 Lacy Road, Durham, NC 27713, USA

Little, Rich *Comedian, Actor*
%Rich Little Enterprises, 21550 Oxnard St, #630, Woodland Hills, CA 91367, USA

Little, Robert A *Chef*
49 Firth St, London W1V 5TE, England

Little, Roberta *Model*
%Click Model Mgmt, 881 7th Ave, New York, NY 10019, USA

Little, Sally *Golfer*
%Endicott Assoc, PO Box 10850, Palm Desert, CA 92255, USA

Little, Tawny *Entertainer*
17941 Sky Park Circle, #F, Irvine, CA 92614, USA

Littler, Gene *Golfer*
PO Box 1949, Rancho Santa Fe, CA 92067, USA

Littles, Gene *Basketball Coach*
%Denver Nuggets, McNichols Arena, 1635 Clay St, Denver, CO 80204, USA

Littleton, Harvey K *Sculptor*
Rt 1, Box 843, Spruce Pine, NC 28777, USA

Litton, Andrew   *Conductor*
%IMG Artists, Media House, 3 Burlington Lane, London W4 2TH, England

Littrell, Gary L   *Vietnam War Army Hero (CMH)*
4302 Belle Vista Dr, St Petersburg, FL 33706, USA

Litwack, Harry   *Basketball Coach*
1818 Oakwynne Road, Huntingdon Valley, PA 19006, USA

Liu, Lee   *Businessman*
%IES Industries, 200 1st St SE, Cedar Rapids, IA 52401, USA

Liut, Mike   *Hockey Player*
127 Old Canal Way, Weatoque, CT 06089, USA

Lively, Penelope M   *Writer*
Duck End, Great Rollright, Chipping, Northern Oxfordshire OX7 5SB, England

Lively, Robyn   *Actress*
541 10th St NW, #302, Atlanta, GA 30318, USA

Livingston, Barry   *Actor*
11310 Blix St, North Hollywood, CA 91602, USA

Livingston, James E   *Vietnam Marine Corps Hero (CMH), General*
3609 Red Oak Court, New Orleans, LA 70131, USA

Livingston, Stanley   *Actor*
PO Box 1782, Studio City, CA 91614, USA

Lizer, Kari   *Actress*
13410 Killion St, Sherman Oaks, CA 91401, USA

LL Cool J (James Todd Smith)   *Rap Artist, Actor*
%Rush Artists, 1600 Varick St, New York, NY 10013, USA

Llewellyn, John A   *Astronaut*
4202 E Fowler Ave, Tampa, FL 33620, USA

Lloyd Webber, Andrew   *Composer*
%Really Useful Group PLC, 20 Greek St, London W1V 5LF, England

Lloyd, Christopher   *Actor*
%Managemint, PO Box 491246, Los Angeles, CA 90049, USA

Lloyd, Clive   *Cricketer*
%Harefield, Harefield Dr, Wilmslow, Cheshire SK9 1NJ, England

Lloyd, Emily   *Actress*
%Malcolm Sheddon Mgmt, 1 Charlotte Square, London W1P 1DH, England

Lloyd, George W S   *Conductor, Composer*
109 Clarence Gate Gardens, Glentworth St, London NW1 6AU, England

Lloyd, Georgina   *Writer*
%Bantam Books, 1540 Broadway, New York, NY 10036, USA

Lloyd, Greg   *Football Player*
215 Pebble Beach Dr, Fayetteville, GA 30215, USA

Lloyd, Kathleen   *Actress*
%House of Representatives, 400 S Beverly Dr, #101, Beverly Hills, CA 90212, USA

Lloyd, Norman   *Actor*
1813 Old Ranch Road, Los Angeles, CA 90049, USA

Lloyd, Robert A   *Opera Singer*
67-B Fortis Green, London SE1 9HL, England

Lloyd-Jones, David M   *Conductor*
94 Whitelands House, Cheltenham Terrace, London SW3 4RA, England

Lo Bianco, Tony   *Actor*
327 Central Park W, #16-B, New York, NY 10025, USA

Loach, Kenneth (Ken)   *Movie Director*
%Judy Daish, 2 St Charles Place, London W10 6EG, England

Lobbia, John E   *Businessman*
%Detroit Edison, 2000 2nd Ave, Detroit, MI 48226, USA

Lobo   *Singer, Songwriter*
707 18th Ave S, Nashville, TN 37203, USA

Lobo, Rebecca   *Basketball Player*
216 Klaus Anderson Road, Southwick, MA 01077, USA

Lobov, Oleg I   *Government Official, Russia*
%Security Council, Secretary's Office, Kremlin, Moscow, Russia

Local, Ivars Godmanis   *Prime Minister, Latvia*
Brivibus Bluv 36, PDP Riga 226170, Latvia

Locane, Amy   *Actress*
%Don Buchwald, 10 E 44th St, New York, NY 10017, USA

Locatelli, Paul L   *Educator*
%Santa Clara University, President's Office, Santa Clara, CA 95053, USA

Locher, Richard (Dick)   *Editorial Cartoonist*
%Chicago Tribune, Editorial Dept, 435 N Michigan Ave, Chicago, IL 60611, USA

Lochhead, Kenneth C — *Artist*
35 Wilton Crescent, Ottawa ON K1S 2T4, Canada
Lochner, Philip R, Jr — *Government Official, Businessman*
%Time Warner Inc, 75 Rockefeller Plaza, New York, NY 10019, USA
Lockard, John A — *Navy Admiral*
Commander, Naval Air Systems Command, Navy Department, Washington, DC 20361, USA
Locke, Gary — *Governor, WA*
%Governor's Office, State Capitol, Olympia, WA 98504, USA
Locke, Sondra — *Actress*
PO Box 69865, Los Angeles, CA 90069, USA
Lockhart, Anne — *Actress*
191 Upper Lake Road, Thousand Oaks, CA 91361, USA
Lockhart, James — *Conductor*
105 Woodcock Hill, Harrow, Middx HA3 0JJ, England
Lockhart, June — *Actress*
%Agency For Performing Arts, 9200 Sunset Blvd, #900, Los Angeles, CA 90069, USA
Lockhart, Keith — *Conductor*
%Boston Pops Orchestra, Symphony Hall, 301 Massachusetts Ave, Boston, MA 02115, USA
Lockhart, Michael D — *Businessman*
%General Signal Corp, 1 High Ridge Park, Stamford, CT 06905, USA
Locklear, Heather — *Actress*
%Creative Artists Agency, 9830 Wilshire Blvd, Beverly Hills, CA 90212, USA
Lockridge, Richard K — *Businessman*
%Dynatech Corp, 3 New England Executive Park, Burlington, MA 01803, USA
Lockwood, Gary — *Actor*
1065 E Loma Alta Dr, Altadena, CA 91001, USA
Lockwood, Julia — *Actress*
112 Castlenan, London SW13, England
Loderbaum, Jeffrey S — *Businessman*
%Mohawk Industries, 1755 The Exchange, Atlanta, GA 30339, USA
Loderer, Eugen — *Businessman*
%Gewerkschaftsfuhrer, Sudetenstr 2, 89518 Heidenheim, Germany
Lodge, David John — *Writer*
%University of Birmingham, English Dept, Birmingham B15 2TT, England
Loe, Harald A — *Dentist*
%National Dental Research Institute, 9000 Rockville Pike, Bethesda, MD 20892, USA
Loeb, David S — *Financier*
%Countrywide Credit, 155 N Lake Ave, Pasadena, CA 91101, USA
Loeb, John L, Jr — *Diplomat, Financier*
%Loeb Partners, 375 Park Ave, #801, New York, NY 10152, USA
Loeb, Lisa — *Singer, Songwriter*
1028 3rd Ave, #A, New York, NY 10021, USA
Loeb, Marshall R — *Editor*
31 Montrose Road, Scarsdale, NY 10583, USA
Lofgren, Nils — *Singer, Songwriter, Guitarist*
%Anson Smith Mgmt, 3 Bethesda Metro Center, #505, Bethesda, MD 20814, USA
Lofton, Fred C — *Religious Leader*
%Progressive National Baptist Convention, 601 50th St NE, Washington, DC 20019, USA
Lofton, James — *Football Player*
5517 Linmore Lane, Plano, TX 75093, USA
Lofton, Kenneth (Kenny) — *Baseball Player*
PO Box 573, Cotano, AZ 85652, USA
Logan, Don — *Publisher*
%Time Inc, Time-Life Building, Rockefeller Center, New York, NY 10020, USA
Logan, Jack — *Singer*
%William Morris Agency, 1325 Ave of Americas, New York, NY 10019, USA
Logan, James M — *WW II Army Hero (CMH)*
801 Emmons, Kilgore, TX 75662, USA
Logan, John (Johnny) — *Baseball Player*
6115 W Cleveland Ave, Milwaukee, WI 53219, USA
Logan, Rayford W — *Writer, Historian*
3001 Veazey Terrace NW, Washington, DC 20008, USA
Logan, Robert — *Actor*
%BDP Assoc, 10637 Burbank Blvd, North Hollywood, CA 91601, USA
Loggia, Robert — *Actor*
544 Bellagio Terrace, Los Angeles, CA 90049, USA
Loggins, Kenny — *Singer, Songwriter*
670 Oak Springs Lane, Santa Barbara, CA 93108, USA

L

Lochhead - Loggins

Lohman, Gordon R *Businessman*
%Amsted Industries, 205 N Michigan Ave, Chicago, IL 60601, USA

Lohman, James J *Businessman*
%Excel Industries, 1120 N Main St, Elkhart, IN 46514, USA

Lohr, Bob *Golfer*
8929 Bay Cove Court, Orlando, FL 32819, USA

Loiola, Jose *Volleyball Player*
%Assn of Volleyball Pros, 330 Washington Blvd, #600, Marina del Rey, CA 90292, USA

Lokoloko, Tore *Governor General, Papua New Guinea*
%Indosuez Niugine Bank, Burns House, Port Moresby, Papua New Guinea

Lolich, Michael S (Mickey) *Baseball Player*
6252 Robin Hill, Washington, MI 48094, USA

Lollobrigida, Gina *Actress*
Via Appia Antica 223, 00178 Rome, Italy

Lom, Herbert *Actor*
%International Creative Mgmt, 76 Oxford St, London W1N 0AX, England

Lomas, Eric J *Businessman*
%Willcox & Gibbs Inc, 150 Alhambra Circle, Coral Gables, FL 33134, USA

Lomax, Alan *Folk Song Collector, Producer*
450 W 41st St, #600, New York, NY 10036, USA

Lomax, Neil V *Football Player*
11510 SW Military Court, Portland, OR 97219, USA

Lombard, Karina *Actress, Model*
%Gersh Agency, 232 N Canon Dr, Beverly Hills, CA 90210, USA

Lombard, Louise *Actress*
%Annette Stone, 9 Newburgh St, London W1V 1LH, England

Lombardi, John V *Educator*
%University of Florida, President's Office, Gainesville, FL 32611, USA

Lombreglio, Ralph *Writer*
%Doubleday, 1540 Broadway, New York, NY 10036, USA

Lonborg, James R (Jim) *Baseball Player*
498 First Parish Road, Scituate, MA 02066, USA

London, Irving M *Physician*
%Harvard-MIT Health Sciences, 77 Massachusetts Ave, Cambridge, MA 02139, USA

London, Jeremy *Actor*
%Gersh Agency, 232 N Canon Dr, Beverly Hills, CA 90210, USA

London, Julie *Actress, Singer*
16074 Royal Oak Road, Encino, CA 91436, USA

London, Lisa *Actress, Model*
8949 Sunset Blvd, #201, Los Angeles, CA 90069, USA

Lone, John *Actor*
%Levine Thall Plotkin, 1740 Broadway, New York, NY 10019, USA

Long, Chuck *Football Player*
28352 Rancho Grande, Laguna Niguel, CA 92677, USA

Long, Dale W *Publisher*
%Working Woman Magazine, 342 Madison Ave, New York, NY 10173, USA

Long, Dallas *Track Athlete*
1337 Galaxy Dr, Newport Beach, CA 92660, USA

Long, David L *Publisher*
%Sports Illustrated Magazine, Rockefeller Center, New York, NY 10020, USA

Long, Elizabeth Valk *Publisher*
%Time Magazine, Rockefeller Center, New York, NY 10020, USA

Long, Francis A *Businessman*
%Pennsylvania Power & Light, 2 N 9th St, Allentown, PA 18101, USA

Long, Franklin A *Chemist*
650 Harrison Ave, #446, Claremont, CA 91711, USA

Long, Grant *Basketball Player*
3257 Belmont Glen Dr, Marietta, GA 30067, USA

Long, Howie *Football Player, Sportscaster, Actor*
514 S Juanita Ave, Redondo Beach, CA 90277, USA

Long, Joan D *Movie Producer*
La Burrage Place, Lindfield 2070 NSW, Australia

Long, Nia *Actress*
%Innovative Artists, 1999 Ave of Stars, #2850, Los Angeles, CA 90067, USA

Long, Richard *Sculptor*
Old School, Lower Failand, Bristol BS8 3SL, England

Long, Robert *Paleontologist*
%University of California, Paleontology Museum, Berkeley, CA 94720, USA

Long, Robert L J — *Navy Admiral*
247 Heaman's Way, Annapolis, MD 21401, USA

Long, Robert M — *Businessman*
%Longs Drug Stores, 141 N Civic Dr, Walnut Creek, CA 94596, USA

Long, Russell B — *Senator, LA*
1455 Pennsylvania Ave NW, Washington, DC 20004, USA

Long, Sharon R — *Molecular Geneticist*
%Stanford University, Biological Sciences Dept, Stanford, CA 94305, USA

Long, Shelley — *Actress*
15237 Sunset Blvd, Pacific Palisades, CA 90272, USA

Longden, Johnny — *Thoroughbred Racing Jockey, Trainer*
5401 Palmer Dr, Banning, CA 92220, USA

Longfield, William H — *Businessman*
%C R Bard Inc, 730 Central Ave, Murray Hill, NJ 07974, USA

Longford (Francis A Pakenham), Earl of — *Government Official, England*
Bernhurst, Hurst Green, East Sussex TN19 7QN, England

Longley, Luc — *Basketball Player*
%Chicago Bulls, 1901 W Madison St, Chicago, IL 60612, USA

Longmire, William P, Jr — *Physician*
10102 Empyrean Way, #8-203, Los Angeles, CA 90067, USA

Longo, Jeannie Ciprelli- — *Cyclist*
9 Rue Massena, 38000 Grenoble, France

Longo, Lenny — *Singer (The Box Tops)*
%Texas Sounds, PO Box 1644, Dickinson, TX 77539, USA

Longo, Robert — *Artist*
%Longo Studio, 224 Center St, New York, NY 10013, USA

Longstreet, Stephen — *Writer*
1133 Miradero Road, Beverly Hills, CA 90210, USA

Longuet-Higgins, H Christopher — *Chemist*
%Experimental Psych Lab, Sussex Univ, Falmer, Brighton BN1 9QG, England

Lonsbrough Porter, Anita — *Swimmer*
6 Rivendell Gardens, Tettendall, Wolverhampton WV6 8SY, England

Loomis, Henry — *Government Official*
4661 Ortega Island Dr, Jacksonville, FL 32210, USA

Looney, Donald L (Don) — *Football Player*
1447 Wakefield Dr, Houston, TX 77018, USA

Lopes, David E (Davey) — *Baseball Player*
17762 Vineyard Lane, Poway, CA 92064, USA

Lopes, Lisa (Left Eye) — *Rap Artist (TLC)*
%William Morris Agency, 1325 Ave of Americas, New York, NY 10019, USA

Lopes-Graca, Fernando — *Composer*
El Mi Paraiso, 2 Avenida da Republica, 2775 Parede, Portugal

Lopez Arellano, Oswaldo — *President, Honduras; Air Force General*
Servico Aereo de Honduras, Apdo 129, Tegucigalpa DC, Honduras

Lopez Rodriguez, Nicolas de Jesus — *Religious Leader*
Archdiocese of Santo Domingo, Santo Domingo, AP 186, Dominican Republic

Lopez Trujillo, Alfonso Cardinal — *Religious Leader*
Arzobispado, Calle 57, N 48-28 , Medellin, Colombia

Lopez, Albert A (Al) — *Baseball Manager*
3601 Beach Dr, Tampa, FL 33629, USA

Lopez, Dan — *Cartoonist*
77 N Ellsworth Ave, San Mateo, CA 94401, USA

Lopez, George — *Comedian*
%Harvey Elkin Mgmt, 6515 Sunset Blvd, #305, Los Angeles, CA 90028, USA

Lopez, Jennifer — *Actress*
%Abrams Artists, 9200 Sunset Blvd, #625, Los Angeles, CA 90069, USA

Lopez, Jose M — *WW II Army Hero (CMH)*
3223 Hatton Dr, San Antonio, TX 78237, USA

Lopez, Lourdes — *Ballerina*
%New York City Ballet, Lincoln Center Plaza, New York, NY 10023, USA

Lopez, Mario — *Actor*
%Metropolitan Talent Agency, 4526 Wilshire Blvd, Los Angeles, CA 90010, USA

Lopez, Nancy — *Golfer*
2308 Tara Dr, Albany, GA 31707, USA

Lopez, Robert S — *Writer, Historian*
41 Richmond Ave, New Haven, CT 06515, USA

Lopez, T Joseph — *Navy Admiral*
CinC Allied Forces Southern Europe, Box 1, PSC 813, FPO, AE 09620, USA

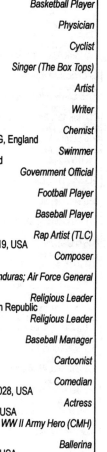

L

Long - Lopez

Lopez, Trini *Singer, Actor, Orchestra Leader*
1139 Abrigo Road, Palm Springs, CA 92262, USA

Lopez-Alegria, Michael E *Astronaut*
%NASA, Johnson Space Center, 2101 NASA Road, Houston, TX 77058, USA

Lopez-Cobos, Jesus *Conductor*
%Terry Harrison Mgmt, 1 Clarendon Court, Charlbury, Oxon OX7 3PS, England

Lopez-Garcia, Antonio *Artist*
%Marlborough Fine Art, 6 Albermarle St, London W1, England

Lorant, Stefan *Writer*
PO Box 803, Lenox, MA 01240, USA

Lord, Jack *Actor*
4999 Kahala Ave, Honolulu, HI 96816, USA

Lord, M G *Editorial Cartoonist*
%Newsday, Editorial Dept, 235 Pinelawn Road, Melville, NY 11747, USA

Lord, Marjorie *Actress*
1110 Maytor Place, Beverly Hills, CA 90210, USA

Lord, Michael *Artist*
14227 71st Ave, Surrey BC V3W 2K9, Canada

Lord, Walter *Writer*
116 E 68th St, New York, NY 10021, USA

Lord, Winston *Diplomat*
740 Park Ave, New York, NY 10021, USA

Loren, Sophia *Actress*
La Concordia Ranch, 1151 Hidden Valley Road, Thousand Oaks, CA 91361, USA

Lorentz, Jim *Hockey Player*
2555 Staley Road, Grand Island, NY 14072, USA

Lorenz, Lee *Cartoonist*
PO Box 131, Easton, CT 06612, USA

Lorenzen, Fred *Auto Racing Driver*
906 Burr Oak Court, Oak Brook, IL 60523, USA

Lorenzoni, Andrea *Astronaut, Italy*
Via B Vergine del Carmelo 168, 00144 Rome, Italy

Loring, Gloria *Singer, Actress*
PO Box 1115, Cedar Glen, CA 92321, USA

Loring, John R *Artist*
860 5th Ave, New York, NY 10021, USA

Loring, Lisa *Actress*
11130 Huston St, #6, North Hollywood, CA 91601, USA

Loring, Lynn *Actress*
506 N Camden Dr, Beverly Hills, CA 90210, USA

Loriod, Yvonne *Concert Pianist*
%Bureau de Concerts, 7 Rue de Richepanse, 75008 Paris, France

Lorring, Joan *Actress*
345 E 68th St, New York, NY 10021, USA

Lorsch, George A *Businessman*
%Armstrong World Industries, 313 W Liberty St, Lancaster, PA 17603, USA

Lorscheider, Aloisio Cardinal *Religious Leader*
%Arquidiocese de Fortaleza, CP D-6, 60.000 Fortaleza, Ceara, Brazil

Lortel, Lucille *Theater Producer*
%Lucille Lortel Theatre, 121 Christopher St, New York, NY 10014, USA

Lortie, Louis *Concert Pianist*
%G Guibord, 4666 De Bullion, Montreal PQ H2T 1Y6, Canada

Loscutoff, Jim *Basketball Player*
166 Jenkins Road, Andover, MA 01810, USA

Losee, Thomas P, Jr *Publisher*
PO Box 471, Cold Spring Harbor, NY 11724, USA

Lott, Felicity A *Opera Singer*
%Lies Askonas Ltd, 186 Drury Lane, London WC2B 5RY, England

Lott, Ronnie *Football Player, Sportscaster*
%Fox-TV, Sports Dept, PO Box 900, Beverly Hills, CA 90213, USA

Loucks, Vernon R, Jr *Businessman*
%Baxter International, 1 Baxter Parkway, Deerfield, IL 60015, USA

Loudon, Dorothy *Actress*
101 Central Park West, New York, NY 10023, USA

Loudon, Rodney *Theoretical Physicist*
3 Gaston St, East Bergholt, Colchester, Essex CO7 6SD, England

Louganis, Greg *Diver*
PO Box 4130, Malibu, CA 90264, USA

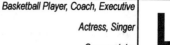

Loughery, Kevin Basketball Player, Coach, Executive
1091 Byrnwyck Road NE, Atlanta, GA 30319, USA
Loughlin, Lori Actress, Singer
9279 Sierra Mar Dr, Los Angeles, CA 90069, USA
Loughlin, Mary Anne Commentator
%WTBS-TV, News Dept, 1050 Techwood Dr NW, Atlanta, GA 30318, USA
Loughran, James Conductor
Rookery, Bollington Cross, Macclesfield, Cheshire SK10 5EL, England
Louis Jin Luxian Religions Leader
Shesshan Catholic Seminary, Beijing, China
Louis, Murray Dancer, Choreographer
%Nikolais/Louis Foundation, 375 W Broadway, New York, NY 10012, USA
Louis-Dreyfus, Julia Actress
131 S Rodeo Dr, #300, Beverly Hills, CA 90212, USA
Louis-Dreyfus, Robert L M Businessman
%Saatchi & Saatchi Co, 83/89 Whitfield St, London W1A 4XA, England
Louisa, Maria Model
%Next Model Mgmt, 23 Watts St, New York, NY 10013, USA
Louise, Tina Actress
310 E 46th St, New York, NY 10017, USA
Louisy, Allan Prime Minister, Saint Lucia
Laborie, Castries, Saint Lucia, West Indies
Lounge, John M (Mike) Astronaut
%Spacelabs Inc, 1215 Jefferson Davis Highway, #150, Arlington, VA 22202, USA
Lourdusamy, Simon Cardinal Religious Leader
Palazzo dei Convertendi, 34 Via della Conciliazione, 00193 Rome, Italy
Lousma, Jack R Astronaut
2722 Roseland St, Ann Arbor, MI 48103, USA
Loutfy, Ali Prime Minister, Egypt
29 Ahmed Hesmat St, Zamalek, Cairo, Egypt
Louvier, Alain Composer
Conservatoire Nat Musique Superieur, 14 Rue de Madrid, 75008 Paris, France
Louvin, Charlie Singer, Songwriter, Guitarist
%Tessier-Marsh, 505 Caton Pass, Madison, TN 37115, USA
Lovano, Joe Jazz Saxophonist
206 W 23rd St, #2, New York, NY 10011, USA
Love, Ben H Association Executive
%Boy Scouts of America, 4407 Eaton Circle, Colleyville, TX 76034, USA
Love, Bob Basketball Player
%Chicago Bulls, 1901 W Madison St, Chicago, IL 60612, USA
Love, Courtney Singer (Hole), Actress, Songwriter
33401 NE 78th St, Carnation, WA 98014, USA
Love, Darlene Singer
%Holiday Entertainment, 8803 Mayne St, Bellflower, CA 90706, USA
Love, Davis, III Golfer
228 Kings Way, Saint Simons Island, GA 31522, USA
Love, Gael Editor
%Connoisseur Magazine, Editorial Dept, 1790 Broadway, New York, NY 10019, USA
Love, John A Governor, CO; Businessman
%Ideal Basic Industries, 950 17th St, Denver, CO 80202, USA
Love, Michael D (Mike) Singer (The Beach Boys)
101 Mesa Lane, Santa Barbara, CA 93109, USA
Love, Nancy Editor
%Mademoiselle Magazine, Editorial Dept, 350 Madison Ave, New York, NY 10017, USA
Love, Susan Surgeon, Oncologist
%University of California Medical Plaza, Breast Center, Los Angeles, CA 90024, USA
Loveless, Patty Singer, Songwriter
%Fitzgerald Hartley Co, 1908 Wedgewood Ave, Nashville, TN 37212, USA
Lovell, A C Bernard Astronomer
Quinta, Swettenham near Congleton, Cheshire, England
Lovell, James A, Jr Astronaut
%Lovell Communications, PO Box 49, Lake Forest, IL 60045, USA
Lovellette, Clyde Basketball Player
7191 W 250 N, Wabash, IN 46992, USA
Lovelock, James E Chemist, Inventor
Coombe Mill, St Giles-on-the-Heath, Launceston, Cornwall PL15 9RY, England
Lover, Seth Inventor, Engineer (Humbucking Pickup)
12752 Adrian Circle, Garden Grove, CA 92840, USA

L

Loughery - Lover

Lovering, Thomas S	*Geologist, Geochemist*
2663 Tallant Road, Santa Barbara, CA 93105, USA	
Lovett, Lyle	*Singer, Songwriter*
%Vector Mgmt, 1500 17th Ave S, Nashville, TN 37212, USA	
Lovitz, Jon	*Actor*
4735 Viviana Dr, Tarzana, CA 91356, USA	
Low, Francis E	*Physicist*
28 Adams St, Belmont, MA 02178, USA	
Low, G David	*Astronaut*
%NASA, Johnson Space Center, 2101 NASA Road, Houston, TX 77058, USA	
Low, Stephen	*Diplomat*
2855 Tilden St NW, Washington, DC 20008, USA	
Lowder, Robert E	*Financier*
%Colonial BancGroup, 1 Commerce St, Montgomery, AL 36104, USA	
Lowe, Chad	*Actor*
%More/Medavoy, 7920 W Sunset Blvd, #400, Los Angeles, CA 90036, USA	
Lowe, Kevin	*Hockey Player*
%New York Rangers, Madison Square Garden, 2 Penn Plaza, New York, NY 10121, USA	
Lowe, Nick	*Singer, Songwriter, Guitarist*
%William Morris Agency, 1325 Ave of Americas, New York, NY 10019, USA	
Lowe, Rob	*Actor*
270 N Canon Dr # 1072, Beverly Hills, CA 90210, USA	
Lowe, Woodrow	*Football Player, Coach*
8327 Tomashaw St, Lenexa, KS 66219, USA	
Lowell, Carey	*Actress, Model*
%International Creative Mgmt, 8942 Wilshire Blvd, Beverly Hills, CA 90211, USA	
Lowenstein, Louis	*Attorney, Educator*
5 Oak Lane, Larchmont, NY 10538, USA	
Lowman, Frank A	*Financier*
%Federal Home Loan Bank, 2 Townsite Plaza, Topeka, KS 66601, USA	
Lown, Bernard	*Cardiologist*
%Harvard University Medical School, 25 Shattuck St, Boston, MA 02115, USA	
Lowry, Mike	*Governor/Senator, WA*
PO Box 4246, Seattle, WA 98104, USA	
Loy, Frank E	*Environmentalist*
%Marshall German Fund, 11 Dupont Circle NW, Washington, DC 20036, USA	
Loynd, Richard B	*Businessman*
%Interco, 101 S Hanley Road, St Louis, MO 63105, USA	
Lozano, Ignacio E, Jr	*Editor*
%La Opinion, 411 W 5th St, Los Angeles, CA 90013, USA	
Lozano, Silvia	*Choreographer*
%Ballet Folklorico, 31 Esq Con Riva Palacio, Mexico City DF, Mexico	
Lu Qihui	*Sculptor*
351 Flats Shuang-Feng Rd, #10-5, Shanghai, China	
Lu, Edward T	*Astronaut*
%NASA, Johnson Space Center, 2101 NASA Road, Houston, TX 77058, USA	
Luan Jujie	*Fencer*
146 Shuang-Le Yuan, #301, Qin-Huai Region, Nanjing, China	
Lubachivsky, Myroslav Cardinal	*Religious Leader*
%Piazza Madonna dei Monti 3, 00184 Rome, Italy	
Lubich Silvia, Chiara	*Evangelist*
%Focolare Movement, 306 Via di Frascati, 00040 Rocca di Papa RM, Italy	
Lubin, Frank J	*Basketball Player*
1214 N Louise St, Glendale, CA 91207, USA	
Lubin, Steven	*Concert Pianist*
%J B Keller, 600 W 111th St, #129, New York, NY 10025, USA	
Lubotsky, Mark	*Concert Violinist*
Overtoom 329 III, 1054 JM Amsterdam, Netherlands	
Lubovitch, Lar	*Dancer, Choreographer*
%Lar Lubovitch Dance Co, 15-17 W 18th St, New York, NY 10011, USA	
Lubs, Herbert A	*Geneticist*
5133 SW 71st Place, Miami, FL 33155, USA	
Lubys, Bronislovas	*Prime Minister, Lithuania*
%Prime Minister's Office, Tuo-Vaizganto 2, Vilnius, Lithuania	
Luc, Tone	*Rap Artist, Actor*
7932 Hillside Ave, Los Angeles, CA 90046, USA	
Lucas, Aubrey K	*Educator*
%University of Southern Mississippi, President's Office, Hattiesburg, MS 39406, USA	

Lucas, Craig	*Lyricist*
%William Morris Agency, 1325 Ave of Americas, New York, NY 10019, USA	
Lucas, Don	*Businessman*
%Cadence Design Systems, 555 River Oaks Parkway, San Jose, CA 95134, USA	
Lucas, George	*Movie Director, Producer*
%LucasFilm, PO Box 2009, San Rafael, CA 94912, USA	
Lucas, Jack H	*WW II Marine Corps Hero (CMH)*
75 Elks Lake Road, Hattiesburg, MS 39401, USA	
Lucas, Jerry R	*Basketball Player*
PO Box 728, Templeton, CA 93465, USA	
Lucas, John H, Jr	*Basketball Player, Coach, Executive*
21 Pin Oaks Estates, Bellaire, TX 77401, USA	
Lucas, Maurice	*Basketball Player, Coach*
5691 Bonita Road, Lake Oswego, OR 97035, USA	
Lucas, Richard J (Richie)	*Football Player*
%Pennsylvania State University, Athletic Dept, University Park, PA 16802, USA	
Lucas, Robert E, Jr	*Nobel Economics Laureate*
5441 S Hyde Park Blvd, Chicago, IL 60615, USA	
Lucas, William	*Government Official*
%Justice Department, Constitution & 10th NW, Washington, DC 20530, USA	
Lucchesini, Andrea	*Concert Pianist*
%Columbia Artists Mgmt Inc, 165 W 57th St, New York, NY 10019, USA	
Lucci, Susan	*Actress*
16 Carteret Place, Garden City, NY 11530, USA	
Luce, Henry, III	*Publisher*
Mill Hill Road, Mill Neck, NY 11765, USA	
Luce, R Duncan	*Psychologist*
20 Whitman Court, Irvine, CA 92612, USA	
Luce, Richard N	*Government Official, England*
%House of Commons, Westminster, London SW1A 0AA, England	
Luce, William (Bill)	*Writer*
PO Box 370, Depoe Bay, OR 97341, USA	
Lucebert (L J Swaanswijk)	*Artist*
Boendermakerhof 10, 1861 TB Bergen N-H, Netherlands	
Lucey, Patrick J	*Governor, WI*
6200 Highway 57, Rt 3, Sturgeon Bay, WI 54235, USA	
Luciano, Robert P	*Businessman*
%Schering-Plough Corp, 1 Giralda Farms, Madison, NJ 07940, USA	
Lucid, Shannon W	*Astronaut, Biophysicist*
1622 Gunwale Road, Houston, TX 77062, USA	
Lucinschi, Petru	*President, Moldova*
%President's Office, 23 Nicolai Iorge Str, 277033 Chisinaud, Moldava	
Luckinbill, Lawrence	*Actor*
RR 3, Flintlock Ridge Road, Katonah, NY 10536, USA	
Luckman, Charles	*Architect*
%Luckman Management Co, 9220 Sunset Blvd, Los Angeles, CA 90069, USA	
Luckman, Sid	*Football Player*
5303 Saint Charles Road, Bellwood, IL 60104, USA	
Luckovich, Mike	*Editorial Cartoonist*
%Atlanta Constitution, Editorial Dept, 72 Marietta St, Atlanta, GA 30303, USA	
Lucky Dube	*Singer*
%Fast Lane Productions, 4856 Haygood Road, #200, Virginia Beach, VA 23455, USA	
Lucky, Robert W	*Electrical Engineer*
48 Gillespie Ave, Fair Haven, NJ 07704, USA	
Luder, Owen H	*Architect*
%Communication in Construction, 2 Smith Square, London SW1P 3H5, England	
Ludlum, Robert	*Writer*
%Henry Morrison, PO Box 235, Bedford Hills, NY 10507, USA	
Ludwig, Christa	*Opera Singer*
Rigistr 14, 6045 Meggen, Switzerland	
Ludwig, Ken	*Writer*
%Steptoe & Johnson, 1330 Connecticut Ave NW, Washington, DC 20036, USA	
Luening, Otto	*Composer*
460 Riverside Dr, New York, NY 10027, USA	
Luers, William H	*Diplomat, Museum Executive*
%Metropolitan Museum of Art, 1000 5th Ave, New York, NY 10028, USA	
Luft, Lorna	*Actress, Singer*
%Golden Goldberg, 9100 Wilshire Blvd, #455, Beverly Hills, CA 90212, USA	

L

Lucas - Luft

Lugbill, Jon — *Kayak Athlete*
%American Canoe Assn, PO Box 1190, Newington, VA 22122, USA

Luikart, John F — *Financier*
%Sutro Co, 201 California St, San Francisco, CA 94111, USA

Luisetti, Angelo (Hank) — *Basketball Player*
131 Winchester Court, Foster City, CA 94404, USA

Luisi, James — *Actor*
22562 Seaver Court, Santa Clarita, CA 91350, USA

Luiso, Anthony — *Businessman*
%International Multifoods, 33 S 6th St, Minneapolis, MN 55402, USA

Lujack, John C (Johnny) — *Football Player*
3700 Harrison St, Davenport, IA 52806, USA

Lujan, Manuel, Jr — *Secretary, Interior*
%Manuel Lujan Agencies, PO Box 3727, Albuquerque, NM 87190, USA

Lukas, D Wayne — *Thoroughbred Racing Trainer*
5699 Happy Canyon Road, Santa Ynez, CA 93460, USA

Lukashenko, Aleksandr — *President, Belarus*
%President's Office, Government House, Dom Urada, 210010 Minsk, Belarus

Luke — *Rap Artist*
%Terry M Hill, 6430 Variel Ave, #101, Woodland Hills, CA 91367, USA

Luke, John A, Jr — *Businessman*
%Westvaco Corp, 299 Park Ave, New York, NY 10171, USA

Lukkarinen, Marjut — *Cross Country Skier*
%Lohja Ski Team, Lohja, Finland

Lulu — *Singer, Actress*
%Susan Angel, 12 D'Arblay St, #100, London W1V 3FP, England

Lumbly, Carl — *Actor*
5875 Carolos Dr, Los Angeles, CA 90068, USA

Lumet, Sidney — *Movie Director*
1 W 81st St, #4-DB, New York, NY 10024, USA

Lumley, Harry — *Hockey Player*
688 4th Ave E, Owen Sound ON N4R 2N4, Canada

Lumley, Joanna — *Actress*
%Inspirational Artiste, PO Box 1AS, London W1A 1AS, England

Lumpp, Ray — *Basketball Player*
21 Hewlett Dr, East Willston, NY 11596, USA

Lumsden, David J — *Conductor, Concert Organist*
Melton House, Soham, Cambridgeshire, England

Luna, Barbara — *Actress*
18026 Rodarte Way, Encino, CA 91316, USA

Lund, Deanna — *Actress*
545 Howard Dr, Salem, VA 24153, USA

Lund, Francis (Pug) — *Football Player*
9999 Wayzata Blvd, Minnetonka, MN 55305, USA

Lundberg, Fred Borre — *Nordic Combined Athlete*
Skogbrynet 11, 9250 Bardu, Norway

Lundberg, George D, II — *Editor, Physician*
%JAMA Magazine, Editorial Dept, 515 N State St, Chicago, IL 60610, USA

Lunden, Joan — *Commentator*
707 Westchester Ave, White Plains, NY 10604, USA

Lundgren, Dolph — *Actor*
1999 Ave of Stars, #2100, Los Angeles, CA 90067, USA

Lundgren, Lauren — *Financier*
%Washington Federal Savings, 425 Pike St, Seattle, WA 98101, USA

Lundquist, Steve — *Swimmer*
3448 Southbay Dr, Jonesboro, GA 30236, USA

Lundquist, Verne — *Sportscaster*
%CBS-TV, Sports Dept, 51 W 52nd St, New York, NY 10019, USA

Lundy, Jessica — *Actress*
%William Morris Agency, 151 S El Camino Dr, Beverly Hills, CA 90212, USA

Lundy, Victor A — *Architect*
%Victor A Lundy Assoc, 701 Mulberry Lane, Bellaire, TX 77401, USA

Luner, Jaime — *Actress*
%Martin Hurwitz, 427 N Canon Dr, #215, Beverly Hills, CA 90210, USA

Lunger, Francis J — *Businessman*
%Nashua Corp, 44 Franklin St, Nashua, NH 03060, USA

Lunghi, Cherie — *Actress*
%Marion Rosenberg, 8428 Melrose Place, #C, Los Angeles, CA 90069, USA

Lunka, Zoltan *Boxer*
Weinheimer Str 2, 69198 Schriesheim, Germany
Lunn, Bob *Golfer*
835 Bali Court, Danville, CA 94526, USA
Luns, Joseph M A H *Government Official, Netherlands*
117 Ave Franklin Roosevelt, 1050 Brussels, Belgium
Lupberger, Edwin A *Businessman*
%Entergy Corp, 639 Loyola Ave, New Orleans, LA 70113, USA
LuPone, Patti *Singer, Actress*
%International Creative Mgmt, 40 W 57th St, New York, NY 10019, USA
Lupu, Radu *Concert Pianist*
%Terry Harrison Mgmt, 3 Clarendon Court, Charlbury, Oxon OX7 3PS, England
Lupus, Peter *Actor*
2401 S 24th St, #110, Phoenix, AZ 85034, USA
Lurie, Alison *Writer*
%Cornell University, English Dept, Ithaca, NY 14850, USA
Lurie, Ranan R *Editorial Cartoonist*
%Cartoonnews International, 9 Mountain Laurel Dr, Greenwich, CT 06831, USA
Lusis, Janis *Track Athlete*
Vesetas 8-3, 1013 Riga, Latvia
Lustiger, Jean-Marie Cardinal *Religious Leader*
Archeveche de Paris, 32 Rue Barbet de Jouy, 75007 Paris, France
Lutali, A P *Governor, AS*
%Governor's Office, Government Offices, Pago Pago, Tutuila, AS 90799, USA
Lutcher, Nellie *Singer*
%Alan Eichler, 1862 Vista del Mar St, Los Angeles, CA 90028, USA
Luter, Joseph W, III *Businessman*
%Smithfield Foods, 501 N Church St, Smithfield, VA 23430, USA
Lutes, Eric *Actor*
%Artists Group, 10100 Santa Monica Blvd, #2490, Los Angeles, CA 90067, USA
Lutz, Bob *Tennis Player*
%US Tennis Assn, 1212 Ave of Americas, New York, NY 10036, USA
Lutz, Robert A *Businessman*
%Chrysler Corp, 12000 Chrysler Dr, Highland Park, MI 48288, USA
LuValle, James *Track Athlete*
3580 Evergreen Dr, Palo Alto, CA 94303, USA
Luxon, Benjamin *Opera Singer*
Lower Cox Street Farm, Detling, Maidstone, Kent ME14 3HE, England
Luyendyk, Arie *Auto Racing Driver*
630 N Lesueur Circle, Mesa, AZ 85203, USA
Luyties, Ricci *Volleyball Player*
%Assn of Volleyball Pros, 330 Washington Blvd, #600, Marina del Rey, CA 90292, USA
Luzhkov, Yuri M *Mayor, Moscow*
%Government of Moscow, Tverskaya Str 13, 103032 Moscow, Russia
Luzinski, Gregory M (Greg) *Baseball Player*
4285 Kings Cross Way, Hoschton, GA 30548, USA
Lyakhov, Vladimir A *Cosmonaut*
%Potchta Kosmonavtov, Moskovskoi Oblasti, 141160 Syvisdny Goroduk, Russia
Lydon, James (Jimmy) *Actor*
1317 Los Arboles Ave NW, Albuquerque, NM 87107, USA
Lydon, John (Johnny Rotten) *Singer, Musician (Sex Pistols)*
%Panacea Entertainment, 2705 Glendower Ave, Los Angeles, CA 90027, USA
Lydon, Thomas J *Judge*
%US Claims Court, 717 Madison Place NW, Washington, DC 20005, USA
Lyght, Todd *Football Player*
2185 Lindsey Court, Tustin, CA 92782, USA
Lyle, Sandy *Golfer*
%Professional Golfer's Assn, PO Box 109601, Palm Beach Gardens, FL 33410, USA
Lyles, Lester L (Les) *Air Force General*
Director, Ballistic Missile Defense, HqUSAF, Pentagon, Washington, DC 20330, USA
Lyman, Richard W *Foundation Executive, Educator*
%Stanford University, Education School, Stanford, CA 94305, USA
Lympany, Moura *Concert Pianist*
%Helen Jennings, 2 Hereford House, Links Road, London W3 OHX, England
Lynch, Allen J *Vietnam War Army Hero (CMH)*
438 Belle Plaine Ave, Gurnee, IL 60031, USA
Lynch, David K *Movie Director*
PO Box 93624, Los Angeles, CA 90093, USA

L

Lunka - Lynch

Lynch, James E (Jim) *Football Player*
1009 W 67th St, Kansas City, MO 64113, USA

Lynch, John M *Prime Minister, Ireland*
21 Garville Ave, Rathgar, Dublin 6, Ireland

Lynch, Kelly *Model, Actress*
1970 Mandeville Canyon Road, Los Angeles, CA 90049, USA

Lynch, Peter S *Financier*
27 State St, Boston, MA 02109, USA

Lynch, Richard *Actor*
%Richard Sindell, 8271 Melrose Ave, #202, Los Angeles, CA 90046, USA

Lynch, Richard (Dick) *Football Player*
203 Manor Road, Douglaston, NY 11363, USA

Lynch, Robert P *Financier*
%Lord Abbett Co, 767 5th Ave, New York, NY 10153, USA

Lynch, Thomas C *Navy Admiral*
1236 Denbigh Lane, Radnor, PA 19087, USA

Lynden-Bell, Donald *Astronomer*
%Institute of Astronomy, Madingley Road, Cambridge CB3 0HA, England

Lynds, Roger *Astronomer*
%Kitt Peak National Observatory, Tucson, AZ 85726, USA

Lyne, Adrian *Movie Director*
9876 Beverly Grove Dr, Beverly Hills, CA 90210, USA

Lynes, George Platt *Photographer*
%Moore Gallery, 724 5th Ave, New York, NY 10019, USA

Lynley, Carol *Actress*
%Don Gerler, 3349 Cahuenga Blvd W, #1, Los Angeles, CA 90068, USA

Lynn Salomon, Janet *Figure Skater*
1716 Grandview Dr, Rochester Hills, MI 48306, USA

Lynn, Cheryl *Singer*
%T-Best Talent, 2001 Wayne Ave, #103, San Leandro, CA 94577, USA

Lynn, Frederic M (Fred) *Baseball Player*
7336 El Fuerte St, Carlsbad, CA 92009, USA

Lynn, James T *Secretary, Housing & Urban Development*
151 Farmington Ave, Hartford, CT 06115, USA

Lynn, Loretta *Singer, Songwriter*
%Loretta Lynn Enterprises, PO Box 120369, Nashville, TN 37212, USA

Lynn, Meredith Scott *Actress*
1530 N Poinsettia Place, #308, Los Angeles, CA 90046, USA

Lynne, Gillian *Dance Director, Choreographer*
%Lean-2 Productions, 18 Rutland St, Knightsbridge, London SW7 1EF, England

Lynne, Gloria *Singer*
%Subrena Artists, 330 W 56th St, #18-M, New York, NY 10019, USA

Lynne, Jeff *Singer, Songwriter*
PO Box 5850, Santa Barbara, CA 93150, USA

Lynne, Shelby *Singer*
%Debbie Doebler Business Mgmt, 1101 17th Ave S, Nashville, TN 37212, USA

Lyon, Lisa *Body Builder, Actress*
%Jungle Gym, PO Box 585, Santa Monica, CA 90406, USA

Lyon, Sue *Actress*
1244 N Havenhurst Dr, Los Angeles, CA 90046, USA

Lyon, Wayne B *Businessman*
%Masco Corp, 21001 Van Born Road, Taylor, MI 48180, USA

Lyon, William *Air Force General, Businessman*
%William Lyon Co, 4490 Von Karman Ave, Newport Beach, CA 92660, USA

Lyons, James A, Jr *Navy Admiral*
9481 Piney Mountain Road, Warrenton, VA 20186, USA

Lysiak, Tom *Hockey Player*
13064 Highway 278 E, Social Circle, GA 30025, USA

Lyst, John H *Editor*
%Indianapolis Star, Editorial Dept, 307 N Pennsylvania, Indianapolis, IN 46204, USA

Lytle, L Ben *Businessman*
%Associated Insurance, 120 Monument Circle, Indianapolis, IN 46204, USA

Lytle, Ronn K *Financier*
%Capstead Mortgage, 2001 Bryan Tower, Dallas, TX 75201, USA

Lyubimov, Yuri P *Theater Director*
%Royal Opera, Covent Garden, 48 Floral St, London WC2E 7QA, England

M'Bow, Amadou-Mahtar — *Government Official, Senegal*
BP 5276, Dakar-Fann, Senegal

Ma, Yo-Yo — *Concert Cellist*
%International Creative Mgmt, 40 W 57th St, New York, NY 10019, USA

Maag, Peter — *Conductor*
Casa Maag, 7504 Pontresina, Switzerland

Maas, Bill — *Football Player*
12415 NE 144th St, Kearney, MO 64060, USA

Maas, Peter — *Writer*
%International Creative Mgmt, 40 W 57th St, New York, NY 10019, USA

Maazel, Lorin — *Conductor, Concert Violinist*
%Pittsburgh Symphony, 600 Pennsylvania Ave, Pittsburgh, PA 15146, USA

Mabee, John — *Thoroughbred Racing Executive*
4346 54th St, San Diego, CA 92115, USA

Mabus, Raymond E, Jr — *Governor, MS*
PO Box 200, Jackson, MS 39205, USA

MacAfee, Ken — *Football Player*
26 W Elm Terrace, Brockton, MA 02401, USA

MacArthur, Douglas, II — *Diplomat*
2101 Connecticut Ave NW, Washington, DC 20008, USA

MacArthur, James — *Actor*
74092 Covered Wagon Trail, Palm Desert, CA 92260, USA

Macaskill, Bridget A — *Financier*
%Oppenheimer Management, 2 World Trade Center, New York, NY 10048, USA

Macauley, Edward C (Easy Ed) — *Basketball Player*
1455 Reauville Dr, St Louis, MO 63122, USA

Maccanico, Antonio — *Government Official, Italy*
%Prime Minister's Office, Piazza Colonna 370, 00187 Rome, Italy

Macchio, Ralph — *Actor*
451 Deerpark Ave, Dix Hills, NY 11746, USA

MacColl, Kristy — *Singer, Songwriter*
%XL Talent, 27-A Penbridge Villas, Studio 7, London W11 3EP, England

MacCorkindale, Simon — *Actor*
%James Sharkey, 21 Golden Square, London W1R 3PA, England

MacCready, Paul B — *Aeronautical Engineer*
%AeroVironment Inc, 222 E Huntington Dr, Monrovia, CA 91016, USA

MacDermot, Galt — *Composer*
%MacDermot Assoc, 12 Silver Lake Road, Staten Island, NY 10301, USA

MacDonald, Gordon J F — *Geophysicist*
%Mitre Corp, 1820 Dolly Madison Blvd, McLean, VA 22102, USA

Macdonald, J Ross — *Physicist*
308 Laurel Hill Road, Chapel Hill, NC 27514, USA

MacDonald, Parker — *Hockey Player*
241 Brandford Road, #252, North Branford, CT 06471, USA

MacDowell, Andie — *Model, Actress*
%Miramax Films, 18 E 48th St New York, NY 10007, USA

MacEachen, Allan J — *Government Official, Canada*
RR 1, Whycocomagh, NS BOE 3MO, Canada

MacGillivary, Charles A — *WW II Army Hero (CMH)*
38 Fallon Circle, Braintree, MA 02184, USA

MacGraw, Ali — *Actress*
27040 Malibu Cove Colony Dr, Malibu, CA 90265, USA

MacGregor, Ian K — *Government Official, England*
Castleton House, Lochgilphead, Argyll, Scotland

MacGregor, John R R — *Government Official, England*
%House of Commons, Westminster, London SW1A 0AA, England

Macharski, Franciszak Cardinal — *Religious Leader*
%Metropolita Krakowski, Ul Franciszkanska 3, 31-004 Krakow, Poland

Machiz, Leon — *Businessman*
%Avnet Inc, 80 Cutter Mill Road, Great Neck, NY 11021, USA

Machlis, Gail — *Cartoonist (Quality Time)*
%Chronicle Syndicate, 870 Market St, San Francisco, CA 94102, USA

Machover, Tod — *Composer*
%Massachusetts Institute of Technology, Media Laboratory, Cambridge, MA 02139, USA

Macht, Stephen — *Actor*
%Paul Kohner, 9300 Wilshire Blvd, #555, Beverly Hills, CA 90212, USA

Machungo, Mario de Graca — *Prime Minister, Mozambique*
%Prime Minister's Office, Avenida Julius Nyerere 1780, Maputo, Mozambique

MacInnis, Al — *Hockey Player*
%St Louis Blues, Kiel Center, 1401 Clark Ave, St Louis, MO 63103, USA

MacIntosh, Craig — *Cartoonist (Sally Forth)*
%King Features Syndicate, 235 E 45th St, New York, NY 10017, USA

MacIsaac, Ashley — *Violinist, Dancer*
%Little Big Man, 39-A Gramercy Park N, #1-C, New York, NY 10010, USA

MacIver, Loren — *Artist*
61 Perry St, New York, NY 10014, USA

Mack, John E — *Psychiatrist*
%Harvard University Medical School, 25 Shattuck St, Boston, MA 02115, USA

Mack, Kevin — *Football Player*
1843 Sperry's Forge, Westlake, OH 44145, USA

Mack, Lonnie — *Singer, Guitarist*
%MM&T, 15001 Mitchell Creek, Fort Bragg, CA 95437, USA

Mack, Warner — *Singer*
2268 E Apple Ave, Muskegon, MI 49442, USA

Mack, William P — *Navy Admiral*
3067 Rundelac Road, Annapolis, MD 21403, USA

Mackay, David — *Movie Director*
%Gersh Agency, 232 N Canon Dr, Beverly Hills, CA 90210, USA

Mackay, Harvey — *Writer*
%Mackay Envelope Corp, 2100 Elm St SE, Minneapolis, MN 55414, USA

Macke, Richard C — *Navy Admiral*
1040 Lunaillo St, #1202, Honolulu, HI 96822, USA

MacKenzie, Gisele — *Singer, Violinist*
11014 Blix Ave, North Hollywood, CA 91602, USA

MacKenzie, John — *Movie Director*
%Peters Fraser Dunlop, Chelsea Harbour, Lots Rd, London SW10 0XF, England

MacKenzie, Kelvin — *Editor*
%The Sun, Editorial Dept, PO Box 481, Virginia St, London EC1 9BD, England

MacKenzie, Warren — *Ceramist*
8695 68th St N, Stillwater, MN 55082, USA

Mackerras, Charles — *Conductor*
10 Hamilton Terrace, London NW8 9UG, England

Mackey, George W — *Mathematician*
25 Coolidge Hill Road, Cambridge, MA 02138, USA

Mackey, John — *Football Player*
1198 Pacific Coast Highway, #506, Seal Beach, CA 90740, USA

Mackie, Robert G (Bob) — *Fashion Designer*
%Bob Mackie Originals, 225 W 39th St, New York, NY 10018, USA

MacKinnon, Catherine — *Attorney, Social Activist*
%University of Michigan, Law School, Ann Arbor, MI 48109, USA

Mackintosh, Cameron A — *Theater Producer*
%Cameron Mackintosh Ltd, 1 Bedford Square, London WC1B 3RA, England

Macklin, David — *Actor*
5410 Wilshire Blvd, #227, Los Angeles, CA 90036, USA

Macklin, J Stanley — *Financier*
%Regions Financial Corp, 417 N 20th St, Birmingham, AL 35203, USA

Macknowski, Stephen — *Canoeist*
462 Kimball Ave, Yonkers, NY 10704, USA

Mackovic, John — *Football Coach*
%University of Texas, Athletic Dept, PO Box 7399, Austin, TX 78713, USA

MacLachlan, Janet — *Actress*
1919 N Taft Ave, Los Angeles, CA 90068, USA

MacLachlan, Kyle — *Actor*
828 Venezia Ave, Venice, CA 90291, USA

MacLaine, Shirley — *Actress*
%MacLaine Enterprises, 25200 Malibu Road, #1, Malibu, CA 90265, USA

MacLane, Saunders — *Mathematician*
5712 S Dorchester Ave, Chicago, IL 60637, USA

MacLean, Don — *Basketball Player*
11528 Odessa Ave, Granada Hills, CA 91344, USA

MacLean, Doug — *Hockey Coach*
%Florida Panthers, Miami Arena, 100 NE 3rd Ave, Miami, FL 33132, USA

MacLean, Steven G — *Astronaut, Canada*
%Astronaut Program, 6767 Rte de l'Aeroport, St-Hubert PQ J3Y 8Y9, Canada

MacLeish, Rick — *Hockey Player*
1415 Marlton Pike, #210, Cherry Hill, NJ 08034, USA

Maclennan, Robert A R — *Government Official, England*
74 Abingdon Villas, London W8 6XB, England

MacLeod, Gavin — *Actor*
%Gage Group, 9255 Sunset Blvd, #515, Los Angeles, CA 90069, USA

MacLeod, John — *Basketball Coach*
51670 Oakbrook Court, Granger, IN 46530, USA

MacLeod, Robert — *Football Player*
110 Malibu Colony Dr, Malibu, CA 90265, USA

MacMahon, Brian — *Epidemiologist*
89 Warren St, Needham, MA 02192, USA

MacMillan, Whitney — *Businessman*
%Cargill Inc, PO Box 9300, Minneapolis, MN 55440, USA

MacNabb, B Gordon — *Missile Engineer*
1406 Prairie Ave, Cheyenne, WY 82009, USA

Macnee, Patrick — *Actor*
PO Box 1685, Palm Springs, CA 92263, USA

MacNeil, Cornell H — *Opera Singer*
%Columbia Artists Mgmt Inc, 165 W 57th St, New York, NY 10019, USA

MacNeil, Robert — *Commentator*
%"MacNeil/Lehrer Newshour" Show, 2700 S Quincy St, Arlington, VA 22206, USA

MacNeish, Richard S — *Archaeologist*
%Andover Archeological Research Foundation, PO Box 83, Andover, MA 01810, USA

MacNelly, Jeffrey K (Jeff) — *Editorial Cartoonist (Pluggers, Shoe)*
333 E Grace St, Richmond, VA 23293, USA

MacNichol, Peter — *Actor*
345 N Maple Dr, #300, Beverly Hills, CA 90210, USA

Macomber, George B H — *Skier*
1 Design Center Place, #600, Boston, MA 02210, USA

Macomber, William B, Jr — *Diplomat, Museum Official*
27 Monomoy Road, Nantucket, MA 02554, USA

Macon, Mark — *Basketball Player*
29600 Franklin Road, #34, Southfield, MI 48034, USA

MacPhail, Leland S (Lee), Jr — *Baseball Executive*
%American League, 350 Park Ave, New York, NY 10022, USA

MacPhee, Donald A — *Educator*
%State University College of New York, President's Office, Fredonia, NY 14063, USA

MacPherson, Duncan I — *Editorial Cartoonist*
%Toronto Daily Star, 1 Yonge St, Toronto ON M5E 1E6, Canada

Macpherson, Elle — *Model*
%Women Inc, 107 Greene St, #200, New York, NY 10012, USA

MacQuitty, Jonathan — *Medical Inventor*
%GenPharm International, 2375 Garcia Ave, Mountain View, CA 94043, USA

MacRae, Meredith — *Actress*
518 Pacific Ave, Manhattan Beach, CA 90266, USA

MacRae, Sheila — *Actress, Singer*
301 N Canon Dr, #305, Beverly Hills, CA 90210, USA

Macy, Bill — *Actor*
%Gold Marshak Liedtke, 3500 W Olive Ave, #1400, Burbank, CA 91505, USA

Macy, Kyle — *Basketball Player*
358 University St, Morehead, KY 40351, USA

Macy, William H — *Actor*
10130 Angelo Circle, Beverly Hills, CA 90210, USA

Madden, D S — *Religious Leader*
%American Baptist Assn, 4605 N State Line, Texarkana, TX 75503, USA

Madden, David — *Writer*
%Louisiana State University, US Civil War Center, Baton Rouge, LA 70803, USA

Madden, Diane — *Dancer*
%Trisha Brown Dance Co, 211 W 61st St, New York, NY 10023, USA

Madden, J Kevin — *Publisher*
%Conde Nast Publications, 360 Madison Ave, #1200, New York, NY 10017, USA

Madden, John E — *Football Coach, Sportscaster*
5955 Coronado Blvd, Pleasanton, CA 94588, USA

Maddox, Lester — *Governor, GA*
3155 Johnson Ferry Road NE, Marietta, GA 30062, USA

Maddox, Rose — *Singer*
749 E Nevada St, Ashland, OR 97520, USA

Maddux, Gregory A (Greg) — *Baseball Player*
3010 Compton Court, Alpharetta, GA 30022, USA

M

Maclennan - Maddux

Mader, Gunther — *Skier*
Am Brenner 28, 6156 Gries, Austria

Madge, Robert — *Businessman*
%Made Networks, 2310 N 1st St, San Jose, CA 95131, USA

Madigan, Amy — *Actress*
22031 Carbon Mesa Road, Malibu, CA 90265, USA

Madigan, John W — *Publisher*
%Tribune Co, 435 N Michigan Ave, Chicago, IL 60611, USA

Madigan, Martha — *Photographer*
%Tyler School of Art, Beech & Penrose Aves, Philadelphia, PA 19126, USA

Madonna — *Singer, Actress*
4519 Cockerham Dr, Los Angeles, CA 90027, USA

Madonna, Jon C — *Businessman*
%KPMG Peat Marwick, 767 5th Ave, New York, NY 10153, USA

Madrazo, Ignacio N — *Surgeon*
%Instituto Mexicano del Seguro Social, Mexico City, Mexico

Madsen, Loren — *Sculptor*
426 Broome St, New York, NY 10013, USA

Madsen, Michael — *Actor*
31336 Broad Beach Road, Malibu, CA 90265, USA

Madsen, Virginia — *Actress*
9354 Claircrest Dr, Beverly Hills, CA 90210, USA

Mae, Vanessa — *Singer*
%Creative Artists Agency, 9830 Wilshire Blvd, Beverly Hills, CA 90212, USA

Maegle, Richard (Dick) — *Football Player*
4047 Aberdeen Way, Houston, TX 77025, USA

Maffie, Michael O — *Businessman*
%Southwestern Gas Corp, 5241 Spring Mountain Road, Las Vegas, NV 89150, USA

Magaw, John W — *Law Enforcement Official*
%Alcohol Tobacco Firearms Bureau, 650 Massachusetts NW, Washington, DC 20001, USA

Magaziner, Henry J — *Architect*
1901 Walnut St, #15-B, Philadelphia, PA 19103, USA

Magee, Dave — *Harness Racing Driver*
55350 Deer Ridge Path, Big Rock, IL 60511, USA

Maggert, Jeff — *Golfer*
66 Pine Song Place, The Woodlands, TX 77381, USA

Magilton, Gerard E (Jerry) — *Astronaut*
%Martin Marietta Astro Space, PO Box 800, Princeton, NJ 08543, USA

Magnus, Edie — *Commentator*
%NBC-TV, News Dept, 30 Rockefeller Plaza, New York, NY 10112, USA

Magnuson, Ann — *Actress*
1317 Maltman Ave, Los Angeles, CA 90026, USA

Magnuson, Keith — *Hockey Player*
265 King Muir Road, Lake Forest, IL 60045, USA

Magoon, Bob — *Powerboat Racing Driver*
1688 Meridian Ave, Miami Beach, FL 33139, USA

Magri, Charles G (Charlie) — *Boxer*
345 Bethnal Green Road, Bethnal Green, London E2 6LG, England

Maguire, Deirdre — *Model*
%Elite Model Mgmt, 111 E 22nd St, #200, New York, NY 10010, USA

Maguire, Paul — *Sportscaster*
%NBC-TV, Sports Dept, 30 Rockefeller Plaza, New York, NY 10112, USA

Magyar, Gabriel — *Concert Cellist*
101 W Windsor Road, #3103, Urbana, IL 61801, USA

Mahaffey, John — *Golfer*
29 Cokeberry St, The Woodlands, TX 77380, USA

Mahaffey, Valerie — *Actress*
%Susan Smith, 121 N San Vicente Blvd, Beverly Hills, CA 90211, USA

Mahal, Taj — *Singer, Songwriter*
%Bill Graham Mgmt, PO Box 429094, San Francisco, CA 94142, USA

Mahan, Larry — *Rodeo Rider*
PO Box 41, Camp Verde, TX 78010, USA

Maharidge, Dale D — *Writer*
%Stanford University, Communications Dept, Stanford, CA 94305, USA

Maharis, George — *Actor*
13150 Mulholland Dr, Beverly Hills, CA 90210, USA

Maharishi Mahesh Yogi — *Religious Leader*
%Institute of World Leadership, Maharishi University, Fairfield, IA 52556, USA

Mahathir Bin Mohamed, Datuk Seri — *Prime Minister, Malaysia*
%Prime Minister's Office, Jalan Dato Onn, 50502 Kuala Lumpur, Malaysia
Maher, Bill — *Commentator, Comedian*
%Brillstein/Grey, 9150 Wilshire Blvd, #350, Beverly Hills, CA 90212, USA
Maher, James R — *Businessman*
%Laboratory Corp Holdings, 358 S Main St, Burlington, NC 27215, USA
Maher, John F — *Financier*
%Great Western Financial Corp, 9200 Oakdale Ave, Chatsworth, CA 91311, USA
Mahfouz, Naguib — *Nobel Literature Laureate*
%American University Press, 113 Sharia Kasr El Aini, Cairo, Egypt
Mahogany, Kevin — *Singer, Saxophonist, Actor*
%WRC Mgmt, 1850 Broadway, #508, New York, NY 10019, USA
Mahoney, David J — *Businessman*
277 Park Ave, New York, NY 10172, USA
Mahoney, John — *Actor*
%International Creative Mgmt, 8942 Wilshire Blvd, Beverly Hills, CA 90211, USA
Mahoney, Joseph A — *Financier*
%Adler Coleman Clearing Corp, 20 Broad St, New York, NY 10005, USA
Mahoney, Robert W — *Businessman*
%Diebold Inc, PO Box 8230, Canton, OH 44711, USA
Mahony, Roger Cardinal — *Religious Leader*
%Archdiocese of Los Angeles, 3424 Wilshire Blvd, Los Angeles, CA 90010, USA
Mahorn, Rick — *Basketball Player*
6425 Glen Oak Dr, Temple Hills, MD 20748, USA
Mahovlich, Frank — *Hockey Player*
27 Glenridge Dr, RR1, Unionville ON L6C 1A2, Canada
Mahre, Phil — *Skier*
White Pass Dr, Naches, WA 98937, USA
Mahre, Steve — *Skier*
2408 N 52nd Ave, Yakima, WA 98903, USA
Maida, Adam J Cardinal — *Religious Leader*
%Archdiocese of Detroit, 1234 Washington Blvd, Detroit, MI 48226, USA
Maiden-Naccarato, Jeanne — *Bowler*
1 Stadium Way N, #4, Tacoma, WA 98403, USA
Maier, Sepp — *Soccer Player*
Parkstr 62, 84405 Anzing, Germany
Mailer, Norman K (Norm) — *Writer*
142 Columbia Heights Place, Brooklyn, NY 11201, USA
Maisel, Jay — *Photographer*
190 The Bowery, New York, NY 10012, USA
Maisky, Mischa M — *Concert Cellist*
%Deutsche Grammaphon Records, 810 7th Ave, New York, NY 10019, USA
Maitland, Beth — *Actress*
%Epstein-Wyckoff, 280 S Beverly Dr, #400, Beverly Hills, CA 90212, USA
Majdarzavyn Ganzorig — *Cosmonaut, Mongolia*
%Academy of Sciences, Peace Ave 54-B, Ulan Bator 51, Mongolia
Majerle, Daniel L (Dan) — *Basketball Player*
2525 E San Miguel Ave, Phoenix, AZ 85016, USA
Majerus, Rick — *Basketball Coach*
%University of Utah, Athletic Dept, Huntsman Center, Salt Lake City, UT 84112, USA
Majewski, Janusz — *Movie Director*
Ul Forteczna 1-A, 01-540 Warsaw, Poland
Major, Clarence L — *Writer*
%University of California, English Dept, Sproul Hall, Davis, CA 95616, USA
Major, John — *Prime Minister, England*
8 Stukley Road, Huntingdon, Cambs, England
Majors, John T (Johnny) — *Football Player, Coach*
4215 Bigelow Blvd, Pittsburgh, PA 15213, USA
Majors, Lee — *Actor*
3000 Holiday Dr, PH #1, Fort Lauderdale, FL 33316, USA
Makarov, Askold A — *Ballet Dancer*
%Askold Makarov's State Ballet, 15 Mayakovsky St, St Petersburg, Russia
Makarov, Oleg G — *Cosmonaut*
%Potchta Kosmonavtov, Moskovskoi Oblasti, 141160 Syvisdny Goroduk, Russia
Makarova, Natalia R — *Ballerina*
%Herbert Breslin, 119 W 57th St, New York, NY 10019, USA
Makeba, Miriam — *Singer*
%Sadiane Corp, 230 Park Ave, #1512, New York, NY 10169, USA

M

Mahathir Bin Mohamed - Makeba

M

Makhalina, Yulia *Ballerina*
%State Kirov Ballet, 1 Ploschad Iskusstr, St Petersburg, Russia

Maki, Fumihiko *Architect*
5-16-22 Higashi-Gotanda, Shinagawaku, Tokyo, Japan

Makk, Karoly *Movie Director*
Hankoczy Jeno Utca 15, 1022 Budapest, Hungary

Mako *Actor*
%Amsel Eisenstadt Frazier, 6310 San Vicente Blvd, #401, Los Angeles, CA 90048, USA

Mako, C Gene *Tennis Player*
430 S Burnside Ave, #M-C, Los Angeles, CA 90036, USA

Maksimova, Yekaterina S *Ballerina*
%Bolshoi Theater, Teatralnaya Pl 1, 103009 Moscow, Russia

Maksymiuk, Jerzy *Conductor*
%BBC Scottish Symphony, Queen Margaret Dr, Glasgow G12 8BC, Scotland

Malandro, Kristina *Actress*
2518 Cardigan Court, Los Angeles, CA 90077, USA

Malara, Anthony C *Television Executive*
%CBS Inc, TV Network, 51 W 52nd St, New York, NY 10019, USA

Malcolm, George J *Concert Harpsichordist*
99 Wimbledon Hill Road, London SW19 4BE, England

Malden, Karl *Actor*
1845 Mandeville Canyon Road, Los Angeles, CA 90049, USA

Malee, Chompoo *Fashion Designer*
%Hino & Malee Inc, 3701 N Ravenswood Ave, Chicago, IL 60613, USA

Maleeva, Katerina *Tennis Player*
Mladostr 1, #45, NH 14, Sofia 1174, Bulgaria

Maleeva-Fragniere, Manuela *Tennis Player*
%Women's Tennis Assn, 133 1st St NE, St Petersburg, FL 33701, USA

Malenick, Donal H *Businessman*
%Worthington Industries, 1205 Dearborn Dr, Columbus, OH 43085, USA

Malerba, Franco E *Astronaut*
Via Cantore 10, 16149 Genova, Italy

Malfitano, Catherine *Opera Singer*
%Metropolitan Opera Assn, Lincoln Center Plaza, New York, NY 10023, USA

Malick, Wendie *Actress*
%Innovative Artists, 1999 Ave of Stars, #2850, Los Angeles, CA 90067, USA

Malicky, Neal *Educator*
%Baldwin-Wallace College, President's Office, Berea, OH 44017, USA

Malietoa Tanumafili II *King, Western Samoa*
%Government House, Vailima, Apia, Western Samoa

Maliponte, Adrianna *Opera Singer*
%Gorlinsky Promotions, 35 Darer, London W1, England

Malkan, Matthew A *Astronomer*
%University of Arizona, Steward Observatory, Tucson, AZ 85721, USA

Malkhov, Vladimir *Ballet Dancer*
%American Ballet Theatre, 890 Broadway, New York, NY 10003, USA

Malkovich, John *Actor*
PO Box 1171, Weston, CT 06883, USA

Mallary, Robert *Sculptor*
PO Box 97, Conway, MA 01341, USA

Mallea, Eduardo *Writer*
Posadas 1120, Buenos Aires, Argentina

Mallender, William H *Businessman*
%Talley Industries, 2702 N 44th St, Phoenix, AZ 85008, USA

Mallette, Alfred J *Army General*
4578 Bedford Court, Evans, GA 30809, USA

Malley, Kenneth C *Navy Admiral*
136 Riverside Road, Edgewater, MD 21037, USA

Mallick, Don *Test Pilot*
42045 N Tilton Dr, Quartz Hill, CA 93536, USA

Mallon, Meg *Golfer*
36800 Woodward Ave, #239, Bloomfield, MI 48304, USA

Malloy, Edward A *Educator*
%University of Notre Dame, President's Office, Notre Dame, IN 46556, USA

Malloy, Patrick E, III *Financier*
%New York Bancorp, 241-02 Northern Blvd, Douglaston, NY 11362, USA

Malo, Raul *Singer (The Mavericks), Songwriter*
%AristoMedia, 1620 16th Ave S, Nashville, TN 37212, USA

Maloff, Sam — *Furniture Designer*
PO Box 51, Alta Loma, CA 91701, USA

Malone, Beverly L — *Labor Leader*
%American Nurses Assn, 800 Maryland Ave SW, Washington, DC 20002, USA

Malone, Brendan — *Basketball Coach*
%New York Knicks, Madison Square Garden, 2 Penn Plaza, New York, NY 10121, USA

Malone, Dorothy — *Actress*
PO Box 7287, Dallas, TX 75209, USA

Malone, James W — *Religious Leader*
%National Catholic Bishops Conference, 1312 Massachusetts, Washington, DC 20005, USA

Malone, Jeff — *Basketball Player*
12520 Guinevere Road, Bowie, MD 20715, USA

Malone, John C — *Television Executive*
%Tele-Communications, 5619 DTC Parkway, Englewood, CO 80111, USA

Malone, Karl — *Basketball Player*
%Utah Jazz, Delta Center, 301 W South Temple, Salt Lake City, UT 84101, USA

Malone, Michael P — *Educator*
%Montana State University, President's Office, Bozeman, MT 59717, USA

Malone, Moses — *Basketball Player*
%San Antonio Spurs, 600 E Market St, #102, San Antonio, TX 78205, USA

Malone, Nancy — *Actress*
11624 Sunshine Terrace, Studio City, CA 91604, USA

Malone, Robert B — *Financier*
%SunBank/South Florida, 501 E Las Olas Blvd, Fort Lauderdale, FL 33301, USA

Malone, Thomas F — *Geophysicist*
300 Woodcroft Parkway, Durham, NC 27713, USA

Malone, Wallace D, Jr — *Financier*
%SouthTrust Corp, 420 N 20th St, Birmingham, AL 35203, USA

Maloney, Dave — *Hockey Player*
1 Vista Ave, Old Greenwich, CT 06870, USA

Maloney, Don — *Hockey Player*
22 Park Dr S, Rye, NY 10580, USA

Maloney, James W (Jim) — *Baseball Player*
7027 N Teilman Ave, #102, Fresno, CA 93711, USA

Maloney, William R — *Marine Corps General*
%Navy Mutual Aid Assn, Henderson Hall, 29 Carpenter Road, Arlington, VA 22204, USA

Malouf, David — *Writer*
%Pantheon/Random House Inc, 201 E 50th St, New York, NY 10022, USA

Maltby, John N — *Businessman*
Broadford House, Stratfield Turgis, Basingstoke, Hants RG27 OAS, England

Maltby, Richard E, Jr — *Lyricist*
1111 Park Ave, #4-D, New York, NY 10128, USA

Maltin, Leonard — *Television Critic*
10424 Whipple St, Toluca Lake, CA 91602, USA

Malyshev, Yuri V — *Cosmonaut*
%Potchta Kosmonavtov, Moskovskoi Oblasti, 141160 Syvisdny Goroduk, Russia

Mamaloni, Solomon S — *Prime Minister, Solomon Islands*
%Prime Minister's Office, Legakilei Ridge, Honiara, Solomon Islands

Mamby, Saoul — *Boxer*
20-17 E Moshulu Parkway, Bronx, NY 10468, USA

Mamet, David A — *Writer*
PO Box 381589, Cambridge, MA 02238, USA

Mamo, Anthony J — *President, Malta*
49 Stella Maris St, Sliema, Malta

Mamohato — *Queen Regent, Lesotho*
%Royal Palace, PO Box 524, Maseru, Lesotho

Mamorsky, Liz — *Artist, Sculptor*
2525 McAlister St, San Francisco, CA 94118, USA

Mamula, Mike — *Football Player*
26 Apple St, Lackawanna, NY 14218, USA

Manakov, Gennadi M — *Cosmonaut*
%Potchta Kosmonavtov, Moskovskoi Oblasti, 141160 Syvisdny Goroduk, Russia

Manarov, Musa C — *Cosmonaut*
Khovanskeya 3, 129 515 Moscow, Russia

Manasseh, Leonard S — *Architect*
6 Bacon's Lane, Highgate, London N6 6BL, England

Manatt, Charles T — *Political Leader*
4814 Woodway Lane NW, Washington, DC 20016, USA

Mancha, Vaughn — *Football Player*
1308 High Road, Tallahassee, FL 32304, USA

Mancham, James R M — *President, Seychelles*
%Lloyd's Bank, 81 Edgware Road, London W2 2HY, England

Manchester, Melissa — *Singer, Songwriter*
15822 High Knoll Road, Encino, CA 91436, USA

Manchester, William — *Writer*
PO Box 329, Wesleyan Station, Middletown, CT 06457, USA

Mancini, Ray (Boom Boom) — *Boxer*
12524 Indianapolis St, Los Angeles, CA 90066, USA

Mancuso, Frank G — *Movie Executive*
%MGM/United Artists, 1350 Ave of Americas, New York, NY 10019, USA

Mancuso, Nick — *Actor*
%Gold Marshak Liedtke, 3500 W Olive Ave, #1400, Burbank, CA 91505, USA

Mandabach, Caryn — *Television Producer*
%Carsey-Warner Productions, 4024 Radford Ave, Building 3, Studio City, CA 91604, USA

Mandan, Robert — *Actor*
4160 Dixie Canyon Road, Sherman Oaks, CA 91423, USA

Mandarich, Tony — *Football Player*
%Indianapolis Colts, 7001 W 56th St, Indianapolis, IN 46254, USA

Mandel, Howie — *Actor*
24710 Robert Guy Road, Hidden Hills, CA 91302, USA

Mandel, Johnny — *Composer*
2401 Main St, Santa Monica, CA 90405, USA

Mandel, Marvin — *Governor, MD*
%Frank A Defilippo, Cross Keys Road, Baltimore, MD 21210, USA

Mandela, N Winnie Madikizela- — *Social Activist*
Orlando West, Soweto, Johannesburg, South Africa

Mandela, Nelson R — *President, South Africa; Nobel Laureate*
%President's Office, Union Buildings, Pretoria 0001, South Africa

Mandelbrot, Benoit B — *Mathematician*
%IBM, PO Box 218, Yorktown Heights, NY 10598, USA

Mandl, Alex J — *Businessman*
%AT&T Co, 295 N Maple Ave, Basking Ridge, NJ 07920, USA

Mandle, E Roger — *Museum Director*
%Rhode Island School of Design, President's Office, Providence, RI 02903, USA

Mandlikova, Hanna — *Tennis Player*
Vymolova 8, 150 00 Prague 5, Czech Republic

Mandrell, Barbara — *Singer*
%Mandrell Mgmt, 605 N Main St, #C, Ashland City, TN 37015, USA

Mandrell, Erline — *Singer*
%Mandrell Mgmt, 605 N Main St, #C, Ashland City, TN 37015, USA

Mandrell, Louise — *Singer*
%Mandrell Mgmt, 605 N Main St, #C, Ashland City, TN 37015, USA

Mandylor, Costas — *Actor*
%Innovative Artists, 1999 Ave of Stars, #2850, Los Angeles, CA 90067, USA

Manekshaw, Sam H F J — *Army Field Marshal, India*
Stavka Springfield, Coonor, Nilgiris, South India, India

Manery, Randy — *Hockey Player*
6587 Garrett Road, Buford, GA 30518, USA

Manetti, Larry — *Actor*
%Epstein-Wyckoff, 280 S Beverly Dr, #400, Beverly Hills, CA 90212, USA

Mangelsdorf, David — *Geneticist*
%Salk Institute, Gene Expression Laboratory, PO Box 85800, San Diego, CA 92186, USA

Mangelsdorf, Paul C — *Geneticist*
510 Caswell Road, Chapel Hill, NC 27514, USA

Mangione, Chuck — *Jazz Trumpeter, Composer*
%Gates Music, 1850 S Winton Road, Rochester, NY 14618, USA

Mangold, James — *Movie Director*
%William Morris Agency, 151 S El Camino Dr, Beverly Hills, CA 90212, USA

Mangold, Sylvia — *Artist*
1 Bull Road, Washingtonville, NY 10992, USA

Maniatis, Thomas P — *Genetics Engineer, Molecular Biolgist*
%Harvard University, Biochemistry Dept, Cambridge, MA 02138, USA

Manilow, Barry — *Singer, Songwriter*
%Stiletto Entertainment, 5443 Beethoven St, Los Angeles, CA 90066, USA

Mankiller, Wilma P — *Social Activist*
%Cherokee Nation, PO Box 948, Tahlequah, OK 74465, USA

Mankowitz, Wolf *Writer*
Bridge House, Ahakista, County Cork, Ireland

Manley, Elizabeth *Figure Skater*
%M A Rosenberg, 73271 Riata Trail, Palm Desert, CA 92260, USA

Mann, Abby *Writer*
%Abby Mann Productions, 602 N Whittier Dr, Beverly Hills, CA 90210, USA

Mann, Aimee *Singer ('Til Tuesday); Songwriter*
%Creative Artists Agency, 9830 Wilshire Blvd, Beverly Hills, CA 90212, USA

Mann, Barry *Composer*
1010 Laurel Way, Beverly Hills, CA 90210, USA

Mann, Carol *Golfer*
6 Cape Chestnut Dr, The Woodlands, TX 77381, USA

Mann, David W *Religious Leader*
10025 Crown Point Dr, Fort Wayne, IN 46804, USA

Mann, Delbert *Movie Director, Producer*
%Caroline Productions, 401 S Burnside Ave, #11-D, Los Angeles, CA 90036, USA

Mann, H Thompson *Swimmer*
1009 Westham Parkway, Richmond, VA 23229, USA

Mann, Herbie *Jazz Flutist*
%Kokopelli Music, PO Box 8200, Santa Fe, NM 87504, USA

Mann, Johnny *Composer, Conductor*
78516 Gorman Lane, Indio, CA 92203, USA

Mann, Larry D *Actor*
%Allen Goldstein Assoc, 5015 Lemona Ave, Sherman Oaks, CA 91403, USA

Mann, Marvin L *Businessman*
%Lexmark International, PO Box 262885, Tampa, FL 33685, USA

Mann, Michael K *Television Producer, Director*
13746 Sunset Blvd, Pacific Palisades, CA 90272, USA

Mann, Robert W *Biomedical Engineer*
5 Pelham Road, Lexington, MA 02173, USA

Mann, Shelley *Swimmer*
315 S Ivy St, Arlington, VA 22204, USA

Mann, Terrence V *Actor*
%Duva-Flack, 200 W 57th St, New York, NY 10019, USA

Mann, Thomas C *Government Official*
2813 22nd St, Lubbock, TX 79410, USA

Manners, David *Actor*
3011 Foothill Road, Santa Barbara, CA 93105, USA

Manning Mims, Madeline *Track Athlete*
7477 E 48th St, #83-4, Tulsa, OK 74145, USA

Manning, Archie *Football Player, Sportscaster*
1420 1st St, New Orleans, LA 70130, USA

Manning, Daniel R (Danny) *Basketball Player*
2805 Tennyson Place, Hermosa Beach, CA 90254, USA

Manning, Irene *Actress*
3165 La Mesa Dr, San Carlos, CA 94070, USA

Manning, Jane *Opera Singer*
2 Wilton Square, London N1, England

Manning, Patrick A M *Prime Minister, Trinidad & Tobago*
%Prime Minister's Office, Central Bank Building, Port of Spain, Trinidad

Manning, Richard E (Rick) *Baseball Player*
12151 New Market, Chagrin Falls, OH 44026, USA

Manning, Robert J *Editor*
191 Commonwealth Ave, Boston, MA 02116, USA

Mannino, Franco *Conductor*
%Studio Mannino, Via Citta di Castello 14, 00191 Rome, Italy

Manoff, Dinah *Actress*
21244 Ventura Blvd, #126, Sherman Oaks, CA 91423, USA

Manoogian, Richard A *Businessman*
%Masco Corp, 21001 Van Born Road, Taylor, MI 48180, USA

Manos, Pete L *Businessman*
%Giant Food Inc, 6300 Sheriff Road, Landover, MD 20785, USA

Mansbach, Peter J *Financier*
%Republic National Bank (NY), 452 5th Ave, New York, NY 10018, USA

Mansell, Nigel *Auto Racing Driver*
Portland House, Station Road, Box 1, Ballasalla, Isle of Man, England

Manser, Michael J *Architect*
%Manser Assoc, 8 Hammersmith Broadway, London W6 7AL, England

M

Mankowitz - Manser

V.I.P. Address Book
423

Mansfield, Michael J (Mike)	*Senator, MT; Diplomat*
1101 Pennsylvania Ave NW, #900, Washington, DC 20004, USA	
Mansholt, Sicco L	*Government Official, Netherlands*
Oosteinde 18, 8351 HB Wapserveen, Netherlands	
Manske, Edgar	*Football Player*
1031 Lanza Court, San Marcos, CA 92069, USA	
Manson, Dave	*Hockey Player*
%Montreal Canadiens, 1260 De la Gauchetiere W, Montreal PQ H3B 5E8, Canada	
Manson, Marilyn	*Singer (Marilyn Manson)*
%Artists & Audience Entertainment, 2112 Broadway, #600, New York, NY 10023, USA	
Mansouri, Lotfi	*Opera Director*
%San Francisco Opera House, 301 Van Ness Ave, San Francisco, CA 94102, USA	
Mantee, Paul	*Actor*
3709 Las Flores Canyon Road, #4, Malibu, CA 90265, USA	
Mantegna, Joe	*Actor*
10415 Sarah St, Toluca Lake, CA 91602, USA	
Mantel, Hillary	*Writer*
%Henry Holt, 115 W 18th St, New York, NY 10011, USA	
Mantha, Mo	*Hockey Player*
8423 Tally Ho Road, Lutherville, MD 21093, USA	
Mantooth, Randolph	*Actor*
PO Box 280, Agoura, CA 91376, USA	
Manuelidis, Laura	*Neuropathologist*
%Yale University Medical School, Neuropathology Dept, New Haven, CT 06520, USA	
Manuella, Tufaga	*Governor General, Tuvalu*
%Government House, Fongafale, Tuvalu	
Manwaring, Kurt D	*Baseball Player*
10938 N 123rd St, Scottsdale, AZ 85259, USA	
Manz, Wolfgang	*Concert Pianist*
Pasteuralle 55, 30655 Hanover, Germany	
Manzarek, Ray	*Keyboardist (The Doors)*
%Goldman & Knell, 1900 Ave of Stars, #1040, Los Angeles, CA 90067, USA	
Manzoni, Giacomo	*Composer*
Viale Papiniano 31, 20123 Milan, Italy	
Mara, Adele	*Actress, Dancer*
1928 Mandeville Canyon Road, Los Angeles, CA 90049, USA	
Mara, Ratu Sir Kamisese K T	*President, Fiji*
%President's Office, Berkeley Parade, 6 Berkeley Crescent, Suva, Fiji	
Mara, Wellington T	*Football Executive*
%New York Giants, Giants Stadium, East Rutherford, NJ 07073, USA	
Maradona, Diego A	*Soccer Player*
%FC Boca Juniors, Brandsen 805, 1161 Capital Federal, Argentina	
Marais, Jean	*Actor*
%Cineart, 34 Ave de Champs-Elysees, 75008 Paris, France	
Maraniss, David	*Journalist*
%Washington Post, Editorial Dept, 1150 15th St NW, Washington, DC 20071, USA	
Marbury, Stephon	*Basketball Player*
%Minnesota Timberwolves, Target Center, 600 1st Ave N, Minneapolis, MN 55403, USA	
Marbut, Robert G	*Publisher*
%Argyle Communications, 100 NE Loop, #1400, San Antonio, TX 78216, USA	
Marc, Alessandra	*Opera Singer*
%Columbia Artists Mgmt Inc, 165 W 57th St, New York, NY 10019, USA	
Marca-Relli, Conrad	*Artist*
%Jaffe Baker Blau Gallery, 608 Banjan Trail, Boca Raton, FL 33431, USA	
Marceau, Marcel	*Mime*
%Compagne de Mime, 32 Rue de Londres, 75009 Paris, France	
Marceau, Sophie	*Actress*
13 Rue Madeleine Michelle, 92200 Neuilly-sur-Seine, France	
March, Barbara	*Actress*
%Judy Schoen, 606 N Larchmont Blvd, #309, Los Angeles, CA 90004, USA	
March, Jane	*Actress*
%Storm Model Mgmt, 5 Jubilee Place, #100, London SW3 3TD, England	
March, Little Peggy	*Singer*
%American Mgmt, 17530 Ventura Blvd, #108, Encino, CA 91316, USA	
Marchais, Georges	*Government Official, France*
%Parti Communiste Francais, 2 Place du Colonel Fabien, 75019 Paris, France	
Marchand, Nancy	*Actress*
205 W 89th St, #6-S, New York, NY 10024, USA	

Marchetti, Gino — *Football Player*
10 Painters Lane, Wayne, PA 19087, USA

Marchetti, Leo V — *Labor Leader*
%Fraternal Order of Police, 5613 Belair Road, Baltimore, MD 21206, USA

Marchibroda, Theodore J (Ted) — *Football Player, Coach*
%Baltimore Ravens, 200 St Paul Place, #2400, Baltimore, MD 21202, USA

Marchuk, Guri I — *Applied Mathematician*
%Computing Math Institute, Leninsky Prosp 32-A, 117334 Moscow, Russia

Marcil, Vanessa — *Actress*
PO Box 691736, West Hollywood, CA 90069, USA

Marcinkevicius, Iustinas M — *Writer*
Mildos Str 33, #6, 232055 Vilnius, Lithuania

Marcinkus, Paul C — *Religious Leader*
%Institute for Religious Work, 00120 Vatican City

Marcis, Dave — *Auto Racing Driver*
%Averys Creek RD-Arden, PO Box 645, Skyland, NC 28776, USA

Marcotte, Don — *Hockey Player*
8 Porter Road, #C, Boxford, MA 01921, USA

Marcovicci, Andrea — *Actress*
3761 Reklaw Dr, Studio City, CA 91604, USA

Marcus, Ken — *Photographer*
6916 Melrose Ave, Los Angeles, CA 90038, USA

Marcus, Rudolph A — *Nobel Chemistry Laureate*
331 S Hill Ave, Pasadena, CA 91106, USA

Marcus, Stanley — *Businessman*
NCNB Center, 4800 Tower II, Dallas, TX 75201, USA

Marcy, Geoffrey W — *Astronomer*
%San Francisco State University, Astronomy Dept, San Francisco, CA 94132, USA

Mardall, Cyril L — *Architect*
5 Boyne Terrace Mews, London W11 3LR, England

Marden, Brice — *Artist*
54 Bond St, New York, NY 10012, USA

Marden, Robert A — *Financier*
%People Heritage Financial, 1 Portland Square, Portland, ME 04101, USA

Mardones, Benny — *Singer*
1303 16th Ave S, Nashville, TN 37212, USA

Maree, Sydney — *Track Athlete*
2 Braxton Road, Rosemont, PA 19010, USA

Margal, Albert M — *Prime Minister, Sierra Leone*
8 Hornsey Rise Gardens, London N19, England

Margaret Rose — *Princess, England*
Kensington Palace, London W8 4PU, England

Margeot, Jean Cardinal — *Religious Leader*
Bonne Terre, Vacoas, Mauritius

Margerison, Richard W — *Businessman*
%Tyler Corp, San Jacinto Tower, 2121 San Jacinto St, Dallas, TX 75201, USA

Margoliash, Emmanuel — *Biochemist*
%University of Chicago, Biological Sciences, 1919 W Taylor St, Chicago, IL 60612, USA

Margolin, Phillip — *Writer*
%Bantam Books, 1540 Broadway, New York, NY 10036, USA

Margolin, Stuart — *Actor*
2809 2nd St, #1, Santa Monica, CA 90405, USA

Margolis, Lawrence S — *Judge*
%US Claims Court, 717 Madison Place NW, Washington, DC 20005, USA

Margrave, John L — *Chemist*
5012 Tangle Lane, Houston, TX 77056, USA

Margrethe II — *Queen, Denmark*
%Amalienborg Palace, 1257 Copenhagen K, Denmark

Margulies, James H (Jimmy) — *Editorial Cartoonist*
%Hackensack Record, Editorial Dept, 150 River St, Hackensack, NJ 07601, USA

Margulies, Julianna — *Actress*
%International Creative Mgmt, 8942 Wilshire Blvd, Beverly Hills, CA 90211, USA

Margulis, Lynn — *Biologist, Botanist*
2 Cummington St, Boston, MA 02215, USA

Mariategui, Sandro — *Prime Minister, Peru*
Congreso Del Peru, #301, Plaza Bolivar, Lima, Peru

Marichal, Juan A S — *Baseball Player*
9458 NW 54 Doral Circle Lane, Miami, FL 33178, USA

M

Marchetti - Marichal

M

Marie — *Princess, Lichtenstein*
%Schloss Vaduz, 9490 Vaduz, Liechtenstein

Marie, Aurelius J B L — *President, Dominica*
Zicack, Portsmouth, Danica

Marie, Lisa — *Model*
%Click Model Mgmt, 881 7th Ave, New York, NY 10019, USA

Marie, Rose — *Actress*
6916 Chisholm Ave, Van Nuys, CA 91406, USA

Marie, Teena — *Singer*
1000 Laguna Road, Pasadena, CA 91105, USA

Marimow, William K — *Journalist*
1025 Winding Way, Baltimore, MD 21210, USA

Marin, Jack — *Basketball Player*
3909 Regent Road, Durham, NC 27707, USA

Marinaro, Edward F (Ed) — *Actor, Football Player*
1466 N Doheny Dr, Los Angeles, CA 90069, USA

Marineau, Philip A — *Businessman*
%Quaker Oats Co, 321 N Clark St, Chicago, IL 60610, USA

Marinella, Sabino — *Businessman*
%Keyport Life Insurance, 125 High St, Boston, MA 02110, USA

Marino, Daniel C (Dan), Jr — *Football Player*
3415 Stallion Lane, Fort Lauderdale, FL 33331, USA

Marino, John — *Cyclist*
%Race Across America, 64 Bennington, Irvine, CA 92620, USA

Mario, Ernest — *Pharmacist, Businessman*
%Alza Corp, 950 Page Mill Road, Palo Alto, CA 94304, USA

Mariotti, Ray — *Editor*
%Austin American-Statesman, Editorial Dept, 166 E Riverside, Austin, TX 78704, USA

Marisol (Escobar) — *Sculptor*
%Marlborough Gallery, 40 W 57th St, New York, NY 10019, USA

Mariucci, Steve — *Football Coach*
%San Francisco 49ers, 4949 Centennial Blvd, Santa Clara, CA 95054, USA

Mark, Hans M — *Government Official, Physicist, Educator*
1715 Scenic Dr, Austin, TX 78703, USA

Mark, Mary Ellen — *Photographer*
%International Center of Photography, 1130 15th Ave, New York, NY 10128, USA

Mark, Reuben — *Businessman*
%Colgate-Palmolive Co, 300 Park Ave, New York, NY 10022, USA

Mark, Robert — *Law Enforcement Official*
Esher, Surrey KT10 8LU, England

Markaryants, Vladimir S — *Government Official, Armenia*
%Council of Ministers, Yerevan, Armenia

Marken, William R — *Editor*
%Sunset Magazine, Editorial Dept, 80 Willow Road, Menlo Park, CA 94025, USA

Markert, Clement L — *Biologist*
4005 Wakefield Dr, Colorado Springs, CO 80906, USA

Markey, Lucille P — *Thoroughbred Racing Breeder*
18 La Gorce Circle Lane, La Gorce Island, Miami Beach, FL 33141, USA

Markham, Monte — *Actor*
PO Box 607, Malibu, CA 90265, USA

Markkula, A C (Mike), Jr — *Businessman*
%Apple Computer, 1 Infinite Loop, Cupertino, CA 95014, USA

Markle, C Wilson — *Film Engineer*
%Colorization Inc, 26 Soho St, Toronto ON M5T 1Z7, Canada

Markle, Peter — *Movie Director*
7510 W Sunset Blvd, #509, Los Angeles, CA 90046, USA

Markov, Victor (Vic) — *Football Player*
5512 NE Windemere Road, Seattle, WA 98105, USA

Markova, Alicia — *Ballerina*
%Barclays Bank Ltd, 137 Brompton Road, London SW3 1QB, England

Markowitz, Harry M — *Nobel Economics Laureate*
1010 Turquoise St, #245, San Diego, CA 92109, USA

Markowitz, Michael — *Artist*
%23rd Street Gallery, 3747 23rd St, San Francisco, CA 94114, USA

Markowitz, Robert — *Movie Director, Producer*
11521 Amanda Dr, Studio City, CA 91604, USA

Marks, Albert J — *Pageant Director*
%Miss American Pageant, 1325 Broadway, Atlantic City, NJ 08401, USA

Marks, Alfred — *Actor*
%Barry Burnett, Grafton House, 2/3 Golden Square, London W1R 3AD, England

Marks, Bruce — *Ballet Dancer, Artistic Director*
%Boston Ballet Co, 19 Clarendon St, Boston, MA 02116, USA

Marks, Leonard H — *Government Official*
2700 Calvert St NW, #714, Washington, DC 20008, USA

Marks, Paul A — *Oncologist, Cell Biologist*
PO Box 1485, Washington Depot, CT 06793, USA

Marks, William L — *Financier*
%Whitney National Bank, 228 St Charles Ave, New Orleans, LA 70130, USA

Markson, Harry — *Boxing Promoter*
10 Sheppard Dr, Middletown, NJ 07748, USA

Markwart, Nevin — *Hockey Player*
218 Harvard St, #203, Brookline, MA 02146, USA

Marlen, John S — *Businessman*
%Ameron Inc, 245 S Los Robles Ave, Pasadena, CA 91101, USA

Marler, Peter R — *Biologist*
Reservoir Road, Staatsburg, NY 12580, USA

Marlette, Douglas N (Doug) — *Editorial Cartoonist*
PO Box 32188, Charlotte, NC 28232, USA

Marley, James E — *Businessman*
%AMP Inc, PO Box 3608, Harrisburg, PA 17105, USA

Marley, Ziggy — *Singer, Songwriter*
Jack's Hill, Kingston, Jamaica

Marlin, Sterling — *Auto Racing Driver*
Rt 8, Columbia, TN 38401, USA

Marm, Walter J, Jr — *Vietnam War Army Hero (CMH)*
PO Box 2017, Fremont, NC 27830, USA

Marohn, William D — *Businessman*
%Whirlpool Corp, 2000 N State St, Rt 63, Benton Harbor, MI 49022, USA

Maroney, Daniel V, Jr — *Labor Leader*
%Amalgamated Transit Union, 5025 Wisconsin Ave NW, Washington, DC 20016, USA

Marotte, Gilles — *Hockey Player*
%Agence Prestige, 4777 Blvd Bourque, Rock Forest PQ J1N 1A6, Canada

Marriner, Neville — *Conductor*
67 Cornwell Gardens, London SW7 4BA, England

Marriott, Alice S — *Businesswoman*
%Marriott International, Marriott Dr, Washington, DC 20058, USA

Marriott, J Willard, Jr — *Businessman*
%Marriott International, Marriott Dr, Washington, DC 20058, USA

Marro, Anthony J — *Editor*
%Newsday, Editorial Dept, 235 Pinelawn Road, Melville, NY 11747, USA

Marron, Donald B — *Financier*
%PaineWebber Group, 1285 Ave of Americas, New York, NY 10019, USA

Marryout, Ronald F — *Navy Admiral*
170 Cranes Crook Lane, Annapolis, MD 21401, USA

Mars, Forrest, Jr — *Businessman*
%Mars Inc, 6885 Elm St, McLean, VA 22101, USA

Mars, Kenneth — *Actor*
10820 Shoshone Ave, Granada Hills, CA 91344, USA

Marsalis, Branford — *Jazz Saxophonist, Composer*
%Wilkins Mgmt, 323 Broadway, Cambridge, MA 02139, USA

Marsalis, Ellis — *Jazz Pianist*
%Management Ark, 118 Village Blvd, Princeton, NJ 08540, USA

Marsalis, Wynton — *Jazz Trumpeter, Composer*
3 Lincoln Center, #2911, New York, NY 10023, USA

Marsden, Charles J — *Businessman*
%Crompton & Knowles Corp, Metro Center, 1 Station Place, Stamford, CT 06902, USA

Marsden, Freddie — *Drummer (Gerry & Pacemakers)*
28-A Manor Road, Bradford BDL 4QU, England

Marsden, Gerard (Gerry) — *Singer, Guitarist (Gerry & Pacemakers)*
28-A Manor Road, Bradford BDL 4QU, England

Marsden, Roy — *Actor*
%London Mgmt, 2-4 Noel St, London W1V 3RB, England

Marsh of Mannington, Richard W — *Government Official, England*
Laurentian House, Barnwood, Gloucs GL4 7RZ, England

Marsh, Brad — *Hockey Player*
RR 2, Mount Laurel, NJ 08054, USA

M

Marks - Marsh

M

Marsh, Graham *Golfer*
%PGA Seniors Tour, 112 T P C Blvd, Ponte Vedra Beach, FL 32082, USA

Marsh, Henry *Track Athlete*
%General Delivery, Bountiful, UT 84010, USA

Marsh, Jean *Actress*
%London Mgmt, 2-4 Noel St, London W1V 3RB, England

Marsh, Linda *Actress*
170 West End Ave, 22-P, New York, NY 10023, USA

Marsh, Marian *Actress*
PO Box 1, Palm Desert, CA 92261, USA

Marsh, Michael (Mike) *Track Athlete*
2425 Holly Hall St, #152, Houston, TX 77054, USA

Marsh, Miles L *Businessman*
%James River Corp, PO Box 2218, Richmond, VA 23218, USA

Marsh, Robert T *Air Force General, Businessman*
%Thiokel Corp, 6327 Manchester Way, Alexandria, VA 22304, USA

Marshall, Barry J *Medical Researcher*
%University of Virginia, Med Center, Immunolgy Dept, Charlottesville, VA 22908, USA

Marshall, Bert *Hockey Player*
23241 Beech St, Dearborn, MI 48124, USA

Marshall, Burke *Attorney*
Castle Meadow Road, Newton, CT 06470, USA

Marshall, Carolyn M *Religious Leader*
%United Methodist Church, 204 N Newlin St, Veedersburg, IN 47987, USA

Marshall, Dale Rogers *Educator*
%Wheaton College, President's Office, Norton, MA 02766, USA

Marshall, Donyell *Basketball Player*
12440 SE 274th St, Auburn, WA 98031, USA

Marshall, E G *Actor*
Bryan Lake Road, RFD 2, Mount Kisco, NY 10549, USA

Marshall, F Ray *Secretary, Labor*
%University of Texas, LBJ Public Affairs School, Austin, TX 78712, USA

Marshall, Frank W *Movie Producer*
%Amblin Entertainment, 100 Universal City Plaza, #477, Universal City, CA 91608, USA

Marshall, Garry K *Movie Director, Actor*
10459 Sarah St, Toluca Lake, CA 91602, USA

Marshall, James *Actor*
30710 Monte Lado Dr, Malibu, CA 90265, USA

Marshall, John *Prime Minister, New Zealand*
%Buddle Findlay Barristers, PO Box 2694, Wellington, New Zealand

Marshall, Margaret A *Opera Singer*
Woodside, Main St, Gargunnock, Stirling FKS 3BP, Scotland

Marshall, Michael A (Mike) *Baseball Player*
601 Furlong Dr, Austin, TX 78746, USA

Marshall, Michael G (Mike) *Baseball Player*
%West Texas A&M, Athletic Dept, Canyon, TX 79016, USA

Marshall, Paula *Actress*
%Innovative Artists, 1999 Ave of Stars, #2850, Los Angeles, CA 90067, USA

Marshall, Penny *Actress, Director*
7150 La Presa Dr, Los Angeles, CA 90068, USA

Marshall, Peter *Television Host*
16714 Oak View Dr, Encino, CA 91436, USA

Marshall, Willard W *Baseball Player*
7 Rockleigh Road, Rockleigh, NJ 07647, USA

Marshall, William *Actor*
PO Box 331212, Pacoima, CA 91333, USA

Martell, Dominic A *Labor Leader*
%Plasterers Cement Masons Int'l Assn, 1125 17th St NW, Washington, DC 20036, USA

Martens, Wilfried *Prime Minister, Belgium*
%Europese Volkspartij, 16 Rue de la Victoire, 1060 Brussels, Belgium

Martika (Marrero) *Singer*
%Lobeline Communications, 8995 Elevado Ave, Los Angeles, CA 90069, USA

Martin (Miss Manners), Judith *Journalist*
1651 Harvard St NW, Washington, DC 20009, USA

Martin, Agnes *Artist*
414 Placitas Road, Taos, NM 87571, USA

Martin, Alastair B *Tennis Contributor*
%Bessemer Trust Co, 630 5th Ave, New York, NY 10111, USA

Martin, Albert C *Architect*
%Albert C Martin Assoc, 811 W 7th St, #800, Los Angeles, CA 90017, USA
Martin, Andrea *Actress*
130 W 42nd St, #1804, New York, NY 10036, USA
Martin, Ann *Commentator*
%KCBS-TV, News Dept, 6121 Sunset Blvd, Los Angeles, CA 90028, USA
Martin, Anne-Marie *Actress*
%Belson & Klass, 144 S Beverly Blvd, #405, Beverly Hills, CA 90212, USA
Martin, Archer J P *Nobel Chemistry Laureate*
47 Roseford Road, Cambridge CB4 2HA, England
Martin, Betsy *Publisher*
%Money Magazine, Rockefeller Center, New York, NY 10020, USA
Martin, David *Commentator*
%CBS-TV, News Dept, 2020 "M" St NW, Washington, DC 20036, USA
Martin, Dewey *Actor*
849 Grammercy Lane, Los Angeles, CA 90005, USA
Martin, Dick *Comedian, Actor*
11030 Chalon Road, Los Angeles, CA 90077, USA
Martin, Edward H *Navy Admiral*
729 Guadalupe Ave, Coronado, CA 92118, USA
Martin, George C *Aeronautical Engineer*
900 University St, #5-P, Seattle, WA 98101, USA
Martin, Henry R *Cartoonist (Good News Bad News)*
100 Dodds Lane, Princeton, NJ 08540, USA
Martin, J Landis *Businessman*
%NL Industries, 2 Greenspoint Dr, 16825 Northchase Dr, Houston, TX 77060, USA
Martin, J Leslie *Architect*
Church Street Barns, Great Shelford, Cambridge, England
Martin, Jacques *Hockey Coach*
%Ottawa Senators, 1000 Prom Palladium Dr, Kanata ON K2V 1A4, Canada
Martin, James G *Governor, NC*
PO Box 32861, Charlotte, NC 28232, USA
Martin, Jared *Actor*
%Paul Kohner, 9300 Wilshire Blvd, #555, Beverly Hills, CA 90212, USA
Martin, Joe *Cartoonist (Mister Boffo)*
%Tribune Media Services, 435 N Michigan Ave, #1500, Chicago, IL 60611, USA
Martin, Kellie *Actress*
5918 Van Nuys Blvd, Van Nuys, CA 91401, USA
Martin, LeRoy *Law Enforcement Official*
%Chicago Police Dept, Superintendent's Office, Chicago, IL 60602, USA
Martin, Marilyn *Singer*
%Atlantic Records, 9229 Sunset Blvd, #900, Los Angeles, CA 90069, USA
Martin, Mark *Auto Racing Driver*
2717 Spruce Creek Blvd, Daytona Beach, FL 32124, USA
Martin, Marsha P *Financier*
%Farm Credit Administration, 1501 Farm Credit Dr, McLean, VA 22102, USA
Martin, Millicent *Actress, Singer*
%London Mgmt, 2-4 Noel St, London W1V 3RB, England
Martin, Nan *Actress*
33604 Pacific Coast Highway, Malibu, CA 90265, USA
Martin, Pamela Sue *Actress*
PO Box 2278, Hailey, ID 83333, USA
Martin, Paul *Government Official, Canada*
%House of Commons, Confederation Building, Ottawa ON K1A 0A6, Canada
Martin, Paul E *Religious Leader*
%American Rescue Workers, 2827 Frankford Ave, Philadelphia, PA 19134, USA
Martin, Preston *Government Official, Financier*
1130 N Lake Shore Dr, #4-E, Chicago, IL 60611, USA
Martin, R Bruce *Chemist*
%University of Virginia, Chemistry Dept, Charlottesville, VA 22903, USA
Martin, Ray *Billiards Player*
11-05 Cadmus Place, Fairlawn, NJ 07410, USA
Martin, Ray *Financier*
%Coast Savings Financial, 1000 Wilshire Blvd, Los Angeles, CA 90017, USA
Martin, Rick *Furniture Maker*
45 N Modlin Lane, Otis, OR 97368, USA
Martin, Rick *Hockey Player*
8441 Sheridan Dr, Williamsville, NY 14221, USA

M

Martin - Martin

Martin, Ronald D *Editor*
%Atlanta Journal-Constitution, Editorial Dept, 72 Marietta, Atlanta, GA 30303, USA

Martin, Slater N *Basketball Player*
4119 Placid St, Houston, TX 77022, USA

Martin, Steve *Comedian*
PO Box 929, Beverly Hills, CA 90213, USA

Martin, Todd *Tennis Player*
%Advantage Int'l, 1025 Thomas Jefferson St NW, #450, Washington, DC 20007, USA

Martin, Tony *Singer, Actor*
10724 Wilshire Blvd, #1406, Los Angeles, CA 90024, USA

Martin, William McChesney, Jr *Government Official, Tennis Contributor*
2861 Woodland Dr NW, Washington, DC 20008, USA

Martindale, Wink *Entertainer, Singer*
5744 Newcastle Lane, Calabasas, CA 91302, USA

Martinez, A *Actor*
6835 Wild Life Road, Malibu, CA 90265, USA

Martinez, Arthur C *Businessman*
%Sears Roebuck Co, Sears Tower, Chicago, IL 60606, USA

Martinez, Conchita *Tennis Player*
%Int'l Management Group, 1 Erieview Plaza, #1300, Cleveland, OH 44114, USA

Martinez, Constantino (Tino) *Baseball Player*
230 Engle St, Tenafly, NJ 07670, USA

Martinez, Daniel J *Artist*
%University of California, Studio Art Dept, Irvine, CA 92717, USA

Martinez, Edgar *Baseball Player*
Bo Maguayo Buzon 1295-RR, Dorado, PR 00646, USA

Martinez, J Dennis *Baseball Player*
9400 SW 63rd Court, Miami, FL 33156, USA

Martinez, Ramon J *Baseball Player*
Bo San Miguel #9, Managuayaba, Santo Domingo, Dominican Republic

Martini, Carlo Maria Cardinal *Religious Leader*
Palazzo Arcivescovile, Piazza Fontana 2, 20122 Milan, Italy

Martino, Al *Singer, Actor*
927 N Rexford Dr, Beverly Hills, CA 90210, USA

Martino, Frank D *Labor Leader*
%Chemical Workers Union, 1655 W Market St, Akron, OH 44313, USA

Martino, Pat *Jazz Guitarist, Composer*
%Frank McDonnell, 27 Pickwick Lane, Newtown Square, PA 19073, USA

Martins, Peter *Ballet Dancer, Artistic Director*
%New York City Ballet, Lincoln Center Plaza, New York, NY 10023, USA

Marton, Eva *Opera Singer*
%Organization of International Opera, 19 Rue Vignon, 75008 Paris, France

Marty, Martin E *Theologian*
239 Scottswood Road, Riverside, IL 60546, USA

Martzke, Rudy *Sportswriter*
%USA Today, Editorial Dept, 1000 Wilson Blvd, Arlington, VA 22209, USA

Marx, Gilda *Fashion Designer*
%Gilda Marx Industries, 11755 Exposition Blvd, Los Angeles, CA 90064, USA

Marx, Gyorgy *Physicist*
%Eotvos University, Atomic Physics Dept, Pushkin 5, 1088 Budapest, Hungary

Marx, Jeffrey A *Journalist*
%Lexington Herald-Leader, Editorial Dept, Main & Midland, Lexington, KY 40507, USA

Marx, Richard *Singer, Songwriter*
%QBQ Entertainment, 341 Madison Ave, #1400, New York, NY 10017, USA

Maryland, Russell *Football Player*
185 Asher Court, Corpus Christi, TX 75019, USA

Marzich, Andy *Bowler*
2709 W 235th St, #D, Torrance, CA 90505, USA

Marzio, Peter C *Museum Director*
%Houston Museum of Fine Arts, 1001 Bissonnet, PO Box 6826, Houston, TX 77265, USA

Masak, Ron *Actor*
5440 Shirley Ave, Tarzana, CA 91356, USA

Masakayan, Liz *Volleyball Player*
3529 Buena Vista St, San Diego, CA 92109, USA

Masco, Judit *Model*
%Next Model Mgmt, 23 Watts St, New York, NY 10013, USA

Mascotte, John P *Businessman*
%Continental Corp, 180 Maiden Lane, New York, NY 10038, USA

Masekela, Hugh R   *Jazz Trumpeter*
%Sadiane Corp, 230 Park Ave, #1512, New York, NY 10169, USA

Mashburn, Jamal   *Basketball Player*
5529 St Andrews Court, Plano, TX 75093, USA

Mashburn, Jesse   *Track Athlete*
8520 S Penn, Oklahoma City, OK 75139, USA

Masiello, Tony   *Mayor*
%Mayor's Office, City Hall, 65 Niagara Square, Buffalo, NY 14202, USA

Masire, Quett K J   *President, Botswana*
%President's Office, State House, Private Bag 001, Gaborone, Botswana

Maske, Henry   *Boxer*
%Sauerland Promotion, Hochstadenstr 1-3, 50674 Cologne, Germany

Maslansky, Paul   *Movie Producer, Director*
%Henry Barnberger, 10866 Wilshire Blvd, #1000, Los Angeles, CA 90024, USA

Masloff, Sophie   *Mayor, Pittsburgh*
%Mayor's Office, City-County Bldg, 414 Grant St, Pittsburgh, PA 15219, USA

Mason of Barnsley, Roy   *Government Official, England*
12 Victoria Ave, Barnsley, S Yorks, England

Mason, Anthony   *Basketball Player*
7818 Sawyer Brown Road, Nashville, TN 37221, USA

Mason, B John   *Meteorologist*
64 Christchurch Road, East Sheen, London SW14, England

Mason, Birny, Jr   *Chemical Engineer*
6 Island Dr, Rye, NY 10580, USA

Mason, Bobbie Ann   *Writer*
PO Box 518, Lawrenceburg, KY 40342, USA

Mason, Dave   *Singer, Songwriter*
%Variety Artists Int'l, 15490 Ventura Blvd, Sherman Oaks, CA 91403, USA

Mason, Jackie   *Comedian*
30 Park Ave, New York, NY 10016, USA

Mason, Marlyn   *Actress, Singer*
27 Glen Oak Court, Medford, OR 97504, USA

Mason, Marsha   *Actress*
320 Galisteo St, #402-B, Santa Fe, NM 87501, USA

Mason, Milla   *Singer*
%Star Keeper, 2100 West End Ave, #109, Nashville, TN 37203, USA

Mason, Monica   *Ballerina*
%Royal Opera House, Convent Garden, Bow St, London WC2, England

Mason, Ron   *Hockey Coach*
%Michigan State University, Athletic Dept, East Lansing, MI 48224, USA

Mason, Steven C   *Businessman*
%Mead Corp, Courthouse Plaza NE, Dayton, OH 45463, USA

Masri, Tahir Nashat   *Prime Minister, Jordan*
PO Box 5550, Amman, Jordan

Massengale, Don   *Golfer*
715 W Davis St, Conroe, TX 77301, USA

Massengale, Rik   *Golfer*
5403 E 103rd Place, #200, Tulsa, OK 74137, USA

Massevitch, Alla G   *Astronomer*
%Astronomical Council, 48 Pjatnitskaja St, 109017 Moscow, Russia

Massey, Anna   *Actress*
%Markham & Froggatt, Julian House, 4 Windmill St, London W1P 1HF, England

Massey, Daniel   *Actor*
35 Tynehan Road, London SW11, England

Massey, Debbie   *Golfer*
545 N Clara Ave, Deland, FL 32720, USA

Massey, T Benjamin   *Educator*
%University of Maryland, President's Office, College Park, MD 20742, USA

Massey, Walter   *Educator*
%Morehouse College, President's Office, Atlanta, GA 30314, USA

Massimino, Rollie   *Basketball Coach*
2000 Prospect Ave E, Cleveland, OH 44115, USA

Mast, Rick   *Auto Racing Driver*
PO Box 15373, Asheville, NC 28813, USA

Masterhoff, Joe   *Writer*
2 Horatio St, New York, NY 10014, USA

Masters, Geoff   *Tennis Player*
De Lorain St, Wavell Heights, QLD 4012, Australia

M

Masekela - Masters

M

Masters, John *Writer*
%McGraw-Hill, 1221 Ave of Americas, New York, NY 10020, USA

Masters, William H *Sex Therapist, Gynecologist*
%Masters & Johnson Institute, Campbell Plaza, 59th & Arsenal, St Louis, MO 63118, USA

Masterson, Chase *Actrss*
%Henderson/Hogan, 247 S Beverly Dr, #102, Beverly Hills, CA 90212, USA

Masterson, Mary Stuart *Actress*
1724 N Vista St, Los Angeles, CA 90046, USA

Masterson, Peter *Writer, Director, Producer*
%Writer's Guild, 555 W 57th St, New York, NY 10019, USA

Masterson, Valerie *Opera Singer*
%Music International, 13 Ardilaun Road, London N5 2QR, England

Masur, Kurt *Conductor*
%New York Philharmonic, Avery Fisher Hall, Lincoln Center, New York, NY 10023, USA

Masur, Richard *Actor*
2847 Mandeville Canyon Road, Los Angeles, CA 90049, USA

Masurok, Yuri *Opera Singer*
%Bolshoi Theater, Teatralnaya Pl 1, 103009 Moscow, Russia

Mata'aho *Queen, Tonga*
%Royal Palace, PO Box 6, Nuku'alofa, Tonga

Matalin, Mary *Political Consultant*
1601 Shenandoah Shores St, Fort Royal, VA 22630, USA

Matalon, David *Entertainment Executive*
%Tri-Star Pictures, 711 5th Ave, New York, NY 10022, USA

Matano, Tsutomo (Tom) *Automotive Designer*
%Mazda Motor, Research/Development Dept, 7755 Irvine Center Dr, Irvine, CA 92618, USA

Matchetts, John *Hockey Player*
2415 Chelton Road, Colorado Springs, CO 80909, USA

Mateo, Manuel M *Financier*
%Golden 1 Credit Union, 6507 4th Ave, Sacramento, CA, 95817, USA

Mather, John C *Astrophysicist*
%Goddard Space Flight Center, Code G-85, Greenbelt, MD 20771, USA

Mathers, Frank *Hockey Executive*
32 Oakglade Dr, Hummelstown, PA 17036, USA

Mathers, Jerry *Actor*
31656 Rancho Viejo Road, #A, San Juan Capistrano, CA 92675, USA

Matheson, Tim *Actor*
830 River Rock Road, Santa Barbara, CA 93108, USA

Mathews, Edwin L (Eddie) *Baseball Player*
13744 Recuerdo Dr, Del Mar, CA 92014, USA

Mathews, F David *Secretary, Health Education & Welfare*
%Charles F Kettering Foundation, 200 Commons Road, Dayton, OH 45459, USA

Mathews, Stanley *Soccer Player*
%English Football Assn, 16 Lancaster Gate, London W2 3LW, England

Mathews, Vince *Track Athlete*
6755 193rd Lane, Flushing Meadows, NY 11365, USA

Mathias, Buster, Jr *Boxer*
4409 Carol Ave SW, Wyoming, MI 49509, USA

Mathias, Charles McC, Jr *Senator, MD; Financier*
3808 Leland St, Chevy Chase, MD 20815, USA

Mathias, Robert B (Bob) *Track Athlete; Representative, CA*
7469 E Pine Ave, Fresno, CA 93727, USA

Mathias, William *Composer*
Y Graigwen Cadnant Road, Menai Bridge, Anglesey, Gwynedd LL59 5NG, Wales

Mathis, Buster, Jr *Boxer*
4409 Carol SW, Wyoming, MI 49509, USA

Mathis, Edith *Opera Singer*
%Ingpen & Williams, 14 Kensington Court, London W8 5DN, England

Mathis, Johnny *Singer*
PO Box 69278, Los Angeles, CA 90069, USA

Mathis, Samantha *Actress*
PO Box 480137, Los Angeles, CA 90048, USA

Mathis, Terance *Football Player*
%Atlanta Falcons, 2745 Burnett Road, Suwanee, GA 30024, USA

Mathis-Eddy, Darlene *Writer*
1409 W Cardinal St, Muncie, IN 47303, USA

Mathwich, Dale F *Businessman*
%American Family Insurance, 6000 American Parkway, Madison, WI 53783, USA

Masters - Mathwich

Matlin, Marlee — *Actress*
10340 Santa Monica Blvd, Los Angeles, CA 90025, USA

Matlock, Jack F, Jr — *Diplomat*
2913 "P" St NW, Washington, DC 20007, USA

Matola, Sharon — *Zoo Director, Conservationist*
%Belize Zoo & Tropical Education Center, PO Box 1787, Belize City, Belize

Matsch, Richard P — *Judge*
%US District Court, 1929 Stout St, Denver, CO 80294, USA

Matson, Ollie — *Football Player, Track Athlete*
1319 S Hudson Ave, Los Angeles, CA 90019, USA

Matson, Randy — *Track Athlete*
1002 Park Place, College Station, TX 77840, USA

Matsui, Kosei — *Pottery Maker*
Ibaraki-ken, Kasama-shi, Kasama 350, Japan

Matsumoto, Shigeharu — *Writer, Association Executive*
%International House of Japan, 11-16 Roppongi, Minatuku, Tokyo, Japan

Matsushita, Hiro — *Auto Racing Driver*
%Pacific Creative Racing, 1606 Avenida Salvador, San Clemente, CA 92672, USA

Matsushita, Masaharu — *Businessman*
%Matsushita Electrical, 1006 Kadoma City, Osaka 571, Japan

Matta del Meskin — *Religious Leader*
Deir el Makarios Monastery, Cairo, Egypt

Matta Echuarren, Roberto S (Matta) — *Artist*
Boissy Sans Avoir, Seine-et-Oise, France

Matte, Thomas R (Tom) — *Football Player*
11309 Old Carriage Road, Glen Arm, MD 21057, USA

Mattea, Kathy — *Singer*
%Titley-Spalding, 900 Division St, Nashville, TN 37203, USA

Mattesich, Rudi — *Skier*
%General Delivery, Troy, VT 05868, USA

Matteson, Thomas T — *Coast Guard Admiral*
%US Coast Guard Academy, Superintendent's Office, New London, CT 06320, USA

Matthaeus, Lothar — *Soccer Player*
%FC Bayern Munich, Sabena Str 51, 81547 Munich, Germany

Matthau, Walter — *Actor*
278 Toyopa Dr, Pacific Palisades, CA 90272, USA

Matthes, Roland — *Swimmer*
Luitpoldstr 35-A, 97828 Marktheidenfeld, Germany

Matthews, Bruce — *Football Player*
3906 E Creek Club Dr, Missouri City, TX 77459, USA

Matthews, Clark J, II — *Businessman*
%Southland Corp, 2711 N Haskell Ave, Dallas, TX 75204, USA

Matthews, Clay, Jr — *Football Player*
6068 Canterbury Dr, Agoura Hills, CA 91301, USA

Matthews, DeLane — *Actress*
12190 1/2 Ventura Blvd, #324, Studio City, CA 91604, USA

Matthews, Ian — *Singer, Guitarist*
%Geoffrey Blumenauer, 11846 Balboa Blvd, #204, Granada Hills, CA 91344, USA

Matthews, Keith — *Astronomer*
%California Institute of Technology, Astronomy Dept, Pasadena, CA 91125, USA

Matthews, Raymond (Rags) — *Football Player*
2501 Oak Hill Circle, #2416, Fort Worth, TX 76109, USA

Matthews, William — *Writer*
523 W 121st St, New York, NY 10027, USA

Matthews, William D — *Businessman*
%Oneida Ltd, Kenwood Ave, Oneida, NY 13421, USA

Matthies, Nina — *Volleyball Player, Coach*
%Pepperdine University, Athletic Dept, Malibu, CA 90265, USA

Matthiessen, Peter — *Writer*
Bridge Lane, Sagaponack, NY 11962, USA

Mattila, Karita M — *Opera Singer*
45-B Croxley Road, London W9 3HJ, England

Mattingly, Donald A (Don) — *Baseball Player*
12641 Browning Road, Evansville, IN 47711, USA

Mattingly, Mack F — *Senator, GA*
4315 10th St, East Beach, St Simons Island, GA 31522, USA

Mattingly, Thomas K, II — *Astronaut, Navy Admiral*
1300 Crystal Dr, #1603, Arlington, VA 22202, USA

M

Mattson, Robin — *Actress*
260 S Beverlt Dr, #210, Beverly Hills, CA 90212, USA

Mattson, Walter E — *Publisher*
%New York Times Co, 229 W 43rd St, New York, NY 10036, USA

Mature, Victor — *Actor*
PO Box 706, Rancho Santa Fe, CA 92067, USA

Matzdorf, Pat — *Track Athlete*
1252 Bainbridge, Naperville, IL 60563, USA

Mauch, Billy (Bill) — *Actor*
538 W Northwest Highway, #C, Palatine, IL 60067, USA

Mauch, Eugene W (Gene) — *Baseball Manager*
71 Princeton Dr, Rancho Mirage, CA 92270, USA

Maucher, Helmut — *Businessman*
%Nestle SA, Ave Nestle, 1800 Vevey, Switzerland

Maugham, R H — *Religious Leader*
%Christian & Missionary Alliance, PO Box 35000, Colorado Springs, CO 80935, USA

Mauldin, Jerry L — *Businessman*
%Entergy Corp, 639 Loyola Ave, New Orleans, LA 70113, USA

Mauldin, William H (Bill) — *Editorial Cartoonist*
%North American Syndicate, 3145 Killarney Lane, Costa Mesa, CA 92626, USA

Maulnier, Thierry — *Writer*
3 Rue Yves-Carriou, 92430 Marnes-la-Coquette, France

Maumenee, Alfred E — *Ophthalmologist*
1700 Hillside Road, Stevenson, MD 21153, USA

Maupin, Robert W — *Businessman*
%Shelter Mutual Insurance, 1817 W Broadway, Columbia, MO 65203, USA

Maura, Carmen — *Actress*
Juan de Austria 13, 28010 Madrid, Spain

Maurer, Gilbert C — *Publisher*
%Hearst Corp, 959 8th Ave, New York, NY 10019, USA

Maurer, Ion Gheorghe — *Premier, Romania*
Bul Aviatorilor 104, Bucharest, Romania

Maurer, Jeffrey S — *Financier*
%United States Trust (NY), 114 W 47th St, New York, NY 10036, USA

Maurer, Robert D — *Inventor (Silica Optical Waveguide)*
6 Roche Dr, Painted Post, NY 14870, USA

Mauriac, Claude — *Writer*
24 Quai de Bethune, 75004 Paris, France

Maurin, Laurence — *Skier, Conservationist*
PO Box 1980, West Bend, WI 53095, USA

Mauroy, Pierre — *Prime Minister, France*
17-19 Rue Voltaire, 59800 Lille, France

Mautner, Hans C — *Financier*
%Corporate Property Investors, 3 Dag Hammarskjold Plaza, New York, NY 10017, USA

Mauz, Henry H (Hank), Jr — *Navy Admiral*
1608 Viscaine Road, Pebble Beach, CA 93953, USA

Mawby, Russell G — *Foundation Executive*
%W K Kellogg Foundation, 1 Michigan Ave E, Battle Creek, MI 49017, USA

Max, Peter — *Artist*
118 Riverside Dr, New York, NY 10024, USA

Maxim, Joey — *Boxer*
2491 Natalie Ave, Las Vegas, NV 89121, USA

Maximova, Ekaterina — *Ballerina*
%Bolshoi Theater, Teatralnaya Pl 1, 103009 Moscow, Russia

Maxson, Robert — *Educator*
%California State University, President's Office, Long Beach, CA 90840, USA

Maxwell, Arthur E — *Oceanographer*
8115 Two Coves Dr, Austin, TX 78730, USA

Maxwell, Charles R (Charlie) — *Baseball Player*
730 Mapleview Ave, Paw Paw, MI 49079, USA

Maxwell, Frank — *Labor Leader*
%Federation of TV-Radio Artists, 260 Madison Ave, New York, NY 10016, USA

Maxwell, Hamish — *Businessman*
%Philip Morris Companies, 120 Park Ave, New York, NY 10017, USA

Maxwell, Ian — *Publisher*
Eaton Terrace, London SW1, England

Maxwell, Kevin F H — *Publisher*
Hill Burn, Hailey near Wallingford, Oxford OX10 6AD, England

Maxwell, Robert D — *WW II Army Hero (CMH)*
1001 SE 15th St, Spc #44, Bend, OR 97702, USA
Maxwell, Vernon — *Basketball Player*
17 Lake Mist Court, Sugar Land, TX 77479, USA
Maxwell, William — *Writer*
%Alfred A Knopf, 201 E 50th St, New York, NY 10022, USA
May, Arthur — *Architect*
%Kohn Pedersen Fox Assoc, 111 W 57th St, New York, NY 10019, USA
May, Billy — *Trumpeter, Conductor, Composer*
4 San Remo, San Clemente, CA 92673, USA
May, Deborah — *Actress*
%Artists Agency, 10000 Santa Monica Blvd, #305, Los Angeles, CA 90067, USA
May, Don — *Basketball Player*
1128 Colwick Dr, Dayton, OH 45420, USA
May, Elaine — *Comedienne, Movie Director*
2017 California Ave, Santa Monica, CA 90403, USA
May, Lee A — *Baseball Player*
9611 Orpin Road, #2, Randallstown, MD 21133, USA
May, Scott — *Basketball Player*
2001 E Hillside Dr, Bloomington, IN 47401, USA
May, Thomas I — *Businessman*
%Boston Edison Co, 800 Boylston St, Boston, MA 02199, USA
May, Torsten — *Boxer*
%Sauerland Promotion, Hans-Bockler-Str 163, 50354 Hurth, Germany
Mayall, John — *Singer, Keyboardist, Composer*
%Monterey Int'l Artists, 200 W Superior, #202, Chicago, IL 60610, USA
Mayall, Nicholas U — *Astronomer*
7206 E Camino Vecino, Tucson, AZ 85715, USA
Mayasich, John — *Hockey Player*
1314 Marquette Ave, #2907, Minneapolis, MN 55403, USA
Mayberry, John C — *Baseball Player*
11115 W 121st Terrace, Overland Park, KS 66213, USA
Mayer, Joseph E — *Chemical Physicist*
2345 Via Siena, La Jolla, CA 92037, USA
Mayer, P Augustin Cardinal — *Religious Leader*
Ecclesia Dei, 00120 Vatican City
Mayes, Rueben — *Football Player*
7306 172nd St SW, Edmonds, WA 98026, USA
Mayfair, Billy — *Golfer*
7666 E Campo Bello Dr, Scottsdale, AZ 85255, USA
Mayfield, Curtis — *Singer, Musician, Songwriter*
%Headline Talent, 1650 Broadway, #508, New York, NY 10019, USA
Mayhew, Patrick B B — *Government Official, England*
%House of Commons, Westminster, London SW1A 0AA, England
Maynard, Andrew — *Boxer*
%Mike Trainer, 3922 Fairmont Ave, Bethesda, MD 20814, USA
Maynard, Don — *Football Player*
6545 Butterfield Dr, El Paso, TX 79932, USA
Maynard, Mimi — *Actress*
%Badgley Connor, 9229 Sunset Blvd, #311, Los Angeles, CA 90069, USA
Mayne, D Roger — *Photographer*
Colway Manor, Colway Lane, Lyme Regis, Dorset DT7 3HD, Canada
Mayne, Ferdinand (Ferdy) — *Actor*
%Lou Coulson, 37 Berwick St, London W1V 3RF, England
Mayne, William — *Writer*
%Harold Ober Assoc, 425 Madison Ave, New York, NY 10017, USA
Maynes, Charles W — *Editor*
%Foreign Policy Magazine, Editorial Dept, 2400 "N" St NW, Washington, DC 20037, USA
Mayo, Virginia — *Actress*
109 E Avenida de las Aboles, Thousand Oaks, CA 91360, USA
Mayo, Whitman — *Actor*
265 Dix Leon Dr, Fairburn, GA 30213, USA
Mayor Zaragoza, Federico — *Government Official, Spain*
%UNESCO, Place de Fonteroy, 75352 Paris, France
Mayr, Ernst — *Biologist, Zoologist*
307 Springs Road, Bedford, MA 01730, USA
Mayron, Melanie — *Actress*
7510 W Sunset Blvd, Los Angeles, CA 90046, USA

Mays, Lyle *Jazz Pianist*
%Ted Kurland, 173 Brighton Ave, Boston, MA 02134, USA

Mays, Willie H *Baseball Player*
51 Mt Vernon Lane, Atherton, CA 94027, USA

Mazach, John J *Navy Admiral*
Commander, Naval Air Force Atlantic, 1279 Franklin St, Norfolk, VA 23511, USA

Mazar, Debi *Actress*
156 W 56th St, New York, NY 10019, USA

Mazeroski, William S (Bill) *Baseball Player*
RR 6, Box 130, Greensburg, PA 15601, USA

Mazowiecki, Tadeusz *Prime Minister, Poland*
%Democratic Union, Al Jerozolimskie 30, 00 24 Warsaw, Poland

Mazur, Jay J *Labor Leader*
%Industrial Textile Employees Needletrades, 1710 Broadway, New York, NY 10019, USA

Mazurok, Yuri A *Opera Singer*
%Boshoi State Theater, Teatralnaya Pl 1, 103009 Moscow, Russia

Mazursky, Paul *Movie Director*
614 26th St, Santa Monica, CA 90402, USA

Mazza, Valeria *Model*
%Ford Model Agency, 344 E 59th St, New York, NY 10022, USA

Mazzo, Kay *Ballerina*
%American Ballet School, 144 W 66th St, New York, NY 10023, USA

Mazzola, Anthony T *Editor*
%Town & Country Magazine, Editorial Dept, 1790 Broadway, New York, NY 10019, USA

Mba, Casimir Oye *Prime Minister, Gabon*
%Prime Minister's Office, Boite Postale 546, Libreville, Gabon

Mbasogo, Teodoro Obiang Nguema *President, Equatorial Guinea*
%President's Office, Malabo, Equatorial Guinea

Mbeki, Thabo *Government Official, South Africa*
%Deputy President's Office, Union Buildings, Pretoria 0001, South Africa

McAdoo, Bob *Basketball Player, Coach*
7685 SW 153rd St, Miami, FL 33157, USA

McAfee, George A *Football Player*
4011 Bristol Road, Durham, NC 27707, USA

McAnally, Mac *Singer, Songwriter*
%TKO Artist Mgmt, 4219 Hillsboro Road, #318, Nashville, TN 37215, USA

McAniff, Nora *Publisher*
%People Magazine, Rockefeller Center, New York, NY 10020, USA

McArdle, Andrea *Actress, Singer*
713 Disston St, Philadelphia, PA 19111, USA

McArthur, Alex *Actor*
10435 Wheatland Ave, Sunland, CA 91040, USA

McArthur, William S (Bill), Jr *Astronaut*
%NASA, Johnson Space Center, 2101 NASA Road, Houston, TX 77058, USA

McBain, Diane *Actress*
156 Keats Circle, Ventura, CA 93003, USA

McBride, Jon A *Astronaut*
%Employers Trust, 525 Vine St, #2310, Cincinnati, OH 45202, USA

McBride, Martina *Singer*
%Bruce Allen, 406-68 Water St, Vancouver BC V6B 1A4, Canada

McBride, Patricia *Ballerina*
%Sharon Wagner Artists, 150 West End Ave, New York, NY 10023, USA

McBride, William J *Rugby Player*
Gorse Lodge, Ballyclare, County Antrim, Northern Ireland

McBroom, Amanda *Singer, Songwriter*
167 Fairview Road, Ojai, CA 93023, USA

McCabe, Eamonn P *Photographer*
58 The Mall, Southgate, London N14, England

McCabe, Frank *Basketball Player*
6202 N Fairlane Dr, Peoria, IL 61614, USA

McCafferty, Donald F (Don), Jr *Football Coach*
167 E Shore Road, Huntington Bay, NY 11743, USA

McCaffrey, Barry R *Army General*
%National Drug Control Policy Office, White House, Washington, DC 20500, USA

McCall, Robert T *Artist*
4816 E Moonlight Way, Paradise Valley, AZ 85253, USA

McCalla, Irish *Actress*
920 Oak Terrace, Prescott, AZ 86301, USA

McCallister, Lon — *Actor*
PO Box 6040, Stateline, NV 89449, USA
McCallum, David — *Actor*
%Hilary Gagan, Caprice House, 3 New Burlington St, London W1X 1FE, England
McCallum, Napoleon A — *Football Player*
314 Doe Run Circle, Henderson, NV 89012, USA
McCambridge, Mercedes — *Actress*
2500 Torrey Pines Road, #1203, La Jolla, CA 92037, USA
McCandless, Bruce, II — *Astronaut*
21852 Pleasant Park Dr, Conifer, CO 80433, USA
McCann, Chuck — *Comedian, Actor*
2941 Briar Knoll Dr, Los Angeles, CA 90046, USA
McCann, David A — *Publisher*
%Town & Country Magazine, 1700 Broadway, New York, NY 10019, USA
McCann, Les — *Jazz Singer, Pianist, Composer*
%DeLeon Artists, 4031 Panama Court, Piedmont, CA 94611, USA
McCants, Keith — *Football Player*
%St Louis Rams, 100 N Broadway, #2100, St Louis, MO 63102, USA
McCarron, Chris — *Thoroughbred Racing Jockey*
218 Windwood Lane, Sierra Madre, CA 91024, USA
McCarron, Douglas J — *Labor Leader*
%Carperters/Joiners Brotherhood, 101 Connecticut Ave NW, Washington, DC 20001, USA
McCartan, Jack — *Hockey Player*
8818 Logan Ave S, Bloomington, MN 55431, USA
McCarthy, Andrew — *Actor*
4708 Vesper Ave, Sherman Oaks, CA 91403, USA
McCarthy, Cormac — *Writer*
%Random House, 201 E 50th St, New York, NY 10022, USA
McCarthy, Donald W — *Astronomer*
%Stewart Observatory, University of Arizona, Tucson, AZ 85721, USA
McCarthy, Eugene J — *Senator, MN*
PO Box 22, Sperryville, VA 22740, USA
McCarthy, Fred — *Cartoonist (Brother Juniper)*
%Field Newspaper Syndicate, 1703 Kaiser Ave, Irvine, CA 92614, USA
McCarthy, Jenny — *Model, Entertainer*
2112 Broadway, Santa Monica, CA 90404, USA
McCarthy, John — *Computer Scientist*
%Stanford University, Computer Science Dept, Stanford, CA 94305, USA
McCarthy, Kevin — *Actor*
14854 Sutton St, Sherman Oaks, CA 91403, USA
McCarthy, Mary Frances — *Writer, Educator*
%Trinity College, English Dept, Washington, DC 20017, USA
McCarthy, Nobu — *Actress*
372 N Encinitas Ave, Monrovia, CA 91016, USA
McCarthy, Paul F, Jr — *Navy Admiral*
16457 Saddle Creek Road, Clarkson Valley, MO 63005, USA
McCarthy, Tony — *Singer, Songwriter*
29/33 Berners Road, London W1P 4AA, England
McCartney, Bill — *Football Coach*
%Promise Keepers, PO Box 18376, Boulder, CO 80308, USA
McCartney, Linda — *Singer, Photographer*
%Joe Dera, 584 Broadway, #1201, New York, NY 10012, USA
McCartney, Paul — *Singer (The Beatles), Songwriter*
%Joe Dera, 584 Broadway, #1201, New York, NY 10012, USA
McCarty, Maclyn — *Bacteriologist, Immunologist*
%Rockefeller University, 66th St & York Ave, New York, NY 10021, USA
McCarty, Walker — *Basketball Player*
%New York Knicks, Madison Square Garden, 2 Penn Plaza, New York, NY 10121, USA
McCarver, J Timothy (Tim) — *Baseball Player, Sportscaster*
1518 Youngford Road, Gladwynne, PA 19035, USA
McCary, Michael — *Singer (Boyz II Men)*
%International Creative Mgmt, 40 W 57th St, New York, NY 10019, USA
McCashin, Constance — *Actress*
PO Box 452, Chatham, MA 02633, USA
McCaskey, Michael B (Mike) — *Football Executive*
%Chicago Bears, Halas Hall, 250 N Washington Road, Lake Forest, IL 60045, USA
McCaskill, Kirk E — *Baseball Player*
PO Box 451, Rancho Santa Fe, CA 92067, USA

McCauley, Barry — *Opera Singer*
8 Pershing St, Emerson, NJ 07630, USA

McCauley, William F — *Navy Admiral*
670 Margarita Ave, Coronado, CA 92118, USA

McCausland, Peter — *Businessman*
%Airgas Inc, 5 Radnor Corporate Center, 100 Matsonford Road, Radnor, PA 19087, USA

McCay, Peggy — *Actress*
2714 Carmar Dr, Los Angeles, CA 90046, USA

McClain, Charly — *Singer*
%John Lantz, PO Box 198888, Nashville, TN 37219, USA

McClain, Katrina — *Basketball Player*
1237 Newbridge Terrace NE, Atlanta, GA 30319, USA

McClanahan, Robert (Rob) — *Hockey Player*
4727 Bouleau Road, White Bear Lake, MN 55110, USA

McClanahan, Rue — *Actress*
%Gersh Agency, 232 N Canon Dr, Beverly Hills, CA 90210, USA

McClatchy, James B — *Publisher*
%McClatchy Newspapers, 2100 "Q" St, Sacramento, CA 95816, USA

McCleery, Finnis D — *Vietnam War Army Hero (CMH)*
826 Veck St, #F, San Angelo, TX 76903, USA

McClelland, David C — *Psychologist*
81 Washington Ave, Cambridge, MA 02140, USA

McClelland, W Craig — *Businessman*
%Union Camp Corp, 1600 Valley Road, Wayne, NJ 07470, USA

McClinton, Delbert — *Singer, Songwriter*
%Harriet Sternberg, 15250 Ventura Blvd, #1215, Sherman Oaks, CA 91403, USA

McCloskey, J Michael — *Environmentalist*
%Sierra Club, 85 2nd St, #200, San Francisco, CA 94105, USA

McCloskey, Jack — *Basketball Coach, Executive*
%Minnesota Timberwolves, Target Center, 600 1st Ave N, Minneapolis, MN 55403, USA

McCloskey, Jim — *Social Activist*
32 Nassau St, #3, Princeton, NJ 08542, USA

McCloskey, Robert J — *Diplomat*
111 Hesketh St, Chevy Chase, MD 20815, USA

McCloud, David J — *Air Force General*
Director, Force Structure, Joint Chiefs of Staff, Washington, DC 20318, USA

McCluggage, Kerry — *Television Executive*
%Paramount Pictures, 5555 Melrose Ave, Los Angeles, CA 90038, USA

McClure, Donald F — *Financier*
%LMSC Federal Credit Union, PO Box 3643, Sunnyvale, CA 94088, USA

McClure, Donald S — *Chemist*
23 Hemlock Circle, Princeton, NJ 08540, USA

McClure, James A — *Senator, ID*
PO Box 2029, McCall, ID 83638, USA

McClurg, Edie — *Actress*
3306 Wonderview Plaza, Los Angeles, CA 90068, USA

McColl, Hugh L, Jr — *Financier*
%NationsBank Corp, 1 NationsBank Plaza, Charlotte, NC 28255, USA

McColl, William (Bill) — *Football Player*
5166 Chelsea St, La Jolla, CA 92037, USA

McComas, Murray K — *Businessman*
%Blair Corp, 220 Hickory St, Warren, PA 16366, USA

McConaughey, Matthew — *Actor*
PO Box 1202, Malibu, CA 90265, USA

McConnell, Harden M — *Chemist*
%Stanford University, Chemistry Dept, Stanford, CA 94305, USA

McConnell, John H — *Businessman*
%Worthington Industries, 1205 Dearborn Dr, Columbus, OH 43085, USA

McConnell, Rob — *Jazz Trombonist, Bandleader*
%Thomas Cassidy, 0366 Horseshoe Dr, Basalt, CO 81621, USA

McConnell, Robert — *Publisher*
%The Gazette, 250 St Antoine St W, Montreal PQ H2Y 3R7, Canada

McConville, Frank — *Labor Leader*
%Union of Plant Guard Workers of America, 25510 Kelly Road, Roseville, MI 48066, USA

McCoo, Marilyn — *Singer, Actress*
2639 Lavery Court, #5, Newbury Park, CA 91320, USA

McCook, John — *Actor*
4154 Colbath Ave, Sherman Oaks, CA 91423, USA

McCool, Richard M — WW II Navy Hero (CMH)
PO Box 11347, Bainbridge Island, WA 98110, USA

McCord, Bob — Hockey Player
47 Craig Dr, West Springfield, MA 01089, USA

McCord, Catherine — Model
%Elite Model Mgmt, 111 E 22nd St, #200, New York, NY 10010, USA

McCord, Kent — Actor
%David Shapira, 15301 Ventura Blvd, #345, Sherman Oaks, CA 91403, USA

McCorkle, Susannah — Singer
%Jerry Kravat Entertainers, 404 Park Ave S, #1000, New York, NY 10016, USA

McCormack, Mark H — Attorney, Sports Executive
%Mark McCormack Enterprises, 1 Erieview Plaza, #1300, Cleveland, OH 44114, USA

McCormack, Mary — Actress
%Gersh Agency, 232 N Canon Dr, Beverly Hills, CA 90210, USA

McCormack, Mike — Football Coach, Executive
%Seattle Seahawks, 11220 NE 53rd St, Kirkland, WA 98033, USA

McCormack, Patricia — Actress
%Paradigm Agency, 10100 Santa Monica Blvd, #2500, Los Angeles, CA 90067, USA

McCormack, Patty — Actress, Model
14723 Magnolia Blvd, Sherman Oaks, CA 91403, USA

McCormick, Charles P, Jr — Businessman
%McCormick Co, 18 Loveton Circle, Sparks, MD 21152, USA

McCormick, Kevin — Cartoonist (Arnold)
%News America Syndicate, 1703 Kaiser Ave, Irvine, CA 92614, USA

McCormick, Maureen — Actress, Singer
2812 Shellcreek Place, Westlake Village, CA 91361, USA

McCormick, Michael F (Mike) — Baseball Player
532 Crawford Dr, Sunnyvale, CA 94087, USA

McCormick, Pat — Diver
PO Box 259, Seal Beach, CA 90740, USA

McCormick, Richard — Educator
%University of Washington, President's Office, Seattle, WA 98195, USA

McCormick, Richard D — Businessman
%US West Inc, 7800 E Orchard Road, Englewood, CO 80111, USA

McCormick, Tim — Basketball Player
2500 Leroy Lane, West Bloomfield, MI 48324, USA

McCormick, William C — Businessman
%Precision Castparts Corp, 4600 SE Harney Dr, Portland, OR 97206, USA

McCormick, William E — Publisher
%Pittsburgh Post-Gazette & Press, 34 Blvd of Allies, Pittsburgh, PA 15230, USA

McCormick, William T, Jr — Businessman
%CMS Energy, Fairlane Plaza South, 330 Town Center Dr, Dearborn, MI 48126, USA

McCovey, Willie L — Baseball Player
PO Box 620342, Woodside, CA 94062, USA

McCowen, Alec — Actor
%Conway Van Gelder Robinson, 18-21 Jermyn St, London SW1Y 6NB, England

McCoy, Charlie — Singer
%Music Park Talent, PO Box 148924, Nashville, TN 37214, USA

McCoy, Dave — Ski Resort Builder
%Mammoth Mountain Chairlifts, PO Box 24, Mammoth Lakes, CA 93546, USA

McCoy, John B — Financier
%Banc One Corp, 17 E Gay St, Columbus, OH 43215, USA

McCoy, Matt — Actor
%Metropolitan Talent Agency, 4526 Wilshire Blvd, Los Angeles, CA 90010, USA

McCoy, Michael P (Mike) — Football Player
551 Exam Court, Lawrenceville, GA 30044, USA

McCoy, Neal — Singer
%Management Associates, 1920 Benson Ave, St Paul, MN 55116, USA

McCracken, Paul W — Economist, Government Official
2564 Hawthorne Road, Ann Arbor, MI 48104, USA

McCraig, Joseph J — Businessman
%Grand Union Co, 201 Willowbrook Blvd, Wayne, NJ 07470, USA

McCraw, Leslie G — Businessman
%Fluor Corp, 3333 Michelson Dr, Irvine, CA 92612, USA

McCray, Curtis L — Educator
%Millikin University, President's Office, Decatur, IL 62522, USA

McCray, Nikki — Basketball Player
288 Center, #6, Collierville, TN 38017, USA

McCrea, William H — *Astrophysicist, Mathematician*
87 Houdean Rise, Lewes, Sussex BN7 1EJ, England

McCready, Mindy — *Singer*
%Moress Nanas Shea, 1209 16th Ave S, Nashville, TN 37212, USA

McCree, Donald H, Jr — *Financier*
%IBJ Schroder Bank/Trust, 1 State St, New York, NY 10004, USA

McCrillis, John W — *Skiing Executive, Writer*
%McCrillis & Eldredge Insurance, 17 Depot St, Newport, NH 03773, USA

McCrone, Walter C — *Microscopologist*
%McCrone Institute, 2820 S Michigan Ave, Chicago, IL 60616, USA

McCrory, Glenn — *Boxer*
Holborn, 35 Station Road, County Durham, England

McCrory, Milton (Milt) — *Boxer*
%Escot Boxing Enterprises, 19244 Bretton Dr, Detroit, MI 48223, USA

McCrossen, Richard G — *Financier*
%Citibank (South Dakota), 701 E 60th St N, Sioux Falls, SD 57104, USA

McCulley, Michael J — *Astronaut*
1112 Tall Pines Dr, Friendswood, TX 77546, USA

McCullin, Donald — *Photographer*
Holly Hill House, Batcombe, Shepton Mallet, Somerset BA4 6BL, England

McCulloch, Ed — *Auto Racing Driver*
44840 Viejo Dr, Hemet, CA 92544, USA

McCulloch, Frank W — *Attorney, Educator, Arbitrator*
5604 Kirkside Dr, Chevy Chase, MD 20815, USA

McCulloch, Frank W — *Editor*
%San Francisco Examiner, Editorial Dept, 110 5th St, San Francisco, CA 94103, USA

McCullough, Colleen — *Writer*
Out Yenna, Norfolk Island 2899, Oceania, Australia

McCullough, David — *Writer*
%Janklow & Nesbit Assoc, 598 Madison Ave, New York, NY 10022, USA

McCullough, Earl — *Track Athlete*
2108 Santa Fe Ave, Long Beach, CA 90810, USA

McCullough, Eugene F, Jr — *Financier*
%BOT Financial Corp, 125 Summer St, Boston, MA 02110, USA

McCullough, Julie — *Actress, Model*
%Gage Group, 9255 Sunset Blvd, #515, Los Angeles, CA 90069, USA

McCumber, Mark — *Golfer*
PO Box 7879, Jacksonville, FL 32238, USA

McCutcheon, Bill — *Actor*
65 Park Terrace W, New York, NY 10034, USA

McCutcheon, Lawrence — *Football Player*
19981 Weems Lane, Huntington Beach, CA 92646, USA

McDaniel Singleton, Mildred — *Track Athlete*
211 W Poppy Field Dr, Altadena, CA 91001, USA

McDaniel, Boyce D — *Physicist*
318 Savage Farm Dr, Ithaca, NY 14850, USA

McDaniel, James — *Actor*
%Innovative Artists, 1999 Ave of Stars, #2850, Los Angeles, CA 90067, USA

McDaniel, Lyndall D (Lindy) — *Baseball Player*
Rt 2, Box 353-A, Hollis, OK 73550, USA

McDaniel, Mel — *Singer, Songwriter*
106 Cranwell Dr, Hendersonville, TN 37075, USA

McDaniel, Randall — *Football Player*
20405 Manor Road, Shorwood, MN 55331, USA

McDaniel, Terry — *Football Player*
3370 Washington Court, Alameda, CA 94501, USA

McDaniel, Xavier — *Basketball Player*
2 Oakmist Court, Blythewood, SC 29016, USA

McDaniels (Darryl M), Darryl — *Rap Artist (Run-DMC)*
%Rush Artists, 1600 Varick St, New York, NY 10013, USA

McDermott, Dyland — *Actor*
320 22nd St, Santa Monica, CA 90402, USA

McDermott, Edward A — *Government Official*
Lake House South, 875 E Camino Real, Boca Raton, FL 33432, USA

McDermott, Richard (Terry) — *Speedskater*
5078 Chainbridge, Bloomfield Hills, MI 48304, USA

McDivitt, James A — *Astronaut, Air Force General*
9146 Cherry Ave, Rapid City, MI 49676, USA

McDonald, Ab	Hockey Player
416 Thompson Dr, Winnipeg MB R3C 3E7, Canada	
McDonald, Audra	Actress
%Peter Strain Assoc, 1501 Broadway, #2900, New York, NY 10036, USA	
McDonald, Charles C	Air Force General
Commader, AF Logistics Command, Wright-Patterson Air Force Base, OH 45433, USA	
McDonald, Country Joe	Singer, Guitarist
PO Box 7054, Berkeley, CA 94707, USA	
McDonald, David L	Navy Admiral
2105 Fleet Landing Blvd, Atlantic Beach, FL 32233, USA	
McDonald, Forrest	Writer, Historian
PO Box 155, Coker, AL 35452, USA	
McDonald, Gail C	Government Official
%Interstate Commerce Commission, 12th & Constitution NW, Washington, DC 20423, USA	
Mcdonald, Gregory C	Writer
%Arthur Greene, 101 Park Ave, New York, NY 10178, USA	
McDonald, John W	Government Official
3800 N Fairfax Dr, Arlington, VA 22203, USA	
McDonald, Lanny	Hockey Player
Box 9, Site 31, RR 2, Calgary AL T3E 3W6, Canada	
McDonald, Michael	Singer, Songwriter
%HK Mgmt, 8900 Wilshire Blvd, #300, Beverly Hills, CA 90211, USA	
McDonald, Paul	Football Player
1815 Tradewinds Lane, Newport Beach, CA 92660, USA	
McDonald, Robert B	Businessman
%Great Lakes Chemical Corp, 1 Great Lakes Blvd, West Lafayette, IN 47906, USA	
McDonald, Thomas F (Tommy)	Football Player
537 W Valley Forge Road, King of Prussia, PA 19406, USA	
McDonald, Wesley	Navy Admiral
5193 Cottingham Place, Alexandria, VA 22304, USA	
McDonnell, John F	Businessman
%McDonnell Douglas Corp, PO Box 516, St Louis, MO 63166, USA	
McDonnell, Mary	Actress
PO Box 6010-540, Sherman Oaks, CA 91413, USA	
McDonnell, Patrick	Cartoonist (Mutts)
%King Features Syndicate, 235 E 45th St, New York, NY 10017, USA	
McDonough, Mary	Actress
%Schiowitz/Clay/Rose, 1680 N Vine St, #614, Los Angeles, CA 90028, USA	
McDonough, Sean	Sportscaster
%CBS-TV, Sports Dept, 51 W 52nd St, New York, NY 10019, USA	
McDonough, Will	Sportswriter
4 Malcolm St, Hingham, MA 02043, USA	
McDonough, William	Architect
410 E Water St, Charlottesvle, VA 22902, USA	
McDonough, William J	Financier
%Federal Reserve Bank, 33 Liberty St, New York, NY 10045, USA	
McDormand, Frances	Actress
333 West End Ave, #12-C, New York, NY 10023, USA	
McDougal, Mike	Hockey Player
3202 Poplar St, Port Huron, MI 48060, USA	
McDougald, Gilbert J (Gil)	Baseball Player
10 Warren Ave, Spring Lake, NJ 07762, USA	
McDougall, Walter A	Writer, Historian
%University of Pennsylvania, History Dept, Philadelphia, PA 19104, USA	
McDowall, Roddy	Actor
3110 Brookdale Road, Studio City, CA 91604, USA	
McDowell, Frank	Plastic Surgeon
100 N Kalaheo Place, #F, Kailua Kona, HI 96734, USA	
McDowell, Jack B	Baseball Player
1949 N Seminary, Chicago, IL 60614, USA	
McDowell, Malcolm	Actor
%Markham & Froggatt, Julian House, 4 Windmill St, London W1P 1HF, England	
McDowell, Ronnie	Singer
%Grand Entertainment Group, 20 Music Square W, #200, Nashville, TN 37203, USA	
McDowell, Samuel E (Sam)	Baseball Player
7479 McClure Ave, Pittsburgh, PA 15218, USA	
McDyess, Antonio	Basketball Player
410 N Thompson Ave, Quitman, MS 39355, USA	

McDonald - McDyess

McEachran, Angus *Editor*
%Memphis Commercial Appeal, Editorial Dept, 495 Union Ave, Memphis, TN 38103, USA

McEldowney, Brooke *Cartoonist (9 Chickwood Lane)*
%United Feature Syndicate, 200 Madison Ave, New York, NY 10016, USA

McElhenny, Hugh *Football Player*
4023 171st Ave SE, Bellevue, WA 98008, USA

McElmury, Jim *Hockey Player*
9122 78th St Court S, Cottage Grove, MN 55016, USA

McElravey, R C *Financier*
%LMSC Federal Credit Union, PO Box 3643, Sunnyvale, CA 94088, USA

McElroy, Joseph P *Writer*
%Georges Borchandt, 136 E 57th St, New York, NY 10022, USA

McElroy, William D *Biochemist*
%University of California, Biology Dept, La Jolla, CA 92067, USA

McElwaine, Guy *Businessman*
%Columbia Pictures Industries, 711 5th Ave, New York, NY 10022, USA

McEnery, Peter *Actor*
%Hutton Mgmt, 200 Fulham Road, London SW10 9PN, England

McEnroe, John P, Jr *Tennis Player*
23712 Malibu Colony Road, Malibu, CA 90265, USA

McEntee, Gerald W *Labor Leader*
%State County Municipal Employees Union, 1625 "L" St NW, Washington, DC 20036, USA

McEntire, Reba *Singer*
%Starstruck Entertainment, 40 Music Square W, Nashville, TN 37203, USA

McEvoy, Marian *Editor*
%Elle Decor Magazine, Editorial Dept, 1633 Broadway, New York, NY 10019, USA

McEwan, Geraldine *Actress*
%Marmont Mgmt, Langham House, 302/8 Regent St, London W1R 5AL, England

McEwan, Ian *Writer*
%Jonathan Cape, 20 Vauxhall Bridge Road, London SW1V 2SA, England

McEwan, Mike *Hockey Player*
19 Main Ave, Sea Cliff, NY 11579, USA

McEwen, Bruce *Neuroscientist*
%Rockefeller University, Immunology Dept, 1230 York Ave, New York, NY 10021, USA

McEwen, Mark *Commentator*
%"Good Morning" Show, CBS-TV, News Dept, 51 W 52nd St, New York, NY 10019, USA

McEwen, Tom *Drag Racing Driver*
17368 Buttonwood St, Fountain Valley, CA 92708, USA

McEwen, Tom *Sportswriter*
%Tampa Tribune, 202 S Parker St, Tampa, FL 33606, USA

McFadden, Gates *Actress*
2332 E Allview Terrace, Los Angeles, CA 90068, USA

McFadden, James (Banks) *Football Player*
253 Riggs Dr, Clemson, SC 29631, USA

McFadden, Mary J *Fashion Designer*
240 W 35th St, #1700, New York, NY 10001, USA

McFadden, Robert D *Journalist*
%New York Times, Editorial Dept, 229 W 43rd St, New York, NY 10036, USA

McFadin, Lewis (Bud) *Football Player*
428 Springwood Dr, Victoria, TX 77905, USA

McFarland, Duncan M *Financier*
%Wellington Management, 75 State St, Boston, MA 02109, USA

McFarlane, Robert C *Government Official*
2010 Prospect St NW, Washington, DC 20037, USA

McFeeley, William S *Writer*
35 Mill Hill Road, Wellfleet, MA 02667, USA

McFerrin, Bobby *Singer, Songwriter*
%Original Artists, 826 Broadway, #400, New York, NY 10003, USA

McGahey, James C *Labor Leader*
%Plant Guard Workers Union, 25510 Kelly Road, Roseville, MI 48066, USA

McGann, Michelle *Golfer*
1200 Singer Dr, Riviera Beach, FL 33404, USA

McGarity, Vernon *WW II Army Hero (CMH)*
4522 Quince Ave, Memphis, TN 38117, USA

McGarrigle, Anne *Singer*
%Concerted Efforts, 59 Parsons St, West Newton, MA 02165, USA

McGarrigle, Kate *Singer*
%Concerted Efforts, 59 Parsons St, West Newton, MA 02165, USA

McGaugh, James L — *Psychobiologist*
2327 Aralia St, Newport Beach, CA 92660, USA

McGavin, Darren — *Actor*
PO Box 2939, Beverly Hills, CA 90213, USA

McGeady, Sister Mary Rose — *Social Activist*
%Covenant House, 460 W 41st St, New York, NY 10036, USA

McGee, Mike — *Football Player, Administrator*
%University of South Carolina, Athletic Dept, Columbia, SC 29208, USA

McGee, Tim D — *Football Player*
8116 Briddlemaker Lane, Cincinnati, OH 45249, USA

McGee, Willie D — *Baseball Player*
668 Turquoise Dr, Hercules, CA 94547, USA

McGeehan, Robert L — *Businessman*
%Kennametal Inc, State Rt 981 S, Latrobe, PA 15650, USA

McGhee, Carla — *Basketball Player*
%Columbus Quest, 7451 State Rt 161, Dublin, OH 43016, USA

McGhee, George C — *Government Official*
36276 Mountville Road, Middleburg, VA 20117, USA

McGill, Archie J, Jr — *Financier*
50 Belmont Ave, Bela Cynwyd, PA 19004, USA

McGill, Billy — *Basketball Player*
5129 W 58th Place, Los Angeles, CA 90056, USA

McGillis, Kelly — *Actress*
303 Whitehead St, Key West, FL 33040, USA

McGinest, Willie — *Football Player*
%New England Patriots, Foxboro Stadium, Rt 1, Foxboro, MA 02035, USA

McGinley, Ted — *Actor*
662 N Van Ness Ave, #305, Los Angeles, CA 90004, USA

McGinnis, Joe — *Writer*
%Morton Janklow Assoc, 598 Madison Ave, New York, NY 10022, USA

McGinty, John J, III — *Vietnam War Marine Corps Hero (CMH)*
75 Eastern Ave, Lynn, MA 01902, USA

McGinty, Kathleen A — *Government Official*
%Environmental Policy, White House, 1600 Pennsylvania Ave, Washington, DC 20500, USA

McGinty, Michael D (Mike) — *Air Force General*
Deputy Chief of Staff Personnel, HqUSAf, Pentagon, Washington, DC 20330, USA

McGirt, James (Buddy) — *Boxer*
195 Suffolk Ave, Brentwood, NY 11717, USA

McGlocklin, Jon — *Basketball Player*
5281 State Road, #83, Heartland, WI 53029, USA

McGlockton, Chester — *Football Player*
%Oakland Raiders, 1220 Harbor Bay Parkway, Alameda, CA 94502, USA

McGlynn, Dick — *Hockey Player*
38 Rock Glen Road, Medford, MA 02155, USA

McGonagle, William L — *Mediterrean Action Navy Hero (CMH)*
500 E Amado Road, #612, Palm Springs, CA 92262, USA

McGoohan, Patrick — *Actor*
16808 Bollinger Dr, Pacific Palisades, CA 90272, USA

McGoon, Dwight C — *Surgeon*
706 12th Ave SW, Rochester, MN 55902, USA

McGough, George — *Financier*
%Sutro Co, 201 California St, San Francisco, CA 94111, USA

McGovern, Elizabeth — *Actress*
17319 Magnolia Blvd, Encino, CA 91316, USA

McGovern, George S — *Senator, SD*
%Stratford Inn, Stratford, CT 06497, USA

McGovern, Jim — *Golfer*
788 Schirra Dr, Oradell, NJ 07649, USA

McGovern, Maureen — *Singer*
%Sterling/Winters, 1900 Ave of Stars, #1640, Los Angeles, CA 90067, USA

McGrady, Tracy — *Basketball Player*
%Toronto Raptors, 20 Bay St, #1702, Toronto ON M5J 2N8, Canada

McGrath, Don J — *Financier*
%Bank of the West, 1450 Treat Blvd, Walnut Creek, CA 94596, USA

McGrath, Eugene R — *Businessman*
%Consolidated Edison (NY), 4 Irving Place, New York, NY 10003, USA

McGrath, Mike — *Bowler*
%Professional Bowlers Assn, 1720 Merriman Road, Akron, OH 44313, USA

M

McGaugh - McGrath

M

McGraw, Frank E (Tug) — *Baseball Player*
2595 Wallingford Road, San Marino, CA 91108, USA

McGraw, Harold W, III — *Publisher*
%McGraw-Hill Inc, 1221 Ave of Americas, New York, NY 10020, USA

McGraw, Harold W, Jr — *Publisher*
%McGraw-Hill Inc, 1221 Ave of Americas, New York, NY 10020, USA

McGraw, Melinda — *Actress*
%Gersh Agency, 232 N Canon Dr, Beverly Hills, CA 90210, USA

McGraw, Tim — *Singer*
%Creative Artists Agency, 3310 West End Ave, #500, Nashville, TN 37203, USA

McGregor, Ewan — *Actor*
%Jonathan Altaras, 27 Floral St, London WC2E 9DP, England

McGregor, Maurice — *Cardiologist*
%Royal Victoria Hospital, 687 Pine Ave W, Montreal PQ H3A 1A1, Canada

McGregor, Scott H — *Baseball Player*
Star Rt 1, Box 2800-1300, Tehachapi, CA 93561, USA

McGriff, Frederick S (Fred) — *Baseball Player*
PO Box 17257, Tampa, FL 33682, USA

McGriff, Hershel — *Auto Racing Driver*
%General Delivery, Green Valley, AZ 85622, USA

McGriff, Jimmy — *Jazz Organist, Bandleader*
%Maxine Harvard, 2227 Highway One, #251, North Brunswick, NJ 08902, USA

McGrory, Mary — *Columnist*
%Washington Post, Editorial Dept, 1150 15th St NW, Washington, DC 20071, USA

McGuane, Thomas F, III — *Writer*
PO Box 25, McLeod, MT 59052, USA

McGuff, Joe — *Sportswriter*
%Kansas City Star, 1729 Grand Ave, Kansas City, MO 64108, USA

McGuinn, Roger — *Singer, Guitarist (Byrds), Songwriter*
%Concerted Efforts, 59 Parson St, West Newton, MA 02165, USA

McGuire, Alfred J (Al) — *Basketball Coach, Sportscaster*
%Al McGuire Enterprises, 1249 E Wisconsin Ave, Pewaukee, WI 53072, USA

McGuire, Christine — *Singer (McGuire Sisters)*
100 Rancho Circle, Las Vegas, NV 89107, USA

McGuire, Dick — *Basketball Player, Coach*
17 Redwood Dr, Dix Hills, NY 11746, USA

McGuire, Dorothy — *Actress*
121 Copley Place, Beverly Hills, CA 90210, USA

McGuire, Dorothy — *Singer (McGuire Sisters)*
100 Rancho Circle, Las Vegas, NV 89107, USA

McGuire, Patricia A — *Educator*
%Trinity College, President's Office, Washington, DC 20017, USA

McGuire, Phyllis — *Singer (McGuire Sisters)*
100 Rancho Circle, Las Vegas, NV 89107, USA

McGuire, Willard H — *Labor Leader*
%National Education Assn, 1201 16th St NW, Washington, DC 20036, USA

McGuire, William Biff — *Actor*
315 W 57th St, #4-H, New York, NY 10019, USA

McGwire, Mark D — *Baseball Player*
1704 Alamo Plaza, #322, Alamo, CA 94507, USA

McHale, Kevin — *Basketball Player, Executive*
20 Blue Jay Lane, North Oaks, MN 55127, USA

McHarg, Ian L — *Landscape Architect*
PO Box 778, Rt 82, Unionsville, PA 19375, USA

McHenry, Donald F — *Diplomat*
%Georgetown University, Foreign Service School, Washington, DC 20057, USA

McIlvaine, Jim — *Basketball Player*
811 Blaine Ave, Racine, WI 53405, USA

McInally, Pat — *Football Player*
PO Box 17791, Fort Mitchell, KY 41017, USA

McInnis, Marty — *Hockey Player*
21 Peter Hobart Dr, Hingham, MA 02043, USA

McIntyre, Donald C — *Opera Singer*
Foxhill Farm, Jackass Lane, Keston, Bromley, Kent BR2 6AN, England

McIntyre, James T, Jr — *Government Official*
%Hansell Post Brandon Dorsey, 1747 Pennsylvania Ave, Washington, DC 20006, USA

McKay, Gardner — *Actor*
252 Lumahai Place, Honolulu, HI 96825, USA

McKay, Heather *Squash, Racquetball Player*
48 Nesbitt Dr, Toronto ON M4W 2G3, Canada
McKay, Jim *Sportscaster*
Battlefield Farm, 2805 Shepperd Road, Monkton, MD 21111, USA
McKay, John A *Businessman*
%Harnischfeger Corp, 2855 S James Dr, New Berlin, WI 53151, USA
McKean, John R *Financier*
%Bay View Federal Bank, 2121 S El Camino Real, San Mateo, CA 94403, USA
McKean, Michael *Actor*
2216 4th St, #8, Santa Monica, CA 90405, USA
McKechnie, Donna *Dancer, Actress*
127 Broadway St, #220, Santa Monica, CA 90401, USA
McKee, E Stanton *Businessman*
%Electronic Arts, 1450 Fashion Island Parkway, San Mateo, CA 94404, USA
McKee, Frank S *Labor Leader*
%United Steelworkers Union, 5 Gateway Center, Pittsburgh, PA 15222, USA
McKee, Kinnaird R *Navy Admiral*
214 Morris St, #614, Oxford, MD 21654, USA
McKee, Maria *Singer*
%William Morris Agency, 1325 Ave of Americas, New York, NY 10019, USA
McKee, Peter B *Businessman*
%FoxMeyer Health Corp, 1220 Senlac Dr, Carrollton, TX 75006, USA
McKee, Todd *Actor*
32362 Lake Pleasant Dr, Westlake Village, CA 91361, USA
McKeel, Sam S *Publisher*
%Chicago Sun-Times, 401 N Wabash Ave, Chicago, IL 60611, USA
McKeever, Jeffrey D *Businessman*
%MicroAge Inc, 2308 S 55th St, Tempe, AZ 85280, USA
McKeever, Marlin *Football Player*
PO Box BK, Los Gatos, CA 95031, USA
McKeithen, John J *Governor, LA*
%McKeithen Wear Ryland Woodard, 221 Wall St, Columbia, LA 71418, USA
McKellar, Danica *Actress*
%Agency For Performing Arts, 9200 Sunset Blvd, #900, Los Angeles, CA 90069, USA
McKellen, Ian *Actor*
25 Earl's Terrace, London W8, England
McKenna, Dave *Jazz Pianist*
%Thomas Cassidy, 0366 Horseshoe Dr, Basalt, CO 81621, USA
McKenna, Quentin C *Businessman*
%Kennametal Inc, State Rt 981 S, Latrobe, PA 15650, USA
McKenna, Virginia *Actress*
67 Glebe Place, London SW3, England
McKenney, Don *Hockey Player*
111 Liberty St, Braintree, MA 02184, USA
McKennitt, Lorena *Singer, Songwriter*
%Quinlan Road, PO Box 933, Stratford ON N5A 7M3, Canada
McKenzie, Andrew *Labor Leader*
%Leather Goods Plastics Novelty Union, 265 W 14th St, New York, NY 10011, USA
McKenzie, Kevin *Ballet Dancer*
%American Ballet Theatre, 890 Broadway, New York, NY 10003, USA
McKenzie, Reginald (Reggie) *Football Player*
1334 100th Ave NE, Bellevue, WA 98004, USA
McKeon, Doug *Actor*
818 6th St, #202, Santa Monica, CA 90403, USA
McKeon, Nancy *Actress*
PO Box 1873, Studio City, CA 91614, USA
McKeown, Bob *Commentator*
%CBS-TV, News Dept, 51 W 52nd St, New York, NY 10019, USA
McKeown, Leslie (Les) *Singer (Bay City Rollers)*
Box 804, Dell D O, Edinburgh E417 7DH, Scotland
McKern, Leo *Actor*
%Richard Hatton, 29 Roehampton Gate, London SW15 5JR, England
McKernan, Leo J *Businessman*
%Clark Equipment, PO Box 8738, Woodcliff Lake, NJ 07675, USA
McKey, Derrick *Basketball Player*
8650 Jaffa Court East Dr, #36, Indianapolis, IN 46260, USA
McKie, Aaron *Basketball Player*
2209 N Delhi St, Philadelphia, PA 19133, USA

M

McKiernan, John S — Governor, RI
95 Hilltop Dr, East Greenwich, RI 02818, USA

McKinley, John — Rower
952 Bloomfield Village, Auburn Hills, MI 48326, USA

McKinney, John R — WW II Army Hero (CMH)
5749 Statesboro Highway, Sylvania, GA 30467, USA

McKinney, Kennedy — Boxer
5900 Sky Pointe Dr, #2134, Las Vegas, NV 89130, USA

McKinney, Rick — Archer
%Hoyt/Easton USA, 549 E Silver Creek, Gilbert, AZ 85296, USA

McKinney, Robert M — Publisher, Diplomat
Wind Fields, 39850 Snickersville Turnpike, Middleburg, VA 20117, USA

McKinney, Tamara — Skier
4935 Parkers Mill Road, Lexington, KY 40513, USA

McKinnon, Bruce — Editorial Cartoonist
%Halifax Herald, Editorial Dept, PO Box 610, Halifax NS B3J 2T2, Canada

McKinnon, Dan — Hockey Player
610 E River Dr, Warroad, MN 56763, USA

McKinzie, Gordon — Aviation Engineer
%Boeing Co, 777 Program, PO Box 3707, Seattle, WA 98124, USA

McKnight, Brian — Singer, Songwriter
%Famous Artists Agency, 1700 Broadway, #500, New York, NY 10019, USA

McKuen, Rod — Writer, Singer, Songwiter
1155 Angelo Dr, Beverly Hills, CA 90210, USA

McKusick, Victor A — Clinical Geneticist
%Johns Hopkins Hospital, Genetics Dept, 600 N Wolfe St, Baltimore, MD 21287, USA

McLachlan, Sarah — Singer, Songwriter
%Nettwerk Productions, 1250 W 6th Ave, Vancouver BC V6H 1A5, Canada

McLaglen, Andrew V — Movie Director
%Stanmore Productions, PO Box 1056, Friday Harbor, WA 98250, USA

McLain, Dennis D (Denny) — Baseball Player
11994 Hyne Road, Brighton, MI 48114, USA

McLane, James (Jimmy) — Swimmer
85 Pinckney St, Boston, MA 02114, USA

McLarty, Thomas F (Mack) — Government Official
%White House, 1600 Pennsylvania Ave NW, Washington, DC 20500, USA

McLaughlin, Ann Dore — Secretary, Labor
%Urban Institute of Washington, 2100 "M" St NW, Washington, DC 20037, USA

McLaughlin, Audrey — Government Official, Canada
%New Democratic Party, House of Commons, Ottawa ON K1A 0A6, Canada

McLaughlin, John — Singer, Songwriter, Guitarist
%International Music Network, 2 Main St, #400, Gloucester, MA 01930, USA

McLaughlin, John J — Commentator
%Oliver Productions, 1211 Connecticut Ave NW, Washington, DC 20036, USA

McLean, Barney — Skier
11745 W 66th Place, #D, Arvada, CO 80004, USA

McLean, Dan D — Businessman
%General Insurance Co, Safeco Plaza, Seattle, WA 98185, USA

McLean, Don — Singer, Songwriter
%Bennett Morgan, 1282 Rt 376, Wappingers Falls, NY 12590, USA

McLean, Jackie — Jazz Saxophonist, Composer
261 Ridgefield St, Hartford, CT 06112, USA

McLean, Rene — Jazz Saxophonist, Flutist
%Brad Simon Organization, 122 E 57th St, New York, NY 10022, USA

McLemore, LaMonte — Singer (The Fifth Dimension)
%Sterling/Winters, 1900 Ave of Stars, #1640, Los Angeles, CA 90067, USA

McLemore, Mark — Baseball Player
2117 Sandell Dr, Grapevine, TX 76051, USA

McLendon, John B, Jr — Basketball Coach
3683 Runnymede Blvd, South Euclid, OH 44121, USA

McLeod, Catherine — Actress
4146 Allott Ave, Van Nuys, CA 91423, USA

McLerie, Allyn Ann — Actress, Dancer
3344 Campanil Dr, Santa Barbara, CA 93109, USA

McLish, Rachel — Actress, Bodybuilder
120 S El Camino Dr, #116, Beverly Hills, CA 90212, USA

McLoughlin, Merrill — Editor
%US News & World Report Magazine, 2400 "N" St NW, Washington, DC 20037, USA

McLure, Charles E, Jr — Government Official
250 Yerba Santa Ana, Los Altos, CA 94022, USA

McMahon, Ed — Entertainer
1050 Summit Dr, Beverly Hills, CA 90210, USA

McMahon, Jim — Football Player
%Zucker Sports Mgmt, 33 N Dearborn St, #19, Chicago, IL 60602, USA

McMahon, Vince — Wrestling Promoter
%World Wrestling Federation, Madison Square Garden, New York, NY 10001, USA

McMath, Sid — Governor, AR
711 W 3rd St, Little Rock, AR 72201, USA

McMeannamin, Michael J — Financier
%Bank One Columbus, 100 E Broad St, Columbus, OH 43215, USA

McMenamin, Mark — Geologist
%Mount Holyoke College, Geology Dept, South Hadley, MA 01075, USA

McMichael, Steve — Football Player
1810 Westlake Dr, Austin, TX 78746, USA

McMichen, Robert S — Labor Leader
%International Typographical Union, PO Box 157, Colorado Springs, CO 80901, USA

McMillan, Howard L, Jr — Financier
%Deposit Guaranty Corp, 210 E Capitol St, Jackson, MS 39201, USA

McMillan, Nate — Basketball Player
17382 SE 54th Place, Bellevue, WA 98006, USA

McMillan, Roy D — Baseball Player
1200 E 9th St, Bonham, TX 75418, USA

McMillan, Terry — Writer
PO Box 2408, Danville, CA 94526, USA

McMillan, William (Bill) — Shooting Athlete
1930 Sandstone Vista, Encinitas, CA 92024, USA

McMillen, C Thomas (Tom) — Basketball Player; Representative, MD
1167 Jeffrey Dr, Crofton, MD 21114, USA

McMonagle, Donald R — Astronaut
%NASA, Johnson Space Center, 2101 NASA Road, Houston, TX 77058, USA

McMullian, Amos R — Businessman
%Flowers Industries, 200 US Highway 19 S, Thomasville, GA 31792, USA

McMurray, W Grant — Religious Leader
%Reorganized Church of Latter Day Saints, PO Box 1059, Independence, MO 64051, USA

McMurtry, James — Singer, Songwriter
%Mark Spector, 44 Post Road W, Westport, CT 06880, USA

McMurtry, Larry — Writer
PO Box 552, Archer City, TX 76351, USA

McNair, Barbara — Singer
%Thomas Cassidy, 0366 Horseshoe Dr, Basalt, CO 81621, USA

McNair, Robert E — Governor, SC
Rt 2, Box 310, Columbia, SC 29212, USA

McNair, Steve — Football Player
%Tennessee Oilers, Hale Hall, Tennessee State University, Nashville, TN 37209, USA

McNair, Sylvia — Concert Singer
%Colbert Artists, 111 W 57th St, New York, NY 10019, USA

McNally, Andrew, III — Publisher
%Rand McNally Co, PO Box 7600, Chicago, IL 60680, USA

McNally, Andrew, IV — Publisher
%Rand McNally Co, PO Box 7600, Chicago, IL 60680, USA

McNally, David A (Dave) — Baseball Player
3305 Ramada Dr, Billings, MT 59102, USA

McNally, Terrence — Writer
218 W 10th St, New York, NY 10014, USA

McNamara, Brian — Actor
11730 National Blvd, #19, Los Angeles, CA 90064, USA

McNamara, Eileen — Journalist
%Boston Globe, Editorial Dept, 135 Morrissey Blvd, Boston, MA 02125, USA

McNamara, John F — Baseball Manager
1206 Beech Hill Road, Brentwood, TN 37027, USA

McNamara, Julianne — Gymnast, Actress
%Gold Marshak Liedtke, 3500 W Olive Ave, #1400, Burbank, CA 91505, USA

McNamara, Kevin J — Businessman
%Chemed Corp, Chemed Center, 225 E 5th St, Cincinnati, OH 45202, USA

McNamara, Robert S — Secretary, Defense
2412 Tracy Place NW, Washington, DC 20008, USA

M

McLure - McNamara

McNamara, William *Actor*
21154 Entrada Road, Topanga, CA 90290, USA
McNary, Gene *Government Official*
%US Immigration & Naturalization Service, 425 "I" St NW, Washington, DC 20001, USA
McNaught, Judith *Writer*
%Pocket Books, 1230 Ave of Americas, New York, NY 10020, USA
McNaughton, Robert F, Jr *Computer Scientist*
2511 15th St, Troy, NY 12180, USA
McNeal, Don *Football Player*
3311 Toledo Plaza, Coral Gables, FL 33134, USA
McNealy, Scott G *Businessman*
%Sun Microsystems, 2550 Garcia Ave, Mountain Valley, CA 94043, USA
McNeice, John A, Jr *Financier*
%Colonial Group, 1 Financial Center, Boston, MA 02111, USA
McNeil, Freeman *Football Player*
94 Abbott Dr, Halesite, NY 11743, USA
McNeil, Kate *Actress*
5640 Rhodes Ave, North Hollywood, CA 91607, USA
McNeil, Lori *Tennis Player*
%Int'l Management Group, 1 Erieview Plaza, #1300, Cleveland, OH 44114, USA
McNeill, Alfred T, Jr *Businessman*
%Turner Corp, 375 Hudson Ave, New York, NY 10014, USA
McNeill, Robert Duncan *Actor*
%Susan Smith Assoc, 121 N San Vicente Blvd, Beverly Hills, CA 90211, USA
McNeill, W Donald *Tennis Player*
2165 15th Ave, Vero Beach, FL 32960, USA
McNeish, Richard *Archaeologist*
%Andover Archaeology Research Foundation, 1 Woodland Road, Andover, MA 01810, USA
McNerney, David H *Vietnam War Army Hero (CMH)*
20322 New Moon Trail, Crosby, TX 77532, USA
McNerney, Walter J *Businessman*
%American Health Properties, 6400 S Fiddler's Green Circle, Englewood, CO 80111, USA
McNichol, Kristy *Actress*
%William Morris Agency, 151 S El Camino Dr, Beverly Hills, CA 90212, USA
McNichols, Stephen L R *Governor, CO*
3404 S Race St, Englewood, CO 80110, USA
McPartland, Marian M *Jazz Pianist*
%Abby Hoffer, 223 1/2 E 48th St, New York, NY 10017, USA
McPeak, Holly *Volleyball Player*
%Women's Pro Volleyball Assn, 840 Apollo St, #204, El Segundo, CA 90245, USA
McPhee, John A *Writer*
475 Drake's Corner Road, Princeton, NJ 08540, USA
McPherson, Don *Football Player*
%Northeastern University, Sports/Society Ctr, 360 Huntington, Boston, MA 02115, USA
McPherson, Frank A *Businessman*
%Kerr-McGee Corp, 123 Robert Kerr Ave, Oklahoma City, OK 73102, USA
McPherson, Harry C, Jr *Government Official*
10213 Montgomery Ave, Kensington, MD 20895, USA
McPherson, James M *Writer, Historian*
15 Randall Road, Princeton, NJ 08540, USA
McPherson, John *Cartoonist (Close to Home)*
%Universal Press Syndicate, 4520 Main St, Kansas City, KS 64111, USA
McPherson, M Peter *Educator*
%Michigan State University, President's Office, East Lansing, MI 48824, USA
McPherson, Mary Patterson *Educator*
%Bryn Mawr College, President's Office, Bryn Mawr, PA 19010, USA
McPherson, Melville P *Government Official*
%Bank of America, 555 California St, San Francisco, CA 94104, USA
McPherson, Rolf K *Religious Leader*
%Church of Foursquare Gospel, 1100 Glendale Blvd, Los Angeles, CA 90026, USA
McQueen, Alexander *Fashion Designer*
%House of Givenchy, 3 Ave St George, 75008 Paris, France
McQueen, Chad *Actor*
8306 Wilshire Blvd, #438, Beverly Hills, CA 90211, USA
McRaney, Gerald *Actor*
%Karg/Weissenbach, 329 N Wetherly Dr, #101, Beverly Hills, CA 90211, USA
McRee, Lisa *Commentator*
%"Good Morning America" Show, 77 W 66th St, New York, NY 10023, USA

McShane, Edward J — *Mathematician*
209 Maury Ave, Charlottesville, VA 22903, USA

McShane, Ian — *Actor*
%International Creative Mgmt, 76 Oxford St, London W1N 0AX, England

McShann, James C (Jay) — *Jazz Pianist*
%New South Productions, 1448 Peachtree St NE, #401, Atlanta, GA 30309, USA

McSorley, Marty — *Hockey Player*
%San Jose Sharks, San Jose Arena, 525 W Santa Clara St, San Jose, CA 95113, USA

McTeer, Robert D, Jr — *Financier, Government Official*
%Federal Reserve Bank, 2200 N Pearl St, Dallas, TX 75201, USA

McTiernan, John — *Movie Director*
%William Morris Agency, 151 S El Camino Dr, Beverly Hills, CA 90212, USA

McVey, Robert — *Hockey Player*
PO Box 1212, Madison, CT 06443, USA

McVie, Christine — *Singer (Fleetwood Mac), Songwriter*
9744 Lloydcrest Dr, Beverly Hills, CA 90210, USA

McVie, John — *Bassist (Fleetwood Mac), Songwriter*
%Stiletto Entertainment, 5443 Beethoven St, Los Angeles, CA 90066, USA

McWethy, John F — *Commentator*
%ABC-TV, News Dept, 1717 De Sales St NW, Washington, DC 20036, USA

McWherter, Ned R — *Governor, TN*
22 Bypass Building, Dresden, TN 38225, USA

McWhirter, Norris D — *Publisher*
Manor House, Kington Langley near Chippenham, Wilts SN15 5NH, England

McWilliam, Edward — *Sculptor*
8-A Holland Villas Road, London W14 8DP, England

McWilliams, Brian — *Labor Leader*
%Longshoremen/Warehousemen Union, 1188 Franklin St, San Francisco, CA 94109, USA

McWilliams, Caroline — *Actress*
%Premiere Artists Agency, 8899 Beverly Blvd, #510, Los Angeles, CA 90048, USA

McWilliams, Fleming — *Singer*
%Michael Dixon Mgmt, 119 Pebble Creek Road, Franklin, TN 37064, USA

Mead, Dana G — *Businessman*
%Tenneco Inc, Tenneco Building, PO Box 2511, Houston, TX 77252, USA

Mead, George W — *Businessman*
%Consolidated Papers Inc, 231 1st Ave N, Wisconsin Rapids, WI 54495, USA

Mead, Shepherd — *Writer*
53 Rivermead Court, London SW6 3RY, England

Meade, Carl J — *Astronaut*
%NASA, Johnson Space Center, 2101 NASA Road, Houston, TX 77058, USA

Meade, Glenn — *Writer*
%St Martin's Press, 175 5th Ave, New York, NY 10010, USA

Meadlock, James W — *Businessman*
%Intergraph Corp, 1 Madison Industrial Park, Huntsville, AL 35894, USA

Meador, Eddie D (Ed) — *Football Player*
%Oro by Jon, PO Box 126, Natural Bridge, VA 24578, USA

Meadow, David L — *Religious Leader*
%Churches of God General Conference, 7176 Glenmeadow Dr, Frederick, MD 21703, USA

Meadows, Bernard W — *Sculptor*
34 Belsize Grove, London NW3, England

Meadows, Jayne — *Actress*
16185 Woodvale Road, Encino, CA 91436, USA

Meadows, Stephen — *Actor*
1760 Courtney Ave, Los Angeles, CA 90046, USA

Meagher, James P — *Editor*
%Barron's Magazine, Editorial Dept, 200 Liberty St, New York, NY 10281, USA

Meagher, John W — *WW II Army Hero (CMH)*
38 Hyannis St, Toms River, NJ 08757, USA

Meagher, Mary T — *Swimmer*
404 Vanderwall, Peachtree City, GA 30269, USA

Meaney, Colm — *Actor*
11921 Laurel Hills Road, Studio City, CA 91604, USA

Means, Natrone — *Football Player*
8907 McMillian Dr, Harrisburg, NC 28075, USA

Means, Russell — *Indian Activist*
444 Crazy Horse Dr, Porcupine, SD 57772, USA

Meara, Anne — *Comedienne, Actress*
118 Riverside Dr, #5-A, New York, NY 10024, USA

Mears, Rick	*Auto Racing Driver*
204 Spyglass Lane, Jupiter, FL 33477, USA	
Mears, Roger, Sr	*Truck Racing Driver*
416 Fairview Road, Bakersfield, CA 93307, USA	
Mears, Walter R	*Journalist*
%Associated Press, Editorial Dept, 2021 "K" St NW, Washington, DC 20006, USA	
Meat Loaf (Marvin Lee Aday)	*Singer*
%Left Bank Mgmt, 6255 Sunset Blvd, #1111, Los Angeles, CA 90028, USA	
Mecham, Evan	*Governor, AZ*
%Mecham Pontiac-AMC-Renault, 4510 W Glendale Ave, Glendale, AZ 85301, USA	
Mechem, Charles S, Jr	*Golf Executive, Businessman*
%United States Show, 1 Eastwood Dr, Cincinnati, OH 45227, USA	
Mechem, Edwin L	*Governor/Senator, NM; Judge*
%US District Court, PO Box 97, Albuquerque, NM 87103, USA	
Meciar, Vladimir	*Prime Minister, Slovakia*
Urad Vlady SR, Nam Slobody 1, 81370 Bratislava, Slovakia	
Mecir, Miloslav	*Tennis Player*
Sevcenkova 9, 85102 Bratislava, Czech Republic	
Mecklenburg, Karl	*Football Player*
6372 S Zenobia Court, Littleton, CO 80123, USA	
Medak, Peter	*Movie Director*
1712 Stanley Ave, Los Angeles, CA 90046, USA	
Medaris, J Bruce	*Clergyman, Army General*
PO Box 415, Fern Park, FL 32751, USA	
Medavoy, Mike	*Entertainment Executive*
9101 Hazen Dr, Beverly Hills, CA 90210, USA	
Medearis, Donald N, Jr	*Pediatrician*
%Massachusetts General Hospital, Children's Services Dept, Boston, MA 02114, USA	
Medina, Patricia	*Actress*
10787 Wilshire Blvd, #1503, Los Angeles, CA 90024, USA	
Medley, Bill	*Singer (Righteous Brothers)*
%Barry Rillera, 9841 Hot Springs Dr, Huntington Beach, CA 92646, USA	
Medley, Charles R O	*Artist*
Charterhouse, Charterhouse Square, London EC1M 6AN, England	
Medlin, John G, Jr	*Financier*
%Wachovia Corp, 301 N Main St, Winston-Salem, NC 27101, USA	
Medoff, Mark H	*Writer*
PO Box 3072, Las Cruces, NM 88003, USA	
Medved, Aleksandr V	*Wrestler*
%Central Soviet Sports Federation, Skatertny p 4, Moscow, Russia	
Medvedev, Andrei	*Tennis Player*
6352 Ellmau/Tirol, Austria	
Medvedev, Zhores A	*Biologist*
4 Osborn Gardens, London NW7 1DY, England	
Medwin, Michael	*Actor*
%International Creative Mgmt, 76 Oxford St, London W1N 0AX, England	
Meehan, Thomas E	*Writer*
Brook House, Obtuse Road, Newtown, CT 06470, USA	
Meek, Phillip J	*Publisher*
%Capital Cities/ABC Inc, 77 W 66th St, New York, NY 10023, USA	
Meely, Cliff	*Basketball Player*
3240 Iris Ave, #204, Boulder, CO 80301, USA	
Meese, Edwin, III	*Attorney General*
1075 Springhill Road, McLean, VA 22102, USA	
Meggett, David	*Football Player*
8 Brisbane Dr, Charleston, SC 29407, USA	
Megson, Claude W	*Architect*
27 Dingle Road, St Hellers, Auckland 5, New Zealand	
Mehl, Lance A	*Football Player*
66766 Graham Road, St Clairsville, OH 43950, USA	
Mehlhaff, Harvey	*Religious Leader*
%North American Baptist Conference, 210 Summit Ave, Oakbridge Terrace, IL 60181, USA	
Mehrabian, Robert	*Educator*
%Carnegie Mellon University, President's Office, Pittsburgh, PA 15213, USA	
Mehregany, Mehran	*Microbiotics Engineer*
%Case Western Reserve University, Electrical Engineer Dept, Cleveland, OH 44106, USA	
Mehringer, David M	*Astronomer*
%University of Illinois, Astronomy Dept, Champaign, IL 61820, USA	

Mehta, Shailesh J *Businessman*
%Providian Corp, 400 W Market St, Louisville, KY 40202, USA
Mehta, Ved *Writer*
139 E 79th St, New York, NY 10021, USA
Mehta, Zubin *Conductor*
%New York Philharmonic, Avery Fisher Hall, Lincoln Center, New York, NY 10023, USA
Meier, Raymond *Photographer*
%Raymond Meier Photography, 532 Broadway, New York, NY 10012, USA
Meier, Richard A *Architect*
%Richard Meier Partners, 475 10th Ave, New York, NY 10018, USA
Meier, Waltraud *Opera Singer*
%Festspielhugel 3, 95445 Bayreuth, Germany
Meigher, S Christopher, III *Publisher*
%Meigher Communications, 100 Ave of Americas, New York, NY 10003, USA
Meinwald, Jerrold *Chemist*
%Cornell University, Chemistry Dept, Ithaca, NY 14853, USA
Meisner, Joachim Cardinal *Religious Leader*
%Archbishop's Diocese, Marzellenstr 32, 50668 Cologne, Germany
Meisner, Randy *Bassist, Singer (Eagles, Poco)*
3706 Eureka Dr, Studio City, CA 91604, USA
Meisner, Sanford *Actor, Director*
%Neighborhood Playhouse School, 340 E 54th St, New York, NY 10022, USA
Mejdani, Rexhap *President, Albania*
%President's Office, Keshilli i Ministrave, Tirana, Albania
Mejia, Paul *Choreographer*
%New York City Ballet, Lincoln Center Plaza, New York, NY 10023, USA
Mekka, Eddie *Actor*
3518 Cahuenga Blvd W, #216, Los Angeles, CA 90068, USA
Melamid, Aleksandr *Artist*
%Ronald Freeman Fine Arts, 31 Mercer St, New York, NY 10013, USA
Melanie *Singer, Songwriter*
53 Baymont St, #5, Clearwater, FL 33767, USA
Melato, Mariangela *Actress*
%William Morris Organization, Via G Carducchi 10, 00187 Rome, Italy
Melcher, John *Senator, MT*
%General Delivery, Forsyth, MT 59327, USA
Melchionni, Bill *Basketball Player*
115 Whitehall Blvd, Garden City, NY 11530, USA
Melchior, Ib *Writer*
8228 Marymount Lane, Los Angeles, CA 90069, USA
Melendez, Bill *Animator*
438 N Larchmont Blvd, Los Angeles, CA 90004, USA
Melendez, Lisette *Singer*
%Famous Artists Agency, 1700 Broadway, #500, New York, NY 10019, USA
Melinda (Saxe) *Illusionist*
%Lady Luck Casino Hotel, Showroom, 206 N 3rd St, Las Vegas, NV 89101, USA
Mellanby, Scott *Hockey Player*
12716 NW 18th Place, Coral Springs, FL 33071, USA
Mellen, Harold J, Jr *Businessman*
%MDU Resources Group, 400 N 4th St, Bismarck, ND 58501, USA
Mellencamp, John *Singer, Songwriter*
5072 W Stevens Road, Nashville, IN 47448, USA
Melles, Carl *Conductor*
Grunbergstr 4, 1130 Vienna, Austria
Mellick, William L *Businessman*
%Twentieth Century Insurance, 6301 Owensmouth Ave, Woodland Hills, CA 91367, USA
Mellinkoff, Sherman M *Physician, Educator*
%University of California, Med Center, 10833 LeConte Ave, Los Angeles, CA 90095, USA
Mellish of Bermondsey, Robert J *Government Official, England*
West India House, Millwall Dock, London E14 9TJ, England
Mellon, Paul *Foundation Executive, Museum Official*
1729 "H" St NW, Washington, DC 20006, USA
Mellor, David *Government Official, England*
%House of Commons, Westminster, London SW1A 0AA, England
Mellor, James R *Businessman*
%General Dynamics, 3190 Fairview Park Dr, Falls Church, VA 22042, USA
Melmon, Kenneth L *Pharmacologist*
51 Cragmont Way, Redwood City, CA 94062, USA

M

Mehta - Melmon

M

Melnick, Bruce E *Astronaut*
%Lockheed Space Operations, 1100 Lockheed Way, Titusville, FL 32780, USA

Melnick, Daniel *Movie, Television Producer*
1123 Sunset Hills Dr, Los Angeles, CA 90069, USA

Melnikov, Vitaly V *Movie Director*
Bucharestskaya Str 23, Korp 1, #193, 192282 St Petersburg, Russia

Melone, Joseph J *Businessman*
%Equitable Life Assurance, 277 Park Ave, New York, NY 10172, USA

Melroy, Pamela A *Astronaut*
%NASA, Johnson Space Center, 2101 NASA Road, Houston, TX 77058, USA

Melton, Sid *Actor*
5347 Cedros Ave, Van Nuys, CA 91411, USA

Melvin, Allan *Actor*
271 N Bowling Green Way, Los Angeles, CA 90049, USA

Melzer, Thomas C *Financier*
%Federal Reserve Bank, PO Box 419440, Kansas City, MO 64141, USA

Men Huifeng *Taiji Master*
%Physical Education Institute, Martial Arts Dept, Beijing, China

Menard, Henry W *Geologist*
%Scripps Institute of Oceanography, Geology Dept, La Jolla, CA 92093, USA

Mendelsohn, Robert V *Businessman*
%Royal Indemnity, 9300 Arrowpoint Blvd, Charlotte, NC 28273, USA

Mendes, Sergio *Pianist*
4849 Encino Ave, Encino, CA 91316, USA

Mendoza, June *Artist*
34 Inner Park Road, London SW19 6DD, England

Menem, Carlos Saul *President, Argentina*
%Casa de Gobierno, Balcarce 50, 1064 Buenos Aires, Argentina

Meneses, Antonio *Concert Cellist*
%International Creative Mgmt, 40 W 57th St, New York, NY 10019, USA

Menges, Carl B *Financier*
%Donaldson Lufkin Jenrette, 140 Broadway, New York, NY 10005, USA

Menges, Chris *Cinematographer*
%Harmony Pictures, 6806 Lexington Ave, Los Angeles, CA 90038, USA

Menken, Alan *Composer*
340 W 55th St, #1-A, New York, NY 10019, USA

Mennea, Pietro *Track Athlete*
Via Cassia 1041, 00189 Rome, Italy

Meno, Chorepiscopus John *Religious Leader*
263 Elm Ave, Teaneck, NJ 07666, USA

Menotti, Gian-Carlo *Composer*
Gilford Haddington, E Lothian EH41 4JF, Scotland

Mentzer, Carl F *Financier*
%SunBank/Miami, 777 Brickell Ave, Miami, FL 33131, USA

Menuhin, Yehudi *Concert Violinist, Conductor*
Chalet Chankly Bore, Buhlstr, 3780 Gstaad-Neuret, Switzerland

Menzel, Jiri *Movie, Theater Director*
%Studio 989, KF A S Jindrisska 34, 112 07 Prague 1, Czech Republic

Menzies, Heather *Actress*
PO Box 1645, Park City, UT 84060, USA

Menzies, James P *Financier*
%Key Bank of New York, 66 S Pearl St, Albany, NY 12207, USA

Meola, Eric *Photographer*
535 Greenwich St, New York, NY 10013, USA

Meola, Tony *Soccer Player*
488 Forest St, Kearny, NJ 07032, USA

Merbold, Ulf *Astronaut, Germany*
Am Sonnenhang 4, 53721 Siegburg, Germany

Mercante, Arthur *Boxing Referee*
135 Wickham Road, Garden City, NY 11530, USA

Mercer, Marian *Actress, Singer*
25901 Piuma Road, Calabasas, CA 91302, USA

Mercer, Ray *Boxer*
501 Gateway Inn, Spring Lake, NC 28390, USA

Mercer, Ron *Basketball Player*
%Boston Celtics, 151 Merrimac St, #500, Boston, MA 02114, USA

Merchant, Ismail N *Movie Producer*
%Merchant-Ivory Productions, 46 Lexington St, London W1P 3LH, England

Merchant, Natalie *Singer, Songwriter*
%Creative Artists Agency, 9830 Wilshire Blvd, Beverly Hills, CA 90212, USA
Merckx, Eddy *Cyclist*
S'Herenweg 11, 1860 Meise, Belgium
Mercure, Alex P *Government Official*
%Department of Agriculture, 14th & Independence SW, Washington, DC 20250, USA
Mercurio, Micole *Actress*
%Innovative Artists, 1999 Ave of Stars, #2850, Los Angeles, CA 90067, USA
Mercurio, Paul *Actor, Singer*
%Beyond Films, 53-55 Brisbane St, Sunnyhills, Sydney NSW 2010, Australia
Meredith, Don *Football Player, Sportscaster*
PO Box 597, Santa Fe, NM 87504, USA
Meredith, Edwin T, III *Publisher*
%Meredith Corp, PO Box 400430, Des Moines, IA 50350, USA
Meredith, James H *Civil Rights Activist*
929 Meadowbrook Road, Jackson, MS 39206, USA
Meredith, Richard *Hockey Player*
7850 Metro Parkway, Minneapolis, MN 55425, USA
Meredith, Thomas C *Educator*
%Western Kentucky University, President's Office, Bowling Green, KY 42101, USA
Meredith, William *Writer*
7373 Swan Point Way, Columbia, MD 21045, USA
Meri, Lennart *President, Estonia*
%President's Office, 39 Weizenberg St, 0100 Tallinn, Estonia
Merigan, Thomas C, Jr *Medical Researcher*
148 Goya Road, Portola Valley, CA 94028, USA
Meriweather, Joe C *Basketball Player*
5316 NW 64th Terrace, Kansas City, MO 64151, USA
Meriwether, Lee *Actress*
12139 Jeanette Place, Granada Hills, CA 91344, USA
Merkerson, S Epatha *Actress*
%Alliance Talent, 9171 Wilshire Blvd, #441, Beverly Hills, CA 90210, USA
Merle, Carole *Skier*
74 Samoens, Haute Savoie, France
Merli, Gino J *WW II Army Hero (CMH)*
605 Gino Merli Dr, Peckville, PA 18452, USA
Merlin, Jan *Actor*
9016 Wonderland Ave, Los Angeles, CA 90046, USA
Merlo, Harry A *Businessman*
%Louisiana-Pacific Corp, 111 SW 5th Ave, Portland, OR 97204, USA
Merow, James F *Judge*
%US Claims Court, 717 Madison Place NW, Washington, DC 20005, USA
Merrifield, R Bruce *Nobel Chemistry Laureate*
43 Mezzine Dr, Cresskill, NJ 07626, USA
Merrill, Catherine *Artist*
%Old Church Pottery, 1456 Florida St, San Francisco, CA 94110, USA
Merrill, Dina *Actress*
524 N Rockingham Ave, Los Angeles, CA 90049, USA
Merrill, John O *Architect*
101 Gardner Place, Colorado Springs, CO 80906, USA
Merrill, Maurice H *Attorney, Educator*
800 Elm Ave, Norman, OK 73069, USA
Merrill, Richard A *Attorney, Educator*
501 Wellington Place, Charlottesville, VA 22903, USA
Merrill, Robert *Opera Singer*
%Robert Merrill Assoc, 79 Oxford Road, New Rochelle, NY 10804, USA
Merritt, C C I *WW II Canadian Army Hero (VC)*
1255 58th Ave W, Vancouver BC V6P 1V9, Canada
Merritt, Jack N *Army General*
%US Army Assn, 2425 Wilson Blvd, Arlington, VA 22201, USA
Merrow, Susan *Association Executive*
%Sierra Club, 85 2nd St, #200, San Francisco, CA 94105, USA
Merson, Michael *Government Official*
%World Health Orgainzation, Ave Appia, 1211 Geneva 27, Switzerland
Merten, Lauri *Golfer*
105 Foulk Road, Wilmington, DE 19803, USA
Mertz, Edwin T *Biochemist*
%Montana State University, Plant Soil/Environmental Sci Dept, Bozeman, MT 59717, USA

M

Merchant - Mertz

M

Mertz, Francis J *Educator*
%Farleigh Dickinson University, President's Office, Rutherford, NJ 07070, USA

Merwin, William Stanley *Writer*
%Atheneum Publishers, 866 3rd Ave, New York, NY 10022, USA

Meschery, Tom *Basketball Player*
PO Box 1297, Truckee, CA 96160, USA

Mese, John *Actor*
%Century Artists, 1148 4th St, #206, Santa Monica, CA 90403, USA

Meselson, Matthew S *Biochemist*
%Harvard University, Fairchild Biochemistry Laboratories, Cambridge, MA 02138, USA

Meskill, Thomas J *Governor, CT; Judge*
218 Stony Mill Lane, East Berlin, CT 06023, USA

Mesnil Du Buisson, Robert Du *Archaeologist*
Chateau de Champobert, Par 61310 Exmes, Orne, France

Messager, Annette *Artist*
%Art Institute of Chicago, Michigan Ave & Adams St, Chicago, IL 60603, USA

Messenger, George L *Businessman*
%Kemper Reinsurance, 1 Kemper Dr, Long Grove, IL 60049, USA

Messer, Thomas M *Museum Director*
1105 Park Ave, New York, NY 10128, USA

Messerschmid, Ernst *Astronaut, Germany*
Der Schone Weg 6, 72766 Reutlingen, Germany

Messerschmidt, J Alexander (Andy) *Baseball Player*
200 Lagunita Dr, Soquel, CA 95073, USA

Messick, Dale *Cartoonist (Brenda Starr)*
%Tribune Media Services, 435 N Michigan Ave, #1500, Chicago, IL 60611, USA

Messier, Mark *Hockey Player*
%Vancouver Canucks, 800 Griffiths Way, Vancouver BC V6B 6G1, Canada

Messina, Jim *Singer, Songwriter*
%Buddy Lee, 38 Music Square E, #300, Nashville, TN 37203, USA

Messina, Jo Dee *Singer, Songwriter*
%Starstruck Entertainment, 40 Music Square W, Nashville, TN 37203, USA

Messner, Reinhold *Explorer, Mountaineer*
Schloss Juval, 39020 Kastelbell/Tschars, Italy

Metcalf, Eric *Football Player*
%San Diego Chargers, Jack Murphy Stadium, Box 609609, San Diego, CA 92160, USA

Metcalf, Joseph, III *Navy Admiral*
4658 Charleston Terrace NW, Washington, DC 20007, USA

Metcalf, Laurie *Actress*
11845 Kling St, North Hollywood, CA 91607, USA

Metcalf, Robert L *Entomologist*
1902 Golfview Dr, Urbana, IL 61801, USA

Metcalf, Shelby *Basketball Coach*
%Texas A&M University, Athletic Dept, College Station, TX 77843, USA

Metheny, Pat *Jazz Guitarist, Composer*
%Ted Kurland, 173 Brighton Ave, Boston, MA 02134, USA

Metrano, Art *Actor*
1330 N Doheny Dr, Los Angeles, CA 90069, USA

Metzger, Henry *Medical Researcher*
3410 Taylor St, Chevy Chase, MD 20815, USA

Mey, Uwe-Jens *Speed Skater*
Vulkanstr 22, 10367 Berlin, Germany

Meyer Reyes, Debbie *Swimmer*
4840 Marconi Ave, Carmichael, CA 95608, USA

Meyer, Armin H *Diplomat*
4610 Reno Road NW, Washington, DC 20008, USA

Meyer, Daniel J *Businessman*
%Cincinnati Milacron, 4701 Marburg Ave, Cincinnati, OH 45209, USA

Meyer, Dina *Actress*
%Innovative Artists, 1999 Ave of Stars, #2850, Los Angeles, CA 90067, USA

Meyer, Jerome J *Businessman*
%Tektronix Inc, 26600 Southwest Parkway, Wilsonville, OR 97070, USA

Meyer, Karl H *Biochemist*
642 Wyndham Road, Teaneck, NJ 07666, USA

Meyer, Larry *Writer, Educator*
19811 Bushard St, Huntington Beach, CA 92646, USA

Meyer, Laurence *Economist, Government*
%Federal Reserve Board, 20th & Constitution NW, Washington, DC 20551, USA

Meyer, Loren	*Basketball Player*
%Phoenix Suns, 201 E Jefferson St, Phoenix, AZ 85004, USA	
Meyer, Raymond J (Ray)	*Basketball Coach*
2518 Cedar Glen Dr, Arlington Heights, IL 60005, USA	
Meyer, Ron	*Entertainment Executive*
%MCA Inc, 100 Universal City Plaza, Universal City, CA 91608, USA	
Meyer, Russ	*Movie Producer, Photographer*
3121 Arrowhead Dr, Los Angeles, CA 90068, USA	
Meyerowitz, Joel	*Photographer*
817 West End Ave, New York, NY 10025, USA	
Meyers Drysdale, Ann	*Basketball Player, Sportscaster*
6621 Doral Dr, Huntington Beach, CA 92648, USA	
Meyers, Ari	*Actress*
%Dove Audio, 301 N Canon Dr, #207, Beverly Hills, CA 90210, USA	
Meyers, Dave	*Basketball Player*
40629 Carmelina Cir, Temecula, CA 92591, USA	
Meyers, John A	*Publisher*
%Time Magazine, Time-Life Building, 1221 Ave of Americas, New York, NY 10020, USA	
Meyfarth, Ulrike Nasse-	*Track Athlete*
Buschweg 53, 51519 Odenthal, Germany	
Mezentseva, Galina	*Ballerina*
%Kirov Ballet Theatre, 1 Ploshchad Iskusstr, St Petersburg, Russia	
Mfume, Kweisi	*Association Executive*
%NAACP, President's Office, 4805 Mount Hope Dr, Baltimore, MD 21215, USA	
Miandad, Javed	*Cricketer*
%Cricket Board of Control, Gaddafi Stadium, Lahore, Pakistan	
Micek, Ernest	*Businessman*
%Cargill Inc, PO Box 9300, Minneapolis, MN 55440, USA	
Miceli, Justine	*Actress*
%Paradigm Agency, 10100 Santa Monica Blvd, #2500, Los Angeles, CA 90067, USA	
Michael	*King, Romania*
Villa Serena, 77 Chemin Louis-Degallier, 1290 Versoix-Geneva, Switzerland	
Michael (Shaheen), Archbishop	*Religious Leader*
%Antiochian Orthodox Christian Archdiocese, 358 Mountain Rd, Englewood, NJ 07631, USA	
Michael, Eugene R (Gene)	*Baseball Manager, Executive*
49 Union Ave, Upper Saddle River, NJ 07458, USA	
Michael, George	*Singer, Songwriter*
2 Elgin Mews, London W9 1NN, England	
Michaels, Alan R (Al)	*Sportscaster*
%ABC-TV, Sports Dept, 77 W 66th St, New York, NY 10023, USA	
Michaels, Brett	*Singer (Poison)*
%Levine/Schneider, 433 N Camden Ave, Beverly Hills, CA 90210, USA	
Michaels, Eugene H	*Association Executive*
%Alzheimer's Disease Research, 15825 Shady Grove Road, Rockville, MD 20850, USA	
Michaels, Jack D	*Businessman*
%HON Industries, 414 E 3rd St, Muscatine, IA 52761, USA	
Michaels, James W	*Editor*
%Forbes Magazine, Editorial Dept, 60 5th Ave, New York, NY 10011, USA	
Michaels, Leonard	*Writer*
438 Beloit Ave, Kensington, CA 94708, USA	
Michaels, Lisa	*Actress*
4942 Vineland Ave, #8, North Hollywood, CA 91601, USA	
Michaels, Lorne	*Television Producer, Screenwriter*
%Broadway Video, 1619 Broadway, #900, New York, NY 10019, USA	
Michaels, Louis A (Lou)	*Football Player*
69 Grace St, Swoyersville, PA 18704, USA	
Michaels, Walter	*Football Player, Coach*
8127 Boca Rio Dr, Boca Raton, FL 33433, USA	
Michaelsen, Kari	*Actress*
280 S Beverly Dr, #400, Beverly Hills, CA 90212, USA	
Michaleczewski, Dariusz	*Boxer*
%Universum Box-Promotion, Am Stadtrand 27, 22047 Hamburg, Germany	
Michals, Duane	*Photographer*
109 E 19th St, New York, NY 10003, USA	
Michel, F Curtis	*Astronaut*
2101 University Blvd, Houston, TX 77030, USA	
Michel, Hartmut	*Nobel Chemistry Laureate*
%Max Planck Biophysik Institut, 60437 Frankfurt/Main, Germany	

Michel, Jean-Louis — *Underwater Scientist*
%IFREMER, Center de Toulon, 83500 La Seyne dur Mer, Toulon, France

Micheler, Elisabeth — *Kayak Athlete*
Gruntenstr 45, 86163 Augsburg, Germany

Michelmore, Lawrence — *Government Official*
4924 Sentinel Dr, Bethesda, MD 20816, USA

Michels, Rinus — *Soccer Coach*
Hotel Breitenbacher Hof, H-Heine-Allee 36, 40213 Dusseldorf, Germany

Michener, Charles D — *Entomologist*
1706 W 2nd St, Lawrence, KS 66044, USA

Michener, James A — *Writer*
2706 Mountain Laurel Lane, Austin, TX 78703, USA

Michie, Donald — *Computer Scientist*
6 Inveralmond Grove, Cramond, Edinburgh EH4 6RA, Scotland

Michiko — *Empress, Japan*
Imperial Palace, 1-1 Chiyoda-ku, Tokyo 100, Japan

Michnik, Adam — *Political Activist, Editor*
Czerha 8/10, 00 732 Warsaw, Poland

Mickal, Abe — *Football Player, Physician*
774 Topaz St, New Orleans, LA 70124, USA

Mickelson, Phil — *Golfer*
2515 McKinney Ave, #940, Dallas, TX 75201, USA

Middendorf, J William, II — *Secretary, Navy*
565 W Main Road, Little Compton, RI 02837, USA

Middlecoff, Cary — *Golfer*
11765 Lost Tree Way, North Palm Beach, FL 33408, USA

Middleton, Mike — *Model*
%Louisa Models, Ebersberger Str 9, 81679 Munich, Germany

Middleton, Rick — *Hockey Player*
47 Edgelawn Ave, #7, North Andover, MA 01845, USA

Midkiff, Dale — *Actor*
4635 Lemona Ave, Sherman Oaks, CA 91403, USA

Midler, Bette — *Singer, Actress*
%All Girl Productions, 100 Universal City Plaza, #507, Universal City, CA 91608, USA

Midori (Goto) — *Concert Violinist*
%Midori Foundation, 850 7th Ave, #705, New York, NY, 10019, USA

Miechur, Thomas F — *Labor Leader*
%Cement & Allied Workers Union, 2500 Brickdale, Elk Grove Village, IL 60007, USA

Mies, Richard W — *Navy Admiral*
Commander, Submarine Force Atlantic, 7958 Blandy Blvd, Norfolk, VA 23551, USA

Mieto, Juha — *Cross Country Skier*
%General Delivery, Mieto, Finland

Mieuli, Franklin — *Basketball Executive*
%Golden State Warriors, 7000 Coliseum Way, Oakland, CA 94621, USA

Mifsud Bonnici, Carmelo — *President, Malta*
%Presidential Palace, Valleta, Malta

Mifune, Toshiro — *Actor*
%Mifune Productions, 9-30-7 Siejyo-Machi, Setagayaku, Tokyo 157, Japan

Migenes, Julia — *Opera Singer*
%Artists Group, 10100 Santa Monica Blvd, #2490, Los Angeles, CA 90067, USA

Mignola, Mike — *Cartoonist (Hellboy)*
%Dark Horse Publishing, 10956 SE Main St, Milwaukie, OR 97216, USA

Miguel, Luis — *Singer*
%Ventura Productions, PO Box 978, Pico Rivera, CA 90660, USA

Mihaly, Andre — *Composer*
Verhalom Ter 9-B, 1025 Budapest II, Hungary

Mikan, George L — *Basketball Player, Executive*
7096 Cahill Road, Minneapolis, MN 55439, USA

Mikhalchenko, Alla A — *Ballerina*
%Bolshoi Theater, Teatralnaya Pl 1, 103009 Moscow, Russia

Mikhalkov, Nikita S — *Movie Director*
Malaya Gruzinskaya 28, #10, 123557 Moscow, Russia

Mikhalkov-Konchalovsky, Andrei S — *Movie Director*
Malaya Gruzinskaya 28, #10, 123557 Moscow, Russia

Miki, Minouri — *Composer*
1-11-6 Higashi Nogawa, Komae-shi, Tokyo 201, Japan

Mikita, Stan — *Hockey Player*
15 Windsor Dr, Oak Park, IL

Mikkelsen, A Verner (Vern) — *Basketball Player*
17715 Breconville Road, Wayzata, MN 55391, USA

Milano, Alyssa — *Actress*
12952 Woodbridge St, Studio City, CA 91604, USA

Milbury, Mike — *Hockey Player, Coach, Executive*
11 Westover Dr, Lynnfield, MA 01940, USA

Milch, David — *Writer*
%International Creative Mgmt, 8942 Wilshire Blvd, Beverly Hills, CA 90211, USA

Mildren, Jack — *Football Player, Representative, OK*
1701 Guilford Lane, Oklahoma City, OK 73120, USA

Miles, Joanna — *Actress*
2062 N Vine St, Los Angeles, CA 90068, USA

Miles, John R (Jack) — *Writer*
3568 Mountain View Ave, Pasadena, CA 91107, USA

Miles, John W — *Geophysicist*
8448 Paseo del Ocaso, La Jolla, CA 92037, USA

Miles, Josephine — *Writer*
2275 Virginia St, Berkeley, CA 94709, USA

Miles, Mark — *Tennis Executive*
%Assn of Tennis Pros, 200 Tournament Players Road, Ponte Vedra Beach, FL 32082, USA

Miles, Sarah — *Actress*
Chithurst Manor, Trotten near Petersfield, Hants GU31 5EU, England

Miles, Sylvia — *Actress*
240 Central Park South, New York, NY 10019, USA

Miles, Vera — *Actress*
PO Box 1704, Big Bear Lake, CA 92315, USA

Milford, Penelope — *Actress*
219 Market St, Venice, CA 90291, USA

Milgram, Stanley — *Social Psychologist*
%City University of New York, Graduate Center, New York, NY 10036, USA

Milius, John F — *Movie Director, Writer*
888 Linda Flora Dr, Los Angeles, CA 90049, USA

Milla, Roger — *Soccer Player*
%Federation Camerounaise de Football, BP 1116, Yaounde, Cameroon

Millar, Jeffrey L (Jeff) — *Cartoonist (Tank McNamara)*
%Universal Press Syndicate, 1301 Spring Oaks Circle, Houston, TX 77055, USA

Millen, Matt — *Football Player, Sportscaster*
3604 Center St, Whitehall, PA 18052, USA

Miller, Alice — *Golfer*
%Ladies Professional Golf Assn, 2570 Volusia Ave, Daytona Beach, FL 32114, USA

Miller, Ann — *Actress, Dancer*
618 N Alta Dr, Beverly Hills, CA 90210, USA

Miller, Arthur — *Writer*
RR 1, Box 320, Tophet Road, Roxbury, CT 06783, USA

Miller, C Arden — *Pediatrician*
908 Greenwood Road, Chapel Hill, NC 27514, USA

Miller, C Ray — *Religious Leader*
%United Brethren in Christ, 302 Lake St, Huntington, IN 46750, USA

Miller, Charles D — *Businessman*
%Avery Dennison Corp, 150 N Orange Grove Blvd, Pasadena, CA 91103, USA

Miller, Cheryl — *Basketball Player, Coach, Sportscaster*
%Phoenix Mercury, Phoenix Suns' Plaza, 201 E Jefferson, Phoenix, AZ 85004, USA

Miller, Creighton E — *Football Player*
1610 Euclid Ave, Cleveland, OH 44115, USA

Miller, David — *Cartoonist (Dave)*
%Tribune Media Services, 435 N Michigan Ave, #1500, Chicago, IL 60611, USA

Miller, Dennis — *Entertainer*
814 N Mansfield Ave, Los Angeles, CA 90038, USA

Miller, Denny — *Actor*
323 E Matilija St, #112, Ojai, CA 93023, USA

Miller, Edward D — *Financier*
%Chemical Banking Corp, 270 Park Ave, New York, NY 10017, USA

Miller, Elizabeth C — *Medical Educator*
5517 Hammersely Road, Madison, WI 53711, USA

Miller, Frank — *Radio Executive*
%CBS Inc, Radio Network, 51 W 52nd St, New York, NY 10019, USA

Miller, Frank — *Cartoonist (Sin City)*
%Dark Horse Publishing, 10956 SE Main St, Milwaukie, OR 97216, USA

M

Miller, Franklin D — *Vietnam War Army Hero (CMH)*
3693 Belle Vista Dr E, St Petersburg, FL 33706, USA

Miller, G William — *Secretary, Treasury; Businessman*
%G William Miller Co, 1215 19th St NW, Washington, DC 20036, USA

Miller, George A — *Psychologist*
16 Willow St, Princeton, NJ 08542, USA

Miller, George D — *Air Force General*
20 Phillips Pond South, Natick, MA 01760, USA

Miller, George T (Kennedy) — *Movie Director*
30 Orwell St, King's Cross, Sydney 2011, Australia

Miller, Harold T — *Publisher*
%Houghton Mifflin Co, 222 Berkeley St, Boston, MA 02116, USA

Miller, Harvey R — *Attorney*
%Weil Gotshal Manges, 767 5th Ave, New York, NY 10153, USA

Miller, James A — *Oncologist*
5517 Hammersely Road, Madison, WI 53711, USA

Miller, James C, III — *Government Official*
%Citizens for Sound Economy, 1250 "H" St NW, Washington, DC 20005, USA

Miller, Jamir — *Football Player*
331 Grenadine Way, Hercules, CA 94547, USA

Miller, Jason — *Writer, Actor*
436 Spruce St, #600, Scranton, PA 18503, USA

Miller, Jeremy — *Actor*
%Gold Marshak Liedtke, 3500 W Olive Ave, #1400, Burbank, CA 91505, USA

Miller, John E — *Army General*
Deputy CG Training & Doctrine Command, Fort Monroe, VA 23651, USA

Miller, John L (Johnny) — *Golfer*
1220 Soda Canyon Road, Napa, CA 94558, USA

Miller, Jonathan W — *Stage, Movie Director*
63 Gloucester Crescent, London NW1, England

Miller, Joyce D — *Labor Leader*
%Amalgamated Clothing & Textile Workers, 1710 Broadway, #3, New York, NY 10019, USA

Miller, Keith H — *Governor, AK*
3605 Arctic Blvd, #1001, Anchorage, AK 99503, USA

Miller, Lajos — *Opera Singer*
Balogh Adam Utca 28, 1026 Budapest, Hungary

Miller, Larry — *Basketball Player*
1300 Paddock Dr, Raleigh, NC 27609, USA

Miller, Larry H — *Basketball Executive, Softball Player*
%Utah Jazz, Delta Center, 301 W South Temple, Salt Lake City, UT 84101, USA

Miller, Lennox — *Track Athlete*
1213 N Lake Ave, Pasadena, CA 91104, USA

Miller, Lenore — *Labor Leader*
%Retail/Wholesale/Department Store Union, 30 E 29th St, New York, NY 10016, USA

Miller, Leonard — *Businessman*
%Lennar Corp, 700 NW 107th Ave, Miami, FL 33172, USA

Miller, Mark — *Singer (Sawyer Brown)*
%TKO Artist Mgmt, 4219 Hillsboro Road, #318, Nashville, TN 37215, USA

Miller, Marvin J — *Labor Leader*
%Baseball Players Assn, 1370 Ave of Americas, New York, NY 10019, USA

Miller, Merton H — *Nobel Economics Laureate*
%University of Chicago, Graduate Business School, 1101 E 58th, Chicago, IL 60637, USA

Miller, Mildred — *Opera Singer*
PO Box 110108, Pittsburgh, PA 15232, USA

Miller, Mitch — *Conductor, Orchestra Leader*
345 W 58th St, New York, NY 10019, USA

Miller, Mulgrew — *Jazz Pianist*
3725 Farmersville Road, Easton, PA 18045, USA

Miller, Nate — *Boxer*
4807 Green St, Philadelphia, PA 19144, USA

Miller, Neal E — *Psychologist*
%Yale University, Psychology Dept, New Haven, CT 06520, USA

Miller, Nicole J — *Fashion Designer*
780 Madison Ave, New York, NY 10021, USA

Miller, Oliver — *Basketball Player*
2912 S Meadow Dr, Fort Worth, TX 76133, USA

Miller, Penelope Ann — *Actress*
%William Morris Agency, 151 S El Camino Dr, Beverly Hills, CA 90212, USA

Miller, Peter North *Businessman*
%Lloyd's of London, Lime St, London EC3M 7HL, England
Miller, Reginald W (Reggie) *Basketball Player*
11116 Catamaran Court, Indianapolis, IN 46236, USA
Miller, Richard B *Attorney*
%Miller Keeton, 909 Fannin, Houston, TX 77010, USA
Miller, Robert (Red) *Football Coach*
3841 S Narcissis Way, Denver, CO 80237, USA
Miller, Robert J (Bob) *Governor, NV*
%Governor's Office, State Capitol, Carson City, NV 89710, USA
Miller, Robert L *Publisher*
%Berlitz Publishing Co, 257 Park Ave S, New York, NY 10010, USA
Miller, Robert S, Jr *Businessman*
%Morrison Knudsen, Morrison Knudsen Plaza, PO Box 73, Boise, ID 83729, USA
Miller, Shannon *Gymnast*
715 E Kelley Ave, Edmond, OK 73003, USA
Miller, Sidney *Actor*
%First Artists, 10000 Riverside Dr, #10, Toluca Lake, CA 91602, USA
Miller, Stanley L *Chemist*
%University of California, Chemistry Dept, La Jolla, CA 92093, USA
Miller, Stephanie *Entertainer*
%Buena Vista-TV, Swanson Building, 5555 Melrose Ave, Los Angeles, CA 90038, USA
Miller, Steve *Singer, Songwriter, Band Leader*
PO Box 12680, Seattle, WA 98111, USA
Miller, Stuart L (Stu) *Baseball Player*
3701 Ocaso Court, Cameron Park, CA 95682, USA
Miller, Ty *Actor*
2118 Wilshire Blvd, #585, Santa Monica, CA 90403, USA
Miller, Warren *Ski Photographer*
505 Pier Ave, Hermosa Beach, CA 90254, USA
Miller, Wiley *Cartoonist (Non Sequitur, Us & Them)*
7 Fairview Knolls NE, Iowa City, IA 52240, USA
Miller, Zell B *Governor, GA*
%Governor's Office, State Capitol Building, #203, Atlanta, GA 30334, USA
Millett, Kate *Feminist Leader, Writer*
20 Old Overlook Road, Poughkeepsie, NY 12603, USA
Millett, Lewis L *Korean War Army Hero (CMH)*
%Korean War Memorial, Patriotic Hall, 1816 Figueroa, #700, Los Angeles, CA 90015, USA
Milligan, Terence A (Spike) *Actor, Writer*
%Spike Milligan Productions, 9 Orme Court, London W2 4RL, England
Milliken, Roger *Businessman*
%Milliken Co, PO Box 3167, Spartanburg, SC 29304, USA
Milliken, William G *Governor, MI*
300 Grandview Parkway, Traverse City, MI 49684, USA
Milling, R King *Financier*
%Whitney National Bank, 228 St Charles Ave, New Orleans, LA 70130, USA
Millo, Aprile *Opera Singer*
%Columbia Artists Mgmt Inc, 165 W 57th St, New York, NY 10019, USA
Mills, Alley *Actress*
444 Carol Canal, Venice, CA 90291, USA
Mills, Chris *Basketball Player*
%Boston Celtics, 151 Merrimac St, #500, Boston, MA 02114, USA
Mills, Curtis *Track Athlete*
328 Lake St, Lufkin, TX 75904, USA
Mills, Donna *Actress*
2260 Benedict Canyon Dr, Beverly Hills, CA 90210, USA
Mills, Frank *Pianist, Composer*
%Rocklands Talent, PO Box 1282, Peterborough ON K9L 7H5, Canada
Mills, Hayley *Actress*
81 High St, Hampton, Middx, England
Mills, John *Actor*
Hill House, Denham Village, Buckinghamshire, England
Mills, Juliet *Actress*
2890 Hidden Valley Lane, Santa Barbara, CA 93108, USA
Mills, Samuel D (Sam), Jr *Football Player*
%Carolina Panthers, Ericsson Stadium, 800 S Mint St, Charlotte, NC 28202, USA
Mills, Stephanie *Singer*
5807 Topanga Canyon Blvd, Woodland Hills, CA 91367, USA

Mills, Terry	*Basketball Player*
PO Box 43658, Detroit, MI 48243, USA	
Mills, William (Billy)	*Track Athlete*
124 Pecos Ave, Raton, NM 87740, USA	
Millsaps, Knox	*Aerospace Engineer*
PO Box 13857, Gainesville, FL 32604, USA	
Milmoe, Caroline	*Actress*
Martin-Smith, Half Moon Chambers, Chapel Walks, Manchester M2 1HN, England	
Milne, John D	*Businessman*
Chilton House, Chilton Candover near Alresford, Hants SO24 9TX, England	
Milner, Martin	*Actor*
14755 Camino Porto Alegre, Del Mar, CA 92014, USA	
Milnes, Sherrill	*Opera Singer*
%Herbert Barrett Mgmt, 1776 Broadway, #1800 New York, NY 10019, USA	
Milosevic, Slobodan	*President, Serbia*
%President's Office, Nemanjina 11, 11000 Belgrade, Serbia	
Milosz, Czeslaw	*Nobel Literature Laureate*
%University of California, Slavic Languages Dept, Berkeley, CA 94720, USA	
Milow, Keith	*Artist*
32 W 20th St, New York, NY 10011, USA	
Milsap, Ronnie	*Singer, Songwriter*
%Ronnie Milsap Enterprises, PO Box 40665, Nashville, TN 37204, USA	
Milstein, Cesar	*Nobel Medicine Laureate*
%Medical Research Council Center, Hills Road, Cambridge CB2 2QH, England	
Milstein, Monroe G	*Businessman*
%Burlington Coat Warehouse, 1839 Rt 130, Burlington, NJ 08016, USA	
Mimieux, Yvette	*Actress*
500 Perugia Way, Los Angeles, CA 90077, USA	
Mimoun, Alain	*Marathon Runner*
27 Ave Edouard-Jenner, 94500 Champigny-sur-Marne, France	
Min, Gao	*Diver*
%Olympic Committee, 9 Tiyuguan Road, Beijing, China	
Minehan, Cathy E	*Financier*
%Federal Reserve Bank, 600 Atlantic Ave, Boston, MA 02210, USA	
Miner, Jan	*Actress*
PO Box 293, Southbury, CT 06488, USA	
Minghella, Anthony	*Movie Director*
%Judy Daish, 2 St Charles Place, London W10 6EG, England	
Miniham, Kenneth A (Ken)	*Air Force General*
%National Security Agency, Director's Office, Fort George G Meade, MD 20755, USA	
Minisi, Anthony S (Skip)	*Football Player*
300 Continental Lane, Paoli, PA 19301, USA	
Minnelli, Liza	*Actress, Singer*
%Black, 150 E 69th St, #21-G, New York, NY 10021, USA	
Minnifield, Frank	*Football Player*
%Baltimore Ravens, 200 St Paul Place, #2400, Baltimore, MD 21202, USA	
Minogue, Kylie	*Singer*
%Terry Blamey Mgmt, 329 Montague St, Albert Park VIC 3206, Australia	
Minor, Ronald R	*Religious Leader*
%Pentecostal Church of God, 4901 Pennsylvania, Joplin, MO 64804, USA	
Minoso, Saturino O (Minnie)	*Baseball Player, Coach*
805 Main Road, Independence, MO 64056, USA	
Minow, Newton N	*Government Official*
179 E Lake Shore Dr, #15-W, Chicago, IL 60611, USA	
Minsky, Marvin L	*Computer Scientist*
%Massachusetts Institute of Technology, Computer Sci Dept, Cambridge, MA 02139, USA	
Minter, Kristin	*Actress*
%Innovative Artists, 1999 Ave of Stars, #2850, Los Angeles, CA 90067, USA	
Mintoff, Dominic	*Prime Minister, Malta*
The Olives, Xintill St, Tarxien, Malta	
Minton, Yvonne F	*Opera Singer*
%Ingpen & Williams, 14 Kensington Court, London W8, England	
Mintz, Shlomo	*Concert Violinist*
%International Creative Mgmt, 40 W 57th St, New York, NY 10019, USA	
Mir, Isabelle	*Skier*
65170 Saint-Lary, France	
Mira, George	*Football Player*
19225 SW 128th Court, Miami, FL 33177, USA	

Mirabella, Grace — *Editor, Publisher*
%Mirabella Magazine, 200 Madison Ave, New York, NY 10016, USA

Mirer, Rick — *Football Player*
%Chicago Bears, Halas Hall, 250 N Washington Road, Lake Forest, IL 60045, USA

Mirikitani, Janice — *Writer*
%Glide Memorial United Methodist Church, 330 Ellis St, San Francisco, CA 94102, USA

Mirisch, Walter M — *Movie Producer*
647 Warner Ave, Los Angeles, CA 90024, USA

Mirren, Helen — *Actress*
%Al Parker, 55 Park Lane, London W1Y 3DD, England

Mirrlees, James A — *Nobel Economics Laureate*
%Cambridge University, Nuffield College, Oxford, England

Mirvish, Edwin (Ed) — *Comedian, Theater Producer*
%Honest Ed's Ltd, 581 Bloor St W, Toronto ON M6G 1K3, Canada

Mirzoev, Akbar — *Prime Minister, Tajikistan*
%Prime Minister's Office, Dushaube, Tajikistan

Mischke, Carl H — *Religious Leader*
1034 Buena Vista Dr, Sun Prairie, WI 53590, USA

Misersky, Antje — *Biathlete*
Grenzgraben 3-A, 98714 Stutzerbach, Germany

Mishin, Vasiliy P — *Space Engineer*
%Aviation Institute, Volokolamskoye Sh 4, 125080 Moscow, Russia

Mitchell, Andrea — *Commentator*
%NBC-TV, News Dept, 4001 Nebraska Ave NW, Washington, DC 20016, USA

Mitchell, Bradford W — *Businessman*
%Harleysville Mutual Insurance, 355 Maple Ave, Harleysville, PA 19438, USA

Mitchell, Brian — *Actor*
5307-B Wilkinson Ave, #20, Valley Village, CA 91607, USA

Mitchell, Don — *Actor*
4139 Cloverdale Ave, Los Angeles, CA 90008, USA

Mitchell, Edgar D — *Astronaut*
242 Seaspray Ave, Palm Beach, FL 33480, USA

Mitchell, Edward E — *Businessman*
%Potomac Electric Power, 1900 Pennsylvania Ave NW, Washington, DC 20068, USA

Mitchell, George J — *Senator, ME*
%Verner Lipfert Bernhard, 901 15th St NW, #700, Washington, DC 20005, USA

Mitchell, George P — *Businessman*
%Mitchell Energy Corp, 2001 Timberloch Place, The Woodlands, TX 77380, USA

Mitchell, Guy — *Singer*
PO Box 42536, Las Vegas, NV 89116, USA

Mitchell, Jack — *Photographer*
1413 Live Oak St, New Smyrna Beach, FL 32168, USA

Mitchell, James F — *Prime Minister, St Vincent & Grenadines*
%Prime Minister's Office, Kingstown, St Vincent, St Vincent & Grenadines

Mitchell, Joni — *Singer, Songwriter*
624 Funchal Road, Los Angeles, CA 90077, USA

Mitchell, Kevin D — *Baseball Player*
3867 Ocean View Blvd, San Diego, CA 92113, USA

Mitchell, Leona — *Opera Singer*
%Columbia Artists Mgmt Inc, 165 W 57th St, New York, NY 10019, USA

Mitchell, Lydell — *Football Player*
702 Reservoir St, Baltimore, MD 21217, USA

Mitchell, Mike — *Basketball Player*
3876 Morgans Creek, San Antonio, TX 78230, USA

Mitchell, Robert C (Bobby) — *Football Player, Executive*
%Washington Redskins, 21300 Redskin Park Dr, Ashburn, VA 20147, USA

Mitchell, Roscoe — *Jazz Reeds Player, Composer*
%SRO Artists, PO Box 9532, Madison, WI 53715, USA

Mitchell, Russ — *Commentator*
%CBS-TV, News Dept, 2020 "M" St NW, Washington, DC 20036, USA

Mitchell, Sasha — *Actor*
%Flick East-West, 9057 Nemo St, #A, West Hollywood, CA 90069, USA

Mitchell, Susan — *Writer*
%Florida Atlantic University, English Dept, Boca Raton, FL 33431, USA

Mitchelson, Marvin — *Attorney*
1801 Century Park East, #1900, Los Angeles, CA 90067, USA

Mitsotakis, Constantine — *Prime Minister, Greece*
%New Democracy Party, Odos Rigillis 18, 106 74 Athens, Greece

M

Mirabella - Mitsotakis

Mittermaier-Neureuther, Rosi — *Skier*
Winkelmoosalm, 83242 Reit Im Winkel, Germany

Mitzelfeld, Jim — *Journalist*
5395 Wild Oak Dr, East Lansing, MI 48823, USA

Mix, Ronald J (Ron) — *Football Player*
2317 Caminto Recodo, San Diego, CA 92107, USA

Mix, Steve — *Basketball Player*
25743 Willowbend Road, Newtown, PA 18940, USA

Mixon, Alan — *Actor*
210 W 16th St, New York, NY 10011, USA

Mixon, Wayne — *Governor, FL*
2219 Demeron Road, Tallahassee, FL 32312, USA

Miyamura, Hiroshi H — *Korean War Army Hero (CMH)*
1905 Mossman Ave, Gallup, NM 87301, USA

Miyazawa, Kiichi — *Prime Minister, Japan*
6-34-1 Jingu-mae, Shibuyaku, Tokyo 150, Japan

Miyori, Kim — *Actress*
%Susan Smith, 121 N San Vicente Blvd, Beverly Hills, CA 90211, USA

Mize, Larry — *Golfer*
106 Graystone Court, Columbus, GA 31904, USA

Mize, Ola Lee — *Korean War Army Hero (CMH)*
211 Hartwood Dr, Gasden, AL 35901, USA

Mizell, Jason — *Rap Artist (Run-DMC)*
%Rush Artists, 1600 Varick St, New York, NY 10013, USA

Mizerak, Steve — *Billiards Player*
140 Alfred St, Edison, NJ 08820, USA

Mizrahi, Isaac — *Fashion Designer*
104 Wooster St, New York, NY 10012, USA

Mladenov, Petar T — *President, Bulgaria*
10 Veliko Turnovo St, Sofia, Bulgaria

Mnouchkine, Ariane — *Theater Director*
%Theatre du Soleil, Cartoucherie, 75012 Paris, France

Mobley, Mary Ann — *Actress*
2751 Hutton Dr, Beverly Hills, CA 90210, USA

Moceanu, Dominique — *Gymnast*
17911 Fall River Circle, Houston, TX 77090, USA

Mochrie Pepper, Dottie — *Golfer*
15 Blazing Star Trail, Landrum, SC 29356, USA

Moco, Marcolino J Carlos — *Prime Minister, Angola*
%Prime Minister's Office, Council of Ministers, Luanda, Angola

Moctezuma, Edwardo Matos — *Archeologist*
%Great Temple Museum, Mexico City, Mexico

Modano, Mike — *Hockey Player*
4720 O'Connor Court, Irving, TX 75062, USA

Modell, Arthur B — *Football Executive*
%Baltimore Ravens, 200 St Paul Place, #2400, Baltimore, MD 21202, USA

Modell, Frank — *Cartoonist*
115 Three Mile Course, Guilford, CT 06437, USA

Modena, Stefano — *Auto Racing Driver*
%Alfa Corse, Via Enrico Fermi 7, 20019 Settimo Milanese, Italy

Modigliani, Franco — *Nobel Economics Laureate*
25 Clark St, Belmont, MA 02178, USA

Modine, Matthew — *Actor*
9696 Culver Blvd, #203, Culver City, CA 90232, USA

Modl, Martha — *Opera Singer*
Perlacherstr 19, 81539 Munich-Grunwald, Germany

Modrow, Hans — *Prime Minister, East Germany*
Bundeskanzlerplatz 2-10, Bonn-Center, 53113 Bonn, Germany

Modrzejewski, Robert J — *Vietnam War Marine Corps Hero (CMH)*
4725 Oporto Court, San Diego, CA 92124, USA

Modzelewski, Ed — *Football Player*
PO Box 4207, 15 Last Wagon Dr, West Sedona, AZ 86340, USA

Modzelewski, Richard (Dick) — *Football Player*
Pier Pointe #1, New Bern, NC 28562, USA

Moe, Douglas E (Doug) — *Basketball Player, Coach*
%Philadelphia 76ers, Veterans Stadium, PO Box 25040, Philadelphia, PA 19147, USA

Moe, Karen — *Swimmer*
151 Miramonte Dr, Moraga, CA 94556, USA

Moe, Thomas S (Tommy) *Skier*
PO Box 100, Girdwood, AK 99587, USA

Moeller, Gary *Football Coach*
%Detroit Lions, Silverdome, 1200 Featherstone Road, Pontiac, MI 48342, USA

Moellering, John H *Army General*
1526 Shipsview Road, Annapolis, MD 21401, USA

Moffatt, Katy *Singer, Songwriter*
PO Box 334, O'Fallon, IL 62269, USA

Moffett, D W *Actor*
450 N Rossmore Ave, #401, Los Angeles, CA 90004, USA

Moffett, James R *Businessman*
%Freeport-McMoRan Inc, 1615 Poydras St, New Orleans, LA 70112, USA

Moffitt, Donald E *Businessman*
%Consolidated Freightways, 3240 Hillview Ave, Palo Alto, CA 94304, USA

Moffo, Anna *Opera Singer*
4 E 66th St, New York, NY 10021, USA

Mogenburg, Dietmar *Track Athlete*
Alter Garfen 34, 51371 Leverkusen, Germany

Mogilny, Alexander *Hockey Player*
1664 Iolanda Place, Point Roberts, WA 98281, USA

Mohn, Reinhard *Publisher*
%Bertelsmann AG, Carl-Bertelsmann-Str 270, 33311 Guetersloh, Germany

Mohns, Doug *Hockey Player*
6 Mitchell Grant Way, Bedford, MA 01730, USA

Mohr, Todd *Singer, Guitarist*
%Morris Bliessner, 1658 York St, Denver, CO 80206, USA

Mohri, Mamoru *Astronaut, Japan*
%NASDA, 2-1-1 Sengen, Tukubashi, Ibaraki 305, Japan

Moi, Daniel Arap *President, Kenya*
%President's Office, Harambee House, PO Box 30510, Nairobi, Kenya

Moise, Patty *Auto Racing Driver*
PO Box 77919, Greensboro, NC 27417, USA

Moiseyev, Igor A *Dance Director, Choreographer*
%Moiseyev Dance Co, 20 R, Triumfalnaya Pl, Moscow, Russia

Mokae, Zakes *Actor*
%Gersh Agency, 232 N Canon Dr, Beverly Hills, CA 90210, USA

Mokhehle, Ntsu *Prime Minister, Lesotho*
%Prime Minister's Office, Military Council, PO Box 527, Maseru, Lesotho

Mokrzynski, Jerzy *Architect*
Ul Marszalkowska 140 M 18, 00 061 Warsaw, Poland

Moldofsky, Philip J *Cancer Researcher*
%Fox Chase Cancer Center, 7701 Burholme Ave, Philadelphia, PA 19111, USA

Molen, Richard L *Businessman*
%Huffy Corp, PO Box 1204, Dayton, OH 45401, USA

Molina, Alfred *Actor*
%Lou Coulson, 37 Berwick St, London W1V 3RF, England

Molina, Mario J *Nobel Chemistry Laureate*
8 Clematis Road, Lexington, MA 02173, USA

Molinari, Susan K *Commentator, Representative, NY*
%CBS-TV, News Dept, 51 W 52nd St, New York, NY 10019, USA

Molinari, William R *Financier*
%Van Kampen/American, 1 Parkview Plaza, Oakbrook Terrace, IL 60181, USA

Molinaro, Al *Actor*
PO Box 9218, Glendale, CA 91226, USA

Molitor, Paul L *Baseball Player*
16 Tudor Gate, Toronto ON M2L 1N4, Canada

Moll, Kurt *Opera Singer*
Billwerder Billdeich, 22033 Hamburg, Germany

Moll, Richard *Actor*
1119 Amalfi Dr, Pacific Palisades, CA 90272, USA

Mollemann, Jurgen W *Government Official, Germany*
Coesfeldweg 59, 48161 Munster, Germany

Moller, Andreas *Soccer Player*
%Borussia Dortmund, Postfach 100509, 44005 Dortmund, Germany

Moller, Frank *Judo Athlete*
%Sportclub Berlin, Weissenseer Weg 51-55, 13051 Berlin, Germany

Moller, Hans *Artist*
2207 W Allen St, Allentown, PA 18104, USA

M

Moe - Moller

Moller-Gladisch, Silke — Track Athlete
Lange Str 6, 18055 Rostock, Germany

Moloney, Paddy — Singer (The Chieftains)
%S L Feldman, 1505 W 2nd Ave, #200, Vancouver BC V6H 3Y4, Canada

Molson, Hartland — Hockey Executive
1555 Notre Dame St E, Montreal PQ H2L 2RS, Canada

Momaday, N Scott — Writer
%University of Arizona, English Dept, Tucson, AZ 85721, USA

Monacelli, Amieto — Bowler
%Professional Bowlers Assn, 1720 Merriman Road, Akron, OH 44313, USA

Monahan, Michael T — Financier
%Comerica Inc, 500 Woodward Ave, Detroit, MI 48226, USA

Monan, J Donald — Educator
%Boston College, President's Office, Chestnut Hill, MA 02167, USA

Monbouquette, William C (Bill) — Baseball Player
Pheasant Run Apts, Building 2, Voorheesville, NY 12186, USA

Moncrief, Sidney — Basketball Player
5700 Landers Road, Pulaski, AR 72117, USA

Mond, Philip — Photographer
PO Box 8906, Fort Lauderdale, FL 33310, USA

Mondale, Walter F — Vice President, Diplomat
%Dorsey & Whitney, 1st National Bank Plaza E, #2200, Minneapolis, MN 55411, USA

Monday, Robert J (Rick) — Baseball Player, Sportscaster
10815 Oirtibello Dr, San Diego, CA 92124, USA

Money, Eddie — Singer
%Bill Graham Mgmt, PO Box 492094, San Francisco, CA 94142, USA

Money, John W — Psychologist
2104 E Madison St, Baltimore, MD 21205, USA

Money, Ken — Astronaut, Canada
%Canadian Space Agency, PO Box 7014, Station V, Vanier ON K1A 8E2, Canada

Monica — Singer
%William Morris Agency, 1325 Ave of Americas, New York, NY 10019, USA

Monicelli, Mario — Movie Director
Via del Babuino 135, 00137 Rome, Italy

Monin, Clarence V — Labor Leader
%Locomotive Engineers Brotherhood, 1370 Ontario St, Cleveland, OH 44113, USA

Monk, Art — Football Player
%Fox-TV, Sports Dept, PO Box 900, Beverly Hills, CA 90213, USA

Monk, Debra — Actress
%Gage Group, 315 W 57th St, #4-H, New York, NY 10019, USA

Monk, Meredith — Choreographer, Composer
%House Foundation for Arts, 131 Varick St, New York, NY 10013, USA

Monkhouse, Bob — Actor
%Peter Prichard, Regent House, 235 Regent St, London W1R 8AX, England

Monreal Luque, Alberto — Government Official, Spain
Zurbaran 10, Madrid 28010, Spain

Monroe, A L (Mike) — Labor Leader
%International Brotherhood of Painters, 1750 New York NW, Washington, DC 20006, USA

Monroe, Earl (The Pearl) — Basketball Player
1130 Minisink Way, Westfield, NJ 07090, USA

Monroe, Richard — Publisher
%Atlanta Journal-Constitution, 72 Marietta St, Atlanta, GA 30303, USA

Montagnier, Luc — Medical Researcher
%Institut Pasteur, 25-28 Rue du Docteur-Roux, 75724 Paris Cedex 15, France

Montagu, Ashley — Anthropologist, Educator
321 Cherry Hill Road, Princeton, NJ 08540, USA

Montague, Diana — Opera Singer
91 St Martin's Lane, London WC2, England

Montague, Lee — Actor
%Conway Van Gelder Robinson, 18-21 Jermyn St, London SW1Y 6NB, England

Montague-Smith, Patrick W — Editor
%Brereton, 197 Park Road, Kingston-upon-Thames, Surrey, England

Montalban, Ricardo — Actor
1423 Oriole Dr, Los Angeles, CA 90069, USA

Montana, Claude — Fashion Designer
Rue de Lille, 75007 Paris, France

Montana, Joseph C (Joe), Jr — Football Player
PO Box 7342, Menlo Park, CA 94026, USA

Montana, Monte — *Actor*
10326 Montana Lane, Aqua Dulce, CA 91350, USA

Montazeri, Ayatollah Hussein Ali — *Religious Leader*
%Madresseh Faizieh, Qom, Iran

Monteiro, Antonio M — *President, Cape Verde*
%President's Office, Cia de la Republica, Sao Tiago, Praia, Cape Verde

Monteith, Larry K — *Educator*
%North Carolina State University, President's Office, Raleigh, NC 27695, USA

Monteveecchi, Liliane — *Singer*
%Buzz Halliday, 8899 Beverly Blvd, #620, Los Angeles, CA 90048, USA

Montez, Chris — *Singer*
%Arsisanian Assoc, 6671 Sunset Blvd, #1502, Los Angeles, CA 90028, USA

Montgomery, Anne — *Sportscaster*
%ESPN-TV, Sports Dept, ESPN Plaza, Bristol, CT 06010, USA

Montgomery, Belinda — *Actress*
335 N Maple Dr, #361, Beverly Hills, CA 90210, USA

Montgomery, Clifford (Cliff) — *Football Player*
362 I U Willets Road, Roslyn Heights, NY 11577, USA

Montgomery, David — *Photographer*
11 Edith Grove, #B, London SW10, England

Montgomery, George — *Actor*
PO Box 2187, Rancho Mirage, CA 92270, USA

Montgomery, Jack C — *WW II Army Hero (CMH)*
2701 Fort Davis Dr, Muskogee, OK 74403, USA

Montgomery, James F — *Financier*
%Great Western Financial Corp, 9200 Oakdale Ave, Chatsworth, CA 91311, USA

Montgomery, Jim — *Swimmer, Coach*
%Indiana University, Athletic Dept, Bloomington, IN 47405, USA

Montgomery, John Michael — *Singer*
%Hallmark Direction, 1905 Broadway, Nashville, TN 37203, USA

Montgomery, John W — *Theologian*
2 Rue de Rome, 67000 Strasbourg, France

Montgomery, Julia — *Actress*
8380 Melrose Ave, #207, Los Angeles, CA 90069, USA

Montgomery, Melba — *Singer*
%Ace Productions, PO Box 428, Portland, TN 37148, USA

Montgomery, Thomas M (Tom) — *Army General*
US Representative, NATO Military Committee, APO, AE 09724, USA

Montgomery, W Burton — *Businessman*
%Nationwide Life Insurance, 1 Nationwide Plaza, Columbus, OH 43215, USA

Monti, Roberto — *Businessman*
%Kmart Corp, 3100 W Big Beaver Road, Troy, MI 48084, USA

Montross, Eric — *Basketball Player*
7965 Lantern Road, Indianapolis, IN 46256, USA

Montsho Este — *Soul/Rap Artist (Arrested Development)*
%William Morris Agency, 1325 Ave of Americas, New York, NY 10019, USA

Montville, Leigh — *Sportswriter*
%Boston Globe, Editorial Dept, 135 Morrissey Blvd, Boston, MA 02125, USA

Moody, James L, Jr — *Businessman*
%Hannaford Bros Co, 145 Pleasant Hill Road, Scarborough, ME 04074, USA

Moody, Orville — *Golfer*
RR 1, Box 146-C, Como, TX 75431, USA

Moody, Ron — *Actor*
%Eric Glass, 28 Berkeley Square, London W1X 6HD, England

Moomaw, Donn D — *Football Player*
3124 Corda Dr, Los Angeles, CA 90049, USA

Moon, H Warren — *Football Player*
1 Lakeside Estates, Missouri City, TX 77459, USA

Moon, Sun Myung — *Religious Leader*
%Unification Church, 4 W 43rd St, New York, NY 10036, USA

Moon, Wallace W (Wally) — *Baseball Player*
11415 Angelina Circle, College Station, TX 77840, USA

Mooney, Edward J — *Businessman*
%Nalco Chemical Co, 1 Nalco Center, Naperville, IL 60563, USA

Mooney, Harold A — *Biologist*
2625 Ramona St, Palo Alto, CA 94306, USA

Mooney, Michael J — *Educator*
%Lewis & Clark College, President's Office, Portland, OR 97219, USA

Moonves, Leslie *Television Producer*
%Warner Bros Television, 100 Television Plaza, Burbank, CA 91505, USA

Moore, Ann S *Publisher*
%People Magazine, Publisher's Office, Time & Life Building, New York, NY 10020, USA

Moore, Arch A, Jr *Governor, WV*
507 Jefferson Ave, Glen Dale, WV 26038, USA

Moore, Archie *Boxer*
3517 East St, San Diego, CA 92102, USA

Moore, Arthur *Labor Leader*
%Sheet Metal Workers Int'l Assn, 1750 New York Ave NW, Washington, DC 20006, USA

Moore, Brian *Writer*
33958 Pacific Coast Highway, Malibu, CA 90265, USA

Moore, Chante *Singer, Songwriter*
%William Morris Agency, 1325 Ave of Americas, New York, NY 10019, USA

Moore, Clayton *Actor*
4720 Park Olivo, Calabasas, CA 91302, USA

Moore, Clyde R *Businessman*
%Thomas & Betts Corp, 1555 Lynnfield Road, Memphis, TN 38119, USA

Moore, Constance *Actress, Singer*
10450 Wilshire Blvd, #1-B, Los Angeles, CA 90024, USA

Moore, D Larry *Businessman*
%Honeywell Inc, PO Box 524, Minneapolis, MN 55440, USA

Moore, Demi *Actress*
%Rufglen Films, 1453 3rd St, #420, Santa Monica, CA 90401, USA

Moore, Dick *Cartoonist (Our Gang)*
%Dick Moore Assoc, 1560 Broadway, New York, NY 10036, USA

Moore, Dickie *Hockey Player*
%Moore Equipments, 4955 Clemin St Francois, St Laurent PQ H4S 1P3, Canada

Moore, Dorothy *Singer*
%Sirius Entertainment, 13531 Clairmont Way, #8, Oregon City, OR 97045, USA

Moore, Dudley *Actor, Comedian*
4727 Wilshire Blvd, #600, Los Angeles, CA 90010, USA

Moore, Francis D *Surgeon*
10 Longwood Dr, #264, Westwood, MA 02090, USA

Moore, George E *Surgeon*
12048 S Blackhawk Dr, Conifer, CO 80433, USA

Moore, Herman *Football Player*
265 Mount Hermon Circle, Danville, VA 24540, USA

Moore, J Jeremy *General, England*
%Lloyds Bank, Cox's & King's Branch, 7 Pall Mall, London SW1, England

Moore, Jackie *Singer*
%Talent Consultants Int'l, 1560 Broadway, #1308, New York, NY 10036, USA

Moore, Jesse W *Space Engineer*
%Ball Aerospace Corp, Boulder Industrial Park, Boulder, CO 80306, USA

Moore, John A *Biologist*
11522 Tulane Ave, Riverside, CA 92507, USA

Moore, John W *Educator*
%Indiana State University, President's Office, Terre Haute, IN 47809, USA

Moore, Joseph G (Joe) *Baseball Player*
PO Box 65, Gause, TX 77857, USA

Moore, Julianne *Actress*
%Creative Artists Agency, 9830 Wilshire Blvd, Beverly Hills, CA 90212, USA

Moore, Leonard E (Lenny) *Football Player*
8815 Stonehaven Road, Randallstown, MD 21133, USA

Moore, Malcolm A S *Medical Researcher*
%Memorial Sloan-Kettering Cancer Center, 1275 York Ave, New York, NY 10021, USA

Moore, Mary Tyler *Actress*
510 E 86th St, #21-A, New York, NY 10028, USA

Moore, Melba *Singer*
7004 Kennedy Blvd E, #325-D, Guttenberg, NJ 07093, USA

Moore, Melissa Ann *Actress*
PO Box 55, Versailles, KY 40383, USA

Moore, Michael *Movie Director*
%"TV Nation" Show, Comedy Central, 1775 Broadway, New York, NY 10019, USA

Moore, Michael K *Prime Minister, New Zealand*
%Labor Party, House of Representatives, Wellington, New Zealand

Moore, Mike *Attorney*
%Attorney General's Office, PO Box 220, Jackson, MS 39205, USA

Moore, Patrick — Astronomer, Writer
Farthings, 39 West St, Selsey, Sussex, England

Moore, Paul, Jr — Religious Leader
55 Bank St, New York, NY 10014, USA

Moore, Ralph — Jazz Saxophonist
%Denon Records, 135 W 50th St, #1915, New York, NY 10020, USA

Moore, Roger — Actor
Chalet Le Fenil, 3783 Grund Bei Staad, Switzerland

Moore, Sam — Singer (Sam & Dave)
%I'ma Da Wife Enterprises, 7119 E Shea Blvd, #109-436, Scottsdale, AZ 85254, USA

Moore, Steve — Cartoonist (In the Bleachers)
%Tribune Media Services, 435 N Michigan Ave, #1500, Chicago, IL 60611, USA

Moore, Susanna — Writer
%Alfred A Knopf, 201 E 50th St, New York, NY 10022, USA

Moore, Terry — Actress
10366 Wilshire Blvd, #5, Los Angeles, CA 90024, USA

Moore, Thomas — Writer
%Harper/Collins Publishers, 10 E 53rd St, New York, NY 10022, USA

Moore, Tom — Movie, Theater Director
8283 Hollywood Blvd, Los Angeles, CA 90069, USA

Moore, W Edward C — Microbiologist
1607 Boxwood Dr, Blacksburg, VA 24060, USA

Moorer, Michael — Boxer
%Main Events, 811 Totowa Road, #100, Totowa, NJ 07512, USA

Moorer, Thomas H — Navy Admiral, Businessman
9707 Old Georgetown Road, Bethesda, MD 20814, USA

Moorman, Thomas S (Tom), Jr — Air Force General
Vice Chief of Staff, HqUSAF, Pentagon, Washington, DC 20330, USA

Moos, Eugene — Financier, Government Official
%Commodity Credit Corp, PO Box 2415, Washington, DC 20013, USA

Mora, James E (Jim) — Football Coach
%NBC-TV, Sports Dept, 30 Rockefeller Plaza, New York, NY 10112, USA

Morahan, Christopher — Movie Director
%Michael Whitehall, 125 Gloucester Road, London SW7 4TE, England

Morales, Pablo — Swimmer
%Cornell University, Law School, Ithaca, NY 14853, USA

Moran, Erin — Actress
%The Agency, 1800 Ave of Stars, #400, Los Angeles, CA 90067, USA

Moran, John — Religious Leader
%Missionary Church, PO Box 9127, Fort Wayne, IN 46899, USA

Moran, Julie — Sportscaster
555 Melrose Ave, Los Angeles, CA 90038, USA

Moran, Peggy — Actress
3101 Village, #3, Camarillo, CA 93012, USA

Moranis, Rick — Actor
101 Central Park West, #12-B, New York, NY 10023, USA

Morath, Ingeborg H (Inge) — Photographer
212 Tophet Road, Roxbury, CT 06783, USA

Morath, Max — Singer
%Producers Inc, 11806 N 56th St, Tampa, FL 33617, USA

Morceanu, Dominque — Gymnast
%Gymnastics & More, 8 Micro Dr, Woburn, MA 01801, USA

Morcott, Southwood J — Businessman
%Dana Corp, PO Box 1000, Toledo, OH 43697, USA

Mordkovitch, Lydia — Concert Violinist
25-A Belsize Ave, London NW3, England

Moreau, Jeanne — Actress
103 Blvd Haussmann, 75008 Paris, France

Moreira Neves, Lucas Cardinal — Religious Leader
CP 1907, Ave 7 de Setembro 309, Campo Grande, 40120 Salvador, Brazil

Moreira, Airto — Jazz Percussionist
%Berkeley Agency, 2608 9th St, Berkeley, CA 94710, USA

Moreno, Rita — Actress, Singer
1620 Amalfi Dr, Pacific Palisades, CA 90272, USA

Moret, Rogelio (Roger) — Baseball Player
RR 1, Box 6742, Guayama, PR 00784, USA

Moretti, Tobias — Actor
%Prima Donna, 2 Schubertstr, 80336 Munich, Germany

M

Moore - Moretti

Morford, John A	*Businessman*
%V T Inc, 8500 Shawnee Mission Parkway, Merriam, KS 66202, USA	
Morgan, Barbara R	*Astronaut*
%Oklahoma State University, Teacher in Space Program, Stillwater, OK 74078, USA	
Morgan, Debbi	*Actress*
207 W 86th St, #1116, New York, NY 10024, USA	
Morgan, Frank	*Jazz Saxophonist*
%Integrity Talent, PO Box 961, Burlington, MA 01803, USA	
Morgan, Gil	*Golfer*
PO Box 806, Edmond, OK 73083, USA	
Morgan, Harry	*Actor*
13172 Boca de Canon Lane, Los Angeles, CA 90049, USA	
Morgan, Jane	*Singer*
27740 Pacific Coast Highway, Malibu, CA 90265, USA	
Morgan, Jaye P	*Singer, Actress*
1185 La Grange Ave, Newbury Park, CA 91320, USA	
Morgan, Joseph L (Joe)	*Baseball Player*
3523 Country Club Place, Danville, CA 94506, USA	
Morgan, Joseph M (Joe)	*Baseball Manager*
15 Oak Hill Dr, Walpole, MA 02081, USA	
Morgan, Lorrie	*Singer*
PO Box 78, Spencer, TN 38585, USA	
Morgan, Marabel	*Writer*
%Total Woman Inc, 1300 NW 167th St, Miami, FL 33169, USA	
Morgan, Michele	*Actress, Singer*
5 Rue Jacques Dulud, 92200 Neuilly-sur-Seine, France	
Morgan, Nancy	*Actress*
8380 Melrose Ave, #207, Los Angeles, CA 90069, USA	
Morgan, Robert B	*Senator, NC*
PO Box 377, Lillington, NC 27546, USA	
Morgan, Robin E	*Editor*
%Ms Magazine, Editorial Dept, 230 Park Ave, New York, NY 10169, USA	
Morgan, Stanley	*Football Player*
9200 Forrest Hill Lane, Germantown, TN 38139, USA	
Morgan, Walter T J	*Biochemist*
57 Woodbury Dr, Sutton, Surrey, England	
Morganna	*Entertainer*
PO Box 20281, Columbus, OH 43220, USA	
Morgenthau, Robert M	*Attorney*
1085 Park Ave, New York, NY 10128, USA	
Morgridge, John P	*Businessman*
%Cisco Systems, 170 W Tasan Dr, San Jose, CA 95134, USA	
Mori, Hanae	*Fashion Designer*
17 Ave Montaigne, 75008 Paris, France	
Moriarty, Cathy	*Actress*
1100 Alta Loma Road, #801, West Hollywood, CA 90069, USA	
Moriarty, Michael	*Actor*
200 W 58th St, #3-B, New York, NY 10019, USA	
Moriarty, Phil	*Swimming Coach*
%Harbour Village, #20-E, Branford, CT 06045, USA	
Morikawa, Toshio	*Financier*
%Sumitomo Bank, 3-2-1 Marunouchi, Chiyodaku, Tokyo 100, Japan	
Morin, Jim	*Editorial Cartoonist*
%Miami Herald, Editorial Dept, Herald Plaza, Miami, FL 33101, USA	
Morinigo, Higinio	*President, Paraguay; Army General*
Calle General Urguiza 625-Acassuso, Buenos Aires, Argentina	
Morison, Patricia	*Actress, Singer*
%Craig Agency, 8485 Melrose Place, #E, Los Angeles, CA 90069, USA	
Morissette, Alanis	*Singer, Songwriter*
%Atlas/Third Rail, 9169 Sunset Blvd, Los Angeles, CA 90069, USA	
Morita, Akio	*Businessman*
%Sony Corp, 6-7-35 Kitashinagawa, Shinagawaku, Tokyo 141, Japan	
Morita, Pat (Noriyuki)	*Actor*
4007 Sunswept Dr, Studio City, CA 91604, USA	
Moritz, Charles F	*Editor*
%Current Biography, H W Wilson Co, 950 University Ave, Bronx, NY 10452, USA	
Moritz, Louisa	*Actress*
%Beverly Hills St Moritz, 120 S Reeves St, Beverly Hills, CA 90212, USA	

Moriya, Gakuji — *Businessman*
%Mitsubishi Heavy Industries, 2-5-1 Marunouchi, Chiyodaku, Tokyo, Japan

Moriyama, Raymond — *Architect*
32 Davenport Road, Toronto ON M5R 1H3, Canada

Morkis, Dorothy — *Equestrian Rider*
17 Farm St, Dover, MA 02030, USA

Morley, Malcolm — *Artist*
%Pace Gallery, 32 E 57th St, New York, NY 10022, USA

Moro, Peter — *Architect*
20 Blackheath Park, London SE3 9RP, England

Moroder, Giorgio — *Composer*
1880 Century Park East, #900, Los Angeles, CA 90067, USA

Morrall, Earl E — *Football Player*
9751 SW 15th Dr, Davie, FL 33324, USA

Morrey, Charles B, Jr — *Mathematician*
210 Yale Ave, Berkeley, CA 94708, USA

Morrice, Norman A — *Ballet Choreographer*
%Royal Ballet, Bow St, London WC2E 9DD, England

Morricone, Ennio — *Composer*
Via Ara Coeli 4, 00186 Rome, Italy

Morris Wingerter, Pam — *Synchronized Swimmer*
PO Box 14381, New Bern, NC 28561, USA

Morris, Bam — *Football Player*
RR 1, Box 182-M, Cooper, TX 75432, USA

Morris, Betty — *Bowler*
%Women's International Bowling Congress, 5301 S 76th St, Greendale, WI 53129, USA

Morris, Charles B — *Vietnam War Army Hero (CMH)*
4624 E 4th St, Tulsa, OK 74112, USA

Morris, Chris — *Basketball Player*
%Utah Jazz, Delta Center, 301 W South Temple, Salt Lake City, UT 84101, USA

Morris, Desmond J — *Writer, Zoologist*
%Jonathan Cape Ltd, 20 Vauxhall Bridge Road, London SW1V 2SA, England

Morris, Garrett — *Actor, Singer*
3740 Barham Blvd, #E-116, Los Angeles, CA 90068, USA

Morris, Gary — *Singer*
%Jeff Wald Entertainment, 8900 Wilshire Blvd, #101, Beverly Hills, CA 90211, USA

Morris, George — *Football Player*
6075 Roswell Road NE, #112, Atlanta, GA 30328, USA

Morris, Howard — *Comedian, Director*
2160 Sunset Crest Dr, Los Angeles, CA 90046, USA

Morris, James P — *Opera Singer*
%Colbert Artists, 111 W 57th St, New York, NY 10019, USA

Morris, Jan — *Writer*
Trefan Morys, Llanystumdwy, Criccieth, Gwymedd, Wales

Morris, Joe — *Football Player*
%Baltimore Ravens, 200 St Paul Place, #2400, Baltimore, MD 21202, USA

Morris, John S (Jack) — *Baseball Player*
527 Prairie Nest Road, Great Falls, MT 59405, USA

Morris, Jon — *Guitarist (Dig)*
%Overland Productions, 156 W 56th St, #500, New York, NY 10019, USA

Morris, Mark W — *Choreographer*
%Mark Morris Dance Group, 225 Lafayette St, #504, New York, NY 10012, USA

Morris, Mercury — *Football Player*
6200 SW 64th Court, Miami, FL 33143, USA

Morris, Nathan — *Singer (Boyz II Men)*
%International Creative Mgmt, 8942 Wilshire Blvd, Beverly Hills, CA 90211, USA

Morris, Oswald (Ossie) — *Cinematographer*
Holbrook, Church St, Fontmell Magna, Dorset, England

Morris, Robert — *Sculptor*
%Hunter College, Art Dept, New York, NY 10021, USA

Morris, Ronald — *Track Athlete*
330 S Reese Place, Burbank, CA 91506, USA

Morris, Seth Irvin — *Architect*
2 Waverly Court, Houston, TX 77005, USA

Morris, Wayna — *Singer (Boyz II Men)*
%International Creative Mgmt, 8942 Wilshire Blvd, Beverly Hills, CA 90211, USA

Morris, William C — *Financier*
%J&W Seligman Co, 100 Park Ave, New York, NY 10017, USA

Morris, William S, III *Publisher*
%Florida Times-Union, 1 Riverside Ave, Jacksonville, FL 32202, USA
Morris, Wright *Writer, Photographer*
341 Laurel Way, Mill Valley, CA 94941, USA
Morrison, Philip *Astronomer*
%Massachusetts Institute of Technology, Astronomy Dept, Cambridge, MA 02139, USA
Morrison, Tommy *Boxer*
PO Box 701107, Tulsa, OK 74170, USA
Morrison, Toni *Nobel Literature Laureate*
%Princeton University, Dickinson Hall, Princeton, NJ 08544, USA
Morrison, Van *Singer, Songwriter*
%Inspirational Artiste, PO Box 1AS, London W1A 1AS, England
Morrissey *Singer, Songwriter*
%Reach Media, 285 W Broadway, #230, New York, NY 10013, USA
Morrissey, Bill *Singer, Songwriter*
%Sage Productions, 258 Harvard St, #283, Brookline, MA 02146, USA
Morrone, Joe *Soccer Coach*
%University of Connecticut, Athletic Dept, Storrs, CT 06269, USA
Morrow (Cousin Brucie), Bruce *Radio Entertainer*
%CBS Radio Network, 51 W 52nd St, New York, NY 10019, USA
Morrow, Bobby *Track Athlete*
PO Box 9, Beeville, TX 78104, USA
Morrow, Byron *Actor*
%Ricky Barr, PO Box 69590, Los Angeles, CA 90069, USA
Morrow, Rob *Actor*
%William Morris Agency, 151 S El Camino Dr, Beverly Hills, CA 90212, USA
Morse, David *Actor*
%William Morris Agency, 151 S El Camino Dr, Beverly Hills, CA 90212, USA
Morse, David E *Publisher*
%Christian Science Monitor, 1 Norway St, Boston, MA 02115, USA
Morse, Ella Mae *Singer*
3232 W 152nd Place, Gardena, CA 90249, USA
Morse, John *Golfer*
1480 Bridlebrook Court, Casselberry, FL 32707, USA
Morse, Philip M *Physicist*
126 Wildwood St, Winchester, MA 01890, USA
Morse, Robert *Actor*
13830 Davana Terrace, Sherman Oaks, CA 91423, USA
Mortensen, J D *Surgeon*
%Cardipulmonics Inc, 5060 W Amelia Earhart Dr, Salt Lake City, UT 84116, USA
Mortier, Gerard *Opera Director*
%Opera National de la Monnaie, 4 Rue Leopold, 1000 Brussels, Belgium
Mortimer Barrett, Angela *Tennis Player*
The Oaks, Coombe Hill, Beverly Lane, Kingston-on-Thames, Surrey, England
Mortimer, John C *Writer*
Turville Heath Cottage, Henley-on-Thames, Oxon, England
Mortimer, Penelope R *Writer*
19 Saint Gabriel's Road, London NW2 4DS, England
Morton, Bruce A *Commentator*
%Cable News Network, News Dept, 820 1st St NE, Washington, DC 20002, USA
Morton, Craig L *Football Player*
19021 35th Place, Lake Oswego, OR 97034, USA
Morton, Gary *Comedian*
40241 Clubview Dr, Rancho Mirage, CA 92270, USA
Morton, Joe *Actor*
%Judy Schoen, 606 N Larchmont Blvd, #309, Los Angeles, CA 90004, USA
Morton, Johnnie *Football Player*
%Detroit Lions, Silverdome, 1200 Featherstone Road, Pontiac, MI 48342, USA
Morton, Rogers C B *Secretary, Interior & Commerce*
Rt 1, Easton, MD 21601, USA
Morton, T Ron *Financier*
%PACCAR Financial Corp, 777 106th Ave NE, Bellevue, WA 98004, USA
Mosbacher, Robert A *Secretary, Commerce*
%Mosbacher Energy Co, 712 Main St, #2200, Houston, TX 77002, USA
Moschen, Michael *Juggler*
41 Popple Swamp Road, Cornwall Bridge, CT 06754, USA
Moschitta, John, Jr *Comedian, Actor*
8033 Sunset Blvd, #41, Los Angeles, CA 90046, USA

Moschner, Albin F — Businessman
%Zenith Electronics, 1000 Milwaukee Ave, Glenview, IL 60025, USA

Mosconi, Alain — Swimmer
%French Swimming Federation, 148 Ave Gambetta, 75020 Paris, France

Mosebar, Donald H (Don) — Football Player
1713 Walnut Ave, Manhattan Beach, CA 90266, USA

Mosel, Tad — Writer
149 East Side Dr, Box 249, #26-B, Concord, NH 03301, USA

Moseley, Mark D — Football Player
16001 Berkeley Dr, Haymarket, VA 20169, USA

Moser, Donald B — Editor
%Smithsonian Magazine, Editorial Dept, 900 Jefferson SW, Washington, DC 20560, USA

Moser, Jurgen K — Mathematician
%Eidgenossische Technische Hochschule, Ramistr, 8092 Zurich, Switzerland

Moser-Proll, Annemarie — Skier
5602 Kleinarl 115, Austria

Moses, Edwin — Track Athlete
%USA Track & Field, PO Box 120, Indianapolis, IN 46206, USA

Moses, Mark — Actor
%Ambrosio/Mortimer, 9150 Wilshire Blvd, #175, Beverly Hills, CA 90212, USA

Moses, Rick — Actor, Singer
%Calder Agency, 19919 Redwing St, Woodland Hills, CA 91364, USA

Moses, Yolanda T — Educator
%City College of New York, President's Office, New York, NY 10031, USA

Mosimann, Anton — Chef
46 Abingdon Villas, London W8, England

Moskow, Michael — Financier
%Federal Reserve Bank, 230 S LaSalle St, Chicago, IL 60604, USA

Moskowitz, Robert — Artist
81 Leonard St, New York, NY 10013, USA

Mosley, J Brooke — Religious Leader
1604 Foulkeways, Gwynedd, PA 19436, USA

Mosley, Roger E — Actor
4470 W Sunset Blvd, #107-342, Los Angeles, CA 90027, USA

Mosley, Walter — Writer
37 Carmine St, #275, New York, NY 10014, USA

Mosmiller, Joseph W — Financier
%Loyola Federal Savings Bank, 120 E Baltimore St, Baltimore, MD 21202, USA

Moss, Cynthia — Elephant Conservationist
%African Wildlife Foundation, Mara Road, PO Box 48177, Nairobi, Kenya

Moss, Elza — Religious Leader
%Primitive Advent Christian Church, 395 Frame Road, Elkview, WV 25071, USA

Moss, Frank E — Senator, UT
1848 S Wasatch Dr, Salt Lake City, UT 84108, USA

Moss, Geoffrey — Cartoonist, Illustrator
315 E 68th St, New York, NY 10021, USA

Moss, Jerry — Record Producer
%A&M Records, 1416 N La Brea Ave, Los Angeles, CA 90028, USA

Moss, Kate — Model
%Women Model Mgmt, 107 Greene St, #200, New York, NY 10012, USA

Moss, Ronn — Actor
%Sutton Barth Vennari, 145 S Fairfax Ave, #310, Los Angeles, CA 90036, USA

Moss, Stirling — Auto Racing Driver
%Stirling Moss Ltd, 46 Shephard St, Mayfair, London W1Y 8JN, England

Mossbauer, Rudolf — Nobel Physics Laureate
Stumpflingstr 6-A, 82031 Grunwald, Germany

Mosser, Jonell — Singer
%Studio One Artists, 7010 Westmoreland Ave, #100, Takoma Park, MD 20912, USA

Mossi, Donald L (Don) — Baseball Player
1340 Sanford Ranch Road, Ukiah, CA 95482, USA

Most, Don — Actor
6643 Buttonwood Ave, Agoura, CA 91301, USA

Mosteller, Frederick — Statistician
%Harvard University, Statistics Dept, Cambridge, MA 02138, USA

Mostow, George D — Mathematician
25 Beechwood Road, Woodbridge, CT 06525, USA

Mota Pinto, Carlos — Prime Minister, Portugal
Rua Gil Vicente 83, 3000 Coimbra, Portugal

M

Moschner - Mota Pinto

M

Mota, Manuel R (Manny) *Baseball Player, Coach*
3926 Los Olivos Lane, La Crescenta, CA 91214, USA

Mota, Rosa *Marathon Athlete*
R Teatro 194 4 Esq, 4100 Porto, Portugal

Motley, Marion *Football Player*
3302 E 145th St, Cleveland, OH 44120, USA

Mott, Stewart R *Political Activist*
515 Madison Ave, New York, NY 10022, USA

Motta, Dick *Basketball Coach*
PO Box 4, Fish Haven, ID 83287, USA

Mottelson, Benjamin *Nobel Physics Laureate*
Nordita, Blegdamsvej 17, 2100 Copenhagen 0, Denmark

Motulsky, Arno G *Geneticist*
4347 53rd St NE, Seattle, WA 98105, USA

Mould, Bob *Guitarist, Songwriter*
%Linda Clark, PO Box 1304, Burbank, CA 91507, USA

Moulton, Alexander E *Bicycle Engineer*
The Hall, Bradford-on-Avon, Wilts, England

Mounsey, Yvonne *Ballerina*
%Westside School of Ballet, 1711 Stewart St, Santa Monica, CA 90404, USA

Mount, Peggy *Actress*
%Richard Stone, 25 Whitehall, London SW1A 2BS, England

Mount, Rick *Basketball Player*
904 Hopkins Road, Lebanon, IN 46052, USA

Mountcastle, Vernon B, Jr *Neurophysiologist*
15601 Carroll Road, Monkton, MD 21111, USA

Mourning, Alonzo *Basketball Player*
7260 W 12th Ave, Hialeah, FL 33014, USA

Mouskouri, Nana *Singer, Songwriter*
12 Rue Gutenberg, 92000 Boulogne, France

Mowat, Farley M *Writer, Naturalist*
25 St John St, Port Hope ON, Canada

Mowerson, Robert *Swimmer*
2601 Kenzie Terrace, #324, Minneapolis, MN 55418, USA

Mowrey, Dude *Singer*
%Debra McCloud, 511 Music Circle S, Nashville, TN 37203, USA

Moxley, John H, III *Physician, Businessman*
8180 Manitoba St, #210, Playa del Rey, CA 90293, USA

Moyer, Alan D *Editor*
%Phoenix Newspaper Inc, Editorial Dept, 120 E Van Buren St, Phoenix, AZ 85004, USA

Moyer, Paul *Commentator*
12742 Highwood St, Los Angeles, CA 90049, USA

Moyers, Bill D *Commentator*
76 4th St, Garden City, NY 11530, USA

Moyet, Alison *Singer*
%Motley Music, 132 Liverpool Road, London N1 3LA, England

Moynihan, Colin B *Government Official, England*
Crown Reach, 16 Grosvenor Road, London SW1V 3JV, England

Moyola of Castledawson, Baron *Prime Minister, Northern Ireland*
Moyola Park, Castledawson, County Derry, Northern Ireland

Mozilo, Angelo R *Financier*
%Countrywide Credit, 1555 N Lake Ave, Pasadena, CA 91104, USA

Mphahlele, Ezekiel *Writer*
5444 Zone 5, Pimville, Johannesburg, South Africa

Msuya, Cleopa D *Prime Minister, Tanzania*
%Prime Minister's Office, PO Box 980, Dodoma, Tanzania

Mswati III *King, Swaziland*
%Royal Palace, PO Box 1, Mbabane, Swaziland

Mubarak, Muhammad Hosni *President, Egypt; Army General*
%Presidential Palace, Abdeen, Cairo, Egypt

Mucke, Manuela *Kayak Athlete*
Charlottenstr 13, 10315 Berlin, Germany

Mudd, Howard *Football Player, Coach*
%Seattle Seahawks, 11220 NE 53rd St, Kirkland, WA 98033, USA

Mudd, Jodie *Golfer*
Buck Creek Road, Finchville, KY 40022, USA

Mudd, Roger H *Commentator*
7167 Old Dominion Dr, McLean, VA 22101, USA

Mota - Mudd

Mueller, Carl M *Financier*
%BT Capital, 280 Park Ave, New York, NY 10017, USA

Mueller, Charles W *Businessman*
%Union Electric Co, 1901 Chouteau Ave, St Louis, MO 63103, USA

Mueller, George E *Electrical Engineer, Missile Scientist*
PO Box 5856, Santa Barbara, CA 93150, USA

Mueller, Leah Poulos *Speed Skater*
11455 N Mulberry Dr, Mequon, WI 53092, USA

Mueller, Pete *Speed Skater, Coach*
11455 N Mulberry Dr, Mequon, WI 53092, USA

Mueller-Stahl, Armin *Actor*
Gartenweg 31, 23730 Sierksdorf, Germany

Muellner, George K *Air Force General*
Deputy for Acquisitions, HqUSAF, Pentagon, Washington, DC 20330, USA

Muench, David *Photographer*
PO Box 30500, Santa Barbara, CA 93130, USA

Muench, John *Artist*
Flying Point, Freeport, ME 04032, USA

Muetterties, Earl L *Chemist*
%University of California, Chemistry Dept, Berkeley, CA 94720, USA

Muetzelfeldt, Bruno *Religious Leader*
%Lutheran World Federation, 150 Rt de Ferney, 1211 Geneva 20, Switzerland

Mugabe, Robert G *President, Zimbabwe*
%President's Office, Munhumutapa Bldg, Samora Machel Ave, Harare, Zimbabwe

Mugler, Thierry *Fashion Designer*
4-6 Rue Aux Ours, 75003 Paris, France

Muhammad, Wallace D *Religious Leader*
%American Muslim Mission, 7351 S Stony Island Blvd, Chicago, IL 60649, USA

Muir DeGraad, Karen *Swimmer*
%Applebosch State Hospital, Ozwatini, Natal, South Africa

Muirsheil of Kilmacolm, Viscount *Government Official, England*
Knapps, Kilmacolm, Renfrewshire, Scotland

Mukai, Chiaki Naito- *Astronaut, Japan*
15836 Seahorse Dr, Houston, TX 77062, USA

Mukhamedov, Irek J *Ballet Dancer*
%Royal Ballet, Bow St, London WC2E 9DD, England

Mukherjee, Bharati *Writer*
%Grove Weidenfeld, 841 Broadway, New York, NY 10003, USA

Mulari, Tarja *Speed Skier*
%Motion Oy, Vanhan Mankkaantie 33, 02180 Espoo, Finland

Muldaur, Diana *Actress*
259 Quadro Vecchio Dr, Pacific Palisades, CA 90272, USA

Muldaur, Maria *Singer, Songwriter*
%Piedmont Talent, 311 Oakdale Road, Charlotte, NC 28216, USA

Muldoon, Patrick *Actor, Model*
%Gallin Morey, 345 N Maple Dr, #300, Beverly Hills, CA 90210, USA

Muldoon, Paul *Writer*
%Farrar Straus Giroux, 19 Union Square W, New York, NY 10003, USA

Muldowney, Shirley *Drag Racing Driver*
79559 North Ave, Armada, MI 48005, USA

Mulgrew, Kate *Actress*
%Metropolitan Talent Agency, 4526 Wilshire Blvd, Los Angeles, CA 90010, USA

Mulkey, Chris *Actor*
%Paradigm Agency, 10100 Santa Monica Blvd, #2500, Los Angeles, CA 90067, USA

Mull, Martin *Actor*
338 Chadbourne Ave, Los Angeles, CA 90049, USA

Mullane, Richard M (Mike) *Astronaut*
1301 Las Lomas Road NE, Albuquerque, NM 87106, USA

Mullaney, Joe *Basketball Coach*
18 Hope St, North Providence, RI 02911, USA

Mullavey, Greg *Actor*
PO Box 46067, West Hollywood, CA 90046, USA

Mullen, Joseph P (Joey) *Hockey Player*
36 Friends Lane, South Dennis, MA 02660, USA

Muller, Egon *Motorcycle Racing Rider*
Dorfstr 17, 24247 Rodenbek/Kiel, Germany

Muller, Gerd *Soccer Player*
Noestr 21, 81479 Munich, Germany

Muller, Henry J *Editor*
%Time Warner Inc, Magazines Division, Rockefeller Center, New York, NY 10020, USA

Muller, Jennifer *Dancer, Choreographer*
%The Muller/Works Foundation, 131 W 24th St, New York, NY 10011, USA

Muller, Jorg *Auto Racing Driver*
%Insert Motorsport, Fassoldshof 1, 95336 Mainleus, Germany

Muller, K Alex *Nobel Physics Laureate*
%IBM Research Laboratory, Saumerstr 4, 8803 Ruschlikon, Switzerland

Muller, Kirk *Hockey Player*
%Florida Panthers, Miami Arena, 100 NE 3rd Ave, Miami, FL 33132, USA

Muller, Marcia *Writer*
%Mysterious Press, Warner Books, 1271 6th Ave, New York, NY 10020, USA

Muller, Peter *Skier*
Haldenstr 18, 8134 Adliswil, Switzerland

Muller, Peter *Architect*
3 Rue Rene Boylesve, 37600 Loches, France

Muller, Richard S *Microbiotics Engineer*
%University of California, Sensor/Acutator Center, Berkeley, CA 94720, USA

Muller, Robby *Cinematographer*
%Smith/Gosnell/Nicholson, 1515 Palisades Dr, #N, Pacific Palisades, CA 90272, USA

Mulley of Manor Park, Frederick W *Government Official, England*
%House of Lords, Westminster, London SW1A 0PW, England

Mulligan, Richard *Actor*
419 N Larchmont Blvd, #129, Los Angeles, CA 90004, USA

Mulligan, Richard C *Molecular Biologist*
11 Sumner Road, Cambridge, MA 02138, USA

Mulligan, Robert P *Movie Director*
%J V Broffman, 5150 Wilshire Blvd, #505, Los Angeles, CA 90036, USA

Mulliken, Bill *Swimmer*
4216 N Keeler Ave, Chicago, IL 60641, USA

Mullin, Christopher P (Chris) *Basketball Player*
4499 Deer Ridge Road, Danville, CA 94506, USA

Mullin, J Stanley *Skier*
%Sheppard Mullin Richter Hampton, 333 S Hope St, Los Angeles, CA 90071, USA

Mullin, Leo F *Businessman*
%Delta Air Lines, Hartsfield International Airport, Atlanta, GA 30320, USA

Mullins, Jeff *Basketball Player, Coach*
3925 Huntcliff Dr, Charlotte, NC 28226, USA

Mullis, Kary B *Nobel Chemistry Laureate*
6767 Neptune Place, #4, La Jolla, CA 92037, USA

Mullova, Viktoria Y *Concert Violinist*
%Harold Holt, 31 Sinclair Road, London W14 0NS, England

Mulloy, Gardner *Tennis Player*
800 NW 9th Ave, Miami, FL 33136, USA

Mulroney, Dermot *Actor*
1180 S Beverly Dr, #618, Los Angeles, CA 90035, USA

Mulroney, M Brian *Prime Minister, Canada*
%Ogilvy Renault, 1981 McGill College Ave, Montreal PQ H3A 3C1, Canada

Mulumba, Etienne Tshisekedi Wa *Prime Minister, Zaire*
%Prime Minister's Office, Kinshasa, Zaire

Muluzi, Bakili *President, Malawi*
%President's Office, Private Bag 361, Capitol City, Lilongwe 3, Malawi

Mulva, James J *Businessman*
%Phillips Petroleum, Phillips Building, 4th & Keeler Sts, Bartlesville, 74004, USA

Mulvey, Grant *Hockey Player*
491 Hampshire Ave, Elmhurst, IL 60126, USA

Mulvoy, Mark *Editor, Publisher*
%Sports Illustrated Magazine, Rockefeller Center, New York, NY 10020, USA

Mumford, David B *Mathematician*
26 Gray St, Cambridge, MA 02138, USA

Mumy, Billy *Actor*
14421 Ventura Blvd, #260, Sherman Oaks, CA 91423, USA

Muna, Solomon Tandeng *Prime Minister, Cameroon*
PO Box 15, Mbengwi, Mono Division, North West Province, Cameroon

Munch, Guido *Astronomer*
%Max Planck Institute, Konigstuhl 17, 69117 Heidelberg, Germany

Munchak, Michael A (Mike) *Football Player*
9155 Saddlebow Dr, Brentwood, TN 37027, USA

Muncie, Chuck — Football Player
HC 65 Box 5913, Bullhead City, AZ 86429, USA

Mundy, Carl E, Jr — Marine Corps General
9308 Ludgate Dr, Alexandria, VA 22309, USA

Munitz, Barry A — Educator
%California State University System, 400 Golden Shore St, Long Beach, CA 90802, USA

Munk, Walter H — Geophysicist
9530 La Jolla Shores Dr, La Jolla, CA 92037, USA

Munn, Stephen P — Businessman
%Carlisle Corp, 250 S Clinton St, Syracuse, NY 13202, USA

Munnell, Alicia — Economist, Government Official
%Council of Economic Advisers, Old Government Office Bldg, Washington, DC 20500, USA

Munoz Vega, Paolo Cardinal — Religious Leader
Casa del Sagrado Corazon, Casilla 17-02-5222, Suc 2, Quito, Ecuador

Munoz, Anthony — Football Player, Sportscaster
%Fox TV, Sports Dept, PO Box 900, Beverly Hills, CA 90213, USA

Munro, Alice — Writer
PO Box 1133, Clinton ON N0M 1L0, Canada

Munro, Caroline — Actress
%International Creative Mgmt, 76 Oxford St, London W1N 0AX, England

Munro, Dana G — Diplomat
PO Box 317, Media, PA 19063, USA

Munro, Ian — Editor
%Annals of Internal Medicine, Editorial Dept, 34 Beacon St, Boston, MA 02108, USA

Munro, J Richard — Publisher
%Time Warner Inc, Rockefeller Plaza, New York, NY 10020, USA

Munsel, Patrice — Opera Singer
PO Box 472, Schroon Lake, NY 12870, USA

Munson, William A (Bill) — Football Player
1212 Lakeside, Birmingham, MI 48009, USA

Muntyan, Mikhail — Opera Singer
16 N Iorga Str, #13, 277012 Kishinev, Moldova

Muradov, Sakhat A — Head of Government, Turkmenistan
%Turkmenistan Mejlis, 17 Gogol St, Ashkhabad, Turkmenistan

Murakami, Masanori — Baseball Player
1-4-15-1506 Nisho Ohi Shinagawa, Tokyo, Japan

Murayama, Makio — Biochemist
5010 Benton Ave, Bethesda, MD 20814, USA

Murayama, Tomiichi — Prime Minister, Japan
3-2-2 Chiyomachi, Oita, Oita 870, Japan

Murchison, Ira — Track Athlete
10113 S Sangamon St, Chicago, IL 60643, USA

Murdoch, J Iris — Writer
Cedar Lodge, Steeple Aston, Oxon, England

Murdoch, K Rupert — Publisher
%News America Publishing, 1211 Ave of Americas, New York, NY 10036, USA

Murdoch, Robert J (Bob) — Hockey Player, Coach
1466-8 Timber Trail, Akron, OH 44313, USA

Murdock, David H — Businessman
%Dole Food Co, 31365 Oak Crest Dr, Westlake Village, CA 91361, USA

Murdock, George — Actor
5733 Sunfield Ave, Lakewood, CA 90712, USA

Murdock, George P — Anthropologist
Wynnewood Plaza, #107, Wynnewood, PA 19096, USA

Murdock, Shirley — Singer
%Rodgers Redding, 1048 Tatnall St, Macon, GA 31201, USA

Muresan, Gheorghe — Basketball Player
%Washington Wizards, Capital Centre, 1 Truman Dr, Landover, MD 20785, USA

Murphey, Michael Martin — Singer, Songwriter
%Wildfire Productions, 207 Paseo Del Pueblo Sur, #K, Taos, NM 87571, USA

Murphy, Austin S — Financier
%River Bank America, 645 5th Ave, New York, NY 10022, USA

Murphy, Ben — Actor
3601 Vista Pacifica, #17, Malibu, CA 90265, USA

Murphy, Bob — Golfer
%Eddie Elias Enterprises, PO Box 5118, Akron, OH 44334, USA

Murphy, Calvin — Basketball Player, Executive
43 Sterling St, Sugar Land, TX 77479, USA

Murphy, Caryle M *Journalist*
%Washington Post, Editorial Dept, 1150 15th St NW, Washington, DC 20071, USA

Murphy, Charles S *Government Official*
100 Bluff View Dr, #503-C, Belleair Bluffs, FL 33770, USA

Murphy, Dale B *Baseball Player*
1603 W Grantville Road, Grantville, GA 30220, USA

Murphy, David Lee *Singer*
%D Mgmt, PO Box 121682, Nashville, TN 37212, USA

Murphy, Donna *Actress, Singer*
%Silver Kass Massetti Agency, 145 W 45th St, #1204, New York, NY 10036, USA

Murphy, Ed *Basketball Coach*
%University of Mississippi, Smith Coliseum, University, MS 38677, USA

Murphy, Eddie *Comedian, Actor*
%Eddie Murphy Productions, Carnegie Tower, 152 W 57th St, #4700, New York, 10019, USA

Murphy, Erin *Actress*
972 Cornell Road, Pasadena, CA 91106, USA

Murphy, John Cullen *Cartoonist (Prince Valiant)*
14 Mead Ave, Cos Cob, CT 06807, USA

Murphy, John J *Businessman*
%Dresser Industries, PO Box 718, Dallas, TX 75221, USA

Murphy, Lawrence T (Larry) *Hockey Player*
%Detroit Red Wings, Joe Louis Arena, 600 Civic Center Dr, Detroit, MI 48226, USA

Murphy, Mark *Singer*
%Prince/SF Productions, 2674 24th Ave, San Francisco, CA 94116, USA

Murphy, Michael *Actor*
PO Box FFF, Taos, NM 87571, USA

Murphy, Mike *Hockey Coach*
17072 Oak View Dr, Encino, CA 91436, USA

Murphy, R Madison *Businessman*
%Murphy Oil, 200 Peach St, El Dorado, AR 71730, USA

Murphy, Raymond G *Korean War Marine Corps Hero (CMH)*
4677 Sutton St NW, Albuquerque, NM 87114, USA

Murphy, Reg *Editor, Publisher*
%National Geographic Society, 1145 17th St NW, Washington, DC 20036, USA

Murphy, Richard W *Diplomat*
16 Sutton Place, #9-A, New York, NY 10022, USA

Murphy, Rosemary *Actress*
220 E 73rd St, New York, NY 10021, USA

Murphy, Sean *Golfer*
1004 June Place, Lovington, NM 88260, USA

Murphy, Terry *Entertainer*
%Sherry Ingram, 3575 Cahuenga Blvd W, #600, Los Angeles, CA 90068, USA

Murphy, Thomas S *Businessman*
%Capital Cities/ABC, 77 W 66th St, New York, NY 10023, USA

Murray of Epping Forest, Lionel (Len) *Union Official*
29 The Crescent, Loughton, Essex, England

Murray, A Brean *Financer*
%Brean Murray Foster, 633 3rd Ave, New York, NY 10017, USA

Murray, Albert *Writer*
45 W 132nd St, New York, NY 10037, USA

Murray, Anne *Singer*
%Bruce Allen Talent, 406-68 Water St, Vancouver BC V6B 14A, Canada

Murray, Bill *Comedian*
RD 1, PO Box 573, Washington Springs Road, Palisades, NY 10964, USA

Murray, Bruce C *Planetary Scientist*
%Jet Propulsion Laboratory, 4800 Oak Grove Dr, Pasadena, CA 91109, USA

Murray, Bryan C *Hockey Coach, Executive*
%Florida Panthers, Miami Arena, 100 NE 3rd Ave, Miami, FL 33132, USA

Murray, Charles A *Social Scientist*
%American Enterprise Institute, 1150 17th St NW, Washington, DC 20036, USA

Murray, Charles P, Jr *WW II Army Hero (CMH)*
5906 Northridge Road, Columbia, SC 29206, USA

Murray, David K *Jazz Saxophonist, Bandleader*
%Joel Chriss, 300 Mercer St, #3-J, New York, NY 10003, USA

Murray, Don *Actor*
1201 La Patera Canyon Road, Goleta, CA 93117, USA

Murray, Doug *Cartoonist (The 'Nam)*
%Marvel Comic Group, 387 Park Ave S, New York, NY 10016, USA

Murray, Eddie C — *Baseball Player*
2330 W Joppa Road, #155, Lutherville, MD 21093, USA

Murray, Elizabeth — *Artist*
%Paula Cooper Gallery, 534 W 21st St, New York, NY 10011, USA

Murray, Iain — *Yachtsman*
%Int'l Management Group, 75490 Fairway Dr, Indian Wells, CA 92210, USA

Murray, Jan — *Comedian*
1157 Calle Vista Dr, Beverly Hills, CA 90210, USA

Murray, Jim — *Sportswriter*
430 Bellagio Terrace, Los Angeles, CA 90049, USA

Murray, John E, Jr — *Educator*
%Duquesne University, President's Office, Pittsburgh, PA 15282, USA

Murray, Joseph E — *Nobel Medicine Laureate*
108 Abbott Road, Wellesley Hills, MA 02181, USA

Murray, Kathryn — *Dancer*
2877 Kalakaua Ave, Honolulu, HI 96815, USA

Murray, Michael — *Concert Organist*
1876 Northwest Blvd, #B, Columbus, OH 43212, USA

Murray, Peg — *Actress*
800 Light House Road, Southold, NY 11971, USA

Murray, Tracy — *Basketball Player*
4337 Marina City Dr, Marina del Rey, CA 90292, USA

Murray, Ty — *Rodeo Rider*
RR 3, Box 160-B, Stephenville, TX 76401, USA

Murtagh, Kate — *Actress*
15146 Moorpark St, Sherman Oaks, CA 91403, USA

Musante, Tony — *Actor*
38 Bedford St, New York, NY 10014, USA

Musburger, Brent W — *Sportscaster*
%ABC-TV, Sports Dept, 77 W 66th St, New York, NY 10023, USA

Muse, William V — *Educator*
%Auburn University, President's Office, Auburn University, AL 36849, USA

Museveni, Yoweri K — *President, Uganda*
%President's Office, State House, PO Box 7006, Kampala, Uganda

Musgrave, F Story — *Astronaut*
426 Biscayne Blvd, Seabrook, TX 77586, USA

Musgrave, R Kenton — *Judge*
%US Court of International Trade, 1 Federal Plaza, New York, NY 10278, USA

Musgrave, Ted — *Auto Racing Driver*
500 Fern Hill Road, Troutman, NC 28166, USA

Musgrave, Thea — *Composer, Conductor*
%Virginia Opera Assn, PO Box 2580, Norfolk, VA 23501, USA

Musial, Stanley F (Stan) — *Baseball Player*
1655 Des Peres Road, #125, St Louis, MO 63131, USA

Musiol, Bogdan — *Bobsled Athlete*
%Fitness-Studio, Talstr 50, 98544 Zella-Mehlis, Germany

Mussa, Michael — *Economist*
%International Monetary Fund, 700 19th St NW, Washington, DC 20431, USA

Musselman, Bill — *Basketball Coach*
%Portland Trail Blazers, 1 N Center Court, #200, Portland, OR, USA

Musser, Warren V — *Businessman*
%Safeguard Scientifics, 435 Devon Park Dr, Wayne, PA 19087, USA

Mussina, Michael C (Mike) — *Baseball Player*
1302 Spruce St, Montoursville, PA 17754, USA

Musso, George F — *Football Player*
604 W High St, Edwardsville, IL 62025, USA

Mussolini, Alessandra — *Government Official, Italy*
%Italian Social Movement (MSI), Chamber of Deputies, 00100 Rome, Italy

Muster, Brad — *Football Player*
%New Orleans Saints, 1500 Poydras St, New Orleans, LA 70112, USA

Muster, Thomas — *Tennis Player*
370 Fetter Ave, Hewlett, NY 11557, USA

Mustin, Henry C — *Navy Admiral*
2347 S Rolfe St, Arlington, VA 22202, USA

Mutalov, Abdulkhashim — *Prime Minister, Uzbekistan*
%Prime Minister's Office, Tashkent, Uzbekistan

Muth, Rene — *Basketball Coach*
%Pennsylvania State University, Athletic Dept, University Park, PA 16802, USA

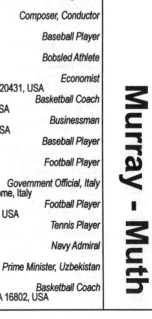

M

Muti, Ornella *Actress*
%Tony Ruggero Initiative, Via Giovanni Bettolo 3, 00195 Rome, Italy

Muti, Riccardo *Conductor*
Via Corti Alle Mura 25, 48100 Ravenna, Italy

Mutombo, Dikembe *Basketball Player*
11513 Lake Potomac Dr, Potomac, MD 20854, USA

Mutschler, Carlfried *Architect*
E-7, 7, 68159 Mannheim, Germany

Mutter, Anne-Sophie *Concert Violinist*
Effnerstr 48, 81925 Munich, Germany

Mutter, Carol A *Marine Corps General*
Deputy CofS Manpower/Reserve Affairs, HqUSMC, 2 Navy Annex, Washington, DC 20380,

Muursepp, Martin *Basketball Player*
%Dallas Mavericks, Reunion Arena, 777 Sports St, Dallas, TX 75207, USA

Mwanawasa, Levy P *Vice President, Zambia*
%Vice President's Office, PO Box 30208, Lusaka, Zambia

Mwinyi, Ali Hassam *President, Tanzania*
%President's Office, State House, PO Box 9120, Dar es Salaam, Tanzania

Mydans, Carl *Photographer*
%Time Inc Magazines, Time & Life Bldg, Rockefeller Center, New York, NY 10020, USA

Myers Tikalsky, Linda *Skier*
RR 5, Box 265-T, Santa Fe, NM 87501, USA

Myers, A Maurice *Businessman*
%America West Airlines, 51 W 3rd St, Tempe, AZ 85281, USA

Myers, Anne M *Religious Leader*
%Church of the Brethren, 1451 Dundee Ave, Elgin, IL 60120, USA

Myers, Barton *Architect*
%Barton Myers Assoc, 9348 Civic Center Dr, Beverly Hills, CA 90210, USA

Myers, Dale D *Space Engineer*
%Dale Myers Assoc, PO Box 232518, Leucadia, CA 92023, USA

Myers, Dee Dee *Government Official*
%"Equal Time" Show, CNBC-TV, 30 Rockefeller Plaza, New York, NY 10112, USA

Myers, Harry J, Jr *Publisher*
46 W Ranch Trail, Morrison, CO 80465, USA

Myers, Jack D *Physician*
%University of Pittsburgh, Scaife Hall, #1291, Pittsburgh, PA 15261, USA

Myers, John *Auto Racing Driver*
4025 Meadowood Dr, Birmingham, AL 35242, USA

Myers, Lisa *Commentator*
%NBC-TV, News Dept, 4001 Nebraska Ave NW, Washington, DC 20016, USA

Myers, Mike *Comedian*
%Brillstein/Grey, 9150 Wilshire Blvd, #350, Beverly Hills, CA 90212, USA

Myers, Minor, Jr *Educator*
%Illinois Wesleyan University, President's Office, Bloomington, IL 61702, USA

Myers, Norman *Environmental Scientist, Conservationist*
Upper Meadow, Old Road, Headington, Oxford OX3 8SZ, England

Myers, Reginald R *Korean War Marine Corps Hero (CMH)*
PO Box 803, Annandale, VA 22003, USA

Myers, Richard B (Dick) *Air Force General*
Assistant to Chairman, Joint Chiefs of Staff, Pentagon, Washington, DC 20318, USA

Myers, Rochelle *Writer*
3827 California St, San Francisco, CA 94118, USA

Myers, Russell *Cartoonist (Broom Hilda)*
%Tribune Media Services, 435 N Michigan Ave, #1500, Chicago, IL 60611, USA

Myers, Walter Dean *Photographer*
%Harcourt Brace, 525 "B" St, San Diego, CA 92101, USA

Myerson, Bess *Consumer Advocate*
2 E 71st St, New York, NY 10021, USA

Myerson, Harvey *Attorney*
%Finley Kumble Wagner Assoc, 425 Park Ave, New York, NY 10022, USA

Myles, Alannah *Singer*
%Goldman Lichetenberg Assoc, 10960 Wilshire Blvd, #2150, Los Angeles, CA 90024, USA

Myrick, Goodwin L *Businessman*
%Alfa Corp, 2108 E South Blvd, Montogmery, AL 36116, USA

Mysen, Bjorn O *Geochemist*
%Carnegie Institution, 5221 Broad Branch Road, Washington, DC 20015, USA

Muti - Mysen

N'Dour, Youssou — *Singer*
%Soundscape, 799 Greenwich St, New York, NY 10014, USA

Naber, John — *Swimmer*
PO Box 50107, Pasadena, CA 91115, USA

Nabers, Drayton, Jr — *Businessman*
%Protective Life Corp, 2801 Highway 280 S, Birmingham, AL 35223, USA

Nabors, Jim — *Actor, Singer*
215 Kulamanu, Honolulu, HI 96816, USA

Nachmansohn, David — *Biochemist*
560 Riverside Dr, New York, NY 10027, USA

Nader, George — *Actor*
893 Camino del Sur, Palm Springs, CA 92262, USA

Nader, Michael — *Actor*
%Paradigm Agency, 10100 Santa Monica Blvd, #2500, Los Angeles, CA 90067, USA

Nader, Ralph — *Consumer Activist*
%Center for Study of Responsive Law, PO Box 19367, Washington, DC 20036, USA

Nadriah — *Soul/Rap Artist (Arrested Development)*
%William Morris Agency, 1325 Ave of Americas, New York, NY 10019, USA

Naehring, Timothy J (Tim) — *Baseball Player*
7300 Pinehurst Dr, Cincinnati, OH 45244, USA

Nagako Kuni — *Empress Mother, Japan*
%Imperial Palace, 1-1 Chiyoda, Chiyoda-ku, Tokyo, Japan

Nagano, Kent — *Conductor*
%Berkeley Symphony Orchestra, 2322 Shattuck Ave, Berkeley, CA 94704, USA

Nagel, Steven R — *Astronaut*
%NASA, Johnson Space Center, 2101 NASA Road, Houston, TX 77058, USA

Nagorske, Lynn A — *Financier*
%TCF Financial Corp, 801 Marquette Ave, Minneapolis, MN 55402, USA

Nagy, Stephen (Steve) — *Baseball Player*
1417 S 57th, Tacoma, WA 98408, USA

Nahan, Stu — *Sportscaster*
11274 Canton Dr, Studio City, CA 91604, USA

Naharin, Ohad — *Choreographer*
%Dance Theater, Scheldeldoekshaven 60, 2511 EN Gravenhage, Netherlands

Naifeh, Steven W — *Writer*
%Connie Clausen Assoc, 250 E 87th St, New York, NY 10128, USA

Naipaul, V S — *Writer*
%Aitken & Stone Ltd, 29 Fernshaw Road, London SW10 0TG, England

Nair, Mira — *Movie Director*
%International Creative Mgmt, 8942 Wilshire Blvd, Beverly Hills, CA 90211, USA

Naisbitt, John — *Writer*
%Universal Press Syndicate, 4520 Main St, Kansas City, KS 64111, USA

Najarian, John S — *Surgeon*
%University of Minnesota Health Center, Surgery Dept, Minneapolis, MN 55455, USA

Najee — *Jazz Saxophonist*
%Associated Booking Corp, 1995 Broadway, #501, New York, NY 10023, USA

Najimy, Kathy — *Actress*
120 W 45th St, #3601, New York, NY 10036, USA

Nakahara, Shin — *Financier*
%Bank of Tokyo Trust, 1251 Ave of Americas, New York, NY 10116, USA

Nakajiim, Tadashi — *Astronomer*
%California Institute of Technology, Astronomy Dept, Pasadena, CA 91125, USA

Nakama, Keo — *Swimmer*
1788 Laukahi St, Honolulu, HI 96821, USA

Nakamura, Kuniwo — *President, Palau*
%President's Office, Babelthuapj, Palau

Nakamura, Tameaki — *Businessman*
%Sumitomo Metal Industries, 5-33-4 Kitahama, Chuoku, Osaka 541, Japan

Nakasone, Robert C — *Businessman*
%Toys "R" Us Inc, 461 From Road, Paramus, NJ 07652, USA

Nakasone, Yasuhiro — *Prime Minister, Japan*
3-22-7 Kamikitazawa, Setagayaku, Tokyo, Japan

Nalder, Eric C — *Journalist*
%Seattle Times, Editorial Dept, Fairview Ave N & John St, Seattle, WA 98111, USA

Nam Duck-Woo — *Prime Minister, South Korea*
395-101 Soekyo-Dong, Mapo-ku Seoul, South Korea

Namath, Joseph W (Joe) — *Football Player*
7 Bay Harbor Road, Tequesta, FL 33469, USA

Namesink, Eric *Swimmer*
114 Hickory St, Butler, PA 16001, USA
Namias, Jerome *Meteorologist*
%Scripps Institute of Oceanography, Sverdrup Hall, La Jolla, CA 92093, USA
Nanne, Louis V (Lou) *Hockey Player, Executive*
6982 Tupa Dr, Edina, MN 55439, USA
Nannini, Alessandro *Auto Racing Driver*
Via del Paradiso 4, 53100 Siena, Italy
Nano, Fatos *Prime Minister, Albania*
%Prime Minister's Office, Keshilli i Ministrave, Tirana, Albania
Nantz, Jim *Sportscaster*
%CBS-TV, Sports Dept, 51 W 52nd St, New York, NY 10019, USA
Napier, Charles *Actor*
Star Route, Box 60-H, Caliente, CA 93518, USA
Napier, John *Stage Designer*
%MLR, 200 Fulham Road, London SW10, England
Napier, John L *Judge*
PO Box 2874, Pawleys Island, SC 29585, USA
Napier, Wilfrid F Cardinal *Religious Leader*
%Archdiocese, 97 Saint John's St, PO Box 65, 4700 Kokstad, South Africa
Napoles, Jose *Boxer*
Cerrada De Tizapan 9-303 Ediciov, Codigo Postel 06080 Mexico City, Mexico
Narasimha Rao, P V *Prime Minister, India*
9 Moti Lal Nehru Marg, New Delhi 11, India
Narayan, R K *Writer*
Soundarya Apts, 1 Eldams Road, #164-A, Alwarpet, Madras 600 018, India
Narayanan, Kocheril Raman *President, India*
%President's Office, Bharat Ka, Rashtrapti Bhavan, New Delhi 110004, India
Narizzano, Silvio *Movie Director*
%Al Parker, 55 Park Lane, London W1Y 3DD, England
Narleski, Raymond E (Ray) *Baseball Player*
1183 Chews Landing Road, Laurel Springs, NJ 08021, USA
Naruhito *Crown Prince, Japan*
%Imperial Palace, 1-1 Chiyoda, Chiyoda-ku, Tokyo, Japan
Narvekar, Prabhakar R *Financier*
%International Monetary Fund, 700 19th St NW, Washington, DC 20431, USA
Narz, Jack *Television Host*
1905 Beverly Place, Beverly Hills, CA 90210, USA
Nasciemento, Milton *Singer, Songwriter*
%Link Producoes, Rua Visconde de Piraja 608, Rio De Janeiro 22410, Brazil
Nash, Cotton *Basketball Player*
600 Summershade Circle, Lexington, KY 40502, USA
Nash, Graham *Singer, Songwriter (Crosby Stills Nash)*
%Jensen Communications, 230 E Union St, Pasadena, CA 91101, USA
Nash, Jack *Financier*
%Odyssey Partners, 31 W 52nd St, New York, NY 10019, USA
Nash, John F *Nobel Economics Laureate*
%Princeton University, Economics Department, Princeton, NJ 08544, USA
Nash, Steve *Basketball Player*
%Phoenix Suns, 201 E Jefferson St, Phoenix, AZ 85004, USA
Nash, William L *Army General*
CG, 1st Armored Division, US Army Europe & 7th Army, APO, AE 09252, USA
Naslund, Mats *Hockey Player*
6963 Pregassona, Switzerland
Naslund, Ron *Hockey Player*
2600 Cheyenne Circle, Minnetonka, MN 55305, USA
Nastase, Ilie *Tennis Player*
Clubul Sportiv Steaua, Calea Plevnei 114, Bucharest, Hungary
Nasution, Abdul Haris *Army General, Indonesia*
Jl Teuku Umar 40, Jakarta Pusat, Indonesia
Natalicio, Diana S *Educator*
%University of Texas at El Paso, President's Office, El Paso, TX 79968, USA
Nater, Swen *Basketball Player*
PO Box 426, Enumclaw, WA 98022, USA
Nathan, Tony C *Football Player, Coach*
15110 Dunbarton Place, Miami Lakes, FL 33016, USA
Nathaniel (Popp), Bishop *Religious Leader*
%Romanian Orthodox Episcopate, 2522 Grey Tower Road, Jackson, MI 49201, USA

Nathans, Daniel — *Nobel Medicine Laureate*
%Johns Hopkins School of Medicine, Microbiology Dept, Baltimore, MD 21205, USA

Natkin, Robert — *Artist*
24 Mark Twain Lane, West Redding, CT 06896, USA

Natori, Josie C — *Fashion Designer*
%Natori Co, 40 E 34th St, New York, NY 10016, USA

Natt, Calvin — *Basketball Player*
4825 S Fraser St, Aurora, CO 80015, USA

Natter, Robert J — *Navy Admiral*
Commander, US 7th Fleet, FPO, AP 96601, USA

Naude, C F Beyers — *Religious Leader*
%Ecumenical Advice Bureau, 185 Smit St, Braamfontein 2001, South Africa

Naughton, David — *Actor*
%Gold Marshak Liedtke, 3500 W Olive Ave, #1400, Burbank, CA 91505, USA

Naughton, James — *Actor, Singer*
3100 Arrowhead Dr, Los Angeles, CA 90068, USA

Naulls, Willie — *Basketball Player*
435 Loring Ave, Los Angeles, CA 90024, USA

Nauman, Bruce — *Artist*
%Leo Castelli Gallery, 420 W Broadway, New York, NY 10012, USA

Navon, Itzhak — *President, Israel*
%Education & Culture Ministry, Jerusalem, Israel

Navratilova, Martina — *Tennis Player*
%Women's Tennis Assn, 133 1st St NE, St Petersburg, FL 33701, USA

Nayden, Denis J — *Businessman*
%Kidder Peabody Group, 10 Hanover Square, New York, NY 10005, USA

Naylor, Gloria — *Writer*
%One Way Productions, 638 2nd St, Brooklyn, NY 11215, USA

Nazam, Hisham — *Govenment Official, Saudi Arabia*
%Ministry of Petroleum & Mineral Resources, Riyadh, Saudi Arabia

Nazarbayev, Nursultan A — *President, Kazakhstan*
%President's Office, Pl Respubliki 4, 480091 Alma Ata, Kazakhstan

NdegeOcello, Me'Shell — *Singer, Bassist*
%Handprint Entertainment, 8436 W 3rd St, #650, Los Angeles, CA 90048, USA

Ndimira, Pascal Firmin — *Prime Minister, Burundi*
%Prime Minister's Office, Bujumbura, Burundi

Ne'eman, Yuval — *Physicist*
%Tel-Aviv University, Physics/Astronomy Dept, Tel-Aviv 69978, Israel

Neagle, Dennis E (Denny) — *Baseball Player*
945 Waugh Chapel Road, Gambrills, MD 21054, USA

Neal, James F — *Attorney*
%Neal & Harwell, 3rd National Bank Building, #800, Nashville, TN 37219, USA

Neal, John E — *Financier*
%Kemper Financial Services, 120 S LaSalle St, Chicago, IL 60603, USA

Neal, Patricia — *Actress*
45 East End Ave, #4-C, New York, NY 10028, USA

Neal, Richard I — *Marine Corps General*
Assistant Commandant, Hq US Marine Corps, Navy Annex, Washington, DC 20380, USA

Neame, Christopher — *Actor*
%Borinstein Oreck Bogart, 8271 Melrose Ave, #110, Los Angeles, CA 90046, USA

Neame, Ronald — *Movie Director*
%Kimridge Corp, 2317 Kimridge Ave, Beverly Hills, CA 90210, USA

Near, Holly — *Singer, Songwriter, Actress*
560 Key Blvd, Richmond, CA 94805, USA

Nebel, Dorothy Hoyt — *Skier*
19 Garwood Trail, Denville, NJ 07834, USA

Neblett, Carol — *Opera Singer*
%Robert Lombardo, Harkness Plaza, 61 W 62nd St, #B-5, New York, NY 10023, USA

Nederlander, James M — *Theater Producer*
%Nederlander Organization, 810 7th Ave, New York, NY 10019, USA

Nedley, Robert E — *Businessman*
%St Joe Paper Co, 1650 Prudential Dr, Jacksonville, FL 32207, USA

Nedomansky, Vaclav — *Hockey Player*
292 Town Center Dr, Troy, MI 48084, USA

Nedved, Petr — *Hockey Player*
%Pittsburgh Penguins, Civic Arena, Centre Ave, Pittsburgh, PA 15219, USA

Needham, Connie — *Actress*
19721 Castlebar Dr, Rowland Heights, CA 91748, USA

N

Nathans - Needham

Needham, Hal — *Movie Director*
%Bandit Productions, 3518 Cahuenga Blvd W, #110, Los Angeles, CA 90068, USA

Needham, Tracey — *Actress*
%Badgley Connor, 9229 Sunset Blvd, #311, Los Angeles, CA 90069, USA

Needleman, Jacob — *Philosopher*
25 San Andreas Way, San Francisco, CA 94127, USA

Neel, James V G — *Geneticist*
2235 Belmont Road, Ann Arbor, MI 48104, USA

Neel, Louis Boyd — *Conductor*
%York Club, 135 St George St, Toronto ON M5B 2L8, Canada

Neel, Louis E F — *Nobel Physics Laureate*
15 Rue Marcel Allegot, 92190 Meudon, France

Neely, Cam — *Hockey Player*
33 Belmont St, Beverly, MA 01915, USA

Neely, Mark E, Jr — *Writer, Historian*
%Oxford University Press, 198 Madison Ave, New York, NY 10016, USA

Neely, Ralph E — *Football Player*
806 Patricia Circle, Quitman, TX 75783, USA

Neeson, Liam — *Actor*
%International Creative Mgmt, 40 W 57th St, New York, NY 10019, USA

Nef, John U — *Writer, Historian*
2726 "N" St NW, Washington, DC 20007, USA

Neff, Francine I — *Government Official*
1509 Sagebrush Trail SE, Albuquerque, NM 87123, USA

Neff, Hildegard — *Actress, Singer*
%Agentur Lentz, Holbeinstr 4, 81679 Munich, Germany

Neff, William D — *Psychologist*
2080 Hideaway Court, Morris, IL 60450, USA

Negoesco, Stephen — *Soccer Coach*
%University of San Francisco, Athletic Dept, San Francisco, CA 94117, USA

Negron, Taylor — *Actor*
%J Michael Bloom, 9255 Sunset Blvd, #710, Los Angeles, CA 90069, USA

Negroponte, John D — *Diplomat*
%US State Department, 2201 "C" St NW, Washington, DC 20520, USA

Neher, Erwin — *Nobel Medicine Laureate*
%Max Planck Biophysical Chemistry Institute, 37083 Gottingen, Germany

Nehmer, Reinhold — *Bobsled Athlete*
Varnkevitz, 18556 Altenkirchen, Germany

Neid, Silvia — *Soccer Player*
Betramstr 18, 60320 Frankfurt/Main, Germany

Neil, Andrew F — *Editor*
%Sunday Times, Editorial Dept, 1 Pennington St, London E1 9XN, England

Neil, Hildegarde — *Actress*
%Vernon Conway, 5 Spring St, London W2 3RA, England

Neill, Mary Gardner — *Museum Director*
%Seattle Art Museum, Volunteer Park, Seattle, WA 98112, USA

Neill, Noel — *Actress*
331 Sage Lane, Santa Monica, CA 90402, USA

Neill, Rolfe — *Publisher*
%Charlotte News-Observer, 600 S Tryon St, Charlotte, NC 28202, USA

Neill, Sam — *Actor*
PO Box 153, Noble Park, VIC 3174, Australia

Neilson, Roger — *Hockey Coach*
1796 Westover Point Road, RR 3, Lakefield ON K0L 2HO, Canada

Neilson-Bell, Sandra — *Swimmer*
3101 Mistyglen Circle, Austin, TX 78746, USA

Neiman, LeRoy — *Artist*
1 W 67th St, New York, NY 10023, USA

Neizvestny, Ernst I — *Artist*
81 Grand St, New York, NY 10013, USA

Nelligan, Kate — *Actress*
%Larry Dalzell Assoc, 17 Broad Court, London WC2B 5QN, England

Nellis, William J — *Physicist*
%University of California, Lawrence Livermore Lab, Livermore, CA 94551, USA

Nelson, Barry — *Actor*
134 W 58th St, New York, NY 10019, USA

Nelson, Byron — *Golfer*
Fairway Ranch, Litsey Road, RR 2, Box 5, Roanoke, TX 76262, USA

Nelson, Cindy *Skier*
%US Ski Assn, PO Box 100, Park City, UT 84060, USA

Nelson, Craig Richard *Actor*
%Borinstein Oreck Bogart, 8271 Melrose Ave, #110, Los Angeles, CA 90046, USA

Nelson, Craig T *Actor*
3518 Cahuenga Blvd W, #304, Los Angeles, CA 90068, USA

Nelson, David *Actor, Television Director*
8544 Sunset Blvd, Los Angeles, CA 90069, USA

Nelson, Deborah *Journalist*
%Seattle Times, Editorial Dept, Fairview Ave N & John St, Seattle, WA 98111, USA

Nelson, Donald A (Nellie) *Basketball Player, Coach, Executive*
%Dallas Mavericks, Reunion Arena, 777 Sports St, Dallas, TX 75207, USA

Nelson, Ed *Actor*
124 Old Pecan Grove Lane, Waveland, MS 39576, USA

Nelson, Gaylord A *Governor/Senator, WI; Environmentalist*
%Wilderness Society, 900 17th St NW, Washington, DC 20006, USA

Nelson, George D *Astronaut*
%University of Washington, Astronomy Dept, Seattle, WA 98195, USA

Nelson, James E *Religious Leader*
%Baha'i Faith, 536 Sheridan Road, Wilmette, IL 60091, USA

Nelson, John Allen *Actor*
%Paradigm Agency, 10100 Santa Monica Blvd, #2500, Los Angeles, CA 90067, USA

Nelson, John C *Financier*
%Norwest Bank Colorado, 1740 Broadway, Denver, CO 80274, USA

Nelson, John W *Conductor*
%IMG Artists, Media House, 3 Burlington Lane, London W4 2TH, England

Nelson, Judd *Actor*
2934 1/2 N Beverly Glen Circle, #57, Los Angeles, CA 90077, USA

Nelson, Judith *Opera Singer*
2600 Buena Vista Way, Berkeley, CA 94708, USA

Nelson, Kent C *Businessman*
%United Parcel Service, 55 Glenlake Parkway NE, Atlanta, GA 30328, USA

Nelson, Kirk N *Businessman*
%Federated Mutual Insurance, 121 E Park Square, Owatonna, MN 55060, USA

Nelson, Larry *Golfer*
421 Oakmont Circle, Marietta, GA 30067, USA

Nelson, Ralph A *Nutritionist*
%Carle Foundation Hospital, 611 W Park St, Urbana, IL 61801, USA

Nelson, Robert T *Admiral, Coast Guard*
%Vice Commandant's Office, US Coast Guard, 2100 2nd SW, Washington, DC 20593, USA

Nelson, Tracy *Actress*
13263 Ventura Blvd, #10, Studio City, CA 91604, USA

Nelson, William (Bill) *Representative, FL; Astronaut*
3000 Rocky Point Road, Melbourne, FL 32905, USA

Nelson, William C *Financier*
%Boatmen's 1st National (KC), 10th & Baltimore, Kansas City, 64114, USA

Nelson, Willie *Singer, Songwriter*
%Pedernails Studio, Rt 1, Briarcliff TT, Spicewood, TX 78669, USA

Nemec, Corin *Actor*
701 N Valley St, Burbank, CA 91505, USA

Nemecek, Bohumil *Boxer*
V Zahradkach 30, 400 00 Usti Nad Labem, Czechoslovakia

Nemecheck, Joe *Auto Racing Driver*
%Nemco Motorsports, PO Box 1131, Mooresville, NC 28115, USA

Nemeth, Miklos *Prime Minister, Hungary*
%European Reconstruction Bank, 175 Bishopgate, London EC2A 2EH, England

Nemov, Alexei *Gymnast*
%Gymnastics Federation, Lujnetskaya Nabereynaya 8, 119270 Moscow, Russia

Nenneman, Richard A *Editor*
PO Box 992, East Brunswick, NJ 08816, USA

Nepote, Jean *Law Enforcement Official*
26 Rue Armengaud, 92210 Saint-Cloud, Hauts-de-Seine, France

Nerette, Joseph *President, Haiti; Judge*
%Supreme Court, Chief Justice's Office, Port-au-Prince, Haiti

Neri Vela, Rodolfo *Astronaut, Mexico*
Playa Copacabana 131, Col Marte, Mexico City DF 08830, Mexico

Neri, Manuel *Artist*
%Anne Kohs Assoc, 251 Post St, #425, San Francisco, CA 94108, USA

Nerlove, Marc L *Economist*
%University of Maryland, Agricultural/Resource Economics, College Park, MD 20742, USA

Nero, Franco *Actor*
%Gersh Agency, 232 N Canon Dr, Beverly Hills, CA 90210, USA

Nero, Peter *Pianist, Conductor*
%Gurtman & Murtha, 450 7th Ave, #603, New York, NY 10123, USA

Nerud, John *Thoroughbred Racing Executive*
%Tartan Farms, 5910 SW 44th Ave, Ocala, FL 34474, USA

Nesbitt, Gregory L *Businessman*
%Central Louisiana Electric, 2030 Donahue Ferry Road, Pineville, LA 71360, USA

Nesmith, Michael *Singer, Guitarist (The Monkees)*
2828 Donald Douglas Loop N, #15, Santa Monica, CA 90405, USA

Nespral, Jackie *Commentator*
%NBC-TV, News Dept, 30 Rockefeller Plaza, New York, NY 10112, USA

Ness, Norman F *Astrophysicist*
9 Wilkinson Dr, Landenberg, PA 19350, USA

Nessen, Ronald H (Ron) *Government Official, Commentator*
6409 Walhonding Road, Bethesda, MD 20816, USA

Nesterenko, Evgeny Y *Opera Singer*
Fruzenskaya Nab 24/1-78, 119146 Moscow, Russia

Netanyahu, Benjamin *Prime Minister, Israel*
%Prime Minister's Office, 3 Rehov Kaplan, Hakirya, Jerusalem 91007, Israel

Nett, Robert B *WW II Army Hero (CMH)*
5417 Kessington Dr, Columbus, GA 31907, USA

Nettelsheim, Christine Cook *Judge*
%US Claims Court, 717 Madison Place NW, Washington, DC 20005, USA

Nettles, Graig *Baseball Player*
11217 Carmel Creek Road, #2, San Diego, CA 92130, USA

Nettleton, Lois *Actress*
%Susan Mann, 11762 Moorpark St, #G, Studio City, CA 91604, USA

Neubauer, Franz *Financier*
%Bayerische Landesbank, 80277 Munich, Germany

Neufeld, Elizabeth F *Biochemist*
%University of California Medical School, Biology Dept, Los Angeles, CA 90024, USA

Neufeld, Ray *Hockey Player*
805 Neipsic Road, Glastonbury, CT 06033, USA

Neuharth, Allen H *Publisher*
%Freedom Forum, 1101 Wilson Blvd, Arlington, VA 22209, USA

Neuhaus, Max *Artist, Composer*
350 5th Ave, #3304, New York, NY 10118, USA

Neuhaus, Richard J *Religious Leader*
%Center on Religion & Society, 152 Madison Ave, New York, NY 10016, USA

Neuhauser, Duncan V B *Epidemiologist*
2655 N Park Ave, Cleveland Heights, OH 44106, USA

Neumann, Gerhard *Aeronautical Engineer*
%General Electric Co, 1000 Western Ave, West Lynn, MA 01905, USA

Neumann, Robert G *Diplomat, Educator*
4986 Sentinel Dr, #301, Bethesda, MD 20816, USA

Neumann, Wolfgang *Opera Singer*
%Metropolitan Opera Assn, Lincoln Center Plaza, New York, NY 10023, USA

Neumeier, John *Choreographer*
%Hamburg Ballet, 54 Caspar-Voght-Str, 20535 Hamburg, Germany

Neuner, Doris *Luge Athlete*
6024 Innsbruck, Austria

Neurath, Hans *Biochemist*
5752 60th NE, Seattle, WA 98105, USA

Neuwirth, Bebe *Actress, Dancer, Singer*
144 Prospect Ave, Princeton, NJ 08540, USA

Neves, Lucas Moreira Cardinal *Religious Leader*
Av Sefa de Setembro 1682, 40080-001 Salvador, Bahia, Brazil

Neville, Aaron *Singer*
5771 Eastover Dr, New Orleans, LA 70128, USA

Neville, John *Actor*
99 Norman St, Stratford ON N5A 5R8, Canada

Neville, Robert C *Theologian*
%Boston University, Theology School, Boston, MA 02215, USA

Nevins, Claudette *Actress*
%Gold Marshak Liedtke, 3500 W Olive Ave, #1400, Burbank, CA 91505, USA

Newbern, George — Actor
%United Talent Agency, 9560 Wilshire Blvd, #500, Beverly Hills, CA 90212, USA

Newbigging, William — Publisher
%Edmonton Journal, 10006 101st St, Edmonton AB T5J 2S6, Canada

Newbury, Mickey — Songwriter, Singer
128 River Road, Hendersonville, TN 37075, USA

Newcomb, Gerry — Artist
1748 26th Ave E, Seattle, WA 98112, USA

Newcomb, Jonathan — Publisher
35 Pierrepont St, Brooklyn, NY 11201, USA

Newcombe, Donald (Don) — Baseball Player
800 W 6th St, Los Angeles, CA 90017, USA

Newcombe, John D — Tennis Player
%John Newcombe's Tennis Ranch, PO Box 310469, New Braunfels, TX 78131, USA

Newell, Homer E — Physicist
2567 Nicky Lane, Alexandria, VA 22311, USA

Newell, Norman D — Palaeontologist, Geologist
%American Museum of Natural History, Central Park W & 79th, New York, NY 10023, USA

Newell, Peter F (Pete) — Basketball Coach
1409 Granvia Ave, Palos Verdes Peninsula, CA 90274, USA

Newgard, Christopher — Biochemist
%Southwestern Medical Center, Biochemistry Dept, Dallas, TX 75237, USA

Newhart, Bob — Comedian, Actor
420 Amapola Lane, Los Angeles, CA 90077, USA

Newhouse, Donald E — Publisher
%Advance Publications, 950 Fingerboard Road, Staten Island, NY 10305, USA

Newhouse, Frederick (Fred) — Track Athlete
816 Bantry Way, Benicia, CA 94510, USA

Newhouse, Robert — Football Player
6847 Truxton Dr, Dallas, TX 75231, USA

Newhouse, Samuel I, Jr — Publisher
%Conde Nast Publications, Conde Nast Bldg, 350 Madison Ave, New York, NY 10017, USA

Newhouser, Harold (Hal) — Baseball Player
2584 Marcy Court, Bloomfield Hills, MI 48302, USA

Newley, Anthony — Singer, Actor, Songwriter
%Peter Charlesworth, 60 Old Brompton Road, London SW7 3LQ, England

Newlin, Mike — Basketball Player
1414 Horseshoe Dr, Sugar Land, TX 77478, USA

Newman, Arnold — Photographer
33 W 67th St, New York, NY 10023, USA

Newman, Barry — Actor
425 N Oakhurst Dr, Beverly Hills, CA 90210, USA

Newman, Bernard — Judge
%US Court of International Trade, 1 Federal Plaza, New York, NY 10278, USA

Newman, Beryl R — WW II Army Hero (CMH)
HC 67, Box 843, Urbanna, VA 23175, USA

Newman, David (Fathead) — Jazz Saxophonist
%Raleigh Group, 1223 Wilshire Blvd, #502, Santa Monica, CA 90403, USA

Newman, Edwin H — Commentator
870 United Nations Plaza, #18-D, New York, NY 10017, USA

Newman, Harry L — Football Player
3145 Palm Aire Dr N, #102, Pompano Beach, FL 33069, USA

Newman, James H — Astronaut
%NASA, Johnson Space Center, 2101 NASA Road, Houston, TX 77058, USA

Newman, Johnny — Basketball Player
%Milwaukee Bucks, Bradley Center, 1001 N 4th St, Milwaukee, WI 53203, USA

Newman, Kevin — Commentator
%"Sunday GMA" Show, ABC-TV, News Dept, 77 W 66th St, New York, NY 10023, USA

Newman, Laraine — Comedienne
10480 Ashton Ave, Los Angeles, CA 90024, USA

Newman, Melvin S — Organic Chemist
2239 Onandaga Dr, Columbus, OH 43221, USA

Newman, Nanette — Actress
Seven Pines, Wentworth, Surrey GU25 4QP, England

Newman, Oscar — Architect, Urban Planner
%Washington University, Architecture Dept, St Louis, MO 63130, USA

Newman, Paul — Actor
555 Long Wharf Dr, New Haven, CT 06511, USA

Newman, Phyllis	*Actress, Singer*
529 W 42nd St, #7-F, New York, NY 10036, USA	
Newman, Randy	*Singer, Songwriter*
1610 San Remo Dr, Pacific Palisades, CA 90272, USA	
Newmar, Julie	*Actress*
204 S Carmelina Ave, Los Angeles, CA 90049, USA	
Newsom, David	*Actor*
7471 Melrose Ave, Los Angeles, CA 90046, USA	
Newsom, David D	*Diplomat*
4990 Sentinel Dr, #102, Bethesda, MD 20816, USA	
Newsome, Ozzie	*Football Player, Executive*
100 Airline St, Muscle Shoals, AL 35661, USA	
Newton, C M	*Basketball Coach, Administrator*
65 Ave of Champions, Nicholasville, KY 40356, USA	
Newton, Christopher	*Theater Director*
%Shakespeare Festival, PO Box 774, Niagara-on-the-Lake ON L0S 1J0, Canada	
Newton, Helmut	*Photographer*
7 Ave St Roman, #T-1008, Monte Carlo, Monaco	
Newton, Juice	*Singer, Songwriter*
PO Box 3035, Rancho Santa Fe, CA 92067, USA	
Newton, Lloyd W	*Air Force General*
Vice Chief of Staff, HqUSAF, Pentagon, Washington, DC 20330, USA	
Newton, Nate	*Football Player*
PO Box 258, Coppell, TX 75019, USA	
Newton, Russell B, Jr	*Financier*
%Alliance Mortgage Co, 4500 Salisbury Road, Jacksonville, FL 32216, USA	
Newton, Wayne	*Singer, Actor*
6629 S Pecos Road, Las Vegas, NV 89120, USA	
Newton-John, Olivia	*Singer, Actress*
PO Box 2710, Malibu, CA 90265, USA	
Ney, Edward N	*Businessman, Diplomat*
%Burson-Marsteller, 230 Park Ave S, New York, NY 10003, USA	
Ney, Richard	*Actor*
800 S San Rafael Ave, Pasadena, CA 91105, USA	
Nezhat, Camran	*Endocrinologist*
%Fertility/Endocrinology Ctr, 5555 Peachtree Dunwoody Road NE, Atlanta, GA 30342, USA	
Nguyen Van Linh	*Chairman, Vietnam*
%Communist Party, Hoang Hoa Tham, Hanoi, Vietnam	
Nguyen Van Thieu	*President, South Vietnam; Army General*
White House, Coombe Park, Kingston-Upon-Thames, Surrey, England	
Nguyen, Dustin	*Actor*
465 N Sierra Bonita Ave, #8, Los Angeles, CA 90036, USA	
Nicely, Olza M (Tony)	*Businessman*
%Geico Corp, 1 Geico Plaza, 5260 Western Ave NW, Washington, DC 20076, USA	
Nicholas (Smisko), Bishop	*Religious Leader*
%American Carpatho, 312 Garfield St, Johnstown, PA 15906, USA	
Nicholas, Denise	*Actress*
932 Longwood Ave, Los Angeles, CA 90019, USA	
Nicholas, Fayard	*Dancer*
23388 Mulholland Dr, #58, Woodland Hills, CA 91364, USA	
Nicholas, Harold	*Dancer*
789 West End Ave, #9-D, New York, NY 10025, USA	
Nicholas, Henry	*Labor Leader*
%Hospital & Health Care Union, 330 W 42nd St, #1905, New York, NY 10036, USA	
Nicholas, Nicholas J, Jr	*Publisher*
%Pluggers Inc, 1000 SW Broadway, #1850, Portland, OR 97205, USA	
Nicholls, Bernie	*Hockey Player*
22 Longledge Dr, Rye Brook, NY 10573, USA	
Nichols, Bobby	*Golfer*
8681 Glenlyon Court, Fort Myers, FL 33912, USA	
Nichols, Dorothy L	*Financier*
%Farm Credit Administration, 1501 Farm Credit Dr, McLean, VA 22102, USA	
Nichols, J D	*Singer, Guitarist (The Commodores)*
%Commodore Entertainment, 1920 Benson Ave, St Paul, MN 55116, USA	
Nichols, John D	*Businessman*
%Illinois Tool Works, 3600 W Lake Ave, Glenview, IL 60025, USA	
Nichols, Kyra	*Ballerina*
%New York City Ballet, Lincoln Center Plaza, New York, NY 10023, USA	

Nichols, Larry *Rubik Cube Designer*
%Moleculon Research Corp, 139 Main St, Cambridge, MA 02142, USA
Nichols, Mike *Movie Director, Comedian*
%Westbury Hotel, 15 E 69th St, New York, NY 10021, USA
Nichols, Nichelle *Actress*
23281 Leonora Dr, Woodland Hills, CA 91367, USA
Nichols, Peter R *Writer*
%Rochelle Stevens, 2 Terrett's Place, Upper St, London N1 19Z, England
Nichols, Stephen *Actor*
3176 Federal Ave, Los Angeles, CA 90066, USA
Nicholson, Jack *Actor*
9911 W Pico Blvd, #PH-A, Los Angeles, CA 90035, USA
Nickel, Herman W *Diplomat*
%US Institute for Peace, 4701 Willard Ave, #1216, Bethesda, MD 20815, USA
Nickerson, Donald A, Jr *Religious Leader*
%Episcopal Church, 815 2nd Ave, New York, NY 10017, USA
Nickerson, Hardy *Football Player*
1181 Livorna Road, Alamo, CA 94507, USA
Nicklaus, Jack W *Golfer*
%Golden Bear International, 11760 US Highway 1, North Palm Beach, FL 33408, USA
Nicks, John *Figure Skating Coach*
%Ice Capades Chalet, 2701 Harbor Blvd, Costa Mesa, CA 92626, USA
Nicks, Michelle *Model*
%Wilhelmina Artists, 300 Park Ave, #200, New York, NY 10022, USA
Nicks, Stevie *Singer, Songwriter*
%Front Line Mgmt, 8900 Wilshire Blvd, #300, Beverly Hills, CA 90211, USA
Nickson, David W *Businessman*
%Scottish & Newcastle Breweries, Holrood Road, Edinburgh EH8 8YS, Scotland
Nickson, Julia *Actress*
1206 S Hudson Ave, Los Angeles, CA 90019, USA
Nicol, Alex *Actor*
1496 San Leandro Park Road, Santa Barbara, CA 93108, USA
Nicol, Donald *Publisher*
%Winnipeg Free Press, 300 Carlton St, Winnipeg MB R3C 3A7, Canada
Nicollier, Claude *Astronaut, Switzerland*
18710 Martinique Dr, Houston, TX 77058, USA
Nicolson, Nigel *Writer*
Sissinghurst Castle, Kent, England
Nidetch, Jean *Businesswoman*
%Weight Watchers International, 3860 Crenshaw Blvd, Los Angeles, CA 90008, USA
Nieberg, Lars *Equestrian Rider*
Gestit Waldershausen, 35315 Homberg, Germany
Nieder, Bill *Track Athlete*
PO Box 310, Mountain Ranch, CA 95246, USA
Niederhoffer, Victor *Squash Player*
%Niederhoffer Cross Zeckhauser, 757 3rd Ave, New York, NY 10017, USA
Niekro, Joseph F (Joe) *Baseball Player*
2707 Fairway Dr S, Plat City, FL 33567, USA
Niekro, Philip H (Phil) *Baseball Player*
6382 Nichols Road, Flowery Branch, GA 30542, USA
Nielsen, Brigitte *Actress, Model*
%Bartels, PO Box 57593, Sherman Oaks, CA 91413, USA
Nielsen, Gifford *Football Player*
3665 Maranatha Dr, Sugar Land, TX 77479, USA
Nielsen, Leslie *Actor*
%Hanson & Schwam, 9350 Wilshire Blvd, #315, Beverly Hills, CA 90212, USA
Nielsen, Rick *Singer, Guitarist (Cheap Trick)*
%Ken Adamay, 3805 County Road "M", Middleton, WI 53562, USA
Niemann, Gunda *Speed Skater*
E Hackel Str 6, 99097 Erfurt, Germany
Niemi, Lisa *Actress*
10960 Dickens St, #302, Sherman Oaks, CA 91423, USA
Nieminen, Toni *Ski Jumper*
%Landen Kanava 99, Vesijarvenkatu 74, 15140 Lahti, Finland
Nierenberg, William A *Physicist*
9581 La Jolla Farms Road, La Jolla, CA 92037, USA
Nierman, Leonardo *Artist*
Amsterdam 43 PH, Mexico City 11 DF, Mexico

Nigh, George P *Governor, OK; Educator*
%University of Central Oklahoma, 100 N University Dr, Edmond, OK 73034, USA
Nigrelli, Ross F *Pathologist*
29 Barracuda Road, East Quogue, NY 11942, USA
Nikolayev, Andrian G *Cosmonaut, Air Force General*
%Potchta Kosmonavtov, Moskovskoi Oblasti, 141160 Syvisdny Goroduk, Russia
Niles, Nicholas H *Publisher*
%Sportng News Publishing Co, 1212 N Lindbergh Blvd, St Louis, MO 63132, USA
Niles, Thomas M T *Diplomat*
PSC 108, Box 560, APO, AE 09842, USA
Nilsen, John *Composer, Guitarist*
%Magic Wing Music, PO Box 222, West Linn, OR 97068, USA
Nilsson, Birgit *Opera Singer*
Hammenhog, 270 50 Hammenhog, Sweden
Nilsson, Lars-Goran *Businessman*
%Home Insurance, 59 Maiden Lane, New York, NY 10038, USA
Nilsson, Lennart *Photographer*
%Pantheon Books, 201 E 50th St, New York, NY 10022, USA
Nilsson, Ulf *Hockey Player*
4 Danbury Ave, Westport, CT 06880, USA
Nimoy, Leonard *Actor*
17 Gateway Dr, Batavia, NY 14020, USA
Nims, Arthur L, III *Judge*
%US Tax Court, 400 2nd St NW, Washington, DC 20217, USA
Nimziki, Joe *Movie Director*
%Paradigm Agency, 10100 Santa Monica Blvd, #2500, Los Angeles, CA 90067, USA
Nin-Culmell, Joaquin M *Composer*
5830 Clover Dr, Oakland, CA 94618, USA
Nininger, Harvey H *Meteoriticist*
PO Box 420, Sedona, AZ 86339, USA
Nipar, Yvette *Actress*
9300 Wilshire Blvd, #410, Beverly Hills, CA 90212, USA
Nipon, Albert *Fashion Designer*
%Leslie Faye Co, Albert Nipon Div, 1400 Broadway, #1600, New York, NY 10018, USA
Nirenberg, Louis *Mathematician*
221 W 82nd St, New York, NY 10024, USA
Nirenberg, Marshall W *Nobel Medicine Laureate*
%National Heart Institute, Biochemical Genetics Laboratory, Bethesda, MD 20014, USA
Nirmala, Sister *Religious Leader*
%Missionaries of Charity, 54-A Lower Circular Road, Calcutta 700016, India
Nisbet, Robert A *Historian, Sociologist*
6131 Purple Aster Lane NE, Albuquerque, NM 87111, USA
Nishizawa, Junichi *Electronics Inventor*
%Semiconductor Research Institute, Sendai, Japan
Nishizuka, Yassutomi *Pharmacologist*
%Kobe University School of Medicine, Pharmacology Dept, Kobe, Japan
Nishkian, Byron *Skier*
150 4th St, #PH, San Francisco, CA 94103, USA
Niskanen, William A, Jr *Government Official, Economist*
%Cato Institute, 1000 Massachusetts Ave NW, #6, Washington, DC 20001, USA
Nissalke, Tom *Basketball Coach*
4569 S Thousand Oaks Dr, Salt Lake City, UT 84124, USA
Nitschke, Raymond E (Ray) *Football Player*
411 Peppermint Court, RR 1, Oneida, WI 54155, USA
Nitze, Paul H *Secretary, Navy; Diplomat*
1619 Massachusetts Ave NW, #811, Washington, DC 20036, USA
Niven, Kip *Actor*
20781 Big Rock Dr, Malibu, CA 90265, USA
Niven, Laurence (Larry) *Writer*
136 El Camino Dr, Beverly Hills, CA 90212, USA
Niwano, Nikkyo *Religious Leader*
Rissho Kosei-kai, 2-11-1 Wada Suginamiku, Tokyo 166, Japan
Nixon, Agnes E *Television Producer, Screenwriter*
774 Conestoga Road, Rosemont, PA 19010, USA
Nixon, Edwin R *Businessman*
Starkes Heath, Rogate near Petersfield, Hants, England
Nixon, Gary *Motorcycle Racing Rider*
%Gary Nixon Enterprises, 2408 Carroll Mill Road, Phoenix, MD 21131, USA

Nixon, Marni — *Singer, Actress*
1747 Van Buren St, #790, Hollywood, FL 33020, USA

Nixon, Norm — *Basketball Player*
345 N Maple Dr, #205, Beverly Hills, CA 90210, USA

Niyazov, Saparmurad — *President, Turkmenistan*
%President's Office, Askkhabad, Turkmenistan

Nkomo, Joshua — *Political Leader, Zimbabwe*
%House of Assembly, Salisbury, Zimbabwe

Noah, Yannick — *Tennis Player, Coach*
1820 Montreux, Switzerland

Noakes, Michael — *Artist*
146 Hamilton Terrace, St John's Wood, London NW8 9UX, England

Nobis, Thomas H (Tommy), Jr — *Football Player, Executive*
40 S Battery Place NE, Atlanta, GA 30342, USA

Noble, Adrian K — *Theater Director*
%Royal Shakespeare Co, Barbican Theater, London EC2, England

Noble, Chelsea — *Actress*
PO Box 8665, Calabasas, CA 91372, USA

Noble, David J — *Businessman*
%Statesman Group, 1400 Des Moines Building, Des Moines, IA 50316, USA

Noble, James — *Actor*
%Paradigm Agency, 10100 Santa Monica Blvd, #2500, Los Angeles, CA 90067, USA

Nodell, Mart — *Cartoonist (The Green Lantern)*
117 Lake Irene Dr, West Palm Beach, FL 33411, USA

Noe, Vergilius Cardinal — *Religious Leader*
Saint Peter's Basilica, 00120 Vatican City

Noel, Philip W — *Governor, RI*
21 Kirby Ave, Warwick, RI 02889, USA

Noguchi, Thomas T — *Pathologist*
1110 Avoca Ave, Pasadena, CA 91105, USA

Noha, Edward J — *Businessman*
%CNA Financial, CNA Plaza, Chicago, IL 60685, USA

Noiret, Philippe — *Actor*
%Le Studio Canal, 17 Rue Dumont Durville, 75118 Paris, France

Nojima, Minoru — *Concert Pianist*
%Hillyer Kazuko International, 250 W 57th St, New York, NY 10107, USA

Nokes, Matthew D (Matt) — *Baseball Player*
15432 Harrow Lane, Poway, CA 92064, USA

Nolan, Christopher — *Writer*
158 Vernon Ave, Clontanf, Dublin 3, Ireland

Nolan, Jeanette — *Actress*
940 Locust Ave, Charlottesville, VA 22901, USA

Nolan, Kathleen (Kathy) — *Actress*
360 E 55th St, #PH, New York, NY 10022, USA

Nolan, Kenneth C — *Artist*
PO Box 125, South Salem, NY 10590, USA

Nolan, Martin F — *Editor*
%Boston Globe, Editorial Dept, 135 Morrissey Blvd, Boston, MA 02125, USA

Nolan, Ted — *Hockey Player, Coach*
269 Queen St E, Sault Sainte Marie ON P6A 1Y9, Canada

Nolan, Thomas B — *Geologist*
2219 California St NW, Washington, DC 20008, USA

Noland, Kenneth — *Artist*
RR 2, Box 125, Kitchawan Road, South Salem, NY 10590, USA

Nolin, Gena Lee — *Actress*
%William Morris Agency, 151 S El Camino Dr, Beverly Hills, CA 90212, USA

Noll, Charles H (Chuck) — *Football Coach*
201 Grant St, Sewickley, PA 15143, USA

Nolte, Claudia — *Government Official, Germany*
Mulgarten 28, 98693 Ilmenau, Germany

Nolte, Nick — *Actor*
6174 Bonsall Dr, Malibu, CA 90265, USA

Nolting, Paul F — *Religious Leader*
%Church of Lutheran Confession, 620 E 50th St, Loveland, CO 80538, USA

Nomellini, Leo — *Football Player*
520 St Claire Dr, Palo Alto, CA 94306, USA

Noonan, Patrick F — *Association Executive, Conservationist*
11901 Glen Mills Road, Potomac, MD 20854, USA

N

Noonan, Peggy *Writer*
%Random House Inc, 201 E 50th St, New York, NY 10022, USA

Noone, Peter *Singer, Actor*
9265 Robin Lane, Los Angeles, CA 90069, USA

Noor Al-Hussein *Queen, Jordan*
%Royal Palace, Amman, Jordan

Nordenstrom, Bjorn *Cancer Radiologist*
%Karolinska Institute, Radiology Dept, Stockholm, Sweden

Nordli, Odvar *Prime Minister, Norway*
Snarveien 4, 2312 Ottestad, Norway

Nordsieck, Kenneth H *Astronaut*
%University of Wisconsin, Space Astronomy Laboratory, Madison, WI 53706, USA

Noren, Irving A (Irv) *Baseball Player*
3154 Camino Crest Dr, Oceanside, CA 92056, USA

Norlander, John *Basketball Player*
511 12th St S, Virginia, MN 55792, USA

Norman, Greg *Golfer*
218 US Highway 1, #302, Tequesta, FL 33469, USA

Norman, Jessye *Concert Singer*
%Shaw Concerts, Lincoln Center Plaza, 1900 Broadway, #200, New York, NY 10023, USA

Norman, Ken *Basketball Player*
19020 Kelzie Ave, Homewood, IL 60430, USA

Norodom Sihanouk, Prince Samdech Preah *King, Cambodia*
%Khemarindra Palace, Phnom Penh, Cambodia

Norrington, Roger A C *Conductor*
%Byers Schwalbe Assoc, 1 5th Ave, New York, NY 10003, USA

Norris, Christopher *Actress*
12747 Riverside Dr, #208, Valley Village, CA 91607, USA

Norris, Chuck *Actor*
PO Box 872, Navasota, TX 77868, USA

Norris, Michael K (Mike) *Baseball Player*
1003 Imperial Dr, Hayward, CA 94541, USA

Norris, Michele *Commentator*
%ABC-TV, News Dept, 1717 De Sales St NW, Washington, DC 20036, USA

Norris, T C *Businessman*
%P H Glatfelter Co, 228 S Main St, Spring Grove, PA 17362, USA

Norris, Terry *Boxer*
1466 Ramsey Road, Alpine, CA 91901, USA

Norsworthy, Lamar *Businessman*
%Holly Corp, 100 Crescent Court, Dallas, TX 75201, USA

North, Andy *Golfer*
3289 High Point Road, Madison, WI 53719, USA

North, Douglass C *Nobel Economics Laureate*
7569 Homestead Road, Benzonia, MI 49616, USA

North, Jay *Actor*
290 NE 1st Ave, Lake Butler, FL 32054, USA

North, Oliver L *Government Official, Marine Officer*
RR 1, Box 560, Bluemont, VA 20135, USA

North, Sheree *Actress*
1467 Palisades Dr, Pacific Palisades, CA 90272, USA

Northam, Jeremy *Actor*
%International Creative Mgmt, 8942 Wilshire Blvd, Beverly Hills, CA 90211, USA

Northrip, Richard A *Labor Leader*
%Cement & Allied Workers Union, 2500 Brickdale, Elk Grove Village, IL 60007, USA

Northrop, Wayne *Actor*
21919 W Canon Dr, Topanga, CA 90290, USA

Northway, Douglas (Doug) *Swimmer*
5751 N Kolb Road, #12101, Tucson, AZ 85750, USA

Norton, Edward *Actor*
%International Creative Mgmt, 8942 Wilshire Blvd, Beverly Hills, CA 90211, USA

Norton, Gerard Ross (Toys) *WW II Rhodesian Army Hero (VC)*
Box 112, PO Banket, Zimbabwe

Norton, James J *Labor Leader*
%Graphic Communications International, 1900 "L" St NW, Washington, DC 20036, USA

Norton, Ken *Boxer, Actor*
16 S Peck Dr, Laguna Niguel, CA 92677, USA

Norton, Ken, Jr *Football Player*
%San Francisco 49ers, 4949 Centennial Blvd, Santa Clara, CA 95054, USA

Norton, Peter — *Computer Software Designer*
225 Arizona Ave, #200-W, Santa Monica, CA 90401, USA

Norville, Deborah — *Commentator*
PO Box 426, Mill Neck, NY 11765, USA

Norvo, Kenneth N (Red) — *Jazz Vibraphonist*
420 Alta Ave, Santa Monica, CA 90402, USA

Norwood, Scott — *Football Player*
14519 Creek Branch Court, Centreville, VA 20120, USA

Nosseck, Noel — *Movie Director*
24124 Malibu Road, Malibu, CA 90265, USA

Notebaert, Richard C — *Businessman*
%Ameritech, 30 S Wacker Dr, Chicago, IL 60606, USA

Noth, Christopher — *Actor*
45 E 9th St, #35, Rancho Santa Margarita, CA 92688, USA

Notkins, Abner L — *Virologist*
%National Institute of Dental Research, 9000 Rockville Pike, Bethesda, MD 20892, USA

Noto, Lore — *Theater Producer, Actor*
%Sullivan Street Playhouse, 181 Sullivan St, New York, NY 10012, USA

Noto, Lucio A — *Businessman*
%Mobil Corp, 3225 Gallows Road, Fairfax, VA 22037, USA

Nott, John W F — *Government Official, England*
%Hillsdown Holdings PLC, 32 Hampstead High St, London NW3 1QD, England

Nottebohm, Andreas — *Artist*
%Weinstein Gallery, 383 Geary St, San Francisco, CA 94102, USA

Nottingham, R Kendall — *Businessman*
%American Life Insurance, 1 Alico Plaza, 600 King St, Wilmington, DE 19801, USA

Nouhak Phoumsavanh — *President, Laos*
%President's Office, Presidential House, Vientiane, Laos

Nouri, Michael — *Actor*
14 W 68th St, #12, New York, NY 10023, USA

Novacek, Jay M — *Football Player*
Rt 1, Box 611-Z, Sanger, TX 76266, USA

Novak Popper, Ilona — *Swimmer*
Il-Orso-Utca 23, Budapest, Hungary

Novak, John R — *Inventor (Air Cleaning Radiator)*
%Engelhard Corp, Automotive Emissions Systems, 101 Wood Ave, Iselin, NJ 08830, USA

Novak, Kim — *Actress*
PO Box 339, Chiloquin, OR 97624, USA

Novak, Michael — *Theologian*
%American Enterprise Institute, 1150 17th St NW, Washington, DC 20036, USA

Novak, Robert D S — *Columnist*
1750 Pennsylvania Ave NW, #1312, Washington, DC 20006, USA

Novello (Fr Guido Sarducci), Don — *Comedian*
%Vesuvio Olive Oil Co, PO Box 245, Fairfax, CA 94978, USA

Novello, Antonia C — *Medical Administrator*
1315 31st St NW, Washington, DC 20007, USA

Novosel, Michael J — *Vietnam War Army Hero (CMH)*
202 Oakwood Dr, Enterprise, AL 36330, USA

Novotna, Jana — *Tennis Player*
%Women's Tennis Assn, 133 1st St NE, St Petersburg, FL 33701, USA

Noyce, Phillip — *Movie Director*
%International Creative Mgmt, 8942 Wilshire Blvd, Beverly Hills, CA 90211, USA

Noyd, R Allen — *Religious Leader*
%General Council, Christian Church, 1294 Rutledge Road, Transfer, PA 16154, USA

Noyes, Albert, Jr — *Chemist*
5102 Fairview Dr, Austin, TX 78731, USA

Noyes, Richard M — *Chemist*
2014 Elk Ave, Eugene, OR 97403, USA

Noyo Sanchez, Aristides — *President, Panama*
%Morgan & Morgan, PO Box 1824, Panama City, Panama

Nozawa, Hiroo — *Financier*
%Bank of California, 400 California St, San Francisco, CA 94104, USA

Nsengiyremeye, Dismas — *Prime Minister, Rwanda*
%Prime Minister's Office, Kigali, Rwanda

Ntombi — *Queen, Swaziland*
%Royal Residence, PO Box 1, Lobamba, Swaziland

Nucatola, John P — *Basketball Referee*
21 Hawthorne Dr, Clark, NJ 07066, USA

Nucci, Danny *Actor*
%Gold Marshak Liedtke, 3500 W Olive Ave, #1400, Burbank, CA 91505, USA

Nucci, Leo *Opera Singer*
%Herbert Breslin, 119 W 57th St, New York, NY 10019, USA

Nugent, Nelle *Theater Producer*
%Foxboro Entertainment, 133 E 58th St, #301, New York, NY 10022, USA

Nugent, Ted *Singer, Guitarist*
%Madhouse Mgmt, PO Box 15108, Ann Arbor, MI 48106, USA

Nujoma, Sam S *President, Namibia*
%President's Office, State House, Mugabe Ave, 9000 Windhoek, Namibia

Numan, Gary *Singer, Songwriter*
%Beggars, 8 Hogarth Rd, London SW5, England

Nunez, Miguel Angel, Jr *Actor*
%Gold Marshak Liedtke, 3500 W Olive Ave, #1400, Burbank, CA 91505, USA

Nunley, Frank *Football Player*
24632 Olive Tree Lane, Los Altos Hills, CA 94024, USA

Nunn, Louie B *Governor, KY*
RR 3, Park, KY 42749, USA

Nunn, Michael *Boxer*
1202 N Stark St, Davenport, IA 52804, USA

Nunn, Trevor R *Theater Director*
%Royal Shakespeare Theater, Stratford-upon-Avon, Warwickshire, England

Nurmi (Vampira), Maila *Actress*
844 1/2 N Hudson, Los Angeles, CA 90038, USA

Nussbaum, Karen *Labor Activist*
%9 to 5 National Assn of Working Women, 614 Superior Ave, Cleveland, OH 44113, USA

Nusslein-Volhard, Christiane *Nobel Medicine Laureate*
%Max Planck Biology Institute, Spenmannstr 35/III, 72076 Tubingen, Germany

Nutt, Jim *Artist*
1035 Greenwood Ave, Wilmette, IL 60091, USA

Nutting, H Anthony *Government Official, England*
7 Ashchurch Park Villas, London W12 9SP, England

Nutting, Wallace H *Army General*
PO Box 96, Biddeford Pool, ME 04006, USA

Nutzle, Futzie *Artist, Cartoonist*
PO Box 325, Aromas, CA 95004, USA

Nuwer, Hank *Writer, Journalist*
18 Bostwick Lane, Richmond, VA 23226, USA

Nuxhall, Joseph H (Joe) *Baseball Player*
5706 Lindenwood Lane, Fairfield, OH 45014, USA

Nuyen, France *Actress*
1800 Franklin Canyon Terrace, Beverly Hills, CA 90210, USA

Nyad, Diana *Swimmer, Sportscaster*
%Uptown Racquet Club, 151 E 86th St, New York, NY 10028, USA

Nyberg, Frederik *Skier*
Kaptensgatan 2-C, 832 00 Froson, Sweden

Nye, Carrie *Actress*
200 W 57th St, #900, New York, NY 10019, USA

Nye, Eric *Businessman*
%Texas Utilities Co, 1601 Bryan St, Dallas, TX 75201, USA

Nye, Louis *Actor*
1241 Corsica Dr, Pacific Palisades, CA 90272, USA

Nye, Robert *Writer*
2 Westbury Crescent, Wilton, Cork, Ireland

Nyerere, Julius K *President, Tanzania*
%Sokiene University, PO Box 3000, Chuo Kikuu, Morogoro, Tanzania

Nyers, Rezso *Secretary General, Hungary*
%Representatives House, Szechenyi Rakpart 19, 1054 Budapest, Hungary

Nygren, Carrie *Model*
%Elite Model Mgmt, 111 E 22nd St, #200, New York, NY 10010, USA

Nykvist, Sven *Cinematographer*
%Dove Films, 6387 Ivarene Ave, Los Angeles, CA 90068, USA

Nyman, Michael *Composer, Pianist*
%Michael Nyman Ltd, PO Box 430, High Wycombe HP13 5QT, England

Nystrom, Joakim *Tennis Player*
Torsgatan 194, 931 00 Skellefteaa, Sweden

O'Bannon, Ed — Basketball Player
19723 Normandale Ave, Cerritos, CA 90703, USA

O'Bannon, Frank — Governor, IN
%Governor's Office, State House, #206, Indianapolis, IN 46204, USA

O'Boyle, Maureen — Entertainer
%"In Person" Show, CBS-TV, 51 W 52nd St, New York, NY 10019, USA

O'Brasky, David — Publisher
%Vanity Fair Magazine, 350 Madison Ave, New York, NY 10017, USA

O'Brian, Hugh — Actor
%Hugh O'Brian Youth Foundation, 10880 Wilshire Blvd, #900, Los Angeles, CA 90024, USA

O'Brian, Patrick — Writer
%W W Norton Co, 500 5th Ave, New York, NY 10110, USA

O'Brien, Brian — Physicist
PO Box 166, North Hollywood, CT 06281, USA

O'Brien, Cathy — Track Athlete
19 Foss Farm Road, Durham, NH 03824, USA

O'Brien, Conan — Entertainer
125 N Wetherly Dr, Los Angeles, CA 90048, USA

O'Brien, Conor Cruise — Writer; Diplomat, Ireland
Whitewater, The Summit, Howth, Dublin, Ireland

O'Brien, Dan — Track Athlete
PO Box 9244, Moscow, ID 83843, USA

O'Brien, Edna — Writer
%Weidenfeld & Nicolson, Orion House, 5 Upper St, London WC2H 9EA, England

O'Brien, George H, Jr — Korean War Marine Corps Hero (CMH)
2001 Douglas St, Midland, TX 79701, USA

O'Brien, Gregory M — Educator
%University of New Orleans, Chancellor's Office, New Orleans, LA 70148, USA

O'Brien, Ken — Football Player
1401 45th St, Sacramento, CA 95819, USA

O'Brien, M Vincent — Thoroughbred Racing Trainer
Ballydoyle House, Cashel, County Tipperary, Ireland

O'Brien, Margaret — Actress
1250 La Peresa Dr, Thousand Oaks, CA 91362, USA

O'Brien, Parry — Track Athlete
73285 Goldflower St, Palm Desert, CA 92260, USA

O'Brien, Pat — Sportscaster
%CBS-TV, Sports Dept, 51 W 52nd St, New York, NY 10019, USA

O'Brien, Raymond F — Businessman
%Consolidated Freightways, 3240 Hillview Ave, Palo Alto, CA 94304, USA

O'Brien, Richard — Composer, Lyricist
%Jonathan Altaras, 27 Floral St, London WC2E 9DP, England

O'Brien, Ron — Diving Coach
%Swimming Hall of Fame, 1 Hall of Fame Dr, Fort Lauderdale, FL 33316, USA

O'Brien, Thomas H — Financier
%PNC Bank Corp, 5th Ave & Wood St, Pittsburgh, PA 15222, USA

O'Brien, Thomas M — Financier
%North Side Savings Bank, 185 W 231st St, Bronx, NY 10463, USA

O'Brien, Tim — Writer
17 Partride Lane, Boxford, MA 01921, USA

O'Brien, Virginia — Actress
PO Box 456, Wrightwood, CA 92397, USA

O'Byrne, Bryan — Actor
9200 Sunset Blvd, #801, Los Angeles, CA 90069, USA

O'Callaghan, John (Jack) — Hockey Player
226 Kenmore Ave, Elmhurst, IL 60126, USA

O'Callaghan, Mike — Governor, NV
%Las Vegas Sun, 800 S Valley View Blvd, Las Vegas, NV 89107, USA

O'Connell, Maura — Singer
%Monterey Artists, 901 18th Ave S, Nashville, TN 37212, USA

O'Connor, Bryan D — Astronaut
%NASA, Johnson Space Center, 2101 NASA Road, Houston, TX 77058, USA

O'Connor, Carroll — Actor
30826 Broad Beach Road, Malibu, CA 90265, USA

O'Connor, Donald — Actor, Dancer
PO Box 20204, Sedona, AZ 86341, USA

O'Connor, Glynnis — Actress
%Bill Treusch, 853 7th Ave, #9-A, New York, NY 10019, USA

O

O'Bannon - O'Connor

O

O'Connor, John J Cardinal — *Religious Leader*
%Archdiocese of New York, 452 Madison Ave, New York, NY 10022, USA

O'Connor, Mark — *Fiddle Player*
%CM Mgmt, 7957 Nita Ave, West Hills, CA 91304, USA

O'Connor, Martin J — *Religious Leader*
Palazzo San Carlo, 00120 Vatican City

O'Connor, Patrick D (Pat) — *Movie Director*
Sutton, Surrey SM2 5TD, England

O'Connor, Sandra Day — *Supreme Court Justice*
%US Supreme Court, 1 1st St NE, Washington, DC 20543, USA

O'Connor, Sinead — *Singer, Songwriter*
35 Harwood Road, Fulham, London W1V 3AT, England

O'Connor, Thom — *Artist*
Moss Road, Voorheesville, NY 12186, USA

O'Connor, Tim — *Actor*
%House of Representatives, 400 S Beverly Dr, #101, Beverly Hills, CA 90212, USA

O'Connor, Timothy J — *Actor*
%Artists Agency, 10000 Santa Monica Blvd, #305, Los Angeles, CA 90067, USA

O'Day, Alan — *Singer, Songwriter*
%Talent Consultants Int'l, 1560 Broadway, #1308, New York, NY 10036, USA

O'Day, Anita — *Singer*
%Alan Eichler, 1862 Vista Del Mar St, Los Angeles, CA 90028, USA

O'Day, George — *Yachtsman*
6 Turtle Lane, Dover, MA 02030, USA

O'Donnell, Annie — *Actress*
%Media Artists Group, 8383 Wilshire Blvd, #954, Beverly Hills, CA 90211, USA

O'Donnell, Chris — *Actor*
1724 N Vista St, Los Angeles, CA 90046, USA

O'Donnell, John J — *Labor Leader*
%Air Line Pilots Assn, 1625 Massachusetts Ave NW, Washington, DC 20036, USA

O'Donnell, Neil — *Football Player*
711 Duncan Ave, #720, Pittsburgh, PA 15237, USA

O'Donnell, Rosie — *Actress*
%Bernie Young Agency, 9800 Topanga Canyon Blvd, #D, Chatsworth, CA 91311, USA

O'Donnell, William (Bill) — *Harness Racing Driver*
7354 Forest Haven Estate, St Louis, MO 63123, USA

O'Donnell, William T — *Labor Leader*
%United Garment Workers, PO Box 239, Hermitage, TN 37076, USA

O'Donovan, Leo J — *Educator*
%Georgetown University, President's Office, Washington, DC 20057, USA

O'Driscoll, Martha — *Actress*
22 Indian Circle Dr, Indian Creek Village, Miami Beach, FL 33154, USA

O'Grady, Gail — *Actress*
%William Morris Agency, 151 S El Camino Dr, Beverly Hills, CA 90212, USA

O'Grady, Lani — *Actress*
%First Artists, 10000 Riverside Dr, #10, Toluca Lake, CA 91602, USA

O'Grady, Mac — *Golfer*
%Professional Golfer's Assn, PO Box 109601, Palm Beach Gardens, FL 33410, USA

O'Grady, Scott — *Air Force Hero*
State Office Building, #1160, Salt Lake City, UT 84114, USA

O'Grady, Sean — *Boxer*
PO Box 770455, Oklahoma City, OK 73177, USA

O'Hara, Jenny — *Actress*
8663 Wonderland Ave, Los Angeles, CA 90046, USA

O'Hara, Maureen — *Actress*
PO Box 1400, Christeansted, St Croix, VI 00851, USA

O'Hara, Terrence J — *Movie Director*
%Armstrong/Hirsch, 1888 Century Park East, #1800, Los Angeles, CA 90067, USA

O'Hare, Dean R — *Businessman*
%Chubb Corp, 15 Mountain View Road, Warren, NJ 07059, USA

O'Hare, Don R — *Businessman*
%Sundstrand Corp, 4949 Harrison Ave, Rockford, IL 61108, USA

O'Hare, Joseph A — *Educator*
%Fordham University, President's Office, Bronx, NY 10458, USA

O'Hare, Michael — *Actor*
%Onoroto/Guillod, 4444 Lankershim Blvd, #203, North Hollywood, CA 91602, USA

O'Herlihy, Daniel — *Actor*
%International Artists, 235 Regent St, London W1R 8AX, England

O'Horgan, Thomas F (Tom) *Composer, Director*
%Carl Goldstein, 9951 Seacrest Circle, #201, Boynton Beach, FL 33437, USA

O'Hurley, John *Actor*
%Metropolitan Talent Agency, 4526 Wilshire Blvd, Los Angeles, CA 90010, USA

O'Keefe, Michael *Actor*
PO Box 216, Malibu, CA 90265, USA

O'Keefe, Miles *Actor*
%Paige Management Group, PO Box 2132, Malibu, CA 90265, USA

O'Koren, Mike *Basketball Player*
%New Jersey Nets, Byrne Meadowlands Arena, East Rutherford, NJ 07073, USA

O'Leary, Brian T *Astronaut*
1993 S Kihei Road, #21200, Kihei, HI 96753, USA

O'Leary, Hazel R *Secretary, Energy*
%Energy Department, 1000 Independence Ave SW, Washington, DC 20585, USA

O'Leary, John *Actor*
%Gage Group, 9255 Sunset Blvd, #515, Los Angeles, CA 90069, USA

O'Leary, Thomas H *Businessman*
%Burlington Resources, PO Box 4239, Houston, TX 77210, USA

O'Leary, William *Actor*
%House of Representatives, 400 S Beverly Dr, #101, Beverly Hills, CA 90212, USA

O'Loughlin, Gerald S *Actor*
PO Box 340832, Arleta, CA 91334, USA

O'Maley, David B *Businessman*
%Ohio National Life Insurance, 1 Financial Way, Cincinnati, OH 45242, USA

O'Malley, Peter *Baseball Executive*
%Los Angeles Dodgers, 1000 Elysian Park Ave, Los Angeles, CA 90012, USA

O'Malley, Robert E *Vietnam War Marine Corps Hero (CMH)*
PO Box 775, Goldthwaite, TX 76844, USA

O'Malley, Susan *Basketball Executive*
%Washington Wizards, Capital Centre, 1 Truman Dr, Landover, MD 20785, USA

O'Malley, Thomas D *Businessman*
%Tosco Inc, 72 Cummings Point Road, Stamford, CT 06902, USA

O'Malley, Thomas P *Educator*
%Loyola Marymount University, President's Office, Los Angeles, CA 90045, USA

O'Mara, Donald J *Businessman*
%Hexcel Corp, PO Box 8181, Pleasanton, CA 94588, USA

O'Mara, Kate *Actress*
%Michael Ladkin, 11 Southwick Mews, London W2 1JG, England

O'Mara, Mark *Harness Racing Driver, Trainer*
6882 NW 65th Terrace, Pompano Beach, FL 33067, USA

O'Meara, Mark *Golfer*
6312 Deacon Circle, Windemere, FL 34786, USA

O'Neal, A Daniel, Jr *Government Official*
1613 Forest Lane, McLean, VA 22101, USA

O'Neal, Bob H *Businessman*
%Stewart & Stevenson, 2707 North Loop W, Houston, TX 77008, USA

O'Neal, Griffin *Actor*
14209 Riverside Dr, Van Nuys, CA 91423, USA

O'Neal, Jermaine *Basketball Player*
%Portland Trail Blazers, 1 N Center Court, #200, Portland, OR 97227, USA

O'Neal, Leslie *Football Player*
5617 Adobe Falls Road, #A, San Diego, CA 92120, USA

O'Neal, Ryan *Actor*
21368 Pacific Coast Highway, Malibu, CA 90265, USA

O'Neal, Shaquille R *Basketball Player*
3110 Main St, #225, Santa Monica, CA 90405, USA

O'Neal, Tatum *Actress*
300 Central Park West, #16-G, New York, NY 10024, USA

O'Neil, Alexander *Singer, Songwriter*
%Richard Walters, 421 S Beverly Dr, #800, Beverly Hills, CA 90212, USA

O'Neil, F J *Actor*
12228 Cantura St, Studio City, CA 91604, USA

O'Neil, John B (Buck) *Baseball Player, Coach*
3049 E 32nd St, Kansas City, MO 64128, USA

O'Neil, Thomas F *Businessman*
%General Tire & Rubber Co, 1 General St, Akron, OH 44329, USA

O'Neil, Tricia *Actress*
%David Shapira, 15301 Ventura Blvd, #345, Sherman Oaks, CA 91403, USA

O'Horgan - O'Neil

O'Neill, Brion *Hockey Executive*
%Hockey Hall of Fame, BCE Place, 30 Yonge St, Toronto ON M5E 1X8, Canada

O'Neill, Dick *Actor*
443 S Oakhurst Dr, PH-401, Beverly Hills, CA 90212, USA

O'Neill, Ed *Actor*
2607 Grand Canal, Venice, CA 90291, USA

O'Neill, Eugene F *Communications Engineer*
17 Dellwood Court, Middletown, NJ 07748, USA

O'Neill, Gail *Model*
%Click Model Mgmt, 881 7th Ave, New York, NY 10019, USA

O'Neill, Jennifer *Actress, Model*
%Oscar Productions, 32356 Mulholland Highway, Malibu, CA 90265, USA

O'Neill, Michael J *Editor*
23 Cayuga Road, Scarsdale, NY 10583, USA

O'Neill, Paul A *Baseball Player*
7785 Hartford Hill Lane, Cincinnati, OH 45242, USA

O'Neill, Paul H *Businessman, Baseball Executive*
%Aluminum Co of America, 1501 Alcoa Building, Pittsburgh, PA 15219, USA

O'Neill, Shane *Television Executive*
%RKO General, 175 Ghent Road, Fairlawn, OH 44333, USA

O'Neill, Terence P (Terry) *Photographer*
8 Warwick Ave, London W2 1XB, England

O'Neill, William A *Governor, CT*
Meeks Point, East Hampton, CT 06424, USA

O'Quinn, John M *Attorney*
%O'Quinn Kerensky McAnich, 2300 Lyric Center, 440 Louisiana, Houston, TX 77002, USA

O'Quinn, Terry *Actor*
%Innovative Artists, 1999 Ave of Stars, #2850, Los Angeles, CA 90067, USA

O'Ree, Willie *Hockey Player*
7961 Anders Circle, La Mesa, CA 91942, USA

O'Reilly, Anthony J F *Businessman, Publisher*
%H J Heinz Co, 600 Grant St, Pittsburgh, PA 15219, USA

O'Reilly, Cyril *Actor*
%Stone Manners, 8091 Selma Ave, Los Angeles, CA 90046, USA

O'Reilly, Harry *Actor*
%Ambrosio/Mortimer, 9150 Wilshire Blvd, #175, Beverly Hills, CA 90212, USA

O'Reilly, Terry *Hockey Player, Coach*
1 Cherry Lane, Georgetown, MA 01833, USA

O'Rourke, Charles C *Football Player*
220 Bedford St, #A-7, Bridgewater, MA 02324, USA

O'Rourke, J Tracy *Businessman*
%Varian Assoc, 3050 Hansen Way, Palo Alto, CA 94304, USA

O'Shea, Kevin *Basketball Player*
87 Aquauista Way, San Francisco, CA 94131, USA

O'Shea, Milo *Actor*
%Bancroft Hotel, 40 W 72nd St, #17-A, New York, NY 10023, USA

O'Sullivan, Gilbert *Singer*
%Laurie Jay, 32 Willesden Land, London NW6 7ST, England

O'Sullivan, Maureen *Actress*
1839 Union St, Schenectady, NY 12309, USA

O'Sullivan, Peter *Editor*
%Houston Post, Editorial Dept, 4747 Southwest Freeway, Houston, TX 77027, USA

O'Sullivan, Richard *Actor*
%Al Mitchell, 5 Anglers Lane, Kentish Town, London NW5 3DG, England

O'Toole, Annette *Actress*
360 Morton St, Ashland, OR 97520, USA

O'Toole, Peter *Actor*
%Veerline Ltd, 8 Baker St, London W1A 1DA, England

Oakley, Charles *Basketball Player*
%New York Knicks, Madison Square Garden, 2 Penn Plaza, New York, NY 10121, USA

Oaks, Robert C (Bob) *Air Force General, Businessman*
%USAir Group Inc, 2345 Crystal Dr, Arlington, VA 22202, USA

Oates, Adam R *Hockey Player*
1480 S County Road, Osterville, MA 02655, USA

Oates, John *Singer (Hall & Oates), Songwriter*
%Creative Artists Agency, 9830 Wilshire Blvd, Beverly Hills, CA 90212, USA

Oates, Johnny L *Baseball Player, Manager*
20222 Eagle Cove Court, Petersburg, VA 23803, USA

Oates, Joyce Carol — *Writer*
%Princeton University, English Dept, Princeton, NJ 08540, USA

Oates, Simon — *Actor*
%International Artistes, 235 Regent St, London W1R 8AX, England

Obame-Nguema, Paulin — *Prime Minister, Gabon*
%Prime Minister's Office, Boite Postale 546, Libreville, Gabon

Obando Bravo, Miguel Cardinal — *Religious Leader*
Arzobispado, Apartado 3050, Managua, Nicaragua

Obasanjo, Olusegun — *President, Nigeria; Army General*
%Obasanjo Farms Nigeria, PO Box 90, Otta, Ogun State, Nigeria

Obato, Gyo — *Architect*
%Hellmuth Obato Kassabaum, 211 N Broadway, #600, St Louis, MO 63102, USA

Oberding, Mark — *Basketball Player*
4 Inwood Autumn, San Antonio, TX 78248, USA

Oberg, Margo — *Surfer*
RR1, Box 73, Koloa, Kaui HI 96756, USA

Oberlin, David W — *Government Official*
800 Independence Ave SW, #814, Washington, DC 20591, USA

Obermeyer, Klaus F — *Fashion Designer*
%Sport Obermeyer, 115 Atlantic Ave, Aspen, CO 81611, USA

Obote, A Milton — *President, Uganda*
%Uganda People's Congress, PO Box 1951, Kampala, Uganda

Obraztsova, Elena V — *Opera Singer*
%Bolshoi Theater, Teatralnaya Pl 1, 103009 Moscow, Russia

Ocasek, Ric — *Singer (The Cars)*
%Rascoff/Zysblat, 110 W 57th St, #300, New York, NY 10019, USA

Ocean, Billy — *Singer, Songwriter*
%Arista Records, 6 W 57th St, New York, NY 10019, USA

Ochirbat, Punsalmaagiyn — *President, Mongolia*
%Presidential Palace, Ulan Bator, Mongolia

Ochman, Wieslaw — *Opera Singer*
Ul Miaczynska 46-B, 02-637 Warsaw, Poland

Ochoa, Ellen — *Astronaut*
%NASA, Johnson Space Center, 2101 NASA Road, Houston, TX 77058, USA

Ockels, Wubbo — *Astronaut, Netherlands*
%ESTEC, Postbus 299, 2200 AG Noordwijk, Netherlands

Oddi, Silvio Cardinal — *Religious Leader*
Via Pompeo Magno 21, 00192 Rome, Italy

Oddsson, David — *Prime Minister, Iceland*
%Prime Minister's Office, Stjo'rnaaroshusio, 150 Reykjavik, Iceland

Odell, Bob — *Football Player, Coach*
35 Beth Ellen Dr, Lewisburg, PA 17837, USA

Odell, Noel E — *Geological Researcher, Mountaineer*
5 Dean Court, Cambridge, England

Odermatt, Robert A — *Architect*
140 Camino Don Miguel, Orinda, CA 94563, USA

Odessa, Devon — *Actress*
%Writers & Artists, 924 Westwood Blvd, #900, Los Angeles, CA 90024, USA

Odetta (Gordon) — *Singer*
200 E 90th St, #3-G, New York, NY 10128, USA

Odjig, Daphne — *Artist*
PO Box 111, Anglemont BC V0E 1A0, Canada

Odomes, Nate — *Football Player*
900 Quail Creek, Columbus, GA 31907, USA

Oduber, Nelson O — *Prime Minister, Aruba*
%Prime Minister's Office, Oranjestad, Aruba

Odum, Eugene P — *Ecologist*
30602 Beech Creek Road, Athens, GA 30606, USA

Oe, Kenzaburo — *Nobel Literature Laureate*
585 Seijo-Machi, Setagayaku, Tokyo, Japan

Oenish, Dean — *Physician*
%Preventive Medical Research Institute, 900 Bridgeway, #2, Sausalito, CA 94965, USA

Oerter, Alfred A (Al) — *Track Athlete*
19435 Doewood Dr, Monument, CO 80132, USA

Offerdahl, John — *Football Player*
3016 Birkdale St, Fort Lauderdale, FL 33332, USA

Offerman, Jose A — *Baseball Player*
Ed 81, Urb Anscaono Moscoso, San Pedro de Marcos, Dominican Republic

O

Oates - Offerman

Ogato, Sadako *Government Official, Japan*
%United Nations Office for Refugees, CP 2500, 1211 Geneva 2, Switzerland

Ogden, Carlos C *WW II Army Hero (CMH)*
8786 Grape Wagon Circle, San Jose, CA 95135, USA

Ogden, Jonathan *Football Player*
%Baltimore Ravens, 200 St Paul Place, #2400, Baltimore, MD 21202, USA

Ogden, Ralph L *Businessman*
%Liberty Life Insurance, PO Box 789, Greenville, SC 29602, USA

Ogi, Adolf *President, Switzerland*
Bundesjause-Nord, Kochergasse 10, 3003 Berne, Switzerland

Ogilvie, Lana *Model*
%Company Models, 270 Lafayette St, #1400, New York, NY 10012, USA

Ogilvy, David M *Businessman*
Chateau de Touffou, 86300 Bonnes, France

Ogilvy, Ian *Actor*
%Michael Whitehall, 125 Gloucester Road, London SW7 4TE, England

Oglivie, Benjamin A (Ben) *Baseball Player*
2019 E Myrna Lane, Tempe, AZ 85284, USA

Ogrodnick, John *Hockey Player*
35774 Fredericksburg, Framington Hills, MI 48331, USA

Oh, Sadaharu *Baseball Player*
%Yomiuri Giants, 1-7-1 Otemachi, Chiyodaku, Tokyo 100, Japan

Oh, Soon-Teck *Actor*
%Artists Group, 10100 Santa Monica Blvd, #2490, Los Angeles, CA 90067, USA

Ohara, Sakae *Businessman*
%Daihatsu Motor Co, 1-1 Daihatsucho, Ikeda City 563, Japan

Ohga, Norio *Businessman*
%Sony Corp, 6-7-35 Kitashinagawa, Shingawaku, Tokyo 141, Japan

Ohlmeyer, Donald W (Don), Jr *Television Executive*
%NBC-TV, 3000 W Alameda Ave, Burbank, CA 91523, USA

Ohlsson, Garrick *Concert Pianist*
%Vincent Ryan, 135 W 16th St, New York, NY 10011, USA

Ohman, Jack *Editorial Cartoonist (Mixed Media)*
%Portland Oregonian, Editorial Dept, 1320 SW Broadway, Portland, OR 97201, USA

Ohnishi, Minoru *Businessman*
%Fuji Photo Film, 26-30 Nishiazabu, Minatoku, Tokyo 106, Japan

Ohno, Susumu *Geneticist*
7329 Oak Dr, Glendora, CA 91741, USA

Ohtani, Ichiji *Businessman*
%Toyobo Co, 2-2-8 Dojimahama, Kitaku, Osaka 530, Japan

Ohtani, Monshu Koshin *Religious Leader*
Horikawa-Dori, Hanayachosagaru, Shimogyoku, Kyoto 600, Japan

Ohyama, Heiichiro *Conductor*
6305 Via Cabrera, La Jolla, CA 92037, USA

Oimeon, Casper *Skier*
540 S Mountain Ave, Ashland, OR 97520, USA

Oistrakh, Igor *Concert Violinist*
Novolesnaya Str 3, Korp 2, #10, Moscow, Russia

Oiter, Bailey *President, Micronesia*
%President's Office, Palikia, Pohnepei FM, 96941 Kolonia, Micronesia

Ojukwu, Chukwuemeka O *President, Biafra; Army General*
75 Marine Road, Apapa, Lagos, Nigeria

Okamoto, Ayako *Golfer*
22627 Ladeene Ave, Torrance, CA 90505, USA

Okamoto, Toshiro *Businessman*
%Isuzu Motors, 6-22-10 Minamioi, Shinagawaku, Tokyo 140, Japan

Okamura, Arthur *Artist*
210 Kale St, Bolinas, CA 94924, USA

Okhotnikoff, Nikolai P *Opera Singer*
Canal Griboedova 109, 190068 St Petersburg, Russia

Okubo, Susumu *Physicist*
1209 East Ave, Rochester, NY 14607, USA

Okuda, Hiroshi *Businessman*
%Toyota Motor, 1 Toyotacho, Toyota City, Aicji Prefecture 471, Japan

Olafsson, Olafur J *Publisher*
%Sony Electronics Publishing USA, 9 W 57th St, New York, NY 10019, USA

Olah, George A *Nobel Chemistry Laureate*
2252 Gloaming Way, Beverly Hills, CA 90210, USA

Olajuwon, Hakeem A *Basketball Player*
%Houston Rockets, Summit, Greenway Plaza, #10, Houston, TX 77046, USA
Olandt, Ken *Actor*
%Gold Marshak Liedtke, 3500 W Olive Ave, #1400, Burbank, CA 91505, USA
Olazabel, Jose Maria *Golfer*
%Sergio Gomez, Apartado 26, 20080 San Sebastian, Spain
Olbermann, Keith *Sportscaster*
%MSNBC-TV, News Dept, 30 Rockefeller Plaza, New York, NY 10112, USA
Old, Lloyd J *Cancer Biologist*
%Ludwig Institute of Cancer Research, 1345 Ave of Americas, New York, NY 10105, USA
Oldenburg, Claes T *Sculptor*
556 Broome St, New York, NY 10013, USA
Oldenburg, Richard E *Museum Director*
%Museum of Modern Art, 11 W 53rd St, New York, NY 10019, USA
Oldendorf, William *Physician*
%University of California, Medical Center, Neurology Dept, Los Angeles, CA 90024, USA
Olderman, Murray *Sportswriter*
832 Inverness Dr, Rancho Mirage, CA 92270, USA
Oldfield, Bruce *Fashion Designer*
27 Beauchamp Place, London SW3, England
Oldfield, Mike *Singer, Songwriter*
%Management Works, Singes House, 32 Galena Road, London W6 OLT, England
Oldfield, Sally *Singer*
100 Chalk Farm Road, London NW1, England
Oldham, Todd *Fashion Designer*
499 7th Ave, #800, New York, NY 10018, USA
Oldman, Gary *Actor, Director*
%Pinewood Studios, Iverheath, Bucks SL0 0NH, England
Olds, Robin *WW II Air Force Hero, Football Player*
PO Box 1478, Steamboat Springs, CO 80477, USA
Oleksy, Jozef *Prime Minister, Poland*
%UI Ursad Rady Ministrow, Ul Wiejska 4/8, 00-583 Warsaw, Poland
Olerud, John G *Baseball Player*
1310 180th Ave NE, Bellevue, WA 98008, USA
Olevsky, Julian *Concert Violinist*
68 Blue Hills Road, Amherst, MA 01002, USA
Oliansky, Joel *Movie Director, Writer*
%Creative Artists Agency, 9830 Wilshire Blvd, Beverly Hills, CA 90212, USA
Olin, Ken *Actor*
522 Arbamar Place, Pacific Palisades, CA 90272, USA
Olin, Lena *Actress*
Strindbergsgatan 49, 115 31 Stockholm, Sweden
Oliphant, Patrick B *Editorial Cartoonist*
%Universal Press Syndicate, 4520 Main St, Kansas City, KS 64111, USA
Olitski, Jules *Artist*
PO Box 440, Marlboro, VT 05344, USA
Oliva, L Jay *Educator*
%New York University, President's Office, New York, NY 10012, USA
Oliva, Pedro (Tony) *Baseball Player*
212 Spring Valley Dr, Minneapolis, MN 55420, USA
Oliva, Sergio *Body Builder*
%Oliva's Gym, 7383 Rogers Ave, Chicago, IL 60626, USA
Olivares, Ruben *Boxer*
%Geno Productions, PO Box 113, Montebello, CA 90640, USA
Oliveira, Elmar *Concert Violinist*
%Shaw Concerts, Lincoln Center Plaza, 1900 Broadway, #200, New York, NY 10023, USA
Oliveira, Nathan *Artist*
785 Santa Maria Ave, Palo Alto, CA 94305, USA
Oliver *Singer*
PO Box 53664, Indianapolis, IN 46253, USA
Oliver, Albert (Al) *Baseball Player*
PO Box 1466, Portsmouth, OH 45662, USA
Oliver, Christian *Actor*
%Michael Slessinger, 8730 Sunset Blvd, #220-W, Los Angeles, CA 90069, USA
Oliver, Covey T *Attorney, Diplomat*
Ingleton-on-Miles, RFD 1, Box 194, Easton, MD 21601, USA
Oliver, Daniel *Government Official*
%Heritage Foundation, 214 Massachusetts Ave NW, Washington, DC 20002, USA

O

O

Oliver, Daniel T	*Navy Admiral*

Deputy CNO Manpower/Personnel, HqUSN, Pentagon, Washinhgton, DC 20370, USA

Oliver, Edith *Theater Critic*
%New Yorker Magazine, Editorial Dept, 20 W 43rd St, New York, NY 10036, USA

Olivero, Magda *Opera Singer*
%Matthews/Napal Ltd, 270 West End Ave, New York, NY 10023, USA

Olivor, Jane *Singer*
%Purple Hat Productions, 23-50 Waters Edge Dr, Bayside, NY 11360, USA

Olkewicz, Walter *Actor*
%Gold Marshak Liedtke, 3500 W Olive Ave, #1400, Burbank, CA 91505, USA

Olmedo, Alex *Tennis Player*
5067 Woodley Ave, Encino, CA 91436, USA

Olmos, Edward James *Actor*
18034 Ventura Blvd, #228, Encino, CA 91316, USA

Olmstead, Bert *Hockey Player*
220 26th Ave SW, #201, Calgary AL T2S 0M4, Canada

Olsen, Ashley *Actress*
8916 Ashcroft Ave, Los Angeles, CA 90048, USA

Olsen, Jack *Writer*
7954 NE Baker Hill Road, Bainbridge Island, WA 98110, USA

Olsen, Kenneth H *Inventor (Magnetic Core Memory)*
%Advanced Modular Solutions, 97 Piper Road, Acton, MA 01720, USA

Olsen, Mary Kate *Actress*
8916 Ashcroft Ave, Los Angeles, CA 90048, USA

Olsen, Merlin J *Football Player, Sportscaster*
6851 Silverlake Dr, Park City, UT 84060, USA

Olsen, Paul E *Geologist*
%Columbia University, Lamont-Doherty Geological Laboratory, New York, NY 10027, USA

Olson, Allen I *Governor, ND*
7386 Howard Lane, Eden Prairie, MN 55346, USA

Olson, Gary G *Financier*
%Norwest Bank South Dakota, PO Box 5128, Sioux Falls, SD 57117, USA

Olson, James *Actor*
250 W 57th St, #2223, New York, NY 10107, USA

Olson, Lute *Basketball Coach*
%University of Arizona, McKale Memorial Center, Tucson, AZ 85721, USA

Olson, Nancy *Actress*
945 N Alpine Dr, Beverly Hills, CA 90210, USA

Olson, Weldon *Hockey Player*
2623 Goldenrod Lane, Findlay, OH 45840, USA

Olsson, Curt G *Financier*
%Skandinaviska Enskilda Banken, 106 40, Stockholm, Sweden

Olstead, Bert *Hockey Player*
220 26th Ave SW, #301, Calgary AB, Canada

Olsten, Stuart P *Businessman*
%Olsten Corp, 175 Broad Hollow Road, Melville, NY 11747, USA

Olszewski, Jan *Prime Minister, Poland*
Biuro Poselskie, Al Ujazdowskie 13, 00-567 Warsaw, Poland

Onanian, Edward *Religious Leader*
%Diocese of Armenian Church, 630 2nd Ave, New York, NY 10016, USA

Ondaatje, Michael *Writer*
%Glendon College, English Dept, 2275 Bayview, Toronto ON M4N 3M6, Canada

Ong Teng Cheong *President, Singapore*
%President's Office, Orchard Road, Istana, Singapore 0922, Singapore

Ong, John D *Businessman*
%B F Goodrich Co, PO Box 5010, Richfield, OH 44286, USA

Ongais, Danny *Auto Racing Driver*
3031 Orange Ave, Santa Ana, CA 92707, USA

Ono, Yoko *Filmmaker, Artist*
%Dakota Hotel, 1 W 72nd St, New York, NY 10023, USA

Onodi, Henrietta *Gymnast*
%Gymnastics Federation, Magyar Torna Szovetseg, 1143 Budapest, Hungary

Onorati, Peter *Actor*
4191 Stansbury St, Sherman Oaks, CA 91423, USA

Ontkean, Michael *Actor*
PO Box 1212, Malibu, CA 90265, USA

Onufriyenko, Yuri *Astronaut*
%Potchta Kosmonavtov, Moskovskoi Oblasti, 141160 Syvisdny Goroduk, Russia

Oliver - Onufriyenko

Oosterhuis, Peter — *Golfer*
%Riviera Country Club, 1250 Capri Dr, Pacific Palisades, CA 90272, USA

Opalinski-Harrer, Janice — *Volleyball Player*
%Women's Pro Volleyball Assn, 840 Apollo St, #204, El Segundo, CA 90245, USA

Ophuls, Marcel — *Movie Director*
10 Rue Ernest Deloison, 92200 Neuilly-sur-Seine, France

Opik, Ernst J — *Astronomer*
%University of Maryland, Physics/Astronomy Dept, College Park, MD 20742, USA

Oppel, Richard A — *Editor*
%Knight-Ridder, National Press Building, 529 14th St NW, Washington, DC 20045, USA

Oppenheim, Dennis A — *Artist*
54 Franklin St, New York, NY 10013, USA

Oppenheim-Barnes, Sally — *Government Official, England*
Quietways, The Highlands, Painswick, Glos, England

Oppenheimer, Allan — *Actor*
%Henderson/Hogan, 247 S Beverly Dr, #102, Beverly Hills, CA 90212, USA

Oppenheimer, Benjamin R — *Astronomer*
%California Institute of Technology, Astronomy Dept, Pasadena, CA 91125, USA

Opperman, Jan — *Auto Racing Driver*
4630 Minnesota Ave, Fair Oaks, CA 95628, USA

Orange, Walter (Clyde) — *Singer, Drummer (The Commodores)*
%Commodores Entertainment, 1920 Benson Ave, St Paul, MN 55116, USA

Orbach, Jerry — *Actor, Singer*
301 W 53rd St, New York, NY 10019, USA

Orbach, Raymond L — *Educator*
%University of California, Chancellor's Office, Riverside, CA 92521, USA

Orbelian, Konstantin A — *Composer*
Demirchyan Str 27, #12, 3750002 Yerevan, Armenia

Ordovos, Jose M — *Medical Researcher*
%Tufts University, Nutrition Research Center, Medford, MA 02155, USA

Orenduff, J Michael — *Educator*
%New Mexico State University, President's Office, Las Cruces, NM 88003, USA

Oresko, Nicholas — *WW II Army Hero (CMH)*
31 Benjamin Road, Tenafly, NJ 07670, USA

Orgad, Ben Zion — *Composer*
14 Bloch St, Tel-Aviv 64161, Israel

Organ, H Bryan — *Artist*
%Redfern Gallery, 20 Cork St, London W1, England

Orlando, George J — *Labor Leader*
%Distillery Wine & Allied Workers, 66 Grand Ave, Englewood, NJ 07631, USA

Orlando, Tony — *Singer*
PO Box 7710, Branson, MO 65615, USA

Orleans, Joan — *Singer*
PO Box 2596, New York, NY 10009, USA

Orme, Stanley — *Government Official, England*
8 Northwood Grove, Sale, Cheshire, England

Ormond, Julia — *Actress*
%Creative Artists Agency, 9830 Wilshire Blvd, Beverly Hills, CA 90212, USA

Ornish, Dean — *Physician*
%Preventive Medicine Research Institute, 900 Bridgeway, #2, Sausalito, CA 94965, USA

Ornstein, Donald S — *Mathematician*
857 Tolman Dr, Stanford, CA 94305, USA

Orr, David A — *Businessman*
Home Farm House, Shackleford, Godalming, Surrey GU8 6AH, England

Orr, James F, III — *Businessman*
%UNUM Corp, 2211 Congress St, Portland, ME 04122, USA

Orr, Johnny — *Basketball Coach, Administrator*
%Iowa State University, Athletic Dept, Ames, IA 50011, USA

Orr, Kay — *Governor, NE*
%Governor's Office, State Capitol, Lincoln, NE 68509, USA

Orr, Robert D — *Governor, IN; Diplomat*
%US Embassy, 30 Hill St, Singapore, Singapore

Orr, Robert G (Bobby) — *Hockey Player*
300 Boylston St, #605, Boston, MA 02116, USA

Orr, Terrence S — *Ballet Dancer*
%American Ballet Theatre, 890 Broadway, New York, NY 10003, USA

Orr-Cahall, Christina — *Museum Director*
%Norton Gallery of Art, 1451 S Olive Ave, West Palm Beach, FL 33401, USA

Orrall, Robert Ellis	*Singer*
3 E 54th St, #1400, New York, NY 10022, USA	
Orser, Brian	*Figure Skater*
1600 James Naismith Dr, Gloucester ON L1B 5N4, Canada	
Ortega Saavedra, Daniel	*President, Nicaragua*
%Frente Sandinista de Liberacion National, Managua, Nicaragua	
Ortenberg, Arthur	*Businessman*
%Liz Claiborne Inc, 1441 Broadway, New York, NY 10018, USA	
Ortiz, Carlos	*Boxer*
2050 Seward Ave, #3-C, Bronx, NY 10473, USA	
Ortiz, Christina	*Concert Pianist*
%Harrison/Parrott, 12 Penzance Place, London W11 4PA England	
Ortiz, Frank V, Jr	*Diplomat*
663 Garcia St, Santa Fe, NM 87501, USA	
Ortlieb, Patrick	*Skier*
%Hotel Montana, Oberlech, 6764 Lech, Austria	
Orvick, George M	*Religious Leader*
%Evangelical Lutheran Synod, 6 Browns Court, Mankato, MN 56001, USA	
Osborn, William A	*Financier*
%Northern Trust Corp, 50 S LaSalle St, Chicago, IL 60603, USA	
Osborne DuPont, Margaret	*Tennis Player*
415 Camino Real, El Paso, TX 79922, USA	
Osborne, Burl	*Editor, Publisher*
%Dallas Morning News, Editorial Dept, Communications Center, Dallas, TX 75265, USA	
Osborne, James A	*Religious Leader*
%Salvation Army, 799 Bloomfield Ave, Verona, NJ 07044, USA	
Osborne, Jeffrey	*Singer, Songwriter*
%Jack Nelson Inc, PO Box 3718, Los Angeles, CA 90078, USA	
Osborne, Joan	*Singer, Songwriter*
PO Box 2596, New York, NY 10009, USA	
Osborne, Richard de J	*Businessman*
%Asarco Inc, 180 Maiden Lane, New York, NY 10038, USA	
Osborne, Tom	*Football Coach*
%University of Nebraska, Athletic Dept, South Stadium, Lincoln, NE 68588, USA	
Osbourne, Ozzy	*Singer, Songwriter*
66 Malibu Colony Road, Malibu, CA 90265, USA	
Osburn, Julie	*Actress*
%J Michael Bloom, 9255 Sunset Blvd, #710, Los Angeles, CA 90069, USA	
Osgood, Charles	*News Commentator*
%CBS-TV, News Dept, 524 W 57th St, New York, NY 10019, USA	
Osgood, Charles E	*Psychologist, Educator*
30 E Main St, Champaign, IL 61820, USA	
Osheroff, Douglas C	*Nobel Physics Laureate*
%Stanford University, Physics Dept, Stanford, CA 94305, USA	
Oshima, Nagisa	*Movie Director*
%Oshima Productions, 2-15-7 Arasaka, Minatoku, Tokyo, Japan	
Oslin, K T	*Singer*
%Moress-Nanas-Shea, 1209 16th Ave S, Nashville, TN 37212, USA	
Osman, Osman Ahmed	*Civil Engineer*
%People's Assembly, Heliopolis, Cairo, Egypt	
Osmond, Cliff	*Actor, Director*
630 Benvenida Ave, Pacific Palisades, CA 90272, USA	
Osmond, Donny	*Singer*
36 Avignon Ave, Newport Beach, CA 92657, USA	
Osmond, Marie	*Singer, Actress*
%United Mgmt, 3325 N University Ave, #150, Provo, UT 84604, USA	
Osnes, Larry G	*Educator*
%Hamline University, President's Office, St Paul, MN 55104, USA	
Osrin, Raymond H	*Editorial Cartoonist*
%Cleveland Plain Dealer, Editorial Dept, 1801 Superior, Cleveland, OH 44114, USA	
Ost, Friedheim	*Government Official, Germany*
Bundestag, Bundeshaus, Gorresstr 15, 53113 Bonn, Germany	
Osteen, Claude W	*Baseball Player*
1959 Wexford Road, Palmyra, PA 17078, USA	
Osteen, H M, Jr	*Financier*
%Bankers First Corp, 1 10th St, Augusta, GA 30901, USA	
Oster, Jeffrey W	*Marine Corps General*
Deputy CofS, Programs/Resources, HqUSMC, 2 Navy Annex, Washington, DC 20380, USA	

Osterbrock, Donald E *Astronomer*
120 Woodside Ave, Santa Cruz, CA 95060, USA
Ostertag, Greg *Basketball Player*
1603 W 15th St, #202-C, Lawrence, KS 66044, USA
Osterwald, Bibi *Actress*
341 Carroll Park West, Long Beach, CA 90814, USA
Ostheim, Michael *Model*
%Louisa Models, Ebersberger Str 9, 81679 Munich, Germany
Ostin, Mo *Record Producer*
%DreamWorks SKG, Music Div, 100 Universal City Plaza, Universal City, CA 91608, USA
Ostos, Javier *Swimmer*
%FINA, Isabel La Catolica 13, Desp 401-2, Mexico City 1 DF, Mexico
Ostriker, Jeremiah P *Astrophysicist*
33 Philip Dr, Princeton, NJ 08540, USA
Ostrom, John H *Vertebrate Paleontologist*
198 Towpath Lane, Cheshire, CT 06410, USA
Oswald, Mark *Auto Racing Driver*
%Championship Quest Motorsports, 125 Charles Road, King, NC 27021, USA
Oswald, Stephen S *Astronaut*
%NASA, Johnson Space Center, 2101 NASA Road, Houston, TX 77058, USA
Otaka, Tadaaki *Conductor*
%Harold Holt, 31 Sinclair Road, London W14 0NS, England
Otis, Carre *Actress, Model*
1900 Ave of Stars, #1040, Los Angeles, CA 90067, USA
Otis, Glenn K *Army General*
97 Normandy Lane, Newport News, VA 23606, USA
Otis, James L (Jim) *Football Player*
14795 Greenleaf Valley Dr, Chesterfield, MO 63017, USA
Otis, Johnny *Singer, Guitarist, Songwriter*
7105 Baker Lane, Sebastopol, CA 95472, USA
Otman Assed, Mohamed *Prime Minister, Libya*
Villa Rissani, Route Oued Akrach, Souissi, Rabat, Morocco
Otsuka, Hisashi *Artist*
%Images International of Hawaii, Ala Moana Shopping Center, Honolulu, HI 96814, USA
Ottey, Merlene *Track Athlete*
%Momentu Sports Mgmt, PO Box 2902, 5001 Aarau, Switzerland
Otto, A T, Jr *Labor Leader*
%Railroad Yardmasters Union, 1411 Peterson Ave, #201, Park Ridge, IL 60068, USA
Otto, Frei *Architect*
Berghalde 19, 7250 Leonberg, 71229 Warmbroun, Germany
Otto, James E (Jim) *Football Player*
00 Estates Dr, Auburn, CA 95602, USA
Otto, Joel *Hockey Player*
RR 1, Box 81-C, Pequot Lakes, MN 56472, USA
Otto, Kristin *Swimmer*
%ZDF Sportedaktion, Postfach 4040, 55100 Mainz, Germany
Otumfuo Nana Opoku Ware II *Ruler, Ghana*
%Asantehene's Palace, Manhyia, Kumasi, Ashanti, Ghana
Otunga, Maurice Cardinal *Religious Leader*
%Cardinal's Residence, PO Box 14231, Nairobi, Kenya
Otwell, Ralph M *Editor*
2750 Hurd Ave, Evanston, IL 60201, USA
Ouattara, Alassane D *Prime Minister, Cote D'Ivoire; Financier*
%International Monetary Fund, 700 19th St NW, Washington, DC 20431, USA
Ouedraogo, Gerard Kango *Prime Minister, Burkina Faso*
01-BP 347, Ouagadougou, Burkina Faso
Ovchinikov, Vladimir P *Concert Pianist*
%Manygate, 13 Cotswold Mews, 30 Battersea Square, London SW11 3RA, England
Overall, Park *Actress*
20 Ironside St, #18, Marina del Rey, CA 90292, USA
Overgard, Robert M *Religious Leader*
%Church of Lutheran Brethren, PO Box 655, Fergus Falls, MN 56538, USA
Overgard, William *Cartoonist (Rudy)*
%United Feature Syndicate, 200 Madison Ave, New York, NY 10016, USA
Overhauser, Albert W *Physicist*
236 Pawnee Dr, West Lafayette, IN 47906, USA
Overholser, Geneva *Editor*
%Des Moines Register, Editorial Dept, Box 957, Des Moines, IA 50304, USA

O

Osterbrock - Overholser

Overstreet, Paul	*Singer, Songwriter*
%Bobby Roberts, 909 Meadowlark Lane, Goodlettesville, TN 37072, USA	
Overstrom, Gunnar S, Jr	*Financier*
%Shawmut National Corp, 1 Federal St, Boston, MA 02110, USA	
Ovitz, Michael S	*Entertainment Executive*
457 Rockingham, Los Angeles, CA 90049, USA	
Ovshinsky, Stanford R	*Ovionics Engineer, Inventor*
%Energy Conversion Devices, 1675 W Maple Road, Troy, MI 48084, USA	
Owen, Bill	*Actor*
%Richard Stone, 25 Whithall, London SW1A 2BS, England	
Owen, David A L	*Government Official, England*
78 Narrow St, Limehouse, London E14, England	
Owen, Edwyn (Bob)	*Hockey Player*
747 SW Randolph Ave, Topeka, KS 66606, USA	
Owen, Henry	*Diplomat*
%Brookings Institute, 1775 Massachusetts Ave NW, Washington, DC 20036, USA	
Owen, Randy Y	*Singer, Guitarist (Alabama)*
PO Box 529, Fort Payne, AL 35968, USA	
Owen, Ray D	*Biologist*
1583 Rose Villa St, Pasadena, CA 91106, USA	
Owens, Billy	*Basketball Player*
%Sacramento Kings, 1 Sports Parkway, Sacramento, CA 95834, USA	
Owens, Buck	*Singer, Songwriter*
%Buck Owens Productions, 3223 Sillect Ave, Bakersfield, CA 93308, USA	
Owens, Gary	*Entertainer*
17856 Via Vallarta, Encino, CA 91316, USA	
Owens, James D (Jim)	*Football Player, Coach*
%Rowan Companies, 2470 First City Tower, 1001 Fannin, Houston, TX 77002, USA	
Owens, Steve E	*Football Player*
4204 Northampton Court, Norman, OK 73072, USA	
Owens, William A	*Navy Admiral*
1355 Caminito Batea, La Jolla, CA 92037, USA	
Owensby, Earl	*Movie, Television Producer*
1 Motion Picture Blvd, Shelby, NC 28152, USA	
Owlsey, Alvin	*Businessman*
%Ball Corp, 345 S High St, Muncie, IN 47305, USA	
Oxenberg, Catherine	*Actress*
1526 N Beverly Dr, Beverly Hills, CA 90210, USA	
Oyakawa, Yoshi	*Swimmer*
4171 Hutchinson Road, Cincinnati, OH 45248, USA	
Oz, Amos	*Writer*
Arad 80700, Arad, Israel	
Oz, Frank R	*Puppeteer, Movie Director*
PO Box 20750, New York, NY 10023, USA	
Ozaki, Masashi	*Golfer*
%Bridgestone Sports, 15320 Industrial Park Blvd NE, Covington, GA 30014, USA	
Ozark, Daniel L (Danny)	*Baseball Executive*
PO Box 6666, Vero Beach, FL 32961, USA	
Ozawa, Ichiro	*Government Official, Japan*
1-11 Kiocho, Chiyodaku, Tokyo, Japan	
Ozawa, Seiji	*Conductor*
%Boston Symphony, Symphony Hall, 301 Massachusetts Ave, Boston, MA 02115, USA	
Ozbek, Rifat	*Fashion Designer*
%Ozbek Ltd, 18 Haunch of Venison Yard, London W1Y 1AF, England	
Ozick, Cynthia	*Writer*
%Alfred A Knopf Inc, 201 E 50th St, New York, NY 10022, USA	
Ozim, Igor	*Concert Violinist*
Briebergstr 6, 50939 Colgone, Germany	
Ozio, David	*Bowler*
%Professional Bowlers Assn, 1720 Merriman Road, Akron, OH 44313, USA	
Ozorkiewicz, Ralph L	*Businessman*
%Wyle Electronics, PO Box 19675, Irvine, CA 92623, USA	
Ozzie, Ray	*Computer Software Designer*
%Lotus Development Corp, 55 Cambridge Plaza, Cambridge, MA 02142, USA	
Ozzie, Raymond	*Computer Software Designer (Notes)*
33 Harbor St, Manchester-by-the-Sea, MA 01944, USA	

Paar, Jack — *Entertainer*
9 Chateau Ridge Dr, Greenwich, CT 06831, USA

Pace, Darrell — *Archer*
4394 Princeton Road, Hamilton, OH 45011, USA

Pace, Judy — *Actress*
4139 Cloverdale Ave, Los Angeles, CA 90008, USA

Pace, Orlando — *Football Player*
%St Louis Rams, 100 N Broadway, #2100, St Louis, MO 63102, USA

Pace, Peter — *Marine Corps General*
Director, Operations, Joint Chiefs of Staff, Pentagon, Washington, DC 20318, USA

Pacheco, Ferdie — *Sportscaster*
%NBC-TV, Sports Dept, 30 Rockefeller Plaza, New York, NY 10112, USA

Pacheco, Manuel T — *Educator*
%University of Arizona, President's Office, Tucson, AZ 85721, USA

Pacino, Al — *Actor*
%Chal Productions, 301 W 57th St, #16-C, New York, NY 10019, USA

Pack, Robert — *Basketball Player*
9071 W Mississippi Ave, Denver, CO 80226, USA

Packer, A William (Billy) — *Sportscaster*
165 Fescue Dr, Advance, NC 27006, USA

Pacquer, Michel — *Businessman*
%Elf-Aquitaine Societe, 75739 Paris Cedex 15, France

Pacula, Joanna — *Actress*
%Gersh Agency, 232 N Canon Dr, Beverly Hills, CA 90210, USA

Padilla, Doug — *Track Athlete*
182 N 555 W, Orem, UT 84057, USA

Padiyara, Anthony Cardinal — *Religious Leader*
Archdiocese Curia, Post Bag 2580, Ernakulam, Cochin-68201, Kerala, India

Paeniu, Bikenibeu — *Prime Minister, Tuvalu*
%Prime Minister's Office, Vaiaku, Funafuti, Tuvalu

Paez, Jorge (Maromero) — *Boxer*
%Decor Depot, 677 Anita St, #D, Chula Vista, CA 91911, USA

Pafko, Andrew (Andy) — *Baseball Player*
1420 Blackhawk Dr, Mount Prospect, IL 60056, USA

Page, Alan C — *Football Player, Judge*
520 Lafayette Road N, St Paul, MN 55155, USA

Page, Anita — *Actress*
929 Rutland Ave, Los Angeles, CA 90042, USA

Page, Bettie — *Model*
PO Box 56176, Chicago, IL 60656, USA

Page, David C — *Geneticist*
%Whitehead Institute, 9 Cambridge Center, Cambridge, MA 02142, USA

Page, Fred — *Hockey Executive*
%Hockey Hall of Fame, BCE Place, 38 Yonge, Toronto ON M5E 1X8, Canada

Page, Genevieve — *Actress*
52 Rue de Vaugirard, 75006 Paris, France

Page, Greg — *Boxer*
%Don King Promotions, 968 Pinehurst Dr, Las Vegas, NV 89109, USA

Page, Harrison — *Actor*
%SDB Partners, 1801 Ave of Stars, #902, Los Angeles, CA 90067, USA

Page, Jimmy — *Singer (The Yardbirds, Led Zeppelin)*
29/33 Berners St, London W1P 4AA, England

Page, LaWanda — *Actress*
%Starwil Talent, 6253 Hollywood Blvd, #730, Los Angeles, CA 90028, USA

Page, Martin — *Singer*
%Famous Artists Agency, 1700 Broadway, #500, New York, NY 10019, USA

Page, Michael — *Equestrian Rider*
PO Box 229, North Salem, NY 10560, USA

Page, Patti — *Singer, Actress*
14923 Caminito Ladera, Del Mar, CA 92014, USA

Page, Pierre — *Hockey Coach, Executive*
%Anaheim Mighty Ducks, PO Box 2000, Gene Autry Way, Anaheim, CA 92803, USA

Page, Tim — *Journalist*
%Washington Post, Editorial Dept, 1150 15th St NW, Washington, DC 20071, USA

Paget, Debra — *Actress*
737 Kuhlman Road, Houston, TX 77024, USA

Pagett, Nicola — *Actress*
22 Victoria Road, Mortlake, London SW14, England

P

Paar - Pagett

Paglia, Camille *Writer, Educator*
%University of the Arts, Humanities Dept, 320 S Broad St, Philadelphia, PA 19102, USA
Pagliarulo, Michael T (Mike) *Baseball Player*
11 Fieldstone Dr, Winchester, MA 01890, USA
Pagonis, William G *Army General*
25190 N Pawnee Road, Barrington, IL 60010, USA
Paige, Elaine *Singer*
DeWalden Court, 85 New Cavendish St, London W1M 7RA, England
Paige, Janis *Actress*
1700 Rising Glen Road, Los Angeles, CA 90069, USA
Paige, Mitchell *WW II Marine Corps Hero (CMH)*
PO Box 2358, Palm Desert, CA 92261, USA
Paik, Kun Woo *Concert Pianist*
%Worldwide Artists, 6 Petersfield Crescent, Coulsdon, Sur CR5 2JP, England
Paik, Nam June *Video Artist*
%Galerie Bonino, 48 Great Jones St, New York, NY 10012, USA
Pailes, William A *Astronaut*
20899 Chippoaks Forest Circle, Sterling, VA 20165, USA
Paisley, Ian R K *Political Leader, Northern Ireland*
%Parsonage, 17 Cyprus Ave, Belfast BT5 5NT, Northern Ireland
Pak, Charles *Medical Researcher*
%University of Texas, Health Sciences Center, Dallas, TX 75235, USA
Pakula, Alan J *Movie Director, Producer*
%Pakula Co, 330 W 58th St, #508, New York, NY 10019, USA
Palade, George E *Nobel Medicine Laureate*
%University of California, Cellular & Molecular Division, La Jolla, CA 92093, USA
Palance, Jack *Actor*
PO Box 6201, Tehachapi, CA 93582, USA
Palau, Luis *Evangelist*
1500 NW 167th Place, Beaverton, OR 97006, USA
Palazzini, Pietro Cardinal *Religious Leader*
Via Proba Petronia 83, 00136 Rome, Italy
Palermo, Stophon M *Baseball Umpire*
7921 W 118th St, Overland Park, KS 66210, USA
Paley, Grace *Writer*
PO Box 620, Thetford Hill, VT 05074, USA
Palillo, Ron *Actor*
5400 Newcastle Ave, #26, Encino, CA 91316, USA
Palin, Michael *Actor, Writer (Monty Python)*
%Gumby Corp, 68-A Delancey St, Camden Town, London NW1 7RY, England
Pall, Olga *Skier*
Fahrenweg 28, 6060 Absam, Austria
Palladino, Vincent *Labor Leader*
%National Assn of Postal Supervisors, 1727 King St, Alexandria, VA 22314, USA
Palley, Stephen W *Television Executive*
%King World Productions, 1700 Broadway, New York, NY 10019, USA
Palmeiro, Rafael C *Baseball Player*
5216 Reims Court, Colleyville, TX 76034, USA
Palmer, Arnold D *Golfer*
PO Box 52, Youngstown, PA 15696, USA
Palmer, Betsy *Actress*
40 Jordan Dr, Riverdale, NJ 07761, USA
Palmer, C R *Businessman*
%Rowan Companies, Transco Tower, 2800 Post Oak Blvd, Houston, TX 77056, USA
Palmer, Dean W *Baseball Player*
916 Hill Roost Road, Tallahassee, FL 32312, USA
Palmer, Geoffrey W R *Prime Minister, New Zealand*
85 Elizabeth St, #7, Wellington, New Zealand
Palmer, James A (Jim) *Baseball Player, Sportscaster*
117 Ardaan Road, Lutherville, MD 21093, USA
Palmer, Reginald Oswald *Governor General, Grenada*
Government House, St George's, Grenada
Palmer, Robert *Singer, Songwriter*
%William Morris Agency, 1325 Ave of Americas, New York, NY 10019, USA
Palmer, Robert B *Businessman*
%Digital Equipment, 111 Powdermill Road, Maynard, MA 01754, USA
Palmer, Sandra *Golfer*
259 Fairview St, Laguna Beach, CA 92651, USA

Palmer, William R *Publisher*
%Detroit News, 615 Lafayette Blvd, Detroit, MI 48226, USA

Palmieri, Eddie *Jazz Pianist, Singer*
%Ralph Mercado Mgmt, 568 Broadway, #806, New York, NY 10012, USA

Palmieri, Paul *Religious Leader*
%Church of Jesus Christ, 6th & Lincoln Sts, Monongahela, PA 15063, USA

Palminteri, Chazz *Actor*
375 Greenwich St, New York, NY 10013, USA

Palms, John M *Educator*
%University of South Carolina, President's Office, Columbia, SC 29208, USA

Paltrow, Bruce W *Television Producer*
304 21st St, Santa Monica, CA 90402, USA

Paltrow, Gwyneth *Actress*
%Creative Artists Agency, 9830 Wilshire Blvd, Beverly Hills, CA 90212, USA

Pamuk, Orhan *Writer*
%Farrar Straus Giroux, 19 Union Square W, New York, NY 10003, USA

Pancetti, John A *Financier*
%Republic Bank for Savings, 415 Madison Ave, New York, NY 10017, USA

Pandit, Korla *Organist*
PO Box 11614, Santa Rosa, CA 95406, USA

Panetta, Leon E *Government Official*
%White House, 1600 Pennsylvania Ave NW, Washington, DC 20500, USA

Panhofer, Walter *Concert Pianist*
Erdbergstr 35/9, 1030 Vienna, Austria

Panic, Milan *Prime Minister, Yugoslavia; Businessman*
%ICN Pharmaceuticals, 3300 Hyland Ave, Costa Mesa, CA 92626, USA

Panichas, George A *Writer*
PO Box AB, College Park, MD 20741, USA

Pankin, Stuart *Actor*
%Brillstein/Grey, 9150 Wilshire Blvd, #350, Beverly Hills, CA 90212, USA

Panoff, Robert *Nuclear Engineer*
1140 Connecticut Ave NW, Washington, DC 20036, USA

Panofsky, Wolfgang K H *Physicist*
25671 Chapin Road, Los Altos, CA 94022, USA

Panov, Valery M *Ballet Dancer*
%Carson Office, 119 W 57th St, #903, New York, NY 10019, USA

Panova, Galina *Ballerina*
%Carson Office, 119 W 57th St, #903, New York, NY 10019, USA

Pantoliano, Joe *Actor*
2313 30th St, Santa Monica, CA 90405, USA

Panton, Verner *Architect*
Kohlenberggasse 21, 4051 Basle, Switzerland

Panza di Biumo, Giuseppe *Art Patron*
Sentiero Vinorum 2, 6900 Massagno, Switzerland

Paola *Queen, Belgium*
%Koninklijk Palais, Rue de Brederode, 1000 Brussels, Belgium

Paolozzi, Eduardo L *Sculptor*
107 Dovehouse, London SW3, England

Papart, Max *Artist*
10 Rue Pernety, 75014 Paris, France

Papas, Irene *Actress*
Xenokratous 39, Athens-Kolonaki, Greece

Papert, Seymour *Mathematician*
%Massachusetts Institute of Technology, 20 Ames St, Cambridge, MA 02142, USA

Papp, Lazlo *Boxer*
Ora-Utca 6, 1125 Budapest, Hungary

Pappalardo, Salvatore Cardinal *Religious Leader*
%Arcivescovado, Corso Vittorio Emanuele 461, 90134 Palermo, Italy

Pappas, George *Bowler*
%George Pappas's Park Lanes, 1700 Montford Dr, Charlotte, NC 28209, USA

Pappas, Milton S (Milt) *Baseball Player*
RR 1, Box 154, Ashland Ave, Beecher, IL 60401, USA

Pappenheimer, John R *Physiologist*
63 Chilton St, Cambridge, MA 02138, USA

Paquin, Anna *Actress*
%Double Happy, PO Box 9585, Wellington, New Zealand

Paradis, Vanessa *Model, Singer*
BP 138, 75223 Paris Cedex 05, France

P

Palmer - Paradis

P

Paradise - Parker

Paradise, Bob — *Hockey Player*
1303 Beechwood Place, St Paul, MN 55116, USA

Parayre, Jean-Paul C — *Businessman*
%Lyonnaise des Eaux-Dumez, 32 Ave Pablo Picasso, 92022 Nanterre, France

Parazynski, Scott E — *Astronaut*
%NASA, Johnson Space Center, 2101 NASA Road, Houston, TX 77058, USA

Parcells, Duane C (Bill) — *Football Coach*
%New York Jets, 1000 Fulton Ave, Hempstead, NY 11550, USA

Pardee, Arthur B — *Biochemist*
30 Codman Road, Brookline, MA 02146, USA

Pare, Michael — *Actor*
15250 Ventura Blvd, #710, Sherman Oaks, CA 91403, USA

Paredes, Marco — *Artist*
%Hospitality House, 146 Leavenworth St, San Francisco, CA 94102, USA

Parent, Bernie — *Hockey Player*
13 Pawtucket Dr, Cherry Hill, NJ 08003, USA

Paret, Peter — *Writer, Historian*
%Institute for Advanced Studies, Historical Studies School, Princeton, NJ 08540, USA

Paretsky, Sara N — *Writer*
5831 S Blackstone Ave, Chicago, IL 60637, USA

Parillaud, Anne — *Actress*
%Artmedia, 10 Ave George V, 75008 Paris, France

Parilli, Vito (Babe) — *Football Player, Coach*
2000 Gene Autry Way, Gate 6, #202, Anaheim, CA 92806, USA

Paris, Mica — *Singer*
%Garfield Group, 325 W Lafayette St, #200, New York, NY 10012, USA

Paris, Twila — *Singer*
%Proper Mgmt, PO Box 23069, Nashville, TN 37202, USA

Parise, Louis — *Labor Leader*
%National Maritime Union, 1125 15th St NW, Washington, DC 20005, USA

Parise, Ronald A — *Astronaut*
15419 Good Hope Road, Silver Spring, MD 20905, USA

Parish, Robert L — *Basketball Player*
20 Stonybrook Road, #1, Framingham, MA 01702, USA

Parizeau, Jacques — *Political Leader, Canada*
%Parti Quebecois, 7370 Rue St Hubert, Montreal PQ H2R 2N3, Canada

Park Choong-Hoon — *President, South Korea; General*
1-36 Seongbukdong, Seonbukku, Seoul, South Korea

Park Yung-Wok — *Businessman*
%Hyundai Corp, 140-2 Kyedong, Chongroku, Seoul, South Korea

Park, Brad — *Hockey Player, Coach*
%Bradan Corp, 22-B Cranes Court, Woburn, MA 01801, USA

Park, Charles R — *Physiologist*
5325 Stanford Dr, Nashville, TN 37215, USA

Park, Merle F — *Ballerina*
21 Millers Court, Chiswick Mall, London W4 2PF, England

Parkening, Christopher — *Concert Guitarist*
%Columbia Artists Mgmt Inc, 165 W 57th St, New York, NY 10019, USA

Parker, Alan W — *Movie Director*
%Parker Film Co, Pinewood Studios, Iver Heath, Bucks, England

Parker, Andrea — *Actress*
%Susan Smith, 121 N San Vicente Blvd, Beverly Hills, CA 90211, USA

Parker, Anthony — *Basketball Player*
%Philadelphia 76ers, Veterans Stadium, PO Box 25040, Philadelphia, PA 19147, USA

Parker, Bob — *Skier*
408 Camino Don Miguel, Santa Fe, NM 87501, USA

Parker, Brant J — *Cartoonist (Wizard of Id)*
6766 Bull Run Post Office Road, Centreville, VA 20120, USA

Parker, Bruce C — *Botanist*
841 Hutcheson Dr, Blacksburg, VA 24060, USA

Parker, Clarence M (Ace) — *Football Player*
210 Snead's Fairway, Portsmouth, VA 23701, USA

Parker, Corey — *Actor*
139 Fraser Ave, Santa Monica, CA 90405, USA

Parker, David G (Dave) — *Baseball Player*
7864 Ridge Road, Cincinnati, OH 45237, USA

Parker, Denise — *Archer*
2160 S 800 E, Salt Lake City, UT 84106, USA

Parker, Edna G	*Judge*
%US Tax Court, 400 2nd St NW, Washington, DC 20217, USA	
Parker, Eleanor	*Actress*
2195 La Paz Way, Palm Springs, CA 92264, USA	
Parker, Eugene N	*Physicist*
1323 Evergreen Road, Homewood, IL 60430, USA	
Parker, Fess	*Actor*
PO Box 898, Los Olivos, CA 93441, USA	
Parker, Frank A	*Tennis Player*
601 E Henry Clay St, Milwaukee, WI 53217, USA	
Parker, Franklin	*Writer*
%Western Carolina University, Education & Psychology Dept, Cullowhee, NC 28723, USA	
Parker, George M	*Labor Leader*
%Glass Workers Union, 1440 S Byrne Road, Toledo, OH 43614, USA	
Parker, Graham	*Singer, Guitarist*
%Chapman, 11 Old Lincoln's Inn, London WC2, England	
Parker, Jack D (Jackie)	*Football Player*
%Edmonton Eskimo, 90211 111th Ave, Edmonton AB T5B 0C3, Canada	
Parker, James T (Jim)	*Football Player*
5448 Wingborne Court, Columbia, MD 21045, USA	
Parker, Jameson	*Actor*
4354 Laurel Canyon Blvd, #306, Studio City, CA 91604, USA	
Parker, Maceo	*Jazz Saxophonist*
%Verve Records, Worldwide Plaza, 825 8th Ave, New York, NY 10019, USA	
Parker, Mary-Louise	*Actress*
%William Morris Agency, 151 S El Camino Dr, Beverly Hills, CA 90212, USA	
Parker, Maynard M	*Editor*
%Newsweek Magazine, Editorial Dept, 251 W 57th St, New York, NY 10019, USA	
Parker, Nathaniel	*Actor*
%Markham & Froggatt, Julian House, 4 Windmill St, London W1P 1HF, England	
Parker, Olivia	*Photographer*
%Brent Sikkema, 252 Lafayette St, #400, New York, NY 10012, USA	
Parker, Patrick S	*Businessman*
%Parker Hannifin Corp, 17325 Euclid Ave, Cleveland, OH 44112, USA	
Parker, Ray, Jr	*Singer, Guitarist*
1025 N Roxbury Dr, Beverly Hills, CA 90210, USA	
Parker, Robert A R	*Astronaut*
%NASA Headquarters, Policy & Plans Division, Washington, DC 20546, USA	
Parker, Robert B	*Writer*
555 W 57th St, #1230, New York, NY 10019, USA	
Parker, Sarah Jessica	*Actress*
PO Box 69646, Los Angeles, CA 90069, USA	
Parker, Scott	*Motorcyle Racing Rider*
6080 Grand Blanc Road, Swartz Creek, MI 48473, USA	
Parker, Suzy	*Model, Actress*
770 Hot Springs Road, Santa Barbara, CA 93108, USA	
Parker, Willard	*Actor*
74580 Fairway Dr, Indian Wells, CA 92260, USA	
Parkhill, Barry	*Basketball Player*
3429 Cesford Grange, Keswick, VA 22947, USA	
Parkins, Barbara	*Actress*
%Contemporary Artists, 1427 3rd St Promenade, #205, Santa Monica, CA 90401, USA	
Parkinson, Dian	*Entertainer, Model*
107 N Reino Road, #180, Thousand Oaks, CA 91320, USA	
Parkinson, Roger P	*Publisher*
%Minneapolis Star Tribune, 425 Portland Ave, Minneapolis, MN 55488, USA	
Parks, Bernard	*Law Enforcement Official*
%Los Angeles Police Department, 150 S Los Angeles St, Los Angeles, CA 90012, USA	
Parks, Cherokee	*Basketball Player*
%Minnesota Timberwolves, Target Center, 600 1st Ave N, Minneapolis, MN 55403, USA	
Parks, Gordon R	*Movie Director, Photographer*
860 United Nations Plaza, New York, NY 10017, USA	
Parks, Hildy	*Actress*
225 W 44th St, New York, NY 10036, USA	
Parks, Maxie	*Track Athlete*
4545 E Norwich Ave, Fresno, CA 93726, USA	
Parks, Michael	*Actor*
%Agency For Performing Arts, 9200 Sunset Blvd, #900, Los Angeles, CA 90069, USA	

P

Parker - Parks

Parks, Rosa L — *Civil Rights Activist*
9336 Wildemere St, Detroit, MI 48206, USA

Parks, Van Dyke — *Composer*
267 S Arden Blvd, Los Angeles, CA 90004, USA

Parks, Wally — *Auto Racing Executive*
%National Hot Rod Assn, 2023 Financial Way, Glendora, CA 91741, USA

Parmelee, Harold J — *Businessman*
%Turner Corp, 375 Hudson St, New York, NY 10014, USA

Parnell, Lee Roy — *Singer*
%Mike Robertson Mgmt, 1227 17th Ave S, #200, Nashville, TN 37212, USA

Parnell, Melvin L (Mel) — *Baseball Player*
700 Turquoise St, New Orleans, LA 70124, USA

Parr, Carolyn Miller — *Judge*
%US Tax Court, 400 2nd St NW, Washington, DC 20217, USA

Parr, Robert G — *Chemist*
701 Kenmore Road, Chapel Hill, NC 27514, USA

Parrish, Lance M — *Baseball Player*
22370 Starwood Dr, Yorba Linda, CA 92887, USA

Parrish, Larry A — *Baseball Player*
2525 Kokomo Road, Haines City, FL 33844, USA

Parry, Natasha — *Actress*
%International Creative Mgmt, 76 Oxford St, London W1N 0AX, England

Parry, Robert T — *Financier*
%Federal Reserve Bank, 101 Market St, San Francisco, CA 94105, USA

Parseghian, Ara — *Football Coach, Sportscaster*
240 Seaview Court, #PH-A, Maroc, FL 34145, USA

Parsky, Gerald L — *Attorney*
%Aurora Capital Partners, 1800 Century Park East, Los Angeles, CA 90067, USA

Parsons, Benny — *Auto Racing Driver*
1691 Old Harmony Dr, Concord, NC 28027, USA

Parsons, David — *Choreographer*
%Parsons Dance Foundation, 476 Broadway, New York, NY 10013, USA

Parsons, Estelle — *Actress*
505 West End Ave, New York, NY 10024, USA

Parsons, Karyn — *Actress*
3208 Cahuenga Blvd W, #16, Los Angeles, CA 90068, USA

Parsons, Nicholas — *Actor*
%Susan Shaper, 174/178 N Gower St, London NW1 2NB, England

Part, Arvo — *Composer*
%Universal Editions, Warwick House, 9 Warrick St, London W1R 5RA, England

Parton, Dolly — *Singer, Actress, Songwriter*
Crockett Road, Rt 1, Brentwood, TN 37027, USA

Parton, Stella — *Singer*
%Stella Parton Productions, PO Box 120295, Nashville, TN 37212, USA

Partridge, John A — *Architect*
20 Old Pye St, Westminster, London SW1, England

Parzybok, William G, Jr — *Businessman*
%Fluke Corp, 6920 Seaway Blvd, Everett, WA 98203, USA

Pasanella, Marco — *Furniture Designer*
%Pasanella Co, 45 W 18th St, New York, NY 10011, USA

Pasarell, Charles — *Tennis Player*
PO Box 2388, Palm Desert, CA 92261, USA

Paschke, Melanie — *Track Athlete*
Asseweg 2, 38124 Braunschweig, Germany

Pascoal, Hermeto — *Jazz Musician*
%Brasil Universo Prod, RVN Vitor Guisard 209, Rio de Janerio 21832, Brazil

Pascual, Camilo A — *Baseball Player*
7741 SW 32nd St, Miami, FL 33155, USA

Pascual, Luis — *Theater Director*
%Theatre de l'Europe, 1 Place Paul Claudel, 75006 Paris, France

Pasdar, Adrian — *Actor*
%International Creative Mgmt, 8942 Wilshire Blvd, Beverly Hills, CA 90211, USA

Paskai, Laszlo Cardinal — *Religious Leader*
Uri Utca 62, 1014 Budapest, Hungary

Pasmore, E J Victor — *Artist*
Dar Gamri, Gudja, Malta

Passeau, Claude W — *Baseball Player*
113 London St, Lucedale, MS 39452, USA

Passer, Ivan — *Movie Director*
%Creative Road Corp, 8222 Melrose Ave, #301, Los Angeles, CA 90046, USA
Pastore, John O — *Governor/Senator, RI*
81 Mountain Laurel Dr, Cranston, RI 02920, USA
Pastorelli, Robert — *Actor*
2751 Holly Ridge Dr, Los Angeles, CA 90068, USA
Pastrana Borrero, Misael — *President, Colombia*
Carrera 4, 92-10, Bogota DE, Colombia
Pastrano, Willie — *Boxer*
5035 Yale St, #3, Metairie, LA 70006, USA
Pataki, George E — *Governor, NY*
%Governor's Office, State Capitol, Albany, NY 12224, USA
Patane, Giuseppe — *Conductor*
Holbeinstr 6, 81679 Munich, Germany
Patasse, Ange-Felix — *President, Central African Republic*
%Palais de Renaissance, Bangui, Central African Republic
Patat, Frederic — *Spatinaut, France*
%Faculte de Medecine, 2 Bis Blvd Tonnelle, 37032 Tours Cedex, France
Pate, James L — *Businessman*
%Pennzoil Co, Pennzoil Place, PO Box 2967, Houston, TX 77252, USA
Pate, Jerry — *Golfer*
%Professional Golfer's Assn, PO Box 109601, Palm Beach Gardens, FL 33410, USA
Pate, Michael — *Actor*
21 Bundarra Road, Bellvue Hill NSW 2023, Australia
Patel, Homi B — *Businessman*
%Hartmarx Corp, 101 N Wacker Dr, Chicago, IL 60606, USA
Paterno, Joseph V (Joe) — *Football Coach*
830 McKee St, State College, PA 16803, USA
Paterson, Bill — *Actor*
%Kerry Gardner, 15 Kensington High St, London W8 5NP, England
Patin, Robert W — *Businessman*
%Washington National, 300 Tower Parkway, Lincolnshire, IL 60069, USA
Patinkin, Mandy — *Actor, Singer*
200 W 90th St, New York, NY 10024, USA
Patitz, Tatjana — *Model, Actress*
%International Creative Mgmt, 8942 Wilshire Blvd, Beverly Hills, CA 90211, USA
Patkin, Max — *Baseball Clown*
PO Box 68, Easton, PA 18044, USA
Paton, T Angus L — *Civil Engineer*
L'Epervier, Rt Orange, St Brelade, Jersey, United Kingdom
Patrell, Oliver L — *Businessman*
%Colonial Penn Group, PO Box 1990, Valley Forge, PA 19482, USA
Patrese, Ricardo — *Auto Racing Driver*
Via Umberto 1, 35100 Padova, Italy
Patric, Jason — *Actor*
501 21st Place, Santa Monica, CA 90402, USA
Patrick, Craig — *Hockey Player, Coach, Executive*
96 Quail Hill Lane, Pittsburgh, PA 15238, USA
Patrick, Dan — *Sportscaster*
%ESPN-TV, Sports Dept, ESPN Plaza, 935 Middle St, Bristol, CT 06010, USA
Patrick, Dennis — *Movie Director, Actor*
%Arlene Dayton Mgmt, 10110 Empyrean Way, #304, Los Angeles, CA 90067, USA
Patrick, Joseph A — *Financier*
%Baird Patrick Co, 20 Exchange Place, New York, NY 10005, USA
Patrick, Ruth — *Educator*
%Academy of Natural Sciences, 19th & Parkway, Philadelphia, PA 19103, USA
Patsatsia, Otar — *Prime Minister, Georgia*
%Prime Minister's Office, Government House, Ul Ingorokva, Tbilisi, Georgia
Patten, Christopher — *Governor General, Hong Kong*
%Foreign & Commonwealth Office, London SW1, England
Patterson, Dick — *Actor*
%Pat Lynn, 10525 Strathmore Dr, Los Angeles, CA 90024, USA
Patterson, Floyd — *Boxer*
PO Box 336, Springtown Road, New Paltz, NY 12561, USA
Patterson, Francine G (Penny) — *Animal Psychologist (Koko Trainer)*
%Gorilla Foundation, PO Box 620-640, Woodside, CA 94062, USA
Patterson, Gary — *Cartoonist (Cats)*
%Patterson International, 25208 Malibu Road, Malibu, CA 90265, USA

Patterson, James *Writer, Businessman*
%J Walter Thompson, 466 Lexington Ave, New York, NY 10017, USA

Patterson, John M *Governor, AL*
%Court of Judiciary, PO Box 30155, Montgomery, AL 36101, USA

Patterson, Lorna *Actress*
23530 Erwin St, Van Nuys, CA 91401, USA

Patterson, Percival J *Prime Minister, Jamaica*
%Prime Minister's Office, 1 Devon Road, PO Box 272, Kingston 6, Jamaica

Patterson, Richard North *Writer*
%McCutchen Doyle Brown Enersen, 3 Embarcadero Center, San Francisco, CA 94111, USA

Patterson, Robert M *Vietnam War Army Air Hero (CMH)*
907 Ironwood Dr, Henderson, KY 42420, USA

Patti, Sandi *Singer*
%Anderson Group, 2200 Madison Square, Anderson, IN 46011, USA

Pattillo, Linda *Commentator*
%ABC-TV, News Dept, 77 W 66th St, New York, NY 10023, USA

Patton, Mel *Track Athlete*
2312 Via Del Aguagate, Fallbrook, CA 92028, USA

Patton, Paul *Governor, KY*
%Governor's Office, State Capitol Building, #101, Frankfort, KY 40601, USA

Patty, J Edward (Budge) *Tennis Player*
La Marne, 14 Ave de Jurigoz, 1006 Lausanne, Switzerland

Patulski, Walter G (Walt) *Football Player*
4899 Abbottsbury Lane, Syracuse, NY 13215, USA

Patz, Arnall *Ophthalmologist*
%Johns Hopkins Hospital, Wilmer Eye Institute, 600 N Wolfe, Baltimore, MD 21287, USA

Patzaichan, Ivan *Canoeist*
SC Sportiv, Unirea Tricolor, Soseaua Stefan Cel Mare 9, Bucharest, Romania

Paul, Alexandra *Actress*
11936 Gorham Ave, #104, Los Angeles, CA 90049, USA

Paul, Arthur *Magazine Designer*
17 E Delaware Place, Chicago, IL 60611, USA

Paul, Billy *Singer*
%Walt Reeder Productions, 1516 Redwood Lane, Wyncote, PA 19095, USA

Paul, Donald (Don) *Football Player*
20100 Delita Dr, Woodland Hills, CA 91364, USA

Paul, Gyorgy *Concert Violinist*
27 Armitage Road, London NW11, England

Paul, Les *Guitarist, Inventor (Recording Methods)*
78 Deerhaven Road, Mahwah, NJ 07430, USA

Paul, Robert *Figure Skater*
10675 Rochester Ave, Los Angeles, CA 90024, USA

Paul, Tommy *Boxer*
340 Commonwealth Ave, Buffalo, NY 14216, USA

Paul, Wolfgang *Soccer Player*
Postfach 1324, 59939 Olsberg-Bigge, Germany

Paula, Alejandro F (Jandi) *Prime Minister, Netherlands Antilles*
%Premier's Office, Fort Amsterdam 17, Willemstad, Netherlands Antilles

Pauley, Jane *Commentator*
271 Central Park West, #10-E, New York, NY 10024, USA

Pauls, Raymond *Jazz Pianist, Composer*
Veidenbaum Str 41/43, #26, 226001 Riga, Latvia

Paulsen, Albert *Actor*
%H David Moss Assoc, 733 N Seward St, #PH, Los Angeles, CA 90038, USA

Paulson, Dennis *Golfer*
1664 Olympus Loop Dr, Vista, CA 92083, USA

Paultz, Billy *Basketball Player*
738 Benedicten Terrace, Sabastian, FL 32958, USA

Paup, Bryce *Football Player*
1112 Moraine Way, Green Bay, WI 54303, USA

Pavan, Marisa *Actress*
4 Allee des Brouillards, 75018 Paris, France

Pavarotti, Luciano *Opera Singer*
Stradelho Nava U 8, 41199 Modena, Italy

Pavin, Corey *Golfer*
6505 Aladdin Dr, Orlando, FL 32818, USA

Paxson, Jim *Basketball Player*
1236 SW Cardinell Dr, #A, Portland, OR 97201, USA

Paxton, Bill	*Actor*
1216 Village Meadows Dr, Lompoc, CA 93436, USA	
Paxton, John	*Editor*
%St Martin's Press, 175 5th Ave, New York, NY 10010, USA	
Paxton, Tom	*Singer, Songwriter*
%Fleming Tamulevich Assoc, 733-5 N Main St, Ann Arbor, MI 48104, USA	
Paycheck, Johnny	*Singer, Songwriter*
%Midnight Special, PO Box 918, Hendersonville, TN 37077, USA	
Payden, Joan A	*Financier*
%Payden & Pagel, 333 S Grand Ave, Los Angeles, CA 90071, USA	
Paymer, David	*Actor*
1506 Pacific St, Santa Monica, CA 90405, USA	
Payne, Anthony E	*Composer*
2 Wilton Square, London N1 3DL, England	
Payne, David L	*Financier*
%Westamerica Bancorp, 1108 5th Ave, San Rafael, CA 94901, USA	
Payne, Freda	*Singer*
10160 Cielo Dr, Beverly Hills, CA 90210, USA	
Payne, Harry C	*Educator*
%Williams College, President's Office, Williamstown, MA 01267, USA	
Payne, Heather	*Model*
%Wilhelmina Artists, 300 Park Ave, #200, New York, NY 10022, USA	
Payne, Henry	*Editorial Cartoonist*
%Scripps-Howard News Service, 1090 Vermont Ave NW, Washington, DC 20005, USA	
Payne, Keith	*Vietnam War Australian Army Hero (VC)*
2 St Bee's Ave, Bucasia QLD 4740, Australia	
Payne, Ladell	*Educator*
%Randolph-Macon College, President's Office, Ashland, VA 23005, USA	
Payne, Roger S	*Biologist, Conservationist*
191 Western Road, Lincoln, MA 01773, USA	
Payne, William P (Billy)	*Sports Executive*
%1996 Olympic Games Committee, 150 Williams St, #6000, Atlanta, GA 30303, USA	
Pays, Amanda	*Actress*
11075 Santa Monica Blvd, #150, Los Angeles, CA 90025, USA	
Payton, Benjamin F	*Educator*
%Tuskegee Institute, President's Office, Tuskegee, AL 36088, USA	
Payton, Gary	*Basketball Player*
14003 SE 43rd St, Bellevue, WA 98006, USA	
Payton, Gary E	*Astronaut*
7835 Belleflower Dr, Springfield, VA 22152, USA	
Payton, Nicholas	*Jazz Trumpeter*
%Management Ark, 116 Village Blvd, Princeton, NJ 08540, USA	
Payton, Walter J	*Football Player*
300 N Martingale Road, #340, Schaumburg, IL 60173, USA	
Paz, Octavio	*Nobel Literature Laureate, Diplomat*
%Revista Vuelta, Leonardo da Vinci 17, Mexico City 03910 DF, Mexico	
Pazienza, Vinny	*Boxer*
64 Waterman Ave, Cranston, RI 02910, USA	
Peabody, Endicott (Chub), III	*Governor, MA; Football Player*
PO Box 803, Hollis, NH 03049, USA	
Peacock, Andrew S	*Government Official, Australia*
30 Monomeath Ave, Canterbury, VIC 3126, Australia	
Peaker, E J	*Actress*
4935 Densmore Ave, Encino, CA 91436, USA	
Pearce, Austin W	*Businessman*
%British Aerospace, Brooklands Road, Weybridge, Surrey KT13 0SJ, England	
Pearlman, Jerry K	*Businessman*
%Zenith Electronics, 1000 Milwaukee Ave, Glenview, IL 60025, USA	
Pearlstein, Philip	*Artist*
361 W 36th St, New York, NY 10018, USA	
Pearlstine, Norman	*Editor*
%Time Warner Inc, Magazines Division, Rockefeller Plaza, New York, NY 10020, USA	
Pearson, David	*Auto Racing Driver*
290 Burnett Road, Spartanburg, SC 29316, USA	
Pearson, Drew	*Football Player*
1701 Eden Valley Lane, Plano, TX 75093, USA	
Pearson, Louis	*Sculptor*
224 12th St, San Francisco, CA 94103, USA	

P

Paxton - Pearson

Pease, Patsy *Actress*
4620 Kester Ave, #108, Sherman Oaks, CA 91403, USA
Pease, Rendel S *Physicist*
The Poplars, West Isley, Newbury, Berks RG16 0AW, England
Peay, Francis *Football Player, Coach*
PO Box 53877, Indianapolis, IN 46253, USA
Peay, J H Binford (Binnie), III *Army General*
Commander in Chief, US Central Command, MacDill Air Force Base, FL 33621, USA
Peca, Michael *Hockey Player*
%Buffalo Sabres, Marine Midland Arena, 1 Seymour Knox Plaza, Buffalo, NY 14210, USA
Pechstein, Claudia *Speed Skater*
%Pollinger Consulting, Wartenberger Str 24, 13053 Berlin, Germany
Peck, Gregory *Actor*
PO Box 837, Beverly Hills, CA 90213, USA
Peck, M Scott *Psychiatrist, Writer*
New Preston Marble Bliss Road, RFD 1, Washington Depot, CT 06793, USA
Peck, Richard E *Educator*
%University of New Mexico, President's Office, Albuquerque, NM 87131, USA
Pecker, David J *Publisher*
%Hachette Filipacchi, 1633 Broadway, New York, NY 10019, USA
Pecker, Jean-Claude *Astronomer*
Pusat-Tasek, 85350 Les Corbeaux, Ile d'Yeu, France
Peddle, Chuck *Computer Designer*
PO Box 91346, Mission Hill, CA 91345, USA
Pedersen, Richard F *Diplomat*
Twilight Park, Haines Falls, NY 12436, USA
Pedersen, William *Architect*
%Kohn Pedersen Fox Assoc, 111 W 57th St, New York, NY 10019, USA
Pederson, Donald O *Electrical Engineer*
1436 Via Loma, Walnut Creek, CA 94598, USA
Pedregon, Cruz *Auto Racing Driver*
%McDonald's Racing, PO Box 52, Moorpark, CA 93020, USA
Pedroni, Simone *Concert Pianist*
%Columbia Artists Mgmt Inc, 165 W 57th St, New York, NY 10019, USA
Peebles, Ann *Singer*
%Absolute Artists, 530 Howard St, #200, San Francisco, CA 94105, USA
Peebles, P J E *Physicist, Educator*
%Princeton University, Physics Dept, Princeton, NJ 08544, USA
Peeples, Nia *Actress, Singer*
PO Box 21833, Waco, TX 76702, USA
Peerce, Larry *Movie Director*
225 W 34th St, #1012, New York, NY 10122, USA
Peery, Troy A, Jr *Businessman*
%Heilig-Meyers Co, 2235 Staples Mill Road, Richmond, VA 23230, USA
Peete, Calvin *Golfer*
128 Garden Gate Dr, Ponte Vedra Beach, FL 32082, USA
Pei, I(eoh) M(ing) *Architect*
%Pei Cobb Freed Partners, 600 Madison Ave, New York, NY 10022, USA
Pekarkova, Iva *Writer*
%Farrar Straus Giroux, 19 Union Square W, New York, NY 10003, USA
Peladeau, Pierre *Editor*
%Quebecor Inc, 612 St Jacques St, Montreal PQ H3C 4M8, Canada
Pele *Soccer Player*
Praca dos Tres Poderes, Palacio de Planalto 70150-900 Brasilia DF, Brazil
Pelen, Perrine *Skier*
31 Ave de l'Eygala, 38700 Corens Mont Fleury, France
Pelikan, Jaroslav J *Writer, Historian*
156 Chestnut Lane, Hamden, CT 06518, USA
Pelikan, Lisa *Actress*
PO Box 57444, Sherman Oaks, CA 91413, USA
Pellegrini, Bob *Football Player*
5124 Haven Ave, Ocean City, NJ 08226, USA
Pellegrino, Edmund D *Physician*
5610 Wisconsin Ave, Chevy Chase, MD 20815, USA
Pelletreau, Robert H, Jr *Diplomat*
%US State Department, 2201 "C" St NW, Washington, DC 20520, USA
Pelli, Cesar A *Architect*
%Cesar Pelli Assoc, 1056 Chapel St, New Haven, CT 06510, USA

Peltz, Nelson — *Businessman*
%Triarc Companies, 900 3rd Ave, New York, NY 10022, USA

Peluso, Lisa — *Actress*
%Shauna Sickenger, PO Box 301, Ramona, CA 92065, USA

Pemberton, Brian — *Businessman*
%Cable & Wireless PLC, Mercury House, Theobald's Road, London WC1, England

Pena, Alejandro — *Baseball Player*
12635 Etris Road, Roswell, GA 30075, USA

Pena, Elizabeth — *Actress*
1768 Rotary Dr, Los Angeles, CA 90026, USA

Pena, Paco — *Concert Guitarist*
%Karin Vaessen, 4 Boscastle Road, London NW5 1EG, England

Penderecki, Krzysztof — *Composer, Conductor*
Ul Cisowa 22, 30-229 Cracow, Poland

Pendergrass, Henry P — *Physician, Educator*
%Vanderbilt University, Medical School, 1621 21st Ave S, Nashville, TN 37212, USA

Pendergrass, Teddy — *Singer, Songwriter*
1505 Flat Rock Road, Narberth, PA 19072, USA

Penders, Tom — *Basketball Coach*
%University of Texas, Athletic Dept, Austin, TX 78713, USA

Pendleton, Moses — *Dancer, Choreographer*
%Momix, PO Box 35, Washington, CT 06794, USA

Pendleton, Terry L — *Baseball Player*
1831 Bally Bunion Dr, Duluth, GA 30097, USA

Penghlis, Thaao — *Actor*
7187 Macapo Dr, Los Angeles, CA 90068, USA

Peniston, CeCe — *Singer*
%Brothers Mgmt, 141 Dunbar Ave, Fords, NJ 08863, USA

Penky, Joseph F — *Chemical Engineer*
%Purdue University, Chemical Engineering Dept, West Lafayette, IN 47907, USA

Penn (Jillette) — *Comedian, Illusionist (Penn & Teller)*
142 W 49th St, New York, NY 10019, USA

Penn, Arthur H — *Movie Director*
%William Morris Agency, 151 S El Camino Dr, Beverly Hills, CA 90212, USA

Penn, Christopher — *Actor*
6728 Zumirez Dr, Malibu, CA 90265, USA

Penn, Irving — *Photographer*
%Irving Penn Studio, 89 5th Ave, New York, NY 10003, USA

Penn, Sean — *Actor, Director*
%Clyde Is Hungary Productions, 22333 Pacific Coast Highway, Malibu, CA 90265, USA

Pennacchio, Len A — *Geneticist*
%Stanford University, Human Genome Center, Stanford, CA 94305, USA

Pennario, Leonard — *Concert Pianist*
1140 Calle Vista Dr, Beverly Hills, CA 90210, USA

Pennington, Weldon J — *Publisher*
%Seattle Times, Fairview Ave N & John St, Seattle, WA 98109, USA

Pennock, Raymond — *Businessman*
%Morgan Grenfell Group, 23 Great Winchester St, London EC2P 2AX, England

Penny, Joe — *Actor*
10453 Sarah St, North Hollywood, CA 91602, USA

Penny, Roger P — *Businessman*
%Bethlehem Steel, 1170 8th Ave, Bethlehem, PA 18018, USA

Penny, Sydney — *Actress*
6894 Parsons Trail, Tujunga, CA 91042, USA

Penske, Roger S — *Auto Racing Driver, Builder; Businessman*
%Penske Corp, 13400 Outer Dr W, Detroit, MI 48239, USA

Penzias, Arno A — *Nobel Physics Laureate*
%AT&T Bell Laboratories, Radiophysics Research Dept, Holmdel, NJ 07733, USA

Peoples, John — *Physicist*
%Fermi Nat Acceleration Lab, CDF Collaboration, PO Box 500, Batavia, IL 60510, USA

Pep, Willie — *Boxer*
130 Hartford Ave, Wethersfield, CT 06109, USA

Pepitone, Joseph A (Joe) — *Baseball Player*
32 Lois Lane, Farmingdale, NY 11735, USA

Pepper, John E, Jr — *Businessman*
%Procter & Gamble Co, 1 Procter & Gamble Plaza, Cincinnati, OH 45202, USA

Peppler, Mary Jo — *Volleyball Player*
2015 Garnet Ave, #R-136, San Diego, CA 92109, USA

P

Perahia, Murray — *Concert Pianist*
%Fine Arts Mgmt, 201 6th Ave, #A, Brooklyn, NY 11217, USA

Perak, Sultan of — *Ruler, Malaysia*
%Sultan's Palace, Istana Bukit Serene, Kuala Lumpur, Malaysia

Peralta, Ricardo — *Astronaut, Mexico*
%Ingeneria Instituto, Ciudad Universitaria, 04510 Mexico City DF, Mexico

Percy, Charles H — *Senator, IL*
%Charles Percy Assoc, 1750 "K" St NW, #1200, Washington, DC 20006, USA

Perdue, Will — *Basketball Player*
%San Antonio Spurs, 600 E Market St, #102, San Antonio, TX 78205, USA

Pereira, Aristides M — *President, Cape Verde*
PO Box 172, Praia, Cape Verde

Perek, Lubos — *Astronomer*
%Astronomical Institute, Budecska 6, Prague 2, Czech Republic

Perelman, Ronald O — *Businessman*
%MacAndrews & Forbes Group, 36 E 63rd St, New York, NY 10021, USA

Perenchio, A Jerrold — *Entertainment Executive*
%Chartwell Partnerships, 1999 Ave of Stars, #3050, Los Angeles, CA 90067, USA

Perenyi, Miklos — *Concert Violinist*
Erdoalja Utca 1/B, 1037 Budapest, Hungary

Peres, Shimon — *Prime Minister, Nobel Peace Laureate*
%Israel Labour Party, 10 Hayarkon St, Tel-Aviv 63571, Israel

Peretokin, Mark — *Ballet Dancer*
%Bolshoi Theater, Teatralnaya Pl 1, 103009 Moscow, Russia

Perez Balladares, Ernesto — *President, Panama*
%President's Office, Valija 50, Panama City 1, Panama

Perez de Cuellar, Javier — *Secretary General, United Nations*
%Republic National Bank, 425 5th Ave, New York, NY 10016, USA

Perez Esquivel, Adolfo — *Nobel Peace Laureate*
%University of Peace, Apdo Postal 199, 1250 Escalzu, Costa Rica

Perez Fernandez, Pedro — *Government Official, Spain*
%Ministerio de Economia, Hacieda y Comercio, Alcala 9, Madrid 14, Spain

Perez Godoy, Ricardo P — *President, Peru; Army General*
Blasco Nunez de Balboa 225, Miraflores, Lima, Peru

Perez, Atanasio R (Tony) — *Baseball Player, Manager*
1717 N Bayshore Dr, #2735, Miami, FL 33132, USA

Perez, Hugo — *Soccer Player*
22018 Newbridge Dr, Lake Forest, CA 92630, USA

Perez, Pascual — *Baseball Player*
%Salvador, Cucurulo #105, Santiago, Dominican Republic

Perez, Rosie — *Actress*
1990 S Bundy Dr, #600, Los Angeles, CA 90025, USA

Perez, Vincent — *Actor*
%Artmedia, 10 Ave George V, 75008 Paris, France

Perick, Christof — *Conductor*
%Shaw Concerts, Lincoln Center Plaza, 1900 Broadway, #200, New York, NY 10023, USA

Perier, Francois — *Actor*
%Artmedia, 10 Ave George V, 75008 Paris, France

Perini, David B — *Businessman*
PO Box 9160, Framingham, MA 01701, USA

Perkins, Carl — *Singer, Songwriter*
%Steve Perkins, 27 Sunnymeade Dr, Jackson, TN 38305, USA

Perkins, David D — *Biologist, Geneticist*
345 Vine St, Menlo Park, CA 94025, USA

Perkins, Edward J — *Diplomat*
%US State Department, 2201 "C" St NW, Washington, DC 20520, USA

Perkins, Elizabeth — *Actress*
%Creative Artists Agency, 9830 Wilshire Blvd, Beverly Hills, CA 90212, USA

Perkins, James B, III — *Navy Admiral*
Commander, Military Sealift Command, 901 "M" St SE, Washington, DC 20398, USA

Perkins, Lawrence B, Jr — *Architect*
%Perkins Eastman Partners, 437 5th Ave, New York, NY 10016, USA

Perkins, Lucian — *Photographer*
%Washington Post, Editorial Dept, 1150 15th St NW, Washington, DC 20071, USA

Perkins, Millie — *Actress*
2511 Canyon Dr, Los Angeles, CA 90068, USA

Perkins, Sam — *Basketball Player*
%Seattle Supersonics, 190 Queen Ave N, PO Box C-900911, Seattle, WA 98109, USA

Perahia - Perkins

Perkins, Thomas J — *Businessman*
%Tandem Computers, 19333 Vallco Parkway, Cupertino, CA 95014, USA

Perkoff, Gerald T — *Physician*
1300 Torrey Pines Dr, Columbia, MO 65203, USA

Perl, Martin L — *Nobel Physics Laureate*
3737 El Centro Ave, Palo Alto, CA 94306, USA

Perle, George — *Composer*
%Queens College, Music Dept, Flushing, NY 11367, USA

Perlegos, George — *Businessman*
%Atmel, 2325 Orchard Parkway, San Jose, CA 95131, USA

Perlemuter, Vlado — *Concert Pianist*
21 Rue Ampere, 75017 Paris, France

Perley, James — *Labor Leader*
%American Assn of University Professors, 1012 14th St NW, Washington, DC 20005, USA

Perlich, Max — *Actor*
%United Talent Agency, 9560 Wilshire Blvd, #500, Beverly Hills, CA 90212, USA

Perlman, Itzhak — *Concert Violinist*
173 Riverside Dr, #3-C, New York, NY 10024, USA

Perlman, Lawrence — *Businessman*
%Ceridian Corp, 8100 34th Ave S, Minneapolis, MN 55425, USA

Perlman, Rhea — *Actress*
PO Box 491246, Los Angeles, CA 90049, USA

Perlman, Ron — *Actor*
335 N Maple Dr, #361, Beverly Hills, CA 90210, USA

Perlmutter, Norman — *Financier*
%Heitman Financial, 180 N LaSalle St, Chicago, IL 60601, USA

Perna, Frank, Jr — *Businessman*
%Magnetek Electric, 400 S Prairie Ave, Waukesha, WI 53186, USA

Peron, Isabelita Martinez de — *President, Argentina*
Moreto 3, Los Jeronimos, Madrid, Spain

Perot, H Ross — *Businessman*
%Perot Group, Lakeside Square, 12377 Merit Dr, #1700, Dallas, TX 75251, USA

Perranoski, Ronald P (Ron) — *Baseball Player*
3805 Indian River Dr, Vero Beach, FL 32963, USA

Perreau, Gigi — *Actress*
4258 Beeman Ave, Studio City, CA 91604, USA

Perreault, Gilbert (Gil) — *Hockey Player*
4 De la Serenite, Victoriaville PQ G6P 6S2, Canada

Perrella, James E — *Businessman*
%Ingersoll-Rand Co, 20 Chestnut Ridge Road, Woodcliff Lake, NJ 07675, USA

Perrin, Charles R — *Businessman*
%Duracell International, Bershire Corporate Park, Bethel, CT 06801, USA

Perrine, Valerie — *Actress*
14411 Riverside Dr, Sherman Oaks, CA 91423, USA

Perron, Jean — *Hockey Coach*
5 Thomas Mellon Circle, San Francisco, CA 94134, USA

Perry, Charles O — *Sculptor*
20 Shorehaven Road, Norwalk, CT 06855, USA

Perry, Felton — *Actor*
PO Box 931359, Los Angeles, CA 90093, USA

Perry, Fletcher (Joe) — *Football Player*
1844 E Chicago St, Chandler, AZ 85225, USA

Perry, Gaylord J — *Baseball Player*
PO Box 1958, Kill Devil Hill, NC 27948, USA

Perry, Gerald — *Football Player*
2940 Dell Dr, Columbia, SC 29209, USA

Perry, James E (Jim) — *Baseball Player*
2608 S Ridgeview Way, Sioux Falls, SD 57105, USA

Perry, Joe — *Guitarist (Aerosmith), Songwriter*
PO Box 2665, Duxbury, MA 02331, USA

Perry, John Bennett — *Actor*
%Judy Schoen, 606 N Larchmont Blvd, #309, Los Angeles, CA 90004, USA

Perry, Kenny — *Golfer*
418 Quail Ridge Road, Franklin, KY 42134, USA

Perry, Linda — *Singer (4 Non Blondes), Songwriter*
%Gerard Mgmt, 601 Van Ness Ave, #E3-347, San Francisco, CA 94102, USA

Perry, Luke — *Actor*
137 N Larchmont Blvd, #117, Los Angeles, CA 90004, USA

Perry, Matthew *Actor*
7204 Chelan Way, #505, Los Angeles, CA 90068, USA

Perry, Michael Dean *Football Player*
19125 Peninsula Point Road, Cornelius, NC 28031, USA

Perry, Robert P *Molecular Biologist*
1808 Bustleton Pike, Churchville, PA 18966, USA

Perry, Roger *Actor*
4363 Ledge Ave, Toluca Lake, CA 91602, USA

Perry, Seymour M *Physician*
%Georgetown Medical School, Community Medicine Dept, Washington, DC 20007, USA

Perry, Steve *Singer (Journey)*
%Premier Talent, 3 E 54th St, #1100, New York, NY 10022, USA

Perry, Troy D *Religious Leader*
%Metropolitan Churches Fellowship, 5300 Santa Monica Blvd, Los Angeles, CA 90029, USA

Perry, William (Refrigerator) *Football Player*
Rt 3, Box 265, Aiken, SC 29801, USA

Perry, William J *Secretary, Defense*
PO Box AA, Stanford, CA 94309, USA

Persoff, Nehemiah *Actor*
5847 Tampa Ave, Tarzana, CA 91356, USA

Person, Chuck *Basketball Player*
%San Antonio Spurs, 600 E Market St, #102, San Antonio, TX 78205, USA

Person, Wesley *Basketball Player*
PO Box 305, Brantley, AL 36009, USA

Persson, Goeran *Prime Minister, Sweden*
%Prime Minister's Office, Rosenbad 4, 103 33 Stockholm, Sweden

Persson, Jorgen *Cinematographer*
Lievagen 23, 183 38 Taby, Sweden

Pertschuk, Michael *Government Official, Political Activist*
%Advocacy Institute, 1730 "M" St NW, #600, Washington, DC 20036, USA

Perutz, Max F *Nobel Chemistry Laureate*
42 Sedley Taylor Road, Cambridge, England

Pesci, Joe *Actor*
PO Box 6, Lavallette, NJ 08735, USA

Pescia, Lisa *Actress*
%Epstein-Wyckoff, 280 S Beverly Dr, #400, Beverly Hills, CA 90212, USA

Pescow, Donna *Actress*
2179 W 21st St, Los Angeles, CA 90018, USA

Pesek, Libor *Conductor*
%IMG Artists, Media House, 3 Burlington Lane, London W4 2TH, England

Pesky, John M (Johnny) *Baseball Player*
2201 Edison Ave, Fort Myers, FL 33901, USA

Peter, Valentine J *Religious Leader, Educator*
%Father Flanagan's Boys Home, Boys Town, NE 68010, USA

Peterdi, Gabor *Artist*
108 Highland Ave, Rowayton, CT 06853, USA

Peters, Bernadette *Actress, Singer*
323 W 80th St, New York, NY 10024, USA

Peters, Bob *Hockey Coach*
%Bemidji State University, Athletic Dept, Bemidji, MN 56601, USA

Peters, Brock *Actor*
1420 Rising Glen Road, Los Angeles, CA 90069, USA

Peters, Charles G, Jr *Editor*
%Washington Monthly, 1611 Connecticut Ave NW, Washington, DC 20009, USA

Peters, Elizabeth *Writer*
%Mysterious Press, Warner Books, 1271 6th Ave, New York, NY 10020, USA

Peters, Floyd *Football Player, Coach*
9222 Hyland Creek Road, Bloomington, MN 55437, USA

Peters, Gary C *Baseball Player*
7121 N Serenoa Dr, Sarasota, FL 34241, USA

Peters, Gretchen *Singer, Songwriter*
%Purple Crayon Mgmt, PO Box 358, Hendersonville, TN 37077, USA

Peters, Jean *Actress*
507 N Palm Dr, Beverly Hills, CA 90210, USA

Peters, Jon *Movie Producer*
9 Beverly Park, Beverly Hills, CA 90210, USA

Peters, Maria Liberia *Prime Minister, Netherlands Antilles*
%Prime Minister's Office, Fort Amsterdam, Willemstad, Netherlands Antilles

Peters, Mary *Track Athlete*
Willowtree Cottage, River Road, Dunmurray, Belfast, Northern Ireland
Peters, Mike *Editorial Cartoonist (Grimmy)*
1269 1st St, #8, Sarasota, FL 34236, USA
Peters, Richard J *Businessman*
%Penske Corp, 13400 Outer Dr W, Detroit, MI 48239, USA
Peters, Roberta *Opera Singer, Actress*
64 Garden Road, Scarsdale, NY 10583, USA
Peters, Tom *Writer, Management Consultant*
%Tom Peters Group, 555 Hamilton Ave, Palo Alto, CA 94301, USA
Petersdorf, Robert G *Physician*
1219 Parkside Dr E, Seattle, WA 98112, USA
Petersen, Paul *Actor, Singer*
14530 Denker Ave, Gardena, CA 90247, USA
Petersen, Raymond J *Publisher*
%Hearst Corp, 959 8th Ave, New York, NY 10019, USA
Petersen, Robert E *Publisher*
%Petersen Publishing Co, 6420 Wilshire Blvd, #100, Los Angeles, CA 90048, USA
Petersen, William L *Actor*
3330 Cahuenga Blvd, #400, Los Angeles, CA 90068, USA
Petersen, Wolfgang *Movie Director*
%Creative Artists Agency, 9830 Wilshire Blvd, Beverly Hills, CA 90212, USA
Peterson, Ben *Wrestler*
%Camp of Champs, PO Box 438, Watertown, WI 53094, USA
Peterson, Bruce *Test Pilot*
43665 21st St W, Lancaster, CA 93536, USA
Peterson, David C *Photographer*
2024 35th St, Des Moines, IA 50310, USA
Peterson, Donald H *Astronaut*
%Aerospace Operations Consultants, 427 Pebblebrook Dr, Seabrook, TX 77586, USA
Peterson, Douglas (Pete) *Representative, FL*
%US State Department, 2201 "C" St NW, Washington, DC 20520, USA
Peterson, Elly *Women's Activist*
1515 "M" St NW, Washington, DC 20005, USA
Peterson, Esther *Consumer Advocate*
3032 Stephenson Place NW, Washington, DC 20015, USA
Peterson, Fred I (Fritz) *Baseball Player*
2525 Old Tavern Road, #17, Lisle, IL 60532, USA
Peterson, John *Wrestler*
457 19th Ave, Comstock, WI 54826, USA
Peterson, Lars *Surgeon*
%Sahlgrenska University Hospital, Goteborg, Sweden
Peterson, Michael *Singer*
%Reprise Records, 3300 Warner Blvd, Burbank, CA 91505, USA
Peterson, Oscar E *Jazz Pianist, Composer*
%Regal Recordings, 2421 Hammond Road, Mississauga ON L5K 1T3, Canada
Peterson, Peter G *Financier, Secretary of Commerce*
%Blackstone Group, 345 Park Ave, New York, NY 10154, USA
Peterson, Ralph *Jazz Drummer*
%Joel Chriss, 300 Mercer St, #3-J, New York, NY 10003, USA
Peterson, Ray *Singer*
201 Odyssey St, Henderson, NV 89014, USA
Peterson, Robert L *Businessman*
%IBP Inc, IBP Ave, Dakota City, NE 68731, USA
Peterson, Russell W *Governor, DE*
11 E Mozart Dr, Wilmington, DE 19807, USA
Peterson, Thomas R *Educator*
%Seton Hall University, President's Office, South Orange, NJ 07079, USA
Peterson, Walter R *Governor, NH; Educator*
PO Box 3100, Peterborough, NH 03458, USA
Petersson, Tom *Singer, Bassist (Cheap Trick)*
%Ken Adamay, 3805 County Road "M", Middleton, WI 53562, USA
Petherbridge, Edward *Actor*
%Jonathan Altaras, 27 Floral St, London WC2E 9DP, England
Petibon, Richard A (Richie) *Football Player, Coach*
%Washington Redskins, 21300 Redskin Park Dr, Ashburn, VA 20147, USA
Petit, Philippe *High Wire Walker*
%Cathedral of Saint John the Devine, 1047 Amsterdam Ave, New York, NY 10025, USA

Petit, Richard G *Businessman*
%Colonial Penn Life Insurance, 1818 Market St, Philadelphia, PA 19103, USA

Petit, Roland *Ballet Dancer, Choreographer*
20 Blvd Gabes, 13008 Marseilles, France

Petraglia, John (Johnny) *Bowler*
%Professional Bowlers Assn, 1720 Merriman Road, Akron, OH 44313, USA

Petrassi, Goffredo *Composer*
Via Ferdinando di Savoia 3, 00196 Rome, Italy

Petrenko, Viktor *Figure Skater*
%International Skating Center, 1375 Hopmeadow St, Simsbury, CT 06070, USA

Petri, Michala *Concert Recorder Player*
Nodde-Hegnet 30, Nodebo, 3480 Fredensborg, Denmark

Petrie, Daniel M, Jr *Movie Director*
%Richland/Wunsch/Hohman Agency, 9220 Sunset Blvd, #311, Los Angeles, CA 90069, USA

Petrie, Daniel M, Sr *Movie, Theater Director*
13201 Haney Place, Los Angeles, CA 90049, USA

Petrie, Geoff *Basketball Player, Executive*
%Sacramento Kings, 1 Sports Parkway, Sacramento, CA 95834, USA

Petrie, George O *Actor*
%Gage Group, 9255 Sunset Blvd, #515, Los Angeles, CA 90069, USA

Petrocelli, Americo P (Rico) *Baseball Player*
19 Townsend Road, Lynnfield, MA 01940, USA

Petrocelli, Daniel *Attorney*
%Mitchell Silverberg Krupp, 11377 W Olympic Blvd, Los Angeles, CA 90064, USA

Petrone, Rocco A *Missile Engineer*
1329 Granvia Altamira, Palos Verdes Estates, CA 90274, USA

Petroske, John *Hockey Player*
PO Box 366, Side Lake, MN 55781, USA

Petrov, Andrei P *Composer*
Petrovskaya Str 42, #75, 197046 St Petersburg, Russia

Petrov, Nikolai A *Concert Pianist*
Kutuzovsky Prosp 26, #23, 121 165 Moscow, Russia

Petrovics, Emil *Composer*
Attila Utca 29, 1013 Budapest, Hungary

Petrucciani, Michel *Jazz Pianist*
%Joel Chriss, 300 Mercer St, #3-J, New York, NY 10003, USA

Petry, Daniel J (Dan) *Baseball Player*
1808 Cartlen Dr, Placentia, CA 92870, USA

Petry, Thomas E *Businessman*
%Eagle-Picher Industries, 580 Walnut St, Cincinnati, OH 45202, USA

Pett, Joel *Editorial Cartoonist*
%Lexington Herald-Leader, Editorial Dept, Main & Midland, Lexington, KY 40507, USA

Pettengill, Gordon H *Planetary Physicist*
%Massachusetts Institute of Technology, Space Research Ctr, Cambridge, MA 02139, USA

Petterson, Donald K *Diplomat*
American Embassy Khartoum, #63900, APO, AE 09829, USA

Pettet, Joanna *Actress*
%Paradigm Agency, 10100 Santa Monica Blvd, #2500, Los Angeles, CA 90067, USA

Pettibon, Raymond *Artist*
%Richard/Bennett Gallery, 10337 Wilshire Blvd, Los Angeles, CA 90024, USA

Pettigrew, L Eudora *Educator*
%State University of New York, President's Office, Old Westbury, NY 11568, USA

Pettijohn, Francis J *Geologist*
11630 Glen Arm Road, #V-51, Glen Arm, MD 21057, USA

Pettit, Robert L (Bob), Jr *Basketball Player*
7 Garden Lane, New Orleans, LA 70124, USA

Pettit, T Christopher *Financier*
%Lehman Brothers, 3 World Financial Center, New York, NY 10281, USA

Pettitte, Andrew E (Andy) *Baseball Player*
1714 N Park Side, Deer Park, TX 77536, USA

Petty, Kyle *Auto Racing Driver*
4941 Finch Farm Road, Trinity, NC 27370, USA

Petty, Lee *Auto Racing Driver*
%Petty Enterprises, 307 Branson Mill Road, Randleman, NC 27317, USA

Petty, Lori *Actress*
12301 Wilshire Blvd, #200, Los Angeles, CA 90025, USA

Petty, Richard *Auto Racing Driver*
PO Box 86, 311 Branson Mill Road, Randleman, NC 27317, USA

Petty, Tom *Singer, Guitarist, Songwriter*
%East End Mgmt, 8209 Melrose Ave, #200, Los Angeles, CA 90046, USA

Peugeot, Roland *Businessman*
%Estab Peugeot Ferres, 75 Ave Grande Armee, 75116 Paris, France

Peyser, Penny *Actress*
%Epstein-Wyckoff, 280 S Beverly Dr, #400, Beverly Hills, CA 90212, USA

Peyton of Yeovil, John W W *Government Official, England*
Old Malt House, Hinton St George, Somerset TA17 8SE, England

Pezzano, Chuck *Bowling Writer*
%Professional Bowlers Assn, 1720 Merriman Road, Akron, OH 44313, USA

Pfaff, Judy *Artist*
%Holly Solomon Gallery, 172 Mercer St, New York, NY 10012, USA

Pfann, George R *Football Player*
120 Warwick Place, Ithaca, NY 14850, USA

Pfeiffer, Carl E *Businessman*
%Quanex Corp, 1900 W Loop S, Houston, TX 77027, USA

Pfeiffer, Doug *Ski Instructor, Editor*
PO Box 1806, Big Bear Lake, CA 92315, USA

Pfeiffer, Eckhard *Businessman*
%Compaq Computer, 20555 State Highway 249, Houston, TX 77070, USA

Pfeiffer, Michelle *Actress*
3727 W Magnolia Blvd, #300, Burbank, CA 91505, USA

Pfeiffer, Norman *Architect*
%Hardy Holzman Pfeiffer, 811 W 7th St, Los Angeles, CA 90017, USA

Pflimlin, Pierre *Prime Minister, France*
24 Ave de la Paix, 67000 Strasbourg, France

Pflug, Jo Ann *Actress*
1270 Peachtree Battle Ave NW, Atlanta, GA 30327, USA

Pfund, Randy *Basketball Coach, Executive*
%Miami Heat, Miami Arena, 100 NE 3rd Ave, Miami, FL 33132, USA

Phair, Liz *Singer, Songwriter*
%Vector Mgmt, 1500 17th Ave S, Nashville, TN 37212, USA

Pham Tuan *Cosmonaut, Vietnam*
4C-1000-Soc Son, Hanoi, Vietnam

Phantog *Mountaineer*
%Wuxi Sports & Physical Culture Commission, Jiagnsu, China

Phelan, Jim *Basketball Coach*
%Mount St Mary's College, Athletic Dept, Emmitsburg, MD 21727, USA

Phelps, Ashton, Jr *Publisher*
%New Orleans Times-Picayune, 3800 Howard Ave, New Orleans, LA 70140, USA

Phelps, Kelly Joe *Singer, Guitarist*
%Mongel Music, 123 Townsend St, #445, San Francisco, CA 94107, USA

Phelps, Michael E *Neuroscientist*
16720 Huerta Road, Encino, CA 91436, USA

Phelps, Richard F (Digger) *Basketball Coach*
%ESPN-TV, Sports Dept, ESPN Plaza, 935 Middle St, Bristol, CT 06010, USA

Philbin, Regis *Entertainer*
955 Park Ave, New York, NY 10028, USA

Philip *Crown Prince, England; Duke of Edinburgh*
%Buckingham Palace, London SW1A 1AA, England

Philip (Saliba), Primate *Religious Leader*
%Antiochian Orthodox Christian Church, 358 Mountain Road, Englewood, NJ 07631, USA

Philipp, Stephanie *Model*
%Agentur Margit de la Berg, 82057 Icking-Isartal, Germany

Philippe *Crown Prince, Belgium*
%Koninklijk Palais, Rue de Brederode, 1000 Brussels, Belgium

Phillip, Andy *Basketball Player*
PO Box 385, Rancho Mirage, CA 92270, USA

Phillips, Bobbie *Actress*
11300 W Olympic Blvd, #300, Los Angeles, CA 90064, USA

Phillips, Caryl *Writer*
%Amherst College, English Dept, Amherst, MA 01002, USA

Phillips, Chynna *Singer, Actress*
10557 Troon Ave, Los Angeles, CA 90064, USA

Phillips, Flip *Jazz Saxophonist*
%Verve Records, Worldwide Plaza, 825 8th Ave, New York, NY 10019, USA

Phillips, Grace *Actress*
%Gersh Agency, 232 N Canon Dr, Beverly Hills, CA 90210, USA

P

Petty - Phillips

Phillips, Graham H *Businessman*
%Ogilvy Group, Worldwide Plaza, 309 W 49th St, New York, NY 10019, USA

Phillips, Harvey *Concert Tuba Player*
%TubaRanch, 4769 S Harrell Road, Bloomington, IN 47401, USA

Phillips, John *Singer (Mamas & Papas), Songwriter*
%Paradise Artists, 108 E Matilija St, Ojai, CA 93023, USA

Phillips, Julia *Movie Producer, Writer*
1100 Alta Loma Road, #1207, Los Angeles, CA 90069, USA

Phillips, Julianne *Actress*
2227 Mandeville Canyon Road, Los Angeles, CA 90049, USA

Phillips, Kate *Writer*
%Houghton Mifflin, 215 Park Ave S, New York, NY 10003, USA

Phillips, Lawrence *Football Player*
%St Louis Rams, 100 N Broadway, #2100, St Louis, MO 63102, USA

Phillips, Lou Diamond *Actor*
11766 Wilshire Blvd, #1470, Los Angeles, CA 90025, USA

Phillips, Mackenzie *Actress*
%SDB Partners, 1801 Ave of Stars, #902, Los Angeles, CA 90067, USA

Phillips, Michelle *Actress, Singer (Mamas & Papas)*
10557 Troon Ave, Los Angeles, CA 90064, USA

Phillips, Norma *Social Activist*
%Mothers Against Drunk Driving, PO Box 819100, Dallas, TX 75381, USA

Phillips, Owen M *Geophysical Engineer*
%Johns Hopkins University, Geophysical Mechanics Dept, Baltimore, MD 21218, USA

Phillips, Peg *Actress*
%Alliance Talent, 9171 Wilshire Blvd, #441, Beverly Hills, CA 90210, USA

Phillips, Robert W *Astronaut*
%National Aviation & Space Agency, Code D-4, 300 "E" St SW, Washington, DC 20546, USA

Phillips, Sam *Singer, Songwriter*
%Direct Mgmt Group, 947 N La Cienega Blvd, #G, Los Angeles, CA 90069, USA

Phillips, Sian *Actress*
8 Alexa Court, 78 Lexham Gardens, London W8 6JL, England

Phillips, Stone *Commentator*
%NBC-TV, News Dept, 30 Rockefeller Plaza, New York, NY 10112, USA

Phillips, Susan M *Financier, Government Official*
%Federal Reserve Board, 20th St & Constitution NW, Washington, DC 20551, USA

Phillips, Warren H *Publisher*
%Bridge Works Publications, PO Box 1798, Bridgehampton, NY 11932, USA

Phillips, Wendy *Actress*
2285 Walker Lane, Salt Lake City, UT 84117, USA

Phillips, William *Editor, Writer*
%Partisan Review, Editorial Dept, 236 Bay State Road, Boston, MA 02215, USA

Phills, Bobby *Basketball Player*
13608 Cadiz Dr, Baker, LA 70714, USA

Phipps, Ogden M *Financier, Thoroughbred Racing Executive*
%Bessemer Group, 100 Woodbridge Center Dr, Woodbridge, NJ 07095, USA

Phoenix, Joaquin *Actor*
1450 Belfast Dr, Los Angeles, CA 90069, USA

Piano, Renzo *Architect*
%Renzo Piano Building Workshop, Via P P Rubens 29, 16158 Genoa, Italy

Piazza, Marguerite *Opera Singer*
5400 Park Ave, #301, Memphis, TN 38119, USA

Piazza, Michale J (Mike) *Baseball Player*
PO Box 864, Oakwood Lane, Valley Forge, PA 19482, USA

Picachy, Lawrence Cardinal *Religious Leader*
%Archbishop's House, 32 Park St, Calcutta 700016, India

Picard, Dennis J *Businessman*
%Raytheon Co, 141 Spring St, Lexington, MA 02173, USA

Picardo, Robert *Actor*
4926 Commonwealth Ave, La Canada, CA 91011, USA

Picasso, Paloma *Jewelry Designer, Actress*
%Lopez-Cambil Ltd, 37 W 57th St, New York, NY 10019, USA

Piccard, Franck *Skier*
%General Delivery, Les Sailses, France

Piccard, Jacques E J *Underwater Scientist*
Place d'Armes, 1096 Cully, Switzerland

Piccoli, Michel *Actor*
11 Rue Des Lions St Paul, 75004 Paris, France

Piccone, Robin — *Fashion Designer*
%Piccone Apparel Corp, 1424 Washington Blvd, Venice, CA 90291, USA

Picerni, Paul — *Actor*
19119 Wells Dr, Tarzana, CA 91356, USA

Pichler, Joseph A — *Businessman*
%Kroger Co, 1014 Vine St, Cincinnati, OH 45202, USA

Pickard, Nancy — *Writer*
2502 W 71st Terrace, Prairie Village, KS 66208, USA

Pickens, Carl — *Football Player*
623 Terrace Ave, Murphy, NC 28906, USA

Pickens, Jo Ann — *Opera Singer*
%Norman McCann Artists, 56 Lawrie Park Gardens, London SE26 6XJ, England

Pickens, T Boone, Jr — *Businessman*
%Mesa Inc, Trammell Crow Center, 2001 Ross Ave, Dallas, TX 75201, USA

Pickering, Byron — *Artist*
6919 NE Highland Dr, Lincoln City, OR 97367, USA

Pickering, Thomas R — *Diplomat*
%US State Department, 2201 "C" St NW, Washington, DC 20520, USA

Pickering, William H — *Scientist, Educator*
292 St Katherine Dr, Flintridge, CA 91011, USA

Pickett, Bobby — *Singer*
%Stuart Hersh Entertainment, PO Box 310, Hartsdale, NY 10530, USA

Pickett, Cindy — *Actress*
662 N Van Ness Ave, #305, Los Angeles, CA 90004, USA

Pickett, Michael D — *Businessman*
%Merisel Inc, 200 Continental Blvd, El Segundo, CA 90245, USA

Pickett, Wilson — *Singer*
%Talent Source, 1560 Broadway, #1308, New York, NY 10036, USA

Pickitt, John L — *Air Force General*
38 Sunrise Point Road, Lake Wylie, SC 29710, USA

Pickles, Christina — *Actress*
137 S Westgate Ave, Los Angeles, CA 90049, USA

Piech, Ferdinand — *Businessman*
%Volkswagenwerk AG, Braunschweiger Str 63, 38179 Schwulper, Germany

Piel, Gerard — *Editor, Publisher*
%Scientific American Magazine, 415 Madison Ave, New York, NY 10017, USA

Piel, Jonathan — *Editor*
%Scientific American Magazine, 415 Madison Ave, New York, NY 10017, USA

Pieper, Roel — *Businessman*
%Tandem Computers, 19333 Vallco Parkway, Cupertino, CA 95014, USA

Pierce, Daniel — *Financier*
%Scudder Stevens Clark, 345 Park Ave, New York, NY 10154, USA

Pierce, David Hyde — *Actor*
4724 Crown Dr, Los Angeles, CA 90026, USA

Pierce, Jill — *Actress*
%Kazarian/Spencer, 11365 Ventura Blvd, #100, Studio City, CA 91604, USA

Pierce, John R — *Electrical Engineer*
4008 El Cerrito Road, Palo Alto, CA 94306, USA

Pierce, Mary — *Tennis Player*
%Nick Bollettieri Tennis Academy, 5500 34th St W, Bradenton, FL 34210, USA

Pierce, Ricky C — *Basketball Player*
%Charlotte Hornets, 1 Hive Dr, Charlotte, NC 28217, USA

Pierce, Samuel R, Jr — *Secretary, Housing & Urban Development*
16 W 77th St, New York, NY 10024, USA

Pierce, W William (Billy) — *Baseball Player*
1321 Baileys Crossing Dr, Lemont, IL 60439, USA

Piercy, Marge — *Writer*
%Moddlemarsh Inc, PO Box 1473, Wellfleet, MA 02667, USA

Pierpoint, Eric — *Actor*
2199 Topanga Skyline Dr, Topanga, CA 90290, USA

Pierpoint, Robert — *Commentator*
%CBS-TV, News Dept, 2020 "M" St NW, Washington, DC 20036, USA

Pierre of Normandy, Abbe — *Religious Leader, Social Activist*
%Monastery, Normandy, France

Pierson, Frank R — *Movie, Television Director, Writer*
1223 Amalfi Dr, Pacific Palisades, CA 90272, USA

Pierson, Markus — *Sculptor*
%OutWest, 7216 Washington St NE, #A, Albuquerque, NM 87109, USA

P

Piccone - Pierson

Pietrangeli, Nicola *Tennis Player*
Via Eustachio Manfredi 15, Rome, Italy
Pietrangelo, Frank *Hockey Player*
11 Buttonwood Lane, Avon, CT 06001, USA
Pietz, Amy *Actress*
%Gersh Agency, 232 N Canon Dr, Beverly Hills, CA 90210, USA
Pigaty, Leo J *Army General*
DCG, Material Readiness, 5001 Eisenhower Ave, Arlington, VA 22304, USA
Pigford, Robert L *Chemical Engineer*
255 Possum Park Road, #317, Newark, DE 19711, USA
Piggott, Lester K *Thoroughbred Racing Jockey*
Florizel, Newmarket, Suffolk, England
Pigliucci, Riccardi *Businessman*
%Perkin-Elmer Corp, 761 Main Ave, Norwalk, CT 06859, USA
Pigott, Charles M *Businessman*
%Paccar Inc, 777 106th Ave NE, Bellevue, WA 98004, USA
Pigott-Smith, Tim *Actor*
%Michael Whitehall, 125 Gloucester Road, London SW7 4TE, England
Pihos, Peter L (Pete) *Football Player*
%M & P Enterprises, 3544 Heathrow Dr, Winston-Salem, NC 27127, USA
Pike, Gary *Singer (The Lettermen)*
%ACT Mgmt, 13090 Hosler Ave, Chico, CA 95973, USA
Pike, Jim *Singer (The Lettermen)*
%ACT Mgmt, 13090 Hosler Ave, Chico, CA 95973, USA
Pike, Larry R *Businessman*
%Union Central Life Insurance, 1876 Waycross Road, Cincinnati, OH 45240, USA
Pilarczyk, Daniel E *Religious Leader*
100 E 8th St, Cincinnati, OH 45202, USA
Pilic, Nicki *Tennis Player*
%DTB, Otto-Fleck-Schneise 8, 60528 Frankfurt/Maim, Germany
Pilkis, Simon J *Physiologist, Biosphysicist*
%State University of New York, Health Sciences Center, Stony Brook, NY 11794, USA
Pillard, Charles H *Labor Leader*
%Electrical Workers Union, 1125 15th St NW, Washington, DC 20005, USA
Pilling, Donald L *Navy Admiral*
Deputy Chief of Naval Operations, HqUSN, Pentagon, Washington, DC 20350, USA
Pilliod, Charles J, Jr *Businessman, Diplomat*
494 Saint Andrews Dr, Akron, OH 44303, USA
Pillow, Ray *Singer*
%Joe Taylor Artist Agency, 2802 Columbine Place, Nashville, TN 37204, USA
Pillsbury, Edmund P *Museum Director*
%Kimbell Art Museum, 3333 Camp Bowie Blvd, Fort Worth, TX 76107, USA
Pilote, Pierre *Hockey Player*
RR 5, Milton ON L9T 2X9, Canada
Pilson, Neal H *Television Producer*
%CBS-TV, Sports Dept, 51 W 52nd St, New York, NY 10019, USA
Pimenta, Simon I Cardinal *Religious Leader*
%Archbishop's House, 21 Nathalal Parekh Marg, Bombay 400 039, India
Pincay, Laffit, Jr *Thoroughbred Racing Jockey*
5200 Los Grandes Way, Los Angeles, CA 90027, USA
Pinchot, Bronson *Actor*
PO Box 15598, Beverly Hills, CA 90209, USA
Pinckney, Ed *Basketball Player*
1315 Club House Road, Gladwyne, PA 19035, USA
Pincus, Lionel I *Financier*
%E M Warburg Pincus Co, 466 Lexington Ave, New York, NY 10017, USA
Pine, Courtney *Jazz Saxophonist*
%Concerted Efforts, 59 Parsons St, West Newton, MA 02165, USA
Pine, Robert *Actor*
11923 Addison St, Valley Village, CA 91607, USA
Pinera, Mike *Singer, Guitarist*
21206 Pacific Coast Highway, Malibu, CA 90265, USA
Pingel, John S *Football Player*
80 Celestial Way, #203, Juno Beach, FL 33408, USA
Pinger, Mark *Swimmer*
5201 Orduna Dr, #6, Coral Gables, FL 33146, USA
Piniella, Louis V (Lou) *Baseball Player, Manager*
1005 Taray De Avila, Tampa, FL 33613, USA

Pinkel, Donald P — *Pediatrician*
2501 Addison Road, Houston, TX 77030, USA

Pinkerton, Guy C — *Financier*
%Washington Federal Savings, 425 Pike St, Seattle, WA 98101, USA

Pinkett, Jada — *Actress*
9560 Wilshire Blvd, #516, Beverly Hills, CA 90212, USA

Pinnock, Trevor — *Conductor*
35 Gloucester Crescent, London NW1 7DL, England

Pinochet Ugarte, Augusto — *President, Chile; Army General*
%Commander in Chief's Office, Military Affairs Office, Santiago, Chile

Pintasilgo, Maria de Lourdes — *Premier, Portugal*
Almeda Santo Antonio dos Capuchos 4-5, 1100 Lisbon, Portugal

Pintauro, Danny — *Actor*
19722 Trull Brook Dr, Tarzana, CA 91356, USA

Pinter, Harold — *Writer*
%Judy Daish, 2 St Charles Place, London W10 6EG, England

Pinter, Michael R — *Businessman*
%Kemper Reinsurance, 1 Kemper Dr, Long Grove, IL 60049, USA

Piore, Emanuel R — *Physicist*
2 5th Ave. #7-A, New York, NY 10011, USA

Piovanelli, Silvano Cardinal — *Religious Leader*
Piazzi S Giovanni 3, 50129 Florence, Italy

Pipes, R Byron — *Educator*
%Rensselaer Polytechnic Institute, President's Office, Troy, NY 12180, USA

Pippard, A Brian — *Physicist*
30 Porson Road, Cambridge CB2 2EU, England

Pippen, Scottie — *Basketball Player*
%Chicago Bulls, 1901 W Madison St, Chicago, IL 60612, USA

Pippig, Uta — *Marathon Runner*
4279 Niblick Dr, Longmont, CO 80503, USA

Piquet, Nelson — *Auto Racing Driver*
9 Ave des Papauns Fontvieille, Monte Carlo, Monaco

Piraro, Dan — *Cartoonist (Bizarro)*
%Chronicle Features, 870 Market St, San Francisco, CA 94102, USA

Pirelli, Leopoldo — *Businessman*
Piazzle Cadorna 5, 20123 Milan, Italy

Pires de Miranda, Pedro — *Businessman*
%Petroleos de Portugal, Rua das Flores 7, 1200 Lisbon, Portugal

Pires, Pedro V R — *Prime Minister, Cape Verde; Army General*
%PAICV, CP 22, Sao Tiago, Cape Verde

Pironio, Eduardo Cardinal — *Religious Leader*
Piazza del S Uffizio 11, 00193 Rome, Italy

Pischetsrider, Bernd — *Businessman*
%Bayerishe Motoren Werke, Petuelring 130, 80788 Munich, Germany

Piscopo, Joe — *Actor*
PO Box 258, Bernardsville, NJ 07924, USA

Pisier, Marie-France — *Actress*
%Gaumont International, 30 Ave Charles de Gaulle, 92200 Neuilly, France

Pister, Karl S — *Educator*
%University of California, Chancellor's Office, Santa Cruz, CA 95064, USA

Pitakaka, Moses — *Governor General, Solomon Islands*
%Government House, Hoinaua, Guadacanal, Solomon Islands

Pitillo, Maria — *Actress*
1724 N Vista St, Los Angeles, CA 90046, USA

Pitino, Richard (Rick) — *Basketball Coach*
%Boston Celtics, 151 Merrimac St, #500, Boston, MA 02114, USA

Pitney, Gene — *Singer*
8901 6 Mile Road, Caledonia, WI 53108, USA

Pitou Zimmerman, Penny — *Skier*
%Penny Pitou Travel, 55 Canal St, Laconia, NH 03246, USA

Pitt, Brad — *Actor*
%Creative Artists Agency, 9830 Wilshire Blvd, Beverly Hills, CA 90212, USA

Pitt, Ingrid — *Actress*
4 Court Lodge, 48 Sloane Square, London SW1, England

Pittman, James A, Jr — *Endocrinologist*
5 Ridge Dr, Birmingham, AL 35213, USA

Pittman, John A — *Korean War Army Hero (CMH)*
303 Grand Ave, Box 331, Greenwood, MS 38930, USA

P

Pinkel - Pittman

Pittman, R F — *Publisher*
%Tampa Tribune, 202 S Parker St, Tampa, FL 33606, USA

Pittman, Richard A — *Vietnam War Marine Corps Hero (CMH)*
9494 Los Coches Road, Lakeside, CA 92040, USA

Pitts, Elijah — *Football Player, Coach*
%Buffalo Bills, 1 Bills Dr, Orchard Park, NY 14127, USA

Pitts, Robert (R C) — *Basketball Player*
12655 E Milburn Ave, Baton Rouge, LA 70815, USA

Pitts, Ron — *Sportscaster*
%Fox-TV, Sports Dept, 205 E 67th St, New York, NY 10021, USA

Pitts, Tyrone S — *Religious Leader*
%Progressive National Baptist Convention, 601 50th St NE, Washington, DC 20019, USA

Pitzer, Kenneth S — *Chemist*
12 Eagle Hill, Kensington, CA 94707, USA

Piza, Arthur Luiz de — *Artist*
16 Rue Dauphine, 75006 Paris, France

Place, Mary Kay — *Actress*
2739 Motor Ave, Los Angeles, CA 90064, USA

Plachta, Leonard E — *Educator*
%Central Michigan University, President's Office, Mount Pleasant, MI 48859, USA

Plager, Bob — *Hockey Player, Coach, Executive*
362 Branchport Dr, Chesterfield, MO 63017, USA

Plain, Belva — *Writer*
%Delacorte Press, 1540 Broadway, New York, NY 10036, USA

Plakson, Suzie — *Actress*
302 N La Brea Ave, #363, Los Angeles, CA 90036, USA

Planchon, Roger — *Theater Director, Writer*
%Artmedia, 10 Ave George V, 75008 Paris, France

Planinc, Milka — *Prime Minister, Yugoslavia*
%Federal Executive Council, Bul Lenjina 2, 11075 Novi Belgrad, Yugoslavia

Plank, Raymond — *Businessman*
%Apache Corp, 2000 Post Oak Blvd, Houston, TX 77056, USA

Plano, Richard J — *Physicist*
14337 Long Channel Dr, Germantown, MD 20874, USA

Plant, Robert — *Singer, Songwriter*
484 Kings Road, London SW10 0LF, England

Plante, William M — *Commentator*
%CBS-TV, News Dept, 2020 "M" St NW, Washington, DC 20036, USA

Plantu (Jean H Plamtureux) — *Editorial Cartoonist*
%Le Monde, Editorial Dept, 7 Rue Falguiere, 75015 Paris, France

Platini, Michel — *Soccer Player*
%Comite d'Org, 90 Ave des Champs-Elysees, 75008 Paris, France

Platon, Nicolas — *Archaeologist*
Leof Alexandras 126, 11471 Athens, Greece

Platt, Kenneth A — *Physician*
11435 Quivas Way, Westminster, CO 80234, USA

Platt, Lewis E — *Businessman*
%Hewlett-Packard Co, 3000 Hanover St, Palo Alto, CA 94304, USA

Platt, Nicholas — *Diplomat*
131 E 69th St, New York, NY 10021, USA

Plavinsky, Dmitri — *Artist*
Arbat Str 51, Kotp 2, #97, 121002 Moscow, Russia

Plavsic, Biljana — *President, Bosnia*
%President's Office, Pale, Bosnia

Player, Gary J — *Golfer*
3930 RCA Blvd, #3001, Palm Beach Gardens, FL 33410, USA

Playten, Alice — *Actress*
33 5th Ave, New York, NY 10003, USA

Pleau, Larry — *Hockey Coach*
6 Still Meadow Lane, Somers, CT 06071, USA

Pleshette, Suzanne — *Actress*
PO Box 1492, Beverly Hills, CA 90213, USA

Pletcher, Eldon — *Editorial Cartoonist*
210 Canberra Court, Slidell, LA 70458, USA

Pletnev, Mikhail V — *Conductor, Concert Pianist*
Starpkonyushenny Per 33, #16, Moscow, Russia

Plettner, Bernhard — *Businessman*
%Siemens AG, Wittelsbacherplatz 2, 80333 Munich, Germany

Plettner, Helmut	*Businessman*
%Bosch-Siemens Hausgerate, Hochstr 17, 81541 Munich, Germany	
Plimpton, Calvin H	*Physician*
%Downstate Medical Center, 450 Clarkson Ave, Brooklyn, NY 11203, USA	
Plimpton, George A	*Writer*
%Paris Review, 541 E 72nd St, New York, NY 10021, USA	
Plimpton, Martha	*Actress*
502 Park Ave, #15-G, New York, NY 10022, USA	
Plisetskaya, Maiya M	*Ballerina*
Tverskaya 25/9, #31, 103050 Moscow, Russia	
Pliska, Paul	*Opera Singer*
%Metropolitan Opera Assn, Lincoln Center Plaza, New York, NY 10023, USA	
Plitt, Henry G	*Entertainment Executive*
%Showscan Film Corp, 3939 Landmark St, Culver City, CA 90232, USA	
Plotkin, Stanley A	*Virologist*
3940 Delancey St, Philadelphia, PA 19104, USA	
Plowright, Joan	*Actress*
%Write on Cue, 15 New Row, #300, London WC2N 4LA, England	
Plowright, Rosalind	*Opera Singer*
%Columbia Artists Mgmt Inc, 165 W 57th St, New York, NY 10019, USA	
Plum, Milton R (Milt)	*Football Player*
1104 Oakside Court, Raleigh, NC 27609, USA	
Plumb, Eve	*Actress*
145 S Fairfax Ave, #310, Los Angeles, CA 90036, USA	
Plummer, Amanda	*Actress*
49 Wampum Hill Road, Weston, CT 06883, USA	
Plummer, Christopher	*Actor, Singer*
49 Wampum Hill Road, Weston, CT 06883, USA	
Plummer, PattiSue	*Track Athlete*
%USA Track & Field, PO Box 120, Indianapolis, IN 46206, USA	
Plunkett, James W (Jim), Jr	*Football Player*
51 Kilroy Way, Atherton, CA 94027, USA	
Plyushch, Ivan S	*Head of State, Ukraine*
%Supreme Soviet, Government Building, Bankivska 11, Kiev 252009, Ukraine	
Pocklington, Peter H	*Hockey Executive*
%Edmonton Oilers, 11230 110th St, Edmonton AB T5G 3GB, Canada	
Podesta, Rossana	*Actress*
Via Bartolomeo Ammanatti 8, 00187 Rome, Italy	
Podewell, Cathy	*Actress*
17328 S Crest Dr, Los Angeles, CA 90035, USA	
Podhoretz, Norman	*Editor, Writer*
%Commentary Magazine, Editorial Dept, 165 E 56th St, New York, NY 10022, USA	
Podres, John J (Johnny)	*Baseball Player*
1 Colonial Court, Glens Falls, NY 12804, USA	
Poe	*Singer, Songwriter*
%Creative Artists Agency, 9830 Wilshire Blvd, Beverly Hills, CA 90212, USA	
Poe, Gregory	*Fashion Designer*
%Dutch Courage, 1950 S Santa Fe Ave, Los Angeles, CA 90021, USA	
Poelker, John S	*Financier*
%Fleet Finance Inc, 211 Perimeter Center Parkway, Atlanta, GA 30346, USA	
Pogorelich, Ivo	*Concert Pianist*
%Kantor Concert Mgmt, 67 Teignmouth Road, London NW2 4EA, England	
Pogrebin, Letty Cottin	*Editor, Writer*
33 W 67th St, New York, NY 10023, USA	
Pogue, L Welch	*Attorney*
5204 Kenwood Ave, Chevy Chase, MD 20815, USA	
Pogue, William R	*Astronaut*
%Vutuara Assoc, 1101 S Old Missouri Road, #30, Springdale, AR 72764, USA	
Pohl, Dan	*Golfer*
11609 S Tusaye Court, Phoenix, AZ 85044, USA	
Pohl, Karl Otto	*Financier*
%Oppenheim Jr Cie, Bockenheimer Landstr 20, 60325 Frankfurt/Main, Germany	
Pohlad, Carl R	*Baseball Executive*
%Minnesota Twins, 501 Chicago Ave S, Minneapolis, MN 55415, USA	
Poile, N R (Bud)	*Hockey Executive*
1509-2004 Fullerton Ave, North Vancouver BC V7P 3G8, Canada	
Poindexter, Buster	*Singer*
%Agency For Performing Arts, 9200 Sunset Blvd, #900, Los Angeles, CA 90069, USA	

P

P

Poindexter, Christian H — *Businessman*
%Baltimore Gas & Electric, 39 W Lexington St, Baltimore, MD 21201, USA

Poindexter, John M — *Navy Admiral, Government Official*
10 Barrington Fare, Rockville, MD 20850, USA

Pointer, Anita — *Singer (The Pointer Sisters)*
12060 Crest Court, Beverly Hills, CA 90210, USA

Pointer, Noel — *Jazz Violinist*
%Headline Talent, 1650 Broadway, #508, New York, NY 10019, USA

Pointer, Priscilla — *Singer (The Pointer Sisters)*
213 16th St, Santa Monica, CA 90402, USA

Pointer, Ruth — *Singer (The Pointer Sisters)*
6408 Trancas Canyon Road, Malibu, CA 90265, USA

Poitier, Sidney — *Actor*
9255 Doheny Road, Los Angeles, CA 90069, USA

Pokelwaldt, Robert N — *Businessman*
%York International, 631 S Richland Ave, York, PA 17403, USA

Polanski, Roman — *Movie Director*
%Agents Associes Beaume, 201 Rue Faubourg St Honore, 75008 Paris, France

Polanyi, John C — *Nobel Chemistry Laureate*
%University of Toronto, Chemistry Dept, Toronto ON M5S 1A1, Canada

Poletti, Ugo Cardinal — *Religious Leader*
Vicario di Roma, Piazza S Giovanni in Laterano 6, 00184 Rome, Italy

Polgar, Laszlo — *Opera Singer*
Abel Jeno Utca 12, 1113 Budapest, Hungary

Polito, Jon — *Actor*
%Innovative Artists, 1999 Ave of Stars, #2850, Los Angeles, CA 90067, USA

Polke, Sigmar — *Artist*
%Michael Werner, 21 E 67th St, New York, NY 10021, USA

Poll, Martin H — *Movie Producer*
%Martin Poll Productions, 8961 Sunset Blvd, #E, Los Angeles, CA 90069, USA

Polla, Dennis L — *Microbiotics Engineer*
%University of Minnesota, Electrical Engineering Dept, Minneapolis, MN 55455, USA

Pollack, Andrea — *Swimmer*
%SSV, Postfach 420140, 34070 Kassel, Germany

Pollack, Daniel — *Concert Pianist*
%University of Southern California, Music Dept, Los Angeles, CA 90089, USA

Pollack, Jim — *Actor*
%Ericka Wain, 1418 N Highland Ave, #102, Los Angeles, CA 90028, USA

Pollack, Joseph — *Labor Leader*
%Insurance Workers Union, 1017 12th St NW, Washington, DC 20005, USA

Pollack, Lester — *Financier*
%Centre Partners, 1 Rockefeller Center, New York, NY 10020, USA

Pollack, Sam — *Hockey Executive*
6811 Monkland Ave, Montreal PQ H4B 1J2, Canada

Pollack, Sydney — *Movie Director*
13525 Lucca Dr, Pacific Palisades, CA 90272, USA

Pollak, Cheryl A — *Actress*
%Gersh Agency, 232 N Canon Dr, Beverly Hills, CA 90210, USA

Pollak, Kevin — *Comedian, Actor*
%Irvin Arthur, 9363 Wilshire Blvd, #212, Beverly Hills, CA 90210, USA

Pollak, Lisa — *Journalist*
%Baltimore Sun, Editorial Dept, 501 N Calvert St, Baltimore, MD 21202, USA

Pollan, Tracy — *Actress*
Lottery Hill Farm, South Woodstock, VT 05071, USA

Pollard, C William — *Businessman*
%ServiceMaster Cos, 1 ServiceMaster Road, Downers Grove, IL 60515, USA

Pollard, Michael J — *Actor*
520 S Burnside Ave, #12-A, Los Angeles, CA 90036, USA

Pollard, Scott — *Basketball Player*
%Detroit Pistons, Palace, 2 Championship Dr, Auburn Hills, MI 48326, USA

Pollay, Richard L — *Financier*
%Chicago Title & Trust, 171 N Clark St, Chicago, IL 60601, USA

Pollen, Arabella R H — *Fashion Designer*
Canham Mews, #8, Canham Road, London W3 7SR, England

Pollicino, Joseph A — *Financier*
%CIT Group Holdings, 650 CIT Dr, Livingston, NJ 07039, USA

Pollin, Abe — *Basketball, Hockey Executive*
%Centre Group, Capital Centre, 1 Truman Dr, Landover, MD 20785, USA

Pollini, Maurizio — Concert Pianist
%RESIA, Via Manzoni 31, 20120 Milan, Italy

Pollock, Alex J — Businessman
%Federal Home Loan Bank, 111 E Wacker Dr, Chicago, IL 60601, USA

Pollock, Michael P — Navy Fleet Admiral, England
Ivy House, Churchstoke, Montgomery, Powys SY15 6DU, Wales

Pollock, Thomas P — Entertainment Executive
%MCA Inc, 100 Universal City Plaza, Universal City, CA 91608, USA

Polyakov, Valery — Cosmonaut
%Health Ministry, Choroshevskoye Chaussee 76-A, 123 007 Moscow, Russia

Polynice, Olden — Basketball Player
PO Box 220339, Newhall, CA 91322, USA

Pomerantz, John J — Businessman
%Leslie Fay Co, 1400 Broadway, New York, NY 10018, USA

Pomerantz, Marvin A — Businessman
%Gaylord Container Corp, 500 Lake Cook Road, Deerfield, IL 60015, USA

Pomeroy, Wardell B — Psychotherapist
1611 Vallejo St, San Francisco, CA 94123, USA

Pommier, Jean Bernard — Concert Pianist
2 Chemin Des Cotes de Montmoiret, 1012 Lausanne, Switzerland

Pomodora, Arnaldo — Sculptor
Via Vigevano 5, 20144 Milan, Italy

Ponazecki, Joe — Actor
%Don Buchwald, 10 E 44th St, New York, NY 10017, USA

Ponce Enrile, Juan — Government Official, Philippines
2305 Morado St, Dasmarinas Village, Makati, Metro Manila, Philippines

Pond, Kirk P — Businessman
%National Semiconductor, 2900 Semiconductor Dr, Santa Clara, CA 95051, USA

Pons, B Stanley — Chemist
%University of Utah, Chemistry Dept, Eyring Building, Salt Lake City, UT 84112, USA

Pons, Juan — Opera Singer
%Deutsche Grammaphon Records, 810 7th Ave, New York, NY 10019, USA

Ponti, Carlo — Movie Producer
Chalet Daniel, Burgenstock, Nidwalden, Switzerland

Ponti, Michael — Concert Pianist
Heubergstr 32, 83565 Eschenlohe, Germany

Ponty, Jean-Luc — Jazz Violinist, Composer
10340 Santa Monica Blvd, Los Angeles, CA 90025, USA

Pool, John L — Cancer Surgeon
560 Belden Hill Road, Wilton, CT 06897, USA

Poole, Brian — Singer (The Tremeloes)
67 Tower Drivem Neath Hill, Milton Keynes MK14 6JX, England

Poole, George (Barney) — Football Player
111 Saratoga Circle, Hattisburg, MS 39401, USA

Poole, William — Government Official, Economist
%Brown University, Economics Dept, Providence, RI 01912, USA

Pooley, Don — Golfer
5251 N Camino Sumo, Tucson, AZ 85718, USA

Poons, Larry — Artist
831 Broadway, New York, NY 10003, USA

Pop, Iggy — Singer, Songwriter, Actor
%Art Collins, PO Box 561, Pine Bush, NY 12566, USA

Popcorn, Faith — Businesswoman
%Brain Reserve Inc, 1 Madison Ave, New York, NY 10010, USA

Pope, Clarence C, Jr — Religious Leader
%Fort Worth Episcopal Church Diocese, 6300 Ridlea Place, Fort Worth, TX 76116, USA

Pope, Edwin — Sportswriter
%Miami Herald, Editorial Dept, 1 Herald Plaza, Miami, FL 33132, USA

Pope, Everett P — WW II Marine Corps Hero (CMH)
Amelia Island Plantation, 4 Water Oak, Fernandina Beach, FL 32034, USA

Pope, Odeon — Jazz Trumpeter, Bandleader
%Brad Simon Organization, 122 E 57th St, New York, NY 10022, USA

Pope, Peter T — Businessman
%Pope & Talbot Inc, 1500 SW 1st Ave, Portland, OR 97201, USA

Popiel, Poul — Hockey Player
2501 Peppermill Ridge, Chesterfield, MO 63005, USA

Popoff, Frank P — Businessman
%Dow Chemical, 2030 Dow Center, Midland, MI 48674, USA

P

Pollini - Popoff

P

Popov, Alexander — *Swimmer*
%Swimming Assn, Sports House, Maitland Road, #7, Hackett 2602, Australia
Popov, Leonid I — *Cosmonaut*
%Potchta Kosmonavtov, Moskovskoi Oblasti, 141160 Syvisdny Goroduk, Russia
Popov, Oleg — *Clown*
%Organization of State Circuses, Pushecnaya 4, Moscow, Russia
Popovich, Gregg — *Basketball Executive, Coach*
%San Antonio Spurs, 600 E Market St, #102, San Antonio, TX 78205, USA
Popovich, Pavel R — *Cosmonaut, Air Force General*
AIUS-Agroressurs, VNIZ, Bolshevitskij Per 11, 101 000 Moscow, Russia
Poppa, Ryal R — *Businessman*
%Storage Technology Corp, 2270 S 88th St, Louisville, CO 80028, USA
Porizkova, Paulina — *Model, Actress*
135 W Haley St, #201, Santa Barbara, CA 93101, USA
Porsche, Ferdinand, II — *Businessman*
%Porsche Dr Ing HCF, Porschenstr 42, 70435 Stuttgart, Germany
Portale, Carl — *Publisher*
%Elle Magazine, Hachette Filipacchi, 1633 Broadway, New York, NY 10019, USA
Porteous, Patrick A — *WW II British Army Hero (VC)*
Christmas Cottage, Church Lane, Funtington, West Sussex PO18 9LQ, England
Porter of Luddenham, George — *Nobel Chemistry Laureate*
%Imperial College, Photomolecular Sciences Center, London SW7 2BB, England
Porter, David H — *Educator*
%Skidmore College, President's Office, Saratoga Springs, NY 12866, USA
Porter, Howard — *Basketball Player*
1034 Iglehart Ave, St Paul, MN 55104, USA
Porter, Keith R — *Cytologist, Educator*
%University of Colorado, Molecular Cellular Dept, Boulder, CO 80309, USA
Porter, Richard W — *Electrical Engineer*
69 Catherine St, Burlington, VT 05401, USA
Porter, Terry — *Basketball Player*
%Minnesota Timberwolves, Target Center, 600 1st Ave N, Minneapolis, MN 55403, USA
Portillo, Michael — *Government Official, England*
%House of Commons, Westminster, London SW1A 0AA, England
Portis, Charles — *Writer*
7417 Kingwood Road, Little Rock, AR 72207, USA
Portman, John C, Jr — *Architect*
%Charles Portman Assoc, 225 Peachtree St NE, #200, Atlanta, GA 30303, USA
Portman, Natalie — *Actress*
%International Creative Mgmt, 8942 Wilshire Blvd, Beverly Hills, CA 90211, USA
Porto, James — *Photographer*
480 Canal St, New York, NY 10013, USA
Portwich, Ramona — *Kayak Athlete*
KC Limmer, Stockhardtweg 3, 30453 Hannover, Germany
Posnick, Adolph — *Businessman*
%Ferro Corp, 1000 Lakeside Ave, Cleveland, OH 44114, USA
Post, Avery D — *Religious Leader*
PO Box 344, Meadowbrook Road, Norwich, VT 05055, USA
Post, Glen F, III — *Businessman*
%Century Telephone, 100 Century Park Dr, Monroe, LA 71203, USA
Post, Markie — *Actress*
10153 1/2 Riverside Dr, #333, Toluca Lake, CA 91602, USA
Post, Mike — *Composer*
%Mike Post Productions, 1007 W Olive Ave, Burbank, CA 91506, USA
Post, Sandra — *Golfer*
%Ladies Professional Golf Assn, 2570 Volusia Ave, Daytona Beach, FL 32114, USA
Post, Ted — *Movie Director*
%Norman Blumenthal, 11030 Santa Monica Blvd, Los Angeles, CA 90025, USA
Poster, Steve — *Cinematographer*
%Smith/Gosnell/Nicholson, 1515 Palisades Dr, #N, Pacific Palisades, CA 90272, USA
Postlethwaite, Pete — *Actor*
%Markham & Froggatt, Julian House, 4 Windmill St, London W1P 1HF, England
Postlewait, Kathy — *Golfer*
220 Raintree Dr, Casselberry, FL 32707, USA
Postman, Marc — *Astronomer*
3311 Greenvale Road, Pikesville, MD 21208, USA
Poston, Tom — *Actor*
2930 Deep Canyon Dr, Beverly Hills, CA 90210, USA

Popov - Poston

Potapenko, Vitaly — *Basketball Player*
%Cleveland Cavaliers, 2923 Statesboro Road, Richfield, OH 44286, USA

Potok, Chaim — *Writer, Artist*
%Alfred A Knopf, 201 E 50th St, New York, NY 10022, USA

Potter, Chris — *Actor*
PO Box 876, Station "F", 50 Charles St E, Toronto ON M4Y 2N9, Canada

Potter, Cynthia — *Diver, Sportscaster*
1188 Ragley Hall Road NE, Atlanta, GA 30319, USA

Potter, Dan M — *Religious Leader*
PO Box 66052, Albany, NY 12206, USA

Potter, Huntington — *Medical Researcher*
%Harvard Medical School, 25 Shattuck St, Boston, MA 02115, USA

Potter, Philip A — *Religious Leader*
3-A York Castle Ave, Kingston 6, Jamaica

Potts, Annie — *Actress*
%Elsboy Mgmt, 1581 N Crescent Heights Blvd, Beverly Hills, CA 90046, USA

Potts, Cliff — *Actor*
PO Box 131, Topanga, CA 90290, USA

Potts, Erwin — *Businessman*
%McClatchy Newspapers, 2100 "Q" St, Sacramento, CA 95816, USA

Potts, Thomas H — *Financier*
%Resource Mortgage Capital, 10500 Little Patuxent Parkway, Columbia, MD 21044, USA

Potvin, Denis — *Hockey Player*
2951 NE 27th Ave, Lighthouse Point, FL 33064, USA

Potvin, Jean — *Hockey Player*
24 Longwood Dr, Huntington Station, NY 11746, USA

Poulin, Dave — *Hockey Player, Coach*
%University of Notre Dame, Athletic Dept, Notre Dame, IN 46556, USA

Pound, Richard W D — *Olympics Official*
87 Arlington Ave, Westmount PQ H3Y 2W5, Canada

Pound, Robert V — *Physicist*
87 Pinehurst Road, Belmont, MA 02178, USA

Pounder, C C H — *Actress*
%Susan Smith, 121 N San Vicente Blvd, Beverly Hills, CA 90211, USA

Poundstone, Paula — *Comedienne, Actress*
1223 Broadway, #162, Santa Monica, CA 90404, USA

Poupard, Paul Cardinal — *Religious Leader*
%Pontificium Consilium Pro Dialogo, 00120 Vatican City

Pousette, Lena — *Actress*
5120 Fairway Oaks Dr, Windermere, FL 34786, USA

Poussaint, Alvin F — *Psychiatrist, Educator*
%Judge Baker Guidance Center, 295 Longwood Ave, Boston, MA 02115, USA

Povich, Maury R — *Commentator, Entertainer*
%Dakota Hotel, 1 W 72nd St, New York, NY 10023, USA

Povich, Shirley L — *Sportswriter*
%Washington Post, Editorial Dept, 1150 15th St NW, Washington, DC 20071, USA

Powell, A J Philip — *Architect*
%Powell Moya Partners, 21 Upper Cheyne Row, London SW3, England

Powell, Anthony — *Writer*
Chantry near Frome, Somerset BA11 3LJ, England

Powell, Brittney — *Actress*
%Amsel Eisenstadt Frazier, 6310 San Vicente Blvd, #401, Los Angeles, CA 90048, USA

Powell, Clifton — *Actor*
%Abrams Artists, 9200 Sunset Blvd, #625, Los Angeles, CA 90069, USA

Powell, Colin L — *Army General*
1663 Prince St, Alexandria, VA 22314, USA

Powell, Don G — *Financier*
%Van Kampen/American, 1 Parkview Plaza, Oakview Terrace, IL 60181, USA

Powell, Earl A (Rusty), III — *Museum Official*
%National Gallery of Art, Constitution Ave & 4th St NW, Washington, DC 20565, USA

Powell, George E, III — *Businessman*
%Yellow Corp, 10990 Roe Ave, Overland Park, KS 66211, USA

Powell, George E, Jr — *Businessman*
%Yellow Corp, 10990 Roe Ave, Overland Park, KS 66211, USA

Powell, J Enoch — *Government Official, England*
33 S Eaton Place, London SW1, England

Powell, James B — *Businessman*
%Laboratory Corp Holdings, 358 S Main St, Burlington, NC 27215, USA

Powell, James R *Inventor (Magnetic Levitation Vehicle)*
%Brookhaven National Laboratory, Upton, NY 11973, USA

Powell, Jane *Singer, Actress*
150 West End Ave, #26-C, New York, NY 10023, USA

Powell, John *Track Athlete*
%John Powell Assoc, 10445 Mary Ave, Cupertino, CA 95014, USA

Powell, John W (Boog) *Baseball Player*
333 W Camden St, Baltimore, MD 21201, USA

Powell, Joseph L (Jody) *Government Official, Journalist*
%Powell Tate, 700 13th St NW, #1000, Washington, DC 20005, USA

Powell, Lewis F, Jr *Supreme Court Justice*
%US Supreme Court, 1 1st St NE, Washington, DC 20543, USA

Powell, Marvin *Football Player*
5441 8th Ave, Los Angeles, CA 90043, USA

Powell, Mel *Composer, Jazz Pianist*
%California School of Arts, Composition Dept, Santa Clarita, CA 91355, USA

Powell, Mike *Track Athlete*
%Team Powell, PO Box 8000-354, Alta Loma, CA 91701, USA

Powell, Monroe *Singer (The Platters)*
%Personality Presents, 880 E Sahara Ave, #101, Las Vegas, NV 89104, USA

Powell, Robert *Actor*
10 Pond Place, London W12 7RJ, England

Power, Taryn *Actress*
621 N Orlando Ave, #8, West Hollywood, CA 90048, USA

Powers, Alexandra *Actress*
12142 Burbank Blvd, #2, Valley Village, CA 91607, USA

Powers, Brian M *Businessman*
%Valassis Communications, 19975 Victor Parkway, Livonia, MI 48152, USA

Powers, J F *Writer*
%Alfred A Knopf, 201 E 50th St, New York, NY 10022, USA

Powers, James B *Religious Leader*
%American Baptist Assn, 4605 N State Line, Texarkana, TX 75503, USA

Powers, Mala *Actress*
10543 Valley Spring Lane, North Hollywood, CA 91602, USA

Powers, Paul J *Businessman*
%Commercial Intertech, 1775 Logan Ave, Youngstown, OH 44505, USA

Powers, Stefanie *Actress*
PO Box 67981, Los Angeles, CA 90067, USA

Powter, Susan *Physical Fitness Instructor*
%Susan Powter Corp, 2220 Colorado Ave, #1, Santa Monica, CA 90404, USA

Pozsgay, Imre *Government Official, Hungary*
%Parliament Buildings, Kossuth Lajos Ter 1, 1055 Budapest, Hungary

Prance, Ghillean T *Botanist*
%Kew Royal Botanic Gardens, Richmond, Surrey TW9 3AE, England

Prange, Laurie *Actress*
1519 Sargent Place, Los Angeles, CA 90026, USA

Prather, Joan *Actress*
31647 Sea Level Dr, Malibu, CA 90265, USA

Pratiwi Sudarmono *Astronaut, Indonesia*
Jalan Pegangsaan, Timur 16, Jakarta, Indonesia

Pratt, Edward T, Jr *Businessman*
%Pratt Hotel Corp, 2 Galleria Tower, 13455 Noel Road, Dallas, TX 75240, USA

Pratt, Everett H (Ev), Jr *Air Force General*
Vice Commander, USAF Europe, Unit 3050, Box 1, APO, AE 09094, USA

Pratt, Jack E, Sr *Businessman*
%Pratt Hotel Corp, 2 Galleria Tower, 13455 Noel Road, Dallas, TX 75240, USA

Pratt, Richard D *Businessman*
%Intelligent Electronics, 411 Eagleview Blvd, Exton, PA 19341, USA

Preate, Ernest D, Jr *Attorney, Government Official*
%Attorney General's Office, 4th & Walnut, Harrisburg, PA 17120, USA

Precourt, Charles J *Astronaut*
%NASA, Johnson Space Center, 2101 NASA Road, Houston, TX 77058, USA

Preer, John R, Jr *Biologist*
1414 E Maxwell Lane, Bloomington, IN 47401, USA

Pregulman, Merv *Football Player*
%Siskin Steel & Supply Co, PO Box 1191, Chattanooga, TN 37401, USA

Prejean, Sister Helen *Writer*
%Vintage Books, 201 E 50th St, New York, NY 10022, USA

Prelog, Vladimir — *Nobel Chemistry Laureate*
Bellariastr 33, 8002 Zurich, Switzerland

Prendergast, G Joseph — *Financier*
%Wachovia Bank, 191 Peachtree St NE, Atlanta, GA 30303, USA

Prentice of Daventry, Reginald — *Government Official, England*
Wansdyke, Church Lane, Mildenhall, Marlborough, Wilts, England

Prentice, Dean — *Hockey Player*
13-220 Salisbury Ave, Cambridge ON N1S 1K5, Canada

Prentiss, Paula — *Actress, Comedienne*
719 N Foothill Road, Beverly Hills, CA 90210, USA

Prescott, John L — *Government Official, England*
365 Saltshouse Road, Sutton-on-Hull, North Humberside, England

Presle, Micheline — *Actress*
6 Rue Antoine Dubois, 75006 Paris, France

Presley, Priscilla — *Actress*
1167 Summit Dr, Beverly Hills, CA 90210, USA

Presnell, Glenn E — *Football Player, Coach*
510 Happy Hollow, Ironton, OH 45638, USA

Press, Frank — *Geophysicist*
%Carnegie Institution, 5241 Broad Branch Road, Washington, DC 20015, USA

Pressey, Paul — *Basketball Player, Coach*
8415 N Indian Creek Parkway, Fox Creek, WI 53217, USA

Pressler, H Paul — *Attorney, Judge*
3711 San Felipe St, #9-J, Houston, TX 77027, USA

Pressler, Menahem — *Concert Pianist*
%Melvin Kaplan Inc, 115 College St, Burlington, VT 05401, USA

Pressman, Edward R — *Movie Producer*
%Edward R Pressman Films, 445 N Bedford Dr, #PH, Beverly Hills, CA 90210, USA

Pressman, Lawrence — *Actor*
15033 Encanto Dr, Sherman Oaks, CA 91403, USA

Pressman, Michael — *Movie, Television Director/Producer*
%William Morris Agency, 151 S El Camino Dr, Beverly Hills, CA 90212, USA

Preston, Billy — *Singer, Songwriter, Keyboardist*
4271 Garthwaite Ave, Los Angeles, CA 90008, USA

Preston, Johnny — *Singer*
%Ken Keene Artists, PO Box 1875, Gretna, LA 70054, USA

Preston, Kelly — *Actress, Model*
15821 Ventura Blvd, #460, Encino, CA 91436, USA

Preston, Simon J — *Concert Organist, Choirmaster*
Little Hardwick, Langton Green, Tunbridge Wells, Kent TN3 OEY, England

Pretre, Georges — *Conductor*
Chateau de Vaudricourt, A Naves, Par Castres 81100, France

Preus, David W — *Religious Leader*
2481 Como Ave, St Paul, MN 55108, USA

Preval, Rene — *President, Haiti*
%President's Office, Palais du Government, Port-au-Prince, Haiti

Previn, Andre — *Conductor, Composer, Jazz Pianist*
%Sherwood Stables, 8 Sherwood Lane, Bedford Hills, NY 10507, USA

Previn, Dory — *Singer, Songwriter*
2533 Zorada Dr, Los Angeles, CA 90046, USA

Prew, William A — *Swimmer, Businessman*
6650 Lahser Road, Bloomfield, MI 48301, USA

Prey, Hermann — *Opera, Concert Singer*
Fichtenstr 14, 82152 Krailling, Germany

Pribilinec, Jozef — *Track Athlete*
Moyzesova 75, 966 22 Lutila, Slovakia

Price, Alan — *Singer, Organist (Animals), Songwriter*
%Crowell Mgmt, 4/5 High St, Huntingdon, Cambs PE18 6TE, England

Price, Antony — *Fashion Designer*
34 Brook St, London W1, England

Price, Charles H, II — *Businessman, Diplomat*
1 W Armour Blvd, #300, Kansas City, MO 64111, USA

Price, Frank — *Movie Executive*
%Price Entertainment, 2425 Olympic Blvd, Santa Monica, CA 90404, USA

Price, Frederick K C — *Religious Leader*
%Crenshaw Christian Church, 7901 S Vermont Ave, Los Angeles, CA 90044, USA

Price, George C — *Prime Minister, Belize*
%House of Representatives, Belmopan, Belize

P

Prelog - Price

Price, Hugh B — *Association Executive*
%Rockefeller Foundation, 420 5th Ave, New York, NY 10018, USA

Price, Kenneth — *Artist*
PO Box 1356, Taos, NM 87571, USA

Price, Larry C — *Photographer*
PO Box 16217, Baltimore, MD 21210, USA

Price, Leontyne M V — *Opera Singer*
9 Van Dam St, New York, NY 10013, USA

Price, Lloyd — *Singer, Pianist, Songwriter*
%Nate Adams, 801 Tilden St, #30-A, Bronx, NY 10467, USA

Price, Marc — *Actor*
8444 Magnolia Dr, Los Angeles, CA 90046, USA

Price, Margaret B — *Opera Singer*
%Harrison/Parrott, 12 Penzance Place, London W11 4PA England

Price, Nick — *Golfer*
900 S US Highway 1, #201, Jupiter, FL 33477, USA

Price, Noel — *Hockey Player*
273 McClelland Road, Nepan ON K2H 8N7, Canada

Price, Paul B — *Physicist*
1056 Overlook Road, Berkeley, CA 94708, USA

Price, Ray — *Singer*
%Musgrave & Doran, 1722 S Glenstone Ave, #UU, Springfield, MO 65804, USA

Price, Reynolds — *Writer*
PO Box 99014, Durham, NC 27708, USA

Price, Richard — *Writer*
%Janklow & Nesbit Assoc, 598 Madison Ave, New York, NY 10022, USA

Price, S H — *Publisher*
%Newsweek Inc, 251 W 57th St, New York, NY 10019, USA

Price, W Mark — *Basketball Player*
%Philadelphia 76ers, Veterans Stadium, PO Box 25040, Philadelphia, PA 19147, USA

Price, Willard D — *Explorer*
814 Via Alhambra, #N, Laguna Hills, CA 92653, USA

Prichard, Peter S — *Editor*
%USA Today, Editorial Dept, 1000 Wilson Blvd, Arlington, VA 22209, USA

Priddy, Nancy — *Actress*
%Cunningham-Escott-Dipene, 10635 Santa Monica Blvd, Los Angeles, CA 90025, USA

Pride, Charlie — *Singer*
%Cecca Productions, 3198 Royal Lane, #200, Dallas, TX 75229, USA

Priesand, Sally J — *Religious Leader*
10 Wedgewood Circle, Eatontown, NJ 07724, USA

Priest, Maxi — *Singer*
%Virgin Records, 1790 Broadway, #2000, New York, NY 10019, USA

Priest, Pat — *Actress*
PO Box 1298, Hatley, ID 83333, USA

Priestley, Jason — *Actor*
1811 Whitley Ave, Los Angeles, CA 90028, USA

Prigogine, V Ilya — *Nobel Chemistry Laureate*
67 Ave Fond'Roy, 1180 Brussels, Belgium

Primack, Joel R — *Astronomer*
%University of California, Astronomy Dept, Santa Cruz, CA 95064, USA

Primakov, Yevgeny M — *Government Official, Russia*
%Foreign Affairs Ministry, Smolenskaya-Sennaya 32/34, Moscow, Russia

Primatesta, Raul Francisco Cardinal — *Religious Leader*
Arzobispado, Ave H Irigoyen 98, 5000 Cordoba, Argentina

Primeau, Keith — *Hockey Player*
%Carolina Hurricanes, 5000 Aerial Center, #100, Morristown, NC 27560, USA

Primis, Lance R — *Publisher*
%New York Times Co, 229 W 43rd St, New York, NY 10036, USA

Prince (Rogers Nelson) — *Singer, Songwriter*
%Paisley Park Enterprises, 7801 Audubon Road, Chanhassen, MN 55317, USA

Prince, Gregory S, Jr — *Educator*
%Hampshire College, President's Office, Amherst, MA 01002, USA

Prince, Harold S (Hal) — *Theater Producer, Director*
%Harold Prince Organization, 10 Rockefeller Plaza, #1009, New York, NY 10020, USA

Prince, William — *Actor*
9061 Keith Ave, #305, Los Angeles, CA 90069, USA

Principal, Victoria — *Actress*
814 Cynthia St, Beverly Hills, CA 90210, USA

Prine, Andrew — Actor
3264 Longridge Ave, Sherman Oaks, CA 91423, USA

Prine, John — Singer, Songwriter
%Al Bunetta Mgmt, 33 Music Square W, #102-B, Nashville, TN 37203, USA

Pringle, Joan — Actress
740 S Burnside Ave, Los Angeles, CA 90036, USA

Prinosil, David — Tennis Athlete
%TC Amberg Am Schanzl, Am Schanzl 3, 92224 Amberg, Germnay

Prinz, Dianne K — Astronaut
%US Naval Research Lab, Code 7660, 4555 Overlook Ave, Washington, DC 20375, USA

Prinze, Freddie, Jr — Actor
%Gersh Agency, 232 N Canon Dr, Beverly Hills, CA 90210, USA

Prior of Brampton, James M L — Government Official, England
36 Morpeth Mansions, London SW1, England

Pritchard, David E — Physicist
%Massachusetts Institute of Technology, Physics Dept, Cambridge, MA 02139, USA

Pritchett, James — Actor
53 W 74th St, New York, NY 10023, USA

Pritchett, Matt — Cartoonist (Matt)
%London Daily Telegraph, 181 Marsh Wall, London E14 9SR, England

Pritkin, Roland I — Eye Surgeon
1008 Washington Blvd, #6, Oak Park, IL 60302, USA

Pritzker, Jay A — Businessman
%Marmon Group, 225 W Washington St, Chicago, IL 60606, USA

Pritzker, Robert A — Businessman
%Marmon Group, 225 W Washington St, Chicago, IL 60606, USA

Prix, Wolf — Architect
%Coop Himmelblau, 3526 Beethoven St, Los Angeles, CA 90066, USA

Probert, Bob — Hockey Player
%Chicago Blackhawks, United Center, 1901 W Madison St, Chicago, IL 60612, USA

Probst, Lawrence — Businessman
%Electronic Arts, 1450 Fashion Island Blvd, San Mateo, CA 94404, USA

Proby, P J — Singer
%British & Int'l Artists, 500 Waterman Ave, #191, East Providence, RI 02914, USA

Prochnow, Jurgen — Actor
Lamontstr 98, 81679 Munich, Germany

Proctor, Charles N — Skier
100 Lockwood Lane, #238, Scotts Valley, CA 95066, USA

Prodi, Romano — Prime Minister, Italy
%Prime Minister's Office, Piazza Colomma 370, 00187 Rome, Italy

Professor Griff — Rap Artist (Public Enemy)
%Rush Artists, 1600 Varick St, New York, NY 10013, USA

Profumo, John D — Government Official, England
28 Commercial St, London E1 6LS, England

Prokhorov, Aleksandr M — Nobel Physics Laureate
%General Physics Institute, 38 Vavilov Str, 117942 Moscow, Russia

Pronovost, Marcel — Hockey Player
4620 Dali Court, Windsor ON N9G 2M8, Canada

Prophet, Elizabeth Clare — Religious Leader
%Church Universal & Triumphant, Box A, Livingston, MT 59047, USA

Propp, Brian — Hockey Player
336 Bay Ave, Ocean City, NJ 08226, USA

Props, Rene — Actress
%Agency For Performing Arts, 9200 Sunset Blvd, #900, Los Angeles, CA 90069, USA

Prosky, Robert — Actor
381 2nd St, #3-R, Jersey City, NJ 07302, USA

Prosser, C Ladd — Physiologist
101 W Windsor Road, #2106, Urbana, IL 61801, USA

Prosser, Robert — Religious Leader
%Cumberland Presbyterian Church, 1978 Union Ave, Memphis, TN 38104, USA

Prost, Alain M P — Auto Racing Driver
%Star Racing Promotion, 2 Rue Neuve, 1450 Sainte-Croix, France

Protopopov, Oleg — Figure Skater
Chalet Hubel, 3818 Grindelwald, Switzerland

Proulx, E Annie — Writer
General Delivery, Vershire, VT 05079, USA

Provine, Dorothy — Actress
8832 Ferncliff NE, Bainbridge Island, WA 98110, USA

Prowse, David — *Actor*
%David Prowse Fitness Centre, 12 Marshalsea Road, London SE1 4YB, England
Prudhomme, Don — *Drag Racing Driver*
1232 Distribution Way, Vista, CA 92083, USA
Prudhomme, Paul — *Chef*
527 Mandeville St, New Orleans, LA 70117, USA
Prueher, Joseph W (Joe) — *Navy Admiral*
CinC, US Pacific Command, Camp H M Smith, HI 96861, USA
Pruett, Jeanne — *Singer, Songwriter*
%J-E Talent Agency, PO Box 4446, Peytonsville Road, Franklin, TN 37064, USA
Pruett, Scott — *Auto Racing Driver*
400 Highway 28, Crystal Bay, NV 89402, USA
Pruitt, Basil A, Jr — *Burn Surgeon*
%US Army Institute of Surgical Research, Fort Sam Houston, TX 78234, USA
Pruitt, Gary B — *Businessman*
%McClatchy Newspapers, 2100 "Q" St, Sacramento, CA 95816, USA
Pruitt, Gregory D (Greg) — *Football Player*
13851 Larchmere Blvd, Shaker Heights, OH 44120, USA
Prunariu, Dumitru D — *Cosmonaut, Romania*
Str Sf Spiridon 12, #4, 70231 Bucharest, Romania
Prunskiene, Kazimiera — *Council of Ministers Chairman, Lithuania*
Blindziu 19-12004 Vilnius, Lithuania
Prusiner, Stanley B — *Nobel Medicine Laureate*
%University of San Francisco, Neurology Dept, San Francisco, CA 94143, USA
Pryce, Jonathan — *Actor, Singer*
%James Sharkey, 21 Golden Square, London W1R 3PA, England
Pryor, Hubert — *Editor, Publisher*
3560 S Ocean Blvd, #607, Palm Beach, FL 33480, USA
Pryor, Nicholas — *Actor*
%SDB Partners, 1801 Ave of Stars, #902, Los Angeles, CA 90067, USA
Pryor, Peter P — *Editor*
%Daily Variety, Editorial Dept, 5700 Wilshire Blvd, #120, Los Angeles, CA 90036, USA
Pryor, Richard — *Comedian*
16847 Bosque Dr, Encino, CA 91436, USA
Pryor, Thomas M — *Editor*
%Daily Variety, Editorial Dept, 5700 Wilshire Blvd, #120, Los Angeles, CA 90036, USA
Ptashne, Mark S — *Molecular Biologist*
%Harvard University, Biochemistry Dept, Cambridge, MA 02138, USA
Pucci, Bert — *Publisher*
%Los Angeles Magazine, 1888 Century Park East, Los Angeles, CA 90067, USA
Puck, Theodore T — *Biophysicist*
10 S Albion St, Denver, CO 80246, USA
Puck, Wolfgang — *Chef*
%Spago Restaurant, 8795 W Sunset Blvd, Los Angeles, CA 90069, USA
Puckett, Gary — *Singer, Songwriter*
11088 Indian Lore Court, San Diego, CA 92127, USA
Puckett, Kirby — *Baseball Player*
6625 West Trail, Minneapolis, MN 55439, USA
Puente, Tito — *Jazz Percussionist, Bandleader*
%Ralph Mercado Mgmt, 568 Broadway, #806, New York, NY 10012, USA
Puenzo, Luis A — *Movie Director*
%Cinematografia Nacional Instituto, Lima 319, 1073 Buenos Aires, Argentina
Puett, Clay — *Thoroughbred Racing Gate Inventor*
%True Center Gate Co, PO Box 32221, Phoenix, AZ 85064, USA
Puett, Tommy — *Actor*
23441 Golden Springs, #199, Diamond Bar, CA 91765, USA
Puff Daddy — *Rap Artist*
%International Creative Mgmt, 40 W 57th St, New York, NY 10019, USA
Pugh, Lawrence R — *Businessman*
%VF Corp, 1047 N Park Road, Wyomissing, PA 19610, USA
Pugsley, Don — *Actor*
6305 Yucca St, #214, Los Angeles, CA 90028, USA
Pulford, Bob — *Hockey Player, Executive*
78 Coventry Road, Northfield, IL 60093, USA
Pulido, Mark A — *Businessman*
%McKesson Corp, 1 Post St, San Francisco, CA 94104, USA
Pullen, Gregory J — *Financier*
%TCF Financial Corp, 801 Marquette Ave, Minneapolis, MN 55402, USA

Pulliam, Eugene S *Publisher*
%Indianapolis Star, 307 N Pennsylvania St, Indianapolis, IN 46204, USA
Pullman, Bill *Actor*
2599 Glen Green, Los Angeles, CA 90068, USA
Pulte, William J *Businessman*
%Pulte Corp, 33 Bloomfield Hills Parkway, Bloomfield Hills, MI 48304, USA
Pulver, Liselotte *Actress*
Villa Bip, 1166 Perroy, Kanton Vaudois, Switzerland
Puppa, Daren *Hockey Player*
4526 Cheval Blvd, Lutz, FL 33549, USA
Purcell, James N *Government Official*
10 Parc Chateau-Banquet, 1202 Geneva, Switzerland
Purcell, Lee *Actress*
%Artists Agency, 10000 Santa Monica Blvd, #305, Los Angeles, CA 90067, USA
Purcell, Patrick B *Publisher, Entertainment Executive*
%News America Publishing Inc, 210 South St, New York, NY 10002, USA
Purcell, Philip J *Businessman*
%Dean Witter Discover Co, 2 World Trade Center, New York, NY 10048, USA
Purcell, Sarah *Actress*
6525 Esplanade St, Playa del Rey, CA 90293, USA
Purdee, Nathan *Actor*
56 W 66th St, New York, NY 10023, USA
Purdy, James *Writer*
236 Henry St, Brooklyn, NY 11201, USA
Purim, Flora *Singer*
PO Box 29242, Oakland, CA 94604, USA
Purkey, Robert T (Bob) *Baseball Player*
5767 King School Road, Bethel Park, PA 15102, USA
Purl, Linda *Actress*
431 Alma Real Dr, Pacific Palisades, CA 90272, USA
Purpur, Clifford (Fido) *Hockey Player*
2108 6th Ave N, Grand Forks, ND 58203, USA
Purpura, Dominick P *Neuroscientist*
%Albert Einstein College of Medicine, 1300 Morris Park Ave, Bronx, NY 10461, USA
Purvis, G Frank, Jr *Businessman*
%Pan-American Life Insurance, 601 Poydras St, New Orleans, LA 70130, USA
Puryear, Martin *Artist*
%Nancy Drysdale Gallery, 700 New Hampshire Ave NW, #917, Washington, DC 20037, USA
Pusch, Alexander *Fencer*
Lindenweg 39, 97941 Tauberbischofsheim, Germany
Pusey, Nathan M *Educator*
200 E 66th St, New York, NY 10021, USA
Putch, John *Actor*
3972 Sunswept Dr, Studio City, CA 91604, USA
Putnam, George *Financier*
%Putnam Investments, 1 Post Office Square, Boston, MA 02109, USA
Puttnam, David T *Movie Producer*
%Enigma Productions, 13/15 Queens Gate Place Mews, London SW7 5BG, England
Puyana, Rafael *Concert Harpsichordist*
88 Rue de Grenelle, 75007 Paris, France
Puzo, Mario *Writer*
866 Manor Lane, Bay Shore, NY 11706, USA
Pye, William B *Sculptor*
43 Hambalt Road, Clapham, London SW4 9EQ, England
Pyle, Denver *Actor*
%Tri Island Land & Cattle Co, 10614 Whipple St, North Hollywood, CA 91602, USA
Pym of Sandy, Francis L *Government Official, England*
Everton Park, Sandy, Beds, England
Pynchon, Thomas *Writer*
%Henry Holt, 115 W 18th St, New York, NY 10011, USA
Pyne, Natasha *Actress*
%Kate Feast, Primrose Hill Studios, Fitzroy Road, London NW1 8TR, England
Pyne, Stephen J *Writer, Historian*
%University of Iowa, History Dept, Iowa City, IA 52242, USA
Pytka, Joseph *Commercials Director*
%Suellen Wagner, 916 Main St, Venice, CA 90291, USA

P

Pulliam - Pytka

Qasimi, Sheikh Sultan bin Muhammad Al- *Ruler, Sharjah*
%Royal Palace, Sharjah, United Arab Emirates
Qin Jiwei *Army General, China*
%Defense Minister's Office, Communist Party, Beijing, China
Quackenbush, H Q (Bill) *Hockey Player*
54 Danielle Court, Lawrenceville, NJ 08648, USA
Quaid, Dennis *Actor*
11718 Barrington Court, #508, Los Angeles, CA 90049, USA
Quaid, Randy *Actor*
PO Box 17372, Beverly Hills, CA 90209, USA
Quant, Mary *Fashion Designer*
%Mary Quant Ltd, 3 Ives St, London SW3 2NE, England
Quarracino, Antonio Cardinal *Religious Leader*
%Archdiocese of Buenos Aires, Buenos Aires, Argentina
Quarrie, Donald (Don) *Track Athlete*
%Jamaican Amateur Athletic Assn, PO Box 272, Kingston 5, Jamaica
Quarry, Jerry *Boxer*
%Jerry Quarry Foundation, 44520 Mayberry Ave, Hemet, CA 92544, USA
Quatro, Suzi *Singer*
%Paul Bridson, 74 Lower Bridge St, Chester CH1 1 RU, England
Quayle, J Danforth (Dan) *Vice President*
%Campaign America, 6263 N Scottsdale Road, #292, Scottsdale, AZ 85250, USA
Queen Latifah (Dana Owens) *Rapper, Actress*
%Flavor Unit Mgmt, 155 Morgan St, Jersey City, NJ 07302, USA
Queler, Eve *Conductor*
%Opera Orchestra of New York, 239 W 72nd St, #2-R, New York, NY 10023, USA
Questel, Mae *Actress*
27 E 65th St, New York, NY 10021, USA
Quick, Diana *Actress*
39 Seymour Walk, London SW10, England
Quick, Richard *Swimming Coach*
%Stanford University, Athletic Dept, Stanford, CA 94305, USA
Quie, Albert H *Governor, MN*
Rt 5, Box 231-A, Faribault, MN 55021, USA
Quigley, Linnea *Actress*
PO Box 43, Newbury Park, CA 91320, USA
Quigley, Philip J (Phil) *Businessman*
%Pacific Telesis Group, 130 Kearny St, San Francisco, CA 94108, USA
Quilley, Denis *Actor*
%Bernard Hunter, 13 Spencer Gardens, London SW14 7AH, England
Quindlen, Anna *Columnist*
%Random House, 201 E 50th St, New York, NY 10022, USA
Quine, Willard V O *Philosopher*
38 Chestnut St, Boston, MA 02108, USA
Quinlan, Kathleen *Actress*
PO Box 861, Rockaway, OR 97136, USA
Quinlan, Michael R *Businessman*
%McDonald's Corp, McDonald's Plaza, 1 Kroc Dr, Oak Brook, IL 60523, USA
Quinn, Aidan *Actor*
%Creative Artists Agency, 9830 Wilshire Blvd, Beverly Hills, CA 90212, USA
Quinn, Anthony *Actor*
PO Box 479, Bristol, RI 02809, USA
Quinn, Jane Bryant *Columnist*
%Newsweek Magazine, Editorial Dept, 251 W 57th St, New York, NY 10019, USA
Quinn, John C *Editor*
%Freedom Forum, 1101 Wilson Blvd, Arlington, VA 22209, USA
Quinn, Martha *Actress*
13903 Hesby St, Sherman Oaks, CA 91423, USA
Quinn, Sally *Journalist*
3014 "N" St NW, Washington, DC 20007, USA
Quinn, William F *Governor, HI*
1365 Laukahi St, Honolulu, HI 96821, USA
Quintero, Jose *Theater Director*
%Thomas Andrews, 39 E 72nd St, #500, New York, NY 10021, USA
Quisenberry, Daniel R (Dan) *Baseball Player*
12208 Buena Vista St, Leawood, KS 66209, USA
Quivar, Florence *Opera Singer*
%Metropolitan Opera Assn, Lincoln Center Plaza, New York, NY 10023, USA

Raabe, Max — *Opera Singer*
%Klimperkasten, Thuyring 63, 12101 Berlin, Germany

Rabb, Maxwell M — *Diplomat*
Wilson Hill Road, Colrain, MA 01340, USA

Rabbitt, Eddie — *Singer, Songwriter*
%Brokaw Co, 1915 Church St, Nashville, TN 37203, USA

Rabin, Stanley A — *Businessman*
%Commercial Metals Co, 7800 N Stemmons Freeway, Dallas, TX 75247, USA

Rabinow, Jacob — *Electrical Engineer*
6920 Selkirk Dr, Bethesda, MD 20817, USA

Rabinowitz, Harry — *Conductor, Composer*
%Honor Music, Walking Bottom, Peaslake, Surrey GU5 9RR, England

Rabinowitz, Jesse C — *Biochemist*
%University of California, Molecular & Cell Biology Dept, Berkeley, CA 94720, USA

Rabkin, Mitchell T — *Physician*
124 Canton Ave, Milton, MA 02186, USA

Rabuka, Sitiveni — *Prime Minister, Fiji; Army General*
%Prime Minister's Office, Victoria Parade, 6 Berkeley Parade, Suva, Fiji

Raby, Stuart — *Physicist*
%Ohio State University, Physics Dept, Columbus, OH 43210, USA

Rachins, Alan — *Actor*
1274 Capri Dr, Pacific Palisades, CA 90272, USA

Racicot, Marc F — *Governor, MT*
%Governor's Office, State Capitol, Helena, MT 59620, USA

Racimo, Victoria — *Actress*
%Marion Rosenberg, 8428 Melrose Place, #C, Los Angeles, CA 90069, USA

Radatz, Richard R (Dick) — *Baseball Player*
%Atlantic Container, PO Box 348, Braintree, MA 02184, USA

Rademacher, Ingo — *Actor*
%SDB Partners, 1801 Ave of Stars, #902, Los Angeles, CA 90067, USA

Rademacher, T Peter (Pete) — *Boxer*
5585 River Styx Road, Medina, OH 44256, USA

Rader, Douglas L (Doug) — *Baseball Manager*
112-7 Cedar Point, Stuart, FL 33494, USA

Rader, Randall R — *Judge*
%US Claims Court, 717 Madison Place NW, Washington, DC 20005, USA

Radford, Mark — *Basketball Player*
3423 NE 22nd Ave, Portland, OR 97212, USA

Radford, Michael — *Movie Director*
3-B Rickering Mews, London W2 5AD, England

Radke, Brad W — *Baseball Player*
%Richard Radke, 3107 Emerson, Tampa, FL 33629, USA

Radojevic, Danilo — *Ballet Dancer*
%American Ballet Theatre, 890 Broadway, New York, NY 10003, USA

Radwanski, George — *Editor*
%Toronto Star, Editorial Dept, 1 Yonge St, Toronto ON M5E 1E6, Canada

Rady, Ernest S — *Businessman*
%WestCorp, 23 Pasteur Road, Irvine, CA 92618, USA

Rae, Cassidy — *Actress*
%SDB Partners, 1801 Ave of Stars, #902, Los Angeles, CA 90067, USA

Rae, Charlotte — *Actress*
10790 Wilshire Blvd, #903, Los Angeles, CA 90024, USA

Rae, Robert K — *Political Leader, Canada*
%Premier's Office, Queen's Park, Toronto ON M7A 1A1, Canada

Rafelson, Bob — *Movie Director*
12899 Mulholland Dr, Beverly Hills, CA 90210, USA

Raffi (Cavoukian) — *Singer*
%International Creative Mgmt, 40 W 57th St, New York, NY 10019, USA

Raffin, Deborah — *Actress*
%Dove Audio, 301 N Canon Dr, #207, Beverly Hills, CA 90210, USA

Rafsanjani, Hojatoleslam H — *President, Iran*
%Expediency Council of Islamic Order, Majalis, Teheran, Iran

Rafter, Patrick — *Tennis Player*
%Assn of Tennis Professionals, 200 Tournament Players Rd, Ponte Vedra, FL 32082, USA

Raftery, S Frank — *Labor Leader*
%Painters & Allied Trades Union, 1750 New York Ave NW, Washington, DC 20006, USA

Ragin, John S — *Actor*
5708 Briarcliff Road, Los Angeles, CA 90068, USA

R

Raabe - Ragin

Rahal, Bobby — *Auto Racing Driver*
5 New Albany Farms Road, New Albany, OH 43054, USA

Rahman Khan, Ataur — *Prime Minister, Bangladesh*
%Bangladesh Jatiya League, 500-A Dhanmondi R/A, Road 7, Dhaka, Bangladesh

Rahn, Helmut — *Soccer Player*
Dittmarstr 1, 45144 Essen, Germany

Raichle, Marcus E — *Neurologist, Radiologist*
%Washington University Medical School, Neurology Dept, St Louis, MO 63130, USA

Railsback, Steve — *Actor*
11684 Ventura Blvd, #581, Studio City, CA 91604, USA

Raimond, Jean-Bernard — *Government Official, France*
203 Ave Daumesnil, 75012 Paris, France

Raimondi, Ruggero — *Opera Singer*
%Columbia Artists Mgmt Inc, 165 W 57th St, New York, NY 10019, USA

Raine, Craig A — *Writer*
%New College, English Dept, Oxford OX1 3BN, England

Raine, Kathleen J — *Writer*
47 Paultons Square, London SW3, England

Rainer, Luise — *Actress*
%Knittel, Vico Morcote, 6911 Lugano, Switzerland

Raines, Franklin D — *Government Official, Financier*
%Office of Management/Budget, Executive Office Building, Washington, DC 20503, USA

Raines, Howell — *Journalist*
%New York Times, Editorial Dept, 229 W 43rd St, New York, NY 10036, USA

Raines, Timothy (Tim) — *Baseball Player*
310 Saddleworth Place, Lake Mary, FL 32746, USA

Rainey, Ford — *Actor*
3821 Carbon Canyon Road, Malibu, CA 90265, USA

Rainey, Wayne — *Motorcyle Racing Rider*
1660 Akron Peninsula Road, #201, Akron, OH 44313, USA

Rainier III — *Prince, Monaco*
%Palais de Monaco, Boite Postale 518, 98015 Monte Carlo Cedex, Monaco

Rainwater, Gregg — *Actor*
PO Box 291830, Los Angeles, CA 90029, USA

Rainwater, Marvin — *Singer*
%Tuff-Stuff Productions, PO Box 520495, Independence, MO 64052, USA

Raitt, Bonnie — *Singer, Songwriter*
1344 N Spaulding Ave, Los Angeles, CA 90046, USA

Raitt, John — *Singer, Actor*
1164 Napoli Dr, Pacific Palisades, CA 90272, USA

Rajna, Thomas — *Concert Pianist, Composer*
10 Wyndover Road, Claremont, Cape 7700, South Africa

Rakhmonov, Emomali — *President, Tajikistan*
%President's Office, Supreme Soviet, Dushanbe, Tajikistan

Rakim — *Rap Artist (Eric B & Rakim)*
%Mean City Mgmt, 1775 Broadway, #700, New York, NY 10019, USA

Rakowski, Mieczyslaw F — *Prime Minister, Poland*
Miesiecznik Dzis, Ul Poznanska 3, 00-680 Warsaw, Poland

Raksin, David — *Composer, Conductor*
6519 Aldea Ave, Van Nuys, CA 91406, USA

Rales, Steven M — *Businessman*
%Danaher Corp, 1250 24th St NW, Washington, DC 20037, USA

Rall, David P — *Toxicologist, Pharmacologist*
5302 Reno Road NW, Washington, DC 20015, USA

Rall, J Edward — *Physician*
3947 Baltimore St, Kensington, MD 20895, USA

Rallis, George J — *Prime Minister, Greece*
4 Kanari St, Athens, Greece

Ralph, Sheryl Lee — *Actress, Singer*
938 S Longwood Ave, Los Angeles, CA 90019, USA

Ralston, Dennis — *Tennis Player*
2005 San Vicente Dr, Concord, CA 94519, USA

Ralston, John — *Football Player, Coach*
1740 Hawkins Dr, Los Altos, CA 94024, USA

Ralston, Joseph W (Joe) — *Air Force General*
%Vice Chairman's Office, Joint Chiefs of Staff, Pentagon, Washington, DC 20318, USA

Ralston, Vera Hruba — *Actress*
4121 Crescienta Dr, Santa Barbara, CA 93110, USA

Ram, C Venkata — *Physician*
%Texas Southwestern Medical Center, 5323 Harry Hines Blvd, Dallas, TX 75235, USA

Rama IX — *King, Thailand*
%Chitralada Villa, Bangkok, Thailand

Rama Rau, Santha — *Writer*
RR 1, Box 200, Leedsville Road, Amenia, NY 12501, USA

Ramage, Rob — *Hockey Player*
16127 Wilson Manor Dr, Chesterfield, MO 63005, USA

Rambahadur Limbu — *Vietnam War Sarawak Army Hero (VC)*
Box 420, Bandar Seri Begawan, Negara Brunei Darussalam, Brunei

Rambert, Charles J J — *Architect*
179 Rue de Courcelles, 75017 Paris, France

Rambis, Kurt — *Basketball Player, Coach*
20 Chatham, Manhattan Beach, CA 90266, USA

Rambo, David L — *Religious Leader*
%Christian & Missionary Alliance, PO Box 35000, Colorado Springs, CO 80935, USA

Rambo, John — *Track Athlete*
1847 Myrtle Ave, Long Beach, CA 90806, USA

Ramey, Samuel E — *Opera Singer*
320 Central Park West, New York, NY 10025, USA

Ramgoolam, Seewosagur — *Prime Minister, Mauritius*
85 Desforges St, Port Louis, Mauritius

Ramirez Vazquez, Pedro — *Architect*
Ave de la Fuentes 170, Mexico City 20 DF, Mexico

Ramirez, Manuel A (Manny) — *Baseball Player*
501 W 168th St, #3-F, New York, NY 10032, USA

Ramirez, Michael P — *Editorial Cartoonist*
%Memphis Commercial Appeal, Editorial Dept, 495 Union Ave, Memphis, TN 38103, USA

Ramirez, Raul — *Tennis Player*
Avenida Ruiz, 65 Sur Ensenada, Baja California, Mexico

Ramis, Harold A — *Actor, Movie Director*
160 Euclid Ave, Glencoe, IL 60022, USA

Ramon, Haim — *Government Official, Israel*
%Ministry of Health, PO Box 1176, 2 Ben-Tabei St, Jerusalem 91010, Israel

Ramos, Del — *Singer (The Association)*
%Variety Artists, 555 Chorro St, #A-1, San Luis Obispo, CA 93405, USA

Ramos, Fidel V — *President, Philippines; Army General*
%President's Office, Malacanang Palace, J P Laurel St, Manila, Philippines

Ramos, Larry, Jr — *Singer, Guitarist (The Association)*
%Variety Artists, 555 Chorro St, #A-1, San Luis Obispo, CA 93405, USA

Ramos, Mando — *Boxer*
16860 Bay View Dr, Huntington Beach, CA 92649, USA

Ramos, Mel — *Artist*
5941 Ocean View Dr, Oakland, CA 94618, USA

Rampal, Jean-Pierre — *Concert Flutist*
15 Ave Mozart, 75016 Paris, France

Rampling, Charlotte — *Actress*
1 Ave Emile Augier, 78290 Croissy-sur-Seine, France

Rampton, Calvin L — *Governor, UT*
2550 Elizabeth St, Salt Lake City, UT 84106, USA

Ramsay, Craig — *Hockey Player*
9701 NW 58th Court, Pompano Beach, FL 33076, USA

Ramsay, John T (Jack) — *Basketball Coach, Executive*
21 Newcastle Road, Ocean City, NJ 08226, USA

Ramsey, Frank V, Jr — *Basketball Player*
Buckner Ridge Lane, Box 363, Madisonville, KY 42431, USA

Ramsey, Garrard (Buster) — *Football Player*
4102 Highway 411-S, Maryville, TN 37801, USA

Ramsey, Logan — *Actor*
12923 Killion St, Van Nuys, CA 91401, USA

Ramsey, Mary — *Singer (10000 Maniacs)*
%New York End, 2525 Michigan Ave, #1-A, Santa Monica, CA 90404, USA

Ramsey, Michael (Mike) — *Hockey Player*
6362 Oxbow Bend, Chanhassen, MN 55317, USA

Ramsey, Norman F, Jr — *Nobel Physics Laureate*
24 Monmouth Court, Brookline, MA 02146, USA

Ramsey, William (Bill) — *Singer, Songwriter*
Elbchaussee 118, 22763 Hamburg, Germany

R

Ram - Ramsey

R

Ramsey, William E — *Navy Admiral*
825 Bayshore Dr, Pensacola, FL 32507, USA

Ran, Shulamit — *Composer*
%University of Chicago, Music Dept, 5845 S Ellis Ave, Chicago, IL 60637, USA

Ranck, Bruce E — *Businessman*
%Browning-Ferris Industries, 757 N Eldridge Parkway, Houston, TX 77079, USA

Rand, Marvin — *Photographer*
%Marvin Rand Assoc, 1310 Abbot Kinney Blvd, Venice, CA 90291, USA

Rand, Mary — *Track Athlete*
1185 Linda Vista Dr, San Marcos, CA 92069, USA

Rand, Robert W — *Neurosurgeon, Educator*
%Good Samaritan Hospital, Neurosciences Institute, Los Angeles, CA 90017, USA

Randall, Claire — *Religious Leader*
13427 Countryside Dr, Sun City West, AZ 85375, USA

Randall, Jon — *Singer*
%M Hitchcock Mgmt, PO Box 159007, Nashville, TN 37215, USA

Randall, Tony — *Actor*
%Beresford, 1 W 81st St, #6-D, New York, NY 10024, USA

Randall, W D (Bo), Jr — *Knife Maker*
%Randall Made Knives, PO Box 1988, Orlando, FL 32802, USA

Randi, James — *Illusionist*
12000 NW 8th St, Fort Lauderdale, FL 33325, USA

Randle, Theresa — *Actress*
1018 Meadowbrook Ave, Los Angeles, CA 90019, USA

Randolph, Boots — *Jazz Saxophonist*
%Gerald Purcell, 954 2nd Ave, New York, NY 10022, USA

Randolph, Jennings — *Senator, WV*
300 3rd St, Elkins, WV 26241, USA

Randolph, John — *Actor*
1850 N Whitney Place, Los Angeles, CA 90028, USA

Randolph, Joyce — *Actress*
295 Central Park West, #18-A, New York, NY 10024, USA

Randolph, Judson G — *Pediatric Surgeon*
111 Michigan Ave NW, Washington, DC 20010, USA

Randolph, Willie L — *Baseball Player*
648 Juniper Place, Franklin Lakes, NJ 07417, USA

Randrup, Michael — *Test Pilot*
10 Fairlawn Road, Lytham, Lanc, England

Rands, Bernard — *Composer*
%Harvard University, Music Dept, Cambridge, MA 02138, USA

Ranford, Bill — *Hockey Player*
%Washington Capitals, USAir Arena, 1 Truman Dr, Landover, MD 20785, USA

Ranieri, Lewis S — *Financier*
%Bank United of Texas, 3200 Southwest Freeway, Houston, TX 77027, USA

Ranki, Dezso — *Concert Pianist*
Kertesz-Utca 50, 1073 Budapest, Hungary

Rankin, Alfred M, Jr — *Businessman*
%NACCO Industries, 5875 Landerbrook Dr, Mayfield Heights, OH 44124, USA

Rankin, Judy — *Golfer*
2715 Racquet Club Dr, Midland, TX 79705, USA

Rankin, Kenny — *Singer, Songwriter, Guitarist*
%Absolute Artists, 530 Howard St, #200, San Francisco, CA 94105, USA

Ranks, Shabba — *Singer*
%Famous Artists Agency, 1700 Broadway, #500, New York, NY 10019, USA

Ranney, Helen M — *Physician*
6229 La Jolla Mesa Dr, La Jolla, CA 92037, USA

Ransey, Kelvin — *Basketball Player*
1205 Gretna Green Ave, Toledo, OH 43607, USA

Ransohoff, Joseph — *Neurosurgeon*
%New York University Medical School, Neurosurgery Dept, New York, NY 10016, USA

Rao, P V Narasimha — *Prime Minister, India*
Lok Sabha, New Delhi, India

Rao, Paul P — *Judge*
%US Court of International Trade, 1 Federal Plaza, New York, NY 10278, USA

Raoul, Alfred — *Prime Minister, Congo; Army Officer*
%Foreign Affairs Ministry, Brazzaville, Congo

Rapaport, Michael — *Actor*
%Innovative Artists, 1999 Ave of Stars, #2850, Los Angeles, CA 90067, USA

Ramsey - Rapaport

Raper, Kenneth B — *Bacteriologist*
602 N Segoe Road, Madison, WI 53705, USA

Raphael (Martos) — *Singer*
%Kaduri Agency, 16125 NE 18th Ave, North Miami Beach, FL 33162, USA

Raphael, Fredric M — *Writer*
Largadelle, St Lauraent la Vallee, 24170 Belves, France

Raphael, Sally Jessy — *Entertainer*
%MultiMedia Entertainment, 8 Elm St, New Haven, CT 06510, USA

Rapping 4-Tay — *Rap Artist*
%William Morris Agency, 1325 Ave of Americas, New York, NY 10019, USA

Rappuoli, Rino — *Medical Researcher*
%Sclavo Research Center, Via Fiorentina 1, 53100, Siena, Italy

Rapson, Ralph — *Architect*
1 Seymour Ave, Minneapolis, MN 55414, USA

Rarick, Cindy — *Golfer*
%Ladies Professional Golf Assn, 2570 Volusia Ave, Daytona Beach, FL 32114, USA

Rasa Don (Donald Jones) — *Soul/Rap Artist (Arrested Development)*
%William Morris Agency, 1325 Ave of Americas, New York, NY 10019, USA

Rasche, David — *Actor*
687 Grove Lane, Santa Barbara, CA 93105, USA

Rashad, Ahmad — *Football Player, Sportscaster*
130 W 42nd St, #2400, New York, NY 10036, USA

Rashad, Phylicia — *Actress*
130 W 42nd St, #2400, New York, NY 10036, USA

Raskin, David — *Composer*
%Robert Light, 6404 Wilshire Blvd, Los Angeles, CA 90048, USA

Rasmussen, Norman C — *Nuclear Engineer*
80 Winsor Road, Sudbury, MA 01776, USA

Rasmussen, Poul N — *Prime Minister, Denmark*
Christiansborg Palace, Prins Jorgens Ganard II, 1218 Copenhagen K, Denmark

Raspberry, Larry — *Singer (The Gentrys)*
%Craig Nowag Attractions, 6037 Haddington Place, Memphis, TN 38119, USA

Raspberry, William J — *Journalist*
%Washington Post, Editorial Dept, 1150 15th St NW, Washington, DC 20071, USA

Ratcliffe, G Jackson, Jr — *Businessman*
%Hubbell Inc, 584 Derby Milford Road, Orange, CT 06477, USA

Ratcliffe, John A — *Radio Astronomer*
193 Huntingdon Road, Cambridge CB3 0DL, England

Ratelle, J G Jean — *Hockey Player*
11 Tophet Road, Lynnfield, MA 01940, USA

Rathbone, Perry T — *Museum Director*
130 Mount Auburn St, #506, University Green, Cambridge, MA 02138, USA

Rather, Dan — *Commentator*
%CBS-TV, News Dept, 51 W 52nd St, New York, NY 10019, USA

Rathmann, Jim — *Auto Racing Driver*
3950 N Riverside Dr, Indialantic, FL 32903, USA

Ratleff, Ed — *Basketball Player*
310 Wisconsin Ave, #7, Long Beach, CA 90814, USA

Ratliff, Floyd — *Biophysicist*
2215 Calle Cacique, Santa Fe, NM 87505, USA

Ratliff, Robert J — *Businessman*
%AGCO Corp, 4830 River Green Parkway, Duluth, GA 30096, USA

Ratliff, Theo — *Basketball Player*
%Detroit Pistons, Palace, 2 Championship Dr, Auburn Hills, MI 48326, USA

Ratnoff, Oscar D — *Physician*
2916 Sedgewick Road, Shaker Heights, OH 44120, USA

Ratterman, George — *Football Player*
750 Crescent Lane, Lakewood, CO 80215, USA

Rattle, Simon — *Conductor*
%Birmingham Symphony, Paradise Place, Birmingham B3 3RP, England

Ratushinskaya, Irina B — *Writer*
15 Crothall Close, Palmers Green, London N13, England

Ratzenberger, John — *Actor*
PO Box 515, Vashon, WA 98070, USA

Ratzinger, Joseph Cardinal — *Religious Leader*
Piazza del Santuffizio 11, 00120 Vatican City

Rau, Johannes — *Government Official, West Germany*
Haroldstr 2, 47057 Dusseldorf, Germany

Rauch, Johnny *Football Player, Coach*
%San Jose State University, Athletic Dept, San Jose, CA 95192, USA

Raum, Arnold *Judge*
%US Tax Court, 400 2nd St NW, Washington, DC 20217, USA

Rauschenberg, Robert *Artist*
%M Knoedler Co, 19 E 70th St, New York, NY 10021, USA

Rautio, Nina *Opera Singer*
%Metropolitan Opera Assn, Lincoln Center Plaza, New York, NY 10023, USA

Raven, Eddy *Singer, Songwriter, Guitarist*
%Crazy Crow, 1071 Bradley Road, Gallatin, TN 37066, USA

Raven, Peter H *Botanist*
%Missouri Botanical Garden, PO Box 299, St Louis, MO 63166, USA

Raven, Robert D *Attorney*
%Morrison & Foerster, 345 California St, #3500, San Francisco, CA 94104, USA

Ravitch, Diane S *Writer, Historian*
%New York University, Press Building, Washington Place, New York, NY 10003, USA

Ravony, Francisque *Prime Minister, Madagascar*
%Prime Minister's Office, Mahazoarivo, Antananarivo, Madagascar

Rawlings, Hunter R, III *Educator*
%Cornell University, President's Office, Ithaca, NY 14853, USA

Rawlings, Jerry J *President, Ghana; Air Force Officer*
%Head of State's Office, The Castle, PO Box 1627, Accra, Ghana

Rawlins, Benjamin W, Jr *Financier*
%Union Planters Corp, 7130 Goodlett Farms Parkway, Cordova, TN 38018, USA

Rawlins, V Lane *Educator*
%University of Memphis, President's Office, Memphis, TN 38152, USA

Rawlinson of Ewell, Peter *Government Official, England*
9 Priory Walk, London SW10 9SP, England

Rawls, Betsy *Golfer*
4613 Sylvanus Dr, Wilmington, DE 19803, USA

Rawls, Lou *Singer, Actor*
109 Fremont Place W, Los Angeles, CA 90005, USA

Ray, Amy *Singer, Songwriter (Indigo Girls)*
%Russell Carter Artist Mgmt, 315 Ponce de Leon Aave, #756, Decatur, GA 30030, USA

Ray, Marguerite *Actress*
1329 N Vista St, #106, Los Angeles, CA 90046, USA

Ray, Norman W (Norm) *Navy Admiral*
USNATO, USM PSC 81, Box 151, APO, AE 09724, USA

Ray, Robert D *Governor, IA*
%Blue Cross/Blue Shield of Iowa, 636 Grand Ave, Des Moines, IA 50309, USA

Ray, Ronald E *Vietnam War Army Hero (CMH)*
PO Box 2839, Winter Haven, FL 33883, USA

Rayburn, Gene *Entertainer*
245 5th Ave, New York, NY 10016, USA

Raye, Collin *Singer*
%Scott Dean Mgmt, 612 Humboldt St, Reno, NV 89509, USA

Rayl, Jim *Basketball Player*
201 West Boulevard, Kokomo, IN 46902, USA

Raymond, Arthur E *Airplane Designer*
73 Oakmont Dr, Los Angeles, CA 90049, USA

Raymond, Gene *Actor*
250 Trino Way, Pacific Palisades, CA 90272, USA

Raymond, Guy *Actor*
550 Erskine Dr, Pacific Palisades, CA 90272, USA

Raymond, Lee R *Businessman*
%Exxon Corp, 5959 Las Colinas Blvd, Irving, TX 75039, USA

Raymond, Paula *Actress*
PO Box 86, Beverly Hills, CA 90213, USA

Rayner, E Charles (Chuck) *Hockey Player*
116-5710 201st St, Langley BC V3A 8A8, Canada

Raz, Kavi *Actor*
%Dale Garrick, 8831 Sunset Blvd, #402, Los Angeles, CA 90069, USA

Razafimahatratra, Victor Cardinal *Religious Leader*
Archeveche, Andohalo, 101 Antananarivo, Madagascar

Razanamasy, Guy *Prime Minister, Madagascar*
%Prime Minister's Office, Mahazoarivo, Antananarivo, Madagascar

Razumovsky, Georgy P *Government Official, Russia*
%Russian Parliament, Kremlin, Moscow, Russia

Re, Edward D *Judge*
%US Court of International Trade, 1 Federal Plaza, New York, NY 10278, USA

Rea, Chris *Singer, Guitarist*
%East-West Records, 46 Kensington Court St, London W8 5DP, England

Rea, Peggy *Actress*
10331 Riverside Dr, #204, Toluca Lake, CA 91602, USA

Rea, Stephen *Actor*
108 Leonard St, London EC2A 4RH, England

Read, James *Actor*
%Pakula/King, 9229 Sunset Blvd, #315, Los Angeles, CA 90069, USA

Readdy, William F *Astronaut*
%NASA, Johnson Space Center, 2101 NASA Road, Houston, TX 77058, USA

Reagan, Nancy *Wife of US President, Actress*
668 St Cloud Road, Bel Air, CA 90077, USA

Reagan, Ronald *President, USA; Actor*
668 St Cloud Road, Bel Air, CA 90077, USA

Reagon, Bernice Johnson *Singer (Sweet Honey in the Rock)*
%American University, History Dept, Washington, DC 20016, USA

Real Roxanne, The *Rap Artist*
%Headline Talent, 1650 Broadway, #508, New York, NY 10019, USA

Reamer, Norton H *Financier*
%United Asset Management, 1 International Plaza, Boston, MA 02110, USA

Reams, Lee Roy *Actor, Singer*
%Ligeti, 415 W 55th St, New York, NY 10019, USA

Reardon, Jeffrey J (Jeff) *Baseball Player*
4 Marlwood Lane, Palm Beach Gardens, FL 33418, USA

Reardon, Kenneth (Ken) *Hockey Player*
568 Grosvenor Ave, West Mont PQ H3Y 2S7, Canada

Reason, J Paul *Navy Admiral*
CinC, US Atlantic Fleet, 1562 Mitscher Ave, Norfolk, VA 23551, USA

Reason, Rex *Actor*
%Roadside Productions, 20105 Rhapsody Road, Walnut Creek, CA 91789, USA

Rebek, Julius, Jr *Chemist*
100 Memorial Dr, #53-A, Cambridge, MA 02142, USA

Recchi, Mark *Hockey Player*
537 Kingsberry Circle, Pittsburgh, PA 15234, USA

Rechter, Yacov *Architect*
150 Arlozorov St, Tel Aviv 62098, Israel

Reckell, Peter *Actor*
%Sterling/Winters, 1900 Ave of Stars, #1640, Los Angeles, CA 90067, USA

Rector, Milton G *Association Executive*
%National Council on Crime & Delinquency, 288 Monroe, River Edge, NJ 07661, USA

Redbone, Leon *Singer*
%Red Shark Inc, 179 Aquetong Road, New Hope, PA 18938, USA

Redd, John S *Navy Admiral*
%Joint Chiefs of Staff, Strategic Plans/Policy, Pentagon, Washington, DC 20318, USA

Redden, Joseph J (Joe) *Air Force General*
Commander, Air University, 55 LeMay Plaza, Maxwell Air Force Base, AL 36112, USA

Reddicliffe, Steven *Editor*
%TV Guide Magazine, Editorial Dept, 100 Matsonford Road, Radnor, PA 19087, USA

Redding, Peter S *Businessman*
%Standard Register Co, 600 Albany St, Dayton, OH 45408, USA

Reddy, D Raj *Computer Scientist*
%Robotics Institute, Carnegie-Mellon University, Pittsburgh, PA 15213, USA

Reddy, Helen *Singer*
%Helen Reddy Inc, 820 Stanford St, Santa Monica, CA 90403, USA

Redfield, James *Writer*
%Warner Books, 1271 6th Ave, New York, NY 10020, USA

Redford, Robert *Actor, Movie Director*
Rt 3, Box 837, Provo, UT 84604, USA

Redgrave, Corin *Actor*
%Kate Feast, Primrose Hill Studios, Fitzroy Road, London NW1 8TR, England

Redgrave, Lynn *Actress*
21342 Colina Dr, Topanga, CA 90290, USA

Redgrave, Vanessa *Actress*
%James Sharkey, 21 Golden Square, London W1R 3PA, England

Reding, Juli *Actress*
PO Box 1806, Beverly Hills, CA 90213, USA

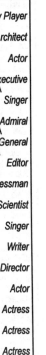

R

Re - Reding

Redington, Joe, Sr *Dog Sled Racer*
%Joe Redington Sled Dog Institute, HC 30, Box 5460, Wasilla, AK 99654, USA

Redman, Dewey *Jazz Reeds Player, Composer*
%Joel Chriss, 300 Mercer St, #3-J, New York, NY 10003, USA

Redman, Joshua *Jazz Saxophonist, Composer*
%Jazz Tree, 211 Thompson St, #1-D, New York, NY 10012, USA

Redman, Joyce *Actress*
%Peters Fraser Dunlop, Chelsea Harbour, Lots Rd, London SW10 0XF, England

Redman, Peter *Financer*
%Cessna Finance Corp, 5800 E Pawnee St, Wichita, KS 67218, USA

Redman, Richard C (Rick) *Football Player*
153 Prospect St, Seattle, WA 98109, USA

Redmond, Marge *Actress*
101 Central Park West, New York, NY 10023, USA

Redmond, Mickey *Hockey Player*
30699 Harlincin Court, Franklin, MI 48025, USA

Redmond, Paul A *Businessman*
%Washington Water Power, East 1411 Mission Ave, Spokane, WA 99202, USA

Redpath, Jean *Singer*
Sunny Knowe, The Promenade, Leven, Fife, Scotland

Redstone, Sumner M *Theater Executive*
%Viacom Inc, 1515 Broadway, New York, NY 10036, USA

Reece, Beasley *Football Player, Sportscaster*
%Premier Sports, 110 E 59th St, #800, New York, NY 10022, USA

Reece, Gabrielle (Gabby) *Volleyball Player, Model*
5111 Ocean Front Walk, Marina del Rey, CA 90292, USA

Reece, Thomas L *Businessman*
%Dover Corp, 280 Park Ave, New York, NY 10017, USA

Reed, Andre D *Football Player*
5218 Fairway Oaks Dr, Windermere, FL 34786, USA

Reed, Carlton D, Jr *Businessman*
%Central Main Power, Edison Dr, Augusta, ME 04336, USA

Reed, Eric *Jazz Pianist*
%Integrity Talent, PO Box 961, Burlington, MA 01803, USA

Reed, Herb *Singer (The Platters)*
%JP Productions, 57 18th Ave, Ronkonkoma, NY 11779, USA

Reed, Ishmael S *Writer*
1446 6th St, #C, Berkeley, CA 94710, USA

Reed, Jerry *Singer, Songwriter*
%Jerry Lee Enterprises, PO Box 3586, Brentwood, TN 37024, USA

Reed, John E *Businessman*
%Mestek Inc, 200 N Elm St, Westfield, MA 01085, USA

Reed, John H *Governor, ME; Diplomat*
410 "O" St SW, Washington, DC 20024, USA

Reed, John S *Financier*
%Citicorp, 399 Park Ave, New York, NY 10022, USA

Reed, Lou *Singer, Songwriter (Velvet Undergound)*
%Sister Ray Enterprises, 584 Broadway, #609, New York, NY 10012, USA

Reed, Margaret *Actress*
%Moress Nanas Wald, 12424 Wilshire Blvd, #840, Los Angeles, CA 90025, USA

Reed, Mark A *Physicist*
%Yale University, Electrical Engineering Dept, PO Box 2157, New Haven, CT 06520, USA

Reed, Oliver *Actor*
Houmit Lane, Houmit Vale, Guernsey, Channel Islands, England

Reed, Pamela *Actress*
1875 Century Park East, #1300, Los Angeles, CA 90067, USA

Reed, Rex *Entertainment Critic*
%Dakota Hotel, 1 W 72nd St, #86, New York, NY 10023, USA

Reed, Richard J *Meteorologist*
%University of Washington, Atmospheric Sciences Dept, Seattle, WA 98195, USA

Reed, Thomas C *Government Official*
%Quaker Hill Development Corp, PO Box 2240, Healdsburg, CA 95448, USA

Reed, Willis, Jr *Basketball Player, Coach, Executive*
44 N Wyoming Ave, South Orange, NJ 07079, USA

Reedy, George E, Jr *Educator, Journalist*
1840 N Prospect Ave, #304, Milwaukee, WI 53202, USA

Rees, Clifford H (Ted), Jr *Air Force General*
3114 Barbard Court, Fairfax, VA 22031, USA

Rees, Merlyn	Government Official, England

Rees, Merlyn — Government Official, England
%House of Commons, Westminster, London SW1A 0AA, England

Rees, Mina — Mathematician
301 E 66th St, New York, NY 10021, USA

Rees, Norma S — Educator
%California State University, President's Office, Hayward, CA 94542, USA

Rees, Roger — Actor
%Gersh Agency, 232 N Canon Dr, Beverly Hills, CA 90210, USA

Rees-Mogg of Hinton Blewett, William — Publisher
3 Smith Square, London SW1, England

Reese, Della — Singer, Actress
1910 Bel Air Road, Los Angeles, CA 90077, USA

Reese, Eddie — Swimming Coach
%University of Texas, Athletic Dept, Austin, TX 78712, USA

Reese, Harold H (Pee Wee) — Baseball Player
1400 Willow Ave, Louisville, KY 40204, USA

Reese, Miranda — Ballerina
%New York City Ballet, Lincoln Center Plaza, New York, NY 10023, USA

Reeve, Christopher — Actor
PO Box 26, Springfield, NJ 07081, USA

Reeves, Bryant — Basketball Player
%Vancouver Grizzlies, 288 Beatty St, #300, Vancouver BC V6B 2M1, Canada

Reeves, Daniel E (Dan) — Football Player, Coach
%Atlanta Falcons, 2745 Burnett Road, Suwanee, GA 30024, USA

Reeves, Del — Singer, Songwriter
%Billy Deaton Mgmt, 1300 Division St, #102, Nashville, TN 37203, USA

Reeves, Dianne — Singer
%Baker Winokur Ryder, 405 S Beverly Dr, #500, Beverly Hills, CA 90212, USA

Reeves, Donna A — Golfer
%Ladies Professional Golf Assn, 2570 Volusia Ave, Daytona Beach, FL 32114, USA

Reeves, Keanu — Actor
%Creative Artists Agency, 9830 Wilshire Blvd, Beverly Hills, CA 90212, USA

Reeves, Khalid — Basketball Player
%Dallas Mavericks, Reunion Arena, 777 Sports St, Dallas, TX 75207, USA

Reeves, Martha — Singer (Martha & The Vandellas)
PO Box 4013, Los Angeles, CA 90078, USA

Reeves, Richard — Columnist
%Universal Press Syndicate, 4520 Main St, Kansas City, KS 64111, USA

Reeves, Scott — Actor
6520 Platt Ave, #634, West Hills, CA 91307, USA

Reeves, Steve — Actor, Bodybuilder
%Classic Images Enterprises, PO Box 807, Valley Center, CA 92082, USA

Regalbuto, Joe — Actor
724 24th St, Santa Monica, CA 90402, USA

Regan, Donald T — Secretary, Treasury; Financier
240 Mclaws Circle, #142, Williamsburg, VA 23185, USA

Regan, Gerald A — Government Official, Canada
PO Box 828, Station B, Ottawa ON K1P 5P9, Canada

Regan, Judith — Writer, Talk Show Host
%New Enterprises, 1211 Ave of Americas, New York, NY 10036, USA

Regan, Larry — Hockey Player
114 Damour St, Aylmer PQ J9H 5V4, Canada

Regan, Philip R — Baseball Player, Manager
1375 108th St, Byron Center, MI 49315, USA

Regazzoni, Clay — Auto Racing Driver
Via Monzoni 13, 6900 Lugano, Switzerland

Regehr, Duncan — Actor
2401 Main St, Santa Monica, CA 90405, USA

Reggiani, Serge — Singer, Actor
%Charley Marouani, 4 Ave Hoche, 75008 Paris, France

Regine — Restauranteur
502 Park Ave, New York, NY 10022, USA

Regis, John — Track Athlete
67 Fairby Road, London SE12, England

Regnier, Charles — Actor, Theater Director
Seestr 6, 82541 Munsing, Germany

Rehm, Jack D — Publisher
%Meredith Corp, PO Box 400430, Des Moines, IA 50350, USA

R

Rehnquist, William H *Supreme Court Chief Justice*
%US Supreme Court, 1 1st St NE, Washington, DC 20543, USA

Reich, Charles A *Attorney, Educator*
%Crown Publishers, 225 Park Ave S, New York, NY 10003, USA

Reich, John *Theater Director*
724 Bohemia Parkway, Sayville, NY 11782, USA

Reich, Robert B *Secretary, Labor*
%"The Long & The Short of It" Show, WGBH-TV, 125 Western Ave, Boston, MA 02134, USA

Reich, Steve M *Composer*
%Helene Cann Reich Music Foundation, 175 5th Ave, #2396, New York, NY 10010, USA

Reichert, Jack F *Businessman*
%Brunswick Corp, 1 N Field Court, Lake Forest, IL 60045, USA

Reichman, Fred *Artist*
1235 Stanyan St, San Francisco, CA 94117, USA

Reichmann, Paul *Businessman*
%Olympia & York Ltd, 2 First Canadian Place, Toronto ON M5X 1B5, Canada

Reid, Antonio (L A) *Songwriter*
%Kear Music, Carter Turner Co, 9229 W Sunset Blvd, West Hollywood, CA 90069, USA

Reid, Beryl *Actress*
%James Sharkey, 21 Golden Square, London W1R 3PA, England

Reid, Daphne Maxwell *Actress*
11342 Dona Lisa Dr, Studio City, CA 91604, USA

Reid, Don S *Singer (Statler Brothers), Songwriter*
%American Major Talent, PO Box 492, Hernando, MS 38632, USA

Reid, Frances *Actress*
400 S Beverly Dr, #216, Beverly Hills, CA 90212, USA

Reid, Harold W *Singer (Statler Brothers), Songwriter*
%American Major Talent, PO Box 492, Hernando, MS 38632, USA

Reid, J R *Basketball Player*
121 Cemetary St, Chester, SC 29706, USA

Reid, James S, Jr *Businessman*
%Standard Products Co, 2130 W 110th St, Cleveland, OH 44102, USA

Reid, Michael B (Mike) *Football Player, Songwriter*
825 Overton Lane, Nashville, TN 37220, USA

Reid, Norman R *Museum Director*
50 Brabourne Rise, Park Langley, Beckenham, Kent, England

Reid, Ogden R *Journalist, Diplomat*
Ophir Hill, Purchase, NY 10577, USA

Reid, Robert *Basketball Player, Coach*
%Washington Wizards, Capital Centre, 1 Truman Dr, Landover, MD 20785, USA

Reid, Robert *Skier*
%Dixfield Health Care Center, Dixfield, ME 04224, USA

Reid, Stephen E (Steve) *Football Player, Physician*
262 Graemere, Northfield, IL 60093, USA

Reid, Tim *Actor, Director*
11342 Dona Lisa Dr, Studio City, CA 91604, USA

Reid, William R *WW II British Royal Air Force Hero (VC)*
Cranford, Ferntower Place, Crieff, Perthshire PH7 3DD, Scotland

Reidy, Carolyn K *Publisher*
%Simon & Schuster, 1230 Ave of Americas, New York, NY 10020, USA

Reig, Oscar Ribas *Head of Government, Andorra*
%Governmental Offices, Andorra la Vella, Andorra

Reightler, Kenneth S, Jr *Astronaut*
%NASA, Johnson Space Center, 2101 NASA Road, Houston, TX 77058, USA

Reilly, Charles Nelson *Actor*
2341 Gloaming Way, Beverly Hills, CA 90210, USA

Reilly, John *Actor*
%Gersh Agency, 232 N Canon Dr, Beverly Hills, CA 90210, USA

Reilly, John P *Businessman*
%Figgie International, 4420 Sherwin Road, Willoughby, OH 44094, USA

Reilly, William K *Government Official*
%Stanford University, International Studies Institute, Stanford, CA 94305, USA

Reimer, Dennis J (Denny) *Army General*
%Chief of Staff, HqUSA, Pentagon, Washington, DC 20310, USA

Reimer, Roland *Religious Leader*
%Mennonite Brethren Churches Conference, 8000 W 21st St N, Wichita, KS 67205, USA

Reina Idiaquez, Carlos Roberto *President, Honduras*
%President's Office, 6 Avda La Calle, Tegucigalpa, Honduras

Reineck, Thomas — *Kayak Athlete*
Graf-Bernadotte-Str 4, 45133 Essen, Germany

Reiner, Carl — *Actor, Writer, Director*
714 N Rodeo Dr, Beverly Hills, CA 90210, USA

Reiner, Rob — *Actor, Director*
%Creative Artists Agency, 9830 Wilshire Blvd, Beverly Hills, CA 90212, USA

Reines, Frederick — *Nobel Physics Laureate*
18 Perkins Court, Irvine, CA 92612, USA

Reinhard, Robert R (Bob) — *Football Player*
37230 NW Soap Creek Road, Corvallis, OR 97330, USA

Reinhardt, John E — *Diplomat*
4200 Massachusetts Ave NW, #702, Washington, DC 20016, USA

Reinhardt, Max — *Publisher*
43 Onslow Square, #2, London SW7 3LR, England

Reinhold, Judge — *Actor, Director*
1341 Ocean Ave, #113, Santa Monica, CA 90401, USA

Reinking, Ann — *Actress, Dancer, Choreographer*
80 Central Park West, #7-G, New York, NY 10023, USA

Reinsdorf, Jerry M — *Baseball Executive*
%Chicago White Sox, 333 W 35th St, Chicago, IL 60616, USA

Reiser, Paul — *Actor*
4243 Colfax Ave, #C, Studio City, CA 91604, USA

Reiss, Howard — *Chemist*
16656 Oldham St, Encino, CA 91436, USA

Reisz, Karel — *Movie Director*
11 Chalcot Gardens, Off England's Lane, London NW3 4YB, England

Reiter, Mario — *Skier*
Hauselweg 5, 6830 Rankweil, Austria

Reiter, Thomas — *Astronaut, Germany*
%Europe Astronaut Center, Linder Hohe, Box 906096, 51127 Cologne, Germany

Reitman, Ivan — *Movie Director, Producer*
%Ivan Reitman Productions, 100 Universal City Plaza, Universal City, CA 91608, USA

Reitz, Bruce — *Surgeon*
%Johns Hopkins Hospital, 600 N Wolfe St, Baltimore, MD 21287, USA

Relman, Arnold S — *Editor, Physician*
%New England Journal of Medicine, 1440 Main St, Waltham, MA 02154, USA

Relph, Michael — *Movie Producer*
The Lodge, Primrose Hill Studios, Fitzroy Road, London NW1, England

Remedios, Alberto T — *Opera Singer*
%Opera & Concert Artists, 75 Albermarle Gardens, London NW6 3AN, England

Remek, Vladimir — *Cosmonaut, Czech Republic*
Veletrzni 17, Prague 7 17000, Czech Republic

Remigino, Lindy — *Track Athlete*
22 Paris Lane, Newington, CT 06111, USA

Remillard, Arthur J, Jr — *Businessman*
%Commerce Group, 211 Main St, Webster, MA 01570, USA

Remington, Deborah W — *Artist*
309 W Broadway, New York, NY 10013, USA

Remini, Leah — *Actress*
%Rick Siegel Mgmt, 1940 Westwood Blvd, #169, Los Angeles, CA 90025, USA

Remnick, David — *Writer*
%New Yorker Magazine, Editorial Dept, 20 W 43rd St, New York, NY 10036, USA

Remsen, Bert — *Actor*
5722 Mammoth Ave, Van Nuys, CA 91401, USA

Renaud, Line — *Singer*
5 Rue de Bois de Boulogne, 75016 Paris, France

Renchard, William S — *Financier*
%Chemical Banking Corp, 30 Rockefeller Plaza, New York, NY 10112, USA

Rendell, Edward G (Ed) — *Mayor*
%Mayor's Office, City Hall, 23 N Juniper St, Philadelphia, PA 19107, USA

Rendell, Ruth — *Writer*
Nussteads, Polstead, Suffolk, Colchester CO6 5DN, England

Rene, France-Albert — *President, Seychelles*
%President's Office, State House, Victoria, Mahe, Seychelles

Reneau, Daniel D — *Educator*
%Louisiana Tech University, President's Office, Ruston, LA 71272, USA

Renfrew of Kaimsthorn, Andrew C — *Archaeologist*
%Cambridge University, Archaeology Dept, Cambridge CB2 3DZ, England

R

Reineck - Renfrew of Kaimsthorn

R

Renfro, Brad — *Actor*
322 Foxboro Dr, Walnut, CA 91789, USA

Renfro, Melvin L (Mel) — *Football Player*
3507 NE Martin Luther King Blvd, #C-205, Portland, OR 97212, USA

Renick, Jesse (Cab) — *Basketball Player*
2656 SE Washington Blvd, Bartlettsville, OK 74006, USA

Renk, Silke — *Track Athlete*
Erhard-Hubner-Str 13, 06132 Halle/S, Germany

Renko, Steven (Steve) — *Baseball Player*
3408 W 35th St, Leawood, KS 68209, USA

Rennebohm, J Fred — *Religious Leader*
%Congregational Christian Churches National Assn, Box 1620, Oak Creek, MI 53154, USA

Rennert, Gunther — *Opera Director*
Schwalbenweg 11-A, 82152 Krailling, Oberbayem, Germany

Rennert, Laurence H (Dutch) — *Baseball Umpire*
Walkers Glen, 2560 46th Road, Vero Beach, FL 32966, USA

Rennert, Wolfgang — *Conductor*
Holbeinstr 58, 12203 Berlin, Germany

Reno, Hunter — *Model*
%Elite Model Mgmt, 111 E 22nd St, #200, New York, NY 10010, USA

Reno, Janet — *Attorney General*
%Justice Department, Constitution Ave & 10th St NW, Washington, DC 20002, USA

Reno, John F — *Businessman*
%Dynatech Corp, 3 New England Executive Park, Burlington, MA 01803, USA

Reno, Nancy — *Volleyball Player*
%Assn of Volleyball Pros, 330 Washington Blvd, #600, Marina del Rey, CA 90292, USA

Reno, William H — *Army General*
Deputy Chief of Staff for Personnel, HqUSA, Washington, DC 20310, USA

Rense, Paige — *Editor*
%Architectural Digest, 5900 Wilshire Blvd, Los Angeles, CA 90036, USA

Rentmeester, Co — *Photographer*
4479 Douglas Ave, Bronx, NY 10471, USA

Renton, R Timothy — *Government Official, England*
%House of Commons, Westminster, London SW1A 0AA, England

Rentzepis, Peter M — *Chemist*
%University of California, Chemistry Dept, Irvine, CA 92717, USA

Renvall, Johan — *Ballet Dancer*
%American Ballet Theatre, 890 Broadway, New York, NY 10003, USA

Renyi, Thomas A — *Financier*
%Bank of New York, 48 Wall St, New York, NY 10005, USA

Repin, Vadim V — *Concert Violinist*
Eckholdtweg 2-A, 23566 Lubeck, Germany

Rerych, Stephen (Steve) — *Swimmer*
445 Baltimore Ave, Asheville, NC 28801, USA

Rescigno, Nicola — *Conductor*
%Robert Lombardo, 61 W 62nd St, #6-F, New York, NY 10023, USA

Resnais, Alain — *Movie Director*
70 Rue Des Plantes, 75014 Paris, France

Resnick, Milton — *Artist*
87 Eldridge St, New York, NY 10002, USA

Resnik, Regina — *Opera Singer*
50 W 56th St, New York, NY 10019, USA

Respert, Shawn — *Basketball Player*
%Toronto Raptors, 20 Bay St, #1702, Toronto ON M5J 2N8, Canada

Ressler, Glenn E — *Football Player*
%Ponderosa Steak Franchise, 328 Blacklatch Lane, Camp Hill, PA 17011, USA

Restani, Jane A — *Judge*
%US Court of International Trade, 1 Federal Plaza, New York, NY 10278, USA

Restani, Kevin — *Basketball Player*
16 Lyndhurst Dr, San Francisco, CA 94132, USA

Reswick, James B — *Engineer*
1003 Dead Run Dr, McLean, VA 22101, USA

Retton, Mary Lou — *Gymnast*
322 Vista Del Mar, Redondo Beach, CA 90277, USA

Retzlaff, Palmer (Pete) — *Football Player*
%Sports Film, 511 Old Lancaster Pike, Berwyn, PA 19312, USA

Reuben, David R — *Psychiatrist, Writer*
%Scott Meredith, 845 3rd Ave, New York, NY 10022, USA

Reuben, Gloria *Actress*
%Gersh Agency, 232 N Canon Dr, Beverly Hills, CA 90210, USA
Reum, W Robert *Businessman*
%Interlake Corp, 550 Warrenville Road, Lisle, IL 60532, USA
Reuschel, Ricky E (Rick) *Baseball Player*
618 E Maude Ave, Arlington Heights, IL 60004, USA
Reuss, Jerry *Baseball Player*
850 Las Vegas Blvd N, Las Vegas, NV 89101, USA
Reutersward, Carl Fredrik *Artist*
6 Rue Montolieu, 1030 Bussigny/Lausanne, Switzerland
Revel, Jean-Francois *Writer*
55 Quai de Bourbon, 75004 Paris, France
Revere, Paul *Singer (Paul Revere & The Raiders)*
PO Box 544, Grangeville, ID 83530, USA
Revill, Clive *Actor*
15029 Encanto Dr, Sherman Oaks, CA 91403, USA
Revollo Bravo, Mario Cardinal *Religious Leader*
Arzobispado, Carrera 7-A N 10-20, Bogota DE, Colombia
Rexrodt, Gunther *Government Official, Germany*
%BM Fur Wirtschaft, Villemombler Str 76, 53123 Berlin, Germany
Reynolds Booth, Nancy *Skier*
3197 Padaro Lane, Carpinteria, CA 93013, USA
Reynolds, A William *Businessman*
%GenCorp, 175 Ghent Road, Fairlawn, OH 44333, USA
Reynolds, Albert *Prime Minister, Ireland*
Mount Carmel House, Dublin Road, Longford, Ireland
Reynolds, Anna *Opera Singer*
Peesten 9, 8656 Kasendorf, Germany
Reynolds, Burt *Actor*
16133 Jupiter Farms Road, Jupiter, FL 33478, USA
Reynolds, David S *Writer, Historian*
16 Linden Lane, Old Westbury, NY 11568, USA
Reynolds, Dean *Commentator*
%ABC-TV, News Dept, 1717 De Sales St NW, Washington, DC 20036, USA
Reynolds, Debbie *Actress, Singer*
305 Convention Center Dr, Las Vegas, NV 89109, USA
Reynolds, Frank *Commentator*
1124 Connecticut Ave NW, Washington, DC 20036, USA
Reynolds, Gene *Actor, Television Producer*
2034 Castillian Dr, Los Angeles, CA 90068, USA
Reynolds, Glenn F *Inventor (Proscar Drug)*
242 Edgewood Ave, Westfield, NJ 07090, USA
Reynolds, Harry (Butch) *Track Athlete*
%Advantage Int'l, 1025 Thomas Jefferson St NW, #450, Washington, DC 20007, USA
Reynolds, J Guy *Navy Admiral*
1605 Fox Hunt Court, Alexandria, VA 22307, USA
Reynolds, James *Actor*
%Progressive Artists Agency, 400 S Beverly Dr, #216, Beverly Hills, CA 90212, USA
Reynolds, Jerry O *Basketball Coach, Executive*
%Sacramento Kings, 1 Sports Parkway, Sacramento, CA 95834, USA
Reynolds, John H *Physicist, Educator*
%University of California, Physics Dept, Berkeley, CA 94720, USA
Reynolds, John T *Television Executive*
PO Box 1738, Beverly Hills, CA 90213, USA
Reynolds, John W *Governor, WI; Judge*
%US District Court, 517 E Wisconsin Ave, Milwaukee, WI 53202, USA
Reynolds, Nick *Singer (Kingston Trio)*
%Fuji Productions, 2480 Williston Dr, Charlottesville, VA 22901, USA
Reynolds, Thomas A, Jr *Attorney*
%Winston & Strawn, 1 First National Plaza, 45 W Wacker Dr, Chicago, IL 60601, USA
Reynolds, W Ann *Educator*
%City University of New York, Chancellor's Office, New York, NY 10021, USA
Reznor, Trent *Singer (Nine Inch Nails)*
%Conservative Mgmt, 2337 W 11th St, #7, Cleveland, OH 44113, USA
Rhame, Thomas G (Tom) *Army General*
%Defense Security Assistance Agency, 1111 J Davis Highway, Arlington, VA 22202, USA
Rhames, Ving *Actor*
%William Morris Agency, 151 S El Camino Dr, Beverly Hills, CA 90212, USA

Rheaume, Manon — *Hockey Player*
PO Box 70065, Las Vegas, NV 89170, USA

Rhines, Peter B — *Oceanographer*
5753 61st Ave NE, Seattle, WA 98105, USA

Rhoades, Barbara — *Actress*
90 Old Redding Road, Weston, CT 06883, USA

Rhoads, George — *Sculptor*
1478 Mecklenburg Road, Ithaca, NY 14850, USA

Rhoden, Richard A (Rick) — *Baseball Player*
PO Box 546, Crescent City, FL 32112, USA

Rhodes, Cynthia — *Actress, Dancer*
15250 Ventura Blvd, #900, Sherman Oaks, CA 91403, USA

Rhodes, James A — *Governor, OH*
2375 Tremont Road, Columbus, OH 43221, USA

Rhodes, Nick — *Keyboardist (Duran Duran)*
PO Box 21, London W10 6XA, England

Rhodes, Ray — *Football Coach*
2 Preamble Dr, Mount Laurel, NJ 08054, USA

Rhodes, Richard L — *Writer*
%Janklow & Assoc, 598 Madison Ave, New York, NY 10022, USA

Rhodes, Rodrick — *Basketball Player*
%Houston Rockets, Summit, Greenway Plaza, #10, Houston, TX 77046, USA

Rhodes, Zandra — *Fashion Designer*
64 Porchester Road, London W2, England

Rhome, Gerald B (Jerry) — *Football Player, Coach*
%St Louis Rams, 100 N Broadway, #2100, St Louis, MO 63102, USA

Rhue, Madlyn — *Actress*
148 S Maple Dr, #D, Beverly Hills, CA 90212, USA

Rhys-Davies, John — *Actor*
1933 Cold Canyon Road, Calabasas, CA 91302, USA

Ri Jong Ok — *Premier, North Korea*
%Vice President's Office, Pyongyang, North Korea

Riady, Mochtar — *Financier*
%Bank Central Asia, 25/26 Jalan Asemka, Jakarta Barat 01, Indonesia

Ribbs, Willy T — *Auto Racing Driver*
2343 Ribbs Lane, San Jose, CA 95116, USA

Ribeiro, Antonio Cardinal — *Religious Leader*
Campo Martires da Patria 45, 1198 Lisbon Codex, Portugal

Ribicoff, Abraham A — *Secretary, Health Education & Welfare*
%Kaye Scholer Fierman Hays Handler, 425 Park Ave, New York, NY 10022, USA

Ricci, Christina — *Actress*
%International Creative Mgmt, 40 W 57th St, New York, NY 10019, USA

Ricci, Ruggiero — *Concert Violinist*
2930 E Delhi Road, Ann Arbor, MI 48103, USA

Ricciarelli, Katia — *Opera Singer*
Via Magellana 2, 20097 Corsica, Italy

Rice, Anne — *Writer*
1239 1st St, New Orleans, LA 70130, USA

Rice, Charles E — *Financier*
%Barnett Banks, 50 N Laura St, Jacksonville, FL 32202, USA

Rice, Donald B — *Businessman, Government Official*
%Teledyne Inc, 2049 Century Park East, Los Angeles, CA 90067, USA

Rice, Gene D — *Religious Leader*
%Church of God, PO Box 2430, Cleveland, TN 37320, USA

Rice, Gigi — *Actress*
14951 Alva Dr, Pacific Palisades, CA 90272, USA

Rice, Glen — *Basketball Player*
9492 Doral Blvd, Miami, FL 33178, USA

Rice, James E (Jim) — *Baseball Player*
96 Castlemere Place, North Andover, MA 01845, USA

Rice, Jerry L — *Football Player*
2 Brittany Meadows, Atherton, CA 94027, USA

Rice, Joseph L, III — *Financier*
%Clayton Dubilier Rice, 126 E 56th St, New York, NY 10022, USA

Rice, Norman B — *Mayor*
%Mayor's Office, Municipal Building, 600 4th Ave, Seattle, WA 98104, USA

Rice, Simeon — *Football Player*
%Arizona Cardinals, 8701 S Hardy Dr, Tempe, AZ 85284, USA

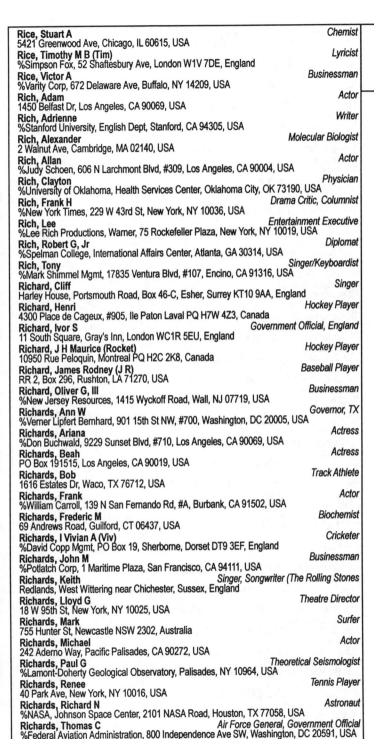

Rice, Stuart A	*Chemist*
5421 Greenwood Ave, Chicago, IL 60615, USA	
Rice, Timothy M B (Tim)	*Lyricist*
%Simpson Fox, 52 Shaftesbury Ave, London W1V 7DE, England	
Rice, Victor A	*Businessman*
%Varity Corp, 672 Delaware Ave, Buffalo, NY 14209, USA	
Rich, Adam	*Actor*
1450 Belfast Dr, Los Angeles, CA 90069, USA	
Rich, Adrienne	*Writer*
%Stanford University, English Dept, Stanford, CA 94305, USA	
Rich, Alexander	*Molecular Biologist*
2 Walnut Ave, Cambridge, MA 02140, USA	
Rich, Allan	*Actor*
%Judy Schoen, 606 N Larchmont Blvd, #309, Los Angeles, CA 90004, USA	
Rich, Clayton	*Physician*
%University of Oklahoma, Health Services Center, Oklahoma City, OK 73190, USA	
Rich, Frank H	*Drama Critic, Columnist*
%New York Times, 229 W 43rd St, New York, NY 10036, USA	
Rich, Lee	*Entertainment Executive*
%Lee Rich Productions, Warner, 75 Rockefeller Plaza, New York, NY 10019, USA	
Rich, Robert G, Jr	*Diplomat*
%Spelman College, International Affairs Center, Atlanta, GA 30314, USA	
Rich, Tony	*Singer/Keyboardist*
%Mark Shimmel Mgmt, 17835 Ventura Blvd, #107, Encino, CA 91316, USA	
Richard, Cliff	*Singer*
Harley House, Portsmouth Road, Box 46-C, Esher, Surrey KT10 9AA, England	
Richard, Henri	*Hockey Player*
4300 Place de Cageux, #905, Ile Paton Laval PQ H7W 4Z3, Canada	
Richard, Ivor S	*Government Official, England*
11 South Square, Gray's Inn, London WC1R 5EU, England	
Richard, J H Maurice (Rocket)	*Hockey Player*
10950 Rue Peloquin, Montreal PQ H2C 2K8, Canada	
Richard, James Rodney (J R)	*Baseball Player*
RR 2, Box 296, Rushton, LA 71270, USA	
Richard, Oliver G, III	*Businessman*
%New Jersey Resources, 1415 Wyckoff Road, Wall, NJ 07719, USA	
Richards, Ann W	*Governor, TX*
%Verner Lipfert Bernhard, 901 15th St NW, #700, Washington, DC 20005, USA	
Richards, Ariana	*Actress*
%Don Buchwald, 9229 Sunset Blvd, #710, Los Angeles, CA 90069, USA	
Richards, Beah	*Actress*
PO Box 191515, Los Angeles, CA 90019, USA	
Richards, Bob	*Track Athlete*
1616 Estates Dr, Waco, TX 76712, USA	
Richards, Frank	*Actor*
%William Carroll, 139 N San Fernando Rd, #A, Burbank, CA 91502, USA	
Richards, Frederic M	*Biochemist*
69 Andrews Road, Guilford, CT 06437, USA	
Richards, I Vivian A (Viv)	*Cricketer*
%David Copp Mgmt, PO Box 19, Sherborne, Dorset DT9 3EF, England	
Richards, John M	*Businessman*
%Potlatch Corp, 1 Maritime Plaza, San Francisco, CA 94111, USA	
Richards, Keith	*Singer, Songwriter (The Rolling Stones*
Redlands, West Wittering near Chichester, Sussex, England	
Richards, Lloyd G	*Theatre Director*
18 W 95th St, New York, NY 10025, USA	
Richards, Mark	*Surfer*
755 Hunter St, Newcastle NSW 2302, Australia	
Richards, Michael	*Actor*
242 Aderno Way, Pacific Palisades, CA 90272, USA	
Richards, Paul G	*Theoretical Seismologist*
%Lamont-Doherty Geological Observatory, Palisades, NY 10964, USA	
Richards, Renee	*Tennis Player*
40 Park Ave, New York, NY 10016, USA	
Richards, Richard N	*Astronaut*
%NASA, Johnson Space Center, 2101 NASA Road, Houston, TX 77058, USA	
Richards, Thomas C	*Air Force General, Government Official*
%Federal Aviation Administration, 800 Independence Ave SW, Washington, DC 20591, USA	

R

Rice - Richards

R	**Richardson of Duntisbourne, William H**	*Financier*
	Kingsley House, 1-A Wimpole St, London W1M 7AA, England	

Richardson of Duntisbourne - Richmond

Richardson of Duntisbourne, William H — *Financier*
Kingsley House, 1-A Wimpole St, London W1M 7AA, England

Richardson of Lee, John S — *Physician*
Windcutter, Lee, North Devon, England

Richardson, Ashley — *Model*
%Laura Danford, 91 5th Ave, #401, New York, NY 10003, USA

Richardson, Cheryl — *Actress*
8900 Amestoy Ave, Northridge, CA 91325, USA

Richardson, Dorothy (Dot) — *Softball Player*
%USC Medical Center, 1200 N State St, #GH-3900, Los Angeles, CA 90033, USA

Richardson, Earl — *Educator*
%Morgan State University, President's Office, Baltimore, MD 21239, USA

Richardson, Elliot L — *Secretary, Defense & HEW*
%Milbank Tweed Hadley McCloy, 1825 "I" St NW, Washington, DC 20006, USA

Richardson, Gordon W H — *Financier*
%Bank of England, London EC2R 8AH, England

Richardson, Hamilton — *Tennis Player*
870 United Nations Plaza, New York, NY 10017, USA

Richardson, Howard — *Writer*
207 Columbus Ave, New York, NY 10023, USA

Richardson, Ian — *Actor*
131 Lavender Sweep, London SW 11, England

Richardson, Joely — *Actress*
%International Creative Mgmt, 76 Oxford St, London W1N 0AX, England

Richardson, Midge T — *Editor*
%Seventeen Magazine, Editorial Dept, 850 3rd Ave, New York, NY 10022, USA

Richardson, Miranda — *Actress*
195 Devonshire Road, London SE23 ENJ, England

Richardson, Natasha — *Actress*
30 Brackenburg Ave, London W6, England

Richardson, Nolan — *Basketball Coach*
2539 E Joyce St, Fayetteville, AR 72703, USA

Richardson, Patricia — *Actress*
196 Granville Ave, Los Angeles, CA 90049, USA

Richardson, Pooh — *Basketball Player*
%Los Angeles Clippers, Sports Arena, 3939 Figueroa St, Los Angeles, CA 90037, USA

Richardson, Robert C — *Nobel Physics Laureate*
%Cornell University, Physics Dept, Clark Hall, Ithaca, NY 14853, USA

Richardson, Robert C (Bobby) — *Baseball Player*
47 Adams Ave, Sumter, SC 29150, USA

Richardson, Sam — *Sculptor*
4121 Sequoyah Road, Oakland, CA 94605, USA

Richardson, Susan — *Actress*
6331 Hollywood Blvd, #924, Los Angeles, CA 90028, USA

Richardson, W Franklyn — *Religious Leader*
%National Baptist Convention, 52 S 6th Ave, Mount Vernon, NY 10550, USA

Richardson, William B (Bill) — *Ambassador to United Nations*
%US Mission, 799 United Nations Plaza, New York, NY 10017, USA

Richer, Stephane — *Hockey Player*
%Montreal Canadiens, 1260 De la Gauchetiere W, Montreal PQ H3B 5E8, Canada

Richey, Nancy — *Tennis Player*
2936 Cumberland Dr, San Angelo, TX 76904, USA

Richey, Ronald K — *Businessman*
%Torchmark Corp, 2001 3rd Ave S, Birmingham, AL 35233, USA

Richie, Lionel — *Singer, Songwriter*
%DeMann Entertainment, 8000 Beverly Blvd, Los Angeles, CA 90048, USA

Richler, Mordecai — *Writer*
1321 Sherbroke St W, #80-C, Montreal PQ H3Y 1J4, Canada

Richman, Caryn — *Actress*
12304 Santa Monica Blvd, #104, Los Angeles, CA 90025, USA

Richman, Peter Mark — *Actor*
5114 Del Moreno Dr, Woodland Hills, CA 91364, USA

Richmond, Branscombe — *Actor*
5706 Calvin Ave, Tarzana, CA 91356, USA

Richmond, Julius B — *Physician*
PO Box 996, West Tisbury, MA 02575, USA

Richmond, Mitch — *Basketball Player*
9908 Wexford Circle, Granite Bay, CA 95746, USA

Richter, Burton *Nobel Physics Laureate*
%Stanford University, Linear Accelerator Center, PO Box 4349, Stanford, CA 94309, USA
Richter, Earl E *Businessman*
%Modine Manufacturing, 1500 DeKoven Ave, Racine, WI 53403, USA
Richter, Gerhard *Artist*
Bismarckstr 50, 50672 Cologne, Germany
Richter, Leslie A (Les) *Football Player*
%National Assn of Stock Car Racing, 1801 Speedway Blvd, Daytona Beach, FL 32114, USA
Richter, Michael T (Mike) *Hockey Player*
2016 Hilltop Road, Flourtown, PA 19031, USA
Richter, Pat *Football Player, Administrator*
45 Cambridge Road, Madison, WI 53704, USA
Richter, Ulrike *Swimmer*
Goethestr 65, 08297 Zwonitz, Germany
Rick, Charles M, Jr *Geneticist*
8 Parkside Dr, Davis, CA 95616, USA
Ricker, Robert S *Religious Leader*
%Baptist General Conference, 2002 S A Heights Road, Arlington Heights, IL 60005, USA
Rickershauser, Charles E, Jr *Businessman*
%PS Group, 4307 La Jolla Village Dr, San Diego, CA 92122, USA
Ricketts, Thomas R *Financier*
%Standard Federal Bank, 36800 S Gratiot Ave, Clinton Township, MI 48035, USA
Rickey, George W *Sculptor*
Rt 2, Box 235, East Chatham, NY 12060, USA
Rickles, Don *Comedian, Actor*
10249 Century Woods Dr, Los Angeles, CA 90067, USA
Rickman, Alan *Actor*
%Creative Artists Agency, 9830 Wilshire Blvd, Beverly Hills, CA 90212, USA
Ridder, Bernard H, Jr *Publisher*
%St Paul Pioneer Press, 345 Cedar St, St Paul, MN 55101, USA
Ridder, Eric *Publisher*
%Knight-Ridder Inc, 1 Herald Plaza, Miami, FL 33132, USA
Ridder, P Anthony *Publisher*
%Knight-Ridder Inc, 1 Herald Plaza, Miami, FL 33132, USA
Riddick, Frank A, Jr *Physician*
1923 Octavia St, New Orleans, LA 70115, USA
Riddick, Steven (Steve) *Track Athlete*
381 Hobson Ave, Hampton, VA 23661, USA
Riddle, D Raymond *Businessman*
%First National Bank of Atlanta, 2 Peachtree St NW, Atlanta, GA 30303, USA
Riddles, Libby *Dog Sled Racer*
PO Box 872901, Wasilla, AK 99687, USA
Ride, Sally K *Astronaut*
%California Space Institute, PO Box 0221, 9500 Gilman Dr, La Jolla, CA 92093, USA
Rider, Isaiah (J R) *Basketball Player*
PO Box 12-1R, Montchanin, DE 19710, USA
Ridge, Thomas J *Governor, Representative, PA*
%Governor's Office, Main Capitol Building, Harrisburg, PA 17120, USA
Ridgeley, Andrew *Singer, Guitarist (Wham!)*
8800 Sunset Blvd, #401, Los Angeles, CA 90069, USA
Ridgley, Bob *Actor*
%Twentieth Century, 15315 Magnolia Blvd, #429, Sherman Oaks, CA 91403, USA
Ridgway, Brunilde S *Archaeologist*
%Bryn Mawr College, Archaeology Dept, Bryn Mawr, PA 19010, USA
Riedel, Lars *Track Athlete*
Reichenbainer Str 154, 01925 Chemnitz, Germany
Riederer, Richard K *Businessman*
%Weirton Steel Corp, 400 Three Springs Dr, Weirton, WV 26062, USA
Riefenstahl, Leni *Movie Director, Photographer*
Tengstr 20, 80798 Munich, Germany
Riegel, Hans *Businessman*
%HARIBO Gmbh, Postfach 1720, 53007 Bonn, Germany
Riegert, Peter *Actor*
25 Sea Colony Dr, Santa Monica, CA 90405, USA
Riegle, Gene *Harness Racing Driver, Trainer*
1143 Fort Jefferson Ave, Greenville, OH 45331, USA
Riesenhuber, Heinz *Government Official, Germany*
%Bundstag, Bundeshaus, Gorresstr 15, 53113 Bonn, Germany

R

Riessen, Marty	*Tennis Player*
PO Box 5444, Santa Barbara, CA 93150, USA	
Rifkin, Jeremy	*Writer, Social Activist*
1660 "L" St NW, #216, Washington, DC 20036, USA	
Rifkin, Joshua	*Concert Pianist*
61 Dana St, Cambridge, MA 02138, USA	
Rifkin, Ron	*Actor*
500 S Sepulveda Blvd, Los Angeles, CA 90049, USA	
Rifkind, Malcolm L	*Government Official, England*
%House of Commons, Westminster, London SW1A 0AA, England	
Rigby McCoy, Cathy	*Gymnast, Actress*
%McCoy/Rigby Entertainment, 110 E Wilshire Ave, #200, Fullerton, CA 92832, USA	
Rigby, Jean P	*Opera Singer*
31 Sinclair Road, London W14 0NS, England	
Rigby, Paul	*Cartoonist*
72 Kenyon Road, Hampton, CT 06247, USA	
Rigg, Diana	*Actress*
%London Mgmt, 2-4 Noel St, London W1V 3RB, England	
Riggin Soule, Aileen	*Diver*
2943 Kalakaua Ave, #1007, Honolulu, HI 96815, USA	
Riggs, Lorrin A	*Psychologist*
80 Lyme Road, #104, Hanover, NH 03755, USA	
Righetti, David A (Dave)	*Baseball Player*
552 Magdalena Ave, Los Altos, CA 94024, USA	
Righi-Lambertini, Egano Cardinal	*Religious Leader*
Piazza della Citta Leonina 9, 00193 Rome, Italy	
Rights, Graham H	*Religious Leader*
%Moravian Church, Southern Province, 459 S Church St, Winston-Salem, NC 27101, USA	
Rigney, William J (Bill)	*Baseball Manager*
3136 Round Hill Road, Alamo, CA 94507, USA	
Riker, Albert J	*Plant Pathologist*
2760 E 8th St, Tucson, AZ 85716, USA	
Riker, Derek	*Model, Actor*
%International Creative Mgmt, 40 W 57th St, New York, NY 10019, USA	
Riker, Drew	*Model*
%International Creative Mgmt, 40 W 57th St, New York, NY 10019, USA	
Riklis, Meshulam	*Businessman*
%McCrory Corp, 667 Madison Ave, New York, NY 10021, USA	
Riley, Bill	*Hockey Player*
12731 Haskell Lane, Bowie, MD 20716, USA	
Riley, Bridget	*Artist*
%Mayor Rowan Gallery, 31-A Bruton Place, London W1X 7A8, England	
Riley, Jack	*Actor*
%House of Representatives, 400 S Beverly Dr, #101, Beverly Hills, CA 90212, USA	
Riley, Jack	*Hockey Player, Coach*
1281 Grouse Dr, Pittsburgh, PA 15243, USA	
Riley, Jeannie C	*Singer*
%Jeannie C Riley Enterprises, 105 Ewingville Dr, Franklin, TN 37064, USA	
Riley, Patrick J (Pat)	*Basketball Player, Coach, Executive*
180 Arvida Parkway, Coral Gables, FL 33156, USA	
Riley, Richard W	*Secretary, Education*
%Education Department, 400 Maryland Ave SW, Washington, DC 20202, USA	
Riley, Robert F	*Financier*
%Dreyfus Corp, 200 Park Ave, New York, NY 10166, USA	
Riley, Teddy	*Songwriter, Singer*
%Future Enterprise Records, 70 Universal City Plaza, Universal City, CA 91608, USA	
Riley, Terry M	*Composer, Musician*
%Shri Moonshine Ranch, 13699 Moonshine Road, Camptonville, CA 95922, USA	
Rilling, Helmuth	*Conductor*
Johann-Sebastian-Bach-Platz, 70178 Stuttgart, Germany	
Rimes, LeAnn	*Singer*
2945 Fondren Circle, Dallas, TX 75205, USA	
Rimington, Stella	*Government Official, England*
PO Box 3255, London SW1P 1AE, England	
Rimmel, James E	*Religious Leader*
%Evangelical Presbyterian Church, 26049 Five Mile Road, Detroit, MI 48239, USA	
Rinaldi, Kathy	*Tennis Player*
%Advantage Int'l, 1025 Thomas Jefferson St NW, #450, Washington, DC 20007, USA	

Riessen - Rinaldi

Rinaldo, Benjamin *Skier*
%Ski World, 3680 Buena Park Dr, North Hollywood, CA 91604, USA

Rindlaub, John V *Financier*
%Seafirst Corp, 701 5th Ave, Seattle, WA 98104, USA

Rinearson, Peter M *Journalist*
%Seattle Times, Editorial Dept, Fairview Ave N & John St, Seattle, WA 98111, USA

Rinehart, Charles R *Publisher*
%Ashai Shimbun, 2-6-1 Yuraku-Cho, Chiyoda-Ku, Tokyo 100, Japan

Rinehart, Charles R *Financier*
%H F Ahmanson Co, 4900 Rivergrade Road, Irwindale, CA 91706, USA

Rinehart, Kenneth *Chemist*
%University of Illinois, Chemistry Dept, Urbana, IL 61801, USA

Rines, John R *Financier*
%General Motors Acceptance, 3044 W Grand Blvd, Detroit, MI 48202, USA

Ringadoo, Veerasamy *President, Mauritius*
Corner of Farquhar & Sir Celicourt Antelme Sts, Quatre-Bornes, Mauritius

Ringer, Jennifer *Ballerina*
%New York City Ballet, Lincoln Center Plaza, New York, NY 10023, USA

Ringler, James M *Businessman*
%Premark International, 1717 Deerfield Road, Deerfield, IL 60015, USA

Ringo, James (Jim) *Football Player*
408 Montross Court, Chesapeake, VA 23323, USA

Ringwald, Molly *Actress*
%Innovative Artists, 1999 Ave of Stars, #2850, Los Angeles, CA 90067, USA

Rinna, Lisa *Actress*
%International Creative Mgmt, 8942 Wilshire Blvd, Beverly Hills, CA 90211, USA

Rintzler, Marius *Opera Singer*
Friedingstr 18, 40625 Dusseldorf, Germany

Riordan, Michael T *Businessman*
%Fort Howard Corp, 1919 S Broadway, Green Bay, WI 54304, USA

Riordan, Mike *Basketball Player*
%Riordan's Saloon, 26 Market Place, Annapolis, MD 21401, USA

Riordan, Richard J *Mayor*
%Mayor's Office, City Hall, 200 N Spring St, Los Angeles, CA 90012, USA

Rios, Alberto *Writer*
%Arizona State University, English Dept, Tempe, AZ 85287, USA

Ripken, Calvin E (Cal), Jr *Baseball Player*
2330 W Joppa Road, #333, Lutherville, MD 21093, USA

Ripken, Calvin E (Cal), Sr *Baseball Manager*
410 Clover St, Aberdeen, MD 21001, USA

Ripley, Alexandra *Writer*
24 Ripley St, Newport News, VA 23603, USA

Ripley, S Dillon *Museum Director, Zoologist*
2324 Massachusetts Ave NW, Washington, DC 20008, USA

Rippey, James F *Financier*
%Columbia Management, 1300 SW 6th St, Portland, OR 97201, USA

Rippey, Rodney Allan *Actor*
3941 Veselich Ave, #4-251, Los Angeles, CA 90039, USA

Ris, Hans *Zoologist*
5542 Riverview Dr, Waunakee, WI 53597, USA

Risen, Arnie *Basketball Player*
3217 Bremerton Road, Cleveland, OH 44124, USA

Rison, Andre *Football Player*
%Kansas City Chiefs, 1 Arrowhead Dr, Kansas City, KS 64129, USA

Risser, Paul G *Educator*
%Miami University, President's Office, Oxford, OH 45056, USA

Ritchie, Clint *Actor*
10000 Riverside Dr, #6, Toluca Lake, CA 91602, USA

Ritchie, Daniel L *Educator, Television Executive*
%University of Denver, Chancellor's Office, Denver, CO 80208, USA

Ritchie, Jim *Sculptor*
%Adelson Galleries, Mark Hotel, 25 E 77th St, New York, NY 10021, USA

Ritchie, Michael B *Movie Director, Producer*
%Miracle Pictures, 22 Miller Ave, Mill Valley, CA 94941, USA

Ritenour, Lee *Jazz Guitarist, Singer, Composer*
11808 Dorothy St, #108, Los Angeles, CA 90049, USA

Ritger, Dick *Bowler*
804 Valley View Dr, River Falls, WI 54022, USA

R

Rinaldo - Ritger

Ritter, John — *Actor*
9545 Dalegrove Dr, Beverly Hills, CA 90210, USA

Rittereiser, Robert P — *Financier*
%Nationar, 330 Madison Ave, New York, NY 10017, USA

Ritts, Herb — *Photographer*
7927 Hillside Ave, Los Angeles, CA 90046, USA

Ritts, Jim — *Golf Executive*
%Ladies Professional Golf Assn, 2570 Volusia Ave, Daytona Beach, FL 32114, USA

Rivera, Chita — *Actress, Singer, Dancer*
99 S Greenbush Road, Blauvelt, NY 10913, USA

Rivera, Geraldo — *Entertainer*
%Geraldo Investigative News Group, 555 W 57th St, #1100, New York, NY 10019, USA

Rivers, Glenn (Doc) — *Basketball Player*
%Cable News Network, Sports Dept, 1050 Techwood Dr NW, Atlanta, GA 30318, USA

Rivers, Joan — *Entertainer*
10 Bay St, #156, Westport, CT 06880, USA

Rivers, Johnny — *Singer, Songwriter*
3141 Coldwater Canyon Lane, Beverly Hills, CA 90210, USA

Rivers, Larry — *Artist*
404 E 14th St, New York, NY 10009, USA

Rivette, Jacques — *Movie Director*
20 Blvd de la Bastille, 75012 Paris, France

Rivlin, Alice M — *Government Official*
%Federal Reserve Board, 20th & Constitution NW, Washington, DC 20551, USA

Rizzotti, Jennifer — *Basketball Player*
%New England Blizzard, 179 Allyn St, #403, Hartford, CT 06103, USA

Rizzuto, Philip F (Phil) — *Baseball Player, Sportscaster*
912 Westminster Ave, Hillside, NJ 07205, USA

Roach, John R — *Religious Leader*
%Archdiocese of St Paul, 226 Summit Ave, St Paul, MN 55102, USA

Roach, John V, II — *Businessman*
%Tandy Corp, 1 Tandy Center, #1800, Fort Worth, TX 76102, USA

Roach, Maxwell (Max) — *Jazz Percussionist*
%Fat City Artists, 1908 Chet Atkins Place, #502, Nashville, TN 37212, USA

Roadman, Charles H (Chip), II — *Air Force General, Physician*
%Surgeon General's Office, 170 Luke Ave, Bolling Air Force Base, DC 20332, USA

Roaf, Willie — *Football Player*
1900 E 38th Ave, Pine Bluff, AR 71601, USA

Roark, Terry P — *Educator*
%University of Wyoming, President's Office, Laramie, WY 82071, USA

Robards, Jason — *Actor*
200 W 57th St, #900, New York, NY 10019, USA

Robbe-Grillet, Alain — *Writer, Director*
18 Blvd Maillot, 92200 Neuilly-sur-Seine, France

Robbins, Frederick C — *Nobel Medicine Laureate*
2626 W Park Blvd, Shaker Heights, OH 44120, USA

Robbins, Harold — *Writer*
601 W Camino Sur, Palm Springs, CA 92262, USA

Robbins, Herbert E — *Mathematician*
%Rutgers University, Mathematics Dept, New Brunswick, NJ 08903, USA

Robbins, Jane — *Actress*
%Scott Marshall Mgmt, 44 Perry Road, London W3 7NA, England

Robbins, Tim — *Actor, Director*
%International Creative Mgmt, 40 W 57th St, New York, NY 10019, USA

Robbins, Tom — *Writer*
PO Box 338, La Conner, WA 98257, USA

Robelot, Jane — *Commentator*
%CBS-TV, News Dept, 51 W 52nd St, New York, NY 10019, USA

Robens of Woldingham, Alfred — *Government Official, England*
2 Laleham Abbey, Staines, Middx TW18 1SZ, England

Roberson, Irvin (Bo) — *Track Athlete*
820 N Raymond Ave, #47, Pasadena, CA 91103, USA

Roberts, Bernard — *Concert Pianist*
Uwchlaw'r Coed, Llanbedr, Gwynedd LL45 2NA, Wales

Roberts, Bert C, Jr — *Businessman*
%MCI Communications, 1801 Pennsylvania Ave NW, Washington, DC 20006, USA

Roberts, Brian L — *Businessman*
%Storer Communications, 1500 Market St, Philadelphia, PA 19102, USA

Roberts, Cecil — *Labor Leader*
%United Mine Workers, 900 15th St NW, Washington, DC 20005, USA

Roberts, Chalmers M — *Journalist*
6699 MacArthur Blvd, Bethesda, MD 20816, USA

Roberts, Corrine (Cokie) — *Commentator*
%ABC-TV, News Dept, 1717 De Sales St NW, Washington, DC 20036, USA

Roberts, David (Dave) — *Track Athlete*
14310 SW 73rd Ave, Archer, FL 32618, USA

Roberts, Doris — *Actress*
6225 Quebec Dr, Los Angeles, CA 90068, USA

Roberts, Eric — *Actor*
2604 Ivanhoe Dr, Los Angeles, CA 90039, USA

Roberts, Eugene L, Jr — *Editor*
%New York Times, Editorial Dept, 229 W 43rd St, New York, NY 10036, USA

Roberts, George R — *Financier*
%Kohlberg Kravis Roberts Co, 2800 Sand Hill Road, Menlo Park, CA 94025, USA

Roberts, H Edward (Ed) — *Computer Designer*
%Bleckley Memorial Hospital, 408 Peacock St, Cochran, GA 31014, USA

Roberts, Jim — *Hockey Player, Coach*
137 Ridgecrest Dr, Chesterfield, MO 63017, USA

Roberts, John — *Commentator*
%CBS-TV, News Dept, 51 W 52nd St, New York, NY 10019, USA

Roberts, John D — *Chemist*
%California Institute of Technology, Chemistry Dept, Pasadena, CA 91125, USA

Roberts, John M — *Anthropologist*
122 Kent Dr, Pittsburgh, PA 15241, USA

Roberts, Julia — *Actress*
%International Creative Mgmt, 8942 Wilshire Blvd, Beverly Hills, CA 90211, USA

Roberts, Kenny — *Motorcycle Racing Rider*
1660 Akron Peninsula Road, #201, Akron, OH 44313, USA

Roberts, Kevin — *Businessman*
%Saatchi & Saatchi Worldwide, 375 Hudson St, New York, NY 10014, USA

Roberts, Loren — *Golfer*
3311 Tournament Dr S, Memphis, TN 38125, USA

Roberts, Marcus — *Jazz Pianist*
%Marcus Roberts Enterprises, 9648 Olive Blvd, #1, St Louis, MO 63132, USA

Roberts, Oral — *Evangelist*
%Oral Roberts University, 7777 S Lewis Ave, Tulsa, OK 74171, USA

Roberts, Paul H — *Mathematician*
PO Box 951567, Los Angeles, CA 90095, USA

Roberts, Pernell — *Actor*
20395 Seaboard Road, Malibu, CA 90265, USA

Roberts, Ralph J — *Businessman*
%Comcast Corp, 1500 Market St, Philadelphia, PA 19102, USA

Roberts, Richard J — *Nobel Medicine Laureate*
%New England Biolabs, 32 Tozer Road, Beverly, MA 01915, USA

Roberts, Richard L — *Educator*
%Oral Roberts University, President's Office, 7777 S Lewis Ave, Tulsa, OK 74171, USA

Roberts, Robin — *Sportscaster*
%ESPN-TV, Sports Dept, ESPN Plaza, Bristol, CT 06010, USA

Roberts, Robin E — *Baseball Player*
504 Terrace Hill Road, Temple Terrace, FL 33617, USA

Roberts, Stanley — *Basketball Player*
1192 Congaree Road, Hopkins, SC 29061, USA

Roberts, Tanya — *Actress*
2126 Ridgemont Dr, Los Angeles, CA 90046, USA

Roberts, Tony — *Actor*
970 Park Ave, #8-N, New York, NY 10028, USA

Roberts, Xavier — *Doll Designer*
%Original Appalachian Artworks, Highway 75, Cleveland, GA 30528, USA

Robertson, Alvin C — *Basketball Player*
3 Birnam Oaks, San Antonio, TX 78248, USA

Robertson, Belinda — *Fashion Designer*
%B R Cashmere, 22 Palmerston Place, Edinburgh EH12 5AL, Scotland

Robertson, Charles T (Tony), Jr — *Air Force General*
Commander, 15th Air Force, 575 Waldron St, Travis Air Force Base, CA 94535, USA

Robertson, Cliff — *Actor*
325 Dunemere Dr, La Jolla, CA 92037, USA

R

Roberts - Robertson

Robertson, Georgina *Model*
%Company Mgmt, 270 Lafayette St, New York, NY 10012, USA

Robertson, Isiah *Football Player*
201 E Mason St, Mabank, TX 75147, USA

Robertson, M G (Pat) *Evangelist*
%Christian Broadcast Network, 100 Centerville Turnpike, Virginia Beach, VA 23463, USA

Robertson, Oscar P *Basketball Player*
621 Tusculum Ave, Cincinnati, OH 45226, USA

Robertson, Robbie *Singer, Guitarist (The Band); Songwriter*
323 14th St, Santa Monica, CA 90402, USA

Robes, Ernest C (Bill) *Ski Jumper*
3 Mile Road, Etna, NH 03750, USA

Robie, Carl *Swimmer*
2525 Sunnybrook Dr, Sarasota, FL 34239, USA

Robinowitz, Joseph R *Editor, Publisher*
%TV Guide Magazine, Editorial Dept, 100 Matsonford Road, Radnor, PA 19087, USA

Robinson of Woolwich, John *Religious Leader*
%Trinity College, Cambridge CB2 1TQ, England

Robinson, Andrew *Actor*
2671 Byron Place, Los Angeles, CA 90046, USA

Robinson, Arnie *Track Athlete*
2904 Ocean View Blvd, San Diego, CA 92113, USA

Robinson, Arthur H *Cartographer*
7802 Courtyard Dr, Madison, WI 53719, USA

Robinson, Brooks C *Baseball Player*
PO Box 1168, Baltimore, MD 21203, USA

Robinson, Charles E *Businessman*
%Pacific Telecom, 805 Broadway, Vancouver, WA 98660, USA

Robinson, Chip *Auto Racing Driver*
3034 Lake Forest Dr, Augusta, GA 30909, USA

Robinson, Chris *Actor*
%Irv Schechter, 9300 Wilshire Blvd, #410, Beverly Hills, CA 90212, USA

Robinson, Chris *Singer (The Black Crowes)*
%Angelus Entertainment, 9016 Wilshire Blvd, #346, Beverly Hills, CA 90211, USA

Robinson, Clifford *Basketball Player*
PO Box 3357, San Ramon, CA 94583, USA

Robinson, Dave *Football Player*
406 S Rose Blvd, Akron, OH 44320, USA

Robinson, David W *Basketball Player*
8 Davenport Lane, San Antonio, TX 78257, USA

Robinson, Dawn *Singer (En Vogue)*
%William Morris Agency, 1325 Ave of Americas, New York, NY 10019, USA

Robinson, Dwight P *Financier*
%Government National Mortgage Assn, 451 7th St SW, Washington, DC 20410, USA

Robinson, E B, Jr *Financier*
%Deposit Guaranty Corp, 210 E Capitol St, Jackson, MS 39201, USA

Robinson, Eddie G *Football Coach*
%Grambling State University, Athletic Dept, Grambling, LA 71245, USA

Robinson, Frank *Baseball Player, Manager*
15557 Aqua Verde Dr, Los Angeles, CA 90077, USA

Robinson, Glenn *Basketball Player*
2444 Harrison St, Gary, IN 46407, USA

Robinson, James H *Financier*
%SunBank/South Florida, 501 E Las Olas Blvd, Fort Lauderdale, FL 33301, USA

Robinson, Jay *Actor*
13757 Milbank Ave, Sherman Oaks, CA 91423, USA

Robinson, Jerry *Football Player*
%Oakland Raiders, 1220 Harbor Bay Parkway, Alameda, CA 94502, USA

Robinson, John *Football Coach*
22410 Rolling Hills Lane, Yorba Linda, CA 92887, USA

Robinson, John C *Businessman*
%Bearings Inc, 3615 Euclid Ave, #1-B, Cleveland, OH 44115, USA

Robinson, Kenneth *Government Official, England*
12 Grove Terrace, London NW5, England

Robinson, Larry *Hockey Player, Coach*
3211 Stevenson St, Plant City, FL 33567, USA

Robinson, Laura *Actress*
3100 Ellington Dr, Los Angeles, CA 90068, USA

Robinson, Leonard (Truck) *Basketball Player, Sportscaster*
10125 Prince Palace, #203, Upper Marlboro, MD 20774, USA
Robinson, Mary *President, Ireland*
'Aras an Uachtarain, Phoenix Park, Dublin 8, Ireland
Robinson, Matthew (Mack) *Track Athlete*
550 McDonald St, Pasadena, CA 91103, USA
Robinson, Patrick *Fashion Designer*
%Ann Klein Co, 11 W 42nd St, #2300, New York, NY 10036, USA
Robinson, Phil Alden *Movie Director*
%Turner Agency, 3000 W Olympic Blvd, #1438, Santa Monica, CA 90404, USA
Robinson, Rumeal *Basketball Player*
%Phoenix Suns, 201 E Jefferson St, Phoenix, AZ 85004, USA
Robinson, Smokey *Singer, Songwriter*
17085 Rancho St, Encino, CA 91316, USA
Robinson, Vicki Sue *Singer*
%Black Coffee Music, PO Box 7481, Wilton, CT 06897, USA
Robinson, Wilkes C *Judge*
%US Claims Court, 717 Madison Place NW, Washington, DC 20005, USA
Robinson-Peete, Holly *Actress*
%William Morris Agency, 151 S El Camino Dr, Beverly Hills, CA 90212, USA
Robisch, Dave *Basketball Player*
1401 Guernes Court, Springfield, IL 62702, USA
Robison, Paula *Concert Flutist*
%Shaw Concerts, Lincoln Center Plaza, 1900 Broadway, #200, New York, NY 10023, USA
Robitaille, Luc *Hockey Player*
121 Ransom Oaks Dr, East Amherst, NY 14051, USA
Robles, Marisa *Concert Harpist*
38 Luttrell Ave, London SW15 6PE, England
Robson, Bryan *Soccer Player*
%Manchester United FC, Old Trafford, Stretford, Manchester, England
Robustelli, Andrew R (Andy) *Football Player*
30 Spring St, Stamford, CT 06901, USA
Roby, Reggie *Football Player*
12004 Wandworth Dr, Tampa, FL 33626, USA
Robyn (Carlsson) *Singer*
%RCA Records, 1540 Broadway, #900, New York, NY 10036, USA
Rocard, Michel L L *Prime Minister, France*
14 Cite Vaneau, 75007 Paris, France
Rocca, Peter *Swimmer*
534 Hazel Ave, San Bruno, CA 94066, USA
Rocco, Alex *Actor*
1755 Ocean Oaks Road, Carpinteria, CA 93013, USA
Rocco, Louis R *Vietnam War Army Hero (CMH)*
3918 San Isidro NW, Albuquerque, NM 87107, USA
Rochberg, George *Composer*
3500 West Chester Pike, #CH-118, Newtown Square, PA 19073, USA
Roche, Anthony D (Tony) *Tennis Player*
5 Kapiti St, St Ives NSW 2075, Australia
Roche, E Kevin *Architect*
%Roche Dinkeloo Assoc, 20 Davis St, Hamden, CT 06517, USA
Roche, Eugene *Actor*
9911 W Pico Blvd, #PH-A, Los Angeles, CA 90035, USA
Roche, John *Basketball Player*
6401 E 6th Ave, Denver, CO 80220, USA
Rochefort, Jean *Actress*
Le Chene Rogneaux, 078125 Grosvre, France
Rochon, Lela *Actress*
%Paradigm Agency, 10100 Santa Monica Blvd, #2500, Los Angeles, CA 90067, USA
Rock, Angela *Volleyball Player*
1205 Saxony Road, Encinitas, CA 92024, USA
Rock, Chris *Comedian, Actor*
%William Morris Agency, 1325 Ave of Americas, New York, NY 10019, USA
Rock, Douglas L *Businessman*
%Smith International, 16740 Hardy St, Houston, TX 77032, USA
Rockburne, Dorothea G *Artist*
140 Grand St, New York, NY 10013, USA
Rockefeller, David *Financier*
30 Rockefeller Plaza, #506, New York, NY 10112, USA

R

Robinson - Rockefeller

Rockefeller, Laurance S *Foundation Executive*
%Rockefeller Bros Fund, 30 Rockefeller Plaza, #5600, New York, NY 10112, USA

Rockwell, Martha *Skier, Coach*
%Dartmouth College, Box 9, Hanover, NH 03755, USA

Rodbell, Martin *Nobel Medical Laureate*
%National Institute of Environment Health Sciences, Research Triangle, NC 27709, USA

Rodd, Marcia *Actress*
11738 Moorpark St, #C, Studio City, CA 91604, USA

Rodenheiser, Richard (Dick) *Hockey Player*
186 State St, Framingham, MA 01702, USA

Rodgers of Quarry Bank, William T *Government Official, England*
48 Patshull Road, London NW3 2LD, England

Rodgers, Guy *Basketball Player*
1447 Hi Point St, Los Angeles, CA 90035, USA

Rodgers, Jimmie *Singer, Songwriter*
PO Box 685, Forsyth, MO 65653, USA

Rodgers, Joan *Opera Singer*
113 Sotheby Road, London N5 2UT, England

Rodgers, Joe M *Diplomat*
%JMR Investments, Vanderbilt Plaza, 2100 West End Ave, Nashville, TN 37203, USA

Rodgers, John *Geologist*
%Yale University, Geology Dept, New Haven, CT 06520, USA

Rodgers, Joseph T *Businessman*
%Quantum, 500 McCarthy Blvd, Milpitas, CA 95035, USA

Rodgers, Robert L (Buck) *Baseball Player, Manager*
5181 West Knoll Dr, Yorba Linda, CA 92886, USA

Rodgers, T J *Businessman*
%Cypress Semiconductor, 3901 N 1st St, San Jose, CA 95134, USA

Rodgers, William H (Bill) *Marathon Runner*
372 Chestnut Hill Ave, Boston, MA 02146, USA

Rodin, Judith S *Psychiatrist, Educator*
%University of Pennsylvania, President's Office, Philadelphia, PA 19104, USA

Rodl, Henrik *Basketball Player*
%ALBA Berlin, Olympischer Platz 4, 14053 Berlin, Germany

Rodman, Dennis *Basketball Player*
4809 Seashore Dr, Newport Beach, CA 92663, USA

Rodnina, Irina *Figure Skater*
480 Cottage Grove Road, Box 939, Lake Arrowhead, CA 92352, USA

Rodrigue, George *Journalist*
%Dallas News, Editorial Dept, Communications Center, Dallas, TX 75265, USA

Rodriguez, Alexander E (Alex) *Baseball Player*
%Seattle Mariners, Kingdome, PO Box 4100, Seattle, WA 98104, USA

Rodriguez, Andres *President, Paraguay; Army General*
Bostra Senora del Carmen y San Rafael, Asuncion, Paraguay

Rodriguez, Arturo S *Labor Leader*
%United Farm Workers, 29700 Woodfoel Tehachapi Road, Keene, CA 93531, USA

Rodriguez, Beatriz *Ballerina*
%Joffrey Ballet, 70 E Lake St, #1300, Chicago, IL 60601, USA

Rodriguez, Ivan (Pudge) *Baseball Player*
E3 Calle 3, Vega Baja, PR 00693, USA

Rodriguez, Johnny *Singer, Songwriter*
%Al Embry, PO Box 23162, Nashville, TN 37202, USA

Rodriguez, Joseph C *Korean War Army Hero (CMH)*
1736 Tommy Aaron Dr, El Paso, TX 79936, USA

Rodriguez, Juan (Chi Chi) *Golfer*
%Eddie Elias Enterprises, PO Box 5118, Akron, OH 44334, USA

Rodriguez, Larry *Religious Leader*
%Metropolitan Churches Fellowship, 5300 Santa Monica Blvd, Los Angeles, CA 90029, USA

Rodriguez, Paul *Actor, Comedian*
435 N Camden Dr, #400, Beverly Hills, CA 90210, USA

Rodriguez, Raul *Float Designer*
%Fiesta Floats, 9362 Lower Azusa Road, Temple City, CA 91780, USA

Rodriguez, Rita M *Financier*
%Export-Import Bank, 811 Vermont Ave NW, Washington, DC 20571, USA

Roe, Elwin C (Preacher) *Baseball Player*
204 Wildwood Terrace, White Plains, MO 65775, USA

Roe, John H *Businessman*
%Bemis Co, Northstar Center, 222 S 9th St, Minneapolis, MN 55402, USA

Roe, Tommy	*Singer*
%Dave Hoffman Mgmt, PO Box 26037, Minneapolis, MN 55426, USA	
Roeder, Kenneth D	*Physiologist*
454 Monument St, Concord, MA 01742, USA	
Roeg, Nicolas J	*Movie Director*
2 Oxford & Cambridge Mansions, Old Marylebone Road, London NW1, England	
Roehm, Carolyne J	*Fashion Designer*
%Carolyn Roehm Inc, 257 W 39th St, #400, New York, NY 10018, USA	
Roelandts, Willem	*Businessman*
%Xilinx, 2100 Logic Dr, San Jose, CA 95124, USA	
Roemer, Charles E (Buddy), III	*Governor, LA*
%Governor's Office, State Capitol Building, Baton Rouge, LA 70804, USA	
Roemer, William F	*Financier*
%Integra Financial Corp, PO Box 837, Pittsburgh, PA 15230, USA	
Roenick, Jeremy	*Hockey Player*
749 Hawthorne St, Elmhurst, IL 60126, USA	
Roenicke, Gary S	*Baseball Player*
11066 Golden Way, Nevada City, CA 95959, USA	
Roessler, Ernest C	*Financier*
%CCB Financial Corp, 111 Corcoran St, Durham, NC 27701, USA	
Rogallo, Francis	*Inventor (Hang Glider)*
91 Osprey Lane, Kitty Hawk, NC 27949, USA	
Roge, Pascal	*Concert Pianist*
17 Ave des Cavaliers, 1224 Geneva, Switzerland	
Roger of Taize, Brother	*Religious Leader*
Taize Community, 71250 Cluny, France	
Rogers, Arthur M, Jr	*Financier*
%J P Morgan Delaware, 902 Market St, Wilmington, DE 19801, USA	
Rogers, Bernard W	*Army General*
1467 Hampton Ridge Dr, McLean, VA 22101, USA	
Rogers, Bill	*Golfer*
710 Patterson Ave, San Antonio, TX 78209, USA	
Rogers, C B, Jr	*Businessman*
%Equifax Inc, PO Box 4472, Atlanta, GA 30302, USA	
Rogers, Charles (Buddy)	*Actor*
1147 Pickfair Way, Beverly Hills, CA 90210, USA	
Rogers, Fred M	*Television Producer, Host*
%Public Broadcasting System, 1329 Braddock Place, Alexandria, VA 22314, USA	
Rogers, George	*Football Player*
100 Stanford Bridge Road, Columbia, SC 29212, USA	
Rogers, James E	*Businessman*
%CINergy Corp, 139 E 4th St, Cincinnati, OH 45202, USA	
Rogers, Jane A	*Actress*
1485 S Beverly Dr, #8, Los Angeles, CA 90035, USA	
Rogers, Julie	*Singer*
%British & Int'l Artists, 500 Waterman Ave, #191, East Providence, RI 02914, USA	
Rogers, Kenny	*Singer, Songwriter, Actor*
Rt 1, Box 100, Colbert, GA 30628, USA	
Rogers, Lynn L	*Wildlife Biologist, Ecologist*
145 W Conan St, Ely, MN 55731, USA	
Rogers, Melody	*Actress*
2051 Nicols Canyon Road, Los Angeles, CA 90046, USA	
Rogers, Mimi	*Actress*
11693 San Vicente Blvd, #241, Los Angeles, CA 90049, USA	
Rogers, O W (Buck)	*Baseball Player, Manager*
3145 Snake Path Road, Blairs, VA 24527, USA	
Rogers, Paul	*Actor*
9 Hillside Gardens, Highgate, London N6 5SU, England	
Rogers, Ralph B	*Businessman*
%Texas Industries, 1341 W Mockingbird Lane, Dallas, TX 75247, USA	
Rogers, Ray	*Labor Leader*
%Corporate Campaign Inc, 80 8th Ave, New York, NY 10011, USA	
Rogers, Richard G	*Architect*
%R Rogers Partnership, Thames Wharf, Rainville Rd, London W6 9HA, England	
Rogers, Rob	*Editorial Cartoonist*
Pittsburgh Post-Gazette, Editorial Dept, 23 Blvd of Allies, Pittsburgh, PA 15230, USA	
Rogers, Robert D	*Businessman*
%Texas Industries, 1341 W Mockingbird Lane, Dallas, TX 75247, USA	

R

Roe - Rogers

Rogers, Rodney *Basketball Player*
%Los Angeles Clippers, Sports Arena, 3939 Figueroa St, Los Angeles, CA 90037, USA

Rogers, Rosemary *Writer*
%Avon Books, 959 8th Ave, New York, NY 10019, USA

Rogers, Roy *Actor, Singer*
15650 Seneca Road, Victorville, CA 92392, USA

Rogers, Roy *Basketball Player*
%Vancouver Grizzlies, 288 Beatty St, #300, Vancouver BC V6B 2M1, Canada

Rogers, Stephen D (Steve) *Baseball Player*
3746 S Madison Ave, Tulsa, OK 74105, USA

Rogers, Suzanne *Actress*
11266 Canton Dr, Studio City, CA 91604, USA

Rogers, Tristan *Actor*
8550 Holloway Dr, #301, Los Angeles, CA 90069, USA

Rogers, Wayne *Actor*
11828 La Grange Ave, Los Angeles, CA 90025, USA

Rogers, William P *Secretary, State; Attorney General*
%Rogers & Wells, 607 14th St NW, #900, Washington, DC 20005, USA

Rogerson, Kate *Golfer*
%Ladies Professional Golf Assn, 2570 Volusia Ave, Daytona Beach, FL 32114, USA

Rogin, Gilbert L *Editor*
43 W 10th St, New York, NY 10011, USA

Rogoff, Ilan *Concert Pianist*
Villa La Puerta, 07170 Valldemosa, Majorca, Baleares, Spain

Rohatyn, Felix G *Financier*
%Lazard Freres Co, 1 Rockefeller Plaza, New York, NY 10020, USA

Rohde, David *Journalist*
%Christian Science Monitor, Editorial Dept, 1 Norway St, Boston, MA 02115, USA

Rohlander, Uta *Track Athlete*
Liebigstr 9, 06237 Leuna, Germany

Rohmer, Eric *Movie Director*
%Les Films du Losange, 26 Ave Pierre-de-Serbie, 75116 Paris, France

Rohrbasser, Markus *Financier*
%UBS North America, 299 Park Ave, New York, NY 10171, USA

Rohrer, Heinrich *Nobel Physics Laureate*
%IBM Research Laboratory, Saumerstr 4, 8803 Ruschlikon, Switzerland

Roizman, Bernard *Virologist*
5555 S Everett Ave, Chicago, IL 60637, USA

Roizman, Owen *Cinematographer*
17533 Magnolia Blvd, Encino, CA 91316, USA

Rojas, Nydia *Singer*
%Silverlight Entertainment, 9171 Wilshire Blvd, #426, Beverly Hills, CA 90210, USA

Roker, Al *Entertainer*
%CNBC-TV, 2200 Fletcher Ave, Fort Lee, NJ 07024, USA

Roland, Ed *Singer, Songwriter (Collective Soul)*
%William Morris Agency, 1325 Ave of Americas, New York, NY 10019, USA

Rolandi, Gianna *Opera Singer*
%Columbia Artists Mgmt Inc, 165 W 57th St, New York, NY 10019, USA

Rolen, Scott *Baseball Player*
%Philadelphia Phillies, Veterans Stadium, PO Box 7575, Philadelphia, PA 19101, USA

Roles, Barbara Ann *Figure Skater*
531 Esplanade St, #212, Redondo Beach, CA 90277, USA

Rolfe Johnson, Anthony *Opera Singer*
%Lies Askonas Ltd, 6 Henrietta St, London WC2E 8LA, England

Rolle, Esther *Actress*
4421 Don Felipe Dr, Los Angeles, CA 90008, USA

Rollin, Betty *Writer, Commentator*
%NS Bienstack Inc, 1740 Broadway, New York, NY 10019, USA

Rollins, Gary W *Businessman*
%Rollins Inc, 2170 Piedmont Road NE, Atlanta, GA 30324, USA

Rollins, Henry *Singer, Songwriter*
%3 Artists Mgmt, 2550 Laurel Pass, Los Angeles, CA 90046, USA

Rollins, Jack *Movie Producer*
%Rollins Joffe Morra Brezner Productions, 130 W 57th St, New York, NY 10019, USA

Rollins, Kenny *Basketball Player*
The Gardens, 220 Hibiscus Way, Parrish, FL 34219, USA

Rollins, R Randall *Businessman*
%Rollins Inc, 2170 Piedmont Road NE, Atlanta, GA 30324, USA

Rollins, Reed C — *Botanist*
19 Chauncy St, Cambridge, MA 02138, USA
Rollins, Sonny — *Jazz Saxophonist, Composer*
Route 9-G, Germantown, NY 12526, USA
Rollins, Wayne (Tree) — *Basketball Player, Coach*
PO Box 541521, Orlando, FL 32854, USA
Rolston, Matthew — *Photographer*
%Bulfinch Press, Little Brown Co, 34 Beacon St, Boston, MA 02108, USA
Roman, Joseph — *Labor Leader*
%Glass & Ceramic Workers Union, 556 E Town St, Columbus, OH 43215, USA
Roman, Petre — *Prime Minister, Romania*
Str Gogol 2, Sector 1, Bucharest, Romania
Roman, Ruth — *Actress*
%Curtis Roberts Enterprises, 9056 Santa Monica Blvd, Los Angeles, CA 90069, USA
Romanenko, Yuri V — *Cosmonaut*
%Potchta Kosmonavtov, Moskovskoi Oblasti, 141160 Syvisdny Goroduk, Russia
Romano, John — *Psychiatrist*
212 Valley Road, Merion Station, PA 19066, USA
Romano, Umberto — *Artist*
162 E 83rd St, New York, NY 10028, USA
Romanos, John J (Jack), Jr — *Publisher*
%Pocket Books, 1230 Ave of Americas, New York, NY 10020, USA
Romansky, Monroe J — *Physician*
5600 Wisconsin Ave, Chevy Chase, MD 20815, USA
Romario (de Souza Faria) — *Soccer Player*
%Futebol Confederacao, Rua da Alfandega 70, 20.070 Rio de Janeiro, Brazil
Romelfanger, Charles — *Labor Leader*
%Pattern Makers League, 4106 34th Ave, Moline, IL 61265, USA
Romeo, Robin — *Bowler*
%Ladies Professional Bowlers Tour, 7171 Cherryvale Blvd, Rockford, IL 61112, USA
Romer, Roy R — *Governor, CO*
%Governor's Office, State Capitol Building, #136, Denver, CO 80203, USA
Romer, Suzanne F C — *Prime Minister, Netherlands Antilles*
%Prime Minister's Office, Willemstad, Curacao, Netherlands Antilles
Romero, Danny, Jr — *Boxer*
531 Veranda Road NW, Albuquerque, NM 87107, USA
Romero, Ned — *Actor*
19438 Lassen Ave, Northridge, CA 91324, USA
Romig, Joseph (Joe) — *Football Player*
1300 Plaza Court N, Lafayette, CO 80026, USA
Romijn, Rebecca — *Model*
%Next Model Mgmt, 23 Watts St, New York, NY 10013, USA
Rominger, Kent V — *Astronaut*
%NASA, Johnson Space Center, 2101 NASA Road, Houston, TX 77058, USA
Romiti, Cesare — *Businessman*
%Fiat SpA, Corso Marconi 10, 10125 Turin, Italy
Ronaldo — *Soccer Player*
%FC Barcelona, Aristides Maillol S/N, 08 028 Barcelona, Spain
Ronan, William J — *Railway Engineer*
525 S Flagler Dr, West Palm Beach, FL 33401, USA
Ronningen, Jon — *Wrestler*
Mellomasveien 132, 1414 Trollasen, Norway
Rono, Peter — *Track Athlete*
%Mount Saint Mary's College, Athletic Dept, Emmitsburg, MD 21727, USA
Ronsch, Hannelore — *Government Official, Germany*
%Bundestag, Bundeshaus, Gorresstr 15, 53113 Bonn, Germany
Ronstadt, Linda — *Singer*
%Peter Asher Mgmt, 644 N Doheny Dr, Los Angeles, CA 90069, USA
Rook, Susan — *Commentator*
%Cable News Network, News Dept, 1050 Techwood Dr NW, Atlanta, GA 30318, USA
Rooke, Ervin J (Erv) — *Air Force General*
%National Defense University, Fort Lesley J McNair, Washington, DC 20319, USA
Rooney, Andrew A (Andy) — *Commentator*
254 Rowayton Ave, Rowayton, CT 06853, USA
Rooney, Daniel M — *Football Executive*
%Pittsburgh Steelers, 3 Rivers Stadium, 300 Stadium Circle, Pittsburgh, PA 15212, USA
Rooney, Mickey — *Actor*
31351 Via Colinas, Westlake Village, CA 91362, USA

R

Rollins - Rooney

R

Rooney, Patrick W — *Businessman*
%Cooper Tire & Rubber Co, Lima & Western Aves, Findlay, OH 45840, USA

Roots, Melvin H — *Labor Leader*
%Plasters & Cement Workers Union, 1125 17th St NW, Washington, DC 20036, USA

Roper, Dee Dee (Spinderella) — *Rap Artist (Salt-N-Pepa)*
%Next Plateau Records, 1650 Broadway, #1103, New York, NY 10019, USA

Rorem, Ned — *Composer, Writer*
PO Box 764, Nantucket, MA 02554, USA

Rosato, Genesia — *Ballerina*
%Royal Ballet, Bow St, London WC2E 9DD, England

Rosberg, Keke — *Auto Racing Driver*
%Opel Team Rosberg, Nactweide 35, 67433 Neustadt/Weinstr, Germany

Rosburg, Bob — *Golfer*
49425 Avenida Club La Quinta, La Quinta, CA 92253, USA

Roschkov, Victor — *Editorial Cartoonist*
1 Yonge St, Toronto ON, Canada 90068, USA

Rose, Charles (Charlie) — *Commentator*
%Rose Communications, 499 Park Ave, New York, NY 10022, USA

Rose, Clarence — *Golfer*
502 Pine Needles Court, Goldsboro, NC 27534, USA

Rose, H Michael — *Army General, England*
%Coldstream Guards, Wellington Barracks, London SW1E 6HQ, England

Rose, Jalen — *Basketball Player*
%Indiana Pacers, Market Square Arena, 300 E Market St, Indianapolis, IN 46204, USA

Rose, Jamie — *Actress*
8380 Melrose Ave, #207, Los Angeles, CA 90069, USA

Rose, Judd — *Commentator*
%ABC-TV, News Dept, 77 W 66th St, New York, NY 10023, USA

Rose, Lee — *Basketball Coach*
%University of South Florida, Athletic Dept, Tampa, FL 33620, USA

Rose, Margot — *Actress*
%Judy Schoen, 606 N Larchmont Blvd, #309, Los Angeles, CA 90004, USA

Rose, Michel — *Businessman*
%Lafarge Corp, 11130 Sunrise Valley Dr, Reston, VA 20191, USA

Rose, Murray — *Swimmer*
401 S Prairie Ave, Inglewood, CA 90301, USA

Rose, Peter E (Pete) — *Baseball Player, Manager.*
8570 Crescent Dr, Los Angeles, CA 90046, USA

Rose, W Axl — *Singer (Guns n' Roses), Songwriter*
%Artists & Audience Entertainment, 2112 Broadway. #600, New York, NY 10023, USA

Roseanne — *Actress, Comedienne*
2029 Century Park East, #3950, Los Angeles, CA 90067, USA

Rosellini, Albert D — *Governor, WA*
5936 6th Ave S, Seattle, WA 98108, USA

Roseman, Saul — *Biochemist*
8206 Cranwood Court, Baltimore, MD 21208, USA

Rosen, Albert (Al) — *Conductor*
Pod Lysinami 21, 14700 Prague 4, Czech Republic

Rosen, Albert L (Al) — *Baseball Player, Executive*
15 Mayfair Dr, Rancho Mirage, CA 92270, USA

Rosen, Benjamin M — *Businessman*
%Compaq Computer, 20555 State Highway 249, Houston, TX 77070, USA

Rosen, Charles W — *Concert Pianist*
101 W 78th St, New York, NY 10024, USA

Rosen, Milton W — *Engineer, Physicist*
5610 Alta Vista Road, Bethesda, MD 20817, USA

Rosen, Nathaniel — *Concert Cellist*
36 Clinton Ave, Nyack, NY 10960, USA

Rosenbaum, Edward E — *Physician*
333 NW 23rd St, Portland, OR 97210, USA

Rosenberg, Alan — *Actor*
%Gersh Agency, 232 N Canon Dr, Beverly Hills, CA 90210, USA

Rosenberg, Claude N, Jr — *Financier*
%RCM Capital Management, 4 Embarcadero Center, San Francisco, CA 94111, USA

Rosenberg, Howard — *Television Critic*
5859 Larboard Lane, Agoura Hills, CA 91301, USA

Rosenberg, Pierre M — *Museum Director*
%Musee du Louvre, 34-36 Quai du Louvre, 75068 Paris, France

Rooney - Rosenberg

Rosenberg, Steven A — *Cancer Researcher, Surgeon*
10104 Iron Gate Road, Potomac, MD 20854, USA

Rosenberg, Stuart — *Movie Director*
1984 Coldwater Canyon Dr, Beverly Hills, CA 90210, USA

Rosenberg, Tina — *Writer*
%New School for Social Research, World Policy Institute, New York, NY 10011, USA

Rosenberger, Roger L — *Businessman*
%John Alden Financial Corp, 7300 Corporate Center Dr, Miami, FL 33126, USA

Rosenblath, Marshall N — *Physicist*
2311 Via Siena, La Jolla, CA 92037, USA

Rosenblatt, Dana — *Boxer*
16 Ivy Road, Malden, MA 02148, USA

Rosenblith, Walter A — *Biophysicist*
54 Devolder Road, Marstons Mills, MA 02648, USA

Rosenbluth, Leonard — *Basketball Player*
14654 SW 140th Court, Miami, FL 33186, USA

Rosenbluth, Marshall N — *Fusion Theorist, Physicist*
2311 Via Siena Lane, La Jolla, CA 92037, USA

Rosenburg, Saul A — *Oncologist*
%Stanford University, Oncology Division, Stanford, CA 94305, USA

Rosenfeld, Arnold S — *Editor*
%Cox Newspapers, PO Box 105720, Atlanta, GA 30348, USA

Rosenfelt, Frank E — *Entertainment Executive*
UIP House, 45 Beadon Road, Hammersmith, London W6, England

Rosenfield, Jack E — *Businessman*
%Hanover Direct Inc, 1500 Harbor Blvd, Weehawken, NJ 07087, USA

Rosenfield, James H — *Television Executive*
%John Blair Communications, 1290 Ave of Americas, New York, NY 10104, USA

Rosenquist, James A — *Artist*
PO Box 4, 420 Broadway, Aripeka, FL 34679, USA

Rosensteel, John W — *Businessman*
%Keyport Life Insurance, 125 High St, Boston, MA 02110, USA

Rosenstein, Samuel M — *Judge*
%US Court of International Trade, 2200 S Ocean Lane, Fort Lauderdale, FL 33316, USA

Rosenthal, Abraham (A M) — *Editor, Columnist*
%New York Times, Editorial Dept, 229 W 43rd St, New York, NY 10036, USA

Rosenthal, Bernard J — *Artist*
1482 York Ave, #4-D, New York, NY 10021, USA

Rosenthal, Harvey — *Businessman*
%Melville Corp, 1 Threall Road, Rye, NY 10580, USA

Rosenthal, Jacob (Jack) — *Journalist*
%New York Times, Editorial Dept, 229 W 43rd St, New York, NY 10036, USA

Rosenthal, Tony — *Sculptor*
173 E 73rd St, New York, NY 10021, USA

Rosenzweig, Barney — *Television Producer*
%Rosenzweig Productions, 130 S Hewitt St, Los Angeles, CA 90012, USA

Rosenzweig, Mark R — *Physiological Psychologist*
%University of California, Psychology Dept, Berkeley, CA 94720, USA

Roses, Allen D — *Neurologist*
%Duke University, Medical Center, Bryan Research Center, Durham, NC 27706, USA

Rosewall, Ken — *Tennis Player*
111 Pentacost Ave, Turramurra NSW 2074, Australia

Rosewoman, Michele — *Jazz Pianist*
%Abby Hoffer, 223 1/2 E 48th St, New York, NY 10017, USA

Rosin, Walter L — *Religious Leader*
%Lutheran Church Missouri Synod, 1333 S Kirkwood Road, St Louis, MO 63122, USA

Rosnes, Renee — *Jazz Pianist*
%Integrity Talent, PO Box 961, Burlington, MA 01803, USA

Ross Fairbanks, Anne — *Swimmer*
10 Grandview Ave, Troy, NY 12180, USA

Ross, Al — *Cartoonist*
2185 Bolton St, Bronx, NY 10462, USA

Ross, Betsy — *Sportscaster*
%Madison Square Garden Network, 4 Pennsylania Plaza, New York, NY 10001, USA

Ross, Charlotte — *Actress*
%Abrams Artists, 9200 Sunset Blvd, #625, Los Angeles, CA 90069, USA

Ross, David A — *Museum Director*
%Whitney Museum of American Art, 945 Madison Ave, New York, NY 10021, USA

R

Rosenberg - Ross

Ross, Diana	*Singer, Actress*
PO Box 11059, Glenville Station, Greenwich, CT 06831, USA	
Ross, Don	*Body Builder*
PO Box 981, Venice, CA 90294, USA	
Ross, Douglas T	*Computer Scientist*
%Softech Inc, 3260 Eagle Park Dr NE, Grand Rapids, MI 49525, USA	
Ross, Herbert D	*Movie Director*
30900 Broad Beach Road, Malibu, CA 90265, USA	
Ross, Ian M	*Electrical Engineer*
%AT&T Bell Laboratories, 101 Crawfords Corner Road, Holmdel, NJ 07733, USA	
Ross, Jerry L	*Astronaut*
%NASA, Johnson Space Center, 2101 NASA Road, Houston, TX 77058, USA	
Ross, Jimmy D	*Army General*
9208 Cross Oaks Court, Fairfax Station, VA 22039, USA	
Ross, Joseph J	*Businessman*
%Federal Signal Corp, 1415 W 22nd St, Oak Brook, IL 60523, USA	
Ross, Karie	*Sportscaster*
%ESPN-TV, Sports Dept, ESPN Plaza, Bristol, CT 06010, USA	
Ross, Katherine	*Actress*
33050 Pacific Coast Highway, Malibu, CA 90265, USA	
Ross, Marion	*Actress*
20929 Ventura Blvd, #47, Woodland Hills, CA 91364, USA	
Ross, Raymond E	*Businessman*
%Cincinnati Milacron, 4701 Marburg Ave, Cincinnati, OH 45209, USA	
Ross, Robert	*Foundation Executive*
%Muscular Dystrophy Assn, 3300 E Sunrise Dr, Tucson, AZ 85718, USA	
Ross, Robert J (Bobby)	*Football Coach*
%Detroit Lions, Silverdome, 1200 Featherstone Road, Pontiac, MI 48342, USA	
Ross, Wilburn K	*WW II Army Hero (CMH)*
PO Box 355, Dupont, WA 98327, USA	
Rossdale, Gavin	*Singer, Songwriter (Bush)*
%International Creative Mgmt, 40 W 57th St, New York, NY 10019, USA	
Rosse, James N	*Publisher*
%Freedom Newspapers Inc, PO Box 19549, Irvine, CA 92623, USA	
Rossellini, Isabella	*Model, Actress*
745 5th Ave, #814, New York, NY 10151, USA	
Rossello, Pedro J	*Governor, PR*
%Governor's Office, State Capitol, San Juan, PR 00936, USA	
Rossen, Carol	*Actress*
1119 23rd St, #8, Santa Monica, CA 90403, USA	
Rosser, James M	*Educator*
%California State University, President's Office, Los Angeles, CA 90032, USA	
Rosser, Ronald E	*WW II Army Hero (CMH)*
36 James St, Roseville, OH 43777, USA	
Rosset, Barnet L, Jr	*Publisher*
%Rosset Co, 61 4th Ave, New York, NY 10003, USA	
Rosset, Marc	*Tennis Player*
%Michel Rosset, Rue Albert Gos 16, 1206 Geneva, Switzerland	
Rossi, Opilio Cardinal	*Religious Leader*
Via Della Scrofa 70, 00186 Rome, Italy	
Rossi, Paolo	*Soccer Player*
%Juventus FC Turin, Piazza Crimea 7, 10131 Turin, Italy	
Rossi, Tino	*Singer, Actor*
40 Blvd Maillot, 92200 Neuilly/Seine, France	
Rossini, Frederick D	*Chemist*
605 S Highway One, #T-900, Juno Beach, FL 33408, USA	
Rosskopf, Joerg	*Table Tennis Player*
%Tischtennisbund, Otto-Fleck-Schneise 12-A, 60528 Frankfurt/Maim, Germany	
Rossner, Judith	*Writer*
263 West End Ave, New York, NY 10023, USA	
Rossner, Petra	*Cyclist*
Goethstr 9, 72124 Pliezhausen, Germany	
Rosso, Louis T	*Businessman*
%Beckman Instruments, 2500 Harbor Blvd, Fullerton, CA 92835, USA	
Rossovich, Rick	*Actor*
%Gersh Agency, 232 N Canon Dr, Beverly Hills, CA 90210, USA	
Rossovich, Timothy J (Tim)	*Football Player, Actor*
%Artists Group, 10100 Santa Monica Blvd, #2490, Los Angeles, CA 90067, USA	

Rosten, Irwin — *Writer, Producer, Director*
2217 Chelan Dr, Los Angeles, CA 90068, USA

Rostow, Eugene V — *Economist*
1315 4th St SW, Washington, DC 20024, USA

Rostow, Walt W — *Economist, Government Official*
1 Wildwind Point, Austin, TX 78746, USA

Rostropovich, Mstislav L — *Concert Cellist, Conductor*
%National Symphony Orchestra, Kennedy Center, Washington, DC 20566, USA

Rostvold, Gerhard N — *Economist*
19712 Oceanaire Circle, Huntington Beach, CA 92648, USA

Roszell, Stephen W — *Financier*
%IDA Advisory Group, 80 S 8th St, Minneapolis, MN 55402, USA

Rota, Gian-Carlo — *Applied Mathematician*
1105 Massachusetts Ave, #8-F, Cambridge, MA 02138, USA

Rotblat, Joseph — *Nobel Peace Laureate, Physicist*
%8 Asmara Road, London NW2 3ST, England

Rote, Tobin C — *Football Player*
7590 Lighthouse Road, Port Hope, MI 48468, USA

Rote, W Kyle — *Football Player*
24700 Deepwater Point Dr, #14, St Michaels, MD 21663, USA

Rotenstreich, Jon — *Businessman*
%TIG Insurance, 5205 N O'Connor Blvd, Irving, TX 75039, USA

Roth, Ann — *Costume Designer*
Road 3, Box 3124, Bangor, PA 18013, USA

Roth, Arnold — *Cartoonist*
%National Cartoonists Society, 9 Ebony Court, Brooklyn, NY 11229, USA

Roth, David Lee — *Singer, Songwriter (Van Halen)*
455 Bradford St, Pasadena, CA 91105, USA

Roth, Geneen — *Writer*
%E P Dutton, 375 Hudson St, New York, NY 10014, USA

Roth, Jesse — *Endocrinologist*
%National Institute of Arthritis, 9000 Rockville Pike, Bethesda, MD 20892, USA

Roth, Joe — *Television Executive*
%Walt Disney Pictures, 500 S Buena Vista Blvd, Burbank, CA 91521, USA

Roth, Mark — *Bowler*
%Professional Bowlers Assn, 1720 Merriman Road, Akron, OH 44313, USA

Roth, Michael I — *Financier*
%Mutual Life Insurance, 1740 Broadway, New York, NY 10019, USA

Roth, Philip — *Writer*
%Houghton Mifflin, 215 Park Ave S, New York, NY 10003, USA

Roth, Tim — *Actor, Director*
%Markham & Froggatt, Julian House, 4 Windmill St, London W1P 1HF, England

Roth, William G — *Businessman*
%Dravo Corp, 915 Penn Ave, Pittsburgh, PA 15222, USA

Rothberg, Patti — *Singer*
%Creative Artists Agency, 9830 Wilshire Blvd, Beverly Hills, CA 90212, USA

Rothenberg, Alan I — *Soccer, Basketball Executive*
%US Soccer Federation, 1801-11 S Prairie Ave, Chicago, IL 60616, USA

Rothenberg, Susan — *Artist*
%Sperone Westwater Gallery, 142 Green St, New York, NY 10012, USA

Rothenberger, Anneliese — *Opera Singer*
Quellenhof, 8268 Salenstein/TG, Switzerland

Rothenburger Luding, Christa — *Speed Skater, Cyclist*
%Dresdener Eisspot-Club, Pieschener Allee 1, 01067 Dresden, Germany

Rothermere of Hemsted, V Harold — *Publisher*
New Carmelite House, Carmelite St, London EC4, England

Rothert, Harlow — *Track Athlete*
2372 Branner Dr, Menlo Park, CA 94025, USA

Rothman, Frank — *Entertainment Executive*
10555 Rocca Place, Los Angeles, CA 90077, USA

Rothrock, Cynthia — *Actress*
4654-B East Ave S, #190, Palmdale, CA 93552, USA

Rothschild, David de — *Financier*
%Rothschild Inc, 1251 Ave of Americas, New York, NY 10020, USA

Rothschild, Miriam — *Naturalist*
%Ashton World, Peterborough, Northants, England

Rothstein, Ronald (Ron) — *Basketball Coach*
%Cleveland Cavaliers, 2923 Statesboro Road, Richfield, OH 44286, USA

R

Rosten - Rothstein

R

Rothwell, Harold J — *Judge*
%Random House, 201 E 50th St, New York, NY 10022, USA

Roubos, Gary L — *Businessman*
%Dover Corp, 280 Park Ave, New York, NY 10017, USA

Rouleau, Joseph-Alfred — *Opera Singer*
32 Lakeshore Road, Beaconsfield PQ H9W 4H3, England

Roundfield, Dan — *Basketball Player*
340 Spring Lake Terrace, Roswell, GA 30076, USA

Roundtree, Richard — *Actor*
28843 Wagon Road, Agoura Hills, CA 91301, USA

Roundtree, Saudia — *Basketball Player*
%Atlanta Glory, 151 Ponce de Leon Ave NE, #200, Atlanta, GA 30308, USA

Rourke, Mickey — *Actor*
9150 Wilshire Blvd, #350, Beverly Hills, CA 90212, USA

Rouse, Christopher — *Composer*
%University of Rochester, Eastman School of Music, Rochester, NY 14604, USA

Rouse, Irving — *Anthropologist*
12 Ridgewood Terrace, North Haven, CT 06473, USA

Rouse, Jeff — *Swimmer*
302 Gerber Dr, Fredericksburg, VA 22408, USA

Roux, Albert H — *Chef*
%Le Gavroche, 43 Upper Brook St, London W1Y 1PF, England

Roux, Jean-Louis — *Theater Director*
4145 Blueridge Crescent, #2, Montreal PQ H3H 1S7, Canada

Roux, Michel A — *Chef*
%Waterside Inn, Ferry Road, Bray, Berks SL6 2AT, England

Rowan, Carl T — *Columnist, Government Official*
%CTR Productions, 3251 Sutton Place NW, #C, Washington, DC 20016, USA

Rowden, William H — *Navy Admiral*
55 Pinewood Court, Lancaster, VA 22503, USA

Rowe, Misty — *Actress*
PO Box 11152, Greenwich, CT 06831, USA

Rowe, Sandra M — *Editor*
%Portland Oregonian, Editorial Dept, 1320 SW Broadway, Portland, OR 97201, USA

Rowell, Lester J, Jr — *Businessman*
%Provident Mutual Life, 1600 Market St, Philadelphia, PA 19103, USA

Rowell, Victoria — *Actress*
%Abrams Artists, 9200 Sunset Blvd, #625, Los Angeles, CA 90069, USA

Rowen, Robert G — *Financier*
%Bell Federal Savings & Loan, 79 W Monroe St, Chicago, IL 60603, USA

Rowland, F Sherwood — *Nobel Chemistry Laureate*
4807 Dorchester Road, Corona del Mar, CA 92625, USA

Rowland, James A — *Royal Air Force Marshal, Australia*
21/171 Walker St, North Sydney 2060, Australia

Rowland, John G — *Governor, CT*
%Governor's Office, State Capitol, 210 Capitol Ave, Hartford, CT 06106, USA

Rowland, John W — *Labor Leader*
%Amalgamated Transit Union, 5025 Wisconsin Ave NW, Washington, DC 20016, USA

Rowland, Landon H — *Businessman*
%Kansas City Southern, 114 W 11th St, Kansas City, MO 64105, USA

Rowland, Robert A — *Government Official*
%Occupational Safety Commission, 1825 "K" St NW, Washington, DC 20006, USA

Rowland, Roland W (Tiny) — *Businessman*
%Lonrho Ltd, Cheapside House, 138 Cheapside, London EC2V 6BL, England

Rowlands, Gena — *Actress*
7917 Woodrow Wilson Dr, Los Angeles, CA 90046, USA

Rowling, Wallace E — *Prime Minister, New Zealand*
PO Box 78, Motueka, Nelson, New Zealand

Roy (Uwe Ludwig Horn) — *Animal Illusionist (Siegfried & Roy)*
%Beyond Belief, 1639 N Valley Dr, Las Vegas, NV 89108, USA

Roy, James D — *Financier*
%Federal Home Loan Bank, 601 Grant St, Pittsburgh, PA 15219, USA

Roy, Patrick — *Hockey Player*
%Colorado Avalanche, McNichols Arena, 1635 Clay St, Denver, CO 80204, USA

Roy, Vesta M — *Governor, NH*
%State Senate, State House, Concord, NH 03301, USA

Royal, Billy Joe — *Singer, Songwriter*
%Mark Ketchum Mgmt, 204 Cherokee Road, Hendersonvlle, TN 37075, USA

Rothwell - Royal

Royo Sanchez, Aristides — *President, Panama*
PO Box 3333, Panama City, Panama

Royse, John N — *Financier*
%Old National Bancorp, 420 Main St, Evansville, IN 47708, USA

Rozanov, Evgeny G — *Architect*
24 Pushkinskaya Ul, 103824 Moscow, Russia

Rozhdestvensky, Gennady N — *Conductor*
%Victor Hochhauser Ltd, 4 Oak Hill Way, London NW3, England

Rozhdestvensky, Valery I — *Cosmonaut*
%Potchta Kosmonavtov, Moskovskoi Oblasti, 141160 Syvisdny Goroduk, Russia

Rozier, Clifford — *Basketball Player*
%Toronto Raptors, 20 Bay St, #1702, Toronto ON M5J 2N8, Canada

Rozier, Mike — *Football Player*
PO Box 1516, Houston, TX 77251, USA

Rubalcaba, Gonzalo — *Jazz Pianist*
%DL Media, 51 Oakland Terrace, Bela Cynwyd, PA 19004, USA

Rubbia, Carlo — *Nobel Physics Laureate*
%Harvard University, Physics Dept, Cambridge, MA 02138, USA

Ruben, Joseph P — *Movie Director*
%United Talent Agency, 9560 Wilshire Blvd, #500, Beverly Hills, CA 90212, USA

Rubenstein, Ann — *Commentator*
%NBC-TV, News Dept, 30 Rockefeller Plaza, New York, NY 10112, USA

Rubenstein, Edward — *Physician*
%Stanford University Medical School, Surgery Dept, Stanford, CA 94305, USA

Rubik, Erno — *Inventor (Rubik Cube)*
Rubik Studio, Varosmajor Utca 74, 1122 Budapest, Hungary

Rubin, Benjamin A — *Inventor (Bifurcated Needle)*
50 Belmont Ave, #601, Bala Cynwyd, PA 19004, USA

Rubin, Ellis — *Attorney*
333 NE 23rd St, Miami, FL 33137, USA

Rubin, Harry — *Biologist*
%University of California, Molecular Biology Dept, Berkeley, CA 94720, USA

Rubin, Louis D, Jr — *Writer*
702 Ginghoul Road, Chapel Hill, NC 27514, USA

Rubin, Robert — *Medical Researcher*
%Massachusetts General Hospital, 32 Fruit St, Boston, MA 02114, USA

Rubin, Robert E — *Secretary, Treasury*
%Treasury Department, 1500 Pennsylvania Ave NW, Washington, DC 20220, USA

Rubin, Stephen E — *Publisher*
%Doubleday, 1540 Broadway, New York, NY 10036, USA

Rubin, Theodore I — *Psychiatrist*
219 E 62nd St, New York, NY 10021, USA

Rubin, Vanessa — *Singer*
%Joel Chriss, 300 Mercer St, #3-J, New York, NY 10003, USA

Rubin, Vera C — *Astronomer*
%Carnegie Institute, 5241 Broad Branch Road NW, Washington, DC 20015, USA

Rubin, William — *Museum Curator*
%Museum of Modern Art, 11 W 53rd St, New York, NY 10019, USA

Rubini, Cesare — *Basetketball Coach*
%Federazione Italian Pallacanestro, Via Fogliano 15, 00199 Rome, Italy

Rubino, Frank A — *Attorney*
2601 S Bayshore Dr, Miami, FL 33133, USA

Rubinstein, John — *Actor*
10531 Collier St, Tarzana, CA 91356, USA

Ruby, Michael — *Editor*
%US News & World Report Magazine, 2400 "N" St NW, Washington, DC 20037, USA

Ruckelshaus, William D — *Businessman, Government Official*
%Browning-Ferris Industries, 757 N Eldridge Parkway, Houston, TX 77079, USA

Rucker, Anja — *Track Athlete*
Wollnitzer Str 42, 07749 Jena, Germany

Rucker, Darius — *Singer (Hootie & The Blowfish)*
%FishCo Mgmt, PO Box 5656, Columbia, SC 29250, USA

Ruckriem, Ulrich — *Sculptor*
%C Grimaldis Gallery, 1006 Morton St, Baltimore, MD 21201, USA

Rudbottom, Roy R, Jr — *Diplomat*
7831 Park Lane, #213-A, Dallas, TX 75225, USA

Rudd, Paul — *Actor*
%International Creative Mgmt, 8942 Wilshire Blvd, Beverly Hills, CA 90211, USA

R

Royo Sanchez - Rudd

Rudd, Ricky — *Auto Racing Driver*
4721-402 Morehead Road, Harrisburg, NC 28075, USA

Ruddle, Francis H — *Biologist, Geneticist*
%Yale University, Biology Dept, New Haven, CT 06511, USA

Rudel, Julius — *Conductor*
101 Central Park West, #11-A, New York, NY 10023, USA

Rudenstine, Neil L — *Educator*
%Harvard University, President's Office, Cambridge, MA 02138, USA

Ruder, David S — *Government Official, Educator*
%Baker & McKenzie, 1 Prudential Plaza, 130 E Randolph Dr, Chicago, IL 60601, USA

Rudi, Joseph O (Joe) — *Baseball Player*
RR 1, Box 186, Baker City, OR 97814, USA

Rudie, Evelyn — *Actress*
%Santa Monica Playhouse, 1211 4th St, Santa Monica, CA 90401, USA

Rudman, Warren B — *Senator, NH*
41 Indian Rock Road, Nashua, NH 03063, USA

Rudner, Rita — *Comedienne*
2447 Benedict Canyon Dr, Beverly Hills, CA 90210, USA

Rudnick, Paul — *Writer*
%Creative Artists Agency, 9830 Wilshire Blvd, Beverly Hills, CA 90212, USA

Rudoff, Sheldon — *Religious Leader*
%Union of Orthodox Jewish Congregations, 333 7th Ave, New York, NY 10001, USA

Rudolph, Alan S — *Movie Director*
15760 Ventura Blvd, #16, Encino, CA 91436, USA

Rudolph, Donald E — *WW II Army Hero (CMH)*
497 Shamrock Dr, Bovey, MN 55709, USA

Rudolph, Frederick — *Writer, Historian*
234 Ide Road, Williamstown, MA 01267, USA

Rudometkin, John — *Basketball Player*
6181 Wise Road, Newcastle, CA 95658, USA

Rudzinski, Witold — *Composer*
Ul Narbutta 50 M 6, 02-541 Warsaw, Poland

Ruehe, Volker — *Government Official, Germany*
%Bundesministerium Der Verteidigung, Hardthoehe, 53125 Bonn, Germany

Ruehl, Mercedes — *Actress*
129 McDougal St, New York, NY 10012, USA

Ruelas, Gabriel (Gabe) — *Boxer*
9537 Rincon St, Arleta, CA 91331, USA

Ruether, Rosemary R — *Theologian*
1426 Hinman Ave, Evanston, IL 60201, USA

Ruffini, Attilio — *Government Official, Italy*
Camera dei Deputati, 00187 Rome, Italy

Rugambwa, Laurian Cardinal — *Religious Leader*
%Archbishop's House, St Joseph, PO Box 167, Dar es Salaam, Tanzania

Ruge, John A — *Cartoonist*
240 Bronxville Road, #B-4, Bronxville, NY 10708, USA

Rugers, Martin — *Astronomer*
%University of Washington, Astronomy Dept, Seattle, WA 98195, USA

Ruijssenaars, Andries — *Businessman*
%Eagle-Picher Industries, 580 Walnut St, Cincinnati, OH 45202, USA

Ruisi, Christopher S — *Businessman*
%USLife Corp, 125 Maiden Lane, New York, NY 10038, USA

Ruiz Garcia, Samuel — *Religious Leader*
%San Cristobal Diocese, 20 De Noviembre 1, San Cristobal de Casas, Mexico

Ruiz, Alejandro R — *WW II Army Hero (CMH)*
32146 Road 124, Visalia, CA 93291, USA

Ruiz, Hilton — *Jazz Pianist*
%Ralph Mercado Mgmt, 568 Broadway, #608, New York, NY 10012, USA

Rukavishnikov, Nikolai N — *Cosmonaut*
%Potchta Kosmonavtov, Moskovskoi Oblasti, 141160 Syvisdny Goroduk, Russia

Rukeyser, Louis R — *Commentator*
PO Box 25527, Alexandria, VA 22313, USA

Rukeyser, William S — *Publisher*
1509 Rudder Lane, Knoxville, TN 37919, USA

Ruklick, Joe — *Basketball Player*
1300 Central St, Evanston, IL 60201, USA

Ruland, Jeff — *Basketball Player, Coach*
%Iona College, Athletic Dept, New Rochelle, NY 10801, USA

Rule, Janice *Actress*
%Susan Smith, 121 N San Vicente Blvd, Beverly Hills, CA 90211, USA
Rummenigge, Karl-Heinz *Soccer Player*
Eichleite 4, 80231 Grunwald, Germany
Rumsfeld, Donald H *Secretary, Defense; Businessman*
400 N Michigan Ave, #405, Chicago, IL 60611, USA
Runcie of Cuddesdon, Robert A K *Archbishop, Canterbury*
26-A Jennings Road, Saint Albans, Herts AL1 4PD, England
Runco, Mario, Jr *Astronaut*
%NASA, Johnson Space Center, 2101 NASA Road, Houston, TX 77058, USA
Rundgren, Todd *Singer, Songwriter*
%Panacea Entertainment, 2705 Glendower Road, Los Angeles, CA 90027, USA
Runge, Edward P (Ed) *Baseball Umpire*
649 Calle de la Sierra, El Cajon, CA 92019, USA
Runnells, Thomas W (Tom) *Baseball Manager*
7023 Westwind Dr, Sylvania, OH 43560, USA
Runyan, Joe *Dog Sled Racer*
%Rt 1, 314.5 Parks Highway, Nenana, AK 99760, USA
Runyan, Paul *Golfer*
PO Box 1908, Pinehurst, NC 28370, USA
Runyon, Edwin *Religious Leader*
%General Assn of General Baptists, 100 Stinson Dr, Popular Bluff, MO 63901, USA
Runyon, Marvin T, Jr *Government Official*
%US Postal Service, 475 L'Enfant Plaza SW, Washington, DC 20260, USA
RuPaul *Entertainer*
%World of Wonder, 1157 N Highland Ave, #100, Los Angeles, CA 90038, USA
Ruscha, Edward *Artist*
13775 Valley Vista Blvd, Sherman Oaks, CA 91423, USA
Ruscio, Al *Actor*
%Paul Kohner, 9300 Wilshire Blvd, #555, Beverly Hills, CA 90212, USA
Rush, Barbara *Actress*
1708 Tropical Ave, Beverly Hills, CA 90210, USA
Rush, Geoffrey *Actor*
%Creative Artists Agency, 9830 Wilshire Blvd, Beverly Hills, CA 90212, USA
Rush, Jennifer *Singer*
%British & Int'l Artists, 500 Waterman Ave, #191, East Providence, RI 02914, USA
Rush, Merrilee *Singer/Songwriter*
%Sterling Talent, PO Box 231059, Tigard, OR 97281, USA
Rush, Richard W *Movie Director, Producer*
821 Stradella Road, Los Angeles, CA 90077, USA
Rush, Robert J (Bob) *Football Player*
8201 Scruggs Drive, Germantown, TN 38138, USA
Rushdie, A Salman *Writer*
%Deborah Rodgers Ltd, 49 Blenhiem Crescent, London W11, England
Ruskin, Uzi *Businessman*
%United Merchants/Manufacturers, 2 Executive Dr, #780, Fort Lee, NJ 07024, USA
Russ, Tim *Actor*
%Stone Manners, 8091 Selma Ave, Los Angeles, CA 90046, USA
Russ, William *Actor*
2973 Passmore Dr, Los Angeles, CA 90068, USA
Russell, Betsy *Actress*
13926 Magnolia Blvd, Sherman Oaks, CA 91423, USA
Russell, Brenda *Singer, Songwriter, Keyboardist*
%Turner Mgmt, 3500 W Olive Ave, #680, Burbank, CA 91505, USA
Russell, Bryon *Basketball Player*
%Utah Jazz, Delta Center, 301 W South Temple, Salt Lake City, UT 84101, USA
Russell, Campy *Basketball Player*
66 Earlmoor Blvd, Pontiac, MI 48341, USA
Russell, Cazzie *Basketball Player*
%Savannah College of Art & Design, Athletic Dept, Savannah, GA 31402, USA
Russell, Charles (Chuck) *Movie Director*
%United Talent Agency, 9560 Wilshire Blvd, #500, Beverly Hills, CA 90212, USA
Russell, Charles T *Businessman*
%Visa International Service, 3125 Clearview Way, San Mateo, CA 94402, USA
Russell, David O *Movie Director*
%United Talent Agency, 9560 Wilshire Blvd, #500, Beverly Hills, CA 90212, USA
Russell, Donald Stuart *Governor/Senator, SC; Judge*
%US Court of Appeals, PO Box 1985, Spartanburg, SC 29304, USA

R

Russell, Frank E — *Businessman*
%Central Newspapers, 135 N Pennsylvania Ave, Indianapolis, IN 46204, USA

Russell, Fred M — *Sportswriter*
500 Elmington Ave, #525, Nashville, TN 37205, USA

Russell, Galen — *Photographer*
%Mountain Light Photography, 1466 66th St, Emeryville, CA 94608, USA

Russell, George A — *Jazz Drummer, Pianist, Composer*
%Joel Chriss, 300 Mercer St, #3-J, New York, NY 10003, USA

Russell, Harold — *Actor, Government Official*
34 Old Town Road, Hyannis, MA 02601, USA

Russell, James S — *Navy Admiral, Hero*
7734 Walnut Ave SW, Tacoma, WA 98498, USA

Russell, Jane — *Actress*
2935 Torito Road, Montecito, CA 93108, USA

Russell, Ken — *Movie Director*
16 Salisbury Place, London W1H 1FH, England

Russell, Keri — *Actress*
520 Salerno Dr, Pacific Palisades, CA 90272, USA

Russell, Kimberly — *Actress*
%Paul Kohner, 9300 Wilshire Blvd, #555, Beverly Hills, CA 90212, USA

Russell, Kurt — *Actor*
229 E Gainsborough Road, Thousand Oaks, CA 91360, USA

Russell, Leon — *Singer, Songwriter*
%Brad Davis, PO Box 158125, Nashville, TN 37215, USA

Russell, Leonard — *Football Player*
752 S Rock Garden Circle, Anaheim, CA 92808, USA

Russell, Mark — *Comedian*
2800 Wisconsin Ave NW, Washington, DC 20007, USA

Russell, Nipsy — *Comedian*
353 W 57th St, New York, NY 10019, USA

Russell, Theresa — *Actress*
9454 Lloydcrest Dr, Beverly Hills, CA 90210, USA

Russell, William E (Bill) — *Baseball Player, Manager*
11430 S Fulton Ave, Tulsa, OK 74137, USA

Russell, William F (Bill) — *Basketball Player, Coach*
PO Box 1200, Mercer Island, WA 98040, USA

Russell, William L — *Geneticist*
130 Tabor Road, Oak Ridge, TN 37830, USA

Russert, Timothy J (Tim) — *Commentator*
%"Meet the Press" Show, NBC-TV, 4001 Nebraska Ave NW, Washington, DC 20016, USA

Russi, Bernhard — *Skier*
Postfach, 6490 Andermatt, Switzerland

Russo, Gianni — *Actor*
%Sanders Agency, 8831 Sunset Blvd, #304, Los Angeles, CA 90069, USA

Russo, Rene — *Actress*
10435 Whipple St, North Hollywood, CA 91602, USA

Russo, Richard — *Writer*
%Random House, 201 E 50th St, New York, NY 10022, USA

Rust, Edward B, Jr — *Businessman*
%State Farm Auto Insurance, 1 State Farm Plaza, Bloomington, IL 61710, USA

Rutan, Elbert L (Burt) — *Airplane Designer*
%Scaled Composites, Mojave Airport, Hangar 78, Mojave, CA 93501, USA

Rutan, Richard G — *Experimental Airplane Pilot, Designer*
%Voyager Aircraft Inc, Mojave Airport, Hangar 77, Mojave, CA 93501, USA

Ruth, Mike — *Football Player*
7 Greenfield Circle, Norton, MA 02766, USA

Rutherford, Ann — *Actress*
826 Greenway Dr, Beverly Hills, CA 90210, USA

Rutherford, John S (Johnny), III — *Auto Racing Driver*
4919 Black Oak Lane, Fort Worth, TX 76114, USA

Rutherford, Kelly — *Actress*
PO Box 492266, Los Angeles, CA 90049, USA

Rutigliano, Sam — *Football Coach*
%Liberty University, Athletic Dept, Lynchburg, VA 24506, USA

Rutledge, William P — *Businessman*
%Teledyne Inc, 2049 Century Park East, Los Angeles, CA 90067, USA

Ruttan, Susan — *Actress*
4312 Babcock Ave, #5, Studio City, CA 91604, USA

Rutter, John M *Composer, Conductor*
Old Lacey's, St John's St, Duxford, Cambridge, England
Ruttgers, Jurgen *Government Official, Germany*
%BM fur Bildung/Technologie, Heinemannstr 2, 53175 Bonn, Germany
Ruud, Birger *Skier, Ski Jumper*
Munstersvei 20, 3600 Kongsberg, Norway
Ruud, Sigmund *Skier, Ski Jumper*
Kirkeveien 57, Oslo 3, Norway
Ruuska Percy, Sylvia *Swimmer*
4216 College View Way, Carmichael, CA 95608, USA
Ruusuvuori, Aarno E *Architect*
Annankatu 15 B 10, 00120 Helsinki 12, Finland
Ruwe, Robert P *Judge*
%US Tax Court, 400 2nd St NW, Washington, DC 20217, USA
Rwigema, Pierre Claver *Prime Minister, Rwanda*
%Prime Minister's Office, Assembly Building, Church St, Kigali, Rwanda
Ryan, Arthur F *Businessman*
%Prudential Insurance, Prudential Plaza, 751 Broad St, Newark, NJ 07102, USA
Ryan, Ashton J, Jr *Financier*
%First National Bank (NO), 210 Baronne St, New Orleans, LA 70112, USA
Ryan, Debbie *Basketball Coach*
%University of Virginia, Athletic Dept, PO Box 3785, Charlottesville, VA 22903, USA
Ryan, Fran *Actress*
22440 Clarendon St, #102, Woodland Hills, CA 91367, USA
Ryan, Frank B *Football Player*
282 Prospect St, New Haven, CT 06511, USA
Ryan, John E *Financier*
%Resolution Trust Corp, 801 17th St NW, Washington, DC 20434, USA
Ryan, John T, III *Businessman*
%Mine Safety Appliances, 121 Gamma Dr, Pittsburgh, PA 15238, USA
Ryan, L Nolan *Baseball Player*
PO Box 670, Alvin, TX 77512, USA
Ryan, Meg *Actress*
11718 Barrington Court, #508, Los Angeles, CA 90049, USA
Ryan, Michael E (Mike) *Air Force General*
Chief of Staff, HqUSAF, Pentagon, Washington, DC 20330, USA
Ryan, Michael M *Actor*
48 E 3rd St, New York, NY 10003, USA
Ryan, Mitchell *Actor*
30355 Mulholland Dr, Cornell, CA 91301, USA
Ryan, Patrick G *Businessman*
%Aon Corp, 123 N Wacker Dr, Chicago, IL 60606, USA
Ryan, Tim *Sportscaster*
%CBS-TV, Sports Dept, 51 W 52nd St, New York, NY 10019, USA
Ryan, William J *Financier*
%People Heritage Financial, 1 Portland Square, Portland, ME 04101, USA
Rybkin, Ivan *Government Official, Russia*
%National Security Council, 4 Staraya Ploschad, 103073 Moscow, Russia
Rydell, Bobby *Singer, Actor*
917 Bryn Mawr Ave, Narbeth, PA 19072, USA
Rydell, Mark *Movie Director*
1 Topsail St, Marina del Rey, CA 90292, USA
Ryder, Winona *Actress*
%Three Arts Entertainment, 9460 Wilshire Blvd, #700, Beverly Hills, CA 90212, USA
Rykiel, Sonia F *Fashion Designer*
175 Blvd St Germain, 75006 Paris, France
Ryman, Robert T *Artist*
17 W 16th St, New York, NY 10011, USA
Rypien, Mark R *Football Player*
%Mark Rypien Motorsports, 177 Knob Hill Road, Mooresville, NC 28115, USA
Rysanek, Leonie *Opera Singer*
83115 Neubeurern, Germany
Rysanek, Sonia *Opera Singer*
%Herbert Breslin, 119 W 57th St, New York, NY 10019, USA
Ryumin, Valery V *Cosmonaut*
%Potchta Kosmonavtov, Moskovskoi Oblasti, 141160 Syvisdny Goroduk, Russia
Ryun, James R (Jim) *Track Athlete; Representative, KS*
Rt 3, PO Box 62-B, Lawrence, KS 66044, USA

R

Rutter - Ryun

Saam, Byrum *Sportscaster*
%Philadelphia Phillies, Veterans Stadium, PO Box 7575, Philadelphia, PA 19101, USA

Saar, Bettye *Artist*
8074 Willow Glen Road, Los Angeles, CA 90046, USA

Saari, Roy *Swimmer*
PO Box 7086, Mammoth Lakes, CA 93546, USA

Saatchi, Charles *Businessman*
%Saatchi & Saatchi Co, 80 Charlotte St, London W1A 1AQ, England

Saban, Louis H (Lou) *Football Player, Coach*
1020 N Broadway, Milwaukee, WI 53202, USA

Sabatini, Gabriela *Tennis Player*
Ap Int 14, Suc 27, 1427 Buenos Aires, Argentina

Sabatino, Michael *Actor*
%Paul Kohner, 9300 Wilshire Blvd, #555, Beverly Hills, CA 90212, USA

Sabato, Antonio, Jr *Actor, Model*
PO Box 12073, Marina del Rey, CA 90295, USA

Sabato, Ernesto *Writer*
Severino Langeri 3135, Santos Lugares, Argentina

Sabattani, Aurelio Cardinal *Religious Leader*
Palazzo del Tribunale, Piazza S Marta, 00120 Vatican City

Saberhagen, Bret W *Baseball Player*
1735 SW MockingbirdDr, Port Saint Lucie, FL 34986, USA

Sabo, Christopher A (Chris) *Baseball Player*
15003 Grandville, Detroit, MI 48223, USA

Sabonis, Arvydas *Basketball Player*
%Portland Trail Blazers, 1 N Center Court, #200, Portland, OR 97227, USA

Sacco, Albert, Jr *Astronaut*
%Northeastern University, Chemical Engineering Dept, Boston, MA 02115, USA

Sachs, Gloria *Fashion Designer*
%Gloria Sachs Designs Ltd, 550 7th Ave, New York, NY 10018, USA

Sachs, Robert G *Physicist*
5490 South Shore Dr, Chicago, IL 60615, USA

Sack, Steve *Cartoonist (Professor Doodle's)*
%Minneapolis Star & Tribune, 425 Portland Ave, Minneapolis, MN 55488, USA

Sacks, Greg *Auto Racing Driver*
4381 S Atlantic Ave, #503, New Smyrna, FL 32169, USA

Sacks, Oliver W *Physician, Neurologist, Writer*
299 W 12th St, New York, NY 10014, USA

Sadat, Jehan El- *Social Activist*
%University of Maryland, Int'l Development Center, College Park, MD 20742, USA

Saddler, Donald E *Choreographer, Dancer*
%Coleman-Rosenberg Agency, 210 E 58th St, New York, NY 10022, USA

Saddler, Sandy *Boxer*
%J Denise Saddler Alicea, Anheuser-Busch, 350 Park Ave, New York, NY 10022, USA

Sade (Adu) *Singer, Songwriter*
41/45 Beak St, London W1R 3LE, England

Sadecki, Raymond M (Ray) *Baseball Player*
4237 E Clovis Ave, Mesa, AZ 85206, USA

Sadik, Nafis *Government Official, Pakistan*
%United Nations Population Fund, 220 E 42nd St, New York, NY 10017, USA

Sadoulet, Bernard *Astronomer*
2824 Forest Ave, Berkeley, CA 94705, USA

Saeki, Akira *Businessman*
%Sharp Corp, 22-22 Nagaikecho, Abenoku, Osaka 543, Japan

Safar, Peter *Surgeon*
%University of Pittsburgh, Medical Center, Surgery Dept, Pittsburgh, PA 15260, USA

Safdie, Moshe *Architect*
100 Properzi Way, Somerville, MA 02143, USA

Safer, Morley *Commentator*
%"Sixty Minutes" Show, CBS-TV, 555 W 57th St, New York, NY 10019, USA

Safire, William *Journalist, Writer*
6200 Elmwood Road, Chevy Chase, MD 20815, USA

Sagal, Katey *Actress*
7095 Hollywood Blvd, #792, Los Angeles, CA 90028, USA

Sagan, Francoise *Writer*
%Equemauville, 14600 Honfleur, France

Sagansky, Jeff *Entertainment Executive*
35 E 76th St, New York, NY 10021, USA

Sagdeev, Roald Z *Physicist*
%Space Research Institute, Profsoyuznaya 84/32, 11780 Moscow B-485, Russia
Sagebrecht, Marianne *Actress*
Kaulbachstr 61, Ruckgeb, 80539 Munich, Germany
Sager, Carole Bayer *Singer, Songwriter*
10761 Bellagio Road, Los Angeles, CA 90077, USA
Sager, Ruth *Geneticist*
%Dana-Farber Cancer Institute, 44 Binney St, Boston, MA 02115, USA
Saget, Bob *Actor*
%Brillstein/Grey, 9150 Wilshire Blvd, #350, Beverly Hills, CA 90212, USA
Sahagun, Elena *Actress*
%William Morris Agency, 151 S El Camino Dr, Beverly Hills, CA 90212, USA
Sahl, Mort *Comedian*
2325 San Ysidro Dr, Beverly Hills, CA 90210, USA
Sahm, Doug *Singer, Songwriter*
%Pilot Mgmt, 209 10th Ave S, #509, Nashville, TN 37203, USA
Said Mohamed Djohar *President, Comoros Islands*
%President's Office, Boite Postale 421, Moroni, Comoros Islands
Sailer, Toni *Skier*
%Gundhabing 19, 6370 Kitzbuhl, Austria
Saimes, George *Football Player, Executive*
%Washington Redskins, 21300 Redskin Park Dr, Ashburn, VA 20147, USA
Sain, John F (Johnny) *Baseball Player*
2 S 707 Ave Latour, Oakbrook, IL 60521, USA
Saint James, Susan *Actress*
%Marlene Fait, 854 N Genesee Ave, Los Angeles, CA 90046, USA
Saint Laurent, Yves *Fashion Designer*
5 Ave du Marceau, 75016 Paris
Saint, Eva Marie *Actress*
%Paul Kohner, 9300 Wilshire Blvd, #555, Beverly Hills, CA 90212, USA
Saint-Jean, Olivier *Basketball Player*
%Sacramento Kings, 1 Sports Parkway, Sacramento, CA 95834, USA
Saint-Subber, Arnold *Theater Producer*
116 E 64th St, New York, NY 10021, USA
Sainte-Marie, Buffy *Singer, Songwriter*
%Einstein Brothers, 20 Duncan St, #200, Toronto ON M5H 3G8, Canada
Saito, Eishiro *Businessman*
%Nippon Steel, 2-6-3 Otemachi, Chiyodaku, Tokyo, Japan
Sajak, Pat *Entertainer*
%"Wheel of Fortune" Show, 3400 Riverside Dr, #201, Burbank, CA 91505, USA
Sakabe, Takeo *Businessman*
%Ashai Glass, 2-1-1 Marunouchi, Chiyodaku, Tokyo 100, Japan
Sakamoto, Ryuichi *Composer*
111 4th Ave, #11-K, New York, NY 10003, USA
Sakamoto, Soichi *Swimming Coach*
768 McCully St, Honolulu, HI 96826, USA
Sakamura, Ken *Computer Inventor*
%University of Tokyo, Information Science Dept, Tokyo, Japan
Sakic, Joe *Hockey Player*
%Colorado Avalanche, McNichols Arena, 1635 Clay St, Denver, CO 80204, USA
Sakmann, Bert *Nobel Medicine Laureate*
%Max Planck Institute, Jahnstr 39, 69120 Heidelberg, Germany
Saks, Gene *Theater Director, Actor*
7095 Hollywood Blvd, Los Angeles, CA 90028, USA
Salaam, Rashaan *Football Player*
8132 Brookhaven Road, San Diego, CA 92114, USA
Salam, Saeb *Prime Minister, Lebanon*
32 Route de Malagnou, 1208 Geneva, Switzerland
Salans, Lester B *Physician*
%Sandoz Research Institute, Rt 10, Hanover, NJ 07936, USA
Salazar, Alberto *Marathon Runner*
%Int'l Management Group, 1 Erieview Plaza, #1300, Cleveland, OH 44114, USA
Saldana, Theresa *Actress*
%David Shapira, 15301 Ventura Blvd, #345, Sherman Oaks, CA 91403, USA
Saldich, Robert J *Businessman*
%Raychem Corp, 300 Constitution Dr, Menlo Park, CA 94025, USA
Saleh, Ali Abdullah *President, Yemen Arab Republic; General*
%President's Office, Zubairy St, Sana'a, Yemen Arab Republic

Saleh, Jaime *Governor, Netherlands Antilles*
Fort Amsterdam 2, Willemstad, Curacao, Netherlands Antilles

Salenger, Meredith *Actress*
%Writers & Artists, 924 Westwood Blvd, #900, Los Angeles, CA 90024, USA

Salerno-Sonnenberg, Nadja *Concert Violinist*
%Columbia Artists Mgmt Inc, 165 W 57th St, New York, NY 10019, USA

Sales, Eugenio de Araujo Cardinal *Religious Leader*
Palacio Sao Joaquim, Rua da Gloria 446, 20241 Rio de Janeiro RJ, Brazil

Sales, Soupy *Comedian*
245 E 35th St, New York, NY 10016, USA

Salgado, Sebastiano *Photographer*
%Aperture Foundation, 20 E 23rd St, New York, NY 10010, USA

Salhany, Lucille S *Television Executive*
%Twentieth Century Fox TV, 10201 W Pico Blvd, Los Angeles, CA 90064, USA

Saliba, Metropolitan Primate Philip *Religious Leader*
%Antiochian Orthodox Christian Diocese, 358 Mountain Road, Englewood, NJ 07631, USA

Saliers, Emily *Singer, Songwriter (Indigo Girls)*
%Ruseel Carter Artist Mgmt, 315 Ponce de Leon Ave, #756, Decatur, GA 30030, USA

Salim, Salim Ahmed *Prime Minister, Tanzania*
%Organization of African Unity, PO Box 3243, Addis Ababa, Ethiopia

Salinger, J(erome) D(avid) *Writer*
RR 3, Box 176, Cornish Flat, NH 03745, USA

Salinger, Matt *Actor*
%Bresler Kelly Assoc, 15760 Ventura Blvd, #1730, Encino, CA 91436, USA

Salinger, Pierre E G *Senator, CA; Journalist*
3904 Hillandale Court NW, Washington, DC 20007, USA

Salizzoni, Frank L *Businessman*
%USAir Group, 2345 Crystal Dr, Arlington, VA 22202, USA

Salkind, Alexander *Movie Producer*
Pinewood Studios, Iver Heath, Iver, Bucks SL0 0NH, England

Salkind, Ilya *Movie Producer*
Pinewood Studios, Iver Heath, Iver, Bucks SL0 0NH, England

Salle, David *Artist*
%Larry Gagosian Gallery, 980 Madison Ave, #PH, New York, NY 10021, USA

Salley, John *Basketball Player*
429 Page Ave NE, Atlanta, GA 30307, USA

Sallinen, Aulis H *Composer*
Runneberginkatu 37-A, 00100 Helsinki 10, Finland

Sallis, Peter *Actor*
%Jonathan Altaras, 27 Floral St, London WC2E 9DP, England

Salminen, Matti *Opera Singer*
%Mariedi Anders Artists Mgmt, 535 El Camino del Mar, San Francisco, CA 94121, USA

Salmons, Steve *Volleyball Player*
1717 N El Dorado Ave, Ontario, CA 91764, USA

Salomon, Mikael *Cinematographer*
PO Box 2230, Los Angeles, CA 90078, USA

Salonen, Esa-Pekka *Conductor*
%Los Angeles Philharmonic, Music Center, 135 N Grand, Los Angeles, CA 90012, USA

Salonga, Lea *Singer, Actress*
%Atlantic Records, 75 Rockefeller Plaza, New York, NY 10019, USA

Salpeter, Edwin E *Physicist*
116 Westbourne Lane, Ithaca, NY 14850, USA

Salt, Jennifer *Actress*
9045 Elevado St, West Hollywood, CA 90069, USA

Saltykov, Aleksey A *Movie Director*
%Institute Mosfilmosvsky Per 4-A #104, 119285 Moscow, Russia

Saltzman, Robert P *Businessman*
%Jackson National Life, 5901 Executive Dr, Lansing, MI 48911, USA

Salvador, Sal *Jazz Guitarist, Composer*
315 W 53rd St, New York, NY 10019, USA

Salzman, Pnina *Concert Pianist*
20 Dubnov St, Tel-Aviv, Israel

Sam the Sham (Domingo S Samudio) *Singer*
3667 Tutwiler Ave, Memphis, TN 38122, USA

Samaranch Torello, Juan Antonio *International Olympics Official*
Avenida Pau Casals 24, 08021 Barcelona 6, Spain

Samaras, Lucas *Sculptor, Photographer*
%Pace Gallery, 32 E 57th St, New York, NY 10022, USA

Sambora, Richie *Singer, Songwriter (Bon Jovi)*
%Bon Jovi Mgmt, 205 W 57th St, #603-5, New York, NY 10019, USA
Samios, Nicholas P *Science Administrator, Physicist*
%Brookhaven National Laboratory, Director's Office, Upton, NY 11973, USA
Sammet, Rolf *Businessman*
%Hoechst, Postfach 800320, 65926 Frankfurt/Main, Germany
Samms, Emma *Actress*
2934 1/2 N Beverly Glen Circle, #417, Los Angeles, CA 90077, USA
Sampaio, Jorge *President, Portugal*
%President's Office, Palacio de Belem, 1300 Lisbon, Portugal
Sample, Joe *Jazz Pianist*
%Performers of the World, 8901 Melrose Ave, #200, West Hollywood, CA 90069, USA
Sample, Steven B *Educator*
%University of Southern California, President's Office, Los Angeles, CA 90089, USA
Sampras, Pete *Tennis Player*
6352 MacLaurin Dr, Tampa, FL 33647, USA
Sampson, Kelvin *Basketball Coach*
%University of Oklahoma, Lloyd Noble Complex, Norman, OK 73019, USA
Sampson, Ralph *Basketball Player, Coach*
3825 Pupert Lane, Richmond, VA 23233, USA
Sampson, Robert *Actor*
%Twentieth Century, 15315 Magnolia Blvd, #429, Sherman Oaks, CA 91403, USA
Sams, David E, Jr *Businessman*
%Connecticut Mutual Life, 140 Garden St, Hartford, CT 06154, USA
Sams, John B, Jr *Air Force General*
Vice Commander, Air Mobility Command, Scott Air Force Base, IL 62225, USA
Samuelson, Don *Governor, ID*
Rt 3, PO Box 300, Sandpoint, ID 83864, USA
Samuelson, Paul A *Nobel Economics Laureate*
94 Somerset St, Belmont, MA 02178, USA
Samuelsson, Bengt I *Nobel Medicine Laureate*
%Karolinska Institute, Chemistry Dept, 171 77 Stockholm, Sweden
Samuelsson, Kjell *Hockey Player*
7 Knottingham Dr, Voorhees, NJ 08043, USA
Samuelsson, Ulf *Hockey Player*
53 Walker Ave, Rye, NY 10580, USA
San Juan, Olga *Actress*
4845 Willowcrest Ave, Studio City, CA 91601, USA
Sanborn, David *Jazz Saxophonist*
%Creative Artists Agency, 9830 Wilshire Blvd, Beverly Hills, CA 90212, USA
Sanchez Vicario, Arantxa *Tennis Player*
Sabino de Arana 28, #6-1-A, 08028 Barcelona, Spain
Sanchez, Emilio *Artist*
333 E 30th St, New York, NY 10016, USA
Sanchez, Emilio *Tennis Player*
Sabiono de Avena 28, Barcelona 46, Spain
Sanchez, Jose Cardinal *Religious Leader*
%Congregation for Evangelization of Peoples, 00120 Vatican City
Sanchez, Poncho *Jazz Drummer*
PO Box 59236, Norwalk, CA 90652, USA
Sanchez-Gijon, Aitana *Actress*
%Alsira Garcia-Maroto, Gran Via 63, 3 Izda, 28013 Madrid, Spain
Sanchez-Vilella, Roberto *Governor, PR*
414 Munoz Rivera Ave #7-A, Stop 31-1/2, Hato Rey, PR 00918, USA
Sand, Paul *Actor*
%Writers & Artists, 924 Westwood Blvd, #900, Los Angeles, CA 90024, USA
Sand, Todd *Figure Skater*
2973 Harbor Blvd, #468, Costa Mesa, CA 92626, USA
Sanda, Dominique *Actress*
%Artmedia, 10 Ave George V, 75008 Paris, France
Sandage, Allan R *Astronomer*
%Hale Observatories, 813 Santa Barbara St, Pasadena, CA 91101, USA
Sandberg, Michael G R *Financier*
54-A Hyde Park Gate, London SW7 5EB, England
Sandberg, Ryne D *Baseball Player*
11809 S Montezuma Court, Phoenix, AZ 85044, USA
Sandbulte, Arend J *Businessman*
%Minnesota Power, 30 W Superior St, Duluth, MN 55802, USA

Sambora - Sandbulte

Sander, Jil	*Fashion Designer*
Osterfeldstr 32-34, 22529 Hamburg, Germany	
Sanderling, Kurt	*Conductor*
Am Iderfenngraben 47, 13156 Berlin, Germany	
Sanders, Barry	*Football Player*
%Detroit Lions, Silverdome, 1200 Featherstone Road, Pontiac, MI 48342, USA	
Sanders, Bill	*Cartoonist*
PO Box 661, Milwaukee, WI 53201, USA	
Sanders, Carl E	*Governor, GA*
1400 Candler Building, Atlanta, GA 30043, USA	
Sanders, Deion L	*Football, Baseball Player*
125 W Meadow Court, Alpharetta, GA 30004, USA	
Sanders, Doug	*Golfer*
%Doug Sanders Enterprises, 8828 Sandringham Dr, Houston, TX 77024, USA	
Sanders, James C	*Government Official*
%Small Business Administration, 1441 "C" St NW, Washington, DC 20416, USA	
Sanders, Jonathan (Jon)	*Yachtsman*
28 Portland St, Redlands 6009 WA, Australia	
Sanders, Lawrence	*Writer*
%G P Putnam's Sons, 200 Madison Ave, New York, NY 10016, USA	
Sanders, Lewis A	*Financier*
%Sanford C Bernstein Co, 767 5th Ave, New York, NY 10153, USA	
Sanders, Marlene	*Commentator*
%WNET-TV, News Dept, 356 W 58th St, New York, NY 10019, USA	
Sanders, Pharoah	*Blues Saxophonist*
%Joel Chriss, 300 Mercer St, #3-J, New York, NY 10003, USA	
Sanders, Richard	*Actor*
PO Box 1644, Woodinville, WA 98072, USA	
Sanders, Steve	*Singer (Oak Ridge Boys)*
329 Rockland Road, Hendersonville, TN 37075, USA	
Sanders, Summer	*Swimmer*
730 Sunrise Ave, Roseville, CA 95661, USA	
Sanders, Tom (Satch)	*Basketball Player, Executive*
114 The Fenway, Boston, MA 02115, USA	
Sanders, W J (Jerry), III	*Businessman*
%Advanced Micro Devices, 1 AMD Place, PO Box 3453, Sunnyvale, CA 94088, USA	
Sanders, Wayne R	*Businessman*
%Kimberly-Clark Corp, PO Box 619100, Dallas, TX 75261, USA	
Sanderson, Derek	*Hockey Player*
267 Manning St, Needham, MA 02192, USA	
Sanderson, Geoff	*Hockey Player*
2710 Plaza Road, Whitefish, MT 59937, USA	
Sanderson, Peter	*Artist*
1105 Shell Gate Plaza, Alameda, CA 94501, USA	
Sanderson, Tessa	*Track Athlete*
%Tee-Dee Promotion, Atlas Bus Center, Oxgate Lane, London NW2 7HU, England	
Sanderson, William	*Actor*
13047 Bloomfield St, Studio City, CA 91604, USA	
Sanderson, Wimp	*Basketball Coach*
%University of Arkansas at Little Rock, Athletic Dept, Little Rock, AR 72204, USA	
Sandeson, William S	*Editorial Cartoonist*
119 W Sherwood Terrace, Fort Wayne, IN 46807, USA	
Sandford (Camp), John	*Writer*
%G P Putnam's Sons, 200 Madison Ave, New York, NY 10016, USA	
Sandiford, L Erskine	*Prime Minister, Barbados*
%Prime Minister's Office, Bay St, Bridgetown, Barbados	
Sandler, Adam	*Actor, Comedian*
5420 Worster Ave, Van Nuys, CA 91401, USA	
Sandler, Herbert M	*Financier*
%Golden West Financial, 1901 Harrison St, Oakland, CA 94612, USA	
Sandler, Marion O	*Financier*
%Golden West Financial, 1901 Harrison St, Oakland, CA 94612, USA	
Sandlund, Debra	*Actress*
%Innovative Artists, 1999 Ave of Stars, #2850, Los Angeles, CA 90067, USA	
Sandman, Mark	*Singer (Morphine)*
%Vertigo Touring, 48 Laight St, New York, NY 10013, USA	
Sandoval, Arturo	*Jazz Trumpeter*
%Turi's Music Enterprises, 101 S Royal Poinciana Blvd, Miami Springs, FL 33166, USA	

Sandoval, Hope *Singer (Mazzy Star)*
%Creative Artists Agency, 9830 Wilshire Blvd, Beverly Hills, CA 90212, USA
Sandoval, Miguel *Actor*
%Paradigm Agency, 10100 Santa Monica Blvd, #2500, Los Angeles, CA 90067, USA
Sandrelli, Stefania *Actress*
%TNA, Viale Parioli 41, 00197 Rome, Italy
Sandrich, Jay H *Television Director*
610 N Maple Dr, Beverly Hills, CA 90210, USA
Sands, Julian *Actor*
1287 Ozeta Terrace, Los Angeles, CA 90069, USA
Sands, Tommy *Singer, Actor*
%Arslanian Assoc, 6671 Sunset Blvd, #1502, Los Angeles, CA 90028, USA
Sandstrom, Sven *Financier*
%World Bank Group, 1818 "H" St NW, Washington, DC 20433, USA
Sandstrom, Tomas *Hockey Player*
145 Iron Run Road, Bethel Park, PA 15102, USA
Sandy B *Singer*
%Pyramid Entertainment, 89 5th Ave, #700, New York, NY 10003, USA
Sandy, Gary *Actor*
12810 Waddell St, North Hollywood, CA 91607, USA
Sanford, Charles S, Jr *Financier*
%Bankers Trust New York Corp, 280 Park Ave, New York, NY 10017, USA
Sanford, Isabel *Actress*
%Lemack Co, 215 S La Cienega Blvd, #203, Beverly Hills, CA 90211, USA
Sanford, Lucius M *Football Player*
8746 Carriage Hill Dr, Columbia, MD 21046, USA
Sanford, Richard D *Businessman*
%Intelligent Electronics, 411 Eagleview Blvd, Exton, PA 19341, USA
Sanford, Terry *Governor/Senator, NC; Educator*
1508 Pinecrest Road, Durham, NC 27705, USA
Sanger, David J *Concert Organist*
Old Wesleyan Chapel, Embleton near Cockermouth, Cumbria CA13 9YA, England
Sanger, Frederick *Nobel Chemistry Laureate*
Far Leys, Fen Lane, Swaffham Bulbeck, Cambridge CB5 0NJ, England
Sanger, Stephen W *Businessman*
%General Mills, PO Box 1113, Minneapolis, MN 55440, USA
Sangueli, Andrei *Prime Minister, Moldova*
%Prime Minister's Office, Piaca Maril Atuner, 277033 Kishineu, Moldova
Sanguinetti Cairolo, Julio Maria *President, Uruguay*
%President's Office, Ave Luis Alberto de Herrera 3350, Montevideo, Uruguay
Sano, Kenjiro *Businessman*
%Isuzu Motors Ltd, 6-26-1 Minamioi, Shinagawaku, Tokyo 140, Japan
Sansom, Bruce *Ballet Dancer*
%Royal Ballet, Bow St, London WC2E 9DD, England
Sansom, Chip *Cartoonist (Born Loser)*
1050 Erie Cliff Dr, Cleveland, OH 44107, USA
Santamaria, Mongo *Jazz Congo Drummer*
%Tropijazz Talent, 568 Broadway, #806, New York, NY 10012, USA
Santana, Carlos *Guitarist, Singer, Songwriter*
%Santana Mgmt, 121 Jordan St, San Rafael, CA 94901, USA
Santana, Manuel *Tennis Player*
%International Tennis Hall of Fame, 194 Bellevue Ave, Newport, RI 02840, USA
Santarelli, Eugene D (Gene) *Air Force General*
Vice Commander, Pacific Air Forces, 25 "E" St, Hickam Air Force Base, HI 96853, USA
Santer, Jacques *Premier, Luxembourg*
69 Rue J P Huberty, 1742 Luxembourg
Santiago, Benito R *Baseball Player*
13240 SW 28th Court, Davie, FL 33330, USA
Santiago, Lina *Singer*
%Famous Artists Agency, 1700 Broadway, #500, New York, NY 10019, USA
Santiago, Saundra *Actress*
%Paul Kohner, 9300 Wilshire Blvd, #555, Beverly Hills, CA 90212, USA
Santo, Ronald E (Ron) *Baseball Player*
1721 Meadow Lane, Bannockburn, IL 60015, USA
Santoni, Reni *Actor*
%Henderson/Hogan, 247 S Beverly Dr, #102, Beverly Hills, CA 90212, USA
Santorini, Paul E *Physicist, Engineer*
PO Box 49, Athens, Greece

S

Sandoval - Santorini

Santos, Joe *Actor*
%Paradigm Agency, 10100 Santa Monica Blvd, #2500, Los Angeles, CA 90067, USA

Saper, Clifford *Neurologist*
%Beth Israel Hospital, Neurogy Dept, 330 Brookline Ave, Boston, MA 02215, USA

Sara, Mia *Actress*
222 N Norton Ave, Los Angeles, CA 90004, USA

Sarafanov, Gennady V *Cosmonaut*
%Potchta Kosmonavtov, Moskovskoi Oblasti, 141160 Syvisdny Goroduk, Russia

Sarandon, Chris *Actor*
9540 Hidden Valley Road, Beverly Hills, CA 90210, USA

Sarandon, Susan *Actress*
%International Creative Mgmt, 40 W 57th St, New York, NY 10019, USA

Sarazen, Eugene (Gene) *Golfer*
%Emerald Beach Apartments, PO Box 667, Marco Island, FL 34146, USA

Sardi, Vincent, Jr *Restauranteur*
%Sardi's Restaurant, 234 W 44th St, New York, NY 10036, USA

Sarfati, Alain *Architect*
28 Rue Barbet Du Jouy, 75007 Paris, France

Sargent, Ben *Editorial Cartoonist*
%Austin American-Statesman, 166 E Riverside Dr, Austin, TX 78704, USA

Sargent, Francis W *Governor, MA*
Farm St, Dover, MA 02030, USA

Sargent, John T *Publisher*
Halsey Lane, Watermill, NY 11976, USA

Sargent, Joseph D *Movie Producer, Director*
33740 Pacific Coast Highway, Malibu, CA 90265, USA

Sarinic, Hrvoje *Prime Minister, Croatia*
%Prime Minister's Office, Opaticka 2, Zagreb, Croatia

Sarner, Craig *Hockey Player*
131 Oak Shore Dr, Burnsville, MN 55306, USA

Sarni, Vincent A *Baseball Executive*
%Pittsburgh Pirates, Three Rivers Stadium, Pittsburgh, PA 15212, USA

Sarnoff, William *Publisher*
%Warner Publishing Inc, 1325 Ave of Americas, New York, NY 10019, USA

Sarofim, Fayez S *Financier*
%Fayez Sarofim Co, 2 Houston Center, Houston, TX 77010, USA

Sarosi, Imre *Swimming Coach*
1033 Bp Harrer Dal Utca 4, Hungary

Sarraute, Nathalie *Writer*
12 Ave Pierre 1 de Serbie, 75116 Paris, France

Sarrazin, Michael *Actor*
9920 Beverly Grove Dr, Beverly Hills, CA 90210, USA

Sartzetakis, Christos *President, Greece*
%Presidential Palace, 7 Vas Georgiou B', Athens, Greece

Sasaki, Sadamichi *Businessman*
%Fuji Heavy Industries, 1-7-2 Nishi-Shinjuku, Shinjukuku, Tokyo 160, Japan

Sasser, Clarence E *Vietnam War Army Hero (CMH)*
13414 FM 521, Rosharon, TX 77583, USA

Sasser, E Rhone *Financier*
%United Carolina Bancshares, 127 W Webster St, Whiteville, NC 28472, USA

Sassoon, David *Fashion Designer*
%Bellville Sassoon, 18 Culford Gardens, London SW3 2ST, England

Sassoon, Vidal *Hair Stylist*
1163 Calle Vista Dr, Beverly Hills, CA 90210, USA

Satanowski, Robert *Conductor*
Ul Madalinskiego 50/52 M 1, 02-581 Warsaw, Poland

Satcher, David *Medical Administrator*
%Surgeon General's Office, 200 Independence Ave SW, Washington DC 20201, USA

Sather, Glen C *Hockey Coach, Executive*
%Edmonton Oilers, 11230 110th St, Edmonton AB T5G 3GB, Canada

Sato, Kazuo *Economist*
300 E 71st St, #15-H, New York, NY 10021, USA

Satowaki, Joseph Cardinal *Religious Leader*
%Archbishop's House, 5-3 Minami Yametecho, Nagasaki 850, Japan

Satre, Philip G *Businessman*
%Promus Companies, 1023 Cherry Road, Memphis, TN 38117, USA

Satriani, Joe *Singer, Guitarist*
%Bill Graham Mgmt, PO Box 429094, San Francisco, CA 94142, USA

Satrum, Jerry R — *Businessman*
%Georgia Gulf Corp, 400 Perimeter Center Terrace, Atlanta, GA 30346, USA

Satterfield, Paul — *Actor*
PO Box 6945, Beverly Hills, CA 90212, USA

Sauer, Henry J (Hank) — *Baseball Player*
207 Vallejo Court, Millbrae, CA 94030, USA

Sauer, Louis — *Architect*
3472 Marlowe St, Montreal PQ H4A 3L7, Canada

Saul, April — *Journalist*
%Philadelphia Inquirer, Editorial Dept, 400 N Broad St, Philadelphia, PA 19130, USA

Saul, Stephanie — *Journalist*
%Newsday, Editorial Dept, 235 Pinelawn Road, Melville, NY 11747, USA

Sauls, Don — *Religious Leader*
%Pentecostal Free Will Baptist Church, PO Box 1568, Dunn, NC 28335, USA

Saunders, Arlene — *Opera Singer*
535 E 86th St, New York, NY 10028, USA

Saunders, Cicely — *Hospice Movement Founder*
%St Christopher's Hospice, 51-53 Lawreie Park Road, Sydenham 6DZ, England

Saunders, George L, Jr — *Attorney*
179 E Lake Shore Dr, Chicago, IL 60611, USA

Saunders, Jennifer — *Actress*
%Peters Fraser Dunlop, Chelsea Harbour, Lots Rd, London SW10 0XF, England

Saunders, John — *Cartoonist (Mary Worth)*
%King Features Syndicate, 235 E 45th St, New York, NY 10017, USA

Saunders, John — *Sportscaster*
%ESPN-TV, Sports Dept, ESPN Plaza, Bristol, CT 06010, USA

Saunders, Phil (Flip) — *Basketball Coach*
%Minnesota Timberwolves, Target Center, 600 1st Ave N, Minneapolis, MN 55403, USA

Saunders, Townsend — *Wrestler*
733 E Chantilly Dr, Sierra Vista, AZ 85635, USA

Saundners, Ernest W — *Businessman*
%Arthur Guinness & Sons, 10 Albermarle St, London W1X 4AJ, England

Saura, Carlos — *Movie Director*
%Direccion General del Libro, Paseo De la Casrellana 109, Madrid 16, Spain

Sauter, Van Gordon — *Television Executive*
1815 Garden Highway, Sacramento, CA 95833, USA

Savage, Chantay — *Singer*
%Pyramid Entertainment, 89 5th Ave, #700, New York, NY 10003, USA

Savage, Elizabeth — *Actress*
%Agency For Performing Arts, 9200 Sunset Blvd, #900, Los Angeles, CA 90069, USA

Savage, Fred — *Actor*
1450 Belfast Dr, Los Angeles, CA 90069, USA

Savage, John — *Actor*
%Artists Agency, 10000 Santa Monica Blvd, #305, Los Angeles, CA 90067, USA

Savage, Randy (Macho Man) — *Wrestler*
%World Wrestling Federation, PO Box 105366, Atlanta, GA 30348, USA

Savant, Doug — *Actor*
1015 E Angeleno Ave, Burbank, CA 91501, USA

Savard, Denis — *Hockey Player*
175 E Kennedy Blvd, #175, Tampa, FL 33602, USA

Savard, Serge — *Hockey Player, Executive*
1790 Place de la Falaise, CP 369, St Bruno PQ J3V 5G8, Canada

Savary, Jerome — *Theater Director*
%Theatre National de Chaillot, 1 Place du Trocadero, 75116 Paris, France

Savidge, Jennifer — *Actress*
2705 Glenower Ave, Los Angeles, CA 90027, USA

Saviers, Grant — *Businessman*
%Adaptec, 691 S Milpitas Ave, Milpitas, CA 95035, USA

Saville, Curtis — *Long Distance Rower, Explorer*
RFD Box 44, West Charleston, VT 05872, USA

Saville, Kathleen — *Long Distance Rower, Explorer*
RFD Box 44, West Charleston, VT 05872, USA

Savimbi, Jonas — *Political Leader, Angola*
%Black Manafort Stone Kelly, 1111 N Fairfax St, Alexandria, VA 22314, USA

Savinykh, Viktor P — *Cosmonaut*
%Moscow State University, Gorochovskii 4, 103 064 Moscow, Russia

Savitskaya, Svetlana Y — *Cosmonaut*
%Russian Association, Khovanskaya Str 3, 129 515 Moscow, Russia

Savitsky, George *Football Player*
350 E Seabright Road, Ocean City, NJ 08226, USA

Savitt, Richard (Dick) *Tennis Player*
19 E 80th St, New York, NY 10021, USA

Savoy, Guy *Chef*
%Restaurant Guy Savoy, 18 Rue Troyon, 75017 Paris, France

Savvina, Iya S *Actress*
%Bolshaya Grunzinskaya St 12, #43, 123242 Moscow, Russia

Saw Maung *Prime Minister, Myanmar; Army General*
%Prime Minister's Office, Yangon, Myanmar

Sawalha, Julia *Actress*
%Associated International Mgmt, 5 Denmark St, London WC2H 8LP, England

Sawallisch, Wolfgang *Conductor*
Hinterm Bichl 2, 83224 Grassau, Germany

Sawaragi, Osamu *Businessman*
%National Steel Corp, 4100 Edison Lakes Parkway, Mishawaka, IN 46545, USA

Sawhill, John C *Government, Association Official*
%Nature Conservancy, 1815 N Lynn St, Arlington, VA 22209, USA

Sawyer, Amos *President, Liberia*
%President's Office, Executive Mansion, PO Box 9001, Monrovia, Liberia

Sawyer, Diane *Commentator*
%ABC-TV, News Dept, 77 W 66th St, New York, NY 10023, USA

Sawyer, Forrest *Commentator*
%"Day One" Show, 147 Columbus Ave, #800, New York, NY 10023, USA

Sawyer, James L *Labor Leader*
%Leather Workers Union, 11 Peabody Square, Peabody, MA 01960, USA

Sax, Stephen L (Steve) *Baseball Player*
7971 Park Dr, Fair Oaks, CA 95628, USA

Saxbe, William H *Attorney General; Senator, OH*
1171 N Ocean Blvd, Gulfstream, FL 33483, USA

Saxe, Adrian *Artist*
4835 N Figueroa St, Los Angeles, CA 90042, USA

Saxon, John *Actor*
2432 Banyan Dr, Los Angeles, CA 90049, USA

Sayed, Mostafa Amr El *Chemist*
579 Westover Dr NW, Atlanta, GA 30305, USA

Sayers, E Roger *Educator*
%University of Alabama, President's Office, Tuscaloosa, AL 35487, USA

Sayers, Gale E *Football Player*
624 Birch Road, Northbrook, IL 60062, USA

Sayles, John T *Movie Director*
225 Lafayette St, #1109, New York, NY 10012, USA

Sayles, Thomas D, Jr *Financier*
%Summit Bancorp, 750 Walnut Ave, Cranford, NJ 07016, USA

Scaasi, Arnold *Fashion Designer*
16 E 52nd St, New York, NY 10022, USA

Scacchi, Greta *Actress*
%Susan Smith, 121 N San Vicente Blvd, Beverly Hills, CA 90211, USA

Scaduto, Al *Cartoonist (They'll Do It Everytime)*
250 Birchwood Park Dr, Jericho Park, NY 11753, USA

Scaggs, Boz *Singer, Songwriter*
%HK Mgmt, 8900 Wilshire Blvd, #300, Beverly Hills, CA 90211, USA

Scales, Prunella M *Actress*
%Conway Van Gelder Robinson, 18-21 Jermyn St, London SW1Y 6NB, England

Scalfaro, Oscar L *President, Italy*
%President's Office, Palazzo del Quirinale, 00187 Rome, Italy

Scalia, Antonin *Supreme Court Justice*
%US Supreme Court, 1 1st St NE, Washington, DC 20543, USA

Scalia, Jack *Actor*
23049 Calvert St, Woodland Hills, CA 91367, USA

Scalise, George *Businessman*
%Apple Computer, 1 Infinite Dr, Cupertino, CA 95014, USA

Scancarelli, Jim *Cartoonist (Gasoline Alley)*
%Mark J Cohen, PO Box 1892, Santa Rosa, CA 95402, USA

Scanga, Italo *Artist*
7127 Olivetas, La Jolla, CA 92037, USA

Scanlan, Hugh P S *Labor Leader*
23 Seven Stones Dr, Broadstairs, Kent, England

Scarabelli, Michele *Actress*
4720 Vineland Ave, #216, North Hollywood, CA 91602, USA
Scarbath, John C (Jack) *Football Player*
736 Calvert Road, Rising Sun, MD 21911, USA
Scarbrough, W Carl *Labor Leader*
%Furniture Workers Union, 1910 Airlane Dr, Nashville, TN 37210, USA
Scardelletti, Robert A *Labor Leader*
%Transportation Communications Union, 3 Research Place, Rockville, MD 20850, USA
Scardino, Albert J *Journalist*
19 Empire House, Thurloe Place, London SW7 2RU, England
Scarfe, Gerald A *Cartoonist*
10 Cheyne Walk, London SW3, England
Scargill, Arthur *Labor Leader*
%National Union of Mineworkers, Holly St, Sheffield S1 2GT, England
Scarwid, Diana *Actress*
PO Box 3614, Savannah, GA 31414, USA
Scates, Al *Volleyball Coach*
8433 Apple Hill Court, Las Vegas, NV 89128, USA
Scavullo, Francesco *Photographer*
212 E 63rd St, New York, NY 10021, USA
Schaal, Richard *Actor*
%Atkins Assoc, 303 S Crescent Heights Blvd, Los Angeles, CA 90048, USA
Schaap, Richard J *Journalist*
%ABC-TV, Sports Dept, 77 W 66th St, New York, NY 10023, USA
Schachman, Howard K *Molecular Biochemist*
%University of California, Molecular Biology Dept, Berkeley, CA 94720, USA
Schadt, James P *Publisher*
%Reader's Digest Assn, Reader's Digest Road, Pleasantville, NY 10570, USA
Schaech, Johnathon *Actor*
1122 S Roxbury Dr, Beverly Hills, CA 90035, USA
Schaefer, Ernst J *Medical Researcher*
%Tufts University, Nutrition Research Center, Medford, MA 02155, USA
Schaefer, George L *Movie Director*
1040 Woodland Dr, Beverly Hills, CA 90210, USA
Schaefer, Henry F, III *Chemist*
%University of Georgia, Computational Quantum Chemistry Center, Athens, GA 30602, USA
Schaeffer, Susan F *Writer*
%Alfred A Knopf Inc, 201 E 50th St, New York, NY 10022, USA
Schaetzel, John R *Writer*
2 Bay Tree Lane, Bethesda, MD 20816, USA
Schafer, Edward T *Governor, ND*
%Governor's Office, State Capitol, 600 "E" Blvd, Bismarck, ND 58501, USA
Schaffel, Lewis *Basketball Executive*
%Miami Heat, Miami Arena, 100 NE 3rd Ave, Miami, FL 33132, USA
Schaffer, Peter L *Writer*
%McNaughton-Lowe Representation, 200 Fulham Road, London SW10, England
Schairer, George S *Aerospace Design Engineer*
4242 Hunts Point Road, Bellevue, WA 98004, USA
Schaller, George B *Zoologist*
90 Sentry Hill Road, Roxbury, CT 06783, USA
Schallert, William *Actor*
14920 Ramos Place, Pacific Palisades, CA 90272, USA
Schally, Andrew V *Nobel Medicine Laureate*
%Veterans Administration Hospital, 1601 Perdido St, New Orleans, LA 70112, USA
Schama, Simon M *Writer, Historian*
%Minda de Gunzburg European Studies Center, Adolphus Hall, Cambridge, MA 02138, USA
Schanberg, Sydney H *Journalist*
164 W 79th St, Apt 12-D, New York, NY 10024, USA
Schank, Roger C *Computer Scientist, Psychologist*
%Northwestern University, Learning Sciences Institute, Evanston, IL 60201, USA
Scharansky, Natan *Social Activist, Computer Scientist*
%Brandeis University, 415 South St, Waltham, MA 02154, USA
Scharer, Erich *Bobsled Athlete*
Grutstrasse 63, 8074 Herrliberg, Switzerland
Scharping, Rudolf *Government Official, Germany*
Wilhelmstr 5, 56112 Lahnstein, Germany
Schatz, Albert *Microbiologist*
%Rutgers University, Research/Endowment Foundation, New Brunswick, NJ 08903, USA

Schatz, Gottfried — *Biochemist*
%Basle University, Klingelbergstr 70 4056 Basle, Switzerland

Schatz, Howard — *Photographer*
435 W Broadway, #2, New York, NY 10012, USA

Schatzberg, Jerry N — *Movie Director*
%International Creative Mgmt, 8942 Wilshire Blvd, Beverly Hills, CA 90211, USA

Schaudt, Martin — *Equestrian Athlete*
Gerhardstr 10/2, 72461 Albstadt, Germany

Schaufuss, Peter — *Ballet Dancer, Director*
%Papoutsis Representation Ltd, 18 Sundial Ave, London SE25 4BX, England

Schaus, Fred — *Basketball Coach*
2032 Georgia Lane, St Louis, MO 63141, USA

Schawlow, Arthur L — *Nobel Physics Laureate*
850 Webster St, #117, Palo Alto, CA 94301, USA

Schayes, Adolph (Dolph) — *Basketball Player*
PO Box 156, DeWitt, NY 13214, USA

Schayes, Danny — *Basketball Player*
3900 E Long Road, Littleton, CO 80121, USA

Scheckter, Jody D — *Auto Racing Driver*
39 Ave Princess Grace, Monte Carlo, Monaco

Schedeen, Anne — *Actress*
%Metropolitan Talent Agency, 4526 Wilshire Blvd, Los Angeles, CA 90010, USA

Scheel, Walter — *President, West Germany*
Lindenstr 22, 5000 Cologne-Marienburg, Germany

Scheffer, Victor B — *Zoologist*
14806 SE 54th St, Bellevue, WA 98006, USA

Scheffler, Steve — *Basketball Player*
%Denver Nuggets, McNichols Arena, 1635 Clay St, Denver, CO 80204, USA

Scheibel, Arnold B — *Medical Researcher*
16231 Morrison St, Encino, CA 91436, USA

Scheider, Roy — *Actor*
PO Box 364, Sagaponack, NY 11962, USA

Scheider, Wilhelm — *Businessman*
%Freid Krupp GmbH, Altendorferstr 103, 45143 Essen, Germany

Schein, Philip S — *Physician*
6212 Robinwood Road, Bethesda, MD 20817, USA

Schell, Jonathan — *Journalist*
%Newsday, Editorial Dept, 235 Pinelawn Road, Melville, NY 11747, USA

Schell, Maria — *Actress*
%Gertrud Rother, Nordstr 5, 83512 Reitmehring, Germany

Schell, Maximilian — *Actor*
%Management Baumbauer, Keplestra 2, 81679 Munich, Germany

Schell, Ronnie — *Actor*
4024 Saphire Dr, Encino, CA 91436, USA

Schellhase, Dave — *Basketball Player*
1510 19 1/2 St S, Moorhead, MN 56560, USA

Schelling, Gunther F K — *Civil Engineer*
%Graz University, Rechbauerstr 12, 8010 Graz, Austria

Schemansky, Norbert — *Weightlifter*
24826 New York St, Dearborn, MI 48124, USA

Schembechler, Glenn E (Bo) — *Football Coach*
1904 Boulder Dr, Ann Arbor, MI 48104, USA

Schenkel, Chris — *Sportscaster*
7101 N Kalorama Road, Leesburg, IN 46538, USA

Schenkenberg, Markus — *Model*
%Boss Models, 1 Gansevoort St, New York, NY 10014, USA

Schenkkan, Robert F — *Writer*
%Dramatist Guild, 234 W 44th St, New York, NY 10036, USA

Schepisi, Frederic A — *Movie Director*
159 Eastern Road, South Melbourne, VIC 3205, Australia

Scheraga, Harold A — *Chemist*
212 Homestead Terrace, Ithaca, NY 14850, USA

Scherbo, Vitali — *Gymnast*
8308 Aqua Spray Ave, Las Vegas, NV 89128, USA

Scherrer, Jean-Louis — *Fashion Designer*
51 Ave du Montaigne, 75008 Paris, France

Scheuer, Paul J — *Chemist*
3271 Melemele Place, Honolulu, HI 96822, USA

Scheuring, Garry J *Financier*
%Midlantic Corp, Metro Park Plaza, PO Box 600, Edison, NJ 08818, USA
Schevill, James *Writer*
1309 Oxford St, Berkeley, CA 94709, USA
Schiavelli, Vincent *Actor*
%Alliance Talent, 9171 Wilshire Blvd, #441, Beverly Hills, CA 90210, USA
Schiavo, Mary *Government Official, Social Activist*
%Ohio State University, Public Policy Dept, Columbus, OH 43210, USA
Schickel, Richard *Writer, Movie Critic*
9051 Dicks St, Los Angeles, CA 90069, USA
Schickele, Peter *Composer, Comedian*
%International Creative Mgmt, 40 W 57th St, New York, NY 10019, USA
Schieffer, Bob *Commentator*
%CBS-TV, News Dept, 2020 "M" St NW, Washington, DC 20036, USA
Schiff, Andras *Concert Pianist*
%Shirley Kirshbaum, 711 West End Ave, #5-KN, New York, NY 10025, USA
Schiffer, Claudia *Model*
Aussenwall 94, 47495 Rheinberg, Germany
Schiffer, Menahem M *Mathematician*
3748 Laguna Ave, Palo Alto, CA 94306, USA
Schiffrin, Andre *Publisher*
%New Press, 201 E 50th St, New York, NY 10022, USA
Schifrin, Lalo *Composer*
710 N Hillcrest Road, Beverly Hills, CA 90210, USA
Schillebeeckx, Edward *Theologian*
%Crossroad Publishing Co, 575 Lexington Ave, New York, NY 10022, USA
Schiller, Harvey W *Sports Executive*
%Turner Sports, 1050 Techwood Dr NW, Atlanta, GA 30318, USA
Schiller, Lawrence J *Television Director*
PO Box 56056, Sherman Oaks, CA 91413, USA
Schilling, William G *Actor*
616 N Valley St, Burbank, CA 91505, USA
Schimberni, Mario *Businessman*
%Motedison, Foro Buonaparte 31, 20121 Milan, Italy
Schimmel, Paul R *Biochemist*
%Massachusetts Institute of Technology, Biology Dept, Cambridge, MA 02139, USA
Schindler, Alexander M *Religious Leader*
%Union of American Hebrew Congregations, 838 5th Ave, New York, NY 10021, USA
Schinkel, Ken *Hockey Player*
19927 Beaulieu Court, Fort Myers, FL 33908, USA
Schirra, Walter M, Jr *Astronaut*
16834 Via de Santa Fe, PO Box 73, Rancho Santa Fe, CA 92067, USA
Schisgal, Murray J *Writer*
%International Creative Mgmt, 40 W 57th St, New York, NY 10019, USA
Schlafly, Phyllis S *Women's Activist*
68 Fairmount Ave, Alton, IL 62002, USA
Schlag, Edward W *Chemist*
Osterwaldstr 91, 80805 Munich, Germany
Schlatter, Charlie *Actor*
13501 Contour Dr, Sherman Oaks, CA 91423, USA
Schlegel, Hans W *Astronaut, Germany*
DLR, Astronautenburo, Postfach 906058, Linder Hohe, 51140 Cologne, Germany
Schlegel, John P *Educator*
%University of San Francisco, President's Office, San Francisco, CA 94117, USA
Schlein, Dov C *Financier*
%Republic New York Corp, 452 5th Ave, New York, NY 10018, USA
Schlesinger, Arthur M, Jr *Writer, Historian*
4 E 62nd St, #1, New York, NY 10021, USA
Schlesinger, Helmut *Financier*
%Deutsche Bundesbank, W-Epstein-Str 14, 60431 Frankfurt/Main, Germany
Schlesinger, James R *Secretary, Defense & Energy*
%Georgetown University, 1800 "K" St NW, #400, Washington, DC 20006, USA
Schlesinger, John R *Movie Director*
1896 Rising Glen Road, Los Angeles, CA 90069, USA
Schlessinger, Laura *Radio Psychologist, Physiologist*
%KFI-Radio, 610 S Ardmore Ave, Los Angeles, CA 90005, USA
Schleyer, Paul Von R *Chemist*
%Friedrich-Alexander-Universitat, Henkestr 41, 91469 Erlangen, Germany

Schlondorff, Volker O — *Movie Director*
Obermaierstr 1, 80538 Munich, Germany

Schloredt, Robert (Bob) — *Football Player*
%Nestle-Beich, 1827 N 167th St, Seattle, WA 98133, USA

Schlosberg, Richard T, III — *Publisher*
%Los Angeles Times, Times Mirror Square, Los Angeles, CA 90053, USA

Schluter, Poul H — *Prime Minister, Denmark*
%Prime Minister's Office, Prins Jorgens Gaard II, 1218 Copenhagen, Denmark

Schmeichel, Peter — *Soccer Player*
%Manchester United, M Busby Way, Old Traford, Manchester M16 0RA, England

Schmeling, Maximilian (Max) — *Boxer*
Sonnenweg 1, 21279 Hollenstedt, Germany

Schmemann, Serge — *Journalist*
%New York Times, Editorial Dept, 229 W 43rd St, New York, NY 10036, USA

Schmid, Rudi — *Physician*
211 Woodland Road, Kentfield, CA 94904, USA

Schmidt, Andreas — *Opera Singer*
%Deutsche Grammaphon Records, 810 7th Ave, New York, NY 10019, USA

Schmidt, Benno C, Jr — *Educator*
%Edison Project, 375 Park Ave, New York, NY 10152, USA

Schmidt, Bill — *Track Athlete*
1809 Devonwood Court, Knoxville, TN 37922, USA

Schmidt, Birgit — *Kayak Athlete*
Kuckuckswald 11, 14532 Kleinmachnow, Germany

Schmidt, Carl F — *Pharmacologist, Physiologist*
%Thomas Wynne Apartments, #1/3-B, Wynne, PA 19096, USA

Schmidt, Eric — *Computer Engineer, Businessman*
%Norvell Inc, 122 E 1700 South, Provo, UT 84606, USA

Schmidt, Helmut — *Chancellor, West Germany*
%Die Zeit, Speersport 1, 20095 Hamburg, Germany

Schmidt, Joseph (Joe) — *Football Player*
29600 Northwestern Highway, Southfield, MI 48034, USA

Schmidt, Kate — *Track Athlete*
4373 Scandia Way, Los Angeles, CA 90065, USA

Schmidt, Maarten — *Astronomer*
%California Institute of Technology, Astronomy Dept, Pasadena, CA 91125, USA

Schmidt, Michael J (Mike) — *Baseball Player*
373 Eagle Dr, Jupiter, FL 33477, USA

Schmidt, Milt — *Hockey Player*
8 Crest Dr W, Dover, MA 02030, USA

Schmidt, Ole — *Conductor, Composer*
Puggaardsgade 17, 1573 Copenhagen, Denmark

Schmidt, Richard — *Orthopedic Surgeon*
%University of Pennsylvania Hospital, 3400 Spruce St, Philadelphia, PA 19104, USA

Schmidt, Wolfgang — *Track Athlete*
Birkheckenstr 116-B, 70599 Stuttgart, Germany

Schmidt-Nielsen, Knut — *Physiologist*
%Duke University, Zoology Dept, Durham, NC 27706, USA

Schmidtke, Fredy — *Cyclist*
Theodor-Fontane-Str 22, 41541 Dormagen, Germany

Schmiege, Robert W — *Businessman*
%Chicago & North Western, 165 N Canal St, Chicago, IL 60606, USA

Schmiege, Sandra Kay — *Artist*
%End of the Road Gallery/Studio, 5822 Stepetz Road, #53, Aurora, MN 55705, USA

Schmitt, Arnd — *Fencer*
Rheinuferweg 59-B, 47495 Bornheim, Germany

Schmitt, Harrison H (Jack) — *Senator, NM; Astronaut*
6053 McKinney Dr NE, Albuquerque, NM 87109, USA

Schmitt, Wolfgang R — *Businessman*
%Rubbermaid Inc, 1147 Akron Road, Wooster, OH 44691, USA

Schnabel, Julian — *Artist*
%Pace Gallery, 32 E 57th St, New York 10022, USA

Schnabel, Karl Ulrich — *Concert Pianist*
305 West End Ave, New York, NY 10023, USA

Schnackenberg, Roy L — *Artist*
1919 N Orchard St, Chicago, IL 60614, USA

Schnarre, Monika — *Model, Actress*
%Artists Group, 10100 Santa Monica Blvd, #2490, Los Angeles, CA 90067, USA

Schneider, Andrew — *Journalist*
%Pittsburgh Press, Editorial Dept, 34 Blvd of Allies, Pittsburgh, PA 15230, USA
Schneider, Fred — *Singer, Songwriter (The B-52s)*
%Monterey Peninsula Artists, 509 Hartnell St, Monterey, CA 93940, USA
Schneider, John — *Actor, Singer*
2644 E Chevy Chase Dr, Glendale, CA 91206, USA
Schneider, Leann — *Businesswoman*
%Showboat Inc, 2800 E Fremont St, Las Vegas, NV 89104, USA
Schneider, Rob — *Comedian, Actor*
%United Talent Agency, 9560 Wilshire Blvd, #500, Beverly Hills, CA 90212, USA
Schneider, Vreni — *Skier*
Dorf, 8767 Elm, Switzerland
Schneider, William (Buzz) — *Hockey Player*
6 Beacon Hill Road, Marblehead, MA 01945, USA
Schneider, William G — *Physical Chemist*
%National Research Council, 65 Whitemarl Dr, #2, Ottawa ON K1L 8J9, Canada
Schneider, William H — *Army General*
69 Granburg Circle, San Antonio, TX 78218, USA
Schneiderhan, Wolfgang — *Concert Violinist*
Kaasgrabengasse 98-A, 1190 Vienna, Austria
Schnelldorfer, Manfred — *Figure Skater*
Seydlitzstr 55, 80993 Munich, Germany
Schnittke, Alfred — *Composer*
Beim Andreasbrunnen 5, 20249 Hamburg, Germany
Schnittker, Dick — *Basketball Player*
2303 E Las Granadas, Green Valley, AZ 85614, USA
Schochet, Bob — *Cartoonist*
Sunset Road, Highland Mills, NY 10930, USA
Schockemohle, Alwin — *Equestrian Rider*
Munsterlandstr 51, 49439 Muhlen, Germany
Schoelen, Jill — *Actress*
%Gold Marshak Liedtke, 3500 W Olive Ave, #1400, Burbank, CA 91505, USA
Schoen, Max H — *Dentist*
5818 S Sherbourne Dr, Los Angeles, CA 90056, USA
Schoendienst, Albert F (Red) — *Baseball Player, Manager*
1105 Jo Carr Dr, Town And Country, MO 63017, USA
Schoenfeld, Gerald — *Theater Producer*
%Shubert Organization Inc, 225 W 44th St, New York, NY 10036, USA
Schoenfield, Al — *Swimming Administrator*
2731 Pecho Road, Los Osos, CA 93402, USA
Schoenfield, Dana — *Swimmer*
10775 Equestrian Dr, Santa Ana, CA 92705, USA
Schoffer, Nicolas — *Sculptor*
Villa Des Arts, 15 Rue Hegesippe-Moreau, 75018 Paris, France
Schofield, George H — *Businessman*
%Zurn Industries, 1 Zurn Place, Erie, PA 16505, USA
Scholder, Fritz — *Artist*
118 Cattletrack Road, Scottsdale, AZ 85251, USA
Scholes, Clarke — *Swimmer*
1360 Somerset, Grosse Pointe Park, MI 48230, USA
Scholl, Hermann — *Businessman*
%BOSCH, Postfach 106050, 70049 Stuttgart, Germany
Schollander, Don — *Swimmer*
3576 Lakeview Blvd, Lake Oswego, OR 97035, USA
Scholten, Jim — *Singer (Sawyer Brown)*
%TKO Artist Mgmt, 4219 Hillsboro Road, #318, Nashville, TN 37215, USA
Schonberg, Claude-Michel — *Composer*
%Theatre Royal Drury Lane, Catherine St, London WC2, England
Schonberg, Harold C — *Music Critic*
160 Riverside Dr, New York, NY 10024, USA
Schonhuber, Franz — *Commentator*
%Europaburo, Fraunhoferstr 23, 80469 Munich, Germany
Schoolnik, Gary — *Medical Researcher*
%Stanford University Medical School, Microbiology Dept, Stanford, CA 94305, USA
Schoomaker, Peter J (Pete) — *Army General*
Commanding General, Special Operations, Fort Bragg, NC 28307, USA
Schopf, J William — *Paleobiologist*
%University of California, Study of Evolution Center, Los Angeles, CA 90024, USA

S

Schneider - Schopf

Schorer, Jane *Journalist*
%Des Moines Register, Editorial Dept, Box 957, Des Moines, IA 50304, USA

Schorr, Bill *Cartoonist (Phoebe's Place)*
%Kansas City Star, Editorial Dept, 1729 Grand Ave, Kansas City, MO 64108, USA

Schorr, Daniel L *Journalist, Writer*
3113 Woodley Road, Washington, DC 20008, USA

Schott, Marge *Baseball Executive*
%Cincinnati Reds, 100 Riverfront Stadium, Cincinnati, OH 45202, USA

Schottenheimer, Martin E (Marty) *Football Coach*
%Kansas City Chiefs, 1 Arrowhead Dr, Kansas City, KS 64129, USA

Schou, Mogens *Psychiatrist*
%Aarhus University, Institute of Psychiatry, Aarhus, Denmark

Schowalter, Edward R, Jr *Korean War Army Hero (CMH)*
913 Bibb Ave, Auburn, AL 36830, USA

Schrader, Ken *Auto Racing Driver*
4001 Windy Road, Concord, NC 28027, USA

Schrader, Paul J *Movie Director*
9696 Culver Blvd, #203, Culver City, CA 90232, USA

Schramm, David *Actor*
%Gersh Agency, 232 N Canon Dr, Beverly Hills, CA 90210, USA

Schramm, David N *Astrophysicist*
150 Pitkin Mesa Dr, Aspen, CO 81611, USA

Schramm, Texas E (Tex) *Football Executive*
6116 N Central Expressway, #518, Dallas, TX 75206, USA

Schranz, Karl *Skier*
Hotel Garni, 6580 St Anton, Austria

Schreiber, Avery *Actor*
6612 Ranchito Ave, Van Nuys, CA 91405, USA

Schreiber, Martin J *Governor, WI*
2700 S Shore Dr, #B, Milwaukee, WI 53207, USA

Schreier, Peter *Opera Singer*
Giesener Str 5, 31157 Sarstedt/Hanover, Germany

Schrempf, Detlef *Basketball Player*
8827 NE 36th St, Bellevue, WA 98004, USA

Schrempp, Jurgen E *Businessman*
%Daimler-Benz AG, Plieningerstrasse, 70546 Stuttgart, Germany

Schreyer, Edward R *Governor General, Canada*
401-250 Wellington Crescent, Winnipeg MB R3M 0B3, Canada

Schrieffer, John R *Nobel Physics Laureate*
%Florida State University, Physics Dept, Tallahassee, FL 32306, USA

Schriesheim, Alan *Applied Chemist*
1440 N Lake Shore Dr, #31-AC, Chicago, IL 60610, USA

Schriever, Bernard A *Air Force General*
2300 "M" St NW, #900, Washington, DC 20037, USA

Schrimshaw, Nevin S *Nutritionist*
Sandwich Notch Farm, Thornton, NH 03223, USA

Schrock, Richard R *Chemist*
%Massachusetts Institute of Technology, Chemistry Dept, Cambridge, MA 02139, USA

Schroeder, Barbet G *Movie Director, Producer*
8033 W Sunset Blvd, #51, Los Angeles, CA 90046, USA

Schroeder, Frederick R (Ted), Jr *Tennis Player*
1010 W Muirlands Dr, La Jolla, CA 92037, USA

Schroeder, Jim *Bowler*
3 Greenhaven Terrace, Tonawanda, NY 14150, USA

Schroeder, John H *Educator*
%University of Wisconsin, Chancellor's Office, Milwaukee, WI 53211, USA

Schroeder, Paul W *Writer, Historian*
%University of Illinois, History Dept, 810 S Wright St, Urbana, IL 61801, USA

Schroeder, Terry *Water Polo Player, Coach*
4901 Lewis Road, Agoura Hills, CA 91301, USA

Schrom, Kenneth M (Ken) *Baseball Player*
713 Roisante, El Paso, TX 79922, USA

Schruefer, John J *Physician*
%Georgetown University Hospital, Ob-Gyn Dept, Washington, DC 20007, USA

Schubert, Mark *Swimming Coach*
%University of Southern California, Athletic Dept, Los Angeles, CA 90089, USA

Schubert, Richard F *Association Executive*
7811 Old Dominion Dr, McLean, VA 22102, USA

Schuchart, John A	*Businessman*
%MDU Resources Group, 400 N 4th St, Bismarck, ND 58501, USA	
Schuck, Anett	*Kayak Athlete*
Defoestry 6-A, 04159 Leipzig, Germany	
Schuck, John	*Actor*
925 Victoria Ave, Venice, CA 90291, USA	
Schueler, Jon R	*Artist*
40 W 22nd St, New York, NY 10010, USA	
Schuh, Harry F	*Football Player*
2309 Massey Road, Memphis, TN 38119, USA	
Schul, Bob	*Track Athlete*
PO Box 267, Dayton, OH 45409, USA	
Schulberg, Budd	*Writer*
Brookside, PO Box 707, Westhampton Beach, NY 11978, USA	
Schuler, Carolyn	*Swimmer*
26552 Via Del Sol, Mission Viejo, CA 92691, USA	
Schull, Rebecca	*Actress*
%Writers & Artists, 924 Westwood Blvd, #900, Los Angeles, CA 90024, USA	
Schuller, Grete	*Sculptor*
8 Barstow Road, #7-G, Great Neck, NY 11021, USA	
Schuller, Gunther	*Composer, Conductor*
%Margun Music, 167 Dudley Road, Newton Centre, MA 02159, USA	
Schuller, Robert H	*Evangelist*
464 S Esplanade St, Orange, CA 92869, USA	
Schult, Jurgen	*Track Athlete*
Drosselweg 6, 19069 Leuna, Germany	
Schulte, David	*Financier*
%Chilmark Partners, 2 N Riverside Plaza, Chicago, IL 60606, USA	
Schultes, Richard E	*Ethnobotanist*
501 Lexington St, #105, Waltham, MA 02154, USA	
Schultz, Dave	*Hockey Player*
7 Bradford Way, West Berlin, NJ 08091, USA	
Schultz, Dave	*Auto Racing Driver*
2365 Lazy River Lane, Fort Myers, FL 33905, USA	
Schultz, Dean	*Financier*
%Federal Home Loan Bank, 1079 Hutchinson Road, Walnut Creek, CA 94598, USA	
Schultz, Dwight	*Actor*
%Paul Kohner, 9300 Wilshire Blvd, #555, Beverly Hills, CA 90212, USA	
Schultz, Frederick H	*Government Official*
PO Box 1200, Jacksonville, FL 32201, USA	
Schultz, Howard H (Howie)	*Basketball, Baseball Player*
1333 McKusick Road Lane W, Stillwater, MN 55082, USA	
Schultz, Michael A	*Movie Director*
%Chrystalite Productions, PO Box 1940, Santa Monica, CA 90406, USA	
Schultz, Peter C	*Inventor (Silica Optical Waveguide)*
%Heraeus Amersil Inc, 3473 Satellite Blvd, #300, Duluth, GA 30096, USA	
Schultz, Peter G	*Chemist*
%University of California, Chemistry Dept, Berkeley, CA 94720, USA	
Schultz, Richard D	*Association Executive*
%US Olympic Committee, 1 Olympia Plaza, Colorado Springs, CO 80909, USA	
Schultz, Theodore W	*Nobel Economics Laureate*
5620 S Kimbark Ave, Chicago, IL 60637, USA	
Schultze, Charles L	*Government Official*
%Brookings Institute, 1775 Massachusetts Ave NW, Washington, DC 20036, USA	
Schulz, Axel	*Boxer*
Zehmplatz 10, 15230 Frankfurt/Oder, Germany	
Schulz, Charles M	*Cartoonist (Peanuts)*
2021 3rd St, #A, Santa Monica, CA 90405, USA	
Schulze, John B	*Businessman*
%Lamson & Sessions Co, 25701 Science Park Dr, Cleveland, OH 44122, USA	
Schulze, Richard M	*Businessman*
%Best Buy Co, 7075 Flying Cloud Dr, Eden Prairie, MN 55344, USA	
Schumacher, Joel	*Movie Director*
%Greenfield & Selvaggi, 11766 Wilshire Blvd, #1610, Los Angeles, CA 90025, USA	
Schumacher, Michael	*Auto Racing Driver*
Forsthausstr 92, 54578 Kerpen-Manheim, Germany	
Schuman, Allan L	*Businessman*
%Ecolab Inc, Ecolab Center, 370 N Wabasha St, St Paul, MN 55102, USA	

Schumann, Jochem *Yachtsman (Soling)*
Birkenstr 88, 48336 Penzberg, Germany

Schumann, Maurice *Government Official, France*
53 Ave Marechal-Lyautey, 75016 Paris, France

Schumann, Ralf *Pistol Marksman*
Steomach 22, 97640 Stockheim, Germany

Schurmann, Petra *Swimmer*
Max-Emanuel-Str 7, 82319 Starnberg, Germany

Schussler Fiorenza, Elisabeth *Writer, Educator*
%Notre Dame University, Theology Dept, Notre Dame, IN 46556, USA

Schutz, Stephen *Graphic Artist*
%Blue Mountain Arts Inc, PO Box 4549, Boulder, CO 80306, USA

Schutz, Susan Polis *Writer*
%Blue Mountain Arts Inc, PO Box 4549, Boulder, CO 80306, USA

Schuur, Diane *Singer*
%Paul Canter Enterprises, 33042 Ocean Ridge, Dana Point, CA 92629, USA

Schwab, Charles R *Financier*
%Charles Schwab Co, 101 Montgomery St, San Francisco, CA 94104, USA

Schwab, John J *Psychiatrist*
6217 Innes Trace Road, Louisville, KY 40222, USA

Schwantner, Joseph *Composer*
%Eastman School of Music, 26 Gibbs St, Rochester, NY 14604, USA

Schwarthoff, Florian *Track Athlete*
Fischweiher 51, 64646 Heppenheim, Germany

Schwartz, Gerard *Conductor*
575 West End Ave, #4-B, New York, NY 10024, USA

Schwartz, Jacob T *Computer Scientist*
%New York University, Courant Math Sciences Institute, New York, NY 10012, USA

Schwartz, Lloyd *Journalist*
27 Pennsylvania Ave, Somerville, MA 02145, USA

Schwartz, Maxime *Medical Administrator*
%Institut Pasteur, 25-28 Rue du Docteur-Roux, 75724 Paris Cedex 15, France

Schwartz, Melvin *Nobel Physics Laureate*
PO Box 5068, Ketchum, ID 83340, USA

Schwartz, Richard J *Businessman*
%Jonathan Logan Co, 980 Ave of Americas, New York, NY 10018, USA

Schwartz, Stephen L *Composer, Lyricist*
%Paramuse Assoc, 1414 Ave of Americas, New York, NY 10019, USA

Schwartz, Tony *Communications Specialist*
455 W 56th St, New York, NY 10019, USA

Schwarz, Gerard R *Conductor*
575 West End Ave, #4-B, New York, NY 10024, USA

Schwarz, John H *Physicist*
%California Institute of Technology, Physics Dept, Pasadena, CA 91125, USA

Schwarz-Schilling, Christian *Government Official, Germany*
%Post-Telecomm Ministry, Heinrich-von-Stephanstr 1, 53175 Bonn, Germany

Schwarzenegger, Arnold *Body Builder, Actor*
3110 Main St, #300, Santa Monica, CA 90405, USA

Schwarzkopf, Elisabeth *Opera Singer*
Rebhusstra 29, 8126 Zunnikon, Zurich, Switzerland

Schwarzkopf, H Norman *Army General*
400 N Ashley Dr, #3050, Tampa, FL 33602, USA

Schwarzman, Stephen A *Financier*
%Blackstone Group, 345 Park Ave, New York, NY 10154, USA

Schwarzschild, Martin *Astronomer*
12 Ober Road, Princeton, NJ 08540, USA

Schwebel, Stephen M *Judge*
%Int'l Court of Justice, Peace Palace, 2517 KJ The Hague, Netherlands

Schweickart, Russell L *Astronaut*
2125 Red Hill Circle, Belvedere, Tiburon, CA 94920, USA

Schweig, Eric *Actor*
%Prime Talent, PO Box 5163, Vancouver BC V6B 1M4, Canada

Schweiker, Richard S *Secretary, Health & Human Services*
%American Council of Life Insurance, 1001 Pennsylvania Ave, Washington, DC 20004, USA

Schweikert, J E *Religious Leader*
%Old Roman Catholic Church, 4200 N Kedvale Ave, Chicago, IL 60641, USA

Schweikher, Paul *Architect*
3222 E Missouri Ave, Phoenix, AZ 85018, USA

Schwery, Henri Cardinal — *Religious Leader*
%Bishoporic of Sion, CP 2068, 1950 Sion 2, Switzerland

Schwimmer, David — *Actor*
1330 Londonberry Place, Los Angeles, CA 90069, USA

Schwinden, Ted — *Governor, MT*
1335 Highland St, Helena, MT 59601, USA

Schygulla, Hanna — *Actress*
%ZBF Agentur, Ordensmeisterstr 15-16, 12099 Berlin, Germany

Scialfa, Patty — *Singer (The E Street Band)*
%Gold Mountain, 3575 Cahuenga Blvd W, #450, Los Angeles, CA 90068, USA

Sciorra, Anabella — *Actress*
%Wolf/Kasteller, 132 S Rodeo Dr, #300, Beverly Hills, CA 90212, USA

Sciutti, Graziella — *Opera Singer*
%RCA Records, 1540 Broadway, #900, New York, NY 10036, USA

Scofield, Dino — *Actor*
3330 Barham Blvd, #103, Los Angeles, CA 90068, USA

Scofield, John — *Jazz Electric Guitarist*
%Sco Biz, 6 Terrace Heights, Katonah, NY 10536, USA

Scofield, Paul — *Actor*
Gables, Balcombe, Sussex RH17 6ND, England

Scoggins, Matt — *Swimmer*
4900 Calhoun Canyon Loop, Austin, TX 78735, USA

Scoggins, Tracy — *Actress*
1131 Alta Loma Road, #515, Los Angeles, CA 90069, USA

Scola, Ettore — *Movie Director*
Via Bertoloni 1/E, 00197 Rome, Italy

Scolari, Peter — *Actor*
%OTML, 500 S Sepulveda Blvd, #500, Los Angeles, CA 90049, USA

Scolnick, Edward — *Cancer Researcher*
%Merck & Co, Research & Development, PO Box 2000, Rahway, NJ 07065, USA

Score, Herbert J (Herb) — *Baseball Player, Sportscaster*
%WKNR-Radio, 9446 Broadview Road, Cleveland, OH 44147, USA

Scorsese, Martin — *Movie Director*
445 Park Ave, #700, New York, NY 10022, USA

Scorupco, Izabella — *Actress, Singer, Model*
%International Creative Mgmt, 8942 Wilshire Blvd, Beverly Hills, CA 90211, USA

Scott Thomas, Kristin — *Actress*
%PMK Public Relations, 955 S Carillo Dr, #200, Los Angeles, CA 90048, USA

Scott, Byron — *Basketball Player*
31815 Camino Capistrano, #C, San Juan Capistrano, CA 92675, USA

Scott, Clyde L (Smackover) — *Football Player, Track Athlete*
12840 Rivercrest Dr, Little Rock, AR 72212, USA

Scott, David K — *Educator*
%University of Massachusetts, President's Office, Amherst, MA 01003, USA

Scott, David R — *Astronaut*
1300 Manhatten Ave, #B, Manhattan Beach, CA 90266, USA

Scott, Debralee — *Actress*
%Fifi Oscard Assoc, 24 W 40th St, #1700, New York, NY 10018, USA

Scott, Dennis — *Basketball Player*
9832 Laurel Valley Dr, Windermere, FL 34786, USA

Scott, Donovan — *Actor*
%Judy Schoen, 606 N Larchmont Blvd, #309, Los Angeles, CA 90004, USA

Scott, Freddie — *Singer*
%Headline Talent, 1650 Broadway, #508, New York, NY 10019, USA

Scott, George — *Baseball Player*
1316 Goodrich St, Greenville, MS 38701, USA

Scott, George C — *Actor*
11766 Wilshire Blvd, #760, Los Angeles, CA 90025, USA

Scott, Irene F — *Judge*
%US Tax Court, 400 2nd St NW, Washington, DC 20217, USA

Scott, Jack — *Singer*
%Jack Grenier Productions, 32500 Concord Dr, #230, Madison Heights, MI 48071, USA

Scott, Jane — *Jazz Critic*
%Cleveland Plain Dealer, 1801 Superior Ave, Cleveland, OH 44114, USA

Scott, Jerry — *Cartoonist (Baby Blues)*
%Creators Syndicate, 5777 W Century Blvd, #700, Los Angeles, CA 90045, USA

Scott, Jimmy — *Singer*
%J's Way Jazz, 175 Prospect St, #20-D, East Orange, NJ 07017, USA

S

Schwery - Scott

Scott, John B — *Businessman*
%Kemper Investors Life, 1 Kemper Dr, Long Grove, IL 60049, USA

Scott, Kathryn Leigh — *Actress*
PO Box 17217, Beverly Hills, CA 90209, USA

Scott, Larry — *Body Builder*
PO Box 162, North Salt Lake City, UT 84011, USA

Scott, Larry R — *Businessman*
%Carolina Freight Corp, PO Box 1000, Cherryville, NC 28021, USA

Scott, Lizabeth — *Actress*
PO Box 69405, Los Angeles, CA 90069, USA

Scott, Martha — *Actress*
14054 Chandler Blvd, Van Nuys, CA 91401, USA

Scott, Melody Thomas — *Actress*
%Save the Earth, 4881 Topanga Canyon Blvd, #201, Woodland Hills, CA 91364, USA

Scott, Michael W (Mike) — *Baseball Player*
28355 Chat Dr, Laguna Nigel, CA 92677, USA

Scott, Paul — *Writer*
33 Drumsheugh Gardens, Edinburgh, Scotland

Scott, Pippa — *Actress*
10850 Wilshire Blvd, #250, Los Angeles, CA 90024, USA

Scott, Ray — *Sportscaster*
PO Box 559, Salisbury, NC 28145, USA

Scott, Richard (Dick) — *Football Player*
9606 Falls Road, Potomac, MD 20854, USA

Scott, Ridley — *Movie Director*
%RSA Films, 6-10 Lexington St, London W1, England

Scott, Robert L, Jr — *WW II Army Air Corps Hero, Writer*
96 Ridgecrest Place, Warner Robins, GA 31088, USA

Scott, Robert S — *WW II Army Hero (CMH)*
312 Camino Encatado, Santa Fe, NM 87501, USA

Scott, Robert W — *Governor, NC; Educator*
%North Carolina Community College System, 200 W Jones St, Raleigh, NC 27603, USA

Scott, Shelby — *Labor Leader*
%American Federation of TV/Radio Artists, 200 Madison Ave, New York, NY 10016, USA

Scott, Stephen — *Jazz Pianist*
%Verve Records, Worldwide Plaza, 825 8th Ave, New York, NY 10019, USA

Scott, Steve — *Track Athlete*
2431 Morina Blvd, San Diego, CA 92110, USA

Scott, Thomas C (Tom) — *Football Player*
215 Lexington Ave, New York, NY 10016, USA

Scott, Tom — *Jazz Saxophonist*
%Performers of the World, 8901 Melrose Ave, #200, West Hollywood, CA 90069, USA

Scott, Tony — *Movie Director*
%Totem Productions, 8009 Santa Monica Blvd, West Hollywood, CA 90046, USA

Scott, Walter, Jr — *Businessman*
%Peter Kiewit Sons, 1000 Kiewit Plaza, Omaha, NE 68131, USA

Scott, Willard H, Jr — *Entertainer*
%NBC-TV, News Dept, 30 Rockefeller Plaza, New York, NY 10112, USA

Scott, Winston E — *Astronaut*
%NASA, Johnson Space Center, 2101 NASA Road, Houston, TX 77058, USA

Scott-Heron, Gil — *Singer, Songwriter*
PO Box 31, Malverne, NY 11565, USA

Scotto, Renata — *Opera Singer*
%Robert Lombardo, Harkness Plaza, 61 W 62nd St, #B-5, New York, NY 10023, USA

Scowcroft, Brent — *Air Force General, Government Official*
1750 "K" St NW, #800, Washington, DC 20006, USA

Scranton, William W — *Governor, PA; Ambassador to UN*
%Northeastern National Bank Building, #231, Penn & Spruce, Scranton, PA 18503, USA

Scrimm, Angus — *Actor*
PO Box 5193, North Hollywood, CA 91616, USA

Scrimshaw, Nevin S — *Nutritionist*
Sandwich Mountain Farm, PO Box 330, Thornton, NH 03223, USA

Scripps, Charles E — *Publisher*
10 Grandin Lane, Cincinnati, OH 45208, USA

Scruggs, Earl — *Singer, Banjoist, Songwriter*
%Louise Scruggs, PO Box 66, Madison, TN 37116, USA

Scudamore, Peter — *Thoroughbred Racing Jockey*
Mucky Cottage, Grangehill, Naunton, Cheltenham, Glos GL54 3AY, England

Scuduto, Al	*Cartoonist*
%King Features Syndicate, 235 E 45th St, New York, NY 10017, USA	
Scully, Joseph C	*Financier*
%St Paul Bancorp, 6700 W North Ave, Chicago, IL 60707, USA	
Scully, Sean P	*Artist*
%David McKee, 745 5th Ave, New York, NY 10151, USA	
Scully, Vincent E (Vin)	*Sportscaster*
1555 Capri Dr, Pacific Palisades, CA 90272, USA	
Scully-Power, Paul D	*Astronaut*
330 Dartmouth St, #B-1, Boston, MA 02116, USA	
Sculthorpe, Peter J	*Composer*
91 Holdsworth St, Woollahra, NSW 2025, Australia	
Scutt, Der	*Architect*
%Der Scutt Architect, 44 W 28th St, New York, NY 10001, USA	
Seaborg, Glenn T	*Nobel Chemistry Laureate*
%University of California, Lawrence Laboratory, Cyclotron Rd, Berkeley, CA 94720, USA	
Seaforth-Hayes, Susan	*Actress*
4528 Beck Ave, North Hollywood, CA 91602, USA	
Seaga, Edward P G	*Prime Minister, Jamaica*
Vale Royal, Kingston, Jamaica	
Seagal, Steven	*Actor*
2282 Mandeville Canyon Road, Los Angeles, CA 90049, USA	
Seagren, Bob	*Track Athlete, Actor*
12840 Gwynne Lane, Bel Air, CA 90077, USA	
Seagrove, Jenny	*Actress*
%Marmont Mgmt, Langham House, 302/8 Regent St, London W1R 5AL, England	
Seal	*Singer, Songwriter*
%Atlas/Third Rail Entertainment, 9169 Sunset Blvd, Los Angeles, CA 90069, USA	
Seale, Bobby	*Political Activist (Black Panthers)*
%Cafe Society, 302 W Chelton Ave, Philadelphia, PA 19144, USA	
Seale, John	*Cinematographer*
%Smith/Gosnell/Nicholson, 1515 Palisades Dr, #N, Pacific Palisades, CA 90272, USA	
Seals, Dan	*Singer, Songwriter*
%Moringstar Productions, 153 Sanders Ferry Road, Hendersonville, TN 37075, USA	
Seals, Son	*Singer*
%Fat City Artists, 1908 Chet Atkins Place, #502, Nashville, TN 37212, USA	
Sealy, Malik	*Basketball Player*
%Detroit Pistons, Palace, 2 Championship Dr, Auburn Hills, MI 48326, USA	
Seaman, Christopher	*Conductor*
25 Westfield Dr, Glasgow G52 2SG, Scotland	
Seamans, Robert C, Jr	*Aeronautical Engineer*
675 Hale St, Beverly Farms, MA 01915, USA	
Searcy, Nick	*Actor*
%Paradigm Agency, 10100 Santa Monica Blvd, #2500, Los Angeles, CA 90067, USA	
Searfoss, Richard A	*Astronaut*
%NASA, Johnson Space Center, 2101 NASA Road, Houston, TX 77058, USA	
Searle, Ronald	*Cartoonist, Animator*
%John Locke Studio, 15 E 76th St, New York, NY 10021, USA	
Searock, Charles J, Jr	*Air Force General*
Vice Commander, AF Material Command, Wright-Patterson Air Force Base, OH 45433, USA	
Sears, Paul B	*Ecologist*
17 Las Milpas, Taos, NM 87571, USA	
Sears, Victor W (Vic)	*Football Player*
2501 Web Chapel Extension 9105, Dallas, TX 75220, USA	
Seau, Tiana (Junior), Jr	*Football Player*
1904 Via Casa Alta, La Jolla, CA 92037, USA	
Seaver, G Thomas (Tom)	*Baseball Player*
Larkspur Lane, Greenwich, CT 06830, USA	
Seavey, David	*Editorial Cartoonist*
%USA Today, Editorial Dept, 1000 Wilson Blvd, Arlington, VA 22209, USA	
Seawright, G William	*Businessman*
%Stanhome Inc, 333 Western Ave, Westfield, MA 01085, USA	
Sebastian, John	*Singer, Songwriter*
%Firstars Mgmt, 14724 Ventura Blvd, #PH, Sherman Oaks, CA 91403, USA	
Sebastian, Tim	*Writer*
%Bantam Books, 1540 Broadway, New York, NY 10036, USA	
Sebestyen, Marta	*Singer (Muzsik)*
%Concerted Efforts, 59 Parsons St, West Newton, MA 02165, USA	

S

Scuduto - Sebestyen

Sebetzki, Gunther		*Hockey Executive*
%Hockey Hall of Fame, Exhibition Place, Toronto ON M6K 3C3, Canada		
Secada, Jon		*Singer, Songwriter*
601 Brickell Key Dr, #200, Miami, FL 33131, USA		
Secchia, Peter		*Diplomat*
%US Embassy, Via Veneto 1119-A, Rome, Italy		
Secombe, Harry		*Actor*
%Willinghurst Ltd, 46 St James's St, London SW1, England		
Secor, Kyle		*Actor*
%Gersh Agency, 232 N Canon Dr, Beverly Hills, CA 90210, USA		
Secord, John		*Singer*
%Making Texas Music, PO Box 1971, Longview, TX 75606, USA		
Sedaka, Neil		*Singer, Songwriter*
%Neil Sedaka Music, 888 7th Ave, #1905, New York, NY 10106, USA		
Seddon, Margaret Rhea		*Astronaut*
%NASA, Johnson Space Center, 2101 NASA Road, Houston, TX 77058, USA		
Sedelmaier, J Josef (Joe)		*Movie, Television Director; Animator*
%Sedelmaier Film Productions, 858 W Armitage Ave, #267, Chicago, IL 60614, USA		
Sedgman, Frank A		*Tennis Player*
26 Bolton Ave, Hampton, VIC 3188, Australia		
Sedgwick, Kyra		*Actress*
%International Creative Mgmt, 8942 Wilshire Blvd, Beverly Hills, CA 90211, USA		
Sedney, Jules		*Prime Minister, Suriname*
%Trade & Industry Assn, PO Box 111, Paramaribo, Suriname		
Sedykh, Yuri		*Track Athlete*
%Sports Council, 4 Skatertny Pereulok, Moscow, Russia		
See, Carolyn		*Writer*
PO Box 107, Topanga, CA 90290, USA		
Seear, Beatrice N S		*Government Official, England*
189-B Kennington Road, London SE11 6ST, England		
Seefehlner, Egon H		*Opera Director*
Weyrgasse 3/10, 1030 Vienna, Austria		
Seefelder, Matthias		*Businessman*
%BASF AG, Carl-Bosch-Str 38, 78351 Ludwigshafen, Germany		
Seegal, Frederick M		*Financier*
%Wasserstein Perella Group, 31 W 52nd St, New York, NY 10019, USA		
Seeger, Pete		*Singer, Songwriter, Guitarist*
PO Box 431, Dutchess Junction, Beacon, NY 12508, USA		
Seelenfreund, Alan		*Businessman*
%McKesson Corp, 1 Post St, San Francisco, CA 94104, USA		
Seeler, Uwe		*Soccer Player*
Gutenbergring 71, 25868 Norderstedt, Germany		
Seeling, Angelle		*Motorcycle Racing Rider*
%Star Performance Suzuki Racing Team, PO Box 1241, Americus, GA 31709, USA		
Seely, Jeannie		*Singer, Songwriter*
%Tessier-Marsh, 505 Canton Pass, Madison, TN 37115, USA		
Seelye, Talcott W		*Diplomat*
5510 Pembroke Road, Bethesda, MD 20817, USA		
Sega, Ronald M		*Astronaut, Electrical Engineer*
%NASA, Johnson Space Center, 2101 NASA Road, Houston, TX 77058, USA		
Segal, Erich		*Writer*
%Wolfson College, English School, Oxford OX2 6UD, England		
Segal, Fred		*Fashion Designer*
%Fred Segal Jeans, 8100 Melrose Ave, Los Angeles, CA 90046, USA		
Segal, George		*Sculptor*
Davidson Mill Road, New Brunswick, NJ 08901, USA		
Segal, George		*Actor*
711 N Bedford Dr, Beverly Hills, CA 90210, USA		
Segal, Irving E		*Mathematician*
25 Moon Hill Road, Lexington, MA 02173, USA		
Segal, Uri		*Conductor*
%Terry Harrison Mgmt, 3 Clarendon Court, Chalbury, Oxon OX7 3PS, England		
Segelstein, Irwin S		*Television Executive*
%National Broadcasting Co, 30 Rockfeller Plaza, New York, NY 10112, USA		
Seger, Bob		*Singer, Songwriter*
%Punch Enterprises, 567 Purdy St, Birmingham, MI 48009, USA		
Segui, David V		*Baseball Player*
2740 N 131st St, Kansas City, KS 66109, USA		

Segui, Diego P *Baseball Player*
7520 King St, #J, Shawnee Mission, KS 66214, USA
Segura, Francisco (Pancho) *Tennis Player*
%La Costa Resort Hotel & Spa, Costa del Mar Road, Carlsbad, CA 92009, USA
Seguso, Robert *Tennis Player*
%Advantage Int'l, 1025 Thomas Jefferson St NW, #450, Washington, DC 20007, USA
Seibert, Peter *Skier*
PO Box 7, Vail, CO 81658, USA
Seibou, Ali *President, Niger; Army General*
%Chairman of Higher Council for National Orientation, Niamey, Niger
Seidelman, Susan *Movie Director*
%Michael Shedler, 225 W 34th St, #1012, New York, NY 10122, USA
Seidenberg, Ivan G *Businessman*
%NYNEX Corp, 1095 Ave of Americas, New York, NY 10036, USA
Seidler, Harry *Architect*
13 Kalang Ave, Killara, NSW 2071, Australia
Seidman, L William *Government Official, Businessman*
1694 31st St NW, Washington, DC 20007, USA
Seifert, Richard (Robin) *Architect*
Eleventrees, Milespit Hill, Mill Hill, London NW7 2RS, England
Seigenthaler, John L *Publisher*
%Tennessean, 1100 Broadway, Nashville, TN 37203, USA
Seigner, Emmanuelle *Actress*
%Agents Associes Beaume, 201 Rue Faubourg St Honore, 75008 Paris, France
Seignoret, Clarence H A *President, Dominica*
%President's Office, Government House, Victoria St, Roseau, Dominica
Seikaly, Ron *Basketball Player*
27 E Dilido Dr, Miami Beach, FL 33139, USA
Seinfeld, Jerry *Comedian*
2971 Bellmore Ave, Bellmore, NY 11710, USA
Seitz, Frederick *Physicist, Educator*
%Rockefeller University, Physics Dept, 1230 York Ave, New York, NY 10021, USA
Seitz, Peter J *Financier*
%Bethpage Credit Union, 899 S Oyster Bay Road, Bethpage, NY 11714, USA
Seitz, Raymond G H *Diplomat*
%United States Embassy, 24 Grosvenor Square, London S1A 1AE, England
Seixas, E Victor (Vic), Jr *Tennis Player*
8 Harbor Point Dr, #207, Mill Valley, CA 94941, USA
Seizinger, Katja *Skier*
Rudolf-Epp-Str 48, 69412 Eberbach, Germany
Selanne, Teemu *Hockey Player*
%Anaheim Mighty Ducks, PO Box 2000, Gene Autry Way, Anaheim, CA 92803, USA
Selby, David *Actor*
%International Creative Mgmt, 8942 Wilshire Blvd, Beverly Hills, CA 90211, USA
Selby, Philip *Composer*
Hill Cottage, Via 1 Maggio 93, 00068 Rignano Flaminio, Rome, Italy
Seldin, Donald W *Physician*
%Texas Southwest Medical Center, 5323 Harry Hines Blvd, Dallas, TX 75235, USA
Seldon, Bruce *Boxer*
%Don King Productions, 968 Pinehurst Dr, Las Vegas, NV 89109, USA
Seles, Monica *Tennis Player*
%Laurel Oak Estates, 7751 Beeridge Road, Sarasota, FL 34241, USA
Seley, Jason *Sculptor*
%Cornell University, Art Dept, Ithaca, NY 14853, USA
Selig, Allan H (Bud) *Baseball Executive*
%Milwaukee Brewers, County Stadium, 201 S 46th St, Milwaukee, WI 53214, USA
Seliger, Mark *Photographer*
%Little Brown Co, 34 Beacon St, Boston, MA 02108, USA
Seligman, Martin E P *Psychologist*
%University of Pennsylvania, Psychology Dept, Philadelphia, PA 19104, USA
Selkirk, George N *Government Official, England*
Rose Lawn Coppice, Wimborne, Dorset, England
Selkoe, Dennis J *Neurologist*
%Brigham & Women's Hospital, 221 Longwood Ave, Boston, MA 02115, USA
Sellars, Peter *Theater Director*
%Creative Artists Agency, 9830 Wilshire Blvd, Beverly Hills, CA 90212, USA
Selleca, Connie *Actress*
%William Morris Agency, 151 S El Camino Dr, Beverly Hills, CA 90212, USA

Selleck, Tom *Actor*
331 Sage Lane, Santa Monica, CA 90402, USA

Seller, Peg *Sychronized Swimmer, Coach*
72 Monkswood Crescent, Newmarket ON L3Y 2K1, Canada

Sellers, Franklin *Religious Leader*
%Reformed Episcopal Church, 2001 Frederick Road, Baltimore, MD 21228, USA

Sellers, Ron *Football Player*
4109 Hickory Dr, Palm Beach Gardens, FL 33418, USA

Sellick, Phyllis *Concert Pianist*
Beverley House, 29-A Ranelagh Ave, Barnes, London SW13 0BN, England

Selmon, Dewey *Football Player*
2725 S Berry, Norman, OK 73072, USA

Selmon, Lee Roy *Football Player*
18255 Wayne Road, Odessa, FL 33556, USA

Selmon, Lucious *Football Player, Coach*
%Jacksonville Jaguars, 1 Stadium Place, Jacksonville, FL 32202, USA

Selten, Reinhold *Nobel Economics Laureate*
Hardtweg 23, 53639 Konigswinter, Germany

Selvy, Franklin D (Frank) *Basketball Player*
206 Honey Horn Dr, Simpsonville, SC 29681, USA

Selzer, Milton *Actor*
%LA Artists Talent Agency, 2566 Overland Ave, #600, Los Angeles, CA 90064, USA

Selzer, Richard *Writer, Surgeon*
6 St Roman Terrace N, Hartford, CT 06511, USA

Semak, Michael W *Photographer*
1796 Spruce Hill Road, Pickering ON L1V 1S4, Canada

Sembello, Michael *Singer, Songwriter*
%Talent Consultants Int'l, 1560 Broadway, #1308, New York, NY 10036, USA

Sembene, Ousmane *Theater Director*
PO Box 8087, Yoff, Senegal

Sembler, Melvin F *Diplomat*
%Sembler Co, 5858 Central Ave, St Petersburg, FL 33707, USA

Semel, Terry S *Movie Executive*
%Warner Bros, 4000 Warner Blvd, Burbank, CA 91522, USA

Semenov, Anatoli *Hockey Player*
%Buffalo Sabres, Marine Midland Arena, 1 Seymour Knox Plaza, Buffalo, NY 14210, USA

Semenyaka, Lyudmila *Ballerina*
%Bolshoi Theater, Teatralnaya Pl 1, 103009 Moscow, Russia

Semiz, Teata *Bowler*
27 Burnside Place, Haskell, NJ 07420, USA

Semizorova, Nina L *Ballerina*
%Bolshoi Theater, Teatralnaya Pl 1, 103009 Moscow, Russia

Semkow, Jerzy G *Conductor*
Ul Dynasy 6 M 1, 00-354 Warsaw, Poland

Semler, Jerry D *Businessman*
%American United Life, 1 American Square, Indianapolis, IN 46282, USA

Sempe, Jean-Jacques *Cartoonist*
4 Rue Du Moulin-Vert, 75014 Paris, France

Semple, Robert B, Jr *Journalist*
%New York Times, Editorial Dept, 229 W 43rd St, New York, NY 10036, USA

Semyonov, Vladilen G *Ballet Dancer*
15/17-504 Roubinshteina St, 191002 St Petersburg, Russia

Sen, Mrinal *Movie Director*
14 Beltola Road, Calcutta 700026, India

Sendak, Maurice B *Writer, Illustrator*
200 Chestnut Hill Road, Ridgefield, CT 06877, USA

Senderens, Alain *Chef*
%Restaurant Lucas Carton, 9 Place De La Madeleine, 75008 Paris, France

Senff, Dina (Nida) *Swimmer*
%D W Couturier-Senff, Praam 122, 1186-TL Amstelveen, Netherlands

Senghor, Leopold Sedar *President, Senegal; Poet*
1 Square de Tocqueville, 75015 Paris, France

Sengstacke, John H H *Publisher*
%Sengstacke Enterprises, 2400 S Michigan Ave, Chicago, IL 60616, USA

Sensi, Giuseppe Cardinal *Religious Leader*
16 Piazza S Calisto, 00153 Rome, Italy

Seow, Yit Kin *Concert Pianist*
8 North Terrace, London SW3 2BA, England

Sepulveda, Charlie — *Jazz Musician*
%Ralph Mercado Mgmt, 568 Broadway, #608, New York, NY 10012, USA

Sequeira, Luis — *Plant Pathologist*
10 Appomattox Court, Madison, WI 53705, USA

Serafini, Tito A — *Neurobiologist*
%University of California, Neurobiology Dept, San Francisco, CA 94143, USA

Seraphim, His Beatitude Archbishop — *Religious Leader*
%Holy Synod of Church of Greece, Athens, Greece

Seraphin, Oliver — *Prime Minister, Dominica*
44 Green's Lane, Goodwill, Dominica

Serebrier, Jose — *Conductor, Composer*
20 Queensgate Gardens, London SW7 5LZ, England

Serebrov, Alexander A — *Cosmonaut*
%Potchta Kosmonavtov, Moskovskoi Oblasti, 141160 Syvisdny Goroduk, Russia

Serembus, John — *Labor Leader*
%Upholsterers Union, 25 N 4th St, Philadelphia, PA 19106, USA

Sereni, Mario — *Opera Singer*
%Eric Semon Assoc, 111 W 57th St, New York, NY 10019, USA

Serious, Yahoo — *Actor*
12/33 E Crescent St, McMahons Point, NSW 2060, Australia

Serkin, Peter A — *Concert Pianist*
RFD 3, Brattleboro, VT 05301, USA

Serlemitsos, Peter J — *Astronomer*
%BBXRT Project, Goddard Space Flight Center, Greenbelt, MD 20771, USA

Serna, Assumpta — *Actress*
8306 Wilshire Blvd, #438, Beverly Hills, CA 90211, USA

Serna, Pepe — *Actor*
127 Ruby Ave, Newport Beach, CA 92662, USA

Serota, Nicholas A — *Museum Director*
%Tate Gallery, Millbank, London SW1P 4RG, England

Serra, Richard — *Sculptor*
173 Duane St, New York, NY 10013, USA

Serrano, Juan — *Concert Guitarist*
%Prince/SF Productions, 2674 24th Ave, San Francisco, CA 94116, USA

Serrault, Michel L — *Actor, Singer*
%MS Productions, 12 Rue Greuze, 75116 Paris, France

Serrin, James B — *Mathematician*
4422 Dupont Ave, S Minneapolis, MN 55409, USA

Servan-Schreiber, Jean-Claude — *Journalist*
147 Bis Rue d'Alesia, 75014 Paris, France

SerVass, Cory J — *Editor*
%Saturday Evening Post Magazine, 1100 Waterway Blvd, Indianapolis, IN 46202, USA

Sessions, William S — *Law Enforcement Official, Judge*
3920 Argyle Terrace NW, Washington, DC 20011, USA

Seter, Mordecai — *Composer*
1 Karny St, Ramat Aviv, Tel-Aviv, Israel

Seth, Vikram — *Writer*
%Phoenix House, Orion House, 5 Upper St, London WC2H 9EA, England

Sethna, Homi N — *Engineer*
Old Yacht Club, Chatrapati Shrivaji Maharaj, Bombay 400 038, India

Setlow, Richard B — *Biophysicist*
4 Beachland Ave, East Quogue, NY 11942, USA

Setzer, Brian — *Singer, Guitarist, Band Leader*
%Dave Kaplan Mgmt, 520 Washington Blvd, #427, Venice Beach, CA 90292, USA

Setzoil, LeRoy I — *Sculptor*
30450 Mariah Lane, Sheridan, OR 97378, USA

Sevastyanov, Vitayl I — *Cosmonaut*
%Potchta Kosmonavtov, Moskovskoi Oblasti, 141160 Syvisdny Goroduk, Russia

Seven, Johnny — *Actor*
11213 McLennan Ave, Granada Hills, CA 91344, USA

Severance, Joan — *Model, Actress*
%Agency For Performing Arts, 9200 Sunset Blvd, #900, Los Angeles, CA 90069, USA

Severeid, Suzanne — *Model, Actress*
%Barry Freed, 2029 Century Park East, #600, Los Angeles, CA 90067, USA

Severino, John C — *Television Executive*
%Prime Ticket Network, 401 S Prairie St, Inglewood, CA 90301, USA

Severinsen, Carl H (Doc) — *Jazz Trumpeter, Band Leader*
4275 White Pine Lane, Santa Ynez, CA 93460, USA

S

Sepulveda - Severinsen

Seward, George C — *Attorney*
%Seward & Kissel, 1 Battery Park Plaza, New York, NY 10004, USA

Sewell, George — *Actor*
%Peter Charlesworth, 68 Old Brompton Road, London SW7 3LQ, England

Sewell, Rufus — *Actor*
%Julian Belfarge, 46 Albermarle St, London W1X 4PP, England

Sexton, Charlie — *Singer, Guitarist*
%Courage Artists, 310 Water St, #201, Vancouver BC V6B 1B6, Canada

Seybold, Jonathan — *Businessman*
%Seybold Seminars, 303 Vintage Park Dr, Fosters, CA 94404, USA

Seymour, Caroline — *Actress*
%Langford Assoc, 17 Westfields Ave, London SW13 0AT, England

Seymour, Jane — *Actress*
PO Box 548, Agoura, CA 91376, USA

Seymour, Lynn — *Ballerina*
%Artistes in Action, 16 Balderton St, London W1Y 1TF, England

Seymour, Stephanie — *Model*
12828 High Bluff Dr, #200, San Diego, CA 92130, USA

Seynhaeve, Ingrid — *Model*
%Elite Model Mgmt, 111 E 22nd St, #200, New York, NY 10010, USA

Sfar, Rachid — *Prime Minister, Tunisia*
278 Ave de Tervuren, 1150 Brussels, Belgium

Sgouros, Dimitris — *Concert Pianist*
Tompazi 28 Str, Piraeus 18537, Greece

Shack, Eddie — *Hockey Player*
686 Oriole Parkway, Toronto ON M4R 2C5, Canada

Shack, William A — *Anthropologist*
2597 Hilgard Ave, Berkeley, CA 94709, USA

Shackelford, Ted — *Actor*
12305 Valley Heart Dr, Studio City, CA 91604, USA

Shafer, R Donald — *Religious Leader*
%Brethren in Christ Church, PO Box 290, Grantham, PA 17027, USA

Shafer, Raymond P — *Governor, PA*
%Dunaway & Cross, 1146 19th St, Washington, DC 20036, USA

Shaffer, David H — *Publisher*
%MacMillan Inc, 1177 Ave of Americas, #1965, New York, NY 10036, USA

Shaffer, Paul — *Orchestra Leader, Keyboardist*
%Panacea Entertainment, 2705 Glendower Ave, Los Angeles, CA 90027, USA

Shaffer, Peter L — *Writer*
173 Riverside Dr, New York, NY 10024, USA

Shaffer, Thomas — *Financier*
%First Los Angeles Bank, 2049 Century Park East, Los Angeles, CA 90067, USA

Shagan, Steve — *Writer*
285 W Via Lola, Palm Springs, CA 92262, USA

Shagari, Alhaji Shehu Usman Aliu — *President, Nigeria*
22 Shehu Crescent, PO Box 162, Adarawa, Sokoto State, Nigeria

Shaggy — *Singer*
%Agency Group, 1775 Broadway, #433, New York, NY 10019, USA

Shah Reza Pahlavi II — *Crown Prince, Iran*
%Kubbeh Palace, Heliopolis, Cairo, Egypt

Shah, Idries — *Writer*
%A P Watt Ltd, 26/28 Bedford Row, London WC1R 4HL, England

Shahabuddin Ahmed — *President, Bangladesh; Judge*
%Supreme Court, Office of Chief Justice, Dhaka, Bangladesh

Shaheen, Jeanne — *Governor, NH*
%Governor's Office, State House, Concord, NH 03301, USA

Shaiman, Marc — *Composer*
8476 Brier Dr, West Hollywood, CA 90046, USA

Shain, Harold — *Publisher*
%Newsweek Magazine, 251 W 57th St, New York, NY 10019, USA

Shakespeare, Frank J, Jr — *Television Executive, Diplomat*
303 Coast Blvd, La Jolla, CA 92037, USA

Shalala, Donna E — *Secretary, Health & Human Services*
%Health & Human Services Dept, 200 Independence Ave SW, Washington, DC 20201, USA

Shales, Thomas W — *Journalist*
%Washington Post, Editorial Dept, 1150 15th St NW, Washington, DC 20071, USA

Shalikashvili, John M (Shali) — *Army General*
Chairman's Office, Joint Chiefs of Staff, Pentagon, Washington, DC 20318, USA

Shalit, Gene	*Movie Critic*
225 E 79th St, New York, NY 10021, USA	
Shamask, Ronaldus	*Fashion Designer*
%Moss Shamask, 39 W 37th St, New York, NY 10018, USA	
Shamir, Yitzhak	*Prime Minister, Israel*
Kiriyat Ben Gurian, Jerusalem 91919, Israel	
Shamoon, Alan	*Financier*
%Apple Bank for Savings, 205 E 42nd St, New York, NY 10017, USA	
Shanahan, Brendan	*Hockey Player*
242 Trumbull St, Hartford, CT 06103, USA	
Shanahan, Edmond M	*Financier*
%Bell Federal Savings & Loan, 79 W Monroe St, Chicago, IL 60603, USA	
Shanahan, Mike	*Football Coach*
%Denver Broncos, 13655 E Dove Valley Parkway, Englewood, CO 80112, USA	
Shanahan, R Michael	*Financier*
%Capital Research & Mgmt, 333 S Hope St, Los Angeles, CA 90071, USA	
Shanahan, William S	*Businessman*
%Colgate-Palmolive Co, 300 Park Ave, New York, NY 10022, USA	
Shandling, Garry	*Comedian, Actor*
%Brillstein/Grey, 9150 Wilshire Blvd, #350, Beverly Hills, CA 90212, USA	
Shandrowsky, Alex	*Labor Leader*
%Marine Engineer Beneficial Assn, 444 N Capitol St NW, Washington, DC 20001, USA	
Shane, Bob	*Singer (Kingston Trio)*
9410 S 46th St, Phoenix, AZ 85044, USA	
Shane, Rita	*Opera Singer*
%Daniel Tritter, 545 5th Ave, New York, NY 10017, USA	
Shanice	*Singer*
%William Morris Agency, 1325 Ave of Americas, New York, NY 10019, USA	
Shank, Bud	*Jazz Saxophonist, Flutist*
PO Box 948, Port Townsend, WA 98368, USA	
Shank, Roger C	*Computer Scientist*
%Northwestern University, Learning Sciences Institute, Evanston, IL 60201, USA	
Shankar, Ravi	*Sitar Player*
17 Warden Court, Gowalia Tank Road, Bombay 36, India	
Shanks, Eugene B, Jr	*Financier*
%Bankers Trust New York Corp, 280 Park Ave, New York, NY 10017, USA	
Shannon	*Singer*
%Famous Artists Agency, 1700 Broadway, #500, New York, NY 10019, USA	
Shannon, Claude E	*Applied Mathematician*
5 Cambridge St, Winchester, MA 01890, USA	
Shannon, Elaine	*Writer*
%Penguin USA, 375 Hudson St, New York, NY 10014, USA	
Shannon, Molly	*Comedienne*
%Innovative Artists, 1999 Ave of Stars, #2850, Los Angeles, CA 90067, USA	
Shantz, Robert C (Bobby)	*Baseball Player*
152 Mount Pleasant Ave, Ambler, PA 19002, USA	
Shapar, Howard K	*Government Official*
4610 Langdrum Lane, Chevy Chase, MD 20815, USA	
Shapiro, Ascher H	*Mechanical Engineer*
111 Perkins St, Jamaica Plain, MA 02130, USA	
Shapiro, Debbie	*Actress*
%Agency For Performing Arts, 9200 Sunset Blvd, #900, Los Angeles, CA 90069, USA	
Shapiro, Harold T	*Educator*
%Princeton University, President's Office, Princeton, NJ 08544, USA	
Shapiro, Helen	*Singer*
%British & Int'l Artists, 500 Waterman Ave, #191, East Providence, RI 02914, USA	
Shapiro, Irving S	*Businessman, Attorney*
%Skadden Arps Slate Meagher Flom, 919 3rd Ave, New York, NY 10022, USA	
Shapiro, Irwin I	*Physicist*
17 Lantern Lane, Lexington, MA 02173, USA	
Shapiro, Joel E	*Artist*
280-290 Lafayette St,, #3-D, New York, NY 10012, USA	
Shapiro, Karl J	*Writer*
211 W 106th St, #11-C, New York, NY 10025, USA	
Shapiro, Marc J	*Financier*
%Texas Commerce Bank, 712 Main St, Houston, TX 77002, USA	
Shapiro, Mary L	*Government Official*
%Securities & Exchange Commission, 450 5th St NW, Washington, DC 20001, USA	

S

Shalit - Shapiro

Shapiro, Maurice M — *Astrophysicist*
205 S Yoakum Parkway, #1514, Alexandria, VA 22304, USA

Shapiro, Mel — *Writer*
%University of California, Theater Film & TV Dept, Los Angeles, CA 90024, USA

Shapiro, Neal — *Equestrian Rider*
4190 Silver Beach Road, Ballston Spa, NY 12020, USA

Shapiro, Robert B — *Businessman*
%Monsanto Co, 800 N Lindbergh Blvd, St Louis, MO 63167, USA

Shapiro, Robert L — *Attorney*
2121 Ave of Stars, #1900, Los Angeles, CA 90067, USA

Shapley, Lloyd S — *Mathematician, Economist*
%University of California, Economics Dept, Los Angeles, CA 90024, USA

Shaposhnikov, Yevgeny I — *Air Marshal, Russia*
%Commonwealth of Independent States Military Command, Moscow, Russia

Share, Charlie (Chuck) — *Basketball Player*
12922 Twin Meadows Court, St Louis, MO 63146, USA

Sharif Zaid Ibin Shaker — *Prime Minister, Jordan*
%Prime Minister's Office, PO Box 80, 35215 Amman, Jordan

Sharif, M M Nawaz — *Prime Minister, Pakistan*
%Pakistan Muslim League, Parliament, Islamabad, Pakistan

Sharif, Omar — *Actor*
%Anne Alvares Correa, 18 Rue Troyon, 75017 Paris, France

Sharma, Rakesh — *Cosmonaut, India*
%Hindustan Aeronautics Ltd, Bangalore 560 037, India

Sharman, Helen — *Cosmonaut*
12 Stratton Court, Adelaide Road, Surbiton, Surrey, England

Sharman, William W (Bill) — *Basketball Player, Coach, Executive*
27996 Palos Verdes Dr E, Rancho Palos Verde, CA 90275, USA

Sharon, Ariel — *Government Official, Israel; Army Genera*
%Knesset, Jerusalem, Israel

Sharp, Dee Dee — *Singer*
%Cape Entertainment, 1161 NW 76th Ave, Fort Lauderdale, FL 33322, USA

Sharp, Marsha — *Basketball Coach*
%Texas Tech University, Athletic Dept, Lubbock, TX 79409, USA

Sharp, Mitchell W — *Government Official, Canada*
33 Monkland Ave, Ottawa ON K1S 1Y8, Canada

Sharp, Phillip A — *Nobel Medicine Laureate*
36 Fairmont Ave, Newton, MA 02158, USA

Sharp, Robert P — *Geologist*
1901 Gibraltar Road, Santa Barbara, CA 93105, USA

Sharp, U S Grant, Jr — *Navy Admiral*
876 San Antonio Place, San Diego, CA 92106, USA

Sharpe, Rochelle P — *Journalist*
2500 "Q" St NW, #315, Washington, DC 20007, USA

Sharpe, Shannon — *Football Player*
204 Jay St, Glennville, GA 30427, USA

Sharpe, Tom — *Writer*
%Richard Scott Simon Ltd, 43 Doughty St, London WC1N 2LF, England

Sharpe, William F — *Nobel Economics Laureate*
25 Doud Dr, Los Altos, CA 94022, USA

Sharpton, Al — *Religious Leader, Social Activist*
1133 Bedford Ave, Brooklyn, NY 11216, USA

Sharqi, Sheikh Hamad Bin Muhammad Al- — *Ruler, Fujairah*
%Royal Palace, Fujairah, United Arab Emirates

Shatalov, Valdimir A — *Cosmonaut*
%Potchta Kosmonavtov, Moskovskoi Oblasti, 141160 Syvisdny Goroduk, Russia

Shatkin, Aaron J — *Scientist*
%Center for Advanced Biotechnology, 679 Hoes Lane, Piscataway, NJ 08854, USA

Shatner, William — *Actor*
3674 Berry Ave, Studio City, CA 91604, USA

Shattuck, Kim — *Singer, Guitarist (The Muffs)*
%International Creative Mgmt, 40 W 57th St, New York, NY 10019, USA

Shattuck, Shari — *Actress*
10641 La Grande Ave, #201, Los Angeles, CA 90025, USA

Shaud, Grant — *Actor*
8738 Appian Way, Los Angeles, CA 90046, USA

Shaud, John A — *Air Force General, Association Executive*
%Air Force Aid Society, 1745 Jefferson Davis Highway, #202, Arlington, VA 22202, USA

Shaughnessy, Charles — *Actor*
534 15th St, Santa Monica, CA 90402, USA

Shavelson, Melville — *Producer, Writer*
11947 Sunshine Terrace, North Hollywood, CA 91604, USA

Shaver, Billy Joe — *Singer, Songwriter*
%Fat City Artists, 1908 Chet Atkins Place, #502, Nashville, TN 37212, USA

Shaver, Helen — *Actress*
%Shaver/Smith, 9171 Wilshire Blvd, #406, Beverly Hills, CA 90210, USA

Shaw, Artie — *Jazz Clarinetist*
2127 W Palos Court, Newbury Park, CA 91320, USA

Shaw, Bernard — *Commentator*
%Cable News Network, News Dept, 820 1st St NE, Washington, DC 20002, USA

Shaw, Brewster H, Jr — *Astronaut*
%NASA, Johnson Space Center, 2101 NASA Road, Houston, TX 77058, USA

Shaw, Brian — *Basketball Player*
540 Brickell Key Dr, #1513, Miami, FL 33131, USA

Shaw, Carolyn Hagner — *Publisher*
%Social Register, 2620 "P" St NW, Washington, DC 20007, USA

Shaw, David L — *Journalist*
%Los Angeles Times, Editorial Dept, Times-Mirror Square, Los Angeles, CA 90053, USA

Shaw, Kenneth A — *Educator*
%Syracuse University, President's Office, Syracuse, NY 13244, USA

Shaw, Marlena — *Singer*
%Berkeley Agency, 2608 9th St, Berkeley, CA 94710, USA

Shaw, Martin — *Actor*
204 Belswin's Lane, Hemel, Hempstead, Herts, England

Shaw, Robert J (Bob) — *Baseball Player*
222 US Highway 1, #208, Tequesta, FL 33469, USA

Shaw, Robert L — *Conductor*
%Atlanta Symphony, 1280 Peachtree St NE, Atlanta, GA 30309, USA

Shaw, Run Run — *Movie Producer*
Shaw House, Lot 220 Clear Water Bay Road, Kowloon, Hong Kong, China

Shaw, Scott — *Photographer*
%Odessa American, Editorial Dept, 222 E 4th St, Odessa, TX 79761, USA

Shaw, Stan — *Actor*
%Innovative Artists, 1999 Ave of Stars, #2850, Los Angeles, CA 90067, USA

Shaw, Tim — *Swimmer, Water Polo Player*
9229 Spring Valley Lake, Victorville, CA 92392, USA

Shaw, William — *Businessman*
%Volt Information Services, 1221 Ave of Americas, New York, NY 10020, USA

Shawcross of Friston, H William — *Judge; Government Official, England*
Friston Place, Sussex, I-1 Albany, Piccadilly, London W1V 9RP, England

Shawn, Wallace — *Writer, Actor*
%Gersh Agency, 232 N Canon Dr, Beverly Hills, CA 90210, USA

Shaye, Robert — *Movie Executive*
%New Line Cinema, 578 8th Ave, New York, NY 10018, USA

Shea, Jack — *Speed Skater*
28 Forest St, Lake Placid, NY 12946, USA

Shea, John — *Actor*
1495 Orlando Road, Pasadena, CA 91106, USA

Shea, Joseph F — *Space Scientist*
15 Dogwood Road, Weston, MA 02193, USA

Shea, Judith — *Artist*
%Barbara Krakow Gallery, 10 Newbury St, Boston, MA 02116, USA

Shear, Jules — *Singer, Songwriter*
%Mike's Artist Mgmt, 147 W Simpson, Tucson, AZ 85701, USA

Shear, Rhonda — *Comedienne*
PO Box 67838, Los Angeles, CA 90067, USA

Shearer, Brad — *Football Player*
1909 Lakeshore Dr, #B, Austin, TX 78746, USA

Shearer, Moira — *Ballerina, Actress*
%Rogers Coleridge White, 2 Powis Mews, London W11 1JN, England

Shearing, George A — *Jazz Pianist, Composer*
%Joan Shulman, 103 Avenue Road, #301, Toronto ON M5R 2G9, Canada

Sheed, Wilfrid J J — *Writer*
%General Delivery, Sag Harbor, NY 11963, USA

Sheedy, Ally — *Actress*
11755 Wilshire Blvd, #2270, Los Angeles, CA 90025, USA

Sheehan, Doug *Actor*
%Innovative Artists, 1999 Ave of Stars, #2850, Los Angeles, CA 90067, USA

Sheehan, John J *Marine Corps General*
%CinC, US Atlantic Command, 1562 Mitscher Ave, Norfolk, VA 23551, USA

Sheehan, Neil *Journalist*
4505 Klingle St NW, Washington, DC 20016, USA

Sheehan, Patty *Golfer*
2300 Skyline Blvd, Reno, NV 89509, USA

Sheehan, Susan *Writer*
4505 Klingle St NW, Washington, DC 20016, USA

Sheehy, Gail H *Writer*
300 E 57th St, #18-D, New York, NY 10022, USA

Sheehy, Tim *Hockey Player*
241 Perkins St, Jamaica Plain, MA 02130, USA

Sheen, Martin *Actor*
6916 Dune Dr, Malibu, CA 90265, USA

Sheerer, Gary *Water Polo Player*
1557 Country Club Dr, Los Altos, CA 94024, USA

Sheffer, Craig *Actor*
5699 Kanan Dr, #275, Agoura, CA 91301, USA

Sheffield, Gary A *Baseball Player*
6731 30th St S, St Petersburg, FL 33712, USA

Sheffield, John M (Johnny) *Actor*
834 1st Ave, Chula Vista, CA 91911, USA

Sheffield, William *Governor, AK*
PO Box 91476, Anchorage, AK 99509, USA

Sheik, Duncan *Singer*
%Creative Artists Agency, 9830 Wilshire Blvd, Beverly Hills, CA 90212, USA

Sheikh Humaid Bin Rashid Al-Nuami *Ruler, Ajman*
%Royal Palace, Ajman, United Arab Emirates

Sheikh Jaber Al-Ahmad Al-Jaber Al Sabah *Emir, Kuwait*
%Sief Palace, Amiry Diwan, Kuwait

Sheikh Martoum Bin Rashid Al-Maktoum *Ruler, Dubai*
%Royal Palace, Dubai, United Arab Emirates

Sheikh Rashid Bin Ahmed Al-Mu'alla *Ruler, Umm Al Quwain*
%Ruler's Palace, Umm Al Quwain, United Arab Emirates

Sheikh Rashid bin Said al-Maktoum *Prime Minister, United Arab Emirates*
%Royal Palace, PO Box 899, Abu Dhubai, United Arab Emirates

Sheikh Saad Al-Abdullah Al-Salem Sabah *Crown Prince & Prime Minister, Kuwait*
%Prime Minister's Office, PO Box 4, Safat, 13001 Kuwait City, Kuwait

Sheikh Saqr Bin Muhammad Al-Qasimi *Ruler, Ras Al Khaimah*
%Ruler's Palace, Ras Al Khaimah, United Arab Emirates

Sheikh Sultan Bin Muhammad Al-Qasimi *Ruler, Sharjah*
%Royal Palace, Sharjah, United Arab Emirates

Sheikh Zayed Bin Sultan Al-Nahayan *Ruler, Abu Dhabi*
%President's Office, Manhal Palace, Abu Dhabi, United Arab Emirates

Sheila E(scovedo) *Singer, Drummer*
8900 Wilshire Blvd, #300, Beverly Hills, CA 90211, USA

Sheinberg, Sidney J *Entertainment Executive*
%MCA Inc, 100 Universal City Plaza, Universal City, CA 91608, USA

Sheiner, David S *Actor*
1827 Veteran Ave, #19, Los Angeles, CA 90025, USA

Sheinfeld, David *Composer*
1458 24th Ave, San Francisco, CA 94122, USA

Sheinkman, Jack *Labor Leader*
%Amalgamated Clothing & Textile Workers, 1710 Broadway, #3, New York, NY 10019, USA

Shelby, Carroll *Auto Racing Driver, Builder*
%Shelby Industries, 19021 S Figueroa St, Gardena, CA 90248, USA

Sheldon, Jack *Jazz Singer, Trumpter*
7095 Hollywood Blvd, #617, Los Angeles, CA 90028, USA

Sheldon, Sidney *Writer*
10250 W Sunset Blvd, Los Angeles, CA 90077, USA

Shell, Art *Football Player, Coach*
2318 Walker Dr, Lawrenceville, GA 30043, USA

Shell, Donnie *Football Player*
2945 Shandon Road, Rock Hill, SC 29730, USA

Shelley, Barbara *Actress*
%Ken McReddie, 91 Regent St, London W1R 7TB, England

Shelley, Carole _Actress_
333 W 56th St, New York, NY 10019, USA
Shelley, Howard G _Concert Pianist, Conductor_
38 Cholmeley Park, London N6 5ER, England
Shelton, Deborah _Actress_
%Michael Slessinger, 8730 Sunset Blvd, #220-W, Los Angeles, CA 90069, USA
Shelton, Henry H (Hugh) _Army General_
%Chairman's Office, Joint Chiefs of Staff, Pentagon, Washington, DC 20318, USA
Shelton, Lonnie _Basketball Player_
860 S 8th Ave, Kingsburg, CA 93631, USA
Shelton, Ricky Van _Singer, Songwriter_
%Michael Campbell Mgmt, 1313 16th Ave S, Nashville, TN 37212, USA
Shelton, Robert M _Religious Leader_
%Cumberland Presbyterian Church, 1978 Union Ave, Memphis, TN 38104, USA
Shelton, Ronald W _Movie Director_
15200 Friends St, Pacific Palisades, CA 90272, USA
Shelton, William E _Educator_
%Eastern Michigan University, President's Office, Ypsilanti, MI 48197, USA
Shenandoh, Joanne _Singer, Songwriter_
%Oneida Indian Territory, PO Box 10, Oneida, NY 13421, USA
Shepard, Alan B, Jr _Astronaut; Navy Admiral_
1512 Bonifacio Lane, Pebble Beach, CA 93953, USA
Shepard, Jean _Singer_
%Ace Productions, PO Box 428, Portland, TN 37148, USA
Shepard, Jewel _Model, Actress_
PO Box 480265, Los Angeles, CA 90048, USA
Shepard, Robert N _Psychologist_
%Stanford University, Psychology Dept, Stanford, CA 94305, USA
Shepard, Samuel K (Sam) _Writer, Actor_
1801 Martha St, Encino, CA 91316, USA
Shephard, Gillian _Government Official, England_
%House of Commons, Westminster, London SW1A 0AA, England
Shephard, Stephen B _Editor_
%Business Week Magazine, 1221 Ave of Americas, New York, NY 10020, USA
Shepheard, Peter F _Architect_
21 Well Road, London NW3 1LH, England
Shepherd, Cybill _Model, Actress_
3930 Valley Meadow Road, Encino, CA 91436, USA
Shepherd, Kenny Wayne _Blues Guitarist_
%Ken Shepherd Co, 509 Market St, #612, Shreveport, LA 71101, USA
Shepherd, Malcolm N _Government Official, England_
29 Kennington Palace Court, Sancroft St, London SE11, England
Shepherd, Morgan _Auto Racing Driver_
PO Box 623, Conover, NC 28613, USA
Shepherd, Sherrie _Cartoonist (Francie)_
%United Feature Syndicate, 200 Madison Ave, New York, NY 10016, USA
Shepherd, William M _Astronaut_
12117 Ticonderoga Road, Houston, TX 77044, USA
Sheppard, Jonathan _Steeplechase Racing Trainer_
%Ashwell Stables, 297 Lamborntown Road, West Grove, PA 19390, USA
Sheppard, T G _Singer_
%R J Kaltenbach, PO Box 490, Kodak, TN 37764, USA
Sheps, Cecil G _Epidemiologist_
388 Carolina Meadows Villa, Chapel Hill, NC 27514, USA
Sher, Antony _Actor_
%Hope & Lyne, 108 Leonard St, London EC2A 4RH, England
Shera, Mark _Actor_
%Karg/Weissenbach, 329 N Wetherly Dr, #101, Beverly Hills, CA 90211, USA
Sherba, John _Violinist (Kronos Quartet)_
%Kronos Quartet, 1235 9th Ave, San Francisco, CA 94122, USA
Sheridan, Bonnie Bramlett _Singer (Delaney & Bonnie), Actress_
18011 Martha St, Encino, CA 91316, USA
Sheridan, Jamey _Actor_
%Sames/Rollnick Assoc, 250 W 57th St, New York, NY 10107, USA
Sheridan, Jim _Movie Director_
%Creative Artists Agency, 9830 Wilshire Blvd, Beverly Hills, CA 90212, USA
Sheridan, Nicolette _Actress_
%Creative Artists Agency, 9830 Wilshire Blvd, Beverly Hills, CA 90212, USA

S

Sheridan, Tony — *Singer*
%Atlantis Artist Agency, 1950 West Lane Road, Ottawa ON K1H 5J6, Canada

Sherlock, Nancy J — *Astronaut*
%NASA, Johnson Space Center, 2101 NASA Road, Houston, TX 77058, USA

Sherman, Bobby — *Singer, Actor*
1870 Sunset Plaza Dr, Los Angeles, CA 90069, USA

Sherman, Cindy — *Photographer*
%Metro Pictures, 519 W 24th St, New York, NY 10011, USA

Sherman, George M — *Businessman*
%Danaher Corp, 1250 24th St NW, Washington, DC 20037, USA

Sherman, Paddy — *Publisher*
%Citizen, Box 5020, Ottawa ON K2C 3M4, Canada

Sherman, Richard M — *Composer, Lyricist*
808 N Crescent Dr, Beverly Hills, CA 90210, USA

Sherman, Robert B — *Songwriter, Writer*
1032 Hilldale Ave, Los Angeles, CA 90069, USA

Sherman, Vincent — *Movie Director*
6355 Sycamore Meadows Dr, Malibu, CA 90265, USA

Sherman, William — *Religious Leader*
%Woodmont Baptist Church, 2100 Woodmont Blvd, Nashville, TN 37215, USA

Shernoff, William M — *Attorney*
600 S Indian Hill Blvd, Claremont, CA 91711, USA

Sherrill, Jackie — *Football Coach*
%Mississippi State University, Athletic Dept, Mississippi State, MS 39762, USA

Sherrod, Blackie — *Sportswriter*
%Dallas Morning News, Editorial Dept, Communications Center, Dallas, TX 75265, USA

Sherry, Paul H — *Religious Leader*
%United Church of Christ, 700 Prospect Ave, Cleveland, OH 44115, USA

Sherwood, Madeline Thornton — *Actress*
32 Leroy St, New York, NY 10014, USA

Shesol, Jeff — *Cartoonist (Thatch)*
%Creators Syndicate, 5777 W Century Blvd, #700, Los Angeles, CA 90045, USA

Shettles, Landrum B — *Obstetrician, Gynecologist*
2209 Pardee Place, Las Vegas, NV 89104, USA

Shevardnadze, Eduard A — *President, Georgia*
%President's Office, State Council, Tbilisi, Georgia

Shevchenko, Arkady N — *Government Official, Russia*
%Alfred A Knopf Inc, 201 E 50th St, New York, NY 10022, USA

Shi, David E — *Educator*
%Furman University, President's Office, Greenville, SC 29613, USA

Shields, Brooke — *Model, Actress*
%Christa Inc, 2300 W Sahara Ave, #630, Las Vegas, NV 89102, USA

Shields, Carol — *Writer*
701-237 Wellington Crescent, Winnipeg MB R3M 0A1, Canada

Shields, Perry — *Judge*
%US Tax Court, 400 2nd St NW, Washington, DC 20217, USA

Shields, Robert — *Mime (Shields & Yarnell)*
%Robert Shields Designs, PO Box 10024, Sedona, AZ 86339, USA

Shields, Will — *Football Player*
%Kansas City Chiefs, 1 Arrowhead Dr, Kansas City, KS 64129, USA

Shiely, John S — *Businessman*
%Briggs & Stratton, PO Box 702, Milwaukee, WI 53201, USA

Shigeta, James — *Actor*
8917 Cynthia St, #1, Los Angeles, CA 90069, USA

Shikler, Aaron — *Artist*
44 W 77th St, New York, NY 10024, USA

Shiley Newhouse, Jean — *Track Athlete*
3189 Barry Ave, Los Angeles, CA 90066, USA

Shilton, Peter — *Soccer Player*
%Plymouth Argyll Football Club, Plymouth, England

Shimerman, Armin — *Actor*
%Innovative Artists, 1999 Ave of Stars, #2850, Los Angeles, CA 90067, USA

Shimkus, Joanna — *Actress*
9255 Doheny Road, Los Angeles, CA 90069, USA

Shimono, Sab — *Actor*
2025 Addison St, Berkeley, CA 94704, USA

Shine, Michael (Mike) — *Track Athlete*
508 Royal Road, State College, PA 16801, USA

Shinefield, Henry R — *Pediatrician*
2705 Larkin St, San Francisco, CA 94109, USA

Shinn, George — *Basketball Executive*
%Charlotte Hornets, 1 Hive Dr, Charlotte, NC 28217, USA

Shinseki, Eric K (Ric) — *Army General*
Deputy CofS, Operations/Plans, Hq USA, Pentagon, Washington, DC 20310, USA

Shipler, David K — *Journalist*
4005 Thornapple St, Bethesda, MD 20815, USA

Shipley, Walter V — *Financier*
%Chase Manhattan Corp, 270 Park Ave, New York, NY 10017, USA

Shipp, E R — *Columnist*
%New York Daily News, Editorial Dept, 220 E 42nd St, New York, NY 10017, USA

Shipp, John Wesley — *Actor*
850 N King's Road, #208, West Hollywood, CA 90069, USA

Shire, David L — *Composer*
%Savitsky Stain Geibelson, 1901 Ave of Stars, #1450, Los Angeles, CA 90067, USA

Shire, Talia — *Actress*
10730 Bellagio Road, Los Angeles, CA 90077, USA

Shirley, George — *Opera Singer*
%University of Michigan, Music School, Ann Arbor, MI 48109, USA

Shirley, J Dallas — *Basketball Referee*
5324 Pommel Dr, Mount Airy, MD 21771, USA

Shirley-Quirk, John — *Opera Singer*
6062 Red Clover Lane, Clarksville, MD 21029, USA

Shlaudeman, Harry W — *Diplomat*
3531 Winfield Lane NW, Washington, DC 20007, USA

Shlyapina, Galina A — *Ballerina*
%Bolshoi Theater, Teatralnaya Pl 1, 103009 Moscow, Russia

Shnayerson, Robert B — *Editor*
118 Riverside Dr, New York, NY 10024, USA

Shoate, Rod — *Football Player*
Rt 2, Box 407, Spiro, OK 74959, USA

Shobert, Bubba — *Motorcycle Racing Rider*
7318 93rd St, Lubbock, TX 79424, USA

Shock, Ernest F — *Labor Leader*
%United Steelworkers Upholstery Division, 25 N 4th St, Philadelphia, PA 19106, USA

Shocked, Michelle — *Singer*
%Little Big Man, 39-A Gramercy Park N, #1-C, New York, NY 10010, USA

Shockley, William — *Actor*
6345 Balboa Blvd, #375, Encino, CA 91316, USA

Shoecraft, John A — *Balloonist*
%Shoecraft Contracting Co, 7430 E Stetson Dr, Scottsdale, AZ 85251, USA

Shoemaker, Carolyn — *Geologist, Astronomer*
%Mount Palomar Observatory, Palomar Mountain, Mount Palomar, CA 92060, USA

Shoemaker, Robert M — *Army General*
Rt 4, Box 4510-K, Belton, TX 76513, USA

Shoemaker, William L (Willie) — *Thoroughbred Racing Jockey, Trainer*
%Vincent Andrews Mgmt, 315 S Beverly Dr, #208, Beverly Hills, CA 90212, USA

Shoemate, C Richard — *Businessman*
%CPC International, International Plaza, Englewood Cliffs, NJ 07632, USA

Shoji, Dave — *Volleyball Coach*
%University of Hawaii, Athletic Dept, Hilo, HI 96720, USA

Sholty, George — *Harness Racing Driver*
3669 Cypress Wood Court, Lake Worth, FL 33467, USA

Shonekan, Ernest A O — *President, Nigeria*
12 Alexander Ave, Ikoyi, Lagos, Nigeria

Shonin, Georgi S — *Cosmonaut, Air Force General*
%Potchta Kosmonavtov, Moskovskoi Oblasti, 141160 Syvisdny Goroduk, Russia

Short, Alonzo E, Jr — *Army General*
Director, Information Systems Agency, 701 S Courthouse Road, Arlington, VA 22204, USA

Short, Bobby — *Singer, Actor, Pianist*
444 E 57th St, #9-E, New York, NY 10022, USA

Short, Martin — *Comedian*
15907 Alcima Ave, Pacific Palisades, CA 90272, USA

Short, Purvis — *Basketball Player*
8111 Fondren Lake Dr, Houston, TX 77071, USA

Short, Thomas C — *Labor Leader*
%Theatrical Stage Employees Int'l Alliance, 1515 Broadway, New York, NY 10036, USA

Shorter, Frank *Marathon Runner*
%Frank Shorter Sports Wear, 89 Willowbrook Road, #D, Boulder, CO 80301, USA

Shorter, Wayne *Jazz Saxophonist, Composer*
%International Music Network, 2 Main St, #400, Gloucester, MA 01930, USA

Shortridge, Steve *Actor*
1707 Clearview Dr, Beverly Hills, CA 90210, USA

Shortway, Richard H *Publisher*
%Vogue Magazine, 350 Madison Ave, New York, NY 10017, USA

Shostakovich, Maxim D *Conductor*
PO Box 273, Jordanville, NY 13361, USA

Show, Grant *Actor*
937 S Tremaine Ave, Los Angeles, CA 90019, USA

Showalter, Max *Actor*
5 Gilbert Hill Road, Chester, CT 06412, USA

Showalter, William N (Buck), III *Baseball Manager*
7501 Jefferson Ave, Century, FL 32535, USA

Shower, Kathy *Model, Actress*
300 W Lakeview Ave, Madison, WI 53716, USA

Showfety, Robert E *Financier*
%Federal Home Loan Bank, 1475 Peachtree St NE, Atlanta, GA 30309, USA

Shreve, Susan R *Writer*
3319 Newark St NW, Washington DC 20008, USA

Shribman, David M *Journalist*
%Boston Globe, Editorial Dept, 1130 Connecticut Ave NW, Washington, DC 20036, USA

Shrimpton, Jean *Model, Actress*
Abbey Hotel, Penzance, Cornwall, England

Shriner, Kin *Actor*
3915 Benedict Canyon Dr, Sherman Oaks, CA 91423, USA

Shriner, Wil *Entertainer*
5313 Quakertown Ave, Woodland Hills, CA 91364, USA

Shriver, Donald W, Jr *Educator*
%Union Theological Seminary, President's Office, New York, NY 10027, USA

Shriver, Duward F *Chemist*
1100 Colfax St, Evanston, IL 60201, USA

Shriver, Eunice Kennedy *Association Executive*
%Joseph P Kennedy Foundation, 1325 "G" St NW, #500, Washington, DC 20005, USA

Shriver, Loren J *Astronaut*
%Space Transportation Systems Operation, Kennedy Space Center, FL 32899, USA

Shriver, Maria *Commentator*
3110 Main St, #300, Santa Monica, CA 90405, USA

Shriver, Pamela H (Pam) *Tennis Player*
%PHS Ltd, 401 Washington Ave, #902, Baltimore, MD 21204, USA

Shriver, R Sargent, Jr *Government Official, Diplomat*
%Fried Frank Harris Shriver Assoc, 1350 New Hampshire NW, Washington, DC 20036, USA

Shrontz, Frank A *Businessman*
2949 81st Place, #P, Mercer Island, WA 98040, USA

Shtokolov, Boris T *Opera Singer*
%Mariinsky Theater, Teatralnaya Pl 1, St Petersburg, Russia

Shuart, James M *Educator*
%Hofstra University, President's Office, Hempstead, NY 11550, USA

Shubin, Neil H *Biologist*
%Harvard University, Biology Dept, Cambridge, MA 02138, USA

Shudlick, Carol Ann *Basketball Player*
%University of Minnesota, Athletic Dept, Minneapolis, MN 55455, USA

Shue, Andrew *Actor*
2617 Outpost Dr, Los Angeles, CA 90068, USA

Shue, Elisabeth *Actress*
PO Box 464, South Orange, NJ 07079, USA

Shue, Gene *Basketball Coach, Executive*
1151 Jeffery Dr, Crofton, MD 21114, USA

Shugart, Alan F *Inventor (Computer Disc Drive)*
%Seagate Technologies, 920 Disc Dr, Scotts Valley, CA 95066, USA

Shukovsky, Joel *Writer*
%Shukovsky-English Ent, 4024 Radford Ave, Studio City, CA 91604, USA

Shula, Don F *Football Coach*
16 Indian Creek Island, Miami, FL 33154, USA

Shuler, Ellie G, Jr *Air Force General*
32 Willow Way W, Alexander City, AL 35010, USA

Shuler, Heath — *Football Player*
%New Orleans Saints, 1500 Poydras St, New Orleans, LA 70112, USA

Shull, Clifford G — *Nobel Physics Laureate*
4 Wingate Road, Lexington, MA 02173, USA

Shull, Richard B — *Actor*
%Cheerieerie Ltd, 130 W 42nd St, #2400, New York, NY 10036, USA

Shulman, Lawrence E — *Biomedical Researcher*
2205 Rogene Dr, #102, Baltimore, MD 21209, USA

Shulman, Robert G — *Biophysicist*
333 Cedar St, New Haven, CT 06510, USA

Shultz, George P — *Secretary, State, Treasury & Labor*
776 Dolores St, Stanford, CA 94305, USA

Shumate, John — *Basketball Player, Coach*
1061 E Magdalena Dr, Tempe, AZ 85283, USA

Shumsky, Oscar — *Concert Violinist*
%Maxim Gershunoff Attractions, 502 Park Ave, New York, NY 10022, USA

Shumway, Norman E — *Heart Surgeon*
%Stanford University, Medical Center, 300 Pasteur Dr, Stanford, CA 94304, USA

Shyer, Charles R — *Writer, Director*
4040 Stansburg Ave, Sherman Oaks, CA 91423, USA

Sias, John B — *Publisher*
%Chronicle Publishing Co, 901 Mission St, San Francisco, CA 94103, USA

Sibbett, Jane — *Actress*
2144 Nichols Canyon Road, Los Angeles, CA 90046, USA

Siberry, Jane — *Singer, Songwriter*
%Agency Group, 1775 Broadway, #433, New York, NY 10019, USA

Sibley, Antoinette — *Ballerina*
%Royal Ballet, Bow St, London WC2E 9DD, England

Sichting, Jerry — *Basketball Player, Executive*
3190 Country Club Road, Martinsville, IN 46151, USA

Sidenbladh, Goran — *Architect*
Narvagen 23, 114 60 Stockholm, Sweden

Sider, Harvey R — *Religious Leader*
%Brethren in Christ Church, PO Box 290, Grantham, PA 17027, USA

Sidey, Hugh S — *Journalist*
%Time Inc, Editorial Dept, 1050 Connecticut Ave NW, Washington, DC 20036, USA

Sidi Mohammed — *Crown Prince, Morocco*
%Royal Palace, Rabat, Morocco

Sidlik, Thomas W — *Financier*
%Chrysler Financial Corp, 27777 Franklin Road, Southfield, MI 48034, USA

Sidney, George — *Movie Director*
910 N Rexford Dr, Beverly Hills, CA 90210, USA

Sidney, Sylvia — *Actress*
%Century Artists, 1148 4th St, #206, Santa Monica, CA 90403, USA

Siebert, Wilfred C (Sonny) — *Baseball Player*
2555 Brush Creek, St Louis, MO 63129, USA

Sieff, Jeanloup — *Photographer*
87 Rue Ampere, 75017 Paris, France

Siegbahn, Kai M B — *Nobel Physics Laureate*
%University of Uppsala, Physics Institute, Uppsala, Sweden

Siegel, Bernie S — *Surgeon, Writer*
61 Oxbow Lane, Woodbridge, CT 06525, USA

Siegel, Herbert J — *Businessman*
%Chris-Craft Industries, 767 5th Ave, New York, NY 10153, USA

Siegel, Ira T — *Publisher*
%Reed Reference Publishers, 121 Chanlon Road, New Providence, NJ 07974, USA

Siegel, L Pendleton (Penn) — *Businessman*
%Potlatch Corp, 1 Maritime Plaza, San Francisco, CA 94111, USA

Siegel, Robert C — *Commentator*
%National Public Radio, News Dept, 2025 "M" St NW, Washington, DC 20036, USA

Siegel, Robert C — *Businessman*
%Stride Rite Corp, PO Box 9191, Lexington, MA 02173, USA

Siegfried (Fischbacher) — *Animal Illusionist (Siegfried & Roy)*
%Beyond Belief, 1639 N Valley Dr, Las Vegas, NV 89108, USA

Siegfried, Larry — *Basketball Player*
4178 Covert Road, Perrysville, OH 44864, USA

Siekevitz, Philip — *Cell Biologist*
290 West End Ave, New York, NY 10023, USA

Siemaszko, Nina — *Actress*
%Gersh Agency, 232 N Canon Dr, Beverly Hills, CA 90210, USA

Siemon, Jeffrey G (Jeff) — *Football Player*
5401 Londonderry, Edina, MN 55436, USA

Siepi, Cesare — *Opera Singer*
12095 Brookfield Club Dr, Roswell, GA 30075, USA

Sierens, Gayle — *Sportscaster*
%NBC-TV, Sports Dept, 30 Rockefeller Plaza, New York, NY 10112, USA

Siering, Lauri — *Swimmer*
3829 Rotterdam Ave, Modesto, CA 95356, USA

Sierra, Ruben A — *Baseball Player*
%Toronto Blue Jays, 300 Bremner Blvd, Toronto ON M5V 3B3, Canada

Siers, Kevin — *Editorial Cartoonist*
%Charlotte Observer, Editorial Dept, 600 S Tryon St, Charlotte, NC 28202, USA

Sievers, Roy E — *Baseball Player*
11505 Bellefontaine Road, Spanish Lake, MO 63138, USA

Sieverts, Thomas C W — *Architect*
Buschstr 20, 53113 Bonn, Germany

Sifford, Charlie — *Golfer*
3214 Woodland View Dr, Kingwood, TX 77345, USA

Sific, Mokdad — *Prime Minister, Algeria*
%Prime Minister's Office, Government Palais, Al-Moradia, Algiers, Algeria

Sigel, Jay — *Golfer*
1284 Farm Road, Berwyn, PA 19312, USA

Sigler, Andrew C — *Businessman*
%Champion International Corp, 1 Champion Plaza, Stamford, CT 06921, USA

Sigman, Carl — *Songwriter*
1036 NE 203rd Lane, North Miami Beach, FL 33179, USA

Sigwart, Ulrich — *Heart Surgeon*
%Centre Hospitalier Universitaire Vaudois, Lausanne, Switzerland

Siilasvuo, Ensio — *Army General, Finland*
Castrenikatu 6-A-17, 00530 Helsinki 53, Finland

Sikes, Alfred C — *Government Official*
%Hearst New Media/Technology Group, 959 8th Ave, New York, NY 10019, USA

Sikes, Cynthia — *Actress*
250 N Delfern Dr, Los Angeles, CA 90077, USA

Sikking, James B — *Actor*
258 S Carmelina Ave, Los Angeles, CA 90049, USA

Silas, James — *Basketball Player*
106 E 6th Sr, t, #645, Austin, TX 78701, USA

Silas, Paul — *Basketball Player, Coach*
21 Five Ponds Dr, Waccabus, NY 10597, USA

Silber, John R — *Educator*
132 Carlton St, Brookline, MA 02146, USA

Silberman, Charles E — *Writer*
535 E 86th St, New York, NY 10028, USA

Silberstein, Diane Wichard — *Publisher*
%New Yorker Magazine, 20 W 43rd St, New York, NY 10036, USA

Silja, Anja — *Opera Singer*
%Cleveland Symphony, Severence Hall, Cleveland, OH 44106, USA

Silk, David (Dave) — *Hockey Player*
41 Lewis St, Newton, MA 02158, USA

Silk, George — *Photographer*
Owenoke Park, Westport, CT 06880, USA

Sillas, Karen — *Actress*
PO Box 725, Wading River, NY 11792, USA

Sillitoe, Alan — *Writer*
%Savage Club, 1 Whitehall Place, London SW1 2HD, England

Sills, Beverly — *Opera Singer, Director*
Rural Farm Delivery, Lambert's Cove Road, Vinegard Haven, MA 02568, USA

Silva Henriquez, Raul Cardinal — *Religious Leader*
Palacio Arzobispal, Casilla 30-D, Santiago, Chile

Silva, Henry — *Actor*
5226 Beckford Ave, Tarzana, CA 91356, USA

Silva, Jackie — *Volleyball Player*
%Marcia Esposito, PO Box 931416, Los Angeles, CA 90093, USA

Silva, Tom — *Television Entertainer*
%"This Old House" Show, PO Box 2284, South Burlington, VT 05407, USA

Silver, Edward J — *Religious Leader*
%Bible Way Church, 5118 Clarendon Road, Brooklyn, NY 11203, USA
Silver, Horace — *Jazz Pianist, Composer*
%Bridge Agency, 35 Clark St, #A-5, Brooklyn, NY 11201, USA
Silver, Joan Macklin — *Movie Director*
%Silverfilm Productions, 477 Madison Ave, New York, NY 10022, USA
Silver, Joel — *Movie Producer*
%Silver Pictures, 4000 Warner Blvd, Burbank, CA 91522, USA
Silver, Robert S — *Mechanical Engineer*
Oakbank, Breadalbane St, Tobermory, Isle of Mull, Scotland
Silver, Ron — *Actor*
6116 Tyndall Ave, Riverside, NY 10471, USA
Silverman, Al — *Publisher*
%Book-of-the-Month Club Inc, Rockefeller Center, New York, NY 10020, USA
Silverman, Howard — *Financier*
%Gruntal Co, 14 Wall St, New York, NY 10005, USA
Silverman, Jonathan — *Actor*
2255 Moutain Oak Dr, Los Angeles, CA 90068, USA
Silverman, Syd — *Publisher*
%Variety, 154 W 46th St, New York, NY 10036, USA
Silvers, Robert J — *Publisher*
%Saturday Evening Post Magazine, 1100 Waterway Blvd, Indianapolis, IN 46202, USA
Silverstein, Abe — *Aeronautical Engineer*
21160 Seabury Ave, Fairview Park, OH 44126, USA
Silverstein, Elliott — *Movie Director*
%Gersh Agency, 232 N Canon Dr, Beverly Hills, CA 90210, USA
Silverstein, Joseph H — *Conductor*
%Utah Symphony Orchestra, 123 W South Temple, Salt Lake City, UT 84101, USA
Silverstein, Shel — *Cartoonist*
%Harper Collins Publishers, 10 E 53rd St, New York, NY 10022, USA
Silverstone, Alicia — *Actress*
PO Box 1847, Burlingame, CA 94011, USA
Silvia — *Queen, Sweden*
Kungliga Slottet, Stottsbacken, 111 30 Stockholm, Sweden
Silvia, Charles — *Swimming Contributor*
20 Maybrook Road, Springfield, MA 01129, USA
Sim, Gerald — *Actor*
%Associated International Mgmt, 5 Denmark St, London WC2H 8LP, England
Simanek, Robert E — *Korean War Marine Corps Hero (CMH)*
25194 Westmoreland Dr, Farmington Hills, MI 48336, USA
Sime, David W — *Track Athlete, Physician*
240 Harbor Dr, Key Biscayne, FL 33149, USA
Simeon II — *King, Bulgaria*
Apartado de Correos 3135, 28080 Madrid, Spain
Simeoni, Sara — *Track Athlete*
Via Castello Rivoli Veronese, 37010 Verona, Italy
Simic, Charles — *Writer*
PO Box 192, Strafford, NH 03884, USA
Simitis, Costas — *Prime Minister, Greece*
%Premier's Office, Leoferos Vassilssis Sophia 15, 106 74 Athens, Greece
Simmonds, Kennedy A — *Prime Minister, St Kitts & Nevis*
%Prime Minister's Office, PO Box 196, Basseterre, St Kitts & Nevis
Simmons, Adele S — *Foundation Executive, Educator*
%Catherine T MacArthur Foundation, 140 S Dearborn St, Chicago, IL 60603, USA
Simmons, Clyde — *Football Player*
%Jacksonville Jaguars, 1 Stadium Place, Jacksonville, FL 32202, USA
Simmons, Floyd (Chunk) — *Track Athlete*
2330 Pembroke Ave, #8, Charlotte, NC 28207, USA
Simmons, Gene — *Singer, Bassist (Kiss)*
%McGhee Entertainment, 8730 Sunset Blvd, #195, Los Angeles, CA 90069, USA
Simmons, Jaason — *Actor*
%"Baywatch" Show, 5433 Beethoven St, Los Angeles, CA 90066, USA
Simmons, Jean — *Actress*
636 Adelaide Place, Santa Monica, CA 90402, USA
Simmons, Joseph — *Rap Artist (Run-DMC)*
%Rush Artists, 1600 Varick St, New York, NY 10013, USA
Simmons, Lionel — *Basketball Player*
108 Wellesley Court, Mount Laurel, NJ 08054, USA

S

Silver - Simmons

Simmons, Richard   *Physical Fitness Instructor*
PO Box 5403, Beverly Hills, CA 90209, USA

Simmons, Richard D   *Publisher*
%International Herald Tribune, 181 Ave C de Gaulle, 92521 Neuilly, France

Simmons, Richard P   *Businessman*
%Allegheny Ludlum, 1000 6 PPG Place, Pittsburgh, PA 15222, USA

Simmons, Roy W   *Financier*
%Zions Bancorp, 1380 Kennecott Building, Salt Lake City, UT 84133, USA

Simmons, Ruth   *Educator*
%Smith College, President's Office, Northampton, MA 01063, USA

Simmons, Ted L   *Baseball Player*
PO Box 26, Chesterfield, MO 63006, USA

Simms, Al   *Hockey Player*
4789 N Cramer St, Whitefish Bay, WI 53211, USA

Simms, Joan   *Actress*
%MGA, Southbank House, Black Prince Road, London SE1 7SJ, England

Simms, Larry   *Actor*
PO Box 55, Grays River, WA 98621, USA

Simms, Phillip (Phil)   *Football Player, Sportscaster*
%David Fishof Productions, 252 W 71st St, New York, NY 10023, USA

Simms, Primate George Otto   *Religious Leader*
62 Cypress Grove Road, Dublin 6, Ireland

Simon, Bob   *Commentator*
%CBS-TV, News Dept, 2020 "M" St NW, Washington, DC 20036, USA

Simon, Carly   *Singer, Songwriter*
135 Central Park W, #6-S, New York, NY 10023, USA

Simon, Claude   *Nobel Literature Laureate*
Place Vieille, Salses, 66600 Rivesaltes, France

Simon, George W   *Astronaut*
2308 Rancho Lane, Alamogordo, NM 88310, USA

Simon, Herbert A   *Nobel Economics Laureate*
%Carnegie-Mellon University, Psychology Dept, Pittsburgh, PA 15260, USA

Simon, John I   *Movie, Drama Critic*
%New York Magazine, Editorial Dept, 444 Madison Ave, New York, NY 10022, USA

Simon, Leonard S   *Financier*
%Rochester Community Savings Bank, 40 Franklin St, Rochester, NY 14604, USA

Simon, Neil   *Writer*
10745 Chalon Road, Los Angeles, CA 90077, USA

Simon, Paul   *Singer, Songwriter*
%Rubenstein Assoc, 1345 Ave of Americas, #300, New York, NY 10105, USA

Simon, Roger M   *Columnist*
%Baltimore Sun, 1627 "K" St NW, Washington, DC 20006, USA

Simon, Scott   *Commentator*
%NBC-TV, News Dept, 30 Rockefeller Plaza, New York, NY 10112, USA

Simon, Simone   *Actress*
5 Rue De Tilsitt, 75008 Paris, France

Simon, William E   *Secretary, Treasury*
Nomis Hill, Sandspring Road, New Vernon, NJ 07976, USA

Simone, Albert J   *Educator*
%Rochester Institute of Technology, President's Office, Rochester, NY 14623, USA

Simone, Nina   *Singer, Songwriter*
7250 Franklin Ave, #115, Los Angeles, CA 90046, USA

Simonini, Edward (Ed)   *Football Player*
20 Overlook Circle, New Braunfels, TX 78132, USA

Simonis, Adrianus J Cardinal   *Religious Leader*
Aartsbisdom, BP 14019, Maliebaan, 3508 SB Utrecht, Netherlands

Simonov, Yuriy I   *Conductor*
%Moscow Conservatory, Gertsema St 13, Moscow, Russia

Simons, Elwyn L   *Anthropologist*
%Duke University, Primate Center, 3705 Erwin Road, Durham, NC 27705, USA

Simons, Lawrence B   *Government Official*
%Powell Goldstein Frazier, 1001 Pennsylvania Ave NW, Washington, DC 20004, USA

Simonsen, Renee   *Model, Actress*
%Ford Model Agency, 344 E 59th St, New York, NY 10022, USA

Simpson Stern, Carol   *Labor Leader*
%American Assn of University Professors, 1012 14th St NW, Washington, DC 20005, USA

Simpson, Alan K   *Senator, WY*
%"The Long & the Short of It" Show, WGBH-TV, 125 Western Ave, Boston, MA 02134, USA

Simpson, Charles R — *Judge*
%US Tax Court, 400 2nd St NW, Washington, DC 20217, USA

Simpson, John R — *Law Enforcement Official*
%US Secret Service, 1800 "G" St NW, Washington, DC 20223, USA

Simpson, John, Sr — *Harness Racing Driver*
Mount Morris Star Route, Waynesburg, PA 15370, USA

Simpson, Louis A — *Businessman*
%Geico Corp, 1 Geico Plaza, 5260 Western Ave NW, Washington, DC 20076, USA

Simpson, Louis A M — *Writer*
186 Old Field Road, Setauket, NY 11733, USA

Simpson, Michael — *Businessman*
%A M Castle Co, 3400 N Wolf Road, Franklin Park, IL 60131, USA

Simpson, O J — *Football Player, Actor, Sportscaster*
360 N Rockingham Ave, Los Angeles, CA 90049, USA

Simpson, Ralph — *Basketball Player*
36461 Jefferson Court, Farmington, MI 48335, USA

Simpson, Scott — *Golfer*
15778 Paseo Hermosa, Poway, CA 92064, USA

Simpson, Tim — *Golfer*
6750 Polo Dr, Cumming, GA 30040, USA

Simpson, Valerie — *Singer (Ashford & Simpson), Songwriter*
%Associated Booking Corp, 1995 Broadway, #501, New York, NY 10023, USA

Simpson, Wayne K — *Baseball Player*
330 Collamer Dr, Carson, CA 90746, USA

Simpson, William A — *Businessman*
%USLife Corp, 125 Maiden Lane, New York, NY 10038, USA

Sims, Frank M — *Businessman*
%Clark Equipment, PO Box 8738, Woodcliff Lake, NJ 07675, USA

Sims, Joan — *Actress, Comedienne*
17 Esmond Court, Thackery St, London W8, England

Sims, Kenneth — *Football Player*
PO Box 236, Kosse, TX 76653, USA

Sin, Jaime L Cardinal — *Religious Leader*
121 Arzobispo St, Entramuros, PO Box 132, Manila, Philippines

Sinatra, Frank — *Actor, Singer*
915 N Foothill Road, Beverly Hills, CA 90210, USA

Sinatra, Frank, Jr — *Singer, Actor*
2211 Florian Place, Beverly Hills, CA 90210, USA

Sinatra, Nancy — *Singer, Actress*
%Bootleggers, PO Box 10235, Beverly Hills, CA 90213, USA

Sinbad — *Actor, Comedian*
21704 Devonshire St, #13, Chatsworth, CA 91311, USA

Sinclair, Clive M — *Businessman, Inventor*
18 Shepherd House, 5 Shepherd St, London W1Y 7LD, England

Sindelar, Joey — *Golfer*
221 Prospect Hill Road, Horseheads, NY 14845, USA

Sinden, Donald — *Actor*
Rats Castle, Isle of Oxney, Kent, England

Sinden, Harry — *Hockey Player, Coach, Executive*
9 Olde Village Dr, Winchester, MA 01890, USA

Sindermann, Horst — *President, East Germany*
Volkskammer, Berlin, Germany

Sinfelt, John H — *Chemist*
%Exxon Research & Engineering, Clinton Township, Rt 22-E, Annandale, NJ 08801, USA

Singer, Isadore M — *Mathematician*
%Massachusetts Institute of Technology, Mathematics Dept, Cambridge, MA 02139, USA

Singer, Lori — *Actress*
%Chuck Binder, 1465 Lindacrest Dr, Beverly Hills, CA 90210, USA

Singer, Marc — *Actor*
11218 Canton Dr, Studio City, CA 91604, USA

Singer, Maxine F — *Biochemist*
5410 39th St NW, Washington, DC 20015, USA

Singer, Robert W — *Businessman*
%Keystone Consolidated, 5430 LBJ Freeway, Dallas, TX 75240, USA

Singer, S Fred — *Geophysicist*
4084 University Dr, #101, Fairfax, VA 22030, USA

Singer, William R (Bill) — *Baseball Player*
242 Santa Barbara, Irvine, CA 92606, USA

Singh, Bipin *Dancer, Choreographer*
%Manipuri Nartanalaya, 15-A Bipin Pal Road, Calcutta 700026, India

Singh, Sukhmander *Civil Engineer*
%Santa Clara University, Civil Engineering Dept, Santa Clara, CA 95053, USA

Singh, Vijay *Golfer*
%Int'l Management Group, 1 Erieview Plaza, #1300, Cleveland, OH 44114, USA

Singh, Vishwanath Pratap *Prime Minister, India*
4 Askok Road, Allahabad, India

Singletary, Michael (Mike) *Football Player*
22 Polo Dr, South Barrington, IL 60010, USA

Singleton, Chris *Football Player*
2488 Princeton Court, Fort Lauderdale, FL 33327, USA

Singleton, Henry E *Businessman*
%Argonaut Group, 1800 Ave of Stars, Los Angeles, CA 90067, USA

Singleton, John D *Movie Director*
PO Box 92547, Pasadena, CA 91109, USA

Singleton, Kenneth W (Kenny) *Baseball Player*
10 Sparks Farm Road, Sparks, MD 21152, USA

Singleton, Margie *Singer*
%Country Music Spectacular, 249 Bluegrass Dr, Hendersonville, TN 37075, USA

Singleton, Penny *Actress*
13419 Riverside Dr, #C, Sherman Oaks, CA 91423, USA

Singleton, William D *Publisher*
%Houston Post, 1560 Broadway, #1450, Denver, CO 80202, USA

Sington, Frederick W (Fred) *Football Player*
1104 Royal Tower Dr, #A, Birmingham, AL 35209, USA

Sinise, Gary *Actor*
PO Box 6704, Malibu, CA 90264, USA

Sinner, George A *Governor, ND*
101 N 3rd St, Moorhead, MN 56560, USA

Sinopoli, Giuseppe *Conductor, Composer*
%Hannelore Tschope, Feilitzschstr 1, 80802 Munich, Germany

Sinowatz, Fred *Chancellor, Austria*
Loewelstr 18, 1010 Vienna, Austria

Sinton, Nell *Artist*
1020 Francisco St, San Francisco, CA 94109, USA

Sinyavskaya, Tamara I *Opera Singer*
%Bolshoi Theatre, Ploshchad Sverdlova, 103009 Moscow, Russia

Siodmak, Curt *Movie Producer, Director*
Old South Fork Ranch, 43422 S Fork Dr, Three Rivers, CA 93271, USA

Siouxsie Sioux *Singer (Siouxsie & The Banshees)*
127 Aldersgate St, London EC1, England

Sipe, Brian *Football Player*
1345 Crest Road, Del Mar, CA 92014, USA

Siphandon, Khamtay *Prime Minister, Laos; Army General*
%Prime Minister's Office, Vientiane, Laos

Sipinen, Arto K *Architect*
Arkkitehtitoimistro Arto Sipinen Ky, Ahertajantie 3, 02100 Espoo, Finland

Sir Mix-A-Lot *Rap Artist*
%William Morris Agency, 1325 Ave of Americas, New York, NY 10019, USA

Siren, Heikki *Architect*
Tiirasaarentie 35, 00200 Helsinki, Finland

Siren, Katri A H *Architect*
Lounaisvayla 8-A, 00200 Helsinki, Finland

Siri Singh Sahib *Religious Leader*
%Sikh, 1649 S Robertson Blvd, Los Angeles, CA 90035, USA

Sirikit *Queen, Thailand*
%Chritrada Villa, Bangkok, Thailand

Sirtis, Marina *Actress*
%Jim Dobson Assoc, 9903 Santa Monica Blvd, Beverly Hills, CA 90212, USA

Sishido, Fukushige *Businessman*
%Fuji Electric, 1-1 Tanabeshinden, Kawasakiku, Kawasaki 210, Japan

Siskel, Gene *Movie Critic*
%Chicago Tribune, 435 N Michigan Ave, Chicago, IL 60611, USA

Sisson, C(harles) H(ubert) *Writer*
Moorfield Cottage, The Hill, Langport, Somerset TA10 9PU, England

Sissons, Kimber *Actress*
PO Box 691748, Los Angeles, CA 90069, USA

Sister Max *Fashion Designer*
%Mount Everest Centre for Buddhist Studies, Katmandu, Nepal
Sites, James W *Publisher*
%American Legion Magazine, 700 N Pennsylvania St, Indianapolis, IN 46204, USA
Sithole, Ndabaningi *Political Leader, Zimbabwe*
%ZANU Party, PO Box UA 525, Harare, Zimbabwe
Sitkovetsky, Dmitri *Concert Violinist*
%Columbia Artists Mgmt Inc, 165 W 57th St, New York, NY 10019, USA
Sitter, Carl L *Korean War Marine Corps Hero (CMH)*
3307 Quail Hill Dr, Midlothian, VA 23112, USA
Sitter, Charles R *Businessman*
%Exxon Corp, 5959 Las Colinas Blvd, Irving, TX 75039, USA
Sittler, Darryl *Hockey Player*
84 Buttonwood Court, East Amherst, NY 14051, USA
Sixx, Nikki *Singer, Bassist, Drummer (Motley Crue)*
936 Vista Ridge Lane, Westlake Village, CA 91362, USA
Sizemore, Jerald G (Jerry) *Football Player*
1730 Whipporwill Trail, Leander, TX 78641, USA
Sizova, Alla I *Ballerina*
%Universal Ballet School, 4301 Harewood Road NE, Washington, DC 20017, USA
Sjoberg, Patrik *Track Athlete*
Hokegatan 17, 416 66 Goteberg, Sweden
Sjogren, Kim *Concert Violinist*
Edlevej 10, 2900 Hellerup, Denmark
Sjoman, Vilgot *Movie Director*
PO Box 27126, 102 52 Stockholm, Sweden
Skaggs, Ricky *Singer, Guitarist*
380 Forest Retreat, Hendersonville, TN 37075, USA
Skah, Khalid *Track Athlete*
Boite Pstale 2577, Fez, Morocco
Skates, Ronald L *Businessman*
%Data General, 4400 Computer Dr, Westboro, MA 01580, USA
Skeggs, Leonard T, Jr *Biochemist*
10212 Blair Lane, Kirtland, OH 44094, USA
Skerritt, Tom *Actor*
PO Box 2095, Santa Monica, CA 90406, USA
Skibniewska, Halina *Architect*
Wydziat Architektury Politechniki , Ul Koszykowa 55, 00-659 Warsaw, Poland
Skiles, Scott *Basketball Player, Coach*
%Phoenix Suns, 201 E Jefferson St, Phoenix, AZ 85004, USA
Skilling, Hugh H *Electrical Engineer*
1981 Montecito Ave, #128, Mountain View, CA 94043, USA
Skinner, Jimmy *Hockey Coach*
2860 Askin Ave, Windsor ON N9E 3H9, Canada
Skinner, Jonty *Swimmer, Coach*
%University of Alabama, Athletic Dept, Tuscaloosa, AL 35487, USA
Skinner, Samuel K *Secretary, Transportation; Businessman*
%Commonwealth Edison, 1 First National Plaza, PO Box 767, Chicago, IL 60690, USA
Skinner, Stanley T *Businessman*
%Pacific Gas & Electric, PO Box 770000, San Francisco, CA 94177, USA
Skinner, Val *Golfer*
78365 Highway 111, #150, La Quinta, CA 92253, USA
Skjvorecky, Josef *Writer*
%Erindale College, English Dept, Toronto ON M5S 1A5, Canada
Skladany, Thomas E (Tom) *Football Player*
6666 Highland Lakes Place, Westerville, OH 43082, USA
Sklenar, Herbert A *Businessman*
%Vulcan Materials Co, 1 Metroplex Dr, Birmingham, AL 35209, USA
Skoblikova, Lydia *Speed Skater*
B Chernizovskaya St 6-2-43, Moscow, Russia
Skol, Michael *Diplomat*
3033 Cleveland Ave NW, Washington, DC 20008, USA
Skold, Per *Businessman*
%Sventskt Stal, PO Box 16344, 103 26 Stockholm, Sweden
Skolimowski, Jerzy *Movie Director*
%Film Polski, Ul Mazowiecka 6/8, 00-048 Warsaw, Poland
Skolnick, Mark H *Geneticist*
%University of Utah, Medical Center, Genetics Dept, Salt Lake City, UT 84112, USA

Skoog, Folke K — *Physiologist*
2820 Marshall Court, Madison, WI 53705, USA

Skoog, Meyer (Whitey) — *Basketball Player, Coach*
1545 Aspen Dr, Saint Peter, MN 56082, USA

Skotheim, Robert A — *Museum Administrator*
%Huntington Library, 1151 Oxford Road, San Marino, CA 91108, USA

Skowron, William J (Moose) — *Baseball Player*
1118 Beachcomber Dr, Schaumberg, IL 60193, USA

Skrebneski, Victor — *Photographer*
1350 N LaSalle Dr, Chicago, IL 60610, USA

Skrepenak, Greg — *Football Player*
325 W Center Hill Road, Dallas, PA 18612, USA

Skrowaczewski, Stanislaw — *Conductor, Composer*
%Minnesota Symphony, 1111 Nicollet Mall, Minneapolis, MN 55403, USA

Skrypnyk, Metropolitan Mstyslav S — *Religious Leader*
%Ukranian Orthodox Church, PO Box 445, South Bound Brook, NJ 08880, USA

Skutt, Thomas J — *Businessman*
%Mutual of Omaha, Mutual of Omaha Plaza, Omaha, NE 68175, USA

Skvorecky, Josef V — *Writer*
487 Sackville St, Montreal ON M4X 1T6, Canada

Skye, Ione — *Actress*
8794 Lookout Mountain Ave, Los Angeles, CA 90046, USA

Slade, Bernard N — *Writer*
345 N Saltair Ave, Los Angeles, CA 90049, USA

Slade, Mark — *Actor*
14332 Riverside Dr, #11, Sherman Oaks, CA 91423, USA

Slade, Roy — *Artist, Museum Director*
%Cranbrook Academy Art Museum, PO Box 801, Bloomfield, MI 48303, USA

Sladkevicius, Vicentas Cardinal — *Religious Leader*
R Carno 31, 234230 Kaisiadorys, Lietuva, Lithuania

Slagle, James R — *Computer Scientist*
2117 W Hoyt Ave, St Paul, MN 55108, USA

Slaney, Mary Decker — *Track Athlete*
1923 Flintrock St, Eugene, OR 97402, USA

Slash (Saul Hudson) — *Singer, Guitarist (Guns n' Roses)*
901 Dove St, #260, Newport Beach, CA 92660, USA

Slate, Jeremy — *Actor*
%CNA Assoc, 1925 Century Park East, #750, Los Angeles, CA 90067, USA

Slater, Christian — *Actor*
%Susan Culley Assoc, 955 Carrillo Dr, #200, Los Angeles, CA 90048, USA

Slater, Helen — *Actress*
%Innovative Artists, 1999 Ave of Stars, #2850, Los Angeles, CA 90067, USA

Slater, Jackie — *Football Player*
PO Box 6411, Orange, CA 92863, USA

Slater, Rodney — *Secretary, Transportation*
%Transportation Department, 400 7th St SW, Washington, DC 20590, USA

Slatkin, Leonard E — *Conductor*
%Washington National Symphony, Kennedy Center, Washington, DC 20566, USA

Slaton, James (Jim) — *Water Polo Player*
PO Box 688, Yosemite National Park, CA 95389, USA

Slattery, John M, Jr — *Actor*
%ABC-TV, 2040 Ave of Stars, Los Angeles, CA 90067, USA

Slattvik, Simon — *Nordic Skier*
Bankgata 22, 2600 Lillehammer, Norway

Slaughter, Enos B — *Baseball Player*
959 Lawson Chapel Church Road, Roxboro, NC 27573, USA

Slaughter, Frank G — *Writer*
PO Box 14, Ortega Station, Jacksonville, FL 32210, USA

Slaughter, John B — *Educator*
%Occidental College, President's Office, Los Angeles, CA 90041, USA

Slavich, Dennis M — *Businessman*
%Morrison Knudsen, Morrison Knudsen Plaza, PO Box 73, Boise, ID 83729, USA

Slavitt, David R — *Writer*
523 S 41st St, Philadelphia, PA 19104, USA

Sledge, Percy — *Singer*
5524 Claresholm St, Gautier, MS 39553, USA

Sleep, Wayne — *Dancer, Actor, Choreographer*
%Inspirational Artiste, PO Box 1AS, London W1A 1AS, England

Slezak, Erika	*Actress*
%International Creative Mgmt, 40 W 57th St, New York, NY 10019, USA	
Slichter, Charles P	*Physicist*
61 Chestnut Court, Champaign, IL 61821, USA	
Slick, Grace	*Singer, Songwriter*
2548 Laurel Pass, Los Angeles, CA 90046, USA	
Sliwa, Curtis	*Founder, Guardian Angels*
%Guardian Angels, 628 W 28th St, New York, NY 10001, USA	
Sliwa, Lisa	*President, Guardian Angels; Model*
%Guardian Angels, 628 W 28th St, New York, NY 10001, USA	
Sloan, Gerald E (Jerry)	*Basketball Player, Coach*
3588 E Oak Rim Way, Salt Lake City, UT 84109, USA	
Sloan, Norm	*Basketball Coach*
%University of Florida, Athletic Dept, Gainesville, FL 32611, USA	
Sloan, Robert L	*Financier*
%Riggs National Corp, 808 17th St NW, Washington, DC 20006, USA	
Sloan, Stephen C (Steve)	*Football Coach, Administrator*
%University of Alabama, Athletic Dept, University, AL 35486, USA	
Sloane, Carol	*Singer*
%Buck Spurr Mgmt, 215 Salem St, Woburn, MA 01801, USA	
Slobodyanik, Alexander	*Concert Pianist*
%Columbia Artists Mgmt Inc, 165 W 57th St, New York, NY 10019, USA	
Slocum, R C	*Football Coach*
%Texas A&M University, Athletic Dept, College Station, TX 77843, USA	
Slotnick, Bernard	*Publisher*
%DC Comics Group, 355 Lexington Ave, New York, NY 10017, USA	
Slotnick, Joey	*Actor*
%Gersh Agency, 232 N Canon Dr, Beverly Hills, CA 90210, USA	
Slotnick, Mortimer H	*Artist*
43 Amherst Dr, Rochelle, NY 10804, USA	
Slotnick, R Nathan	*Surgeon*
825 Fairfax Ave, Norfolk, VA 23507, USA	
Slowinski, David	*Computer Scientist*
%Cray Research, Highway 178 N, Chippewa Falls, WI 54729, USA	
Sloyan, James	*Actor*
13740 Albers St, Van Nuys, CA 91401, USA	
Sluman, Jeff	*Golfer*
8 Tartan Ridge Road, Burr Ridge, IL 60521, USA	
Slusarski, Tadeusz	*Track Athlete*
Ul Atenska 2 M 154, 03-978 Warsaw, Poland	
Slutsky, Lorie A	*Foundation Executive*
%New York Community Trust, 2 Park Ave, New York, NY 10016, USA	
Smagorinsky, Joseph	*Meteorologist*
21 Duffield Place, Princeton, NJ 08540, USA	
Smale, John G	*Businessman*
%General Motors, 3044 W Grand Blvd, Detroit, MI 48202, USA	
Smale, Stephen	*Mathematician*
68 Highgate Road, Berkeley, CA 94707, USA	
Small, Lawrence W	*Financier*
%Federal National Mortgage Assn, 3900 Wisconsin Ave NW, Washington, DC 20016, USA	
Small, Marya	*Actress*
%Shirley Wilson Agency, 5410 Wilshire Blvd, #227, Los Angeles, CA 90036, USA	
Small, William N	*Navy Admiral*
1605 Bluecher Court, Virginia Beach, VA 23454, USA	
Smalley, Richard E	*Nobel Chemistry Laureate*
%Rice University, Chemistry Dept, PO Box 1892, Houston, TX 77251, USA	
Smalley, Roy F, Jr	*Baseball Player*
256 Timber Trace Dr, Saint Albans, MO 63073, USA	
Smarr, Larry L	*Physicist*
%University of Illinois, Supercomputing Applications Center, Champaign, IL 61820, USA	
Smart, Jean	*Actress*
4545 Noeline Ave, Encino, CA 91436, USA	
Smarth, Rosny	*Prime Minister, Haiti*
%Prime Minister's Office, Palais du Gouvernement, Port-au-Prince, Haiti	
Smathers, George A	*Senator, FL*
Alfred I du Pont Building, 169 E Flagler St, Miami, FL 33131, USA	
Smeal, Eleanor C	*Women's Activist*
900 N Stafford St, #1217, Arlington, VA 22203, USA	

S

Slezak - Smeal

Smedley, Geoffrey	*Sculptor*
Rt 3, Gambier Island, Gibsons, BC V0N 1V0, Canada	
Smialek, Robert I	*Businessman*
%Insilco Corp, 425 Metro Place N, Dublin, OH 43017, USA	
Smigel, Irwin	*Dentist*
%Smigel Research 635 Madison Ave, New York, NY 10022, USA	
Smight, Jack	*Movie Director*
225 Tigertail Road, Los Angeles, CA 90049, USA	
Smiley, Jane G	*Writer*
%Alfred A Knopf Inc, 201 E 50th St, New York, NY 10022, USA	
Smiley, John P	*Baseball Player*
208 W 3rd Ave, Trappe, PA 19426, USA	
Smirnoff, Yakov	*Comedian, Actor*
%Comrade in America, 1990 S Bundy Dr, #200, Los Angeles, CA 90025, USA	
Smirnov, Nikolai I	*Navy Fleet Admiral, Russia*
%Ministry of Defence, Kremlin, 4 Staraya Ploshchad, 103073 Moscow, Russia	
Smith Court, Margaret	*Tennis Player*
65 The Esplanade, Nedlands WA 6009, Australia	
Smith Osborne, Madolyn	*Actress*
%United Talent Agency, 9560 Wilshire Blvd, #500, Beverly Hills, CA 90212, USA	
Smith, Adrian	*Basketball Player*
2829 Saddleback Dr, Cincinnati, OH 45244, USA	
Smith, Albert C	*Biologist*
2474 Aha Aina Place, Honolulu, HI 96821, USA	
Smith, Alexander J C	*Financier*
%Marsh & McLennan Cos, 1166 Ave of Americas, New York, NY 10036, USA	
Smith, Alexis	*Artist*
1907 Lincoln Blvd, Venice, CA 90291, USA	
Smith, Alfred J	*Labor Leader*
%Mechanics Educational Society, 15300 E Seven Mile Road, Detroit, MI 48205, USA	
Smith, Allison	*Actress*
%Innovative Artists, 1999 Ave of Stars, #2850, Los Angeles, CA 90067, USA	
Smith, Amber	*Model, Actress*
%Next Model Mgmt, 23 Watts St, New York, NY 10013, USA	
Smith, Andrea	*Artist*
313 Lakau, Lahaina, HI 96761, USA	
Smith, Ann	*Tennis Player*
734 Summerwood Dr, New Braunfels, TX 78130, USA	
Smith, Anna Deavere	*Actress*
%Creative Artists Agency, 9830 Wilshire Blvd, Beverly Hills, CA 90212, USA	
Smith, Anna Nicole	*Model, Actress*
7600 W Tidwell Road, Houston, TX 77040, USA	
Smith, Anne Mollegen	*Editor*
451 W 24th St, New York, NY 10011, USA	
Smith, April	*Writer*
427 7th St, Santa Monica, CA 90402, USA	
Smith, Arthur K, Jr	*Educator*
%University of Utah, President's Office, Salt Lake, City, UT 84112, USA	
Smith, Bernard R	*Financier*
%Bethpage Credit Union, 899 S Oyster Bay Road, Bethpage, NY 11714, USA	
Smith, Bill	*Swimmer*
46-049 Alii Anela Place, #1726, Kaneohe, HI 96744, USA	
Smith, Billy	*Hockey Player*
260 SE Mizner Blvd, #606, Boca Raton, FL 33432, USA	
Smith, Billy Ray, Jr	*Football Player*
3790 Via de la Valle, #204, Del Mar, CA 92014, USA	
Smith, Bobby	*Hockey Player*
10073 Lee Dr, Eden Prairie, MN 55347, USA	
Smith, Bruce P	*Football Player*
4584 Winding Woods Lane, Hamburg, NY 14075, USA	
Smith, Buffalo Bob	*Actor*
500 Overlook Dr, Flat Rock, NC 28731, USA	
Smith, C Reginald (Reggie)	*Baseball Player*
6186 Coral Pink Circle, Woodland Hills, CA 91367, USA	
Smith, Calvin	*Track Athlete*
16703 Sheffield Park Dr, Lutz, FL 33549, USA	
Smith, Carl R	*Air Force General*
%Armed Forces Benefit Assn, 909 N Washington St, Alexandria, VA 22314, USA	

Smith, Carleton	*Foundation Executive, Art Expert*
Chalet le Stop, 1882 Gryon, Switzerland	
Smith, Charles	*Basketball Player*
%San Antonio Spurs, 600 E Market St, #102, San Antonio, TX 78205, USA	
Smith, Charles	*Basketball Player*
%Miami Heat, Miami Arena, 100 NE 3rd Ave, Miami, FL 33132, USA	
Smith, Charles A (Bubba)	*Football Player, Actor*
5178 Sunlight Place, Los Angeles, CA 90016, USA	
Smith, Charles Martin	*Actor*
31515 Germaine Lane, Westlake Village, CA 91361, USA	
Smith, Chesterfield	*Attorney*
5915 Ponce de Leon Blvd, #63, Coral Gables, FL 33146, USA	
Smith, Clint	*Hockey Player*
501-199 Bellview Ave, West Vancouver BC V7V 1B7, Canada	
Smith, Connie	*Singer*
%Ace Productions, PO Box 428, Portland, TN 37148, USA	
Smith, Cotter	*Actor*
15332 Antioch St, #800, Pacific Palisades, CA 90272, USA	
Smith, Darden	*Singer, Songwriter*
%AGF Entertainment, 30 W 21st St, #700, New York, NY 10010, USA	
Smith, Dean E	*Basketball Coach*
%University of North Carolina, PO Box 2126, Chapel Hill, NC 27515, USA	
Smith, Del	*Sculptor*
Cascade Head Ranch, 2750 Four Creeks Road, Otis, OR 97368, USA	
Smith, Derek	*Hockey Player*
201 Bramblewood Lane, East Amherst, NY 14051, USA	
Smith, Dick	*Diving Coach*
PO Box 304, The Woodlands, TX 77383, USA	
Smith, Doug	*Basketball Player*
21930 Winchester St, Southfield, MI 48076, USA	
Smith, Elmore	*Basketball Player*
33065 Cedar Road, Mayfield Heights, OH 44124, USA	
Smith, Emil L	*Biochemist, Biophysicist*
%University of California, Medical School, Los Angeles, CA 90024, USA	
Smith, Emmitt J, III	*Football Player*
%Dallas Cowboys, 1 Cowboys Parkway, Irving, TX 75063, USA	
Smith, F Dean	*Track Athlete*
Ivan Star Rt Box 71, Breckenridge, TX 76424, USA	
Smith, Floyd	*Hockey Player*
138 Stonehenge Dr, Orchard Park, NY 14127, USA	
Smith, Francis G	*Astronomer*
Old School House, Henbury, Macclesfield, Cheshire SK11 9PH, England	
Smith, Frederick W	*Businessman*
%FDX Inc, PO Box 727, Memphis, TN 38194, USA	
Smith, Gerard	*Publisher, Tennis Executive*
%World Tennis Assn, 133 1st St NE, St Petersburg, FL 33701, USA	
Smith, Gerard C	*Government Official*
2425 Tracy Place NW, Washington, DC 20008, USA	
Smith, Gregory White	*Writer*
129 1st Ave SW, Aiken, SC 29801, USA	
Smith, Guinn	*Track Athlete*
2164 Hyde St, #306, San Francisco, CA 94109, USA	
Smith, Hamilton O	*Nobel Medicine Laureate*
8222 Carrbridge Circle, Baltimore, MD 21204, USA	
Smith, Harry	*Commentator*
%CBS-TV, News Dept, 51 W 52nd St, New York, NY 10019, USA	
Smith, Harry	*Bowler*
%Professional Bowlers Assn, 1720 Merriman Road, Akron, OH 44313, USA	
Smith, Harry E (Blackjack)	*Football Player*
805 Leawood Terrace, Columbia, MO 65203, USA	
Smith, Hedrick L	*Journalist*
4204 Rosemary St, Chevy Chase, MD 20815, USA	
Smith, Hoke L	*Educator*
%Towson State University, President's Office, Towson, MD 21204, USA	
Smith, Howard G	*Publisher*
%Newsweek Magazine, 251 W 57th St, New York, NY 10019, USA	
Smith, Howard K	*Commentator*
6450 Brooks Lane, Washington, DC 20016, USA	

S

Smith - Smith

Smith, Hubert G (Hugh)	*Army General*
Deputy CinC, US Transportation Command, Scott Air Force Base, IL 62225, USA	
Smith, Hulett C	*Governor, WV*
2105 Harper Road, Beckley, WV 25801, USA	
Smith, Ian D	*Prime Minister, Rhodesia*
Gwenoro Farm, Selukwe, Zimbabwe	
Smith, J T	*Football Player*
11 Autumn Oaks, Austin, TX 78738, USA	
Smith, Jaclyn	*Actress*
10398 Sunset Blvd, Los Angeles, CA 90077, USA	
Smith, James (Bonecrusher)	*Boxer*
355 Keith Hills Road, Lillington, NC 27546, USA	
Smith, James F, Jr	*Financier*
%First American Corp, First American Center, Nashville, TN 37237, USA	
Smith, Jay R	*Publisher*
%Atlanta Journal-Constitution, 72 Marietta St, Atlanta, GA 30303, USA	
Smith, Jeff	*Writer, Food Expert*
%Frugal Gourmet, 88 Virginia Ave, #2, Seattle, WA 98101, USA	
Smith, Jim Ray	*Football Player*
7049 Cliffbrook Dr, Dallas, TX 75240, USA	
Smith, Jimmy O	*Jazz Organist*
2125 Kincaid Way, Sacramento, CA 95825, USA	
Smith, Joe	*Basketball Player*
7639 Leafwood Dr, Norfolk, VA 23518, USA	
Smith, John	*Track Athlete, Coach*
%University of California, Athletic Dept, Los Angeles, CA 90024, USA	
Smith, John Coventry	*Religious Leader*
%World Council of Churches, 150 Rt de Ferbey, 1211 Geneva 20, Switzerland	
Smith, John F (Jack), Jr	*Businessman*
%General Motors, 3044 W Grand Blvd, Detroit, MI 48202, USA	
Smith, John W	*Wrestler, Coach*
1509 Fairway Dr, Stillwater, OK 74074, USA	
Smith, Kathy	*Physical Fitness Instructor*
12424 Wilshire Blvd, #740, Los Angeles, CA 90025, USA	
Smith, Katie	*Baaketball Player*
%Columbus Quest, 7451 State Rt 161, Dublin, OH 43016, USA	
Smith, Keith	*Financier*
%Dreyfus Corp, 200 Park Ave, New York, NY 10166, USA	
Smith, Kurtwood	*Actor*
635 Fronenac Ave, Los Angeles, CA 90065, USA	
Smith, Lane	*Actor*
%Artists Agency, 10000 Santa Monica Blvd, #305, Los Angeles, CA 90067, USA	
Smith, Lawrence Leighton	*Conductor*
%Louisville Symphony, 611 W Main St, Louisville, KY 40202, USA	
Smith, Lee A	*Baseball Player*
%Baltimore Orioles, 333 W Camden Ave, Baltimore, MD 21201, USA	
Smith, Ley S	*Businessman*
%Upjohn Co, 7000 Portage Road, Kalamazoo, MI 49001, USA	
Smith, Lonnie Liston, Jr	*Jazz Keyboardist*
%Associated Booking Corp, 1995 Broadway, #501, New York, NY 10023, USA	
Smith, Loren A	*Judge*
%US Claims Court, 717 Madison Place NW, Washington, DC 20005, USA	
Smith, M Elizabeth (Liz)	*Columnist*
160 E 38th St, New York, NY 10016, USA	
Smith, Madeline	*Actress*
%George Heathcote, 12 Neals Yard, London WC2H 9DP, England	
Smith, Maggie	*Actress*
%International Creative Mgmt, 76 Oxford St, London W1N 0AX, England	
Smith, Margo	*Singer, Songwriter*
%C&S Music, 1802 Williamson Court, #200, Brentwood, TN 37027, USA	
Smith, Marilyn	*Golfer*
2503 Bluebonnet Dr, Richardson, TX 75082, USA	
Smith, Martha	*Actress, Model*
9690 Heather Road, Beverly Hills, CA 90210, USA	
Smith, Marvin (Smitty)	*Jazz Drummer*
%Joel Chriss Co, 300 Mercer St, #3-J, New York, NY 10003, USA	
Smith, Mel	*Comedian*
%Talkback, 33 Percy St, London W1P 9FG, England	

Smith, Michael	*Nobel Chemistry Laureate*
300-2455 W 3rd Ave, Vancouver BC V6K 1L8, Canada	
Smith, Michael J	*Businessman*
%Lands' End Inc, 1 Lands' End Lane, Dodgeville, WI 53595, USA	
Smith, Michael W	*Singer, Songwriter*
%Blanton/Harrell, 2910 Poston Ave, Nashville, TN 37203, USA	
Smith, Michelle	*Swimmer*
%Swimming Assn, House of Sports, Longmile Road, Dublin 12, Ireland	
Smith, Mike	*Assocaition Executive*
%Names Project Foundation, 310 Townsend St, San Francisco, CA 94017, USA	
Smith, Moishe	*Artist*
PO Box 747, Hyde Park, UT 84318, USA	
Smith, Neil	*Football Player*
333 E 46th Tr, Kansas City, MO 64112, USA	
Smith, Norman R	*Educator*
%Wagner College, President's Office, Staten Island, NY 10301, USA	
Smith, O C	*Singer*
%Headline Talent, 1650 Broadway, #508, New York, NY 10019, USA	
Smith, Orlando (Tubby)	*Basketball Coach*
%University of Kentucky, Athletic Dept, Lexington, KY 40536, USA	
Smith, Osborne E (Ozzie)	*Baseball Player, Sportscaster*
PO Box 8787, St Louis, MO 63101, USA	
Smith, Pat	*Wrestler*
%Oklahoma State University, Athletic Dept, Stillwater, OK 47078, USA	
Smith, Patti	*Singer, Songwriter*
%Beverly Smith, PO Box 188, Mantua, NJ 08051, USA	
Smith, Phil	*Basketball Player*
3334 Avenida Sierra, Escondido, CA 92029, USA	
Smith, R Jackson	*Diver*
1 Deepwoods Lane, Old Greenwich, CT 06870, USA	
Smith, Ralph	*Cartoonist*
%King Features Syndicate, 235 E 45th St, New York, NY 10017, USA	
Smith, Randy	*Basketball Player*
1542 Amherst Ave, Buffalo, NY 14214, USA	
Smith, Ray E	*Religious Leader*
%Open Bible Standard Churches, 2020 Bell Ave, Des Moines, IA 50315, USA	
Smith, Ray F	*Entomologist*
3092 Hedaro Court, Lafayette, CA 94549, USA	
Smith, Raymond W	*Businessman*
%Bell Atlantic, 1717 Arch St, Philadelphia, PA 19103, USA	
Smith, Rex	*Actor*
%Agency For Performing Arts, 9200 Sunset Blvd, #900, Los Angeles, CA 90069, USA	
Smith, Richard A	*Publisher*
%Harcourt General, 27 Boylston St, Chestnut Hill, MA 02167, USA	
Smith, Richard E (Dick)	*Make-up Artist*
27 Wilford Ave, Branford, CT 06405, USA	
Smith, Richard M	*Editor*
%Newsweek Magazine, Editorial Dept, 251 W 57th St, New York, NY 10019, USA	
Smith, Riley	*Football Player*
2765 Government Blvd, Mobile, AL 36606, USA	
Smith, Robert C	*Editor*
%TV Guide Magazine, Editorial Dept, 100 Matsonford Road, Radnor, PA 19087, USA	
Smith, Robert Gray (Graysmith)	*Editorial Cartoonist*
%San Francisco Chronicle, 901 Mission St, San Francisco, CA 94103, USA	
Smith, Robyn	*Thoroughbred Racing Jockey*
1155 San Ysidro Dr, Beverly Hills, CA 90210, USA	
Smith, Roger	*Actor*
2707 Benedict Canyon Dr, Beverly Hills, CA 90210, USA	
Smith, Roger Guenveur	*Actor*
%William Morris Agency, 151 S El Camino Dr, Beverly Hills, CA 90212, USA	
Smith, Rolland	*Commentator*
%CBS-TV, News Dept, 524 W 57th St, New York, NY 10019, USA	
Smith, Ronnie Ray	*Track Athlete*
752 Athens Blvd, Los Angeles, CA 90044, USA	
Smith, Samuel H	*Educator*
%Washington State University, President's Office, Pullman, WA 99164, USA	
Smith, Shawnee	*Actress*
1025 Indiana Ave, Venice, CA 90291, USA	

S

Smith - Smith

Smith, Shelley — *Model, Actress*
182 S Mansfield Ave, Los Angeles, CA 90036, USA

Smith, Sherwood H, Jr — *Businessman*
%Carolina Power & Light, 411 Fayetteville St Mall, Raleigh, NC 27601, USA

Smith, Sinjin — *Volleyball Player*
%Assn of Volleyball Pros, 330 Washington Blvd, #600, Marina del Rey, CA 90292, USA

Smith, Stanley R (Stan) — *Tennis Player*
%ProServe, 1101 Woodrow Wilson Blvd, #1800, Arlington, VA 22209, USA

Smith, Steven D (Steve) — *Basketball Player*
3762 Waterlilly Way SE, Marietta, GA 30067, USA

Smith, Steven L — *Astronaut*
%NASA, Johnson Space Center, 2101 NASA Road, Houston, TX 77058, USA

Smith, Taran Noah — *Actor*
%Full Circle Mgmt, 12665 Kling St, North Hollywood, CA 91604, USA

Smith, Tommie — *Track Athlete*
3300 W 78th Place, Los Angeles, CA 90043, USA

Smith, Tony — *Artist*
%Pace Gallery, 32 E 57th St, New York, NY 10022, USA

Smith, Vince — *Singer, Songwriter*
%Process Talent Mgmt, 439 Wiley Ave, Franklin, PA 16323, USA

Smith, Wallace B — *Religious Leader*
%Reorganized Church of Latter Day Saints, Box 1059, Independence, MO 64051, USA

Smith, Walter — *Computer Software Designer*
%Microsoft Corp, 1 Microsoft Way, Redmond, WA 98052, USA

Smith, Walter H F — *Oceanographer, Cartologist*
%Nat Oceanic/Atmospheric Administration, Commerce Dept, Washington, DC 20230, USA

Smith, Wayne T — *Businessman*
%Humana Corp, 500 W Main St, Louisville, KY 40202, USA

Smith, Will — *Actor, Singer, Rap Artist*
%NBC Productions, 330 Bob Hope Dr, Burbank, CA 91523, USA

Smith, William — *Actor*
3250 W Olympic Blvd, #67, Santa Monica, CA 90404, USA

Smith, William D — *Navy Admiral*
7025 Fairway Oaks, Fayetteville, PA 17222, USA

Smith, William Jay — *Writer*
RR 1, Box 151, 62 Luther Shaw Road, Cummington, MA 01026, USA

Smith, William R, Jr — *Attorney*
1 Harbour Place, PO Box 3239, Tampa, FL 33601, USA

Smith, William Y — *Army General*
%Institute for Defense Analyses, 1801 N Beauregard St, Alexandria, VA 22311, USA

Smithburg, William D — *Businessman*
%Quaker Oats Co, 321 N Clark St, Chicago, IL 60610, USA

Smithers, William — *Actor*
2202 Anacapa St, Santa Barbara, CA 93105, USA

Smithies, Oliver — *Geneticist*
%University of North Carolina, Genetics Dept, Chapel Hill, NC 27599, USA

Smithson, Peter D — *Architect*
Cato Lodge, 24 Gilston Road, London SW10 9SR, England

Smitrovich, Bill — *Actor*
5075 Amestoy Ave, Encino, CA 91316, USA

Smits, Jimmy — *Actor*
%El Sendero, PO Box 49922, Barrington Station, Los Angeles, CA 90049, USA

Smits, Rik — *Basketball Player*
8554 Moore Road, Indianapolis, IN 46278, USA

Smolan, Rick — *Photographer*
%Workman Publishers, 708 Broadway, New York, NY 10003, USA

Smoltz, John A — *Baseball Player*
111 Royal Dornoch Dr, Duluth, GA 30097, USA

Smoot, George F, III — *Astrophysicist*
%Lawrence Berkeley Laboratory, 1 Cyclotron Blvd, Berkeley, CA 94720, USA

Smothers, Dick — *Comedian (Smothers Brothers)*
%SmoBro Productions, 8489 W 3rd St, #1078, Los Angeles, CA 90048, USA

Smothers, Tom — *Comedian (Smothers Brothers)*
%SmoBro Productions, 8489 W 3rd St, #1078, Los Angeles, CA 90048, USA

Smyl, Stan — *Hockey Player*
202-130 W 5th St, North Vancouver BC V7M 1J8, Canada

Smylie, Robert E — *Governor, ID*
1436 Lewis St, Boise, ID 83712, USA

Smyth, Charles P — *Physical Chemist*
245 Prospect Ave, Princeton, NJ 08540, USA

Smyth, Joe — *Singer (Sawyer Brown)*
%TKO Artist Mgmt, 4219 Hillsboro Road, #318, Nashville, TN 37215, USA

Smyth, Patty — *Singer*
%Stiefel-Phillips, 9255 W Sunset Blvd, #610, Los Angeles, CA 90069, USA

Smyth, Randy — *Yachtsman*
17136 Bluewater Lane, Huntington Beach, CA 92649, USA

Smythe, Quenton G M — *WW II South Africa Army Hero (VC)*
54 Seadoone Road, Amanzimtoti 4126, Natal, South Africa

Smythe, Reginald (Reggie) — *Cartoonist (Andy Capp)*
Whitegates, 96 Caledonian Road, Hartlepool, England

Snead, Jesse Caryle (J C) — *Golfer*
PO Box 782170, Wichita, KS 67278, USA

Snead, Norman B (Norm) — *Football Player*
6012 Radio Road, Naples, FL 34104, USA

Snead, Samuel J (Sam) — *Golfer*
PO Box 839, Hot Springs, VA 24445, USA

Sneider, Richard L — *Diplomat*
211 Central Park West, New York, NY 10024, USA

Snell, Esmond E — *Biochemist*
5001 Greystone Dr, Austin, TX 78731, USA

Snell, Matthews (Matt) — *Football*
%Snell Construction Co, 585 Washington, New York, NY 10014, USA

Snell, Peter — *Track Athlete*
6452 Dunston Lane, Dallas, TX 75214, USA

Snell, Richard — *Businessman*
%Pinnacle West Capital, 400 E Van Buren St, Phoenix, AZ 85004, USA

Snellings, Ronald L — *Financier*
%Pentagon Credit Union, PO Box 1432, Arlington, VA 22210, USA

Sneva, Tom — *Auto Racing Driver*
3301 E Valley Vista Lane, Paradise Valley, AZ 85253, USA

Snider, Edward M (Ed) — *Hockey Executive*
726 Williamson Road, Bryn Mawr, PA 19010, USA

Snider, Edwin D (Duke) — *Baseball Player*
3037 Lakemont Dr, Fallbrook, CA 92028, USA

Snider, R Michael — *Medical Researcher*
%Pfizer Pharmaceuticals, Eastern Point Road, Groton, CT 06340, USA

Snider, Todd — *Singer*
%Magnolia Way, 233 Lauderdale Road, Nashville, TN 37205, USA

Snipes, Wesley — *Actor*
%Endeavor Talent Agency, 9701 Wilshire Blvd, #1000, Beverly Hills, CA 90212, USA

Snipstead, Richard — *Religious Leader*
%Free Lutheran Congregations Assn, 402 W 11th St, Canton, SD 57013, USA

Snodgrass, William D — *Writer*
RD 1, Erieville, NY 13061, USA

Snodgress, Carrie — *Actress*
3025 Surry St, Los Angeles, CA 90027, USA

Snoop Doggy Dogg (Calvin Broadus) — *Rap Artist*
%International Creative Mgmt, 40 W 57th St, New York, NY 10019, USA

Snow — *Singer, Songwriter*
%S L Feldman, 1505 W 2nd Ave, #200, Vancouver BC V6H 3Y4, Canada

Snow, Hank — *Singer, Songwriter*
PO Box 1084, Nashville, TN 37202, USA

Snow, Jack T (JT) — *Baseball Player*
401 Purdue Circle, Seal Beach, CA 90740, USA

Snow, John W — *Businessman*
%CSX Corp, James Center, PO Box 85629, Richmond, VA 23285, USA

Snow, Percy — *Football Player*
122 Hartford Ave SE, Canton, OH 44707, USA

Snow, Phoebe — *Singer, Songwriter*
%Agency Group, 1775 Broadway, #433, New York, NY 10019, USA

Snowdon (A C R Armstrong-Jones), Earl of — *Photographer*
22 Launceston Place, London W8 5RL, England

Snyder, Dick — *Basketball Player*
4621 E Mockingbird Lane, Paradise Valley, AZ 85253, USA

Snyder, Gary S — *Writer*
18442 Macnab Cypress Road, Nevada City, CA 95959, USA

Smyth - Snyder

Snyder, Joan — *Artist*
%Hirschi & Adler Modern, 21 E 70th St, New York, NY 10021, USA

Snyder, Richard E — *Publisher*
Linden Farm, Boutonville Road, PO Box 175, Cross River, NY 10518, USA

Snyder, Robert C — *Businessman*
%Quanex Corp, 1900 West Loop S, Houston, TX 77027, USA

Snyder, Solomon H — *Psychiatrist, Pharmacologist*
3801 Canterbury Road, #1001, Baltimore, MD 21218, USA

Snyder, Tom — *Commentator*
1225 Beverly Estates Dr, Beverly Hills, CA 90210, USA

Snyder, William D — *Photographer*
%Dallas Morning News, Communications Center, Dallas, TX 75265, USA

Soares, Joao Clemente Baena — *Government Official*
%Organization of American States, 17th & Constitution NW, Washington, DC 20006, USA

Soares, Mario A N L — *President, Portugal*
Rua Dr Joao Soares #2-3, 1600 Lisbon, Portugal

Sobers, Garfield S (Gary) — *Cricketer*
%Cricket Board, 9 Appleblossom, Petit Valley, Diego Martin, Trinidad

Soble, Ron — *Actor*
%Tyler Kjar, 10643 Riverside Dr, Toluca Lake, CA 91602, USA

Sobral, Maria de Souza — *Basketball Player*
%Richmond Rage, 7650 E Parham Road, #260, Richmond, VA 23294, USA

Sobule, Jill — *Singer, Songwriter*
%Kusnick Passick Mgmt, 3 E 28th St, #600, New York, NY 10016, USA

Socol, Jerry M — *Businessman*
%J Baker Inc, 555 Turnpike St, Canton, MA 02021, USA

Sodano, Angelo Cardinal — *Religious Leader*
%Office of Secretary of State, 00120 Vatican City

Soderberg, E Loren — *Photographer*
PO Box 313, Sausalito, CA 94966, USA

Soderbergh, Steven A — *Movie Director*
%Outlaw Productions, 827 Hilldale Ave, Los Angeles, CA 90069, USA

Soderstrom, Elisabeth — *Opera Singer*
19 Hersbyvagen, 181 42 Lidingo, Sweden

Soeda, Takao — *Financier*
%Tokai Bank of California, 300 S Grand Ave, #7, Los Angeles, CA 90071, USA

Sofaer, Abraham D — *Attorney*
%Hughes Hubbard Reed, 1300 "I" St NW, Washington, DC 20005, USA

Sohn Kee Chung — *Marathon Runner*
%Korean Olympic Committee, International PO Box 1106, Seoul, South Korea

Sokol, Marilyn — *Actress*
24 W 40th St, #1700, New York, NY 10018, USA

Sokoloff, Louis — *Physiologist, Neurochemist*
%National Mental Health Institute, 9000 Rockville Pike, Bethesda, MD 20892, USA

Sokolove, James G — *Attorney*
1 Boston Place, Boston, MA 02108, USA

Sokomanu, George — *President, Vanuatu*
BP 105, D-5 Noumea Cedex, New Caledonia

Soleri, Paolo — *Architect*
%Cosanti Foundation, 6433 Doubletree Road, Scottsdale, AZ 85253, USA

Soles, P J — *Actress*
20940 Almazan Rd, Woodland Hills, CA 91364, USA

Solh, Rashid — *Prime Minister, Lebanon*
%Chambre of Deputes, Place de l'Etoile, Beirut, Lebanon

Solomon, Arthur K — *Biophysicist*
27 Cragie St, Cambridge, MA 02138, USA

Solomon, David H — *Medical Scientist*
%University of California VA Wadsworth, Geriartics Dept, Los Angeles, CA 90024, USA

Solomon, Edward I — *Chemist*
%Stanford University, Chemistry Dept, Stanford, CA 94305, USA

Solomon, Freddie — *Football Player*
803 Turtle River Court, Plant City, FL 33567, USA

Solomon, Yonty — *Concert Pianist*
43 Belsize Park Gardens, London NW3 4JJ, England

Solovyev, Anatoli Y — *Cosmonaut*
%Potchta Kosmonavtov, Moskovskoi Oblasti, 141160 Syvisdny Goroduk, Russia

Solovyev, Vladimir A — *Cosmonaut*
Khovanskaya Ul D 3, Kv 28, 129 515 Moscow, Russia

Solow, Robert M — *Nobel Economics Laureate*
528 Lewis Wharf, Boston, MA 02110, USA

Solso, Theodore M — *Businessman*
%Cummins Engine Co, PO Box 3005, Columbus, IN 47202, USA

Soltan, Jerzy — *Architect*
6 Shady Hill Square, Cambridge, MA 02138, USA

Soltau, Gordy — *Football Player*
1111 Hamilton Ave, Palo Alto, CA 94301, USA

Solvay, Jacques — *Businessman*
%Solvay & Cie, Rue du Prince Albert 33, 1050 Brussels, Belgium

Solymosi, Zoltan — *Ballet Dancer*
%Royal Ballet, Bow St, London WC2E 9DD, England

Solzhenitsyn, Aleksandr I — *Nobel Literature Laureate*
%Farrar Straus Giroux, 19 Union Square W, New York, NY 10003, USA

Somare, Michael T — *Prime Minister, Papua New Guinea*
Karan, Murik Lakes, East Sepik, Papua New Guinea

Sombrotto, Vincent R — *Labor Leader*
%National Letter Carriers Assn, 100 Indiana Ave NW, Washington, DC 20001, USA

Somers, Brett — *Actress*
315 W 57th St, #4-H, New York, NY 10019, USA

Somers, Gwen — *Actress, Model*
%Alice Fries Agency, 1927 Vista Del Mar Ave, Los Angeles, CA 90068, USA

Somers, Suzanne — *Actress*
23852 Pacific Coast Highway, #916, Malibu, CA 90265, USA

Somerset, Willie — *Basketball Player*
PO Box 314, Monmouth Junction, NJ 08852, USA

Sommars, Julie — *Actress*
%Century Artists, 1148 4th St, #206, Santa Monica, CA 90403, USA

Sommaruga, Cornelio — *International Official, Switzerland*
%International Red Cross, 12 Grand-Mezel Place, 1204 Geneva, Switzerland

Sommer, Elke — *Actress*
Atzelsberger Str 46, 91080 Marloffstein, Germany

Sommers, Gordon L — *Religious Leader*
%Moravian Church, Northern Province, 1021 Center St, Bethlehem, PA 18018, USA

Sommers, Joanie — *Singer*
1862 Vista Del Mar, Los Angeles, CA 90028, USA

Somogyi, Jeannie R — *Ballerina*
%New York City Ballet, Lincoln Center Plaza, New York, NY 10023, USA

Somogyi, Jozsef — *Sculptor*
Marton Utca 3/5, 1038 Budapest, Hungary

Somorjai, Gabor A — *Chemist*
%University of California, Chemistry Dept, Berkeley, CA 94720, USA

Sondheim, Stephen J — *Composer, Lyricist*
300 Park Ave, #1700, New York, NY 10022, USA

Songaila, Antoinette — *Astronomer*
%University of Hawaii, Astronomy Dept, Honolulu, HI 96822, USA

Sonja — *Queen, Norway*
Det Kongelige Slott, Drammensveien 1, 0010 Oslo, Norway

Sonnenfeld, Barry — *Movie Director*
%United Talent Agency, 9560 Wilshire Blvd, #500, Beverly Hills, CA 90212, USA

Sonnenschein, Hugo F — *Educator*
%University of Chicago, President's Office, Chicago, IL 60637, USA

Sonsini, Larry W — *Attorney*
%Wilson Sonsini Goodrich Rosati, 650 Page Mill Road, Palo Alto, CA 94304, USA

Sontag, Susan — *Writer*
470 W 24th St, New York, NY 10011, USA

Soose, Billy — *Boxer*
PO Box 127, Tafton, PA 18464, USA

Sophia — *Queen, Spain*
%Palacio de la Zarzuela, 28071 Madrid, Spain

Sorato, Bruno F — *Financier*
%Union Bank of Switzerland, Bahnhofstr 45, 8000 Zurich, Switzerland

Sorbo, Kevin — *Actor*
8924 Clifton Way, #103, Beverly Hills, CA 90211, USA

Sorel, Edward — *Artist*
Rt 301, Carmel, NY 10512, USA

Sorel, Louise — *Actress*
10808 Lindbrook Dr, Los Angeles, CA 90024, USA

S

Solow - Sorel

S

Sorel, Nancy *Actress*
%Paul Kohner, 9300 Wilshire Blvd, #555, Beverly Hills, CA 90212, USA

Soren, Tabitha *Entertainer*
%MTV, News Dept, 10 Universal City Plaza, #3000, Universal City, CA 91608, USA

Sorensen, Jacki F *Physical Fitness Expert*
%Jacki's Inc, 129 1/2 N Woodland Blvd, #5, Deland, FL 32720, USA

Sorensen, Theodore C *Government Official, Attorney*
%Paul Weiss Rifkind Assoc, 1285 Ave of Americas, New York, NY 10019, USA

Sorenson, Paul *Actor*
%Don Schwartz, 6922 Hollywood Blvd, #508, Los Angeles, CA 90028, USA

Sorenson, Richard K *WW II Marine Corps Hero (CMH)*
3393 Skyline Blvd, Reno, NV 89509, USA

Sorenstam, Annika *Golfer*
%Int'l Management Group, 1 Erieview Plaza, #1300, Cleveland, OH 44114, USA

Sorkin, Arleen *Actress*
3226 N Knoll Dr, Los Angeles, CA 90068, USA

Sorlie, Donald M *Test Pilot*
14612 44th Ave NW, Gig Harbor, WA 98332, USA

Soros, George *Financier*
%Soros Fund Mgmt, 888 7th Ave, #3300, New York, NY 10106, USA

Sorrell, Martin S *Businessman*
%WPP Group, 27 Farm St, London W1X 6RD, England

Sorrento, Paul A *Baseball Player*
14470 Mark Dr, Largo, FL 33774, USA

Sorsa, T Kalevi *Prime Minister, Finland*
%Bank of Finland, PO Box 160, 00101 Helsinki, Finland

Sorvino, Mira *Actress*
%William Morris Agency, 151 S El Camino Dr, Beverly Hills, CA 90212, USA

Sorvino, Paul *Actor*
110 E 87th St, New York, NY 10128, USA

Sosa, Damuel (Sammy) *Baseball Player*
Mello Centro, San Pedro de Macoris, Dominican Republic

Sosa, Mercedes *Singer, Songwriter*
%Blue Moon Art Mgmt, 270 Ave of Americas, New York, NY 10014, USA

Sothern, Ann *Actress*
PO Box 2285, Ketchum, ID 83340, USA

Sotin, Hans *Singer*
Schulheide 10, 21227 Bendestorf, Germany

Sotirhos, Michael A *Diplomat*
%American Embassy, A Leoforos Vassilissis Sofias 91, 106 60 Athens, Greece

Sotkilava, Zurab L *Opera Singer*
%Bolshoi Theater, Teatralnaya Pl 1, 103009 Moscow, Russia

Soto, Jock *Ballet Dancer*
%New York City Ballet, Lincoln Center Plaza, New York, NY 10023, USA

Soto, Mario M *Baseball Player*
Joachs-Lachaustegui #42, Sur-Bani, Dominican Republic

Soto, Talisa *Actress, Model*
%Agency For Performing Arts, 9200 Sunset Blvd, #900, Los Angeles, CA 90069, USA

Sotomayor, Antonio *Artist*
3 Le Roy Place, San Francisco, CA 94109, USA

Sotomayor, Javier *Track Athlete*
Miramar, Havana, Cuba

Sottile, Benjamin J *Businessman*
%Gibson Greetings Inc, 2100 Section Road, Cincinnati, OH 45237, USA

Sottsass, Ettore, Jr *Industrial Designer*
Via Manzoni 14, 20121 Milan, Italy

Soul, David *Actor*
4201 Hunt Club Lane, Westlake Village, CA 91361, USA

Soulages, Pierre *Artist*
18 Rue des Trois-Portes, 75005 Paris, France

Soule, Charles E, Sr *Businessman*
%Paul Revere Insurance Group, PO Box 15123, Worcester, MA 01615, USA

Sousa, Mauricio de *Cartoonist (Monica)*
%Mauricio de Sousa Producoes, Rua do Curtume 745, Sao Paulo SP, Brazil

Soutar, Dave *Bowler*
PO Box 230, Gravois Mills, MO 65037, USA

Soutar, Judy *Bowler*
%Women's International Bowling Congress, 5301 S 76th St, Greendale, WI 53129, USA

Sorel - Soutar

Soutendijk, Renee — *Actress*
%Marion Rosenberg, 8428 Melrose Place, #C, Los Angeles, CA 90069, USA

Souter, David H — *Supreme Court Justice*
%US Supreme Court, 1 1st St NE, Washington, DC 20543, USA

South, Joe — *Singer, Songwriter, Guitarist*
3051 Claremont Road NE, Atlanta, GA 30329, USA

Southern, Silas (Eddie) — *Track Athlete*
1045 Rosewood Dr, De Soto, TX 75115, USA

Souza, Francis N — *Artist*
148 W 67th St, New York, NY 10023, USA

Souzay, Gerard — *Singer*
26 Rue Freycinet, 75116 Paris, France

Sowell, Arnold — *Track Athlete*
1647 Waterstone Lane, #1, Charlotte, NC 28262, USA

Soyer, David — *Cellist (Guarneri String Quartet)*
6 W 77th St, New York, NY 10024, USA

Spacek, Sissy — *Actress*
Beau Val Farm, Box 22, #640, Cobham, VA 22929, USA

Spacey, Kevin — *Actor*
7083 Hollywood Blvd, Los Angeles, CA 90028, USA

Spade, David — *Comedian, Actor*
%Brillstein/Grey, 9150 Wilshire Blvd, #350, Beverly Hills, CA 90212, USA

Spader, James — *Actor*
9530 Heather Road, Beverly Hills, CA 90210, USA

Spahn, Warren E — *Baseball Player*
RR 2, Hartshorne, OK 74547, USA

Spain, James W — *Writer*
42 Galle Face Court II, #42, Colombo 3, Sri Lanka

Spanarkel, Jim — *Basketball Player*
436 Edgewood Place, Rutherford, NJ 07070, USA

Spander, Art — *Sportswriter*
%San Francisco Examiner, Editorial Dept, 110 5th Ave, San Francisco, CA 94118, USA

Spano, Joe — *Actor*
%E C Assoc, 5140 Colfax Ave, #150, North Hollywood, CA 91601, USA

Spano, Vincent — *Actor*
%More/Medavoy, 7920 W Sunset Blvd, #400, Los Angeles, CA 90036, USA

Spark, Muriel S — *Writer*
%David Higham, 5-8 Lower John St, Golden Square, London W1R 4H4, England

Sparlis, Al — *Football Player*
13206 Mindanao Way, Marina del Rey, CA 90292, USA

Sparv, Camilla — *Actress*
957 N Cole Ave, Los Angeles, CA 90038, USA

Spassky, Boris V — *Chess Player*
%State Committee for Sports, Skatertny Pereulok 4, Moscow, Russia

Speaks, Ruben L — *Religious Leader*
%African Methodist Episcopal Zion Church, PO Box 32843, Charlotte, NC 28232, USA

Spear, Laurinda H — *Architect*
550 Brickell Ave, #200, Miami, FL 33131, USA

Spears, Billie Jo — *Singer*
%Joe Taylor Artist Agency, 2802 Columbine Place, Nashville, TN 37204, USA

Spears, William D — *Football Player*
63 Waterbridge Place, Ponte Vedra, FL 32082, USA

Spector, Elisabeth (Lisa) — *Government Official*
%Resolution Trust Corp, 801 17th St NW, Washington, DC 20434, USA

Spector, Phil — *Record Producer*
1210 S Arroyo Parkway, Pasadena, CA 91105, USA

Spector, Ronnie — *Singer*
%GreenSpec Properties, 39-B Mill Plain Road, #233, Danbury, CT 06811, USA

Spedding, Frank H — *Chemist, Physicist*
520 Oliver Circle, Ames, IA 50014, USA

Speech (Todd Thomas) — *Soul/Rap Artist (Arrested Development)*
%William Morris Agency, 1325 Ave of Americas, New York, NY 10019, USA

Speed, Lake — *Auto Racing Driver*
4025 Old Salisbury Road, Kannapolis, NC 28083, USA

Speight, Francis — *Artist*
508 E 9th St, Greenville, NC 27858, USA

Spelling, Aaron — *Movie, Television Producer*
%Aaron Spelling Productions, 5700 Wilshire Blvd, #575, Los Angeles, CA 90036, USA

Spelling, Randy	*Actor*
%Spelling Productions, 5700 Wilshire Blvd, #575, Los Angeles, CA 90036, USA	
Spelling, Tori	*Actress*
594 N Mapleton Dr, Los Angeles, CA 90024, USA	
Spellman, Alonzo	*Football Player*
2352 Magnolia, Buffalo Grove, IL 60089, USA	
Spellman, John D	*Governor, WA*
%Carney Stephenson Badley, Columbia Center, 701 5th Ave, Seattle, WA 98104, USA	
Spence, Dave	*Labor Leader*
%Horseshoers Union, Rt 2, Box 71-C, Englishtown, NJ 07726, USA	
Spence, Gerry	*Attorney*
%Spence Moriarity Schuster, 15 S Jackson St, Jackson, WY 83001, USA	
Spence, Jonathan D	*Writer, Historian*
691 Forest Road, New Haven, CT 06516, USA	
Spence, Roger F	*Religious Leader*
%Reformed Episcopal Church, 2001 Frederick Road, Baltimore, MD 21228, USA	
Spencer, Bud	*Actor*
%Mistral Film Group, Via Archimede 24, 00187 Rome, Italy	
Spencer, Donald C	*Mathematician*
943 County Road 204, Durango, CO 81301, USA	
Spencer, Elizabeth	*Writer*
402 Longleaf Dr, Chapel Hill, NC 27514, USA	
Spencer, Elmore	*Basketball Player*
1770 Foxlair Trail, Atlanta, GA 30349, USA	
Spencer, F Gilman	*Editor*
%Denver Post, Editorial Dept, 1560 Broadway, Denver, CO 80202, USA	
Spencer, Felton	*Basketball Player*
%Golden State Warriors, 7000 Coliseum Way, Oakland, CA 94621, USA	
Spencer, Frank Cole	*Surgeon, Educator*
560 1st Ave, New York, NY 10016, USA	
Spencer, John	*Actor*
%Abrams Artists, 9200 Sunset Blvd, #625, Los Angeles, CA 90069, USA	
Spencer, Melvin J	*Religious Leader, Attorney*
5910 N Shawnee Ave, Oklahoma City, OK 73112, USA	
Spencer, Susan	*Commentator*
%CBS-TV, News Dept, 2020 "M" St NW, Washington, DC 20036, USA	
Spencer-Devlin, Muffin	*Golfer*
1561 S Congress Ave, #141, Delray Beach, FL 33445, USA	
Spender, Percy C	*Judge*
Headingley House, 11 Wellington St, Woolhara, Sydney NSW 2025, Australia	
Sperber Carter, Paula	*Bowler*
9895 SW 95th St, Miami, FL 33186, USA	
Sperber, Wendie Jo	*Actress*
12121 Ventura Blvd, Calabasas, CA 91302, USA	
Sperling, Gene	*Government Official*
%National Economic Council, 1600 Pennsylvania Ave NW, Washington, DC 20506, USA	
Spethmann, Dieter	*Businessman*
%Thyssen AG, Karl-Theodor-Str 6, 40213 Dusseldorf, Germany	
Spice 1	*Rap Artist*
%KKR Entertainment, 1300 Clay St, Oakland, CA 94612, USA	
Spicer, William E, III	*Physicist*
785 Mayfield Road, Palo Alto, CA 94305, USA	
Spiegelman, Art	*Illustrator, Writer*
%Raw Books & Graphics, 27 Greene St, New York, NY 10013, USA	
Spielberg, David	*Actor*
11338 Cashmere St, Los Angeles, CA 90049, USA	
Spielberg, Steven	*Movie Director*
%DreamWorks SKG, 100 Universal City Plaza, Universal City, CA 91608, USA	
Spielman, Chris	*Football Player*
2094 Edgemont Road, Columbus, OH 43212, USA	
Spier, Peter E	*Artist*
PO Box 566, Shoreham, NY 11786, USA	
Spiers, Ronald I	*Diplomat*
RR 1, Box 54-A, Middletown Road, South Londonderry, VT 05155, USA	
Spilhaus, Athelstan F	*Meteorologist, Oceanographer*
PO Box 1063, Middlesburg, VA 22117, USA	
Spillane, Mickey	*Writer, Actor*
PO Box 265, Murrells Inlet, SC 29576, USA	

Spindler, Marc	*Football Player*
%New York Jets, 1000 Fulton Ave, Hempstead, NY 11550, USA	
Spinella, Stephen	*Actor*
%William Morris Agency, 1325 Ave of Americas, New York, NY 10019, USA	
Spiner, Brent	*Actor*
6922 1/2 Paseo del Serra, Los Angeles, CA 90068, USA	
Spinetti, Victor	*Actor*
15 Devonshire Place, Brighton, Sussex, England	
Spinks, Michael	*Boxer*
Centerville Road, Wilmington, DE 19808, USA	
Spittka, Marko	*Judo Athlete*
%Judo Club 90, Zielona-Gora-Str 9, 15230 Frankfurt/Ober, Germany	
Spitz, Mark A	*Swimmer*
383 Dalehurst Ave, Los Angeles, CA 90024, USA	
Spitzer, Lyman, Jr	*Astrophysicist*
659 Lake Dr, Princeton, NJ 08540, USA	
Spivakovsky, Tossy	*Concert Violinist*
29 Burnham Hill, Westport, CT 06880, USA	
Splittorff, Paul W	*Baseball Player*
4204 Hickory Lane, Blue Spring, MO 64015, USA	
Spock, Benjamin M	*Pediatrician, Social Activist, Rower*
PO Box 1268, Camden, ME 04843, USA	
Spohr, Arnold T	*Ballet Director*
%Royal Winnipeg Ballet, 289 Portage Ave, Winnipeg MB R3B 2B4, Canada	
Sponable, Jess M	*Astronaut*
1 Chaco Court, Sandia Park, NM 87047, USA	
Sponenburgh, Mark	*Sculptor*
5562 NW Pacific Coast Highway, Waldport, OR 97376, USA	
Spong, John S	*Religious Leader*
24 Rector St, Newark, NJ 07102, USA	
Spoon, Alan G	*Businessman*
%Washington Post Co, 1150 15th St NW, Washington, DC 20071, USA	
Spooner, John	*Writer, Financier*
%Houghton Mifflin Co, 215 Park Ave S, New York, NY 10003, USA	
Spotswood, Denis	*Royal Air Force Marshal, England*
Coombe Cottage, Hambleden, Oxon RG9 6SD, England	
Spradlin, G D	*Actor*
%Gersh Agency, 232 N Canon Dr, Beverly Hills, CA 90210, USA	
Sprague, Edward N	*Baseball Player*
4677 Pine Valley Circle, Stockton, CA 95219, USA	
Sprague, George F	*Geneticist, Agronomist*
494 W 10th Ave, #208, Eugene, OR 97401, USA	
Sprague, Peter J	*Businessman*
%National Semiconductor, 2900 Semiconductor Dr, Santa Clara, CA 95051, USA	
Sprayberry, James M	*Vietnam War Army Hero*
426 Holiday Dr, Titus, AL 36080, USA	
Sprewell, Latrell	*Basketball Player*
27097 Greenhaven Road, Hayward, CA 94542, USA	
Spriggs, Larry	*Basketball Player*
14250 Point Reyes St, Fontana, CA 92336, USA	
Spring, Sherwood C	*Astronaut*
%Army Space Program Office, DAMO/FDX, 2810 Old Lee Highway, Fairfax, VA 22031, USA	
Springer, Jerry	*Entertainer, Mayor*
%"Jerry Springer Show", 454 N Columbia Dr, #200, Chicago, IL 60611, USA	
Springer, Michael	*Golfer*
1838 E Oak Creek Circle, Fresno, CA 93720, USA	
Springer, Robert C	*Astronaut*
4205 Willow Bend Circle SE, Decatur, AL 35603, USA	
Springfield, Dusty	*Singer*
7 Oak Thorpe Road, Palmer's Green, London N13 5HV, England	
Springfield, Rick	*Singer, Actor*
15456 Cabrito Road, Van Nuys, CA 91406, USA	
Springs, Alice	*Photographer*
7 Ave Saint-Ramon, #T-1008, Monte Carlo, Monaco	
Springsteen, Bruce	*Singer, Songwriter*
1224 Benedict Canyon Dr, Beverly Hills, CA 90210, USA	
Sprinkel, Beryl W	*Government Official*
20140 St Andrews Dr, Olympia Fields, IL 60461, USA	

S

Spindler - Sprinkel

Sprinkle, Edward A (Ed)	*Football Player*
%Motor Vacations Unlimited, Rt 20, Elgin, IL 60120, USA	
Spungin, Joel D	*Businessman*
%United Stationers, 2200 E Golf Road, Des Plaines, IL 60016, USA	
Spurrier, Steve O	*Football Player, Coach*
12115 NW 1st lane, Gainesville, FL 32607, USA	
Spyridon, Archbishop	*Religious Leader*
%Greek Orthodox Church, 8-10 E 79th St, New York, NY 10021, USA	
Squier, Billy	*Singer, Songwriter*
%Dera Assoc, 584 Broadway, #1201, New York, NY 10012, USA	
Squires, John	*Computer Disc Drive Engineer*
%Conner Peripherals, 3081 Zanker Road, San Jose, CA 95134, USA	
Srb, Adrian M	*Geneticist*
411 Cayuga Heights Road, Ithaca, NY 14850, USA	
St Clair, Robert B (Bob)	*Football Player*
3312 Parker Hill Road, Santa Rosa, CA 95404, USA	
St Cyr, Lili	*Exotic Dancer*
624 N Plymouth Blvd, #7, Los Angeles, CA 90004, USA	
St George, William R	*Navy Admiral*
862 San Antonio Place, San Diego, CA 92106, USA	
St Jacques, Robert J	*Businessman*
%Life Insurance of Georgia, 5780 Powers Ferry Road NW, Atlanta, GA 30327, USA	
St James, Lyn	*Auto Racing Driver*
PO Box 4147, Ormond Beach, FL 32175, USA	
St Jean, Garry	*Basketball Coach, Executive*
%Golden State Warriors, 7000 Coliseum Way, Oakland, CA 94621, USA	
St John of Fawsley, Norman A F	*Government Official, England*
27 Charles St, London W1X 7HD, England	
St John, H Bernard	*Prime Minister, Barbados*
3 Enterprise, Christchurch, Barbados	
St John, Jill	*Actress*
%Borinstein Oreck Bogart, 8271 Melrose Ave, #110, Los Angeles, CA 90046, USA	
St John, Kristoff	*Actor*
7101 Farralone Ave, #114, Canoga Park, CA 91303, USA	
Staats, Elmer B	*Government Official*
%Truman Scholarship Foundation, 712 Jackson Place NW, Washington, DC 20006, USA	
Stabler, Ken M (Kenny)	*Football Player*
%Stabler Co, 260 N Joachim St, Mobile, AL 36603, USA	
Stacey Q	*Singer*
%Headline Talent, 1650 Broadway, #508, New York, NY 10019, USA	
Stack, Allen M	*Swimmer*
PO Box 76, Honolulu, HI 96810, USA	
Stack, Robert	*Actor*
321 St Pierre Road, Los Angeles, CA 90077, USA	
Stackhouse, Jerry	*Basketball Player*
805 Arrow Dr, Kinston, NC 28501, USA	
Stacomb, Kevin	*Basketball Player*
8 Old Walcott Ave, Jamestown, RI 02835, USA	
Stacy, Hollis	*Golfer*
%Blackman Financial Services, 386 Columbus Ave, New York, NY 10024, USA	
Stadler, Craig R	*Golfer*
1 Cantitoe Lane, Englewood, CO 80110, USA	
Stadler, Sergei V	*Concert Violinist*
Kaiserstr 43, 80801 Munich, Germany	
Stadtman, Earl R	*Biochemist*
16907 Redland Road, Derwood, MD 20855, USA	
Stafford, Harrison	*Football Player*
Rt 1, Box 216-H, Edna, TX 77957, USA	
Stafford, Jim	*Singer, Songwriter*
PO Box 6366, Branson, MO 65615, USA	
Stafford, Jo	*Singer*
2339 Century Hill, Los Angeles, CA 90067, USA	
Stafford, John R	*Businessman*
%American Home Products, 5 Giralda Farms, Madison, NJ 07940, USA	
Stafford, Michelle	*Actress*
%Paul Kohner, 9300 Wilshire Blvd, #555, Beverly Hills, CA 90212, USA	
Stafford, Nancy	*Actress*
13080 Mindanao Way, #69, Marina del Rey, CA 90292, USA	

Stafford, Robert T — *Governor/Senator, VT*
1 Sugarwood Hill Road, RR 1, Box 3954, Rutland, VT 05701, USA
Stafford, Thomas P — *Astronaut, Air Force General*
3212 E Interstate 240, Oklahoma City, OK 73135, USA
Stafford-Clark, Max — *Theater Director*
7 Gloucester Crescent, London NW1, England
Stager, Gus — *Swimming Coach*
%University of Michigan, Athletic Dept, Ann Arbor, MI 48104, USA
Staheli, Donald L — *Businessman*
%Continental Grain, 277 Park Ave, New York, NY 10172, USA
Stahl, Dale E — *Businessman*
%Gaylord Container Corp, 500 Lake Cook Road, Deerfield, IL 60015, USA
Stahl, Lesley R — *Commentator*
%CBS-TV, News Dept, 51 W 52nd St, New York, NY 10019, USA
Stahle, Hans — *Businessman*
%Alfa-Laval, PO Box 12150, 102 24, Stockhom, Sweden
Stahr, Elvis J, Jr — *Conservationist*
16 Martin Dale N, Greenwich, CT 06830, USA
Staley, Dawn — *Basketball Player*
1228 Callowhill St, #603, Philadelphia, PA 19123, USA
Staley, Walter — *Equestrian Rider*
214 W Teal Lake Road, Mexico, MO 65265, USA
Stallings, George — *Religious Leader*
%African American Catholic Congregation, 1015 "I" St NE, Washington, DC 20002, USA
Stallone, Sylvester — *Actor, Director*
100 SE 32nd Road, Coconut Grove, FL 33129, USA
Stallones, Reuel — *Scientist*
12414 Modena Trail, Austin, TX 78729, USA
Stallworth, John — *Football Player*
695 Dughill Road, Brownsboro, AL 35741, USA
Stamler, Jonathan — *Hematologist*
%Duke University, Medical Center, Hematology Dept, Durham, NC 27708, USA
Stamos, John — *Actor*
2319 St George St, Los Angeles, CA 90027, USA
Stamos, Theodoros — *Artist*
%Louis Meisel Gallery, 141 Prince St, New York, NY 10012, USA
Stamp, Terence — *Actor*
%Markham & Froggatt, Julian House, 4 Windmill St, London W1P 1HF, England
Stanat, Dug — *Artist*
2835 23rd St, San Francisco, CA 94110, USA
Standiford, Les — *Writer*
%Harper/Collins, 10 E 53rd St, New York, NY 10022, USA
Stanfel, Dick — *Football Player, Coach*
1104 Juniper Parkway, Libertyville, IL 60048, USA
Stanfill, Dennis C — *Movie Executive*
908 Oak Grove Ave, San Marino, CA 91108, USA
Stanfill, William T (Bill) — *Football Player*
2307 Tara Dr, Albany, GA 31707, USA
Stang, Arnold — *Actor*
PO Box 786, New Canaan, CT 06840, USA
Stanich, George — *Track Athlete*
15816 Marigold Ave, Gardena, CA 90249, USA
Stanier, John W — *Army Field Marshal, England*
%Coutts & Co, 440 The Strand, London SC2R 0QS, England
Stankovic, Borislav (Boris) — *Basketball Executive*
%FIBA, PO Box 70067, Kistlerhofstr 168, 81379 Munich, Germany
Stankowski, Paul — *Golfer*
2515 McKinney Ave, #940, Dallas, TX 75201, USA
Stanky, Edward R (Eddie) — *Baseball Manager*
2100 Spring Hill Road, Mobile, AL 36607, USA
Stanley, Allan H — *Hockey Player*
RR 3, Fennelon Falls ON K0M 1N0, Canada
Stanley, Florence — *Actress*
PO Box 48876, Los Angeles, CA 90048, USA
Stanley, Frank — *Cinematographer*
PO Box 2230, Los Angeles, CA 90078, USA
Stanley, Julian C, Jr — *Psychologist*
%Johns Hopkins University, Blumberg Center, Baltimore, MD 21218, USA

S

Stafford - Stanley

Stanley, Kim	*Actress*
1501 Montano St, #6, Santa Fe, NM 87501, USA	
Stanley, Marianne Crawford	*Basketball Coach*
%University of California, Athletic Dept, Berkeley, CA 94720, USA	
Stanley, Paul	*Singer, Guitarist (Kiss)*
%McGhee Mgmt, 8730 Sunset Blvd, #195, Los Angeles, CA 90069, USA	
Stanley, Ralph	*Guitarist*
%Rebel Records, PO Box 3057, Roanoke, VA 24015, USA	
Stanley, Steven M	*Paleobiologist*
115 Overhill Road, Baltimore, MD 21210, USA	
Stans, Maurice H	*Secretary, Commerce*
211 S Orange Grove Ave, Pasadena, CA 91105, USA	
Stansfield Smith, Colin	*Architect*
Three Ministers House, 76 High St, Winchester, Hants SO23 8UL, England	
Stansfield, Lisa	*Singer, Songwriter*
PO Box 59, Ashwell, Herts SG7 5NG, England	
Stansky, Robert	*Financier*
%Fidelity Magellan Fund, 82 Devonshire St, Boston, MA 02109, USA	
Stantis, Scott	*Editorial Cartoonist (The Buckets)*
%Memphis Commerical-Appeal, Editorial Dept, 495 Union Ave, Memphis, TN 38103, USA	
Stanton, Donald S	*Educator*
%Oglethorpe University, President's Office, Atlanta, GA 30319, USA	
Stanton, Frank	*Broadcast Executive*
25 W 52nd St, New York, NY 10019, USA	
Stanton, Harry Dean	*Actor*
14527 Mulholland Dr, Los Angeles, CA 90077, USA	
Stanton, Jeff	*Motorcycle Racing Rider*
1137 Athens Road, Sherwood, MI 49089, USA	
Stanton, Paul	*Hockey Player*
23 Linda St, Foxboro, MA 02035, USA	
Stanton, Susan	*Businesswoman*
%Payless Cashways, 2301 Main St, Kansas City, MO 64108, USA	
Staples, Mavis	*Singer*
2772 E 75th St, Chicago, IL 60649, USA	
Stapleton, Jean	*Actress*
250 W Main St, #100, Charlottesvle, VA 22902, USA	
Stapleton, Maureen	*Actress*
1-14 Morgan Manor, Lenox, MA 01240, USA	
Stapp, John P	*Aerospace Scientist*
%New Mexico Research Institute, PO Box 553, Alamogordo, NM 88311, USA	
Starbird, Kay	*Basketball Player*
%Seattle Reign, 400 Mercer St, #408, Seattle, WA 98109, USA	
Starfield, Barbara H	*Physician*
%Johns Hopkins University, Hygiene School, 624 N Broadway, Baltimore, MD 21205, USA	
Stargell, Wilver D (Willie)	*Baseball Player*
813 Tarpon Dr, Wilmington, NC 28409, USA	
Stark, Freya M	*Writer, Explorer*
Via Canova, Asolo, Treviso, Italy	
Stark, Jurgen K	*Religious Leader*
%Church of Christ Scientist, 175 Huntington Ave, Boston, MA 02115, USA	
Stark, Koo	*Actress*
%Rebecca Blond Assoc, 52 Shaftesbury Ave, London W1V 7DE, England	
Stark, Nathan J	*Lawyer*
RR 1, Box 178, Punxsutawney, PA 15767, USA	
Stark, Ray	*Movie Producer*
%MGM Studios, 10232 W Washington Blvd, Culver City, CA 90232, USA	
Stark, Rohn T	*Football Player*
107 Sebago Lake Dr, Sewickley, PA 15143, USA	
Starker, Janos	*Concert Cellist*
1241 Winfield Road, Bloomington, IN 47401, USA	
Starks, John	*Basketball Player*
1061 N Willow Ave, Broken Arrow, OK 74012, USA	
Starling, Marlon	*Boxer*
141 Fairview Dr, South Windsor, CT 06074, USA	
Starn, Douglas	*Photographer*
%Stux Gallery, 163 Mercer St, #1, New York, NY 10012, USA	
Starn, Mike	*Photographer*
%Stux Gallery, 163 Mercer St, #1, New York, NY 10012, USA	

Starnes, Vaughn A *Surgeon*
%Stanford University, Med Center, Heart/Lung Transplant Dept, Stanford, CA 94305, USA

Starr, Albert *Cardiac Surgeon*
5050 SW Patton Road, Portland, OR 97221, USA

Starr, B Bartlett (Bart) *Football Player*
2065 Royal Fern lane, Birmingham, AL 35244, USA

Starr, Blaze *Exotic Dancer*
%Carrolltown Mall, Eldersburg, MD 21784, USA

Starr, Edwin *Singer*
1161 NW 78th Ave, Fort Lauderdale, FL 33322, USA

Starr, Kay *Singer*
%General Artists, 16810 Baijo Road, Encino, CA 91436, USA

Starr, Kenneth W *Government Official, Judge*
%Pepperdine University, Law School, Malibu, CA 90265, USA

Starr, Leonard *Cartoonist (Annie, Kelly Green)*
46 Post Road E, Westport, CT 06880, USA

Starr, Paul E *Sociologist*
%Princeton University, Sociology Dept, Green Hall, Princeton, NJ 08544, USA

Starr, Ringo *Singer (The Beatles), Actor*
%David Fishof Presents, 252 W 71st St, New York, NY 10023, USA

Starzl, Thomas E *Physician*
%University of Pittsburgh Medical School, Surgery Dept, Pittsburgh, PA 15261, USA

Stassen, Harold E *Governor, MN, Educator*
431 E Haskell St, #1, West St Paul, MN 55118, USA

Stastny, Peter *Hockey Player*
26 McGuire Lane, West Orange, NJ 07052, USA

Stata, Ray *Businessman*
%Analog Devices, 1 Technology Way, Norwood, MA 02062, USA

Staton, Candi *Singer*
%Capital Entertainment, 1201 "N" St NW, #A-5, Washington, DC 20005, USA

Staton, Dakota *Jazz Singer*
%Arthur Shafman, PO Box 352, Pawling, NY 12564, USA

Staub, Daniel J (Rusty) *Baseball Player*
21509 17th Ave, Flushing, NY 11360, USA

Staubach, Roger T *Football Player*
6912 Edelweiss Circle, Dallas, TX 75240, USA

Stauffer, William A (Bill) *Basketball Player*
3920 Grand Ave, #301, Des Moines, IA 50312, USA

Stautner, Ernest A (Ernie) *Football Player, Coach*
801 Greenvalley Lane, Highland Village, TX 75067, USA

Staveley, William D M *Royal Navy Fleet Admiral, England*
%N Thames Health Authority, 40 Eastbourne Terrace, London W2 3QR, England

Stavropoulos, William S *Businessman*
%Dow Chemical, 2020 Dow Center, Midland, MI 48674, USA

Stayskal, Wayne *Editorial Cartoonist*
PO Box 191, Tampa, FL 33601, USA

Stead, Eugene A, Jr *Physician*
5113 Townsville Road, Bullock, NC 27507, USA

Steadman, J Richard *Sports Orthopedic Surgeon*
%Steadman Hawkins Clinic, 181 W Meadows Dr, #400, Vail, CO 81657, USA

Stebbins, George L *Geneticist*
216 "F" St, #165, Davis, CA 95616, USA

Stecher, Renate *Track Athlete*
Haydnstr 11, #526/38, 07749 Jena, Germany

Stecher, Theodore P *Astronomer*
%UIT Project, Goddard Space Flight Center, Greenbelt, MD 20771, USA

Steding, Katy *Basketball Player*
11440 SW Roberts Court, Tualatin, OR 97062, USA

Steel, Amy *Actress*
%Innovative Artists, 1999 Ave of Stars, #2850, Los Angeles, CA 90067, USA

Steel, Danielle F *Writer*
330 Bob Hope Dr, Burbank, CA 91523, USA

Steel, David M S *Government Official, England*
Aikwood Tower, Ettrick Bridge, Selkirkshire, Scotland

Steel, Dawn *Movie Executive*
%Atlas Entertainment, 9169 W Sunset Blvd, West Hollywood, CA 90069, USA

Steele, Barbara *Actress*
2460 Benedict Canyon Dr, Beverly Hills, CA 90210, USA

S

Steele, Larry *Basketball Player*
139 SW Del Prado St, Lake Oswego, OR 97035, USA
Steele, Martin R *Marine Corps General*
Deputy CofS, Plans/Policies/Ops, Hq USMC, Navy Annex, Washington, DC 20380, USA
Steele, Richard *Boxing Referee*
2438 Antler Point Dr, Henderson, NV 89014, USA
Steele, Shelby *Writer*
%San Jose State University, English Dept, San Jose, CA 95192, USA
Steele, Tommy *Singer, Actor*
%IMG, Media House, 3 Burlington Lane, London W4 2TH, England
Steele, William M (Mike) *Army General*
Commanding General, US Army Pacific, Fort Shafter, HI 96853, USA
Steele-Perkins, Christopher H *Photographer*
5 Homer House, Rushcroft Road, London, England
Steen, Jessica *Actress*
%Don Buchwald, 9229 Sunset Blvd, #710, Los Angeles, CA 90069, USA
Steenburgen, Mary *Actress*
165 Copper Cliff Lane, Sedona, AZ 86336, USA
Steere, William C, Jr *Businessman*
%Pfizer Inc, 235 E 42nd St, New York, NY 10017, USA
Stefan, Greg *Hockey Player*
37648 Baywood Dr, #33, Farmington Hills, MI 48335, USA
Stefani, Gwen *Singer, Songwriter (No Doubt)*
%MOB Agency, 6404 Wilshire Blvd, #700, Los Angeles, CA 90048, USA
Stefanich, Jim *Bowler*
1025 N Prairie, Joliet, IL 60435, USA
Stefanko, Robert A *Businessman*
%A Schulman Inc, 3550 W Market St, Akron, OH 44333, USA
Stefanopolous, Constantine (Costis) *President, Greece*
%Presidential Palace, Odos Zalokosta 10, Athens, Greece
Steffensen, Dwight A *Businessman*
%Bergen Brunswig Corp, 4000 Metropolitan Dr, Orange, CA 92868, USA
Steffes, Kent *Volleyball Player*
11106 Ave de Cortez, Pacific Palisades, CA 90272, USA
Steffy, Joe *Football Player*
%Broadway Buick, 259 Broadway, Newburgh, NY 12550, USA
Stegemeier, Richard J *Businessman*
%Unocal Corp, 2101 Rosecrans Ave, #1200, El Segundo, CA 90245, USA
Steger, Joseph A *Educator*
%University of Cincinnati, President's Office, Cincinnati, OH 45221, USA
Steger, Will *Arctic Explorer*
%International Artic Project, 990 3rd St E, St Paul, MN 55106, USA
Steig, William *Writer, Artist*
301 Berkeley St, #4, Boston, MA 02116, USA
Steiger, Janet D *Government Official*
%Federal Trade Commission, Pennsylvania Ave & 6th St NW, Washington, DC 20580, USA
Steiger, Rod *Actor*
6324 Zumirez Dr, Malibu, CA 90265, USA
Stein, Bob *Basketball Executive*
%Minnesota Timberwolves, Target Center, 600 1st Ave N, Minneapolis, MN 55403, USA
Stein, Elias M *Mathematician*
132 Dodds Lane, Princeton, NJ 08540, USA
Stein, Gilbert (Gil) *Hockey Executive*
%National Hockey League, 650 5th Ave, #3300, New York, NY 10019, USA
Stein, Herbert *Government Official, Economist*
%American Enterprise Institute, 1150 17th St NW, Washington, DC 20036, USA
Stein, Horst *Conductor*
%Mariedi Anders Mgmt, 535 El Camino Del Mar, San Francisco, CA 94121, USA
Stein, Howard *Financier*
%Dreyfus Corp, 200 Park Ave, New York, NY 10166, USA
Stein, J Dieter *Businessman*
%BASF Corp, 3000 Continental Dr N, Mt Olive, NJ 07828, USA
Stein, Joseph *Writer*
1130 Park Ave, New York, NY 10128, USA
Stein, Mark *Singer, Keyboardist (Vanilla Fudge)*
%Future Vision, 280 Riverside Dr, #12-L, New York, NY 10025, USA
Stein, Paul E *Air Force General*
%US Air Force Academy, Superintendent's Office, Colorado Springs, CO 80840, USA

Steele - Stein

Stein, Robert — Editor
%McCall's Magazine, Editorial Dept, 375 Lexington Ave, New York, NY 10017, USA

Steinbach, Alice — Journalist
%Baltimore Sun, Editorial Dept, 501 N Calvert St, Baltimore, MD 21202, USA

Steinbach, Terry L — Baseball Player
750 Boone Ave N, Golden Valley, MN 55427, USA

Steinberg, David — Comedian, Television Director
4909 Woodley Ave, Encino, CA 91436, USA

Steinberg, Joseph S — Businessman
%Leucadia National Corp, 315 Park Ave S, New York, NY 10010, USA

Steinberg, Leigh — Sports Attorney
2727 Dunleer Place, Los Angeles, CA 90064, USA

Steinberg, Leo — Writer, Art Historian
165 W 66th St, New York, NY 10023, USA

Steinberg, Robert M — Businessman
%Reliance Group Holdings, 55 E 52nd St, New York, NY 10055, USA

Steinberg, Saul — Artist, Cartoonist
%New Yorker Magazine, 20 W 43rd St, New York, NY 10036, USA

Steinberg, Saul P — Businessman
%Reliance Group Holdings, 55 E 52nd St, New York, NY 10055, USA

Steinberg, William R — Labor Leader
%American Radio Assn, 26 Journal Square, #1501, Jersey City, NJ 07306, USA

Steinberger, Jack — Nobel Physics Laureate
25 Chemin des Merles, 1213 Onex, Geneva, Switzerland

Steinbrenner, George M, III — Baseball Executive
River Ave & E 16th, New York, NY 10002, USA

Steinem, Gloria — Social Activist, Editor
118 E 73rd St, New York, NY 10021, USA

Steiner, George — Writer
32 Barrow Road, Cambridge, England

Steiner, Jeffrey J — Businessman
%Fairchild Corp, 3800 W Service Road, Chantilly, VA 22021, USA

Steinfeld, Jake — Actor, Body Builder
622 Toyopa Dr, Pacific Palisades, CA 90272, USA

Steinhardt, Richard — Biologist
%University of California, Biology Dept, Berkeley, CA 94720, USA

Steinhart, Ronald G — Financier
%Bank One Texas, 1717 Main St, Dallas, TX 75201, USA

Steinhauer, Sherri — Golfer
PO Box 13584, Tucson, AZ 85732, USA

Steinkraus, William (Bill) — Equestrian Rider
PO Box 3038, Noroton, CT 06820, USA

Steinkuhler, Dean — Football Player
General Delivery, Palmyra, NE 68418, USA

Steinsaltz, Adin — Religious Leader
%Israel Talmudic Publications Institute, PO Box 1458, Jerusalem, Israel

Steinseifer, Carrie — Swimmer
8197 E Sunnyside Dr, Scottsdale, AZ 85260, USA

Stella, Frank P — Artist
17 Jones St, New York, NY 10014, USA

Stelle, Kellogg S — Physicist
%Imperial College, Prince Consort Road, London SW7 2BZ, England

Stempel, Robert C — Businessman
%Energy Conversion Devices, 1647 W Maple Road, Troy, MI 48084, USA

Stenerud, Jan — Football Player
%Howard Needles Tammen Bergendoff, 1201 Walnut, #700, Kansas City, MO 64106, USA

Stenmark, Ingemar — Skier
Slalomvagen 9, 920 64 Tarnaby, Sweden

Stent, Gunther S — Molecular Biologist
145 Purdue Ave, Kensington, CA 94708, USA

Stepan, F Quinn — Businessman
%Stepan Co, 22 W Frontage Road, Northfield, IL 60093, USA

Stepanian, Ira — Financier
%Bank of Boston Corp, 100 Federal St, Boston, MA 02110, USA

Stephanie — Princess, Monaco
Maison Clos St-Martin, St Remy de Provence, France

Stephanopoulos, George R — Journalist, Government Official
%White House, 1600 Pennsylvania Ave NW, Washington, DC 20500, USA

S

Stein - Stephanopoulos

Stephens, Olin James, II   *Naval Architect, Yacht Designer*
%Sparkman & Stephens, 79 Madison Ave, New York, NY 10016, USA

Stephens, Sanford (Sandy)   *Football Player*
1930 E 86th St, #111, Bloomington, MN 55425, USA

Stephens, W Thomas   *Businessman*
%Manville Corp, Ken-Caryl Ranch, PO Box 5108, Denver, CO 80217, USA

Stephens, Woodford C (Woody)   *Thoroughbred Racing Trainer*
15534 Cairnyan Ct, Miami Lakes, FL 33014, USA

Stephenson, Dwight E   *Football Player*
6301 Hutchinson Road, Miami Lakes, FL 33014, USA

Stephenson, Gordon   *Architect*
55/14 Albert St, Claremont WA 6010, Australia

Stephenson, Jan L   *Golfer*
1231 Garden St, #204, Titusville, FL 32796, USA

Stephenson, Pamela   *Actress*
%John Reid, Singes House, 32 Galena Road, London W6 0LT, England

Stepnoski, Mark M   *Football Player*
1131 Meadow Creek Dr, #C-1108, Irving, TX 75038, USA

Steppling, John   *Writer*
%William Morris Agency, 151 S El Camino Dr, Beverly Hills, CA 90212, USA

Sterban, Richard A   *Singer (Oak Ridge Boys)*
329 Rockland Road, Hendersonville, TN 37075, USA

Sterling, Annette   *Singer (Martha & Vandellas)*
%Soundedge Personal Mgmt, 332 Southdown Road, Lloyd Harbor, NY 11743, USA

Sterling, Jan   *Actress*
3959 Hamilton St, #11, San Diego, CA 92104, USA

Sterling, Philip   *Actor*
4114 Benedict Canyon Dr, Sherman Oaks, CA 91423, USA

Sterling, Robert   *Actor*
121 S Bentley Ave, Los Angeles, CA 90049, USA

Sterling, Tisha   *Actress*
PO Box 788, Ketchum, ID 83340, USA

Stern, Andrew L   *Labor Leader*
%Service Employees International Union, 1313 "L" St NW, Washington, DC 20005, USA

Stern, Daniel   *Actor*
PO Box 6788, Malibu, CA 90264, USA

Stern, David J   *Basketball Executive*
%National Basketball Assn, Olympic Tower, 122 E 55th St, New York, 10022, USA

Stern, Fritz R   *Writer, Historian*
15 Claremont Ave, New York, NY 10027, USA

Stern, Gary H   *Financier*
%Federal Reserve Bank, 250 Marquette Ave, Minneapolis, MN 55401, USA

Stern, Howard A   *Entertainer*
29 Pinetree Lane, Old Westbury, NY 11568, USA

Stern, Isaac   *Concert Violinist*
211 Central Park West, New York, NY 10024, USA

Stern, Leonard B   *Television, Movie Producer*
1709 Angelo Dr, Beverly Hills, CA 90210, USA

Stern, Mike   *Jazz Guitarist*
%Tropix International, 163 3rd Ave, #143, New York, NY 10003, USA

Stern, Richard G   *Writer*
%University of Chicago, English Dept, Chicago, IL 60637, USA

Stern, Robert A M   *Architect*
%Robert Stern Architects, 211 W 61st St, #500, New York, NY 10023, USA

Sternbach, Leo H   *Medical Chemist*
10 Woodmont Road, Upper Montclair, NJ 07043, USA

Sterner, George R   *Navy Admiral*
Commander, Naval Sea Systems, Navy Department, Washington, DC 20350, USA

Sternfeld, Reuben   *Financier*
%Inter-American Development Bank, 1300 New York Ave NW, Washington, DC 20577, USA

Sternhagen, Frances   *Actress*
152 Sutton Manor Road, New Rochelle, NY 10801, USA

Sterrett, Samuel B   *Judge*
%US Tax Court, 400 2nd St NW, Washington, DC 20217, USA

Sterzinsky, Georg Maximilian Cardinal   *Religious Leader*
%Archdiocese of Berlin, Wundstr 48/50, 14057 Berlin, Germany

Stetter, Karl   *Microbiologist*
%Universtat Regensburg, Universitatsstr 31, 93053 Regensburg, Germany

Stevens (Yusef Islam), Cat	*Singer, Songwriter*
Ariola Steinhauser Str 3, 81667 Munich, Germany	
Stevens, Andrew	*Actor*
3965 Valley Meadow Road, Encino, CA 91436, USA	
Stevens, Brinke	*Actress*
8033 Sunset Blvd, #556, Los Angeles, CA 90046, USA	
Stevens, Chuck	*Photographer*
1720 Mission St, #B, San Francisco, CA 94103, USA	
Stevens, Connie	*Singer, Actress*
8721 Sunset Blvd, #PH-1, Los Angeles, CA 90069, USA	
Stevens, Craig	*Actor*
1308 N Flores St, Los Angeles, CA 90069, USA	
Stevens, Dodie	*Singer*
%British & Int'l Artists, 500 Waterman Ave, #191, East Providence, RI 02914, USA	
Stevens, Dorit	*Actress, Model*
11524 Amanda Dr, Studio City, CA 91604, USA	
Stevens, Fisher	*Actor*
%William Morris Agency, 151 S El Camino Dr, Beverly Hills, CA 90212, USA	
Stevens, Gary	*Jockey*
%Thoroughbred Racing Assn, 3000 Marcus Ave, Lake Success, NY 11042, USA	
Stevens, George, Jr	*Movie Producer*
%New Liberty Productions, John F Kennedy Center, Washington, DC 20566, USA	
Stevens, John Paul	*Supreme Court Justice*
%US Supreme Court, 1 1st St NE, Washington, DC 20543, USA	
Stevens, Kaye	*Singer, Actress*
%Ruth Webb, 13834 Magnolia Blvd, Sherman Oaks, CA 91423, USA	
Stevens, Kevin M	*Hockey Player*
38 Bay Pond Road, Duxbury, MA 02332, USA	
Stevens, Ray	*Singer, Songwriter*
%Kathy Gangwisch, 207 Westport Road, #202, Kansas City, MO 64111, USA	
Stevens, Rise	*Opera Singer*
930 5th Ave, New York, NY 10021, USA	
Stevens, Roger L	*Theater Producer*
%President's Arts/Humanities Commission, Kennedy Center, Washington, DC 20566, USA	
Stevens, Ronnie	*Actor*
%Caroline Dawson, 47 Courtfield Road, #9, London SW7 4DB, England	
Stevens, Scott	*Hockey Player*
234 Columbia Ave, Fort Lee, NJ 07024, USA	
Stevens, Shadoe	*Actor, Radio Personality*
2570 Benedict Canyon Dr, Beverly Hills, CA 90210, USA	
Stevens, Shakin'	*Singer, Songwriter*
%Mgmt Gerd Kehren, Postfach 1455, 41804 Erkelenz, Germany	
Stevens, Stella	*Actress, Model*
2180 Coldwater Canyon Dr, Beverly Hills, CA 90210, USA	
Stevens, Warren	*Actor*
14155 Magnolia Blvd, #27, Sherman Oaks, CA 91423, USA	
Stevenson, Adlai E, III	*Senator, IL*
225 W Wacker Dr, #2250, Chicago, IL 60606, USA	
Stevenson, Juliet	*Actress*
%Markham & Froggatt, Julian House, 4 Windmill St, London W1P 1HF, England	
Stevenson, Parker	*Actor*
10100 Santa Monica Blvd, #400, Los Angeles, CA 90067, USA	
Stevenson, Teofilo	*Boxer*
%Comite Olimppicu, Hotel Havana, Libre, Havana, Cuba	
Stever, H Guyford	*Aeronautical, Space Engineer*
588 Russell Ave, Gaithersburg, MD 20877, USA	
Stevie B	*Singer*
%Famous Artists Agency, 1700 Broadway, #500, New York, NY 10019, USA	
Steward, H Leighton	*Businessman*
%Louisiana Land & Exploration, 909 Poydras St, New Orleans, LA 70112, USA	
Stewart of Fulham, R Michael M	*Government Official, England*
Combe, Newbury, Berks, England	
Stewart, Al	*Singer, Songwriter*
%Chapman Co, PO Box 5549, Santa Monica, CA 90409, USA	
Stewart, C Jim, II	*Businessman*
%Stewart & Stevenson, 2707 North Loop W, Houston, TX 77008, USA	
Stewart, Catherine Mary	*Actress*
350 DuPont St, Toronto ON M5R 1Z9, Canada	

S

Stevens (Yusef Islam) - Stewart

Stewart, David A (Dave) *Keyboardist, Guitarist (Eurythmics)*
PO Box 245, London N89 QG, England

Stewart, David K (Dave) *Baseball Player*
1038 Canton Circle, Claremont, CA 91711, USA

Stewart, Donald W *Senator, AL*
9003 Teddy Rae Court, Springfield, VA 22152, USA

Stewart, Elaine *Actress*
1011 N Roxbury Dr, Beverly Hills, CA 90210, USA

Stewart, Gary *Singer*
%Entertainment Artists, 903 18th Ave S, Nashville, TN 37212, USA

Stewart, Ian *Government Official, England*
%House of Commons, Westminster, London SW1A 0AA, England

Stewart, J W *Businessman*
%BJ Services, 5500 NW Central Dr, Houston, TX 77092, USA

Stewart, James B *Journalist*
%Simon & Schuster Inc, 1230 Ave of Americas, New York, NY 10020, USA

Stewart, Jermaine *Singer*
%Richard Walters, 421 S Beverly Dr, #800, Beverly Hills, CA 90212, USA

Stewart, John *Singer (Kingston Trio)*
%Fuji Productions, 2480 Williston Dr, Charlottesville, VA 22901, USA

Stewart, John Y (Jackie) *Auto Racing Driver*
24 Route de Divonne, 1260 Nyon, Switzerland

Stewart, Jon *Comedian*
%William Morris Agency, 151 S El Camino Dr, Beverly Hills, CA 90212, USA

Stewart, Kordell *Football Player*
%Pittsburgh Steelers, 3 Rivers Stadium, 300 Stadium Circle, Pittsburgh, PA 15212, USA

Stewart, Lisa *Singer*
%Turner Co, 1018 17th Ave S, #6, Nashville, TN 37212, USA

Stewart, Martha *Entertainer, Publisher*
Lily Pond Lane, Hampton, CT 06247, USA

Stewart, Mary *Writer*
House of Letterawe, Lock Awe, Argyll PA33 1AH, Scotland

Stewart, Melvin, Jr *Swimmer*
1311 Lake Lauden Blvd, Knoxville, TN 37916, USA

Stewart, Norm *Basketball Coach*
%University of Missouri, Athletic Dept, Columbia, MO 65211, USA

Stewart, Patrick *Actor*
2263 Moreno Dr, Los Angeles, CA 90039, USA

Stewart, Payne *Golfer*
9209 Charles E Limpus Road, Orlando, FL 32836, USA

Stewart, Peggy *Actress*
11139 Hortense St, North Hollywood, CA 91602, USA

Stewart, Redd *Singer, Songwriter*
%Tessier-Marsh Talent, 505 Canton Pass, Madison, TN 37115, USA

Stewart, Robert L *Astronaut, Army General*
815 Sun Valley Dr, Woodland Park, CO 80863, USA

Stewart, Rod *Singer, Songwriter*
23 Beverly Park, Los Angeles, CA 90210, USA

Stewart, Ron *Hockey Player*
17200 W Ball Road, #606, Surprise, AZ 85374, USA

Stewart, S Jay *Businessman*
%Morton International, 100 N Riverside Plaza, Chicago, IL 60606, USA

Stewart, Thomas *Opera Singer*
%Columbia Artists Mgmt Inc, 165 W 57th St, New York, NY 10019, USA

Stewart, Thomas D *Physical Anthropologist*
1191 Crest Lane, McLean, VA 22101, USA

Stich, Michael *Tennis Player*
Ernst-Barlach-Str 44, 25336 Elmshorn, Germany

Stickel, Fred A *Publisher*
%Portland Oregonian, 1320 SW Broadway, Portland, OR 97201, USA

Stickler, Alfons Cardinal *Religious Leader*
Biblioteca Apostolica Vaticina, 00120 Vatican City

Stickney, Dorothy *Actress*
13 E 94th St, New York, NY 10128, USA

Stieb, David A (Dave) *Baseball Player*
PO Box 7422, Incline Village, NV 89452, USA

Stieber, Tamar *Journalist*
%Albuquerque Journal, Editorial Dept, 7777 Jefferson NE, Albuquerque, NM 87109, USA

Stiefel, Ethan — *Ballet Dancer*
%New York City Ballet, Lincoln Center Plaza, New York, NY 10023, USA

Stiegler, Josef (Pepi) — *Skier*
PO Box 290, Teton Village, WY 83025, USA

Stiers, David Ogden — *Actor*
%GKAC, 12304 Santa Monica Blvd, #119, Los Angeles, CA 90025, USA

Stigers, Curtis — *Singer, Saxophonist*
%C Winston Simone Mgmt, 1790 Broadway, #1000, New York, NY 10019, USA

Stiglitz, Joseph E — *Economist*
2942 Ordway St NW, Washington, DC 20008, USA

Stigwood, Robert C — *Movie, Theater, Music Producer*
%Barton Manor, Isle of Wight, Whippingham, East Cowes, PO32 6LB, England

Stihl, Hans-Peter — *Businessman*
%DIHT, Vadstr 115, 71307 Waiblingen, Germany

Stiles, Alan — *Publisher*
%Esquire Magazine, 2 Park Ave, New York, NY 10016, USA

Stilgoe, Richard — *Lyricist*
%Noel Gray Artists, 24 Denmark St, London WC2H 8NJ, England

Still, Art — *Football Player*
9891 Point Peter Road, Gowanda, NY 14070, USA

Still, Ray — *Concert Oboist*
%Chicago Symphony Orchestra, 220 S Michigan Ave, Chicago, IL 60604, USA

Still, Susan Leigh — *Astronaut*
%NASA, Johnson Space Center, 2101 NASA Road, Houston, TX 77058, USA

Stiller, Ben — *Comedian, Director*
%Creative Artists Agency, 9830 Wilshire Blvd, Beverly Hills, CA 90212, USA

Stiller, Jerry — *Comedian, Actor*
118 Riverside Dr, #5-A, New York, NY 10024, USA

Stillings, Floyd — *Rodeo Performer*
2118 S Baldwin Ave, Arcadia, CA 91007, USA

Stillman, Royle E — *Baseball Player*
PO Box 984, New Castle, CO 81647, USA

Stillman, Whit — *Movie Director*
%United Talent Agency, 9560 Wilshire Blvd, #500, Beverly Hills, CA 90212, USA

Stills, Stephen — *Singer, Guitarist (Crosby Stills & Nash)*
191 N Phelps Ave, Winter Park, FL 32789, USA

Stillwagon, Jim — *Football Player*
890 Gatehouse Lane, Columbus, OH 43235, USA

Stillwell, Roger — *Football Player*
25 Woodland Court, Novato, CA 94947, USA

Stilwell, Richard D — *Opera Singer*
1969 Rockingham St, McLean, VA 22101, USA

Stine, R L — *Writer*
%Scholastic Book Services, 555 Broadway, New York 10012, USA

Stine, Richard — *Editorial Cartoonist*
8100 Hidden Cove Road, Bainbridge Island, WA 98110, USA

Sting (Gordon Summer) — *Singer, Actor, Bassist, Songwriter*
%Outlandos, 2 The Grove, Highgate Village, London N16, England

Stingley, Darryl — *Football Player, Executive*
%New England Patriots, Foxboro Stadium, Rt 1, Foxboro, MA 02035, USA

Stinnette, Joe L, Jr — *Businessman*
%Fireman's Fund Insurance, 777 San Marin Dr, Novato, CA 94998, USA

Stipe, Michael — *Singer (REM), Songwriter*
%REM/Athens Ltd, 250 W Clayton St, Athens, GA 30601, USA

Stiritz, William P — *Businessman*
%Ralston Purina Co, Checkerboard Square, St Louis, MO 63164, USA

Stirling, Linda — *Actress*
4717 Laurel Canyon Blvd, #2068, North Hollywood, CA 91607, USA

Stith, Bryant — *Basketball Player*
RR 1, Box 380-A, Freeman, VA 23856, USA

Stitzlein, Lorraine — *Bowling Executive*
%Professional Bowlers Assn, 1720 Merriman Road, Akron, OH 44313, USA

Stobart, John — *Artist*
Beach Road, Edgartown, MA 02539, USA

Stock, Barbara — *Actress*
13421 Cheltenham Dr, Sherman Oaks, CA 91423, USA

Stockdale, James B — *Vietnam War Navy Hero (CMH), Admiral*
547 "A" Ave, Coronado, CA 92118, USA

Stockhausen, Karlheinz — *Composer*
Stockhausen-Verlag, 51515 Kurten, Germany

Stockman, David A — *Government Official, Financier*
%Blackstone Group, 345 Park Ave, New York, NY 10154, USA

Stockman, Shawn — *Singer (Boyz II Men)*
%BIV Entertainment, 5 Bishop Road, Vincentown, NJ 08088, USA

Stockton, Dave K — *Golfer*
32373 Tres Lagos St, Mentone, CA 92359, USA

Stockton, Dick — *Sportscaster*
%Fox-TV, Sports Dept, PO Box 900, New York, NY 90213, USA

Stockton, John H — *Basketball Player*
%Utah Jazz, Delta Center, 301 W South Temple, Salt Lake City, UT 84101, USA

Stockwell, Dean — *Actor*
9630 Keokuk Ave, Chatsworth, CA 91311, USA

Stockwell, Guy — *Actor*
6652 Coldwater Canyon Ave, North Hollywood, CA 91606, USA

Stoddard, Brandon — *Television Executive*
240 N Glenroy Ave, Los Angeles, CA 90049, USA

Stoitchkov, Hristo — *Soccer Player*
%FC Barcelona, Aristides Maillol S/N, 08 028 Barcelona, Spain

Stojko, Elvis — *Figure Skater*
PO Box 69029, Rosedale PO, 1900 King St E, Hamilton ON L8K 6R4, Canada

Stokes, J J — *Football Player*
%San Francisco 49ers, 4949 Centennial Blvd, Santa Clara, CA 95054, USA

Stokkan, Bill — *Auto Racing Executive*
%Championship Auto Racing Teams, 755 W Big Beaver Road, #800, Troy, MI 48084, USA

Stoklos, Randy — *Volleyball Player*
%Assn of Volleyball Pros, 330 Washington Blvd, #600, Marina del Rey, CA 90292, USA

Stolle, Frederick S — *Tennis Player*
%Turnberry Isle Yacht & Racquet Club, 19735 Turnberry Way, North Miami, FL 33180, USA

Stolley, Paul D — *Physician*
6424 Brass Knob, Columbia, MD 21044, USA

Stolley, Richard B — *Editor*
%Time Inc, Time-Life Building, Rockefeller Center, New York, NY 10020, USA

Stolojan, Theodor — *Prime Minister, Romania*
%Int'l Bank of Reconstruction/Development, 1818 "H" St NW, Washington, DC 20433, USA

Stoltenberg, Gerhard — *Government Official, Germany*
Grauheindorferstr 108, 53111 Bonn, Germany

Stoltz, Eric — *Actor*
7575 Mulholland Dr, Los Angeles, CA 90046, USA

Stoltzman, Richard L — *Concert Clarinetist*
%Frank Saloman Assoc, 201 W 54th St, #4-C, New York, NY 10019, USA

Stolze, Lena — *Actress*
%Agentur Carola Studlar, Neuroeder Str 1-C, 82152 Planegg, Germany

Stone, Albert L — *Thoroughbred Racing Executive*
700 Central Ave, PO Box 8427, Louisville, KY 40208, USA

Stone, Andrew L — *Movie Director*
10478 Wyton Dr, Los Angeles, CA 90024, USA

Stone, Christopher — *Actor*
23035 Cumorah Crest Dr, Woodland Hills, CA 91364, USA

Stone, Dee Wallace — *Actress*
23035 Cumorah Crest Dr, Woodland Hills, CA 91364, USA

Stone, Doug — *Singer, Songwriter*
%Hallmark Direction, 1905 Broadway, Nashville, TN 37203, USA

Stone, Edward C, Jr — *Space Physicist*
%Jet Propulsion Laboratory, 4800 Oak Grove Dr, #180-904, Pasadena, CA 91109, USA

Stone, Jack — *Religious Leader*
%Church of Nazarene, 6401 The Paseo, Kansas City, MO 64131, USA

Stone, James L — *Korean War Army Hero (CMH)*
1279 Cedarland Plaza Dr, Arlington, TX 76011, USA

Stone, Marvin L — *Editor, Government Official*
6318 Crosswoods Circle, Lake Barcroft, Falls Church, VA 22044, USA

Stone, Oliver W — *Movie Director, Screenwriter*
%Ixtlan Corp, 201 Santa Monica Blvd, #610, Santa Monica, CA 90401, USA

Stone, Peter H — *Writer*
160 E 71st St, New York, NY 10021, USA

Stone, Robert A — *Writer*
%Donadio & Ashworth, 121 W 27th St, #704, New York, NY 10001, USA

Stone, Roger D — *Political Consultant*
34 W 88th St, New York, NY 10024, USA

Stone, Roger W — *Businessman*
%Stone Container Corp, 150 N Michigan Ave, Chicago, IL 60601, USA

Stone, Sharon — *Actress, Model*
PO Box 7304, North Hollywood, CA 91603, USA

Stone, Sly — *Singer, Songwriter, Keyboardist*
%Avenue Mgmt, 250 W 57th S, #407, New York, NY 10107, USA

Stone, Steven M (Steve) — *Baseball Player, Sportscaster*
%WGN-TV, 435 N Michigan Blvd, Chicago, IL 60611, USA

Stone, W Clement — *Businessman*
PO Box 649, Lake Forest, IL 60045, USA

Stonecipher, Harry C — *Businessman*
%McDonnell Douglas Corp, PO Box 516, St Louis, MO 63166, USA

Stoneman, Roni — *Banjoist*
111 Redberry Road, Smyrna, TN 37167, USA

Stones, Dwight — *Track Athlete*
4790 Irvine Blvd, #105, Irvine, CA 92620, USA

Stookey, John H — *Businessman*
%Quantum Chemical, 11500 Northlake Dr, Cincinnati, OH 45249, USA

Stookey, Paul — *Singer (Peter Paul & Mary), Songwriter*
%Newworld, Rt 175, South Blue Hill Falls, ME 04615, USA

Stoppard, Tom S — *Writer*
%Peters Fraser Dunlop, Chelsea Harbour, Lots Rd, London SW10 0XF, England

Storaro, Vittorio — *Cinematographer*
Via Divino Amore 2, 00040 Frattocchie Merino, Italy

Storch, Larry — *Actor*
336 West End St, #17-F, New York, NY 10023, USA

Storer, Peter — *Broadcast Executive*
%Storer Broadcasting Co, 1177 Kane Concourse, Miami Beach, FL 33154, USA

Storey, David M — *Writer*
2 Lyndhurst Gardens, London NW3, England

Stork, Gilbert — *Chemist*
459 Next Day Hill Dr, Englewood, NJ 07631, USA

Storm, Gale — *Actress, Singer*
23831 Bluehill Bay, Dana Point, CA 92629, USA

Storm, Hannah — *Sportscaster*
%NBC-TV, Sports Dept, 30 Rockefeller Plaza, New York, NY 10112, USA

Storm, Tempest — *Exotic Dancer*
PO Box 10845, Beverly Hills, CA 90213, USA

Storr, Anthony — *Psychiatrist, Therapist, Writer*
%Peters Fraser Dunlop, Chelsea Harbour, Lots Rd, London SW10 0XF, England

Story, Liz — *Jazz/Pop Pianist*
%SRO Artists, PO Box 9532, Madison, WI 53715, USA

Story, Ralph — *Commentator*
3425 Wonderview Dr, Los Angeles, CA 90068, USA

Stossel, John — *Commentator*
211 Central Park West, #15-K, New York, NY 10024, USA

Stott, Kathryn L — *Concert Pianist*
Mire House, West Marton near Skipton, Yorks BD23 3UQ, England

Stottlemyre, Melvin L (Mel) — *Baseball Player*
9 S 3rd St, Yakima, WA 98901, USA

Stoudamire, Damon — *Basketball Player*
2605 NE 9th Ave, Portland, OR 97212, USA

Stouder, Sharon — *Swimmer*
144 N Loucks, Los Altos, CA 94022, USA

Stover Irwin Russ, Juno — *Diver*
512 Lanai Circle, Union City, CA 94587, USA

Stowe, David H, Jr — *Businessman*
%Deere Co, John Deere Road, Moline, IL 61265, USA

Stowe, Madeleine — *Actress*
%United Talent Agency, 9560 Wilshire Blvd, #500, Beverly Hills, CA 90212, USA

Stowers, James E, Jr — *Financier*
%American Century Investments, 4500 Main, Kansas City, MO 64111, USA

Stoyanov, Krasimir M — *Cosmonaut, Bulgaria*
%Potchta Kosmonavtov, Moskovskoi Oblasti, 141160 Syvisdny Goroduk, Russia

Stoyanov, Petar — *President, Bulgaria*
%President's Office, 2 Dondukov Blvd, 1123 Sofia, Bulgaria

S

Stone - Stoyanov

Stracey, John — Boxer
Van Laeken 4, Norsey Road, Billericay, Essex CM11 2AD, England

Strachan, Rod — Swimmer
11632 Ranch Hill, Santa Ana, CA 92705, USA

Straight, Beatrice — Actress
30 Norfolk Road, Southfield, MA 01259, USA

Strain, Julie — Model, Actress
602 De La Vista Ave, Santa Barbara, CA 93103, USA

Strain, Sammy — Singer (O'Jays)
%Associated Booking Corp, 1995 Broadway, #501, New York, NY 10023, USA

Strait, George — Singer
%Erv Woolsey Mgmt, 1000 18th Ave S, Nashville, TN 37212, USA

Stram, Henry L (Hank) — Football Coach, Sportscaster
194 Belle Terre Blvd, Covington, LA 70433, USA

Strand, Mark — Writer
%University of Utah, English Dept, Salt Lake City, UT 84112, USA

Strand, Robin — Actor
4118 Elmer Ave, North Hollywood, CA 91602, USA

Strange, Curtis N — Golfer
137 Thomas Dale, Williamsburg, VA 23185, USA

Strasberg, Susan — Actress
PO Box 847, Pacific Palisades, CA 90272, USA

Strasser, Robin — Actress
60 W 66th St, #24-A, New York, NY 10023, USA

Strassman, Marcia — Actress
5115 Douglas Fir Road, #E, Calabasas, CA 91302, USA

Stratas, Teresa — Opera Singer
%Metropolitan Opera Assn, Lincoln Center Plaza, New York, NY 10023, USA

Stratton, Frederick P, Jr — Businessman
%Briggs & Stratton, PO Box 702, Milwaukee, WI 53201, USA

Stratton, William G — Governor, IL
%Chicago Bank of Commerce, 200 E Randolph Dr, Chicago, IL 60601, USA

Straub, Peter F — Writer
53 W 85th St, New York, NY 10024, USA

Straub, Robert W — Governor, OR
2087 Orchard Heights Road NW, Salem, OR 97304, USA

Straus, Robert — Behavioral Scientist
%University of Kentucky, Behavioral Science Dept, Lexington, KY 40536, USA

Straus, Roger W, Jr — Editor, Publisher
%Farrar Straus Giroux, 19 Union Square W, New York, NY 10003, USA

Straus, William L, Jr — Physical Anthropologist
7111 Park Heights Ave, #506, Baltimore, MD 21215, USA

Strauss, Peter — Actor
%Gersh Agency, 232 N Canon Dr, Beverly Hills, CA 90210, USA

Strauss, Robert S — Political Leader, Diplomat
%Akin Gump Strauss Hauer Feld, 1700 Pacific Ave, #4100, Dallas, TX 75201, USA

Strausz-Hupe, Robert — Diplomat
White Horse Farm, 864 Grubbs Mill Road, Newtown Square, PA 19073, USA

Straw, Syd — Singer
%Agency Group, 1775 Broadway, #433, New York, NY 10019, USA

Strawberry, Darryl E — Baseball Player
1419 Red Bluff Court, San Dimas, CA 91773, USA

Strawbridge, Francis R, III — Businessman
%Strawbridge & Clothier, 801 Market St, Philadelphia, PA 19107, USA

Strawbridge, Peter S — Businessman
%Strawbridge & Clothier, 801 Market St, Philadelphia, PA 19107, USA

Strawser, Neil — Commentator
130 "E" St SE, Washington, DC 20003, USA

Streep, Meryl — Actress
%Creative Artists Agency, 9830 Wilshire Blvd, Beverly Hills, CA 90212, USA

Street, George L, III — WW II Navy Hero (CMH)
22 Linda Road, Andover, MA 01810, USA

Street, Picabo — Skier
PO Box 25809, Portland, OR 97298, USA

Street, Rebecca — Actress
255 1/2 S Elm Dr, Beverly Hills, CA 90212, USA

Streetman, Ben G — Electrical Engineer
3915 Glengarry Dr, Austin, TX 78731, USA

Strehler, Giorgio — Theater Director
%Piccolo Theatro di Milano, Via Ravello 2, 20121 Milan, Italy
Streisand, Barbra — Singer, Actress, Director
301 N Carolwood Dr, Los Angeles, CA 90077, USA
Streisinger, George — Biologist
%University of Oregon, Molecular Biology Institute, Eugene, OR 97403, USA
Streit, Clarence K — Journalist
2853 Ontario Road NW, Washington, DC 20009, USA
Streitwieser, Andrew, Jr — Chemist
%University of California, Chemistry Dept, Berkeley, CA 94720, USA
Strekalov, Gennady M — Cosmonaut
%Potchta Kosmonavtov, Moskovskoi Oblasti, 141160 Syvisdny Goroduk, Russia
Strenger, Hermann-Josef — Businessman
Domblick 3, 51381 Leverkusen, Germany
Stretton, Ross — Ballet Dancer
%American Ballet Theatre, 890 Broadway, New York, NY 10003, USA
Stricker, Steve — Golfer
1629 N Golf Glen, Madison, WI 53704, USA
Strickland de la Hunty, Shirley — Track Athlete
22 Fraser Road, Applecross WA 6153, Australia
Strickland, Amzie — Actress
1329 N Ogden Dr, Los Angeles, CA 90046, USA
Strickland, David — Actor
%Banner Entertainment, 9201 Wilshire Blvd, #301, Beverly Hills, CA 90210, USA
Strickland, Gail — Actress
14732 Oracle Place, Pacific Palisades, CA 90272, USA
Strickland, Robert L — Businessman
%Lowe's Companies, State Highway 268 E, North Wilksboro, NC 28659, USA
Strickland, Rod — Basketball Player
114 W Glenview Dr, #300, San Antonio, TX 78228, USA
Stricklyn, Ray — Actor
6240 Lindenhurst Ave, Los Angeles, CA 90048, USA
Strider, Marjorie V — Artist
7 Worth St, New York, NY 10013, USA
Stringer, C Vivian — Basketball Coach
%Rutgers University, Athletic Dept, New Brunswick, NJ 08903, USA
Stringer, Howard — Television Executive
186 Riverside Dr, New York, NY 10024, USA
Stritch, Elaine — Singer, Actress
%Michael Whitehall, 125 Gloucester Road, London SW7 4TE, England
Strobel, Eric — Hockey Player
6617 129th St W, Apple Valley, MN 55124, USA
Strock, Don — Football Player, Coach
120 Old Plantation Way, Pikesville, MD 21208, USA
Strolz, Hubert — Skier
6767 Warth 19, Austria
Strom, Brock T — Football Player
4301 W 110th St, Leawood, KS 66211, USA
Strom, Everald H — Religious Leader
%Church of Lutheran Brethren, 1007 Westside Dr, Fergus Falls, MN 56537, USA
Strominger, Jack L — Biochemist
%Harvard University, Biochemistry Dept, Cambridge, MA 02138, USA
Strong, Derek — Basketball Player
5434 Hillcrest Dr, Los Angeles, CA 90043, USA
Strong, Maurice F — Government Official, Canada
%Ontario Hydro, 700 University Ave, Toronto ON M5G 1X6, Canada
Strother, Charles — Businessman
%Target Therapeutics, 47201 Lakeview Blvd, Fremont, CA 94538, USA
Stroud, Carlos — Physicist
%Rockefeller University, Physics Dept, 1230 York Ave, New York, NY 10021, USA
Stroud, Don — Actor
17020 W Sunset Blvd, #20, Pacific Palisades, CA 90272, USA
Stroud, Joe H — Editor
%Detroit Free Press, Editorial Dept, 321 W Lafayette Blvd, Detroit, MI 48226, USA
Strouse, Charles — Composer
171 W 57th St, New York, NY 10019, USA
Struchkova, Raisa S — Ballerina
%Sovetskiy Ballet, Tverskaya 22-B, 103050 Moscow, Russia

Strudler - Suarez Gonzalez

Strudler, Robert J	*Businessman*
%US Home Corp, 1800 West Loop S, Houston, TX 77027, USA	
Struever, Stuart M	*Anthropologist*
2000 Sheridan Road, Evanston, IL 60201, USA	
Strug, Kerri	*Gymnast*
2801 N Camino Principal, Tucson, AZ 85715, USA	
Strugnell, John	*Theologian*
%Harvard University, Divinity School, 45 Francis Ave, Cambridge, MA 02138, USA	
Strummer, Joe	*Singer, Guitarist (Clash)*
%Clash, 268 Camden Road, London NW1, England	
Struthers, Sally	*Actress*
%David Shapira, 15301 Ventura Blvd, #345, Sherman Oaks, CA 91403, USA	
Struver, Sven	*Golfer*
Kottwitzstr 60, 20253 Hamburg, Germany	
Stuart, Barbara	*Actress*
11156 Valley Spring Lane, North Hollywood, CA 91602, USA	
Stuart, Gloria	*Actress*
884 S Bundy Dr, Los Angeles, CA 90049, USA	
Stuart, Lyle	*Publisher*
1530 Palisade Ave, #6-L, Fort Lee, NJ 07024, USA	
Stuart, Marty	*Singer, Songwriter, Guitarist*
%Rothbaum & Garner, 119 17th Ave S, Nashville, TN 37203, USA	
Stuart, Mary	*Actress*
30 E 68th St, New York, NY 10021, USA	
Stuart, Maxine	*Actress*
%SDB Partners, 1801 Ave of Stars, #902, Los Angeles, CA 90067, USA	
Stubbs, Imogen	*Actress*
%International Creative Mgmt, 76 Oxford St, London W1N 0AX, England	
Stubbs, Levi	*Singer (Four Tops)*
%International Creative Mgmt, 40 W 57th St, New York, NY 10019, USA	
Studeman, William O	*Navy Admiral*
%National Security Agency, Director's Office, Fort George Meade, MD 20755, USA	
Studenroth, Carl W	*Labor Leader*
%Molders & Allied Workers Union, 1225 E McMillan St, Cincinnati, OH 45206, USA	
Studer, Cheryl	*Opera Singer*
%International Performing Artists, 125 Crowfield Dr, Knoxville, TN 37922, USA	
Studi, Wes	*Actor*
%Michael Mann Mgmt, 8380 Melrose Ave, #207, Los Angeles, CA 90069, USA	
Studstill, Patrick L (Pat)	*Football Player*
2235 Linda Flora Dr, Los Angeles, CA 90077, USA	
Stuiver, Minze	*Geological Scientist*
%University of Washington, Geological Sciences Dept, Seattle, WA 98195, USA	
Stumpf, Kenneth E	*Vietnam War Army Hero (CMH)*
PO Box 94, Sparta, WI 54656, USA	
Stumpf, Paul K	*Biochemist*
764 Elmwood Dr, Davis, CA 95616, USA	
Sturckow, Frederick W (Rick)	*Astronaut*
%NASA, Johnson Space Center, 2101 NASA Road, Houston, TX 77058, USA	
Sturdivant, John N	*Labor Leader*
%American Government Employees Federation, 80 "F" St NW, Washington, DC 20001, USA	
Sturdivant, Thomas V (Tom)	*Baseball Player*
1324 SW 71st St, Oklahoma City, OK 73159, USA	
Sturges, Shannon	*Actress*
1223 Wilshire Blvd, #577, Santa Monica, CA 90403, USA	
Sturgess, Thomas W	*Businessman*
%United Stationers, 2200 E Golf Road, Des Plaines, IL 60016, USA	
Sturm, John F	*Association Executive*
%Newspaper Assn of America, 1921 Gallows Road, #4, Vienna, VA 22182, USA	
Sturman, Eugene	*Sculptor*
1108 W Washington Blvd, Venice, CA 90291, USA	
Sturtevant, Julian M	*Chemist*
%Yale University, Chemistry Dept, PO Box 6066, New Haven, CT 06520, USA	
Stuzin, Charles B	*Financier*
%CSF Holdings, 1100 W McNab Road, Fort Lauderdale, FL 33309, USA	
Styron, William	*Writer*
12 Rucum Road, Roxbury, CT 06783, USA	
Suarez Gonzalez, Adolfo	*Prime Minister, Spain*
Sagasta, 33 Madrid 4, Spain	

Suau, Anthony — *Photographer*
%Denver Post, PO Box 1709, Denver, CO 80201, USA

Subotnick, Morton — *Composer*
121 Coronado Lane, Santa Fe, NM 87501, USA

Subroto — *Government Leader, Indonesia*
%OPEC, Obere Donaustr 93, 1020 Vienna, Austria

Suchet, David — *Actor*
%Brunskill, 169 Queen's Gate, #8, London SW7 5EH, England

Suchocka, Hanna — *Prime Minister, Poland*
%Prime Minister's Office, Ul Wiejska 48, 00-583 Warsaw, Poland

Sudersham, Ennackel — *Theoretical Physicist*
%University of Texas, Physics Dept, Austin, TX 78713, USA

Sudharmono — *Government Official, Indonesia; General*
%Vice President's Office, Jalan Merdeka Selatan 6, Jakarta, Indonesia

Sudol, Edward L (Ed) — *Baseball Umpire*
415 Rivilo Blvd, Daytona Beach, FL 32118, USA

Sues, Alan — *Actor*
9014 Dorrington Ave, Los Angeles, CA 90048, USA

Suess, Hans E — *Geochemist*
%University of California, Chemistry Dept, La Jolla, CA 92093, USA

Sugar, Bert Randolph — *Writer, Editor*
6 Southview Road, Chappaqua, NY 10514, USA

Sugar, Leo T — *Football Player*
816 Coutant, Flushing, MI 48433, USA

Sugarman, Burt — *Movie Producer*
%Giant Group, 9000 W Sunset Blvd, #16, Los Angeles, CA 90069, USA

Sugarmann, Josh — *Social Activist*
1650 Harvard St NW, Washington, DC 20009, USA

Suggs, Louise — *Golfer*
2000 S Ocean Blvd, #X-2, Delray Beach, FL 33483, USA

Suharto — *President, Indonesia; Army General*
%President's Office, 15 Jalan Merdeka Utara, Jakarta, Indonesia

Suhey, Matt — *Football Player*
550 Carriage Way, Deerfield, IL 60015, USA

Suhl, Harry — *Physicist*
%University of California, Physicis Dept, San Diego, CA 92093, USA

Suhor, Yvonne — *Actress*
%J Michael Bloom, 9255 Sunset Blvd, #710, Los Angeles, CA 90069, USA

Suhr, August R (Gus) — *Baseball Player*
341 Hazel Ave, Millbrae, CA 94030, USA

Sui, Anna — *Fashion Designer*
%Anna Sui Corp, 275 W 39th St, New York, NY 10018, USA

Suitner, Otmar — *Conductor*
Platanestr 13, 13156 Berlin-Niederschonhausen, Germany

Suk, Josef — *Concert Violinist*
Karlovo Namesti 5, 12000 Prague 2, Czech Republic

Sukova, Helena — *Tennis Player*
1 Ave Grande Bretagne, Monte Carlo, Monaco

Sukowa, Barbara — *Actress*
%Management Jovanovic, 24 Kathi-Kobus-Str, 80797 Munich, Germany

Sulaiman, Jose — *Boxing Official*
%World Boxing Council, Genova 33, Colonia Juarez, Cuahtetemoc 0660, Mexico

Suleymanoglu, Naim — *Weightlifter*
%Olympic Committee, Sisli, Buyukdere Cad 18 Tankaya, Istanbul, Turkey

Suliotis, Elena — *Opera Singer*
Villa il Poderino, Via Incontri 38, Florence, Italy

Sullivan, Brendan V, Jr — *Attorney*
%Williams & Connolly, 725 12th St NW, Washington, DC 20005, USA

Sullivan, Charles A — *Businessman*
%Interstate Bakeries Corp, 12 E Armour Blvd, Kansas City, MO 64111, USA

Sullivan, Daniel J — *Businessman*
%Roadway Services, PO Box 5459, Akron, OH 44334, USA

Sullivan, Danny — *Auto Racing Driver*
414 E Cooper St, #201, Aspen, CO 81611, USA

Sullivan, Dennis P — *Mathematician*
%Queens College, Mathematics Dept, 33 W 42nd St, #706, New York, NY 10036, USA

Sullivan, Joseph P — *Businessman*
%Vigoro Corp, 225 N Michigan Ave, Chicago, IL 60601, USA

S

Suau - Sullivan

Sullivan, Kathleen *Commentator*
1025 N Kings Road, #202, West Hollywood, CA 90069, USA
Sullivan, Kathryn D *Astronaut*
2610 N Key Blvd, Arlington, VA 22201, USA
Sullivan, Leon H *Religious Leader*
%Zion Baptist Church, 3600 N Broad St, Philadelphia, PA 19140, USA
Sullivan, Louis W *Secretary, Health & Human Services*
%Morehouse School of Medicine, 720 Westview Dr SW, Atlanta, GA 30310, USA
Sullivan, Michael J (Mike) *Governor, WY*
1124 S Durbin St, Casper, WY 82601, USA
Sullivan, Pat *Football Player, Coach*
4775 Overton Woods Dr, Fort Worth, TX 76109, USA
Sullivan, Susan *Actress*
8642 Allenwood Road, Los Angeles, CA 90046, USA
Sullivan, Timothy J *Educator*
%College of William & Mary, President's Office, Williamsburg, VA 23187, USA
Sullivan, William J *Educator*
%Seattle University, President's Office, Seattle, WA 98122, USA
Sultan Qaboos Bin Said *Sultan, Oman*
%Royal Palace, PO Box 252, Muscat, Oman
Sultan Salman Al-Saud *Astronaut, Saudi Arabia*
PO Box 18368, Riyadh 11415, Saudi Arabia
Sultan, Donald K *Artist*
45 White St, New York, NY 10013, USA
Sulzberger, Arthur O, Jr *Publisher*
%New York Times, 229 W 43rd St, New York, NY 10036, USA
Summer, Donna *Singer*
18171 Eccles St, Northridge, CA 91325, USA
Summerall, George A (Pat) *Sportscaster*
10036 Sawgrass Dr, Ponte Vedra, FL 32082, USA
Summerfield, Eleanor *Actress*
%Saraband, 245 Liverpool Road, Islington, London N1 1LX, England
Summers, Carol *Artist*
2817 Smith Grade, Santa Cruz, CA 95060, USA
Summers, Dana *Cartoonist (Lug Nuts, Bound & Gagged)*
%Orlando Sentinel, 633 N Orange Ave, Orlando, FL 32801, USA
Summitt, Pat Head *Basketball Coach*
3720 River Trace Lane, Knoxville, TN 37920, USA
Sumners, Rosalynn *Figure Skater*
%Barbara Kindness, 9912 225th Place SW, Edmonds, WA 98020, USA
Sun Yun-Hsuan *Prime Minister, Taiwan*
1 Chung Hsiao E Road, Taipei 110, Taiwan
Sundance, Robert *Social Activist*
%California Indian Alcoholism Commission, 225 W 8th St, Los Angeles, CA 90014, USA
Sundin, Mats *Hockey Player*
%Toronto Maple Leafs, 60 Carlton St, Toronto ON M5B 1L1, Canada
Sundlun, Bruce G *Governor, RI*
PO Box 15248, Riverside, RI 02915, USA
Sundquist, Donald K (Don) *Governor, Representative, TN*
%Governor's Office, State Capitol Building, Nashville, TN 37219, USA
Sundquist, Ulf *Businessman*
Ergo Consult Oy, Nordic Law, Mikonkatu 2, 00100 Helsinki, Finalnd
Sununu, John H *Governor, NH; Government Official*
24 Samoset Dr, Salem, NH 03079, USA
Supernaw, Doug *Singer, Songwriter*
%Senior Mgmt, PO Box 218200, Nashville, TN 37221, USA
Suquia Goicoechea, Angel Cardinal *Religious Leader*
El Cardenal Arxobispo, San Justo 2, 28074 Madrid, Spain
Sura, Bob *Basketball Player*
%Cleveland Cavaliers, 2923 Statesboro Road, Richfield, OH 44286, USA
Surhoff, William J (B J) *Baseball Player*
12999 Jerome Jay Dr, Cockeysville, MD 21030, USA
Surin, Bruny *Track Athlete*
PO Box 2, Succ St Michel, Montreal PQ H2A 3L8, Canada
Surtees, Bruce *Cinematographer*
25535 Hacienda Place, Carmel, CA 93923, USA
Surtees, John *Auto Racing Driver*
%Team Surtees, Station Road, Edenbridge, Kent TN8 6HL, England

Susa, Conrad — *Composer*
433 Eureka St, San Francisco, CA 94114, USA

Suschitzky, Wolfgang — *Cinematographer*
Douglas House, 6 Maida Ave, #11, London W2 1TG, England

Susman, Todd — *Actor*
11462 Poema Place, #34-102, Chatsworth, CA 91311, USA

Sutcliffe, Richard L (Rick) — *Baseball Player*
25911 99th St, Lee's Summit, MO 64086, USA

Suter, Bob — *Hockey Player*
4332 McConnell St, Madison, WI 53711, USA

Suter, Gary — *Hockey Player*
5337 Comanche Way, Madison, WI 53704, USA

Sutherland, Donald — *Actor*
%Creative Artists Agency, 9830 Wilshire Blvd, Beverly Hills, CA 90212, USA

Sutherland, Joan — *Opera Singer*
%Ingpen & Williams, 14 Kensington Court, London W8, England

Sutherland, Kiefer — *Actor*
9056 Santa Monica Blvd, #100, Los Angeles, CA 90069, USA

Sutherland, Peter D — *Government Official, Ireland*
68 Eglinton Road, Dublin 4, Ireland

Sutter, Brent — *Hockey Player*
2 S 551 Thaddeis Circle, Glen Ellyn, IL 60137, USA

Sutter, Brian — *Hockey Player, Coach*
2485 Peppermill Ridge Dr, Chesterfield, MO 63005, USA

Sutter, Darryl — *Hockey Coach*
%San Jose Sharks, San Jose Arena, 525 W Santa Clara St, San Jose, CA 95113, USA

Sutter, Duane — *Hockey Player, Coach*
1566 Coloma Court S, Wheaton, IL 60187, USA

Sutter, H Bruce — *Baseball Player*
1368 Hamilton Road, Kennesaw, GA 30152, USA

Sutter, Ron — *Hockey Player*
%St Louis Blues, Kiel Center, 1401 Clark Ave, St Louis, MO 63103, USA

Sutton, Donald H (Don) — *Baseball Player, Sportscaster*
1145 Mountain ivy Dr, Roswell, GA 30075, USA

Sutton, Eddie — *Basketball Coach*
%Oklahoma State University, Athletic Dept, Stillwater, OK 74078, USA

Sutton, George P — *Aeronautical Engineer*
725 Barrington Ave, #110, Los Angeles, CA 90049, USA

Sutton, Hal — *Golfer*
8308 Brockington Dr, Shreveport, LA 71107, USA

Suwa, Gen — *Anthropologist*
%University of California, Human Evolutionary Science Lab, Berkeley, CA 94720, USA

Suzman, Janet — *Actress*
%William Morris Agency, 31/32 Soho Square, London W1V 5DG, England

Suzuki, Robert — *Educator*
%California State University, President's Office, Bakersfield, CA 93311, USA

Suzy (Aileen Mehle) — *Columnist*
18 E 68th St, #1-B, New York, NY 10021, USA

Svare, Harland — *Football Player, Coach*
3095 Caminito Sagunto, Del Mar, CA 92014, USA

Svedberg, Bjorn — *Businessman*
%L M Ericsson Telephone, Telefonaktiebiolaget, 126 11 Stockholm, Sweden

Svendsen, Louise A — *Museum Curator*
16 Park Ave, New York, NY 10016, USA

Svenson, Bo — *Actor*
15332 Antioch St, #356, Pacific Palisades, CA 90272, USA

Svetlanov, Yevgeni F — *Conductor*
Stanislavsky Str 14, #14, 103009 Moscow, Russia

Sviridov, Georgi V — *Composer*
Bolshaya Gruzinskaya Str 36-62, 123056 Moscow, Russia

Svoboda, Josef — *Architect*
%Laterna Magika, Lilova 9, 11000 Prague 1, Czech Republic

Swados, Elizabeth A — *Writer, Composer*
360 Central Park West, #16-G, New York, NY 10025, USA

Swagerty, Jane — *Swimmer*
162 James Ave, Atherton, CA 94027, USA

Swaggart, Jimmy L — *Evangelist*
8919 World Ministry Ave, Baton Rouge, LA 70810, USA

Swaminathan, Monkombu S _Geneticist_
%M S Swaminathan Foundation, 3 Cross St, Taramani, Madras 600113, India

Swan, John W D _Premier, Bermuda_
%Cabinet Office, 105 Front St, Hamilton HM12, Bermuda

Swan, Richard G _Mathematician_
700 Melrose Ave, #M-3, Winter Park, FL 32789, USA

Swank, Hilary _Actress_
%Metropolitan Talent Agency, 4526 Wilshire Blvd, Los Angeles, CA 90010, USA

Swann, Lynn C _Football Player, Sportscaster_
%Swann Inc, 600 Grant St, #4800, Pittsburgh, PA 15219, USA

Swanson, August G _Physician_
3146 Portage Bay Pl E, #H, Seattle, WA 98102, USA

Swanson, Dennis _Television Executive_
%Capital Cities/ABC, 77 W 66th St, New York, NY 10023, USA

Swanson, Jackie _Actress_
847 Iliff St, Pacific Palisades, CA 90272, USA

Swanson, Kristy _Actress_
2934 1/2 N Beverly Glen Circle, #416, Los Angeles, CA 90077, USA

Swartz, Jacob T _Scientist_
New York University, 251 Mercer St, New York, NY 10012, USA

Swayze, Patrick _Actor_
%Wolf/Kasteller, 132 S Rodeo Dr, #300, Beverly Hills, CA 90212, USA

Swe, U Ba _Prime Minister, Myanmar_
84 Innes Road, Yangon, Myanmar

Sweat, Keith _Songwriter, Singer_
PO Box 1002, Bronx, NY 10466, USA

Sweat, Keith _Singer, Songwriter_
%International Creative Mgmt, 40 W 57th St, New York, NY 10019, USA

Swedberg, Heidi _Actress_
%Writers & Artists, 924 Westwood Blvd, #900, Los Angeles, CA 90024, USA

Sweeney, D B _Actor_
%International Creative Mgmt, 8942 Wilshire Blvd, Beverly Hills, CA 90211, USA

Sweeney, John J _Labor Leader_
%AFL-CIO, 815 16th St NW, Washington, DC 20006, USA

Sweeney, Walter F (Walt) _Football Player_
%Touchdown Ink, 1742 Garnet Ave, #130, San Diego, CA 92109, USA

Sweet, Sharon _Opera Singer_
%Metropolitan Opera Assn, Lincoln Center Plaza, New York, NY 10023, USA

Swenson, Inga _Actress_
3475 Cabrillo Blvd, Los Angeles, CA 90066, USA

Swenson, Rick _Dog Sled Racer_
%Trot-A-Long Kennel, Manley, AK 99756, USA

Swenson, Ruth Ann _Opera Singer_
%Metropolitan Opera Assn, Lincoln Center Plaza, New York, NY 10023, USA

Swensson, Earl S _Architect_
%Earl Swensson Assoc, 2100 W End Ave, #1200, Nashville, TN 37203, USA

Swett, James E _WW II Marine Corps Hero (CMH)_
PO Box 327, Trinity Center, CA 96091, USA

Swift, Clive _Actor_
%Roxane Vacca Mgmt, 8 Silver Place, London W1R 3LJ, England

Swift, Graham _Writer_
%Alfred A Knopf Inc, 201 E 50th St, New York, NY 10022, USA

Swift, Hewson H _Biologist_
%University of Chicago, Molecular Genetics/Cell Biology Dept, Chicago, IL 60637, USA

Swift, Richard J _Businessman_
%Foster Wheeler Corp, Perryville Corporate Park, Clinton, NJ 08809, USA

Swift, Stephen J _Judge_
%US Tax Court, 400 2nd St NW, Washington, DC 20217, USA

Swift, William C (Bill) _Baseball Player_
5880 E Sapphire Lane, Paradise Valley, AZ 85253, USA

Swilling, Pat _Football Player_
%Oakland Raiders, 1220 Harbor Bay Parkway, Alameda, CA 94502, USA

Swinburne, Nora _Actress_
52 Crammer Court, Whitehead's Grove, London SW3, England

Swindell, F Gregory (Greg) _Baseball Player_
3771 Elmora St, Houston, TX 77005, USA

Swindells, William, Jr _Businessman_
%Willamette Industries, 3800 First Interstate Tower, Portland, OR 97201, USA

Swindoll, Charles R	*Evangelist, Writer*
%Insight for Living, 211 E Imperial Highway, Fullerton, CA 92835, USA	
Swing, William L	*Diplomat*
%US State Department, 2201 "C" St NW, Washington, DC 20520, USA	
Swingley, Doug	*Dog Sled Racer*
General Delivery, Simms, MT 59477, USA	
Swink, James E (Jim)	*Football Player*
1201 8th Ave, Fort Worth, TX 76104, USA	
Swisher, Carl C	*Anthropologist*
%Institute of Human Origins, 1288 9th St, Berkeley, CA 94710, USA	
Swit, Loretta	*Actress*
%Artists Group, 10100 Santa Monica Blvd, #2490, Los Angeles, CA 90067, USA	
Switzer, Barry	*Football Coach*
916 Meadow Lane Dr, #3102, Irving, TX 75063, USA	
Swofford, Ken	*Actor*
144 S Beverly Dr, #405, Beverly Hills, CA 90212, USA	
Swoopes, Sheryl	*Basketball Player*
PO Box 43021, Lubbock, TX 79409, USA	
Swope, Richard T (Dick)	*Air Force General*
%Inspector General's Office, HqUSAF, Pentagon, Washington, DC 20330, USA	
Swygert, H Patrick	*Educator*
%Howard University, President's Office, Washington, DC 20059, USA	
Syberberg, Hans-Jurgen	*Movie Director*
Genter Str 15-A, 80805 Munich, Germany	
Sybil	*Singer*
%Silva Gandhi, 1600 Broadway, #910, New York, NY 10019, USA	
Sykes, Eric	*Actor*
%Norma Farnes, 9 Orme Court, London W2 4RL, England	
Sykes, Lynn R	*Geologist*
RFD 1, Box 248, Washington Spring Road, Palisades, NY 10964, USA	
Sykes, Phil	*Hockey Player*
2312 Hill Lane, Redondo Beach, CA 90278, USA	
Sylbert, Anthea	*Costume Designer*
13949 Ventura Blvd, #309, Sherman Oaks, CA 91423, USA	
Sylvester, George H	*Air Force General*
Rt 1, Box 345-G, Mount Jackson, VA 22842, USA	
Sylvester, Michael	*Opera Singer*
%Columbia Artists Mgmt Inc, 165 W 57th St, New York, NY 10019, USA	
Symms, Steven D	*Senator, ID*
210 Cameron St, Alexandria, VA 22314, USA	
Syms, Sylvia	*Actress*
%Barry Brown, 47 West Square, London SE11 4SP, England	
Synge, Richard L M	*Nobel Chemistry Laureate*
19 Meadow Rise Road, Norwich NR2 3QE, England	
Syse, Jan P	*Prime Minister, Norway*
Camilla Colletts Vei 3, 0258 Oslo, Norway	
Sytsma, John F	*Labor Leader*
%Locomotive Engineers Brotherhood, 1370 Ontario Ave, Cleveland, OH 44113, USA	
Szabo, Bence	*Fencer*
Nagyszombat 6 25, 1034 Budapest, Hungary	
Szabo, Istvan	*Movie Director*
%Objektiv Fil Studio-MAFILM, Rona Utca 174, 1149 Budapest, Hungary	
Szasz, Thomas S	*Psychiatrist*
4739 Limberlost Lane, Manlius, NY 13104, USA	
Szekely, Eva	*Swimmer*
Szepvolgyi Utca 4/B, 1025 Budapest, Hungary	
Szekessy, Karen	*Photographer*
Haynstr 2, 20249 Hamburg, Germany	
Szep, Paul M	*Editorial Cartoonist*
7 Stetson St, Brookline, MA 02146, USA	
Szigmond, Vilmos	*Cinematographer*
PO Box 2230, Los Angeles, CA 90078, USA	
Szoka, Edmund C Cardinal	*Religious Leader*
%Prefecture for Economic Affairs, 00120 Vatican City	
Szymborska, Wislawa	*Nobel Literature Laureate*
Ul Krolewska 82/89, 30-079 Cracow, Poland	

T (Lawrence Tero), Mr — *Actor*
395 Green Bay Road, Lake Forest, IL 60045, USA

Tabackin, Lew — *Jazz Flutist*
38 W 94th St, New York, NY 10025, USA

Tabitha 'Masentle — *Princess, Lesotho*
%Royal Palace, PO Box 524, Maseru, Lesotho

Tabone, Censu — *President, Malta*
%President's Office, The Palace, Valletta, Malta

Tabori, Kristoffer — *Actor*
172 E 95th St, New York, NY 10128, USA

Tabori, Laszlo — *Track Athlete*
2221 W Olive Ave, Burbank, CA 91506, USA

Taco — *Singer*
%British & Int'l Artists, 500 Waterman Ave, #191, East Providence, RI 02914, USA

Taddei, Giuseppe — *Opera Singer*
%Metropolitan Opera Assn, Lincoln Center Plaza, New York, NY 10023, USA

Tagliabue, Paul J — *Football Executive*
%National Football League, 280 Park Ave, #12-W, New York, NY 10017, USA

Taglianetti, Peter — *Hockey Player*
67 Merion Court, Bridgeville, PA 15017, USA

Tait, John E — *Businessman*
%Penn Mutual Life, Independence Square, Philadelphia, PA 19172, USA

Takacs-Nagy, Gabor — *Concert Violinist*
5265 Centennial Trail, Boulder, CO 80303, USA

Takagaki, Tasuku — *Financier*
%Bank of Tokyo, 3-2-1 Nihombashi Hongokucho, Chuoku, Tokyo, Japan

Takahashi, Michiaki — *Immunologist*
%Osaka University, Microbe Diseases Research Institute, Osaka, Japan

Takamatsu, Shin — *Architect*
%Shin Takamatsu Assoc, 36-4 Jobodaiincho Takeda, Fushimiku, Kyoto, Japan

Takano, Atsushi — *Financier*
%Fuji Bank & Trust, 2 World Trade Center, New York, NY 10048, USA

Takeda, Yutaka — *Businessman*
%Nippon Steel, 2-6-3 Otemachi, Chiyodaku, Tokyo 100, Japan

Takei, George — *Actor*
425 S Rimpau Blvd, Los Angeles, CA 90020, USA

Takeshita, Noboru — *Prime Minister, Japan*
3-5-9 Daisawa, Setagayaku, Tokyo, Japan

Tal, Josef — *Composer*
3 Dvira Haneviyah St, Jerusalem, Israel

Talbot, Don — *Swimming Coach*
%Canadian Sports Fed, 333 River Road, Vanier, Ottawa ON K1L 8B9, Canada

Talbot, Nita — *Actress*
3420 Merrimac Road, Los Angeles, CA 90049, USA

Talbott, Michael — *Actor*
10340 Santa Monica Blvd, Los Angeles, CA 90025, USA

Talese, Gay — *Writer*
154 E Atlantic Blvd, Ocean City, NJ 08226, USA

Taliaferro, George — *Football Player*
%Innovative Health Systems, 3013 Stratfield Dr, Bloomington, IN 47401, USA

Tallchief, Maria — *Ballerina*
%Chicago Lyric Opera, 20 N Wacker Dr, Chicago, IL 60606, USA

Talley, Darryl V — *Football Player*
8713 Lake Tibet Court, Orlando, FL 32836, USA

Talmadge, Herman E — *Governor/Senator, GA*
%Barnett & Alagia, 15 Circle Dr, Hampton, GA 30228, USA

Talu, Naim — *Prime Minister, Turkey; Financier*
%Akbank TAS, Findukh, Istanbul, Turkey

Tamayo Mendez, Arnaldo — *Cosmonaut, Cuba*
Calle 16, #504, c/5A y 7MA, Miramar, Ciudad Havana 11300, Cuba

Tamberlane, John — *Financier*
%Republic Bank for Savings, 415 Madison Ave, New York, NY 10017, USA

Tamblyn, Russ — *Actor, Dancer*
1221 N King's Road, #PH-405, West Hollywood, CA 90069, USA

Tambor, Jeffrey — *Actor*
5526 Calhoun Ave, Van Nuys, CA 91401, USA

Tamia — *Singer*
%William Morris Agency, 1325 Ave of Americas, New York, NY 10019, USA

Tamm, Peter — *Publisher*
%Axel Springer Verlag, Kochstr 50, 10969 Berlin, Germany

Tan, Amy R — *Writer*
%G P Putnam's Sons, 200 Madison Ave, New York, NY 10016, USA

Tanana, Frank D — *Baseball Player*
28492 S Harwich Dr, Farmington Hills, MI 48334, USA

Tananbaum, Andrew H — *Financier*
%Century Business Credit, 119 W 40th St, New York, NY 10018, USA

Tananbaum, Stanley — *Financier*
%Century Business Credit, 119 W 40th St, New York, NY 10018, USA

Tandon, Sirjang Lal — *Businessman*
%Tandon Corp, 301 Science Dr, #8025, Moorpark, CA 93021, USA

Tanen, Ned S — *Entertainment Executive*
%Paramount Pictures, 5555 Melrose Ave, Los Angeles, CA 90038, USA

Tanford, Charles — *Physiologist*
Tarlswood, Back Lane, Easingwold, York YO6 3BG, England

Tange, Kenzo — *Architect*
%Kenzo Tange Assoc, 7-2-21 Akasaka, Minato-ku, Tokyo, Japan

Taniguchi, Tadatsugu — *Molecular Biologist*
%University of Osaka, Molecular & Cellular Biology Dept, Osaka, Japan

Tanksley, Steven D — *Plant Geneticist*
%Cornell University, Plant Genetics Dept, Ithaca, NY 14853, USA

Tannenwald, Theodore, Jr — *Judge*
%US Tax Court, 400 2nd St NW, Washington, DC 20217, USA

Tanner, Alain — *Movie Director*
Chemin Point-du-Jour 12, 1202 Geneva, Switzerland

Tanner, Charles W (Chuck) — *Baseball Manager*
34 Maitland Lane E, New Castle, PA 16105, USA

Tanner, Joseph R — *Astronaut*
%NASA, Johnson Space Center, 2101 NASA Road, Houston, TX 77058, USA

Tanner, Roscoe — *Tennis Player*
General Delivery, Rising Fawn, GA 30738, USA

Tannous, Afif I — *Government Official*
6912 Oak Court, Annandale, VA 22003, USA

Tanumafili, Malietoa, II — *Head of State, Western Samoa*
%Government House, Valima, Apia, Western Samoa

Taofinu'u, Pio Cardinal — *Religious Leader*
%Cardinal's Office, PO Box 532, Apia, Western Samoa

Tape, Gerald F — *Physicist*
4970 Sentinel Dr, #502, Bethesda, MD 20816, USA

Tapia, Johnny — *Boxer*
2009 Foothill Dr SW, Albuquerque, NM 87105, USA

Tarantino, Quentin — *Movie Director*
%A Band Apart Production, 10202 W Washington Blvd, Culver City, CA 90232, USA

Tarbell, Dean S — *Chemist*
6033 Sherwood Dr, Nashville, TN 37215, USA

Tardif, Marc — *Hockey Player*
%Laurier Pontiac, 3001 Rue Kepler, Ste-Foy PQ G1X 3V4, Canada

Tarkanian, Jerry — *Basketball Coach*
%Fresno State University, Athletic Dept, Fresno, CA 93740, USA

Tarkenton, Francis A (Fran) — *Football Player, Businessman*
%Tarkenton Co, 3340 Peachtree Road NE, #444, Atlanta, GA 30326, USA

Tarnow, Robert L — *Businessman*
%Goulds Pumps Inc, 300 Willow Brook Office Park, Fairport, NY 14450, USA

Tarpley, Roy — *Basketball Player*
2250 Justin Road, #108-303, Highland Village, TX 75067, USA

Tarr, Curtis W — *Government Official, Businessman*
%Intermet Corp, 5445 Corporate Dr, #200, Troy, MI 48098, USA

Tarr, Robert J, Jr — *Publisher*
%Harcourt General, 27 Boylston St, Chestnut Hill, MA 02167, USA

Tarski, Alfred — *Mathematician*
462 Michigan Ave, Berkeley, CA 94707, USA

Tartabull, Danilio (Dan) — *Baseball Player*
26115 Idlewild Way, Malibu, CA 90265, USA

Tarver, Jackson W — *Publisher*
%Atlanta Journal-Constitution, 72 Marietta St, Atlanta, GA 30303, USA

Tasker, Steven J (Steve) — *Football Player*
44 Gypsy Lane, East Aurora, NY 14052, USA

T

Tamm - Tasker

Tate, Frank — *Boxer*
12731 Water Oak Dr, Missouri City, TX 77489, USA

Tate, Jeffrey P — *Conductor*
%Royal Opera House, Convent Garden, Bow St, London WC2E 7QA, England

Tate, John — *Boxer*
PO Box 6230, Knoxville, TN 37914, USA

Tatiana (Sorokko) — *Model*
%Ford Model Agency, 344 E 59th St, New York, NY 10022, USA

Tatishvili, Tsisana R — *Opera Singer*
%Tbilsi State Opera, Tbilisi, Georgia

Tatrai, Vilmos — *Concert Violinist*
%Zenemuveszeti Foiskola, Liszt Ference Ter 2, 1136 Budapest XIII, Hungary

Tatum, Jack — *Football Player*
10620 Mark St, Oakland, CA 94605, USA

Taube, Henry — *Nobel Chemistry Laureate*
441 Gerona Road, Stanford, CA 94305, USA

Taubman, A Alfred — *Businessman*
%Taubman Co, 200 E Long Lake Road, Bloomfield Hills, MI 48304, USA

Taufa'ahau Tupou IV — *King, Tonga*
%The Palace, PO Box 6, Nuku'alofa, Tonga

Taupin, Bernie — *Singer, Songwriter*
PO Box 176, Los Olivos, CA 93441, USA

Tauscher, Hansjorg — *Skier*
Schwand 7, 87561 Oberstdorf, Germany

Tavard, Georges H — *Theologian*
330 Market St, Brighton, MA 02135, USA

Tavener, John — *Football Player*
197 N Main St, Johnstown, OH 43031, USA

Tavener, John — *Composer*
%Chester Music, 8-9 Firth St, London W1V 5TZ, England

Taverner, Sonia — *Ballerina*
PO Box 129, Stony Plain AB, Canada

Tavernier, Bertrand R M — *Movie Director*
%Little Bear Productions, 7-9 Rue Arthur Groussier, 75010 Paris, France

Taya, Maawiya Ould Sid'Ahmed — *President, Mauritania; Army Officer*
%President's Office, Boite Postale 184, Nouakchott, Mauritania

Taylor, Alan — *Writer, Historian*
%Alfred A Knopf, 201 E 50th St, New York, NY 10022, USA

Taylor, Billy — *Jazz Pianist, Composer*
555 Kappock St, Bronx, NY 10463, USA

Taylor, Buck — *Actor*
206 Via Colinas, Westlake Village, CA 91362, USA

Taylor, Carl E — *Physician*
Bittersweet Acres, 1201 Hollins Lane, Baltimore, MD 21209, USA

Taylor, Cecil P — *Jazz Pianist, Composer*
%PSI/Soul Note Records, 810 7th Ave, New York, NY 10019

Taylor, Charles (Ghankay) — *President, Liberia*
%Executive Mansion, PO Box 9001, Capitol Hill, Monrovia, Liberia

Taylor, Charley — *Football Player, Executive*
242 Oakgrove Ave, Atherton, CA 94027, USA

Taylor, Clarice — *Actress*
380 Elkwood Terrace, Englewood, NJ 07631, USA

Taylor, Dave — *Hockey Player, Executive*
18920 Pasadero Dr, Tarzana, CA 91356, USA

Taylor, Delores — *Actress*
PO Box 25355, Los Angeles, CA 90025, USA

Taylor, Don — *Movie Director, Actor*
1111 San Vicente Blvd, Santa Monica, CA 90402, USA

Taylor, Elizabeth — *Actress*
PO Box 55995, Sherman Oaks, CA 91413, USA

Taylor, Eric — *Artist*
13 Tredgold Ave, Branhope near Leeds, West Yorkshire LS16 9BS, England

Taylor, Fred R — *Basketball Coach*
3144 Derby Road, Columbus, OH 43221, USA

Taylor, Gerard H — *Businessman*
%MCI Communications, 1801 Pennsylvania Ave NW, Washington, DC 20006, USA

Taylor, Glen — *Basketball Executive*
%Minnesota Timberwolves, Target Center, 600 1st Ave N, Minneapolis, MN 55403, USA

Taylor, Gregory F — *Financier*
%Stifel Financial Group, 500 N Broadway, St Louis, MO 63102, USA

Taylor, Henry S — *Writer*
PO Box 23, Lincoln, VA 20160, USA

Taylor, J Herbert — *Botanist*
1414 Hilltop Dr, Tallahassee, FL 32303, USA

Taylor, James — *Singer, Songwriter*
%Peter Asher Mgmt, 644 N Doheny Dr, Los Angeles, CA 90069, USA

Taylor, James (Jim) — *Football Player*
7840 Walden Road, Baton Rouge, LA 70808, USA

Taylor, James A — *Vietnam War Army Hero (CMH)*
793 Hagemann Dr, Livermore, CA 94550, USA

Taylor, Johnnie — *Singer*
%Rodgers Redding, 1048 Tatnall St, Macon, GA 31201, USA

Taylor, Johnny — *Basketball Player*
%Orlando Magic, Orlando Arena, 1 Magic Place, Orlando, FL 32801, USA

Taylor, Joseph H, Jr — *Nobel Physics Laureate*
272 Hartley St, Princeton, NJ 08540, USA

Taylor, Judson H — *Educator*
%State University of New York College, President's Office, Cortland, NY 13045, USA

Taylor, Kenneth N — *Publisher*
1515 E Forest Ave, Wheaton, IL 60187, USA

Taylor, Koko — *Singer*
%Alligator Artists Mgmt, 1441 W Devon, Chicago, IL 60660, USA

Taylor, Lauriston S — *Physicist*
10450 Lottsford Road, #3011, Mitchellville, MD 20721, USA

Taylor, Lawrence — *Football Player*
122 Canterburg Place, Williamsburg, VA 23188, USA

Taylor, Lili — *Actress*
%William Morris Agency, 151 S El Camino Dr, Beverly Hills, CA 90212, USA

Taylor, Livingston — *Singer*
%Fat City Artists, 1908 Chet Atkins Place, #502, Nashville, TN 37212, USA

Taylor, Marianne — *Actress*
%Jack Scagnatti, 5118 Vineland Ave, #102, North Hollywood, CA 91601, USA

Taylor, Maurice — *Basketball Player*
%Los Angeles Clippers, Sports Arena, 3939 Figueroa St, Los Angeles, CA 90037, USA

Taylor, Meldrick — *Boxer*
1158 N York Road, Warminster, PA 18974, USA

Taylor, Meshach — *Actor*
369 E Calaveras St, Altadena, CA 91001, USA

Taylor, Nicole R (Niki) — *Model*
8362 Pines Blvd, #334, Hollywood, FL 33024, USA

Taylor, Paul B — *Dancer, Choreographer*
%Paul Taylor Dance Co, 552 Broadway, New York, NY 10012, USA

Taylor, Regina — *Actress*
%William Morris Agency, 151 S El Camino Dr, Beverly Hills, CA 90212, USA

Taylor, Renee — *Actress*
16830 Ventura Blvd, #326, Encino, CA 91436, USA

Taylor, Richard E — *Nobel Physics Laureate*
%Stanford University, Linear Accelerator Center, Box 4349, Stanford, CA 94309, USA

Taylor, Rip — *Comedian*
1133 N Clark Dr, Los Angeles, CA 90035, USA

Taylor, Robert — *Track Athlete*
221 W Bryan St, Tyler, TX 75702, USA

Taylor, Rod — *Actor*
2375 Bowmont Dr, Beverly Hills, CA 90210, USA

Taylor, Roger — *Tennis Player*
39 Newstead Way, Wimbledon SW19, England

Taylor, Samuel A — *Writer*
Meadow Rue, East Blue Hill, ME 04629, USA

Taylor, Telford — *Attorney, Writer*
54 Morningside Dr, New York, NY 10025, USA

Taylor, William O — *Publisher*
%Affiliated Publications, 135 Morrissey Blvd, Boston, MA 02125, USA

Taylor, Wilson H — *Businessman*
%Cigna Corp, 1 Liberty Place, Philadelphia, PA 19103, USA

Taylor-Young, Leigh — *Actress*
%Don Buchwald, 9229 Sunset Blvd, #710, Los Angeles, CA 90069, USA

T

Taylor - Taylor-Young

Tcherina, Ludmila — *Ballerina*
42 Cours Albert 1er, 75008 Paris, France

Tcherkassky, Marianna — *Ballerina*
%American Ballet Theatre, 890 Broadway, New York, NY 10003, USA

Te Kanawa, Kiri — *Opera Singer*
%Jules Haefliger Impressario, Postfach 4113, 6002 Lucerne, Switzerland

Teagle, Terry — *Basketball Player*
65 Hessenford St, Sugar Land, TX 77479, USA

Teannaki, Teatao — *President, Kiribati*
%President's Office, PO Box 68, Bairiki, Tarawa Atoll, Kiribati

Tear, Robert — *Opera Singer*
11 Ravenscourt Court, London W6, England

Teasdale, Joseph P — *Governor, MO*
800 W 47th St, Kansas City, MO 64112, USA

Tebaldi, Renata — *Opera Singer*
Piazzetta della Guastella 1, 20122 Milan, Italy

Tebbetts, George R (Birdie) — *Baseball Player, Manager*
229 Oak Ave, Anna Maria, FL 33501, USA

Tebbit of Chingford, Norman B — *Government Official, England*
%House of Lords, Westminster, London SW1A 0PW, England

Tebbutt, Arthur R — *Statistician*
1511 Pelican Point Dr, Sarasota, FL 34231, USA

Teets, John W — *Businessman*
%Dial Corp, 1850 N Central Ave, Phoenix, AZ 85004, USA

Tegart Dalton, Judy — *Tennis Player*
72 Grange Road, Toorak, VIC 3142, Australia

Teich, Malvin C — *Electrical Engineer*
%Columbia University, Electrical Engineering Dept, New York, NY 10027, USA

Teicher, Louis (Lou) — *Pianist (Ferrante & Teicher)*
%Avant-Garde Records, 12224 Avila Dr, Kansas City, MO 64145, USA

Teichner, Helmut — *Skior*
4250 Marine Dr, #2101, Chicago, IL 60613, USA

Tcitelbaum, Philip — *Psychologist*
%University of Florida, Psychology Dept, Gainesville, FL 32611, USA

Teitell, Conrad L — *Attorney*
16 Marlow Court, Riverside, CT 06878, USA

Tekulve, Kenton C (Kent) — *Baseball Player*
1531 Sequoia Dr, Pittsburgh, PA 15241, USA

Telegdi, Valentine L — *Physicist*
Eidgenossische Technische Hochschule, Houggerberg, Zurich, Switzerland

Tellep, Daniel M — *Businessman*
%Lockheed Corp, PO Box 5118, Thousand Oaks, CA 91359, USA

Teller — *Comedian, Illusionist (Penn & Teller)*
142 W 49th St, New York, NY 10019, USA

Teller, Edward — *Physicist*
%University of California Livermore Laboratory, PO Box 808, Livermore, CA 94551, USA

Telnack, John J (Jack) — *Automobile Designer*
%Ford Motor Co, American Road, Dearborn, MI 48121, USA

Teltscher, Eliot — *Tennis Player, Coach*
%Pepperdine University, Athletic Dept, Malibu, CA 90265, USA

Temesvari, Andrea — *Tennis Player*
%ProServe, 1101 Woodrow Wilson Blvd, #1800, Arlington, VA 22209, USA

Temirkanov, Yuri — *Conductor*
%St Petersburg Philharmonic, Ul Brodskogo 2, St Petersburg, Russia

Temko, Allan B — *Journalist*
%San Francisco Chronicle, Editorial Dept, 901 Mission, San Francisco, CA 94103, USA

Templeton, Ben — *Cartoonist (Motley's Crew)*
%Tribune Media Services, 435 N Michigan Ave, #1500, Chicago, IL 60611, USA

Templeton, Christopher — *Actress, Singer*
11333 Moorpark St, North Hollywood, CA 91602, USA

Templeton, Garry L — *Baseball Player*
13552 Del Pomonte Road, Poway, CA 92064, USA

Templeton, John M — *Financier*
Lyford Cay Club, Box N-7776, Nassau, Bahamas

Tenace, F Gene — *Baseball Player*
15358 Midland Road, Poway, CA 92064, USA

Tenet, George — *Government Official*
%Central Intelligence Agency, Director's Office, Washington, DC 20505, USA

Tengbom, Anders   *Architect*
Kornhamnstorg 6, 111 27 Stockholm, Sweden
Tennant, Veronica   *Ballerina*
%National Ballet of Canada, 157 King St E, Toronto ON M5C 1G9, Canada
Tennant, Victoria   *Actress*
PO Box 929, Beverly Hills, CA 90213, USA
Tenney, Charles H, II   *Businessman*
%Bay State Gas, 300 Friberg Parkway, Westborough, MA 01581, USA
Tenney, Jon   *Actor*
9818 Craigmitchell Lane, Sunland, CA 91040, USA
Tennille, Toni   *Singer (The Captain & Tennille)*
7123 Franktown Road, Carson City, NV 89704, USA
Tennstedt, Klaus   *Conductor*
Rothenbaumchaussee 132-174, 20149 Hamburg, Germany
Tenorio, Pedro   *Governor, CM*
%Governor's Office, Capitol Hill, Saipan, CM 96950, USA
Tenoso, Edwin E (Ed)   *Air Force General*
Commander, 21st Air Force, 1907 E Arnold Ave, McGuire Air Force Base, NJ 08641, USA
Tenuta, Judy   *Comedienne*
13504 Contour Dr, Sherman Oaks, CA 91423, USA
Ter Horst, Jerald F   *Government Official, Journalist*
7815 Evening Lane, Alexandria, VA 22306, USA
Ter-Petrosyan, Levon   *President, Armenia*
%President's Office, Parliament Building, Yerevan, Armenia
Teraoka, Masami   *Artist*
41-048 Kaulu St, Waimanalo, HI 96795, USA
Tereschenko, Sergei A   *Prime Minister, Kazakhstan*
%Prime Minister's Office, Dom Pravieelstra, 148008 Alma-Ata, Kazakhstan
Tereshkova, Valentina V   *Cosmonaut*
%Soviet Woman's Committee, 6 Nemirovich-Danchenko, 103009 Moscow, Russia
Terfel, Bryn   *Opera Singer*
%Deutsche Grammaphon Records, 810 7th Ave, New York, NY 10019, USA
Terkel, Louis (Studs)   *Writer*
850 W Castlewood Terrace, Chicago, IL 60640, USA
Terminator X   *Rap Artist (Public Enemy)*
%Rush Artists, 1600 Varick St, New York, NY 10013, USA
Terranova, Phil   *Boxer*
30 Bugardus Place, New York, NY 10040, USA
Terrasson, Jacky   *Jazz Pianist*
%Joel Chriss, 300 Mercer St, #3-J, New York, NY 10003, USA
Terreri, Chris   *Hockey Player*
41 Rhode Island Ave, Warwick, RI 02889, USA
Terrile, Richard   *Astronomer*
2121 E Woodlyn Road, Pasadena, CA 91104, USA
Terry, Clark   *Jazz Trumpeter, Singer*
24 Westland Dr, Glen Cove, NY 11542, USA
Terry, Hilda   *Cartoonist (Teena)*
8 Henderson Place, New York, NY 10028, USA
Terry, John Q   *Architect*
Old Exchange, Dedham, Colchester, Essex, England
Terry, Megan   *Writer*
2309 Hanscom Blvd, Omaha, NE 68105, USA
Terry, Randall A   *Anti-Abortion Activist*
%Operation Rescue National, PO Box 360221, Melbourne, FL 32936, USA
Terry, Richard E   *Businessman*
%Peoples Energy Corp, 130 E Randolph Dr, Chicago, IL 60601, USA
Terry, Ronald A   *Financier*
%First Tennessee National, 165 Madison Ave, Memphis, TN 38103, USA
Terry, Ruth   *Singer, Actress*
622 Hospitality Dr, Rancho Mirage, CA 92270, USA
Terry, Tony   *Singer*
%Famous Artists Agency, 1700 Broadway, #500, New York, NY 10019, USA
Terzian, Jacques   *Sculptor*
PO Box 883753, San Francisco, CA 94188, USA
Tesh, John   *Composer, Pianist, Entertainer*
%Agency For Performing Arts, 9200 Sunset Blvd, #900, Los Angeles, CA 90069, USA
Teshoian, Nishan   *Businessman*
%Keystone International, 9600 W Gulf Bank Dr, Houston, TX 77040, USA

T

Tengbom - Teshoian

Tessier-Lavigne, Marc — *Neurobiologist*
1768 Lexington Ave, San Mateo, CA 94402, USA

Testaverde, Vinny — *Football Player*
936 Crenshaw Lake Road, Lutz, FL 33549, USA

Testi, Fabio — *Actor*
Via Siacci 38, 00197 Rome, Italy

Tetley, Glen — *Ballet Director, Choreographer*
15 W 9th St, New York, NY 10011, USA

Tetzlaff, Christian — *Concert Violinist*
%Virgin Classics Records, 1790 Broadway, #2000, New York, NY 10019, USA

Tewes, Lauren — *Actress*
2739 31st Ave S, Seattle, WA 98144, USA

Tewkesbury, Joan F — *Movie Director, Screenwriter*
%Creative Artists Agency, 9830 Wilshire Blvd, Beverly Hills, CA 90212, USA

Tews, Andreas — *Boxer*
Hamburger Allee 1, 19063 Schwerin, Germany

Thacker, Brian M — *Vietnam War Army Hero (CMH)*
11413 Monterey Dr, Wheaton, MD 20902, USA

Thackery, Jimmy — *Guitarist*
%Blue Sky Artist Mgmt, 761 N Washington Ave, Minneapolis, MN 55401, USA

Thagard, Norman E — *Astronaut, Physician*
%NASA, Johnson Space Center, 2101 NASA Road, Houston, TX 77058, USA

Than Shwe — *Head of State, Myanmar; Army General*
%State Law Restoration Council, Signal Pagoda Road, Yangon, Myanmar

Tharp, Twyla — *Dancer, Choreographer*
%MPL Productions, 170 W 74th St, New York, NY 10023, USA

Thatcher of Lincolnshire, Margaret H — *Prime Minister, England*
11 Dulwich Gate, Dulwich, London SE12, England

Thaves, Bob — *Cartoonist (Frank & Ernest)*
PO Box 67, Manhattan Beach, CA 90267, USA

Thaw, John — *Actor*
%Associated International Mgmt, 5 Denmark St, London WC2H 8LP, England

Thaxter, Phyllis — *Actress*
716 Riomar Dr, Vero Beach, FL 32963, USA

Thayer, Brynn — *Actress*
1511 Amalfi Dr, Pacific Palisades, CA 90272, USA

Thayer, W Paul — *Businessman, Government Official*
10200 Hollow Way, Dallas, TX 75229, USA

Theauwes, Felix — *Businessman*
%Alza Corp, 950 Page Mill Road, Palo Alto, CA 94304, USA

Theberge, James D — *Diplomat*
4462 Cathedral Ave NW, Washington, DC 20016, USA

Theile, David — *Swimmer*
84 Woodville St, Hendea, Brisbane QLD 4011, Australia

Theismann, Joseph R (Joe) — *Football Player, Sportscaster*
%JRT Assoc, 5661 Columbia Pike, #100-B, Falls Church, VA 22041, USA

Theodorakis, Mikis — *Composer*
Epifanous 1, Akropolis, Athens, Greece

Theodorescu, Monica — *Equestrian Athlete*
Gestit Lindenhof, 48336 Sassenberg, Germany

Theodosius (Lazor), Primate Metropolitan — *Religious Leader*
%Orthodox Church in America, PO Box 675, Rt 25-A, Syosset, NY 11791, USA

Theroux, Paul E — *Writer*
35 Elsynge Road, London SW18 2NR, England

Thesiger, Wilfred P — *Explorer*
15 Shelley Court, Tite St, London SW3 4JB, England

Theus, Reggie — *Basketball Player*
%New Jersey Nets, Byrne Meadowlands Arena, East Rutherford, NJ 07073, USA

Thewlis, David — *Actor*
%International Creative Mgmt, 76 Oxford St, London W1N 0AX, England

Thiandoum, Hyacinthe Cardinal — *Religious Leader*
Archeveche, BP 1908, Dakar, Senegal

Thibaudet, Jean-Yves — *Concert Pianist*
255 W 88th St, #10-B, New York, NY 10024, USA

Thibiant, Aida — *Fashion Expert*
%Institut de Beaute, 449 N Canon Dr, Beverly Hills, CA 90210, USA

Thicke, Alan — *Actor*
10505 Sarah St, Toluca Lake, CA 91602, USA

Thiebaud, Wayne — *Artist*
1617 17th Ave, Sacramento, CA 95814, USA

Thielemans, Toots — *Jazz Harmonica Player, Guitarist*
%Peter Levinson Communications, 2575 Palisade Ave, #11-H, Bronx, NY 10463, USA

Thiemann, Charles Lee — *Financier*
%Federal Home Loan Bank, PO Box 598, Cincinnati, OH 45201, USA

Thiess, Ursula — *Actress*
1940 Bel Air Road, Los Angeles, CA 90077, USA

Thiessen, Tiffani-Amber — *Actress*
3523 Wrightwood Court, Studio City, CA 91604, USA

Thigpen, Lynne — *Actress*
35 W 20th St, New York, NY 10011, USA

Thimann, Kenneth V — *Biologist*
3815 Walnut St, Philadelphia, PA 19104, USA

Thimmesch, Nicholas — *Journalist*
6301 Broad Branch Road, Chevy Chase, MD 20815, USA

Thinnes, Roy — *Actor*
1725-B Madison Ave, #634, Memphis, TN 38104, USA

Thirsk, Robert — *Astronaut, Canada*
%Astronaut Program, 6767 Rt de l'Aeroport, St-Hubert PQ J3Y 8Y9, Canada

Thiry, Kent — *Businessman*
%Vivra, 400 Primrose, Burlingame, CA 94010, USA

Thode, Henry G — *Chemist*
%McMaster University, Nuclear Research Dept, Hamilton ON L8S 4M1, Canada

Thoma, Georg — *Nordic Skier*
Bisten 6, 79856 Hinterzarten, Germany

Thomalla, Georg — *Actor*
Hans Nefer, 5640 Bad Gastein, Austria

Thomas, Aurelius — *Football Player*
PO Box 091157, Columbus, OH 43209, USA

Thomas, B J — *Singer, Songwriter*
%Marathon Attractions, 24 Music Square W, #208, Nashville, TN 37203, USA

Thomas, Barbara S — *Government Official*
%News International, 1 Virginia St, London E1 9XY, England

Thomas, Betty — *Actress, Director*
PO Box 1892, Studio City, CA 91614, USA

Thomas, Billy M — *Army General*
8249 Clifton Farm Court, Community, VA 22306, USA

Thomas, Carla — *Singer*
%Talent Consultants Int'l, 1560 Broadway, #1308, New York, NY 10036, USA

Thomas, Caroline Bedell — *Physician*
830 W 40th St, #259, Baltimore, MD 21211, USA

Thomas, Clarence — *Supreme Court Justice*
%US Supreme Court, 1 1st St NE, Washington, DC 20543, USA

Thomas, D(onald) M(ichael) — *Writer*
Coach House, Rashleigh Vale, Tregolls Rd, Truro, Cornwall TR1 1TJ, England

Thomas, David — *Concert Singer*
74 Hyde Vale, Greenwich, London SE10 8HP, England

Thomas, David Clayton — *Singer (Blood Sweat & Tears)*
%United Concert Productions, 308 E 6th St, #13, New York, NY 10003, USA

Thomas, Debra J (Debi) — *Figure Skater*
22 E 71st St, New York, NY 10021, USA

Thomas, Derrick — *Football Player*
1029 Hanover Dr, Beverly Hills, CA 90210, USA

Thomas, Dominic R — *Religious Leader*
%Church of Jesus Christ, 6th & Lincoln Sts, Monongahela, PA 15063, USA

Thomas, Donald A — *Astronaut*
%NASA, Johnson Space Center, 2101 NASA Road, Houston, TX 77058, USA

Thomas, E Donnall — *Nobel Medicine Laureate*
%Hutchinson Cancer Research Center, 1124 Columbia St, Seattle, WA 98104, USA

Thomas, Elizabeth Marshall — *Writer*
80 E Mountain Road, Peterborough, NH 03458, USA

Thomas, Frank E — *Baseball Player*
3312 Midwest Road, Oak Brook, IL 60523, USA

Thomas, Frank J — *Baseball Player*
118 Doray Dr, Pittsburgh, PA 15237, USA

Thomas, Fred — *Law Enforcement Official*
%Metropolitan Police Dept, 300 Indiana Ave NW, Washington, DC 20001, USA

T

Thiebaud - Thomas

Thomas, Garet G — *Financier*
%Bankers Trust Delaware, 1011 Centre Road, 7#200, Wilmington, DE 19805, USA

Thomas, Gareth — *Engineer*
%University of California, Materials Science Dept, Berkeley, CA 94720, USA

Thomas, Heather — *Actress*
1433 San Vicente Blvd, Santa Monica, CA 90402, USA

Thomas, Helen A — *Journalist*
2501 Calvert St NW, Washington, DC 20008, USA

Thomas, Henry L, Jr — *Football Player*
16811 Southern Oaks Dr, Houston, TX 77068, USA

Thomas, Irma — *Singer*
%Emile Jackson, PO Box 26126, New Orleans, LA 70186, USA

Thomas, Isiah L, III — *Basketball Player, Executive*
710 Lone Pine Road, Bloomfield Hills, MI 48304, USA

Thomas, J Gorman — *Baseball Player*
759 Tallwood Road, Charleston, SC 29412, USA

Thomas, Jack Ward — *Government Official, Biologist*
%University of Montana, Biology Dept, Missoula, MT 59812, USA

Thomas, Jay — *Actor*
%The Agency, 1800 Ave of Stars, #400, Los Angeles, CA 90067, USA

Thomas, Jean — *Ceramist*
1427 Summit Road, Berkeley, CA 94708, USA

Thomas, Jim — *Basketball Executive*
%Sacramento Kings, 1 Sports Parkway, Sacramento, CA 95834, USA

Thomas, John — *Track Athlete*
51 Mulberry St, Brockton, MA 02402, USA

Thomas, John — *Basektball Player*
%New York Knicks, Madison Square Garden, 2 Penn Plaza, New York, NY 10121, USA

Thomas, Jonathan Taylor — *Actor*
PO Box 64846, Los Angeles, CA 90064, USA

Thomas, Kurt — *Gymnast*
%George Wallach, 1400 Braeridge Dr, Beverly Hills, CA 90210, USA

Thomas, Kurt — *Basketball Player*
1826 Brook Terrace Trail, Dallas, TX 75232, USA

Thomas, Lee M — *Government Official*
%Enviromental Protection Agency, 401 "M" St SW, Washington, DC 20024, USA

Thomas, Leon — *Jazz Singer*
%Abby Hoffer, 223 1/2 E 48th St, New York, NY 10017, USA

Thomas, Llewellyn H — *Theoretical Physicist*
3012 Wycliff Road, Raleigh, NC 27607, USA

Thomas, Marlo — *Actress*
420 E 54th St, #22-F, New York, NY 10022, USA

Thomas, Mary — *Singer (The Crystals)*
%Mars Talent, 168 Orchid Dr, Pearl River, NY 10965, USA

Thomas, Michael Tilson — *Conductor, Concert Pianist*
%San Francisco Symphony, Davies Symphony Hall, San Francisco, CA 94102, USA

Thomas, Pat — *Football Player*
612 Middle Cove, Plano, TX 75023, USA

Thomas, Philip Michael — *Actor*
Miamiway Theatre, 12615 W Dixie Highway, North Miami, FL 33161, USA

Thomas, R David (Dave) — *Businessman*
%Wendy's International, 4288 W Dublin-Granville Road, Dublin, OH 43017, USA

Thomas, Richard — *Actor*
4963 Los Feliz Blvd, Los Angeles, CA 90027, USA

Thomas, Richard L — *Financier*
%First Chicago Corp, 1 First National Plaza, Chicago, IL 60670, USA

Thomas, Robert D — *Publisher*
223 Mariomi Road, New Canaan, CT 06840

Thomas, Rozonda (Chili) — *Rap Artist (TLC)*
%William Morris Agency, 1325 Ave of Americas, New York, NY 10019, USA

Thomas, Rufus — *Singer, Songwriter*
%Talent Consultants Int'l, 1560 Broadway, #1308, New York, NY 10036, USA

Thomas, Serena Scott — *Actress*
%International Creative Mgmt, 76 Oxford St, London W1N 0AX, England

Thomas, Steve — *Television Entertainer*
%"This Old House" Show, PO Box 2284, South Burlington, VT 05407, USA

Thomas, Thurman — *Football Player*
18 Greenlaw, Sugar Land, TX 77479, USA

Thomas, Tim — *Basketball Player*
%Philadelphia 76ers, Veterans Stadium, PO Box 25040, Philadelphia, PA 19147, USA
Thomas, Tracy Y — *Mathematician*
1323 17th St, #26, Santa Monica, CA 90404, USA
Thomas, Wayne — *Hockey Player*
288 W Lincoln Ave, Libertyville, IL 60048, USA
Thomas, William R — *Financier*
%Capital Southwest Corp, 12900 Preston Road, Dallas, TX 75230, USA
Thomason, Harry Z — *Television Producer*
10732 Riverside Dr, North Hollywood, CA 91602, USA
Thome, James H (Jim) — *Baseball Player*
1827 S Crest Dr, Peoria, IL 61605, USA
Thomerson, Tim — *Actor*
%Innovative Artists, 1999 Ave of Stars, #2850, Los Angeles, CA 90067, USA
Thomopoulos, Anthony — *Television Executive*
1280 Stone Canyon Road, Los Angeles, CA 90077, USA
Thompson, Andrea — *Actress*
%Gersh Agency, 232 N Canon Dr, Beverly Hills, CA 90210, USA
Thompson, Clifford — *Hockey Player, Coach*
9 Robin Road, Reading, MA 01867, USA
Thompson, D Gary — *Financier*
%Wachovia Bank (Georgia), 181 Peachtree St NE, Atlanta, GA 30303, USA
Thompson, Daley — *Track Athlete*
%Olympic Assn, 1 Wadsworth Plain, London SW18 1EH, England
Thompson, David — *Basketball Player, Executive*
5045 Strawberry Hill Dr, #C, Charlotte, NC 28211, USA
Thompson, David C — *Coast Guard Admiral*
%US Coast Guard, Atlantic, Governors Island, New York, NY 10004, USA
Thompson, David R — *Judge*
%US Court of Appeals, 940 Front St, San Diego, CA 92101, USA
Thompson, Edward K — *Editor*
%Smithsonian Magazine, Editorial Dept, 900 Jefferson Dr, Washington, DC 20560, USA
Thompson, Edward T — *Editor*
3 Hunt Farm, Waccabuc, NY 10597, USA
Thompson, Emma — *Actress*
%Lorraine Hamilton, 19 Denmark St, London WC2H 8NA, England
Thompson, G Lee — *Businessman*
%Smith Corona Corp, PO Box 2090, Cortland, NY 13045, USA
Thompson, G Ralph — *Religious Leader*
%Seventh-Day Adventists, 12501 Old Columbia Pike, Silver Spring, MD 20904, USA
Thompson, Gary — *Basketball Player*
2531 Park Vista Circle, Ames, IA 50014, USA
Thompson, Gina — *Singer*
%Famous Artists Agency, 1700 Broadway, #500, New York, NY 10019, USA
Thompson, Homer A — *Archaeologist*
Meadow Lakes, #30-06, Highstown, NJ 08520, USA
Thompson, Hugh L — *Educator*
%Washburn University, President's Office, Topeka, KS 66621, USA
Thompson, Hunter S — *Journalist, Writer*
PO Box 220, Woody Creek, CO 81656, USA
Thompson, J Lee — *Movie Director*
9595 Lime Orchard Road, Beverly Hills, CA 90210, USA
Thompson, Jack — *Actor*
%Michael McLean, 12754 Sarah St, Studio City, CA 91604, USA
Thompson, Jack E — *Businessman*
%Homestake Mining, 650 California St, San Francisco, CA 94108, USA
Thompson, James B, Jr — *Geologist*
20 Richmond Road, Belmont, MA 02178, USA
Thompson, James R — *Governor, IL*
35 W Wacker Dr, Chicago, IL 60601, USA
Thompson, James R, Jr — *Space Administrator*
%Orbital Sciences Corp, 620 Discovery Dr, #120, Huntsville, AL 35806, USA
Thompson, Jason D — *Baseball Player*
26351 Sorrell Place, Laguna Hills, CA 92653, USA
Thompson, John B — *Basketball Coach*
4881 Colorado Ave NW, Washington, DC 20011, USA
Thompson, Kenneth L — *Computer Scientist*
366 Ridge Road, Watchung, NJ 07060, USA

T

Thompson, LaSalle — *Basketball Player*
%Indiana Pacers, Market Square Arena, 300 E Market St, Indianapolis, IN 46204, USA

Thompson, Lea — *Actress*
7966 Woodrow Wilson Dr, Los Angeles, CA 90046, USA

Thompson, Linda — *Actress*
3365 Cahuenga Blvd W, #450, Los Angeles, CA 90068, USA

Thompson, Max — *WW II Army Hero (CMH)*
Rt 3, PO Box 56, Canton, NC 28716, USA

Thompson, Melvin E — *Governor, GA*
509 N Patterson St, Valdosta, GA 31601, USA

Thompson, Mike — *Editorial Cartoonist*
%State Journal Register, Editorial Dept, 1 Copley Plaza, Springfield, IL 62701, USA

Thompson, N David — *Businessman*
%North American Reinsurance, 237 Park Ave, New York, NY 10017, USA

Thompson, Paul H — *Educator*
%Weber State University, President's Office, Ogden, UT 84408, USA

Thompson, Richard — *Singer, Songwriter, Guitarist*
%Metropolitan Entertainment, 2 Penn Plaza, #2600, New York, NY 10121, USA

Thompson, Richard C — *Publisher*
%US News & World Report Magazine, 2400 "N" St NW, Washington, DC 20037, USA

Thompson, Robert G K — *Army General, England*
Pitcott House, Winsford Minehead, Somerset, England

Thompson, Sada — *Actress*
PO Box 490, Southbury, CT 06488, USA

Thompson, Starley L — *Climatologist*
%National Atmospheric Research Center, PO Box 3000, Boulder, CO 80307, USA

Thompson, Sue — *Singer*
%Terry M Hill, 6430 Variel Ave, #101, Woodland Hills, CA 91367, USA

Thompson, Tommy G — *Governor, WI*
%Governor's Office, State Capitol, PO Box 7863, Madison, WI 53707, USA

Thompson, Wilbur (Moose) — *Track Athlete*
11372 Martha Ann, Los Alamitos, CA 90720, USA

Thompson, William P — *Religious Leader*
%World Council of Churches, 475 Riverside Dr, New York, NY 10115, USA

Thomson of Fleet, Kenneth R — *Publisher*
%Thomson Newspapers, 65 Queen St W, Toronto ON M5H 2M8, Canada

Thomson, Anna — *Actress*
%Innovative Artists, 1999 Ave of Stars, #2850, Los Angeles, CA 90067, USA

Thomson, H C (Hank) — *Harness Racing Official*
PO Box 38, Mullett Lake, MI 49761, USA

Thomson, James A — *Research Company Executive*
%Rand Corp, 1700 Main St, Santa Monica, CA 90401, USA

Thomson, June — *Commentator*
%KNBC-TV, News Dept, 3000 W Alameda Ave, Burbank, CA 91523, USA

Thomson, Meldrim, Jr — *Governor, NH*
Mount Cube Farm, Orford, NH 03773, USA

Thomson, Peter W — *Golfer*
Carmel House, 44 Mathoura Road, Toorak, VIC 3142, Australia

Thomson, Robert B (Bobby) — *Baseball Player*
122 Sunlit Dr, Watchung, NJ 07060, USA

Thon, William — *Artist*
%General Delivery, Port Clyde, ME 04855, USA

Thone, Charles — *Governor, NE*
%Erickson & Sederstrom, 301 S 13th St, #400, Lincoln, NE 68508, USA

Thoni, Gustav — *Skier, Coach*
39026 Prato Allo Stelvio-Prao BZ, Italy

Thora — *Actress*
1414 N Fairfax Ave, Los Angeles, CA 90046, USA

Thorburn, Clifford C D (Cliff) — *Snooker Player*
31 West Side Dr, Markham ON, Canada

Thorgren, Aya — *Model*
%Ford Model Agency, 344 E 59th St, New York, NY 10022, USA

Thorn, George W — *Physician*
16 Gurney St, Cambridge, MA 02138, USA

Thorn, Rod — *Basketball Player*
20 Loewen Court, Rye, NY 10580, USA

Thorn, Tracey — *Singer (Everything But the Girl)*
%Atlantic Records, 75 Rockefeller Plaza, New York, NY 10019, USA

Thornburgh, Richard L (Dick) *Attorney General; Governor, PA*
%Kirkpatrick & Lockhart, 1800 "M" St NW, #900, Washington, DC 20036, USA
Thorne, Kip S *Physicist*
%California Institute of Technology, Physics Dept, Pasadena, CA 91125, USA
Thorne-Smith, Courtney *Actress*
11033 Massachusetts Ave, #19, Los Angeles, CA 90025, USA
Thornhill, Arthur H, Jr *Publisher*
50 S School St, Portsmouth, NH 03801, USA
Thornton, Andre *Baseball Player*
PO Box 395, Chagrin Falls, OH 44022, USA
Thornton, Billy Bob *Actor, Director*
%International Creative Mgmt, 8942 Wilshire Blvd, Beverly Hills, CA 90211, USA
Thornton, Kathryn C *Astronaut*
%NASA, Johnson Space Center, 2101 NASA Road, Houston, TX 77058, USA
Thornton, Michael E *Vietnam War Navy Air Hero (CMH)*
118 Toler Place, Norfolk, VA 23503, USA
Thornton, Sigrid *Actress*
%William Morris Agency, 151 S El Camino Dr, Beverly Hills, CA 90212, USA
Thornton, William E *Astronaut*
%NASA, Johnson Space Center, 2101 NASA Road, Houston, TX 77058, USA
Thornton, Winfred L *Businessman*
%St Joe Paper Co, 1650 Prudential Dr, Jacksonville, FL 32207, USA
Thornton-Sherwood, Madeleine *Actress*
32 Leroy St, New York, NY 10014, USA
Thorogood, George *Singer, Guitarist*
%Michael Donahue Mgmt, PO Box 807, Lewisburg, VA 24901, USA
Thorpe, J Jeremy *Government Official, England*
2 Orme Square, Bayswater, London W2, England
Thorpe, James *Library, Art Gallery Director*
%Huntington Library, 1650 Oxford Road, San Marino, CA 91104, USA
Thorpe, Jim *Golfer*
845 Preserve Terrace, Heathrow, FL 32746, USA
Thorpe, Otis H *Basketball Player*
PO Box 400, Canfield, OH 44406, USA
Thorsell, William *Editor*
%Toronto Globe & Mail, 444 Front St W, Toronto M5V 2S9, Canada
Thorsen, Howard B *Coast Guard Admiral*
Commander, Atlantic Area, US Coast Guard, Governors Island, New York, NY 10004, USA
Thorsness, Leo K *Vietnam Air Force Hero (CMH)*
PO Box 47, Indianola, WA 98342, USA
Thorson, Linda *Actress*
145 W 45th St, #1204, New York, NY 10036, USA
Threadgill, Henry L *Jazz Saxophonist, Composer*
%Joel Chriss, 300 Mercer St, #3-J, New York, NY 10003, USA
Threatt, Sedale *Basketball Player*
5359 Newcastle Lane, Calabasas, CA 91302, USA
Threlkeld, Richard D *Commentator*
%CBS-TV, News Dept, 51 W 52nd St, New York, NY 10019, USA
Threshie, R David, Jr *Publisher*
%Orange County Register, 625 N Grand Ave, Santa Ana, CA 92701, USA
Throne, Malachi *Actor*
11805 Mayfield Ave, #306, Los Angeles, CA 90049, USA
Thulin, Ingrid *Actress*
Kevingestrand 7-B, 182 31 Danderyd, Sweden
Thunder, Johnny *Singer*
%Stormin Norman Productions, 2 W Front St, Red Bank, NJ 07701, USA
Thunell, Lars H *Businessman*
%Home Insurance, 59 Maiden Lane, New York, NY 10038, USA
Thunman, Nils R *Navy Admiral*
1516 S Willemore Ave, Springfield, IL 62704, USA
Thuot, Pierre J *Astronaut*
%NASA, Johnson Space Center, 2101 NASA Road, Houston, TX 77058, USA
Thurman, Dennis *Football Player*
3447 W 59th Place, Los Angeles, CA 90043, USA
Thurman, Uma *Actress*
%Flick East-West, 9057 Nemo St, #A, West Hollywood, CA 90069, USA
Thurman, William E *Air Force General*
10 Firestone Dr, Pinehurst, NC 28374, USA

Thornburgh - Thurman

Thurmond, Nate — *Basketball Player, Executive*
5094 Diamond Heights Blvd, #B, San Francisco, CA 94131, USA

Thurow, Lester C — *Economist*
%Massachusetts Institute of Technology, Economics Dept, Cambridge, MA 02139, USA

Thurston, Frederick C (Fuzzy) — *Football Player*
1261 Monroe, Green Bay, WI 54301, USA

Thyssen, Greta — *Actress*
444 E 82nd St, New York, NY 10028, USA

Thyssen-Bornemisza, Hans-Heinrich — *Businessman, Art Collector*
Villa Favorita, 6796 Castagnola di Lugano, Switzerland

Tiainen, Juha — *Track Athlete*
%Olympic Committee, Topeliuksenkatu 41 a A, Helsinki 25, Finland

Tian Jiyun — *Government Official, China*
%Vice Premier's Office, State Council, Beijing, China

Tiant, Luis C — *Baseball Player*
1121 N Pine Island Road, Fort Lauderdale, FL 33322, USA

Tibbets, Paul W — *WW II Army Air Corps Hero*
5574 Knollwood Dr, Columbus, OH 43232, USA

Tice, George A — *Photographer*
323 Gill Lane, #9-B, Iselin, NJ 08830, USA

Tichnor, Alan — *Religious Leader*
%United Synagogue of America, 155 5th Ave, New York, NY 10010, USA

Tickner, Charlie — *Figure Skater*
5410 Sunset Dr, Littleton, CO 80123, USA

Ticotin, Rachel — *Actress*
%International Creative Mgmt, 8942 Wilshire Blvd, Beverly Hills, CA 90211, USA

Tidwell, Moody R, III — *Judge*
%US Claims Court, 717 Madison Place NW, Washington, DC 20005, USA

Tiegs, Cheryl — *Model*
%Barbara Shapiro, 2 Greenwich Plaza, #100, Greenwich, CT 06830, USA

Tiemann, Norbert T — *Governor, NE*
7511 Pebblestone Dr, Dallas, TX 75230, USA

Tierney, Lawrence — *Actor*
2352 Penmar Ave, Venice, CA 90291, USA

Tierney, Maura — *Actress*
%Gersh Agency, 232 N Canon Dr, Beverly Hills, CA 90210, USA

Tiffany (Renee Darwish) — *Singer*
%Dick Scott Entertainment, 888 7th Ave, #2900, New York, NY 10106, USA

Tiffin, Pamela — *Actress*
15 W 67th St, New York, NY 10023, USA

Tigar, Kenneth — *Actor*
642 Etta St, Los Angeles, CA 90065, USA

Tiger, Lionel — *Social Scientist, Anthropologist*
248 W 23rd St, #400, New York, NY 10011, USA

Tigerman, Stanley — *Architect*
%Tigerman & McCurry, 444 N Wells St, #206, Chicago, IL 60610, USA

Tighe, Kevin — *Actor*
PO Box 453, Sedro Wooley, WA 98284, USA

Tilberis, Elizabeth J — *Editor*
%Harper's Bazaar Magazine, Editorial Dept, 1700 Broadway, New York, NY 10019, USA

Tilelli, John H, Jr — *Army General*
CinC, United Nations Combined Forces Korea, APO, AP 96205, USA

Tiller, Nadja — *Actress*
Via Tamporiva 26, 6976 Castagnola, Switzerland

Tilley, Patrick L (Pat) — *Football Player, Coach*
5332 Goodgoin Road, Ruston, LA 71270, USA

Tillis, Mel — *Singer, Songwriter*
PO Box 1626, Branson, MO 65615, USA

Tillis, Pam — *Singer, Songwriter*
%Mike Robertson Mgmt, PO Box 120073, Nashville, TN 37212, USA

Tillotson, Johnny — *Singer*
%American Mgmt, 17530 Ventura Blvd, #108, Encino, CA 91316, USA

Tilly, Jennifer — *Actress*
270 N Canon Dr, #1582, Beverly Hills, CA 90210, USA

Tilly, Meg — *Actress*
321 S Beverly Dr, #M, Beverly Hills, CA 90212, USA

Tilson, Joseph (Joe) — *Artist*
Old Rectory, Christian Malford, Wilts SN15 4BW, England

Tilton, Charlene	*Actress*
22059 Galvez St, Woodland Hills, CA 91364, USA	
Tilton, Martha	*Singer, Actress*
760 Lausanne Road, Los Angeles, CA 90077, USA	
Tilton, Robert	*Evangelist*
%Robert Tilton Ministries, PO Box 819000, Dallas, TX 75381, USA	
Timakata, Fred	*President, Vanuatu*
%President's Office, Port Vila, Vanuatu	
Timbers, Stephen B	*Financier*
%Kemper Corp, 1 Kemper Dr, Long Grove, IL 60049, USA	
Timerman, Jacobo	*Publisher*
%Alfred A Knopf, 201 E 50th St, New York, NY 10022, USA	
Timme, Robert	*Architect*
%Taft Architects, 2444 Times Blvd, #320, Houston, TX 77005, USA	
Timmermann, Ulf	*Track Athlete*
Ahrenshooper Str 4, 13051 Berlin, Germany	
Timmins, Cali	*Actress*
%The Agency, 1800 Ave of Stars, #400, Los Angeles, CA 90067, USA	
Timmins, Margo	*Singer (Cowboy Junkies)*
%New York End, 2575 Michigan Ave, #A-1, Santa Monica, CA 90404, USA	
Timmons, Michael	*Guitarist (Cowboy Junkies), Songwriter*
%New York End, 2525 Michigan Ave, #A-1, Santa Monica, CA 90404, USA	
Timmons, Richard F (Rich)	*Army General*
Commanding General, 8th US Army/UN Combined Forces Korea, APO, AE 96205, USA	
Timofeyeva, Nina V	*Ballerina*
%Bolshoi Theater, Teatralnaya Pl 1, 103009 Moscow, Russia	
Timpe, Ronald E	*Businessman*
%Standard Insurance, 1100 SW 6th Ave, Portland, OR 97204, USA	
Tindemans, Leo	*Prime Minister, Belgium*
Jan Verbertlei 24, 2520 Edegem, Belgium	
Tindle, David	*Artist*
4 Rue Nande, 56260 Quemerie Sur Scorff Morbihan, France	
Ting, Samuel C C	*Nobel Physics Laureate*
15 Moon Hill Road, Lexington, MA 02173, USA	
Ting, Walasse	*Artist*
100 W 25th St, New York, NY 10001, USA	
Tinker, Grant A	*Television Executive*
531 Barnaby Road, Los Angeles, CA 90077, USA	
Tinkham, Michael	*Physicist*
98 Rutledge Road, Belmont, MA 02178, USA	
Tinsley, Bruce	*Editorial Cartoonist*
%USA Today, Editorial Dept, 1000 Wilson Blvd, Arlington, VA 22209, USA	
Tinsley, Gaynell C (Gus)	*Football Player*
14343 Highland Road, Rt 3, PO Box 485, Baton Rouge, LA 70810, USA	
Tinsley, Jackson B (Jack)	*Editor*
%Fort Worth Star-Telegram, Editorial Dept, 400 W 7th St, Fort Worth, TX 76102, USA	
Tinstman, Robert A	*Businessman*
%Morrison Knudsen, Morrison Knudsen Plaza, PO Box 73, Boise, ID 83729, USA	
Tippett, Andre	*Football Player*
17 Knob Hill St, Sharon, MA 02067, USA	
Tippett, Michael K	*Composer, Conductor*
%Schott & Co, 48 Great Marlborough St, London W1V 2BN, England	
Tippin, Aaron	*Singer, Songwriter*
%Starstruck Publicity, 40 Music Square W, Nashville, TN 37203, USA	
Tipton, Daniel	*Religious Leader*
%Churches of Christ in Christian Union, Box 30, Circleville, OH 43113, USA	
Tipton, Eric G (The Red)	*Football Player*
125 Nina Lane, Williamsburg, VA 23188, USA	
Tiriac, Ion	*Tennis Player, Coach*
%Ion Tiriac/TV Enterprises, 251 E 49th St, New York, NY 10017, USA	
Tirico, Mike	*Sportscaster*
%ESPN-TV, News Dept, ESPN Plaza, 935 Middle St, Bristol, CT 06010, USA	
Tirimo, Martino	*Concert Pianist*
2 Combemartin Road, London SW18 5PR, England	
Tisch, James S	*Businessman*
%Loews Corp, 655 Madison Ave, #800, New York, NY 10021, USA	
Tisch, Laurence A	*Businessman*
%CBS Inc, 51 W 52nd St, New York, NY 10019, USA	

Tisch, Preston R *Government Official, Football Executive*
%Loews Corp, 655 Madison Ave, #800, New York, NY 10021, USA

Tisch, Steve *Writer*
14454 Sunset Blvd, Pacific Palisades, CA 90272, USA

Tisdale, Wayman *Basketball Player*
10617 S 70th E Ave, Tulsa, OK 74133, USA

Tito, Teburoro *President, Kiribati*
%President's Office, Tarawa, Kiribati

Titov, Gherman S *Cosmonaut; Air Force General*
3 Hovanskaya Str, #8, 129515 Moscow, Russia

Titov, Vladimir G *Cosmonaut*
%Potchta Kosmonavtov, Moskovskoi Oblasti, 141160 Syvisdny Goroduk, Russia

Tittle, Yelberton A (Y A) *Football Player*
%Rollins Burdick Hunter Insurance, 2595 E Bayshore Blvd, Palo Alto, CA 94303, USA

Titus-Carmel, Gerard *Artist*
La Grand Maison, 02210 Oulchy Le Chateau, France

Tizard, Catherine A *Governor General, New Zealand*
Government House, Private Bag, Wellington, New Zealand

Tizon, Albert *Journalist*
%Seattle Times, Editorial Dept, Fairview Ave N & John St, Seattle, WA 98111, USA

Tjeknavorian, Loris-Zare *Composer*
44 Coconut Row, #B-603, Palm Beach, FL 33480, USA

Tkachuk, Keith *Hockey Player*
63 Lyman Ave, Medford, MA 02155, USA

Tkaczuk, Ivan *Religious Leader*
%Ukrainian Orthodox Church, 3 Davenport Ave, #2-A, New Rochelle, NY 10805, USA

Toal, Lawrence J *Financier*
%Dime Bancorp, 589 5th Ave, New York, NY 10017, USA

Tober, Barbara D *Editor*
%Bride Magazine, Editorial Dept, 140 E 45th St, New York, NY 10017, USA

Tobey, David (Dave) *Basketball Referee*
%Naismith Basketball Hall of Fame, 1150 W Columbus Ave, Springfield, MA 01105, USA

Tobey, Kenneth *Actor*
14155 Magnolia Blvd, #34, Sherman Oaks, CA 91423, USA

Tobian, Gary *Diver*
9171 Belted Kingfisher Road, Blaine, WA 98230, USA

Tobias, Andrew *Writer*
%Micro Education Corp of America, 285 Riverside Ave, Westport, CT 06880, USA

Tobias, Randall L *Businessman*
%Eli Lilly Co, Lilly Corporate Center, Indianapolis, IN 46285, USA

Tobias, Robert M *Labor Leader*
%National Treasury Employees Union, 901 "E" St NW, Washington, DC 20004, USA

Tobiasse, Theo *Artist*
3 Quai Rauba Coupa, 06 Nice, France

Tobin, Don *Cartoonist (The Little Woman)*
24441 Calle Sonora, #324, Laguna Hills, CA 92653, USA

Tobin, James *Nobel Economics Laureate*
117 Alden Ave, New Haven, CT 06515, USA

Tocchet, Rick *Hockey Player*
%Phoenix Coyotes, Renaissance Square, 2 N Central Ave, #1930, Phoenix, AZ 85004, USA

Tocklin, Adrian M *Businessman*
%Continental Corp, 180 Maiden Lane, New York, NY 10038, USA

Toczyska, Stefania *Opera Singer*
%Columbia Artists Mgmt Inc, 165 W 57th St, New York, NY 10019, USA

Todd of Trumpington, Alexander R *Nobel Chemistry Laureate*
9 Parker St, Cambridge, England

Todd, Beverly *Actress*
488 Valley Ridge Ave, Los Angeles, CA 90043, USA

Todd, James A, Jr *Businessman*
%Birmingham Steel Corp, 1000 Urban Center Dr, Birmingham, AL 35242, USA

Todd, Mark *Equestrian*
PO Box 507, Cambridge, New Zealand

Todd, Rachel *Actress*
8899 Beverly Blvd, #808, Los Angeles, CA 90048, USA

Todd, Richard *Actor*
Chinham Farm, Faringdon, Oxon SN7 8EZ, England

Todd, Virgil H *Religious Leader*
%Memphis Theological Seminary, 168 E Parkway S, Memphis, TN 38104, USA

Todea, Alexandru Cardinal	*Religious Leader*
Archdiocese of Alba Julia, Str P P Aron 2, 3175 Blaj, Romania	
Todorov, Stanko	*Prime Minister, Bulgaria*
Narodno Sobranie, Sofia, Bulgaria	
Toennies, Jan Peter	*Physicist*
Ewaldstr 7, 37075 Gottingen, Germany	
Tofani, Loretta A	*Journalist*
%Philadelphia Inquirer, Editorial Dept, 400 N Broad St, Philadelphia, PA 19130, USA	
Toffler, Alvin	*Writer*
%Random House, 201 E 50th St, New York, NY 10022, USA	
Toft, Richard P	*Financier*
%Chicago Title & Trust, 171 N Clark St, Chicago, IL 60601, USA	
Tognini, Michel	*Cosmonaut, France*
%CNES, 2 Place Maurice Quentin, 75039 Paris, France	
Tokody, Ilona	*Opera Singer*
%Hungarian State Opera, Andrassy Utca 22, 1062 Budapest, Hungary	
Tolan, Robert (Bobby)	*Baseball Player*
4145 Olympiad Dr, Los Angeles, CA 90043, USA	
Toland, John W	*Writer*
101 Long Ridge Road, Danbury, CT 06810, USA	
Tolbert, Berlinda	*Actress*
1800 Ave of Stars, #400, Los Angeles, CA 90067, USA	
Toles, Thomas G (Tom)	*Editorial Cartoonist*
%Buffalo News, Editorial Dept, 1 News Plaza, Buffalo, NY 14203, USA	
Tolkan, James	*Actor*
%Paradigm Agency, 10100 Santa Monica Blvd, #2500, Los Angeles, CA 90067, USA	
Toller, William R	*Businessman*
%Witco Corp, 1 American Lane, Greenwich, CT 06831, USA	
Tolleson, John C	*Financier*
%First USA, 2001 Bryan Tower, Dallas, TX 75201, USA	
Tom, Heather	*Actress*
%Somers Teitelbaum David, 1925 Century Park East, #2320, Los Angeles, CA 90067, USA	
Tom, Nicholle	*Actress*
%Savage Agency, 6212 Banner Ave, Los Angeles, CA 90038, USA	
Tomasson, Helgi	*Ballet Dancer, Director*
%San Francisco Ballet, 819 Lorraine Ave, Ardmore, PA 19003, USA	
Tomaszewski, Henryk	*Choreographer*
Al Debowa 16, 53-121 Wroclaw, Poland	
Tomba, Alberto	*Skier*
Castel dei Britti, 40100 Bologna, Italy	
Tomczak, Mike	*Football Player*
108 Bell Acres Estate, Sewickley, PA 15143, USA	
Tomei, Concetta	*Actress*
7920 Sunset Blvd, #350, Los Angeles, CA 90046, USA	
Tomei, Marisa	*Actress*
%Altman Greenfield Selvaggi, 120 W 45th St, #3600, New York, NY 10036, USA	
Tominac, John J	*WW II Army Hero (CMH)*
3234 Taylor Road, Carmel, CA 93923, USA	
Tomita, Stan	*Photographer*
2439 St Louis Dr, Honolulu, HI 96816, USA	
Tomjanovich, Rudolph (Rudy)	*Basketball Player, Coach*
107368 Paulwood Dr, Houston, TX 77046, USA	
Tomko, Jozef Cardinal	*Religious Leader*
Villa Betania, Via Urbano VIII-16, 00165 Rome, Italy	
Tomlin, Lily	*Comedienne, Actress*
%Omnipotent Theatricalz, PO Box 27700, Los Angeles, CA 90027, USA	
Tomlinson, Charles	*Writer*
%Bristol University, English Dept, Bristol BS8 1TH, England	
Tomlinson, David	*Actor*
Brook Cottage, Mursley, Bucks, England	
Tomlinson, John	*Opera Singer*
%Music International, 13 Ardilaun Road, Highbury, London N5 2QR, England	
Tomlinson, Mel A	*Ballet Dancer*
1216 Bunche Dr, Raleigh, NC 27610, USA	
Tomowa-Sintow, Anna	*Opera Singer*
%Columbia Artists Mgmt Inc, 165 W 57th St, New York, NY 10019, USA	
Tompkins, Angel	*Actress*
9612 Vidor Dr, #101, Los Angeles, CA 90035, USA	

T

Todea - Tompkins

Tompkins, Darlene — *Actress*
15413 Hall Road, #230, Macomb, MI 48044, USA

Toms, David — *Golfer*
820 S MacArthur Blvd, #105-383, Coppell, TX 75019, USA

Tomsic, Ron — *Basketball Player*
448 Isabella Terrace, Corona del Mar, CA 92625, USA

Toneff, Robert (Bob) — *Football Player*
18 Dutch Valley Lane, San Anselmo, CA 94960, USA

Tonegawa, Susumu — *Nobel Medicine Laureate*
%Massachusetts Institute of Technology, Biology Dept, Cambridge, MA 02139, USA

Toner, Mike — *Journalist*
%Atlanta Journal-Constitution, Editorial Dept, 72 Marietta, Atlanta, GA 30303, USA

Toney, Andrew — *Basketball Player*
%Philadelphia 76ers, Veterans Stadium, PO Box 25040, Philadelphia, PA 19147, USA

Too Short — *Rap Artist*
%Pyramid Entertainment, 89 5th Ave, #700, New York, NY 10003, USA

Tooker, Gary L — *Businessman*
%Motorola Inc, 1303 E Algonquin Road, Schaumburg, IL 60196, USA

Tooker, George — *Artist*
PO Box 385, Hartland, VT 05048, USA

Toomey, Bill — *Track Athlete*
1185 Linda Vista Dr, San Marcos, CA 92069, USA

Toon, Malcolm — *Diplomat*
375 PeeDee Road, Southern Pines, NC 28387, USA

Topol, Chaim — *Actor*
%Brian Eagles, 236 Grays Inn Road, London WC1X 8HB, England

Topper, John — *Singer (Blues Traveler)*
%Monterey Peninsula Artists, 509 Hartnell St, Monterey, CA 93940, USA

Topping, Lynne — *Actress*
%Sekura/A Talent, PO Box 931779, Los Angeles, CA 90093, USA

Topping, Seymour — *Editor*
5 Heathcote Road, Scarsdale, NY 10583, USA

Torborg, Jeffrey A (Jeff) — *Baseball Player, Manager*
5208 Siesta Cove Dr, Sarasota, FL 34242, USA

Torgensen, Paul E — *Educator*
%Virginia Polytechnic Institute, President's Office, Blacksburg, VA 24061, USA

Tork, Peter — *Singer, Bassist (The Monkees)*
%16 Magazine, 233 Park Ave S, New York, NY 10003, USA

Torme, Mel — *Singer, Songwriter*
%International Ventures, 1734 Coldwater Canyon Dr, Beverly Hills, CA 90210, USA

Torn, Rip — *Actor*
%Gersh Agency, 232 N Canon Dr, Beverly Hills, CA 90210, USA

Torp, Niels A — *Architect*
Industrigaten 59, PO Box 5387, 0304 Oslo, Norway

Torrance, Thomas F — *Religious Leader, Educator*
37 Braid Farm Road, Edinburgh EH10 6LE, Scotland

Torre, Joseph P (Joe) — *Baseball Player, Manager*
Premium Point Central Dr, New Rochelle, NY 10801, USA

Torrence, Dean — *Singer (Jan & Dean), Songwriter*
18932 Gregory Lane, Huntington Beach, CA 92646, USA

Torrence, Gwen — *Track Athlete*
PO Box 361965, Decatur, GA 30036, USA

Torres, Jose — *Boxer*
364 Greenwich St, #B, New York, NY 10013, USA

Torres, Liz — *Singer, Actress*
%Hecht Harman Vukas, 1206 N Havenhurst Dr, Los Angeles, CA 90046, USA

Torretta, Gino — *Football Player*
2466 La Canada Court, Pinole, CA 94564, USA

Torrey, Bill — *Hockey Executive*
%Florida Panthers, Miami Arena, 100 NE 3rd Ave, Miami, FL 33132, USA

Torrey, Rich — *Cartoonist (Hartland)*
%King Features Syndicate, 235 E 45th St, New York, NY 10017, USA

Torrissen, Birger — *Nordic Skier*
PO Box 216, Lakeville, CT 06039, USA

Tortelier, Yan Pascal — *Conductor*
%M A de Valmalete, Building Gaceau, 11 Ave Delcasse, 75635 Paris, France

Torvill, Jayne — *Ice Dancer*
PO Box 16, Beeston, Nottingham NG9, England

Toski, Bob *Golfer*
160 Essex St, Newark, OH 43055, USA

Totenberg, Nina *Commentator*
%National Public Radio, News Dept, 615 Main Ave NW, Washington, DC 20024, USA

Totten, Robert *Movie Director*
13819 Riverside Dr, Sherman Oaks, CA 91423, USA

Totter, Audrey *Actress*
1945 Glendon Ave, #301, Los Angeles, CA 90025, USA

Touraine, Jean-Louis *Immunologist*
%Edouard-Herriot Hospital, Place d'Arsonval, 69437 Lyons Cedex 03, France

Tournier, Michel *Writer*
Le Presbytere, Choisel, 78460 Chevreuse, France

Tousey, Richard *Physicist*
4941 N Via Velazquez, Tucson, AZ 85750, USA

Toussaint, Allen *Jazz Pianist, Composer*
%Encore Booking Agency, 3530 Rue Delphine, New Orleans, LA 70131, USA

Toussaint, Beth *Actress*
%Don Buchwald, 9229 Sunset Blvd, #710, Los Angeles, CA 90069, USA

Tower, Horace L, III *Businessman*
%Stanhome Inc, 333 Western Ave, Westfield, MA 01085, USA

Tower, Joan P *Composer*
%Bard College, Music Dept, Annandale-on-Hudson, NY 12504, USA

Towers, Constance *Actress*
10263 Century Woods Dr, Los Angeles, CA 90067, USA

Towers, Kenneth *Editor*
%Chicago Sun-Times, Editorial Dept, 401 N Wabash, Chicago, IL 60611, USA

Towle, Steve *Football Player*
255 Snowfields Run, Heathrow, FL 32746, USA

Towne, Monte *Basketball Player*
%University of North Carolina/Ashville, Athletic Dept, Asheville, NC 28804, USA

Towne, Robert *Movie Director, Screenwriter*
1417 San Remo Dr, Pacific Palisades, CA 90272, USA

Towner, Ralph N *Jazz Guitarist, Pianist*
%Ted Kurland, 173 Brighton Ave, Boston, MA 02134, USA

Townes, Charles H *Nobel Physics Laureate*
%University of California, Physics Dept, Berkeley, CA 94720, USA

Townes, Harry *Actor*
201 Queensbury Dr SW, #1, Huntsville, AL 35802, USA

Townsend, Colleen *Actress*
%National Presbyterian Church, 4101 Nebraska Ave NW, Washington, DC 20016, USA

Townsend, Greg *Football Player*
%Oakland Raiders, 1220 Harbor Bay Parkway, Alameda, CA 94502, USA

Townsend, Ken W *Financier*
%Boatmen's 1st National, PO Box 25189, Oklahoma City, OK 73125, USA

Townsend, Robert *Actor*
2934 1/2 N Beverly Glen Circle, #407, Los Angeles, CA 90077, USA

Townsend, Roscoe *Religious Leader*
%Evangelical Friends, 2018 Maple St, Wichita, KS 67213, USA

Townshend, Peter *Singer, Songwriter, Guitarist (The Who)*
Boathouse, Ranelagh Dr, Twickenham, Middx TW1 1QZ, England

Townson, Ron *Singer (The Fifth Dimension)*
%Sterling/Winters, 1900 Ave of Stars, #1640, Los Angeles, CA 90067, USA

Toy, Sam *Businessman*
35 Stanhope Terrace, Lancaster Gate, London W2 2UA, England

Toyada, Eiji *Businessman*
%Toyota Motor, 1 Toyotacho, Toyota City, Aichi Prefecture 471, Japan

Toye, Wendy *Choreographer, Ballerina, Director*
%London Mgmt, 2-4 Noel St, London W1V 3RB, England

Toyoda, Shoichiro *Businessman*
%Toyota Motor, 1 Toyotacho, Toyota City, Aichi Prefecture 471, Japan

Tozzi, Giorgio *Opera Singer*
%RCA Records, 1540 Broadway, #900, New York, NY 10036, USA

Trabert, Tony *Tennis Player*
115 Knotty Pine Trail, Ponte Vedra, FL 32082, USA

Tracey, Margaret *Ballerina*
%New York City Ballet, Lincoln Center Plaza, New York, NY 10023, USA

Tracey, Patricia A *Navy Admiral*
CinC, Education & Training, HqUSN, Pentagon, Washington, DC 20370, USA

Trachta, Jeff — *Actor*
1040 N Maple St, Burbank, CA 91505, USA

Trachte, Don — *Cartoonist (Henry)*
%King Features Syndicate, 235 E 45th St, New York, NY 10017, USA

Trachtenberg, Stephen J — *Educator*
%George Washington University, President's Office, Washington, DC 20052, USA

Tracy, Arthur — *Singer, Actor*
350 W 57th St, New York, NY 10019, USA

Tracy, Michael C — *Artistic Director, Dancer*
%Pilobolus Dance Theater, PO Box 388, Washington Depot, CT 06794, USA

Tracy, Paul — *Auto Racing Driver*
%Newman/Haas Racing, 500 Tower Parkway, Lincolnshire, IL 60069, USA

Trafton, Stephen J — *Financier*
%Glendale Federal Savings, 700 N Brand Blvd, Glendale, CA 91203, USA

Trager, Milton — *Physical Therapist*
%Trager Institute, 21 Locust Ave, Mill Valley, CA 94941, USA

Trager, William — *Parasitologist*
%Rockefeller University, Parasitology Lab, 1230 York Ave, New York, NY 10021, USA

Train, Harry D, II — *Navy Admiral*
401 College Place, #10, Norfolk, VA 23510, USA

Train, Russell E — *Government Official, Environmentalist*
%World Wildlife Fund, 1250 24th St NW, Washington, DC 20037, USA

Trainor, Bernard E — *Marine Corps General*
80 Potter Pond, Lexington, MA 02173, USA

Trainor, Edward J — *Businessman*
%Standex International, 6 Manor Parkway, Salem, NH 03079, USA

Tramiel, Jack — *Businessman*
%Atari Corp, 455 S Mathilda Ave, Sunnyvale, CA 94086, USA

Tramiel, Sam — *Businessman*
%Atari Corp, 455 S Mathilda Ave, Sunnyvale, CA 94086, USA

Trammell, Alan S — *Baseball Player*
7346 Sandy Creek Lane, Battle Creek, MI 48010, USA

Trammell, Terry — *Sports Orthopedic Surgeon*
%Orthopedics-Indianapolis, 1801 N Senate Blvd, #200, Indianapolis, IN 46202, USA

Tranchell, Peter A — *Composer*
%Caius College, Music Dept, Cambridge CB2 1TA, England

Trani, Eugene P — *Educator*
%Virginia Commonwealth University, President's Office, Richmond, VA 23284, USA

Trask, Thomas E — *Religious Leader*
%Assemblies of God, 1445 Boonville Ave, Springfield, MO 65802, USA

Traub, Charles — *Photographer*
39 E 10th St, New York, NY 10003, USA

Trautmann, Richard — *Judo Athlete*
Horemansstr 29, 80636 Munich, Germany

Trautwig, Al — *Sportscaster*
%ABC-TV, Sports Dept, 77 W 66th St, New York, NY 10023, USA

Travalena, Fred — *Comedian*
4515 White Oak Place, Encino, CA 91316, USA

Travanti, Daniel J — *Actor*
1077 Melody Road, Lake Forest, IL 60045, USA

Travell, Janet G — *Physician*
40 Norfolk Ave, Northampton, MA 01060, USA

Travers, Mary — *Singer (Peter Paul & Mary)*
PO Box 135, Bearsville, NY 12409, USA

Travers, Pat — *Singer, Guitarist*
%American Bands Mgmt, PO Box 840607, Houston, TX 77284, USA

Travis, Cecil H — *Baseball Player*
2260 Highway 138, Riverdale, GA 30296, USA

Travis, Kylie — *Model, Actress*
2925 Trudy Dr, Beverly Hills, CA 90210, USA

Travis, Nancy — *Actress*
231 S Cliffwood Ave, Los Angeles, CA 90049, USA

Travis, Randy — *Singer, Songwriter, Guitarist*
%Libby Hatcher, 1610 16th Ave S, Nashville, TN 37212, USA

Travis, Stacey — *Actress*
%Geddes Agency, 1201 Greenacre Blvd, West Hollywood, CA 90046, USA

Travolta, John — *Actor*
1504 Live Oak Lane, Santa Barbara, CA 93105, USA

Traylor, Susan *Actress*
%Abrams-Rubaloff Lawrence, 8075 W 3rd St, #303, Los Angeles, CA 90048, USA
Treach *Rap Artist (Naughty By Nature)*
%Flavor Unit Mgmt, 155 Morgan St, Jersey City, NJ 07302, USA
Treadway, Edward A *Labor Leader*
%Elevator Constructors Union, 5565 Sterret Place, Columbia, MD 21044, USA
Treadway, James C, Jr *Government Official*
Laurel Ledge Farm, Croton Lake Road, RD 4, Mount Kisco, NY 10549, USA
Treadway, Kenneth *Swimming Contributor*
%Phillips Petroleum Co, Adams Building, Bartlesville, OK 74003, USA
Trebek, Alex *Entertainer*
3405 Fryman Road, Studio City, CA 91604, USA
Trebelhorn, Thomas L (Tom) *Baseball Manager*
4344 SE 26th Ave, Portland, OR 97202, USA
Tree, Michael *Violinist (Guarneri String Quartet)*
45 E 89th St, New York, NY 10128, USA
Treen, David C *Governor, LA*
%Deutsch Kerrigan Stile, 755 Magazine St, New Orleans, LA 70130, USA
Treiman, Sam B *Physicist*
60 McCosh Circle, Princeton, NJ 08540, USA
Trejos Fernandez, Jose J *President, Costa Rica*
Apartado 10 096, 1000 San Jose, Costa Rica
Trelford, Donald G *Editor*
20 Richmond Crescent, London N1 0LZ, England
Tremayne, Les *Actor*
901 S Barrington Ave, Los Angeles, CA 90049, USA
Tremblay, Mario *Hockey Player, Coach*
714 Mistassini, Lachenaie PQ J6W 5H2, Canada
Tremblay, Michael *Writer*
294 Carre St Louis, #5-E, Montreal PQ H2X 1A4, Canada
Tremlett, David R *Artist*
Broadlawns, Chipperfield Road, Bovingdon, Herts, England
Tremont, Ray C *Religious Leader*
%Volunteers of America, 3939 N Causeway Blvd, #400, Metairie, LA 70002, USA
Trenet, Charles *Singer, Songwriter*
2 Rue Anatole-France, 11100 Narbonne, France
Trent, Gary *Basketball Player*
%Portland Trail Blazers, 1 N Center Court, #200, Portland, OR 97227, USA
Tretiak, Vladislav *Hockey Player, Coach*
%Transglobal Sports, 94 Festival Dr, Toronto ON M2R 3V1, Canada
Tretyak, Ivan *Army General, Russia*
%Ministry of Defense, 34 Nanerezhnaya M Thoreza, Moscow, Russia
Trever, John *Editorial Cartoonist*
%Albuquerque Journal, 717 Silver Ave SW, Albuquerque, NM 87102, USA
Trevi, Gloria *Singer*
%Leisil Ent, Ave del Parque 67 Col Napoles, Mexico City DF 03810, Mexico
Trevino, Lee B *Golfer*
1901 W 47th Place, #200, Westwood, KS 66205, USA
Trevino, Rick *Singer*
%Dan Goodman Mgmt, PO Box 120775, Nashville, TN 37212, USA
Trevor, Claire *Actress*
%Pierre Hotel, 2 E 61st St, New York, NY 10021, USA
Trevor, William *Writer*
%Viking Press, 27 Wright's Lane, London W8, England
Treybig, James G *Businessman*
%Tandem Computers, 19333 Vallco Parkway, Cupertino, CA 95014, USA
Tribbitt, Sherman W *Governor, DE*
39 Hazel Road, Dover, DE 19901, USA
Tribe, Laurence H *Attorney, Educator*
%Harvard University, Law School, Griswold Hall, Cambridge, MA 02138, USA
Trickey, Paula *Actress*
%Halpern Assoc, 12304 Santa Monica Blvd, #104, Los Angeles, CA 90025, USA
Trickle, Dick *Auto Racing Driver*
3979 English Oak Dr, Lincolnton, NC 28092, USA
Tricky *Rap Artist, Singer, Songwriter*
%Little Big Man, 39-A Grammercy Park N, #1-C, New York, NY 10010, USA
Trigere, Pauline *Fashion Designer*
498 Fashion Ave, #10-B-5, New York, NY 10018, USA

Trigger, Sarah *Actress*
%Paradigm Agency, 10100 Santa Monica Blvd, #2500, Los Angeles, CA 90067, USA

Trillin, Calvin M *Writer*
%New Yorker Magazine, Editorial Dept, 20 W 43rd St, New York, NY 10036, USA

Trimble, Vance H *Editor*
1013 Sunset Ave, Kenton Hills, KY 41011, USA

Trinh, Eugene *Astronaut*
%Jet Propulsion Laboratory, 4800 Oak Grove Dr, Pasadena, CA 91109, USA

Trintignant, Jean-Louis *Actor*
%Artmedia, 10 Ave George V, 75008 Paris, France

Triplet, Kirk *Golfer*
29860 N 77th Place, Scottsdale, AZ 85262, USA

Trippi, Charles L (Charley) *Football Player*
125 Riverhill Court, Athens, GA 30606, USA

Tripplehorn, Jean *Actress*
350 5th Ave, #3505, New York, NY 10118, USA

Tripucka, Kelly *Basketball Player*
310 N Kings Dr, Charlotte, NC 28204, USA

Tritt, Travis *Singer, Songwriter*
PO Box 440099, Kennesaw, GA 30144, USA

Troger, Christian *Swimmer*
%I Muncher SC, Josefstr 26, 82941 Deisenhofen, Germany

Troisgros, Pierre E R *Restauranteur*
%Place Jean Troisgros, 42300 Roanne, France

Troitskaya, Natalia L *Opera Singer*
Klostergasse 37, 1170 Vienna, Austria

Trost, Barry M *Chemist*
24510 Amigos Court, Los Altos Hills, CA 94024, USA

Trost, Carlisle A H *Navy Admiral*
10405 Windsor View Dr, Rockville, MD 20854, USA

Trotman, Alexander J *Businessman*
%Ford Motor Co, American Road, Dearborn, MI 48121, USA

Trottler, Bryan J *Hockey Player, Executive, Coach*
165 Thousand Oaks Dr, Pittsburgh, PA 15241, USA

Troup, Bobby *Songwriter, Actor*
16074 Royal Oak St, Encino, CA 91436, USA

Troutt, William E *Educator*
%Belmont University, President's Office, Nashville, TN 37212, USA

Trovoada, Miguel A C L *President, Sao Tome & Principe*
%President's Office, Prago do Povo, Sao Tome, Sao Tome & Principe

Trowbridge, Alexander B, Jr *Secretary, Commerce*
1823 23rd St NW, Washington, DC 20008, USA

Trower, Robin *Singer, Guitarist*
%Stardust Mgmt, 4600 Franklin Ave, Los Angeles, CA 90027, USA

Troxel, Gary *Singer (The Fleetwoods)*
1119 Marihugh Road, Mount Vernon, WA 98273, USA

Troyat, Henri *Writer*
%Academie Francaise, 23 Quai de Conti, 75006 Paris, France

Truax, Billy *Football Player*
PO Box 96, Gulfport, MS 39502, USA

Trubshaw, Brian *Test Pilot, Businessman*
%British Aerospace, Filton, Bristol, England

Trucks, Virgil O (Fire) *Baseball Player*
36 Santarem Circle, Punta Gorda, FL 33983, USA

Trudeau, Garry B *Cartoonist (Doonesbury)*
459 Columbus Ave, #113, New York, NY 10024, USA

Trudeau, Pierre E *Prime Minister, Canada*
%Heenan Blaikie, 1250 Boul Rene-Levesque, Montreal PQ H3B 4Y1, Canada

Truitt, Anne D *Sculptor*
3506 35th St NW, Washington, DC 20016, USA

Truly, Richard H *Astronaut, Space Administrator, Admiral*
%Georgia Tech Research Institute, 400 10th St, Atlanta, GA 30332, USA

Truman, David B *Political Scientist*
Tory Hill Road, Box 308, Hillsdale, NY 12529, USA

Truman, James *Editor*
%Conde Nast Publications, 350 Madison Ave, New York, NY 10017, USA

Trump, Donald J *Businessman*
%Trump Organization, 725 5th Ave, New York, NY 10022, USA

Trump, Ivana *Businesswoman, Model*
500 Park Ave, #500, New York, NY 10022, USA

Trump, Ivanka *Model*
500 Park Ave, #500, New York, NY 10022, USA

Trumpy, Robert T (Bob), Jr *Football Player, Sportscaster*
%NBC-TV, Sports Dept, 30 Rockefeller Plaza, New York, NY 10112, USA

Trundy, Natalie *Actress*
6140 Lindenhurst Ave, Los Angeles, CA 90048, USA

Trusel, Lisa *Actress*
2350 Allview Terrace, Los Angeles, CA 90068, USA

Tryggvason, Bjarni V *Astronaut, Canada*
%Astronaut Program, 6767 Rt de l'Aeroport, St Hubert PQ J3Y 8Y9, Canada

Trynin, Jennifer *Singer, Songwriter, Guitarist*
%Rascoff/Zysblat, 110 W 57th St, #300, New York, NY 10019, USA

Trzaskoma, Richard J *Air Force General*
Commander, 22nd Air Force, Travis Air Force, CA 94535, USA

Tsang, David *Businessman*
%Oak Technology, 139 Kifer Court, Sunnyvale, CA 94086, USA

Tsao, I Fu *Chemical Engineer*
%University of Michigan, Chemical Engineering Dept, Ann Arbor, MI 48109, USA

Tschetter, Kris *Golfer*
%Ladies Professional Golf Assn, 2570 Volusia Ave, Daytona Beach, FL 32114, USA

Tschudi, Hans-Peter *President, Switzerland*
%Int'l Croix-Rouge Committee, Ave de la Paix 17, 1211 Geneva, Switzerland

Tsibliyev, Vasily *Cosmonaut*
%Potchta Kosmonavtov, Moskovskoi Oblasti, 141160 Syvisdny Goroduk, Russia

Tsoucalas, Nicholas *Judge*
%US Court of International Trade, 1 Federal Plaza, New York, NY 10278, USA

Tsui, John K *Financier*
%First Hawaiian Bank, 999 Bishop St, Honolulu, HI 96813, USA

Tsutsumi, Yoshiaki *Businessman*
%Seibu Railway, 16-15-1 Minami Ikebukuro, Toshimaku, Tokyo 171, Japan

Tubbs, Billy *Basketball Coach*
%Texas Christian University, Athletic Dept, Fort Worth, TX 76129, USA

Tucci, Stanley *Actor, Director*
%William Morris Agency, 151 S El Camino Dr, Beverly Hills, CA 90212, USA

Tuchman, Maurice *Museum Curator*
%Los Angeles Museum of Art, 5905 Wilshire Blvd, Los Angeles, CA 90036, USA

Tuck, Jessica *Actress*
%Writers & Artists, 924 Westwood Blvd, #900, Los Angeles, CA 90024, USA

Tucker, J Walter, Jr *Businessman*
%Keystone Consolidated, 5430 LBJ Freeway, Dallas, TX 75240, USA

Tucker, Marcia *Museum Official*
%New Museum of Contemporary Art, 583 Broadway, New York, NY 10012, USA

Tucker, Michael *Actor*
197 Oakdale Ave, Mill Valley, CA 94941, USA

Tucker, Robert (Bob) *Football Player*
8 Hunter Road, Hazleton, PA 18201, USA

Tucker, Tanya *Singer*
%Tanya Tucker Inc, 5200 Maryland Way, #202, Brentwood, TN 37027, USA

Tucker, William E *Educator*
%Texas Christian University, Chancellor's Office, Fort Worth, TX 76129, USA

Tuckwell, Barry E *Concert French Hornist, Conductor*
13140 Fountain Head Road, Hagerstown, MD 21742, USA

Tudjman, Franjo *President, Croatia*
%President's Office, Presidential Palace, Zagreb, Croatia

Tudor, John T *Baseball Player*
31 Upton Hills Lane, Middleton, MA 01949, USA

Tuerff, James R *Businessman*
%American General Corp, 2929 Allen Parkway, Houston, TX 77019, USA

Tugwell, John *Financier*
%National Westminster Bank, 10 Exchange Place, Jersey City, NJ 07302, USA

Tully, Daniel P *Businessman*
%Merrill Lynch Co, World Financial Center North, 32 Vesey St, New York, NY 10007, USA

Tully, Darrow *Publisher*
9862 Bridgeton Dr, Tampa, FL 33626, USA

Tumanishvili, Mikhail I *Theater Director*
Barnova Str 126-A, #8, 380079 Tbilsi, Georgia

Tumi, Christian W Cardinal *Religious Leader*
Archeveche, BP 272, Douala, Cameroon

Tune, Thomas J (Tommy) *Dancer, Actor, Theater Director*
1501 Broadway, #1508, New York, NY 10036, USA

Tunney, John V *Senator, CA*
106 Esparta Way, Santa Monica, CA 90402, USA

Tunney, Robin *Actress*
%William Morris Agency, 1325 Ave of Americas, New York, NY 10019, USA

Tunnick, George *Association Executive*
%National Assn of Female Executives, 127 W 24th St, New York, NY 10011, USA

Tupouto'a *Crown Prince, Tonga*
%The Palace, PO Box 6, Nuku'alofa, Tonga

Tupper, C John *Physician, Educator*
PO Box 2007, El Macera, CA 95618, USA

Turco, Paige *Actress*
%Gersh Agency, 232 N Canon Dr, Beverly Hills, CA 90210, USA

Turco, Richard P *Atmospheric Scientist*
%R&D Assoc, 4640 Admiralty Way, Marina del Rey, CA 90292, USA

Turcotte, Ron *Thoroughbred Racing Jockey*
PO Box 215, Van Buren, ME 04785, USA

Tureck, Rosalyn *Concert Pianist*
%Tureck Bach Institute, 215 E 68th St, New York, NY 10021, USA

Turgeon, Pierre *Hockey Player*
%St Louis Blues, Kiel Center, 1401 Clark Ave, St Louis, MO 63103, USA

Turkel, Ann *Actress*
9877 Beverly Grove Dr, Beverly Hills, CA 90210, USA

Turkevich, Anthony L *Chemist*
175 Briarwood Loop, Briarwood Lakes, Hinsdale, IL 60523, USA

Turley, Robert L (Bob) *Baseball Player*
PO Box 607, Jasper, GA 30143, USA

Turley, Stewart *Businessman*
%Eckerd Corp, PO Box 4689, Clearwater, FL 33758, USA

Turman, Glynn *Actor*
%Paradigm Agency, 10100 Santa Monica Blvd, #2500, Los Angeles, CA 90067, USA

Turnbull, David *Physicist*
29 Concord Ave, #715, Cambridge, MA 02138, USA

Turnbull, Renaldo *Football Player*
88 Oriole St, New Orleans, LA 70124, USA

Turnbull, William *Artist*
%Waddington Galleries, 11 Cork St, London W1, England

Turner, Cathy *Speed Skater*
PO Box 67747, Rochester, NY 14617, USA

Turner, Clyde (Bulldog) *Football Player*
10240 FM 116, Gatesville, TX 76528, USA

Turner, Edwin L *Astrophysicist*
%Princeton University, Astrophysical Sciences Dept, Princeton, NJ 08544, USA

Turner, Eric *Football Player*
2719 Yucca Dr, Camarillo, CA 93012, USA

Turner, Francis J *Geologist*
2525 Hill Court, Berkeley, CA 94708, USA

Turner, Guinevere *Actress*
%Gersh Agency, 130 W 42nd St, #1804, New York, NY 10036, USA

Turner, Ike *Singer, Songwriter*
905 Viewpoint Dr, San Marcos, CA 92069, USA

Turner, James A (Jim) *Football Player*
14155 W 59th Place, Arvada, CO 80004, USA

Turner, James R *Baseball Player*
1004 Woodmont Blvd, Nashville, TN 37204, USA

Turner, James T *Judge*
%US Claims Court, 717 Madison Place NW, Washington, DC 20005, USA

Turner, Janine *Actress*
8301 Boat Club Road, #1211, Fort Worth, TX 76179, USA

Turner, John G *Businessman*
%NWNL Companies, 20 Washington Ave S, Minneapolis, MN 55401, USA

Turner, John N *Prime Minister, Canada*
27 Dunloe Road, Toronto ON M4V 2W4, Canada

Turner, Kathleen *Actress*
163 Amsterdam Ave, #210, New York, NY 10023, USA

Turner, Morrie *Cartoonist (Wee Pals)*
2761 Dohr St, Berkeley, CA 94702, USA
Turner, Norv *Football Coach*
%Washington Redskins, 21300 Redskin Park Dr, Ashburn, VA 20147, USA
Turner, R Gerald *Educator*
%University of Mississippi, Chancellor's Office, University, MS 38677, USA
Turner, Robert E (Ted), III *Communications, Sports Executive*
%Time Warner Inc, 75 Rockefeller Plaza, New York, NY 10019, USA
Turner, Sammy *Singer*
%British & Int'l Artists, 500 Waterman Ave, #191, East Providence, RI 02914, USA
Turner, Sherri *Golfer*
5001 Millstaff Dr, Oak Ridge, NC 27310, USA
Turner, Stansfield *Navy Admiral, Government Official*
1320 Skipwith Road, McLean, VA 22101, USA
Turner, Tina *Singer, Actress*
%Creative Artists Agency, 9830 Wilshire Blvd, Beverly Hills, CA 90212, USA
Turner, William B *Financier*
%Synovus Financial Corp, 901 Front St, Columbus, GA 31901, USA
Turner, William C *Diplomat*
4350 Camelback Road, #240-B, Phoenix, AZ 85018, USA
Turnesa, Mike *Golfer*
68 Hartsdale Road, Elmsford, NY 10523, USA
Turnesa, Willie *Golfer*
28 Barksdale Road, White Plains, NY 10607, USA
Turnley, David C *Photographer*
%Detroit Free Press, 321 W Lafayette Blvd, Detroit, MI 48226, USA
Turnquest, Orville A *Governor General, Bahamas*
%Government House, Government Hill, PO Box N-8301, Nassau NP, Bahamas
Turow, Scott F *Writer*
%Sonnenschein Carlin Nath Rosenthal, Sears Tower, #8000, Chicago, IL 60606, USA
Turpin, Melvin *Basketball Player*
606 N Center St, Clinton, IL 61727, USA
Turre, Steve *Jazz Trombonist*
%Brad Simon Organization, 122 E 57th St, #400, New York, NY 10022, USA
Turrell, James *Artist*
%Skystone Foundation, 9000 Hutton Ranch Road, Flagstaff, AZ 86004, USA
Turrentine, Stanley W *Jazz Saxophonist*
%La Place Music, PO Box 44555, Fort Washington, MD 20749, USA
Turro, Nicholas J *Chemist*
125 Downey Dr, Tenafly, NJ 07670, USA
Turteltaub, Jon *Movie Director*
%Endeavor Talent Agency, 9701 Wilshire Blvd, #1000, Beverly Hills, CA 90212, USA
Turturro, John *Actor*
16 N Oak St, Ventura, CA 93001, USA
Turturro, Nicholas *Actor*
%Abrams Artists, 9200 Sunset Blvd, #625, Los Angeles, CA 90069, USA
Tusher, Thomas W *Businessman*
%Levi Strauss Assoc, 1155 Battery St, San Francisco, CA 94111, USA
Tushingham, Rita *Actress*
%Lip Service, 4 Kingly St, London W1R 5LF, England
Tusquets Blanca, Oscar *Architect*
%Tusquets Diaz Assoc, Cavallers 50, 08034 Barcelona, Spain
Tutin, Dorothy *Actress*
%Michael Whitehall, 125 Gloucester Road, London SW7 4TE, England
Tutone, Tommy *Singer, Dancer*
%International Creative Mgmt, 40 W 57th St, New York, NY 10019, USA
Tuttle, O Frank *Geochemist*
PO Box 16, Greer, AZ 85927, USA
Tuttle, William G T, Jr *Army General*
%Logistics Management Institute, 2000 Corporate Ridge, Mc Lean, VA 22102, USA
Tutu, Desmond M *Nobel Peace Laureate, Religious Leader*
Bishopscourt, Claremont Cape 7700, South Africa
Twain, Shania *Singer, Songwriter*
%Mary Bailey Mgmt, 4 Al Wende Ave, Kirkland Lakes ON P2N 3J5, Canada
Twardzik, Dave *Basketball Player, Executive*
%Golden State Warriors, 7000 Coliseum Way, Oakland, CA 94621, USA
Tway, Bob *Golfer*
PO Box 4030, Edmond, OK 73083, USA

Tweed, John N — *Religious Leader*
%Reformed Presbyterian Church, 1117 E Devonshire Ave, Phoenix, AZ 85014, USA

Tweed, Shannon — *Actress, Model*
2650 Benedict Canyon Dr, Beverly Hills, CA 90210, USA

Twibell, Roger — *Sportscaster*
%ABC-TV, Sports Dept, 77 W 66th St, New York, NY 10023, USA

Twiggy (Leslie Lawson) — *Model, Actress*
%Shulman, St George's House, 15 Hanover Square, London W1R 9AJ, England

Twilley, Dwight — *Singer, Songwriter*
%Paradise Artists, 108 E Matilija St, Ojai, CA 93023, USA

Twilley, Howard — *Football Player*
3109 S Columbia Circle, Tulsa, OK 74105, USA

Twohy, Robert — *Cartoonist*
%New Yorker Magazine, Editorial Dept, 20 W 43rd St, New York, NY 10036, USA

Twombly, Cy — *Artist*
%Leo Castelli Gallery, 420 W Broadway, New York, NY 10012, USA

Twomey, William P — *Businessman*
%LTV Corp, 200 Public Square, Cleveland, OH 44114, USA

Twyman, John K (Jack) — *Businessman, Basketball Player*
%Super Food Services, 3233 Newmark Dr, Miamisburg, OH 45342, USA

Tyabji, Hatim A — *Businessman*
%VeriFone, 3 Lagoon Dr, Redwood City, CA 94065, USA

Tydings, Joseph D — *Senator, MD*
%Anderson Kill Olick, 2000 Pennsylvania NW, #7500, Washington, DC 20006, USA

Tyers, Kathy — *Writer*
%Martha Millard Agency, 204 Park Ave, Madison, NJ 07940, USA

Tygart, W Barger — *Businessman*
%J C Penney Co, PO Box 10001, Dallas, TX 75301, USA

Tyler, Anne — *Writer*
222 Tunbridge Road, Baltimore, MD 21212, USA

Tyler, Bonnie — *Singer, Songwriter*
%Station Agency, 132 Liverpool Road, London N1 1LA, England

Tyler, Harold R, Jr — *Attorney*
%Patterson Belknap Webb Tyler, 30 Rockefeller Plaza, New York, NY 10112, USA

Tyler, Liv — *Actress*
%Creative Artists Agency, 9830 Wilshire Blvd, Beverly Hills, CA 90212, USA

Tyler, Robert — *Actor*
%Innovative Artists, 1999 Ave of Stars, #2850, Los Angeles, CA 90067, USA

Tyler, Steven — *Singer (Aerosmith), Songwriter*
%Collins Mgmt, 101 Huntington Ave, #2575, Boston, MA 02199, USA

Tyler, Wendell — *Football Player*
2647 Ryans Place, Lancaster, CA 93536, USA

Tylo, Hunter — *Actress*
%Innovative Artists, 1999 Ave of Stars, #2850, Los Angeles, CA 90067, USA

Tyner, Charles — *Actor*
%Dade/Schultz, 11846 Ventura Blvd, #100, Studio City, CA 91604, USA

Tyner, McCoy — *Jazz Pianist, Composer*
%JLM, 590 Broadway, #1005, New York, NY 10012, USA

Tyra, Charlie — *Basketball Player*
901 Stoneykirk Dr, Louisville, KY 40223, USA

Tyrrell, Susan — *Actress*
1489 Scott Ave, Los Angeles, CA 90026, USA

Tyson, Cathy — *Actress*
%Peters Fraser Dunlop, Chelsea Harbour, Lots Rd, London SW10 0XF, England

Tyson, Cicely — *Actress*
315 W 70th St, New York, NY 10023, USA

Tyson, Michael G (Mike) — *Boxer*
6740 Tomiyasu Lane, Las Vegas, NV 89120, USA

Tyson, Richard — *Actor*
%Parker Public Relations, 11500 W Olympic Blvd, #400, Los Angeles, CA 90064, USA

Tyus, Wyomia — *Track Athlete*
1102 Keniston Ave, Los Angeles, CA 90019, USA

Tyzack, Margaret — *Actress*
%Joyce Edwards, 275 Kennington Road, London SE1 6BY, England

Udvari, Frank — Hockey Referee
504-250 Glenridge Dr, Waterloo ON N2J 1H8, Canada
Ueberroth, Peter V — Baseball Executive, Olympics Official
%Adia Services, 100 Redwood Shores Parkway, Redwood City, CA 94065, USA
Uelses, John — Track Athlete
3846 Exception Place, Escondido, CA 92025, USA
Uemura, Ko — Financier
%Fuji Bank & Trust, 1 World Trade Center, New York, NY 10048, USA
Uggams, Leslie — Singer, Actress
3 Lincoln Center, New York, NY 10023, USA
Uhry, Alfred F — Writer
%Marshall Purdy, 226 W 47th St, #900, New York, NY 10036, USA
Ujiie, Junichi — Financier
%Nomura Securities, 2 World Financial Center, 200 Liberty St, New York, NY 10281, USA
Ulanova, Galina S — Ballerina
%Bolshoi Theater, Teatralnaya Pl 1, 103009 Moscow, Russia
Ulland, Olav — Skier
2664 W Lake Sammamish Parkway SE, Bellevue, WA 98008, USA
Ullman, Norman — Hockey Player
25 Austin Dr, #819, Unionville ON L3R 8H4, Canada
Ullman, Tracey — Comedienne
3800 La Crescenta Ave, #209, La Crescenta, CA 91214, USA
Ullmann, Liv — Actress
101 W 79th St, #8-F, New York, NY 10024, USA
Ullsten, Ola — Prime Minister, Sweden
%Folkpartiet, PO Box 6508, 113 83 Stockholm, Sweden
Ulmanis, Guntis — President, Latvia
%President's Office, Supreme Council, 11 Jeraba St, Riga 22681 PDP, Latvia
Ulrich, Kim Johnston — Actress
%SDB Partners, 1801 Ave of Stars, #902, Los Angeles, CA 90067, USA
Ulrich, Robert J — Businessman
%Dayton Hudson, 777 Nicollet Mall, Minneapolis, MN 55402, USA
Ulrich, Skeet — Actor
%International Creative Mgmt, 8942 Wilshire Blvd, Beverly Hills, CA 90211, USA
Ulrich, Thomas — Boxer
Brunsbutteler Damm 29, 13581 Berlin, Germany
Ultmann, John E — Physician
5632 S Harper St, Chicago, IL 60637, USA
Ulusu, Bulent — Prime Minister, Turkey; Navy Admiral
Ciftehavuzlar Yesilbahar 50-K 8/27, Kadikoy/Istanbul, Turkey
Ulvaeus, Bjorn — Singer (ABBA), Composer
%Gorel Hanser, Sodra Brobanken 41A, Skeppsholmen, 111 49 Stockholm, Sweden
Ulvang, Vegard — Cross Country Skier
Fjellveien 53, 9900 Kirkenes, Norway
Umar Bin Hassan — Rap Artist (The Last Poets)
%Agency Group, 1775 Broadway, #433, New York, NY 10019, USA
Unanue, Emil R — Pathologist
%Washington University Medical School, Pathology Dept, St Louis, MO 63110, USA
Underwood, Benton J — Psychologist
1745 Stevens Dr, Glenview, IL 60025, USA
Underwood, Blair — Actor
4116 W Magnolia Blvd, #101, Burbank, CA 91505, USA
Underwood, Cecil H — Governor, WV
609 13th Ave, Huntington, WV 25701, USA
Underwood, Jay — Actor
%Paul Kohner, 9300 Wilshire Blvd, #555, Beverly Hills, CA 90212, USA
Ung Huot — Prime Minister, Cambodia
%Prime Minister's Office, Supreme National Council, Phnom Penh, Cambodia
Ungaro, Emanuel M — Fashion Designer
2 Ave du Montaigne, 75008 Paris, France
Ungaro, Susan Kelliher — Editor
%Family Circle Magazine, Editorial Dept, 110 5th Ave, New York, NY 10011, USA
Unger, Deborah Kara — Actress
%International Creative Mgmt, 8942 Wilshire Blvd, Beverly Hills, CA 90211, USA
Unger, Jim — Cartoonist (Herman)
%Universal Press Syndicate, 4520 Main St, Kansas City, KS 64111, USA
Unger, Kay — Fashion Designer
%Saint Gillian Sportswear, 498 7th Ave, New York, NY 10018, USA

Unger, Leonard *Diplomat*
31 Amherst Road, Belmont, MA 02178, USA

Ungers, Oswald M *Architect*
Belvederestr 60, 50933 Cologne, Germany

Unitas, John C (Johnny) *Football Player*
5607 Patterson Road, Baldwin, MD 21013, USA

Unseld, Westley S (Wes) *Basketball Player, Coach, Executive*
2210 Cedar Circle Dr, Baltimore, MD 21228, USA

Unser, Alfred (Al) *Auto Racing Driver*
7625 Central Ave NW, Albuquerque, NM 87121, USA

Unser, Alfred (Al), Jr *Auto Racing Driver*
6847 Rio Grande Blvd, Albuquerque, NM 87107, USA

Unser, Robert W (Bobby) *Auto Racing Driver*
656 N MacDonald St, Mesa, AZ 85201, USA

Upbin, Hal J *Businessman*
%Kellwood Co, 600 Kellwood Parkway, St Louis, MO 63017, USA

Updike, John H *Writer*
675 Hale St, Beverly Farms, MA 01915, USA

Uphoff-Becker, Nicole *Equestrian Rider*
Freiherr-von-Lanen-Str 15, 48231 Warendorf, Germany

Upshaw, Dawn *Opera Singer*
%Columbia Artists Mgmt Inc, 165 W 57th St, New York, NY 10019, USA

Upshaw, Eugene (Gene) *Football Player, Labor Leader*
1102 Pepper Tree Dr, Great Falls, VA 22066, USA

Upton, Arthur C *Physician*
401 E 86th St, #12-B, New York, NY 10028, USA

Urbanchek, Jon *Swimming Coach*
%University of Michigan, Athletic Dept, Ann Arbor, MI 48109, USA

Ure, Midge *Singer, Guitarist*
%International Talent Group, 729 7th Ave, #1600, New York, NY 10019, USA

Urich, Robert *Actor*
10061 Riverside Dr, #1026, Toluca Lake, CA 91602, USA

Uris, Leon M *Writer*
PO Box 1559, Aspen, CO 81612, USA

Urist, Marshall R *Orthopedic Surgeon*
%University of California, Medical Center, Ortho/Bone Lab, Los Angeles, CA 90024, USA

Urkal, Oklay *Boxer*
Bautzener Str 4, 10829 Berlin, Germany

Urmanov, Aleksei *Figure Skater*
%Union of Skaters, Luzhnetskaya Nab 8, Moscow 119871, Russia

Urmson, Claire *Model*
%Ford Model Agency, 344 E 59th St, New York, NY 10022, USA

Urquhart, Brian E *Diplomat*
131 E 66th St, New York, NY 10021, USA

Urquhart, Lawrence M *Businessman*
%Burmah Oil, Burmah House, Pipers Way, Swindon, Wilts SN3 1RE, England

Urshan, Nathaniel A *Religious Leader*
%United Pentecostal Church International, 8855 Dunn Road, Hazelwood, MO 63042, USA

Ursi, Corrado Cardinal *Religious Leader*
Via Capodimonte 13, 80136 Naples, Italy

Usachev, Yuri *Cosmonaut*
%Potchta Kosmonavtov, Moskovskoi Oblasti, 141160 Syvisdny Goroduk, Russia

Usery, William J, Jr *Secretary, Labor*
2400 Virginia Ave, Washington, DC 20037, USA

Usher, Thomas J *Businessman*
%USX Corp, 600 Grant St, Pittsburgh, PA 15219, USA

Ustinov, Peter *Actor*
11 Rue de Silly, 92100 Boulogne, France

Ut, Nick *Photographer*
%Associated Press, Photo Dept, 221 S Figueroa St, #300, Los Angeles, CA 90012, USA

Uteem, Cassam *President, Mauritius*
%President's Office, Le Reduit, Port Louis, Mauritius

Utley, Garrick *Commentator*
%ABC-TV, News Dept, 8 Carburton St, London W1P 7DT, England

Utley, Stan *Golfer*
PO Box 6024, Columbia, MO 65205, USA

Utzon, Jorn *Architect*
%General Delivery, 3150 Hellebaek, Denmark

Vacariou, Nicolae — *Prime Minister, Romania*
%Prime Minister's Office, Piata Victoriei 1, 71201 Bucharest, Romania

Vaccaro, Brenda — *Actress*
17641 Tarzana St, Encino, CA 91316, USA

Vachon, Louis-Albert Cardinal — *Religious Leader*
%Seminaire de Quebec, 1 Rue des Remparts, Quebec QC G1R 5LY, Canada

Vachon, Rogatien R (Rogie) — *Hockey Player, Coach, Executive*
7033 Trolleyway St, Playa Del Rey, CA 90293, USA

Vachss, Andrew H — *Writer*
299 Broadway, #1800, New York, NY 10007, USA

Vadim, Roger P — *Movie Director*
316 Alta Ave, Santa Monica, CA 90402, USA

Vaduva, Leontina — *Opera Singer*
%Royal Opera House, Covent Garden, Bow St, London WC2, England

Vaea of Houma, Baron — *Prime Minister, Tonga*
%Prime Minister's Office, Nuku'alofa, Tonga

Vagelos, P Roy — *Businessman, Biochemist*
1 Crossroads Dr, 500 Building "A", Bedminster, NJ 07921, USA

Vago, Pierre — *Architect*
Le Valparon, 77123 Noisy-sur-Ecole, France

Vahi, Tiit — *Prime Minister, Estonia*
%Tallinn City Council, Tallinn, Estonia

Vail, Thomas — *Editor*
%Cleveland Plain Dealer, Editorial Dept, 1801 Superior, Cleveland, OH 44114, USA

Vajiralongkorn — *Crown Prince, Thailand*
%Chitralada a Villa, Bangkok, Thailand

Vajna, Andrew — *Movie Producer*
%Cinergi Productions, 2308 Broadway, Burbank, CA 90404, USA

Vajpayee, Atal Bihari — *Prime Minister, India*
6 Raisina Road, New Delhi 110011, India

Valar, Paul — *Skier*
PO Box 906, Franconia, NH 03580, USA

Valdez, Luis — *Writer*
%El Teatro Capesino, 705 4th St, San Juan Bautista, CA 95045, USA

Vale, Jerry — *Singer*
1100 N Alta Loma Road, #1404, Los Angeles, CA 90069, USA

Valen, Nancy — *Actress*
15535 Riverside Dr, #4, Sherman Oaks, CA 91423, USA

Valente, Benita — *Opera Singer*
%Anthony Checchia, 135 S 18th St, Philadelphia, PA 19103, USA

Valente, Catarina — *Singer*
Via ai Ronci 12, 6816 Bissone, Switzerland

Valenti, Carl M — *Publisher*
%Information Services, Dow Jones Telerate, 200 Liberty St, New York, NY 10281, USA

Valenti, Jack J — *Association Executive*
%Motion Picture Assn, 1600 "I" St NW, Washington, DC 20006, USA

Valentic, Nikica — *Prime Minister, Croatia*
%Prime Minister's Office, Radicev Tug 7, 41000 Zagreb, Croatia

Valentine, Darnell — *Basketball Player*
7546 SW Ashford St, Tigard, OR 97224, USA

Valentine, DeWain — *Artist*
59-230 Alapio Road, Haleiwa, HI 96712, USA

Valentine, Karen — *Actress*
PO Box 1410, Washington Depot, CT 06793, USA

Valentine, Raymond C — *Agronomist*
%University of California, Plant Growth Laboratory, Davis, CA 95616, USA

Valentine, Robert J (Bobby) — *Baseball Player, Manager*
4102 Flower Garden Dr, Arlington, TX 76016, USA

Valentine, Scott — *Actor*
662 N Van Ness Ave, #305, Los Angeles, CA 90004, USA

Valentine, William N — *Physician*
PO Box 4698, Sun River, OR 97707, USA

Valentini Terrani, Lucia — *Opera Singer*
Piazza Cavour 4, 35100 Padova, Italy

Valentino (Garavani) — *Fashion Designer*
Palazzo Mignanelli, Piazza Mignanelli 22, 00187 Rome, Italy

Valenzuela, Fernando — *Baseball Player*
3004 N Beachwood Dr, Los Angeles, CA 90068, USA

V

Vacariou - Valenzuela

Valeriani, Richard G — *Commentator*
23 Island View Dr, Sherman, CT 06784, USA

Valet, Julia — *Model*
%Ford Model Agency, 344 E 59th St, New York, NY 10022, USA

Vallee, Bert L — *Biochemist, Physician*
56 Browne St, Brookline, MA 02146, USA

Vallee, Roy — *Businessman*
%Avnet Inc, 80 Cutter Mill Road, Great Neck, NY 11021, USA

Valletta, Amber — *Model*
%Boss Models, 1 Gansevoort St, New York, NY 10014, USA

Valley, Mark — *Actor*
%Gersh Agency, 232 N Canon Dr, Beverly Hills, CA 90210, USA

Valli, Alida — *Actress*
%G Perrone Elisabetta Morea, Viale Liegi 42, 00198 Rome, Italy

Valli, Frankie — *Singer*
5603 N Winton Court, Calabasas, CA 91302, USA

Vallone, Raf — *Actor*
%Anne Alvares, Correa Panis, 18 Rue Troyon, 75017 Paris, France

Valo, Elmer W — *Baseball Player*
571 Columbia Ave, Palmerton, PA 18071, USA

Valot, Daniel L — *Businessman*
%Total Petroleum, 900 19th St, Denver, CO 80202, USA

Valtman, Edmund S — *Editorial Cartoonist*
80 Loeffler Road, #G-301, Bloomfield, CT 06002, USA

Van Allan, Richard — *Opera Singer*
18 Octavia St, London SW11 3DN, England

Van Allen, James A — *Physicist*
5 Woodland Mounds Road, RFD 6, Iowa City, IA 52245, USA

Van Almsick, Franziska (Franzi) — *Swimmer*
Wandsbeker Zolistr 82-90, 22041 Hamburg, Germany

Van Amerongen, Jerry — *Cartoonist (The Neighborhood)*
%King Features Syndicate, 235 E 45th St, New York, NY 10017, USA

Van Andel, Jay — *Businessman*
%Amway Corp, 7575 E Fulton St E, Ada, MI 49355, USA

Van Ark, Joan — *Actress*
10950 Alta View Dr, Studio City, CA 91604, USA

Van Arsdale, Dick — *Basketball Player, Executive*
6422 N 30th Place, Phoenix, AZ 85016, USA

Van Arsdale, Tom — *Basketball Player*
7510 N Eucalyptus Dr, Scottsdale, AZ 85253, USA

Van Auken, John A — *Tennis Contributor*
%Canadian Tennis Technology, PO Box 1538, Sydney NS B1P 6R7, Canada

Van Basten, Marco — *Soccer Player*
%AC Milan, Via Turati 3, 20121 Milan, Italy

Van Breda Kolff, Bill (Butch) — *Basketball Coach*
1005 Warwick Court, Sun City Center, FL 33573, USA

Van Buren (Pauline Phillips), Abigail — *Columnist (Dear Abby)*
%Phillips-Van Buren Inc, 1900 Ave of Stars, #2710, Los Angeles, CA 90067, USA

Van Buren, Steve W — *Football Player*
4726 Benner St, Philadelphia, PA 19135, USA

Van Citters, Robert L — *Physiologist, Biophysicist*
%University of Washington Medical School, Physiology Dept, Seattle, WA 98815, USA

Van Dam, Jose — *Opera Singer*
%Zurich Artists, Rutistr 52, 8044 Zurich-Gockhausen, Switzerland

Van Damme, Jean-Claude — *Actor*
PO Box 4149, Chatsworth, CA 91313, USA

Van Dantzig, Rudi — *Choreographer*
Emma-Straat 27, Amsterdam, Netherlands

Van de Ven, Monique — *Actress*
%Marion Rosenberg, 8428 Melrose Place, #C, Los Angeles, CA 90069, USA

Van de Wetering, John E — *Educator*
%State University of New York, President's Office, Brockport, NY 14420, USA

Van den Berg, Lodewijk — *Astronaut*
%EG&G Corp, 130 Robin Hill Road, Goleta, CA 93117, USA

Van den Haag, Ernest — *Attorney, Writer*
118 W 79th St, New York, NY 10024, USA

Van der Klugt, Cor J — *Businessman*
%Phillip Gloeilampenfabrieken, 5621 CT Eindhoven, Netherlands

Van der Meer, Simon *Nobel Physics Laureate*
4 Chemin des Corbillettes, 1218 GD-Saconnex, Switzerland
Van Deventer, Neill *Publisher*
%Cleveland Plain Dealer, 1801 Superior Ave, Cleveland, OH 44114, USA
Van Devere, Trish *Actress*
3211 Retreat Court, Malibu, CA 90265, USA
Van Dien, Casper *Actor*
11837 Courtleigh Dr, #5, Los Angeles, CA 90066, USA
Van Doren, Mamie *Actress*
428 31st St, Newport Beach, CA 92663, USA
Van Dreelen, John *Actor*
%Paul Kohner, 9300 Wilshire Blvd, #555, Beverly Hills, CA 90212, USA
Van Dusen, Granville *Actor*
2161 Ridgemont Dr, Los Angeles, CA 90046, USA
Van Duyn, Mona J *Writer*
7505 Teasdale Ave, St Louis, MO 63130, USA
Van Dyke, Barry *Actor*
27800 Blythdale Road, Agoura, CA 91301, USA
Van Dyke, Dick *Actor*
%William Morris Agency, 151 S El Camino Dr, Beverly Hills, CA 90212, USA
Van Dyke, Jerry *Actor*
1705 Jameson St, Benton, AR 72015, USA
Van Dyke, Leroy *Singer*
%Leroy Van Dyke Enterprises, 29000 Highway V, Smithton, MO 65350, USA
Van Dyke, William G *Businessman*
%Donaldson Co, 1400 W 94th St, Minneapolis, MN 55431, USA
Van Eeghen, Mark *Football Player*
90 Woodstock Lane, Cranston, RI 02920, USA
Van Excel, Nick *Basketball Player*
4209 50th St, #2, Kenosha, WI 53144, USA
Van Halen, Alex *Drummer (Van Halen)*
12024 Summit Circle, Beverly Hills, CA 90210, USA
Van Halen, Eddie *Singer, Guitarist (Van Halen)*
31736 Broad Beach Road, Malibu, CA 90265, USA
Van Hamel, Martine *Ballerina*
%Peter S Diggins Assoc, 133 W 71st St, New York, NY 10023, USA
Van Hellmond, Andy *Hockey Referee*
75 International Blvd, #300, Rexdale ON M9W 6L9, Canada
Van Hoften, James C D A *Astronaut*
%Bechtel Defense & Space Organization, 50 Beale St, San Francisco, CA 94105, USA
Van Horn, Keith *Basketball Player*
%New Jersey Nets, Byrne Meadowlands Arena, East Rutherford, NJ 07073, USA
Van Meter, Victoria (Vicki) *Pilot*
%James Van Meter, 902 Grove St, Meadville, PA 16335, USA
Van Pallandt, Nina *Actress, Singer*
845 E 6th St, Los Angeles, CA 90021, USA
Van Patten, Dick *Actor*
13920 Magnolia Blvd, Sherman Oaks, CA 91423, USA
Van Patten, Jimmy *Actor*
14111 Riverside Dr, #15, Sherman Oaks, CA 91423, USA
Van Patten, Joyce *Actress*
9220 Sunset Blvd, #206, Los Angeles, CA 90069, USA
Van Patten, Nels *Actor*
12439 Magnolia Blvd, #197, North Hollywood, CA 91607, USA
Van Patten, Timothy *Actor*
7461 Beverly Blvd, #400, Los Angeles, CA 90036, USA
Van Patten, Vincent *Actor*
13926 Magnolia Blvd, Sherman Oaks, CA 91423, USA
Van Peebles, Mario *Actor*
853 7th Ave, #3-E, New York, NY 10019, USA
Van Pelt, Brad *Football Player*
501 State St, Santa Barbara, CA 93101, USA
Van Riper, Paul K *Marine Corps General*
CG, Combat Development Command, 300 Russell Road, Quantico, VA 22134, USA
Van Runkle, Theodora *Fashion Designer*
8805 Lookout Mountain Road, Los Angeles, CA 90046, USA
Van Ryn, John *Tennis Player*
315 S Lake Dr, Palm Beach, FL 33480, USA

V

Van der Meer - Van Ryn

Van Sant, Gus, Jr — *Movie Director*
%Addis-Wechsler, 955 S Carillo Dr, Los Angeles, CA 90048, USA

Van Sant, R William — *Businessman*
%Lukens Inc, 50 S 1st Ave, Coatesville, PA 19320, USA

Van Staveren, Petra — *Swimmer*
%Olympic Committee, Surinamestraar 33, 2585 Le Harve, Netherlands

Van Stekelenburg, Mark — *Businessman*
%Rykoff-Sexton Inc, 761 Terminal St, Los Angeles, CA 90021, USA

Van Tamelen, Eugene E — *Chemist*
23570 Camino Hermoso Dr, Los Altos Hills, CA 94024, USA

Van Tuyl, Cecil — *Businessman*
%V T Inc, 8500 Shawnee Mission Parkway, Merriam, KS 66202, USA

Van Ummerson, Claire A — *Educator*
%Cleveland State University, President's Office, Cleveland, OH 44115, USA

Van Valkenburgh, Deborah — *Actress*
2025 Stanley Hills Dr, Los Angeles, CA 90046, USA

Van Voreen, Monique — *Actress*
165 E 66th St, New York, NY 10021, USA

Van Wachem, Loedwijk C — *Businessman*
Royal Dutch/Shell, 30 Carel van Bylandtaan, 2596 HR The Hague, Netherlands

Van Zant, Steve — *Singer, Songwriter*
322 W 57th St, New York, NY 10019, USA

Van, Allen — *Hockey Player*
4890 Ashley Lane, #206, Inver Grove Heights, MN 55077, USA

Vanbiesbrouck, John — *Hockey Player*
272 W Thatch Palm Dr, Boca Raton, FL 33432, USA

Vance, Cyrus R — *Secretary, State*
%Simpson Thatcher Bartlett, 425 Lexington Ave, New York, NY 10017, USA

Vandenburgh, Jane — *Writer*
%North Point Press, 1563 Solano Ave, #353, Berkeley, CA 94707, USA

Vander Jagt, Guy — *Representative, MI*
%Baker & Hostetler, 1050 Connecticut Ave NW, Washington, DC 20036, USA

Vanderberg Shaw, Helen — *Synchronized Swimming Coach*
%Heaven's Fitness, 301 14th St NW, Calgary AL T2N 2A1, Canada

Vanderbilt, Gloria — *Fashion Designer*
62 W 47th St, New York, NY 10036, USA

Vanderhoef, Larry N — *Educator*
%University of California, President's Office, Davis, CA 95616, USA

Vanderhoof, John D — *Governor, CO*
%Club Twenty, 845 Grand, Grand Junction, CO 81501, USA

Vandermeersch, Bernard — *Anthropologist*
%University of Bordeaux, Anthropology Dept, Bordeaux, France

Vanderstar, Cornelius C — *Businessman*
%International Aluminum Corp, 767 Monterey Pass Road, Monterey Park, CA 91754, USA

Vanderveen, Loet — *Sculptor*
Lime Creek 5, Big Sur, CA 93920, USA

VanDerveer, Tara — *Basketball Coach*
1036 Cascade Dr, Menlo Park, CA 94025, USA

Vandeweghe, Ernie — *Basketball Player, Physician*
101 Copley Place, Beverly Hills, CA 90210, USA

Vandiver, S Ernest — *Governor, GA*
109 Hartwell Dr, Lavonia, GA 30553, USA

Vandross, Luther — *Singer, Songwriter*
%Alive Enterprises, 3264 S Kihei Road, Kihei, HI 96753, USA

Vane, John R — *Nobel Medicine Laureate*
White Angles, 7 Beech Dell, Keston, Kent BR2 6EP, England

Vanek, John — *Basketball Referee*
9th St, RD 1, Nesquehoning, PA 18240, USA

Vaness, Carol — *Opera Singer*
%Metropolitan Opera Assn, Lincoln Center Plaza, New York, NY 10023, USA

Vangelis — *Composer*
%Aptel Co, 55 Welbeck St, London W1M 7RD, England

Vanilla Ice (Robby Van Winkle) — *Rap Artist*
%Famous Artists Agency, 1700 Broadway, #500, New York, NY 10019, USA

Vanity (Denise Matthews) — *Singer, Actress*
1871 Messino Dr, San Jose, CA 95132, USA

Vann, Joey — *Singer (The Duprees)*
%Stormin Norman Productions, 2 W Front St, Red Bank, NJ 07701, USA

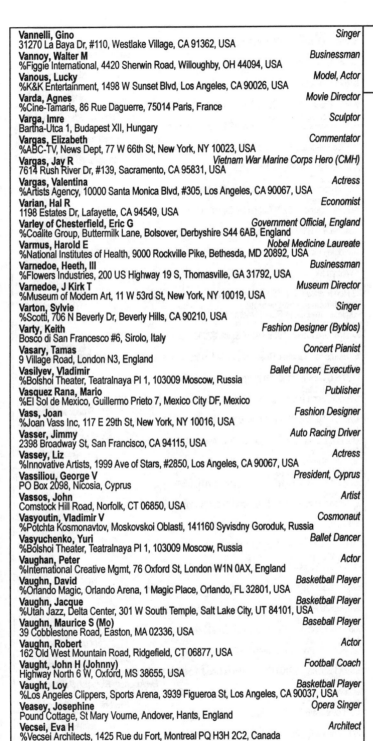

Vannelli, Gino — *Singer*
31270 La Baya Dr, #110, Westlake Village, CA 91362, USA
Vannoy, Walter M — *Businessman*
%Figgie International, 4420 Sherwin Road, Willoughby, OH 44094, USA
Vanous, Lucky — *Model, Actor*
%K&K Entertainment, 1498 W Sunset Blvd, Los Angeles, CA 90026, USA
Varda, Agnes — *Movie Director*
%Cine-Tamaris, 86 Rue Daguerre, 75014 Paris, France
Varga, Imre — *Sculptor*
Bartha-Utca 1, Budapest XII, Hungary
Vargas, Elizabeth — *Commentator*
%ABC-TV, News Dept, 77 W 66th St, New York, NY 10023, USA
Vargas, Jay R — *Vietnam War Marine Corps Hero (CMH)*
7614 Rush River Dr, #139, Sacramento, CA 95831, USA
Vargas, Valentina — *Actress*
%Artists Agency, 10000 Santa Monica Blvd, #305, Los Angeles, CA 90067, USA
Varian, Hal R — *Economist*
1198 Estates Dr, Lafayette, CA 94549, USA
Varley of Chesterfield, Eric G — *Government Official, England*
%Coalite Group, Buttermilk Lane, Bolsover, Derbyshire S44 6AB, England
Varmus, Harold E — *Nobel Medicine Laureate*
%National Institutes of Health, 9000 Rockville Pike, Bethesda, MD 20892, USA
Varnedoe, Heeth, III — *Businessman*
%Flowers Industries, 200 US Highway 19 S, Thomasville, GA 31792, USA
Varnedoe, J Kirk T — *Museum Director*
%Museum of Modern Art, 11 W 53rd St, New York, NY 10019, USA
Varton, Sylvie — *Singer*
%Scotti, 706 N Beverly Dr, Beverly Hills, CA 90210, USA
Varty, Keith — *Fashion Designer (Byblos)*
Bosco di San Francesco #6, Sirolo, Italy
Vasary, Tamas — *Concert Pianist*
9 Village Road, London N3, England
Vasilyev, Vladimir — *Ballet Dancer, Executive*
%Bolshoi Theater, Teatralnaya Pl 1, 103009 Moscow, Russia
Vasquez Rana, Mario — *Publisher*
%El Sol de Mexico, Guillermo Prieto 7, Mexico City DF, Mexico
Vass, Joan — *Fashion Designer*
%Joan Vass Inc, 117 E 29th St, New York, NY 10016, USA
Vasser, Jimmy — *Auto Racing Driver*
2398 Broadway St, San Francisco, CA 94115, USA
Vassey, Liz — *Actress*
%Innovative Artists, 1999 Ave of Stars, #2850, Los Angeles, CA 90067, USA
Vassiliou, George V — *President, Cyprus*
PO Box 2098, Nicosia, Cyprus
Vassos, John — *Artist*
Comstock Hill Road, Norfolk, CT 06850, USA
Vasyoutin, Vladimir V — *Cosmonaut*
%Potchta Kosmonavtov, Moskovskoi Oblasti, 141160 Syvisdny Goroduk, Russia
Vasyuchenko, Yuri — *Ballet Dancer*
%Bolshoi Theater, Teatralnaya Pl 1, 103009 Moscow, Russia
Vaughan, Peter — *Actor*
%International Creative Mgmt, 76 Oxford St, London W1N 0AX, England
Vaughn, David — *Basketball Player*
%Orlando Magic, Orlando Arena, 1 Magic Place, Orlando, FL 32801, USA
Vaughn, Jacque — *Basketball Player*
%Utah Jazz, Delta Center, 301 W South Temple, Salt Lake City, UT 84101, USA
Vaughn, Maurice S (Mo) — *Baseball Player*
39 Cobblestone Road, Easton, MA 02336, USA
Vaughn, Robert — *Actor*
162 Old West Mountain Road, Ridgefield, CT 06877, USA
Vaught, John H (Johnny) — *Football Coach*
Highway North 6 W, Oxford, MS 38655, USA
Vaught, Loy — *Basketball Player*
%Los Angeles Clippers, Sports Arena, 3939 Figueroa St, Los Angeles, CA 90037, USA
Veasey, Josephine — *Opera Singer*
Pound Cottage, St Mary Vourne, Andover, Hants, England
Vecsei, Eva H — *Architect*
%Vecsei Architects, 1425 Rue du Fort, Montreal PQ H3H 2C2, Canada

V

Vannelli - Vecsei

Vecsey, George S *Columnist*
%New York Times, Editorial Dept, 229 W 43rd St, New York, NY 10036, USA

Vedder, Eddie *Singer (Pearl Jam), Songwriter*
799 44th Ave SW, Seattle, WA 98136, USA

Vee, Bobby *Singer, Songwriter*
%Rockhouse Studio, PO Box 41, Sauk Rapids, MN 56379, USA

Vega, Suzanne *Singer, Songwriter*
%AGF Entertainment, 30 W 21st St, #700, New York, NY 10010, USA

Veiga, Carlos A Wahnon de C *Prime Minister, Cape Verde*
%Prime Minister's Office, Praca, 12 Septembre, Sao Tiago, Cape Verde

Veil, Simone *Government Official, France*
11 Place Vauban, 75007 Paris, France

Velasquez, Jorge L, Jr *Thoroughbred Racing Jockey*
770 Allerton Ave, Bronx, NY 10467, USA

Velasquez, Patricia *Model*
%International Management Group, 170 5th Ave, #1000, New York, NY 10010, USA

Velez, Lauren *Actress*
%Gersh Agency, 232 N Canon Dr, Beverly Hills, CA 90210, USA

Velikhov, Yevgeni P *Physicist*
Moscow V-71, Leninski Prospekt 14, 117901 Moscow, Russia

Veljohnson, Reginald *Actor*
%Badgley McQueeney Connor, 9229 Sunset Blvd, #607, Los Angeles, CA 90069, USA

Vendela *Model*
%William Morris Agency, 151 S El Camino Dr, Beverly Hills, CA 90212, USA

Venet, Philippe *Fashion Designer*
62 Rue Francois 1er, 75008 Paris, France

Venkataraman, Ramaswamy *President, India*
Pothigai, Greenways Road, Madras 600 028, India

Venora, Diane *Actress*
%Innovative Artists, 1999 Ave of Stars, #2850, Los Angeles, CA 90067, USA

Venter, J Craig *Molecular Biologist*
%Institute for Genomic Research, 9712 Medical Center Dr, Rookville, MD 20850, USA

Venturi, Ken *Golfer*
1320 S Calle De Maria, Palm Springs, CA 92264, USA

Venturi, Robert *Architect*
%Venturi Scott Brown Assoc, 4236 Main St, Philadelphia, PA 19127, USA

Venza, Jac *Broadcast Producer*
%WNET-TV, 356 W 58th St, New York, NY 10019, USA

Vera, Billy *Singer, Songwriter, Actor*
%Gold Marshak Liedtke, 3500 W Olive Ave, #1400, Burbank, CA 91505, USA

Verbeek, Pat *Hockey Player*
3821 Wentwood Dr, Dallas, TX 75225, USA

Verchota, Philip (Phil) *Hockey Player*
5852 County Road 9 NE, Willmar, MN 56201, USA

Verdi, Bob *Sportswriter*
%Chicago Tribune, 435 N Michigan Ave, Chicago, IL 60611, USA

Verdon, Gwen *Dancer, Actress*
26 Latimer Lane, Bronxville, NY 10708, USA

Verdugo, Elena *Actress*
PO Box 2048, Chula Vista, CA 91912, USA

Verdy, Violette *Ballerina*
44 W 62nd St, #44-C, New York, NY 10023, USA

Vereen, Ben *Actor, Dancer, Singer*
%MPI Talent Agency, 9255 Sunset Blvd, #804, Los Angeles, CA 90069, USA

Verhoeven, Paul *Movie Director*
%Riverside Pictures, 1075 AA Amsterdam, Netherlands

Verhoogen, John *Geophysicist*
306 Santa Ana Ave, San Francisco, CA 94127, USA

Verity, C William, Jr *Secretary, Commerce*
120 Spanish Point Dr, Beaufort, SC 29902, USA

Verma, Inder M *Molecular Biologist*
%Salk Institute, 10010 N Torrey Pines Road, La Jolla, CA 92037, USA

Vermeij, Geerat J *Evolutionary Biologist, Paleontologist*
%University of California, Geology Dept, Davis, CA 95616, USA

Vermeil, Dick *Football Coach, Sportscaster*
%St Louis Rams, 100 N Broadway, #2100, St Louis, MO 63102, USA

Verna, Tony *Television Executive*
500 Ocampo Dr, Pacific Palisades, CA 90272, USA

Verne, Richard — Radio Executive
%NBC-Radio, 30 Rockefeller Plaza, New York 10112, USA

Vernier-Palliez, Bernard M A — Diplomat, France
25 Grande Rue, 78170 La Celle St Cloud, France

Vernon, Glen — Actor
11123 Aqua Vista St, #103, North Hollywood, CA 91602, USA

Vernon, Harvey — Actor
%Paradigm Agency, 10100 Santa Monica Blvd, #2500, Los Angeles, CA 90067, USA

Vernon, James B (Mickey) — Baseball Player
100 E Rose Valley Road, Wallingford, PA 19086, USA

Vernon, John — Actor
15125 Mulholland Dr, Los Angeles, CA 90077, USA

Vernon, Kate — Actress
%Innovative Artists, 1999 Ave of Stars, #2850, Los Angeles, CA 90067, USA

Vernon, Richard — Actor
%Julian Belfarge, 46 Albermarle St, London W1X 4PP, England

Veronis, John J — Publisher
%Veronis Suhler Assoc, 350 Park Ave, New York, NY 10022, USA

Verplank, Scott — Golfer
1800 Oak Forest Dr, Edmond, OK 73003, USA

Verrell, Cec — Actress
%Michael Slessinger Assoc, 8730 Sunset Blvd, #220-W, Los Angeles, CA 90069, USA

Verrett, Shirley — Opera Singer
%International Management Group, 22 E 71st St, New York, NY 10021, USA

Versace, Dick — Basketball Coach
%Turner Broadcast System, Sports Dept, 1050 Techwood Dr, Atlanta, GA 30318, USA

Versace, Donatella — Fashion Designer
%Gianni Versace SpA, Via Gesu 12, 20121 Milan, Italy

Verzetnitsch, Fritz — Businessman
%Gewerkschaftsfuhrer, Hohenstauffengasse 10-12, 1010 Vienna, Austria

Vesely, David L (Dave) — Air Force General
Assistant Vice Chief of Staff, HqUSAF, Pentagon, Washington, DC 20330, USA

Vessels, Billy W — Football Player
4701 Santa Maria St, Coral Gables, FL 33146, USA

Vessey, John W, Jr — Army General
Star Rt, Box 136-A, Garrison, MN 56450, USA

Vest, Charles M — Educator
%Massachusetts Institute of Technology, President's Office, Cambridge, MA 02138, USA

Vest, George S — Diplomat
5307 Iroquois Road, Bethesda, MD 20816, USA

Vest, Jake — Cartoonist (That's Jake)
1709 Carol Woods Dr, Apopka, FL 32703, USA

Vest, R Lamar — Religious Leader
%Church of God, PO Box 2430, Cleveland, TN 37320, USA

Vetri, Victoria — Actress
7045 Hawthorn Ave, #206, Los Angeles, CA 90028, USA

Vetrov, Aleksandr — Ballet Dancer
%Bolshoi Theater, Teatralnaya Pl 1, 103009 Moscow, Russia

Vettori, Ernst — Ski Jumper
Fohrenweg 1, 6060 Absam-Eichat, Austria

Vettrus, Richard J — Religious Leader
%Church of Lutheran Brethren, 707 Crestview Dr W, Union, IA 52175, USA

Vickers, Jonathan S (Jon) — Opera Singer
%John Coast Agency, 1 Park Close, London SW1X 7PQ, England

Vickers, Steve — Hockey Player
21 Greenville Road, Scarsdale, NY 10583, USA

Victoria — Crown Princess, Sweden
%Royal Palace, Kung Slottet, Stottsbacken, 111 30 Stockholm, Sweden

Victorin (Ursache), Archbishop — Religious Leader
%Romanian Orthodox Church, 19959 Riopelle St, Detroit, MI 48203, USA

Vida, J D — Test Pilot (SR-71)
%OL Det 6, 2762LS/FT, Edwards Air Force Base, CA 93523, USA

Vidal, Gore — Writer
La Rondinaia Amalfi Ravello, Salerno, Italy

Vidal, Ricardo J Cardinal — Religious Leader
Chancery, PO Box 52, Cebu City 6401, Philippines

Vidali, Lynn — Swimmer
14750 Mosegard, Morgan Hill, CA 95037, USA

Vidmar, Peter — *Gymnast*
23832 Via Roble, Coto De Caza, CA 92679, USA

Vie, Richard C — *Businessman*
%Unitrin Co, 1 E Wacker Dr, Chicago, IL 60601, USA

Viehboeck, Franz — *Cosmonaut, Austria*
Brunnerbergstr 3021, 2380 Perchtoldsdorf, Austria

Vieillard, Roger — *Artist*
7 Rue de l'Estrapade, 75005 Paris, France

Vieira, Joao Bernardo — *Head of State, Guinea-Bissau; General*
Conselho de Estado, Bissau, Guinea-Bissau

Vieira, Meredith — *Commentator*
%ABC-TV, News Dept, 77 W 66th St, New York, NY 10023, USA

Viereck, Peter — *Writer, Historian*
12 Silver St, South Hadley, MA 01075, USA

Vigil, Selene — *Singer (7 Year Bitch)*
%Talent House, 1407 E Madison St, #41, Seattle, WA 98122, USA

Vigoda, Abe — *Actor*
8500 Melrose Ave, #208, West Hollywood, CA 90069, USA

Viguerie, Richard A — *Publisher*
%Viguerie Co, 7777 Leesburg Pike, Falls Church, VA 22043, USA

Viklund, William E — *Financier*
%Long Island Savings Bank, 201 Old Country Road, Melville, NY 11747, USA

Viktorenko, Alexander S — *Cosmonaut*
%Potchta Kosmonavtov, Moskovskoi Oblasti, 141160 Syvisdny Goroduk, Russia

Vila, Bob — *Home Repair Entertainer*
PO Box 749, Marstons Mills, MA 02648, USA

Vilar, Tracy — *Actress*
%Abrams Artists, 9200 Sunset Blvd, #625, Los Angeles, CA 90069, USA

Vilas, Guillermo — *Tennis Player*
%Guy Cromwell Betz, Pembroke One Building, #525, Virginia Beach, VA 23462, USA

Vilenkin, Alex — *Physicist, Astronomer*
%Tufts University, Physics & Astronomy Dept, Medford, MA 02155, USA

Viljoen, Marais — *President, South Africa*
PO Box 5555, Pretoria 0001, South Africa

Villa, Carlos — *Artist*
1664 Grove St, San Francisco, CA 94117, USA

Villani, Edmond D — *Financier*
%Scudder Stevens Clark, 345 Park Ave, New York, NY 10154, USA

Villarroel, Vernoica — *Opera Singer*
%Columbia Artists Mgmt Inc, 165 W 57th St, New York, NY 10019, USA

Villas Boas, Claudio — *Anthropologist, Explorer*
Parque Nacional do Xingu, Rua Capital Federal 309, 01259 Sao Paulo, Brazil

Villas Boas, Orlando — *Anthropologist, Explorer*
Parque Nacional do Xingu, Rua Capital Federal 309, 01259 Sao Paulo, Brazil

Villella, Edward J — *Ballet Dancer, Choreographer*
%Miami City Ballet, 905 Lincoln Road, Miami Beach, FL 33139, USA

Villeneuve, Jacques — *Auto Racing Driver*
%Forsythe-Green Inc, 7615 Zionsville Road, Indianapolis, IN 46268, USA

Villiers, Christopher — *Actor*
%Michael Whitehall, 125 Gloucester Road, London SW7 4TE, England

Villiers, James — *Actor*
%International Creative Mgmt, 76 Oxford St, London W1N 0AX, England

Vimond, Paul M — *Architect*
91 Ave Niel, 75017 Paris, France

Vince, Pruitt Taylor — *Actor*
%Gersh Agency, 232 N Canon Dr, Beverly Hills, CA 90210, USA

Vincent, Jan-Michael — *Actor*
%David Krieff, 11693 San Vicente Blvd, #296, Los Angeles, CA 90049, USA

Vincent, Jay — *Basketball Player*
63 E Howell Road, Mason, MI 48854, USA

Vincent, Richard F — *Army Field Marshal, England*
%Midland Bank, Shaftesbury, Dorset SP7 8JX, England

Vincent, Sam — *Basketball Player*
4031 Shoals Dr, Okemos, MI 48864, USA

Vinci, Charles (Chuck) — *Weightlifter*
17906 Midvale Ave, Cleveland, OH 44145, USA

Vines, C Jerry — *Religious Leader*
%First Baptist Church, 124 W Ashley St, Jacksonville, FL 32202, USA

Vining, David — *Gastroenterologist*
%Bowman Gray Med School, Wake Forest University, Winston-Salem, NC 27103, USA

Vinnie — *Rap Artist (Naughty By Nature)*
%Flavor Unit Mgmt, 155 Morgan St, Jersey City, NJ 07302, USA

Vinogradov, Pavel — *Cosmonaut*
%Potchta Kosmonavtov, Moskovskoi Oblasti, 141160 Syvisdny Goroduk, Russia

Vinoly, Rafael — *Architect*
1016 5th Ave, New York, NY 10028, USA

Vinson, James S — *Educator*
%University of Evansville, President's Office, Evansville, IN 47722, USA

Vint, Jesse Lee, III — *Actor*
%Film Artists, 7080 Hollywood Blvd, #1118, Los Angeles, CA 90028, USA

Vinton, Bobby — *Singer*
%MPI Talent Agency, 9255 Sunset Blvd, #804, Los Angeles, CA 90069, USA

Vinton, Will — *Animator*
%Will Vinton Productions, 2580 NW Upshur St, Portland, OR 97210, USA

Viola, Bill — *Sculptor*
282 Granada Ave, Long Beach, CA 90803, USA

Viola, Frank J, Jr — *Baseball Player*
106 Coves Rub, Oyster Bay Cove, NY 11791, USA

Virata, Cesar E — *Prime Minister, Philippines*
63 E Maya Dr, Quezon City, Philippines

Virdon, William C (Bill) — *Baseball Manager*
1311 River Road, Springfield, MO 65804, USA

Viren, Lasse — *Track Athlete*
Suomen Urheilulitto Ry, Box 25202, 00250 Helsinki 25, Finland

Virolainen, Johannes — *Prime Minister, Finland*
Kirkniemi, Lohja, Finland

Viry, Alain — *Businessman*
%Willcox & Gibbs Inc, 150 Alhambra Circle, Coral Gables, FL 33134, USA

Viscardi Johnston, Catherine — *Publisher*
%Mirabella Magazine, 200 Madison Ave, New York, NY 10016, USA

Viscuso, Sal — *Actor*
6491 Ivarene Ave, Los Angeles, CA 90068, USA

Vise, David A — *Journalist*
%Washington Post, Editorial Dept, 1150 15th St NW, Washington, DC 20071, USA

Vishnevskaya, Galina P — *Opera Singer*
%Bolshoi Theater, Teatralnaya Pl 1, 103009 Moscow, Russia

Visitor, Nana — *Actress*
1516 N Genesee Ave, Los Angeles, CA 90046, USA

Viso, Michel — *Spatinaut, France*
7 Domaine Chateau-Gaillard, 94700 Maisons-d'Alfort, France

Visscher, Maurice B — *Physiologist*
120 Melbourne Ave SE, Minneapolis, MN 55414, USA

Visser, Lesley — *Sportscaster*
%ABC-TV, Sports Dept, 77 W 66th St, New York, NY 10023, USA

Vitale, Alberto A — *Publisher*
%Random House, 201 E 50th St, New York, NY 10022, USA

Vitale, Dick — *Sportscaster*
%ESPN-TV, Sports Dept, ESPN Plaza, Bristol, CT 06010, USA

Vitez, Michael — *Journalist*
%Philadelphia Inquirer, Editorial Dept, 400 N Broad St, Philadelphia, PA 19130, USA

Vittadini, Adrienne — *Fashion Designer*
%Adrienne Vittadini Inc, 575 7th Ave, New York, NY 10018, USA

Vitti, Monica — *Actress*
%IPC, Via F 38, Siacci, 00197 Rome, Italy

Vittoria, Joseph V — *Businessman*
%Avis Inc, 900 Old Country Road, Garden City, NY 11530, USA

Viviano, Joseph P — *Businessman*
%Hershey Foods Corp, 100 Crystal A Dr, Hershey, PA 17033, USA

Vizquel, Omar E — *Baseball Player*
Blvd Del Cafetel, Res Adroana 6 Pisa, Caracas, Venezuela

Vladeck, Judith P — *Attorney*
%Vladeck Waldman Elias Engelhard, 1501 Broadway, New York, NY 10036, USA

Vlug, Dirk J — *WW II Army Hero (CMH)*
1464 Seymour Ave NW, Grand Rapids, MI 49504, USA

Vo Nguyen Giap — *Army General, Vietnam*
Dang Cong San Vietnam, 1-C Blvd Hoang Van Thu, Hanoi, Vietnam

Vo Van Kiet *Prime Minister, Vietnam*
%Prime Minister's Office, Hoang Hoa Thum, Hanoi, Vietnam

Vogel, Darlene *Actress*
%Michael Slessinger, 8730 Sunset Blvd, #220-W, Los Angeles, CA 90069, USA

Vogel, Hans-Jochen *Government Official, West Germany*
Stresemanstr 6, 53123 Bonn-Bad Godesberg, Germany

Vogel, Matt *Swimmer*
1430 S Michael Court, Visalia, CA 93292, USA

Vogelstein, Bert *Geneticist*
%Johns Hopkins University Medical School, Oncology Center, Baltimore, MD 21218, USA

Vogt, Carl W *Government Official*
%National Transportation Safety Board, 490 L'Enfant Plz SW, Washington, DC 20594, USA

Vogt, Peter K *Virologist*
%Univ of Southern California, Med School, 2011 Zonal Ave, Los Angeles, CA 90033, USA

Vogt, Rochus E *Physicist, Astronomer*
%California Institute of Technology, Bridge Laboratory, Pasadena, CA 91125, USA

Vogts, Berti *Soccer Player*
Mozartweg 2, 41352 Korschenbroich, Germany

Voight, Deborah *Opera Singer*
%RCA Records, 1540 Broadway, #900, New York, NY 10036, USA

Voight, Jon *Actor*
13340 Galewood Dr, Sherman Oaks, CA 91423, USA

Voinovich, George V *Governor, OH*
%Governor's Office, State House, 77 S High St, Columbus, OH 43215, USA

Voiselle, William S (Bill) *Baseball Player*
105 Lowell St, Ninety Six, SC 29666, USA

Volberding, Paul *Cancer Researcher*
%General Hospital AIDS Activities Dept, 995 Potrero Ave, San Francisco, CA 94110, USA

Volcker, Paul A *Government Official*
%James D Wolfensohn Inc, 599 Lexington Ave, New York, NY 10022, USA

Voldstad, John *Actor*
%Halpern Assoc, 12304 Santa Monica Blvd, #104, Los Angeles, CA 90025, USA

Volk, Igor P *Cosmonaut*
%Potchta Kosmonavtov, Moskovskoi Oblasti, 141160 Syvisdny Goroduk, Russia

Volk, Patricia *Writer*
%Raines & Raines, 71 Park Ave, New York, NY 10016, USA

Volker, Sandra *Swimmer*
%Olympiastutzpunkt, Am Dulsbergbad 1, 22049 Hamburg, Germany

Volkmann, Elisabeth *Opera Singer*
Sonnenstr 20, 80331 Munich, Germany

Volkov, Alexander A *Cosmonaut*
%Potchta Kosmonavtov, Moskovskoi Oblasti, 141160 Syvisdny Goroduk, Russia

Vollbracht, Michaele *Fashion Designer, Artist*
%General Delivery, Safety Harbor, FL 34695, USA

Vollenweider, Andreas *Concert Harpist*
Sempacher Str 16, 8032 Zurich, Switzerland

Vollrath, Frederick E (Fred) *Army General*
Deputy Chief of Staff Personnel, HqUSA, Pentagon, Washington, DC 20310, USA

Volpe, Joseph (Joe) *Opera Executive*
%Metropolitan Opera Assn, Lincoln Center Plaza, New York, NY 10023, USA

Volynov, Boris V *Cosmonaut*
%Potchta Kosmonavtov, Moskovskoi Oblasti, 141160 Syvisdny Goroduk, Russia

Volz, Nedra *Actress*
5606 E Fairfield St, Mesa, AZ 85205, USA

Von Aroldingen, Karin *Ballerina*
%New York City Ballet, Lincoln Center Plaza, New York, NY 10023, USA

Von der Heyden, Karl I M *Businessman*
%Mettalgellschaft Corp, 520 Madison Ave, New York, NY 10022, USA

Von Dohnanyi, Christoph *Conductor*
%Cleveland Orchestra, Severance Hall, Cleveland, OH 44106, USA

Von Furstenberg, Betsy *Actress*
230 Central Park West, New York, NY 10024, USA

Von Furstenberg, Diane *Fashion Designer*
389 W 12th St, New York, NY 10014, USA

Von Furstenberg, Egon *Fashion Designer*
50 E 72nd St, New York, NY 10021, USA

Von Gerkan, Manon *Model*
%Elite Model Mgmt, 111 E 22nd St, #200, New York, NY 10010, USA

Von Grunigen, Michael
Chalet Sunneblick, 3778 Schonried, Switzerland
Skier

Von Habsburg-Lothringem, Otto
Hindenburgstr 14, 82343 Pocking, Germany
Government Official, Germany

Von Hartz, Maria del Carmen
%Ford Model Agency, 344 E 59th St, New York, NY 10022, USA
Model

Von Klitzing, Klaus
%Max Planck Institute, Heisenbergstr 1, 70569 Stuttgart, Germany
Nobel Physics Laureate

Von Kuenheim, Eberhard
%Bayerische Motoren Werke, Petuelring 13, 80788 Munich, Germany
Businessman

Von Otter, Sophie
%Columbia Artists Mgmt Inc, 165 W 57th St, New York, NY 10019, USA
Opera Singer

Von Oy, Jenna
19 Saddle Ridge Road, Newtown, CT 06470, USA
Actress

Von Runkle, Theodora
8805 Lookout Mountain Road, Los Angeles, CA 90046, USA
Costume Designer

Von Saltza Olmstead, Chris
7060 Fairway Place, Carmel, CA 93923, USA
Swimmer

Von Schack, Wesley W
%DQE Inc, 1 Oxford Center, 301 Grant St, Pittsburgh, PA 15219, USA
Businessman

Von Stade, Frederica
1200 San Antonio Ave, Alameda, CA 94501, USA
Opera Singer

Von Sydow, Max
Avd C-G Risberg, Strandvegen B, 114 56 Stockholm, Sweden
Actor

Von Trier, Lars
%Dansk Filminstitutet, Store Sondervoldsstrede 4, 1419 Copenhagen, Denmark
Movie Director

Von Trotta, Margarethe
Turkenstr 91, 80799 Munich, Germany
Movie Director

Von Weizsacker, Carl-Friedrich
Aplenstr 15, 83139 Socking, Germany
Philosopher

Von Weizsacker, Richard
Meisenstr 6, 14195 Berlin, Germany
President, Germany

Vonderschmitt, Bernard
%Xilinx, 2100 Logic Dr, San Jose, CA 95124, USA
Businessman

Vonk, Hans
%St Louis Symphony, 1824 Garden St, Belleville, IL 62226, USA
Conductor

Vonnegut, Kurt, Jr
PO Box 27, Sagaponack, NY 11962, USA
Writer

Voorhees, John J
3965 Waldenwood Dr, Ann Arbor, MI 48105, USA
Dermatologist

Voris, R M (Butch)
%Blue Angels NAVFLIGHTDEMRON, 390 San Carlos Road, #A, Pensacola, FL 32508, USA
Navy Aviator (Blue Angels)

Vos Savant, Marilyn
%Parade Publications, 711 3rd Ave, New York, NY 10017, USA
Writer

Voss, James S
%NASA, Johnson Space Center, 2101 NASA Road, Houston, TX 77058, USA
Astronaut

Voss, Janice E
%NASA, Johnson Space Center, 2101 NASA Road, Houston, TX 77058, USA
Astronaut

Voulkos, Peter
951 62nd St, Oakland, CA 94608, USA
Artist

Voznesensky, Andrei A
Kotelnicheskaya Nab 1/15, Bl W, #62, 109240 Moscow, Russia
Writer

Vraa, Sanna
%Irv Schechter, 9300 Wilshire Blvd, #410, Beverly Hills, CA 90212, USA
Model, Actress

Vranes, Danny
7105 Highland Dr, Salt Lake City, UT 84121, USA
Basketball Player

Vrankovic, Stoyko
%Minnesota Timberwolves, Target Center, 600 1st Ave N, Minneapolis, MN 55403, USA
Basketball Player

Vu Van Mau
132 Suon Nguyet Anh, Ho Chi Minh City, Vietnam
Prime Minister, Vietnam

Vuarnet, Jean
Chalet Squaw Peak, 74110 Auoriaz, France
Skier

Vuitton, Henri-Louis
78 Bis Ave Marceau, 75000 Paris, France
Fashion Designer

Vuono, Carl E
5796 Westchester St, Alexandria, VA 22310, USA
Army General

V

Von Grunigen - Vuono

W

Waakataar, Paar   *Singer, Guitarist (A-Ha)*
%Terry Slater, Thatched Cottage, Hollow Lane, Headley Downs, Hamp, England

Wachner, Linda J   *Businesswoman*
%Warnaco Group, 90 Park Ave, New York, NY 10016, USA

Wachtel, Christine   *Track Athlete*
Helmut-Just-Str 5, 17036 Neubrandenburg, Germany

Wachter, Anita   *Skier*
Gantschierstr 579, 6780 Schruns, Austria

Waddell, John Henry   *Artist*
Star Route 2273, Oak Creek Village Road, Cornville, AZ 86325, USA

Waddington of Read, David   *Governor General, Bermuda*
Government House, 11 Langton Hill, Pembroke HM13, Bermuda

Waddington, Leslie   *Art Dealer*
%Waddington Galleries, 11 Cork St, London W1X 1PD, England

Waddington, Steven   *Actor*
%Kerry Gardner, 15 Kensington High St, London W8 5NP, England

Wade, Adam   *Singer*
118 E 25th St, #600, New York, NY 10010, USA

Wade, Edgar L   *Religious Leader*
4466 Elvis Presley Blvd, #222, Memphis, TN 38116, USA

Wade, S Virginia   *Tennis Player*
Sharstead Court, Sittingbourne, Kent, England

Wade, William J (Bill), Jr   *Football Player*
PO Box 210124, Nashville, TN 37221, USA

Wadhams, Wayne   *Singer, Keyboardist (The Fifth Estate)*
73 Hemenway, Boston, MA 02115, USA

Wadkins, Bobby   *Golfer*
5815 Harbour Hill Place, Midlothian, VA 23112, USA

Wadkins, Lanny   *Golfer*
6002 Kettering Court, Dallas, TX 75248, USA

Wadlow, Joan K   *Educator*
%University of Alaska, Chancellor's Office, Fairbanks, AK 99775, USA

Wadsworth, Charles W   *Chamber Pianist*
%Chamber Music Society, 225 E 79th St, New York, NY 10021, USA

Waelsch, Salome G   *Geneticist*
90 Morningside Dr, New York, NY 10027, USA

Wages, Robert E   *Labor Leader*
%Oil Chemical Atomic Workers International Union, PO Box 2812, Denver, CO 80201, USA

Waggoner, J Virgil   *Businessman*
%Sterling Chemicals, 1200 Smith St, Houston, TX 77002, USA

Waggoner, Lyle   *Actor*
4606 Pine Valley Place, Westlake Village, CA 91362, USA

Waggoner, Paul E   *Agronomist*
314 Vineyard Road, Guilford, CT 06437, USA

Wagner, Chuck   *Actor, Singer*
50 Balsam Ave, Toronto ON M4E 3B4, Canada

Wagner, Gerrit A   *Businessman*
%Royal Dutch/Shell Group, 30 Carel Van Bylandtlaan, The Hague, Netherlands

Wagner, Harold A   *Businessman*
%Air Products & Chemicals Inc, 7201 Hamilton Blvd, Allentown, PA 18195, USA

Wagner, Jack   *Actor, Singer*
1134 Alta Loma Road, #115, West Hollywood, CA 90069, USA

Wagner, John   *Cartoonist (Maxine)*
%Hallmark Cards, Shoebox Division, 101 McDonald Dr, Lawrence, KS 66044, USA

Wagner, Lindsay   *Actress*
121 Strand St, #A, Santa Monica, CA 90405, USA

Wagner, Lisa   *Bowler*
%Ladies Professional Bowlers Tour, 7171 Cherryvale Blvd, Rockford, IL 61112, USA

Wagner, Mike   *Football Player*
800 Wyngold Dr, Pittsburgh, PA 15237, USA

Wagner, Philip M   *Columist*
32 Montgomery St, Boston, MA 02116, USA

Wagner, Robert   *Actor*
1500 Old Oak Road, Los Angeles, CA 90049, USA

Wagner, Robert T   *Educator*
%South Dakota State University, President's Office, Brookings, SD 57007, USA

Wagner, Robin S A   *Stage, Set Designer*
%Robin Wagner Studio, 890 Broadway, New York, NY 10003, USA

Wagner, Wolfgang M M — *Opera Director*
Festspielhugel #3, 95445 Bayreuth, Germany

Wagoner, Dan — *Dancer, Choreographer*
%Contemporary Dance Theater, 17 Duke's Road, London WC1H 9AB, England

Wagoner, David R — *Writer*
5416 154th Place SW, Edmonds, WA 98026, USA

Wagoner, Harold E — *Architect*
331 Lindsey Dr, Berwyn, PA 19312, USA

Wagoner, Porter — *Singer, Songwriter*
%Porter Wagoner Enterprises, PO Box 290785, Nashville, TN 37229, USA

Wahl, Ken — *Actor*
480 Westlake Blvd, Malibu, CA 90265, USA

Wahlberg (Marky Mark), Mark — *Singer, Actor, Model*
63 Pilgrim Road, Braintree, MA 02184, USA

Wahlberg, Donnie — *Singer, Actor*
27 Dudley St, Roxbury, MA 02119, USA

Wahlen, George E — *WW II Navy Hero (CMH)*
3437 W 5700 South, Roy, UT 84067, USA

Wahlgren, Olof G C — *Editor*
Nicoloviusgatan 5-B, 217 57 Malmo, Sweden

Wahlstrom, Jarl H — *Religious Leader*
Borgstrominkuja 1-A-10, 00840 Helsinki 84, Finland

Waigel, Theodor — *Government Official, Germany*
%Finance Ministry, Graurheindorfer Str 108, 53117 Bonn, Germany

Waihee, John D, III — *Governor, HI*
1164 Bishop St, #800, Honolulu, HI 96813, USA

Wain, Bea — *Singer*
9955 Durant Dr, #305, Beverly Hills, CA 90212, USA

Wainwright, James — *Actor*
7060 Hollywood Blvd, #610, Los Angeles, CA 90028, USA

Wainwright, Loudon, III — *Singer, Songwriter*
%Teddy Wainwright, 31 Katonah Ave, Katonah, NY 10536, USA

Waite, John — *Singer, Songwriter*
%Rascoff/Zysblat, 110 W 57th St, #300, New York, NY 10019, USA

Waite, Ralph — *Actor*
93-317 Ironwood St, Palm Desert, CA 92260, USA

Waite, Ric — *Cinematographer*
%Smith/Gosnell/Nicholson, 1515 Palisades Dr, #N, Pacific Palisades, CA 90272, USA

Waite, Terence H (Terry) — *Religious Leader*
%Travellers' Club, 106 Pall Mall, London SW1Y 5EP, England

Waits, Tom — *Singer, Songwriter, Pianist*
PO Box 498, Valley Ford, CA 94972, USA

Waitz, Grete — *Track Athlete*
Birgitte Hammers Vei 15-G, 1169 Oslo, Norway

Wajda, Andrzej — *Movie Director*
Ul Jozefa Hauke Bosaka 14, 01-540 Warsaw, Poland

Wajed, Hasina — *Prime Minister, Bangladesh*
%Prime Minister's Office, Tejgada, Dhaka, Bangladesh

Wakata, Koichi — *Astronaut*
%NASA, Johnson Space Center, 2101 NASA Road, Houston, TX 77058, USA

Wakefield, Samuel N — *Army General*
Commanding General, US Combined Arms Support Command, Fort Lee, VA 23801, USA

Wakefield, Timothy S (Tim) — *Baseball Player*
2827 Choctaw Dr, Melbourne, FL 32935, USA

Wakeham of Maldon, John — *Government Official, England*
%House of Lords, Westminster, London SW1A 0PW, England

Wakeman, Rick — *Keyboardist, Songwriter*
Bajonor House, 2 Bridge St, Peel, Isle of Man, United Kingdom

Walcott, Derek A — *Nobel Literature Laureate*
%University of Boston, English Dept, Boston, MA 02215, USA

Walcott, Gregory — *Actor*
22246 Saticoy St, Canoga Park, CA 91303, USA

Wald, Jeff — *Talent Agent*
1467 Chastain Parkway W, Pacific Palisades, CA 90272, USA

Wald, Richard C — *Television Executive*
35 Orchard Road, Larchmont, NY 10538, USA

Waldegrave, William — *Government Official, England*
%House of Commons, Westminster, London SW1A 0AA, England

W

Wagner - Waldegrave

Walden - Walker

Walden, Lynette — *Actress*
%Metropolitan Talent Agency, 4526 Wilshire Blvd, Los Angeles, CA 90010, USA

Walden, Robert — *Actor*
1450 Arroyo View Dr, Pasadena, CA 91103, USA

Waldheim, Kurt — *President, Austria; Sec-Gen, UN*
1 Lobkowitz Platz, 1010 Vienna, Austria

Waldie, Marc — *Volleyball Player*
305 Pinecrest Place, Andover, KS 67002, USA

Waldner, Jan-Ove — *Table Tennis Player*
%Banda, Skjulstagatan 1O, 632 29 Eskilstuna, Sweden

Walenberg, Alan — *Publisher*
%Redbook Magazine, 224 W 57th St, New York, NY 10019, USA

Wales, Ross — *Swimmer*
2730 Walsh Road, Cincinnati, OH 45208, USA

Walesa, Lech — *Nobel Peace Laureate; President, Poland*
Ul Pilotow 17 D/3, Gdansk-Zaspa, Poland

Walken, Christopher — *Actor*
8969 Sunset Blvd, Los Angeles, CA 90069, USA

Walker, Alan — *Anthropologist*
%Johns Hopkins Medical School, Cell Biology/Anatomy Dept, Baltimore, MD 21205, USA

Walker, Alice M — *Social Activist, Writer*
327 25th Ave, #3, San Francisco, CA 94121, USA

Walker, Ally — *Actress*
%Moore, 7920 Sunset Blvd, #400, Los Angeles, CA 90046, USA

Walker, Antoine — *Basketball Player*
%Boston Celtics, 151 Merrimac St, #500, Boston, MA 02114, USA

Walker, Arnetia — *Actress*
%Paul Kohner, 9300 Wilshire Blvd, #555, Beverly Hills, CA 90212, USA

Walker, Billy — *Singer*
%Billy Walker Enterprises, 1122 Longview Dr, Hendersonville, TN 37075, USA

Walker, Bree — *Commentator*
PO Box 681143, Park City, UT 84068, USA

Walker, Brian — *Cartoonist (I li & Lois)*
%King Features Syndicate, 235 E 45th St, New York, NY 10017, USA

Walker, Catherine — *Fashion Designer*
65 Sydney St, Chelsea, London SW3 6PX, England

Walker, Charles B — *Businessman*
%Ethyl Corp, PO Box 2189, Richmond, VA 23218, USA

Walker, Chet — *Basketball Player*
124 Fleet St, Marina del Rey, CA 90292, USA

Walker, Chris — *Actor*
%Rolf Kruger, 121 Gloucester Place, London W1H 3PJ, England

Walker, Clay — *Singer*
%Erv Woolsey Agency, 1000 18th Ave S, Nashville, TN 37212, USA

Walker, Clint — *Actor*
Rodeo Flat Road, Auburn, CA 95603, USA

Walker, Colleen — *Golfer*
%Ladies Professional Golf Assn, 2570 Volusia Ave, Daytona Beach, FL 32114, USA

Walker, Darrell — *Basketball Player, Coach*
16122 Patriot Dr, Little Rock, AR 72212, USA

Walker, David M — *Astronaut*
%NASA, Johnson Space Center, 2101 NASA Road, Houston, TX 77058, USA

Walker, E Cardon — *Movie Executive*
%Walt Disney Co, 500 S Buena Vista St, Burbank, CA 91521, USA

Walker, E Doak, Jr — *Football Player*
PO Box 773329, Steamboat Springs, CO 80477, USA

Walker, George T, Jr — *Composer*
323 Grove St, Montclair, NJ 07042, USA

Walker, Greg — *Cartoonist (Hi & Lois)*
%King Features Syndicate, 235 E 45th St, New York; NY 10017, USA

Walker, Herschel — *Football Player*
%Dallas Cowboys, 1 Cowboys Parkway, Irving, TX 75063, USA

Walker, James E — *Educator*
%Middle Tennessee State University, President's Office, Murfreesboro, TN 37132, USA

Walker, James L (Jimmy) — *Labor Leader*
%Int'l Fireman & Oilers Brotherhood, 1100 Circle 75 Parkway, Atlanta, GA 30339, USA

Walker, Jeffrey C — *Financier*
%Chemical Venture Partners, 270 Park Ave, New York, NY 10017, USA

Walker, Jerry Jeff — Singer, Songwriter, Guitarist
%Tried & True Music, PO Box 39, Austin, TX 78767, USA

Walker, Jimmie (J J) — Comedian
%Global Entertainment, 322 Southdown Road, Lloyd Harbor, NY 11743, USA

Walker, Jimmy — Basketball Player
1216 Lake Point Lane, Stone Mountain, GA 30088, USA

Walker, Joe Louis — Singer, Guitarist
%Rick Bates, 714 Brookside Lane, Sierra Madre, CA 91024, USA

Walker, John — Track Athlete
Jeffs Road, RD Papatoetoe, New Zealand

Walker, Joseph P — Businessman
%CTS Corp, 905 West Blvd N, Elkhart, IN 46514, USA

Walker, Justin — Actor
%Agency For Performing Arts, 9200 Sunset Blvd, #900, Los Angeles, CA 90069, USA

Walker, K Grahame — Businessman
%Dexter Corp, 1 Elm St, Windsor Locks, CT 06096, USA

Walker, Larry K R — Baseball Player
2001 Blake St, Denver, CO 80205, USA

Walker, LeRoy T — Track Coach, Executive, Educator
1208 Red Oak Ave, Durham, NC 27707, USA

Walker, Marcy — Actress
%Leslie Bader, 10225 Donna Ave, Northridge, CA 91324, USA

Walker, Martin D — Businessman
%M A Hanna Co, 200 Public Square, Cleveland, OH 44114, USA

Walker, Mort — Cartoonist (Beetle Bailey, Sarge)
61 Studio Court, Stamford, CT 06903, USA

Walker, Peter E — Government Official, England
Abbots Morton Manor, Grooms Hill, Abbots Morton, Worc WR7 4LT, England

Walker, Polly — Actress
%Markham & Froggatt, Julian House, 4 Windmill St, London W1P 1HF, England

Walker, Robert M — Physicist
3 Romany Park Lane, St Louis, MO 63132, USA

Walker, Robert, Jr — Actor
%TOPS, 23410 Civic Center Way, #C-1, Malibu, CA 90265, USA

Walker, Ronald — Publisher
%Smithsonian Magazine, 900 Jefferson Dr, Washington, DC 20560, USA

Walker, Samaki — Basketball Player
%Dallas Mavericks, Reunion Arena, 777 Sports St, Dallas, TX 75207, USA

Walker, Sandra — Opera Singer
%Columbia Artists Mgmt Inc, 165 W 57th St, New York, NY 10019, USA

Walker, Sarah E B — Opera Singer
152 Inchmery Road, London SE6 1DF, England

Walker, Tonja — Actress
4138 Augusta Dr, Crown Point, IN 46307, USA

Walker, Wally — Basketball Player
154 Lombard St, #58, San Francisco, CA 94111, USA

Walker, Zena — Actress
%Frazer-Skemp Mgmt, 34 Bramerton St, Chelsea, London SW3 5LA, England

Wall, Akure — Model
%Elite Model Mgmt, 111 E 22nd St, #200, New York, NY 10010, USA

Wall, Art — Golfer
22 Hedge Row Run, Clarks Summit, PA 18411, USA

Wall, Brian A — Sculptor
306 Lombard St, San Francisco, CA 94133, USA

Wall, David — Ballet Dancer
%Royal Ballet, Bow St, London WC2E 9DD, England

Wall, Frederick T — Physical Chemist
2468 Via Viesta, La Jolla, CA 92037, USA

Wall, M Danny — Financier
1031 Chartwell Court, Salt Lake City, UT 84103, USA

Wall, Shannon J — Labor Leader
%National Maritime Union, 346 W 17th St, New York, NY 10011, USA

Wall, William — Businessman
%Novellus Systems, 3970 N 1st St, San Jose, CA 95134, USA

Wallace, Anthony F C — Anthropologist
%University of Pennsylvania, Anthropology Dept, Philadelphia, PA 19014, USA

Wallace, Bruce — Geneticist
940 McBryde Dr, Blacksburg, VA 24060, USA

W

Walker - Wallace

Wallace, Craig K — *Physician*
%National Institutes of Health, 9000 Rockville Pike, Bethesda, MD 20892, USA

Wallace, David Foster — *Writer*
%Illinois State University, English Dept, Normal, IL 61761, USA

Wallace, George C — *Governor, AL; Educator*
3140 Fitzgerald Road, Montgomery, AL 36106, USA

Wallace, Ian — *Opera Singer*
%Peters Fraser Dunlop, Chelsea Harbour, Lots Rd, London SW10 0XF, England

Wallace, Jane — *Entertainer*
%"Under Scrutiny" Show, Fox-TV, PO Box 900, Beverly Hills, CA 90213, USA

Wallace, Kenny — *Auto Racing Driver*
PO Box 3050, Concord, NC 28025, USA

Wallace, Marcia — *Actress*
1312 S Genesee Ave, Los Angeles, CA 90019, USA

Wallace, Mike — *Commentator*
%CBS-TV, News Dept, 524 W 57th St, New York, NY 10019, USA

Wallace, Rasheed — *Basketball Player*
501 Harrier Court, Durham, NC 27713, USA

Wallace, Rusty — *Auto Racing Driver*
PO Box 1656, Cornelius, NC 28031, USA

Wallace, Steve — *Football Player*
394 Ferrell Tatum Road, LaGrange, GA 30240, USA

Wallach, Eli — *Actor*
%Paradigm Agency, 10100 Santa Monica Blvd, #2500, Los Angeles, CA 90067, USA

Wallach, Timothy C (Tim) — *Baseball Player*
10762 Holly Dr, Garden Grove, CA 92840, USA

Wallechinsky, David — *Writer*
%William Morrow, 1350 Ave of Americas, New York, NY 10016, USA

Wallenberg, Peter — *Businessman*
%Skandinaviska Enskilda Banken, 106 40 Stockholm, Sweden

Waller, Gordon — *Singer (Peter & Gordon)*
7 Passage St, Powey, Cornwell PL23 1DE, England

Waller, Michael — *Editor*
%Hartford Courant Co, 285 Broad St, Hartford, CT 06115, USA

Waller, Robert James — *Writer*
%Del Norte Ranch, Alpine, TX 79830, USA

Waller, William L — *Governor, MS*
220 S President, Jackson, MS 39201, USA

Wallin, Winston R — *Businessman*
%Medtronic Inc, 7000 Central Ave NE, Minneapolis, MN 55432, USA

Walling, Cheves T — *Chemist*
PO Box 537, Jaffrey, NH 03452, USA

Wallis, Shani — *Actress*
15460 Vista Haven, Sherman Oaks, CA 91403, USA

Walliser, Maria — *Skier*
Selfwingert, 7208 Malans, Switzerland

Walls, Everson — *Football Player*
5927 Tree Shadow Court, Dallas, TX 75252, USA

Walmsley, Jon — *Actor*
7101 Woodrow Wilson Dr, Los Angeles, CA 90068, USA

Walsh, Don — *Underwater Explorer*
%International Maritime Inc, HC 86, Box 101, Myrtle Point, OR 97458, USA

Walsh, Donnie — *Basketball Coach, Executive*
%Indiana Pacers, Market Square Arena, 300 E Market St, Indianapolis, IN 46204, USA

Walsh, Dylan — *Actor*
%International Creative Mgmt, 8942 Wilshire Blvd, Beverly Hills, CA 90211, USA

Walsh, Gwynyth — *Actress*
12304 Santa Monica Blvd, #104, Los Angeles, CA 90025, USA

Walsh, Joe — *Singer, Songwriter, Guitarist (Eagles)*
%David Spero Mgmt, 1679 S Belvoir Blvd, Cleveland, OH 44121, USA

Walsh, John — *Television Host*
%"Most Wanted" Show, Fox-TV, 5151 Wisconsin Ave NW, Washington, DC 20016, USA

Walsh, John, Jr — *Museum Curator*
%J Paul Getty Art Museum, 17985 Pacific Coast Highway, Malibu, CA 90265, USA

Walsh, Kenneth A — *WW II Marine Air Corps Hero (CMH)*
1008 Riviera Dr, Santa Ana, CA 92706, USA

Walsh, Lawrence E — *Government Official, Attorney*
1902 Bedford St, Oklahoma City, OK 73116, USA

Walsh, M Emmet — *Actor*
4173 Motor Ave, Culver City, CA 90232, USA

Walsh, Martin — *Association Executive*
%National Organization on Disability, 910 16th St NW, Washington, DC 20006, USA

Walsh, Patrick C — *Urologist*
%Johns Hopkins Hospital, Brady Urological Institute, Baltimore, MD 21205, USA

Walsh, Sydney — *Actress*
%Innovative Artists, 1999 Ave of Stars, #2850, Los Angeles, CA 90067, USA

Walsh, William (Bill) — *Football Coach, Administrator*
12 Vinegard Hill Road, Woodside, CA 94062, USA

Walsh, William B — *Medical Administrator*
5101 Westpath Way, Bethesda, MD 20816, USA

Walston, Ray — *Actor*
423 S Rexford Dr, #205, Beverly Hills, CA 90212, USA

Walter, James W — *Businessman*
%Walter Industries, 1500 N Dale Mabry Highway, Tampa, FL 33607, USA

Walter, Jessica — *Actress*
10530 Strathmore Dr, Los Angeles, CA 90024, USA

Walter, Paul H L — *Labor Leader*
3 Benedictine Retreat, Savannah, GA 31411, USA

Walter, Tracy — *Actress*
257 N Rexford Dr, Beverly Hills, CA 90210, USA

Walter, Ulrich — *Astronaut, Germany*
%DLR, Astronautenburo, Linder Hohe, 51147 Cologne, Germany

Walters, Barbara — *Commentator*
33 W 60th St, New York, NY 10023, USA

Walters, Harry N — *Government Official*
%DHC Holdings Corp, 125 Thomas Dale, Williamsburg, VA 23185, USA

Walters, Jamie — *Actress, Singer*
4702 Ethel Ave, Sherman Oaks, CA 91423, USA

Walters, Julie — *Actress*
%International Creative Mgmt, 76 Oxford St, London W1N 0AX, England

Walters, Kirk W — *Financier*
%Northeast Savings, PO Box 2599, Hartford, CT 06146, USA

Walters, Roger T — *Architect*
46 Princess Road, London NW1 8JL, England

Walters, Susan — *Actress*
939 8th Ave, #400, New York, NY 10019, USA

Walters, Vernon A — *Government Official, Army General*
2295 S Ocean Blvd, Palm Beach, FL 33480, USA

Walton, Cedar A, Jr — *Jazz Pianist*
%Bridge Agency, 35 Clark St, #A-5, Brooklyn, NY 11201, USA

Walton, Jess — *Actress*
4702 Ethel Ave, Sherman Oaks, CA 91423, USA

Walton, Joseph (Joe) — *Football Coach*
%Robert Morris College, Athletic Dept, Corapolis, PA 15108, USA

Walton, William T (Bill), III — *Basketball Player*
1010 Myrtle Way, San Diego, CA 92103, USA

Waltrip, Darrell L — *Auto Racing Driver*
110 Deerfield, Franklin, TN 37064, USA

Waltrip, Robert L — *Businessman*
%Service Corp International, 1929 Allen Parkway, Houston, TX 77019, USA

Waltz, Lisa — *Actress*
%Writers & Artists, 924 Westwood Blvd, #900, Los Angeles, CA 90024, USA

Walworth, Arthur — *Writer*
North Hill, 865 Central Ave E, #206, Needham, MA 02192, USA

Walz, Carl E — *Astronaut*
%NASA, Johnson Space Center, 2101 NASA Road, Houston, TX 77058, USA

Wambaugh, Joseph — *Writer*
3520 Kellogg Way, San Diego, CA 92106, USA

Wan Li — *Government Official, China*
%State Council, People's Congress, Tian An Men Square, Beijing, China

Wang Junxia — *Track Athlete*
%Athletic Assn, 9 Tiyuguan Road, 10061 Beijing, China

Wang Tian-Ren — *Sculptor*
Shaanxi Sculpture Institute, Longshoucun, Xi'am, Shaanxi 710016, China

Wang, Charles B — *Businessman*
%Computer Associates Int'l, 1 Computer Associates Plaza, Islandia, NY 11788, USA

Wang, Garrett *Actor*
1440 Veteran Ave, #212, Los Angeles, CA 90024, USA

Wang, Henry Y *Chemical Engineer*
%University of Michigan, Chemical Engineering Dept, Ann Arbor, MI 48109, USA

Wang, Taylor G *Astronaut, Physicist*
%Vanderbilt University, Microgravity Research Center, Nashville, TN 37235, USA

Wang, Vera *Fashion Designer*
%Vera Wang Bridal House, 225 W 39th St, #1000, New York, NY 10018, USA

Wang, Wayne *Movie Director*
%International Creative Mgmt, 8942 Wilshire Blvd, Beverly Hills, CA 90211, USA

Wang, Y C *Businessman*
%Formosa Plastics Corp, 39 Chung Shang 3rd Road, Kaohsiung, Taiwan

Wangchuk, Jigme Singye *King, Bhutan*
%Royal Palace, Tashichhodzong, Thimphu, Bhutan

Wannstedt, David R (Dave) *Football Coach*
%Chicago Bears, Halas Hall, 250 N Washington Road, Lake Forest, IL 60045, USA

Wanzer, Bobby *Basketball Player*
40 Fairhill Dr, Rochester, NY 14618, USA

Wapner, Joseph A *Judge, Actor*
16616 Park Lane Place, Los Angeles, CA 90049, USA

Ward, Benjamin *Law Enforcement Official*
%New York Police Commissioner's Office, 1 Police Plaza, New York, NY 10038, USA

Ward, Burt *Actor*
1461 Rockinghorse Lane, La Habra, CA 90631, USA

Ward, Charlie *Basketball, Football Player*
312 Plum St, Thomasville, GA 31792, USA

Ward, David *Opera Singer*
1 Kennedy Crescent, Lake Wanaka, New Zealand

Ward, David *Educator*
%University of Wisconsin, President's Office, Madison, WI 53706, USA

Ward, Douglas Turner *Actor, Writer*
%Negro Ensemble Co, 1540 Broadway, New York, NY 10036, USA

Ward, Fred *Actor*
1215 Cabrillo Ave, Venice, CA 90291, USA

Ward, Harvie *Golfer*
%Grand Cyprus Golf Club, 1 N Jacaranda Dr, Orlando, FL 32836, USA

Ward, Mary B *Actress*
%Innovative Artists, 1999 Ave of Stars, #2850, Los Angeles, CA 90067, USA

Ward, Megan *Actress*
%Innovative Artists, 1999 Ave of Stars, #2850, Los Angeles, CA 90067, USA

Ward, Michael P *Mountaineer, Surgeon*
%St Andrews's Hospital, Bow St, London E3 3NT, England

Ward, Milton H *Businessman*
%Cyprus Minerals Co, 9100 E Mineral Circle, Englewood, CO 80112, USA

Ward, R Duane *Baseball Player*
4505 Pacific St, Framington, MA 87402, USA

Ward, Rachel *Actress*
%Judy Cann, 110 Queen St, Woollahra NSW 2025, Australia

Ward, Robert *Composer*
The Forest, 2701 Pickett Road, #4029, Durham, NC 27705, USA

Ward, Robert R (Bob) *Football Player*
515 N Academy St, Greensboro, MD 21639, USA

Ward, Rodger *Auto Racing Driver*
1329 Craigmont St, El Cajon, CA 92019, USA

Ward, Ron *Hockey Player*
3178 W 140th St, Cleveland, OH 44111, USA

Ward, Sela *Actress*
289 S Robertson Blvd, #469, Beverly Hills, CA 90211, USA

Ward, Simon *Actor*
%International Creative Mgmt, 76 Oxford St, London W1N 0AX, England

Ward, Sterling *Religious Leader*
%Brethren Church, 524 College Ave, Ashland, OH 44805, USA

Ward, Vincent *Movie Director*
PO Box 423, Kings Cross, Sydney NSW 2011, Australia

Wardeborg, George E *Businessman*
%Wicor Inc, 306 N Milwaukee St, Milwaukee, WI 53202, USA

Warden, Jack *Actor*
23604 Malibu Colony Road, Malibu, CA 90265, USA

Ware, Andre *Football Player*
3910 Wood Park, Sugar Land, TX 77479, USA

Ware, Herta *Actress*
PO Box 151, Topanga Canyon, CA 90290, USA

Wareham, James L *Businessman*
%Wheeling-Pittsburgh, 1134 Market St, Wheeling, WV 26003, USA

Wareham, John P *Businessman*
%Beckman Instruments, 2500 Harbor Blvd, Fullerton, CA 92835, USA

Warfield, Marsha *Actress*
PO Box 691713, Los Angeles, CA 90064, USA

Warfield, Paul D *Football Player*
15476 NW 77th Court, #347, Hialeah, FL 33016, USA

Warfield, Ronald *Businessman*
%Country Life Insurance, 1711 General Electric Road, Bloomington, IL 61704, USA

Warfield, William C *Opera Singer*
247 E Chestnut St, #701, Chicago, IL 60611, USA

Wargo, Tom *Golfer*
2801 Putter Lane, Centralia, IL 62801, USA

Wariner, Steve *Singer, Songwriter*
%Steve Wariner Productions, PO Box 1647, Franklin, TN 37065, USA

Waring, Todd *Actor*
%Don Buchwald, 10 E 44th St, New York, NY 10017, USA

Warioba, Joseph *Prime Minister, Tanzania*
%Regional Administration Minister's Office, Dar es Salaam, Tanzania

Wark, Robert R *Museum Curator*
%Huntington Library & Art Gallery, 1151 Oxford Road, San Marino, CA 91108, USA

Warlock, Billy *Actor*
6822 Lasaine Ave, Van Nuys, CA 91406, USA

Warmerdam, Cornelius (Dutch) *Track Athlete*
3976 N 1st St, Fresno, CA 93726, USA

Warnecke, John Carl *Architect*
300 Broadway St, San Francisco, CA 94133, USA

Warnecke, Mark *Swimmer*
Am Schichtmeister 100, 58453 Witten, Germany

Warner, Chris *Cartoonist (Black Cross)*
%Dark Horse Publishing, 10956 SE Main St, Milwaukie, OR 97216, USA

Warner, Dave *Businessman*
%Electronics for Imaging, 2855 Campus Dr, San Mateo, CA 94403, USA

Warner, David *Actor*
%Julian Belfarge, 46 Albermarle St, London W1X 4PP, England

Warner, Douglas A, III *Financier*
%J P Morgan Co, 60 Wall St, New York, NY 10005, USA

Warner, Julie *Actress*
%Creative Artists Agency, 9830 Wilshire Blvd, Beverly Hills, CA 90212, USA

Warner, Malcolm-Jamal *Actor*
PO Box 69646, Los Angeles, CA 90069, USA

Warner, Margaret *Commentator*
%"MacNeil/Lehrer Newshour" Show, WNET-TV, 2700 S Quincy St, Arlington, VA 22206, USA

Warner, Philip G *Editor*
%Houston Chronicle, Editorial Dept, 801 Texas Ave, Houston, TX 77002, USA

Warner, T C *Actress*
%SDB Partners, 1801 Ave of Stars, #902, Los Angeles, CA 90067, USA

Warner, Todd *Sculptor*
155 NW 11th St, Boca Raton, FL 33432, USA

Warner, Tom *Television Producer*
%Carsey-Warner Productions, 4024 Radford Ave, Building 3, Studio City, CA 91604, USA

Warner, William W *Writer*
2243 47th St NW, Washington, DC 20007, USA

Warnes, Jennifer *Singer, Songwriter*
%Donald Miller, 12746 Kling St, Studio City, CA 91604, USA

Warnke, Paul C *Government Official*
5037 Garfield St NW, Washington, DC 20016, USA

Warnock, John *Businessman*
%Adobe Systems, 345 Park Ave, San Jose, CA 95110, USA

Warren G (Griffin Warren III) *Rap Artist*
%Richard Walters, 421 S Beverly Dr, #800, Beverly Hills, CA 90212, USA

Warren, Fran *Singer*
%Richard A Barz, Rt 1, Box 91, Tannersville, PA 18372, USA

Warren, Frederick M — *Architect*
65 Cambridge Terrace, Christchurch 1, New Zealand

Warren, Gloria — *Singer, Actress*
16872 Bosque Dr, Encino, CA 91436, USA

Warren, Jennifer — *Actress*
1675 Old Oak Road, Los Angeles, CA 90049, USA

Warren, Kenneth S — *Physician*
%Picower Medical Research Institute, 350 Community Dr, Manhasset, NY 11030, USA

Warren, L D — *Editorial Cartoonist*
1815 William Howard Taft Road, #203, Cincinnati, OH 45206, USA

Warren, Lesley Ann — *Actress*
%Passionflower, 2934 Beverly Glen Circle, #372, Los Angeles, CA 90077, USA

Warren, Michael (Mike) — *Actor, Basketball Player*
189 Greenfield Ave, Los Angeles, CA 90049, USA

Warren, Thomas L — *Association Executive*
%National Wildlife Federation, 8925 Leesburg Pike, Vienna, VA 22184, USA

Warren, Tom — *Triathlete*
2393 La Marque St, Pacific Beach, CA 92109, USA

Warren, W Michael, Jr — *Businessman*
%Energen Corp, 2101 6th Ave N, Birmingham, AL 35203, USA

Warren, William D — *Businessman*
%National Re Corp, PO Box 10167, Stamford, CT 06904, USA

Warrick, Ruth — *Actress*
903 Park Ave, New York, NY 10021, USA

Warwick, Dionne — *Singer*
1583 Lindacrest Dr, Beverly Hills, CA 90210, USA

Was, Don — *Composer, Bassist (Was Not Was)*
12831 Mulholland Dr, Beverly Hills, CA 90210, USA

Washburn, Barbara — *Mapologist*
1010 Waltham St, #F-22, Lexington, MA 02173, USA

Washburn, Beverly — *Actress*
15 White Tail Court, Henderson, NV 89014, USA

Washburn, H Bradford, Jr — *Museum Official, Explorer*
1010 Waltham St, #F-22, Lexington, MA 02173, USA

Washburn, Sherwood L — *Anthropologist*
2797 Shasta Road, Berkeley, CA 94708, USA

Washington, Baby — *Singer, Pianist*
%Headline Talent, 1650 Broadway, #508, New York, NY 10019, USA

Washington, Claudell — *Baseball Player*
12 Charles Hill Road, Orinda, CA 94563, USA

Washington, Denzel — *Actor*
4701 Sencola Ave, Toluca Lake, CA 91602, USA

Washington, Dwayne (Pearl) — *Basketball Player*
12 Percy Place, #1, Cambridge, MA 02139, USA

Washington, Gene A — *Football Player*
%National Football League, 280 Park Ave, #12-W, New York, NY 10017, USA

Washington, Grover, Jr — *Jazz Saxophonist*
%Zane Mgmt, Bellevue, Broad & Walnut, #600, Philadelphia, PA 19102, USA

Washington, Joe — *Football Player*
2141 Cashmere Ave, Port Arthur, TX 77640, USA

Washington, Kermit — *Basketball Player*
14223 SW Amberwood Circle, Lake Oswego, OR 97035, USA

Washington, MaliVai — *Tennis Player*
%ProServe, 1101 Woodrow Wilson Blvd, #1800, Arlington, VA 22209, USA

Wasim Akram — *Cricketer*
%Lancashire Cricket Club, Old Trafford, Manchester M16 0PX, England

Wasmeier, Markus — *Skier*
83727 Schliersee, Germany

Wasmosy, Juan Carlos — *President, Paraguay*
%Palacio de Gobierno, Ave Mariscal Lopez, Asuncion, Paraguay

Wass, Ted — *Actor*
11733 Valleycrest Road, Studio City, CA 91604, USA

Wasserburg, Gerald J — *Geophysicist*
1207 Arden Road, Pasadena, CA 91106, USA

Wasserman, Dale — *Writer*
Casa Blanca Estates, #37, Paradise Valley, AZ 95253, USA

Wasserman, Dan — *Editorial Cartoonist*
%Boston Globe, Editorial Dept, 135 Morrissey Blvd, Boston, MA 02125, USA

Wasserman, Lew R — *Entertainment Executive*
911 N Foothill Road, Beverly Hills, CA 90210, USA

Wasserman, Rob — *Jazz Bassist*
%Steep Productions, 64 Molino Ave, Mill Valley, CA 94941, USA

Wasserman, Robert H — *Physiologist, Veterinarian*
%Cornell University, Veterinary Medicine College, Ithaca, NY 14853, USA

Wasserstein, Bruce — *Financier*
%Wasserstein Perella Group, 31 W 52nd St, #2700, New York, NY 10019, USA

Wasserstein, Wendy — *Writer*
%Royce Carlton Inc, 866 United Nations Plaza, #4030, New York, NY 10017, USA

Wasson, Craig — *Actor*
%J Michael Bloom, 9255 Sunset Blvd, #710, Los Angeles, CA 90069, USA

Watanabe, Milio — *Computer Scientist*
%Nippon Electric Co, Computer Labs, 5-33-1 Shiba, Tokyo, Japan

Watanabe, Moriyuki — *Businessman*
%Mazda Motor Corp, 3-1 Shinchi, Fuchucho, Akigun, Hiroshima 730-91, Japan

Watanabe, Sadao — *Jazz Saxophonist*
%International Music Network, 2 Main St, #400, Gloucester, MA 01930, USA

Watanabe, Takeo — *Businessman*
%Mitsubishi Oil, 1-2-4 Toranomon, Minatoku, Tokyo 100, Japan

Watanabe, Youji — *Architect*
1-6-13 Hirakawacho, Chiyodaku, Tokyo, Japan

Waterman, Denis — *Actor*
%International Creative Mgmt, 76 Oxford St, London W1N 0AX, England

Waterman, Felicity — *Actress*
160 E Mountain Dr, Santa Barbara, CA 93108, USA

Waters, Crystal — *Singer*
%AM/PM Entertainment, 415 63rd St, #200, Brooklyn, NY 11220, USA

Waters, John — *Movie Director*
10 W Highfield Road, Baltimore, MD 21218, USA

Waters, John B — *Government Official*
405 Burridge Waters Edge, Sevierville, TN 37862, USA

Waters, Lou — *Commentator*
%Cable News Network, News Dept, 1050 Techwood Dr NW, Atlanta, GA 30318, USA

Waters, Richard — *Publisher*
20 Somerset Downs, St Louis, MO 63124, USA

Waters, Roger — *Singer, Bassist (Pink Floyd)*
%Ten Tenths Mgmt, 106 Gifford St, London N1 ODF, England

Waterston, Sam — *Actor*
RR Box 197, Easton St, West Cornwall, CT 06796, USA

Wathan, John D — *Baseball Manager*
1401 Deer Run Trail, Blue Springs, MO 64015, USA

Watkin, David — *Cinematographer*
6 Sussex Mews, Brighton BN2 1GZ, England

Watkins, Dean A — *Businessman*
%Watkins-Johnson Co, 3333 Hillview Ave, Palo Alto, CA 94304, USA

Watkins, Tasker — *WW II British Army Hero (VC), Judge*
5 Pump Court, Middle Temple, London EC4, England

Watkins, Tionne (T-Boz) — *Rap Artist (TLC)*
%William Morris Agency, 1325 Ave of Americas, New York, NY 10019, USA

Watkinson of Woking, Harold A — *Government Official, England*
Tyma House, Bosham near Chichester, Sussex, England

Watley, Jody — *Singer*
PO Box 6339, Beverly Hills, CA 90212, USA

Watling, Jack — *Actor*
%London Mgmt, 2-4 Noel St, London W1V 3RB, England

Watrous, Bill — *Jazz Trombonist*
%Thomas Cassidy, 0366 Horseshoe Dr, Basalt, CO 81621, USA

Watson Richardson, Lillian (Pokey) — *Swimmer*
4960 Maunalani Circle, Honolulu, HI 96816, USA

Watson, Albert M — *Photographer*
777 Washington St, New York, NY 10014, USA

Watson, Alberta — *Actress*
400 S Beverly Dr, #216, Beverly Hills, CA 90212, USA

Watson, Alexander F — *Diplomat*
%US State Department, 2201 "C" St NW, Washington, DC 20520, USA

Watson, Bobby — *Jazz Saxophonist*
%Split Second Timing, 104 W 70th St, #11-C, New York, NY 10023, USA

W

Wasserman - Watson

W

Watson, Bobs — *Actor*
2700 Montrose Ave, Montrose, CA 91020, USA

Watson, Cecil J — *Physician*
%Abbott Northwestern Hospital, 2727 Chicago Ave, Minneapolis, MN 55407, USA

Watson, Dale — *Singer*
%Cross Three Mgmt, 33 Music Square W, #100, Nashville, TN 37203, USA

Watson, Doc — *Singer, Guitarist, Banjoist*
%Greenhill Mgmt, 1671 Appian Way, Santa Monica, CA 90401, USA

Watson, Elizabeth M — *Law Enforcement Official*
%Houston Police Department, Chief's Office, 61 Riesner St, Houston, TX 77002, USA

Watson, Emily — *Actress*
%International Creative Mgmt, 76 Oxford St, London W1N 0AX, England

Watson, Gene — *Singer*
%Sound & Serenity Mgmt, PO Box 22105, Nashville, TN 37202, USA

Watson, Harry (Moose) — *Hockey Player*
20 Jonquil Crescent, Markham ON L3P 1T4, Canada

Watson, James D — *Nobel Medicine Laureate*
Bungtown Road, Cold Spring Harbor, NY 11724, USA

Watson, James L — *Judge*
%US Court of International Trade, 1 Federal Plaza, New York, NY 10278, USA

Watson, Kenneth M — *Physicist, Oceanographer*
PO Box 9726, Rancho Santa Fe, CA 92067, USA

Watson, Martha — *Track Athlete*
5509 Royal Vista Lane, Las Vegas, NV 89129, USA

Watson, Mills — *Actor*
2824 Dell Ave, Venice, CA 90291, USA

Watson, Ned G — *Businessman*
%Jacobs Engineering Group, 251 S Lake Ave, Pasadena, CA 91101, USA

Watson, Paul — *Environmental Activist*
%Sea Shepherd Conservation Society, 1314 2nd St, Santa Monica, CA 90401, USA

Watson, Paul — *Photographer*
%Toronto Star, Editorial Dept, 1 Yonge St, Toronto ON M5E 1E6, Canada

Watson, Raymond L — *Entertainment Executive*
%Walt Disney Co, 500 S Buena Vista St, Burbank, CA 91521, USA

Watson, Stephen E — *Businessman*
%Dayton Hudson, 777 Nicollet Mall, Minneapolis, MN 55402, USA

Watson, Thomas S (Tom) — *Golfer*
1901 W 47th Place, #200, Shawnee Mission, KS 66205, USA

Watson, Wayne — *Singer*
%Atkins-Muse, 1808 W End Ave, #1600, Nashville, TN 37203, USA

Watt, Ben — *Guitarist, Singer, Songwriter*
%Atlantic Records, 75 Rockefeller Plaza, New York, NY 10019, USA

Watt, James G — *Secretary, Interior*
1800 N Spirit Dance Road, Jackson Hole, WY 83001, USA

Watters, Rickey — *Football Player*
560 Mill Creek Lane, Santa Clara, CA 95054, USA

Watters, Tim — *Hockey Player*
804 Oak Grove Parkway, Houghton, MI 49931, USA

Watterson, Bill — *Cartoonist (Calvin & Hobbes)*
%Universal Press Syndicate, 4520 Main St, Kansas City, KS 64111, USA

Watterson, John B (Brett) — *Astronaut*
2508 Via Anacapa, Palos Verdes Estates, CA 90274, USA

Wattleton, A Faye — *Association Executive, Entertainer*
%Fischer-Ross Agency, 250 W 57th St, New York, NY 10107, USA

Watts, Andre — *Concert Pianist*
205 W 57th St, New York, NY 10019, USA

Watts, Charles R (Charlie) — *Drummer (The Rolling Stones)*
%Rupert Lowenstein, 2 King St, London SW1Y 6QL, England

Watts, Claudius E, III — *Educator, Army General*
%The Citadel, President's Office, Charleston, SC 29409, USA

Watts, Ernie — *Art Director, Stage Designer*
%International Creative Mgmt, 40 W 57th St, New York, NY 10019, USA

Watts, Ernie — *Jazz Saxophonist*
%Cameron Organization, 201 W Magnolia Blvd, Burbank, CA 91502, USA

Watts, Glenn E — *Labor Leader*
%Communications Workers of America, 501 3rd St NW, Washington, DC 20001, USA

Watts, Heather — *Ballerina*
%New York City Ballet, Lincoln Center Plaza, New York, NY 10023, USA

Watts, Helen J — *Opera Singer*
Rock House, Wallis, Ambleston, Haverford-West, Dyfed SA62 5RA, Wales

Watts, Quincy — *Track Athlete*
%First Team Marketing, PO Box 67581, Los Angeles, CA 90067, USA

Watts, Stanley H (Stan) — *Basketball Coach*
205 E 2950th St N, Provo, UT 84604, USA

Waugh, Auberon A — *Writer*
Combe Florey House, Combe Florey, Taunton, Somerset, England

Waugh, John S — *Chemist*
%Massachusetts Institute of Technology, Chemistry Dept, Cambridge, MA 02139, USA

Waxenberg, Alan M — *Publisher*
%Good Housekeeping Magazine, 959 8th Ave, New York, NY 10019, USA

Waxman, Al — *Actor*
87 Forest Hill Road, Toronto ON M4V 2L6, Canada

Way, Kenneth L — *Businessman*
%LSS Holding Corp, 10 Hanover Square, New York, NY 10005, USA

Wayans, Damon — *Actor*
12140 Summit Court, Beverly Hills, CA 90210, USA

Wayans, Keenen Ivory — *Movie Director, Actor*
16405 Mulholland Dr, Los Angeles, CA 90049, USA

Wayda, Stephen — *Photographer*
%Playboy Magazine, Reader Service, 680 N Lake Shore Dr, Chicago, IL 60611, USA

Wayland, Len — *Actor*
%Sutton Barth Vennari, 145 S Fairfax Ave, #310, Los Angeles, CA 90036, USA

Wayne, June — *Artist*
1108 N Tamarind Ave, Los Angeles, CA 90038, USA

Wayne, Patrick — *Actor*
10502 Whipple St, North Hollywood, CA 91602, USA

Wazzan, Chafiq al- — *Prime Minister, Lebanon*
Rue Haroun El-Rashid, Immeuble Wazzan, Bierut, Lebanon

Weah, George — *Soccer Player*
%AC Milan, Via Turati 3, 20221 Milan, Italy

Weatherly, Shawn — *Actress*
12203 Octagon St, Los Angeles, CA 90049, USA

Weathers, Carl — *Actor*
17552 Sunset Blvd, Pacific Palisades, CA 90272, USA

Weatherspoon, Clarence — *Basketball Player*
PO Box 117, Crawford, MS 39743, USA

Weatherspoon, Teresa — *Basketball Player*
%New York Liberty, Madison Square Garden, 2 Penn Plaza, New York, NY 10121, USA

Weaver, Dennis — *Actor*
13867 Country Road 1, Ridgway, CO 81432, USA

Weaver, DeWitt — *Golfer*
PO Box 580, Zepplinstrauss Road, Helen, GA 30545, USA

Weaver, Earl S — *Baseball Manager*
501 Cypress Pointe Dr W, Hollywood, FL 33027, USA

Weaver, Fritz — *Actor*
161 W 75th St, New York, NY 10023, USA

Weaver, James — *Cartoonist*
6251 Winthrop Ave, #12, Indianapolis, IN 46220, USA

Weaver, Sigourney — *Actress*
200 W 57th St, #1306, New York, NY 10019, USA

Weaver, Sylvester L (Pat), Jr — *Television Executive*
564 Crocker Sperry Dr, Santa Barbara, CA 93108, USA

Weaver, Warren E — *Chemist*
7607 Horsepen Road, Richmond, VA 23229, USA

Webb, Carl B — *Financier*
%First Nationwide Bank, 135 Main St, San Francisco, CA 94105, USA

Webb, Chloe — *Actress*
50 Dudley Ave, Venice, CA 90291, USA

Webb, Coyt — *Businessman*
%Southwestern Public Service, Tyler & 6th, Amarillo, TX 79170, USA

Webb, Jimmy — *Songwriter, Singer*
1560 N Laurel Ave, #109, Los Angeles, CA 90046, USA

Webb, Kerrie — *Golfer*
%Int'l Management Group, 1 Erieview Plaza, #1300, Cleveland, OH 44114, USA

Webb, Lucy — *Comedienne*
1360 N Crescent Heights, #38, Los Angeles, CA 90046, USA

Webb, Russell (Russ) — *Water Polo Player*
2493 N Mountain Lane, Upland, CA 91784, USA

Webb, Susan Cordelia — *Sculptor*
%Quartersaw Gallery, 528 NW 12th, Portland, OR 97209, USA

Webb, Tamilee — *Physical Fitness Instructor*
%ESPN-TV, ESPN Plaza, Bristol, CT 06010, USA

Webb, Veronica — *Model, Actress*
%Ford Model Agency, 344 E 59th St, New York, NY 10022, USA

Webb, Wellington E — *Mayor*
%Mayor's Office, City-County Building, 1437 Bannock St, Denver, CO 80202, USA

Webber, Chris — *Basketball Player*
%Washington Wizards, Capital Centre, 1 Truman Dr, Landover, MD 20785, USA

Weber, Bruce — *Photographer*
%Robert Miller Gallery, 41 E 57th St, New York, NY 10022, USA

Weber, Dick — *Bowler*
1305 Arlington Dr, Florissant, MO 63033, USA

Weber, Eberhard — *Jazz Bassist, Cellist, Composer*
%Ted Kurland, 173 Brighton Ave, Boston, MA 02134, USA

Weber, Eugen — *Writer, Historian*
11579 Sunset Blvd, Los Angeles, CA 90049, USA

Weber, Mary E — *Astronaut*
%NASA, Johnson Space Center, 2101 NASA Road, Houston, TX 77058, USA

Weber, Pete — *Bowler*
1305 Arlington Dr, Florissant, MO 63033, USA

Weber, Robert M (Bob) — *Cartoonist*
%New Yorker Magazine, 20 W 43rd St, New York, NY 10036, USA

Weber, Stephen L — *Educator*
%State University of New York, President's Office, Oswego, NY 13126, USA

Weber, Steven — *Actor*
2991 Hollyridge Dr, Los Angeles, CA 90068, USA

Weber-Koszto, Monika — *Fencer*
Am Steinbach 6, 53229 Bonn, Germany

Webster, Alexander (Alex) — *Football Player*
8461 SE Palm Hammock Lane, Hobe Sound, FL 33455, USA

Webster, Marvin — *Basketball Player*
165 Essex Ave, #305-10, Metuchen, NJ 08840, USA

Webster, Mike — *Football Player, Coach*
220 W Rittenhouse Square, #15-B, Philadelphia, PA 19103, USA

Webster, R Howard — *Publisher, Baseball Executive*
%Toronto Globe & Mail, 444 Front St W, Toronto ON M5V 2S9, Canada

Webster, Robert (Bob) — *Diver*
800 Energy Center Blvd, #3414, Northport, AL 35473, USA

Webster, Tom — *Hockey Player, Coach*
1001 Kingsway Dr, Apex, NC 27502, USA

Webster, William H — *Law Enforcement Official*
4777 Dexter St NW, Washington, DC 20007, USA

Wechsler, Herbert — *Attorney, Educator*
179 E 70th St, New York, NY 10021, USA

Wecker, Andreas — *Gymnast*
Am Dorfplatz 1, 16766 Klein-Ziethen, Germany

Weddington, Sarah R — *Attorney*
709 W 14th St, Austin, TX 78701, USA

Wedel, Dieter — *Movie Director*
%Tonndorfer Strand 2, 22045 Hamburg, Germany

Wedemeyer, Herman C — *Football Player*
%Servco Pacific Inc, 900 Fort Street Mall, #500, Honolulu, HI 96813, USA

Weder, Gustav — *Bobsled Athlete*
Haltenstr 2, Stachen/TG, Switzerland

Wedgeworth, Ann — *Actress*
70 Riverside Dr, New York, NY 10024, USA

Wedgwood, C Veronica — *Writer, Historian*
Whitegate, Alciston near Polegate, Sussex BN26 6UN, England

Wedman, Scott — *Basketball Player*
7912 NW Scenic Dr, Kansas City, MO 64152, USA

Weed, Maurice James — *Composer*
Givens Estates, Villa 21-F, Sweeten Creek Road, Asheville, NC 28803, USA

Weege, Reinhold — *Television Producer*
9736 La Jolla Farms Road, La Jolla, CA 92037, USA

Weekly, John W — *Businessman*
%Mutual of Omaha, Mutual of Omaha Plaza, Omaha, NE 68175, USA

Weeks, Charles R — *Financier*
%Citizens Banking Corp, 1 Citizens Banking Center, Flint, MI 48502, USA

Weeks, John R — *Architect*
39 Jackson's Lane, Highgate, London N6 5SR, England

Weese, Harry M — *Architect*
314 W Willow St, Chicago, IL 60614, USA

Weese, Miranda — *Ballerina*
%New York City Ballet, Lincoln Center Plaza, New York, NY 10023, USA

Wefald, Jon — *Educator*
%Kansas State University, President's Office, Manhattan, KS 66506, USA

Wegman, William G — *Artist, Photographer*
239 W 18th St, New York, NY 10011, USA

Wegner, Hans — *Furniture Designer*
Tinglevej 17, 2820 Gentof'tte, Denmark

Wehling, Ulrich — *Ski Jumper*
%Skiverband, Hubertusstr 1, 81477 Munich, Germany

Wehmeier, Helge H — *Businessman*
%Bayer Corp, Mellon Center, 500 Grant St, Pittsburgh, PA 15219, USA

Weibel, Robert — *Pediatrician*
%University of Pennsylvania Med School, Pediatrics Dept, Philadelphia, PA 19104, USA

Weibring, D A — *Golfer*
1315 Garden Grove Court, Plano, TX 75075, USA

Weidemann, Jakob — *Artist*
Ringsveen, 2600 Lillehammer, Norway

Weidenbaum, Murray L — *Government Official, Economist*
6231 Rosebury Ave, St Louis, MO 63105, USA

Weidenfeld of Chelsea, Arthur G — *Publisher*
9 Chelsea Embankment, London SW3, England

Weider, Joe — *Publisher*
%Weider Health & Fitness, 21100 Erwin St, Woodland Hills, CA 91367, USA

Weidlinger, Paul — *Civil Engineer*
301 E 47th St, New York, NY 10017, USA

Weidman, Jerome — *Writer*
1230 Park Ave, New York, NY 10128, USA

Weidner, William P — *Businessman*
%Pratt Hotel Corp, 2 Galleria Tower, 13455 Noel Road, Dallas, TX 75240, USA

Weikl, Bernd — *Opera Singer*
%Lies Askonas Ltd, 186 Drury Lane, London WC2B 5QD, England

Weiland, Scott — *Singer (Stone Temple Pilots), Songwriter*
%Steve Stewart Mgmt, 8225 Santa Monica Blvd, West Hollywood, CA 90046, USA

Weill, Claudia B — *Movie Director*
2800 Seattle Dr, Los Angeles, CA 90046, USA

Weill, David (Dave) — *Track Athlete*
120 Mountain Spring Ave, San Francisco, CA 94114, USA

Weill, Richard L — *Financier*
%MBIA Inc, 113 King St, Armonk, NY 10504, USA

Weill, Sanford I — *Businessman, Lawyer*
%Travelers Inc, 388 Greenwich St, New York, NY 10013, USA

Wein, George — *Musical Producer*
%Festival Productions, 311 W 74th St, New York, NY 10023, USA

Weinberg, Alvin M — *Physicist*
111 Moylan Lane, Oak Ridge, TN 37830, USA

Weinberg, John L — *Financier*
%Goldman Sachs Co, 85 Broad St, New York, NY 10004, USA

Weinberg, Robert A — *Cancer Researcher, Biochemist*
%Whitehead Institute, 9 Cambridge Center, Cambridge, MA 02142, USA

Weinberg, Steven — *Nobel Physics Laureate*
%University of Texas, Physics Dept, Austin, TX 78712, USA

Weinberger, Caspar W — *Secretary, Defense & HEW; Publisher*
%Forbes Magazine, 60 5th Ave, New York, NY 10011, USA

Weinbrecht, Donna — *Skier*
%General Delivery, West Milford, NJ 07480, USA

Weiner, Art — *Football Player*
404 Kimberly Dr, Greensboro, NC 27408, USA

Weiner, Gerry — *Government Official, Canada*
%Cab du Ministre du Multiculturalisme, Ottawa ON K1A 0M5, Canada

Weiner, Timothy E — *Journalist*
%New York Times, Editorial Dept, 1627 "I" St NW, Washington, DC 20006, USA

Weiner, Walter H — *Financier*
%Republic New York Corp, 452 5th Ave, New York, NY 10018, USA

Weingarten, Reid — *Attorney*
%Steptoe & Johnson, 1330 Connecticut Ave NW, Washington, DC 20036, USA

Weinmeister, Arnie — *Football Player*
PO Box 70149, Seattle, WA 98107, USA

Weinstein, Arnold A — *Writer, Lyricist*
%Columbia University, English Dept, New York, NY 10027, USA

Weinstein, Harvey — *Movie Producer*
%Miramax Films, 7920 Sunset Blvd, Los Angeles, CA 90046, USA

Weinstein, Irwin M — *Internist, Hematologist*
9509 Heather Road, Beverly Hills, CA 90210, USA

Weinstein, Robert (Bob) — *Movie Producer*
%Miramax Films, 7920 Sunset Blvd, Los Angeles, CA 90046, USA

Weintraub, Jacob — *Art Gallery Owner*
%Weintraub Gallery, 965 Madison Ave, New York, NY 10021, USA

Weintraub, Jerry — *Movie Producer*
%Jerry Weintraub Productions, Lorimar Plaza, Burbank, CA 91505, USA

Weir, Gillian C — *Concert Organist, Harpsichordist*
78 Robin Way, Tilehurst, Berks RG3 5SW, England

Weir, Judith — *Composer*
%Chester Music, 8/9 Frith St, London W1V 5TZ, England

Weir, Peter L — *Movie Director*
Post Office, Palm Beach NSW 2108, Australia

Weisberg, Ruth — *Artist*
2421 3rd St, Santa Monica, CA 90405, USA

Weisberg, Tim — *Jazz Flutist*
%Pyramid Entertainment, 89 5th Ave, #700, New York, NY 10003, USA

Weisel, Heidi — *Fashion Designer*
%Heidi Weisel Inc, 260 W 35th St, New York,NY 10001, USA

Weiser, Irving — *Financier*
%Inter-Regional Financial, 60 S 6th St, Minneapolis, MN 55402, USA

Weisgall, Hugo D — *Composer, Conductor*
RR 1, Box 5265, Lincolnville, ME 04849, USA

Weiskantz, Lawrence — *Psychologist*
%Oxford University, Experimental Psychology Dept, Oxford OX1 3UD, England

Weiskopf, Tom — *Golfer*
7580 E Gray Road, Scottsdale, AZ 85260, USA

Weisman, Ben — *Composer*
4527 Alla Road, #3, Marina del Rey, CA 90292, USA

Weisman, Neil J — *Financier*
%Chilmark Capital Corp, 139 W Saddle River Road, Saddle River, NJ 07458, USA

Weisner, Maurice F — *Navy Admiral*
351 Woodbine Dr, Pensacola, FL 32503, USA

Weiss, Kenneth C — *Financier*
%Hyperian Capital Managment, 520 Madison Ave, New York, NY 10022, USA

Weiss, Melvyn I — *Attorney*
%Milberg Weiss Bershad, 1 Pennsylvania Plaza, New York, NY 10119, USA

Weiss, Michael — *Businessman*
%Limited Inc, 184 E Willow St, Columbus, OH 43206, USA

Weiss, Michael T — *Actor*
%Innovative Artists, 1999 Ave of Stars, #2850, Los Angeles, CA 90067, USA

Weiss, Morry — *Businessman*
%American Greetings Corp, 1, American Road, Cleveland, OH 44144, USA

Weiss, Theodore R — *Writer*
%Princeton University, QRL Poetry Series, 26 Haslet St, Princeton, NJ 08540, USA

Weiss, Walter W — *Baseball Player*
7220 S Flanders St, Aurora, CO 80016, USA

Weissenberg, Alexis — *Concert Pianist*
%Columbia Artists Mgmt Inc, 165 W 57th St, New York, NY 10019, USA

Weissflog, Jens — *Ski Jumper*
Markt 2, 09484 Kurort Oberwiesenthal, Germany

Weisskopf, Victor F — *Physicist*
20 Bartlett Terrace, Newton, MA 02159, USA

Weitz, Bruce — *Actor*
18826 Erwin St, Reseda, CA 91335, USA

Weitz, John — *Fashion Designer*
%John Weitz Designs, 600 Madison Ave, New York, NY 10022, USA

Weitz, Paul J — *Astronaut*
3086 N Tam Oshanter Dr, Flagstaff, AZ 86004, USA

Weitzman, Howard L — *Attorney*
%Katten Muchin Zavis Weitzman, 1999 Ave of Stars, #1400, Los Angeles, CA 90067, USA

Weizman, Ezer — *President, Israel; Air Force General*
2 Haddekel St, Caesarea, Israel

Welch, Elisabeth — *Actress, Singer*
4-A Carpenters Close, London SW1, England

Welch, John F (Jack), Jr — *Businessman*
%General Electric, 3135 Easton Turnpike, Fairfield, CT 06431, USA

Welch, Kevin — *Singer, Songwriter*
%Press Network, 1018 17th Ave S, #1, Nashville, TN 37212, USA

Welch, Lenny — *Singer*
%Brothers Mgmt, 141 Dunbar Ave, Fords, NJ 08863, USA

Welch, Raquel — *Actress*
9903 Santa Monica Blvd, #514, Beverly Hills, CA 90212, USA

Welch, Robert L (Bob) — *Baseball Player*
10800 E Cactus Road, #33, Scottsdale, AZ 85259, USA

Welch, Tahnee — *Actress*
134 Duane St, #400, New York, NY 10013, USA

Weld, Tuesday — *Actress*
PO Box 367, Valley Stream, NY 11582, USA

Weldon, Fay — *Writer*
24 Ryland Road, London NW5 3EA, England

Weldon, Virginia V — *Businesswoman, Physician*
%Monsanto Co, 800 N Lindbergh Blvd, St Louis, MO 63141, USA

Weller, Freddie — *Singer, Songwriter*
%Cape Entertainment, 1161 NW 76th Ave, Fort Lauderdale, FL 33322, USA

Weller, Michael — *Writer*
%Rosenstone/Wender, 3 E 48th St, New York, NY 10017, USA

Weller, Peter — *Actor*
8401 Cresthill Road, West Hollywood, CA 90069, USA

Weller, Ronny — *Weightlifter*
AC 1892 Mutterstadt, Waldstr 61, 67112 Mutterstadt, Germany

Weller, Thomas H — *Nobel Medicine Laureate*
56 Winding River Road, Needham, MA 02192, USA

Weller, Walter — *Conductor*
Doblinger Hauptstr 40, 1190 Vienna, Austria

Welling, Paul A — *Coast Guard Admiral*
Commander, Atlantic Area, Governor's Island, New York, NY 10004, USA

Wellman, Mark — *Rock Climber*
%Visitor's Bureau, Yosemite National Park, CA 95389, USA

Wellman, William, Jr — *Actor*
410 N Barrington Ave, Los Angeles, CA 90049, USA

Wells, A Stanton — *Businessman*
%Barnes Group, 123 Main St, Bristol, CT 06010, USA

Wells, Annie — *Photographer*
%Press Democrat, Editorial Dept, 427 Mendocino Ave, Santa Rosa, CA 95401, USA

Wells, Dawn — *Actress*
4616 Ledge Ave, North Hollywood, CA 91602, USA

Wells, J Lyle — *Financier*
%UMB Financial Corp, 1010 Grand Ave, Kansas City, MO 64106, USA

Wells, James M, III — *Financier*
%Crestar Financial Corp, 919 E Main St, Richmond, VA 23219, USA

Wells, Junior — *Singer, Harmonica Player*
%Marty Saltzman Mgmt, 3051 W Logan Road, Chicago, IL 60647, USA

Wells, Kitty — *Singer*
%Wright's Enterprises, 240 Old Hickory Blvd, Madison, TN 37115, USA

Wells, Mark — *Hockey Player*
27619 Harrison Woods Lane, Harrison Turnpike, MI 48045, USA

Wells, Thomas B — *Judge*
%US Tax Court, 400 2nd St NW, Washington, DC 20217, USA

Welser-Most, Franz — *Conductor*
%Artists Management Co, Bildgass, 9494 Schaan, Liechtenstein

Welsh, Moray M — *Concert Cellist*
28 Somerfield Ave, Queens Park, London NW6 6JY, England

Welsh, Stephanie *Photographer*
%Palm Beach Post, Photo Dept, 2751 S Dixie Highway, West Palm Beach, FL 33405, USA

Welsome, Eileen *Journalist*
%Albuquerque Tribune, Editorial Dept, 7777 Jefferson NE, Albuquerque, NM 87109, USA

Welting, Ruth L *Opera Singer*
%Robert Lombardo, Harkness Plaza, 61 W 62nd St, #B-5, New York, NY 10023, USA

Welty, Eudora *Writer*
%Russell & Volkening, 50 W 29th St, New York, NY 10001, USA

Welty, John D *Educator*
4411 N Van Ness Blvd, Fresno, CA 93704, USA

Wences, Senor *Ventriloquist, Comedian*
204 W 55th St, #701-A, New York, NY 10019, USA

Wendelin, Rudolph A *Cartoonist (Smokey the Bear)*
4516 7th St N, Arlington, VA 22203, USA

Wendelstedt, Harry H, Jr *Baseball Umpire*
88 S St Andrews Dr, Ormond Beach, FL 32174, USA

Wenden, Michael *Swimmer*
%Palm Beach Currumbin Center, Thrower Dr, Palm Beach Queens, Australia

Wenders, Wim *Movie Director*
%Road Movies Filmproduktion, Potsdamerstr 199, 10785 Berlin, Germany

Wendt, Gary C *Financier*
%General Electric Capital, 260 Long Ridge Road, Stamford, CT 06927, USA

Wendt, George *Actor*
3856 Vantage Ave, Studio City, CA 91604, USA

Wenge, Ralph *Commentator*
%Cable News Network, News Dept, 1050 Techwood Dr NW, Atlanta, GA 30318, USA

Wenner, Jann S *Publisher*
%Straight Arrow Publications, 1290 Ave of Americas, New York, NY 10104, USA

Went, Frits W *Botanist*
Lodestar Lane 3450, Reno, NV 89503, USA

Wente, Jean R *Businessman*
%California State Automobile Assn, PO Box 422940, San Francisco, CA 94142, USA

Wentworth, Alexandra *Comedienne*
%Creative Artists Agency, 9830 Wilshire Blvd, Beverly Hills, CA 90212, USA

Wentz, Howard B, Jr *Businessman*
%Tambrands Inc, 777 Westchester Ave, White Plains, NY 10604, USA

Wenzel, Andreas *Skier*
Oberhul 151, Liechtenstein-Gamprin, Liechtenstein

Wenzel, Hanni *Skier*
Fanalwegle 4, 9494 Schaan, Liechtenstein

Werbach, Adam *Environmentalist*
%Sierra Club, 85 2nd St, #200, San Francisco, CA 94105, USA

Werber, William M (Bill) *Baseball Player*
11812 Quail Village Way, Naples, FL 34119, USA

Werner, Helmut *Businessman*
%Daimler-Benz AG, Mercedesstr 136, 70327 Stuttgart, Germany

Werner, Michael *Art Dealer*
%Michael Werner Ltd, 21 E 67th St, New York, NY 10021, USA

Werner, Pierre *Prime Minister, Luxembourg*
2 Rond-Point Robert Schuman, Luxembourg

Werner, Roger L, Jr *Television Executive*
%Prime Sports Ventures, 10000 Santa Monica Blvd, Los Angeles, CA 90067, USA

Werth, Isabell *Equestrian Rider*
Winterswicker Feld 4, 47495 Rheinberg, Germany

Wertheim, Jorge *Association Executive*
%UNESCO, Director's Office, UN Plaza, New York, NY 10017, USA

Wertheimer, Fredric M *Association Executive*
3502 Macomb St NW, Washington, DC 20016, USA

Wertheimer, Linda *Commentator*
%National Public Radio, News Dept, 2025 "M" St NW, Washington, DC 20036, USA

Wertheimer, Thomas *Entertainment Executive*
%MCA Inc, 100 Universal City Plaza, Universal City, CA 91608, USA

Werthen, Hans L O *Businessman*
%AB Electrolux, 105 45 Stockholm, Sweden

Wertmuller, Lina *Movie Director*
Piazza Clotilde, 00196 Rome, Italy

Werts, Jo *Artist*
2050 Emmons Road, Cambria, CA 93428, USA

Wesker, Arnold — Writer
37 Ashley Road, London N19 3AG, England

Wesselmann, Tom — Artist
RD 1, Box 36, Long Eddy, NY 12760, USA

Wessels, Leon — Government Official, South Africa
%Foreign Affairs Ministry, Private Bag X-152, Pretoria 001, South Africa

West, Adam — Actor
PO Box 3477, Ketchum, ID 83340, USA

West, Cornel — Theologian, Sociologist
%Harvard University, Afro-American Studies Dept, Cambridge, MA 02138, USA

West, Doug — Basketball Player
15 Holly Road, Wheeling, WV 26003, USA

West, Ernest E — Korean War Army Hero (CMH)
912 Adams Ave, Wurtland, KY 41144, USA

West, Jake — Labor Leader
%International Assn of Iron Workers, 1750 New York Ave NW, Washington, DC 20006, USA

West, Jerome A (Jerry) — Basketball Player, Executive
1210 Moraga Dr, Los Angeles, CA 90049, USA

West, Joel — Model
%Boss Models, 1 Gansevoort St, New York, NY 10014, USA

West, John C — Governor, SC
PO Drawer 13, Hilton Head Island, SC 29938, USA

West, Leslie — Singer, Guitarist
%Skyline Music, PO Box 31, Lancaster, NH 03584, USA

West, Mark — Basketball Player
715 E Forest Hills Dr, Phoenix, AZ 85022, USA

West, Michael — Businessman
%Octel Communications, 1001 Murphy Ranch Road, Milpitas, CA 95035, USA

West, Morris L — Writer
PO Box 102, Avalon NSW 2107, Australia

West, Robert H — Businessman
%Butler Manufacturing, BMA Tower, Penn Valley Park, Kansas City, MO 64141, USA

West, Sam — Actor
%Peters Fraser Dunlop, Chelsea Harbour, Lots Rd, London SW10 0XF, England

West, Shelly — Singer
%West Hood Entertainment, PO Box 210168, Nashville, TN 37221, USA

West, Thomas L, Jr — Businessman
%Variable Annuity Life, 2929 Allen Parkway, Houston, TX 77019, USA

West, Timothy — Actor
%James Sharkey, 21 Golden Square, London W1R 3PA, England

Westbrook, Michael — Football Player
%Washington Redskins, 21300 Redskin Park Dr, Ashburn, VA 20147, USA

Westbrook, Peter — Fencer
15 Washington Place, #1-F, New York, NY 10003, USA

Westerberg, Verne E — Publisher
%Vogue Magazine, 350 Madison Ave, New York, NY 10017, USA

Westerfield, Putney — Publisher
10 Greenview Lane, Hillsborough, CA 94010, USA

Westfall, Ed — Hockey Player
PO Box 39, Locust Valley, NY 11560, USA

Westhead, Paul — Basketball Coach
2217 Via Alamitos, Palos Verdes Estates, CA 90274, USA

Westheimer, David K — Writer
11722 Darlington Ave, #2, Los Angeles, CA 90049, USA

Westheimer, Frank H — Chemist
3 Berkeley St, Cambridge, MA 02138, USA

Westheimer, Ruth S — Sex Therapist, Psychologist
900 W 190th St, New York, NY 10040, USA

Westin, Av — Television Executive, Journalist
%King World Productions, 1700 Broadway, New York, NY 10019, USA

Westin, Dave — Television Executive
%ABC-TV, News Dept, 77 W 66th St, New York, NY 10023, USA

Westlake, Donald E — Writer
%Knox Burger Assoc, 39 1/2 Washington Square S, New York, NY 10012, USA

Westling, Jon — Educator
135 Ivy St, Brookline, MA 02146, USA

Westmoreland, James — Actor
8019 1/2 W Norton Ave, Los Angeles, CA 90046, USA

Westmoreland, William C — *Army General*
107 1/2 Tradd St, Charleston, SC 29401, USA

Weston, Randy — *Jazz Pianist*
PO Box 749, Maplewood, NJ 07040, USA

Westphal, James A — *Space Scientist*
%California Institute of Technology, Planetary Sciences Dept, Pasadena, CA 91125, USA

Westwood, Vivienne — *Fashion Designer*
The Lanterns, #3, Old School House, Bridge Lane, London SW11 3AD, England

Wetherbee, James D — *Astronaut*
%NASA, Johnson Space Center, 2101 NASA Road, Houston, TX 77058, USA

Wetherill, George W — *Geophysicist*
%Carnegie Institution, Terrestrial Magnetism Dept, Washington, DC 20015, USA

Wethington, Charles T, Jr — *Educator*
%University of Kentucky, President's Office, Lexington, KY 40506, USA

Wetter, Friedrich Cardinal — *Religious Leader*
Kardinal-Faulhaber-Str 7, 80333 Munich, Germany

Wettig, Patricia — *Actress*
5855 Topanga Canyon Blvd, #410, Woodland Hills, CA 91367, USA

Wetzel, Gary G — *Vietnam War Army Hero (CMH)*
PO Box 84, Oak Creek, WI 53154, USA

Wetzel, John — *Basketball Coach*
9180 SW Woodbridge Court, Wilsonville, OR 97070, USA

Wetzel, Rosemarie — *Model*
%Elite Model Mgmt, 111 E 22nd St, #200, New York, NY 10010, USA

Wexler, Anne — *Government Official*
1317 "F" St NW, #600, Washington, DC 20004, USA

Wexler, Haskell — *Cinematographer*
1341 Ocean Ave, #111, Santa Monica, CA 90401, USA

Wexler, Jacqueline G — *Educator*
222 Park Ave S, New York, NY 10003, USA

Wexner, Leslie H — *Businessman*
%Limited Inc, 184 E Willow St, Columbus, OH 43206, USA

Weyand, Frederick C — *Army General*
2121 Ala Wai Blvd, PH 1, Honolulu, HI 96815, USA

Weyerhaeuser, George H — *Businessman*
%Weyerhaeuser Co, 33663 32nd Ave S, Tacoma, WA 98023, USA

Whalen, Laurence J — *Judge*
%US Tax Court, 400 2nd St NW, Washington, DC 20217, USA

Whalley, Joanne — *Actress*
1435 Lindacrest Dr, Beverly Hills, CA 90210, USA

Whalum, Kirk — *Jazz Saxophonist*
%Variety Artists Int'l, 15490 Ventura Blvd, Sherman Oaks, CA 91403, USA

Wharton, David — *Swimmer*
%Ohio State University, Athletic Dept, Columbus, OH 43210, USA

Whatley, Ennis — *Basketball Player*
%Portland Trail Blazers, 1 N Center Court, #200, Portland, OR 97227, USA

Wheat, Francis M — *Attorney*
%Gibson Dunn Crutcher, 333 S Grand Ave, #4400, Los Angeles, CA 90071, USA

Wheatley, E H — *Publisher*
%Vancouver Sun, 2250 Granville St, Vancouver BC V6H 3G2, Canada

Wheatley, Tyrone — *Football Player*
%New York Giants, Giants Stadium, East Rutherford, NJ 07073, USA

Wheaton, David — *Tennis Player*
4430 Manitou Road, Tonka Bay, MN 55331, USA

Wheaton, Wil — *Actor*
2603 Seapine Lane, La Crescenta, CA 91214, USA

Wheeler, C E — *Labor Leader*
%Railway Carmen Brotherhood, 4929 Main St, Kansas City, MO 64112, USA

Wheeler, Daniel S — *Editor*
%American Legion Magazine, 700 N Pennsylvania St, Indianapolis, IN 46204, USA

Wheeler, H Anthony — *Architect*
Hawthornbank House, Dean Village, Edinburgh EH4 3BH, Scotland

Wheeler, Harold A — *Radio Engineer*
4900 Telegraph Road, #523, Ventura, CA 93003, USA

Wheeler, John A — *Physicist*
1904 Meadow Lane, Highstown, NJ 08520, USA

Wheeler, Thomas B — *Businessman*
%Massachusetts Mutual Life, 1295 State St, Springfield, MA 01111, USA

Wheeler-Bennett, R C	*Businessman*
%Thomas Borthwick & Sons, St John's Lane, London EC1M 4BX, England	
Whelan, Bill	*Composer*
%William Morris Agency, 31/32 Soho Square, London W1V 5DG, England	
Whelan, Wendy	*Ballerina*
%New York City Ballet, Lincoln Center Plaza, New York, NY 10023, USA	
Whelchel, Lisa	*Actress*
30408 Olympic St, Castaic, CA 91384, USA	
Whinnery, Barbara	*Actress*
%Baier/Kleinman, 3575 Cahuenga Blvd, #500, Los Angeles, CA 90068, USA	
Whinnery, John R	*Electrical Engineer*
1804 Wales Dr, Walnut Creek, CA 94595, USA	
Whipple, Fred L	*Astronomer*
35 Elizabeth Road, Belmont, MA 02178, USA	
Whirry, Shannon	*Actress*
%Stone Manners, 8091 Selma Ave, Los Angeles, CA 90046, USA	
Whishaw, Anthony	*Artist*
7-A Albert Place, Victoria Road, London W8 5PD, England	
Whiston, Don	*Hockey Player*
2 Jeffreys Neck, Ipswich, MA 01938, USA	
Whitacre, Edward E, Jr	*Businessman*
%Southwestern Bell Corp, 175 E Houston, San Antonio, TX 78205, USA	
Whitaker, Forest	*Actor*
10345 W Olympic Blvd, #200, Los Angeles, CA 90064, USA	
Whitaker, Jack	*Sportscaster*
PO Box 342, Bridgehampton, NY 11932, USA	
Whitaker, Louis R (Lou)	*Baseball Player*
803 Pipe St, Martinsville, VA 24112, USA	
Whitaker, Meade	*Judge*
%US Tax Court, 400 2nd St NW, Washington, DC 20217, USA	
Whitaker, Pernell	*Boxer*
4752 Berrywood Road, Virginia Beach, VA 23464, USA	
Whitbread, Fatima	*Track Athlete*
5 Hemley Road, Orsett, Essex, England	
Whitcomb, Edgar D	*Governor, IN*
PO Box 23, Hayden, IN 47245, USA	
Whitcomb, Ian	*Singer, Songwriter*
%British & Int'l Artists, 500 Waterman Ave, #191, East Providence, RI 02914, USA	
White of Rhymney, Eirene L	*Government Official, England*
64 Vandon Court, Petty France, London SW1H 9HF, England	
White, Alvin S (Al)	*Test Pilot*
14254 N Fawnbrooke Dr, Tucson, AZ 85737, USA	
White, Barry	*Singer, Songwriter*
3395 S Jones Blvd, #176, Las Vegas, NV 89102, USA	
White, Betty	*Actress, Comedienne*
PO Box 491965, Los Angeles, CA 90049, USA	
White, Bryan	*Singer, Songwriter*
%GC Mgmt, 1114 17th Ave S, #102, Nashville, TN 37212, USA	
White, Byron R (Whizzer)	*Supreme Court Justice, Football Player*
6801 Hampshire Road, McLean, VA 22101, USA	
White, Charles	*Football Player, Administrator*
51 Foxtail Lane, Dove Canyon, CA 92679, USA	
White, Danny	*Football Player*
12644 N Central Expressway, #115, Dallas, TX 75243, USA	
White, Edmund V	*Writer*
%Maxine Groffsky, 2 5th Ave, New York, NY 10011, USA	
White, Frank	*Baseball Player*
5335 W 96th St, Shawnee Mission, KS 66207, USA	
White, Frank	*Governor, AR*
1 Andover Dr, #7, Little Rock, AR 72227, USA	
White, Gilbert F	*Geographer*
624 Pearl St, #302, Boulder, CO 80302, USA	
White, Jaleel	*Actor*
8916 Ashcroft Ave, Los Angeles, CA 90048, USA	
White, John H	*Photographer*
%Chicago Sun-Times, 401 N Wabash Ave, Chicago, IL 60611, USA	
White, Josh, Jr	*Singer*
%URIM Too Productions, 19191 Lancershire, Rosedale Park, MI 48223, USA	

W

Wheeler-Bennett - White

V.I.P. Address Book   707

White, Joy Lynn — *Singer*
%Buddy Lee, 38 Music Square E, #300, Nashville, TN 37203, USA

White, Judith M — *Biologist*
%University of San Francisco, Biology Dept, San Francisco, CA 94117, USA

White, Julie — *Actress*
%Silver Massetti Szatmary, 8730 Sunset Blvd, #480, Los Angeles, CA 90069, USA

White, Karyn — *Singer*
%William Morris Agency, 1325 Ave of Americas, New York, NY 10019, USA

White, Kate — *Editor*
%Redbook Magazine, Editorial Dept, 224 W 57th St, New York, NY 10019, USA

White, Lari — *Singer, Songwriter*
%Carter Career Mgmt, 1028 18th Ave S, #B, Nashville, TN 37212, USA

White, Lorenzo — *Football Player*
3450 NW 7th St, Fort Lauderdale, FL 33311, USA

White, Marco P — *Chef*
The Restaurant, Knightsbridge, London SW1, England

White, Marilyn — *Track Athlete*
9605 6th Ave, Inglewood, CA 90305, USA

White, Martha G — *Publisher*
%London Free Press, 369 York St, London ON N6A 4G1, Canada

White, Michael R — *Mayor*
%Mayor's Office, City Hall, 60I Lakeside Ave E, Cleveland, OH 44113, USA

White, Michael S — *Movie, Theater Producer*
13 Duke St, St James's, London SW1 6DB, England

White, Nera — *Basketball Player*
RR 3, Box 165, Lafayette, TN 37083, USA

White, Randy — *Football Player*
Rt 1, Box 187, Prosper, TX 75078, USA

White, Raymond P, Jr — *Oral Surgeon*
1506 Velma Road, Chapel Hill, NC 27514, USA

White, Reginald H (Reggie) — *Football Player*
PO Box 10628, Green Bay, WI 54307, USA

White, Robert L — *Labor Leader*
%National Postal Employees Alliance, 1644 11th St NW, Washington, DC 20001, USA

White, Robert M — *Test Pilot, Air Force General*
PO Box 2488, APO, AE, NY 09063, USA

White, Robert M — *Meteorologist*
Somerset House II, 5610 Wisconsin Ave, #1506, Bethesda, MD 20815, USA

White, Robert M, II — *Journalist*
1824 Phelps Place NW, #1813, Washington, DC 20008, USA

White, Roy H — *Baseball Player*
297-101 Kinderkamack Road, Oradell, NJ 07649, USA

White, Sherman E — *Football Player*
PO Box 1856, Pebble Beach, CA 93953, USA

White, Steven A — *Navy Admiral, Businessman*
%Stone & Webster Engineering Corp, 245 Summer St, Boston, MA 02210, USA

White, Tim D — *Anthropologist*
%University of California, Human Evolutionary Studies Lab, Berkeley, CA 94720, USA

White, Vanna — *Entertainer, Model*
2600 Larmar Road, Los Angeles, CA 90068, USA

White, Willard W — *Opera Singer*
10 Montague Ave, London SE4 1YP, England

White, William D (Bill) — *Baseball Player, Executive*
3721 Darrell Lane, Tyler, TX 75701, USA

White, Willye B — *Track Athlete*
7221 S Calumet Ave, Chicago, IL 60619, USA

Whitehead, Alfred K — *Labor Leader*
%International Assn of Fire Fighters, 1750 New York Ave NW, Washington, DC 20006, USA

Whitehead, George W — *Mathematician*
25 Bellevue Road, Arlington, MA 02174, USA

Whitehead, Jerome — *Basketball Player*
1543 Merritt Dr, El Cajon, CA 92020, USA

Whitehead, John C — *Government Official, Financier*
%AEA Investors, 65 E 55th St, New York, NY 10022, USA

Whitehead, John C — *Research Executive*
%Brookings Institute, 1775 Massachusetts Ave NW, Washington, DC 20036, USA

Whitehead, Richard F — *Navy Admiral*
%American Cage & Machine Co, 135 S LaSalle St, Chicago, IL 60603, USA

Whitelaw of Penrith, William S A — *Government Official, England*
%House of Lords, Westminster, London SW1A 0PW, England

Whitelaw, Billie — *Actress*
Rose Cottage, Plum St, Glensford, Suffolk C010 7PX, England

Whiteley, Benjamin R — *Businessman*
%Standard Insurance, 1100 SW 6th Ave, Portland, OR 97204, USA

Whitemore, Willet F, Jr — *Cancer Researcher*
2 Hawthorne Lane, Plandome, NY 11030, USA

Whitfield, Lynn — *Actress*
%Progressive Artists Agency, 400 S Beverly Dr, #216, Beverly Hills, CA 90212, USA

Whitfield, Mal — *Track Athlete*
1322 28th St SE, Washington, DC 20020, USA

Whiting, Margaret — *Singer*
41 W 58th St, #5-A, New York, NY 10019, USA

Whiting, Val — *Basketball Player*
%San Jose Lasers, 1530 Parkmoor Ave, #A San Jose, CA 95128, USA

Whitlam, E Gough — *Prime Minister, Australia*
Westfield Towers, 100 William St, Sydney NSW 2011, Australia

Whitley, Chris — *Singer, Songwriter*
%Creative Artists Agency, 9830 Wilshire Blvd, Beverly Hills, CA 90212, USA

Whitman, Christine Todd — *Governor, NJ*
%Governor's Office, State House, 125 W State St, Trenton, NJ 08608, USA

Whitman, Marina Von Neumann — *Economist*
%University of Michigan, Business Administration Dept, Ann Arbor, MI 48109, USA

Whitman, Slim — *Singer*
3830 Old Jennings Road, Middleburg, FL 32068, USA

Whitman, Stuart — *Actor*
749 San Ysidro Road, Santa Barbara, CA 93108, USA

Whitmore, James — *Actor*
4990 Puesta del Sol, Malibu, CA 90265, USA

Whitmore, James, Jr — *Actor*
1284 La Brea St, Thousand Oaks, CA 91362, USA

Whitney, CeCe — *Actress*
2055 N Nutmeg St, Escondido, CA 92026, USA

Whitney, Hassler — *Educator*
%Institute for Advanced Study, Olden Lane, Princeton, NJ 08540, USA

Whitney, Jane — *Entertainer*
5 TV Place, Needham, MA 02194, USA

Whitney, Ruth R — *Editor*
%Glamour Magazine, Editorial Dept, 350 Madison Ave, New York, NY 10017, USA

Whitsitt, Robert J — *Basketball Executive*
%Seattle Supersonics, 190 Queen Ave N, PO Box C-900911, Seattle, WA 98109, USA

Whittaker, James (Jim) — *Mountaineer*
2023 E Sims Way, #277, Port Townsend, WA 98368, USA

Whittaker, Roger — *Singer, Songwriter*
PO Box 1655, London W8 5HZ, England

Whittingham, Charles A — *Publisher*
11 Woodmill Road, Chappaqua, NY 10514, USA

Whittingham, Charles E (Charlie) — *Thoroughbred Racing Trainer*
1000 Chestnut St, #2=-B, San Francisco, CA 94109, USA

Whitton, Margaret — *Actress*
%William Morris Agency, 151 S El Camino Dr, Beverly Hills, CA 90212, USA

Whitwam, David R — *Businessman*
%Whirlpool Corp, 2000 N State St, Rt 63, Benton Harbor, MI 49022, USA

Whitworth, Kathrynne A (Kathy) — *Golfer*
5990 Lindenshire Lane, #101, Dallas, TX 75230, USA

Whitworth, William — *Editor*
%Atlantic Monthly Magazine, Editorial Dept, 745 Boylston St, Boston, MA 02116, USA

Whyte, William H — *Writer*
175 E 94th St, New York, NY 10128, USA

Wiatt, James A — *Entertainment Executive*
%International Creative Mgmt, 8942 Wilshire Blvd, Beverly Hills, CA 90211, USA

Wiberg, Kenneth B — *Chemist*
160 Carmalt Road, Hamden, CT 06517, USA

Wiberg, Pernilla — *Skier*
Katterunsvagen 32, 60 210 Norrkopping, Sweden

Wiborg, James H — *Businessman*
%Univar Corp, 6100 Carillon Point, Kirkland, WA 98033, USA

Wichmann, Herbert — *Government Official, Germany*
Ohnhorstr 29, 22609 Hamburg, Germany
Wichterle, Otto — *Chemist, Inventor (Soft Contact Lens)*
U Andelky 27, 162 00 Prague 6, Czech Republic
Wick, Charles Z — *Government Official*
%US Information Agency, 400 "C" St SW, Washington, DC 20024, USA
Wickenheiser, Robert J — *Educator*
%St Bonaventure University, President's Office, St Bonaventure, NY 14778, USA
Wicker, Thomas G (Tom) — *Writer, Journalist*
169 E 80th St, New York, NY 10021, USA
Wickham, John A, Jr — *Army General*
13590 N Fawnbrooke Dr, Tucson, AZ 85737, USA
Wickremesinghe, Ranil — *Prime Minister, Sri Lanka*
%Prime Minister's Office, 150 R A De Mel Mawatha, Colombo 3, Sri Lanka
Wicks, Ben — *Editorial Cartoonist*
38 Yorkville Ave, Toronto ON M4W 1L5, Canada
Wicks, Sidney — *Basketball Player*
1030 S La Jolla Ave, Los Angeles, CA 90035, USA
Widdoes, Kathleen — *Actress*
%"As the World Turns" Show, CBS-TV, 524 W 57th St, #5330, New York, NY 10019, USA
Wideman, John Edgar — *Writer*
%University of Massachusetts, English Dept, Amherst, MA 01003, USA
Widman, Herbert (Herb) — *Water Polo Player*
4730 La Villa Marina, #G, Marina del Rey, CA 90292, USA
Widmark, Richard — *Actor*
PO Box 232, Woodland Hills, CA 91365, USA
Widom, Benjamin — *Chemist*
%Cornell University, Chemistry Dept, Ithaca, NY 14853, USA
Widseth, Edwin C (Ed) — *Football Player*
1666 Coffman St, #117, St Paul, MN 55108, USA
Wiebe, Susanne — *Fashion Designer*
Amalienstr 39, 80799 Munich, Germany
Wiedemann, Josef — *Architect*
Im Eichgeholz 11, 80997 Munich, Germany
Wiederkehr, Joseph A — *Labor Leader*
%Roofers Waterproofers & Allied Workers, 1125 17th NW, Washington, DC 20036, USA
Wiedorfer, Paul J — *WW II Army Hero (CMH)*
2506 Moore Ave, Baltimore, MD 21234, USA
Wiese, John P — *Judge*
%US Claims Court, 717 Madison Place NW, Washington, DC 20005, USA
Wiesel, Elie — *Writer, Nobel Peace Laureate*
200 E 64th St, New York, NY 10021, USA
Wiesel, Torsten N — *Nobel Medicine Laureate*
%Rockefeller University, Neurobiology Lab, York & 66th, New York, NY 10013, USA
Wiesen, Bernard — *Movie Director*
Weisgerberstr 2, 80805 Munich, Germany
Wiesenthal, Simon — *War Crimes Activist*
%Jewish Documentation Center, Salztorgasse 6, 1010 Vienna, Austria
Wiesner, Kenneth (Ken) — *Track Athlete*
3601 Meta Lake Road, Eagle River, WI 54521, USA
Wiest, Dianne — *Actress*
59 E 54th St, #22, New York, NY 10022, USA
Wigdale, James B — *Businessman*
%M&I Marshall & Ilsley Bank, 770 N Water St, Milwaukee, WI 53202, USA
Wiggin, Paul — *Football Player, Coach*
5013 Ridge Road, Edina, MN 55436, USA
Wiggins, Audrey — *Singer*
%William Morris Agency, 2100 West End Ave, #1000, Nashville, TN 37203, USA
Wiggins, James Russell — *Editor, Diplomat*
Carlton Cove, HC 63, Box 436, Brooklin, ME 04616, USA
Wiggins, John — *Singer*
%William Morris Agency, 2100 West End Ave, #1000, Nashville, TN 37203, USA
Wigglesworth, Marian McKean — *Skier*
%General Delivery, Wilson, WY 83014, USA
Wightman, Arthur S — *Mathematician, Physicist*
16 Balsam Lane, Princeton, NJ 08540, USA
Wightman, Donald E — *Labor Leader*
%Utility Workers Union, 815 16th Ave NW, Washington, DC 20006, USA

Wigle, Ernest D — *Cardiologist*
101 College St, Toronto ON M56 1L7, Canada

Wiik, Sven — *Skier*
PO Box 774484, Steamboat Springs, CO 80477, USA

Wijdenbosch, Jules — *President, Suriname*
%Presidential Palace, Onafhankelikheidsplein 1, Paramaribo, Suriname

Wilander, Mats — *Tennis Player*
%Einar Wilander, Vickersvagen 2, Vaxjo, Sweden

Wilbraham, John H G — *Concert Cornetist, Trumpeter*
9 D Cuthbert St, Wells, Somerset BA5 2AW, England

Wilbur, Doreen — *Archery Athlete*
1401 W Lincoln Way, Jefferson, IA 50129, USA

Wilbur, Richard C — *Judge*
%US Tax Court, 400 2nd St NW, Washington, DC 20217, USA

Wilbur, Richard P — *Writer*
87 Dodswell Road, Cummington, MA 01026, USA

Wilbur, Richard S — *Physician, Association Executive*
PO Box 70, Lake Forest, IL 60045, USA

Wilby, James — *Actor*
%International Creative Mgmt, 76 Oxford St, London W1N 0AX, England

Wilcox, Christopher — *Editor*
%Reader's Digest Magazine, Reader's Digest Road, Pleasantville, NY 10570, USA

Wilcox, David — *Singer, Songwriter*
%The Agency, 41 Britain St, #200, Toronto ON M5A 1R7, Canada

Wilcox, Larry — *Actor*
10 Appaloosa Lane, Bell Canyon, Canoga Park, CA 91307, USA

Wilcox, Lisa — *Actress*
%Stone Manners, 8091 Selma Ave, Los Angeles, CA 90046, USA

Wilcutt, Terence W — *Astronaut*
%NASA, Johnson Space Center, 2101 NASA Road, Houston, TX 77058, USA

Wild, Earl — *Concert Pianist*
2233 Fernleaf Lane, Worthington, OH 43235, USA

Wild, Jack — *Actor*
%London Mgmt, 2-4 Noel St, London W1V 3RB, England

Wilde, Kim — *Singer, Songwriter*
Big M House, 1 Stevenage Road, Knebworth, Herts SG3 6AN, England

Wilde, Patricia — *Ballerina, Artistic Director*
%Pittsburgh Ballet Theater, 2900 Liberty Ave, Pittsburgh, PA 15201, USA

Wildenstein, Daniel L — *Art Historian, Dealer*
%Wildenstein Co, 57 Rue la Boetie, 75008 Paris, France

Wilder, Billy — *Movie Director*
10375 Wilshire Blvd, Los Angeles, CA 90024, USA

Wilder, Gene — *Actor, Movie Director*
10930 Chalon Road, Los Angeles, CA 90077, USA

Wilder, James — *Football Player*
1706 Cape Bend Ave, Tampa, FL 33613, USA

Wilder, James — *Actor*
%Metropolitan Talent Agency, 4526 Wilshire Blvd, Los Angeles, CA 90010, USA

Wilder, L Douglas — *Governor, VA*
2509 E Broad St, Richmond, VA 23223, USA

Wildman, Valerie — *Actress*
%Moress Nanas Wald, 12424 Wilshire Blvd, #840, Los Angeles, CA 90025, USA

Wildmon, Donald — *Social Activist*
%National Federation of Decency, PO Box 1398, Tupelo, MS 38802, USA

Wildung, Richard K (Dick) — *Football Player*
10368 Rich Road, Bloomington, MN 55437, USA

Wiles, Andrew — *Mathematician*
%Princeton University, Mathematics Dept, Princeton, NJ 08544, USA

Wiley, Don C — *Biochemist*
%Children's Hospital, Molecular Medicine Lab, 320 Longwood Ave, Boston, MA 02115, USA

Wiley, Lee — *Singer*
%Country Crossroads, 7787 Monterey St, Gilroy, CA 95020, USA

Wiley, Richard E — *Government Official*
3818 Woodrow St, Arlington, VA 22207, USA

Wiley, William T — *Artist*
PO Box 654, Woodacre, CA 94973, USA

Wilford, John Noble, Jr — *Journalist*
232 W 10th St, New York, NY 10014, USA

W

Wigle - Wilford

W

Wilhelm, Charles E *Marine Corps General*
Cmd General, Marine Forces Atlantic, PSC Box 20115, Camp Lejeune, NC 28542, USA
Wilhelm, J Hoyt *Baseball Player*
PO Box 2217, Sarasota, FL 34230, USA
Wilkening, Laurel L *Educator*
%University of California, Chancellor's Office, Irvine, CA 92717, USA
Wilkens, Leonard R (Lenny), Jr *Basketball Player, Coach*
2660 Peachtree Road NW, #39-F, Atlanta, GA 30305, USA
Wilkerson, Bobby *Basketball Player*
814 Rustic Road, Anderson, IN 46013, USA
Wilkerson, Isabel *Journalist*
%New York Times, Editorial Dept, 229 W 43rd St, New York, NY 10036, USA
Wilkes, Glen *Basketball Coach*
%Stetson University, Athletic Dept, Campus Box 8359, DeLand, FL 32720, USA
Wilkes, Jamaal *Basketball Player*
7846 W 81st St, Playa del Rey, CA 90293, USA
Wilkes, Maurice V *Computer Engineer*
%Olivetti Research Ltd, 24-A Trumpington St, Cambridge CB2 1QA, England
Wilkie, David *Swimmer*
Oaklands, Queens Hill, Ascot, Berkshire, England
Wilkin, Richard E *Religious Leader*
%Winebrenner Theological Seminary, 701 E Melrose Ave, Findlay, OH 45840, USA
Wilkins, Mac *Track Athlete*
328 Coldbrook Lane, Box 1058, Soquel, CA 95073, USA
Wilkins, Maurice H F *Nobel Medicine Laureate*
30 St John's Park, London SE3, England
Wilkins, Roger *Journalist*
%George Mason University, 207 East Building, Fairfax, VA 22030, USA
Wilkinson, Geoffrey *Nobel Chemistry Laureate*
%Imperial College, Chemistry Dept, London SW7 2AY, England
Wilkinson, John *Businessman*
%Connecticut General Life, 900 Cottage Grove Road, Bloomfield, CT 06002, USA
Wilkinson, Joseph B, Jr *Navy Admiral*
340 Chesapeake Dr, Great Falls, VA 22066, USA
Wilkinson, June *Model, Actress*
1025 N Howard St, Glendale, CA 91207, USA
Wilkinson, Signe *Editorial Cartoonist*
%Philadelphia Daily News, Editorial Dept, 400 N Broad, Philadelphia, PA 19130, USA
Will, George F *Columnist*
1208 30th St NW, Washington, DC 20007, USA
Will, Maggie *Golfer*
308 Country Club Way, Venice, FL 34292, USA
Willard, Fred C *Actor, Comedian*
%William Morris Agency, 151 S El Camino Dr, Beverly Hills, CA 90212, USA
Willard, Kenneth H (Ken) *Football Player*
%Ken Willard Assoc, 3071 Viewpoint Road, Midlothian, VA 23113, USA
Willcocks, David V *Concert Organist*
13 Grange Road, Cambridge CB3 9AS, England
Willebrands, Johannes Cardinal *Religious Leader*
%Council for Promoting Christian Unity, Via dell'Erba I, 00120 Rome, Italy
Willem-Alexander *Crown Prince, Netherlands*
%Huis ten Bosch, The Hague, Netherlands
Willes, Mark H *Publisher, Businessman*
%Times Mirror Co, Times Mirror Square, Los Angeles, CA 90053, USA
Willet, E Crosby *Stained Glass Artist*
%Willet Stained Glass Studios, 10 E Moreland Ave, Philadelphia, PA 19118, USA
Willey, Gordon R *Archaeologist*
25 Gray Gardens E, Cambridge, MA 02138, USA
William *Prince, England*
%Kensington Palace, London W8, England
William, David *Actor, Theater Director*
194 Langarth St E, London ON N6C 1Z5, Canada
William, Edward *Religious Leader*
%Bible Way Church, 5118 Clarendon Road, Brooklyn, NY 11203, USA
Williams of Crosby, Shirley V T B *Government Official, England*
%Social & Liberal Democrats, 4 Cowley St, London SW1P 3NB, England
Williams of Elvel, Charles C P *Government Official, England*
48 Thurloe Square, London SW7 2SX, England

Williams, A C _Medical Researcher_
%University of Birmingham, School of Medicine, Birmingham, England
Williams, Alfred _Football Player_
2506 Autumnshore Court, Katy, TX 77450, USA
Williams, Andy _Singer_
161 Berms Circle, #3, Branson, MO 65616, USA
Williams, Anson _Actor_
24615 Skyline View Dr, Malibu, CA 90265, USA
Williams, Barbara _Actress_
%Innovative Artists, 1999 Ave of Stars, #2850, Los Angeles, CA 90067, USA
Williams, Barry _Actor, Singer_
3646 Reina Court, Calabasas, CA 91302, USA
Williams, Bernabe (Bernie) _Baseball Player_
PO Box 203, Vega Alta, PR 00692, USA
Williams, Betty _Nobel Peace Laureate_
PO Box 725, Valparaiso, FL 32580, USA
Williams, Billy _Cinematographer_
%Coach House, Hawkshill Place, Esher, Surrey KT10 9HY, England
Williams, Billy Dee _Actor_
9255 W Sunset Blvd, #404, Los Angeles, CA 90069, USA
Williams, Billy L _Baseball Player_
586 Prince Edward Road, Glen Ellyn, IL 60137, USA
Williams, Bob _Football Player_
602 Stone Barn Road, Towson, MD 21286, USA
Williams, Brian _Basketball Player_
%Detroit Pistons, Palace, 2 Championship Dr, Auburn Hills, MI 48326, USA
Williams, Brian _Commentator_
%NBC-TV, News Dept, 4001 Nebraska Ave NW, Washington, DC 20016, USA
Williams, Bruce _Radio Entertainer_
PO Box 547, Elfers, FL 34680, USA
Williams, Cara _Actress_
146 S Peck Dr, Beverly Hills, CA 90212, USA
Williams, Charles L (Buck) _Basketball Player_
1532 Fountain St, Rocky Mount, NC 27801, USA
Williams, Cindy _Actress_
2187 SW Kings Court, Portland, OR 97205, USA
Williams, Clarence, III _Actor_
%Flick East-West, 9057 Nemo St, #A, West Hollywood, CA 90069, USA
Williams, Clarke M _Businessman_
%Century Telephone, 100 Century Park Dr, Monroe, LA 71203, USA
Williams, Clyde _Religious Leader_
%Christian Methodist Episcopal Church, 4466 E Presley Blvd, Memphis, TN 38116, USA
Williams, Colleen _Commentator_
%KNBC-TV, News Dept, 3000 W Alameda Ave, Burbank, CA 91523, USA
Williams, Dafydd R (David) _Astronaut_
%NASA, Johnson Space Center, 2101 NASA Road, Houston, TX 77058, USA
Williams, Darnell _Actor_
%Stone Manners, 8091 Selma Ave, Los Angeles, CA 90046, USA
Williams, Dave H _Businessman_
%Alliance Capital Mgmt, 1345 Ave of Americas, New York, NY 10105, USA
Williams, Deniece _Singer_
1414 Seabright Dr, Beverly Hills, CA 90210, USA
Williams, Dick Anthony _Actor_
%Abrams Artists, 9200 Sunset Blvd, #625, Los Angeles, CA 90069, USA
Williams, Don _Singer, Songwriter_
PO Box 422, Branson, MO 65615, USA
Williams, Donald E _Astronaut_
%Science Applications Int'l, 17049 El Camino Real, #202, Houston, TX 77058, USA
Williams, Doug L _Football Player, Coach_
%Morehouse College, Athletic Dept, Atlanta, GA 30314, USA
Williams, Dudley _Ballet Dancer_
%Alvin Ailey Dance Theatre, 1519 Broadway, New York, NY 10036, USA
Williams, E Virginia _Artistic Director, Choreographer_
%Boston Ballet, 19 Clarendon St, Boston, MA 02116, USA
Williams, Easy _Actor_
%Don Schwartz, 6922 Hollywood Blvd, #508, Los Angeles, CA 90028, USA
Williams, Edy _Model, Actress_
1638 Blue Jay Way, Los Angeles, CA 90069, USA

Williams, Elmo *Movie Director, Producer*
1249 Iris St, Brookings, OR 97415, USA

Williams, Eric *Basketball Player*
%Denver Nuggets, McNichols Arena, 1635 Clay St, Denver, CO 80204, USA

Williams, Esther *Swimmer, Actress*
9377 Readcrest Dr, Beverly Hills, CA 90210, USA

Williams, Freeman *Basketball Player*
450 W 41st Place, Los Angeles, CA 90037, USA

Williams, Gary *Basketball Coach*
%University of Maryland, Athletic Dept, College Park, MD 20742, USA

Williams, Hal *Actor*
%Susan Smith, 121 N San Vicente Blvd, Beverly Hills, CA 90211, USA

Williams, Hank, Jr *Singer, Songwriter*
%Hank Williams Jr Ents, PO Box 850, Highway 79 E, Paris, TN 38242, USA

Williams, Harold M *Museum Executive*
%J Paul Getty Museum, 17985 Pacific Coast Highway, Malibu, CA 90265, USA

Williams, Harrison A, Jr *Senator, NJ*
PO Box 2, Holland Road, Bedminster, NJ 07921, USA

Williams, Herb *Basketball Player*
1465 Zenner Dr, Columbus, OH 43207, USA

Williams, Hershel W *WW II Marine Corps Hero (CMH)*
3491 Wire Branch Road, Ona, WV 25545, USA

Williams, Hosea *Religious Leader, Civil Rights Activist*
PO Box 170188, Atlanta, GA 30317, USA

Williams, Howard E (Howie) *Basketball Player*
1940 Hamilton Lane, Carmel, CA 46032, USA

Williams, J Kelley *Businessman*
%First Mississippi Corp, 700 North St, Jackson, MS 39202, USA

Williams, J McDonald *Businessman*
%Trammell Crow Co, Trammell Crow Center, 2001 Ross Ave, Dallas, TX 75201, USA

Williams, Jack K *Medical Administrator*
%Texas Medical Center, 1133 M D Anderson Blvd, Houston, TX 77047, USA

Williams, James *Football Player*
%Chicago Bears, Halas Hall, 250 N Washington Road, Lake Forest, IL 60045, USA

Williams, James *Jazz Pianist*
%Joanne Klein Entertainment, 130 W 28th St, New York, NY 10001, USA

Williams, James (Froggy) *Football Player*
296 Sugarberry Circle, Houston, TX 77024, USA

Williams, James A *Army General*
8928 Maurice Lane, Annandale, VA 22003, USA

Williams, James B *Financier*
%SunTrust Banks, 25 Park Place NE, Atlanta, GA 30303, USA

Williams, James D *Navy Admiral*
6552 Jay Miller Dr, Falls Church, VA 22041, USA

Williams, James Elliott *Vietnam War Navy Hero (CMH)*
20 Perrotti Lane, Palm Coast, FL 32164, USA

Williams, Jayson *Basketball Player*
%New Jersey Nets, Byrne Meadowlands Arena, East Rutherford, NJ 07073, USA

Williams, Jerome *Basketball Player*
%Detroit Pistons, Palace, 2 Championship Dr, Auburn Hills, MI 48326, USA

Williams, JoBeth *Actress*
%Pasquin, 3529 Beverly Glen Blvd, Sherman Oaks, CA 91423, USA

Williams, Joe *Singer*
3337 Knollwood Court, Las Vegas, NV 89121, USA

Williams, John *Concert Guitarist*
%Harold Holt, 31 Sinclair Road, London W14 0NS, England

Williams, John (Hot Rod) *Basketball Player*
%Phoenix Suns, 201 E Jefferson St, Phoenix, AZ 85004, USA

Williams, John A *Writer*
693 Forest Ave, Teaneck, NJ 07666, USA

Williams, John C *Archery Athlete*
718 David Road, Santa Maria, CA 93455, USA

Williams, John T *Conductor, Composer*
%Boston Pops Orchestra, Symphony Hall, 301 Massachusetts Ave, Boston, MA 02115, USA

Williams, Joseph R *Publisher*
%Memphis Commerical Appeal, 495 Union Ave, Memphis, TN 38103, USA

Williams, Kelli *Actress*
%Innovative Artists, 1999 Ave of Stars, #2850, Los Angeles, CA 90067, USA

Williams, Kimberly — *Actress*
415 S Camden Dr, #200, Beverly Hills, CA 90212, USA

Williams, Lucinda — *Singer*
%Monterey Peninsula Artists, 509 Hartnell St, Monterey, CA 93940, USA

Williams, Mark — *Bowler*
%Professional Bowlers Assn, 1720 Merriman Road, Akron, OH 44313, USA

Williams, Mary Alice — *Commentator*
%NYNEX Corp, Public Relations Dept, 1113 Westchester Ave, White Plains, NY 10604, USA

Williams, Mason — *Singer, Guitarist*
PO Box 25, Oakbridge, OR 97463, USA

Williams, Matt — *Writer*
%Zeiderman, 211 E 48th St, New York, NY 10017, USA

Williams, Matthew D (Matt) — *Baseball Player*
7101 E Caron Dr, Paradise Valley, AZ 85253, USA

Williams, Maurice J — *Association Executive*
%Overseas Development Council, 1875 Connecticut Ave NW, Washington, DC 20009, USA

Williams, Michael — *Actor*
%Julian Belfarge, 46 Albermarle St, London W1X 4PP, England

Williams, Micheal — *Basketball Player*
1415 Reynoldston Lane, Dallas, TX 75232, USA

Williams, Montel — *Entertainer, Actor*
%"Montel Williams Show", 1481 Broadway, New York, NY 10036, USA

Williams, Natalie — *Basketball, Volleyball Player*
%Portland Power, Memorial Coliseum, 1 Center Court, Portland, OR 97227, USA

Williams, O L — *Religious Leader*
%United Free Will Baptist Church, 1101 University St, Kinston, NC 28501, USA

Williams, Otis — *Singer (Temptations)*
%Star Directions, 9200 W Sunset Blvd, #PH 20, Los Angeles, CA 90069, USA

Williams, Patrick M — *Composer*
3156 Mandeville Canyon Road, Los Angeles, CA 90049, USA

Williams, Paul — *Songwriter, Actor*
8545 Franklin Ave, Los Angeles, CA 90069, USA

Williams, Phillip L — *Publisher*
%Times Mirror Co, Times Mirror Square, Los Angeles, CA 90053, USA

Williams, Prince Charles — *Boxer*
%Champs Gym, 1243 N 26th St, Philadelphia, PA 19121, USA

Williams, Randy — *Track Athlete*
6580 N Tracy Ave, Fresno, CA 93722, USA

Williams, Redford B, Jr — *Internist*
%Duke University Medical School, Box 3708, Durham, NC 27706, USA

Williams, Reggie — *Basketball Player*
2016 Calloway St, Temple Hills, MD 20748, USA

Williams, Reginald (Reggie) — *Football Player*
540 Madison Ave, #3200, New York, NY 10022, USA

Williams, Richard E — *Cartoonist (Pink Panther)*
3193 Cahuenga Blvd W, Los Angeles, CA 90068, USA

Williams, Richard H (Dick) — *Baseball Manager*
146 Tyler Court, Henderson, NV 89014, USA

Williams, Robert C — *Businessman*
%James River Corp, PO Box 2218, Richmond, VA 23218, USA

Williams, Robin — *Comedian*
1100 Wall Road, Napa, CA 94558, USA

Williams, Roger — *Pianist*
16150 Clear Valley Place, Encino, CA 91436, USA

Williams, Ron — *Bowler*
5700 Westchase Dr, North Richland Heights, TX 76180, USA

Williams, Roy — *Basketball Coach*
%University of Kansas, Athletic Dept, Allen Field House, Lawrence, KS 66045, USA

Williams, Scott — *Basketball Player*
%Philadelphia 76ers, Veterans Stadium, PO Box 25040, Philadelphia, PA 19147, USA

Williams, Simon — *Actor*
%Jonathan Altaras, 27 Floral St, London WC2E 9DP, England

Williams, Stephanie E — *Actress*
%Silver Massetti Szatmary, 8730 Sunset Blvd, #480, Los Angeles, CA 90069, USA

Williams, Stephen — *Anthropologist*
1017 Foothills Trail, Santa Fe, NM 87505, USA

Williams, Steven — *Actor*
%Geddes Agency, 1201 Greenacre Blvd, West Hollywood, CA 90046, USA

W

Williams - Williams

Williams, T Franklin — *Physician*
%Monroe Community Hospital, Director's Office, Rochester, NY 14620, USA

Williams, Theodore — *Businessman*
%Bell Industries, PO Box 49053, Los Angeles, CA 90049, USA

Williams, Theodore S (Ted) — *Baseball Player, Manager*
2448 N Essex Ave, Hernando, FL 34442, USA

Williams, Thomas S Cardinal — *Religious Leader*
Viard, 21 Eccleston Hill, PO Box 198, Wellington 1, New Zealand

Williams, Tonya Lee — *Actress*
%Artists Agency, 10000 Santa Monica Blvd, #305, Los Angeles, CA 90067, USA

Williams, Treat — *Actor*
215 W 78th St, #10-A, New York, NY 10024, USA

Williams, Ulis — *Track Athlete*
2511 29th St, Santa Monica, CA 90405, USA

Williams, Van — *Actor*
PO Box 6679, Ketchum, ID 83340, USA

Williams, Vanessa — *Actress, Singer, Model*
PO Box 858, Chappaque, NY 10514, USA

Williams, Victoria — *Singer, Songwriter*
%Monterey Peninsula Artists, 509 Hartnell St, Monterey, CA 93940, USA

Williams, W Clyde — *Religious Leader*
%Christian Methodist Episcopal Church, 2805 Shoreland Dr, Atlanta, GA 30331, USA

Williams, Walt — *Basketball Player*
3240 Beaumont St, Temple Hills, MD 20748, USA

Williams, Walter — *Singer (O'Jays)*
%Associated Booking Corp, 1995 Broadway, #501, New York, NY 10023, USA

Williams, Walter Ray, Jr — *Bowler*
%Professional Bowlers Assn, 1720 Merriman Road, Akron, OH 44313, USA

Williams, Wendy Lian — *Diver*
%Advantage Int'l, 1025 Thomas Jefferson St NW, #450, Washington, DC 20007, USA

Williams, Wendy O — *Actress, Singer (The Plasmatics)*
%The Plasmatics, 527 Madison Ave, #700, New York, NY 10022, USA

Williams, William A — *Astronaut*
%Environmental Protection Agency, 200 SW 35th St, Corvallis, OR 97333, USA

Williams-Dourdan, Roshumba — *Model*
%Bethann Model Mgmt, 36 N Moore St, #36-N, New York, NY 10013, USA

Williamson, Corliss — *Basketball Player*
%Sacramento Kings, 1 Sports Parkway, Sacramento, CA 95834, USA

Williamson, Ernest L — *Businessman*
%Louisiana Land & Exploration, 909 Poydras St, New Orleans, LA 70112, USA

Williamson, Fred — *Actor, Football Player*
%H David Moss, 733 N Seward St, #PH, Los Angeles, CA 90038, USA

Williamson, Keith — *Air Force Marshal, England*
%National Westminster Bank, Fakenham, Norfolk, England

Williamson, Marianne — *Psychotherapist*
%Los Angeles Center for Living, 8265 W Sunset Blvd, Los Angeles, CA 90046, USA

Williamson, Mykelti T — *Actor*
%United Talent Agency, 9560 Wilshire Blvd, #500, Beverly Hills, CA 90212, USA

Williamson, Nicol — *Actor*
%Jonathan Altaras, 27 Floral St, London WC2E 9DP, England

Williamson, Samuel R, Jr — *Educator*
%University of the South, President's Office, Sewanee, TN 37375, USA

Willingham, Tyrone — *Football Coach*
%Stanford University, Athletic Dept, Stanford, CA 94395, USA

Willis, Bruce — *Actor*
%Rufglen Films, 1453 3rd St, #420, Santa Monica, CA 90401, USA

Willis, Gordon — *Cinematographer*
11849 W Olympic Blvd, #100, Los Angeles, CA 90064, USA

Willis, Kelly — *Singer*
%ATS Mgmt, 8306 Appalachian Dr, Austin, TX 78759, USA

Willis, Kevin A — *Basketball Player*
4970 Carriage Lake Dr, Roswell, GA 30075, USA

Willis, William K (Bill) — *Football Player*
1158 S Waverly St, Columbus, OH 43227, USA

Willoch, Kare I — *Prime Minister, Norway*
Blokkaveien 6-B, 0282 Oslo, Norway

Willoughby, H William — *Financier*
%CRI Inc, 11200 Rockville Pike, Rockville, MD 20852, USA

Wills Moody Roark, Helen N — *Tennis Player*
PO Box 22095, Carmel, CA 93922, USA
Wills, Garry — *Writer*
%Northwestern University, History Dept, Evanston, IL 60201, USA
Wills, Maurice M (Maury) — *Baseball Player*
1723 Stanford Way, Redondo Beach, CA 90278, USA
Wilmer, Harry A — *Psychiatrist*
%Texas Health Science Center, Psychiatric Dept, San Antonio, TX 78284, USA
Wilmers, Robert G — *Financier*
%Manufacturers & Traders, 1 M&T Plaza, Buffalo, NY 14203, USA
Wilmut, Ian — *Geneticist, Embryologist*
%Roslin Institute, Development/Reproduction Dept, Midlothian, Scotland
Wilson of Tillyorn, David C — *Government Official, England, Diplomat*
%House of Lords, Westminster, London SW1A 0PW, England
Wilson, A N — *Writer*
21 Arlington Road, London NW1 7ER, England
Wilson, Al — *Singer*
%Al Lampkin Entertainment, 359 E Magnolia Blvd, #B, Burbank, CA 91502, USA
Wilson, Alexander G (Sandy) — *Composer*
2 Southwell Gardens, #4, London SW7 4SB, England
Wilson, Allan B — *Molecular Biologist*
%University of California, Molecular Biology Dept, Berkeley, CA 94724, USA
Wilson, Ann — *Singer (Heart)*
%Borman Entertainment, 1250 6th St, #401, Santa Monica, CA 90401, USA
Wilson, August — *Writer*
600 1st Ave, #301, Seattle, WA 98104, USA
Wilson, Blenda J — *Educator*
%California State University, President's Office, Northridge, CA 91330, USA
Wilson, Brian D — *Singer (The Beach Boys), Songwriter*
14042 Aubrey Road, Beverly Hills, CA 90210, USA
Wilson, C Kemmons — *Businessman*
3615 S Galloway Dr, Memphis, TN 38111, USA
Wilson, Carl D — *Singer (The Beach Boys), Songwriter*
8860 Evanview Dr, Los Angeles, CA 90069, USA
Wilson, Carnie — *Singer (Wilson Phillips), Songwriter*
13601 Ventura Blvd, #286, Sherman Oaks, CA 91423, USA
Wilson, Cassandra — *Jazz Singer*
%Dream Street Mgmt, 1460 4th St, #205, Santa Monica, CA 90401, USA
Wilson, Colin A St John — *Architect*
Highbury Crescent Rooms, 70 Ronalds Road, London N5 1XW, England
Wilson, Colin H — *Writer*
Tetherdown, Trewallock Lane, Gorran Haven, Cornwall, England
Wilson, Craig — *Water Polo Player*
1423 Lake Blvd, Davis, CA 95616, USA
Wilson, Daniel A (Dan) — *Baseball Player*
1933 E Blaien St, Seattle, WA 98112, USA
Wilson, David Mackenzie — *Museum Director*
%The Lifeboat House, Castletown, Isle of Man
Wilson, Donald M — *Publisher*
4574 Province Line Road, Princeton, NJ 08540, USA
Wilson, Doug — *Hockey Player*
1200 Lammy Place, Los Altos, CA 94024, USA
Wilson, Earl L — *Baseball Player*
PO Box 662, Ponchatoula, LA 70454, USA
Wilson, Earle L — *Religious Leader*
%Wesleyan Church, PO Box 50434, Indianapolis, IN 46250, USA
Wilson, Edward O — *Zoologist, Writer*
9 Foster Road, Lexington, MA 02173, USA
Wilson, Eric C T — *WW II British Army Hero (VC)*
Woodside Cottage, Stowell, Sherborne, Dorset, England
Wilson, Eugene — *Skier*
PO Box 912, Coleraine, NH 55722, USA
Wilson, F Paul — *Writer*
PO Box 33, Allenwood, NJ 08720, USA
Wilson, F Perry — *Chemical Engineer*
11656 Lake House Court, North Palm Beach, FL 33408, USA
Wilson, Flip — *Comedian, Actor*
21970 Pacific Coast Highway, Malibu, CA 90265, USA

W

Wills Moody Roark - Wilson

W

Wilson, Gahan *Cartoonist, Writer*
%New Yorker Magazine, Editorial Dept, 20 W 43rd St, New York, NY 10036, USA
Wilson, George B (Mike), Jr *Football Player, Army General*
1062 Lancaster Ave, Rosemont, PA 19010, USA
Wilson, Gerald S *Jazz Trumpeter, Composer*
4625 Brynhurst Ave, Los Angeles, CA 90043, USA
Wilson, Harold E *Korean War Marine Corps Hero (CMH)*
125 Shadydale Dr, Lexington, SC 29073, USA
Wilson, Harry C *Religious Leader*
%Wesleyan Church Int'l Center, 6060 Castleway West Dr, Indianapolis, IN 46250, USA
Wilson, J Lawrence *Businessman*
%Rohm & Haas Co, 100 Independence Mall W, Philadelphia, PA 19106, USA
Wilson, J Tylee *Businessman*
PO Box 2057, Ponte Vedra, FL 32004, USA
Wilson, James B *Navy Admiral*
40 Windermere Way, Kennet Square, PA 19348, USA
Wilson, James M *Geneticist*
%Univ of Pennsylvania, Medical Center, Genetics Dept, Philadelphia, PA 19104, USA
Wilson, James Q *Educator*
%University of California, Graduate Management School, Los Angeles, CA 90024, USA
Wilson, James R *Businessman*
%Thiokol Corp, 2475 Washington Blvd, Ogden, UT 84401, USA
Wilson, Jean D *Physician*
%Southwestern Internal Medical Center, 5323 Harry Hines Blvd, Dallas, TX 75235, USA
Wilson, Jeannie *Actress*
General Delivery, Ketchum, ID 83340, USA
Wilson, Johnnie E *Army General*
Commanding General, US Material Command, Alexandria, VA
Wilson, Kenneth G *Nobel Physics Laureate*
%Ohio State University, Physics Dept, Columbus, OH 43210, USA
Wilson, Lanford *Writer*
%International Creative Mgmt, 40 W 57th St, New York, NY 10019, USA
Wilson, Lawrence F (Larry) *Football Player, Executive*
11834 N Blackheath Road, Scottsdale, AZ 85254, USA
Wilson, Louis H, Jr *WW II Marine Corps Hero (CMH); General*
1338 Wembly Road, San Marino, CA 91108, USA
Wilson, Malcolm *Governor, NY*
50 Main St, #7, White Plains, NY 10606, USA
Wilson, Marc D *Football Player*
10820 157th Ave NE, Woodinville, WA 98072, USA
Wilson, Mary *Singer (The Supremes)*
163 Amsterdam Ave, #125, New York, NY 10023, USA
Wilson, Mary *Singer (Heart)*
%Borman Entertainment, 1250 6th St, #401, Santa Monica, CA 90401, USA
Wilson, Melanie *Actress*
12946 Dickens St, Studio City, CA 91604, USA
Wilson, Michael H *Government Official, Canada*
%Industry & Science Dept, 235 Queen's St, Ottawa ON K1A OH5, Canada
Wilson, Nancy *Singer*
%John Levy Enterprises, 2820 W Charleston Blvd, #C-22, Las Vegas, NV 89102, USA
Wilson, Neal C *Religious Leader*
%Seventh-Day Adventists, 12501 Old Columbus Pike, Silver Spring, MD 20904, USA
Wilson, Olin C *Astronomer*
1508 Circa Del Lago, B-110, San Marcos, CA 92069, USA
Wilson, Peta *Actress*
12754 Sarah St, Studio City, CA 91604, USA
Wilson, Pete *Governor, Senator, CA*
%Governor's Office, State Capitol Building, #100, Sacramento, CA 95814, USA
Wilson, Rita *Actress*
PO Box 1650, Pacific Palisades, CA 90272, USA
Wilson, Robert E (Bobby) *Football Player*
811 W Lubbock St, Brenham, TX 77833, USA
Wilson, Robert M *Actor*
%Byrd Hoffman Foundation, 131 Varick St, #908, New York, NY 10013, USA
Wilson, Robert R *Physicist*
230 Savage Farm Dr, Ithaca, NY 14850, USA
Wilson, Robert W *Nobel Physics Laureate*
9 Valley Point Dr, Holmdel, NJ 07733, USA

Wilson - Wilson

Wilson, Ron — Hockey Player, Coach
6714 E Yosemite Ave, Orange, CA 92867, USA

Wilson, Samuel W — Army General, Educator
%Hampden-Sydney College, President's Office, Hampden-Sydney, VA 23943, USA

Wilson, Sarah — Religious Leader
%Friends United Meeting, 101 Quaker Hill Dr, Richmond, IN 47374, USA

Wilson, Sheree J — Actress
7218 S Jan Mar Court, Dallas, TX 75230, USA

Wilson, Sloan — Writer
PO Box 510, Colonial Beach, VA 22443, USA

Wilson, Tom — Cartoonist (Ziggy)
%Universal Press Syndicate, PO Box 419149, Kansas City, MO 64141, USA

Wilson, Willie J — Baseball Player
3905 W 110th St, Leawood, KS 66211, USA

Wilson-Johnson, David R — Opera Singer
28 Englefield Road, London N1 4ET, England

Wiltshire, Richard W — Businessman
%Home Beneficial Life, 3901 W Broad St, Richmond, VA 23230, USA

Wiltshire, Richard W, Jr — Businessman
%Home Beneficial Life, 3901 W Broad St, Richmond, VA 23230, USA

Wilzig, Siggi B — Financier
%Trust Co of New Jersey, 35 Journal Square, Jersey City, NJ 07306, USA

Wimmer, Brian — Actor
3375 Creek Road, Salt Lake City, UT 84121, USA

Winans, BeBe — Singer
%Sparrow Communications Group, 101 Winners Circle, Brentwood, TN 37027, USA

Winans, CeCe — Singer
%CL Entertainment, 1420 Coleman Road, Franklin, TN 37064, USA

Winbergh, Gosta — Opera Singer
%Columbia Artists Mgmt Inc, 165 W 57th St, New York, NY 10019, USA

Winbush, Angela — Singer, Songwriter
%Ron Weisner Entertainment, 9200 Sunset Blvd, #PH-15, Los Angeles, CA 90069, USA

Wincer, Simon G — Movie Director
PO Box 241, Toorak, VIC 3142, Australia

Wincott, Michael — Actor
%International Creative Mgmt, 8942 Wilshire Blvd, Beverly Hills, CA 90211, USA

Winders, Wim — Movie Director
%Paul Kohner, 9300 Wilshire Blvd, #555, Beverly Hills, CA 90212, USA

Windle, William F — Anatomist
229 Cherry St, Granville, OH 43023, USA

Windlesham (D J G Hennessy), Baron — Government Official, England
Brasenose College, Oxford OX1 4AJ, England

Windom, William — Actor
PO Box 1067, Woodacre, CA 94973, USA

Windsor, Marie — Actress
9501 Cherokee Lane, Beverly Hills, CA 90210, USA

Winfield, David M (Dave) — Baseball Player
14970 Hickory Greens Court, Fort Myers, FL 33912, USA

Winfield, Paul — Actor
5693 Holly Oak Dr, Los Angeles, CA 90068, USA

Winfield, Rodney M — Artist
444 Laclede Place, St Louis, MO 63108, USA

Winfrey, Oprah — Entertainer
%Harpo Productions, 110 N Carpenter St, Chicago, IL 60607, USA

Wing, Toby — Actress
29923 Big Range Road, Canyon Lake, CA 92587, USA

Winger, Debra — Actress
20220 Inland Ave, Malibu, CA 90265, USA

Winkler, Hans-Gunter — Equestrian Rider
Dr Rau Allee 48, 48231 Warendorf, Germany

Winkler, Henry — Actor, Television Director
PO Box 49914, Los Angeles, CA 90049, USA

Winkler, Irwin — Movie Producer
%Irwin Winkler Productions, 211 S Beverly Dr, #220, Beverly Hills, CA 90212, USA

Winkles, Bobby B — Baseball Manager
78452 Calle Huerta, La Quinta, CA 92253, USA

Winn, George M — Businessman
%Fluke Corp, 6920 Seaway Blvd, Everett, WA 98203, USA

W

Wilson - Winn

W

Winner, Michael R — *Movie Director, Producer*
31 Melbury Road, London W14 8AB, England

Winningham, Mare — *Actress*
PO Box 19, Beckworth, CA 96129, USA

Winograd, Shmuel — *Mathematician, Computer Scientist*
235 Glendale Road, Scarsdale, NY 10583, USA

Winokur, Herbert S, Jr — *Businessman*
%Dyncorp, 2000 Edmund Halley Dr, Reston, VA 20191, USA

Winpisinger, William W — *Labor Leader*
%Machinists & Aerospace Union, 9000 Machinists Place, Upper Marlboro, MD 20772, USA

Winship, Thomas — *Editor*
Old Concord Road, South Lincoln, MA 01773, USA

Winslet, Kate — *Actress*
%Peters Fraser Dunlop, Chelsea Harbour, Lots Rd, London SW10 0XF, England

Winslow, Kellen — *Football Player*
5173 Waring Road, #312, San Diego, CA 92120, USA

Winslow, Michael — *Comedian, Actor*
18653 Ventura Blvd, #635, Tarzana, CA 91356, USA

Winsor, Jackie — *Artist*
%Paula Cooper Gallery, 534 W 21st St, New York, NY 10011, USA

Winsor, Kathleen — *Writer*
115 E 67th St, New York, NY 10021, USA

Winston, George — *Pianist, Composer*
%Dancing Cat Productions, PO Box 639, Santa Cruz, CA 95061, USA

Winston, Hattie — *Actress*
13025 Jarvis Ave, Los Angeles, CA 90061, USA

Winston, Patrick H — *Computer Scientist*
%Massachusetts Institute of Technology, Technology Square, Cambridge, MA 02139, USA

Winston, Roland — *Physicist (Nonimaging Optics)*
5217 S University Ave, #C, Chicago, IL 60615, USA

Winter, Edgar — *Singer, Keyboardist*
%Hooker Enterprises, 5958 Busch Dr, Malibu, CA 90265, USA

Winter, Edward D — *Actor*
181 N Saltair Ave, Los Angeles, CA 90049, USA

Winter, Fred (Tex) — *Basketball Coach*
%Chicago Bulls, 1901 W Madison St, Chicago, IL 60612, USA

Winter, Frederick T — *Thoroughbred Racing Jockey, Trainer*
Montague House, Eastbury, Newbury, Berks RG16 7JL, England

Winter, Johnny — *Singer, Guitarist*
%Slatus Mgmt, 208 E 51st St, #151, New York, NY 10022, USA

Winter, Olaf — *Kayak Athlete*
An der Pirschheide 28, 14471 Potsdam, Germany

Winter, William F — *Governor, MS*
633 N State St, Jackson, MS 39202, USA

Winters, Jonathan — *Comedian*
945 Lilac Dr, Santa Barbara, CA 93108, USA

Winters, Shelley — *Actress*
15 W 72nd St, New York, NY 10023, USA

Wintour, Anna — *Editor*
%Vogue Magazine, Editorial Dept, 350 Madison Ave, New York, NY 10017, USA

Wintour, Charles V — *Editor*
60 East Hatch, Tisbury, Wilts SP3 6PH, England

Winwood, Steve — *Singer, Songwriter, Keyboardist*
%Ron Weisner Entertainment, 9200 Sunset Blvd, #PH-15, Los Angeles, CA 90069, USA

Winzenried, Jesse D — *Financier*
%Securities Investor Protection, 805 15th St NW, Washington, DC 20005, USA

Wirahadikusuman, Umar — *Government Official, Indonesia; General*
Jalan Teuku Umar 61, Jarkata 10310, Indonesia

Wirth, Billy — *Actor*
12711 Ventura Blvd, #490, Studio City, CA 91604, USA

Wirtz, W Willard — *Secretary, Labor*
1211 Connecticut Ave NW, Washington, DC 20036, USA

Wirtz, William W (Bill) — *Hockey Executive*
181 DeWindt Road, Winnetka, IL 60093, USA

Wisdom, Norman — *Comedian*
%Johnny Mans, Maltings, Brewery Road, Hoddesdon, Herts EN11 8HF, England

Wise, Ray — *Actor*
12329 Emelita St, Valley Village, CA 91607, USA

Winner - Wise

Wise, Robert E — *Movie Director, Producer*
2222 Ave of Stars, #2303, Los Angeles, CA 90067, USA

Wise, Willie — *Basketball Player*
2431 134th Ave NE, Bellevue, WA 98005, USA

Wiseman, Joseph — *Actor*
382 Central Park West, New York, NY 10025, USA

Wish Bone — *Rap Artist (Bone Thugs-N-Harmony)*
%Pyramid Entertainment, 89 5th Ave, #700, New York, NY 10003, USA

Wishart, Leonard P, III — *Army General*
%Non-Legislative/Financial Srvcs, House of Representatives, Washington, DC 20515, USA

Wisoff, Peter J K — *Astronaut*
%NASA, Johnson Space Center, 2101 NASA Road, Houston, TX 77058, USA

Wistert, Albert A (Ox) — *Football Player*
256 Gunnell Road, Grants Pass, OR 97526, USA

Wistert, Alvin — *Football Player*
10250 W Seven Mile Road, Northville, MI 48167, USA

Withers, Bill — *Singer, Songwriter*
%Associated Booking Corp, 1995 Broadway, #501, New York, NY 10023, USA

Withers, Googie — *Actress*
%Larry Dalzall, 17 Broad Court, London WC2B 5QN, England

Withers, Jane — *Actress*
3676 Longridge Ave, Sherman Oaks, CA 91423, USA

Witherspoon, Reese — *Actress*
%International Creative Mgmt, 8942 Wilshire Blvd, Beverly Hills, CA 90211, USA

Witherspoon, Tim — *Boxer*
161 Liberty Dr, Langhorne, PA 19047, USA

Witkin, Joel-Peter — *Photographer*
1707 Five Points Road SW, Albuquerque, NM 87105, USA

Witkop, Bernhard — *Chemist*
3807 Montrose Driveway, Chevy Chase, MD 20815, USA

Witt, Alicia — *Actress*
%International Creative Mgmt, 8942 Wilshire Blvd, Beverly Hills, CA 90211, USA

Witt, Katarina — *Figure Skater*
%Arts & Promotions, Bergerstr 295, 60385 Frankfurt/Main, Germany

Witt, Paul J — *Writer*
16032 Valley Vista Blvd, Encino, CA 91436, USA

Witten, Edward — *Theoretical Physicist*
%Institute for Advanced Study, Olden Lane, Princeton, NJ 08540, USA

Witter, Karen — *Actress, Model*
%Innovative Artists, 1999 Ave of Stars, #2850, Los Angeles, CA 90067, USA

Wobst, Frank — *Financier*
%Huntington Bancshares, Huntington Center, Columbus, OH 43287, USA

Wockel-Eckert, Barbel — *Track Athlete*
Im Bangert 61, 64750 Lutzelbach, Germany

Woessner, Mark M — *Businessman, Publisher*
%Bertelsmann AG, Carl-Bertelsmann-Str 270, 39264 Gutersloh, Germany

Woetzel, Damian — *Ballet Dancer, Choreographer*
%New York City Ballet, Lincoln Center Plaza, New York, NY 10023, USA

Wogan, Gerald N — *Toxicologist*
%Massachusetts Institute of Technology, Toxicology Div, Cambridge, MA 02139, USA

Wohl, Dave — *Basketball Coach, Executive*
%Miami Heat, Miami Arena, 100 NE 3rd Ave, Miami, FL 33132, USA

Wohlers, Mark E — *Baseball Player*
310 Dewpoint Lane, Alpharetta, GA 30022, USA

Wohlhuter, Rick — *Track Athlete*
1558 Brittany Court, Wheaton, IL 60187, USA

Woit, Dick — *Physical Fitness Expert*
%Lehman Sports Center, 2700 N Lehmann Court, Chicago, IL 60614, USA

Woiwode, Larry — *Writer*
%State University of New York, English Dept, Binghamton, NY 13901, USA

Wojtowicz, R P — *Labor Leader*
%Railway Carmen Union, 3 Research Place, Rockville, MD 20850, USA

Wolaner, Robin P — *Publisher*
%Sunset Publishing Corp, 80 Willow Road, Menlo Park, CA 94025, USA

Wolf, Dale E — *Governor, DE*
Lieutenant Governor's Office, Legislative Hall, Legislative Ave, Dover, DE 19901, USA

Wolf, David A — *Astronaut*
%Kennedy Space Center, Code TP-TMS-A, NASA, Kennedy Space Center, FL 32899, USA

W

Wolf, Frank — *Publisher*
%Seventeen Magazine, 850 3rd Ave, New York, NY 10022, USA

Wolf, Naomi — *Writer*
%Random House, 201 E 50th St, New York, NY 10022, USA

Wolf, Peter — *Singer (J Geils Band)*
%Premier Talent, 3 E 54th St, #1100, New York, NY 10022, USA

Wolf, Scott — *Actor*
6930 Calhoun Ave, Van Nuys, CA 91405, USA

Wolf, Sigrid — *Skier*
6652 Elbigenalp 45-A, Austria

Wolf, Stephen M — *Businessman*
%USAir Group, 2345 Crystal Dr, Arlington, VA 22202, USA

Wolfbein, Seymour L — *Government Official, Economist*
East 706 Parktown, 2200 Benjamin Franklin Parkway, Philadelphia, PA 19130, USA

Wolfe, George C — *Theater Director*
%Shakespeare Festival, 425 Lafayette St, New York, NY 10003, USA

Wolfe, Kenneth L — *Businessman*
%Hershey Foods Corp, 100 Crystal A Dr, Hershey, PA 17033, USA

Wolfe, Naomi — *Writer*
%Royce Carlton Inc, 866 United Nations Plaza, New York, NY 10017, USA

Wolfe, Ralph S — *Microbiologist*
%University of Illinois, Microbiology Dept, Burrill Hall, Urbana, IL 61801, USA

Wolfe, Thomas K (Tom), Jr — *Writer*
21 E 79th St, New York, NY 10021, USA

Wolfensohn, James D — *Financier*
%World Bank Group, 1818 "H" St NW, Washington, DC 20433, USA

Wolfenstein, Lincoln — *Physicist*
%Carnegie-Mellon University, Physics Dept, Pittsburgh, PA 15213, USA

Wolfermann, Klaus — *Track Athlete*
%Puma Sportschu, Postfach 1420, 91074 Herzogenrauroch, Germany

Wolff, Hugh — *Conductor*
%Affiliate Artists, 37 W 65th St, #601, New York, NY 10023, USA

Wolff, Jon A — *Geneticist*
1122 University Bay Dr, Madison, WI 53705, USA

Wolff, Sanford I — *Labor Leader*
8141 Broadway, New York, NY 10023, USA

Wolff, Tobias — *Writer*
%Syracuse University, English Dept, Syracuse, NY 13244, USA

Wolff, Torben — *Biologist, Zoologist*
2900 Hellerup, Denmark

Wolford, Will — *Football Player*
15 Barnaby Court, Brownsburg, IN 46112, USA

Wollenberg, Richard P — *Businessman*
%Longview Fibre Co, PO Box 639, Longview, WA 98632, USA

Wollman, Harvey — *Governor, SD*
RR 1, Box 43, Hitchcock, SD 57348, USA

Wolper, David L — *Movie Producer*
1833 Rising Glen Road, Los Angeles, CA 90069, USA

Wolpert, Julian — *Geographer*
4588 Provinceline Road, Princeton, NJ 08540, USA

Wolszczan, Alexander — *Astronomer*
%Pennsylvania State University, Astronomy Dept, University Park, PA 16802, USA

Wolters, Kara — *Basketball Player*
137 Westfield Dr, Holliston, MA 01746, USA

Woltz, H O, III — *Businessman*
%Insteel Industries, 1373 Boggs Dr, Mount Airy, NC 27030, USA

Woltz, Howard O, Jr — *Businessman*
%Insteel Industries, 1373 Boggs Dr, Mount Airy, NC 27030, USA

Womack, Bobby — *Singer, Songwriter*
%Rodgers Redding, 1048 Tatnall St, Macon, GA 31201, USA

Wonder, Stevie — *Singer, Songwriter*
%Steveland Morris Music, 4616 W Magnolia Blvd, Burbank, CA 91505, USA

Wong, Albert — *Computer Engineer*
26796 Vista Terrace, Lake Forest, CA 92630, USA

Woo, John — *Movie Director*
%Garth Productions, 20th Century Fox, 10201 W Pico Blvd, Los Angeles, CA 90064, USA

Woo, Peter K C — *Businessman*
%Hongkong & Kowloon Wharf, 7 Canton Road, Kowloon, Hong Kong, China

Wolf - Woo

Wood, C Norman — *Air Force General*
5440 Mount Corcoran Place, Burke, VA 22015, USA

Wood, Carolyn — *Swimmer*
4380 SW 86th Ave, Portland, OR 97225, USA

Wood, David C — *Financier*
%Norwest Financial, 206 8th St, Des Moines, IA 50309, USA

Wood, Elijah — *Actor*
%Brillstein/Grey, 9150 Wilshire Blvd, #350, Beverly Hills, CA 90212, USA

Wood, James — *Businessman*
%Great Atlantic/Pacific Tea, 2 Paragon Dr, Montvale, NJ 07645, USA

Wood, James N — *Museum Director*
%Art Institute of Chicago, 111 S Michigan Ave, Chicago, IL 60603, USA

Wood, Janet — *Actress*
%Acme Talent, 6310 San Vicente Blvd, #520, Los Angeles, CA 90048, USA

Wood, Kimba M — *Judge*
%US District Court House, Foley Square, 40 Centre St, New York, NY 10007, USA

Wood, Lana — *Actress*
868 Masterson Dr, Thousand Oaks, CA 91360, USA

Wood, Leon — *Basketball Player*
3436 Fela Ave, Long Beach, CA 90808, USA

Wood, Maurice — *Physician*
RR 2, Box 543-B, Hot Springs, VA 24445, USA

Wood, Nigel — *Astronaut, England*
Church Crookham, Aldershot, England

Wood, Robert E — *Publisher*
%Peninsula Times Tribune, 435 N Michigan Ave, #1609, Chicago, IL 60611, USA

Wood, Robert J — *Astronaut*
%McDonnell Douglas Corp, PO Box 516, St Louis, MO 63166, USA

Wood, Ron — *Guitarist (The Rolling Stones)*
Sandy Mount House, County Kildare S, Ireland

Wood, Sharon — *Mountaineer*
PO Box 1482, Canmore AB T0L 0M0, Canada

Wood, Sidney B B — *Tennis Player*
300 Murray Place, Southampton, NY 11968, USA

Wood, Thomas H — *Publisher*
%Atlanta Constitution, 72 Marietta St NW, Atlanta, GA 30303, USA

Wood, Wilbur F — *Baseball Player*
3 Elmsbrook Road, Bedford, MA 01730, USA

Wood, William B, III — *Biologist*
%University of Colorado, Molecular Biology Dept, Boulder, CO 80309, USA

Wood, William V (Willie) — *Football Player*
%Willie Wood Mechanical Systems, 7941 16th St NW, Washington, DC 20012, USA

Wood, Willis B, Jr — *Businessman*
%Pacific Enterprises, 633 W 5th St, Los Angeles, CA 90071, USA

Woodard, Alfre — *Actress*
602 Bay St, Santa Monica, CA 90405, USA

Woodard, Charlayne — *Actress, Writer*
%Agency For Performing Arts, 9200 Sunset Blvd, #900, Los Angeles, CA 90069, USA

Woodard, Lynette — *Basketball Player*
%Cleveland Rockers, 1 Center Court, Cleveland, OH 44115, USA

Woodbridge, Todd — *Tennis Player*
%Advantage International, PO Box 3297, North Burnley, VIC 3121, Australia

Woodcock, Leonard F — *Labor Leader, Diplomat*
2404 Vinewood Blvd, Ann Arbor, MI 48104, USA

Wooden, John R — *Basketball Player, Coach*
17711 Margate St, #102, Encino, CA 91316, USA

Woodhead, Cynthia — *Swimmer*
PO Box 1193, Riverside, CA 92502, USA

Woodhouse, John F — *Businessman*
%Sysco Corp, 1390 Enclave Parkway, Houston, TX 77077, USA

Woodhull, John R — *Businessman*
%Logicon Inc, 3710 Skypark Dr, Torrance, CA 90505, USA

Woodiwiss, Kathleen E — *Writer*
%Avon Books, 959 8th Ave, New York, NY 10019, USA

Woodling, Eugene R (Gene) — *Baseball Player*
926 Remsen Road, Medina, OH 44256, USA

Woodring, Wendell P — *Geologist, Paleontologist*
6647 El Colegio Road, Goleta, CA 93117, USA

W

Wood - Woodring

W

Woodruff, Bob — *Singer, Songwriter*
%Bobby Roberts, 909 Meadowlark Lane, Goodlettesville, TN 37072, USA

Woodruff, John — *Track Athlete*
9-J Dennison Dr, East Windsor, NJ 08250, USA

Woodruff, Judy C — *Commentator*
%Cable News Network, News Dept, 820 1st St NE, Washington, DC 20002, USA

Woods, Aubrey — *Actress*
%James Sharkey, 21 Golden Square, London W1R 3PA, England

Woods, Barbara Alyn — *Actress*
%David Shapira, 15301 Ventura Blvd, #345, Sherman Oaks, CA 91403, USA

Woods, Donald — *Social Activist*
%Atheneum Publishers, 866 3rd Ave, New York, NY 10022, USA

Woods, George — *Track Athlete*
7631 Green Hedge Road, Edwardsville, IL 62025, USA

Woods, J Mark — *Businessman*
%Anacomp Inc, 11550 N Meridian St, Indianapolis, IN 46240, USA

Woods, James — *Actor*
%J/P/L, 760 N La Cienega Blvd, Los Angeles, CA 90069, USA

Woods, James D — *Businessman*
%Baker Hughes Inc, 3900 Essex Lane, Houston, TX 77027, USA

Woods, John W — *Financier*
%AmSouth Bancorp, 1900 5th Ave N, Birmingham, AL 35203, USA

Woods, Michael — *Actor*
%David Shapira, 15301 Ventura Blvd, #345, Sherman Oaks, CA 91403, USA

Woods, Phil — *Jazz Clarinetist, Saxophonist*
PO Box 278, Delaware Water Gap, PA 18327, USA

Woods, Rose Mary — *Presidential Secretary*
1194 W Cambridge St, Alliance, OH 44601, USA

Woods, Tiger — *Golfer*
6704 Teakwood St, Cypress, CA 90630, USA

Woodson, Abraham B (Abe) — *Football Player*
1598 Gold Dust Ave, Las Vegas, NV 89119, USA

Woodson, Mike — *Basketball Player*
19918 Parsons Green Court, Katy, TX 77450, USA

Woodson, Robert R — *Businessman*
%John H Harland Co, 2939 Miller Road, Decatur, GA 30035, USA

Woodson, Roderick K (Rod) — *Football Player*
434 Heights Dr, Gibsonia, PA 15044, USA

Woodson, Warren B — *Football Coach*
7087 Regalview Circle, Dallas, TX 75248, USA

Woodward, C Vann — *Writer, Historian*
83 Rogers Road, Hamden, CT 06517, USA

Woodward, Edward — *Actor, Singer*
Ravens Court, Calstock, Cornwall PL18 9ST, England

Woodward, Joanne — *Actress*
555 Long Wharf Dr, New Haven, CT 06511, USA

Woodward, John F — *Navy Admiral, England*
%Navy Secretary, Defense Ministry, Whitehall, London SW1A 2BE, England

Woodward, Kirsten — *Fashion Designer*
%Kirsten Woodward Hats, 26 Portobello Green Arcade, London W10, England

Woodward, Robert U (Bob) — *Journalist*
%Washington Post, Editorial Dept, 1150 15th St NW, Washington, DC 20071, USA

Woodward, Roger — *Concert Pianist*
%LH Productions, 2/37 Hendy Ave, Coogee NSW 2034, Australia

Woolard, Edgar S, Jr — *Businessman*
%E I Du Pont de Nemours Co, 1007 N Market St, Wilmington, DE 19801, USA

Wooldridge, Dean E — *Businessman*
4545 Via Esperanza, Santa Barbara, CA 93110, USA

Woolery, Chuck — *Entertainer*
4444 Woodley Ave, Encino, CA 91436, USA

Wooley, Sheb — *Singer, Songwriter, Actor*
Rt 3, PO Box 231, Sunset Island Trail, Gallatin, TN 37066, USA

Woolley, Catherine — *Writer*
PO Box 71, Higgins Hollow Road, Truro, MA 02666, USA

Woolley, Kenneth F — *Architect*
26 Lang Road, Centennial Park NSW 2021, Australia

Woolsey, Clinton N — *Neurophysiologist*
106 Virginia Terrace, Madison, WI 53705, USA

Woolsey, Elizabeth D — *Skier*
Trail Creek Ranch, Wilson, WY 83014, USA

Woolsey, R James — *Law Enforcement Official*
%Shea & Gardner, 1800 Massachusetts Ave NW, Washington, DC 20036, USA

Woosnam, Ian H — *Golfer*
Dyffryn, Morda Road, Oswestry, Shropshire SY11 2AY, Wales

Wooten, Jim — *Commentator*
%ABC-TV, News Dept, 1717 De Sales St NW, Washington, DC 20036, USA

Wootten, Morgan — *Basketball Coach*
%De Matha High School, Athletic Dept, Hyattsville, MD 20781, USA

Wootton, Charles G — *Diplomat*
%Chevron Corp, 555 Market St, San Francisco, CA 94105, USA

Wopat, Tom — *Actor, Singer*
2614 Woodlawn Dr, Nashville, TN 37212, USA

Word, Weldon R — *Engineer (Paveway Smart Bomb)*
Brookhaven, Northshore Dr, Rt 2, Box 293-BB, Hawkins, TX 75765, USA

Worden, Alfred M — *Astronaut*
%B F Goodrich Research Center, 9921 Brecksville Road, Brecksville, OH 44141, USA

Worgull, David — *Religious Leader*
%Wisconsin Evangelical Lutheran Synod, 1270 N Dobson Road, Chandler, AZ 85224, USA

Worley, Jo Anne — *Actress*
4714 Arcola Ave, North Hollywood, CA 91602, USA

Worndl, Frank — *Skier*
Burgsiedlung 19-C, 87527 Sonthofen, Germany

Woronov, Mary — *Actress*
4350 1/4 Beverly Blvd, Los Angeles, CA 90004, USA

Worsham, James E — *Businessman, Aeronautical Engineer*
%Asia Pacific-Guinness, 5632 Ocean Terrace Dr, Rancho Palos Verdes, CA 90274, USA

Worsley, Lorne (Gump) — *Hockey Player*
421 Bonaire Ave, Beloeil PQ H3G 1L1, Canada

Worth, Irene — *Actress*
333 W 56th St, New York, NY 10019, USA

Worthen, John E — *Educator*
%Ball State University, President's Office, Muncie, IN 47306, USA

Worthington, Melvin L — *Religious Leader*
%Free Will Baptists National Assn, 5233 Mt View Road, Antioch, TN 37013, USA

Worthy, James — *Basketball Player*
11666 Goshen Ave, #316, Los Angeles, CA 90049, USA

Wottle, Dave — — *Track Athlete*
9245 Forest Hill Lane, Germantown, TN 38139, USA

Wouk, Herman — *Writer*
%BSW Literary Agency, 3255 "N" St NW, Washington, DC 20007, USA

Woytowicz-Rudnicka, Stefania — *Concert Singer*
Al Przyjaciol 3 M 13, 00-565 Warsaw, Poland

Wozniak, Steve — *Computer Designer*
475 Alberto Way, Los Gatos, CA 95032, USA

Wray, Fay — *Actress*
2160 Century Park East, #1901, Los Angeles, CA 90067, USA

Wray, Marc F — *Businessman*
%Joy Technologies, 301 Grant St, Pittsburgh, PA 15219, USA

Wregget, Ken — *Hockey Player*
1778 McMillan Road, Pittsburgh, PA 15241, USA

Wright Penn, Robin — *Actress, Model*
%Creative Artists Agency, 9830 Wilshire Blvd, Beverly Hills, CA 90212, USA

Wright, Ben — *Sports Commentator*
%CBS-TV, Sports Dept, 51 W 52nd St, New York, NY 10019, USA

Wright, Betty — *Singer*
%Rodgers Redding, 1048 Tatnall St, Macon, GA 31201, USA

Wright, Charles Alan — *Attorney*
5304 Western Hills Dr, Austin, TX 78731, USA

Wright, Chely — *Singer*
%International Mgmt Services, 818 19th Ave S, Nashville, TN 37203, USA

Wright, Clyde — *Baseball Player*
528 Jeanine Ave, Anaheim, CA 92806, USA

Wright, Cobina, Jr — *Actress*
1326 Dove Meadow Road, Solvang, CA 93463, USA

Wright, Donald C (Don) — *Editorial Cartoonist*
PO Box 1176, Palm Beach, FL 33480, USA

Wright, Donald F — *Publisher*
%Los Angeles Times, Times Mirror Square, Los Angeles, CA 90053, USA

Wright, Felix E — *Businessman*
%Leggett & Platt Inc, PO Box 757, Carthage, MO 64836, USA

Wright, Gary — *Singer, Songwriter*
%Air Tight Mgmt, 115 West Road, Winchester Center, CT 06098, USA

Wright, Gerald — *Theater Director*
%Guthrie Theatre, 725 Vineland Place, Minneapolis, MN 55403, USA

Wright, Irving S — *Physician*
25 East End Ave, New York, NY 10028, USA

Wright, J Oliver — *Diplomat, England*
Burstow Hall, Horley, Surrey H6 9SR, England

Wright, James C, Jr — *Representative, TX; Speaker*
Lanham Federal Office Building, 819 Taylor St, Fort Worth, TX 76102, USA

Wright, Jay — *Writer*
%General Delivery, Piermont, NH 03779, USA

Wright, Jenny — *Actress*
245 W 104th St, New York, NY 10025, USA

Wright, Lawrence A — *Judge*
%US Tax Court, 400 2nd St NW, Washington, DC 20217, USA

Wright, Lorenzen — *Basketball Player*
%Los Angeles Clippers, Sports Arena, 3939 Figueroa St, Los Angeles, CA 90037, USA

Wright, Louis B — *Writer, Historian*
3702 Leland St, Chevy Chase, MD 20815, USA

Wright, Max — *Actor*
%Bresler Kelly Assoc, 15760 Ventura Blvd, #1730, Encino, CA 91436, USA

Wright, Michelle — *Singer*
%Savannah Music, 209 10th Ave S, #528, Nashville, TN 37203, USA

Wright, Mickey — *Golfer*
2972 Treasure Island Road, Port St Lucie, FL 34952, USA

Wright, Pat — *Singer (The Crystals)*
%Mars Talent, 168 Orchid Dr, Pearl River, NY 10965, USA

Wright, Rayfield — *Football Player*
PO Box 30513, Phoenix, AZ 85046, USA

Wright, Raymond R — *Vietnam War Army Hero (CMH)*
490 Joyce St, Mineville, NY 12956, USA

Wright, Robert C — *Television Executive*
%National Broadcasting Co, 30 Rockefeller Plaza, New York, NY 10112, USA

Wright, Sharone — *Basketball Player*
%Toronto Raptors, 20 Bay St, #1702, Toronto ON M5J 2N8, Canada

Wright, Stan — *Track Coach*
2330 Mossy Bank Dr, #1, Sacramento, CA 95833, USA

Wright, Teresa — *Actress*
948 Rowayton Wood Dr, Norwalk, CT 06854, USA

Wrightson, Bernie — *Diver*
924 Birch Ave, Escondido, CA 92027, USA

Wrigley, William — *Businessman*
%William Wrigley Jr Co, 410 N Michigan Ave, Chicago, IL 60611, USA

Wroughton, Philip L — *Financier*
%Marsh & McLennan Cos, 1166 Ave of Americas, New York, NY 10036, USA

Wszola, Jacek — *Track Athlete*
Ul Chrzanowskiego 7 m 70, 04-381, Warsaw, Poland

Wu Cheng-Chung, John B Cardinal — *Religious Leader*
%Catholic Diocese Center, 16 Caine Road, Hong Kong, China

Wu Xiuquan — *Government Official, China; Army Officer*
%Beijing Institute for International Strategic Studies, Beijing, China

Wu, Chien-Shiung — *Physicist*
15 Claremont Ave, New York, NY 10027, USA

Wu, Vivian — *Actress*
%Abrams Artists, 9200 Sunset Blvd, #625, Los Angeles, CA 90069, USA

WuDunn, Sheryl — *Journalist*
%New York Times, Editorial Dept, 229 W 43rd St, New York, NY 10036, USA

Wuerffel, Danny — *Football Player*
%New Orleans Saints, 1500 Poydras St, New Orleans, LA 70112, USA

Wuhl, Robert — *Actor*
10590 Holman Ave, Los Angeles, CA 90024, USA

Wulff, Kai — *Actor*
%Barr Agency, PO Box 69590, Los Angeles, CA 90069, USA

Wulsin, Henry H	*Businessman*
%Colonial Penn Group, PO Box 1990, Valley Forge, PA 19482, USA	
Wunderlich, Hermann	*Businessman*
%Bayer Corp, Mellon Center, 500 Grant St, Pittsburgh, PA 15219, USA	
Wunderlich, Paul	*Artist*
Haynstr 2, 20949 Hamburg, Germany	
Wunsch, Carl I	*Oceanographer*
78 Washington Ave, Cambridge, MA 02140, USA	
Wuorinen, Charles P	*Composer*
%Howard Stokar Mgmt, 870 West End Ave, New York, NY 10025, USA	
Wurtell, C Angus	*Businessman*
%Valspar Corp, 1101 3rd St S, Minneapolis, MN 55415, USA	
Wyatt, J Whitlow (Whit)	*Baseball Player*
PO Box 56, Buchanan, GA 30113, USA	
Wyatt, Jane	*Actress*
651 Siena Way, Los Angeles, CA 90077, USA	
Wyatt, Joe B	*Educator*
%Vanderbilt University, Chancellor's Office, Nashville, TN 37240, USA	
Wyatt, Oscar S, Jr	*Businessman*
%Coastal Corp, 6955 Union Park Ave, #540, Midvale, UT 84047, USA	
Wyatt, Sharon	*Actress*
24549 Park Grande, Calabasas, CA 91302, USA	
Wyeth, Andrew	*Artist*
%Brintons Bridge Road, Chadds Ford, PA 19317, USA	
Wyeth, James Browning	*Artist*
%Frank Fowler, PO Box 247, Lookout Mountain, TN 37350, USA	
Wyle, Noah	*Actor*
5133 Auckland Ave, North Hollywood, CA 91601, USA	
Wyler, Gretchen	*Actress*
15115 Weddington St, Van Nuys, CA 91411, USA	
Wylie, Paul	*Figure Skater*
70 Kirkland St, Cambridge, MA 02138, USA	
Wyludda, Ilke	*Track Athlete*
%LAC Chemnitz, Reichenhainer Str 154, 09125 Chemnitz, Germany	
Wyman, Bill	*Bassist (The Rolling Stones)*
%Rascoff/Zysblat, 110 W 57th St, #300, New York, NY 10019, USA	
Wyman, Jane	*Actress*
56 Kavenidsh Dr, Rancho Mirage, CA 92270, USA	
Wyman, Louis C	*Senator, NH; Judge*
121 Shaw St, Manchester, NH 03104, USA	
Wyman, Thomas H	*Financier*
%S G Warburg Co, Equitable Center, 787 7th Ave, New York, NY 10019, USA	
Wymore, Patrice	*Actress*
Port Antonio, Jamaica, British West Indies	
Wynalda, Eric	*Soccer Player*
2313 Stormcroft Court, Westlake Village, CA 91361, USA	
Wyner, George	*Actor*
3450 Laurie Place, Studio City, CA 91604, USA	
Wynette, Tammy	*Singer*
%Tammy Wynette Enterprises, PO Box 121926, Nashville, TN 37212, USA	
Wynn, Bob	*Golfer*
78455 Calle Orense, La Quinta, CA 92253, USA	
Wynn, Early	*Baseball Player*
PO Box 3969, Venice, FL 34293, USA	
Wynn, Stephen A	*Businessman*
%Mirage Resorts, 3400 Las Vegas Ave S, Las Vegas, NV 89109, USA	
Wynter, Dana	*Actress*
Glenmacnass, Glendalough, County Wicklow, Ireland	
Wyse, Henry W (Hank)	*Baseball Player*
1105 Karen Ave, Pryor, OK 74361, USA	
Wysocki, Charles	*Artist*
PO Box 688, Cedar Glen, CA 92321, USA	
Wyss, Amanda	*Actress*
%Badgley Connor, 9229 Sunset Blvd, #311, Los Angeles, CA 90069, USA	

W

Wulsin - Wyss

X-Y

Xenakis - Yanofsky

Xenakis, Iannis *Composer, Architect, Engineer*
9 Rue Chaptal, 75009 Paris, France

Xie Bingxin *Writer*
%Central Nationalities Institute, Residental Qtrs, Beijing 100081, China

Xie Jin *Movie Director*
%Shanghai Film Studio, 595 Caoxi Beilu, Shagnhai, China

Xu Shuyang *Sculptor*
%Zhejiang Academy of Fine Arts, PO Box 169, Hangzhou, China

Xuxa (Maria da Graca Meneghel) *Entertainer*
%"El Show de Xuxa", KMEX-TV, 6255 Sunset Blvd, #1600, Los Angeles, CA 90028, USA

Yablans, Frank *Movie Producer*
100 Bull Path, East Hampton, NY 11937, USA

Yaeger, Andrea *Tennis Player*
PO Box 10970, Aspen, CO 81612, USA

Yaffe, Martin *Biophysicist*
%University of Toronto, Biophysics Dept, Toronto ON M4W 1J3, Canada

Yago, Bernard Cardinal *Religious Leader*
Arceveche, Ave Jean-Paul II, 01 BP 1287, Abidjan 01, Cote d'Ivoire

Yalow, Rosalyn S *Nobel Medicine Laureate*
%Veterans Administration Medical Center, 130 W Kingsbridge Road, Bronx, NY 10468, USA

Yamaguchi, Kristi T *Figure Skater*
3650 Montecito Dr, Fremont, CA 94530, USA

Yamaguchi, Roy *Restauranteur*
%Roy's Restaurant, Kai Corporate Plaza, 6600 Kalaniaole Hwy, Honolulu, HI 96825, USA

Yamaguchi, Tamotsu *Financier*
%Union Bank, 350 California St, San Francisco, CA 94104, USA

Yamaji, Hiroyuki *Financier*
%Daiwa Bank Trust, 75 Rockefeller Plaza, New York, NY 10019, USA

Yamamoto, Kenichi *Businessman*
%Mazda Motor Corp, 4-6-19 Funairi-Minami, Minamiku, Hiroshima, Japan

Yamamoto, Masashi *Financier*
%Fuji Bank & Trust, 2 World Trade Center, New York, NY 10048, USA

Yamamoto, Takuma *Businessman*
%Fujitsu Ltd, 1-6-1 Marunouchi, Chiyodaku, Tokyo 100, Japan

Yamanaka, Tsuyoshi *Swimmer*
6-10-33-212 Akasaka, Minatoku, Tokyo, Japan

Yamani, Sheikh Ahmed Zaki *Government Official, Saudi Arabia*
Chermignon near Crans-Montana, Valais, Switzerland

Yamaoka, Seigen H *Religious Leader*
%Buddhist Churches of America, 1710 Octavia St, San Francisco, CA 94109, USA

Yamashita, Yasuhiro *Judo Athlete, Coach*
640 Sanada, Hiratsuka, Kanagawa 259-12, Japan

Yancey, James D *Financier*
%Synovus Financial Corp, 901 Front St, Columbus, GA 31901, USA

Yancy, Emily *Actress*
%Henderson/Hogan, 247 S Beverly Dr, #102, Beverly Hills, CA 90212, USA

Yandarbiyev, Zelimkahn *President, Chechen Republic*
%President's Office, Grozny, Chechen Republic

Yang Shangkun *President, China; Army General*
%Overseas Chinese Affairs Committee, Beijing, China

Yang, Chen Ning *Nobel Physics Laureate*
3 Victoria Court, St James, NY 11780, USA

Yang, Chuan-Kwang (C K) *Track Athlete*
PO Box 7855-39, Tsoying, Kaohsking, Taiwan

Yang, Henry T *Educator*
%University of California, Chancellor's Office, Santa Barbara, CA 93106, USA

Yankelovich, Daniel *Social Scientist*
%Public Agenda Foundation, 6 E 39th St, #900, New York, NY 10016, USA

Yankovic, Al (Weird Al) *Comedian, Singer, Songwriter*
8842 Hollywood Blvd, Los Angeles, CA 90069, USA

Yankovic, Frankie *Accordionist*
4853 Bostonian Loop, Heritage Lake, New Port Richey, FL 34655, USA

Yannas, I V *Mechanical Engineer, Medical Researcher*
%Massachusetts Institute of Technology, Engineering School, Cambridge, MA 02139, USA

Yanni (Chryssomallis) *Keyboardist, Songwriter*
6714 Villa Madera Dr SW, Tacoma, WA 98499, USA

Yanofsky, Charles *Biologist*
725 Mayfield Ave, Stanford, CA 94305, USA

Yarborough, Cale — *Auto Racing Driver*
724 Scott Dr, Fredricksburg, VA 22405, USA

Yarborough, William P — *Army General*
160 Hillside Road, Southern Pines, NC 28387, USA

Yarbrough, Curtis — *Religious Leader*
%General Baptists Assn, 100 Stinson, Popular Bluff, MO 63901, USA

Yarbrough, Glenn — *Singer, Songwriter (The Limelighters)*
2835 Woodstock Ave, Los Angeles, CA 90046, USA

Yard, Mollie — *Women's Activist*
1000 16th St NW, Washington, DC 20036, USA

Yardley, George — *Basketball Player*
%George Yardley Co, 17260 Newhope, Fountain Valley, CA 92708, USA

Yarmolinsky, Adam — *Government Official, Attorney*
3700 33rd Place NW, Washington, DC 20008, USA

Yarnell, Celeste — *Actress*
3349 Cahuenga Blvd W, #1, Los Angeles, CA 90068, USA

Yarnell, Lorene — *Mime (Shields & Yarnell)*
7615 W Norton Ave, #1, Los Angeles, CA 90046, USA

Yarrow, Peter — *Singer (Peter Paul & Mary), Songwriter*
27 W 67th St, #5-E, New York, NY 10023, USA

Yary, A Ronald (Ron) — *Football Player*
18 Kenilworth Dr, Cresskill, NJ 07626, USA

Yasbeck, Amy — *Actress*
2170 Century Park East, #1111, Los Angeles, CA 90067, USA

Yasinsky, John B — *Businessman*
%GenCorp, 175 Ghent Road, Fairlawn, OH 44333, USA

Yastrzemski, Carl M — *Baseball Player*
4621 S Ocean Blvd, Highland Beach, FL 33487, USA

Yasufuka, Terayoshi — *Financier*
%Sanwa Bank California, 444 Market St, San Francisco, CA 94111, USA

Yasuma, Susumu — *Financier*
%Industrial Bank of Japan, 245 Park Ave, New York, NY 10167, USA

Yates, Albert C — *Educator*
%Colorado State University, President's Office, Fort Collins, CO 80523, USA

Yates, Brock W — *Sportswriter*
%Car & Driver Magazine, Editorial Dept, 2002 Hogback Road, Ann Arbor, MI 48105, USA

Yates, Cassie — *Actress*
520 Washington Blvd, #175, Marina del Rey, CA 90292, USA

Yates, Edward D — *Businessman*
%DENTSPLY International, 570 W College Ave, York, PA 17404, USA

Yates, Jim — *Auto Racing Driver*
%Commonwealth Service & Supply, 4740 Eisenhower Ave, Alexandria, VA 22304, USA

Yates, Marvin L — *Educator*
%Southern University, President's Office, Baton Rouge, LA 70813, USA

Yates, Peter J — *Movie Director*
334 Caroline Ave, Culver City, CA 90232, USA

Yates, Sandra — *Publisher*
%Ms Magazine, 119 W 40th St, New York, NY 10018, USA

Yauch, Adam (MCA) — *Rapper (The Beastie Boys)*
%Gold Mountain, 3575 Cahuenga Blvd W, #450, Los Angeles, CA 90068, USA

Yeager, Bunny — *Photographer, Model*
9301 NE 6th Ave, #C-311, Miami, FL 33138, USA

Yeager, Charles E (Chuck) — *Test Pilot, Air Force General*
PO Box 128, Cedar Ridge, CA 95924, USA

Yeager, Cheryl L — *Ballerina*
%American Ballet Theatre, 890 Broadway, New York, NY 10003, USA

Yeager, Jeana — *Experimental Airplane Pilot*
PO Box 352, Campbell, TX 75422, USA

Yeager, Stephen W (Steve) — *Baseball Player*
PO Box 34184, Granada Hills, CA 91394, USA

Yearley, Douglas C — *Businessman*
%Phelps Dodge Corp, 2600 N Central Ave, Phoenix, AZ 85004, USA

Yearwood, Trisha — *Singer*
4636-316 Lebanon Pike, Nashville, TN 37076, USA

Yeliseyev, Alexei S — *Cosmonaut*
%Bauman Higher Technical School, Baumanskaya Ul 5, 107 005 Moscow, Russia

Yellen, Janet L — *Financier, Government Official*
%Council of Economic Advisers, Old Executive Office Bldg, Washington, DC 20505, USA

Y

Yarborough - Yellen

Yellen, Linda B — *Television Producer, Director*
3 Sheridan Square, New York, NY 10014, USA

Yeltsin, Boris N — *President, Russian Federation*
%Russian Central Committee, 4 Staraya Ploshchad, 103073 Moscow, Russia

Yendo, Masayoshi — *Architect*
%Nakajima Building, 5-6-8 Ginza, Chuoku, Tokyo 104, Japan

Yeohlee (Teng) — *Fashion Designer*
%Yeohlee, 530 7th Ave, New York, NY 10018, USA

Yeoman, William F (Bill) — *Football Coach*
%University of Houston, Athletic Dept, Houston, TX 77204, USA

Yeosock, John J — *Army General*
411 Taberon Road, Peachtree City, GA 30269, USA

Yepremian, Garabed S (Garo) — *Football Player*
1 E Mount Vernon St, Oxford, PA 19363, USA

Yerkovich, Anthony — *Television Producer*
1802 Ashland Ave, Santa Monica, CA 90405, USA

Yerman, Jack — *Track Athlete*
753 Camellia, Paradise, CA 95969, USA

Yeston, Maury — *Composer*
%Flora Roberts, 157 W 57th St, New York, NY 10019, USA

Yeutter, Clayton K — *Secretary, Agriculture*
%Republican National Committee, 3110 1st St SE, Washington, DC 20003, USA

Yevtushenko, Yevgeny A — *Writer*
Kutuzovski Prospekt 2/1, #101, 121248 Moscow, Russia

Yhombi-Opango, Jacques — *Prime Minister, Congo*
%Prime Minister's Office, Brazzaville, Congo

Yilmaz, A Mesut — *Prime Minister, Turkey*
%Motherland Party, Balgat, Ankara, Turkey

Yma Sumac — *Singer*
%Alan Eichler, 1862 Vista Del Mar St, Los Angeles, CA 90028, USA

Yo-Yo — *Rap Artist*
%William Morris Agency, 1325 Ave of Americas, New York, NY 10019, USA

Yoakam, Dwight — *Singer, Songwriter*
%Borman Entertainment, 1250 6th St, #401, Santa Monica, CA 90401, USA

Yock, Robert J — *Judge*
%US Claims Court, 717 Madison Place NW, Washington, DC 20005, USA

Yoder, Hatten S, Jr — *Petrologist*
%Geophysical Laboratory, 5251 Broad Branch Road NW, Washington, DC 20015, USA

Yodh, Arjun — *Physicist*
%University of Pennsylvania, Physics Dept, Philadelphia, PA 19104, USA

Yodoyman, Joseph — *Prime Minister, Chad*
%Prime Minister's Office, N'Djamena, Chad

Yoken, Mel B — *Writer*
261 Carroll St, New Bedford, MA 02740, USA

Yokich, Stephen P — *Labor Leader*
%United Auto Workers Union, 800 E Jefferson Ave, Detroit, MI 48214, USA

York, Francine — *Actress*
12725 Ventura Blvd, #F, Studio City, CA 91604, USA

York, Herbert F — *Physicist*
6110 Camino de la Costa, La Jolla, CA 92037, USA

York, John J — *Actor*
4804 Laurel Canyon Blvd, #212, Valley Village, CA 91607, USA

York, Lila — *Choreographer*
%Paul Taylor Dancer Co, 552 Broadway, New York, NY 10012, USA

York, Michael — *Actor*
9100 Cordell Dr, Los Angeles, CA 90069, USA

York, Michael M — *Journalist*
%Lexington Herald-Leader, Editorial Dept, Main & Midland, Lexington, KY 40507, USA

York, Susannah — *Actress*
%Jonathan Altaras, 27 Floral St, London WC2E 9DP, England

Yorke, Thom — *Singer (Radiohead)*
%Creative Artists Agency, 9830 Wilshire Blvd, Beverly Hills, CA 90212, USA

Yorkin, Alan (Bud) — *Movie Producer, Director*
%Bud Yorkin Productions, 345 N Maple Dr, #206, Beverly Hills, CA 90210, USA

Yorkin, Peg — *Feminist Activist*
%Fund for Feminist Majority, 1600 Wilson Blvd, #704, Arlington, VA 22209, USA

Yorzyk, William — *Swimmer*
162 W Sturbridge Road, #7, East Brookfield, MA 01515, USA

Yoshida, Kanetake _Financier_
%Union Bank, 350 California St, San Francisco, CA 94104, USA
Yoshimura, Junzo _Architect_
8-6-3 Mejiro, Toshimaku, Tokyo, Japan
Yost, Edward F J (Eddie) _Baseball Player_
48 Oak Ridge Road, Wellesley, MA 02181, USA
Yost, Paul A, Jr _Coast Guard Admiral_
%James Madison Memorial Foundation, 200 "K" St NW, Washington, DC 20001, USA
Yothers, Tina _Actress_
15521 Kennard St, Hacienda Heights, CA 91745, USA
Youdelman, Robert A _Businessman_
%Allen Group, 25101 Chagrin Blvd, Beachwood, OH 44122, USA
Youman, Roger J _Editor_
%TV Guide Magazine, Editorial Dept, 100 Matsonford Road, Radnor, PA 19087, USA
Younce, Leonard A (Len) _Football Player_
111 N Holmes St, Enterprise, OR 97828, USA
Young of Farnworth, Janet M _Government Official, England_
%House of Lords, Westminster, London SW1A 0PW, England
Young, A Thomas _Businessman_
%Martin Marietta Corp, 6801 Rockledge Dr, Bethesda, MD 20817, USA
Young, Alan _Actor_
%Artists Group, 10100 Santa Monica Blvd, #2490, Los Angeles, CA 90067, USA
Young, Andrew _Ambassador; Mayor, Atlanta_
%Law International Inc, 1000 Abernathy Road NE, Atlanta, GA 30328, USA
Young, Boyd _Labor Leader_
%United Paperworkers Union, 3340 Perimeter Hill Dr, Nashville, TN 37211, USA
Young, Bryant _Football Player_
601 Primrose Lane, Matteson, IL 60443, USA
Young, Burt _Actor_
%Agency For Performing Arts, 9200 Sunset Blvd, #900, Los Angeles, CA 90069, USA
Young, Chris _Actor_
5959 Triumph St, Commerce, CA 90040, USA
Young, Connie Paraskevin- _Cyclist_
%US Cycling Federation, 1750 E Boulder St, Colorado Springs, CO 80909, USA
Young, Dean _Cartoonist (Blondie)_
%King Features Syndicate, 235 E 45th St, New York, NY 10017, USA
Young, Earl _Track Athlete_
12576 Montego Plaza, Dallas, TX 75230, USA
Young, Eric O _Baseball Player_
35 S Talmadge St, New Brusnwick, NJ 08901, USA
Young, Frank E _Research Scientist, Government Official_
%Health & Human Services Dept, 200 Independence Ave SW, Washington, DC 20201, USA
Young, Fredd _Football Player_
4200 Real Del Sur, Las Cruces, NM 88011, USA
Young, George _Track Athlete_
8926 N Cox Road, Casa Grande, AZ 85222, USA
Young, Gerald O _Vietnam War Air Force Hero (CMH)_
317 Eden Road, Anacortes, WA 98221, USA
Young, H Edwin _Religious Leader_
%Southern Baptist Convention, 901 Commerce St, Nashville, TN 37203, USA
Young, J Warren _Publisher_
%Boys Life Magazine, 1325 Walnut Hill Road, Irving, TX 75038, USA
Young, Jerry _Religious Leader_
%Grace Brethren Church Fellowship, 855 Turnbull St, Delona, FL 32725, USA
Young, Jesse Colin _Singer, Songwriter_
%Skyline Music, PO Box 31, Lancaster, NH 03584, USA
Young, Jewell _Basketball Player_
4480 Fairways Blvd, Building 8, #203, Bradenton, FL 34209, USA
Young, John W _Astronaut_
%NASA, Johnson Space Center, 2101 NASA Road, Houston, TX 77058, USA
Young, John Zachary _Zoologist_
1 The Crossroads, Brill, Bucks HP18 9TL, England
Young, Karen _Actress_
%Gersh Agency, 232 N Canon Dr, Beverly Hills, CA 90210, USA
Young, Keone _Actor_
%Gage Group, 9255 Sunset Blvd, #515, Los Angeles, CA 90069, USA
Young, Kevin _Track Athlete_
8860 Corban Ave, Northridge, CA 91324, USA

Young, Lawrence J — *Businessman*
%Angelica Corp, 424 S Woods Mill Road, Chesterfield, MO 63017, USA

Young, Lewis H — *Editor*
%Business Week Magazine, 1221 Ave of Americas, New York, NY 10020, USA

Young, Loretta — *Actress*
1705 Ambassador Dr, Beverly Hills, CA 90210, USA

Young, Martin D — *Parasitologist*
610 NW 89th St, Gainesville, FL 32607, USA

Young, Mighty Joe — *Singer, Guitarist*
%Jay Reil, 3430 Bayberry Dr, Northbrook, IL 60062, USA

Young, Neil — *Singer, Songwriter*
2644 30th St, #100, Santa Monica, CA 90405, USA

Young, Otis — *Actor*
6716 Zumirez Dr, Malibu, CA 90265, USA

Young, Paul — *Singer*
%Agency For Performing Arts, 9200 Sunset Blvd, #900, Los Angeles, CA 90069, USA

Young, Richard E — *Space Scientist*
%Jet Propulsion Laboratory, 4800 Oak Grove Dr, Pasadena, CA 91109, USA

Young, Richard S — *Space Administrator, Educator*
137 Saint Croix Ave, Cocoa Beach, FL 32931, USA

Young, Robert — *Actor*
31589 Saddletree Dr, Westlake Village, CA 91361, USA

Young, Robert (Bob) — *Track Athlete*
4265 Country Club Dr, Bakersfield, CA 93306, USA

Young, Robert A, III — *Businessman*
%Arkansas Best, PO Box 10048, Fort Smith, AR 72917, USA

Young, Sean — *Actress*
PO Box 20547, Sedona, AZ 86341, USA

Young, Sheila — *Speed Skater, Cyclist*
%Danskin Inc, 111 W 40th St, #1800, New York, NY 10018, USA

Young, Steve — *Labor Leader*
%American Federation of Musicians, 1501 Broadway, #800, New York, NY 10036, USA

Young, Steven (Steve) — *Football Player*
261 E Broadway, Salt Lake City, UT 84111, USA

Young, Tom — *Basketball Coach*
%Old Dominion University, Athletic Dept, Norfolk, VA 23508, USA

Young, Walter R, Jr — *Businessman*
%Champion Enterprises, 2710 University Dr, Auburn Hills, MI 48326, USA

Young, William Allen — *Actor*
5519 S Holt Ave, Los Angeles, CA 90056, USA

Young-Herries, Michael — *Financier*
%Royal Bank of Scotland, 36 St Andrew Square, Edinburgh EH2 2YB, Scotland

Youngblood, Jim — *Football Player*
534 N Manhattan Place, Los Angeles, CA 90004, USA

Younger, Paul (Tank) — *Football Player, Executive*
%St Louis Rams, 100 N Broadway, #2100, St Louis, MO 63102, USA

Youngerman, Jack — *Artist*
PO Box 508, Bridgehampton, NY 11932, USA

Youngman, Henny — *Comedian*
77 W 55th St, New York, NY 10019, USA

Younis, Waqar — *Cricketer*
%Surrey County Cricket Club, Kennington Oval, London SE11 5SS, England

Yount, Robin R — *Baseball Player*
5001 E Arabian Way, Paradise Valley, AZ 85253, USA

Yow, Kay — *Basketball Coach*
%North Carolina State University, Athletic Dept, Raleigh, NC 27695, USA

Yu Chuan Yong — *Architect*
%Urban/Rural Construction Committee, 149 Guangming Road, Weihai PR, China

Yu Kuo-Hwa — *Financier*
%Central Bank of China, 2 Roosevelt Road, Section 1, Taipei, Taiwan

Yulin, Harris — *Actor*
1630 Crescent Place, Venice, CA 90291, USA

Yunick, Smokey — *Auto Racing Builder*
%Smokey's Automotive Service, 957 N Beach St, Daytona Beach, FL 32117, USA

Yunis, Jorge J — *Geneticist, Pathologist*
%Thomas Jefferson University, Jefferson Medical College, Philadelphia, PA 19107, USA

Yzerman, Steve — *Hockey Player*
%Detroit Red Wings, Joe Louis Arena, 600 Civic Center Dr, Detroit, MI 48226, USA

Zabaleta, Nicanor — *Concert Harpist*
Villa Izar, Aldapeta, 20009 San Sebasatian, Spain
Zabel, Mark — *Kayak Athlete*
Grosse Fischerei 18-A, 39240 Calbe/Saale, Germany
Zable, Walter J — *Businessman*
%Cubic Corp, 9333 Balboa Ave, San Diego, CA 92123, USA
Zaborowski, Robert R J M — *Religious Leader*
%Mariavite Old Catholic Church, 2803 10th St, Wynadotte, MI 48192, USA
Zacharias, Donald W — *Educator*
%Mississippi State University, President's Office, Mississippi State, MS 39762, USA
Zadeh, Lofti A — *Computer Scientist (Fuzzy Logic)*
904 Mendocino Ave, Berkeley, CA 94707, USA
Zadora, Pia — *Actress, Singer*
%Par-Par Productions, 9560 Wilshire Blvd, Beverly Hills, CA 90212, USA
Zaentz, Saul — *Movie Producer*
%Saul Zaentz Co, 2600 10th St, Berkeley, CA 94710, USA
Zaffaroni, Alejandro C — *Biochemist*
%Alza Corp, 950 Page Mill Road, Palo Alto, CA 94304, USA
Zahn, Geoffrey C (Geof) — *Baseball Player*
1114 Lariat Loop, #206, Ann Arbor, MI 48108, USA
Zahn, Paula — *Commentator*
%"Evening News" Show, CBS-TV, News Dept, 51 W 52nd St, New York, NY 10019, USA
Zahn, Wayne — *Bowler*
%Professional Bowlers Assn, 1720 Merriman Road, Akron, OH 44313, USA
Zaklinsky, Konstantin — *Ballet Dancer*
%Kirov Ballet Theatre, 1 Ploshchad Iskusstv, St Petersburg, Russia
Zaks, Jerry — *Theater Director*
%Helen Merrill, 337 W 22nd St, New York, NY 10011, USA
Zalapski, Zarley — *Hockey Player*
308 Kingsberry Circle, Pittsburgh, PA 15234, USA
Zamba, Frieda — *Surfer*
2706 S Central Ave, Flagler Beach, FL 32136, USA
Zamfir, Gheorghe — *Conductor*
Dr Teohari Str 10, Bucharest, Romania
Zamora Rivas, Ruben I — *Government Official, El Salvador*
%National Constituent Assembly, San Salvador, El Salvador
Zampetis, Theodore K — *Businessman*
%Standard Products Co, 2130 W 110th St, Cleveland, OH 44102, USA
Zander, Robin — *Singer, Guitarist (Cheap Trick)*
%Ken Adamay, 3805 County Road "M", Middleton, WI 53562, USA
Zander, Thomas — *Wrestler*
Grundfeldstr 23, 73432 Aalen, Germany
Zane, Billy — *Actor*
450 N Rossmore Ave, #1001, Los Angeles, CA 90004, USA
Zane, Lisa — *Actress*
209 S Orange Dr, Los Angeles, CA 90036, USA
Zanes, Dan — *Singer, Songwriter*
%Harriet Sternberg Mgmt, 4268 Hazeltine Ave, Sherman Oaks, CA 91423, USA
Zankel, Arthur S — *Financier*
%First Manhattan Co, 437 Madison Ave, New York, NY 10022, USA
Zanuck, Lili Fini — *Movie Producer, Director*
%Zanuck Co, 202 N Canon Dr, Beverly Hills, CA 90210, USA
Zanuck, Richard D — *Movie Producer*
%Zanuck Co, 202 N Canon Dr, Beverly Hills, CA 90210, USA
Zanuso, Marco — *Architect*
Piazza Castello 20, Milan, Italy
Zanussi, Krzysztof — *Movie Director*
Kaniowska 114, 01-529, Warsaw, Poland
Zapata, Carmen — *Actress*
6107 Ethel Ave, Van Nuys, CA 91401, USA
Zapf, Hermann — *Book, Type Designer*
2 Hammarskjold Plaza, New York, NY 10017, USA
Zappa, Dweezil — *Singer, Guitarist, Actor*
7885 Woodrow Wilson Dr, Los Angeles, CA 90046, USA
Zappa, Moon Unit — *Singer, Actress*
10377 Oletha Lane, Los Angeles, CA 90077, USA
Zarate, Carlos — *Boxer*
%Gene Aguilera, PO Box 113, Montebello, CA 90640, USA

Zarb, Frank G *Government Official, Financier*
%Alexander & Alexander Services, 1211 Ave of Americas, New York, NY 10036, USA

Zariski, Oscar *Mathematician*
122 Sewall Ave, Brookline, MA 02146, USA

Zarkhi, Aleksandr G *Movie Director*
Cherniachovskogo Str 4, #105, 125319 Moscow, Russia

Zarkin, Herbert J *Businessman*
%Waban Inc, 1 Mercer Road, Natick, MA 01760, USA

Zarnas, August C (Gust) *Football Player*
850 Jennings St, Bethlehem, PA 18017, USA

Zasloff, Michael *Geneticist*
%National Child Health Institute, 9000 Rockville Pike, Bethesda, MD 20892, USA

Zaslow, Jeffrey L (Jeff) *Columnist*
%Chicago Sun-Times, Editorial Dept, 401 N Wabash, Chicago, IL 60611, USA

Zaslow, Michael *Actor*
%Silver Massetti Szatmary, 8730 Sunset Blvd, #480, Los Angeles, CA 90069, USA

Zatopek, Emil *Track Athlete*
Nad Kazankov 3, 171 00 Prague 7, Czech Republic

Zatopkova, Dana *Track Athlete*
Nad Kazankov 3, 171 00 Prague 7, Czech Republic

Zawinul, Josef (Joe) *Jazz Synthesizer, Composer*
%International Music Network, 112 Washington St, Marblehead, MA 01945, USA

Zawoluk, Robert (Zeke) *Basketball Player*
2438 Seymour Ave, Bronx, NY 10469, USA

Zayak, Elaine *Figure Skater*
298 McHenry Dr, Paramus, NJ 07652, USA

Zeamer, Jay *WW II Army Air Corps Hero (CMH)*
123 Commercial St, PO Box 602, Boothbay Harbor, ME 04538, USA

Zech, Lando *Government Official*
%Nuclear Regulatory Commission, 1717 "H" St NW, Washington, DC 20555, USA

Zech, Ronald H *Businessman*
%GATX Corp, 500 W Monroe, Chicago, IL 60661, USA

Zedillo Ponce de Leon, Ernesto *President, Mexico*
%President's Office, Palacio de Gobierno, Mexico City DF, Mexico

Zeffirelli, G Franco *Theater, Movie Director*
Via Appia Pignatelli 448, 00178 Rome, Italy

Zeh, Geoffrey N *Labor Leader*
%Maintenance of Way Employees Brotherhood, 12050 Woodward, Detroit, MI 48203, USA

Zeien, Alfred M *Businessman*
%Gillette Co, Prudential Tower Building, Boston, MA 02199, USA

Zeile, Todd E *Baseball Player*
%Los Angeles Dodgers, 1000 Elysian Park Ave, Los Angeles, CA 90012, USA

Zeitlin, Zvi *Concert Pianist*
204 Warren Ave, Rochester, NY 14618, USA

Zelensky, Igor *Ballet Dancer*
%New York City Ballet, Lincoln Center Plaza, New York, NY 10023, USA

Zelezny, Jan *Track Athlete*
Rue Armady 683, Boleslav, Czech Republic

Zell, Samuel *Businessman*
%Itel Corp, 2 N Riverside Plaza, Chicago, IL 60606, USA

Zellweger, Renee *Actress*
%Gallin-Morey Assoc, 345 N Maple Dr, #300, Beverly Hills, CA 90210, USA

Zeman, Jacklyn *Actress*
6930 Dume Dr, Malibu, CA 90265, USA

Zembriski, Walter *Golfer*
PO Box 617557, Orlando, FL 32861, USA

Zemeckis, Robert L *Movie Director*
PO Box 5218, Santa Barbara, CA 93150, USA

Zenawi, Hailu *Prime Minister, Ethiopia*
%Prime Minister's Office, Addis Ababa, Ethiopia

Zender, Hans *Conductor, Composer*
Am Risebheck, 65812 Bad Soden, Germany

Zentner, Si *Trombonist*
4825 Fairfax Ave, Las Vegas, NV 89120, USA

Zerbe, Anthony *Actor*
245 Chateaux Elise, Santa Barbara, CA 93109, USA

Zerhusen, Al *Soccer*
2048 Rockdale Ave, Simi Valley, CA 93063, USA

Zernial, Gus E Baseball Player
687 Coventry Ave, Clovis, CA 93611, USA

Zeroul, Lamine President, Algeria; Army General
%President's Office, Al-Mouradia, Algiers, Algeria

Zevi, Bruno Architect
Via Nomentana 150, 00162 Rome, Italy

Zevon, Warren Singer, Songwriter
%Peter Asher Mgmt, 644 N Doheny Dr, Los Angeles, CA 90069, USA

Zhamnov, Alexei Hockey Player
%Chicago Blackhawks, United Center, 1901 W Madison St, Chicago, IL 60612, USA

Zhang Aiping Government Official, China; Army General
%Ministry of Defense, State Council, Beijing, China

Zhang Xian Writer
%Jiangsu Branch, Chinese Writers' Assn, Nanjing, China

Zhang Xianliang Writer
%Ningxia Writers' Assn, Yinchuan City, China

Zhang Yimou Movie Director
%Xi'an Film Studio, Xi'an City, Shanxi Province, China

Zhao Yanxia Opera Singer
%Beijing Opera Theatre, Beijing, China

Zhao Ziyang Prime Minister, China
1 Zhong Nan Hai, Beijing, China

Zheng Haixia Basketball Player
%Los Angeles Sparks, Forum, 3900 W Manchester Ave, Inglewood, CA 90305, USA

Zheng, Wei Astronomer
%Johns Hopkins Universities, Astronomy Dept, Baltimore, MD 21218, USA

Zhirinovsky, Vladimir V Government Leader, Russia
%Liberal Democratic Party, Rybnikov Per 1, 103045 Moscow, Russia

Zhitnik, Alexei Hockey Player
%Buffalo Sabres, Marine Midland Arena, 1 Seymour Knox Plaza, Buffalo, NY 14210, USA

Zholobov, Vitali M Cosmonaut
Ul Yanvarskovo Vostaniya D 12, 252 010 Kiev, Ukraine

Zhu Rongji Government Official, China
%Vice Premier's Office, State Council, Xi Changan Jie, Beijing, China

Zia, B Khaleda Prime Minister, Bangladesh
%Bangladesh National Party, Parliament Building, Dhaka, Bangladesh

Zidek, George Basketball Player
1803 Paseao del Mar, Palos Verdes Estates, CA 90274, USA

Ziegler, Dolores Opera Singer
%Lynda Kay, 2702 Crestworth Lane, Buford, GA 30519, USA

Ziegler, Henri A L Aviation Engineer, Businessman
55 Blvd Lannes, 75116 Paris, France

Ziegler, Jack Cartoonist
%New Yorker Magazine, Editorial Dept, 20 W 43rd St, New York, NY 10036, USA

Ziegler, John A, Jr Hockey Executive
1 Detroit Center, 500 Woodward Ave, #4000, Detroit, MI 48226, USA

Ziegler, Larry Golfer
6209 Dartmoor Court, Orlando, FL 32819, USA

Ziegler, Ronald L Government Official, Journalist
%National Assn of Chain Drug Stores, 413 N Lee St, Alexandria, VA 22314, USA

Ziegler, William, III Businessman
%American Maize-Products, 1100 Indianapolis Blvd, Hammond, IN 46320, USA

Ziering, Ian Actor
2700 Jalmia Dr, West Hollywood, CA 90046, USA

Ziff, William B, Jr Publisher
%Ziff-Davis Publishing Co, 1 Park Ave, New York, NY 10016, USA

Ziffren, Kenneth Attorney
%Ziffren Brittenham Branca, 1801 Century Park West, Los Angeles, CA 90067, USA

Ziglar, Zig Businessman
%Success '94 Seminars, General Delivery, Hawkins, TX 75765, USA

Zigler, Edward F Educator
%Yale University, Bush Child Development Center, New Haven, CT 06520, USA

Zikarsky, Bengt Swimmer
%SV Wurzburg 05, Oberer Bogenweg 1, 97074 Wurzburg, Germany

Zikarsky, Bjorn Swimmer
30 Via Lucca F 306, Irvine, CA 92612, USA

Zikes, Les Bowler
%Beverly Lanes, 8 S Beverly Lane, Arlington Heights, IL 60004, USA

Z

Zernial - Zikes

Z

Zimbalist, Efrem, Jr — *Actor*
1448 Holsted Dr, Solvang, CA 93463, USA

Zimbalist, Stephanie — *Actress*
%Innovative Artists, 1999 Ave of Stars, #2850, Los Angeles, CA 90067, USA

Zimerman, Krystian — *Concert Pianist*
%Columbia Artists Mgmt Inc, 165 W 57th St, New York, NY 10019, USA

Zimm, Bruno H — *Chemist*
2522 Horizon Way, La Jolla, CA 92037, USA

Zimmer, David R — *Businessman*
%CORE Industries, 500 N Woodward Ave, Bloomfield Hills, MI 48304, USA

Zimmer, Donald W (Don) — *Baseball Manager*
10124 Yacht Club Dr, St Petersburg, FL 33706, USA

Zimmer, Hans — *Composer*
1547 14th St, Santa Monica, CA 90404, USA

Zimmer, Kim — *Actress*
25561 Almendra Dr, Santa Clarita, CA 91355, USA

Zimmerer, Wolfgang — *Bobsled Athlete*
Schwaigangerstr 22, 82418 Murnau, Germany

Zimmerman, Gary — *Football Player*
16490 Amberstone, Parker, CO 80134, USA

Zimmerman, Howard E — *Chemist*
1 Oconto Court, Madison, WI 53705, USA

Zimmerman, James M — *Businessman*
%Federated Department Stores, 7 W 7th St, Cincinnati, OH 45202, USA

Zimmerman, John T — *Neuroscientist*
%University of Colorado Medical School, Neurology Dept, Denver, CO 80202, USA

Zimmerman, Kent — *Publisher*
%Friendly Exchange Magazine, 1999 Shepard Road, St Paul, MN 55116, USA

Zimmerman, Mary Beth — *Golfer*
%Ladies Professional Golf Assn, 2570 Volusia Ave, Daytona Beach, FL 32114, USA

Zimmerman, Philip (Phil) — *Computer Software Designer*
%PGP Inc, 555 Twin Dolphin Dr, #570, Redwood City, CA 94065, USA

Zimmermann, Egon — *Skier*
%Hotel Kristberg, 67644 Am Arlberg, Austria

Zimmermann, Udo — *Conductor*
%Operhaus Leipzig, Augustusplatz, 04109 Leipzig, Germany

Zindel, Paul — *Writer*
%Harper Collins Publishers, 10 E 53rd St, New York, NY 10022, USA

Zinder, Norton D — *Geneticist*
450 E 63rd St, New York, NY 10021, USA

Zindler, Marvin — *Commentator*
%KTRK-TV, News Dept, 3310 Bissonnet, Houston, TX 77005, USA

Zinke, Olaf — *Speed Skater*
Johannes Bobrowski Str 22, 12627 Berlin, Germany

Zinkernagel, Rolf M — *Nobel Medicine Laureate*
%University of Zurich, Schmelzbergstr 12, 8091 Zurich, Switzerland

Zinman, David J — *Conductor*
%Baltimore Symphony, 1212 Cathedral St, Baltimore, MD 21201, USA

Zinni, Anthony C — *Marine Corps General*
Deputy CinC, US Central Command, Offutt Air Force Base, NE 68113, USA

Zisk, Richard W (Richie) — *Baseball Player*
4231 NE 26th Terrace, Lighthouse Point, FL 33064, USA

Zlatoper, Ronald J (Zap) — *Navy Admiral*
824 Caldwell Road, Wayne, PA 19087, USA

Zmed, Adrian — *Actor*
4345 Freedom Dr, #E, Calabasas, CA 91302, USA

Zmievskaya, Galina — *Figure Skating Coach*
%International Skating Rink, 1375 Hopmeadow St, Simsbury, CT 06070, USA

Zoeller, Frank (Fuzzy) — *Golfer*
418 Deer Run Trace, Floyd's Knobs, IN 47119, USA

Zoffinger, George R — *Financier*
%CoreStates (NJ) Bank, 370 Scotch Road, Pennington, NJ 08534, USA

Zollman, Ronald — *Conductor*
%Konsart AB, Kungsgatan 32, 111 35 Stockholm, Sweden

Zook, John E — *Football Player*
145 Farm Track, Roswell, GA 30075, USA

Zoran — *Fashion Designer*
157 Chambers St, #1200 , New York, NY 10007, USA

Zimbalist - Zoran

Zorich, Chris — Football Player
1429 S Clark St, Chicago, IL 60605, USA

Zorich, Louis — Actor
%Susan Smith, 121 N San Vicente Blvd, Beverly Hills, CA 90211, USA

Zorina, Vera — Actress, Ballet Dancer
247 E 61st St, New York, NY 10021, USA

Zorn, Jim — Football Player, Coach
9930 SE 40th St, Mercer Island, WA 98040, USA

Zorrilla, Alberto — Swimmer
580 Park Ave, New York, NY 10021, USA

Zou Jiahua — Government Official, China
%Communist Central Committee, Zhonganahai, Beijing, China

Zoubi, Mahmoud — Prime Minister, Syria
%Prime Minister's Office, Shahbander St, Damascus, Syria

Zoungrana, Paul Cardinal — Religious Leader
Archeveche, BP 1472, Ouagadougou 01, Burkina Faso

Zsigmond, Vilmos — Cinematographer
%Feinstein & Shorr, 16133 Ventura Blvd, #800, Encino, CA 91436, USA

Zubak, Kresimir — Co-President, Bosnia-Herzegovina
%Presidency, Marsala Titz 7-A, 71000 Sarajevo, Bosnia-Herzegovina

Zubrod, C Gordon — Physician
177 Ocean Lane Dr, Key Biscayne, FL 33149, USA

Zucaro, A C — Businessman
%Old Republic International, 307 N Michigan Ave, Chicago, IL 60601, USA

Zucker, David — Movie Producer, Director
%Zucker Productions, Sony, 10202 W Washington Blvd, Culver City, CA 90232, USA

Zucker, Jerry — Movie Director
481 Denslow Ave, Los Angeles, CA 90049, USA

Zuckerman, Mortimer B — Publisher
%Boston Properties, 599 Lexington Ave, New York, NY 10022, USA

Zuckert, Bill — Actor
%Allen Goldstein Assoc, 5015 Lemona Ave, Sherman Oaks, CA 91403, USA

Zudov, Vyachselav D — Cosmonaut
%Potchta Kosmonavtov, Moskovskoi Oblasti, 141160 Syvisdny Goroduk, Russia

Zukerman, Eugenia — Concert Flutist
%Brooklyn College of Music, Bedford & "H" Aves, Brooklyn, NY 11210, USA

Zukerman, Pinchas — Concert Violinist
%Shirley Kirshbaum Assoc, 711 West End Ave, #5-KN, New York, NY 10025, USA

Zukofsky, Paul — Concert Violinist
%University of Southern California, Schoenberg Institute, Los Angeles, CA 90089, USA

Zumwalt, Elmo R, Jr — Navy Admiral
%Admiral Zumwalt Consultants, 1500 Wilson Blvd, #3105, Arlington, VA 22209, USA

Zuniga, Daphne — Actress
%Murphy, 2401 Main St, Santa Monica, CA 90405, USA

Zuniga, Jose — Actor
%Paradigm Agency, 10100 Santa Monica Blvd, #2500, Los Angeles, CA 90067, USA

Zurbriggen, Pirmin — Skier
%Hotel Larchenhof, 3905 Saas-Almagell, Switzerland

Zwanzig, Robert W — Chemical Physicist
5314 Sangamore Road, Bethesda, MD 20816, USA

Zweig, George — Theoretical Physicist
%Los Alamos National Laboratory, MS B276, PO Box 1663, Los Alamos, NM 87544, USA

Zweig, Martin E — Financier
%Zweig Companies, 900 3rd Ave, New York, NY 10022, USA

Zwerling, Darrell — Actor
%FPA, 12701 Moorpark St, #205, Studio City, CA 91604, USA

Zwick, Edward M — Movie Director, Producer
%Skywalker Sound, 1861 S Bundy, #314, Los Angeles, CA 90025, USA

Zwilich, Ellen Taaffe — Composer
%Music Assoc of America, 224 King St, Englewood, NJ 07631, USA

Zych, Leonard A — Financier
%Chemical Financial Services, 250 W Huron Road, Cleveland, OH 44113, USA

Zydeco, Buckwheat — Singer, Accordionist
%Ted Fox, PO Box 561, Rhinebeck, NY 12572, USA

Zykina, Lyudmila G — Singer, Theater Director
Kotelnicheskaya Nab Y-15 Korp B, #64, Moscow, Russia

Zylis-Gara, Teresa — Opera Singer
16-A Blvd de Belgique, Monaco-Ville, Monaco

Listees of previous editions of the V.I.P. Address Book and the **V.I.P. Address Book Update** whose deaths have been reported prior to close of the compilation are listed below.

Akii-Bua, John	*Track Athlete*	Damsel, Richard A	*Businessman*
Allison, Luther	*Guitarist*	Danilova, Alexandra	*Dancer, Choreographer*
Ames, Louise Bates	*Child Psychologist*	Davis, Gail	*Actress*
Amsterdam, Morey	*Comedian*	Day, J Edward	*Postmaster General*
Anderson, Eugenia	*Diplomat*	De Almeida, Antonio	*Conductor*
Annabella	*Actress*	De Kooning, Willem	*Artist*
Ashburn, D Richie	*Baseball Player*	Dean, Charles H, Jr	*Government Official*
Awdry, R	*Writer*	Debre, Michel	*Prime Minister, France*
Ayres, Lew	*Actor*	Dederich, Chuck	*Drug Rehabiliation Expert*
Baker, Lavern	*Singer*	Deng Xiaoping	*Chairman, Chinese Party*
Bao Dai	*Emperor, Vietnam*	Denver, John	*Singer, Songwriter*
Barney, Rex	*Baseball Player*	DeStevens, George	*Inventor*
Battista, Orlando A	*Inventor, Businessman*	Devaney, Bob	*Football Coach*
Beal, John	*Actor*	Diana	*Princess of Wales, England*
Bernard, Jason	*Actor*	Dickey, James L	*Writer*
Bernardin, Joseph L Cardinal	*Religious Leader*	Dixon, Jeane L	*Psychic, Columnist*
Berry, Richard	*Composer*	Dodd, Lamar	*Artist*
Bing, Rudolf	*Opera Producer*	Dorris, Michael	*Writer, Antropologist*
Blackstone, Harry B, Jr	*Illusionist*	Doyle, David	*Actor*
Blackwell, Ewell	*Baseball Player*	Durenberger, David F	*Senator, MN*
Bloomfield, Coleman	*Businessman*	Eccles, John Carew	*Nobel Medicine Laureate*
Blos, Peter	*Psychoanalyst*	Edel, J Leon	*Writer, Educator*
Blum, Michael S	*Financier*	Edwards, Earle	*Football Coach*
Bokassa, Jean-Bedel	*President, Ctrl African Rep*	Elia, Claudio	*Businessman*
Boorda, Jeremy M (Mike)	*Navy Admiral*	Endo, Shusaku P	*Writer*
Bradbury, Norris E	*Physicist*	Engen, Alf	*Skier*
Brennan, William J, Jr	*Supreme Court Justice*	Ervine-Andrews, Harold M	*WW II British Hero (VC)*
Bristol, Harvey	*Photographer*	Esau, Katherine	*Botanist*
Brown, Roger	*Basketball Player*	Essex, Harry	*Movie Director, Writer*
Brown, Ronald H	*Publisher*	Fairstein, Linda	*Writer, Attorney*
Brown, Willard J	*Baseball Player*	Fassi, Carlo	*Figure Skating Coach*
Buckley, Jeff	*Singer, Songwriter*	Fenneman, George	*Entertainer*
Burroughs, William S	*Writer*	Ferreri, Marco	*Movie Director*
Caen, Herb	*Columnist, Writer*	Flavin, Dan	*Artist*
Caesar, Irving	*Lyricist*	Flemming, Arthur S	*Secretary, HEW*
Cairns, Theodore L	*Organic Chemist*	Foa, Joseph V	*Aeronautical Engineer*
Calvin, Melvin	*Nobel Chemistry Laureate*	Frankl, Viktor E	*Psychiatrist, Writer*
Carne, Marcel	*Movie Director*	Fujita, Nobuo	*WW II Air Force Hero, Japan*
Casares, Maria	*Actress*	Gairy, Eric M	*Prime Minister, Grenada*
Caselotti, Adriana	*Actress*	Geisel, Ernesto	*President, Brazil; Army General*
Celibidache, Sergiu	*Conductor, Composer*	Gian Singh	*WW II Indian Army Hero (VC)*
Chandler, Dorothy	*Philanthropist*	Gilpatric, Roswell L	*Government Official*
Cheatham, Adolphus A (Doc)	*Jazz Trumpeter*	Ginsberg, Allen	*Writer*
Cherrill, Virginia	*Actress*	Goldschmidt, Berthold	*Composer*
Collins, Pat	*Hypnotist*	Goldsmith, James M	*Businessman*
Collinson, John T	*Businessman*	Gordon, Irving	*Composer*
Connolly, Brian	*Singer (Sweet)*	Graham, Robert K	*Optometrist, Inventor*
Cooke, Jack Kent	*Sports Executive*	Grim, Robert A (Bob)	*Baseball Player*
Copeland, Johnny (Clyde)	*Singer, Guitarist*	Harriman, Pamela D C	*Diplomat*
Cousteau, Jacques-Yves	*Oceanographer*	Hayes, Charles A	*Representative, IL*
Cronenweth, Jordan E	*Cinematographer*	Helms, Bobby	*Singer*

738

Helmsley, Harry B	Businessman	Meredith, Burgess	Actor
Hershey, Alfred D	Nobel Medicine Laureate	Michener, James A	Writer
Herzog, Chaim	President, Israel; Historian	Mitchum, Robert	Actor
Hickey, William	Actor	Mobutu Sese Seko	President, Zaire
Hinton, John D	WW II Army Hero (VC)	Mohammmed Fadhil Jamali	Prime Minister, Iraq
Hiss, Alger	Attorney	Moore, Alvy	Actor
Hoelscher, Ludwig	Concert Cellist	Mosbacher, Emil (Bus), Jr	Yachtsman
Hogan, Ben	Golfer	Mulhare, Edward	Actor
Hooker, Evelyn G	Psychiatrist	Nance, Jack	Actor
Huggins, Charles B	Nobel Medicine Laureate	Nannen, Henri	Editor
Hughes, Harold E	Governor/Senator, IA	Notorious BIG (Biggie Smalls)	Rap Artist
Hutson, Donald (Don)	Football Player	Nusrat Fateh Ali Khan	Singer
Huxley, Elspetha J	Writer	Nyro, Laura	Singer, Songwriter
Irsay, Robert (Bob)	Football Executive	O'Connor, James J	Businessman
Jacobs, Helen Hull	Tennis Player	O'Toole, John E	Businessman
Jaeckel, Richard	Actor	Olszewski, John	Football Player
Jaffe, Leo	Movie Executive	Oslin, George	Inventor
Jagan, Cheddi	President, Guyana	Overcash, Reece A, Jr	Businessman
James, Dennis	Television Host	Packard, Vance O	Writer
Jeffries, Carson D	Physicist	Parker, Tom	Agent
Johnson, Blaine	Auto Racing Driver	Patterson-Tyler, Audrey (Mickey)	Track Athlete
Johnson, U Alexis	Diplomat	Paulsen, Pat	Comedian
Kampen, Emerson	Businessman	Payton, Lawrence	Singer (Four Tops)
Karmal, Babrak	President, Afghanistan	Peacock, Eulace	Track Athlete
Keck, William	Architect	Peng Zhen	Government Official, China
Keith, Brian	Actor	Peterson, Dave	Hockey Coach
Kelley, Clarence M	Director, FBI	Picard, Henry	Golfer
Kellner, Alexander R (Alex)	Baseball Player	Pieroni, Leonard J	Businessman
Kempton, Murray	Journalist	Pittendrigh, Colin S	Biologist
Khan, Nusrat Fateh Ali	Singer	Porter, Don	Actor
Kilkenny, John F	Judge	Pramoj, Mom Rachawongse	Premier, Thailand
Krainik, Ardis	Opera Executive	Preston, Lewis T	Financier
Kuralt, Charles B	Commentator	Pritchett, Victor S	Writer
Kurtz, Frank	Diver	Prysock, Arthur	Singer, Songwriter
Lacoste, Rene	Tennis Player	Ratner, Max	Businessman
Lane, Burton	Songwriter	Reynolds, Robert (Bob)	Football Player
Lane, Ronnie	Bassist, Songwriter	Richter, Sviatoslav T	Concert Pianist
Lawrence, Rosina	Actress	Roberts, Richard H	Businessman
Leakey, Mary D	Archeologist	Rollins, Howard E, Jr	Actor
Learoyd, Roderick	WW II British RAF Hero (VC)	Rosten, Leo	Political Scientist, Writer
Lee, Laurie	Writer	Royko, Michael (Mike)	Columnist
Leonard, Sheldon	Actor, Producer	Rozelle, Alvin R (Pete)	Football Executive
Lichtenstein, Roy	Artist	Rudolf, Max	Conductor
Liman, Arthur L	Attorney	Rudolph, Paul M	Architect
Lukas, J Anthony (Tony)	Journalist, Writer	Russ, Robert D	Air Force General
Manley, Michael N	Prime Minister, Jamaica	Russell, James S	Navy Admiral, Hero
Mapelli, Roland L	Businessman	Ruttman, Troy	Auto Racing Driver
Marr, Dave	Golfer	Sacco, Ubaldo (Uby)	Boxer
Mastroianni, Marcello	Actor	Sagan, Carl E	Astronomer, Educator
McAfee, Jerry	Businessman	Salam, Abdus	Nobel Physics Laureate
McCosky, W Barney	Baseball Player	Sanchez Vilella, Roberto	Governor, PR
McKinney, Horace (Bones)	Basketball Player	Savio, Mario	Student Activist
Melvin, Harold	Singer (The Blue Notes)	Schapiro, Meyer	Art Historian

Schauer, Henry	WW II Army Hero (CMH)	Van der Post, Laurens J	Explorer, Write
Scott, Ronnie	Jazz Saxophonist	Van Zandt, Townes	Singer, Songwrite
Serber, Robert	Physicist	VanderMeer, John S (Johnny)	Baseball Playe
Shanker, Albert	Labor Leader	Vasarely, Victor	Artis
Sheinwold, Alfred	Bridge Expert, Columnist	Velazquez, Fidel	Labor Offici
Shoemaker, Eugene M	Geologist, Astronomer	Versace, Gianni	Fashion Designe
Sinclair, Jo	Writer	Vickery, William	Nobel Economics Laureat
Slattery, Richard X	Actor	Von Erich, Fritz	Wrestle
Sleet, Moneta, Jr	Photographer	Vonnegut, Bernard	Atmospheric Physici
Smith, Mary Louise	Government Official	Wald, George M	Nobel Medicine Laureat
Solti, Georg	Conductor	Warner, Karl	Track Athlet
Spinola, Antonio S R de	President, Portugal	Weaver, Robert C	Secretary, HU
Steuber, Robert J (Bob)	Football Player	Weis, Sigfried	Businessma
Stewart, James (Jimmy)	Actor	Werner, Charles G	Editorial Cartoonis
Stone, Toni	Baseball Player	Westwood, Jean	Government Offici
Tanaka, Tomoyuki	Movie Producer	White, Gordon L	Businessma
Tartikoff, Brandon	Television Executive	White, Jesse	Acto
Tejeda, Frank	Representative, TX	Widerberg, Bo	Movie Directo
Teresa, Mother	Nobel Peace Laureate	Williams, Tony	Jazz Drummer, Compose
Tikhonov, Nikolai A	Prime Minister, USSR	Wirtz, Arthur M, Jr	Hockey Executiv
Tiny Tim	Singer, Songwriter	Witherspoon, Jimmy	Singer, Bassis
Tombaugh, Clyde W	Astronomer	Yepes, Narciso	Concert Guitaris
Tonnemaker, F Clayton	Football Player	Young, Faron	Singer, Songwrite
Trampler, Walter	Concert Violist	Zale, Tony	Boxe
Tsongas, Paul E	Senator, MA	Zinnemann, Fred	Movie Directo
Turnbull, William, Jr	Architect		

INDEX OF BUSINESS & FINANCIAL INSTITUTIONS

AM International
Brady, Jerome D
AMC Entertainment
Durwood, Stanley H
AMR Corp
Crandall, Robert L
AT&T Co
Allen, Robert E
Mandl, Alex J
Abbott Laboratories
Burnham, Duane L
Hodgson, Thomas R
Adolph Coors Co
Coors, Joseph
Coors, William K
Advanced Micro Devices
Sanders, W J (Jerry), III
Advent International
Brooke, Peter A
Aetna Life & Casualty
Compton, Ronald E
Agway Inc
Heffner, Ralph H
Air Express International
Hartong, Hendrik J, Jr
Air Products & Chemicals Inc
Wagner, Harold A
Airborne Freight Corp
Cline, Robert S
Alberto-Culver
Lavin, Leonard H
Alex Brown & Sons
Krongard, A B
Alexander & Baldwin Inc
Couch, John C
Alleghany Corp
Kirby, F M
Allegheny Ludlum
Simmons, Richard P

Allen & Co
Allen, Herbert A
Keough, Donald R
Allen Group
Colburn, Philip Wm
Allergan Inc
Herbert, Gavin S, Jr
AlliedSignal Inc
Bossidy, Lawrence A
Allstate Insurance
Choate, Jerry D
Aluminum Co of America
O'Neill, Paul H
Alza Corp
Theauwes, Felix
AmSouth Bancorp
Woods, John W
Amdahl Corp
Lewis, John C, Jr
Amerada Hess
Hess, Leon
American Bankers Insurance
Landon, R Kirk
American Brands Inc
Hays, Thomas C
American Business Products
Carmody, Thomas R
American Century
Stowers, James E, Jr
American Express Co
Golub, Harvey
American Greetings Corp
Weiss, Morry
American Home Assurance
Greenberg, Jeffrey W
American Home Products
Laporte, William F
Stafford, John R
American Life Insurance

Nottingham, R Kendall
American Maize-Products
Ziegler, William, III
American President Cos
Lillie, John M
American Re
Jobe, Edward B
American Savings Bank
Antoci, Mario J
American Standard
Kampouris, Emmanuel A
Ameritech
Notebaert, Richard C
Ametek Inc
Blankley, Walter E
Amoco Corp
Fuller, H Laurance
Amway Corp
DeVos, Richard M
Van Andel, Jay
Analog Devices
Stata, Ray
Anheuser-Busch Cos
Busch, August A, III
Apache Corp
Plank, Raymond
Apple Computer
Markkula, A C (Mike), Jr
Archer Daniels Midland
Andreas, Dwayne O
Arkansas Best
Young, Robert A, III
Armstrong World Industries
Lorsch, George A
Arthur Guinness & Sons
Saundners, Ernest W
Arvin Industries
Baker, James K
Asarco Inc

Osborne, Richard de J
Ashland Oil
Hall, John R
Atlantic Energy
Huggard, E Douglas
Atlantic Richfield
Bowlin, Michael R
Cook, Lodwrick M
Avery Dennison Corp
Miller, Charles D
Avnet Inc
Machiz, Leon
Vallee, Roy
B F Goodrich Co
Ong, John D
BASF Corp
Stein, J Dieter
BBC/Lionheart TV
Frank, Sarah
BIC Corp
Bich, Bruno
Backe Group
Backe, John D
Baird Patrick Co
Patrick, Joseph A
Baker Hughes Inc
Woods, James D
Ball Corp
Owsley, Alvin
Banc One Corp
McCoy, John B
Bank Leumi Trust
Friedmann, David
Bank One Dayton
Kasle, Donald H
Bank One Texas
Steinhart, Ronald G
Bank United of Texas
Burkholder, Barry C

Kelly Services
Kelly, William R
Kemper Corp
Kenyon, Alfred K
Timbers, Stephen B
Kennametal Inc
McGeehan, Robert L
McKenna, Quentin C
Kerr-McGee Corp
McPherson, Frank A
KeyCorp
Gillespie, Robert W
Keyport Life Insurance
Rosensteel, John W
Keystone Consolidated
Singer, Robert W
Keystone Group
Elfner, Albert H, III
Keystone International
Clark, Malcolm D
LeBlanc, Raymond A
Teshoian, Nishan
Kidder Peabody Group
Nayden, Denis J
Kimberly-Clark Corp
Sanders, Wayne R
King World Productions
King, Michael
King, Roger
Palley, Stephen W
Westin, Av
Kmart Corp
Hall, Floyd D
Monti, Roberto
Koch Industries
Koch, Charles G
Kohlberg Co
Kohlberg, Jerome, Jr
Kohlberg Kravis Roberts Co
Kravis, Henry
Roberts, George R
Kohler Co
Kohler, Herbert V, Jr
Kroger Co
Bere, Richard L
Pichler, Joseph A
L M Ericsson Telephone
Svedberg, Bjorn
LDDS Communications
Ebbers, Bernard J
LSI Logic
Corrigan, Wilfred J
LTV Corp
Hoag, David H
Twomey, William P
Lafarge Corp
Rose, Michel
Lands' End Inc
Comer, Gary C
Smith, Michael J
Lazard Freres Co
David-Weill, Michel
Rohatyn, Felix G
Lee Enterprises
Gottlieb, Richard D
Leggett & Platt Inc
Cornell, Harry M, Jr
Wright, Felix E
Lehman Brothers
Fuld, Richard S, Jr
Pettit, T Christopher
Leucadia National Corp
Cumming, Ian M
Steinberg, Joseph S
Levi Strauss Assoc
Tusher, Thomas W
Liberty Mutual Insurance
Countryman, Garl L
Kelly, Edmund F
Limited Inc
Wexner, Leslie H
Litton Industries
Brann, Alton J
Leonis, John M

Liz Claiborne Inc
Ortenberg, Arthur
Lloyd's of London
Miller, Peter North
Lockheed Corp
Tellep, Daniel M
Lockheed Marietta Corp
Augustine, Norman R
Loews Corp
Tisch, James S
Longs Drug Stores
Long, Robert M
Lonrho Ltd
Rowland, Roland W
Loral Corp
Lanza, Frank C
Louisiana Land/Exploration
Steward, H Leighton
Lowe's Companies
Herring, Leonard G
Strickland, Robert L
Lubrizol Corp
Coleman, Lester E
Lyondell Petrochemical
Gower, Bob G
Lyonnaise des Eaux-Dumez
Parayre, Jean-Paul C
M A Hanna Co
Walker, Martin D
M&I Marshall & Ilsley Bank
Wigdale, James B
MBIA Inc
Weill, Richard L
MBNA Corp
Lerner, Alfred
MCA Inc
Biondi, Frank J, Jr
Meyer, Ron
Pollock, Thomas P
Sheinberg, Sidney J
Wertheimer, Thomas
MCI Communications
Roberts, Bert C, Jr
Taylor, Gerard H
MGM/United Artists
Mancuso, Frank G
MNBA America Bank
Cawley, Charles W
MacAndrews & Forbes
Perelman, Ronald O
Magma Copper Co
Donahue, Donald J
Manville Corp
Stephens, W Thomas
Mapco Inc
Barnes, James E
Marine Midland Banks
Cleave, James H
Knox, Northrup R
Marmon Group
Pritzker, Jay A
Pritzker, Robert A
Marriott International
Marriott, Alice S
Marriott, J Willard, Jr
Mars Inc
Mars, Forrest, Jr
Martin Marietta Corp
Young, A Thomas
Masco Corp
Lyon, Wayne B
Manoogian, Richard A
Mattel Inc
Amerman, John W
Maytag Corp
Hadley, Leonard A
McDonald's Corp
Cantalupo, James R
Quinlan, Michael R
McDonnell Douglas Corp
McDonnell, John F
Stonecipher, Harry C
McKesson Corp
Pulido, Mark A

Seelenfreund, Alan
Mead Corp
Mason, Steven C
Media General Inc
Bryan, J Stewart, III
Medtronic Inc
George, William W
Wallin, Winston R
Mellon Bank Corp
Cahouet, Frank V
Melville Corp
Goldstein, Stanley P
Rosenthal, Harvey
Merck Co
Gilmartin, Raymond V
Meredith Corp
Kerr, William T
Merrill Lynch Co
Tully, Daniel P
Metropolitan Life Insurance
Kamen, Harry P
Microsoft Corp
Gates, William H (Bill), III
Midlantic Corp
Scheuring, Garry J
Minnesota Mining (3-M)
DeSimone, Livio D
Mobil Corp
Noto, Lucio A
Mohawk Industries
Kolb, David L
Loderbaum, Jeffrey S
Monsanto Co
Shapiro, Robert B
Weldon, Virginia V
Montgomery Ward
Brennan, Bernard F
Morgan Stanley Group
Fisher, Richard B
Morrison Knudsen
Miller, Robert S, Jr
Tinstman, Robert A
Motorola Inc
Galvin, Robert W
Tooker, Gary L
Mutual of Omaha
Skutt, Thomas J
Weekly, John W
NBC Productions
Agoglia, John
NBC-TV
Ebersol, Dick
Ohlmeyer, Donald W, Jr
NCH Corp
Levy, Irvin L
Levy, Lester A
NEC Corp
Kaneko, Hisashi
NL Industries
Martin, J Landis
NYNEX Corp
Seidenberg, Ivan G
Nashua Corp
Baute, Joseph A
Clough, Charles E
Lunger, Francis J
National Broadcasting Co
Frank, Reuven
Goodman, Julian
Segelstein, Irwin S
Verne, Richard
Wright, Robert C
National Medical Enterprises
Barbakow, Jeffrey C
National Re Corp
Warren, William D
National Semiconductor
Halla, Brian
Sprague, Peter J
National Service Industries
Hubble, Don W
National Steel Corp
Goodwin, V John
Sawaragi, Osamu

National-Standard Co
Guth, John E, Jr
NationsBank Corp
McColl, Hugh L, Jr
Navistar International
Cotting, James C
Netscape Communications
Barksdale, James (Jim)
Clark, James (Jim)
New York Bancorp
Malloy, Patrick E, III
New York Life Insurance
Hohn, Harry G
Newell Co
Ferguson, Daniel C
Newmont Mining
Cambre, Ronald C
Nicor Inc
Cline, Richard G
Nike Inc
Bowerman, William J (Bill)
Knight, Philip H
Nissan Motor
Ishihara, Takashi
Nissan Motor Co
Kume, Yutaka
Nomura Securities
Chapman, Max C, Jr
Ujiie, Junichi
Norfolk Southern Corp
Goode, David R
Nortek Inc
Bready, Richard L
North American Reinsurance
Thompson, N David
Northern Trust Corp
Osborn, William A
Northrop Corp
Kresa, Kent
Northwest Airlines
Checchi, Alfred
Nucor Corp
Iverson, F Kenneth
Nynex Corp
Ferguson, William C
OMI Corp
Klebanoff, Michael
Occidental Petroleum
Irani, Ray R
Odyssey Partners
Levy, Leon
Nash, Jack
Ogden Corp
Ablon, Ralph E
Ohio Edison
Holland, Willard R, Jr
Olin Corp
Griffin, Donald W
Johnstone, John W, Jr
Olsten Corp
Liguori, Frank N
Olsten, Stuart P
Olympia & York Ltd
Reichmann, Paul
Oneida Ltd
Matthews, William D
Oppenheimer Management
Fossel, Jon S
Macaskill, Bridget A
Oshkosh Truck
Goodson, R Eugene
Outboard Marine
Bowman, Harry W
Owens-Corning Fiberglas
Hiner, Glen H
Owens-Illinois Inc
Lemieux, Joseph H
Oxford Industries
Lanier, J Hicks
PNC Bank Corp
O'Brien, Thomas H
PPG Industries
Dempsey, Jerry E
Paccar Inc

Willamette Industries	Bailey, Keith E	**Woolworth Corp**	**Xerox Corp**
Swindells, William, Jr	**Winn-Dixie Stores**	Hennig, Frederick E	Allaire, Paul A
Willcox & Gibbs Inc	Davis, A Dano	**Worthington Industries**	**Yellow Corp**
Lomas, Eric J	Kufeldt, James	Malenick, Donal H	Powell, George E, III
Viry, Alain	**Winnebago Industries**	McConnell, John H	Powell, George E, Jr
William Wrigley Jr Co	Dohrmann, Fred G	**Wyle Electronics**	**Zenith Electronics**
Wrigley, William	**Witco Corp**	Clough, Charles M	Moschner, Albin F
Williams Companies	Toller, William R	Ozorkiewicz, Ralph L	Pearlman, Jerry K

U.S. SENATE

The men and women below are current members of the U.S. Senate. They can all be reached by writing them in care of **U.S. Senate, Washington, DC 20510.**

Letters should be addressed

The Honorable Jane/John Doe
U.S. Senator from - - -

Salutations in letters should be

Dear Mr./Ms. Senator - - -:

Alabama	Sessions, Jeff	Montana	Baucus, Max S
Alabama	Shelby, Richard C	Montana	Burns, Conrad
Alaska	Murkowski, Frank H	Nebraska	Hagel, Chuck
Alaska	Stevens, Theodore F	Nebraska	Kerry, J Robert (Bob)
Arizona	Kyl, Jon L	Nevada	Bryan, Richard H
Arizona	McCain, John S, III	Nevada	Reid, Harry M
Arkansas	Bumpers, Dale	New Hampshire	Gregg, Judd A
Arkansas	Hutchinson, Tim	New Hampshire	Smith, Robert C
California	Boxer, Barbara	New Jersey	Lautenberg, Frank R
California	Feinstein, Dianne	New Jersey	Torricelli, Robert G
Colorado	Allard, Wayne	New Mexico	Bingaman, Jeff
Colorado	Campbell, Ben Nighthorse	New Mexico	Domenici, Pete V
Connecticut	Dodd, Christopher J	New York	D'Amato, Alfonse M
Connecticut	Lieberman, Joseph I	New York	Moynihan, Daniel Patrick
Delaware	Biden, Joseph R, Jr	North Carolina	Faircloth, Duncan M (Lauch)
Delaware	Roth, William V, Jr.	North Carolina	Helms, Jesse
Florida	Graham, D Robert (Bob)	North Dakota	Conrad, Kent
Florida	Mack, Corneilus M (Connie)	North Dakora	Dorgan, Byron L
Georgia	Cleland, Max	Ohio	DeWine, Michael
Georgia	Coverdell, Paul D	Ohio	Glenn, John H, Jr
Hawaii	Akaka, Daniel K	Oklahoma	Inhofe, James M
Hawaii	Inouye, Daniel K	Oklahoma	Nickles, Donald L
Idaho	Craig, Larry E	Oregon	Smith, Gordon
Idaho	Kempthorne, Dirk A	Oregon	Wyden, Ron
Illinois	Durbin, Richard J	Pennsylvania	Santorum, Richard J (Rick)
Illinois	Moseley-Braun, Carol	Pennsylvania	Specter, Arlen
Indiana	Coats, Daniel R	Rhode Island	Chafee, John H
Indiana	Lugar, Richard G	Rhode Island	Reed, John F
Iowa	Grassley, Charles E	South Carolina	Hollings, Ernest F (Fritz)
Iowa	Harkin, Thomas R	South Carolina	Thurmond, J Strom
Kansas	Brownback, Sam	South Dakota	Daschle, Thomas A
Kansas	Roberts, Pat	South Dakota	Johnson, Tim
Kentucky	Ford, Wendell H	Tennessee	Frist, Bill
Kentucky	McConnell, Mitch	Tennessee	Thompson, Fred Dalton
Louisiana	Breaux, John B	Texas	Gramm, W. Phillip (Phil)
Louisiana	Landrieu, Mary L	Texas	Hutchison, Kay Bailey
Maine	Collins, Susan	Utah	Bennett, Robert F (Rob)
Maine	Snowe, Olympia J	Utah	Hatch, Orrin G
Maryland	Mikulski, Barbara A	Vermont	Jeffords, James M (Jim)
Maryland	Sarbanes, Paul S	Vermont	Leahy, Patrick J
Massachusetts	Kennedy, Edward M (Ted)	Virginia	Robb, Charles S
Massachusetts	Kerry, John F	Virginia	Warner, John W
Michigan	Abraham, Spencer	Washington	Gorton, Slade
Michigan	Levin, Carl	Washington	Murray, Patty
Minnesota	Grams, Rodney D (Rod)	West Virginia	Byrd, Robert C.
Minnesota	Wellstone, Paul D	West Virginia	Rockefeller, John D, IV
Mississippi	Cochran, Thad	Wisconsin	Feingold, Russell D
Mississippi	Lott, Trent	Wisconsin	Kohl, Herbert H
Missouri	Ashcroft, John	Wyoming	Enzi, Michael B
Missouri	Bond, Christopher (Kit)	Wyoming	Thomas, Craig

U.S. HOUSE OF REPRESENTATIVES

The men and women below are current members of the U.S. House of Representatives. They can all be reached by writing them in care of U.S. House of Representatives, Washington, DC 20512. Letters should be addressed to

The Honorable Jane/John Doe
U.S. Representative from - - -

Salutations in letters should be

Dear Mr./Ms. Representative - - -:

Alabama	Aderholt, Robert	California	Riggs, Frank
Alabama	Bachus, Spencer T, III	California	Rogan, James E
Alabama	Callahan, H L (Sonny)	California	Rohrabacher, Dana
Alabama	Cramer, Robert E (Bud), Jr	California	Roybal-Allard, Lucille
Alabama	Everett, Terry	California	Royce, Edward R (Ed)
Alabama	Hilliard, Earl F	California	Sanchez, Loretta
Alabama	Riley, Bob	California	Sherman, Brad
Alaska	Young, Donald E	California	Stark, Fortney N (Pete)
Arizona	Hayworth, J D	California	Tauscher, Ellen O
Arizona	Kolbe, James T (Jim)	California	Thomas, William M
Arizona	Pastor, Ed	California	Torres, Esteban E
Arizona	Salmon, Matt	California	Waters, Maxine
Arizona	Shadegg, John	California	Waxman, Henry A
Arizona	Stump, Bob	California	Woolsey, Lynn C
Arkansas	Berry Marion	Colorado	Hefley, Joel M
Arkansas	Dickey, Jay W, Jr	Colorado	McInnis, Scott S
Arkansas	Hutchinson, Asa	Colorado	Schaefer, Daniel L (Dan)
Arkansas	Snyder, Vic	Colorado	Schaffer, Bob
California	Becerra, Xavier	Colorado	Skaggs, David E
California	Berman, Howard L	Connecticut	DeLauro, Rosa L
California	Bilbray, Brian P	Connecticut	Gejdenson, Samuel
California	Bono, Sonny	Connecticut	Johnson, Nancy L
California	Brown, George E, Jr	Connecticut	Kennelly, Barbara Bailey
California	Calvert, Ken	Connecticut	Maloney, James H
California	Campbell, Tom	Connecticut	Shays, Christopher
California	Capps, Walter H	Delaware	Castle, Michael N
California	Condit, Gary A	Florida	Bilirakis, Michael
California	Cox, C Christopher	Florida	Boyd, Allen
California	Cunningham, Randall (Duke)	Florida	Brown, Corrine
California	DeGette, Diana	Florida	Canady, Charles T
California	Dellums, Ronald V	Florida	Davis, Jim
California	Dixon, Julian C	Florida	Deutsch, Peter
California	Dooley, Calvin M, Jr	Florida	Diaz-Balart, Lincoln
California	Doolittle, John T	Florida	Foley, Mark
California	Dreier, David T	Florida	Fowler, Tillie K
California	Eshoo, Anna G	Florida	Goss, Porter J
California	Farr, Sam	Florida	Hastings, Alcee L
California	Fazio, Vic	Florida	McCollum, I William (Bill), Jr
California	Filner, Robert (Bob)	Florida	Meek, Carrie P
California	Gallegly, Elton W	Florida	Mica, John L
California	Harman, Jane	Florida	Miller, Dan
California	Herger, Wally W, Jr	Florida	Ros-Lehtinen, Ileana
California	Horn, J Stephen	Florida	Scarborough, Joe
California	Hunter, Duncan L	Florida	Shaw, E Clay, Jr
California	Kim, Jay	Florida	Stearns, Clifford B (Cliff)
California	Lantos, Thomas P	Florida	Thurman, Karen L
California	Lewis, Jerry	Florida	Weldon, Dave
California	Lofgren, Zoe	Florida	Wexler, Robert
California	Martinez, Matthew G, Jr	Florida	Young, C W (Bill)
California	Matsui, Robert T	Georgia	Barr, Bob
California	McDonald, Juanita M	Georgia	Bishop, Sanford D, Jr
California	McKeon, Howard P (Buck)	Georgia	Chambliss, Saxby
California	Miller, George	Georgia	Collins, Michael A (Mac)
California	Packard, Ronald	Georgia	Deal, John Nathan
California	Pelosi, Nancy	Georgia	Gingrich, Newton L (Newt)
California	Pombo, Richard W	Georgia	Kingston, Jack
California	Radanovich, George P	Georgia	Lewis, John R

Georgia	Linder, John E	Maryland	Ehrlich, Robert L, Jr
Georgia	McKinney, Cynthia A	Maryland	Gilchrest, Wayne T
Georgia	Norwood, Charles, Jr	Maryland	Hoyer, Steny H
Hawaii	Abercrombie, Neil	Maryland	Morella, Constance A
Hawaii	Mink, Patsy Takemoto	Maryland	Wynn Albert R
Idaho	Chenoweth, Helen	Massachusetts	Delahunt, William D
Idaho	Crapo, Michael D	Massachusetts	Frank, Barney
Illinois	Jackson, Jesse L, Jr	Massachusetts	Kennedy, Joseph P, II
Illinois	Blagojevich, Rod R	Massachusetts	Markey, Edward J
Illinois	Costello, Jerry F	Massachusetts	McGovern, James P
Illinois	Crane, Philip M	Massachusetts	Meehan, Martin T
Illinois	Davis, Danny K	Massachusetts	Moakley, John Joseph
Illinois	Evans, Lane A	Massachusetts	Neal, Richard E
Illinois	Ewing, Thomas W	Massachusetts	Olver, John W
Illinois	Fawell, Harris W	Massachusetts	Tierney, John F
Illinois	Gutierrez, Luis V	Michigan	Barcia, James A
Illinois	Hastert, J Dennis	Michigan	Bonior, David E
Illinois	Hyde, Henry J	Michigan	Camp, Dave
Illinois	LaHood, Ray	Michigan	Conyers, John, Jr
Illinois	Lipinski, William O	Michigan	Dingell, John D, Jr
Illinois	Manzullo, Donald A	Michigan	Ehlers, Vernon J
Illinois	Porter, John E	Michigan	Hoekstra, Peter
Illinois	Poshard, Glenn W	Michigan	Kildee, Dale E
Illinois	Rush, Bobby L	Michigan	Kilpatrick, Carolyn Cheeks
Illinois	Shimkus, John M	Michigan	Knollenberg, Joseph (Ken)
Illinois	Weller, Gerald C (Jerry)	Michigan	Levin, Sander M
Illinois	Yates, Sidney R	Michigan	Rivers, Lynn Nancy
Indiana	Burton, Dan L	Michigan	Smith, Nick
Indiana	Buyer, Stephen E	Michigan	Stabenow, Debbie
Indiana	Carson, Julia M	Michigan	Stupak, Bart T
Indiana	Hamilton, Lee H	Michigan	Upton, Frederick S
Indiana	Hostettler, John N	Minnesota	Gutknecht, Gil
Indiana	McIntosh David M	Minnesota	Luther, William P (Bill)
Indiana	Pease, Edward A	Minnesota	Minge, David
Indiana	Roemer, Timothy J	Minnesota	Oberstar, James L
Indiana	Souder, Mark Edward	Minnesota	Peterson, Collin C
Indiana	Visclosky, Peter J	Minnesota	Ramstad, Jim
Iowa	Boswell, Leonard L	Minnesota	Sabo, Martin O
Iowa	Ganske, Greg	Minnesota	Vento, Bruce F
Iowa	Latham, Tom	Mississippi	Parker, Michael (Mike)
Iowa	Leach, James A S (Jim)	Mississippi	Pickering, Charles W (Chip), Jr
Iowa	Nussle, James A (Jim)	Mississippi	Taylor, Gene
Kansas	Moran, Jerry	Mississippi	Thompson, Bennie G
Kansas	Ryun, Jim	Mississippi	Wicker, Roger F
Kansas	Snowbarger, Vince	Missouri	Blunt, Roy
Kansas	Tiahrt, Todd	Missouri	Clay, William (Bill), Sr
Kentucky	Baesler, Scotty	Missouri	Danner, Patsy Ann (Pat)
Kentucky	Bunning, James P D (Jim)	Missouri	Emerson, Jo Ann
Kentucky	Lewis, Ron	Missouri	Gephardt, Richard A
Kentucky	Northup, Anne M	Missouri	Hulshof, Kenny
Kentucky	Rogers, Harold (Hal)	Missouri	McCarthy, Karen
Kentucky	Whitfield, Edward	Missouri	Skelton, Isaac Newton (Ike), IV
Louisiana	Baker, Richard H	Missouri	Talent, James M
Louisiana	Cooksey, John	Montana	Hill, Rick
Louisiana	Fields, Cleo	Nebraska	Barrett, William E (Bill)
Louisiana	Jefferson, William J (Jeff)	Nebraska	Bereuter, Douglas K
Louisiana	John, Chris	Nebraska	Christensen, Jon
Louisiana	Livingston, Robert L (Bob), Jr	Nevada	Ensign, John
Louisiana	Tauzin, Wilbert J (Billy)	Nevada	Gibbons, Jim
Maine	Allen, Thomas H	New Hampshire	Bass, Charles
Maine	Baldacci, John	New Hampshire	Sununu, John E
Maryland	Bartlett, Roscoe G	New Jersey	Andrews, Robert E
Maryland	Cardin, Benjamin L	New Jersey	Franks, Robert D (Bob)
Maryland	Cummings, Elijah E	New Jersey	Frelinghuysen, Rodney

State	Representative
New Jersey	LoBiondo, Frank A
New Jersey	Menendez, Robert
New Jersey	Pallone, Frank, Jr
New Jersey	Pappas, Mike
New Jersey	Pascrell, William J, Jr
New Jersey	Payne, Donald M
New Jersey	Rothman, Steven R
New Jersey	Roukema, Margeret S
New Jersey	Saxton, H James
New Jersey	Smith, Christopher H
New Mexico	Redmond, Bill
New Mexico	Schiff, Steven H
New Mexico	Skeen, Joseph R
New York	Ackerman, Gary L
New York	Boehlert, Sherwood L
New York	Engel, Eliot L
New York	Flake, Floyd H
New York	Forbes, Michael P
New York	Gilman, Benjamin A
New York	Hinchey, Maurice D, Jr
New York	Houghton, Amory, Jr
New York	Kelly, Sue W
New York	King, Peter T
New York	LaFalce, John J
New York	Lazio, Rick A
New York	Lowey, Nita M
New York	Maloney, Carolyn B
New York	Manton, Thomas J
New York	McCarthy, Carolyn
New York	McHugh, John M
New York	McNulty, Michael R
New York	Nadler, Jerrold L (Jerry)
New York	Owens, Major R O
New York	Paxon, L William (Bill)
New York	Quinn, Jack
New York	Rangel, Charles B
New York	Schumer, Charles E
New York	Serrano, José E
New York	Slaughter, Louise M
New York	Solomon, Gerald B H
New York	Towns, Edolphus
New York	Velazquez, Nydia M
New York	Walsh, James T
North Carolina	Ballenger, T Cass
North Carolina	Burr, Richard M
North Carolina	Clayton, Eva M
North Carolina	Coble, Howard
North Carolina	Etheridge, Bob
North Carolina	Hefner, W G (Bill)
North Carolina	Jones, Walter B, Jr
North Carolina	McIntyre, Mike
North Carolina	Myrick, Sue
North Carolina	Price, David E
North Carolina	Taylor, Charles H
North Carolina	Watt, Melvin L
North Dakota	Pomeroy, Earl R
Ohio	Boehner, John A
Ohio	Brown, Sherrod
Ohio	Chabot, Steve
Ohio	Gillmor, Paul E
Ohio	Hall, Tony P
Ohio	Hobson, David L
Ohio	Kaptur, Marcy
Ohio	Kasich, John R
Ohio	Kucinich, Dennis J
Ohio	LaTourette, Steven C
Ohio	Ney, Bob
Ohio	Oxley, Michael G
Ohio	Portman, Rob
Ohio	Pryce, Deborah
Ohio	Regula, Ralph
Ohio	Sawyer, Thomas C
Ohio	Stokes, Louis
Ohio	Strickland, Ted
Ohio	Traficant, James A, Jr
Oklahoma	Coburn, Tom
Oklahoma	Istook, Ernest J (Jim), Jr
Oklahoma	Largent, Steve
Oklahoma	Lucas, Frank D
Oklahoma	Watkins, Wes
Oklahoma	Watts, J C, Jr
Oregon	Blumenauer, Earl
Oregon	DeFazio, Peter A
Oregon	Hooley, Darlene
Oregon	Smith, Robert F (Bill)
Oregon	Witt, Bill
Pennsylvania	Borski, Robert A, Jr
Pennsylvania	Coyne, William J
Pennsylvania	Doyle, Mike
Pennsylvania	English, Phil
Pennsylvania	Fattah, Chaka
Pennsylvania	Foglietta, Thomas M
Pennsylvania	Fox, Jon D
Pennsylvania	Gekas, George W
Pennsylvania	Goodling, William F
Pennsylvania	Greenwood, James C
Pennsylvania	Holdon, Tim
Pennsylvania	Kanjorski, Paul E
Pennsylvania	Klink, Ron
Pennsylvania	Mascara, Frank R
Pennsylvania	McDade, Joseph M
Pennsylvania	McHale, Paul
Pennsylvania	Murtha, John P
Pennsylvania	Peterson, John E
Pennsylvania	Pitts, Joseph R
Pennsylvania	Shuster, E G (Bud)
Pennsylvania	Weldon, W Curtis
Rhode Island	Kennedy, Patrick J
Rhode Island	Weygand, Robert A
South Carolina	Clyburn, James E
South Carolina	Graham, Lindsey
South Carolina	Inglis, Robert D (Bob)
South Carolina	Sanford, Mark
South Carolina	Spence, Floyd D
South Carolina	Spratt, John M, Jr
South Dakota	Thune, John R
Tennessee	Bryant, Ed
Tennessee	Clement, Bob
Tennessee	Duncan, John J, Jr
Tennessee	Ford, Harold E, Jr
Tennessee	Gordon, Bart
Tennessee	Hilleary, Van
Tennessee	Jenkins, William L (Bill)
Tennessee	Tanner, John S
Tennessee	Wamp, Zach
Texas	Archer, William R (Bill), Jr

Texas	Armey, Richard K	Virginia	Bateman, Herbert H (Herb)
Texas	Barton, Joe L	Virginia	Bliley, Thomas J (Tom), Jr
Texas	Bensten, Ken	Virginia	Boucher, Frederick C (Rick)
Texas	Bonilla, Henry	Virginia	Davis, Thomas M, III
Texas	Brady, Kevin	Virginia	Goode, Virgil H, Jr
Texas	Combest, Larry	Virginia	Goodlatte, Robert W (Bob)
Texas	DeLay, Thomas D (Tom)	Virginia	Moran, James P, Jr
Texas	Doggett, Lloyd	Virginia	Pickett, Owen B
Texas	Edwards, Chet	Virginia	Scott, Robert C (Bobby)
Texas	Frost, J Martin	Virginia	Sisisky, Norman
Texas	Gonzalez, Henry B	Virginia	Wolf, Frank R
Texas	Granger, Kay	Washington	Baird, Brian
Texas	Green, Gene	Washington	Dicks, Norman D
Texas	Hall, Ralph M	Washington	Dunn, Jennifer B
Texas	Hinojosa, Ruben	Washington	Hastings, Doc
Texas	Johnson, Eddie Bernice	Washington	McDermott, James A (Jim)
Texas	Johnson, Samuel (Sam)	Washington	Nethercutt, George R, Jr
Texas	Lampson, Nick	Washington	Quigley, Kevin
Texas	Lee, Sheila Jackson	Washington	Smith, Adam
Texas	Ortiz, Solomon P	Washington	White, Rick
Texas	Paul, Ron	West Virginia	Mollohan, Alan B
Texas	Reyes, Silvestre	West Virginia	Rahall, Nick Joe, II
Texas	Sandlin, Max	West Virginia	Wise, Robert E, Jr
Texas	Sessions, Pete	Wisconsin	Barrett, Thomas M
Texas	Smith, Lamar S	Wisconsin	Johnson, Jay
Texas	Stenholm, Charles W	Wisconsin	Kind, Ron
Texas	Tejeda, Frank	Wisconsin	Kleczka, Gerald D
Texas	Thornberry, William M (Mac)	Wisconsin	Klug, Scott L
Texas	Turner, Jim	Wisconsin	Neumann, Mark W
Utah	Cannon, Christopher B	Wisconsin	Obey, David R
Utah	Cook, Merrill	Wisconsin	Petri, Thomas E
Utah	Waldholtz, Enid Greene	Wisconsin	Sensenbrenner, F James, Jr
Vermont	Sanders, Bernard (Bernie)	Wyoming	Cubin, Barbara

ADDITIONAL ADDRESSES

AGENCY ADDRESSES

Abrams Artists & Associates	420 Madison Ave, #1400	New York, NY 10017, USA
Abrams Artists & Associates	9200 Sunset Blvd, #625	Los Angeles, CA 90069, USA
Abrams-Rubaloff & Lawrence	8075 W 3rd St, #303	Los Angeles, CA 90048, USA
Aces Agency	6820 Katherine Ave	Van Nuys, CA 91405, USA
Addis-Wechsler	955 S Carillo Dr, #300	Los Angeles, CA 90048, USA
Advantage International	1025 Thomas Jefferson NW #450	Washington, DC 20007, USA
Agency, The	1800 Ave of Stars, #400	Los Angeles, CA 90067, USA
Agency For Performing Arts	888 7th Ave	New York, NY 10106, USA
Agency For Performing Arts	9000 Sunset Blvd, #1200	Los Angeles, CA 90069, USA
Agents Artistiques Beaume/Bonnet	4 Rue De Ponthieu	75008 Paris, France
Agentur Killer	54 Harthauser Str	81545 Munich, Germany
Agentur Mattes	14 Merzstr	81679 Munich, Germany
Alliance Talent	9171 Wilshire Blvd., #441	Beverly Hills, CA 90210, USA
Alliance Talent	1501 Broadway, #404	New York, NY 10036, USA
Ambrosio/Mortimer & Associates	165 W 46th St, #1214	New York, NY 10036, USA
Ambrosio/Mortimer & Associates	9150 Wilshire Blvd, #175	Beverly Hills, CA 90212, USA
Amsel Eisenstadt & Frazier	6310 San Vicente Blvd, #401	Los Angeles, CA 90048, USA
Arthur, (Irvin) Associates	9363 Wilshire Blvd, #212	Beverly Hills, CA 90210, USA
Artists Agency	10000 Santa Monica Blvd, #305	Los Angeles, CA 90067, USA
Artists Group	10100 Santa Monica Blvd, #2490	Los Angeles, CA 90067, USA
Artmedia	10 Ave George V	75008 Paris, France
Assniated Booking Agency	1995 Broadway, #501	New York, NY 10023, USA
Assniated Talent International	1320 Armacost Ave, #2	Los Angeles, CA 90025, USA
Atkins & Associates	303 S Crescent Heights Blvd	Los Angeles, CA 90048, USA
Badgley Connor	9229 Sunset Blvd, #311	Los Angeles, CA 90069, USA
Baier/Kleinman Int'l	3575 Cahuenga Blvd, #500	Los Angeles, CA 90068, USA

Baldwin Talent	500 S Sepulveda Blvd, #400	Los Angeles, CA 90049, USA
Ball Talent Agency	4342 Lankershim Blvd	Universal City, CA 91602, USA
Barr, (Ricky) Agency	PO Box 69590	Los Angeles, CA 90069, USA
Barrett Benson McCartt Weston	9320 Wilshire Blvd, #3	Los Angeles, CA 90212, USA
Barz, (Richard A) Associates	Rt 1, Box 91	Tannersville, PA 18372, USA
Bauman Hiller & Associates	250 W 57th St, #2223	New York, NY 10107, USA
Bauman Hiller & Associates	5750 Wilshire Blvd, #512	Los Angeles, CA 90036, USA
Beall, (Harry) Management	PO Box 4	Shutesbury, MA 01072, USA
Belfrage, Julian	46 Albermarle St	London W1X 4PP, England
Belson & Klass Associates	144 S Beverly Blvd, #405	Beverly Hills, CA 90212, USA
Bennett Morgan Associates	1282 Rt 376	Wappingers Falls, NY 12590, USA
Berkeley Agency	2608 9th St	Berkeley, CA 94712, USA
Bethann Model Management	36 N Moore St, #36-N	New York, NY 10013, USA
Big J Productions	PO Box 24455	New Orleans, LA 70184, USA
Bikoff, (Yvette) Agency	621 N. Orlando, #8	Los Angeles, CA 90048, USA
Blake Agency	415 N Camden Dr, #121	Beverly Hills, CA 90210, USA
Blanchard, (Nina) Enterprises	957 N Cole Ave	Los Angeles, CA 90038, USA
Bloom, (J Michael) Ltd	9255 Sunset Blvd, #710	Los Angeles, CA 90069, USA
Bloom, (J Michael) Ltd	233 Park Ave S, #1000	New York, NY 10007, USA
Bloom, Lloyd	1440 S Sepulveda Blvd, #110	Los Angeles, CA 90025, USA
Borinstein Oreck Bogart Agency	8271 Melrose Ave, #110	Los Angeles, CA 90046, USA
Borman Sternberg	9220 Sunset Blvd, #320	Los Angeles, CA 90069, USA
Bresler Kelly & Associates	15760 Ventura Blvd, #1730	Encino, CA 91436, USA
Breslin, (Herbert)	119 W 57th St	New York, NY 10019, USA
Brewis, (Alex) Agency	12429 Laurel Terrace Dr	Studio City, CA 91604, USA
Brillstein-Grey Entertainment	9150 Wilshire Blvd, #350	Beverly Hills, CA 90212, USA
Brooke Dunn Oliver	9169 Sunset Blvd, #202	Los Angeles, CA 90069, USA
Brothers Management	141 Dunbar Ave	Fords, NJ 08863, USA
Buchwald, (Don) & Associates	9229 Sunset Blvd, #710	Los Angeles, CA 90069, USA
Buchwald, (Don) & Associates	10 E 44th St	New York, NY 10017, USA
Burton, (Iris) Agency	1450 Belfast Dr	Los Angeles, CA 90069, USA
Calder Agency	19919 Redwing St	Woodland Hills, CA 91364, USA
Camden ITG Talent Agency	822 S. Robertson Blvd, #200	Los Angeles, CA 90035, USA
Carlyle, (Phyllis) Management	5300 Melrose Ave, #305-E	Los Angeles, CA 90038, USA
Carroll, (William) Agency	139 N San Fernando Rd, #A	Burbank, CA 91502, USA
Cassidy, (Thomas) Inc	0366 Horseshoe Dr	Basalt, CO 81621, USA
Cavaleri & Associates	405 Riverside Dr, #200	Burbank, CA 91506, USA
Century Artists	1148 4th St, #206	Santa Monica, CA 90403, USA
Charter Management	8383 Wilshire Blvd, #614	Beverly Hills, CA 90211, USA
Chasin Agency	8899 Beverly Blvd, #716	Los Angeles, CA 90048, USA
Chatto & Linnit	Prince of Wales, Coventry St	London W1V 7FE, England
Circle Talent Associates	433 N Camden Dr, #400	Beverly Hills, CA 90210, USA
Click Model Management	881 7th Ave	New York, NY 10019, USA
C.L.Inc. Talent Agency	843 N Sycamore Ave	Los Angeles, CA 90038, USA
CNA & Associates	1925 Century Park E, #750	Los Angeles, CA 90067, USA
Coast To Coast Talent Group	4942 Vineland Ave, #200	North Hollywood, CA 91601, USA
Colbert Artists Management	111 W 57th St	New York, NY 10019, USA
Columbia Artists Management Inc	165 W 57th St	New York, NY 10019, USA
Commercials Unlimited	9601 Wilshire Blvd, #620	Beverly Hills, CA 90210, USA
Conner, (Hall) Agency	9169 Sunset Blvd	Los Angeles, CA 90069, USA
Contemporary Artists	1427 3rd St Promenade, #205	Santa Monica, CA 90401, USA
Conway Van Gelder Robinson	18-21 Jermyn St	London SW1Y 6HB, England
Cosden Agency	3518 Cahuenga Blvd W, #216	Los Angeles, CA 90068, USA
Craig Agency	8485 Melrose Place, #E	Los Angeles, CA 90069, USA
Creative Artists Agency	9830 Wilshire Blvd	Beverly Hills, CA 90212, USA
Creative Entertainment Associates	2011 Ferry Ave, #U-19	Camden, NJ 08104, USA
Cumber, (Lil) Attractions Agency	6363 Sunset Blvd, #701	Los Angeles, CA 90028, USA
Cunningham-Escott-Dipene	10635 Santa Monica Blvd, #130	Los Angeles, CA 90025, USA
Cunningham-Escott-Dipene	257 Park Ave S, #900	New York, NY 10010, USA
Curtis Brown	162-168 Regent St	London W1R 5TB, England
Dade/Schultz Agency	11846 Ventura Blvd, #100	Studio City, CA 91604, USA

Daish, (Judy) Associates	2 St. Charles Pl	London M10 6EG, England
DeLeon Artists	4031 Panama Court	Piedmont, CA 94611, USA
DH, Talent Agency	1800 N Highland Ave, #300	Los Angeles, CA 90028, USA
Diamond Artists	170 West End Ave, #3-K	New York, NY 10023, USA
Diamond Artists	215 N Barrington Ave	Los Angeles, CA 90049, USA
Doty, (Patricia) Associates	13455 Ventura Blvd, #210	Sherman Oaks, CA 91423, USA
Douglas Gorman, et al	1650 Broadway	New York, NY 10019, USA
Duncan Heath Associates	Paramount House, 162 Wardour	London W1V 3AT, England
Durkin Artists Agency	127 Broadway, #210	Santa Monica, CA 90401, USA
Elite Model Management	111 E 22nd St, #200	New York, NY 10010, USA
Elite Model Management	345 N Maple Dr, #397	Beverly Hills, CA 90210, USA
Endeavor Talent Agency	9701 Wilshire Blvd, #1000	Beverly Hills, CA 90212, USA
Entertainment Talent Agency	PO Box 1821	Ojai, CA 93024, USA
Epstein-Wyckoff & Associates	280 S Beverly Dr, #400	Beverly Hills, CA 90212, USA
Epstein-Wyckoff & Associates	311 W 43rd St, #1401	New York, NY 10036, USA
Famous Artists Agency	1700 Broadway, #500	New York, NY 10019, USA
Farrell/Coulter Talent Agency	PO Box 15189	North Hollywood, CA 91615, USA
Felber, (William) Agency	2126 Cahuenga Blvd	Los Angeles, CA 90068, USA
Film Artists Associates	7080 Hollywood Blvd, #1118	Los Angeles, CA 90028, USA
First Artists Agency	10000 Riverside Dr, #10	Toluca Lake, CA 91602, USA
Flick East-West Talents	9057 Nemo St, #A	West Hollywood, CA 90069, USA
Flick East-West Talents	Carnegie Hall, 818 7th Ave, #1110	New York, NY 10019, USA
Ford Model Agency	344 E 59th St	New York, NY 10022, USA
F.P.A.	12701 Moorpark, #205	Studio City, CA 91604, USA
Freed (Barry) Company	2029 Century Park East, #600	Los Angeles, CA 90067, USA
Front Line Management	8900 Wilshire Blvd, #300	Beverly Hills, CA 90211, USA
Gage Group	315 W 57th St, #4H	New York, NY 10019, USA
Gage Group	9255 Sunset Blvd, #515	Los Angeles, CA 90069, USA
Garrick, (Dale) International	8831 Sunset Blvd, #402	Los Angeles, CA 90069, USA
Garrick, (Dale) International	117 W 48th St	New York, NY 10020, USA
Geddes Agency	1201 Greenacre Blvd	West Hollywood, CA 90046, USA
Geller, (Susan) Associates	335 N Maple Dr. #254	Beverly Hills, CA 90210, USA
Gerler (Don) Agency	3349 Cahuenga Blvd W, #1	Los Angeles, CA 90068, USA
Gersh Agency	130 W 42nd St, #1804	New York, NY 10036, USA
Gersh Agency	232 N Canon Dr	Beverly Hills, CA 90210, USA
Gewald, (Robert) Management	58 W 58th St	New York, NY 10019, USA
Gibson, (J Carter) Agency	9000 Sunset Blvd, #801	Los Angeles, CA 90069, USA
Gilla Roos, Ltd	9744 Wilshire Blvd, #203	Beverly Hills, CA 90212, USA
Gold/Marshak/Liedtke	3500 W Olive Ave, #1400	Burbank, CA 91505, USA
Gordon (Michelle) & Associates	260 S Beverly Dr, #308	Beverly Hills, CA 90212, USA
Gordon/Rosson Co	12700 Ventura Blvd, #340	Studio City, CA 91604, USA
Gores/Fields Agency	10100 Santa Monica Blvd, #2500	Los Angeles, CA 90067, USA
Gorfaine/Schwarz/Roberts	3301 Barham Blvd, #201	Los Angeles, CA 90068, USA
Grady, (Mary) Agency	4444 Lankershim Blvd, #207	North Hollywood, CA 91602, USA
Gray/Goodman	211 S Beverly Dr, #100	Beverly Hills, CA 90212, USA
Greene & Associates	8899 Beverly Blvd, #705	Los Angeles, CA 90048, USA
Greenevine Agency	110 E 9th St, #C-1005	Los Angeles, CA 90079, USA
Halliday (Buzz) & Associates	8899 Beverly Blvd,#620	Los Angeles, CA 90048, USA
Hallmark Entertainment	8033 Sunset Blvd, #1000	Los Angeles, CA 90046, USA
Halpern & Associates	12304 Santa Monica Blvd, #104	Los Angeles, CA 90025, USA
Halsey, (Jim) Co	3225 S Norwood Ave	Tulsa, OK 74135, USA
Hart, Vaughn D	8899 Beverly Blvd, #815	Los Angeles, CA 90048, USA
Hatcher, (Lib) Management	1610 16th Ave S	Nashville, TN 37212, USA
Henderson/Hogan Agency	247 S Beverly Dr, #102	Beverly Hills, CA 90210, USA
Henderson/Hogan Agency	850 7th Ave, #1003	New York, NY 10019, USA
Hill, (Terry M) Associates	6430 Variel Ave, #101	Woodland Hills, CA 91367, USA
Hoffer, (Abby) Entertainment	223 1/2 E 48th St	New York, NY 10017, USA
House of Representatives	400 S. Beverly Dr, #101	Beverly Hills, CA 90212, USA
Howard Talent West	11712 Moorpark St, #205B	Studio City, CA 91604, USA
HTM/Headliner Talent Mgmt	7200 France Ave S, #330	Edina, MN 55435, USA
Hurwitz (Martin) Associates, Inc	427 N Canon Dr, #215	Beverly Hills, CA 90210, USA

Hutton Management	200 Fulham Rd	London SW10 9PN, England
HWA Talent Representatives, Inc	1964 Westwood Blvd, #400	Los Angeles, CA 90025, USA
IFA Talent Agency	8730 Sunset Blvd, #490	Los Angeles, CA 90069
Innovative Artists	1999 Ave of Stars, #2850	Los Angeles, CA 90067, USA
Innovative Artists	1776 Broadway, #1810	New York, NY 10010, USA
International Creative Management	Oxford House, 76 Oxford St	London W1N 0AX, England
International Creative Management	40 W 57th St	New York, NY 10019, USA
International Creative Management	8942 Wilshire Blvd	Beverly Hills, CA 90211, USA
Jennings, (Thomas) & Associates	28035 Dorothy Dr, #210-A	Agoura, CA 91301, USA
Joyce Agency	370 Harrison Ave	Harrison, NY 10528, USA
Karg/Weissenbach Associates	329 N Wetherly Dr, #101	Beverly Hills, CA 90211, USA
Katz, (Raymond) Enterprises	345 N Maple Dr, #205	Beverly Hills, CA 90210, USA
Kazarian/Spencer Associates	11365 Ventura Blvd, #100	Studio City, CA 91604, USA
Kemp (Sharon) Talent Agency	8383 Wilshire Blvd, #516	Beverly Hills, CA 90211, USA
Kjar, (Tyler) Agency	10643 Riverside Dr	Toluca Lake, CA 91602, USA
Kohner, (Paul) Inc	9300 Wilshire Blvd, #555	Beverly Hills, CA 90212, USA
Kosden, (Robert) Agency	7135 Hollywood Blvd, #PH-2	Los Angeles, CA 90046, USA
Kurland, (Ted) Associates	173 Brighton Ave	Boston, MA 02134, USA
LA Talent	8335 Sunset Blvd, #200	Los Angeles, CA 90069, USA
Lantz Office	888 7th Ave, #2500	New York, NY 10106, USA
Lee, (Buddy) Attractions	38 Music Sq E, #300	Nashville, TN 37203, USA
Lemond/Zetter Inc	8370 Wilshire Blvd, #310	Beverly Hills, CA 90211, USA
Levine/Schneider	433 N Camden Ave	Beverly Hills, CA 90210, USA
Lichtman (Terry) Company	4439 Wortser Ave	Studio City, CA 91604, USA
London Management	2-4 Noel St	London W1V 3RB, England
Lookout Management	506 Santa Monica Blvd	Santa Monica, CA 90401, USA
Lovell Associates	7095 Hollywood Blvd, #1006	Los Angeles, CA 90028, USA
MacMillan Inc	1177 Ave of Americas, #1965	New York, NY 10036, USA
Majestic Tours	29701 Kinderkarmack Rd	Oradell, NJ 07649, USA
Management Javonovic	24 Kathi-Kobus-Str	80797 Munich, Germany
Markham & Froggatt	Julian House, 4 Windmill St	London W1P 1HF, England
Marshak Wycoff Associates	280 S Beverly Dr, #400	Beverly Hills, CA 90212, USA
MAX Agency	166 N Canon Dr	Beverly Hills, CA 90210, USA
MCA Concerts	100 Universal City Plaza	Universal City, CA 91608, USA
McHugh, (James) Agency	8150 Beverly Blvd, #303	Los Angeles, CA 90048, USA
Media Artists Group, Inc	8383 Wilshire Blvd, #954	Beverly Hills, CA 90211, USA
Metropolitan Talent Agency	4526 Wilshire Blvd	Los Angeles, CA 90010, USA
MEW Inc	8489 W 3rd St, #1100	Los Angeles, CA 90048, USA
Miskin Agency	2355 Benedict Canyon	Beverly Hills, CA 90210, USA
Monarch Productions	8803 Mayne St	Bellflower, CA 90706, USA
Monterey Peninsula Artists	509 Hartnell St	Monterey, CA 93940, USA
Morris, (William) Agency	151 S El Camino Dr	Beverly Hills, CA 90212, USA
Morris, (William) Agency	31/32 Soho Square	London W1V 5DG, England
Morris, (William) Agency	1325 Ave of Americas	New York, NY 10019, USA
Morris, (William) Agency	2325 Crestmoor Rd	Nashville, TN 37215, USA
Moss, (H David) & Associates	733 N Seward St, #PH	Los Angeles, CA 90038, USA
Moss, (Burton) Agency	8827 Beverly Blvd, #L	Los Angeles, CA 90048, USA
Nathe, (Susan) & Associates	8281 Melrose Ave, #200	Los Angeles, CA 90046, USA
Nationwide Entertainment Svs	2756 N. Green Valley Pkwy, #449	Las Vegas, NV 89014, USA
Next Model Management	23 Watts St	New York, NY 10013, USA
Orange Grove Group, Inc	12178 Ventura Blvd, #205	Studio City, CA 91604, USA
Paradigm Agency	10100 Santa Monica Blvd, #2500	Los Angeles, CA 90067, USA
Paradigm Agency	200 W 57th St, #900	New York, NY 10019, USA
Pauline's Model Management	379 W Broadway	New York, NY 10012, USA
Pecoraro, (George) Productions	3680 Madrid St	Las Vegas, NV 89121, USA
Peters, A D	10 Buckingham St	London WC2H 6BO, England
Peters Fraser Dunlop	Chelsea Harbour, Lots Rd	London SW10 0XF, England
PMK Public Relations	1776 Broadway, #800	New York, NY 10019, USA
PMK Public Relations	955 S Carillo Dr, #200	Los Angeles, CA 90048, USA
Premier Talent Agency	3 E 54th St, #1100	New York, NY 10022, USA
Producers Inc	11806 N 56th St	Tampa, FL 33617, USA

Progressive Artists Agency	400 S Beverly Dr, #216	Beverly Hills, CA 90212, USA
ProServe	1100 Woodrow Wilson Blvd, #1800	Arlington, VA 22209, USA
Ramsay, M	14-A Goodwins Ct, St Martin's Ln	London WC2N 4LL, England
Rapp Enterprises	9200 Sunset Blvd, #620	Los Angeles, CA 90069, USA
Rascoff/Zysblat Organization	110 W 57th St, #300	New York, NY 10019, USA
Redway, (John) Associates	5 Denmark St	London WC2H 8LP, England
Reid, (John) Ent	Singes House, 32 Galena Rd	London W6 0LT, England
Rich, (Elaine) Management	2400 Whitman Place	Los Angeles, CA 90068, USA
Robinson, (Dolores) Management	10683 Santa Monica Blvd	Los Angeles, CA 90025, USA
Rogers & Cowan Agency	1888 Century Park E, #500	Los Angeles, CA 90067, USA
Rollins Joffe Morra Brezner	10201 Pico Blvd, #58	Los Angeles, CA 90064, USA
Rose, (Jack) Agency	9255 Sunset Blvd, #603	Los Angeles, CA 90069, USA
Rosenberg, (Marion) Office	8428 Melrose Place, #C	Los Angeles, CA 90069, USA
Rothberg, Arlyne	850 S Devon Ave	Los Angeles, CA 90024, USA
Rothschild, (Charles) Productions	330 E 48th St	New York, NY 10017, USA
Ruffalo, (Joseph) Management	9655 Wilshire Blvd, #850	Beverly Hills, CA 90212, USA
Rush Artists Management	1600 Varick St	New York, NY 10013, USA
Russo, Lynne	3624 Mound View Ave	Studio City, CA 91604, USA
Sanders Agency	1204 Broadway, #304	New York, NY 10001, USA
Sanders Agency	8831 Sunset Blvd, #304	Los Angeles, CA 90069, USA
Sanford-Beckett-Skouras	1015 Gayley Ave, #300	Los Angeles, CA 90024, USA
Savage Agency	6212 Banner Ave	Los Angeles, CA 90038, USA
Schechter, (Irv) Co	9300 Wilshire Blvd, #410	Beverly Hills, CA 90212, USA
Schiffman Ekman Morrison Marx	156 5th Ave	New York, NY 10010, USA
Schiowitz/Clay/Rose	1680 N Vine St, #614	Los Angeles, CA 90028, USA
Schnarr (Sandie) Agency	8281 Melrose Ave, #200	Los Angeles, CA 90046, USA
Schoen, (Judy) & Associates	606 N Larchmont Blvd, #309	Los Angeles, CA 90004, USA
Schut, (Booh) Agency	11350 Ventura Blvd, #206	Studio City, CA 91604, USA
Schwartz, (Don) Associates	6922 Hollywood Blvd, #508	Los Angeles, CA 90028, USA
Scotti Bros	2114 Pico Blvd	Santa Monica, CA 90405, USA
SDB Partners, Inc	1801 Ave of Stars, #902	Los Angeles, CA 90067, USA
Sekura/A Talent Agency	PO Box 931779	Los Angeles, CA 90093, USA
Selected Artists Agency	3900 W Alameda Ave, #1700	Burbank, CA 91505, USA
Shapira, (David) & Associates	15301 Ventura Blvd, #345	Sherman Oaks, CA 91403, USA
Shapiro-Lichtman Agency	8827 Beverly Blvd	Los Angeles, CA 90048, USA
Sharkey, (James) Associates	21 Golden Sq	London W1R 3PA, England
Shaw Concerts	Lincoln Plz, 1900 Broadway, #200	New York, NY 10023, USA
Shepherd Agency	9034 Sunset Blvd, #100	Los Angeles, CA 90069, USA
Sherrell, (Lew) Agency	1354 Los Robles	Palm Springs, CA 92262, USA
Shriver, (Evelyn) PR	1313 16th Ave S	Nashville, TN 37212, USA
Silver Massetti & Szatmary	8730 Sunset Blvd, #480	Los Angeles, CA 90069, USA
Sindell (Richard) & Associates	8271 Melrose Ave, #202	Los Angeles, CA 90046, USA
Slessinger, (Michael) & Associates	8730 Sunset Blvd, #220W	Los Angeles, CA 90069, USA
Smith, (Susan) & Associates	121 N San Vicente Blvd	Beverly Hills, CA 90211, USA
Smith/Gosnell/Nicholson	1515 Palisades Dr, #N	Pacific Palisades, CA 90272, USA
Special Artists Agency	335 N Maple Dr, #302	Beverly Hills, CA 90210, USA
St James's Management	22 Groom Pl	London SW1, England
Starwil Talent	6253 Hollywood Blvd, #730	Los Angeles, CA 90028, USA
Stein & Stein	9200 Sunset Blvd, #707	Los Angeles, CA 90069, USA
Sterling/Winters	1900 Ave of Stars, #1640	Los Angeles, CA 90067, USA
Stone Manners Agency	8091 Selma Ave	Los Angeles, CA 90046, USA
Subrena Artists	330 W 56th St, #18-M	New York, NY 10019, USA
Sun Agency	8961 Sunset Blvd, #V	Los Angeles, CA 90069, USA
Sutton, Barth & Vennari	145 S Fairfax Ave, #310	Los Angeles, CA 90036, USA
Talent Group Inc	6300 Wilshire Blvd, #2110	Los Angeles, CA 90048, USA
Tannen, (Herb) & Associates	8370 Wilshire Blvd, #209	Beverly Hills, CA 90211, USA
Thomas, (Robert) Agency	28051 Dequindre Road	Madison Heights, MI 48071USA
Tisherman Agency	6767 Forest Lawn Dr, #115	Los Angeles, CA 90068, USA
Tobias, (Herb) Agency	8571 Holloway Dr, #1	Los Angeles, CA 90069, USA
Twentieth Century Artists	15315 Magnolia Blvd, #429	Sherman Oaks, CA 91403, USA
United Talent Agency	9560 Wilshire Blvd, #500	Beverly Hills, CA 90212, USA

Variety Artists International	15490 Ventura Blvd	Sherman Oaks, CA 91403, USA
Wain, (Ericka) Agency	1418 N Highland Ave, #102	Los Angeles, CA 90028, USA
Wallis Agency	1126 Hollywood Way, #203-A	Burbank, CA 91505, USA
Webb, (Ruth) Enterprises	13834 Magnolia Blvd	Sherman Oaks, CA 91423, USA
Wilder Agency	3151 Caheunga Blvd W, #310	Los Angeles, CA 90068, USA
Wilhelmina Artists	300 Park Ave, #200	New York, NY 10022, USA
Wilhelmina Artists	8383 Wilshire Blvd, #650	Beverly Hills, CA 90211, USA
Wolf/Kasteller	132 S Rodeo Dr, #300	Beverly Hills, CA 90212, USA
Wolfman Jack Entertainment	Rt 1, PO Box 56	Belvidere, NC 27919, USA
Writers & Artists Agency	19 W 44th St, #1000	New York, NY 10036, USA
Writers & Artists Agency	924 Westwood Blvd, #900	Los Angeles, CA 90024, USA
Yusem, (Gene) Associates	PO Box 67-B-69	Los Angeles, CA 90067, USA
ZBF Agentur	Ordensmeisterstr 15-16	12099 Berlin, Germany
Zealous Artists	139 S Beverly Dr, #222	Beverly Hills, CA 90212, USA

SYNDICATE ADDRESSES

Associated Press	50 Rockefeller Plaza	New York, NY 10020, USA
Creators Syndicate	5777 W Century Blvd, #700	Los Angeles, CA 90045, USA
King Features Syndicate	235 E 45th St	New York, NY 10017, USA
Times-Mirror Syndicate	Times-Mirror Square	Los Angeles, CA 90053, USA
Tribune Media Services	435 N Michigan Ave, #1500	Chicago, IL 60611, USA
United Feature Syndicate	200 Madison Ave	New York, NY 10016, USA
United Media Syndicate	200 Park Ave	New York, NY 10166, USA
United Press International	2 Pennsylvania Plaza, #1800	New York, NY 10121, USA
Universal Press Syndicate	4900 Main St, #900	Kansas City, KS 64112, USA
Universal Press Syndicate	4400 Fairway Dr	Fairway, KS 66205, USA
Universal Press Syndicate	Time-Life Building	New York, NY 10020, USA
Universal Press Syndicate	1301 Spring Oaks Cir	Houston, TX 77055, USA

MAJOR TELEVISION STATION ADDRESSES

American Broadcasting System

WSB-TV	1801 W Peachtree St NE	Atlanta, GA 30309, USA
WCVB-TV (Boston)	5 TV Place	Needham, MA 02194, USA
WLS-TV	190 N State St	Chicago, IL 60601, USA
WFAA-TV	606 Young St	Dallas, TX 75202, USA
WXYZ-TV (Detroit)	20777 W Ten-Mile Rd	Southfield, MI 48037, USA
KTRK-TV	3310 Bissonnet Dr	Houston, TX 77005, USA
KABC-TV	4151 Prospect Ave	Los Angeles, CA 90027, USA
WPLG-TV	3900 Biscayne Blvd	Miami, FL 33137, USA
WVUE-TV	1025 S Jefferson Davis Pkwy	New Orleans, LA 70125, USA
WABC-TV	7 Lincoln Square	New York, NY 10023, USA
WPIV-TV	4100 City Line Ave	Philadelphia, PA 19131, USA
KGO-TV	900 Front St	San Francisco, CA 94111, USA
WJLA-TV	3007 Tilden St NW	Washington, DC 20008, USA

Columbia Broadcasting System

WBZ-TV	1170 Soldiers Field Rd	Boston, MA 02134, USA
WBBM-TV	630 N McClurg Ct	Chicago, IL 60611, USA
KHOU-TV	1945 Allen Pkwy	Houston, TX 77019, USA
KCBS-TV	6121 Sunset Blvd	Los Angeles, CA 90028, USA
WCIX-TV	8900 NW 18th Terr	Miami, FL 33172, USA
WWL-TV	1024 N Rampart St	New Orleans, LA 70116, USA
WCBS-TV	524 W 57th St	New York, NY 10019, USA
KYW-TV	101 S Independence Mall E	Philadelphia, PA 19106, USA
KPIX-TV	855 Battery St	San Francisco, CA 94111, USA
WUSA-TV	4100 Wisconsin Ave NW	Washington, DC 20016, USA

Fox Television

WAGA-TV	1551 Briarcliff Rd NE	Atlanta, GA 30306, USA
WFXT-TV (Boston)	1000 Providence Hwy	Dedham, MA 02026, USA
WFLD-TV	205 N Michigan Ave	Chicago, IL 60601, USA
KDFW-TV	400 N Griffin St	Dallas, TX 75202, USA
WJBK-TV (Detroit)	16550 W Nine-Mile Rd	Southfield, MI 48075, USA
KRIV-TV	3935 Westheimer Rd	Houston, TX 77027, USA

MAJOR TELEVISION STATION ADDRESSES

KTTV-TV	5746 W Sunset Blvd	Los Angeles, CA 90028, USA
WSVN-TV	1401 79th St Cswy	Miami, FL 33141, USA
WNOL-TV	1661 Canal St	New Orleans, LA 70112, USA
WNYW-TV	205 E 67th St	New York, NY 10021, USA
WTXF-TV	330 Market St	Philadelphia, PA 19106, USA
KTVU-TV (San Francisco)	PO Box 22222	Oakland, CA 94623, USA
WTTG-TV	5151 Wisconsin Ave NW	Washington, DC 20016, USA
	National Broadcasting Company	
WXIA-TV	1611 W Peachtree St NE	Atlanta, GA 30309, USA
WMAG-TV	454 N Columbus Dr	Chicago, IL 60611, USA
KXAS-TV	3900 Barnett St	Fort Worth, TX 76103, USA
WDIV-TV	550 W Lafayette Blvd	Detroit, MI 48231, USA
KPRC-TV	8181 Southwest Frwy	Houston, TX 77074, USA
KNBC-TV (Los Angeles)	3000 W Alameda Ave	Burbank, CA 91523, USA
WTVJ-TV	316 N Miami Ave	Miami, FL 33128, USA
WDSU-TV	520 Royal St	New Orleans, LA 70130, USA
WNBC-TV	30 Rockefeller Plaza	New York, NY 10112, USA
WMGM-TV (Philadelphia)	1601 New Rd	Linwood, NJ 08221, USA
KRON-TV	1001 Van Ness Ave	San Francisco, CA 94109, USA
WRC-TV	4001 Nebraska Ave NW	Washington, DC 20016, USA

TELEVISION CHANNEL ADDRESSES

American Christian Television	6350 West Frwy	Fort Worth, TX 76150, USA
Arts & Entertainment	235 E 45th St	New York, NY 10017, USA
Black Entertainment Network	1232 31st St NW	Washington, DC 20007, USA
British Broadcasting Company	Wood Ln	London W12 8Q,. England
C-SPAN	400 N Capitol St NW	Washington, DC 20001, USA
Cable News Network	100 Int'l Blvd NW	Atlanta, GA 30303, USA
Canadian Broadcasting Company	1500 Bronson Ave	Ottawa ON K1G 3J5, Canada
Canadian Television Network	42 Charles St E	Toronto ON M4Y 1T5, Canada
Capital Cities/ABC	77 W 66th St	New York, NY 10023, USA
Cartoon Network	1050 Techwood Dr NW	Atlanta, GA 30318, USA
Christian Broadcasting Network	1000 Centerville Tpk	Virginia Beach, VA 23463, USA
Cinemax	1100 6th Ave	New York, NY 10036, USA
Columbia Broadcasting System	51 W 52nd St	New York, NY 10019, USA
Comedy Central	1775 Broadway	New York, NY 10019, USA
Consumer News & Business	2200 Fletcher Ave	Fort Lee, NJ 07024, USA
Country Music Television	2806 Opryland Dr	Nashville, TN 37214, USA
Discovery Channel	7700 Wisconsin Ave	Bethesda, MD 20814, USA
Disney Channel	3800 W Alameda Ave	Burbank, CA 91505, USA
E! (Entertainment Television)	5670 Wilshire Blvd	Los Angeles, CA 90036, USA
ESPN (Entertainment & Sports)	ESPN Plaza, 935 Middle St	Bristol, CT 06010, USA
Family Channel	PO Box 64549	Virginia Beach, VA 23467, USA
Fox Broadcasting Co	10201 W Pico Blvd	Los Angeles, CA 90035, USA
FX (Fox Net)	PO Box 900	Beverly Hills, CA 90213, USA
Granada Television	36 Golden Square	London W1R 2AX, England
Home Box Office (HBO)	1100 6th Ave	New York, NY 10036, USA
Home Shopping Network	PO Box 9090	Clearwater, FL 34618, USA
Learning Channel	7700 Wisconsin Ave	Bethesda, MD 20814, USA
Lifetime	309 W 49th St	New York, NY 10019, USA
Madison Square Garden Network	2 Pennsylvania Plaza	New York, NY 10001, USA
Movie Channel (TMC)	1633 Broadway	New York, NY 10019, USA
MTV (Music Television)	1515 Broadway	New York, NY 10036, USA
Nashville Network (TNN)	2806 Opryland Dr	Nashville, TN 37214, USA
National Broadcasting Company	30 Rockefeller Plaza	New York, NY 10112, USA
Nickelodeon	1515 Broadway	New York, NY 10036, USA
PBS (Public Broadcasting System)	1320 Braddock Place	Alexandria, VA 22314, USA
Playboy Channel	9242 Beverly Blvd	Beverly Hills, CA 90210, USA
Prime Ticket Network	10000 Santa Monica Blvd	Los Angeles, CA 90067, USA
QVC Inc	1365 Enterprise Dr	West Chester, PA 19380, USA
Sci-Fi Channel	1230 Ave of Americas	New York, NY 10020, USA
Showtime Network	1633 Broadway	New York, NY 10019, USA

TELEVISION CHANNEL ADDRESSES

TBN (Trinity Broadcast Network)	PO Box A	Tustin, CA 92711, USA
TBS (Turner Broadcasting System)	100 Int'l Blvd NW	Atlanta, GA 30303, USA
Telemundo Group	1740 Broadway	New York, NY 10019, USA
TNT (Turner Network Television)	1050 Techwood Dr NW	Atlanta, GA 30318, USA
TVA	1600 de Maisonneuve Blvd E	Montreal PQ H2L 4P2, Canada
Univision Network	605 3rd Ave	New York, NY 10158, USA
USA Cable Network	1230 Ave of Americas	New York, NY 10020, USA
VH-1 (Video Hits One)	1515 Broadway	New York, NY 10036, USA
Viewer's Choice	909 3rd Ave	New York, NY 10022, USA
Weather Channel	2600 Cumberland Pkwy NW	Atlanta, GA 30339, USA

RECORD COMPANY ADDRESSES

A&M Records	1416 N La Brea Ave	Los Angeles, CA 90028, USA
Angel Records	1750 N Vine St	Los Angeles, CA 90028, USA
Angel Records	810 7th Ave	New York, NY 10019, USA
Arista Records	8370 Wilshire Blvd, #300	Beverly Hills, CA 90211, USA
Arista Records	6 W 57th St	New York, NY 10019, USA
Asylum Records	9229 Sunset Blvd, #718	Los Angeles, CA 90069, USA
Asylum Records	75 Rockefeller Plaza	New York, NY 10019, USA
Atlantic Records	9229 Sunset Blvd, #900	Los Angeles, CA 90069, USA
Atlantic Records	75 Rockefeller Plaza	New York, NY 10019, USA
Blue Note Records	6920 Sunset Blvd	Los Angeles, CA 90028, USA
Capitol Records	1750 N Vine St	Los Angeles, CA 90028, USA
Capitol Records	810 7th Ave	New York, NY 10019, USA
Chrysalis Records	8730 Sunset Blvd	Los Angeles, CA 90069, USA
Chrysalis Records	810 7th Ave, #4	New York, NY 10019, USA
Sony/Columbia/CBS Records	2100 Colorado Ave	Santa Monica, CA 90404, USA
Sony/Columbia/CBS Records	51 W 52nd St	New York, NY 10019, USA
Deutsche Grammaphon Records	810 7th Ave	New York, NY 10019, USA
Elektra Records	75 Rockefeller Plaza	New York, NY 10019, USA
EMI America Records	6920 Sunset Blvd	Los Angeles, CA 90028, USA
EMI America Records	810 7th Ave	New York, NY 10019, USA
Epic Records	1211 S Highland Ave	Los Angeles, CA 90019, USA
Epic Records	550 Madison Ave	New York, NY 10022, USA
Geffen Records	9100 Sunset Blvd	Los Angeles, CA 90069, USA
Geffen Records	1755 Broadway	New York, NY 10019, USA
Island Records	8920 Sunset Blvd, #200	Los Angeles, CA 90069, USA
Island Records	400 Lafayette St, #500	New York, NY 10003, USA
London Records	810 7th Ave	New York, NY 10019, USA
MCA Records	70 Universal City Plaza	Universal City, CA 91608, USA
MCA Records	1755 Broadway	New York, NY 10019, USA
Mercury Records	810 7th Ave	New York, NY 10019, USA
Motown Records	6255 Sunset Blvd	Los Angeles, CA 90028, USA
Nonesuch Records	75 Rockefeller Plaza	New York, NY 10019, USA
Phillips Records	810 7th Ave	New York, NY 10019, USA
Polygram Records	3800 W Alameda Ave, #1500	Burbank, CA 91505, USA
Polygram Records	Worldwide Plaza, 825 8th Ave	New York, NY 10019, USA
Polydor Records	3800 W Alameda Ave	Burbank, CA 91505, USA
Polydor Records	810 7th Ave	New York, NY 10019, USA
RCA Records	6363 Sunset Blvd, #429	Los Angeles, CA 90028, USA
RCA Records	1540 Broadway, #900	New York, NY 10036, USA
Reprise Records	3300 Warner Blvd	Burbank, CA 91505, USA
Reprise Records	75 Rockefeller Plaza	New York, NY 10019, USA
Rhino Records	10635 Santa Monica Blvd	Los Angeles, CA 90025, USA
Sire Records	3300 Warner Blvd	Burbank, CA 91505, USA
Sire Records	75 Rockefeller Plaza	New York, NY 10019, USA
Verve Records	Worldwide Plaza, 825 8th Ave	New York, NY 10019, USA
Virgin Records	338 N. Foothill Rd	Beverly Hills, CA 90210, USA
Virgin Records	1790 Broadway, #2000	New York, NY 10019, USA
Warner Bros Records	3300 Warner Blvd	Burbank, CA 91505, USA
Warner Bros Records	75 Rockefeller Plaza	New York, NY 10019, USA
Windham Hill Records	1416 N La Brea Ave	Los Angeles, CA 90028, USA

Atheneum Publishers	866 3rd Ave	New York, NY 10022, USA
Ballantine Books	201 E 50th St	New York, NY 10022, USA
Bantam Books	1540 Broadway	New York, NY 10036, USA
Crown Publishers	225 Park Ave S	New York, NY 10003, USA
Delacorte Press	1540 Broadway	New York, NY 10036, USA
Dodd Mead Co	6 Ram Ridge Rd	Spring Valley, NY 10977, USA
Doubleday Co	1540 Broadway	New York, NY 10036, USA
Dutton, (E P) Co	375 Hudson St	New York, NY 10014, USA
Farrar Straus Giroux	19 Union Square W	New York, NY 10003, USA
Grove Press	841 Broadway	New York, NY 10003, USA
Harcourt Brace Jovanovich	525 "B" St	San Diego, CA 92101, USA
Harper Collins Publishers	10 E 53rd St	New York, NY 10022, USA
Holt, (Henry) Inc	115 W 18th St	New York, NY 10011, USA
Houghton Mifflin Co	215 Park Ave S	New York, NY 10003, USA
Knopf, (Alfred A) Inc	201 E 50th St	New York, NY 10022, USA
Little Brown Co	34 Beacon St	Boston, MA 02108, USA
McGraw Hill Book Co	1221 Ave of Americas	New York, NY 10011, USA
MacMillan Inc	1177 Ave of Americas, #1965	New York, NY 10036, USA
Morrow, (William) Co	1350 Ave of Americas	New York, NY 10016, USA
New American Library	1633 Broadway	New York, NY 10019, USA
Norton, (W W) Co	500 5th Ave	New York, NY 10110, USA
Pocket Books	1230 Ave of Americas	New York, NY 10020, USA
Prentice-Hall Inc	Rt 9-W	Englewood Cliffs, NJ 07632, USA
Putnam's Sons, G P	200 Madison Ave	New York, NY 10016, USA
Random House Inc	201 E 50th St	New York, NY 10022, USA
Scribner's Sons, Charles	866 3rd Ave	New York, NY 10022, USA
Simon & Schuster Inc.	1230 Ave of Americas	New York, NY 10020, USA
St Martin's Press	175 5th Ave	New York, NY 10010, USA
Viking Press	375 Hudson St	New York, NY 10014, USA

PROFESSIONAL SPORTS TEAM ADDRESSES
BASEBALL

Atlanta Braves	County Stadium, PO Box 4064	Atlanta, GA 30302, USA
Baltimore Orioles	333 W Camden Ave	Baltimore, MD 21201, USA
Boston Red Sox	Fenway Park, 4 Yawkey Wy	Boston, MA 02215, USA
Anaheim Angels	Anaheim Stadium, PO Box 2000	Anaheim, CA 92803, USA
Chicago Cubs	1060 W Addison St	Chicago, IL 60613, USA
Chicago White Sox	333 W 35th St	Chicago, IL 60616, USA
Cincinnati Reds	100 Riverfront Stadium	Cincinnati, OH 45202, USA
Cleveland Indians	Cleveland Stadium	Cleveland, OH 44114, USA
Colorado Rockies	2001 Blake St	Denver, CO 80205, USA
Detroit Tigers	Tiger Stadium, 2121 Trumbell	Detroit, MI 48216, USA
Florida Marlins	100 NE 3rd Ave	Fort Lauderdale, FL 33301, USA
Houston Astros	Astrodome, PO Box 288	Houston, TX 77001, USA
Kansas City Royals	PO Box 419969	Kansas City, MO 64141, USA
Los Angeles Dodgers	1000 Elysian Park Ave	Los Angeles, CA 90012, USA
Milwaukee Brewers	County Stadium, 201 S 46th St	Milwaukee, WI 53214, USA
Minnesota Twins	501 Chicago Ave S	Minneapolis, MN 55415, USA
Montreal Expos	PO Box 500, Station "M"	Montreal PQ H1V 3P2, Canada
New York Mets	Shea Stadium	Flushing, NY 11368, USA
New York Yankees	Yankee Stadium, 161st & River	Bronx, NY 10451, USA
Oakland Athletics	Oakland Coliseum	Oakland, CA 94621, USA
Philadelphia Phillies	Veterans Stadium, PO Box 7575	Philadelphia, PA 19101, USA
Pittsburgh Pirates	Three Rivers Stadium	Pittsburgh, PA 15212, USA
San Diego Padres	PO Box 2000	San Diego, CA 92112, USA
San Francisco Giants	Candlestick Park	San Francisco, CA 94124, USA
Seattle Mariners	Kingdome, PO Box 4100	Seattle, WA 98104, USA
St Louis Cardinals	250 Stadium Plaza	St Louis, MO 63102, USA
Texas Rangers	PO Box 901111	Arlington, TX 76004, USA
Toronto Blue Jays	300 Bremner Blvd	Toronto ON M5V 3B3, Canada

PROFESSIONAL SPORTS TEAMS ADDRESSES

MEN'S BASKETBALL

Atlanta Hawks	1 CNN Center, South Tower	Atlanta, GA 30303, USA
Boston Celtics	151 Merrimac St, #500	Boston, MA 02114, USA
Charlotte Hornets	1 Hive Dr	Charlotte, NC 28217, USA
Chicago Bulls	1901 W. Madison St	Chicago, IL 60612, USA
Cleveland Cavaliers	2923 Statesboro Rd	Richfield, OH 44286, USA
Dallas Mavericks	Reunion Arena, 777 Sports St	Dallas, TX 75207, USA
Denver Nuggets	McNichols Arena, 1635 Clay St	Denver, CO 80204, USA
Detroit Pistons	Palace, 2 Championship Dr	Auburn Hills, MI 48326, USA
Golden State Warriors	7000 Coliseum Way	Oakland, CA 94621, USA
Houston Rockets	Summit, Greenway Place, #10	Houston, TX 77046, USA
Indiana Pacers	Market Sq Arena, 300 E Market St	Indianapolis, IN 46204, USA
Los Angeles Clippers	Sports Arena, 3999 Figueroa St	Los Angeles, CA 90037, USA
Los Angeles Lakers	Forum, PO Box 10	Inglewood, CA 90306, USA
Miami Heat	Miami Arena, 100 NE 3rd Ave	Miami, FL 33301, USA
Milwaukee Bucks	Bradley Center, 1001 N 4th St	Milwaukee, WI 53203, USA
Minnesota Timberwolves	Target Center, 600 1st Ave N	Minneapolis, MN 55403, USA
New Jersey Nets	Byrne Meadowlands Arena	East Rutherford, NJ 07073, USA
New York Knicks	Madison Sq Grdn, 4 Penn Plz	New York, NY 10001, USA
Orlando Magic	Orlando Arena, 1 Magic Place	Orlando, FL 32801, USA
Philadelphia 76ers	Veterans Stadium, PO Box 25040	Philadelphia, PA 19147, USA
Phoenix Suns	201 E Jefferson St	Phoenix, AZ 85004, USA
Portland Trail Blazers	1 N Center Court St, #200	Portland, OR 97227, USA
Sacramento Kings	1 Sports Pkwy	Sacramento, CA 95834, USA
San Antonio Spurs	600 E Market St, #102	San Antonio, TX 78205, USA
Seattle Supersonics	190 Queen Ave N, POB C-900911	Seattle, WA 98109, USA
Toronto Raptors	20 Bay St, #1702	Toronto ON M5J 2N8, Canada
Utah Jazz	Delta Center, 301 W South Temple	Salt Lake City, UT 84101, USA
Vancouver Grizzlies	288 Beatty St, #300	Vancouver BC V6B 2M1, Canada
Washington Wizards	Capital Centre, 1 Truman Dr	Landover, MD 20785, USA

WOMEN'S BASKETBALL (WNBA)

Charlotte Sting	2709 Water Ridge Pkwy	Charlotte, NC 28217, USA
Cleveland Rockers	Gund Arena, 1 Center Ct	Cleveland, OH 44115, USA
Houston Comets	2 Greenway Plaza, #400	Houston, TX 77046, USA
Los Angeles Sparks	Forum, 3900 W. Manchester Blvd	Inglewood, CA 90306, USA
New York Liberty	Madison Sq Grdn, 2 Penn Plaza	New York, NY 10121, USA
Phoenix Mercury	Phoenix Suns Plz, 201 E. Jefferson	Phoenix, AZ 85004, USA
Sacramento Monarchs	Arco Arena, 1 Sports Pkwy	Sacramento, CA 95834, USA
Utah Starzz	Delta Ctr, 301 W. South Temple	Salt Lake City, UT 84101, USA

WOMEN'S BASKETBALL (ABL)

Atlanta Glory	151 Ponce de Leon Ave NE, #200	Atlanta, GA 30308, USA
Colorado Xplosion	800 Grant St, #410	Denver, CO 80203, USA
Columbus Quest	7451 State Rt 161	Dublin, OH 43016, USA
Long Beach StingRays	6378 E Pacific Coast Hwy, #D	Long Beach, CA 90803, USA
New England Blizzard	179 Allyn St, #403	Hartford, CT 06103, USA
Portland Power	1 Center Court St	Portland, OR 97227, USA
Richmond Rage	7650 E Parham Rd, #260	Richmond, VA 23294, USA
San Jose Lasers	1530 Parkmoor Ave, #A	San Jose, CA 95128, USA
Seattle Reign	400 Mercer St, #408	Seattle, WA 98109, USA

FOOTBALL

Arizona Cardinals	8701 S Hardy Dr	Tempe, AZ 85284, USA
Atlanta Falcons	2745 Burnett Rd	Suwanee, GA 30174, USA
Baltimore Ravens	200 St Paul Place, #2400	Baltimore, MD 21202, USA
Buffalo Bills	1 Bills Dr	Orchard Park, NY 14127, USA
Carolina Panthers	800 S Mint St	Charlotte, NC 28202, USA
Chicago Bears	Halas Hall, 250 N Washington Rd	Lake Forest, IL 60045, USA
Cincinnati Bengals	1 Bengals Dr	Cincinnati, OH 45204, USA
Dallas Cowboys	1 Cowboys Pkwy	Irving, TX 75063, USA
Denver Broncos	13655 E Dove Valley Parkway	Englewood, CO 80112, USA
Detroit Lions	Silverdome, 1200 Featherstone Rd	Pontiac, MI 48342, USA
Green Bay Packers	1265 Lombardi Ave	Green Bay, WI 54304, USA

PROFESSIONAL SPORTS TEAMS ADDRESSES

Indianapolis Colts	7001 W 56th St	Indianapolis, IN 46254, USA
Jacksonville Jaguars	1 Stadium Place	Jacksonville, FL 32202, USA
Kansas City Chiefs	1 Arrowhead Dr	Kansas City, KS 64129, USA
Miami Dolphins	7500 SW 30th St.	Davie, FL 33314, USA
Minnesota Vikings	9520 Viking Dr	Eden Prairie, MN 55344, USA
New England Patriots	Foxboro Stadium, Rt 1	Foxboro, MA 02035, USA
New Orleans Saints	1500 Poydras St	New Orleans, LA 70112, USA
New York Giants	Giants Stadium	East Rutherford, NJ 07073, USA
New York Jets	1000 Fulton Ave	Hempstead, NY 11550, USA
Oakland Raiders	1220 Harbor Bay Pkwy	Alameda, CA 94502, USA
Philadelphia Eagles	3501 S Broad St	Philadelphia, PA 19148, USA
Pittsburgh Steelers	3 Rivers Stadium, 300 Stadium Cir	Pittsburgh, PA 15212, USA
San Diego Chargers	Jack Murphy Stadium	San Diego, CA 92160, USA
San Francisco 49ers	4949 Centennial Blvd	Santa Clara, CA 95054, USA
Seattle Seahawks	11220 NE 53rd St	Kirkland, WA 98033, USA
St Louis Rams	100 N Broadway, #2100	St Louis, MO 63102, USA
Tampa Bay Buccaneers	1 Buccaneer Place	Tampa, FL 33607, USA
Tennessee Oilers	Hale Hall, Tennessee State Univ	Nashville, TN 37209, USA
Washington Redskins	21300 Redskin Park Dr	Ashburn, VA 20147, USA

ICE HOCKEY

Anaheim Mighty Ducks	PO Box 2000, Gene Autry Way	Anaheim, CA 92803, USA
Boston Bruins	1 Fleet Ctr	Boston, MA 02114, USA
Buffalo Sabres	1 Seymour H Knox III Plaza	Buffalo, NY 14203, USA
Calgary Flames	PO Box 1540, Station "M"	Calgary AB T2P 3B9, Canada
Carolina Hurricanes	5000 Aerial Center, #100	Morrisville, NC 27560, USA
Chicago Blackhawks	United Ctr, 1901 W Madison St	Chicago, IL 60612, USA
Colorado Avalanche	McNichols Arena, 1635 Clay St	Denver, CO 80204, USA
Dallas Stars	211 Cowboys Parkway	Irving, TX 75063, USA
Detroit Red Wings	Joe Louis Arena, 600 Civic Center	Detroit, MI 48226, USA
Edmonton Oilers	Edmonton Coliseum, 7424-118 Ave	Edmonton AB T5B 4M9, Canada
Florida Panthers	100 NE 3rd Ave, #200	Miami, FL 33301, USA
Los Angeles Kings	Forum, PO Box 10	Inglewood, CA 90308, USA
Montreal Canadiens	1260 de La Gauchetiere St W	Montreal PQ H3H 5E8, Canada
New Jersey Devils	Continental Arena, PO Box 504	East Rutherford, NJ 07073, USA
New York Islanders	Nassau Veterans Coliseum	Uniondale, NY 11553, USA
New York Rangers	Madison Sq Grdn, 2 Penn Plz	New York, NY 10121, USA
Ottawa Senators	1000 Prom Palladium Dr	Kanata ON K2V 1A4, Canada
Philadelphia Flyers	1 CoreStates Complex	Philadelphia, PA 19148, USA
Phoenix Coyotes	2 N Central, #1930	Phoenix, AZ 85004, USA
Pittsburgh Penguins	Civic Arena, Centre Ave	Pittsburgh, PA 15219, USA
San Jose Sharks	525 W Santa Clara St	San Jose, CA 95113, USA
St Louis Blues	1401 Clark Ave	St Louis, MO 63103, USA
Tampa Bay Lightning	401 Channelside Dr	Tampa, FL 33602, USA
Toronto Maple Leafs	60 Carlton St	Toronto ON M5B 1L1, Canada
Vancouver Canucks	800 Griffiths Way	Vancouver BC V6B 6G1, Canada
Washington Capitals	USAir Arena	Landover, MD 20785, USA

OTHER SPORTS ORGANIZATION ADDRESSES

Amateur Athletic Union	3600 W 86th St	Indianapolis, IN 46268, USA
Amateur Softball Assn	2801 NE 50th St	Oklahoma City, OK 73111, USA
American Basketball League	1900 Embarcadero Road, #110	Palo Alto, CA 94303
American Bicycle Assn	PO Box 718	Chandler, AZ 85226, USA
American Bowling Congress	5301 S 76th St	Greendale, WI 53129, USA
American Horse Show Assn	220 E 42nd St	New York, NY 10017, USA
American Hot Rod Assn	111 N. Hayford Rd	Spokane, WA 99204, USA
American Kennel Club	51 Madison Ave	New York, NY 10010, USA
American League (Baseball)	350 Park Ave	New York, NY 10022, USA
American Motorcycle Assn	PO Box 6114	Westerville, OH 43086, USA
American Power Boat Assn	17640 E Nine Mile Rd	East Detroit, MI 48021, USA
American Prof Soccer League	122 "C" St, NW	Washington, DC 20001, USA
American Water Ski Assn	799 Overlook Dr, SE	Winter Haven, FL 33882, USA
Assn of Int'l Amateur Boxing	Postamt Volkrdstr, Postlagernd	1137 Berlin, Germany

OTHER SPORTS ORGANIZATION ADDRESSES

Assn of Int'l Marathon/Road Races	20 Trongate	Glasgow G1 5ES, England
Assn of Ski Racing Professionals	148 Porters Point Rd	Colchester, VT 05446, USA
Assn of Surfing Professionals	16691 Gothard St	Huntington Beach, CA 92648, USA
Assn of Tennis Professionals	200 Tournament Players Rd	Ponte Vedra, FL 32082, USA
Assn of Volleyball Professionals	330 Washington Blvd, #600	Marina del Rey, CA 90292, USA
Canadian Football League	110 Eglinton Ave	Toronto, ON M4R 1A3, Canada
Canadian Nat'l Sports/Rec Ctr	1600 James Naismith Dr	Gloucestor ON KJB 5N4, Canada
Fedn de Int'l Hockey	Avenue des Arts 1 (bte 5)	1040 Brussels, Belgium
Fedn de Int'l Ski	Worbstrasse 210, 3073 Gumligen B	Berne, Switzerland
Fedn Int'l de Canoe	G Massaia 59	50134 Florence, Italy
Fedn Int'l de Football Assn	PO Box 85, Hitzigweg 11	8030 Zurich, Switzerland
Fedn Int'l de Tir a l'Arc (Archery)	Via Cerva 30	20122 Milan, Italy
Fedn of Int'l Volleyball	Ave de la Gare 12	1001 Lausanne, Switzerland
Fedn of Int'l Amateur Cycling	Via Cassia N 490	00198 Rome, Italy
Fedn of Int'l Basketball	PO Box 700607, Kistlerhofstr 168	8000 Munich 70, Germany
Fedn of Int'l Bobsleigh/Toboggan	Via Piranesi 44/b	20137 Milan, Italy
Fedn of Int'l du Sport Automobiles	8 Place de la Concorde	75008 Paris, France
Fedn of Int'l Equestrian	PO Box 3000, Bolligenstrasse 54	Berne 32, Switzerland
Fednal Int'l de Gymnastics	Juraweg 12	3250 Lyss, Switzerland
FIFA Women's Football Assn	37 Sussex Rd, Ickenham	Middx UB10 8PN, England
Formula One Driver's Assn	2 Rue Jean Jaures	1836 Luxembourg
Indy Car Racing	390 Enterprise Ct	Bloomfield Hills, MI 48302, USA
Int'l Badminton Fedn	24 Winchcombe House	Cheltenham, Glos GL52 2NA, England
Int'l Baseball Assn	201 S Capitol Ave, #490	Indianapolis, IN 46225, USA
Int'l Boxing Fedn	134 Evergreen Place	East Orange, NJ 07018, USA
Int'l Cricket Council	Lord's Cricket Ground	London NW8 8QN, England
Int'l Curling Fedn	2 Coates Cres	Edinburgh EH3 7AN, England
Int'l Game Fish Assn	1301 E Atlantic Blvd	Pompano Beach, FL 33060, USA
Int'l Hot Rod Assn	PO Box 3029	Bristol, TN 37625, USA
Int'l Ice Hockey Fedn	Bellevuestrasse 8	A-1190 Vienna, Austria
Int'l Jai Alai Assn	5 Calle Aldamar	San Sebastian 3, Spain
Int'l Judo Fedn	Avenida del Trabajo 2666,	CP 1406, Buenos Aires, Argentina
Int'l Luge Fedn	Olympiadestrasse 168	8786 Rottenmann, Austria
Int'l Motorsports Assn	PO Box 10709	Tampa, FL 33679, USA
Int'l Olympic Committee	Chateau de Vidy	1007 Lausanne, Switzerland
Int'l Roller Skating Fedn	1500 S 70th St	Lincoln, NE 68506, USA
Int'l Rugby Football Board	PO Box 902	Auckland, New Zealand
Int'l Skating Union	Promenade 73	7270 Davos-Platz, Switzerland
Int'l Sled Dog Racing Assn	PO Box 446	Nordman, ID 83848
Int'l Softball Fedn	2801 NE 59th St	Oklahoma City, OK 73111, USA
Int'l Sport Automobile Fed	8 Rue de la Concorde	70008-E Paris, France
Int'l Surfing Assn	Winston Ave, Branksome People	Dorset, England
Int'l Table Tennis Fedn	53 London Rd, St Leonards-on-Sea	East Sussex TN37 6AY, England
Int'l Tennis Fedn	Palliser Rd, Barons Ct	London W14 9EN, England
Int'l Volleyball Fedn	Avenue de la Gare 12	1003 Lausanne, Switzerland
Int'l Weightlifting Fedn	Rosemberg Hp U1	1374 Budapest PF 614, Hungary
Int'l Yacht Racing Union	60 Knightsbridge, Westminster	London SWEX 7JX, England
Ladies Professional Bowlers Tour	7171 Cherryvales Blvd	Rockford, IL 61112, USA
Ladies Professional Golf Assn	2570 Volusra Ave	Daytona Beach, FL 32114, USA
Little League Baseball	PO Box 3485	Williamsport, PA 17701, USA
Major Indoor Lacrosse League	2310 W 75th St	Prairie Village, KS 66208, USA
Major League Baseball	350 Park Ave	New York, NY 10022, USA
National Archery Assn	1 Olympic Plaza	Colorado Springs, CO 80909, USA
National Assn/Intercoll Athletics	1221 Baltimore Ave	Kansas City, MO 64105, USA
National Assn of Stock Car Racing	1801 Speedway Blvd	Daytona Beach, FL 32015, USA
National Basketball Assn	645 5th Ave	New York, NY 10022, USA
National Collegiate Athletic Assn	6201 College Ave	Overland Park, KS 66211, USA
National Football League	410 Park Ave	New York, NY 10022, USA
National Hockey League	650 5th Ave	New York, NY 10019, USA
National Hot Rod Assn	2023 Financial Way	Glendora, CA 91741, USA
National League (Baseball)	350 Park Ave	New York, NY 10022, USA

OTHER SPORTS ORGANIZATION ADDRESSES

National Prof Soccer League	229 3rd St NW	Canton, OH 44702, USA
National Rifle Assn	11250 Waples Mill Rd	Fairfax, VA 22030, USA
National Tractor Pullers Assn	6969 Worthington-Galena Rd	Worthington, OH 43085, USA
PGA Seniors Tour	112 TPC Blvd	Ponte Vedra Beach, FL 32082, USA
Professional Bowlers Assn	1720 Merriman Rd	Akron, OH 44313, USA
Professional Golfers Assn	PO Box 109601	Palm Beach Gardens, FL 33410, USA
Professional Rodeo Cowboys Assn	101 Pro Rodeo Dr	Colorado Springs, CA 80919, USA
Special Olympics	1350 New York Ave NW	Washington, DC 20005, USA
Thoroughbred Racing Assn	420 Fair Hill Dr	Elkton, MD 21921, USA
Union Int'l de Tir (Rifle)	Bavariaring 21	8000 Munich 2, Germany
US Auto Club	4910 W 16th St	Speedway, IN 46224, USA
US Bobsled & Skeleton Assn	PO Box 828	Lake Placid, NY 12946, USA
US Cycling Fedn	1750 E Boulder St	Colorado Springs, CO 80909, USA
US Figure Skating Assn	20 1st St	Colorado Springs, CO 80906, USA
US Luge Assn	PO Box 651	Lake Placid, NY 12946, USA
US Olympic Committee	1 Olympic Plaza	Colorado Springs, CO 80909, USA
US Polo Assn	120 Mill St	Lexington, KY 40507, USA
US Skiing Assn	PO Box 100	Park City, UT 84060, USA
US Tennis Assn	Flushing Meadow	Flushing, NY 11368, USA
US Trotting Assn	750 Michigan Ave	Columbus, OH 43215, USA
US Youth Soccer Assn	PO Box 18404	Memphis, TN 38181, USA
USA Rugby	830 N Tejon	Colorado Springs, CO 80903, USA
USA Track & Field	PO Box 120	Indianapolis, IN 46206, USA
Virginia Slims Women's Tennis	3135 Texas Commerce Tower	Houston, TX 77002, USA
Women's Basketball Assn	4011 N. Bennington	Kansas City, MO 64117, USA
Women's Int'l Bowling Congress	5301 S 76th St	Greendale, WI 53129, USA
Women's Int'l Surfing Assn	PO Box 512	San Juan Capistrano, CA 92675, USA
Women's National Basketball Assn	645 5th Ave	New York, NY 10022
Women's Pro Volleyball Assn	840 Apollo St, #204	El Segundo, CA 90245, USA
Women's Tennis Assn	133 1st St NE	St Petersburg, FL 33701, USA
World Boardsailing Assn	Feldafinger Platz 2	81477 Munich, Germany
World Boxing Assn	Rodrigo Sazagy, Apartado	4070 Panama City, Panama
World Boxing Council	Genova 33, Colonia Juarez	Cuahtemoc 0660, Mexico
World Taekwondo Fedn	San 76 Yuksam-Dong	Kangnam-Ku, Seoul, Korea
World Team Tennis	445 N Wells St	Chicago, IL 60610, USA
World Union of Karate Orgs	1-15-16 Toranomon, Minato-ku	Tokyo 105, Japan
World Wrestling Fedn	1055 Summer St	Stamford, CT 06905, USA

HALLS OF FAME ADDRESSES

Academy of Sports	4 rue de Teheran	75008 Paris, France
Amateur Athletic Foundation of LA	2141 W Adams Blvd	Los Angeles, CA 90018, USA
American Water Ski Hall of Fame	799 Overlook Dr SE	Winter Park, FL 33884, USA
Auto Racing Hall of Fame	4790 W 16th St	Speedway, IN 46224, USA
College Football Hall of Fame	5540 Kings Island Dr	Kings Island, OH 45034, USA
Hockey Hall of Fame	Exhibition Place	Toronto, ON M6K 3C3, Canada
Int'l Boxing Hall of Fame	PO Box 425	Canastota, NY 13032, USA
Int'l Gymnastics Hall of Fame	227 Brooks St	Oceanside, CA 92054, USA
Int'l Motor Sports Hall of Fame	PO Box 1018	Talladega, AL 35160, USA
Int'l Surfing Hall of Fame	5580 La Jolla Blvd, #373	La Jolla, CA 92037, USA
Int'l Swimming Hall of Fame	1 Hall of Fame Dr	Fort Lauderdale, FL 33316, USA
Int'l Tennis Hall of Fame	194 Bellevue Ave	Newport, RI 02840, USA
Int'l Women's Sports Hall of Fame	342 Madison Ave, #728	New York, NY 10173, USA
Lacrosse Hall of Fame Foundation	White, Jr. Athletic Ctr, Homewood	Baltimore, MD 21218, USA
Lawn Tennis Museum	All England Lawn Tennis Club	Wimbledon, England
LPGA Hall of Fame	2570 Volusia Ave	Daytona Beach, FL 32114, USA
Naismith Basketball Hall of Fame	1150 W Columbus Ave	Springfield, MA 01105, USA
Nat'l Baseball Hall of Fame	PO Box 590	Cooperstown, NY 13326, USA
Nat'l Bowling Museum/Hall of Fame	111 Stadium Plaza	St. Louis, MO 63102, USA
Nat'l Cowboy Hall of Fame	Heritage Ctr, 1700 NE 63rd St	Oklahoma City, OK 73111, USA
Nat'l Football Found Hall of Fame	1865 Palmer Ave	Larchmont, NY 10538, USA
Nat'l Museum of Racing	Union Ave	Saratoga Springs, NY 12866, USA
Nat'l Ski Hall of Fame	PO Box 191, Poplar & Mather	Ishpeming, MI 49849, USA

SPORTS HALLS OF FAME ADDRESSES

Nat'l Softball Hall of Fame	2801 NE 50th St	Oklahoma City, OK 73111, USA
Nat'l Sportcaster/Sportswriter HOF	322 E Innes St	Salisbury, NC 28144, USA
Nat'l Sprint Car Hall of Fame	1402 N Lincoln Ave	Knoxville, IA 50138, USA
Nat'l Track & Field Hall of Fame	PO Box 120	Indianapolis, IN 46206, USA
Nat'l Wrestling Hall of Fame	405 W Hall of Fame Ave	Stillwater, OK 74074, USA
PGA Tour Hall of Fame	112 Tournament Players Club Blvd	Ponte Vedra, FL 32082, USA
PGA World Golf Hall of Fame	PGA Blvd, PO Box 1908	Pinehurst, NC 28374, USA
Pro Football Hall of Fame	2121 George Halas Dr, NW	Canton, OH 44708, USA
Pro Rodeo Hall of Champions	101 Pro Rodeo Dr	Colorado Springs, CO 80919, USA
Professional Bowlers Assn HOF	1720 Merriman Rd	Akron, OH 44313, USA
Professional Golfers Assn HOF	100 Ave of Champions	Palm Beach Gardens, FL 33418, USA
Trapshooting Hall of Fame	601 W Vandalia Rd	Vandalia, OH 45377, USA
Trotter Horse Museum & HOF	PO Box 590	Goshen, NY 10924, USA
US Bicycling Hall of Fame	PO Box 8535, 1 W Main St	Somerville, NJ 08876, USA
US Figure Skating Assn HOF	20 1st St	Colorado Springs, CO 80906, USA
US Golf Assn Museum	Golf House	Far Hills, NJ 07931, USA
US Hockey Hall of Fame	PO Box 657, Hat Trick Ave	Eveleth, MN 55734, USA
US Olympic Committee HOF	1750 E Boulder St	Colorado Springs, CO 80909, USA
Volleyball Hall of Fame	PO Box 1895, 444 Dwight St	Holyoke, MA 01040, USA
Women's Bowling Hall of Fame	5301 S 76th St	Greendale, WI 53129, USA
Yachting Hall of Fame	PO Box 129	Newport, RI 02840, USA

INTERNET USERS

Visit our website

at

VIPADDRESS.COM

For Pricing & Ordering Information

BIBLIOGRAPHY

Academy Players Directory, Academy of Motion Picture Arts/Sciences, 8949 Wilshire Blvd, Beverly Hills, CA 90211
African Who's Who, African Journal Ltd, 54-A Tottenham Court Rd, London W1P 08T, England
Biographical Dictionary of Governors of the US, Meckler Publishing, Ferry Ln W, Westport, CT 06880
Biographical Dictionary of US Executive Branch, Greenwood Press, 51 Riverside Ave, Westport, CT 06880
Celebrity Access, Celebrity Access Publications, 20 Sunnyside Ave, Mill Valley, CA 94941
Congressional Directory, Superintendent of Documents, US Government Printing Office, Washington, DC 20402
Contemporary Architects, St Martin's Press, 175 5th Ave, New York, NY 10010
Contemporary Designers, Gale Research Co, Book Tower, Detroit, MI 48226
Contemporary Theatre, Film & Television, Gale Research Co, Book Tower, Detroit, MI 48226
Corporate 1000, Washington Monitor, 1301 Pennsylvania Ave NW, Washington, DC 20004
Editor & Publisher International Yearbook, 575 Lexington Ave, New York, NY 10022
International Directory of Films & Filmmakers, St James Press, 175 5th Ave, New York, NY 10010
International Who's Who, Europa Publications Ltd, 18 Bedford Sq, London WC1B 3JN, England
International Who's Who in Music, Biddles Ltd, Walnut Tree House, Guildford, Surrey GU1 1DA, England
Kraks BlaBog, Nytorv 17, 1450 Copenhagen K, Denmark
Major Companies of the Far East, Graham & Trotman Ltd, 66 Wilton Rd, London SW1V 1DE, England
Major Companies of Europe, Graham & Trotman Ltd, 66 Wilton Rd, London SW1V 1DE, England
Martindale-Hubbell Law Directory, Reed Publishing, Summit, NJ 07902
Moody's International Manual, Moody's Investors Service, 99 Church St, New York, NY 10007
Notable Australians, Paul Hamlyn Pty Ltd, 31 176 S Creek Rd, Dee Why, WA 2099, Australia
Notable New Zealanders, Paul Hamlyn Pty Ltd, 31 Airedale St, Auckland, New Zealand
Prominent Personalities in USSR, Scarecrow Press, Metuchen, NJ 08840
US Court Directory, Government Printing Office, Washington, DC 20401
US Gov't Manual, National Archives & Records Service, General Services Administration, Washington, DC 20408
VIP Autogramm-Magazin, Postfach 11 05, D-35112 Fronhausen, Germany
Who's Who, A & C Black Ltd, St Martin's Press, 175 5th Ave, New York, NY 10010
Who's Who in America, Marquis Who's Who, 200 E Ohio St, Chicago, IL 60611
Who's Who in American Art, R R Bowker Co, 1180 Ave of Americas, New York, NY 1003
Who's Who in American Politics, R R Bowker Co, 1180 Ave of Americas, New York, NY 10036
Who's Who in Canada, Global Press, 164 Commanden Blvd, Agincourt ON M1S 3C7, Canada
Who's Who in France, Editions Jacques Lafitte SA, 75008 Paris, France
Who's Who in Germany, Verlag AG Zurich, Germany
Who's Who in Israel, Bronfman Publishers Ltd, 82 Levinsky St, Tel Aviv 61010, Israel
Who's Who in Poland, Graphica Comense Srl, 22038 Taverreiro, Italy
Who's Who in Scandinavia, A Sutter Druckerei GmbH, 4300 Essen, Germany
Who's Who in Switzerland, Nagel Publishers, 5-5 bis de l'Orangeris, Geneva, Switzerland
Who's Who in the Theatre, Pitman Press, 39 Parker St, London WC2B 5PB, England
Who's Who in Washington, Tiber Reference Press, 4340 East-West Hwy, Bethesda, MD 20814

Book design by Lee Ann Nelson.
Cover logo is Corvinus Skyline.
Body type is Swiss Narrow.
Production by Nelson Design
1 Annabelle Lane
San Ramon, California 94583, USA

V.I.P. ADDRESS BOOK UPDATE
& MULTIPLE COPY DISCOUNTS

Keep Up To Date With the
V.I.P. Address Book Update
Only $24.95!

Every year 20% of people change residences
- Athletes get traded
- Entertainers change agents
- Business people change jobs
- Politicians leave or change office

Changed Addresses   The mid-year V.I.P. ADDRESS BOOK UPDATE lists changes since publication of the basic volume.

Bad Addresses   The UPDATE identifies addresses which are no longer accurate and for which corrections are not available.

New Addresses   The UPDATE even has addresses for new entrants!

Deaths   And a list of people who have died since the V.I.P. ADDRESS BOOK was published is included.

Foreign orders add $4.00 for overseas shipping.

Multiple Copy Discounts

The V.I.P. ADDRESS BOOK offers the following multiple copy discounts:

1 - 2 Copies	$94.95 each
3 - 5 Copies	$85.45 each
6 - 12 Copies	$80.71 each
13 - 49 Copies	$75.96 each
50 - 99 Copies	$71.21 each
100 - 199 Copies	$66.47 each
200 Copies or More	$56.97 each

Foreign orders, write for shipping information.

Order Information

Use your MasterCard, Visa or American Express
or a company purchase order and call toll-free
1-800-258-0615

Or send your check or money order to:

Associated Media Companies
P.O. Box 489
Gleneden Beach, OR 97388-0489
Phone/Fax Number - (541) 764-4233
Internet Users - VIPADDRESS.COM

An Invitation To Join The

The Universal Autograph Collector's Club is the largest organization of its kind in the world with members in over thirty countries. Our journal, *The Pen and Quill*, is published six times a year and features articles in all fields of autograph collecting as well as information useful to today's collector. Members are also given opportunities to purchase through the club autographic material at far below Dealer prices. The UACC also sponsors shows around the world and publishes low cost reference works to aid the collector in their autograph quests. Best of all, the UACC is an organization of collectors and run by collectors.

For membership information, please write:

UACC Dept. V.
P.O. Box 6181
Washington, DC 20044-6181

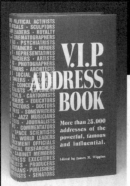